THE

ARCHITECTURAL HISTORY

OF THE

UNIVERSITY OF CAMBRIDGE

THE

ARCHITECTURAL HISTORY

OF THE

UNIVERSITY OF CAMBRIDGE,

AND OF THE

COLLEGES OF CAMBRIDGE AND ETON.

BY THE LATE

ROBERT WILLIS, M.A., F.R.S.

JACKSONIAN PROFESSOR IN THE UNIVERSITY OF CAMBRIDGE,
AND SOMETIME FELLOW OF GONVILLE AND CAIUS COLLEGE.

EDITED WITH LARGE ADDITIONS,

AND BROUGHT UP TO THE PRESENT TIME,

BY

JOHN WILLIS CLARK, M.A.

LATE FELLOW OF TRINITY COLLEGE, CAMBRIDGE.

VOL. II.

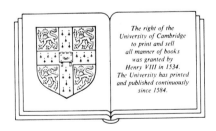

The right of the University of Cambridge to print and sell all manner of books was granted by Henry VIII in 1534. The University has printed and published continuously since 1584.

CAMBRIDGE UNIVERSITY PRESS

CAMBRIDGE

NEW YORK   NEW ROCHELLE   MELBOURNE   SYDNEY

Published by the Press Syndicate of the University of Cambridge
The Pitt Building, Trumpington Street, Cambridge CB2 1RP
32 East 57th Street, New York, NY 10022, USA
10 Stamford Road, Oakleigh, Melbourne 3166, Australia

Introduction © Cambridge University Press 1988

First published 1886
Reprinted with a new Introduction 1988

Printed in Great Britain at the University Press, Cambridge

British Library cataloguing in publication data
Willis, Robert, 1800–1875
The architectural history of the University of
Cambridge and of the colleges of Cambridge and Eton.
1. University of Cambridge – Buildings – History
2. Eton College – Buildings – History
I. Title   II. Willis, Clark John
727'.3'0942659   LF110

Library of Congress cataloguing in publication data
Willis, Robert, 1800–1875
The architectural history of the University of Cambridge and of
the colleges of Cambridge and Eton by Robert Willis: edited with
large additions and brought up to the present time by John Willis
Clark.
p.   cm.
Reprint. Originally published: Cambridge: University Press,
1886. With new introd.
ISBN 0 521 35323 8 (set).   ISBN 0 521 35851 5 (pbk set)
1. University of Cambridge – Buildings – History.   2. Eton College –
Buildings – History.   I. Clark, John Willis, 1833–1910.   II. Title.
LF110.W7 1988
727'.3'0942659–do 19   87-37555

ISBN 0 521 35320 3 hard covers (vol. 1)
ISBN 0 521 35848 5 paperback (vol. 1)
ISBN 0 521 35321 1 hard covers (vol. 2)
ISBN 0 521 35849 3 paperback (vol. 2)
ISBN 0 521 35322 X hard covers (vol. 3)
ISBN 0 521 35850 7 paperback (vol. 3)
ISBN 0 521 35323 8 hard covers (the set)
ISBN 0 521 35851 5 paperback (the set)

CONTENTS

OF THE

SECOND VOLUME.

VIII. QUEENS' COLLEGE.

IX. S. CATHARINE'S HALL.

X. JESUS COLLEGE.

XI. CHRIST'S COLLEGE.

XII. S. JOHN'S COLLEGE.

LIST OF ILLUSTRATIONS

IN THE

SECOND VOLUME.

QUEENS' COLLEGE.

JESUS COLLEGE.

CHRIST'S COLLEGE.

S. JOHN'S COLLEGE.

MAGDALENE COLLEGE.

TRINITY COLLEGE.

ERRATA IN THE SECOND VOLUME.

P. 19,	line	22,	for	1602	read	1598
54	,,	5	,,	1608—9	,,	1609—10
69	,,	5	,,	Small-bridge	,,	Small-bridges
75	note	3	,,	lease	,,	deed
101	line	22	,,	fourteen	,,	thirteen
103	,,	7	,,	Gosling	,,	Gostling's
106	note	1	,,	the same year	,,	1704
121	,,	6	,,	north	,,	west
122	,,	1	,,	views	,,	view
128	line	25	,,	westen	,,	western
140	,,	13	,,	existed	,,	had existed
152	,,	28	,,	Wales	,,	Wailes
154	,,	26	,,	Ely	,,	Ely Cathedral
165	,,	22	,,	48 feet	,,	fifty feet, seven inches
166	,,	8	,,	plans	,,	plan
166	,,	22	,,	gate	,,	gate of entrance
176	,,	25	,,	this	,,	the older
187	,,	2	,,	Preacher	,,	Preachers
189	,,	17	,,	Preacher	,,	Preachers
189	,,	25	,,	Preacher	,,	Preachers
189	note	1	,,	that	,,	the
215	line	26	,,	the gate	,,	that gate
215	,,	36	,,	Parlour,	,,	Parlour, now divided into hall and study,
224	note	1	,,	print	,,	portrait
256	line	6	,,	Simons	,,	Symons
280	,,	4	,,	South	,,	North
297	,,	10	,,	he	,,	Professor Willis
319	,,	4	,,	Kerdall	,,	Kendall
333	,,	15	,,	century	,,	century in which they flourished
367	,,	28	,,	It	,,	The building
367	,,	37	,,	1668	,,	1665
377	,,	35	,,	1762	,,	1763
446	note	3	,,	p. 65	,,	p. 43
547	,,	9	,,	1842—66	,,	1841—66
674	,,	35	,,	1746	,,	1747
718	,,	27	,,	extended	,,	entered

VIII.

The Queens' College of S. Margaret and S. Bernard,

COMMONLY CALLED

Queens' College[1].

CHAPTER I.

[HISTORY OF THE SITE.

HE site on which the founder, King Henry VI., intended in the first instance to place this College, then called the College of S. Bernard, was a strip of ground extending from Trumpington Street on the east, to "the highway leading to the Carmelites," otherwise part of Milne Street, on the west. On the south some dwelling-houses separated it from the street then called Smallbridges Street, now Silver Street; on the north it was bounded by other houses which, together with the site in question, became afterwards part

---

[1] [The History of this College has been written by the Rev. W. G. Searle, M.A., late Fellow. His work entitled "The History of the Queens' College of S[t] Margaret and S[t] Bernard in the University of Cambridge," Cambridge Antiquarian Society, Octavo Publications, Nos. IX. XIII., has rendered the labours of those who succeed him comparatively easy. It will be understood that when I cite him I am referring to this work. Professor Willis had made notes for the history of this site, but he had not written out a connected narrative. For this reason I have included this chapter between square brackets. For the facts here related I am indebted to Mr Searle's work, and also to some of the original conveyances, preserved in the College Treasury. I have to thank my friends Dr Phillips, President, and Dr Campion, Fellow and Senior Tutor, for their kindness in allowing me to study these and all the other College records.]

of S. Catharine's Hall. This property, which was 277½ feet long, by 75 feet wide at the east end, and 72 feet wide at the west end, had been conveyed to the King by Richard Andrewe, burgess of Cambridge, 8 November 1446; as we learn from his foundation-charter, dated 3 December in the same year. In Hammond's plan (fig. 2) the western portion of it is shewn as a garden.

The Society however (which then consisted of the President Andrew Doket, and four Fellows) soon found difficulties in the way of establishing themselves on this site; and with the King's leave returned the charter, praying him to accept instead of it and all it conveyed to them "a site which should be more manageable and better able to provide for the extension of the buildings and grounds of such a College as he desired to found[1]." In consequence a new charter was issued, dated 21 August 1447, confirming to them the site they had selected for themselves[2].

The College is now bounded on the south by Silver Street, on the east by Queens' Lane, anciently the commencement of Milne Street, on the north by King's College, and on the west by the river Cam. Two-thirds of this extensive ground were occupied at the time we are considering, as the plan shews, by the Carmelite Friary, which formed the northern boundary of the ground acquired by Andrew Doket. The rest consisted in the main of a messuage and garden conveyed to him, 24 July 1447, by John Morys of Trumpington, Esquire, and Elizabeth his wife. It extended from Milne Street on the east to the river on the west; and it had at its south-west corner four pieces of property in the following order, beginning from the west. The corner house, "*angulare mesuagium*," belonged to John Morys. Next to this were four tenements and their gardens belonging to the same conjointly with John Battisford of Chesterton; beyond them a piece of ground, not built upon, belonging to Corpus Christi College; and eastward of this again the dwelling-house of John Forster, which extended round the last-mentioned piece so as to form its northern boundary. Of these the four tenements and their gardens became the property of the College two days after the larger property to the north of them (26 July 1447), and

<hr />

[1] [The words thus translated are "pro placabiliori situ ac elargatione edificiorum et habitationis huiusmodi Collegii."]

[2] [This charter is printed by Mr Searle, pp. 8—15.]

were conveyed to the King in the same deed. There is no documentary evidence to shew when the corner-house was acquired[1].
The deed by which John Botwright, Master of Corpus Christi
College, conveys the piece east of the four tenements is dated
thirteen years later, 12 January 1460. The western abuttal is
therein described as Queens' College (*collegium Reginale*), and the
eastern as "a tenement lately belonging to John Forster, now
dead;" but it is not stated that this latter had become the property of the College, and we do not know when it was acquired.
As, however, we shall find that the contract for building the
Hall-range is dated 6 March 1448—49, these different pieces
of property must all have been situated to the west of it, and
have formed a portion of the site of the Pump Court.

Between the College and the Carmelites there was a small
interval, bounded by a ditch and wall; and for a certain distance
a public lane also extended from Milne Street in the direction of
the river. A difference respecting the wall having arisen, the
Convent sold it to the College, together with the ground on
which it stood, 12 February 1536—37, for £1. 3s. 4d., engaging
neither to reclaim it at any time, nor in any way to damage it[2].
In less than two years after this transaction, the dissolution of
religious houses being plainly imminent, and being perhaps
under the impression that better terms would be obtainable
from the College than from the Crown, the Carmelites surrendered their house to Dr Mey, President, and the fellows of
Queens' College, by a deed dated 8 August, 1538, from which
the following passage may be extracted:

"Be it knowen to all men, that we George Legat prior of the howse
of friers Carmelites in Cambridge, comonlie called the White Friers, and

---

[1] [In the conveyance of the four tenements dated 26 July, 25 Hen. VI. (1447), it is
described as "nuper mei dicti Johannis Morys et Elizabeth uxoris mee iacens iuxta
Ripariam ibidem," which shews that it had already changed hands; but whether the
College had then acquired it or not no evidence has been preserved to shew.]

[2] [Searle's History, p. 194. Mag. Jour. 1509—10. f. 225, Item...laboranti
in venella inter collegium et fratres. Ibid. 1511—12. f. 241 *b*, Martino Jonson pro
emendacione muri lapidei ultra capellam ad assignacionem magistri Vicepresidentis
vj s. viij d. 1518—19. fo. 22, It' duobus laborantibus pro labore ij dierum cum di°
circa purgacionem cuiusdam venelle a tergo librarii et camere magistri versus
Fratres Carmelitas xx s. 1524—27. fo. 93 *b*, Item Richardo Bycharstaf purganti
fossam inter fratres et collegium iiij d. 1541—42. f. 87, labourers are paid for
cleaning "angiportum intra fratrum muros et collegium."]

the covent of the same howse...gladly ffrely and willynglie do giue and graunt and surrender in to the hands of the right worshipfull Mr William Mey, doct^r. in law civill...all that owr howse and grownd called the White friers in Cambridge, with all and singular the appertinences therof and thervnto belongyng.

And we also by these presents do testifie that when we shalbe required thervnto we shall depart from the seid howse and grownd and give place vnto them, and also shalbe redie at all tymes to make writyngs, and seale to all such wrytyngs as shalbe devised by ther learned cownsell to lie in vs for the confirmation and assuraunce of this owr gift and dede towards them: so that this owr fact and dede be nothyng preiudiciall, but alowed and approved of and by owr most dred and soueraigne lord the Kyng, In whose graces power and pleasure, beyng the supreme hed of this catholik churche of Englond, whe confesse and acknowledge that it is to alow or disalowe this owr fact or dede[1]."

This amicable transaction was interrupted by the issue of a Royal Commission to Dr Daye, Provost of King's, Dr Mey, President of Queens', and two of the fellows of the same College, on 17 August in the same year, to the following effect :

"Forasmuch as we vnderstande, that the house of the White freers within that our towne and vniuersitie of Cambridge remayneth at this present in suche state, as it is neyther vsed to the honour of God nor to the benefite of our commen wealth, Myndyng for the conversion of it to a better purpose to take it into our own handes;

We latt you witt that having speciall trust in your approved wisedoms and dexterities, We haue named and appointed you, that repayring vnto the said howse immedyately vppon the receipt hereof, ye shall receve of the priour ther in our name, and to our vse, such sufficient writing vnder the convent seale of the said howse, as by your discretion shalbe thought mete and convenyent for the surrendre of the same;

The which surrendre so made, we wooll that ye shall take possession of the said howse, and soo to kepe the same to our vse tyll further knowleage of our pleasour, taking a true and a perfite Inuentory of all the goodes of the saide howse, the which our pleasour is ye shall send vnto vs incontynently, to thentent our further mynde maye theruppon be declared vnto you with more speed and celeritie."

The last article of the royal injunctions was exactly obeyed, for the deed of surrender is dated 28 August, and the inventory of all the moveables belonging to the friars was taken 6 September. A number of entries in the Bursar's Accounts for this and following years shew that the College set to work at once to

---

[1] [Printed by Mr Searle; from whose most interesting account of the suppression of the Carmelite Friary, pp. 220—233, I have extracted the following particulars.]

pull the Convent to pieces; although it was not until 28 November 1541 that Dr Mey formally purchased, of the King's officers of the revenues of the augmentation of his crown in the counties

Fig. 2. Queens' College, reduced from Hammond's map of Cambridge, 1592.

of Cambridge and Huntingdon, all the stone, slate, tile, timber, iron, and glass of the late house of the Carmelites for the moderate sum of £20. From a study of the accounts Mr Searle has shewn that the Convent possessed a church and cloister, chapter-house, bell-tower, hall, dormitory, and kitchen. The site was granted by the King to John Eyre of Bury, Esquire (12 September, 1544), who soon after sold it to Dr Mey, for his conveyance of it to the College is dated 30 November in the same year[1].

By this acquisition the site of the College on the east of the Cam was brought to its present dimensions. The island, or, as it appears at present, the peninsula, which contains the brew-house, stables, fellows' garden and grove, was sold to the College by the town of Cambridge at the instance of King Edward the Fourth, the Queen, and Prince Edward their eldest son, for 40 marks, 6 October, 1475. Its original condition will be understood from Hammond's map (fig. 2). It is described as bounded on the east by the stream (*communis riparia*) which comes down from the mills called "Kings mylle and bischopys mylle:" and on the west by a similar stream coming down from "Newenham mylle." The southern limit was a line of stakes fixed at a certain distance to the north of the road leading from Cambridge to Newnham "between the two bridges called le smale brigges." The space that intervened between the road and this line of stakes, which was 28 feet broad at the east end, and 63 feet broad at the west end, was to be reserved to the town to discharge rubbish on, and to be separated from the College ground by a ditch to be made at the College expense. Furthermore, the College undertook to lengthen the easternmost of the two bridges by twelve feet, and to widen the stream, so that it might be fifty-one feet broad; and the town gave them leave to construct a bridge over the eastern arm of the river, the arches of which might be as wide as those of the bridge at King's College[2].]

---

[1] [It is uncertain how far Dr Mey had acted for the College, and how far on his own account, in these transactions with the Carmelites. The following passage in his will (7 August, 1560), "Item I do give all manner of righte interest tytle or state that I or myne heire have or myghte have or claime in the cittie or circute as hit is now distincted of the late suppressed house of the Whitefriers besides the quenes Colledge in Cambridge to the saide Colledge for ever," implies that he had been the real possessor of the property. Mr Searle's History, p. 293.]

[2] [The deed is printed by Mr Searle, p. 85.]

CHAPTER II.

HISTORY OF THE BUILDINGS DERIVED FROM THE COLLEGE RECORDS.

[WE may now proceed to investigate the history of the buildings that occupy the site, premising that subsequent to the acquisition of the portion on which the courts stand Queen Margaret had petitioned the King her husband to grant to her "the foundation and determination" of the College; which she proposed to call "the Quenes collage of sainte Margarete and saint Bernard;" and that he had acceded to her request. Her charter of foundation is dated 15 April, 1448. She had intended to lay the first stone in person, but being prevented from doing so by various reasons, as she herself says, she commissioned her chamberlain Sir John Wenlock to act as her representative and to lay the said stone. This he did on the very day on which her charter was executed. The place selected was the south-east corner of the Chapel, and the stone is said to have borne this inscription: "*Erit domine nostre regine Margarete dominium in refugium et lapis iste in signum.*" It has been variously translated, but Mr Searle suggests, with much probability, that it means "The power of our lady Queen Margaret shall be our refuge, and this stone (laid in her name) the sign of her protection[1]."]

The only other historical records of the first buildings extant are two contracts. The Bursar's Account Book, called in this College "Magnum Journale," does not begin until 1484, in which year the first President, Andrew Doket, died (4 November). It is probable that during his lifetime he kept the accounts in his own possession. The first of these contracts, dated 14 April, 1448, the day before the laying of the first stone, between the President and fellows of the College on the one hand, and John Veyse of Elesnam (Elsenham) in Essex, draper, and Thomas Sturgeon of the same town and shire, carpenter, on the other

---

[1] [The authority for this inscription is a brief MS history of the College written about 1470 (Mr Searle's History, p. 44). It has hitherto been printed as follows: "Erit dominæ nostræ Reginæ Margaretæ Dominus in refugium et lapis iste in signum:" upon which Fuller (162) makes sundry pious reflections. The Queen's commission to Sir John Wenlock is printed by Mr Searle, p. 42.]

hand, binds the latter parties in one hundred pounds to make "an howse within the seid College as in werk of Carpentre," and to provide all the timber for the roof, the midelwalles (or partitions), stairs, and floor-boards. This house is to be 240 feet in length and 20 feet broad. The scantlings of the beams are given, but no other particulars. For this work a hundred pounds is to be paid by instalments; to wit £54. 13s. 4d. at the next feast of St George (April 23), £20 at the nativity of St John Baptist (June 24), and £25. 6s. 8d. at the feast of St Michael (Sept. 29); the work therefore was expected to occupy about five months. This first indenture is as follows:

"This indenture made the xiiij^{the} day of Aprile the yer of the reign of our sovreign lord the king Herry the sixt six and twenty betwen master Andrew Dokett president of the Quene college of seynt Margret and seynt Barnard and the Felowes of the seid college of the one party, and John Veyse of Elesnam in the shire of Essex draper and Thomas Sturgeon of the seides town and shire carpenter on the other party bereth witteness that—thogh the seides John Veyse and Thomas Sturgeon be holden and strongely by their obligacion bownden to the forseid master Andrewe Dokett in an hundred pound of good and lawfull money of Inglond to be paied to hym his heires or to his successours in the fest of the natiuite of seynt John Baptiste next folowyng the forseid,—yet master Andrewe president and of the seid college Felowes wollen, and by thies presentes indentures graunten that—yef the seides John Veyse and Thomas Sturgeon or other of them or elles any other in their name make or do for to be made well and sufficiauntely an hovse with in the seid college as in werk of carpentre [find]yng also all the tymber that shall nede to the rofe of the seid howse and also lathes and all maner of tymber that shall be ocupyed on the [flore]s and on the Midelwalles and on the steires with all the bord the wich shall be of oke that to the seid flores and steires shall resonable nede of the propre costis and expensez of the seides John and Thomas vndir maner and forme as her foloweth, that is for to say:

the seid house shall conteyne in lengthe xij^{xx} foot of the standard, and in brede xx foote of the standard; and the Someres of the seid hows shall be one side xij inch squar and on the other part xiiij inch squar; and all the Gistes shall be on the one part squar vj inches and on the other part viij inches; and all the bemes shall be squar on the one part x inches and on the other part viij inches; and the walplates on the one part ix inch and on the other part vij inches; And all the bemes that lyen by hemself they shull be squar on the one side x inch and on the other xv inch; And all the sparres shall conteyne in brede at the netherend squar vij inch and at the overend vi inches and in thiknesse on the other part at the nether end vj inch and at the over end v inches; and all the sowthelases and the asshelers shull accord in brede with the sparres and on the other part thes shull be iiij inches squar; and all the wynbemes shull conteyne in brede squar vj inches and in the other part v inches; And al the stoddes shall be in brede viij inch squar and on the other part v inche squar; and the space betwyn all the sparres all the stoddes and all the gystes shull be but x inch;

and all thies covenauntez beforrehersed be plenerly fulfilled and done by the seides John and Thomas or by any other for theym,—that then the forseid obligacion of an C li stand in non strenketh nor effect, and elles yef hit be not fulfilled that then hit stand in strenketh and vertu. Purveid alwey that the seides John and Thomas shall haue of the forseides master Andrewe his successores and of his felowes of the seid College for the forseid Tymbir bord lath and werkmanship that shall pertene to the seid hows an C li of lawfull money of Inglond to be payed at dayes here expressed, that is for to say, at the fest of seynt George next after the date present liiij li xiij s iiij d and at the fest of the natiuite of seynt John Baptiste xx li and at the fest of seynt Michaell the archangell then next folowyng xxv li vi s viij d in pleyn payment of the C li aforseid.

In witteness whereof bothe partyes to thies presentes indenturez alternatly haue putt to her seales. This wittenesseth Richard Andrewe, John Batisford, Benet Morys and mo other. Yeven at Cambrigge day and yer aboven seid."

[Towards the expenses of this building King Henry VI. contributed £200, as the following document dated 4 March, 1449, nearly one year after the contract above quoted, shews:

" It is shewed unto us by our welbeloved the President and Felowes of the College of saint Margarete and saint Bernard in our universite of Cambrigge which is of the foundation of our moost dere and best beloved wyfe the Quene, how that, for as much as the seid president and felowes have not wherwith to edifie the seid College in housing and other necessaries but only of almesse of Cristes devoute people therto putting theire hands and dedes meritorye nor that the seid edification is not to be perfourmed at any wise withoute that the supportation of our moste noble and benygne grace be shedded unto them in this partie —we have yeven them CC^{li}[1]."]

The second contract is dated 6 March, 1448—49. It is between the same parties, and binds Veyse and Sturgeon in £80 to make the roof of the Hall within the said College, finding all the timber. The Hall is to be 50 feet long and 23 feet broad. They are also to make the roofs of the buttery, pantry, and kitchen, with their floors, etc., "the which houses extend in length from the hall to the highway;" with a return of the chambers, each of them containing in length 25 feet, and in breadth 20 feet. It is further provided that all the timbers as enumerated "that shall nede to the seides howses shall accord

---

[1] [MSS. Baker xxv. 449, quoted by Mr Searle, p. 62.]

wyth the other syde the wich is now redy framed next to the freres;" that is, with the north side next to the Carmelites. For this work £80 is to be paid. This second indenture is to the following effect[1] :

"This indenture made the sext day of March the zere of the reigne of our souereigne lord the kyng Herry the sext xxvij[the] between maister Andrew Dokett presidente of the Quenes colage of sente Margrett and sente Barnard of Cambrigge maistere Pers Hirford and maistere Thomas Heywod of the seide colage felowes on the on party, and John Weyse of Elesnam in the shire of Essex draper and Thomas Sturgeon of the seides town and shire carpenter on the other party bereth witteness that —thogh the seides John Weyse and Thomas Sturgeon be howlden and strangly by there obligacions bownden to the forseid master Andrew Dokett, mastre Pers Hirford and to maister Thomas Heywod in iiij[xx]li of good and lawfull money of Inglond to be payed to the seydes master Andrew, master Pers, and master Thomas to there heires successores or to their certeyn attorney in the fest of the natiuite of our Lord next followyng after the dat present the forreherseid,—yet master Andrew master Pers master Thomas wollen and by thies present indentures granten that—yef the seid John Weyse and Thomas Sturgeon or otheir of them or elles any othire in their name make or do for to be made well and sufficiauntly the rofe of the hall within the seid collage being, fyndyng all tymber that shall perteyn ther to,

the wich hall shalbe and conteyn in lenketh L fete of the standard and in brede xxviii fete and the walplates of the seid hall shalbe viij inches of brede and vij inches of Thiknes with jopees from bem to bem and v bemes and every bem shalbe xv inch of brede and x inch thik, and every sparre shalbe in the fote viij inch of brede and vij inch thik and in the topp vij inch of brede and v inch thik, and the principalles shalbe xj inch in breede and x inch thik with a purlyn in the Middes from one principall to a nother with a crown tree ix inch of brede viij inch thik,—and all the tymbere with warkmanshipp that shalbe nedfull to the benches in the seid hall, and also thei shull make the Rofes of botry pantry and kechen with the flores to them longyng with all the Midilwalles and greses to the seid houses perteynyng fyndyng tymber to them nedfull, the wich howses extenden in lenketh from the hall in to the hei way with a return of the Chambers ich of ham conteynyng in lenketh xxv foote and in brede xx; and all the sowtlases, asshalers, walplatz and jopees that shull nede to the seides howses shull accord with the other syde the wich is now redy framed next the Freres, fyndyng all tymber and borde of oke to the seid Flores with all lathes tymber for gresynges and Midelwalles to the seides howses perteynyng; and the space betwen all the stoddes all the sparres and all the Gistes shul be but x inch,

and all thies couauntes beforehesed be planarly fulfilled and doon by the seides John Weyse and Thomas Sturgeon or by any other for them,— that then the forseid obligacion of iiij[xx] li stande in no strenketh nor

---

[1] The parchment of the first indenture is decayed in one or two places. The words supplied are included in square brackets.

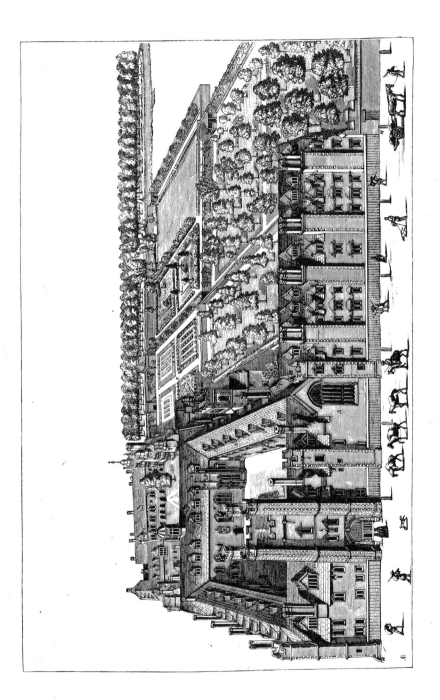

Fig. 3. Queens' College, reduced from Loggan's print, taken about 1688. A, Chapel; B, Library; C, Hall; D, President's Lodge; E, Kitchen; F, President's Garden; G, Fellows' Garden.

affect, and elles yef hit be not performed that then hit stand in strenketh
and vertu.   Purveid alvey that the seides John and Thomas shull haue
of the forseides master Andrew, master Pers, and master Thomas for the
tymber bord lath and werkmanshipp that shall perteyn to the howses
aforseid iiij^{xx} li of lawfull money of Inglond to be payed at daies here
expressed, that is for to sey: at Estern next comyng xx li, at Estern twel-
month after xx li, at sent Thomas day of Caunterbury then next x li, at the
exaltacion of the Holycross then next x li, at the reysing of the rofes of
the seid howses x li, and x li when thei haue plenarly performed all
ther couaunentz beforseid; and this to be done in as hasty wise as thei
may goodly after the walles of the seid howses be redy.

In witteness wherof bothe partyes to thies present indentures alternatly have putto her sealles.   This wittenesse Rychard Andrew, John
Batysford and moo other.   Yeven at Cambrigge, day and zere aboven
seid."

It will be impossible to interpret these contracts, which it
will be observed are for timber-work only, without understanding
the arrangements of the principal quadrangle.   These we will
describe in the next chapter, by the help of the plan (fig. 1), and
then collect the notices that illustrate the history of the rest of
the buildings.

CHAPTER III.

DESCRIPTION OF THE BUILDINGS AND COMPARISON OF THEM WITH THE ACCOUNTS.

THE Quadrangle of Queens' College is of moderate dimensions, measuring 99 feet from east to west, by 84 feet from north
to south, which is less than that of Corpus Christi College.   It is
built, however, of excellent architecture, in red brick, with a noble
gateway, flanked by octagonal turrets, and it has a square tower
at each external angle of the court.   The effect of these towers
is greatly increased by the care with which they are diminished
upwards.   The employment of the towers is a peculiarity which
offers presumptive evidence that the architect of the other two
royal colleges of King's and Eton was employed to design the
buildings of this smaller foundation.

The details of the architecture have suffered less from modern
meddling than in most of the colleges.   The cusps have been
scraped from the windows it is true, and battlements have been
substituted for the eaves which still existed when Loggan's print

was taken (fig. 3), but the ancient character would still be maintained were it not for the overbearing dimensions of a wooden campanile erected a few years since, which bestrides the roof above the entrance to the Chapel. This is, in fact, the earliest remaining quadrangle in Cambridge that can claim attention for real architectural beauty, and fitness of design. Plastering, ashlaring, and patching, rendered necessary by the rough construction and perishable materials of the earlier colleges, and of many of the later ones, have entirely metamorphosed them, but Queens' College is one of the few that still preserve the aspect and character impressed by the original architect.

The Quadrangle is entered on the east side by the gate-way tower above-mentioned [which, like most similar medieval structures, is not in the centre of the range, either towards the court or towards the street, as the plan (fig. 1) shews]. There are chambers to the right and left of the gate, and also along the whole of the south side. The west side is occupied by the Hall, Butteries, and Kitchen, of which the latter extends to Silver Street. The north side has the Library next to the Hall, followed by the Chapel, which extends to Queens' Lane, thus completing this side of the court. In the angle between the Hall and the Library is the Combination Room, over which is part of the President's Lodge.

In the middle of the south range, at a distance of 33 feet from the inner eastern angle of the court (G, fig. 1), the brickwork shews unmistakeable evidence, both within the court and in Silver Street, of an interruption in the work, namely, that the portions to the right and left of the seam were built at different periods. The western half of these is therefore the "return of the chambers" mentioned in the second contract, being, as there described, in continuation of the kitchen. The Hall is actually 52 feet 6 inches long, including the screens, by 27 feet 9 inches broad, measured on the inside, which sufficiently agrees with the contract. There is no room, however, in the College for a house or building 240 feet long, as the first contract describes it, if measured in a straight line. But, if we take the meaning to be, 240 feet length of roofing with flooring to correspond, the dimensions will agree exceedingly well with the sum obtained by adding together the north side, the east side (omitting the gate-house), and the

remainder of the south side; for the total length of the Library
and Chapel, measured from the Hall to the street, is 123 feet;
that of the east side, measured from the Chapel to Silver Street, is
105 feet; or, subtracting 15 feet for the gate-tower, is 90 feet; to
which if we add 33 feet of chambers on the south side, extending
from the inner corner to the joint in the brickwork, we obtain
a total length of 243 feet; a sufficiently close coincidence with
the 240 feet of the contract. The second contract asserts that
this part of the work is "now redy framed next to the Freres,"
that is, the Carmelites, whose ground was to the north of the
College at the time it was drawn up. [We may therefore conclude that the north and east ranges, together with the easternmost portion of the south range, were undertaken first, and were
ready for the woodwork at the date of the first contract (April,
1448). The masonry would be wrought, as usual, by day-work;
but no accounts of it have been preserved. The western range
was ready for the woodwork in about a year after the first
(March 1449).]

The north range of building is finished with a gable-wall close
to the Hall (HI, fig. 1), which would not have been the case if
the primary building had included the Combination Room and
its upper chamber, for then the same roof would have been continued over the latter. This gable is not in the same line with
the wall of the Hall, neither is the gable of the Hall in the same
line with the south wall of the Library. The result is, that at the
angle of the court a small space intervenes between the Hall
and the Library, in which there is a window from the Combination Room, and another over it from the Lodge.

Between the west side of the Hall-range and the river are
placed two other courts, the Cloister Court, and the Pump Court.
The former, to the north, is irregular in shape, having no right
angle. The west side measures 74 feet 5 inches, the east side
66 feet, the north side 102 feet 4 inches, and the south side
79 feet. The Hall and Combination Room occupy the east
side; a cloister the south side; and cloisters with buildings above
them, the west and north sides. The western range, next to
the river, is a long structure of red brick, in two floors, about
twenty feet wide between walls. The ground floor is partly
occupied by the cloister-walk, six feet wide. This cloister con-

sists of plain four-centered arches of brickwork, of three chamfered orders. The arches are fenced below by a low sill-wall,
with the exception of the central one, which is open to the grass.
The windows of the upper story are exactly like those of the
great quadrangle, and the building was probably erected very
soon after that quadrangle was finished, by way of providing
additional chambers. It was originally about 130 feet long, but
was shorn of about 25 feet in 1756, to make way for the new
building in the Pump Court. It is shewn in its original state by
Loggan (fig. 3). This building is now principally occupied by
the President's Lodge; and a gallery belonging to the latter
also extends over the whole cloister on the north side; but the
south cloister has no building above it, and is in continuation
of the Hall screens.

The western building existed as a complete edifice before
the lateral cloisters were built, for its plinth runs along behind
the abutments of the latter, and shews its ends within them.
The last arch also of each lateral cloister merely abuts against
the corresponding arch of the western building, so as to shew
unmistakeably that these side-cloisters were not contemplated
when the former was erected. Their arcades also, although the
same in form as in the previous building, are in two orders only,
of chamfered bricks, instead of in three, as the arcades of the
western cloister are. The south ambulatory, which leads directly
from the Hall door, now commences with a brick porch against
that door with arches on all the three sides. This porch, however, is a subsequent intrusion; the southern and western arches
are elliptical, and have both been closed with doors of which the
hinges remain, leaving only the north door into the cloister-garth
open.

[It is much to be regretted that no precise record of the
erection of these lateral cloisters should have been preserved.
A cloister (*claustrum*) is first mentioned in 1494—95[1]. Large
quantities of lime and sand are bought for it; but there is no
mention of bricks, nor are any payments made to workmen[2].

[1] [The word "claustrum" certainly means "cloister" and not "court," for which
"curia" is always used, as in the following passage (Mag. Jour. 1500—1, f. 150 b):
"Item...pro mundatione aule et claustri et curiarum collegii...iiij*d.*"]

[2] [The following extracts shew the nature of the items recorded (Mag. Jour. i. 92):

It is therefore impossible to decide whether it is a repair or a new work, but probably the latter, as the word does not occur in the accounts between 1484 and 1494, but frequently afterwards. There was a door in it leading into the lane between the College and the Carmelites; and the central space was occupied during the sixteenth century by a garden, of which a single tree remained when Loggan's view was taken[1].]

The Pump Court is on the south of this, bounded by the Butteries and Kitchen on the east; the south and west sides are formed by a modern range of chambers in three floors, built in white brick. It sometimes bears the name of "Erasmus' Court" because that eminent scholar occupied chambers in the turret which rises at the south-east angle (fig. 4). [An account of his residence here was written from tradition in 1680 by Andrew Paschal, Fellow, and Rector of Chedsey in Somersetshire:

"The staires which rise up to his studie at Queen's College in Cambr. doe bring into two of the fairest chambers in the ancient building; in one of them, which lookes into the hall and chief court, the Vice-President kept in my time; in that adjoyning, it was my fortune to be, when fellow. The chambers over are good lodgeing roomes; and to one of them is a square turret adjoyning, in the upper part of which is the study of Erasmus; and over it leads. To that belongs the best prospect about the colledge, viz. upon the river, into

"Inprimis sol' pro vno bigatu de ly lyme pro claustro ijs. vjd. Item sol' Johanni Messand pro bigatu de sabulo pro eodem claustro iiijd. Item pro duobus baskettis ad portandum sabulum cum aliis rebus iijd. Item sol' simoni sympson pro duodecem bigatis sabuli pro eodem claustro iiijs. Item sol' pro communis laborancium in claustro ijs. Item sol' Ricardo Jhonson pro operibus quinque dierum in eodem claustro xxd. Item sol' uxori eius pro dimidio vnius diei in eodem claustro ijd. Item pro clauis pro hostio in claustro nouiter fact' jd. Item sol' uxori Ricardi Jhonson pro portacione lapidum in claustro jd. Item sol' Gilbarto Smyth pro pare de hyngis et hukys pond' xij pownd xviijd. Item sol' predicto viro pro latchys et annulo ferreo eiusdem hostii ijd. Item sol' vni mulieri et duobus scolaribus laborantibus in predicto claustro iiijd. Item duobus scolaribus mundantibus predictum claustrum ijd. Item Rob' loksmyth pro emendacione vnius clauis hostii iuxta pontem jd. Item pro claue hostii iuxta pontem iijd. Item sol pro ly hukys pro hostio eiusdem claustri viijd."]

[1] [Mag. Jour. 1531—32, f. 159. After a payment "circa purgationem venelle versus fratres," we find "Item.. pro claui et sera ad ostium venelle in claustro viij d." 1532—33, f. 177, "Item...pro sera et claui ad ostium in claustro vergenti ad fratres xvj d." 1555—56, f. 235 b, "Item...pro claue ad ostium quod ducit ad cloacam inter fratres et conclaue iiij d." 1568—69, f. 71, "for a keie for ye gate by ye Cloisters into ye freares xij d." For the garden (Ibid. 1528—29, f. 111 b): "Item Ricardo Bikerstaff per duos dies mundanti columbarium et fodienti in horto claustrali viij d." " ...laboranti in horto infra claustrum per vj dies ij s."]

the corne-fields, and countrey adjoyning.   So yᵗ it might very well consist
with the civility of the House to that great man (who was no fellow,
and I think stayed not long there) to let him have that study.   His
sleeping-rome might be either the Vice-President's, or to be neer to him,
the next.   The room for his servitor that above it, and through it he
might goe to that studie, which for the height, and neatnesse and prospect, might easily take his phancy[1]."]

Fig. 4. South-east corner of the Pump Court, shewing Erasmus' turret, the porch of the Hall,
and the south cloister.

The history of the Italian building along the south and west
sides of this court shall be related in the words of Dr Plumptre
(President 1760—1788) :

[1] ["Letters written by eminent persons, publ. from the originals in the Bodleian
Library and Ashmolean Museum," 8°.   Lond. 1813. ii. 340 ; quoted by Mr Searle,
p. 154. The study is still quite unaltered. In the "Life of Erasmus," by S. Knight,
8vo. Cambridge 1726, p. 124, there is a view of the Pump Court, looking East, with
the porch to the staircase as it then was, and the old building on the south side.]

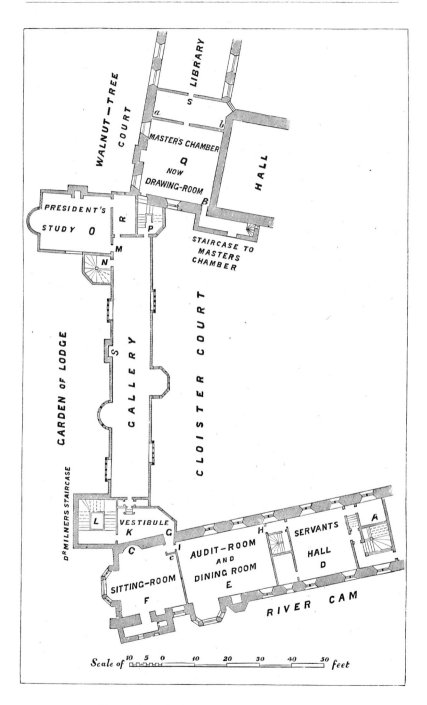

Fig. 5. Plan of the first floor of the President's Lodge.

"In the year 1756 the Clunch building extending from the Lodge Staircase by the Town-bridge to the College Kitchen, on the *outside*, and forming nearly two sides of the Court called Erasmus's Court *within*, being very much decay'd, was taken down, and the present useful and ornamental building begun in its place. It was planned and executed by Mr Essex an eminent Architect and man of good understanding and character in Cambridge; and was finish'd (except the fitting up of the Rooms) before the death of Mr Sedgwick in 1760. Towards defraying the expence of it, he had advanc'd £1000 on the condition of receiving an Annuity for life from the College, about a year and half before his death[1]."

[The building was begun in September 1756, and finished in September 1760, when a payment of £21 "to Mr Essex for surveying the new Building" marks the conclusion of the work. It was at that time intended to rebuild the whole of the river-front, including the Lodge; and the part erected is only one wing of a more extensive design. The opposite wing would have been exactly similar; the central block would have been set in advance of the rest. It was surmounted by a pediment, and access to the bridge was provided through a lofty classical doorway, over which was a smaller pediment[2]. The Lodge staircase mentioned by Dr Plumptre still exists (A, fig. 1).

The "clunch building" which was then pulled down is shewn by Loggan (fig. 3); and his map of Cambridge exhibits still more clearly its relations to the rest of the College. From these indications it has been laid down in block on the plan (fig. 1). It extended along Silver Street from the south-west corner of the Hall-range to the river, and a return of it, which bounded on the west the small court mentioned by Dr Plumptre, extended up to the cloister, overlapping the west side of the Cloister Court by about 25 feet. There can be little doubt that this is the new building (*novum edificium*) the erection of which was begun in 1564. In June of that year William Packet, Bursar, goes to Barrington to buy stone, of course clunch, and twenty-two loads are brought to Cambridge. In September the woodwork is charged for, and the ironwork at the end of that year and at the beginning of the next. It therefore occupied only seven months in building.]

[1] [MS. History of Queens', p. 62. It is preserved in the President's Lodge.]
[2] [The design, which was much admired at the time, will be found in the Cambridge Guide for 1796.]

On the north side of the Principal Quadrangle is the "Walnut Tree Court." The building that forms the east side of it was erected during the Mastership of Dr Davenant (1614—22) [when the College

"was well paid, and grew in reputation very much; and because they wanted room to entertain the numbers that flocked to them, built that goodly Fabrick that contains many fair Lodgings both for Schollars and Fellows, towards *Kings* Colledge[1]"].

The erection of this building was already proceeding in 1617, when (15 November) the Master and Fellows agreed to employ a sum of one hundred pounds which had been given by John Josselyn, Fellow[2], about 1580, together with two hundred pounds derived from the sale of land at Babraham, towards erecting a new building "in the Friers," as the Carmelites' ground was still called in remembrance of the ancient neighbours of the College. [The accounts shew that the purchase of building-materials began in November 1616; and the date 1617, inscribed on the east front, probably denotes the year in which the first stone was laid. The final payment to the architects, dated 9 March, 1618, is signed by them, so that we learn that they were Gilbert Wigge and Henry Mann. The former had been employed upon the second court of S. John's College in 1602. Their work had probably been limited to the brickwork, for "the Plumbers bill for lead in ye new building 4*li*. 18*s*. 2*d*." is charged in September 1618; and that "to ye Mason for a thousand and halfe of tyles" in January 1619. From "a note of money laid out for ye Building," it appears that the total cost was £886. 9*s*. 0*d*. This is dated 20 January, 1619, so that the work had occupied rather less than two years.]

The building is a stack of brick chambers 106 feet in length, standing next to Queens' lane in prolongation of the east front of the College, and forming one side of the Walnut Tree Court. No contracts for it have been preserved. It was built originally in two stories, and a half story with small garrets above, as shewn in Loggan's print (fig. 3); and it had four chambers on a floor.

---

[1] [Life of Dr John Preston, by Tho. Ball; quoted by Mr Searle, p. 406.]

[2] [Comp. History of Corpus, i. 242. The following particulars are from Mr Searle, History, p. 436, the "Old Parchment Register," f. 8, and the "Magnum Journale."]

[3] [On 13 January, 1778, it was agreed "to sequester four Fellowships...towards rebuilding the Walnut-tree Court, the time and circumstances of the Building to be

Having suffered from a fire it was partially rebuilt between 1778 and 1782[3], upon which occasion the gablets were removed, and the upper story added. The present aspect of the building is due to a further repair in 1823, as the following order shews :

"17 January, 1823. Agreed that a new Roof be placed on the Building in the Walnut Tree Court, the walls repaired, and an embattled parapet be raised on each side under the direction of Mr Woods, Clerk of the Works of Downing."

[There was originally a dial on this building, no doubt on the side next to the court[1]. It was probably removed when the parapet was made.]

Fig. 6. North-west corner of the President's Lodge, shewing the oriels, and part of the modern staircase.

left to future consideration and conveniency." On 12 January, 1780, two Fellowships were sequestered for the same purpose among others; and on 13 January, 1780, £1400 of a benefaction left by David Hughes, B.D., was applied "towards rebuilding the 12 Sets of Chambers in the Walnut-tree Court." Lastly, 8 January, 1782, it was agreed to sequester three Fellowships for the same purpose. It is therefore uncertain at what time the work was taken in hand. There is no reference to it in the Accounts, probably because the cost of it was defrayed out of special funds.]

¹ [Mag. Jour. 1624—25, f. 18 (June). "For the stoneworke ouer the Dyall in the new court x^s."]

CHAPTER IV.

HISTORY OF THE PRESIDENT'S LODGE.

THE Lodge now occupies the north and west sides of the Cloister Court (fig. 1). With the exception of the kitchen and some other offices on the ground-floor of the western building, it is wholly on the first and second floors. We will first describe the existing arrangements, by the help of the accompany-

Fig. 7. Part of the north side of the gallery of the President's Lodge, with the oriels of the north wing; taken from the garden.

ing plan of the first floor (fig. 5), on which the letters referred to will be found, unless it is otherwise stated ; and afterwards we will attempt to determine the dates of the different portions ; a task of no little difficulty.

At the south end of the western cloister a wide staircase (A, figs. 1 and 5) leads to an ante-chamber, now the servants' hall (D). Beyond this, separated from it by a passage, and a staircase leading to the garrets, is the Audit-room of the

College (E), used by the President as a dining-room, beyond which again is a sitting-room (F), terminating the western range. This room, and the room over it, have oriels facing north (fig. 6); and on the west side there is a small projecting building which supplies each with a closet. On the east side of this sitting-room is a small vestibule (K) leading to the gallery which extends along the north side of the court, and also to the head of the modern staircase (L). At the north-east corner of the gallery a door (M) leads into a room now used as the President's study (O), which occupies the first floor of a northern wing, with a semicircular oriel looking north (fig. 7). At the junction of this wing with the gallery, a turret-stair (N) leads down to the garden [which it enters through an exceedingly picturesque door, with a wooden door-case and pediment (fig. 8)][1].

At the east end of the gallery there is a second, but smaller, vestibule (P), out of which a flight of nine steps leads up to a room over the Combination Room, now used as a drawing-room (Q). At the south-west corner of this room there is a door (B) still retaining its ancient form and moldings, which formerly opened into a small passage leading to a spiral stair or vice which still exists in the oblong projection on the west side of the Hall (D, fig. 1), and originally gave access to the court below or to the bed-room above. This room, and the whole second floor, is now approached by the staircase the first flight of which leads to the drawing-room. [This staircase was evidently made after the turret in which it is enclosed, as shewn in the woodcut (fig. 9), representing its uppermost flight. The two main beams at the top have been cut through, and the steps constructed across the original windows. It is probable that when this was done the small room (R) was also contrived. The plan (fig. 5) shews that the space occupied by it and by the staircase was

---

[1] [This staircase is sometimes called "Kidman's staircase," from a tradition that Richard Kidman, who robbed several colleges of their plate, for which he was sentenced to transportation for life in 1801, had intended to rob Queens' College also. He entered the Lodge by this staircase, but it happened that the President, Dr Milner, was sitting up late in the gallery, reading. Kidman saw the reflexion of his lamp under the door, and did not venture to proceed. This story is given on the authority of the present President. Compare Cooper's Annals, iv. 470, and Gunning's Reminiscences, ii. 118, ed. 1855.]

originally part of the gallery. The floor over the gallery, study, and western sitting-room is wholly occupied by bedrooms.]

The College Statutes give no information respecting the residence of the President; but in early times it was doubtless limited to the great chamber over the College Parlour, with the bed-chamber above[1]. The first of these, before the present partition (*ab*), forming the east end of the modern drawing-room, was set up, was of the same size as the Combination Room below. At the north-west corner there was probably a small study in the turret, of which the lower portion still exists (C, fig. 1), and is used as a closet; but the upper part was destroyed to make way for the gallery. A door in the east wall (S), still used, gave access to the Library, and through it to the Chapel; and the turret-staircase at the south-west corner (B), to the Hall[2]. It will be readily seen that this situation was admirably adapted for the convenience of the President, who was thus enabled to survey the whole College, or to approach any one of the principal buildings without crossing the court. His bed-chamber, equal in size to the room below, occupied the north end of the hall-range, immediately under the roof. It is now subdivided by modern partitions, but retains its coeval windows, of two small lights, in the north gable[3].

We will now return to the western building. This, the exterior of which was described in the last chapter, was probably appropriated to the use of the President in the reign of Henry the Eighth[4]. The whole of the fittings and arrangements belong

---

[1] [Mag. Jour. 1495—96, f. 100. "Item pro reparacione trium fenestrarum in inferiori camera magistri presidis et j fenestre in camera eius vj s. vj d." The lower room was used as a bedroom also: Ibid. 1528—29, f. 112. "Item pro funiculis lecti presidentis qui est in eius cubiculo inferiori vocat' li parler xviij d."]

[2] The course of the steps, which are of wood, has been altered, and access to the landing cut off, so that the vice leads continuously up to the roof, and the chamber door (B, fig. 5) opens into a small side-room.

[3] [Mag. Jour. 1515—16, f. 287. "Item pro factura fenestrarum in camera magistri, in superiori cubiculo, scilicet latyswyndows, continent' in longitudine xij pedes, precium pedis ij d. ob: ij^s. vj^d."]

[4] [The rooms at the north corner of the western building are certainly referred to in the following extract from the Magnum Journale: 1538—39, f. 47 b. "Item Joanni Grays pro resartione tegulaturæ illius partis Cubiculi magistri nostri que aquis est propria per 6 dies iij s. vj d." The older room is distinguished as follows in an extract referring to one of the small windows in the staircase leading up to it from the court: Ibid. 1551—52, f. 202 b. "Item pro pede noui vitri ad fenestrellam in gradibus qui ducunt ad cubiculum magistri super conclave viij d."]

Fig. 8. Door leading into the garden of the President's Lodge.

Fig. 9. Upper portion of the staircase leading to the President's original bed-chamber
from the vestibule (P) at the east end of the gallery.

to the period of Elizabeth or James the First; and that the present distribution of the apartments is the result of alteration, is plainly shewn by the molded beams of the ceilings, and by the windows; for the spacing of these members of the original structure runs counter to the actual distribution of the rooms and passages in several instances.   It is greatly to be regretted

Fig. 10.   Portion of the Chimney-piece in the Audit-Room, now
the President's dining-room.

that no distinct record of this change can be found in the College books, for this suite of apartments is an exceedingly valuable specimen of the domestic architecture of its period, and of the Cambridge Master's Lodge especially[1].

[1] The form of the beam which crosses the Audit-Room shews that a partition stood under it, and once divided this room, conjointly with its southern passage, into

[It is probable that some room in this building may have been originally the public reception-room of the College, referred to simply as the "large room" (*magna camera*), and afterwards as the "queen's room" (*camera regine*), for the two apartments seem to be the same. In 1500—01, we meet with an interesting enumeration of the principal offices of the College, in a payment for repairs to the windows. They are set down in the following order, "hall, chambers of the President, chapel, parlour, queen's room, library." This list shews that the room in question did not then form part of the Lodge. In 1505—6 the "queen's room" is prepared for an expected visit of Henry the Seventh ; in 1519 the "large room" for Queen Catherine of Aragon ; and in the following year for Cardinal Wolsey, who spent several days in the College[1]. The "Queen's kitchen" is mentioned in 1523—24, and occasionally in subsequent years. In 1691 the Queen's room had apparently become part of the Lodge, for after a payment for four pieces of tapestry hangings "for ye great room in ye Lodgeings," we find "for a bed for ye Queen's chamber £36. 7. 0." No hint of the position of these rooms is given. Before the gallery on the north side of the court was built, the western building would be approached by the hexagonal stair-turret at the north-east angle of the range (fig. 3), the ground-plan of which has been laid down from conjecture on the plan (fig. 1); and the recess in the sitting-room (C, fig. 5) most likely represents the door through which the whole suite was then entered, the staircase at the opposite end (A) having probably been made when the rooms were subdivided as at present, and annexed to the Lodge.]

The ante-chamber (D), which has a modern plaster ceiling, is now lined with the rich panelling originally put up in the Hall in 1531, whence it was removed in 1734. The audit-

---

two equal chambers. The junction of the woodwork of the Audit-Room with the window in the passage (H, fig. 5) is a further proof of these changes.

[1] [Mag. Jour. 1500—01, f. 147. "Item ... pro reparacione diuersarum fenestrarum in aula, in cameris M' presidentis, et in capella, parlorio, camera Regine, libraria, et in diuersis aliis locis collegii : in grosso iij s. iiij d." 1505—6, f. 186. "Item fabro pro clausura fenestrarum vitrearum in Camera regine erga aduentum domini Regis iij s :" 1519—20, f. 21. "Item—laborantibus circa preparacionem magne camere per sex dies erga aduentum Regine iiij s." Ibid. f. 22. "Item ... pro opere ij dierum circa albefaccionem magne camere erga aduentum D. Cardinalis xij d."]

room (E) is a beautiful specimen of Jacobean panelling in oak, unpainted[1], and in excellent preservation, with a rich chimney-piece, of which a portion is here figured (fig. 10). [The western window was made in 1711, the stonework being paid for by the College, the glass and woodwork by the President, Dr James[2].] The sitting-room beyond (F), has panel-work in a plainer style [and of an earlier date. This panelwork was originally carried right round the south and east walls, and a low door admitted to the audit-room. When however the present communication (G) was made, a portion of this panelling was set at right angles to the walls, so as to provide a way from the vestibule (K) into the audit-room, without passing through the other room. The original small door is still to be seen in the panelling (c). The doors at H, I are modern, and were no doubt put in when this change was made. It was probably part of the work done in 1791—93, when the present staircase (L) was built[3].] The staircase (A) in the western cloister is now disused as a main entrance to the Lodge, which is entered through a door at the north end of that ambulatory (B, fig. 1).

We now come to the gallery, the most beautiful specimen of that class of room remaining in the University. It rests upon the walls of the north cloister, as the section (fig. 11) shews, and overhangs it about two feet on each side. It is supported by a series of ornamental brackets or consoles (fig. 12), the disposition of which with reference to the arches of the cloister shews that the cloister and gallery were built independently. The gallery is eighty feet long, twelve feet broad, and nine feet high, built wholly of wood, as are also the two vestibules (K, P), and the staircase (N). It has one

---

[1] [It had however once been painted; Mag. Jour. 1634—35, f. 61 b: "For painting the Audit Chamber 1. 13. 0." The paint was removed in consequence of the following order: "29 May, 1822. Agreed and ordered that the Paint be taken off and the Oak Wainscot restored in the Audit Room." This was part of a complete new furnishing of the Lodge, for on the same day it was further ordered "that the Lodge be furnished according to the Master's Discretion," and in September, 1823, we find "Elliott Smith's Bill for Furniture for the Lodge £475. 0. 0."]

[2] [MSS. Cole. Add. MSS. Mus. Brit. 5858, p. 309.]

[3] [College Order, 10 June, 1789. "Agreed that a new Stair Case be built in, and new Entrance made into, the Lodge according to the Plan proposed by Mr Carter." The first payments were made in 1791—92, and in 1792—93 Mr Carter received £10. 10s. "for Surveying Lodge Stair Case." The total cost was £210.]

large and two small oriels on the side next to the court, and
the same number on the north side. It will be observed that
the latter are not opposite to the former. The large oriel
next the court, and those that light the two vestibules, all of
which are carried up as high as the roof, are supported on
pillars of wood. Originally, as Loggan shews (fig. 13), these
were single shafts, as that in the north-west angle is still;
but the central oriel is now supported on two square wooden
piers (fig. 12), probably for the sake of additional security.

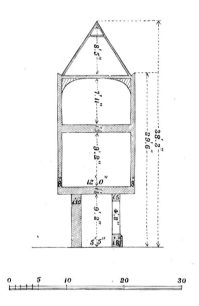

Fig. 11. Vertical section of the Gallery of the President's Lodge.

The gallery (fig. 14) has a flat ceiling of plaster, but its sides
are richly panelled and ornamented with fluted and carved
pilasters, with lions-head masks in the cornice above them.
The study has similar pilasters and panels. The gallery has
been wonderfully well preserved[1]; the length has been diminished by about three feet at the west end in order to make
room for the modern staircase; but otherwise it has been

[1] [The panelwork was once concealed by white paint, which was removed by the
present President immediately after his election in 1857.]

scarcely changed, and even the fire-place (S), on the north side, which has a four-centred stone arch with a panelled chimney-piece above, has not received the common addition of a mantle-shelf.   The fireplace in the study may have been of a similar character, but there the chimney-piece has been cut and patched, and the panelling altered in many places.

Fig. 12.   South side of the President's Lodge.

The story above the gallery, eight feet high, is divided into chambers.   Those at the east end retain some ancient panelwork that may be original, besides some of the original braces of the roof (fig. 11).   There is a fireplace of stone exactly similar in design to the one below, with a panelled and carved chimney-piece. · Besides these there are some very curious specimens of early wainscot, with ancient doors, removed from elsewhere, and also a transverse partition with "linen" panelling like that in the ante-chamber (D) below, probably part of the woodwork transferred from the Hall. The room over the study also is wainscoted with "coachmold" panels.

As originally constructed, the oriel in the centre on the court side, and those in the vestibules at each end of the gallery, were carried above the roof in the form of turrets, surmounted by a receding story, a conical roof, and lofty vanes of rich ironwork. The two intermediate oriels were carried up only as far as the eaves, and had gables above. The semicircular oriel in the President's study still preserves the semi-domical capping (fig. 7), so often seen in Jacobean houses[1], but the others have been cut down to the level of the eaves (fig. 12). [The original aspect of the whole Lodge, as shewn by Loggan, is here given on an enlarged scale (fig. 13), in order to supply the fullest evidence available for a comparison of the ancient with the modern appearance of this most interesting house. Besides the changes noticed above, it should be observed that the oriels in the vestibules had originally windows on the first and second floors closely resembling those of the central oriel; these have been replaced by a single sash-window (figs. 9, 12). Sash-windows have also been introduced into the upper floor above the intermediate oriels, and elsewhere.]

The garden side of the gallery, or rather of the cloister beneath, is covered by a low range of offices built at the College expense in the summer of 1761, in lieu of some taken down to make room for the new building in the Pump Court[2].

There are several entries in the accounts which shew that a gallery of some kind for the master existed before the present one. [A gallery is first mentioned in July 1510, in a payment for cleaning "the president's chamber, the gallery, and the queen's chamber;" and it is again mentioned in another in

---

[1] John Thorpe's designs for wooden houses shew somewhat similar terminations. [This study was called "The Essex Chamber" in the seventeenth century, and the arms of the Earl of Essex, in stained glass of the time, are in the window.]

[2] [Dr Plumptre's MS., p. 73. College Order, 11 March, 1761.]

the same year for repairing " the cloister, the gallery, and the master's room," which shews that it could not then have been in building.   Again, in 1511—12, we find a payment 'for rushes laid down in the chamber and gallery[1].'   This gallery, however, was certainly not the present one, for in 1515—16 the lead roof of the north cloister is repaired[2].

In 1532—33 there are a number of entries having reference to the Lodge. In January 1533 the tiled roof of the " President's chapel is repaired ;" in the following month the lead roof of his gallery (*deambulatorium*) is either made for the first time or repaired, probably the latter; new hangings are bought for his parlour (*conclaue*); and in July work is done to the spouts over his library.   In May his gallery is wainscoted, and a carpenter does work to the windows.   In July his bed-chamber (*cubiculum*) is wainscoted, and in the same month the purchase of a quantity of lead, timber, brick, lime, lath, and "eves-bord" 's recorded.   In the following year the plaster-work of his bed-room and gallery is repaired[3].

---

[1] [Mag. Jour. 1509—10, f. 225, "Item eidem Jacobo in septimana sancti Jacobi per quinque dies in mundacione camere magistri presidentis, et le galere, et cameram Regine xx d." "Item Henrico Smyth per quinque dies pro Reparacione Claustri et le galere et camere magistri ... ij s. jd." Ibid. 1511—12, f. 245 b. "Pro cirpis expositis in camera et galery ij s. ix d."]

[2] [Ibid. 1515—16, f. 213. "Item eidem [thome curle plumbario] pro xxxj libris et tribus quartis de ly sowdre et ferriminacione earundem in tegmine turris [the great gate] et super plumbum claustri in parte boreali xiij s. viij d."]

[3] [Ibid. 1532—33, f. 177 b. "Item xv⁰ Januarii Johanni Sawnders ly Tiler laboranti cum seruo suo per duos dies cum d' super sacellum presidentis xxiij d." "Item xviij⁰ Januarii henrico plummer in parte solucionis pro ly casting of ledde pro deambulatorio presidentis xij d." f. 178 b. "Item 15⁰ Februarii henrico plummer in plena solucione pro ly leddis super deambulatorium presidentis. xxxiij s. iiij d. Item pro ligno consumpto tempore quo reparabatur deambulatorium presidentis vij s. f. 179. Item solui pictori Warde pro depictione ly hangingis pro conclaui presidentis xx s. Item Thome Ferrer vehenti ly wanscotis a M⁰. Walter de lyne [King's Lynn] ad Collegium xij d." f. 179 b. "Item 4⁰. Maii Johanni Alway laboranti super Sylyng in deambulatorio presidentis per duos dies xij d." Further payments are entered extending over twelve days. f. 180. "Item xix⁰ Maii Roberto Joyner laboranti circa fenestras in deambulatorio presidentis per duos dies x d." f. 180 b. "Item xxiiij⁰ Julii henrico plummer laboranti...super canale quod est super librariam presidentis...vj s. viij d. Item 27⁰ Julii Johanni bonywall laboranti circa by Sylyng in cubiculo presidentis cum seruo suo per 4ᵒʳ dies iiij s." Ibid. 1533—34, f. 193. "Item 28⁰ Januarii Joanni tegulatori emendanti implastrationem cubiculi et ambulatorii presidentis per tres dies xviij d."]

In 1537, when a certain wall was purchased from the Carmelites, as mentioned in Chapter I., a clause was inserted in the

Fig. 13. General view of the President's Lodge, enlarged from Loggan.

document drawn up between the Convent and the College that may be thus translated :

"Moreover, whereas the President and Fellows of the aforesaid College have decided, and do now purpose, to make three or four windows, more or less, on the north side of a certain ambulatory called *ly Galari*, adjacent to the demesne of the aforesaid Carmelites ; we the aforesaid Prior and Convent undertake on behalf of ourselves and our successors, that neither we nor they will build or erect, or suffer to be built or erected, any wall or building that may impede, obstruct, divert, or keep off the light from the aforesaid windows[1]."

Fig. 14.   Interior of the Gallery of the President's Lodge, looking east.

The document is dated 12 February, and on the 15th a payment occurs "for three windows of hewn stone in the master's gallery, and for ironwork for the same ;" and in March following the glazier is paid "for thirty feet of glass in the President's new gallery," and the carpenters "for six new window-frames[2]." There are also payments for bricks and tiles, but

---

[1] [The original is printed in Mr Searle's History, p. 194.]

[2] [Mag. Jour. 1536—37, f. 23 a. "Item xv° Februario mr°. Cobb pro tribus fenestris erectis ex quadrato lapide in deambulatorio magistri et ferramentis omnibus ad easdem

their destination is not recorded. In 1542, two workmen are employed for four days "in mending the tiles on the master's gallery, and other places on the north side of the college[1]." In June, 1545, a brick wall is built round the Master's garden, which is described as part of the convent ground (*in fratribus*), and is therefore most probably his present garden; and a mason is paid "for six days' work on the steps that go down from the master's bedroom to his garden[2]." This entry no doubt refers to the turret which at that time existed at the west end of the gallery, from the employment of a mason; and the words "in fratribus" very likely denote the conveyance of stone from the convent; but in 1546, "the door at the head of the stairs in the master's gallery[3]" may possibly refer to the staircase of wood (N), that also goes down to the garden. In 1560, immediately after the election of Dr John Stokes (President 1560—1568), numerous entries occur for "constructing the master's upper chambers[4]." We meet with the purchase of studdes, planks, and beams; but as there are no payments to tilers or plumbers, the work could not have included any change in the roof, and therefore was probably nothing more than a rearrangement of part of the upper story.

This is the last extract referring to the Lodge which appears to imply a new construction, or an extensive alteration of existing rooms. In subsequent years we meet only with charges for small alterations, or for new furniture. With regard to the panelwork in the audit-room and gallery, we find no charges sufficiently extensive during the period when, from its marked

---

liij s. iiij d. Item (ultimo Martii) Rogerio Yownge vitriario pro triginta pedibus vitri in nouo presidentis deambulatorio xij s. vjd. Item Lamberto pro sex ligneis fabricis in fenestris nouis in deambulatorio magistri vj s."]

[1] [Ibid. 1541—42, f. 86 b. "Item 8° Aprilis edoardo greene et Johanni gybson pro 4ᵒʳ dierum opera in resartiendis tegulis deambulatorii magistri et aliis locis in boreali parte collegii iij s. iiij d."]

[2] [Ibid. 1544—45, f. 117 b. "Item eodem tempore accepit Andreas bannocke mason pro opere vj dierum in fratribus circa gradus qui descendunt a cubiculo magistri in hortum eiusdem vj s." The account for the wall is too long for quotation.]

[3] [Ibid. 1545—46, f. 130. "Item Nicholao Ott pro duobus pessulis ad ostium supra gradus in ambulatorio magistri."]

[4] [Ibid. 1559—60, f. 271. [August] "Item Matheo Bruer pro. 13. le studdes ad ædificanda superiora cubicula magistri 8. ped' long' vj s. vj d." This is the first entry referring to the work.]

style, it must have been put up, to be referred to it. We are
therefore left to conclude, from the evidence afforded by the
style, that it is that mentioned in the will of Dr Humphrey
Tindall (President 1579—1614) ; and, from the terms employed,
the cost appears to have been defrayed partly by subscription,
partly by donations, which will explain the absence of all allusion to it in the Bursar's accounts :

> "Item I give to the president and Fellows of Queens college in
> Cambridge to my successors use all the seeling and wainscoting of
> my chambers and lodging I have which (I take) amounteth to two
> hundred and fifty pounds or thereabouts more than I have received from
> the college or any other benefactors towards the same[1]."

The conclusion to which the extracts we have collected leads
is that the present gallery was erected at some period between
1516 and 1541, but probably not before 1537. The absence
of any direct allusion to the work in the accounts is no doubt
remarkable ; but it should be borne in mind that it was the
custom at that period to buy building materials from year to
year, some of the payments for which we have noticed, and lay
them up to season. When wanted for use, they were put together by daywork ; and the wages of the men employed do
not amount to a large sum. It is possible, too, in this instance,
that some of the materials obtained from the Carmelite convent may have been made use of; and in fact we find that in
February, 1537, twelve waggon-loads of wood and a thousand
tiles[2] were bought from the brethren before the convent was
suppressed. After the suppression the supply would of course
be far greater, and the College, having paid only £20 for the
whole of the conventual buildings, could afford to keep a
quantity of the materials for use at home.

It remains for us to attempt to determine the position of the
gallery referred to previous to 1516. We may be sure that
in this college, as in others, the Master's gallery would be close
to his Lodge ; and, as it has been proved that it was not over
the north cloister, a glance at the plan (fig. 1) will shew that
the only possible place for it was on the ground where the

---

[1] [Mr Searle's History, p. 363.]

[2] [Mag. Jour. 1536—37, f. 27. "Item xxij° Februarii pro vectura xij plaustrorum
ruderum et mille tegularum que emebantur a Carmelitis xxij d."]

President's study now is (*a b c d*, fig. 1). An examination of
the lower part of this building shews that the west side (*a b*)
rests on an ancient wall about two feet thick, built of large
blocks of clunch. The north wall has been so much altered
that its original construction cannot be ascertained. The east
wall is now of red brick, but is as thick as the west wall. Is it
not at least probable that we have in these walls the foundations
of the original gallery, and that the three windows of stone
made in 1537 were inserted in its north wall? If by stone
clunch is meant, these windows would soon require renewal;
and the oriel, which Professor Willis decides to be Jacobean,
and which probably belongs to the period of the panelwork,
may have been put in to replace them, and make this part of
the gallery uniform with the rest.]

CHAPTER V.

History of the Chapel, Hall, Combination Room, Library, etc.

CHAPEL. We have seen that the foundation-stone of the
Chapel was laid in 1448. On 12 December, 1454, a license
to celebrate divine worship in chapels and oratories within the
College, or the Hostel of S. Bernard belonging thereto, was
granted by William Gray, Bishop of Ely[1]. No record of a
consecration has been preserved, but that ceremony can scarcely
have been omitted, for Andrew Doket, the first President,
desired by his will[2] dated 2 November, 1484, "that his body
should be buried in the choir of the chapel, in the place where
the lessons are read."

The Chapel is 70 feet long including the antechapel, which
now occupies about 17 feet of the total length. It has three
windows on the south side and two on the north side. There

---

[1] [His license is printed by Mr Searle, p. 44.]

[2] [Printed by Mr Searle, p. 56. It must be remembered, however, that the earth
in graves was frequently consecrated, when the rest of the ground had not been
formally set apart for sacred uses.]

was originally a vestry on that side which projected northwards, like those of Christ's and S. John's, with the organ-chamber over it. [Its tiled roof and chimney are shewn by Loggan (fig. 3). The vestry has been added to the set of rooms on the ground floor of the building in the Walnut Tree Court which abuts against the Chapel, as the organ-chamber was added in 1744 to the set on the first floor. The following curious Order directed this latter alteration:

"12 November 1744. Agreed yᵗ yᵉ Gatekeeper's place should no longer be discharged by yᵉ Schollars, but yᵗ Richard Brooks and Thomas Barker should look after yᵉ Gates alternately; yᵗ yᵉ Income of yᵉ Gate-room should be pᵈ by yᵉ Bursar; yᵗ to supply yᵉ rent of 40 shs. per

Fig. 15.   Clunch window in the Chapel.

annum customarily paid from yᵉ Gate-room to yᵉ Bibleclerks, one pound should be charg'd to yᵉ rent of yᵉ Room next yᵉ Chapel up one pair of Stairs on yᵉ North side, in consideration of yᵉ Organ loft being added to it; and yᵗ yᵉ Room now Burton's should be allow'd for yᵉ other one pound.

At yᵉ same time yᵉ Fellows agreed, yᵗ in consideration of yᵉ Master's giving up yᵉ Organ Loft, yᵉ usual seat in Chappel for yᵉ Family in yᵉ Lodge, they would provide some other proper Seat whenever there was a Family in yᵉ Lodge which should have occasion for one."

The vestry-door may still be seen in the bed-room of the above-mentioned set of rooms (e, fig. 1), and the staircase leading to the organ-chamber was eastward of it. A square clunch window of good design (fig. 15) lighted the latter from the

Chapel. It was still in its old position in 1858, when, in order to preserve it, it was placed in the south wall near the altar. Loggan also shews the original east window, of five lights, and divided by a transom at about one-third of its height.]

The College records contain many curious entries relating to the fittings and furniture of the Chapel and its altars, with inventories of the ornaments and plate (*jocalia*), the first of which was made by order of Andrew Doket in 1472; but nothing relating to the architecture. [There was of course a high altar, and from a payment for repairs in 1507—8 it appears that there were at least two side-altars[1]. One of the windows on the north side contained a representation of S. Margaret and S. Bernard, which seems to have been given by the Lady Margery Roos before 1477; and another, but on which side is not mentioned, was called S. Paul's window[2].

The alterations in the Chapel, consequent on the accession of Edward the Sixth, were unusually gradual. The images were removed in 1547, and the walls whitewashed in May, 1548; but the altars were not pulled down until July, 1549, though a communion-table seems to have been made at a somewhat earlier date; and new service-books are not charged for before 1551—52[3]. In February, 1554, the three altars were set up again[4]; and in the following October and November the desks and organ were repaired, and a gilt cross bought. In June, 1559, a smith is paid "for taking downe ye highe aultare;" in

---

[1] [Mag. Jour. 1507—8, f. 201 b. "Hugoni Wydder carveyr in partem solucionis pro reparacionibus factis circa inferiora altaria vocat' syde alterse in capella vj^s. viij^d." [To the same] "pro waynscote et labore eius fact' circa vnum duorum altarium inferiorum ex parte senestra (*sic*) xx s."]

[2] [She desires by her will, dated 30 August, 1477, to be buried in the chapel "beatorum Margarete et Bernardi Cantebr' in choro ex parte boriali sub fenestra mea sanctorum predictorum." Mr Searle's History, p. 73. Mag. Jour. 1504—5, f. 177 b. "[Cornelio Glasyer] pro noua plumbacione vj pedum Fenestræ sancti Pauli."]

[3] [Ibid. 1547—48, f. 155. "Item 6 maii [1548] pro dealbacione murorum in sacello 4 diebus ij s. viij d." f. 157. "Item 22 octobris [1547] georgio smythe pro labore suo in sacello quum Imagines et tabula auferebantur vij d." 1548—49, f. 163 b. "Item dowseo et 2. filiis pro confectione mense in sacello ij s. iiij. d." f. 169 [July, 1549]. "Item…demolientibus altaria et resartientibus loca vbi erant ij s. iij d." 1551—52, f. 208 b. "Item pro .2. libris communionis x s."]

[4] [Ibid. 1553—54, f. 220 [February]. The same workmen are paid "pro fabricatione altaris et erectione theatri xj s. iij d."; and in April (f. 221) "pro fabricatione .3. altarium iij^s."]

July a communion-table is once more purchased; and between
Michaelmas and the end of the year the other altars were
finally removed and their places occupied by desks[1].   The
organ was not taken away until January, 1570[2].   In 1573 new
seats were made[3], and in 1599 a door and cover for the pulpit,
the mention of which additions shews that a pulpit was there
already.   In 1631—32 a "Reparation of the Chappell" took
place, but no particulars are given.   From the cost however it
was evidently of considerable extent[4].

The notorious William Dowsing has left the following record
of his proceedings in 1643:

> "At Queens College, *Decemb.* 26.
> We beat down a 110 superstitious pictures besides Cherubims and
> Ingravings, where none of the fellows would put on their Hatts in all the
> time they were in the Chapell, and we digged up the Steps for three
> hours and brake down 10 or 12 Apostles and Saints within the hall."

These ravages were repaired immediately after the Restoration, but apparently entirely by private munificence, as no
mention of work done to the Chapel occurs in the accounts.   The
principal donations are recorded as follows by Dr Plumptre.
The date of the first is 1661, which shews that a restoration of
the east end was then in progress:

> "Mr Henry Coke of Thorington in Suffolk Son of Sir Edw'd Coke
> gave to his antient and intimate Friend Dr Martin [President] (1661)
> the Cedar with which the East end of the Chapel was wainscoted, till
> the refitting the whole in the years 1774 and 1775.
> Mr Charles Smith gave in 1673 (having then lately vacated his
> Fell'p) the Velvet covering of the Communion table.   In the same year
> Sir Henry Pickering gave the Velvet Cushions for it.   Mr Catlin
> Fellow of the College gave the covering of a Desk at which the Litany
> us'd to be sung or said[5]."

---

[1] [Mag. Jour. 1558—59, 1559—60, f. 265.   "Item Roberto Belle fabro lignario
pro opera 6 dierum in capella Collegii diruenti altaria in inferiori parte, et erigenti
ibidem pluteos, et efficienti in postico vectes et januam v. s."]

[2] [Ibid. 1569—70, f. 75 b (January).   "Item to Thomas yᵉ virginall maker for
taking down thorgans iij s. iiij d."]

[3] [Ibid. 1572—73 (April), f. 94.   "Item for waynscotte in the chappell and ye
removeinge the olde seates xxxviij s. viij d."]

[4] [The total spent was £88. 0s. 2d., of which "Ashly the joyner" received
£31. 6s. 4d.]

[5] Dr Plumptre notes: "At the new fitting up of the Chapel, these and the Velvet
covering were given to St Botolph's Church [where part is still preserved as the altar-
frontal].   The Litany Desk has been annihilated some years past."

Soon afterwards, in 1678—79, the celebrated Thamar[1] was employed to repair the organ; and in 1710 an entirely new instrument was bought, but the maker's name is not recorded[2].] The appearance of the Chapel after these various changes has been preserved by Cole. His original description is dated 22 February, 1742, but in 1768 and 1773 he made notes of the works that were proceeding, which are subjoined:

"Come we now to the Chapel, wch as I said before, takes up ye better half of ye S. side of ye 1st Quadrangle, and has a Tower at ye W. end of it: ye Altar is rail'd round and stands on an Eminence of 3 Steps, and is intirely covered with Crimson Velvet wth a gold Fringe at all ye joynings of it: in ye Front of it in a Glory is I. H. S., finely wrought with gold; on an Eminence on ye Altar ag^st ye Wall is placed an handsom silver gilt Bason, wth two large Candlesticks of ye same sort, and on y^m is wrote at ye bottom: *Deo et Sacris Reginalibus Cantabr: Edw: Martin Presid:* on ye Bason ye same except ye Presidents name. . . .

The upper end of ye Chapel is entirely wainscoted wth Cedar, from ye Pulpit, wch is a small one of old workmanship and stands in an Arch of ye S. Wall, on one side, and from ye Vestry Door wch exactly fronts ye Pulpit, on ye other side. Over this Door stands ye Organ Loft supported by two Iron Pillars in ye Chapel; and ye Organ, wch is a very handsome one, stands sideways in ye N. Wall of ye Chapel and has a way up to it by ye Vestry. The Chapel is furnished on both sides with 2 Ranges of Stalls and wainscoted in ye old manner, but very neatly: ye Roof is arch'd and wainscoted, and finely gilt and painted. There are more Monuments in this Chapel than one w^d have expected to have met with considering ye Bigness of it, some of which are very curious ones and of good Antiquity. . . .

[The Chapel] is divided from ye Anti Chapel as all other College Chapels are, viz.: by a Screen ag^st wch ye Master or President's Stall is plac'd on ye S. Side and ye Vice-Presidents on ye North: you ascend 2 steps into ye Choir out of ye Antichapel in wch lie some Grave-stones of Antiquity. . . .

Going into this Chapel July 2, 1768, I observed all the Brass of Dr Stokes's Monument reaved, as to his Portrait, except a small Peice of the upper Part of the Face and Cap.[3] . . .

Under the North Wall, and on the steps going up to the Altar, and exactly under the Organ Loft, which used to be supported by 2 Iron

[1] [Compare History of King's College, i. 519.]

[2] [Mag. Jour. 1709—10 (September, 1710). "Charges about making an intire new Organ in ye Chappell £164. 06. 10½."]

[3] [Dr John Stokes was President 1560—68. Mr Searle says, p. 298, "His monument, a stone with his effigy habited as a doctor, an inscription beneath his feet, and a marginal inscription, all on brass plates, was formerly at the east end of the chapel; since the alterations of 1777 it has lain in the antechapel. The lower half of the figure was torn away in Cole's time; it is now quite gone."]

Pillars, now removed, is erected a square large modern Pew for the Master's Family, which comes in by the Vestry Door; so that the Organ is taken away, and the Gallery of it stopt up, and this modern Pew, I hope the only one of the sort in the University, much in the Way up to the Altar and quite disfigures the Uniformity of the Room.

[Tuesday 30 March 1773.] The Chapel in the Spring of 1773 was entirely taken to Peices and new modelled, tho' it seemed to want it very little; every old and modern Tomb Stone being taken up from the Floor, the Altar Peice taken away, with the Stalls and the blew coved Ceiling taking down in order to refit it entirely....In the middle was sunk a square vault . . . in the finest Bed of Gravel I ever saw. A few leaden Coffins were lit upon, but for whom, I believe, is not certainly known. The Ceiling being altered from a Cove to a flat one, the East Window was forced to be lowered. All the Monuments and Stones were taken away and those on the Walls put in different Positions to answer one another. The West End was enlarged[1] and a curious painted Room above the Entrance into it, converted into a Gallery for the Master's Family. [In this room] when the Wainscote was pulled down, they found the Sides all covered with Coats of Arms on the Wall in Water Colours, as I apprehend, for I did not much observe them, being the Arms of all the Sees in England and of all the Colleges in both Universities, except Sidney College. Emmanuel was there: so I suppose it was painted between the years 1584 and 1596.[2]"

[Cole's notice of the alteration of 1773—75 may well be supplemented by the series of College Orders that sanctioned it:

"23 Dec. 1772. Agreed to fit up the inside of the Chapel anew according to the Plan given in by M[r] Essex; to make a Gallery for the Master's family out of part of the rooms late M[r] Thwaites's, and to take the remaining part into the Library; that M[r] Essex be appointed Surveyor of the work at the Salary of 5 p[r] Cent on what is laid out on it, and that the Chapel be shut up at Lady day next in order to begin the work.

22 February 1773. Agreed to have the room over the Butteries fitted up to be us'd as a Chapel while the Chapel is shut up for refitting.

16 Mar. 1773. Agreed in refitting the Chapel to make a vault under it for burying in—to fit up the Antichapel with the Cedar wainscot that is now about the Communion table—that the Pew now us'd for the Master's family be set up in S[t] Botolph's Chancel opposite to that now there—and that the Room which was formerly the Vestry be again us'd as such.

12 Apr. 1773. Agreed that the new Pavement of the Chapel be of Ketton Stone with black dotts.

[1] [About three feet was gained by setting back the screen. In 1858 some of the coats of arms mentioned by Cole were found on the wall within the chapel. The gallery for the use of the President was entirely open until 1858. It was then closed, the central part only being left open, and fitted with oak framework of suitable design.]

[2] [MSS. Cole, ii. 13—18. Add. MSS. Mus. Brit. 5803.]

5 July 1774. Agreed to new pave the Chapel passage with York-shire Stone...And to wash the plain parts of the Cieling and Walls in the Chapel a Naples yellow.

16 Jan. 1775. Agreed that the Area of the Communion table in the Chapel be inclos'd with wooden palisades in imitation of iron with a Mahogany rail upon them. To change away the Candlesticks belonging to the Communion table and the flaggons; to have new Pattens for the bread and a new bason for collecting the Alms, all of Silver Gilt, and the present two Cups new gilt. That the furniture of the Communion table be entirely new, and that the old furniture be given to St Botolph's parish.

1 May 1775. Agreed to open the Chapel on friday the eighth Instant. To have an Entertainment on the occasion not exceeding £2. 10s. at the Fellows table besides the Commons, and 5s. per Mess at the Scholars table besides their Commons; and to give five Guineas among the Workmen that have work'd at it."

These arrangements remained until 1845, when the plaster ceiling was removed, and a new roof of oak constructed, in exact imitation of the old one, the beams of which were found to be much shrunken and out of repair. The original colouring was imitated as closely as possible. Between 1846 and 1848[1] the east window was restored and filled with stained glass by Mr Barnett of York, the cost being defrayed by a subscription of members of the College. Notwithstanding these improvements, however, the Chapel could be described as "still a miserable place;" and in 1858 the complete reconstruction of the interior was entrusted to Mr Bodley, architect, and completed in 1861. A set of rooms on the ground floor at the south-east corner was sacrificed to form an organ-chamber, which opens into the Chapel through a wide and lofty arch. The altar platform was raised on three steps, and by blocking about four feet of the east window, space was obtained for a reredos. This, and the rest of the decoration, may be described as follows[2]:

"The reredos consists of a heavy overhanging cornice, rather wider than the altar, and carved in a row of leaves in high relief. It is supported on stunted Romanesque shafts, of polished Galway marble, with suitable capitals and bases. The intervening space, above the altar, is quite flat,

[1] [College Order, 7 May, 1846. "Agreed that the East Window of the Chapel be restored under the direction of the Rev. Geo. Phillips, the Bursar, and the Dean." 12 January, 1848. "Agreed that the College make up the deficiency between the amount of money received and the actual cost of the erection, putting up, and completing the Window."]

[2] [This description is, in the main, given in the Ecclesiologist, Vol. XXIII. p. 17.]

with a panel sunk in it, the surface of which is inlaid with a large cross. The same style of decoration incrusts the east wall to the north and south of the altar and the north and south walls of the 'sacrarium.' The ground throughout is polished alabaster, inlaid with encaustic tiles, and marbles of various colours in patterns, while the foliage is most judiciously gilt. The pavement of the east end is of rich encaustic tiles; and there is a brass standard on either side of the altar.

The organ-case is thoroughly novel in design, and very good. It is simply a frame to carry the pipes, worked in an early, half Romanesque, style, with a seat beneath for the player. The pipes, of spotted metal, ascend one above the other, as they used to do in the old organs, from which the idea of this one has evidently been taken.

The old deal wood-work, of a very mean character, being found on examination to be rotten, was removed. The new is on the same plan, namely a row of stalls, returned across the west end, with a bench beneath them. In his design, Mr Bodley has blended together the Romanesque and Pointed styles very happily. The stalls are panelled in pointed arches with a circle sunk in the spandrils, in which a flower, or some other device, is painted, and the cornice above them is a suit of deeply cut moldings. In the lower part there is more Romanesque work; the open tracery between the stalls and the bench consists of Romanesque arches, and the details betray a similar origin."

The windows on the south side have been filled with stained glass by Hardman: the central one to the memory of Dr Joshua King, President (1832—57), by his widow, the other two by James Newton Goren, M.A., Fellow, in 1860 and 1879 respectively. The glass for the westernmost window on the north side was given by Thomas Beevor, M.A., Fellow, in 1849; that for the easternmost by subscription of members of the College, in 1850. The lectern, an eagle carved in oak, was given by Edward Ind Welldon, M.A., Fellow, in memory of Alfred Paul Jodrell Mills, M.A., Fellow.

We learn from several entries in the accounts for the sixteenth century, of which the most important are given below, that besides the public Chapel there were two private chapels or oratories, called the chapel of Mr Garret, and the chapel of Lady Roos respectively: but it is impossible to determine where they were situated, or to what use they were put[1].]

[1] [Mag. Jour. 1529—30, f. 126 b, "pro claue hostii Sacelli in quo Mʳ Garret divina celebrare solet." 1534—35, f. 208 b. "Item...in sartiendo pinnaculum eius muri qui includit sacellum magistri garet iiijˢ." f. 209. "Item xvjᵒ Augusti henrico plumbatori pro tegenda turri sacelli m' garret iijˢ. iiijᵈ." 1536—37, f. 22 b. "Item ...pro purgatione turrium super sacellum mʳⁱ garrad (sic) et Walteri et super aulam

HALL. [The foundation and the dimensions of the Hall have been already recorded. It has an oriel on the east side only. On the west side there is an original fireplace. At the north-west angle is a door (K, fig. 1) leading into a coeval building of red brick, which originally contained the staircase to the Master's chamber, but which is now used only as a passage to the Combination Room. There are two windows on the west side, one on each side of the fireplace, and two on the east side, south of the oriel. There was originally a third window on this side, north of the oriel, of two lights only, at a higher level than the others, as Loggan shews (fig. 3). It was probably blocked when the present panelling was put up.

The architecture of the Hall was respected until the last century, and therefore the accounts up to that time record payments for repairs only. There are however several interesting notices of fittings and furniture. In 1501—2, John Love, a painter, receives £4 for painting the canvas hangings; and in 1504—5 the further decoration of them with sentences or texts (*scriptura*) is mentioned. In this year a portion of them was sent to London to be repainted by a painter in Southwark, who received fourpence for his pains[1]. There was panelwork of some kind in the Hall at this time, but perhaps merely a crest of woodwork above the hangings[2]. In September 1531 however the decoration of it with the panelling that has since been removed to the Lodge began. This woodwork, about eight feet high, consisted, so far as we can judge, of "linen" panels surmounted by a frieze containing arms of benefactors in relief, alternating with grotesque heads richly carved, in the usual manner of that time. The illustration (fig. 16) shews a single compartment of the panelwork, with one of the coats of arms.

---

xij^d." 1548—49, f. 164 b. "Item plumbario pro resartione tecti sacelli domine le rose...viij^d."]

[1] [Mag. Jour. 1501.—2, f. 158. "Johanni love pictori pro coloribus et pro labore suo circa pannos pro ornament' aule Collegii iiij li. ijd." 1504—5, f. 177 b. "...pictori pro pictura et scriptura de ly borders in aula xiij^s iiij^d. Item Ade Bell pro sutura Anabatr' Aule collegii iijd. Item Roberto Sympson vectori pro veccione eiusdem Anabatr' londonias vt ibi pingeretur ac pro reveccione eiusdem Cantabrigiam ij^s." f. 179. "Pictori mamenti in Southwark qui pingebat anabatra aule in regardo iiijd."]

[2] [Ibid. 1511—12, f. 242 b, "pro glutino exposito in Aula super defectum ly Crest j d."]

The compartment next to it is precisely similar, with the exception that the arms are replaced by a head. The detailed payments for this woodwork, from the beginning to the end of the work, have fortunately been preserved in the "Magnum Journale," and form so curious a record that the account has been printed entire in the appendix. The first payments were made 30 September, 1531, and the last 10 September, 1532, so that the work occupied rather more than eleven months. The wood was fetched from Lynn, and sawn up on the spot. Two or three carpenters only were employed during each week, and they rarely worked for more than five days. The arms and the heads were executed by Giles Fambeler, a carver, and Dyrik Harrison. A painter named John Ward was employed upon the "skochyns," by which the tinctures of the coats of arms are possibly to be understood ; and towards the end of the work an Augustinian Friar is paid for painting the borders, by which the hangings put up before may perhaps be meant. Unfortunately very little is said in the account that can give

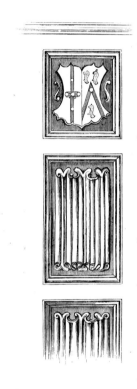

Fig. 16.   One compartment in the Hall.

any idea of the style of the work. So many yards of "antyk crest" and "antyk border" are paid for ; and from the mention of 25 columns to ornament the high table, and 64 for the sides of the Hall, it would appear that the plainness of the panel-work was originally relieved by some enrichment. The total cost of this work, as appears from the account above-mentioned,

was £50. 5s. 3½d. The screen was made in 1548, but doors
were not added to it until 1628[1].]

The Hall was new wainscoted and thoroughly Italianized, or
as the contemporary Dr Plumptre (President 1760—88) phrases
it, "fitted up in its present neat and elegant manner," in the
days of William Sedgwick (President 1731—60), under the
direction of Sir James Burrough, who introduced a flat ceiling
under the original open-timbered roof, with an Italian cornice,
and a lofty composition of wainscot over the high table consisting
of coupled Corinthian columns supporting an entablature and
pediment with side-panels in the same style; so that had not
the pointed windows been retained, the whole would have appeared uniform. The oriel remained intact, but the tracery-
heads of the lateral windows were removed[2]. The work was
begun in 1732, and concluded at the end of 1734, as the following order shews:

"January ye 15th 1734—35. Agreed that ye College should present
Mr Burroughs with 25 Guineas or some thing of yt Value in Consideration of his trouble in laying ye Plan for fitting up ye Hall and overseeing ye Execution of it.

Agreed at ye same time yt Mr Woodward ye Carver should be paid
ten Guineas he giving ye College a full Discharge."

The new woodwork had been put up by Essex[3], but his share
in the work is not specially commemorated. Cole, writing 22
February, 1742, thus describes the alterations:

"[The Hall] very lately was elegantly fitted up according to ye present tast and is now by much ye neatest Hall of any in ye University
being compleatly wainscoted and painted wth handsom fluted Pillars
behind ye Fellows Table at ye upper end of it over wch are neatly carved
ye Arms of ye Foundress: at ye lower end of it over ye two neat Iron
Doors of ye Screens wch front ye Butteries and Kitchin is a small Gallery
for Musick occasionally.[4]"

[The Music-gallery is entered by a door in the centre out
of the rooms immediately to the south of the Hall, over the

---

[1] [Mag. Jour. 1547—8, f. 153 b. "Item 2 Martii Roberto Rychardson pro 8
le waynscot ad le skrene. xvj.d." Ibid. 1627—28, f. 30 b. "Joyner's bill for the
Hall doores 1. 18. 3."]

[2] [There is an engraving of the interior in this state in Le Keux, i. 249.]

[3] [The payments to him are "for wainscotting the Hall."]

[4] [MSS. Cole, ii. 12. Add. MSS. Mus. Brit. 5803.]

Buttery. These were altered, probably for this purpose, in 1779[1].
In 1780, doors were added to the screen[2].

The three pictures over the dais, representing Queen Elizabeth Woodville, Erasmus, and Sir Thomas Smith, by Hudson,
were given in 1766 by the three sons of Harry, fourth Earl of
Stamford. They are works of that period.

Between 1819 and 1822 the oriel was "ornamented with the
arms of the foundresses, masters, and other distinguished personages of the college, beautifully blazoned and stained in glass
by the late Charles Muss, enamel painter to the King[3];" and in
1846 the ceiling was removed and the roof restored to view
under the direction of Mr Dawkes, architect, who unfortunately
thought proper to construct a louvre[4], for which there was no
authority, and which the presence of an original fireplace shews
to have been unnecessary. The ceiling had been attached to
the tiebeams, which were uninjured, but the braces had been
cut away. These were replaced, and the lateral windows, which
were then subdivided into three lights by plain mullions without
tracery, were fitted with new stonework and tracery, at the
expense of Robert Moon, M.A., Fellow[5]. In 1854 the oriel
was restored and filled with stained glass by Hardman by the
same benefactor[6], the older glass being removed to the Audit
Room, and the Gallery of the Lodge. By that time Mr Moon
had become dissatisfied with the tracery which Mr Dawkes had

---

[1] [College Order, 4 January, 1779. "Agreed that the Set of Rooms over the
Butteries be alter'd according to the Plan given in by Mr Essex; and that the principal
Room be wainscoted, and the other Rooms wainscoted Chair high."]

[2] [College Order, 1 November, 1780.]

[3] [Cambridge Guide, 1830. Mag. Jour. 1818—19. "To Mr Muss on Acct of
Painted Glass £50. 0. 0." 1820—21. "Paid Mr Muss for Painted Glass £202. 5. 0."
On 7 June, 1822, it was "Agreed and ordered that the Oriel Window in the Hall be
completed by Mr Muss according to his Plan," and in that year £202. 5. 0 was paid
to him. This marks the conclusion of the work, which had therefore cost £454. 10. 0.]

[4] [The charges for repairs to the louvre which occur frequently in the "Magnum
Journale" refer to the turret over the screens (fig. 3) which contained a bell.]

[5] [College Order, 14 January, 1847. "Agreed to present the thanks of the Society
to Mr Moon for his handsome donation to the ornamental repairs of the hall." A view
of the west side of the Hall by Le Keux shews the windows subdivided into three
lights by two plain mullions, but devoid of tracery.]

[6] [Ibid. 15 November, 1854. "Agreed that the thanks of the Society be presented
to Mr Moon for his liberality in restoring the bay-window of our Hall, and in filling
the same with stained glass."]

inserted in the lateral windows, and obtained leave to replace it by the present tracery, designed by Mr Johnson, architect, and to raise the windows themselves to their present height. He further filled them with stained glass by Hardman. In 1861 the classical fireplace was taken down, and the original opening, a four-centered arch, discovered behind it. Mr Moon then gave the beautiful decorative achievements above it, worked in alabaster and encaustic tiles, from a design by Mr Bodley, whom he further employed at the same time to lay down the floor in tiles and stonework. In 1875 the same architect was employed for the woodwork that surmounts the fireplace, and for the decoration of the whole Hall, the cost of which was defrayed by William Magan Campion, D.D., and George Pirie, M.A., Fellows.

Over the door leading into the screens are the arms of the College carved on a stone shield, set within an ornamental framework consisting of a bracket on which rest two pillars supporting a pediment (fig. 3). This composition was first set up in June, 1575. The following entries [1] illustrate the work:

"Item of free stone to grave the colledge armes on iiij*s*.

Item to Thomas Graye for makyng pillars to the colledg armes thirtene dayes xiij*s*.

Item his man twelve dayes x*s*.

Item to Theodore for gravyng the colledg armes and lyeng on the colors l.*s*.

Item to the same Theodore for gravyng the pillars, gildyng and castyng on there colors xlv*s*.

Item for cariag of the stones belonging to the armes viij*d*."

The arms and their surroundings have been frequently repainted in subsequent years, but without alteration.]

COMBINATION ROOM. The situation of this room has been already described. The pointed windows that still remain unaltered in the upper gable shew that it was built soon after the foundation of the College; but, as explained in the third chapter, it is evident that it was not part of the first buildings. [Like the range on the west side of the Cloister Court, there is no evidence to shew when it was built. A parlour (*parloria*) is

---

[1] [Mag. Jour. 1574—75, f. 108 b, f. 109.]

mentioned in the accounts for 1493—94[1], and in subsequent years a room, evidently the present one, is frequently alluded to. In 1531—32 a repair to the walls is mentioned, which shews that the room could not even then have been new[2]; and in 1533 it was wainscoted by one of the workmen who had previously been employed upon the Hall. A repair done to the hangings in this year is an additional proof that it must have been in existence for some years[3]. In August, 1545, one at least of the windows was glazed with Normandy glass[4]. In the same year further payments occur for woodwork, possibly a chimney-piece, and in 1548 the hearth was laid down in stone[5].

The present panelling was put up in 1686 by Austin, whose work at Clare Hall and King's College we have already noticed. The cost was defrayed out of a donation of £100 given by Anthony Sparrow, D.D., President (1662—67), and afterwards Bishop of Exeter, "for wainscoting and adorning the Combination-Room." The residue of the money was spent in providing chairs and cushions[6].] It was at this time, immediately after the Restoration, that the windows with the cross mullions were inserted in the walls, for they are exactly the same as those of Sir Christopher Wren's vestry at Emmanuel, begun in 1668. [The stained glass in the central window, representing

---

[1] [Mag. Jour. 1493—94. *Reparaciones.* "Item sol' Simoni fabro pro duobus repagulis fenestr' in parloria' ij^d."]

[2] [Ibid. 1531—32, f. 158. "Item...laboranti per tres dies cum seruiente circa reparationem murorum in Conclaui ij^s vj^d."]

[3] [Ibid. 1532—33, f. 177 b. "Item xviij° Januarii Lamberto Joyner in plena solucione pro ly sylyng in Conclaui xl^s." f. 187 b. "Item matri marget et Johanni Sawer laborantibus purgando conclaue comitatis per diem iiij^d. Item Johanni boyman assuenti ly hangingis in conclaui viijd."]

[4] [Ibid. 1544—45, f. 119. "Item 9° Augusti Rogerio Young vitriario pro xxvij pedibus vitri normandie pro fenestra in conclaue et accepit pro singulo pede vj^d. xiij^s. vj^d." f. 125 b. "Item 7° Septembris solui Georgio Raye pro duplici fenestrali in fenestra conclauis iij^s iiij^d."]

[5] [Ibid. 1545—46, f. 129 b (September). "Item...Richardo Wood distringenti asseres ly wanescott in conclaui." f. 130. "Item Ricardo Ashe pictori pingenti postes in conclaui rubro colore xiiij^d. Item Richardo Wood fabricanti li wanescot in conclaui iuxta pactum suum x^s." f. 130 b. "Item Edwardo kynge lavanti li waynescot in conclaui post eius contabulationem." f. 131. "Item pictori lavanti conclaue circa caminum cum le sise water iiij^d."]

[6] [Ibid. 1685—86, f. 226—7. Austin was paid £64 for the panelling; the chairs cost £15. 15. 0; and various other charges made up the rest of the sum. The woodwork here, as elsewhere in the College, was painted. It was ordered, 8 June, 1764, "y^t ye Wainscot in ye Parlour be repair'd and painted."]

the armorial bearings of the two royal Foundresses, was placed there in 1822[1].]

LIBRARY. The old part of the Library, a room forty-three feet long by twenty feet wide, on the first floor of the north side of the Principal Court, is shewn by a row of six equidistant windows to have been intended for that purpose from the first. The book-cases have been altered and patched from time to time in order to obtain more shelf-room. The original medieval desks may be detected as the foundation of each class; on which, in the time of James the First, a handsome superstructure was set, [the work of Andrew Chapman[2],] and this has since been lifted higher by the interposition of plain boards and additional shelves, so as to destroy all ornamental appearance. There are six stalls on each side, but the whole Library is lamentably too small for the valuable collections that have been accumulated.

In 1772 "the Library was enlarged by taking into it the principal part of a set of rooms that were between it and the chapel," to quote Dr Plumptre[3]; and subsequently the rooms on the ground floor below have also been appropriated for the reception of additional benefactions and purchases.

In 1804 the Bell-tower shewn by Loggan (fig. 3) was taken down[4], and in its place a plain projection of white brick was erected containing a staircase to the Library. The little sun-dial on the south face of the upper stage of this tower had been put up in 1538[5]. Cole describes this part of the College as follows:

[1] [The beautiful shield, bearing the arms of Margaret of Anjou, now in this window, was found a few years since in one of the windows of the Buttery.]

[2] [Mag. Jour. 1612—13, f. 147 b (July). " To Andrew Chapman for other woorke in yᵉ librarie x li." The older shelves were in existence in 1529—30. Ibid. f. 126. "Item Joanni...pro claue pluteorum qui sunt in nostra bibliotheca super quibus libri imponuntur vj d."]

[3] [The change was directed by a College Order, 23 Dec., 1772, quoted above, p. 41.]

[4] [College Order, 15 June, 1804. "Agreed that among the other repairs of the College, the tower containing the bell and the clock, being now in considerable danger of falling down, requires immediate attention, and that the necessary works in the way of alteration or repair be done in the ensuing summer under the inspection of the Bursar."]

[5] [Mag. Jour. 1537—38, f. 42 b. "Item 7° Septembris pro horologio...adfixo campanæ (sic) sacelli ijˢ ijᵈ."]

"Over yᵉ W. end [of the Chapel] is a small Tower and agst yᵉ side of it wᶜʰ fronts yᵉ Court is lately placed a very handsome Clock, 1733, and directly under it on yᵉ Wall of yᵉ Chapel and over yᵉ Door wᶜʰ leads to it is also lately painted a very elegant SunDial with all yᵉ signs. This is no small ornamᵗ to yᵉ Court to enliven it."

The dial is still in existence. It is usually ascribed to Sir Isaac Newton, but as he died in 1728, the precise statement of Cole shews that the tradition is inaccurate. [The dial he mentions, however, replaced an older one, made in 1642, about which we find the following entries[1]:

" For stone and worke about ye chappell diall	I.	14.	o
For giult for yᵉ Diall	o.	4.	6
To yᵉ painter for diall	o.	5.	o
For yᵉ cock of yᵉ diall	o.	18.	o
For oyle and white lead and hire of haire cloths	o.	6.	o"

The old tower was replaced by a clock-turret, classical in character, which occupied the same position as the present one. The base was square, and finished at the level of the ridge of the roof by a balustrade. Above this rose a lofty square cupola, surmounted by a small dome, terminating in a weather-cock. It had pilasters at each angle, and on each side a clock-face. This lasted until 1848[2], when the present wooden turret was erected under the direction of Mr Brandon, Architect.

GENERAL REPAIRS. It was mentioned in the third chapter that the windows in the older parts of the College had been altered. They were originally, as at present, of two lights; but the lights were foliated. One, in the original condition, from the north side of the Library, is here figured (fig. 17). The alteration was made at different times during the last century. A College Order dated 5 July, 1774, directs "to Scrape and paint a Stone Colour all the Stone window Frames in the First Court;" a second, dated 1 May, 1775, to treat in a similar manner " the Windows on the north side of the Library;" and a third, seven years later, is as follows:

" 29 June 1782. Order'd the Window Frames on the south side of the College as far as the new building, and on the east side as far as to

---

[1] [Mag. Jour. 1641—42, f. 102 b (May). f. 103 (July).]

[2] [College Order, 12 January, 1848. "Agreed that the Bursar be empowered to erect a new Clock and Bell Tower according to plans to be approved of by the President and Resident Fellows."]

the Walnut-tree Court Building, to be scraped (or chipp'd where wanting) during the Vacation."]

At some period subsequent to 1688 the eaves in the interior of the principal Court were replaced by parapets, but no record of this change has been preserved. The College has fortunately escaped the worse fate that was prepared for it at the end of the last century, when it was proposed to stucco the whole, and to cut the windows down to square heads.

[The east front was restored in 1875, under the direction of W. M. Fawcett, M.A., architect, so as to present, as nearly as possible, the appearance shewn by Loggan.]

GROUND ON THE EAST SIDE OF THE CAM, BOWLING GREEN, TENNIS COURT, etc. [A comparison of Loggan's view (fig. 3) with the modern ground-plan (fig. 1) shews that the arrangement of the ground on the right bank of the Cam was substantially the same then as now. It was laid out almost as soon as the suppression of the Carmelite Friary had put the College into possession of it. We have seen that the President's gar-

Fig. 17. Window on the north side of the Library.

den was laid out, and a wall of clunch and brick built round it, in 1545. In the same year the wall along the river-bank was continued as far as King's College, and also along the east side of the ground opposite to S. Catharine's Hall[1]. In May, 1553, payments begin for a paling "in the freres[2]." The length speci-

---

[1] [The entries referring to these walls in the Magnum Journale are too long for quotation. We find in the account for 1544—45 payments "pro exstructione parietis circa hortum magistri nostri;" "circa parietem in fratribus occidentem versus iuxta aquas;" and in that for 1545—46 "pro magno pariete in fratribus iuxta aulam Katherinæ;" and "iuxta plateam qua itur ad scolas."]

[2] [Mag. Jour. 1552—53, f. 214 b (May). "Item 27º to thomas Watson carpender for yͤ squarynge, framynge, and settynge up in yͤ freres, a wall of eght skore foote of timbre after vᵈ yͤ foote, as Mʳ Stokes yͤ president dyd agre with him for yͤ same iij li. vij s. vj d." f. 216. "Wylᵒ Raynald pro .4. oneribus plaustri lignorum que ad murum pertinebant circa nouum hortum viijˢ."]

fied, 160 feet, which is exactly the length of the wall separating the "Fellows' Garden" from the "Kitchen Garden" (EF, fig. 1), taken in connexion with allusions to a "new garden" in the same account, shew that in this year the garden for the Fellows north of the President's garden was laid out. In June, 1555, this garden was connected with the grove or island by a separate bridge (fig. 2; plan of the site of King's, Vol. I. p. 568) which remained until 1793, when it was ordered to be sold[1].

Until the Walnut-Tree Court was built, the whole of the ground east of these two gardens was probably used as a kitchen-garden or orchard; and the Walnut-Tree which gave its name to the new Court was one of the trees growing in it. The wall that extends along the north side of that Court is probably coeval with the building. In 1688 the Court had numerous trees in it, surrounded by a quickset hedge. These were lime trees which had been planted in 1672, and the hedge in 1683[2]. The row on the south side, with one tree of that on the west side, was cut down in 1761, and the remainder in 1788, when the passage into the Cloister Court was arranged as it is at present[3].

There was once a garden, or at least trees, in the Principal Court also. The quick is mentioned in 1675 and in 1677; but it had apparently been removed before Loggan's time, for he shews only a single tree. There was also a railing in the first Court[4], such as Loggan shews in other colleges, to separate

---

[1] [Mag. Jour. 1554—55, f. 233 (October). "Item Joanni Frost et altro pro . 6. dierum opera portantibus rubbyshe e fratribus ad nouum pontem viij^s. Item...pro . 8 . oneribus le grauel ad tegendum novum pontem v^s. iiij d." College Order, 10 January, 1793. "Agreed that the Bridge from the Bowling green to the Grove be sold to the Best bidder and be removed."]

[2] [Ibid. 1672—73, f. 159 b (November). "For trees set in ye New-court 01. 16. 00." 1673—74, f. 163 b (October). "To Mr Cage for planting ye lime-trees o. 3. o." 1682—83, f. 209 (February). "For 2000 and ½ of Quicksetts in ye New Court o. 12. 6."]

[3] [College Order, 28 February, 1761. "Agreed and order'd that the Row of Lime Trees in the Walnut tree Court next the Library, as likewise the first of the other Row, opposite the Master's Study, be cut down." Ibid. 21 March, 1788. "To cut down the remaining Lime Trees in the Walnut Tree Court, and to make the alteration of the passage under the Master's Study according to his proposal."]

[4] [Mag. Jour. 1603—4, f. 98 b (September, 1604). "Imprimis to the Carpenter for three dayes about ye rayles in ye court and about ye payles iij^s." 1640—41, f. 95 (March). "To Bell and his man Leuying ye Court within ye Railes £0. 4. 0." 1674—75, f. 169 b. "To Billops for mending ye rayls in ye first Court £05. 08. 06."]

the cultivated portion from that which might be walked over. The gate-house and the central alley, called "Regent-walk[1]," were flagged. The Court was first paved in 1515.

The Bowling-green, which occupies about half the Fellows' Garden (fig. 3), is mentioned as already in existence in 1608—9. The Tennis Court, repairs to which frequently occur, stood at the east end of the garden opposite to the great gate, as Hammond shews (fig. 2). This garden, as we learn from a lease of it granted to Catharine Hall in 1707[2], was then called "Tennis Court Garden." It had originally been an orchard. The cultivation of it is alluded to in 1511—12; in 1519—20 fruit-trees and a vine were planted in it; and in 1523—24 a portion was used for the cultivation of saffron[3]. Shortly afterwards it was assigned to the President by the following curious Order[4], dated 20 September, 1532:

"M[d] y[t] the said yer and day it is thus agreid also, and by the hole assent and consent of the said Master and felowse determynd That wheras the president of this College hath before y[is] tyme no garden appointid seueralli for hymself, nother for frute, nor to walk in, but in comen with the felowse both in walkis and in diuident of frute; Now at the desire of the said President the felowship or cumpani of this College wholli hath agreid and grawnted y[t] the said president shall have, enioy, and take from hensforth the Garden or ortzard ouer ageinst the College brode gaates w[t] all the frutes growing within y[e] same to his own propir vse. Vnder y[is] condicion y[t] the said president from hensforthe, shall have no parte nor diuident of suche frutes as growithe within the Colleges grett ortzard.

Teste Simone Heynes, manu propria."

The President having acquired a more convenient garden close to his Lodge, this other garden was probably given back to the College, and used for recreation. Besides tennis, archery was practised there, from a payment in 1587 "for castinge down the buttes in the Tenis court yarde."

---

[1] [This name appears in a list of repairs at the end of the account for 1684—85.]

[2] [See History of S. Catharine's Hall, Chapter I.]

[3] [Mag. Jour. 1511—12, f. 241 b. "Johanni Wanflett excidendo arbores in orto iuxta viam regiam per quatuor dies xij d." Ibid. 1519—20. "In primis Thome Meryk et Nicholao Soffham pro eorum labore per quinque dies circa plantacionem arborum et scissionem vinee in orto ex opposito magne porte collegii iij[s]. iiij[d]." Ibid. 1524—25, f. 69 b. "Item...laboranti in orto ultra collegium quum denudavit terram croci et purgavit ab extramentis...xx[d]."]

[4] [Ibid. 1531—32, f. 172.]

It should be further noticed that a special building for the performance of plays existed in some part of the College. It was built in 1638, when we meet with payments for timber-work and tiles "for yᵉ new Stagehouse[1]." Before this time the plays had been acted in the Hall. The press in which the actors' dresses were kept[2] is still preserved in the Muniment Room, which occupies the first floor over the gate of entrance; a room which has been set apart for that use from the earliest times.

BRIDGES, GROUND WEST OF THE CAM. Hammond's plan (fig. 1) shews that in the sixteenth century there were three Bridges: (1) from the Cloister Court to the opposite bank; (2) from the Fellows' Garden to the Grove; (3) from the high-way between the "Small Bridges" into the College grounds. To these was added before the end of the seventeenth century that from the extreme northern end of the grove to the common, after the row of trees called "Erasmus' walk," shewn in the same plan, had been planted.

There are a number of entries in the accounts referring to these bridges; but it is often impossible to discover which is referred to. The bridge out of the cloisters is frequently alluded to, as in January, 1582—83, when "the entrie from yᵉ great brydge to the cloysters" was paved, but there is no record as to when it was first built. It was rebuilt of wood in 1700[3]; but whether in the old position, or in a new one, is not stated. This bridge did not last quite half a century, as Dr Plumptre records:

"The present bridge from the Cloisters to the Stable-yard was built in the year 1749 and the Wall along the side of the River, as far as the College boundaries extend was carried on[4], and the Grove alter'd from its then nearly natural state to its present one (excepting some few additional improvements since made) in the 3 following years. This, and

[1] [Mag. Jour. 1637—38. Ibid. 1640—41, f. 97 (August). "For mending yᵉ walls over yᵉ Acting Chamber o. 5. 10."]

[2] [Ibid. 1640—41, f. 93 a (October). "To Mʳ Ward for a press for yᵉ Acting cloaths o. 7. 8."]

[3] [Ibid. 1699—1700, f. 37 (January). "To the College Carpenter for the New Bridge going out of the Cloysters £72. 00. 00." (February) "The Bricklayer's bill for the New Bridge £02. 12. 06."]

[4] [It was ordered, 20 March, 1750, that a brick wall should be built between the two Bridges "like that above the new Bridge;" and, 2 January, 1751, that the said wall should be continued to the lower end of the Grove.]

some considerable improvements in the Gardens of the College, and in the Cloister Court, were principally contriv'd, and the work carried on under the direction of John Forlin[1] the then College Gardiner, a man of excellent skill in the ordinary parts of his business, and of some taste and knowledge in these superior parts; qualities which were useful and pleasing, to which he added the more important ones to his Masters and himself, of being an honest and faithful Servant."

The bridge here commemorated is that still in use. It is of one arch, with a span of forty feet, and is wholly built of timber-work, resting on stone piers at either end. The design, due to a Mr Etheridge, was executed by Essex, whence it is sometimes called "the Essex Bridge." It was begun in July 1749, and finished in September, 1750[2].

The ground on the left bank of the Cam was called the "pondyard" in early times, and the existence of a mud-wall round a portion of it is recorded in 1499—1500. We find part of this ground laid out as garden, part as orchard, in 1504—5; and a hedge was made round it in 1511—12[3]. The ground beyond the limits of the orchard was levelled in 1539, and walks were laid out in the garden and orchard[4]. This is the first notice of using any part of the College ground for exercise or recreation. Hammond's plan (fig. 2) shews the arrangement here alluded to. There is an inner plot of ground divided unequally by a hedge into two portions, of which the larger may be identified with the orchard, and the western part of the smaller with the garden. Beyond, there is an irregular strip fenced by a hedge or palisade. In 1547 the ditch along the

---

[1] [Dr Plumptre notes "John Forlin died in 1783 after having been Gardiner upwards of 40 years."]

[2] [Mag. Jour. 1748—49, f. 236 (October). "Mr Etheridge for the Design and Model of the Bridge £21. 00. 00." f. 237 b (July). "Paid for five men for digging the River bank £01. 11. 06." Ibid. 1749—50, f. 241 b (September). "Cook for a Supper on finishing the Bridge to Mr Essex's Men. 0. 17. 9."]

[3] [Ibid. 1496—97, f. 111 b, "le pondyerd" is mentioned. 1499—1500, f. 135. "Item pro iij bigat' argille pro reparacione murorum circa stagna xvjd." 1504—5, f. 177. "M'yrlond erga aduentum matris regis ad collegium pro solucione laborant' in orto et pomerio...xxˢ." 1511—12, f. 245. "Willelmo harwy equitand' versus Eusden ad bigas conducendas ad vehend' spinas pro magno sepe ortum pomarium ambiente ij d."]

[4] [Ibid. 1538—39, f. 47. "Item G. Carter 9° Martii pro opera sua in æquanda area ultra pomerium et salicibus detondendis atque eradicandis, et fodiend' ambulacris in horto .6. diebus ijˢ. Item Jacobo Nicolsono pro .10. plaustris harene in pomarium ad obducenda ambulacra iijˢ. iiij d."]

south side was deepened, so as to convert the whole into an island, as the plan shews, by which appellation it is usually referred to afterwards. The brick wall which still surrounds the orchard was built between 1667 and 1672, probably on the site of the older fence. There are also numerous entries in each year having reference to the cultivation of flowers, vegetables, and fruit-trees, to which great attention has always been paid in this College. It would be beside our present purpose to quote these, curious and interesting as they are; but in connexion with the general aspect of the grounds it should be mentioned that in February, 1630, seventy-two ash-trees were planted, and in January, 1634, twenty-eight elm-trees. A walk called "the Queen's Walk" was planted in 1686[1], but the position is not recorded. The trees planted 1630—34 are probably those which had grown into a grove by the middle of the eighteenth century, when, as Dr Plumptre has recorded, the walks were altered; a work which lasted from 1749 to 1752. In May, 1752, we meet with a payment "for gravel for the walks in the Grove," but no new trees appear to have been planted at that time. In January, 1732, forty lime-trees, bought at a distance from Cambridge, were paid for. These are probably the trees still growing along the river bank from the bridge to the north end of the grove. No further changes appear to have taken place until the autumn of 1812, when some extensive work was undertaken, which was not completed until September, 1815. From a payment for shrubs it was probably a replanting, together with a rearrangement of the walks[2]. Before the erection of King's College new bridge in 1818[3], the view hence, looking north, must have been extensive and beautiful. Dyer, writing in 1814[4], thus commends it:

"Let no one leave these grounds without going to the end of that walk by the side of the river, and let him thence look to the view on the

---

[1] [Ibid. 1686—87, f. 230 (October). "To Hosea Tine for planting yᵉ Queen's walk and other places 0. 10. 0."]

[2] [These details are taken from the Magnum Journale for the years mentioned. The sum spent in 1812—15 was £308. 10. 0.]

[3] [The erection of King's new bridge (see Vol. I. 573) was a very sore point with Dr Milner, then President, and nearly brought about a rupture between him and Mr Simeon. Knight's Memoir of Rev. H. Venn. 8vo. Lond. 1880, p. 12.]

[4] [Dyer's Cambridge, ii. 162.]

opposite side; nor let him say, it is the best in Cambridge, or is *well enough for Cambridge;* though it has not hill and dale, perhaps, of the kind, it is one of the best anywhere; for it has grand objects, which amply compensate for the want of other beauties; a small home view, with the accompaniment of magnificent edifices, and agreable scenery. The west front of King's College Chapel, with its south perspective, the east and south perspective of Clare Hall, the elegant bridge over the Cam, Clare Hall piece, with its plantation of venerable old elms, King's Meadow, with passengers passing and repassing on one side of the river, and Queens' Close on the other, form a most delightful picture."

In December, 1684, the making of the walk since called "Erasmus' Walk," along the south side of the ditch separating the common west of Queens' College from King's College is thus recorded:

"For making yᵉ walk on yᵉ Common, yᵉ Fellows of King's College planting yᵗ side next ye ditch, and wee yᵉ other; for bushing yᵉ trees, levellinge yᵉ ground £4. 2. 6."

It was probably at this time that the fourth bridge, from the College ground to this walk, was constructed. Dr Plumptre remarks on the tradition connecting it with Erasmus:

"The walk call'd Erasmus's walk was (I believe) *first made* in his time [the Presidentship of Henry James (1675—1717)] viz, in the year 1685. For in the Accounts of that year it is spoken of as *made* and as *planted*, not *replanted;* and King's College was at the expence of planting the side next the ditch, Queens of that next the Common. The title was probably given it therefore in honour of that distinguish'd Member of the College, rather than on account of its being a favorite walk of his. If it was so, he enjoy'd I doubt no other shade here than what arose from the adjoining Grove of Kings College; for I find no *direct mention*, nor any thing which may seem to *imply* the plantation or forming of any walk here till this time."

The Brewhouse was first built in 1533—34, and the "New Stables" in 1697. These offices have been always in the same place, and are shewn on each side of an enclosure by Hammond (fig. 2). The relative extent of these offices in 1688 and at the present time is shewn on the plan (fig. 1). It was in this part of the College that Mr Milner, afterwards President, was allowed to build a Laboratory. The Order is as follows:

"28 February, 1782. Granted leave to Mʳ Milner to build a Chemical Laboratory in the Stable yard adjoinyng to the Coal house."

There was also a Pigeon House, but the position of it cannot be now ascertained.]

CHRONOLOGICAL SUMMARY.

1446.	8 November. King Henry the Sixth acquires the first site from Richard Andrewe, burgess of Cambridge.
,,	3 December. Charter granted to the College of S. Bernard.
1447.	21 August. New charter, confirming to the President and Fellows the new site they had selected.
1448.	14 April. First building contract signed.
,,	15 April. New Charter granted by Queen Margaret, and the name of the College changed to "the Queen's college of S. Margaret and S. Bernard." First stone of the buildings laid in her name by Sir John Wenlock.
1449.	4 March. King Henry the Sixth gives £200 for the buildings.
,,	6 March. Second building contract signed.
1454.	12 December. License from the Bishop of Ely for service in a chapel or oratory within the College or the Hostel of S. Bernard.
1475.	6 October. The Town of Cambridge sells to the College the ground west of the Cam.
1484.	4 November. Death of Andrew Doket, the first President. The Bursar's Account-Book, called *Magnum Journale*, begins.
1494—95.	Work done to the Cloister.
1510.	The term "gallery" occurs for the first time in the accounts.
1515—16.	Repairs done to the lead roof of the north cloister.
1531—32.	Panel-work made for the Hall.
1533.	Combination Room wainscoted.
1533—34.	Brewhouse built.
1537.	12 February. The Carmelites sell to the College a wall between themselves and the College; and agree not to obstruct the windows of a certain ambulatory called *ly Galari* about to be built. Payment for three windows of hewn stone in the master's gallery (15 Feb.) and for glass and window-frames (March).
1538.	8 August. The Carmelites surrender their convent to Dr Mey, the President, and the Fellows of Queens' College.
1539.	Walks laid out in the garden and orchard west of the river Cam.
1541.	Dr Mey buys the Carmelite convent from the Augmentation Office.
1544.	Dr Mey sells the site of it to the College for £36 [Dr Plumptre].
1545.	June. Brick wall built round the Master's garden.
1548.	Hall-screen made.
1553.	May. Fellows' Garden laid out and walled.
1555.	June. Bridge built from the Fellows' Garden to the Grove.
1560.	Payments for the master's upper chambers.
1564.	A range of chambers built in the Pump Court.
1575.	June. College Arms set up over the entrance to the Hall.
1579—1614.	Panel-work in the President's Lodge put up, partly by gift of Dr Humphrey Tindall, partly by subscription.
1612—13.	Work done in the Library by Andrew Chapman.

1616—19.	Building along the east side of the Walnut-Tree Court erected.
1628.	Doors added to the Hall-screen.
1642.	Dial put up on the Chapel.
1661.	Restoration of the Chapel.
1666—72.	Brick wall built round Orchard.
1684.	Walk called "Erasmus' Walk" laid out and planted.
1636.	Combination Room wainscoted by Austin.
1697.	Stables built.
1732.	Lime-trees planted in the Grove.
1733.	Dial in the Principal Court mentioned by Cole as "lately painted."
1732—34.	Hall new wainscoted, and ceiling put up, under the direction of Burrough, by Essex.
1749—50.	Bridge from the Cloisters to the Grove built by Essex, from a design by Etheridge. Wall built along the river bank. Walks and gardens altered.
1756—60.	New Building erected by Essex.
1768.	Alterations in the Chapel. Pew made for the President's family.
1772.	Library enlarged by taking into it a set of rooms at the east end.
1773—75.	Further alterations in the Chapel under the direction of Essex. Flat ceiling put up.
1774.	5 July. Windows in the First Court ordered to be scraped.
1775.	1 May. Windows on the north side of the Library ordered to be scraped.
1778—82.	Building on the east side of the Walnut-Tree Court rebuilt after a fire.
1782.	29 June. The window-frames on the south side of the College ordered to be scraped.
1791—92.	New staircase to President's Lodge made.
1793.	10 January. Bridge between the Fellows' Garden and the Grove ordered to be taken down.
1804.	Bell-turret west of the Chapel taken down.
1819—22.	Oriel of Hall ornamented with the arms of the foundresses, etc.
1823.	Building along east side of Walnut-Tree Court altered; parapets added.
1845.	Ceiling of the Chapel removed.
1846.	Ceiling of Hall removed, and louvre made, under the direction of Dawkes. Side-windows restored at expense of Robert Moon, M.A., Fellow.
1848.	Wooden turret west of the Chapel erected under the direction of Brandon.
1854.	Oriel of Hall restored; side-windows altered; the glass of both executed by Hardman; the whole at the expense of Mr Moon.
1858—61.	Complete renovation of the Chapel under the direction of Bodley. Organ-chamber made.
1861.	Fireplace of Hall decorated, and pavement laid down, under the direction of Bodley, at the expense of Mr Moon.
1875.	Fireplace of Hall further ornamented with woodwork, and the whole Hall decorated, under the direction of Bodley, at the expense of Dr Campion and Mr Pirie, Fellows.
.,	Restoration of the east front of the College by Fawcett.

APPENDIX.

ACCOUNT FOR WAINSCOTING THE HALL.

(Magnum Journale, 1531—32.)

Reparationes Collegii et Vtensilium eiusdem.

f. 152.   In primis Matheo Blunt vltimo die septembris laboranti circa ly selyng
aule collegii per quinque dies ....iijs. iiijd.

Item Roberto Cave Joyner pro consimili.................................iijs. iiijd.

Item 9° mensis octobris Matheo Blunt pro sex diebus circa opus pre-
dictum ....iiijs.

Item 17° die octobris Matheo Blunt laboranti circa opus predictum per
sex dies ....iiijs.

Item Roberto Cave pro consimili...iiijs.

Item 20 die octobris pro necessariis suis quum dictus matheus nauigabat
ad lyne pro ly wanscottis ....vijs.

Item 22° die mensis octobris seruo magistri Walters pro vectione ly wanscottis a lyne ad Cantabrigiam..viijs.

Item 24° die mensis octobris Willelmo Lychfyld pro tribus libris ly
glew ....xijd.

Item eodem die hawkes Chaundeler pro quatuor libris candelarum vjd.

Summa xxxvs. ijd.

f. 152 b.   Item Matheo Blunt xxx° die mensis octobris per quinque dies laboranti ....iijs. iiijd.

Item Roberto Cave pro consimili...iijs. iiijd.

Item Ellys Sterne Sawer vna cum seruo suo xxx° die mensis octo-
bris...viijs. jd.

Item 5° die mensis nouembris Matheo Blunt per 4ᵒʳ dies laboranti
ijs. viijd.

Item 5° die mensis nouembris Roberto Cave pro consimili ....ijs. viijd.

Item 11° die mensis nouembris Matheo Blunt per sex dies laboranti ...iiijs.

Item Roberto Cave pro consimili..................................... ....iiijs.

Item Ellys Sterne Sawer pro ly sawing ....xjd.

Item uxori hawkes pro tribus libris candelarum 11° die mensis nouem-
bris ....iijd. ob.

Item 18° die mensis nouembris Matheo Blunt per quinque dies labo-
ranti ....iijs. iiijd.

Item Roberto Cave per sex dies laboranti ....iiijs.

Item 18° die mensis nouembris dyrik harison per sex dies laboranti...iiijs.

Item uxori Hawkes 22° nouembris pro 4ᵒʳ libris candelarum pro operariis
predictis ....vd.

Item Matheo Blunt 25° die mensis nouembris laboranti per quinque dies ....iij*s*. iiij*d*.

Item Roberto Cave per sex dies ....iiij*s*.

Item dyrik harison eodem die pro consimili ....iiij*s*.

Item 2° die decembris Matheo Blunt laboranti per quinque dies iij*s*. iiij*d*.

Item Roberto Cave pro consimili ....iij*s*. iiij*d*.

Item dyrik harison pro consimili.. iij*s*. iiij*d*.

Item vxori hawkes pro 4ᵒʳ libris candelarum 2° die decembris ....v*d*.

Summa pagine lxij*s*. ix*d*. ob.

f. 153.   Item Roberto Cave 9° die decembris laboranti per 4ᵒʳ dies ....ij*s*. viij*d*.

Item Matheo Blunt pro consimili...ij*s*. viij*d*.

Item Dyrik harison pro consimili ....ij*s*. viij*d*.

Item Johanni Ward pictori pro octo ly skochyns ....xvj*d*.

Item 16° die decembris Matheo Blunt laboranti per sex dies ....iiij*s*.

Item Roberto Cave eodem die pro consimili ....iiij*s*.

Item dyrik harison pro consimili ....iiij*s*.

Item Lamberto eodem die pro consimili.................... ....iiij*s*.

Item Ellys Sterne eodem die pro se et seruo suo........................vij*s*. j*d*.

Item vxori hawkes pro six libris candelarum eodem die...............vij*d*. ob.

Item Johanni Warde pro 4ᵒʳ ly skochinges ....viij*d*.

Item Roberto Cave xxiij° decembris laboranti per quinque dies ...iij*s*. iiij*d*.

Item dyrik harison eodem die pro consimili ....iij*s*. iiij*d*.

Item lamberto eodem die pro consimili ....iij*s*. iiij*d*.

Item Arnoldo eodem die pro consimili ....iij*s*. iiij*d*.

Item vxori hawkes eodem die ....vij*d*. ob.

Item Roberto Cave xxx° die decembris laboranti per vnum diem ......viij*d*.

Item dyrik harison pro consimili...viij*d*.

Item lamberto pro consimili... ....viij*d*.

Item Arnoldo pro consimili................. ....viij*d*.

Item Roberto Cave 1° die Januarii laboranti per 4ᵒʳ dies ....ij*s*. viij*d*.

Item lamberto pro consimili ....ij*s*. viij*d*.

Item Arnoldo pro consimili ....ij*s*. viij*d*.

Item dyrik harison pro consimili ....ij*s*. viij*d*.

Item vxori hawkes eodem die pro candelis............................... vij*d*. ob.

Summa pagine iij*li* xix*d*. ob.

f. 153 b.   Item xiij° die mensis Januarii lamberto laboranti per sex dies............iiij*s*.

Item Roberto Cave eodem die pro consimili ....iiij*s*.

Item dyrike harison pro consimili..iiij*s*.

Item Arnoldo pro consimili ....iiij*s*.

Item Ellis Sterne pro se et seruo........................... ....vij*s*.

Item vxori hawkes pro candelis ....v*d*.

Item xx° Januarii Egidio Fambeler Carver pro xvij capitibus de ly Antyk precium cuiuslibet capitis xvj*d*. : summa...........................xxij*s*. viij*d*.

Item lamberto xx° Januarii laboranti per sex dies ....iiij*s*.

Item Roberto Cave pro consimili..iiij*s*.

Item Petro Joyner pro consimili ....iiij*s*.

Item vxori hawkes pro candelis..iij*d*. ob. q'.

Item Ellis Sterne pro se et seruo ....xx*d*.

Item xxvij° Januarii Arnoldo Joner (*sic*) laboranti per sex dies ....iiij*s*.

Item xxviij° Januarii lamberto pro consimili ....iiij*s*.
Item Petro Joyner pro consimili ....iiij*s*.
Item Roberto Cave pro consimili..iiij*s*.
Item Egidio Fambeler Carver pro nouem capitibus xxviij° Januarii ...xij*s*.
Item Ellis Sterne Sawer pro se et seruo predicto die.................vj*s*. ix*d*.
Item vxori hawkes pro candelis ....iij*d*. ob. q'.
Item Roberto Caue 3° februarii laboranti per quinque dies ....iij*s*. iiij*d*.
Item lamberto pro consimili ....iij*s*. iiij*d*.
Item Arnoldo pro consimili ....iij*s*. iiij*d*.
Item Petro pro consimili..iij*s*. iiij*d*.
Item Egidio Fambeler pro tresdecem capitibus 3° februarii ......xvij*s*. iiij*d*.
Item vxori hawkes pro candelis ....i¦*d*. ob.

Summa pagine vj^{li} vj*s*.

f. 154. Item Roberto Cave laboranti per sex dies xj° februarii....................iiij*s*.
Item lamberto pro consimili ....iiij*s*.
Item Arnoldo pro consimili ....iiij*s*.
Item petro pro consimili ....iiij*s*.
Item Ellis Sterne pro se et seruo ....xxij*d*.
Item vxori hawkes pro candelis ....ij*d*. ob.
Item Roberto Cave xvij° februarii laboranti per quinque dies ......iij*s*. iiij*d*.
Item lamberto pro consimili ....iij*s*. iiij*d*.
Item Arnold pro consimili..iij*s*. iiij*d*.
Item petro Joner (*sic*) pro consimili ....iij*s*. iiij*d*.
Item Dyrik harison pro tribus paruis capitibus ....iiij*s*.
Item Roberto Cave xxiiij° februarii laboranti per sex dies ....iiij*s*.
Item lamberto pro consimili ....iiij*s*.
Item Petro pro consimili ....iiij*s*.
Item Arnold pro consimili ....iiij*s*.
Item Dyrik harison pro 4^{or} capitibus que spectant ad superiorem men-
   sam ....vj*s*. viij*d*.
Item Johanni Vesy pro duabus libris ly glew ....vj*d*.
Item lamberto 2° marcii laboranti per sex dies ....iiij*s*.
Item petro Joner (*sic*) pro consimili ....iiij*s*.
Item Arnoldo pro consimili ....iiij*s*.
Item Roberto Cave pro consimili..iiij*s*.
Item Dyrik harison pro septem capitibus maioribus ....xj*s*. viij*d*.
Item pro parua sera vna cum lys hyngis pro paruo ostio in aula ...ij*s*. vj*d*.
Item lamberto 9° marcii laboranti per sex dies ....iiij*s*.

Summa pagine iiij^{li} xij*s*. viij*d*. ob.

f. 154 b. Item petro pro consimili ....iiij*s*.
Item Arnoldo pro consimili .... iiij*s*.
Item Roberto Cave pro consimili..iiij*s*.
Item Dyrik harison pro 4^{or} maioribus skochyngis et armis.........vj*s*. viij*d*.
Item Roberto batman Sawer pro se et seruo ....xxij*d*.
Item Roberto Cave xvj marcii per sex dies laboranti ....iiij*s*.
Item lamberto laboranti per quinque dies xvj° marcii ....iij*s*. iiij*d*.
Item Arnoldo pro sex diebus..iiij*s*.
Item petro pro consimili..iiij*s*.
Item Ellis Sterne pro se et seruo ....xxj*d*.

Item Dyrik harison pro 4ᵒʳ magnis capitibus et armis ....vjs. viijd.

Item Johanni vesy pro ly glew ....xiijd.

Item Roberto Cave laboranti per quinque dies [23° martii, marginal note]..iijs. iiijd.

Item lamberto per sex dies laboranti .... iiijs.

Item petro pro consimili ....iiijs.

Item Arnold pro consimili..iiijs.

Item Dyrik et gylis pro quinque magnis capitibus et armis......viijs. iiijd.

Item Roberto Cave xxix° marcii laboranti per tres dies ....ijs.

Item lamberto pro consimili ....ijs.

Item petro pro consimili ....ijs.

Item Arnoldo pro consimili ....ijs.

Item Dyrik harison pro sex capitibus minoribus...........................viijs.

Item lamberto vj° die Aprilis pro duobus diebus...........................xvjd.

Item Arnoldo pro consimili   ....xvjd.

                              [Summa pagine iiijˡⁱ vijs. ixd.

f. 155. Item petro pro consimili ....xvjd.

Item Roberto Cave pro consimili ....xvjd.

Item Roberto Smyth Sawer pro se et seruo ....iiijs. viijd.

Item lamberto xij° Aprilis laboranti per sex dies............................iiijs.

Item petro pro consimili ....iiijs.

Item Roberto Cave pro consimili........................... ....iiijs.

Item Arnold pro consimili................... ....iiijs.

Item xix° Aprilis lamberto pro sex diebus   ....iiijs.

Item petro pro consimili ....iiijs.

Item Arnold pro consimili................... ....iiijs.

Item dyrik harison pro vno magno scuto ....xxd.

Item Roberto Smyth Sawer ....viis. viijd.

Item xxvij° Aprilis Lamberto laboranti per 4ᵒʳ dies..................ijs. viijd.

Item Arnold pro consimili ....ijs. viijd.

Item petro pro consimili ....ijs. viijd.

Item dyrik pro consimili ....ijs. viijd.

Item v° maij dyrik pro 4ᵒʳ diebus...................................ijs. viijd.

Item lamberto pro consimili...ijs. viijd.

Item Arnold pro consimili............................... ....ijs. viijd.

Item petro pro consimili ....ijs. viijd.

Item vndecimo maij lamberto pro quinque diebus ....iijs. iiijd.

Item Arnold pro consimili............................... ....iijs. iiijd.

Item petro pro consimili ....iijs. iiijd.

Item Roberto Smyth sawer pro se et seruo ....xxijd.

                              Summa pagine iijˡⁱ. xvijs. xd.

f. 155 b. Item xviij° Maij lamberto pro sex diebus.....................................iiijs.

Item petro pro consimili ....iiijs.

Item Arnoldo pro consimili ....iiijs.

Item eodem die lamberto pro quinque scutis ....vjs. viijd.

Item xxv^to maij lamberto pro duobus diebus   ....xvjd.

Item Arnaldo (sic) pro consimili................... ....xvjd.

Item petro pro consimili ....xvjd.

Item Roberto Sawer xxviij° maij .... xvjd.

Item primo Junii lamberto pro 5 diebus ....iij*s.* iiij*d.*
Item Arnoldo pro consimili ....iij*s.* iiij*d.*
Item petro pro consimili ....iij*s.* iiij*d.*
Item vij° Junij lamberto pro sex diebus ....iiij*s.*
Item Arnoldo pro consimili ....iiij*s.*
Item petro pro consimili ....iiij*s.*
Item eodem die Roberto Smyth Sawer ....iiij*s.*
Item eodem die Dyrik harison pro vna virga de ly Antik Crest......viij*d.*
Item eidem x° Junij pro duobus virgis ....xvj*d.*
Item xv° Junij lamberto pro sex diebus ....iiij*s.*
Item Arnoldo pro consimili..iiij*s.*
Item petro pro consimili .... iiij*s.*
Item Batman sawer eodem die..xxiij*d.*
Item dirik harison pro tribus virgis ....ij*s.*
Item eodem die lamberto pro duobus magnis ly vautis et duobus par-
uis ....xxij*s.*
Item xvij° Junii pro vno parvo ly vawlt ....v*s.*
Item xxiij° Junii lamberto pro quatuor parvis ly vawltis ....xx*s.*
Item eodem die lamberto pro quinque diebus ....iij*s.* iiij*d.*
Item eodem die pro ly glew...xij*d.*
Item petro eodem die pro quinque diebus ....iij*s.* iiij*d.*
Item Arnoldo pro consimili ....iij*s.* iiij*d.*

[Summa pagine vj*li* v*s.* iiij*d.*

f. 156.   Item eodem die Batman Sawer ....xvj*d.*
Item eodem die dyrik harison pro 4^or virgis de ly Antyk Crest
ij*s.* viij*d.*
Item xxviij° Junij dyrik pro duobus scutis ....ij*s.* viij*d.*
Item xxx° Junij lamberto pro quatuor diebus ....ij*s.* viij*d.*
Item Arnoldo pro consimili..ij*s.* viij*d.*
Item petro pro consimili ....ij*s.* viij*d.*
Item vj° Julij dyrik harison pro nouem virgis de ly Antyk cum di-
midio...vj*s.* iiij*d.*
Item eodem die lamberto pro sex diebus................................. iiij*s.*
Item petro pro consimili ....iiij*s.*
Item dyrik harison pro duabus virgis de ly Antyk border..............xvj*d.*
Item henrico veysey pro vna libra de byse ....ij*s.* viij*d.*
Item xiij° die Julij lamberto pro sex diebus..............................iiij*s.*
Item petro pro consimili ....iiij*s.*
Item henrico vesey pro d' libre de ly Byse................................xxij*d.*
Item fratri Augustiniensium pro pingendo ly Borders ....v*s.*
Item xx° Julij dyrike harison pro quinque virgis de Antyk Border
ij*s.* iiij*d.*
Item eodem die dyrik harison pro sex virgis ....iiij*s.*
Item xxj Julij Lamberto pro quinque diebus ....ij*s.* iiij*d.*
Item petro pro consimili ....ij*s.* iiij*d.*
Item eodem die dyrik harison in fine Laboris ex iussu presidentis...viij*d.*
Item xxvj° Julij Lamberto pro 4^or diebus .... ij*s.* viij*d.*
Item petro pro consimili ....ij*s.* viij*d.*
Item Johanni Veysey pro duabus libris ly wergresse ....ij*s.* ij*d.*

Item 4º Augusti Lamberto pro sex diebus ....iiij*s*.
Item petro pro consimili ....iiij*s*.
Item Johanni Vesey pro tribus libris wergrese ....iij*s*. vj*d*.

[Summa pagine iiij^li ij*s*. xj*d*.

f. 156 b.   Item Johanni Saunders pro xxvij ly waynskottis ....xxxvj*s*.
Item Johanni Batman Sawer pro se et seruo vij° Augusti ....ij*s*.
Item xviij° Augusti lamberto laboranti per quinque dies ....iij*s*. iiij*d*.
Item petro pro consimili ....iij*s*. iiij*d*.
Item eidem Lamberto pro lxiiij^or paruis columnis pro lateribus aule vij*s*.
Item eidem Lamberto pro extremis partibus de ly crestis ....viij*d*.
Item fratri augustiniensium pro 4^or libris ly generall et quatuor quartis
oley et aliis necessariis ....iiij*s*. iiij*d*.
Item predicto Lamberto pro viginti quinque columnis que ornant supe-
riorem mensam ....iiij*s*. ij*d*.
Item xxix° Augusti lamberto pro quinque diebus.....................iij*s*. iiij*d*.
Item petro pro consimili ....iij*s*. iiij*d*.
Item primo septembris lamberto pro sex diebus ....iiij*s*.
Item petro pro consimili ....iiij*s*.
Item Johanni vesey pro tribus libris de ly glew..........................xv*d*.
Item x° Septembris lamberto pro quinque diebus.....................iij*s*. iiij*d*.
Item petro pro consimili ....iij*s*. iiij*d*.
Item mylone Brakin fabro ferraio (*sic*) pro ly hingis et boltis pro camino
in Aula et Staples...iij*s*. x*d*.
Item eidem pro clauis et ij C ly brads ....iij*s*. xj*d*.
Item Mrs Walters de lyne pro C. et. lx. ly waynskottis .... ix*li*.

Summa pagine xiij^li. xij*s*. ij*d*.

[Cole's account of the coats of arms, dated " Monday, Apr. 21, 1777 " (MSS. Cole,
Vol. 47, p. 326. Add. MSS. Mus. Brit. 5848), is as follows:

"Dining with the President or Master of Queen's College on Thursday April 17,
1777, I took these Arms down in my Pocket Book, being the Top Range of the
Wainscote in the Vestibule, or Antichamber, before you enter the Audit or Dining
Room: the said Arms are placed between Heads carved on the Wainscote, and go on
a Range all round the Room, and some are in the Passage between the Vestibule
or [and?] Audit Room: and no Doubt many are lost, or placed in other Parts of the
College or Lodge, as the Wainscote came originally from the Hall, before it was new
fitted up: but as, no Doubt, the Arms are those of Benefactors to the College, I was
willing to preserve what remain of them. The wainscote is about 8 Feet high, or
rather more, and was very handsome and ornamental in its Time.

"The Arms of Roos and Spencer are repeated 6 or 7 Times; but I shall give it
only once: it is in my Vol. 2 p. 19, having been painted on the Wall of the Chapel,
behind the Wainscote, where I saw them as they were fitting up the Chapel about
3 years ago."

The passage referred to is as follows. It occurs at the end of the note on the
chapel printed above, p. 41, after the words "in order to refit it entirely."

"I observed on the South Wall there had been a coat of Arms painted, but
cheifly obliterated; it had been covered for these 2 Centuries probably by the
Wainscote, being just under where I remember the Organ to have stood, which has
been removed, I suppose, these 20 or 30 years. The Arms were these as well as

I could distinguish them, being painted on the Wall: viz: Argent a Fess Gules, inter 3 Water Bougets Sable, impaling, Quarterly Argent and .... in the 2^d and 3^d Quarter a Fret, over all a Bend Sable, charged with ..... Probably for Spencer. The Sheild of the Make of the Time of Henry 8."

His account of the Hall panelling proceeds thus. The shields are numbered for convenience of reference.

... "The Arms on the Wainscote painted, tho' they are carved on the Wood, are as follow.

[1] Gules a Bar between 3 Water Bougets Or, for Roos, impales, Quarterly, Argent and Gules, on the Gules 2 Frets, Argent, over all on a Bend Sable 3 Mullets Argent.
       This is repeated 6 or 7 Times being Roos and Spencer.

[2] Argent on a Cross Sable 3 Plates, impales Argent on a Cheveron between 3 Griffons Heads erased Sable an Annulet Argent. Repeated twice again.

[3] Or on a Pale Gules 3 Eaglets displayed Argent. Repeated.

[4] Argent 3 Lions passant guardant Gules impales Quarterly 1 and 4 Sable a Saltire engrailed Argent, 2 & 3 Sable a Lion rampant Or.

[5] Spencer impales Sable a Cheveron between 3 Leopards Faces Or. Repeated.

[6] Sable a Saltire engrailed Argent impales Spencer. Repeated.

[7] Gules a Lion rampant parted per Fesse Argent & Sable crowned Or.

[8] Argent on a Cross Sable 5 Plates.

[9] Sable a Lion rampant parted per Fesse Argent and Sable crowned Or impales Argent 3 Birds Sable. Repeated.

[10] Argent a Lion rampant Gules impales Sable a Saltire engrailed Argent.

[11] Royal Arms of France and England quartered, crowned.

[12] Argent on a Cross Sable 3 Plates, impales Spencer.

[13] Argent 3 Lions passant guardant Gules impales Sable a Saltire engrailed Argent."

The frieze, as before mentioned (p. 44), is divided into compartments, of which there are now 57; 51 being in the room, and 6 in the passage. As a general rule, the compartments are eleven inches square, but eleven of them are fifteen inches long by eleven inches broad. In one of these the Royal Arms occur, whence it may be conjectured that this portion of the woodwork was over the dais in the Hall. Of these compartments, 36 contain heads, the remainder contain shields in the following order, supposing the compartments to be counted from the S. E. corner of the room towards the right:

[1] Occurs in compartment 6.
[2]   ,,   ,,   ,,   3. 16. 42.
[3]   ,,   ,,   ,,   1. 19.
[4]
[5]   ,,   ,,   ,,   22. 55.
[6]   ,,   ,,   ,,   14. 25. 29. 50. 53.
[7]
[8]   ,,   ,,   ,,   39.
[9]   ,,   ,,   ,,   12. 37. 47. 57.
[10]
[11]   ,,   ,,   ,,   32.
[12]
[13]   ,,   ,,   ,,   10. 34.

From this enumeration it will be seen that 4 of the shields described by Cole are no longer to be found. Their absence is the more remarkable as the woodwork is continued right round the room without any interruption, so that it is difficult to conceive where any other shields could have been placed. He is wrong too in saying that the arms of Roos and Spencer are "repeated 6 or 7 Times." The arms of Roos occur only once.

Cole has shewn that [1] is for Roos and Spencer. The Lady Margery Roos, a considerable benefactress to the College in 1469 (Mr Searle's History, p. 73), was the daughter and heir of Sir Philip Spencer of Nettlestead, Suffolk, and granddaughter of Robert Tibetot, or Tiptoft (Gage's Hist. and Antiq. of Suffolk, 4° Lond. 1837, p. 4). Her second husband was Sir Roger Wentworth. This explains the presence of the shields numbered [5], [6], [12]. That numbered [4] may be for Holland, Powis, and Tiptoft; that numbered [10] for Powis and Tiptoft; and that numbered [13] for Holland and Tiptoft, but the tinctures are wrong. The woodwork has however been so frequently repainted that mistakes of this kind can easily be explained by the ignorance of a workman. The correct arms of Tiptoft are: Argent, a saltire engrailed gules: of Powis; Or, a lion rampant gules: of Holland; Gules, three lions of England, within a bordure argent. The presence of these shields may be thus explained: the Lady Joan Ingoldsthorpe founded a fellowship in 1491 (Mr Searle's History, p. 119). She was daughter and co-heiress of John, Lord Tiptoft and Charlton, by Joyce, daughter and co-heiress of Edward, Lord Charlton and Powis, by Lady Alianore Holland. These arms occur in Pott-Shrigley Church, East Cheshire, where Lady Joan Ingoldsthorpe is buried. See Earwaker's East Cheshire, ii. 327; and, for the brass of her mother, at Enfield, a paper on "The Monumental Brasses of London and Middlesex," by Rev. Charles Boutell (Trans. Lond. and Midd. Archæol. Soc. i. 67). The shields numbered [7], [9] are for John Grene, esquire, who founded a fellowship by will about 1479 (Mr Searle's History, p. 93). He married Edith, daughter and heir of Thomas Rolfe, whose arms were Argent, 3 ravens sable [9]. (Visitation of Essex, Harl. Soc. Publ. xiii. 57, 58.) John Grene had 3 daughters only: 1. Elizabeth, Abbess at Dartford: 2. Agnes, married Sir William Fyndereux, by whom she had a daughter Anne, married to Sir Roger Wentworth: 3. Margaret, married Henry Tay. The shield numbered [2] is apparently for St Aubyn and Tilney, and [8] for St Aubyn alone. That numbered [3] resembles the quarter in the arms of the College for Lorraine, but the charges in that are on a bend instead of on a pale as here.]

IX.

𝕾. 𝕮𝖺𝖙𝖍𝖆𝖗𝖎𝖓𝖊'𝖘 𝕳𝖆𝖑𝖑.

CHAPTER I.

[HISTORY OF THE SITE[1].

THE site of S. Catharine's Hall is bounded on the east by Trumpington Street, on the north by part of King's College[2], on the west by Queens' Lane, the commencement of the street anciently called Milne Street, on the south partly by Small-bridge Street, now Silver Street, partly by a block of houses at the south-east angle of the site, of which some only are the property of the College.

The acquisition of this site was unusually gradual, and the relations of several of the pieces composing it to each other are extremely intricate and obscure. They have been laid down on

---

[1] [Professor Willis had collected materials for this chapter, but he had not written it out for press. He records in a note the assistance he had derived from a series of extracts from the College documents selected and written out for his use by Henry Philpott, D.D., then Master, now Lord Bishop of Worcester. Similar assistance has been rendered to me, not only by the loan of all the papers written out by Dr Philpott when he was arranging the muniments of his College, but also by unrestricted access to the originals, through the kindness of my friend, the Rev. C. K. Robinson, D.D., the present Master. All quotations from conveyances and other documents have in consequence been carefully compared with the originals. The help that my friend the Rev. G. F. Browne, B.D., formerly Fellow, has so kindly given me on all occasions, has already been gratefully recorded in the preface.]

[2] [The Bull Hotel is actually the north boundary of the site, but, as it belongs to this College, the real boundary is King's College.]

the plan (fig. 1)[1] as accurately as is now possible; but in some cases it has been found impossible to accommodate the medieval measurements to the known dimensions of the ground.

The Founder, Dr Robert Wodelarke, Provost of King's College, began the acquisition of his site by purchasing (10 Sept., 38 Hen. VI. 1459), from John Botwright, John Ansty, and Richard Brocher, who acted as his agents, two tenements on the east side of Milne Street, "over against the late Carmelites then newly Queens' College," as Fuller[2] says. The description of them in the conveyance from the aforesaid parties may be thus translated:

"Situated together in the parishes of S. Edward and S. Botulph, between the tenement of John Rasour to the south, and a tenement belonging to Michael House to the north. The eastern end of one of the aforesaid tenements abuts partly on the aforesaid tenement of John Rasour, partly on a tenement belonging to the College of Corpus Christi and S. Mary called "le George;" the eastern end of the other abuts only on the latter tenement. At their western end they both abut upon the King's high-way called Millestrete. Their northern border, from Millestrete to "le George," along the tenement of Michael House aforesaid, measures 90 feet of assize; their southern border, along that of John Rasour, 107 feet 2 inches. These two tenements we lately acquired from Thomas Lolleworth burgess of Cambridge, dyer, as appears from his conveyance, dated 8 November, 33 Hen. VI. (1454)."

The position of this piece of ground, upon which, according to a record in the College Register[3] made 29 March, 4 Hen. VIII. 1513, "the College is built," can be determined with

---

[1] [The authorities for this plan are the original conveyances of the different pieces, most of which are preserved in the Treasury; a chartulary called "Memoriale Nigrum Magistri Roberti Wodelarke prepositi Collegii Regalis beate Marie et Sancti Nicholai de Cantebrig'," compiled by Wodelarke himself, containing lists of the estates, notices of the buildings, and other interesting particulars; the College Registers; and two plans drawn by James Essex in 1745 and 1765, of which the first shews "the houses next Trumpington Street, as they stood in the year of our Lord 1745;" the second, "the additions" to the College "according to Mrs Ramsden's Will, as they were finish'd in y⁵ Year 1765."]

[2] [Fuller, 168.]

[3] [This, and some other notes respecting the College buildings, are found in a list in the Register, i. 119, headed "Memoriale fact' Anno regni regis henrici octaui iiijᵗᵒ vicesimo die mensis marcii [25 March 1513] de omnibus perquisicionibus factis per magistrum Robertum Wodlark fundatorem huius Collegii et per magistrum et Socios Collegii siue Aule Sancte katerine vt plenius patet per euidencias in turre."]

tolerable accuracy. The reasons for the determination will be seen after the history of the other pieces has been related.

In the following year (9 Sept., 39 Hen. VI. 1460), the Founder obtained from the Master and Scholars of Michael House a lease for ninety-nine years of the tenement mentioned above, at an annual rent of eight shillings. It did not however become the property of the Founder until 13 Sept., 11 Edw. IV. 1471. The dimensions are not stated in the conveyance, nor is the eastern abuttal given. It is simply described as

"A tenement with a garden adjoyning it, in the street (*vicus*) called Millestrete, between a tenement of Robert Wodelarke on the south, and a tenement or hostelry called 'le Black bull' on the north."

On this piece of ground, according to the Register above quoted, "the Library is built."

Twelve years after his purchase of the two tenements above described, viz. on Michaelmas Day, 1472, Dr Wodelarke obtained a lease of a tenement and garden, afterwards called "Wodhows," at some distance to the south of his former acquisitions. It belonged to a chantry of S. Mary and S. Nicholas in the Church of S. Clement, and is described as

"A tenement with two chambers on the ground floor[1], and a garden adjoining, situated in le Milnestrete in the parish of S. Botulph over against the White Friars, between a garden belonging to Queen's College on the south, and the land of John Rasour on the north: containing in length thirty six yards and a half. One head, towards the east, abuts upon land belonging to the said Queen's College, and upon a tenement where Thomas Middilton, tailor, now lives. It there measures ten yards in breadth, and at the other head, towards the west along the street, it measures also ten standard yards[2]."

Had the Founder been able to acquire the property intervening between his first and last purchase—a brewery belonging to John Rasour—he would have completed the frontage of his College towards Milne Street, and would also have obtained

---

[1] [The words thus rendered are "unum tenementum cum duabus bassis cameris... erga fratres albos." The term "Wodhows" occurs in the Register, i. 119.]

[2] [This description is translated from the original lease preserved in the College Treasury. It was granted to Dr Wodelarke by Robert Blakamore, perpetual chaplain of the chantry aforesaid, with consent of John Damlette, Vicar, and of his parishioners. It was for 99 years, with a condition that on its expiration a new lease for the same period should be granted, and so on for ever. The ground must have measured about 4 ft. more along the south border than along the north, as the plan shews.]

an approach from Trumpington Street, as the plan (fig. 1) shews. That such was his intention, and that he had carried negotiations for the purchase of the property so far forward as to feel certain of it, is proved by the following extract from the "Memoriale Nigrum," where, after enumerating the acquisitions already described, the writer proceeds:

"And also another property lately acquired from John Rasour, as will appear more clearly from certain documents agreed upon between the aforesaid John, and Robert Wodelarke, respecting a certain portion of the purchase money to be paid in advance[1].

On these pieces of property the aforesaid Robert founded, built, and at his own cost and outlay erected and maintained to the honour of God, the most blessed Virgin Mary, and Saint Catherine, virgin, a certain House or Hall called the Hall of S. Catherine, commonly spoken of as *Saynt Kateryns Hall of Cambrige.*"

It is impossible now to discover the cause of Wodelarke's failure; but as from the list of documents given in the note below[2], it appears that the property did not pass into the hands of John Rasour until 1482, ten years at least after Wodelarke may be supposed to have tried to purchase it, it may be conjectured that the sale to the one depended upon the sale to the other. The College bought it at last 31 July, 1516, for £50, from Alice Ray, widow of John Ray, Burgess of

---

[1] [The passage, which it is impossible to translate quite literally, is as follows: (Memoriale Nigrum, fo. 49 b) "Ac eciam de alio fundo nuper perquisit' de Johanne Rasour, ut per certas Euidencias inter predictum Johannem et Robertum Wodelarke super certis Arris inter eosdem conuentum est plenius apparebit."]

[2] [1. 9 May, 8 Hen. VI. (1429—30). John Erlham conveys the estate to Thomas Wodewarde, brewer.

2. Date uncertain. Rose Wodewarde, his widow, to Andrew Dokett.

3. 4 May, 5 Edw. IV. (1465). Andrew Dokett to John Chapman and others.

4. 10 July, 22 Edw. IV. (1482). John Chapman, the others being dead, to John Rasour, Thomas Conyngton and others.

5. 2 Jan., 2 Hen. VII. (1487). Thomas Conyngton, Rasour being dead, to Robert Ryplingham, Clerk.

6. 21 Dec., 3 Hen. VII. (1487). Ryplingham leases it for 7 years to Thomas Conyngton, at an annual rent of £4. 0. 0.

It is described in both conveyance and lease as "situatum in parochia Sancti Botulphi inter tenementum Collegii Corporis Christi...ac tenementum nuper Roberti Woodlarke ex parte boriali, et tenementum quondam Johannis Topclyff nuper Thome Drysett ac tenementum pertinens cantarie Sancti Nicholai in ecclesia Sancti Clementis Cantabrigie ex parte australi; et abuttat ad vnum caput super Regiam viam vocat' le hyghstrete et aliud caput abuttat super Regiam viam vocat' le Millestrete."]

Cambridge. No abuttals are given in the conveyance, but the property is described generally as

"all that Tenement or Inne called the Swanne as it is set and buylded in the parisshe of Saynt butholl in Cambrygge afore said with Thappertenaunces to gether with all the Brewyng leadys ymplementis and vtensillis belongyng to brewyng beyng within the said Tenement; ...and also...a voyde Grownde lying and beyng byhynd the said Tenement called the Swane[1]."

The College kept the "voyde Grownde" and built upon it, as will be shewn in the next chapter; but they attached at that time so little importance to an approach from Trumpington Street, that in 1556 they sold the Swan Inn to John Mere, Master of Arts, and Esquire Bedell, for £50, together with the house to the south of it, which had been acquired in the interval, but at what precise time is not known. By comparing the abuttals given in the lease granted in 1487 by Robert Ryplingham, cited below (No. 6), with those given in the conveyance to Mere in 1556, the situation of the whole property, of which part was then sold, becomes clear, as the plan (fig. 1) shews. In 1487 the whole estate is described as extending from Milne Street to High Street, between a tenement of Corpus Christi College and a tenement late of Robert Wodelarke (then S. Catharine's Hall) on the north; and a tenement formerly of John Topcliff, and a tenement of the chantry of S. Nicholas on the south. In 1556 the Swan Inn is described as in Trumpington Street, next to a tenement of Corpus Christi College, called the "George," in the tenure of John Cook, Innholder or Carrier, on the north; and the house adjoining it on the south is described as formerly John Topcliff's, lately Robert Drysett's, now in the tenure of Robert Jenkinson. It is also worth noticing that at this time the Swan abutted westward on a stable with a room over it (*stabulum cum solario*) belonging to S. Catharine's Hall, and that Jenkinson's house abutted on a brick wall and garden belonging to the same[2]. This property consisted, therefore, of two distinct portions; a brewery, afterwards the Swan Inn, which faced the High Street; and a narrow strip of ground, not built upon, which extended to

[1] [Register i. 91. There are no title-deeds between 1487 and 1516.]
[2] [The conveyance to Mere is in the College Register, i. 83.]

Milne Street, and separated the Founder's first purchases from the chantry-ground which he acquired in 1472.

After Mere's death his executors, Thomas Wylson, B.D., and John Ebden, M.A., sold "The Swan," and the property to the south of it. The former was bought 16 February, 1560, by John and Nicholas Wilson, from whom in 1578 the College obtained, for £5, a piece measuring 12 feet in length, by 20 feet in breadth, on which a "hayhouse" stood. It was situated at the western end of the Inn yard, with a messuage of Thomas Hobson to the north, and the College stable above-mentioned to the west and south[1].

It will be convenient, for the sake of clearness, to narrate the subsequent history of this property at once. Nicholas Wilson sold "The Swan" to William Archer in 1580, and William Archer in turn to Cornelius Archer in 1615, from whom the College purchased it for £210 in 1676. The conveyance of 1580 notes that the tenement to the north had formerly belonged to Corpus Christi College, but then belonged to Helen Hobson, widow; in that of 1615, Helen Hobson is replaced by Thomas Hobson, the carrier of famous memory. It is uncertain into whose hands the property to the south of the Swan Inn passed when sold by Mere's executors. In the history of the next acquisitions, however, we shall find it in the possession of Mrs Margaret Hobson.

These were due to the energy of Mr Thomas Buck, Fellow and Bursar of the College, Esquire Bedell, and University Printer. He obtained in 1622 (24 October) a lease of the property which lay immediately to the south of the Swan; and two years afterwards (15 June, 1624) leased to the College the western half. The lease recites that, Margaret Hobson and others having leased to him, for twenty-one years from Michaelmas, 1622, "their tenement...in the parish of S. Botulph...betwene the Tenement and building of Mr Archer in parte, and of Katherine Hall ground in parte on the north side, and the tenement and grounds in the tenure of John Royse on the south side, the east hed abutting upon

[1] [The conveyance, executed by Nicholas Wilson, and Amy Chapman, alias Wilson, his mother, is endorsed "Butler's house, 20 Eliz:" with the following memorandum: "It is agreed between the said Nicholas and Amie, and the said Master Fellows and Scholars, that the wall, which standeth east, and separateth the house of the said Nicholas and Amie and the said Hay house, shall be to the use of the said Master, Fellows, and Scholars and their Successors for ever. Nicholas Willson."]

the strete and the west hed upon *the buildings belonging to Katherine Hall latelie built by Sir John Claypole, Knight,* which said building, yards, and gardeines doe conteine all together in lengtht from the strete vnto the outside of the said building latelie founded by Sir John Claypoole, Knight, eightscore and six foote, and in bredthe thoroughout six and twentie foote[1],"

he lets to the College for nineteen years from the Feast of the Nativity of S. John the Baptist next coming

"all that parcell of ground, heretofore a garden-ground, lieing next *the buildings belonging to the said College or hall, latelie built by the said Sir John Claypole,* conteining in lengthe three score and fiftene foote and eight inches, and in bredthe thoroughout six and twentie foote[2]."

At the expiration of this lease, the College obtained a second for twenty-one years from Cornelius Archer, who had bought the property in 1623 from Margaret Hobson (22 March, 1648). The ground is then described as "*with a house thereon built, as it is now used and enjoyed by the Master and Fellows:*" and they covenant to erect at the end of their term "*a sufficient wall of good materials on the north side of the said ground to fence and sever it from the College court and yard.*" It was finally bought by the College for £30 (3 May, 1662)[3].

In the same year (14 Oct., 20 James I. 1622) in which Buck obtained his lease, he purchased for £6. 13s. 4d., from Cornelius Archer, into whose hands the Swan Inn had now passed, as above related, two small pieces of ground described as

"One little pece of ground conteining in bredthe towards the north two foote, and in bredthe towards the south three foote and nine inches, and in lengthe from north to south twentie foote and three inches, which pece of ground lieth next a certeine house of the said Cornelius Archer oute of which the said pece of ground was lately taken towards the east, and next the ground belonging to the Master and Fellowes of the said Hall of S. Katherine, *whereupon a new building is now erecting towards the west:* one hed thereof abutts on the yard of Thomas Hobson towards the north, and thother hed upon a pece of ground belonging

---

[1] [As these and the following deeds give the only indications now obtainable of the position of these buildings, they are quoted at length; and the sentences relating to buildings are printed in italics.]

[2] [College Register, iii. 22. The lease is in the College Treasury, endorsed "M^r. Thomas Buck, his lease to Katherine Hall of land between Archer's court and Buck's building, 1624." The rent was £3, and is entered regularly every year in the Collector's Accounts, as for "the new Court;" "Rosamond Payne's Court;" "the Court behind the Chapel;" "the back Court by Archer's House."]

[3] [The lease is endorsed "the purchase of Archer's court."]

to the said Cornelius Archer, whereupon a brick wall now is built towards the south ; *upon moste parte of which pre-bargained pece of ground a brick wall is alredie erected by the said Master and Fellows :*

And also one other pece of ground conteining on the north side in lengthe eleauen foote, seauen inches and a halfe ; and on the south side in lengthe twelue foote and in bredth thorowout tenn foote, which last-mentioned pece of ground lieth next the ground of Margaret Hobson and Giles Lagden now in the occupacion of William Dickinson, Butcher, towards the south, *and next the ground of the said Master and Fellowes whereupon the said new Building is now erecting towards the north :* one hed thereof abutts on the ground of the said Cornelius Archer whereupon a brick wall is now built towards the east, and thother hed upon the ground belonging to the said Master and Fellows towards the weste ; both which pre-bargained peces of ground were before thensealing hereof belonging to the Capitall Messuage or tenement of the said Cornelius Archer."

In the following year (5 August, 1623), a third small piece was purchased from Thomas Hobson. It lay to the north of the ground previously acquired, and is described (no dimensions however being given) as

"all that parcell of ground lieing one the sowth parte of the yard of me the said Thomas Hobsone, and some tyme parcell of the said yard, *whereuppon parte of a Bricke wall and two Stockes of Chymneyes belonginge to the said Colledge are now with the licence and consente of me the said Thomas Hobsone, lately erected and builded.*"

These four pieces have been laid down to scale, according to the descriptions given above, and placed westward of the wall laid down on the map made by James Essex in 1745 ; but we cannot now ascertain when that wall was built ; nor assign a reason for the peculiar direction taken by it at the north-eastern corner of the garden[1].

In 1626, John Gostlin, M.D., Master of Caius College, bequeathed[2] to Catharine Hall the Bull Inn, which then occu-

---

[1] [The lease to Mr Buck gives the width of the garden as 26 feet throughout ; and yet the plan made 1745 shews that the eastern end was not then more than 18 feet broad. The only probable explanation is that the wall was built in this shape at some period subsequent to the transactions we are now noticing in order to suit the convenience of the lessees of the Swan Inn.]

[2] [His will is dated 9 Oct. 1626, and he died in the same month. He had visited the College shortly before his death, for in the accounts for 1626—27 we find " For a supper to enterteyne Mr Gostlin 1. 01. 0. Item for wine, tobacco, and apples then 0. 05. 3." The inheritance came to the College at once, but the profits were to be paid for seven years to William Gostlyn, the testator's executor. He, however, made over all his claims to the College, 10 April, 1630, on condition of receiving £40 a year for the next 3½ years. College Register, iii.]

pied a considerable space (as the plan shews), adjacent to
the north boundary of the College, and extended from Milne
Street to Trumpington Street. It came into the possession
of the Society in 1630; but a certain portion of it had been
ceded to them in the spring of the preceding year, for in the
accounts for 1628—29, the following item occurs for the first
time :

"For the rent of p^t of the Bull grownd from Lady day till
Midsummer [1].. 4.0.0"

The extent of this piece is shewn by the following extract
from the next lease of the Inn granted 7 July, 7 Charles I.
(1631), in which an exception from what the old leases had
demised is introduced :

"except and alwayes reserued...vnto the said Master and Fellowes...
all that part of the said Bull and Bull yard, whereon is now erected
a faire building of stone and brick, inclosed with a brickwall on the
north and east syde ; And also seuuentene foote of ground in length
and seuuentene foote and a half in breadth, lying without the said
brickwall, hereafter to be inclosed with a wall and a necessarie howse
thereon to be erected for the use of the said Master and Fellowes...;
which said parcell of ground hath heretofore bene part and parcell of
the bowleing Alley and Garden aunciently belonging to the said Inn[2]."

The extent of these pieces is shewn on the plan. By producing the south boundary line of the Bull Hotel to Milne Street,
a frontage of about fifty feet is given to the first-mentioned
of them. It is nowhere stated that the whole of the ground
was required for the new building ; and if we assume that it
was, it will be necessary to make the original site so narrow
that it is almost impossible to imagine that a College ever
could have occupied it.

In the year before this arrangement was made between
Dr Gostlin's representative and the College, there was obtained
from the Town of Cambridge by a lease for 500 years, dated
16 August, 1629, at an annual rent of twelve pence,

"One peece or parcell of Comon wast ground, lying behynd the
messuage or Inn called the Bull,...whereon part of the new buildings of

---

[1] [In the three following years the same entry occurs, rather differently worded.

1629—30.   For ye rent of ye bull-ground in ye newe court   £8   o   o
1630—31.   For ye rent of Dr Gostlin's courte for the 3. last quarters   4   o   o
1631—32.   For the rent of Dr Goslins court   4   o   o]

[2] [College Register, iii. 3⅓]

the said Hall or Colledge are sett and builded, conteyning in breadth at the end next the Bull gate fower foote and a halfe, and in length from the said Bull gate to the ould buildings of the said Hall one hunderd Sixtie eight foote[1]."

The probable situation of this strip of ground will be pointed out in the next Chapter.

It will be remembered that the northern boundary of " The White Swan" was an Inn called "The George," which originally belonged to Corpus Christi College, and afterwards became the property and residence of Thomas Hobson. The boundary between the two houses coincided with that between the Parishes of S. Botulph and S. Benedict, as we learn from the survey made by Essex in 1745. "The George" had a frontage of sixty feet to Trumpington Street, while its large yard and stables extended back over the north-east quarter of the present College Court, and over the site of the Chapel. Thomas Hobson died 1 Jan. 1630—31, leaving his house to his grandson and namesake, from whom the College acquired it in or about 1637, in which year and the following various sums are charged for clearing away the barns and stables in "Hobson's yard." The house, called "Sadler's House," from a subsequent tenant, remained until 1760[2].

On the accession of Dr Eachard to the Mastership in 1676, a scheme for rebuilding the College was determined upon, for which an extension of the Milne Street portion of the site towards the south was necessary. Application was therefore made to Queens' College for the lease of a strip of the garden which, as we have already seen, extended along the southern

---

[1] [College Register, iii. 35. The yearly rent was to be 12 pence. The reversion of this ground was conveyed to the College 7 Feb. 1839.]

[2] [No conveyance exists, and the date of this acquisition can only be inferred from entries in the accounts, the first of which occurs in 1636—37 :

1636—37.	Mending the lock of Hobson's house		0	0	4
	A dog of iron and brads for a house in Hobson's yard		0	6	0
	A lock for the backgate toward Hobsons		0	7	0
	For taking downe the barne and stables in Hobson's ground and making the brickwall with other work, ut patet per billam		13	17	0
	Recepta casualia. For the old timber of the barne and stables		25	0	0
1637—38.	Harrow for 21 load of sand to paue ye street before Hobson's gate		00	17	06
	Edwards ye shoemaker for repairing Hobson's house		01	10	00

For further particulars of Hobson, and his will, see Cooper's Annals, iii. 230.]

boundary of the College. The Society of Queens' College made, it is said, "many frivolous objections[1]," but at last returned the following answer:

"Q. C. Febr: 17th 1676. This is to certify those whome it may concern, That a Meeting being called of the Fellows of Queens Col: in Cambr: by the consent of the Master (then out of Town) and there being then present 15 of those 19 Fell: which in all belong to the said Coll: it was agreed by 14 of them who thereto subscribed their names, That a Lease should be made to the Master and Fellows of S[t] Catherines Hall for the convenience of their new Building, of 10 feet of ground in breadth and about 36 yards in length (being part of a Garden given to Qu: Coll: by M[r] Andrew Docket first President there) upon conditions to be agreed upon between the 2 Colledges, and likewise provided, that the said Master and Fellows of S[t] Cath. Hall do at their own charge procure the handes of 6 Sergeants at Law, or the Kinge's Counsel, to satisfy Queens Col: that it may be lawfully done, and shall further procure his Majesties Royall leave for the greater satisfaction and security to the Society of Queens Col: afores[d]."

Seven lawyers[2] were accordingly consulted, and they agreed that Queens' College might safely grant the lease. A separate opinion, however, signed by five of them, concluded with the following piece of advice, which unfortunately was disregarded by those to whom it was addressed:

"But I confesse it will concerne the Master and Fellows of S[t] Catherine's Hall to be well assured before they build, that the Colledge will not afterwards avoid the lease, as they may doe, untill eleven years are passed, and a new lease made at the Rent that shall then have bin p[d] for the greatest parte of one and twenty years."

The Society of S. Catharine's further procured, at the beginning of 1677, the following letter from King Charles the Second, addressed to Queens' College[3]:

[1] [These words are used in the case submitted to the Attorney General, in 1799.]

[2] [They were Francis Pemberton, Thomas Waller, Thomas Hanmer, John King, Thomas Exton, William Jones, and Lestrange Calthorpe.]

[3] [A copy of it, endorsed "To our Trusty and Well beloved the Master and Fellows of Q[ueens] C[ollege]" in our University of Cambridge" is in S. Catharine's College Muniment Room. The following extracts from the accounts of the rebuilding refer to this controversy:

167¾—167⅞.	To S[r] William Jones about Queens Coll. garden	1 1 6
167⅞—167⅞.	S[r] W[m] Jones hand for y[e] Kings letter about Queens College	
	garden besides w[t] he formerly had	2 3 0
	To y[e] Secretary and servants for y[e] same letter	7 2 6
	To Secretary Cook about Garden	1 1 6
167⅞—1681.	To M[r] Baron for writings for Queens Coll. garden	1 10 0]

"CH. R.

Trusty and well beloved, we greet you well.

Whereas the Master and Fellows of St Katherine Hall in that our University have by their humble Petition represented un[to Us]

That in consideracion of the ruinous condicion of their late buildings they have [with] the assistance of their friends begun a new structure which they hope by [the muni]ficence of those who shall be disposed to such a work in some time to [bring] to good perfection ;

But that to make ye Court to the said intended structure convenient and regular they have occasion to use a small parcel of ground adjoyning, viz. 10 foot in breadth and about 36 yards in length being part of a Garden devized to your College by A[ndrew] D[okett] heretofore President of the same ; of which they are therefore desyrous to have a lease from you for a term of yeares

And to that end forasmuch as it hath been doubted whether you could graunt such lease thereof without prejudice to the Will of your said Benefactor, They have consulted as well our Attorney Generall as our Advocate and other Councell learned thereupon, Who have declared their opinion it is no way disagreable to the Will of your said Benefactor if you shall graunt the Lease desyred ;

We have upon the humble Request of the said Master and Fellows, and for the advancing of so good a work, thought fitt to recommend it unto you (as we doe hereby in very particular manner recommend it) that you graunt them a lease of the Premises for such number of yeares and under such yearly rent as shall be agreed on between you and them.

So not doubting of your compliance in a matter so legal in it selfe and so usefull to your neighbours we bid you farewell.

Given at our Court at Whitehall, May 30, 1677, in the 29th year of our Reign.

By his Majesties Command

H. COVENTRY."

A lease or covenant of some sort must have been granted immediately afterwards, as the south wall of the Master's Lodge was built upon the ground in question, though none such has been entered in the Register ; and it is known on other evidence that a lease for twenty-one years was granted in 1685 or 1686[1]. The first lease extant is that granted 25 Feb. 1706—7, by which a rent of 20s. a-year is agreed to be paid for

"all that piece of ground on which the Master's lodging and some other part of their structure towards the street is erected, containing by

[1] [The original opinion of the lawyers was examined at that time, for it is endorsed by Sir W. Jones, who dates his opinion 15 Sept., 1685; and in the Collector's accounts for Mich. 1686 occurs the item "for drawing the lease of Queens' College and Garden and sealing money £1. 6. 8."]

estimation Eleven feet in breadth, and thirty six yards in length, being parcel of a garden called Tennis Court Garden in the parish of S. Botulph; and abutting towards other parcel of the said garden south, towards S. Catharine's Hall north, and lying east on the other parcel of the said garden, and west on the aforesaid street."

The events that next followed shall be told in an extract from the Case submitted in 1799 for the opinion of Mr John Mitford, then Attorney General:

"In 1729 Queens College granted to Catharine Hall another Lease of the above piece of Ground, together with another piece being $123\frac{1}{2}$ Feet long, and 7 Feet 2 Inches broad next the Laboratory, and 8 Feet 9 Inches broad the rest of the length, for 21 years, at the Yearly Rent of Two Pounds.

In 1751 another Lease was granted of both the above pieces of Ground exactly upon the same Terms as that in 1729.

About the Year 1789, the two Colleges not being upon very good Terms, Queens College insisted upon Catharine Hall's taking a new Lease, the old one having been expired many Years, and at an *advanced* Rent. The Society of Catharine Hall was willing to take a new Lease, but objected to any advancement of the Rent, on the ground that from the whole tenor of the proceedings respecting the Ground in question as well at the time when the business was first settled and the first Lease granted as also at the periods when the subsequent Leases were granted; and no alteration having then been made in the Rent it was considered by both parties as fixed and unalterable, and it was in fact much more than the intrinsic worth of the Ground granted. After much disagreeable altercation Catharine Hall at last agreed to take a Lease from Queens College for 21 Years from Michaelmas 1789, at the advanced Rent of one Shilling, and such a Lease was granted accordingly.

The late Land Tax Bills having enabled Queens College to alienate this parcel of ground, the Master and Fellows of Catharine Hall, being desirous of preventing any unpleasant Dispute in future between the two Societies proposed to the Master and Fellows of Queens College to purchase it at a fair Valuation. Queens College listened to the proposal, but when they gave in their Terms the Demand they made for those two Slips of Ground was £530.

It appears from the Calculation subjoined that they contain together 252 Square Yards or about $\frac{1}{20}$th part of an Acre, and therefore the Demand by the Society of Queens College for the Sale of the premises in Lease to the Society of Catharine Hall according to the above Estimate is at the Rate of upwards of Ten thousand Pounds per Acre!

The Master and Fellows of Catharine Hall of course rejected this most extravagant and absurd Demand, but offered to refer the Matter with respect to the price of the Ground under all the Circumstances to one or more either Universitymen or Architects, or in short to any indifferent person or persons and in any way or manner that the Society of Queens College should prefer; but to this fair proposal that Society will not accede.

As it is evident to the Master and Fellows of Catharine Hall from the above facts and other Circumstances that the Society of Queens College is determined to avail themselves to the utmost of the advantage they have gained over the Society of Catharine Hall by the negligence or confidence of the Predecessors in that Society they wish to be prepared for the worst against the time of the Expiration of their present Lease.

It may be proper to observe that there is hardly a College in the University, some part of which does not stand upon Ground belonging to some other College or Corporate Body, but no advantage has ever before, we believe, been attempted to be taken of that Circumstance. The Decision therefore of this Question involves in it not only the Peace and Harmony but the very Existence of almost every Society in the University.

The Society of Catharine Hall wish to have your Opinion upon the following points:

1st. If at the Expiration of the present Lease the Society of Queens College should demand a further extention of the Rent, will Catharine Hall be obliged to pay the same, or deliver up Possession of the Premises comprized in the Lease, or can they justify resisting such Demand *in toto*?

2d. If the Society of Queens College should resolve to pursue their Claim to the utmost, and should proceed to take possession of the Premises and pull down such part of the Lodge and other Buildings belonging to Catharine Hall as stand upon their ground, whether a Court of Equity will not interfere to inhibit their proceedings?

3d. What line of Conduct would you advise the Society of Catharine Hall to adopt either now, or, if nothing can be done now, at the time when the present Lease shall expire?"

His opinion must have disheartened his clients:

"The Society of Catharine Hall do not appear to have obtained any contract with Queens College that the lease shall from time to time be renewed, or to have acquired a right, by any means, to compel that College to grant any term beyond the term of 21 years granted by the lease of 1789. Except, therefore, during the remainder of that term, they are wholly in the power of Queens College, who may refuse to renew on any terms, or sell a new term at their own price, either by way of rent or fine.

If therefore they should demand an increased rent, the Society of Catharine Hall must submit, or deliver up the possession at the expiration of the existing term, leaving the buildings in as good state as the same were in at the commencement of the present lease, reasonable wear excepted. When Queens College shall have obtained possession, they may pull down the buildings now standing on their ground, and convert it as they shall think fit for the benefit of their own Society; and a Court of Equity would not, on behalf of Catharine Hall, interfere to prevent this destruction of the buildings.

I think, therefore, the Society of Catherine Hall have only two lines of conduct which they can pursue ; viz. either to wait patiently the termination of the lease for 21 years, and abide the event, taking upon themselves the hazard of more liberal conduct in those who shall then direct the affairs of Queens College, or to submit to the extravagant demand made by Queens College for the ground ; and probably upon reflection the Society of Catherine Hall will find it most prudent, not only for their ease and convenience, but perhaps also with a view to economy, to submit to this extortion.

If upon calculation they shall find submission adviseable, it will probably also be prudent for them to avoid all observation on the conduct of Queens College in the meantime. For however unconscionable the demand may be, considering the relation which exists between the two bodies, and the liberality shewn by other Colleges in similar cases, yet it is easy to imagine that it will cost Catharine Hall more than 530*l.* to procure for themselves elsewhere the same accommodation which they now enjoy by means of the ground in question, supposing that accommodation could be procured by building on another spot for the same purposes [1]."

The Society of Catharine Hall selected the first line of conduct suggested by their adviser, and waited until the lease expired in 1810. Two years and a half were then spent in negociations, as it would appear, for it was not till shortly after Lady-Day, 1813, that the matter was finally settled [2]. Catharine Hall paid to Queens' College £152. 6s. 0d., as rent for the two years and a half that had elapsed since the expiration of the lease; and Queens' College conveyed to them (25 May, 1813) the two pieces in dispute, together with a third piece, described as "a parcel of ground now used as a garden to the Master of Catharine Hall's Lodge, and adjoining the other pieces to the south (as shewn in the plan), together with the wall standing thereon adjoining the Printing Office Garden." The price paid for the whole was £1372.

The acquisition of the second of these two pieces in 1729 had been rendered necessary in order to provide an access to the garden, which Dr Thomas Crosse (Master, 1719—1736)

---

[1] [The Case and Opinion, dated 5 August, 1799, are in the Muniment Room of S. Catharine's College.]

[2] [The following Order was made by Queens' College at this time : " 12 January, 1813. It was at the same time recommended to the Master and Bursar to bring the Dispute between the College and Catharine Hall to as speedy a termination as possible, and according to the best of their Judgments ; and likewise to make terms with any other applicants for the renewal of leases."]

had purchased in the same year (6 November), together with
the house between it and the street, an Inn called "The Three
Horse Shoes." The retention of this garden for the use of
the Master, rent free, is especially stipulated in a conveyance
which was executed by him 4 December, 1730; with the
following condition, that "If the Master and Fellows of the
said Colledge or Hall, or Hall of Saint Katherine, shall at any
Time or Times hereafter think fitt and Convenient to finish the
Building of the said College or Hall which is at present Left
unfinished, and should think it necessary or convenient upon
finishing the said Building...to make use of the said Peice
of Ground ... that then they [his devisees] shall ... permitt
and suffer the said Master and Fellows ... to make use of
imploy or dispose of the said peece of ground or any Part
or Parcell thereof To and for the uses and purposes herein
before mencioned."

No further additions were made to the site after it had reached
the dimensions above described until after the benefaction of
Mrs Mary Ramsden, who by her will, dated 3 Nov. 1743, left
her estates to the College for erecting a building for the reception of six Fellows and ten Scholars (to be called Skerne's
Fellows and Scholars, after her relative Robert Skerne, who
had founded six Scholarships in 1661); for their maintenance;
and for other purposes.

In the "Rules and Orders" appended to her will, she directs:

I. "After all the other purposes of my will are completely executed
and finished, my desire is that with the clear annual rents and profits
of my whole estate may be purchased the houses and ground lying
between the now erected college and Trumpington S^t, in order to erect
thereupon a new building for the reception of the fellows and scholars
of my foundation; but if such houses and ground cannot be purchased
at a reasonable rate, I then desire that the said building may be erected
upon any ground already belonging to the college, or that a purchase
may be made of any other convenient spot adjoining to the said college, on which such buildings may be erected most ornamentally for the
said college.

II. A convenient site being procured and the whole expence in
procuring of it defrayed, then with the said net annual produce I would
have the said building erected, with sufficient distinct apartments for
each fellow and each scholar, if it may be, to front Trumpington S^t, if
not, to be placed, as above said, in such manner as may be most convenient and ornamental to the said college."

In consequence of these directions, the College employed an attorney to acquire the pieces of ground that intervened between "The White Swan" and "The Three Horse Shoes." They first bought (28 May, 1754) from Alice Appleyard for £416 the eastern portion of the ground which has been already described as leased to Thomas Buck in 1622[1]. On the following day the house to the north of "The Three Horse Shoes" was conveyed to them by George Riste for £160: and on 14 June the tenement west of the last purchase by Anne Benwell for £140. Three years afterwards, they obtained from Queens' College the intervening property on the condition of paying an annuity of £8 per annum for ever.

In 1809, the Town of Cambridge leased to the College for 999 years, from Michaelmas 1808, at an annual rent of one guinea,

"certain void Ground in the Street on the West side of their College ...the same being and extending as followeth Videlicet in length before the front of their College ten score and seven feet, Videlicet, at the south end thereof for the first twelve feet to begin with a cant two feet and an half in breadth and from thence northward to the College Gate three feet in breadth and at the North end thereof being at the Bull Inn Back Gate for the first twelve feet there to begin with a cant two feet and a half in breadth and from thence Southward to the College Gate three feet in breadth for them to set a pale thereon before their College."

This is the narrow strip between the west wall of the College buildings and Queens' Lane, extending, as the plan shews, from the northern border of the piece first acquired from Queens' College, as far as the gate of the Bull Hotel[2].

The buildings that occupied the south-west angle of the present site were conveyed to the College 2 April, 1836. They consisted of the University Printing-House and School of Anatomy, together with a row of Almshouses, the property of Queens'

---

[1] [In 1674 this house became the property of Robert Grumball, or Grumbold, Freemason, with whose work we are so familiar. In the accounts for 1683—84 we find "To Jn. Howard for ye Wall between ye Coll. and Mr Grumbold's yard 2. 18. 0." His grandson, Robert Grumball, sold it in 1731 to David Appleyard and Alice his wife for £110. They therefore made £306 by the transaction.]

[2] [The reversion of this ground, and that of the other piece leased in 1629, was purchased from the Town in 1839 (7 Feb.), for £31. 10s. 0d. The Town had leased it in 1724 for 40 years at a yearly rent of 7s. At that time a lease granted in 1780 was surrendered.]

College. The whole stood upon part of the ground intended by King Henry VI. for the site of S. Bernard's College. The price paid, including expenses, was £7,965. 2s. 10d., towards which the Master, Dr Procter, and the Senior Fellow, Mr Burrell, each gave £1000.

In 1871 the house and yard, which occupies the centre of the block at the south-eastern angle of the site, was purchased from Mr C. Balls; and in 1875 two other houses fronting Silver Street, so as to provide a more commodious space for the new Master's Lodge, as the plan shews.]

CHAPTER II.

HISTORY OF THE BUILDINGS OF THE OLD COLLEGE
(1473—1658).

[HAVING traced the gradual acquisition of the site, we will now attempt to determine the plan and arrangement of the buildings that occupied it previous to the general rebuilding of the College at the end of the seventeenth century. The notices that have come down to us are so few, and so conflicting, that this is a task of no small difficulty.]

The founder records the completion of the first buildings in the following terms:

"On this property Robert Wodelarke founded, built, and at his own cost and outlay erected and established to the honour of God, the most blessed Virgin Mary, and saint Katerine the virgin, a certain house or hall, called the hall of saint Katerine, or commonly *Saint Kateryn's Hall of Cambridge*, for one master and a certain number of fellows, to last for ever to the praise of God, and the establishment of the faith.

This work, as aforesaid, was accomplished and fully finished on the festival of Saint Katerine the Virgin [25 November] in the year of our Lord 1473: and on the morrow of the festival Peter Weld M.A, and John Wardall B.A, entered into commons as fellows, together with James Wylborde M.A, Edmund Bacton M.A, and others as fellow-commoners, as will be more fully set forth afterwards[1]."

---

[1] [Memoriale Nigrum, fol. 49. Mention is also made of the materials which the founder had collected. He had bought the timber of certain houses at Coton "memorandum de meremio empto in certis domibus framiatis," together with unwrought

Wodelarke's little College fronted Milne Street, from which was its chief entrance, for it was hemmed in on the east by the gardens and back premises of the houses in High Street.

The Chapel and Library were not finished for several years. In 1475 (28 June), Wodelarke received forty pounds from the executors of William Coote towards the completion of these two buildings[1]; and a benefaction, the amount of which is not recorded, from Clement Denston for the same object.

The Bishop of Ely, William Gray, gave a general license to celebrate divine service in the Chapel in the next year (15 January, 1475—76); but a similar document from William Pykenham, Vicar-General during a vacancy of the See, is dated two years later (26 September, 1478); and as the license granted by it is made to depend on the condition that the Chapel be "suitable and proper and arranged for divine service," we ought perhaps to conclude that the building was not ready before the later date[2].

[The founder also obtained permission (22 August, 1477), from Andrew Doket, President of Queens' College, to build upon the south side of the garden adjoining that belonging to his College; a proceeding which indicates an extension of the buildings in that direction[3].]

After this no record occurs respecting College buildings until 26 October, 1505; when the executors of William Taylard, Esquire, gave a hundred pounds to the "building, repair, and maintenance" of the College[4]. In 1517 (29 April), Dr Thomas Greene (Master, 1507—1529), gave £10 "towards a new structure of four chambers to be built on the south side of the College." This was in the year after the purchase of the "void ground" which completed the Milne Street site, and shews both the importance of that purchase, and that it was at once taken advantage of[5].

---

timber from other persons. A supply of clunch was secured by the hire of six roods of land at Hinton. Sand was also provided.]

[1] [Register of S. Catharine's, i. 13. Denston's name is recorded in Woodelarke's deed of Commemoration, dated 28 June, 1475.]

[2] [Ibid. i. 77.]　　　　　　　　[3] [Ibid. i. 119.]

[4] [Ibid. i. 18. The same sum was given in 1523 by Alice Lupsett, widow of Thomas Lupsett, goldsmith of London, for the same purposes. Ibid. i. 32.]

[5] [Ibid. i. 64.]

Shortly before 1577, a fire had occurred in the College, doing considerable damage. We learn this from a remarkable document by which John Mey, Master or Keeper, and the Fellows grant to Mr Marmaduke Momson, Master of Arts, and sometime Fellow, a lease of his chamber for twenty-one years[1]. The document is also interesting from the description it gives of the arrangement of College rooms at that time. It is dated 23 April, 1577, and after the usual preamble, proceeds thus:

"ye said m^r and fellowes, in consideracion y^t the said marmaduke and som of his kinsfolk and frends have bestowed a somm of monye towardes the bricking vp of certayne chambers consumed by fyer belonging to ye said colledg or Hall; and in consideracion also of his goodwyll alway borne vnto the said colledg, have demysed graunted and to fearme letten, and by thes presentes doe demise graunt and to fearme let vnto the foresaid marmaduke one chamber, being above and over a chamber which Mr Edward Croft pensioner of ye same house hath of the colledg; being also betwixt the queenes colledg lytle orchard of the south end, and a chamber which Mr Jhon Furmarie fellow of the said colledg or Hall is in of the north end of the foresaid chamber; with one lytle bed chamber and one studye in the south end of the chamber, and one other lytle studye in the north end of the chamber; with one vpper chamber also having a study in the south end of y^t chamber and one lytle colehouse in the north end thereof:

to have and to hould the said chamber with the bed chamber, two studyes, and the vpper chamber with the study and colehouse…from the day of the date hereof vntyll the end and tearme of xxj yeares then next folowing, and fully to be compleat and ended if the said marmaduke doe lyve so longe, yeilding and payinge yearely for the same vnto the said m^r and fellowes…the somm of xx^s of good and lawfull monye of England at the feast of thannunciacion of ye virgin marye…….

And the said master and fellowes…doe covenant and grant to and with the said marmaduke…y^t he…and his assigns shall at all tymes during the tearme of this lease have fre accesse with ingresse egresse and regresse to the said chambers so y^t he or they com in and out in such tymes as ther locall statutis do permyt ther gates to stand open on. And the said master and fellowes…do covenant and grant to and with the said marmaduke…that y^ei…shall beare all necessarie reparacions of the sayd chambers during all the said tearme and doo further graunt… y^t if the said marmaduke do chaunce to dye before the said xxj yeares be expired y^t it shalbe lawfull for his executours and assignes to hould and enioy the said chambers for one whole yeare after his death and they to have fre ingresse egresse and regresse into the same chambers paying the rent for ye yeare as he in the fore said lease is bound to pay for the tearme of xxj yeares, videlicet xx.s."

A representation of the College at this time, the end of

---

[1] [Register, i. fol. c.]

the sixteenth century, given by Hammond (fig. 2), shews a small court with buildings on all four sides of it. The north side of this court is nearly in a line with the south wall of

Fig. 2. S. Catharine's Hall and Queens' College, reduced from Hammond's map of Cambridge, 1592.

Queens' College Fellows' Garden. A large building, probably intended to represent the Chapel, stands outside the court on the east. The range of buildings on the south side of the court

is also prolonged beyond it eastward. To the south of this court
there is a garden, with buildings along the west and east sides.
The garden must represent the chantry-ground and Rasour's
tenement; while the small court must stand upon the ground
obtained by the founder in 1459 and 1471. The building on
the west side of the garden may be assigned to the range of
chambers built by Dr Green, one of which we know looked
into Queens' orchard; the eastern building may be intended
to represent the "stable with a room over it," mentioned in
the conveyance of the Swan Inn, in 1556: or the "gallery"
which Mr Cragge, Fellow and Bursar, is known to have built
in this position [1].

The next addition to the College buildings was commenced
in 1611. In April of that year (18 April, 1611), the Master
and Fellows made a contract [2] with John Atkinson, of the
town of Cambridge, to erect a good and substantial range of
building "so long as is between the chapel of the College
and the utmost part of their ground towards Queens' College
Orchard, to be set up in the place where the gallery now
standeth;" the building to be two stories high, each story being
nine feet from floor to ceiling, and the breadth eighteen
feet from the inside of the brick wall unto the outside of the
groundsill in the lower rooms, and the second story as broad as
the said brick wall will suffer it to be; the case of stairs without the building to be of such convenient size as to carry
a fair pair of stairs up to every one of the six rooms; each
of which is to have a fair bay window on the College side; at
the end there is to be a bay window; and convenient lights on
the other side by clerestories; each of the six rooms is to have
partitions for study and bed-chamber. The builder is to take
down and use the gallery, which Mr Cragg built; and to take
down John Royse's house, and instead thereof make a wall,
whereupon the building shall run. The whole work is to be

---

[1] In Speed's plan of Cambridge Catharine Hall is not named, and has no reference,
as the other Colleges have. Its place is shewn by a large building standing a little
to the north-east of the chapel of Queens' College, and forming the south side of a
small court, which has a low building on the west side next Milne Street, and a
larger building in continuation of the range on the same side.

[2] [The contract is printed in the Appendix, No. 1., from the original in the
College Treasury.]

completed within twenty days after next Michaelmas: and the builder is to be paid £60 at the time of sealing, and 100 marks on October 22, or £126. 13s. 4d. in all.

It is unfortunate that the whole length of the building should not have been given, as we should then have known the exact position of the Chapel. If however we compare this contract with that made by the same builder in 1617, for the Perse Building at Caius College, we shall find that the height and breadth of the ground-floor rooms is the same in both: and moreover that the number of rooms in each floor was to be the same[1]. We may therefore assign the same length to the entire building, which will give a total of sixty-three feet, which exactly fills up the width allowed on the plan (fig. 1) for the Chantry-ground, and the "voyde grownde" bought in 1516. It of course stood west of Mr Buck's garden, which was not leased to the College until 1624. John Royse was one of the previous occupiers of the house to the south of this, obtained from Queens' College in 1757. The contract further proves that the Chapel must have stood at the east end of the building on the south side of the court, and not on the north side as Hammond shews; and Blomefield, writing in 1751, confirms the propriety of assigning this site to it, for he says, referring to the existing Court,

"The ancient Chapel belonging to this College, stood in the middle of the Court, where the Garden now is, and the Bones were removed and buried in the new one."

The chambers contracted for above were those to which Sir John Claypoole contributed nearly the whole sum required, in, or just before, 1613, when he gave "one hundred and twenty pounds of lawful English money for and toward the edifying and erecting of certain lodgings and chambers commonly called the New Buildings[2]." This is proved by the lease of Mr Buck's garden, quoted in the previous chapter, in which the garden is described as abutting west on buildings "latelie built by Sir John Claypoole."

---

[1] [History of Caius College, Vol. i. p. 204.]

[2] [By Indenture dated 31 December, 1613, the College agreed to maintain two scholars, and to allow them £5. 6. 8 out of the rents of the above chambers.]

Another building was erected about the same time in consequence of the benefaction of Mrs Rosamond Payne, whose executors paid to the College one hundred pounds in 1610, for the maintenance of two scholars, each of whom was to receive five marks annually. The building is occasionally mentioned in the accounts, but no indication of its position is given. It could not have occupied any portion of Buck's garden; for that was not leased to the College for fourteen years after the date of her bequest. It may however have run westward from the Claypoole building; just as the Perse and Legge buildings at Caius were placed at right angles to each other. The following entries in the accounts refer to it:

"1624—25 7^{lb} of pebbles to paue ye gutter in Ross:
        Paynes Court   0 . 2 . 11
  1626—27 To the Glazier for glazeing ye Library, the
        hall, ye kichin, ye buttry, ye Stairehead
        windowes both in Cleipooles and Payns   0 . 19 . 0"
        buildings

Another range of chambers was in progress in October, 1622, when the two small pieces of ground next Archer's house were bought for the College by Mr Buck. The conveyances quoted in the last chapter speak of the "new building now erecting towards the west;" and the "parte of a brick wall and two stockes of chymneys," which stood on the strip bought of Hobson in the following year, were probably the north side of the same range.

A volume of Bursar's[1] Accounts, beginning in 1622—23, has fortunately been preserved. The items of expenditure are set down under the head of the part of the College in which work is being done. Among those in the first year preserved we find "The Little Court" —"The Garden"—"The Old Buildings "—"The Court next ye Streete"—"The New Courte."

The "New Courte" can be no other than that of which the east side was formed by the building that was being erected in 1622; and which was afterwards called after the person to whose energy the College was indebted for the ground it stood upon. This is proved by the following entries, the first of which occurs regularly every year:

---

[1] [The Bursar in this College was called "Collector reddituum."]

"1623—24 To Mr Bucke for the yeares rent for ye ground
                of ye New Court .... 3 . 0 . 0
   1648—49 Towards the inlarging and makeing out the
                window in the further chamber of Mr Buck's
                building toward ye Bowling-greene .... 1 . 0 . 0"

The second extract shews that this building extended across
the ground as far as Hobson's yard, and also that the College
took immediate advantage of their purchase of the latter in
1637, to lay out a Bowling-green for themselves on the south-
western part of it[1].

This court was also sometimes called "The back Court
by Archer," as is proved by this designation taking the place
of the former one in the accounts, while the rent remains the
same, and also "The Court behind the chappell[2]." A court
called "The Pump Court[3]," to which it is difficult to assign
a separate place in the College, may possibly be this court
under another name.

[1] ["1637—38. For 2 keyes to ye bowling-greene   00 02 00
                    For painting ye seats in ye Bowl: [and other charges] 01 03 00
                    To the Carpent^r for making the Seats   00 06 00
                    Making ye bowling greene   05 00 00
                    Mending ye backe gate of ye Bowl: and a key to the
                          same for ye M^r 00 01 02
                    More to be added for the Bowlingreene   7 00 00
       1639—40. A latch for the bowling greene railes   0 2 6
       1640—41. For boards to the seats in the bowling ally   0 1 8
                    For painting the seats in the bowling greene   0 1 0
       1642—43. Payd for making up ye bowling greene   2 7 9
                    For making up ye doore to ye bowling ally and mend-
                          ing ye rowle   00 1 06
       1645—46. For mending and new laying the bowling green March 12   2 12 8"]
    [2] [The following extracts shew clearly that one and the same place is meant by
these various designations:
"1626—27.   To Mr Bucke for ye newe court   3 0 0
 1627—28.   To Mr Bucke for the new court   3 0 0
 1628—29.   For the rent of the court behind the chappell   3 0 0
 1630—31.   For rent of the backe court by Archer   3 0 0
 1631—32.   For rent of the back court by Archer's house   3 0 0
 1648—49.   To the Carpenter for mending a window in Archer's-Court   0 2 0
 1676—77.   Pump in Archer's court   1 8 10"]
     [3] ["1624—25. A grate for ye sinke in ye pumpe court   0 1 6
       1637—38.   Sadler for nayles and binding for ye pumpe-court   00 00 10
       1638—39.   For wooden barres to the windows in the Pumpe court 00 00 06
       1663—64.   To John Howard for work and materials in raising and new
                          paving ye street and the pump court, per billam Nov. 2^d. 18 17 8"]

The "Old Buildings" are probably the stable already mentioned, the "Storehouse," and perhaps other offices[1]. Their position is confirmed by the length of the piece of ground bought from the town in 1629, and by the terms of the conveyance. The piece is 168 feet long, and extends from the entry of the Bull to "the ould buildings" of the College. This measures exactly the distance from the south-west corner of the Bull Yard (where the entrance may be assumed to have been) to the stable; and the width, four feet, would suit very well for a back foot-way.

"The Little Court" may be the court enclosed by the buildings originally constructed by Wodelarke: and "The Court next the Street," that which had Dr Greene's building on the west, and the Payne and Claypoole building on the east. The Garden, as Hammond shews (fig. 2), was in this court; and in 1622 there was also a Dovehouse in it[2].

Besides these courts there was a cloister-court or building, to which the following entries refer. The position of it is nowhere indicated. As however we have already accounted for all the space within the College, it could only have stood on part of Hobson's ground; a theory which is strengthened by the fact that no entries concerning it are met with before 1636—37:

"1636—37 For a new key for the cloyster doore   o . o . 6
1639—40 Setting up the seate in the cloisters etc
1640—41 For whiting and painting the Cloisters   .. .. o . 6 . 4
            For a dog of iron for the bench in the cloisters o . 2 . o

[1] ["1637—38. For mending the Storehouse wall next yᵉ bowling-
             greene   oo 02 07
      1683—84. Mʳ Chaplain a bill for nayles, scuttles, etc. used about
                 casing yᵉ old building at yᵉ end of yᵉ Chappel   o 19 o
      1688—89. To John Howard for worke don about the chimneys and
                 tyling the old building at the end of the Chappel   2 11 9"]
[2] ["1622—23. In the Garden. For mending yᵉ Douehouse dore   o 2 o
The following entries are worth quoting as shewing the way in which College
courts were planted in the seventeenth century.
      1626—27. For plancks deales and studdes for yᵉ seat in yᵉ Garden, etc. o 14 o
      1630—31. For timber for railes of yᵉ garden   2 12 10
      1638—39. For 3 hookes for the sweete briar in the court   oo oo 09
      1640—41. To the Gardiner for rosemary sweetbriers and worke   o 6 o
      1646—47. To Bell for dressing the Garden and the Court-trees   o 7 7
                 To the gardener for weeding yᵉ garden and the walkes o 3 6"]

1646—47   To the glasier for mending windowes in the
          Cloyster   0 . 8 . 0
1648—49   Allowed Mr Lynford for ye Income of the⎫
          middle study in the furthest chamb^r of y^e⎬ 4 . 2 . 6
          Cloister building ....⎭
1677—78   For a window mending ith' Cloyster   0 . 1 . 8
1685—86   Repairing the chambers in the Cloysters   0 . 10 . 6 "]

All these courts, except the last, were included in a space
less than the area of the present quadrangle and its buildings,
as the plan (fig. 1) shews, where the probable extent and position
has been laid down.

The "faire building of stone and brick enclosed with a
brick wall on the north and east side," which the lease of the
Bull, granted in 1631, describes as "now erected," is still in
existence. It is a range of chambers eighty-seven feet in
length, having the kitchen on the ground-floor, and constitutes
the northern extremity of the College towards Queens' Lane.
It forms the western side of a little court, which is still enclosed
with a wall in conformity with the description in the lease.
The external aspect, as shewn by Loggan (fig. 3), has been
changed by repairs and restorations, especially on the side next
the lane, in which new stone window-frames have been inserted,
to suit the style of the more modern building to the south of it,
but within the court, and in the internal fittings and staircase,
its date is unmistakeably preserved. The staircase is a valuable
example of singular arrangement[1]; and the chamber to which it
leads still preserves its richly panelled outer and inner doors.
[The small room with a quaint projecting oriel shewn by Loggan
over the entry to the Bull Inn was a study, as the following entry
shews :

" 1640—41.   To Masons and Labourers for worke on the
            wall built to support the studdy over the Bull-
            gate .... 2 . 5 . 4 "]

The expression " whereon is now erected[2] " in the above
lease might be taken to mean that the building was then
finished ; [and we have already seen that the College entered

---

[1] It was engraved for Richardson's examples of this period at my request.
[2] The College borrowed £377 in 1630, and £100 in 1635.

into possession of the ground at Lady-Day, 1629; but the accounts shew that no work was undertaken before 1631—32, when the ground was walled in, as we learn from the following entries. The court was then called Dr Gostlin's Court.

"1631—32 To Mr Wilkinson for pavinge the back entrie
              of the bull, and building the wall towards the
              garden   7 . 13 . 4
              For sweepinge Dr Gostlin's court   0 . 0 . 6
              For carriage of 170 loade of earth out of ye
              new court   2 . 2 . 6 "]

The heading "The New Building" occurs for the first time in the accounts for 1634—35. In that year materials are paid for: viz. Slate, tiles, lead, timber, 47,840 bricks, &c.: together with wages to smiths, masons, glaziers and other workmen; the whole charge amounting to £260. 5s. 10d.: [but from the entries quoted below, it would appear not to have been finished for rather more than two years.

"1633—34 Feb. 10.   Pd ye Gardiner for quick sett to
                ye new court   oo . 5 . oo
  1636—37 For red oker for the new building............   o . 1 . o
                For three load of sand and six hundred of
                bricks' att 1s. 10 per hundred for the new
                building ....   o . 13 . 6
                For 5 day's work to Cowel for mending
                the tiling of the new building ....   o . 7 . 6 "

Some notices referring to particular buildings of the old College may be collected, but they are remarkably few and uninteresting.

CHAPEL.—The position of the Chapel has been already discussed. Its dimensions are not stated, but it was large enough to have an Antechapel; and a Belfry was attached to it. It is worth remarking that a window looked into it from one of the adjoining chambers[1]. When the College was rebuilt in 1673 the Chapel was preserved, and repaired to make it fit for service until

---

[1] ["1623—24. Six pesses for the Chappell   o 1 4
         1636—37. For a wainscot cupboard in the outward chappell   o 5 o
         1639—40. A locke for the bellfrey in ye Chapel   o 5 o
                       20 foote of Inch boarde for ye windowe looking into
                           ye chappell   o 2 6"]

there were funds sufficient to provide a new one.   The following entries occur in the building-accounts :

" Lady Williamson, Hales, Norf. gave towards the repaireing⎫
    the old Chappell   ⎬ 50 .   0 . 0
For a Carpet for the Chappel   4 . 16 . 0
For Wainscot and railing in yᵉ Communion Table   4 .   0 . 0"

LIBRARY.—It has been already mentioned that the Library was on the north side of Wodelarke's quadrangle ; and from a catalogue[1] in the College Register of the books that he gave to it, we learn that it had seven "stalls" or bookcases.   We may assume that these were set at right angles to the walls, as was usual in medieval libraries, with a window between each pair of cases.   The Library was therefore about thirty feet long[2].

MASTER'S LODGE.—An inventory of the "Stuffe in the Master's Lodginge," made in 1623, enumerates, at any rate, the principal rooms.   They are "the Master's great chamber ;" "the chamber next the Library ;" " the Master's bed-chamber ;" "the gallery ;" "the old rome at the stayers foote leadinge to the Library."   The Lodge was therefore next to the Library, on the north side of the court, and from a passage in the Founder's Statutes we learn that another of his rooms was over the Hall, which was therefore on the same side[3].

In 1638—39, we find "Expences in the Enlarging of the Chappell and Lodge."   The sum spent was £93. 2s. 2d., but few details are given.   Again, in 1657—58, a sum of £60. 3s. 8d. was spent as follows :

"in the Extraordinary repaires of the Colledg. viz. for slating and sparring yᵉ chappell, ripping both buildings in yᵉ old Court, part of yᵉ Lodging, cloysters, and building in Archers Court ; ripping all the new building, and taking down yᵉ Chimnys, new running and repairing the leads in the new building, etc."]

Fuller[4], speaking of Catharine Hall at this period, calls it " Aula Bella," by which he clearly means to indicate prettiness that depends on smallness of size, and declares that

---

[1] [Printed in the Quarto Publications of the Cambridge Antiquarian Society, No. 1, 1840 ; by Rev. G. E. Corrie.]   [2] [See the Chapter on College Libraries.]
   [3] [Printed by Dr Philpott in "Documents relating to Sᵗ Catharine's College," p. 19 : "reservata soli magistro...camera principali et etiam meliori super aulam, cum alia camera intercepta inter prædictam cameram et librariam."]
   [4] Fuller, 168.

"Lowness of endowment and littleness of receipt is all that can be cavilled at in this foundation, otherwise proportionably most complete in chapel, cloisters, library, hall etc.   Indeed this house was long town-bound (which hindered the growth thereof) till Dr Goslin that good physician cured. it of that disease, by giving the Bull Inn thereunto, so that since it hath flourished with buildings, and students, lately more numerous than in greater colleges."

CHAPTER III.

THE REBUILDING (1673—1704). THE RAMSDEN BUILDING (1757). ALTERATIONS AND ADDITIONS IN THE PRESENT CENTURY.

NOTWITHSTANDING the language of Fuller, it is evident that this "pretty Hall" was a mass of irregularly disposed buildings of different dates, and that the early parts of it were ill-constructed and sinking from age.   Consequently in the last quarter of the seventeenth century it was determined to pull down the whole [except the north wing built in 1634], and to build an entirely new College, the architectural history of which will be better understood by first describing its arrangements as it exists.

It occupies three sides of a spacious quadrangle, measuring 110 feet from north to south, by about 200 feet from east to west. It is on its eastern side open to Trumpington Street, from which it is separated by a space having a mean breadth of 54 feet, occupied by a grove of trees. The north range has, at the west end, the Hall and Buttery on the ground floor; the Combination Room over the Buttery and the Screens on the first floor ; and the Library over the Combination Room and Hall. The Chapel is at the east end of this range, in continuation of the above rooms (fig. 3). The south range contains the Lodge opposite to the Hall, and to the east of this, opposite to the Chapel, a building in continuation of the above, erected for the accommodation of Fellows and Scholars of the Skerne Foundation. Owing to the irregularity of the area, which has an acute angle at the south-west corner,

Fig. 3. S. Catharine's Hall, reduced from Loggan's print, taken about 1688. A, Chapel; B, Library; C, Hall; D, Master's Lodge; E, Kitchen.

Vol. II.

the south range is longer than the north, the former being 162 feet, and the latter 147 feet, in length. Neither of them are extended to the railing which bounds the quadrangle eastward, and which is 195 feet from the centre of the western gateway. The western side of the quadrangle, which stands in Queens' Lane, consists wholly of chambers in three stories surmounted by garrets, and has, in the centre of the court, a gateway of entrance from the lane. The building of 1634, already described, continues the range northwards, on the west side of the "Bull Court," which might well preserve its ancient designation, " Dr Gostlin's Court." The eastern side of the quadrangle is closed merely by a handsome palisade of iron with entrance gates between stone piers in the centre.

According to the original design, engraved by Loggan (fig. 3), this side was to have been occupied by a building in two stories with a gateway tower in the centre, the upper story containing the College Library. The quadrangle itself in this design measured only about 120 feet from east to west, and its eastern front, instead of facing the main street, was placed in a lane running parallel to it behind the back yards of the street houses[1]. A short lane from Trumpington Street gave access to the eastern gateway. Evidently the College was still supposed to stand in Milne Street as of old, and the Trumpington Street entrance was to be the back gate[2].

The realization of the project of reconstructing the College was, if the epitaph in the ante-chapel may be trusted, wholly due to the energy, industry and zeal of Dr Eachard, Master from 1675 to 1697, "who partly supplied the funds himself, partly obtained them from others—from the Learned through friendship, from the Rich through persuasive eloquence, wherein he greatly excelled. He finished the new building to a certain point ; and had the Fates spared him a little longer, he would have left an elegant, magnificent, and complete College, in the place of that sordid and ruinous structure scarce worthy of the name which he had found there." These florid expressions

---

[1] The extremities of the sides of the present Quadrangle stand at the same distance from Trumpington Street as in this original design. The difference between the length of the quadrangle as planned and as now is due to the omission of the eastern building and the position of the iron railing in advance of the gables of the wings.

[2] [These arrangements are shewn in Loggan's plan of Cambridge.]

are selected from his epitaph, for which the usual allowance must be made[1]. The inscription, however, under Loggan's engraving, written during the lifetime of this Master, omits his name altogether, and gives the credit of originating the work to another. After enumerating the ancient benefactors, the writer proceeds to add that others remain to be recorded by whose liberality the buildings represented in the plate had been constructed, in the place of a confined hovel (*tugurium*), frail from the beginning and ill-timbered. After rehearsing twelve names, he concludes with "the venerable Matthew Scrivener, a most learned and most worthy *alumnus* of the College, who was not only the first author of the construction of these new edifices, but who gave an ample estate to be especially reserved for the use of the future chapel[2]."

May we suppose that the writer of this account was the Master himself, who with commendable modesty omitted his own name? There is no real inconsistency in the two histories. The credit of suggesting the entire reconstruction of the College may well be due to Scrivener, and that of soliciting subscriptions and carrying out the work in detail to the Master.

[The rebuilding of the College was commenced on February 23, 1673—74, as we learn from the account book of receipts and disbursements kept by Dr Eachard. In attempting to estimate his share of the credit of the work, it must be remembered that he did not become Master until after the death of Dr John Lightfoot (Master, 1650—1675), in December, 1675. Mr Scrivener may have suggested the plan originally to Dr Lightfoot. He and his Fellows had greatly exerted themselves, and large sums had been collected before Dr Eachard's Mastership began[3]. During the twenty-two years however for which he

---

[1] [The Epitaph is printed in the Appendix.]

[2] Having narrated the foundation by Wodelarke, and the principal benefactors previous to the rebuilding, the writer proceeds—"Sunt et alii singularis erga hanc Aulam liberalitatis Viri, qui loco Tugurii admodum exigui, male materiati, et vel ab initio caduci, quas cernis ædes suis sumptibus extruxerunt. Quorum munificentissimi tantùm hic recensentur...et nunquam non celebrandus venerabilis vir Matth: Scrivener, doctissimus et dignissimus hujus Coll: alumnus qui non modo ædificia hæc nova struendi primus Autor fuit, Sed in honorem Dei (utpote in usum potissimum sacelli futuri) prædium peramplum dedit et consecravit." [Matthew Scrivener, Vicar of Haslingfield, entered the college as a Sizar in 1639, and died in 1687.]

[3] [Dr Lightfoot's interest in the work continued to the end of his life, for he went

held it, he appears to have worked with the utmost energy to obtain funds; and the language of the epitaph in this particular is fully justified by the memoranda that have come down to us. He not only sacrificed his own means, but he appears to have been successful in inciting the Fellows of the College to do likewise. This is shewn by the following extract from one of his account-books, dated London, March 29, 1697, and drawn up shortly before his death:

"The state of ye Accompts relating ye Building and my own accompts very nigh guessed at.

It is very probable y^t upon ye casting up of ye Books there may be 2 or 3 hundred pounds more rec^d then as yet is sett down as laid out, wch in reason ought to be allowed to Dr Eachard and placed to ye disbursements: For y^t since he was master besides all his own Revenue wch he was always ready to fling in, and besides what has been allow'd and placed to accompt towards horses, iourneys, treating Benefactors etc. out of Batchelour Feasts, Fellows Feasts, Fines, plate sold, and ye like, he has spent as tis guessed ye above mentioned sum of 2 or 3 hundred pounds."]

The accounts shew that the work went on without interruption from the commencement to Sept. 29, 1687, or for a little more than fourteen years. The total sum collected, by subscription and by loan, was £8,972. 14*s.* 2*d.*[1]; the sum spent was £8,946. 18*s.* 7*d.* The buildings included in this outlay were the whole of the west side of the quadrangle, the Hall and Combination Room with the Library above, and the Master's Lodge opposite thereto; or, in other words, the whole of the present College with the exception of the Chapel on the north side, and the Skerne building on the south. All the above-described work was completed in the lifetime of Dr Eachard, who died July 7, 1697, having, as it thus appears, witnessed the completion of more than half of the buildings comprehended in the original design. No name of an Architect is mentioned in the College records[2]: [unless payments at the beginning of the accounts to a "Mr Elder, Surveyor, for his journey from

to London on some business connected with it not many months before his death, as is shewn by the following extract from the building accounts: 1673-74—1676-77. "Journey to London Dr Lightfoot, Mr Eachard Mr Calamy 13 6 6."]

[1] [This is the amount arrived at by Dr Philpott from a careful study of the accounts.]
[2] 1673-74—1676-77. "To Mr Elder surveyour for his journey from

London and charges here   8   0   4
To Robert Grumbold for Surveying   2   3   0 "

London ;" and to Robert Grumbold, who had been employed at Clare Hall in 1669, imply that they were responsible for the design :] neither was the building erected by contract, the materials being paid for as they were supplied.

[The accounts unfortunately give but little information respecting the progress of the work. The Hall, Butteries, Combination Room and Library, were finished first, as is shewn by the following entries, which occur in the accounts between 1673—74 and 1676—77. The Hall was opened at Whitsuntide, 1675.

"To ye joyner for Wainscotting ye butteries	5 . 13 . 5
To Cornelius Austin for Wainscotting ye Hall, combination room, and room over that, and other work [1]	159 . 4 . 6
Laid out for wine at opening ye Hall, and commencement, and Sturbich fair following, besides wt was paid by ye College [2]	30 . 0 . 0 "

The Lodge was ready between 1676 and 1678; for the following charges can hardly refer to any other part of the College, though it is not specially stated that they were incurred for it. The furnishing was not completed before 1687—95, under which date the last entry is made :

"167$\frac{6}{7}$—167$\frac{8}{9}$.	To Mr Asgill for gilded Leather	11 . 1 . 3
	To Mr Duckfield for Tapestry hangings and other furniture	12 . 15 . 0
167$\frac{8}{9}$—1681.	To Mr Asgill for chairs and gilded leather to hang withdrawing room, and carpets etc.	63 . 2 . 9
	To the Upholster for bed and Fringe	14 . 11 . 0
1687—1695.	To Mr Reynolds upholster for Bed and chaires for ye Lodgings	23 . 13 . 6 "

The range of chambers next the street was probably the last work completed, for the last division of the accounts, from 26 February, 1683—84 to 29 September, 1687, contains wages to carpenters, joiners, plasterers, etc., with a charge of £36. 13s. 4d. for casements : entries which imply the fitting up of rooms :

---

[1] [An entry at this time "Bought of Mr Wrag Hangings £4. 10. 0" may perhaps refer to the Hall. The Combination Room was not furnished until 1678—1681, when we find "Curtains for Combination, £1. 8. 0."]

[2] [The total of the expenses at the opening of the Hall was £119. 14. 11. A stone with the date "MAY VIITH MDCLXXIIII" carved on it was found in repairing the steps to the screens, and is now used for the scraper of the Master's Lodge. This probably denotes the date of the foundation.]

but the front at any rate had been finished in 1679, as we are told in an amusing letter from James Bonnell to Strype, dated Nov. 17, 1679:

"I went to Cambridge as I intended, and returned ye same night, staying there…3 hours tho much importuned not to return y^t night, wch some circumstances of my hors w^d not permit me to comply with: by ill fortune it provd Gosling day and Mr Blackal preacht; I came when he had done; and was taken up in company all ye time, at a long dinner of ill drest meat (under ye rose) and a formality of being servd by gownd waiting men, little dirty pawd sizers, wth greazy old fash'nd glasses, and trenchers y^t w^d hold no sawce: but this only for merriment between y^o and I: ye end of ye Colledg next Queens, is finisht, and ye gate is plain next ye street; but very hansom of ye inside; they talk of going on, but whether next Spring or no, I cant tell: you will know before this I suppose that Dr Each^d is V. Chancell^r…[1]."

A row of wooden railings was at first set up along the front towards Milne Street[2]; this was afterwards replaced by the "Range of noble Palisadoes of cast iron" still in existence, through the munificence of Dr Thomas Sherlock, Master 1714—19, afterwards Bishop of London[3].

The building accounts terminate on S. Thomas's Day, 1695, up to which date £10,620. 11s. 11d. had been spent; but very little work had been done in the interval between September 29, 1687, and that date. The sum expended during that period (£1673. 13s. 4d.) was chiefly for interest on money that had been borrowed. On the whole, the expenditure had exceeded the receipts by £1647. 17s. 9d. To meet this deficit the College had to make extraordinary exertions. Besides the sacrifices already mentioned, they sold three parcels of plate from the Treasury, which realised £197. 6s. 0d.; and on 22 Nov. 1688, the College Seal was put to a deed of sale to Sir Charles Cæsar, of Bennington, in the County of Hertford, Knight, whereby sundry silver tankards and pieces of plate, weighing

---

[1] [University Library, Add. MS. i. 41. I owe this quotation to the Rev. G. F. Browne.]

[2] [Building Accounts: 1681—1683-84. "To ye Carpenter for ye rails in ye street   22 . 11 . 1"]

[3] [Cantabrigia Depicta, 1763: p. 60. By a codicil to his Will, dated 26 June, 1760, he directed that the surplus of the rents of the property that he had devised to the College should be spent "in repairs of the library and keeping the rooms sweet and clean, and in keeping up the iron rails and painting them, as often as they shall want it."]

altogether 402 ounces, were conveyed to him, in discharge of a loan of £100[1].

On Dr Eachard's death, in 1697, the building funds were found to be in a sadly embarrassed condition, as the following statement, which was circulated in January, 1698—99, sets forth[2].

"*The State of St. Katharine's Hall In Cambridge.*

Whereas the Reverend and Worthy D[r] John Eachard, Late Master of Katharin Hall in the University of Cambridge, out of his great Zeal to promote Learning and Piety, did Design to Rebuild the said College or Hall, which through length of Time, was very much gone to Decay; and being thereto Encourag'd not only by the concurrent Advice and Approbation, but the Generous and Charitable Contributions of many Worthy Gentlemen and Divines, as well such as had been Students of the same College, and his own Pupils, as others in divers parts of the Kingdom; and having through his own indefatigable Industry, and great Expence, added to the liberality of other Contributors, made considerable progress towards the accomplishment of his intended Building, was still encouraged by the repeated Advice, and renew'd Promises, and large Subscriptions of many Prudent, Pious, and Charitably dispos'd Persons, to go on in a Work so greatly tending to the advancement of Learning and Piety: Accordingly, in the latter end of the Reign of King Charles the Second, he undertook a very Large and Chargeable Building, hoping that the Continuance of his own Care, Pains, and Expence, and the Promises and Subscriptions of others, who had engag'd themselves to be Benefactors, would enable him to finish this Great and Costly Work, as well as what he had formerly begun: But the sudden and unexpected Death of that Prince, and the Measures

---

[1] [This deed, shewing so remarkably that plate was at that time looked upon as a fund that might be resorted to in an emergency, and not merely as an ornamental luxury, is printed in the Appendix, No. II. The following extract by Cole, Add. MSS. Mus. Brit. 5866, p. 221, from an account-book of Dr James, President of Queens' 1675—1717, illustrates the way in which money was raised: "July 9, 1694. Paid to D[r] Eachard, Master of S[t] Katherine's Hall towards building their new Chapel, £50, for which I am to receive 5*l.* yearely during my Life, from the said College, viz. 50*s.* every Halfe yeare, and the first 50*s.* to be paid at the Feast of S[t] Thomas next, and soe on &c. The said D[r] has promised, that in Case I die within 2 yeares, he will pay to any poor Relation, such as I, or my Executor shall name, ten Pounds. M[r] Lea Fellow of the College, and the Master are engaged to see good security given for the Payment of £5 yearely." On which Cole remarks: "Dr James made a good Bargain here: for he had the Annuity 22 years, not dying till 1716: so that he gained double his money."]

[2] [The Statement is undated, but D[r] Philpott notes that "there is a memorandum in the College Order Book made by the Master, Sir William Dawes, Jan. 2, 1698-99 of his expenditure for the College, in which the following entry appears: 'For printing 100 of College cases, 12*s.*'" From the abrupt way in which the statement ends, it would appear that intending subscribers were to sign and return it.]

which his Successour took, in particular relating to the University's, raised such just Fears in the Hearts of Such, who otherwise were forward to promote This, and every good Work, least their well-meant Charity should be abus'd to serve the ends of Popish Superstition and Idolatry, as gave occasion to some to withdraw their Subscriptions, and others grew very cold and indifferent: Whereby it came to pass that a very great Debt was contracted, towards the discharging of which, notwithstanding his utmost Care and Pains, and the entire expence of all the proffits of his own Estate, his Mastership, and all his Preferments, he could make but slow advances. For the mighty charge which lay upon the Nation, towards the carrying on a long and rigorous War; and the great necessity of a very large Charity towards the support and relief of our Persecuted Brethren from abroad, rendered such as were willing, less able to assist and further him in his work. When therefore all other ways fail'd, 'twas at length, (not inconsiderately and rashly) but upon Mature Deliberation, Resolv'd to Engage in the building of a Chappel, this being thought the best Expedient, not only to discharge the old Debt, but likewise successfully to carry on and finish his intended work. Pursuant hereto, such Funds were thought upon, and in some part settled and compleated, as gave great hopes and encouragement. But the great difficulties which soon arose from the non-currency of Money; and the stop which was put to his own diligence and endeavours, by his lingering sickness, and at last his immature, and much lamented Death have unfortunately occasion'd that a very great Debt remains: Towards the clearing of which, the late Reverend Doctor (valuing the Public Good, more than the Private Interest of his Relations and Friends) has by Will, intirely bequeath'd his whole Estate of Inheritance, to the value of a Thousand Pounds and upwards; but this falling very short, we whose Names are here under written, being extremely sorry that a Series of unforeseen unlucky Accidents should have retarded and hindered so good a Work, and not willing that any discouragement should ly in the way of any future Patrons of Learning, and Benefactors to Mankind, do, as well towards the discharging of the said Debt, as carrying on the said Chappel, contribute in manner following."

The appeal was successful; various contributions were made with little delay, amounting in all to £764. 14s. 6d.; and the building of the Chapel was at once proceeded with. It was consecrated 1 September, 1704, by Simon Patrick, Bishop of Ely, who has left the following account of the ceremony:

"In the next month (August 1704) I was desired to consecrate a new Chapel built in Catherine Hall, Cambridge. Accordingly I considered of a form wherein to do it, and upon the 1st of September went thither, accompanied with the heads of several colleges and other worthy persons, dedicated it to the worship and service of God, to which it was set apart, with prayers and a sermon and the Holy Communion. The Master of the College, Sir William Dawes, and the

Fellows, desired the form of Consecration might be printed, with the Sermon preached by Mr Leng, a worthy Fellow of that College. Unto which I consented, and both were printed at Cambridge, a little after[1]."

The accounts, which are exceedingly brief, inform us that the woodwork was executed by John Austin, who received £353. 0s. 0d. for it, after a design furnished by Mr Taylor, of London[2]. The carving, by Thomas Woodward, cost £30. 0s. 0d. A payment of £100. 0s. 0d. to " Robin Grumbold, the stonecutter " may indicate that he designed the structure.]

The College now remained without further alteration for about fifty years, until Mrs Ramsden's benefaction in 1743, under the conditions related in Chapter I. This led to the erection of the building adjoining the Master's Lodge, and opposite to the Chapel. [It was at first called " The Yorkshire Building," because the Fellows and Scholars for whom it was intended were to be Yorkshiremen. The Architect was the celebrated James Essex, but he had upon this occasion no room for the display of his invention otherwise than by judiciously copying the details of the building of which his new work is merely a prolongation : and the gable is copied from that of the Chapel opposite[3]. The foundation was laid 1 July, 1757, and the contract for the brick-work, with Simon Barker of Cambridge, is dated 9 July in the same year. The estimate for the cost of all the works was £7,300. Carter, writing in 1753, says :

" The College is now purchasing several Tenements in Trumpington Street...to make room for a new Building wherein are to be Apartments for the new fellows and scholars, *with a Library in front*[4]."

From this it would seem that the idea of closing the quadrangle eastward was revived, but happily not carried out,

---

[1] [Bishop Patrick's Autobiography, Oxford, 1839, p. 187. It was the last service used on such an occasion in Cambridge until the consecration of S. John's Chapel in 1869, when it was taken by the Bishop of Ely as the groundwork of the service then used. Mr Leng's sermon was printed at the University Press in the same year.]

[2] [" P^d. M^r. Taylor, a London Joyner, for the draught of the Wainscot for ye Chappel £01 : 01 : 06."]

[3] [The first intention of the College had been to employ Burrough, from the following Order : "February 10th, 1757. It is agreed to take Advice of Mr Burrough Master of Caius College concerning the new Buildings of Mrs Ramsden's Benefaction."]

[4] Carter, 199. Compare also Dyer's Cambridge, ii. 178. [In the order made by the Court of Quarter Sessions of Cambridge, held 16 July, 1772, it is stated that the Ramsden Building had never yet been inhabited. Borough Rate Report, p. 44.]

when the Ramsden building was projected. The houses next Trumpington Street which had been purchased in 1754 were upon the occasion of these works pulled down, and the College was completely laid open to the street as at present. The merit of this arrangement must be assigned to Essex. The appearance of the court a short time before is thus described by Carter, whose history was published in 1753 :

"The Flower-Garden, where stood the old Chapel (and the Bones which were there dug up, we buried in the present Chapel), is a small but pretty spot, and kept very neat, and on a Pedestal in the Center stood a Statue of Charity, with a Child at her Breast, and two more by her Side ; but was a few Years ago taken away, tho' I think it was an Ornament to the Garden ; but I submit to the superior Judgment of that learned Society, who doubtless thought otherwise[1]."

Two tenements also, which had formed part of the Bull Inn property, adjoining the south side of the Bull, were now pulled down, for the purpose of erecting the present stables : the old stables having been removed for erecting the new building and completing the court and grove. At the same time the boundary line between the College and the Bull Inn was altered, some part of the ground taken from the yard in 1630 being restored to it, and other parts of the yard on which the offices behind the Chapel now stand being taken into the College.

The appearance of the principal court was greatly altered in 1868 by changes in the Hall and Library. An oriel window, projecting into the court, was added to the Hall ; and the windows, together with those in the Butteries and Library, were removed, and replaced by others filled with Gothic tracery. In the following year the interior of the Hall was wainscoted with oak. These alterations were carried out under the super-

---

[1 History of the University of Cambridge, p. 204. The petition of the Master and Fellows to the Bishop of Ely, praying him to consecrate their new chapel, dated 1 September, 1704, sets forth that "the said College or Hall was, by Length of Time, so very much decayed in most of its Buildings (the Chappel as well as others) that it was necessary to rebuild the same, and the same could not be built in a regular and uniform manner, without altering the situation of the Chappel of the said College :" and further that they have "erected a Chappel, in a new place, much more convenient and decent for the publick worship of God." The petition and the Act of Consecration are printed in Cooper's Annals, iv. 67.]

intendance of W. M. Fawcett, M.A., Architect. The cost of the whole was £1770.

The new Lodge was commenced in 1875, on the site acquired from Queens' College, as already recorded, in 1836. The buildings then standing upon it were removed in 1837, and in their places nine dwelling-houses were erected at a cost of £4,378. These were pulled down in 1875, to clear the site for the Lodge. It is a handsome red-brick structure from designs by Mr Fawcett. The external details are closely copied from the front of Sawston Hall, near Cambridge, a good example of a sixteenth century house. The panelling of the dining-room of the Lodge was brought from "Cromwell House" at the Castle End, when that curious old house was pulled down by the Trustees of Storey's Charity. The panelling in the Master's study was removed from the walls of the Buttery, where its features had long been hidden under many coats of paint. The size of the panels, and the style of their ornamentation, prove that this woodwork had been originally made in the reign of Queen Elizabeth. It was therefore probably brought from some part of the old College when the Buttery was built in the 17th century. The cost of erecting the Lodge was about £9,000. The old Lodge has been converted into three sets of rooms for Fellows.]

CHRONOLOGICAL SUMMARY.

1454.	10 September. The Founder, Dr Robert Wodelarke, buys two tenements in Milne Street.
1460.	9 September. The Founder obtains from Michael House a lease of the ground on which the Library is built.
1472.	25 September. The Founder obtains a lease of ground belonging to a chantry of S. Mary and S. Nicholas in S. Clement's Church.
1473.	15 November. Completion of the first buildings.
1475.	28 June. Bequest of £40 from William Coote for completion of the Chapel and Library.
1476.	15 January. License from the Bishop of Ely for service in the chapel.
1477.	22 August. The Founder obtains leave from Andrew Doket, President of Queens' College, to build on the south side of the garden adjoining the garden of his college.
1478.	26 September. License from William Pykenham for service in the chapel.
1516.	Purchase of "The Swan" Inn and "a voyde grownde" behind it.
1517.	29 April. Dr Greene gives £10 to build a structure of four chambers on the south side of the college.
1556.	Sale to John Mere of "The Swan" Inn and the house to the south of it.
1578.	Purchase of a piece of ground 12 ft. long by 20 ft. broad at the west end of the yard of "The Swan" Inn.
1610.	Mrs Rosamond Payne's building built or begun.
1611.	18 April. Contract with John Atkinson for a range of chambers called afterwards Sir John Claypoole's building.
1622.	Michaelmas. Mr Thomas Buck obtains a lease for 21 years of the garden of the messuage south of "The Swan" Inn.
,,	14 October. The same buys from Cornelius Archer two small pieces of ground, part of the yard of "The Swan" Inn.
,,	Building work in what was afterwards called "Archer's Court."
1623.	5 August. Purchase of a small piece of ground from Thomas Hobson.
1624.	15 June. Lease from Mr Thomas Buck of the garden leased to him in 1622.
1626.	Bequest of "The Bull" Inn from Dr John Gostlin, M.D.
1629.	30 August. Lease from the Town for 500 years of a strip of ground extending from "the Bull Gate to the old buildings" of the college.
1630.	Possession obtained of "The Bull" Inn.
1634—36.	The range of chambers on the west side of Dr Gostlin's Court is built.
1637.	Purchase of "The George" Inn from the grandson of Thomas Hobson.
1662.	3 May. Purchase of the garden leased from Thomas Buck in 1624.

1673—74.	23 February. Commencement of the rebuilding by Dr Eachard.
1675.	Whitsuntide. New Hall opened.
1676.	Master's Lodge ready for furniture.
,,	17 February. Queens' College agree to lease a piece of their garden.
.,	16 December. Purchase of " The Swan " Inn from Cornelius Archer.
1677.	30 May. Letter of King Charles II.
1679.	17 November. West side of college mentioned as finished.
1685—86.	Queens' College lease the piece of garden asked for in 1676.
1687.	29 September. Completion of the rebuilding of the college.
1704.	1 September. Consecration of new Chapel.
1729.	Lease of a second piece of the same garden from Queens' College.
1730.	4 December. Conveyance of a garden from Dr Crosse, Master, together with " The Three Horse Shoes " Inn.
1743.	3 November. Mrs Ramsden's Will executed.
1754.	Purchase of houses in Trumpington St. from Alice Appleyard, George Riste, and Anne Benwell.
1757.	1 February. Purchase of house in Trumpington St. from Queens' College.
,,	1 July. Foundation laid of Mrs Ramsden's building.
1809.	Lease from the Town for 999 years of a strip of ground along the west boundary of the college.
1813.	25 May. Purchase of 3 pieces of garden-ground from Queens' College.
1836.	Purchase of the University Printing House and School of Anatomy from Queens' College.
1839.	Purchase from the Town of the strip leased in 1809.
1868.	South front of Hall and Library altered.
1871.	Purchase of Mr Balls' house.
1875.	Purchase of houses from Mr Roe and Mr Jones to complete the site of the Master's Lodge.
,,	New Master's Lodge commenced.

APPENDIX.

I.   *Contract with John Atkinson*, 1611.

Articles of agreement made betweene the Right woorshipfull M^r. D^r. Hills master of S^t. Katherines Hall within the vniuersitie of Cambr' and the fellows of the said Coll: on thone partie, and John Atkinson of the same towne on thother partye, the 18th daie of Aprill 1611.

Imprimis the said John Atkinson...doth...agree to and with the said M^r and fellows of S^t. Katherines Hall to buyld them a good and substantiall Range of buyldinge so longe as ys betweene the Chappell of ye said Coll: and the vtmost part of their grownd towards Queens Coll: ortchyard; to be sett vpp in the place wheare the gallerye now standeth.

Item the said Jo: Atkinson covenaunteth ... that the foresaid buyldinge shall be a girt howse of two stories highe, eyther of them to be nyne foote from the floare to the seelinge, the studds to be 12 inches distant, the breadth 18 foote from the inside of the brick wall vnto the outside of the groundsill in the lower roomes, and the second storye so broade as the said bricke wall will suffer it.

Item the said Joh: Atkinson covenaunteth ..to make a Case of Staires without the buyldinges of such convenient biggnes as to carrye a faire paire of Staires vpp to every of the six roomes, and that in every of the said six roomes there shall be a faire baye windowe on the Coll: side, and in the end a baye windowe; and convenient lightes on thotherside by Cleriestories; and that the windowes shall be well and sufficientlie glased, 14 Iron Casements placed in the most convenient places; and all the said windowes to be colored with white lead and oyle.

Item the said Jo: Atkinson covenaunteth...to make in every of the said six roomes partitions for a studdy and a bedchamber, with sufficient doares, locks, hingells, and stapells.

Item the said Jo: Atkinson covenaunteth...that the severall floares in the said roomes shallbe borded with good and seasoned board, eyther of oke or dealbord; and all the said six roomes shallbe seeled with lime and haire within and without, the whole frame to be rough cast or smooth at the eleccion of ye said M^r. and fellows.

Item the said Jo: Atkinson covenaunteth...to make in the sayd buyldinge 2 stackes of chimneys with 3 fiers in eyther stacke well wrought for continuaunce and for cast of smoke for annoyaunce.

Item the said Jo: Atkinson covenaunteth...to remove Jo: Royse his howse and in stead therof make a wall whearvppon the buyldinge shall run and so provide by a cripple rooffe that the water shall not annoye eyther buyldinge.

Item the said Jo: Atkinson covenaunteth...to make a faire doare for entrance by M^r. Copingers chambers ende, with locke and keye, and thother appurtenaunces; and the whole passage to be throughecast with lime and haire.

Item the said Atkinson covenaunteth...that all and every the timber wch shallbe vsed in the said buyldinge shallbe sound, firme, stronge, and of a good scantlinge; and all the stone, tyle, glasse, iron, morter, brick, and whatsoever thing else is necessary, shallbe of ye best for continuaunce and to make it a strong seemly buyldinge and habitable; And that all the said buyldinge and every the particulars shallbe honestlie performed and ended within xx^{tie} daies after the feast of S^t. Michell the archangell next ensuinge.

For and in consideration of wch covenaunts and performaunce thearof the M^r and fellows of the said Coll: for them and their successors doe covenaunt graunt and agree to and with the said John Atkinson...to paie...vnto the said John Atkinson...at or before the insealing of these covenaunts the somme of three score pownds of lawfull Englishe monie, and in and vppon the xxijth. daie of October next ensuinge one hundreth markes of like currant monie.

And we further covenaunt that the said John Atkinson, in consideracion of the performaunce of ye said premisses, shall and maie have, take downe, and vse, the gallerie wch M^r. Cragg buylt and now standeth in the said Coll: to his owne proper vse comodity and behoofe, with all thappurtenaunces, viz: timber, tyle, glasse, iron, wainscott and claye with all the payle postes and rayles that now compasseth in the fellows garden in the said Coll: to have and enioye them for him his heirs and executours for ever.

In witnesse whearof the parties abouvesaid to these present articles have sett their handes and seale the daie and yeare first aboue written.

JOHN ATKINSON.

Sealed in the presence of
    Henry Kyng and
        Edward Hilles.

II. *Epitaph on Dr Eachard in the ante-chapel of S. Catharine's Hall.*

Tibi habeas, Katharina, hoc mortale depositum
Et in Penetralibus tuis requiescere sinas
Viri vere magni
Tenues hasce Exuvias.
Si quæras cujæ sunt; vix Lapides tacere poterunt
Fundatorem suum
Iohannem Eachard S.T.P.
Academiæ Cantabrigiensis bis Procancellarium,
Hujus Aulæ Custodem vigilantissimum,
De utrâque optime meritum.
Videsne Lector, novam hanc Collegii Faciem?
Quam pulchra ex Ruinis assurgit!
Totum hoc Musarum non indecorum
Domicilium,
Secundus hujus Romæ Romulus
Posset vocare suum.
Huic operi intentus, Liberalitate partim suâ
Illâque maximâ (cum pauperis instar Viduæ
In hoc Gazophylacium totum suum conjecisset)
Partim alienâ quam vel Amicitia inter doctiores
Vel Suadela (qua plurimum pollebat)
Inter divitiores undequaque acciverat,
Hucusque restauravit collegium.
Et si diutius Fata pepercissent,
Antiqua ædificia diruendo,
Nova extruendo
Nullum non movendo Lapidem
(Quæ erat optimi Hominis indefessa industria)
Quod sordidum, ruinosum,
Et vix Collegii nomine indigitandum
Invenerat;
Elegans, magnificum,
Et ab omni parte perfectum
Reliquisset.
Obiit Jul. 7mo 1697.
Ætat. 61.

III.

Grant of plate to Sir Charles Cæsar in discharge of a debt of £200.
Register of S. Catharine's Hall iii. 176.

To all to whom this present writing shall come Wee John Eachard, doctor in divinity Master or Keeper of the Colledge or Hall of St Katherine the Virgin...Greeting,

Whereas Wee the said Master or Keeper and Fellowes of the said Colledge or Hall have borrowed and received of S^r. Charles Cæsar of Bennington in the County of Hertford, Knight, the summe of two hundred pownds of lawfull money of England for the vse of the said Colledge and have expended the same in and towards the new Buildings thereof and which said summe...is now iustly due and owing by us vnto the said S^r. Charles Cæsar, Now Know Yee;

That Wee...for and in satisfaction and discharge of one hundred pownds parcell of the said debt of two hundred pownds by vs owing... Have given granted bargained and sold...unto the said S^r. Charles Cæsar,

All and singuler the Silver Tankards and peeces of plate herein after mentioned; that is to say One Silver Tankard called M^r. Soothbys tankard weighing twenty five Ounces and ten peny weight; One great two eared Silver plate weighing thirty ounces, One Silver Tankard called S^r. John Rouses tankard weighing fifty ounces, One silver tankard called M^r. Peter Pheasants tankard weighing twenty nine ounces and ten peny weight, One Silver tankard called M^r. Robert Brookes tankard weighing twenty four ounces and ten peny weight, One silver two eared plate called M^r. Potts his plate weighing twenty ounces, One other silver two eared plate with the Colledge Arms on it weighing one and twenty ounces, One other silver tankard called M^r. Boothbys tankard weighing nineteene ounces and ten peny weight, One silver tankard called M^r. Rolts tankard weighing twenty ounces and ten peny weight, One Silver Tankard called M^r. Pierces tankard weighing forty three ounces, One Silver tankard called M^r. Peter Husseys tankard weighing forty five ounces, One Silver tankard called M^r. John Whiting's tankard weighing nineteene ounces & ten peny weight, One Silver tankard called M^r. Robert Faggs tankard weighing twenty two ounces and ten peny weight, One other Silver two eared plate with the Colledge Arms on it weighing twenty two ounces, and one Silver drum Salt with the Colledge Arms on it weighing nine ounces and ten peny weight,

To have and to hold all the said Tankards and peeces of plate vnto the said S^r. Charles Cæsar...as his...owne propper Goods and Chattells for ever...

In Witnes whereof the said Master or Keeper and Fellowes...have hereunto sett the Comon Seale of the Colledge or Hall aforesaid.

22 November. 4 James II. (1688).

X.

𝔍𝔢𝔰𝔲𝔰 𝔠𝔬𝔩𝔩𝔢𝔤𝔢.

CHAPTER I.

HISTORY OF THE SITE. HISTORY AND DESCRIPTION OF
THE BUILDINGS ERECTED BY THE FOUNDER AND HIS
IMMEDIATE SUCCESSORS.

[HE site of Jesus College[1], which until 1497 was that of
the Benedictine nunnery of S. Mary and S. Rhadegund, is bounded on the south by Jesus Lane, on the
east and north by common ground anciently called
Grenecroft, but now Midsummer Common, Jesus Green, and
Butt Green, and on the west by a narrow street formerly called
"Garlic Fair Lane" in commemoration of a Fair granted to the
nuns in 1438, but now known by the meaningless name of Park
Street[2]. This street is partly built over the King's Ditch, so
called because made by King Henry the Third in 1267 for the
defence of the town. This therefore was once the limit of the

---

[1] [The materials for the history of this College are (1) the annual volumes of
accounts which extend from 1557 to the present day with no interruption at the time
of the Civil War; (2) the "Conclusion Books"; (3) a compilation made in the 17th
century, partly from documents, partly from tradition, by John Sherman, D.D.,
Fellow. He was of Queens' College, where he was admitted B.A. 1649. He migrated to Jesus, where he proceeded to A.M. 1653, D.D. 1665. He died 1671.
His MS., entitled "Historia Collegii Jesu Adornata Studio Johannis Sherman Collegii Præsidentis &c.," has been most obligingly lent to me by my friend G. E. Corrie,
D.D., Master. A grossly inaccurate transcript of part of it was published by J. O.
Halliwell, London, 1840.]

[2] [Le Keux, ed. Cooper, i. 359. The editor notes that the fair was originally
held in the Nuns' close, near the spot now occupied by the Master's garden. The
position is rendered certain by numerous entries in the Audit-Books. 1577—78.
Reparaciones. "Item for ledding ij paynes in the sowth wyndowe there [in the Chapel]
next to the garlicke fayre closse iij^s. vj^d." There was a gate out of it into Jesus Lane.
Ibid 1654—55. "Mending ye high way from Garlick fair gate to ye Col: gate
00. 05. 10." The Fair was subsequently held in Garlic Fair Lane, and was in existence
as late as 1808.]

site in that direction, as Loggan's plan (fig. 1) shews, so that
the nunnery, and afterwards the College, was surrounded by
water on all sides except towards the south. It is still
separated from the common by a watercourse.]

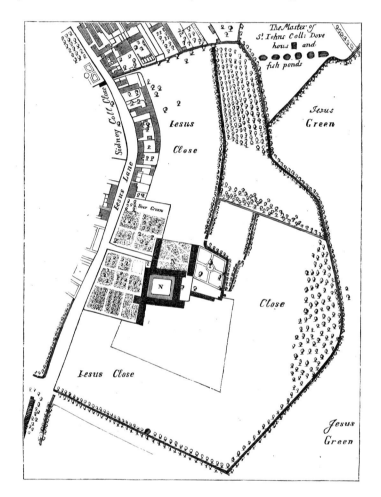

Fig. 1.   Ground-plan of Jesus College, from Loggan's ground-plan of Cambridge.

The Nunnery was founded at the beginning of the twelfth
century, but its history has little to do with that of the College

which took its place. The foundation of the latter by John Alcock, Bishop of Ely, has been already related[1]. The royal charter granted to him is dated 12 June, 1497; and in the following year the first Master, William Chubbes, was appointed. He entered cordially into the schemes of his patron and carried out his views respecting the foundation of a college. In 1499 E. Greigson and W. Plumme were admitted as the first Fellows, and the latter was chosen by the Founder to be the Curator or Supervisor of the buildings then undertaken. By Grace of the Senate he was allowed to absent himself from all congregations, exequiæ, general processions, and the like, in order that his time might be devoted uninterruptedly to the special work for which he had been selected[2].

Bishop Alcock died 1 October, 1500. The extent of the work he had lived to carry out is stated as follows by Nicholas West, Bishop of Ely 1515—1533, in the preamble to the Statutes which he drew up, or amended, twenty years or more after the Founder's death:

"We find the College established and founded for one master, 11 fellows, and 6 boys, or, to speak more correctly, begun to be founded, and built and constructed afresh almost from the foundations upwards by the same Reverend Father[3]."

According to Sherman, however, the Bishop began to alter the buildings of the nunnery before he had obtained a formal

---

[1] [See the Historical Introduction.]

[2] [1497—98. "Conceditur eciam magistro Plumme ut non artetur interesse congregacionibus nec generalibus processionibus nec sepulturis mortuorum quamdiu versatur circa edificacionem collegii Jhesu." Liber Gratiarum, B. 115.]

[3] Commis. Doc. iii. 94. "Collegium scholarium de uno magistro et undecim sociorum ac sex puerorum numero erectum et fundatum, seu ut verius dicatur, fundari coeptum, et pene ab ipsis fundamentis noviter per eundem reverendum patrem aedificatum et constructum comperimus." The previous statutes had been given by Bishop West's predecessor in the see of Ely, Bishop Stanley. Bishop Alcock was himself a zealous promoter of architectural work, if not a practical architect, besides holding the office of Comptroller of the royal works and buildings under King Henry the Seventh. We find him throughout the course of his various preferments leaving buildings that mark this taste, among which may be mentioned the Church of Westbury in Worcestershire, a Chapel at Kingston-upon-Hull, where his parents were buried, a hall and "solarium" at his palace at Ely, his own sepulchral chapel there at the east end of the north aisle of the Presbytery of the Cathedral, in addition to the buildings of his College, the plan of which is full of ingenious contrivance. He also contributed to Great S. Mary's Church, Cambridge.

charter from the king.   The following passages, translated from his work, contain all the information that he could collect respecting the share taken by the Founder or his immediate successors respectively in building the College :

"The college was built by Bishop Alcock from the foundation up-wards on a ground-plan which even to this day recalls that of the nunnery; and in a position most agreeable to the Muses, who delight in quiet and seclusion; a position, namely, as far removed as possible from the noise and confusion of the Town.

*   *   *   *   *

It was in about the eleventh year of the reign of King Henry the Seventh [1495—96] that the reverend father of blessed memory began to build the fabric; and in about the fifteenth year of the same reign [1499—1500], he introduced a master or keeper, five fellows, and six boys (*pueri*), to be maintained out of the revenues formerly belonging to the monastery of S. Rhadegund.

*   *   *   *   *

The foundations of fellowships and scholarships having been related, other persons deserve mention as benefactors.   Among these the first to be named is Sir John Rysley, who built the cloisters and the nave of the church at his own expense, and covered them with lead[1].

*   *   *   *   *

The Lady Joan[2], wife of Sir Richard Hastings, afterwards Lord Wells and Willoughby, whose arms are put up in the Master's Oratory, and the Lady Catherine, widow of Sir Reginald Bray[3], gave contribu-tions to the erection of the buildings situated between the tower and the fellows' garden.   In these buildings the grammar-school was situ-ated, where the schoolmaster and the usher, appointed on the Stanley foundation, discharged their duties.   The nomination of the aforesaid schoolmaster was granted to the Lady Catherine Bray, for the term of

---

[1] [The Commemoration Book records his work in the following terms: " Sir John Rysley covered the Cloisters with timber and lead and completed the Roof and Battlements at the West end of the Church."]

[2] [She was daughter to Lord Welles and Willoughby.   Her father and her only brother, Sir Robert Welles, were both beheaded by Edward IV., who bestowed their titles on her husband, Richard Hastings.   His will is dated 18 March, 1502—3.]

[3] [Sir Reginald Bray died 5 Aug. 1503, and his widow, in December, 1507, or in January, 1507—8.   Sir Reginald directed the works at S. George's Chapel, Windsor, during a great part of the reign of King Henry the Seventh, and provided for their continuance after his death.   He built the royal palaces at Greenwich and Richmond, and laid the foundation of King Henry the Seventh's Chapel at West-minster, 24 January, 1502—3, of which he is said to have been the architect.   Among other offices, he held a post in the household of the Lady Margaret, through whom he may have been led to take an interest in Cambridge.   Manning and Bray, Hist. of Surrey, i. 516.   Lives of the Speakers of the House of Commons.   By J. A. Manning. 8vo. London.   1850.   Cooper's Athenæ Cantabrigienses.   Davis and Tighe, Annals of Windsor, i. 421.]

her life, in consideration of the large and generous donations contributed by her."

To these may be added an extract from the will of Sir John Rysley, dated 13 September, 1511, and proved 14 May, 1512, which shews that the buildings were still unfinished at the former date:

"Item I bequeth towards the making of the cloyster and glasyng of the werke by me made at Jesus College in Cambridge, if I performe it not in my life, clx*li*; whereof is paid to doctour Egliston of the same college for the glasying xx*li*."

We will now compare these scanty records with the buildings themselves. A study of the ground-plans (figs. 1, 2) shews at once that their distribution differs entirely from that of every other college in the University, and that it has been wholly governed by the structural arrangements of the Nunnery, of which the College is a mere adaptation.

The distinctive features of this College are the cloister round that which was the principal quadrangle when Bishop Alcock founded the College, by means of which a dry communication is provided between all the apartments and offices; the entrance court; and the long road leading from the highway to the tower-gate between the parallel boundary walls of the Master's garden and of the Fellows' garden, by which additional privacy is obtained. This latter feature is probably derived from the nunnery. The cloistered quadrangle, universal in monasteries, is possessed by no other college either in Cambridge or Oxford, although many have cloisters in their secondary courts. Wolsey appreciated the convenience of it, and intended to have given a cloister to Christ Church, of which the respond-shafts and wall-ribs still adhere imploringly to the sides of that noble quadrangle, and stamp its architectural effect with the character of an abortive design, notwithstanding the lame attempt to disguise the original purpose of the shafts by continuing them upwards to the string-course.

The church of the nunnery was cruciform, having a nave and side-aisles, choir, central tower, and transepts, each with an eastern chapel. The cloister was on the north side of the nave, surrounded of course in the usual way by the chapter-house, dormitory, refectory, and other offices, which the nuns are accused of having allowed to fall into a state of dilapidation. Bishop

Alcock adapted their church to the purposes of a college chapel by a curious and ingenious transformation, in the course of which a new nave, in length equal only to a transept, was built at the expense of Sir John Rysley, and at the west end of it a range of chambers, assigned to the Master, which extended as far as the west end of the original nave, thus preserving the outline of the old church. The chapter-house, a building not required for a college, was probably pulled down in the course of these works[1].

Bishop Alcock retained the cloister, which was rebuilt at the expense of Sir John Rysley in the old position, but the area was made larger than that of the nuns' cloister by all the space previously occupied by the destroyed north aisle of the church. The deambulatory was enclosed by a wall, pierced, on the north side, with four perpendicular square-headed windows of three lights, as shewn by Loggan (fig. 3), a treatment which was probably carried out on the other sides also. The Bishop placed his Hall on the north side of this new cloister, probably on the foundations of the nuns' refectory, which is proved to have been a thatched building, by certain entries for repairs in their accounts for 1449—50, and 1450—51, which have fortunately been preserved. He erected ranges of chambers on the west side, and on that part of the east side which was not occupied by the wall of the north transept of the church[2]. These chambers are all in three floors, with a nearly flat leaded roof, as in the old court of King's College. The Library occupies the uppermost floor of the western range; the Kitchen a prolongation of this range to the north of the quadrangle. The position of these different offices and ranges of buildings will be understood from the ground-plan (fig. 2).

---

[1] Some years ago, when the plaster was stripped off the east wall of the cloister, the remains of arches were disclosed, which may have been portions of the Chapter-house doorway, or of the entrance to the usual passage between the Chapter-house and transept gable. [The outline of these arches may still be traced by cracks in the plaster. One of the round windows that are supposed to light the bedrooms just cuts into them.]

[2] [The following curious entries occur in the Audit-Book for 1572—73: *Reparaciones:* "Item to Barraker for a hundreth sclaiting latthes bestowed ouer the cloystre ende in the woddyarde xvj^d. Item...for an eaves latthe of x. fote long layde vppon y^e sparres feete vppon the Cloystre ende towardes the woddyarde v^d." Is it possible that the building east of the Hall did not exist at this time?]

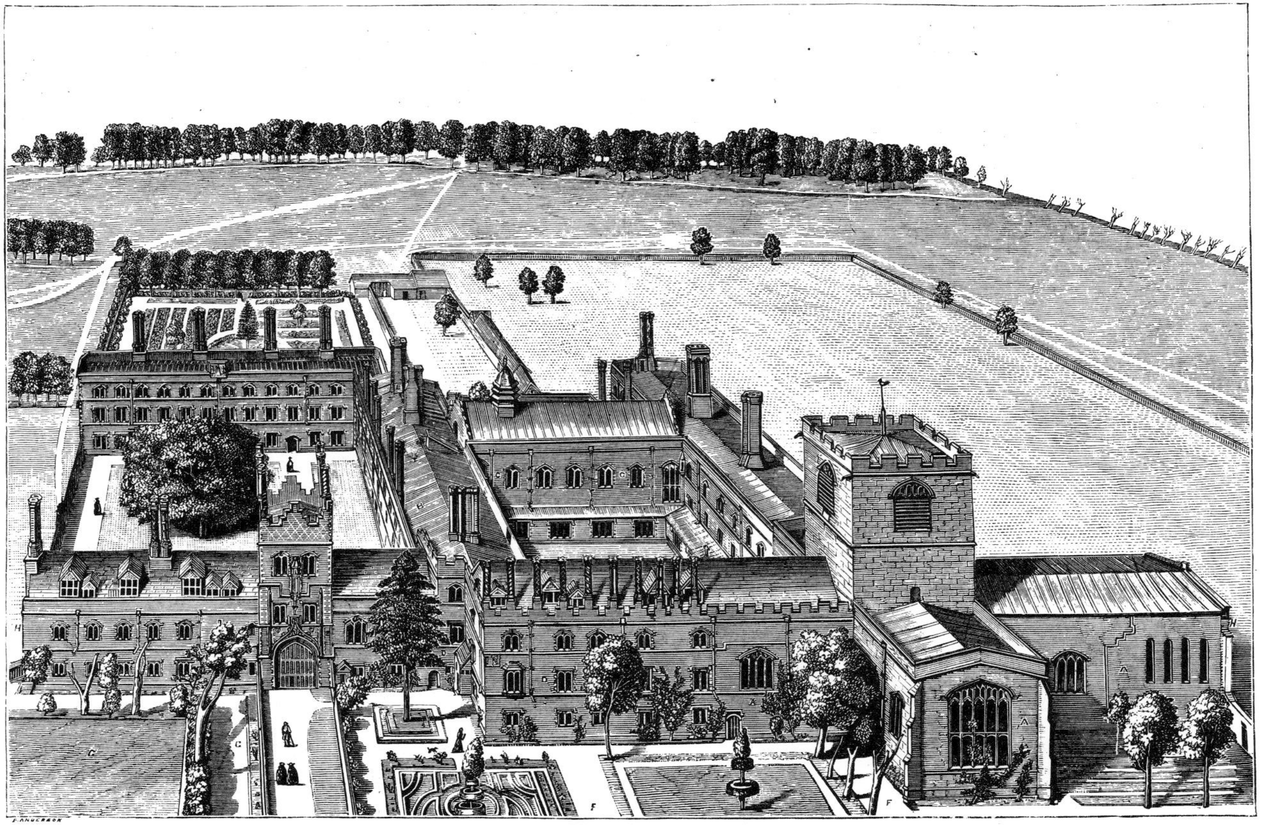

Fig. 3. Jesus College, reduced from Loggan's print, taken about 1688. A, Chapel; B, Library; C, Hall; D, Master's Lodge; E, Kitchen; F, Master's Garden; G, Fellows' Garden.

The floor of the Hall is considerably raised above the level of
the quadrangle, and has the butteries and cellars beneath it, so
that the usual arrangement of the screens is not to be found
here.   The Combination Room is at the east end of the Hall,
entered through a door at the south end of the dais.

Fig. 4.   Doorway at the north end of the passage from Principal Court to Cloister Court.

The range of buildings containing the tower-gateway on the
west of the principal quadrangle forms the south boundary of an
entrance court, probably in the same position as the "curia" of

the Nunnery, a monastic feature which we have already found at Trinity Hall. From this court the cloister-quadrangle is entered through a passage marked by a handsome perpendicular door-case[1] (fig. 4), now opening into it at the north-west angle of the cloister. Formerly however it was placed nearer to the southern extremity of the western range, as Loggan shews (fig. 1).

[The range westward of the tower was built between 1503, in which year Sir Reginald Bray died, and 1507, in which year his widow, who contributed to it, died. The history of the tower itself, and of the range eastward of it, is unfortunately unknown, and they can only be attributed to the Founder by internal evidence. Loggan's print (fig. 3) shews that the chamber on the first floor of this range next to the tower had a large window of three lights with tracery, which may indicate that it was intended for some official purpose.

We have now related the history, and described the position, of the buildings erected by the Founder and his immediate successors. In the next chapter we shall investigate the archi-tectural history of the conventual Church, tracing the steps by which it was converted into a College Chapel. In the third the subsequent history of the chapel down to the present time will be related. The fourth chapter will contain the history of the rest of the buildings.]

CHAPTER II.

History of the Conventual Church.

THE following facts have been ascertained respecting the history of the conventual church.

In 1254 Walter de Suffield, Bishop of Norwich, granted a relaxation of 25 days' penance to all benefactors to the nunnery,

---

[1] Drawings of this doorcase were published by Mr Pugin in his Specimens of Gothic Architecture. 2 vols. 4to. London, 1821. [This illustration (fig. 4) and that of the Great Gate (fig. 21), are from An Application of Heraldry to the Illustration of various University and Collegiate Antiquities, by H. A. Woodham : Camb. Antiq. Soc. Quarto Publications, Nos. 4, 5 (1841—42). The doorcase is not shewn in Loggan's general views (fig. 3) ; an additional proof that it had been moved to its present position after his time. See below, p. 170.]

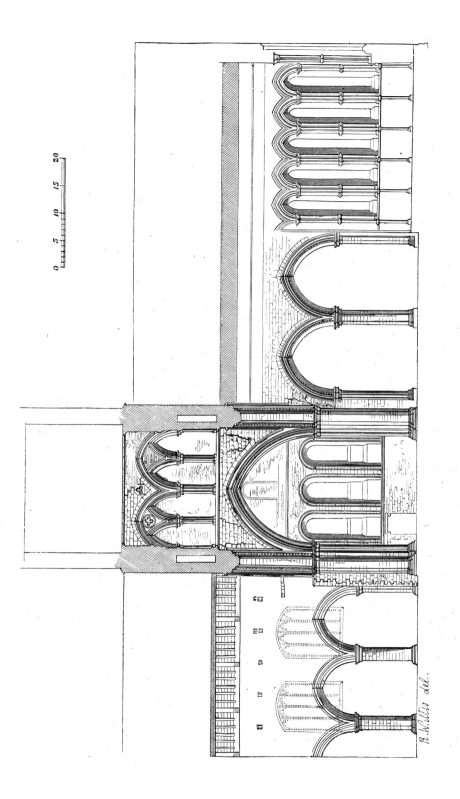

0 5 10 15 20

B. N. Willis del.

Fig. 5. Longitudinal section of Jesus College Chapel, looking north, shewing the piers and pier-arches discovered in 1845. The windows inserted by Bishop Alcock are indicated by dotted lines. Measured and drawn by Professor Willis.

either for the sustenance of the nuns or for building their church; and on 21 May, 1268, the Bishop of Lincoln granted the nuns permission to collect alms for the same purpose[1]. It is clear therefore, that at this time the charge of the fabric of the church had been regularly undertaken by the sisterhood, with such support as they could get from general subscriptions   On 27 April, 1277, the Bishop of Norwich issued an indulgence for the special purpose of enabling the nuns to collect money to pay for the repair of the tower of their church, which had at that date fallen and become little better than a ruin.   Again in 1313 the official to the Archdeacon of Ely recommends them to the clergy of the diocese, as objects of charity who had lost their house and all their substance by fire.   In the following year, 1314, John de Keton, Bishop of Ely, confirmed certain indulgences granted by his brother bishops for this rebuilding; but in little more than half a century the nuns were in trouble again, and in 1376 Thomas de Arundel, Bishop of Ely, granted a relaxation of 40 days' penance to those who would contribute to a fund for making good the losses which they had sustained by another fire.   Fourteen years later a storm of wind blew down part of their habitation, to repair which an indulgence was issued in 1390 by the Archbishop of Canterbury; and in 1456 William Gray, Bishop of Ely, granted them help "for the repair of the bell-tower of the Church of S. Rhadegund," and for other purposes[2].

The church to which these documents refer, presented, when complete, an arrangement totally different from that of the chapel of Jesus College at the present day.   It was planned in the form of a cross, with a tower in the centre, and had, in addition to a north and a south transept, aisles on the north and south sides of the eastern limb, flanking it along half the extent of its walls, and forming chapels which opened to the chancel by two pier-arches in each wall (fig. 2).   The structure was completed by a nave of seven piers with two side-aisles.   It will be well worth while to inquire into the proportions and details of the

---

[1] [This document, with those of 1277, 1313, 1314, 1376, and 1390, is printed in the Appendix from originals in the treasury of Jesus College.]

[2] [Register of Bishop Gray, transcribed in MSS. Cole xix. 155 b.   The words are, "pro reparatione campanilis et vtensilium ecclesie sanctæ Radegundis Cantebrigiæ."]

whole building, for it was an admirable specimen of the architecture of its period, and two of the best-preserved remaining
portions, the series of lancet windows on the north and south
sides of the eastern limb, and the arcade that ornaments the
inner surface of the tower-walls, will always attract attention
and admiration for the beauty of their composition. Before
attempting, however, to trace the architectural history of the
church, it should be mentioned that under the direction of
Bishop Alcock the side-aisles both of the chancel and of the
nave were entirely removed, the pier-arches by which they had
communicated with the remaining central portion of the building were walled up, and the place of each arch was occupied
by a perpendicular window of the plainest description. The
walls were raised, a flat roof was substituted for the high-
pitched roof of the original structure, large perpendicular windows were inserted in the gables of the chancel and south
transept, the latter of which is shewn by Loggan (fig. 3), and
lastly, two-thirds of the nave were cut off from the church by
a wall, and fitted up partly as a Lodge for the Master, partly
as rooms for fellows and students.

As for the portion set apart for the Chapel of the College,
the changes were so skilfully effected and so completely concealed by plaster within and without, that all trace and even
knowledge of the old aisles was lost; but in the course of the
preparations for repairs in 1846, the removal of some of the
plaster made known the fact that the present two south windows
of the chancel were inserted in walls which were themselves
merely the filling up of a pair of pier-arches, and that these
arches, together with the piers upon which they rested, and
the responds whence they sprang, still existed in the walls.
When this key to the secret of the original plan of the
church had been supplied, it was resolved to push the inquiry to
the uttermost; all the plaster was stripped off the inner face of
the walls, piers and arches were brought to light again in all
directions; old foundations were sought for on the outside of
the building, and a complete and systematic examination of the
plan and structure of the original church was set on foot which
led to very satisfactory results. [The description of these will
be made, it is hoped, perfectly clear by the help of the accom-

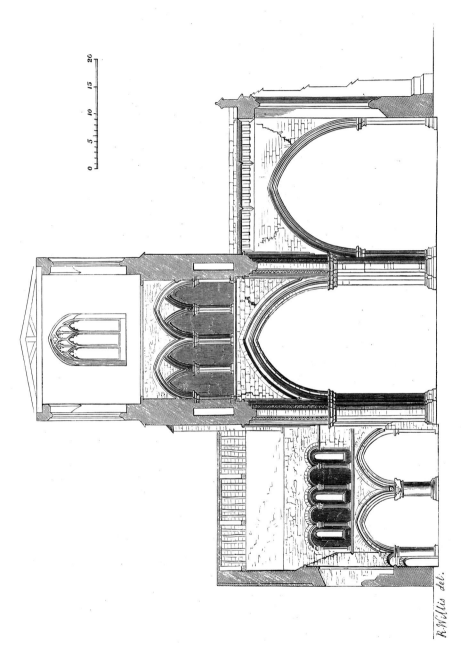

0 5 10 15 20

R.Willis del.

Fig. 6. Transverse section of Jesus College Chapel, on a line drawn through the transepts from north to south. Measured and drawn by Professor Willis.

Vol. II.

panying illustrations, which have been prepared from drawings made by Professor Willis while the restoration was in progress. The original plan of the church has been indicated on that of the College Chapel (fig. 2).]

The conventual church, if its architectural details and structure are taken as a guide, was erected between the years 1150 and 1245, some repairs of the tower only excepted; but during that period the work was carried on at several different times, and with changes of plan, each of which was on a more enlarged scale of dimensions than its predecessor, and shewed the increased and increasing wealth of the builders.

The north transept, which is manifestly the earliest portion, had, in its northern gable, a noble triplet of round-headed Norman windows, which have unfortunately been walled up (fig. 5), and its eastern wall is pierced by two low pointed pier-arches, which meet and rest upon a short cylindrical pillar (fig. 6). These arches opened into an aisle or chapels, the foundations of which were discovered on the outside and are shewn in the general plan (fig. 2). This aisle was destroyed by Bishop Alcock, who further walled up the arches and inserted in each of them a window of three lights. In the course of the restoration of 1845—47 it was thought expedient to build an organ-chamber and vestry upon the old foundations, and the arches, though restored, have been partly filled up with excessively heavy tracery, for the purpose of strengthening the old wall and tower-piers.

Above these arches are three round-headed windows, pierced in the wall of a gallery, having towards the transept an arcade of five round-headed arches (fig. 6). It is easy to see that this was an original clerestory, and that therefore the roof of the chapels was at first so low as to join this wall below the cill of the windows; but, when the church was increased in scale, the adjacent chancel was rebuilt, as we shall presently shew, and then the roof of the chapels must have been raised, probably in the form given to it in the above restoration, so as to shut out the light from the clerestory windows in question[1].

The west wall of this transept has been so mutilated by

---

[1] [In the view of the antechapel in Ackermann's Cambridge, drawn by Mackenzie, dated 1814, these windows, as well as those below, are filled with glass.]

Bishop Alcock's windows, and by the insertion of a door of entrance from the cloister (B, fig. 2), that its original arrangement can only be guessed at. Traces of windows still remain of the same mold as those in the gable, and there must have been an arch opening to the aisle of the nave in place of the present door; but this arch has not been merely filled up as most of the others were, but has been wholly taken out, piers and all.

There is a small square-headed door (fig. 5) with its lintel on corbels in the west corner of this transept, which probably led to a vestry or some such chamber outside the gable-wall.

The high cills[1] of the windows now concealed in the north wall shew that some building stood in the space between the transept and the chapter-house of the nunnery. In the north-east angle there is an octagonal turret-staircase (L, fig. 2), which communicates with the gallery of the clerestory, and probably also gave access to the dormitory, if this chamber was placed, as usual, partly over the chapter-house, and partly beyond it.

The nave of the church, which comes next in order of antiquity, had seven pier-arches on each side, resting on cylindrical and octagonal piers alternately (figs. 2, 5). The pier-arches were pointed and their moldings plain. The proportions and moldings of these arches are precisely the same as those of the pier-arches of the north transept; but the proportions of their piers are essentially different, although the bases and capitals of each are exactly the same. The shaft of the nave pier is four diameters in height; but that of the transept-pier is barely two, and this peculiarity gives an appearance of antiquity to the latter, which may be partly correct, for naves were often built after transepts; but, as the moldings and details of the two arches are the same, we may feel tolerably sure that there is no great difference between their ages, and that the loftier proportions of the nave-arches are due to the fact that in the transept clerestory windows were introduced, whereas in the nave no such windows were employed, and therefore the arches were carried up to a greater height.

The remains of the nave are, however, exceedingly few, for the side-aisle walls have been entirely removed, with the exception of a small portion of the western end of the north wall,

---

[1] [They have been obliterated since Professor Willis wrote.]

which has been retained as a partition-wall in the Master's Lodge (*ab*, fig. 2). The foundation of the remainder of this north wall was exposed by digging against the wall of the present cloister, and the width of the original north aisle was thus determined. A search was made for the foundation of the south aisle-wall, but nothing was found, and it seems to have been entirely destroyed. The existence of this aisle is therefore only proved by the existence of the southern piers and arches of the nave. The two northern and the two southern piers of the nave next to the tower, which were included in that part of the nave which was allowed to remain attached to the chapel, still exist entire, but embedded in the walls of Bishop Alcock's work. They stand, not in the middle of these walls, but close to their inner face (fig. 2), and they were once sufficiently disimmured by pulling down the rubble on each side of them to make it easy to ascertain their position and magnitude, as shewn in the section of the church (fig. 5). Above the abacus, about three feet and a half in height of the arch-moldings remain, and from the curvature of this fragment the form of the entire arch was ascertained; but the remainder of the arches and the whole of the superincumbent wall had been taken down by Alcock or Rysley, to make way for their windows, which are shewn by dotted lines in the section, and from their position it was evidently impossible to save the higher parts of the walls.

In the western part of this series of piers a still greater destruction took place, for as a domestic building, namely the Lodge, was built on the site, the numerous floors and windows seem to have forbidden the preservation of the pillars, which were allowed to stand only when it would have caused more trouble if they had been taken down. On the south side the lower part of the second pillar from the west was discovered embedded in the chimney of one of the offices, and appeared to be circular in plan, and thus to agree with the rule pointed out by those remaining in the eastern part of the nave, namely, that the piers were alternately octagonal and cylindrical; but the position of the windows in the more modern building shews that the remaining piers must have been cut off very close to the ground, for all these windows are extremely low (fig. 3). On the north side the piers may still remain in the walls; the north-west respond is to be seen in a cellar, and the thickness of the western wall of the Lodge (fig. 2) seems to mark the west front of the church, although it is now cased externally with brick. It is possible that a fine western door may at some future time be found in this wall.

The four piers and arches of the central tower are in a more advanced style of architecture, both in form and moldings, than the north transept and nave, as well as on a more lofty and noble scale of magnitude. These facts, as well as the distinct traces of the junction of two different samples of masonry which, when the plaster was stripped off, were seen at the places where these piers are connected with the nave and transepts, prove that this tower was built to replace an older one, probably that which fell down in 1277. Moreover, when the repairs of this part of the church were begun, it was found that the piers had been ashlared with old materials that had Norman moldings on their edges.

The tower-piers and arches are constructed with variations of ornament that may have depended on caprice, or on the slow and unsystematic progress of the work. These differences will be understood from the plan of the four piers here given (fig. 7). The south-western pier, for example, differs from the others in having a strip of large pierced pyramids or dog-tooth work running up on each side of its small shafts (ibid. D, _a_). The westen arch and the northern arch have each a band of the same ornament; but in the eastern and southern arch no such form of decoration exists. Every arch has a crack in its haunches, and an upper course of voussoirs (figs. 5, 6). The masonry of the spandrils over these arches differs as decidedly as the decoration of the voussoirs, for over the western arch the spandril is filled up with rubble-work having only a small patch of ashlar in the south corner, which appears to have been a repair, while the eastern and southern spandrils are built of good ashlar[1]. The northern spandrils are of rubble made up with large stones not laid in courses. Thus there is a regular progression from the rough small rubble to the good ashlar. The south-eastern pier

---

[1] [Many of the details here recorded by Professor Willis have been obliterated by alterations since he wrote.]

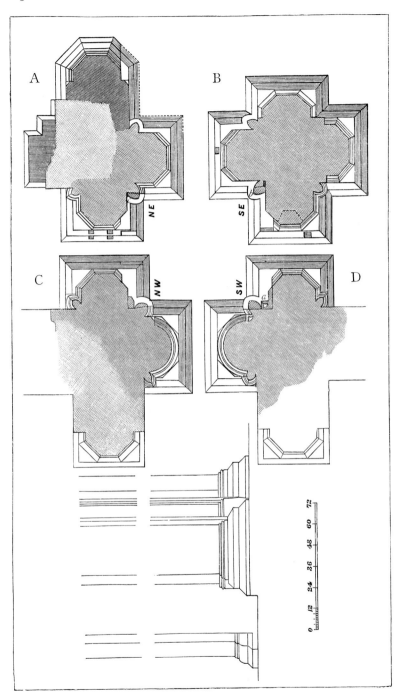

Fig. 7. Plan of the four piers of the tower; reduced from a drawing by Professor Willis.

(fig. 7, B) is the only one of the four that was erected complete
on all its sides; for it was connected with the eastern wall of the
south transept, and it appears that when it was set up the
southern chapel was planned, with the great arch opening from
that chapel to the transept (fig. 2), and the double arch connecting it with the chancel. This is apparent from the complete
plan of the pier here given, which was made when the plaster
was first stripped off, and before the repairs were begun.

Fig. 8.   Perspective section of the north-eastern pier of the tower; from a drawing by Professor Willis.

The north-western pier (fig. 7, C) was originally joined to the
respond of the nave, and the line of junction of the two pieces
of work was distinctly to be seen on the flat face of the wall
(fig. 5). The union between this pier and the north transept
wall was obliterated by Bishop Alcock, as we have previously
shewn. The south-western pier (fig. 7, D) was similar to that
opposite, but in a much more ruinous condition. The north-
eastern pier (ibid. A, fig. 8) was, until 1845—47, a singular
example of the heedless manner in which medieval architects

were accustomed to alter their buildings by merely running up new masonry against old. Two threatening cracks extended from the base to the capital, and somewhat higher, completely disconnecting Bishop Alcock's new wall from the earlier structure. These were filled up, and partly covered, by the buttresses and additions erected under the direction of Augustus Welby Pugin, Architect, in 1847. In the plan of the pier (fig. 7, A), the lightest hatching represents what, from the peculiar tooling

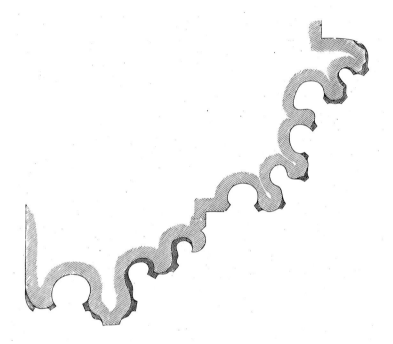

Fig. 9.   Section of the arch-molds of the east and west sides of the roof-story gallery: reduced from the originals by Rev. D. J. Stewart.

shewn on the exposed surfaces, was probably a fragment of the tower-pier of an early Norman church, embedded in portions of three later structures. The darker horizontal lines distinguish the remains of a subsequent addition, coeval possibly with the north gable of the north transept; but the perspective section (fig. 8) shews that this is only a new facing applied to existing work, for there is no bond between these two members of the

pier, and the beds of their masonry are at different levels. The
same process was obviously repeated when the area of the piers
was increased to admit of the construction of the present tower-
arches, and again, when Bishop Alcock's eastern extension was
made. Before the restoration of 1845—47 the shaft in the north-
west angle of the south-eastern pier (fig. 7, B, *b*), and the corresponding shaft in the opposite pier (ibid. A, *c*) had been cut
away in order to admit a gallery which blocked the eastern
tower-arch. The portion cut away has been distinguished on
the plan by hatching in a different direction from that of the rest
of the pier. Traces of this gallery were found on the piers;
and also mortices (now filled up), which proved the existence
of screens which once separated the transepts from the quire.
The quire of the Nuns' church therefore extended, as usual in
monasteries, for some distance into the nave. The date of the
first construction of the eastern gallery is unknown; but a doorway on the exterior of the south side of the chancel, which once
led up to it, and of which a portion still remains (W, fig. 2), was
a good example of the style of the Renaissance. The masonry
of the north face of the south-eastern pier was much discoloured
by fire or by weather.

The roof-story gallery above the pier-arches is a composition
of great beauty, and full of interest for students of the progress
of English Architecture. The pillars of this gallery were evidently built with the work on which they stand, for their capitals
follow the variations of the two patterns of the abacus of the
capitals of the tower-piers below, those on the west and north
being plainer than those on the south and east. The arch-mold,
however, of the gallery is of a much richer type, exactly corresponding to that of the windows of the chancel or presbytery,
and it is curious to observe that the arches of this gallery have
suffered a ruin, and have been repaired with a simpler mold of
the same period, which does not coincide in section with the
earlier and original design. Sections of the two molds are here
given (fig. 9), the earlier one, distinguished by the darker hatching, from the west wall, and the later and simpler one from the
east wall. The earlier mold resembles that used for the pier-
arches of the Presbytery of Ely Cathedral, built by Bishop Hugh
de Northwold between the years 1235 and 1252, and the later

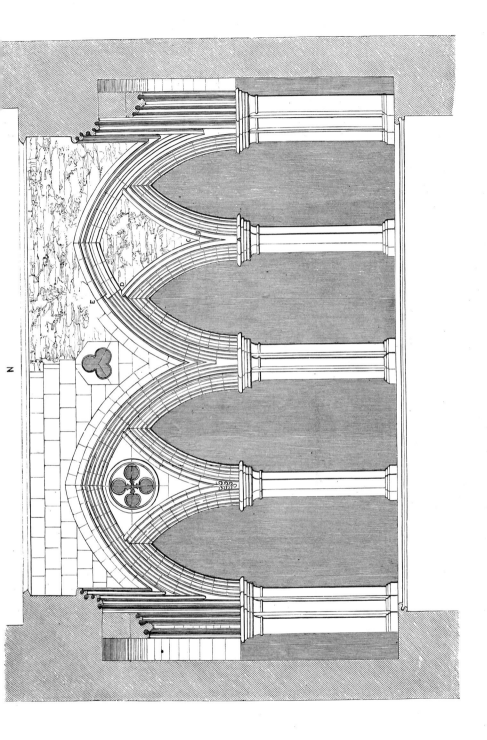

N

Fig. 11. North arcade of the roof-story gallery in Jesus College Chapel, as it appeared in 1846. Measured and drawn by Professor Willis.

one, adopted for the repair of the original work, has much the same character as that used in the presbytery of Worcester Cathedral, built 1269, or seventeen years after that at Ely. In the south gallery the two molds are curiously intermixed, for three of the subarches have been renewed with the later one, and the greater part of the ashlar has been also added; but in the eastern compartment of the north wall the two molds are used together—the later one butting against its predecessor (fig. 11). In the elevation of the north arcade this junction of the two molds is shewn by the letters ABCDE. The earlier form of arch-mold is a good specimen of the Early English style; the moldings are grouped in rectangular masses, and the large rounds have both narrow fillets or wings, and sharp edges or keels, worked on them, as in the molds at Ely referred to above. In the later work both the fillets and keels are used very sparingly, and consequently the rounds and hollows unite with fewer angles, as in the example cited from Worcester.

These changes of design are evidently repairs undertaken in consequence of some actual or threatened ruin of the tower during the thirteenth century; and the documentary evidence quoted above is quite sufficient to prove that the structure was seriously injured by various occurrences during that period. The repairs of the tower were probably begun as soon as funds had been collected to pay for them; and it is possible that the masons employed were the same, or some of the same, who had been engaged at Worcester eight years previously; for we know that it was customary to send long distances to select and hire men for special purposes, as was done in the case of Eton[1], and that each school of workmen followed its own fashions and traditions wherever it might happen to find occupation.

The upper part of the tower (figs. 3, 6) is obviously the work of Bishop Alcock, who could have had very little doubt of the soundness of the piers, or he would not have put a fresh weight upon them. The mere existence, however, of the structure in this the nineteenth century is a convincing proof of the soundness of his judgment. The insecure state in which the piers were found a few years ago was probably chiefly due to such causes as want of drainage, damp, and the general neglect of all old buildings

---

[1] [See Vol. i. p. 384.]

in the last century. The present battlement is worked in Ketton stone. It has therefore probably been repaired at some later date, for Bishop Alcock always used stone from Weldon.

The Chancel, an elevation of the north side of which in its original state is shewn in the section-plate (fig. 5), is an excellent specimen of the architecture of the first half of the

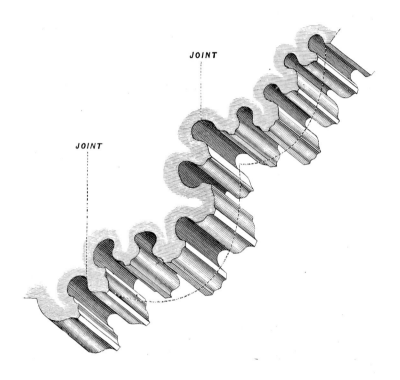

Fig. 10. Section of the arch-mold of the windows in the north wall of the presbytery or chancel : reduced from the original by the Rev. D. J. Stewart.

thirteenth century. The north side, however, differs from the south side in many particulars. Each side has next to the tower two pier-arches which rest on a single pier, but on the south side it is evident that the arch is of one work with the tower-pier from which it springs, whereas on the north side the respond or half-pier against the tower-pier is evidently

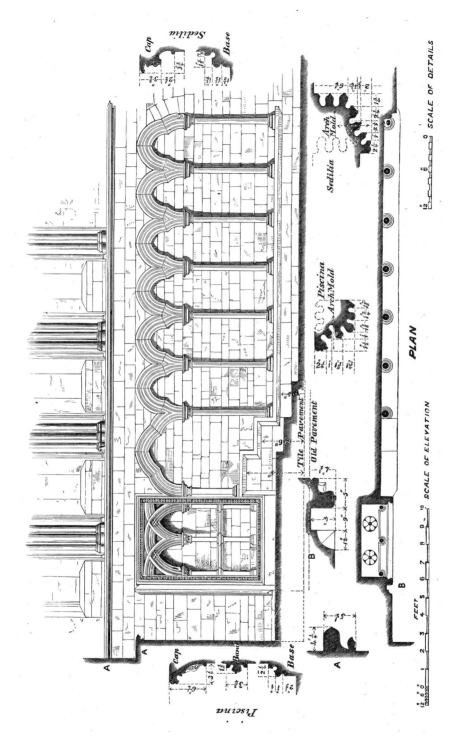

Fig. 12.   South wall of the chancel of Jesus College Chapel, shewing the piscina, the sedilia, the arcade, and the lower portion of the four lancet windows.

the work of a different and subsequent period. The central pier
on the south side is a simple octagon, that on the north
is an elegant fourfold pillar. The moldings on the north
side differ from those on the south side, and are enriched
with an excellently wrought band of the dogtooth ornament[1].
The walls to the east of these arches are pierced with lancet
windows, the jambs and heads of which are ornamented with
triple shafts and rich moldings (fig. 10). On the north side there
are five lancet lights, of which the cills are much nearer to the
pavement than those on the south side, and the wall below
them has no arcade, but is beautifully relieved by having
the central shafts of the windows brought down upon its face.
On the south side there are only four lancet lights (fig. 12), with
moldings the same as those used on the opposite side; but
their cills are placed on a much higher level above the pavement, and the wall-space thus left below is occupied by a
double piscina at the eastern extremity, and in the space that
intervenes between it and the pier-arches by an arcade of seven
trefoiled arches. These arches are close to the wall, and of
course rested originally upon a bench-table in the usual manner; but, as this table projected so far in front of the wall as to
be in the way of the wainscot with which the chapel was lined
in later times, it has been pared off close to the bases of the
pillars[2]. The arch next to the piscina is considerably broader
than the others, and the bench-table rises up two steps beneath
it, whence we may infer that this arch and the seat below
answered the purpose of the usual sedilia; but the wall and the
levels of the floor and bases have been so thoroughly altered
that the original arrangement can no longer be recovered.

The piscina was discovered by removing the modern wainscot
from the north side of the chapel upon the occasion of a repair
in 1815, and it was not only allowed to remain visible, but was
restored by the care of the Rev. William Hustler, then Bursar of
the College. In the Gentleman's Magazine for October in that
year there is the following letter on the subject:

[1] [The wall on the south side has since been repaired, so that the details here
described by Professor Willis are covered up.]

[2] [Since Professor Willis wrote the bench-table has been widened, as the plan
(fig. 12) shews.]

"*Cambridge, Sept.* 14.

Mr URBAN,

The communication of the recovery of a curious and elegant relick of antient Architecture will not perhaps be deemed by you intrusive; and the insertion of it in your Miscellany will, no doubt, afford pleasure to many of your Readers, who, having left this University, still cherish with reverential fondness the recollection of its various architectural beauties.

Fig. 13. Piscina, S. John's College Chapel, as discovered; from Professor Babington's work on the Chapel.

On removing the wainscot from the South side of the Chapel at Jesus College, near the altar, a beautiful niche, formed of the Saxon and Gothic arches united, with their transoms complete, was discovered. It is almost needless to remind your Readers that the Chapel is part of the Conventual Church belonging to a Convent of Benedictine Nuns, instituted in the reign of Henry I., and the niche originally contained the holy water; the two Gothic arches having two small fonts for that purpose.

This newly-discovered relick is formed of a Saxon arch, bisected by two segments of a circle, which form two elegantly Pointed Gothic arches within the Saxon one.

The arches are supported by three small pillars of Purbeck-stone, whose capitals are ornamented with flowers. The whole is surrounded with a beautiful architrave of fretwork. We are indebted for the recovery of this elegant niche to the present Bursar of that learned Foundation (the Rev. Mr Hustler), who has had such parts of it as were decayed restored; and the whole will now remain a specimen of his correct taste, and a beautiful though silent tribute to the architecture of a former day. The Chapel itself is undergoing a thorough repair, and is tastefully painting in the chaste style of antient wainscoting, by a Gentleman who has evidenced much ability in this peculiar line of his profession, and, when completed, will present an elegant model of Gothic Architecture.

Yours &c.,

A Lover of Antient Architecture."

The piscina thus fortunately preserved must have been looked upon as a work of unusual merit even in the thirteenth century, for the design was apparently copied in the parish church of Histon near Cambridge, and by the brethren of the ancient Hospital of S. John, a foundation of the reign of Henry II., which stood on part of the site afterwards occupied by S. John's College. When the new chapel of that College was begun in 1863, the old chapel and some of the adjoining buildings were taken down to make way for it. The walls that were uncovered in the course of these operations turned out to be partly those of the Infirmary of the Hospital, partly those of a chapel of somewhat later date, both of which had been altered to suit the wants of the College which replaced the Hospital in the sixteenth century. At the east end of the south wall of this Infirmary the workmen found, below a coating of white-washed plaster, the remains of a double piscina (fig. 13), the general features of which correspond closely with those of the piscina in the chapel of Jesus College.

A section of the arch-mold of each work is here given (fig. 14, C, D), and if the two be compared it will be seen that the hollows

are much smaller in comparison with the ridges in the specimen at S. John's, and that a half-mold (B) is employed;
peculiarities suggestive of later workmanship.   Moreover, in the
S. John's piscina there are variations in the section of the arch-
mold which are the result of defects in the original design, and

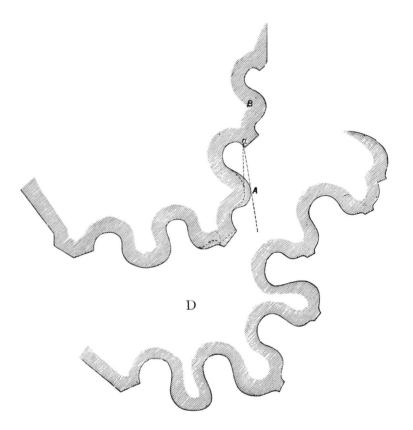

Fig. 14.   Sections of the arch-molds of the piscina at S. John's College (C), at Jesus College (D).

shew its inferiority to the relic in Jesus College chapel.   The
section at the abacus does not coincide, as it ought to do, with
the section at the intersection of the arches ; but the contour of
the leading member (A) is adjusted, by flattening it and cutting
it back as it approaches the point of intersection, so that the edge

(*a*) may disengage itself, and a clumsy botch be avoided. The
dotted line shews this modification of the original outline. The
charming specimen which Bishop Alcock preserved is evidently
the work of skilled masons who could foresee how a design
might be worked out without such expedients[1].

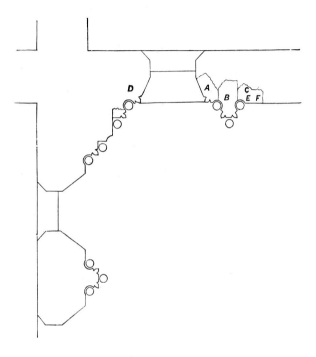

Fig. 15. Plan of the piers at the north-east angle of the quire: reduced from a drawing by
Professor Willis.

Although Bishop Alcock treated the north and south walls
of the east arm of the Nuns' church with the conservative
spirit of an accomplished architect, he thought it necessary
to pull down the east wall and to rebuild it in the style
peculiar to the time in which he lived. In making this change,
however, he adopted the economical plan of using the materials

[1] [The piscina was restored a few years ago under the direction of the Rev.
E. H. Morgan, Fellow.]

of which the old building had been constructed, and embedded
in his new wall so much of the masonry of the thirteenth century
that it was an easy matter to reproduce the original design which
he had destroyed from the fragments of it which his masons
had preserved. The plan of the north-east angle of the quire
(fig. 15) is intended to shew how the design of the eastern
triplet was recovered when the inserted work of the Bishop
was disturbed in the course of the works begun in 1845.
The letters A B C D indicate portions of the old piers
and window-jawms, which were re-arranged in their original
relative positions on the spot, as they were taken out of
the jawm of the Bishop's window. The wrought surface E F
proved incontestably that blank panels existed between the
windows provided by the original design. The caps and arch-
molds were imitated from those of the arcade in the north wall
described above.

The original floor of the church was no doubt destroyed
by Bishop Alcock, just as his arrangements were upset by
subsequent changes. In the course of the restoration of 1845—47
a pavement of tiles was uncovered, two inches below the floor
which then existed, and it was traced in one unbroken level from
the western tower-piers to the east wall, where a marble pavement had been laid in three steps eighteen inches above it.
The bench-tables of the arcades were fifteen inches above
this tile-pavement on the south side and seventeen on the
north, while the sedilia were three feet four inches and two
feet six inches above it. The pavement was obviously too low
for the piscina and sedilia, and was probably that laid down by
Alcock, for the piscina and sedilia were not suited to a college
chapel, and were most likely covered up by his fittings. The
old pavement of the church was four inches below the tiles, and
the bases and footstalls shewed that the whole of the piers stood
on this lower level when first erected, as far, at least, as the
eastern responds; but the arcades and piscina indicate a higher
level for the rest of the area (fig. 12)[1].

The orientation of the walls of the chapel is rather peculiar:
the nave and chancel are very nearly in the same straight line,

[1] [The pavement of which Prof. Willis is here speaking may however be that laid
down in 1644 : see p. 142.]

but the north transept makes an angle of 91° 30′ with the chancel, and has its walls not quite parallel, while the south transept, built with parallel walls, makes the same angle—91° 30′—with the chancel. The tower is in plan a trapezium; the east wall agrees in direction with the east wall of the south transept, the south wall with the direction of the south walls of the presbytery and nave; the west wall is nearly parallel to its east wall, and the north wall is square to the east and west walls.

CHAPTER III.

[HISTORY OF THE COLLEGE CHAPEL.

FOR the history of the Chapel between Bishop Alcock's time and our own we must content ourselves with a few scattered notices taken principally from the audit-books. These we will preface by a translation of Sherman's somewhat highly coloured description of the interior before the Bishop's arrangements had been altered:

"The parish church of S. Rhadegund, which was built on the plan of a cathedral, and dedicated to the name of Jesus, was adapted to the purposes of a chapel, when the nunnery was turned into a college. Before the reign of Edward the Sixth, besides the high altar, there was one on the north side of S. Catharine, and another on the south side of S. Margaret, at both of which masses for the commemoration of benefactors were celebrated. Even subsequent to that period the windows of the chapel were decorated with figures of the Saviour, the Blessed Virgin Mary, the Apostles, the Fathers, and all the hierarchy of heaven, executed with wonderful beauty of workmanship[1]. The altar of God glittered with splendid furniture; in a word, the whole chapel seemed no unworthy spot, wherein priests might supplicate the Almighty."

In 1549 the Visitors of King Edward the Sixth destroyed as many as six altars in "the bodye of the churche[2]." In 1559—

[1] [This statement must have been made from tradition, for the Audit-Books give evidence only of the figures of Christ and S. Peter in the east window, and of S. Ignatius in a window on the north side. Audit-Book, 1580—81. *Reparationes.* "Item...for new leaddinge of vj feete in the easte ende [of the chapel] about the picture of Christe; other six feete in yᵉ picture of sct Peter. Item...leaddinge and mendinge a great hole made by the workemans man ower the northe syde of yᵉ chappell in yᵉ picture of Ignatius."]

[2] [Lamb, Documents, etc., p. 111.]

60 "a communion table" was purchased, and in 1561—62 the Commandments were set up[1]. In 1582—83 the case of the organ was sold, and the pipes in the following year[2]. A pulpit is mentioned as already in existence in 1594—95[3].

In 1634 Robert Dallam of Westminster was employed to set up a new organ at an estimated cost of £200[4]. It was completed in 1637; but six years afterwards, when the Civil War broke out, it was taken down, and apparently concealed, from a subsequent entry in the Accounts for the Michaelmas quarter, 1652: "For discovery of the Organs £1. 00. 00."

In 1636 a new floor was laid down at the east end of the chancel, and new hangings, Litany-desk, etc., provided, and in 1638 a new alms-dish and candlesticks were made for the use of the altar[5].

In November, 1644, we meet with a charge "for levelling yᵉ chappel[6]." This had no doubt been rendered necessary by the

---

[1] [Audit-Book 1559—60. *Templum.* "Imprimis for a communion table vijˢ." Ibid. 1561—62. *Exp. necess.* "for pastinge yᵉ table of the x comaundementes ij d."]

[2] [Ibid. 1582—83. *Recepta forinseca.* "Receyved of Mʳ Lansdall [one of the Fellows] for yᵉ case of the Orgaines vjˢ. viijᵈ." Ibid. 1583—84. *Ibid.* "Item of Robert Lawrence for yᵉ rest of yᵉ organ pipes weyinge 28ˡⁱ after vᵈ. yᵉ li. xjˢ. viijᵈ."]

[3] [Ibid. 1594—95. *Exp. necess.* "Item to Fuller for making a new desk for yᵉ pulpitt."]

[4] [This rests on the authority of Dr Worthington (Master 1650—60) whose notes from the Audit-books and records have been preserved by Baker, MSS. vi. 62. "An. 1634. Oct. 18. An agreement between the Coll. and Rob. Dallam of Westminster, touching the Organs for the Chappell. The College to pay him 200 lib." The following curious order was made at this time respecting the organist's salary, and the blowing of the instrument: "1634. Nov. 28. Decretum est ut in stipendium Organistæ singuli quorum nomina in Albo fuerint (exceptis sizatoribus) pendant singulis Trimestribus 12ᵈ. Sizatores autem singuli suis vicibus ad inflandum Organum Operam impendant hebdomadatim." "An. 1635. Jul. 27. Datæ sunt Robto. Dallam pro Peds. etc. 12 lib. ultra summam de quâ pepigerat." Audit-Book 1638—39. "To Mʳ Dallam for tuneing the Organ May 15 : 1638. vˢ." A maker of the same name had been employed at King's College in 1606 (Vol. i. p. 518).]

[5] [Dr Worthington's extracts, 23 August, 1636 : "Taken out of the Treasury to pay for yᵉ Rail, Floor, Freez, Hangings, etc., about the Altar, and for yᵉ Letany Desk £37. 16. 9." College Order 28 May, 1638. "Consensum est ut duo magni inaurati Crateres nuper facti mutentur in pelvim et duo Candelabra in usum Altaris." Audit-Book, 1638—39. "Bringing the communion plate, vzᵗ. yᵉ bason and candlesticks, from London and to the Colledge July 22. vˢ. iiijᵈ."]

[6] [Ibid. 1642—43. *Exp. necess.* "For taking down the organs o . xv . o." Ibid. 1644—45. *In capella.* "For levelling yᵉ chappel, tiles lime sand and labourers

proceedings of William Dowsing, who visited it in December, 1643, as his diary records :

"Dec. 28. Mr *Boleston*, Fellow, being present, we digged up the Steps, and broke down of superstitiows Saints and Angels 120 at least."

After the Restoration the damage done by Dowsing and others was repaired, as stated in the Commemoration Book :

" The sacred place wherein we are now assembled having been in the time of the Great Rebellion much defaced and by Fanatic Outrage despoiled of the utensils and ornaments provided for decency in Divine Worship, was, upon the happy Restoration of the Church and Monarchy, restored to its former comeliness by the assistance of the Benefactors following :

John Pearson, D.D., then Master [Master 1660—62], afterwards Lord Bishop of Chester, and Mr Thomas Buck, Esquire Bedell of the University, gave each of them £20.

Sir John Goodrick, and Sir John Dawney, Baronets (sometime Fellow Commoners), Joseph Beaumont, D.D., Master [Master 1662 —63], Dr George Evans and Mr Henry Beale, Fellows, and Dr Thomas Stephens sometime Scholar here, gave each of them £10.

Several other sums were advanced by Dr Robert Morgan, Lord Bishop of Bangor, Sir William Doyley, Sir John Poley, Dr Edward Wynn, Dr Henry Hitch, Mr Leonard Letchford, Mr Paul Lawrence, Mr George Payne, Mr Hugh Lloyd, Mr William Martin, Mr John Knight, and Mr Edward Blackstone.

Dr Edmund Boldero, Master [Master 1663—79] gave a large silver Bason and Chalice, which together with two silver flaggons, formerly given by Mr Thomas Newcome, are now used at the Communion."

The sums here specially mentioned amount to £100. As no part of the repair was paid for by the College, it was not thought necessary to enter the receipts and expenses in the Audit-Book, and we are therefore without information respecting the details of the work done[1]. It included, on the authority of Sherman, a restoration of the organ at the expense of Dr Boldero[2], done probably under the direction of Thamar, the

wages per billam Nov. 14. iij^li. vj^s. v^d." Soldiers were lodged in the college at this time, as we have seen was the case at King's. Ibid. 1643—44. *Exp. necess.* "To soldiers y^t came to be billetted Octob. 20. 1643. o. vij^s. j^d. For mending windows locks bedsteads etc broken by ye souldiers, billetted in ye colledge o. xvij^s. o."]

[1] [The only entry having reference to the chapel at this time is the following: Audit-Book 1663—64. *In Capellâ.* "For clearing ye Cherubims and setting y^m up oo . 03 . o6."]

[2] ["Organa pneumatica temporum discordiâ difflata instauravit, et super altare domini 'pateris libavit et auro'."]

celebrated organ-builder of Peterborough, as he is employed in 1669—70 to tune it, and in the following year to execute some trifling repairs. This organ was either replaced by a new one, or extensively repaired, in 1688[1], and in 1693 René Harris was engaged to keep it in order at a yearly salary of £3[2]. This sum was regularly paid for the maintenance of the organ until 1764, at the end of which year it was agreed that the payment should be discontinued. After this the organ gradually fell into a state of ruin, and in 1790 the remains of it were given to All Saints Church[3].

A note at the end of the Audit-Book for 1675—76 gives the following information respecting further improvements:

"Dr Sherman sometimes Fellow of this Coll. gave by his last will and Testament the summe of one hundred pounds towards ye paving of the Chappell wth black and white marble.

Mr Charles Gibson sometimes Fellow of this Coll. gave by his last will and Testament the summe of one hundred pounds, wch by ye consent of the Master and Major part of ye Fellows was assigned for the adorning and beautifying of the Chappell, as much as was necessary. An Act for wch two hundred pounds was given by Mr Lewis then Bursar, as followeth:

Imprimis for 673 foot of black and white marble at two shilling two pence per foot.............................	72 12 00
Item for Steppings 70 and ½ foot at seven shillings per foot	24 13 06
Purbeck and Dunkirk 67 foot at one shilling and six pence per foot	05 00 06
For taking up and carrying away the old pavement...	00 05 00
Given Page at laying ye first stone......................	00 02 06
For ye addition of new seats per billam..................	35 00 00
For whiting the inner Chappel and painting ye seats per billam	06 10 00
To ye Mason per billam	01 16 04
To Page per billam	02 09 06
For paving ye outward Chappell wth Free-Stone and other work per billam	16 12 06
For seats set up at ye West-end of ye Chappel	00 16 00
For removing ye stone and Rubbish	00 02 00
	165 19 10 "

[1] [Audit-Book 1688—89. Christmas—Lady-Day. "Wine at ye Opening of ye Organ 00 . 07 . 00."]

[2] [For René Harris see Vol. i. 519. He was first employed to tune the organ in 1691 —92. The agreement with him, dated 18 December, 1693, is in the College Treasury.]

[3] [College Order, 15 January, 1790. "Agreed to make a present of the remains of our Organ to the Parish of All Saints in Cambridge."]

In 1679 Dr William Saywell (Master 1679—1701) "bestowed twenty pounds in wainscoting the east end of the Chapel and left by Will £100 for the fabric," to quote the Commemoration Book; but no further particulars are given.

Fig. 16. View of the interior of the Chapel, previous to the restoration of 1845—47: reduced from a lithograph in The Cambridge Portfolio.

We now come to the extensive work undertaken between 1789 and 1792 in consequence of a gift of £300 from the Rev. Robert Tyrwhitt, M.A., formerly Fellow. The choir was completely altered in accordance with the taste then prevalent; the oak-roof was concealed by a plaster ceiling; and the tower arcades by another ceiling, so placed that the bases of their shafts were hidden by it. Mr Tyrwhitt's benefaction is entered in the Audit-Book for 1789—90, and the sums paid appear in that and the two following years, but unfortunately they are entered in gross, so that it is impossible to ascertain the exact nature of the work done in each year. The whole sum spent was £817. 11s. 10¼d., of which the balance, after deducting Mr Tyrwhitt's gift, was defrayed by the College. The largest item in the accounts is a sum of £290 paid according to estimate to Averley, carpenter. This was probably partly for stall-work, partly for the ceilings, and the screen with which the eastern arch of the tower was filled. The appearance to which the choir was brought by these alterations will be understood from the accompanying view of the interior (fig. 16), reduced from a lithograph taken about 1840, and from the following description :

"The eastern arch of the tower is walled up, above the gallery and entrance of the choir, which is adorned with Ionic pillars[1]. The ceiling of the Chapel is plain and flat; on each side are three flat-arched windows of three mullions, but beyond these a very beautiful series of lancet-windows; and on the south side in the chancel, elegant pillared niches in the walls, under them. The wainscot of the seats is entirely plain, but the chancel has an air of great elegance and beauty, being finished by a large eastern window flat-arched, divided into two tiers of compartments, and filled with beautiful glass, displaying portraits and armorial bearings, the gift of William Hustler, Esq., Fellow of this College, and University Registrary[2]. Below this window is a small but fine painting of 'The Presentation in the Temple' by *Jouvenet*, a French Painter, presented in 1796 by Dr Pearce, the late Master of the College. The chancel is the only part at present used for divine service[3]."

[1] [The Master's family occupied a pew in the gallery. The pillars and the pediment which they supported may still be seen at the entrance to a yard opposite Magdalene College.]

[2] [The thanks of the College for this glass were given to Mr Hustler by an Order dated 30 April, 1826. A coloured engraving of the lower lights forms the frontispiece to Dr Woodham's paper quoted above.]

[3] [Cambridge Guide, 1830. A view of the Chancel-arch in this condition, from the Antechapel, is given by Ackermann. Storer figures the choir, with the woodwork and windows described in the text, but he imagines the plaster ceiling removed, so as to shew the wooden roof. Our illustration (fig. 16) is from The Cambridge Portfolio, p. 352.]

The original stall-work, profusely adorned with Bishop Alcock's badge and crest, was nearly all removed, and part of it found its way into the Church of Landbeach, of which the Rev. Robert Masters, the well-known antiquary, was then Rector.

In 1815 an agreement was signed with John and Peter Bernasconi, who engaged to cover the exterior with Roman cement at a cost of £440. The battlements and the moldings of the windows were to be repaired with this material, and the external walls were to be encased in it, "all to be coloured and finished as stonework[1]." In 1828 the north and south pier-arches were repaired[2]. By these works the exterior and interior were brought to the appearance they presented when the restoration of 1845—47 was begun.

This had been contemplated so far back as 1832, when the Rev. William Hustler, Fellow, and the Rev. Joseph Studholme, Fellow, each bequeathed £100 to the College "in aid of a fund for the restoration of the chapel." At the audit of 1844 it was found that these sums, with the accumulated interest, amounted to nearly £260. Thereupon, "in consideration of the number of years that must elapse before this fund can become adequate to the object proposed, and of the very deep interest taken in the subject by many members of the College[3]," it was determined to attempt the immediate commencement of the work. Accordingly the College voted £500 towards it, and agreed that an appeal should be made to the present and former members for assistance. At the same meeting it was further agreed to employ Mr Salvin as Architect. In 1845 the Rev. John Gibson, M.A., Fellow, was made treasurer of this fund, and in 1846 the actual work was begun. The partition which blocked the eastern tower-arch was taken down, and the evidences of the original arrangements of the chapel were brought to light, as related above. It was at first intended to place the new screen and stalls in such a position that the transepts might be included in the choir, but this scheme was unfortunately abandoned. The first new work undertaken was the chapel eastward of the north

---

[1] [The agreement is preserved in the College Treasury.]

[2] [College Order, 20 May, 1828. Agreed to accept Mr Clayton's tender (£59. 9. 4) for restoring the columns and arches on the South and North sides of the Chapel.]

[3.] [These words are quoted from a circular issued in 1845.]

transept, together with the north aisle of the choir, which, as the plan (fig. 2) shews, communicate with each other. These were constructed on the old foundations discovered in the course of the investigations, and were completed by the end of the year. Mr Salvin was then requested to retire[1], and Mr Pugin was consulted, through the influence of Mr, afterwards Sir John, Sutton, a Fellow-Commoner of the College, who materially assisted the restoration by his architectural knowledge and generosity. At this time the reconstruction of the corresponding south aisle was projected, but it was never executed.

The work done under the direction of Mr Pugin in the north transept is thus criticised by a writer in The Ecclesiologist for 1849 :

"The opening of the aisle to the east of the north transept, and that north of the choir, of course deprived the north-east lantern pier of much of its support :—added to this, it had been re-ashlared in a most unscientific way. The consequence was, that it showed signs of imme-diate ruin. In place of shoring up the tower, and then rebuilding this pier, as Mr Cottingham had done at Armagh and at Hereford, (a far larger and more difficult undertaking), Mr Pugin, who was called in, has tried to palliate the evil by expedients, filling the arches of the tran-sept with heavy tracery, tying together those of the choir-aisle with a low solid stone screen, and building a buttress in the aisle against the north-east angle of this pier. How far all these expedients may suffice to keep up what is intrinsically unsound remains to be seen [2]."

At the meeting held 18 December, 1846, it was further agreed to proceed with the stall-work and screen; the east window and gable; the roof of the choir; the central tower; and the pointing and plastering of the walls. These works proceeded under the direction of Mr Pugin. The low-pitched wooden roof of Alcock's period, which existed above the plaster ceiling, was taken down, and a new roof was constructed, the pitch of which was regulated by the water-line on the eastern

---

[1] [College Order, 18 December, 1846. Agreed that, as the structure of the new north aisle of the Chapel, for which Mr Salvin furnished the working plans, is now completed, the College does not think it necessary to require his further services, and that application be made to him for the amount of his charges.]

[2] [Mr Pugin, after noticing the above criticisms, thus defends himself in a letter to Mr Sutton : " You will remember that I was told that the funds were at a low ebb, and it would have cost the college *hundreds* of pounds if the whole tower had been shored up and the pier and angles taken out and rebuilt. I do not think we could have done better under the circumstances. Indeed had we begun to rebuild, we must have rebuilt the whole transept."]

face of the tower, the side-walls being lowered to what appeared to be their original height. The timber of the older roof was used, where sufficiently sound, for the moldings, panels, and bosses of the new one. Mr Pugin's care, however, was not limited to the fabric; he superintended the decoration of the roof, and designed the pavement, communion-table, brass lectern, stalls, and screen[1]. The lectern and the screen were given by Mr Sutton, who also designed and gave the organ. An attempt was made to recover from Landbeach Church those portions of the original stall-work which still existed there; but the Churchwardens declined, and it was not until 1879 that some of them were obtained by the College[2].

At the end of 1849 the Chapel was again opened for service. The following description, written at the time, records the most important points of the restoration:

On All Saints'-day the choir of the chapel of Jesus College, Cambridge, was reopened, with full choral service, Holy Communion, and a sermon. The sermon was preached by the Rev. O. Fisher, M.A., one of the Fellows, and the anthem was composed for the occasion by Dr Walmisley, who presided at the organ.

"This chapel has been under restoration for the last four years; but the choir and tower are the only portions as yet completed. It will doubtless be in the recollection of many that the choir was formerly fitted with painted deal seats and panelling of a very inferior Grecian design, and was separated from the transepts by a lath and plaster partition. The roof of the choir was of late Perpendicular design, but had been cieled beneath with a plain flat plaster cieling. Those who have explored the building will also remember a series of fine Early English arches, of an unusual character, in the triforium of the tower,

---

[1] [Mr Pugin discusses the colours and patterns of the pavement in several of his letters, preserved in the College; about the ceiling and table he writes to Mr Sutton: " I am very glad to hear that the ceiling is so successful. I thought it would have a good effect, and not over rich."..." I send you the design for the Communion Table, which I have kept of the same character as the stall-work; the top 3 in. thick, as I know you like solid tops."]

[2] [The Vicar of Landbeach, Rev. John Tinkler, writes, 10 Feb., 1846, to Jesus College: " The Church Wardens of our Parish have given me authority to state that they cannot, from a sense of duty, allow any thing to be removed from our Parish Church." Landbeach Church was restored in 1878, and certain pieces of woodwork —consisting of stall-ends, panelwork, and other fragments—which were then discarded by the architect employed, were purchased by Jesus College. A good deal, however, still remains there, including the pulpit, and portions of the screens. See a paper on Landbeach Church, by the Rev. B. Walker, Rector, in Camb. Antiq. Soc. Comm., No. 21.]

but concealed from view from below by a flat cieling above the great
pier arches. These disfigurements have now been all cleared away,
and the following works completed:—A north aisle has been built to
the choir and north transept on the foundations of one existing during
the time of the nunnery, and communicating with the choir by two very
fine arches, which were found complete (as were also two on the south
side), imbedded in the masonry of the wall. Other arches, communicating with the north transept, were discovered and opened; but have
been filled with stone screen work for the sake of strength. In the
choir itself, the east window, a modern one with glass by Willement,
has been removed, and a lancet window of three lights and two panels,
supposed to be an exact reproduction of the original one, has been substituted for it. The side walls have been brought down to their ancient
height, and a high pitched roof of trussed rafters of early character has
been raised upon them. This roof is boarded beneath with oak, all cut
from the roof which was removed, and its section forms a semidodeca-
gon. It is divided into square panels by larger and smaller ribs, the
latter having bosses at their intersections. The tympanum formed by
the roof above the east window is filled with a fine pentagonal window, and internally with two medallions, containing floriated crosses.
The whole of the roof is varnished, and the ribs and bosses decorated
with vermilion and gold; but the portion above the sacrarium is still
further enriched with sacred devices on the panels in green, vermilion,
white and gold. The aisle roof is blue, with stars in white, and the
rafters oak colour, the principals being relieved with vermilion. The
choir is furnished with stalls and misereres in the upper row, and seats
in the two lower, there being a double row of book boards with standards, the upper ones of very singular and handsome design, surmounted
with sitting figures of academical and ecclesiastical personages. The
stalls have no canopies, but a rich panelling behind them. The whole
arrangement is thought to be almost identical with that of the founder's
stall-work, and indeed, two of the old standards, which had been preserved in the college, are worked in. The floor is of black and red tiles
between the stalls, and of black and white marble, mixed with encaustic
tiles, in the sacrarium, three black marble steps forming the ascent to
the altar. There is a magnificent lectern of brass in the centre of the
stalls [with two branches for lights, and a figure of S. John the Evangelist above it] and two noble brass candlesticks upon the altar steps.
The Litany desk is an old one, which was found in the college, of
Elizabethan design. The covering of the altar is of green velvet,
superbly embroidered. The organ, which is placed in the north aisle,
is a fine instrument of most beautiful tone, built on the old models by
Messrs Bishop, of London, containing, however, two stops of Father
Smith's, one of which, a flute, is from the old organ in Durham Cathedral. It has two rows of keys. The case is extremely elegant, and has
doors folding over the front, painted on the outside with a representation of a choir of angels. It is a unique specimen, harmonizing with
the other beauties of this richly decorated chapel. Painted windows
for the east end are in course of preparation, and money is ready for
placing stained glass also in the two south windows of the choir. With-

out the screen the tower piers have been repaired and cleaned, as likewise the very fine and dignified triforium, which has a grand effect, as
seen from the choir below.   An inspection of the proportions of this
chapel will, we think, be sufficient to show that the college exercised a
sound discretion in confining the choir to the east of the chancel arch,
and not bringing it partially under the tower, as was at one time recommended in a public journal[1]."

To the above account may be appended a description of the
treatment of the east end of the choir:

"It remains to add that the old tradition of reredos-hangings in
Jesus Chapel is continued; there being a rich woven stuff suspended, as
a dossel, behind the altar.   The altar candles are coloured in patterns;
and in addition to the altar candlesticks, there are two fine standard
candlesticks of brass at the angles of the footpace.   A carpet, of good
design, is laid on the sanctuary steps rising to the altar.   The frontal,
when we saw it, was of green, handsomely embroidered in a cross with
the Evangelistic symbols[2]."

The outlay, as added up at audit, 1848, had been £3189. 2s. 1d.;
and the receipts £2740. 9s. 10d.   Of the latter sum the College
had contributed £1477. 10s. 0d., partly from the residue of the
Tyrwhitt benefaction, and the accumulations of the legacies
above mentioned, partly from the corporate funds; the subscriptions of the Fellows and others had amounted to £1119. 3s. 0d.;
and £143. 16s. 10d. had been realised by the sale of old materials.
Subsequently, however, an additional outlay of £1769. 5s. 10d.
was incurred; so that the total outlay was £4958. 7s. 11d.[3], of
which the College paid £3695. 8s. 1d.

The glazing of the windows had not been forgotten during
the progress of the other works.   In January, 1846, the Master,
Dr French, offered to fill the five lancet-windows on the north
side[4].   Subsequently, however, his intentions were altered, and

---

[1] [The Guardian, 1849, p. 733.   An opposite opinion to that expressed in the
last paragraph will be found in The Ecclesiologist, ix. 146.   The portion of the
above description between inverted commas had been communicated to the journal,
probably by a member of the College.]

[2] [The Ecclesiologist, 1851, p. 324.]

[3] [These particulars are derived from a study of the accounts, which have been
lent to me by my friend the Rev. E. H. Morgan, Fellow of Jesus College.]

[4] [Dr French writes to Mr Gibson 14 January, 1846: "I beg through you, as
Treasurer of the Fund for the Restoration of our College Chapel, to communicate to
the Fellows my wish that I may be allowed, at my own expense, to fill the five
Lancet Windows on the North Side of the Chapel with stained glass.   The pattern
I would adopt, if there be no objection in any quarter, is that of the 'Five Sisters'

he gave the glass for the eastern triplet instead. The design
was furnished by Mr Pugin, who devoted much time and thought
both to the selection of subjects, and to their treatment, in the
hope of producing a work that should be suitable to the early
style of the architecture of the chancel[1]. The execution of the
glass was entrusted to Messrs Hardman of Birmingham. They
took as much pains with their part of the work as Mr Pugin had
taken with his; and some delay ensued in order that "the colours
peculiar to this style of glass" might be exactly reproduced.
The windows were ordered in March, 1849, but they were not
put up until February, 1850[2]. Meanwhile the cinquefoil above
the triplet, designed by Mr Pugin, had been filled with stained
glass at the expense of Mr Sutton. This, representing the
"Agnus Dei" adored by angels, was also designed by Mr Pugin,
and executed by Messrs Hardman. The subjects in the three
large lancets are as follows. They occupy circular medallions,
between which are ovals, of smaller size, containing figures of
angels.

NORTH LIGHT.	CENTRAL LIGHT.	SOUTH LIGHT.
Judas and the Elders.	Mary at the Sepulchre.	Christ bearing the Cross.
The Flagellation of Christ.	The Preparation for the Tomb.	Christ mocked by the Soldiers.
Christ before Pilate.		
The Agony in the Garden.	The Deposition.	Pilate washing his hands.
	The Crucifixion.	The Betrayal of Christ.
	The Last Supper.	

The two windows, each of three lights, which had been inserted in the south wall of the chancel by Bishop Alcock, were

in York Minster." In June following he consulted Mr Wales, and apparently asked
him for a design. (Letter of Dr French to Dr Woodham, 19 June, 1846.)]

[1] [Mr Pugin writes to Mr Sutton (without date, but probably in May, 1849), "I
have just returned from Chartres, where I have been for the express purpose of
examining the early windows for your chapel; and I have not only got most
accurate details, but actually a lot of the real glass from a glazier; and Mr Hardman is
going to match the tints exactly, so I have every expectation of producing the *real thing*.
I have had my cartoons done over again, for there is a peculiar treatment about
this early glass which is exceedingly difficult to attain. We shall now get on very
fast, and I can assure you that every exertion shall be made to complete the 3
windows as speedily as possible; but *I* must be perfectly satisfied before I let them
go."]

[2] [When they were ready to be sent off, Mr Pugin writes: "The 3 last windows
are compleated, and will be fixed in a few days. As I have done them twice over,
and taken all possible pains, I shall be very anxious to learn how they look when
fixed."]

glazed next, at the expense of the undergraduate members of the College, in 1852[1]. The subjects are "The Adoration of the Magi," and "Christ among the Doctors," treated in the style of the fifteenth century. In the course of the following year the four lancet-windows on the same side were glazed, like the former, at the expense of the undergraduates. The stone work was restored at the same time, and an external buttress (M, fig. 2) erected[2]. The subjects, treated in the same style as those of the eastern triplet, are the following, the windows being numbered from east to west:

I.	II.	III.	IV.
S. Peter and S. John at the Sepulchre.	The Agony in the Garden.	S. Peter and S. John healing a cripple.	S. John writing his Gospel.
S. John leading the Virgin home.	Christ raising Jairus' daughter.	The Petition of the mother of S. James and S. John.	The Martyrdom of S. John.
The Crucifixion.	The Transfiguration.	The Call of S. James and S. John.	S. John with the Chalice.

The five lancet-windows on the north side were restored in 1858, and glazed in that year, or shortly afterwards, in memory of the Rev. Robert Parker Bowness, sometime Fellow, by his sister[3]. The subjects, treated in the same style as those last mentioned, are, the windows being numbered from west to east:

I.	II.	III.	IV.	V.
The Performance of Acts of Mercy.	The New Jerusalem. S. Michael overcoming the Dragon.	S. Paul preaching at Athens.	The first Council at Jerusalem.	The Ascension.
The Rejection of an Earthly for a Heavenly Crown.	The Angel of Incense offering the Prayers of the Saints.	The Martyrdom of S. Stephen.	The Vision of S. Peter.	The Resurrection.
The Release of Captives.	The Ancients adoring, and casting their Crowns before the Throne.	The first Sermon of S. Peter.	The Conversion of S. Paul.	Christ bearing the Cross.
The Marriage of Radigunda with Clothaire.		Christ in the Synagogue at Nazareth.	The Descent of the Holy Spirit.	The Annunciation.

[1] [The subscription was set on foot by Christopher Smyth, B.A. 1850, M.A. 1853, now Rector of Woodford, near Thrapston. The glass, by Hardman, was exhibited in the Great Exhibition of 1851.]

[2] [College Order, 30 May, 1853. "Agreed to restore the stonework of the four south Lancet Windows of the Chapel to prepare them for the reception of stained glass windows about to be presented by Undergraduate Members of the College; and to build a buttress against the south wall of the choir." The subscription was set on foot by Lachlan Mackintosh Rate, B.A. 1854, M.A. 1857. The glass cost £75. The architect employed was Mr R. Reynolds Rowe, of Cambridge.]

[3] [Messrs Rattee were paid 15 September, 1858, but the thanks of the College to Mrs Watson "for the gift of the stained glass in the North Windows of the Chapel" were not given until 1861.]

All these windows were designed by Mr Pugin, and executed by Messrs Hardman.   It should be further mentioned that there are three lancet windows in the north aisle of the quire, or organ-chamber.   Of these two are by Messrs Hardman, and one by M. Gerente, of Paris.   The subjects are small single figures bearing instruments of music.

At the beginning of 1862 the College became alarmed at the condition of the central tower[1].   Mr G. F. Bodley, Architect, was consulted, and made a detailed report, dated 18 February, 1862, on the state of that portion of the fabric.   After describing the cracks in the arches and in the piers, especially the north-eastern and the south-eastern piers, he advised that the upper stage of the tower, the weight of which, in his opinion, was causing the mischief, should be taken down, and replaced by a light belfry of wood covered with lead; that the four tower-piers, and above all the north-eastern pier, which he held to be the weakest, should be strengthened; that the internal buttress (O, fig. 2) should be bonded "with hard Yorkshire stones to the body of the wall," and be carried up to a greater height; and lastly, that tie-rods of wrought-iron should be added to the tower internally.   In consequence of this report the Master and Fellows decided to take down the upper stage of the tower. Subsequently, however, the Rev. Osmond Fisher, M.A., some-time Fellow, having expressed a strong opinion on the stability of the tower, it was agreed to consult Mr Bacon, clerk of the works at Ely.   After examination of the building, he confirmed Mr Fisher's opinion.   The former decision was therefore re-scinded, and Mr Bodley was requested to prepare plans for restoring and strengthening the tower without taking down any part of it.   It was further decided at the Audit of 1863 that the work of restoring the transepts and ante-chapel, or nave, should be proceeded with at the same time, and a circular was issued by the Dean, dated 4 February, 1864, soliciting subscriptions.   The College promised to contribute £500, besides defraying the entire cost of the necessary repairs to the fabric. In consequence of this alteration in the wishes of the College

---

[1] [The following details have been derived from a study of Mr Bodley's Reports and letters, and of the various circulars issued while the works were in progress.]

Mr Bodley made a second report, dated 30 May, 1864, from which the following passage may be quoted:

"I am glad to say that having on many different occasions examined the state of the cracks in the Tower piers, Triforium, etc. since I last reported on the state of the building, I have found no change whatever of any importance. From what I have since heard too I think some of the signs of failure were of longer standing than I was led to suppose. Having marked where the cracks stopped I find they have not at all increased.

The need of increasing the strength of the Tower and other parts, however, is as great as before. I should recommend that the wrought-iron ties, etc., should be put on as I before recommended, together with the proper restoration of the stone-work, and the added heights given to the internal buttress in the organ-aisle."

The work was put in hand with as little delay as possible, and by February, 1867, the tower had been repaired, refaced[1], and strengthened by solid stone buttresses at the north-east and south-east angles; an iron girder had been fixed above the choir-screen; the roofs of the nave and south transept had been thoroughly restored; the ceiling of the nave had been panelled, and was in course of decoration by Mr Leach, directed by Messrs Morris; the ceiling of the interior of the tower, above the arcades, had been panelled, and painted by the same artists; and the wall in the north transept had been renewed and faced with stone. The following works were next undertaken:

I. The rebuilding of the wall in the archway on the east side of the south transept, through which access had been originally obtained to the south choir-aisle. This had been recommended by Mr Bodley in the following terms:

"The large arch in the east wall of the south transept, blocked up at the end of the 15th century, is of such fine proportions and character that it would seem a pity to hide it out of sight by plastering the wall. I propose, if I find on further examination that it would be no risk to the strength of the building, to take out the filling in of this arch, and build a thicker wall, strengthened by a buttress as shown (P, fig. 2), which will allow the arch to be seen to half its thickness; that is,

---

[1] [When the contractors (Messrs Rattee and Kett) had removed the cement placed on the tower in 1815, Mr Kett writes that "the face of the walls in the Belfry Stage was originally built with a mixture of hard and very durable rag-stone with a portion of clunch. The rag is generally in a sound condition, but the clunch is very much decayed, and I presume it was on this account that it was plastered over; for we found upon removing the old plaster that the face of the clunch is worn away and the surface of the walls is very uneven." Mr Kett to the Master, October, 1865.]

showing it as a recessed arch.   The two 15th century windows I should rebuild."

II.   The restoring and plastering of the walls throughout the transepts and nave.

III.   The excavation of the floor to such a level as would expose the bases of the piers, and the laying down of a new pavement, on a bed of concrete, with materials suited to the different parts.

IV.   The panelling of the nave with oak, and fitting it with seats.

After the completion of these works, which occupied about three years, the south-west tower-pier, being in an unsound state, was under-pinned and reset (in 1869), and further strengthened by an external buttress (fig. 2, X).

It was next determined to glaze all the windows in the transepts and nave[1].   After full discussion, the execution of the glass was entrusted to Morris, Faulkner and Company; and it was wisely decided to set out the complete scheme of the whole series from the beginning.   In the words of a circular issued in 1873 for the purpose of soliciting subscriptions:

"To effect this work satisfactorily, it has been decided to commence the glazing on a plan which may perhaps be a long time in the process of execution, but which when completed shall secure the harmony of each Window with all the rest, and with the other decorative works in the building.   By this means that patchwork appearance will be avoided which so often mars the effect of decorations in Cathedrals and Parish Churches when executed at different times, and as separate and independent works of art.

The windows in the Nave are 4 in number; in the North Transept there are 2; in the South Transept 4 side-windows, and a very large Perpendicular window.   This last named window is already ordered from the Artists whom it is purposed to employ, and, as being the most costly as well as a very important feature in the building, the Master and Fellows of the College have undertaken to glaze it at a cost of £550.

It is intended that each light in the South Transept and Nave Windows should contain a single figure above, and underneath a subject-painting of an incident connected with this figure: each light therefore will be, as it were, a complete window, although the colours in the three or four lights will be so arranged as to produce an harmonious effect.   This separation into parts complete in themselves,

---

[1] [The cost of the works undertaken since 1863 had been nearly £3000, of which sum the necessary repairs, paid for by the College, had cost £880.]

will afford to donors who could not undertake the glazing of an entire window opportunity for presenting a complete and separate work of art[1]."

The following list gives the subjects with their legends[2]. The numbers affixed shew the position of the figures and the subjects by reference to the accompanying diagram.   The windows in the transepts have each three lights, those in the nave have four.   For convenience of reference the windows have been numbered, beginning with the north-east window in the south transept.   It should be further premised that the south window of that transept has five lofty lights, foliated, with tracery above (fig. 3).   It is divided horizontally by a transom into two equal divisions; which, for convenience of decorative treatment, are again equally subdivided, so that there are four rows of figures. The tracery in this window contains small figures of angels bearing musical instruments; in the others, it is filled with foliage and fruit.   The glass first executed was that in Window II.; and the second that in Window VII.   In these two windows the smaller pictures were designed by Mr Madox Brown; in the rest all the subjects were designed by Mr Burne Jones, Mr Morris being responsible for the general execution.

5	6	7	8
1	2	3	4

SOUTH TRANSEPT.

I. NORTH WINDOW, EAST WALL.

The Incarnation.

Sibylla persica   5

The Annunciation   1

Et rex adveniet per secla futurus.

[1] [The estimated cost of these windows was £2290.]

[2] [All the passages which are not from Scripture will be found in the chapter on the Sibyls in S. Augustine's De Civitate Dei, lib. xviii. cap. 23.]

Sanctus Matthæus 6
    The Nativity 2
    Gloria in excelsis deo et in terra pax. [Luke ii. 14]
Sibylla cumana 7
    The Adoration of the Magi 3
    Et coram hic domino reges sistentur ad unum.

II.   South Window, East Wall.

The Passion.

Sibylla delphica 5
    The Agony in the Garden 1
    Dabunt deo alapas manibus incestis.
Sanctus Lucas 6
    The Flagellation of Christ 2
    Posuit dominus in eo iniquitatem omnium nostrum. [Isaiah liii. 6]
Sibylla cimmeria 7
    Christ bearing the Cross 3
    Et impurato ore exspuent venenatos sputus.

III.   Window in the South Wall.

Uppermost Row.

Seraphim, Cherubim, Throni, Potestates, Dominationes.

Second Row.

Principatus, Virtutes, Archangeli, Angeli, Imago Dei.

Third Row.

S. Ursula, S. Dorothea, S. Radegunda, S. Cecilia, S. Catherina.

Fourth Row.

S. Hieronymus, S. Gregorius, Joh. Alcock Ep. Eliensis, S. Ambrosius,
S. Augustinus.

IV.   South Window, West Wall.

The Resurrection.

Sibylla phrygia 4
    Christ recognized by Mary Magdalen 1
    Tetri portas effringet Averni.
Sanctus Marcus 5
    The Incredulity of S. Thomas 2
    Beati qui non viderunt et crediderunt. [Joh. xx. 29]
Sibylla libyssa 6
    The Supper at Emmaus 3
    Ab inferis regressus ad lucem veniet primus.

V.   North Window, West Wall.

The Ascension.

Sibylla erythræa 5
    The Vision of S. Stephen 1
    Animæ cum carne aderunt quas judicat ipse.

Sanctus Ioannes 6
   The Adoration of the Lamb   2
   Deum cernent celsum cum sanctis.
Sibylla tiburtina 7
   The Descent of the Holy Spirit 3
   Ego sum in patre meo et vos in me et ego in vobis. [Joh. xiv. 20]

NAVE.

VI.   East Window, South Wall.

Adam 5
   The Fall   1
   In sudore vultus tui vesceris panem tuum. [Gen. iii. 19]
Enoch 6
   An Angel leading him   2
   Qui mane vigilant ad me invenient me. [Prov. viii. 17]
Noe patriarcha 7
   The Lord shews to Noah the pattern of the Ark   3
   Ponamque fœdus meum tecum. [Gen. xvii. 2]
Abram heres mundi 8
   The Sacrifice of Isaac 4
   In Isaac vocabitur tibi semen. [Gen. xxi. 12]

VII.   West Window, South Wall.

In memory of Benedict Laurence Chapman, sometime Fellow.

Moyses Propheta   5
   The burning Bush   1
   Notas fecit vias suas Moysi. [Psal. cii. 7]
Samuel Propheta   6
   Eli and Samuel in the Temple 2
   Suscitabo mihi sacerdotem fidelem. [1 Sam. ii. 35]
David Rex 7
   David cutting off Goliath's head 3
   Ecce o filia Sion Salvator tuus venit. [Isaiah lxii. 11]
Solomon Rex   8
   The building of the Temple   4
   Tabernaculum Dei cum hominibus. [Psal. lxxvii. 60]

VIII.   West Window, North Wall.

Isaias Propheta 5
   The destruction of Sennacherib 1
   Omne vas quod factum est contra te non dirigetur.
Jeremia Propheta   6
   The punishment of Nebuchadnezzar   2
   Domini est regnum et ipse dominabitur gentium.
Ezechiel Propheta   7
   The resurrection of dry bones   3
   Dedero spiritum meum vobis et vixeritis. [Ezek. xxxvii. 5]
Daniel Propheta   8
   Daniel in the Lions' Den 4
   Jacta super dominum onus tuum et ipse te enutriet. [Psal. liv. 23]

IX. East Window, North Wall.

Temperantia	.	.	.	.	.	5	Fortitudo	.	.	.	.	. 7
Ira	.	.	.	.	.	1	Timiditas	.	.	.	.	. 3
Justitia	.	.	.	.	.	6	Prudentia	.	.	.	.	. 8
Injuria	.	.	.	.	.	2	Stultitia	.	.	.	.	. 4

NORTH TRANSEPT, WEST WALL.

X. South Window.	XI. North Window.
Given by Frederick Orme, M.A.	Given by Lachlan Mackintosh Rate, M.A.
Spes 5	Patientia 5
Fides 6	Obedientia 6
Caritas 7	Docilitas 7

The windows were completed by the end of 1877.]

CHAPTER IV.

History of separate buildings:

Hall.   Library.   Master's Lodge, &c.

HALL.—The Hall is a very handsome and well-proportioned Refectory, still retaining an open roof and ancient stone corbels, but it is marred in effect by later panelling and screen. The oriel on the north side is an exceedingly elegant specimen of the architecture of Alcock's period, and the rich panelling of the soffit of the arch which separates it from the hall is especially beautiful[1]. Opposite to it, on the south side of the high table, is a large window of three lights, divided by a transom. The rest of the windows were originally small, of two lights each, like those we have found employed at Pembroke and elsewhere. They are shewn in this condition as late as Loggan's time (fig. 3); but have since been made longer, by lowering the cills about three feet. [This was done in consequence of the following Order :

"10 December, 1801. Agreed, that the Hall be new painted, the windows altered, and such other Alterations be made in it, as may be agreed upon by the Master and Resident Society."

[1] [This was restored in 1871, under the direction of Mr Waterhouse.]

The total cost of the work then done was £722. 4s. 8d., of which sum nearly £200 was paid to the carpenter[1]. When the Hall was altered in 1875 the roof was found to be of Spanish chestnut, patched with deal. The latter had probably been inserted in 1801.]

The present screen is a regular Italian composition of the Corinthian order, probably part of the work done in 1703, when the Hall was paved with freestone and wainscoted, and a new Bell-turret set up[2]. An older screen, by Woodroffe[3], had been made in 1610—11. The work in 1703 was executed, in part at least, by Grumbald, the mason whom we have found employed at Clare Hall and elsewhere; but, as the cost was principally defrayed by benefactions, which amounted to £250, no details respecting it can be recovered[4]. The wooden panelling along the north and south sides is probably part of this work, as is the screen behind the high table, which is in the same style as that at the other end. A large original fireplace, much mutilated, remains in the north wall behind the panel-work, and there are also traces of an entrance on the same side. There was originally a louvre, which was removed in 1871, being then in a rotten and dangerous state.

[It should be mentioned that this Hall, like others, was originally hung with tapestry, which appears not to have been limited, as usual, to the space over the dais, but to have covered part at least of the side walls, for in 1597—98 we find a charge for mending "yᵉ peece of Arresse over yᵉ chymneye." These hangings were first put up in 1569—70, and were repaired in subsequent years. They are mentioned last in 1614—15.]

---

[1] [The sums paid, as set down in the Audit-Book for 1801—2, are : Painter and Glazier, £94. 6. 2½ ; Coe, Whitesmith, £37. 12. 0 ; Averley, Carpenter, £199. 13. 9; Tomson, Mason, £139. 18. 8; Bradwell, Bricklayer, £152. 9. 8; Scott, Painter, £54. 6. 3; Slate, &c. £63. 18. 1½. Total, £722. 4. 8.]

[2] [These details are taken from the Commemoration Book.]

[3] [Audit-Book, 1610—11. "Item to Woodrofe for yᵉ skrene in yᵉ hall iijˡⁱ. Item for nailes to set it vp. xiijᵈ." A previous screen is alluded to in 1567. "Item the xxiiijᵗʰ of nouember for iij daies to Robert Nicholles mendinge the skrene in yᵉ hall." For Woodroffe see Hist. of King's College, i. 521.]

[4] [The Commemoration Book records the following gifts : William Saywell, D.D., late Master, left by will £100; Henry Poley, sometime Fellow, gave £50; William Cook, LL.D., then Fellow, £50; the Right Hon. Thomas Willoughby, Lord Middleton, £20; James Gardiner, sometime Fellow, £30.]

The entrance to the Hall from the cloister was, until 1875, through a square-headed door-arch (A, fig. 2, *a*, fig. 19), an admirable specimen of Alcock's work, which opened into the space between the screen and the gable-wall of the Hall. This space contained a flight of nine steps, very unskilfully arranged, which led to a landing in front of the screen-doors. Another flight of steps descended on the opposite side through a door (*b*) into a lateral appendage (*d*) vaulted with a rich lierne vault, possibly part of the staircase to the refectory-pulpit of the Nuns, and thence led down to a passage which passed from the cloister along the outside of the gable-wall of the Hall into the court beyond, and contained the doors of the buttery, kitchen and pantry.

[In 1875 the great increase in the number of students rendered considerable alterations necessary in the Hall, the Kitchen, and the Buttery. A new staircase was built on the north side of the Hall (fig. 2); the Hall itself was lengthened by the space gained by the removal of the stairs above described; and an Ante-hall, entered from the new staircase, was contrived over the passage (RQ, fig. 2). The Hall is now entered from the Ante-hall through two doors, pierced in the western gable-wall, which replace a single large arch, through which, by ascending four steps (fig. 19), access was obtained to the muniment-room which looked into the cloister-court, to the rooms over the larder, and to a staircase leading to the rooms above on the same level as the Library. As it was important to have the Hall, the Ante-hall, and a serving-room which it was agreed to make out of the rooms over the larder, all on the same level; and as it had become necessary to lay down a new floor to the Hall, the old Ketton stone slabs being in places quite worn through, it was determined to lay down a new floor of oak twelve inches above the level of the old one, supported on joists resting upon it. By this expedient the required uniformity of level was obtained; and also sufficient headway for the through passage beneath. In consequence of the above alteration in the level of the floor of the Hall the woodwork had to be taken down, and the panels and styles shortened. It was found that the panels were of deal, and therefore they were again painted as before. The screen also was taken down, and turned round, the side which had

previously been the exterior one being fixed against the west
wall.   At the same time the roof was cleaned of paint.

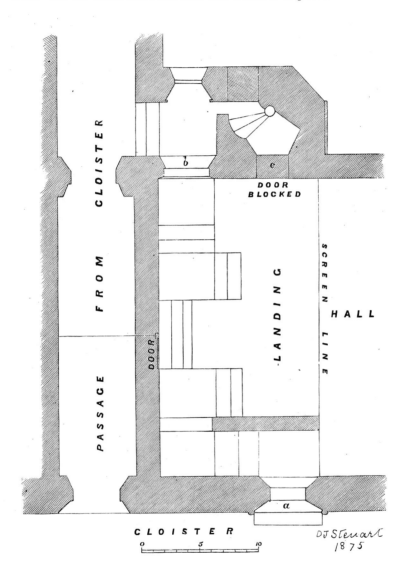

Fig. 19.   Plan of the west end of the Hall, previous to 1875.

The ancient circular staircase or " vice " on the north side of the Hall was removed to make room for the new staircase above described, but the lierne vault (*d*, fig. 19) was preserved, and placed over the vestibule by which the new staircase is approached from the court (*e*, fig. 2). A new servants' hall was built, projecting further into the court than the old one had done, with a lecture-room and muniment-room over it. The Buttery, under the Hall, was increased by the same amount of space as the Hall ; and the larder, on the opposite side of the passage, by the width of a staircase which originally provided direct access to the Library through a door of Alcock's period (S, fig. 2). In the course of the removal of this staircase a lancet window (ibid. T) was discovered in what is now the south wall of the larder. This window was proved to have looked southwards from the direction of the splay, and from the presence of iron hinges to carry the shutter. The wall in which it is contained had therefore once been an outside wall. Access to the Library is now provided by a new staircase entered from the south end of the Ante-hall, through a vestibule formed in the north-west angle of the cloister-court.

COMBINATION ROOM. — The room eastward of the Hall has been used as the College Parlour from very ancient times[1]. It was altered in 1692, the cost being defrayed out of a legacy of £150 bequeathed by Dr William Lewis[2]; and again in 1762 in consequence of a gift of £100 from Francis, Lord Middleton ; but as usual in the case of benefactions the details of the work done are not recorded. The builder employed was Essex[3].

---

[1] [It is first mentioned in the Audit-Book for 1595—96. "Item for 2 longe casmonts for yᵉ hall and an other for yᵉ parlor vˢ. iiijᵈ."]

[2] [Mr William Hussey (B.A. 1683, M.A. 1687), Bursar, records in a memorandum apparently torn out of an Audit-Book, and preserved in Jesus College Treasury, "Octob. 5ᵗʰ, 1691. Dʳ Wᵐ Lewis gave to yᵉ College by his Will and Testament yᵉ summ of one hundred and fifty pounds..." : and "December 15ᵗʰ, 1692. The Charges of altering yᵉ College Parlour coming to 37. 02. 01. it was ordered by yᵉ Mʳ and Fellows at yᵉ Audit Dec. 15ᵗʰ, 1692 yᵗ this sum should be paid out of Dʳ Lewis' Legacy..."]

[3] [College Order, 22 December, 1762. "Order'd that £100 the Gift of Francis late Lord Middleton be laid out in new fitting up the Combination Room." Audit-Book, 1762—63. "Essex for a plan for Parlʳ. window 0. 10. 6." In the following year there are only a few charges for furniture, etc.]

The room is not part of the hall-range, but of that which forms the east side of the cloister-court (fig. 2); and though the floor is now on the same level as that of the Hall, it clearly was once on that of the rooms to the north and south of it, which are three feet higher than its present level; for the floor of the cellar beneath it has been lowered by the same number of feet in order to obtain sufficient height; and the door by which it was once entered may still be seen by ascending the staircase at the north-west angle of the cloister (V, fig. 2)[1]. This door is on the same level as that of the room opposite. The present ceiling has been made at some time subsequent to an older ceiling of wood and plaster which still exists above it. The room between this ceiling and the roof is now used as a lumber-room, being too low for use as a chamber. The more modern ceiling is evidently, from its position, of the same date as the panel-work, which, from its style, was probably put up in 1762.]

LIBRARY.—The Library is a low room on the second floor of the west side of the quadrangle, which retains its oak roof, un-painted, and in good original condition. The fittings are of wainscot, and, although they are of much later date, the whole preserves a venerable air of undisturbed antiquity. The room is 48 feet long and 25 feet broad, and has seven classes on each side. There is no record of the construction of them in the Audit-Books, but to judge from their style, they are those referred to in an inscription above the Library door, which records that Edmund Boldero, Master 1663—79, "rebuilt these book-cases at his own expense[2]."

[It should be remarked that the building containing the Library is of white brick, while that adjoining it on the south, containing the Lodge, is of red brick. There is a very distinct line of demarcation between the two (h, fig. 2).

MASTER'S LODGE.—The Lodge at present occupies the building eastward of the gate of entrance, the south side of the

---

[1] [The passage to this staircase is called "Cow-lane."]

[2] [The text of the inscription is: "Edmundus Boldero, S. T. P. hujus collegii ab anno MDCLXIII Magister, quum armaria hæcce sumtibus propriis de novo exstruxisset, operam haud mediocrem in classibus ordinandis posuit, et, pro cumulo suorum erga nos beneficiorum, quicquid sibi librorum esset, id omne novissimo testamento Biblio-thecæ legavit."]

Cloister Court as far as the west wall of the Chapel (*c d*, fig. 2), and the ground floor of the west side of the same court as far as the northernmost staircase on that side (ibid. G). On the first floor there is a set of college chambers both north and south of this staircase, so that the first floor of the Lodge is bounded by the wall *e f* (figs. 2, 20). On the upper floor the Lodge extends as far as the College Library, the south wall of which is laid down on the same plans (ibid. *g h*).

The Lodge is now entered through a modern door[1] at the end of the south walk of the cloister (fig. 2, F), but there is a more ancient door in the same walk (ibid. H), with a doorcase of Alcock's period. This is now used as the servants' entrance. The garden to the south, which appears to have been assigned to the Master from the earliest times, is now entered through a door in the angle between the east and west wings (ibid. I). In Loggan's time (fig. 3) this door was placed a few feet farther to the west (K, fig. 2). It gave access to a passage about ten feet wide, separated from the dining-room by a stud-partition, which has since been taken down, so as to enlarge the dining-room. There is now a second door into the garden (ibid. L) where Loggan shews a window.]

The building east of the gate was originally in two floors only, without garrets. That westward of the present chapel, however, had in Loggan's time three floors, as at present, with garrets in the roof. At the south-west corner there was a small oriel-window. The parapet was a battlement of ten crests, each crest consisting of three steps finished by a richly molded single chimney-shaft, so that the whole southern wall was crowned by a row of ten equidistant chimneys of various patterns in the shafts, but precisely similar in height, caps, and bases, and resembling a row of pinnacles. This picturesque and unique arrangement was unfortunately destroyed during the last century. The chimneys were altered to their present aspect about 1871.

[The alteration to the building next to the gate was made between 1718 and 1720. A memorandum headed " Charges of ye New-Building between ye Master's Lodge and ye Turret[2],"

---

[1] [The windows on either side of this door were found in the wall, and there is evidence that similar windows exist all round the cloister.]

[2] [This paper is preserved, together with the workmen's bills, in the College Treasury.]

shews that the amount then expended was £266. 16s. 9d. Of this sum £100 was defrayed by a legacy from Charles Proby, D.D., Fellow. With regard to the balance, Dr Charles Ashton, Master 1701—52, has left the following note:

"The remaining summ of £166. 16s. 9d. I paid out of my own money, chusing to have that for my share in the expense of a work so much for the use and ornament of yᵉ College; so that yᵉ College doth owe me nothing upon yᵉ account of that New Building. Dec. 23, 1720.   C. ASHTON."

It is probable that the third floor, which rises to within about three feet of the upper stringcourse of the gateway, was added at this time. The windows are now large rectangular openings with stone jambs, fitted with sashes, but whether they were put in by Dr Ashton, or subsequently, when the rest of the south front of the College was similarly treated, cannot now be discovered.

The steps by which the Lodge was brought to its present dimensions must now be investigated.

The position assigned to the Master's Lodge by Bishop Alcock is not known, and the Statutes merely assign to the Master "those chambers which the Masters have usually in-habited[1]." From this language however we may be sure that it has always occupied a portion at least of the present site, though at first, like other Lodges, it was probably limited to one or two rooms. The Audit-Books contain numerous references to various rooms that formed part of it at different times. In 1561—62 "our maysters chamber" is mentioned; in the following year "one of our master's chambers," which implies that even then the Lodge consisted of several rooms; in 1568—69 "our master's parler;" in 1569—70 "the window in the lower part of [the] master's lodging," when workmen are paid "for slatinge our masters chambre," and "for pargeting our master's hall," a room which is again mentioned in 1573—74, and in 1600—1601; in 1573—74 a payment is made "to our master for sixe wyndowes (after xijᵈ. a wyndowe) in the Tower chambre," a room often alluded to in subsequent years; in 1578—79 "our master's nether parlour," which in the following year is wainscoted; in

[1 " Chapter X. Magister cameram sive cameras eas habebit quas magistri hactenus habere consueverunt, quas etiam magistro assignamus."]

1581—82 "our master's upper chambre," which in the next year
is "seeled," and fitted with wood to carry the hangings; his
"pantre" in the same year; in 1595—96 "our master his grene
chamber and wanscott chamber," "our master his studye," "yᵉ
bukrome chamber in our master his lodginge;" and in 1609--10
"our master's great chamber[1]."

The Lodge has been so frequently altered that it is impossible to identify all these rooms. The enumeration of them,

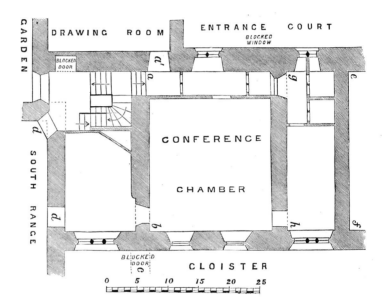

Fig. 20.   Plan of the first floor of the north wing of the Master's Lodge.

however, shews that during the sixteenth century the Lodge
was divided into several apartments, and was at least in two
floors. By the "Tower-chamber" the lower of the two rooms
over the gate of entrance is meant[2]. This room communicated
with that next to it on the first floor of the building to the east

---

[1] [A room called "the Founder's Chamber" is alluded to in terms which indicate
that it was part of the Lodge. Audit-Book, 1667—68. "For flooring and wainscotting yᵉ Lodging Parlour and garret over yᵉ Founders Chamber 7. 00. 00."]

[2] [In the passage above quoted, "window" probably means "light." Each of
the two rooms in the tower has two windows looking north, and one looking south,
each of two lights.]

of the gate by a staircase which is still in existence, but disused. This room, now the drawing-room[1], had a large window of three lights (fig. 3), and is possibly "the great chamber," and that beneath it, now the dining-room, is certainly the "nether parlour." It is lined with panelwork that may well have been put up in 1580. Both these rooms have windows, now blocked, in their north wall. The "tower chamber" was exchanged in 1636—37 for "the chamber under the Conference Chamber[2]." The latter is a large room 20 feet long by 21 feet broad, on the first floor of the north wing of the Lodge, or west range of the Cloister Court (fig. 20). There is a tradition that it was formerly used as the Audit-Room of the college. It was once approached from the court by an external staircase, the door leading to which, now blocked (c, fig. 20), may still be seen above the roof of the west cloister, into which the stairs evidently descended, for the wooden ceiling of that cloister is interrupted at this point and pieced with panelwork of a different and more modern pattern. The "Conference Chamber" is decorated with rich and beautiful panelwork, including an elaborate chimneypiece, closely resembling that of the Audit-Room at Queens' College, but the precise date of its construction has unfortunately been lost. It is clear that the room originally occupied the whole breadth of the range, and that the present partition on the west side has been placed where it is in order to provide a passage to the room beyond. This, which was once entered through a door of fifteenth century work (g, fig. 20), is probably the room to which Sherman refers when he relates that John Reston (Master 1546—1549) "consecrated as an Oratory the room next to the Master's dining-room on the north, and directly over the passage into the cloister[3]." We

[1] [It was brought to its present dimensions by Dr Corrie.]

[2] [Audit-Book, 1636-37. "To Mr Boylston Aprill 14th for the income of the Chamber vnder the Conference Chamber exchanged with the Master for the Vpper Tower iij^li. vij^s. vj^d." We ought perhaps to understand from this statement that both the Tower chambers were once assigned to the Master.]

[3] "Cameram juxta Magistri cœnaculum a parte Boreali sitam cui immediate subjicit introitus in claustrum vir pius sibi in oratorium consecrari fecit." [The Oratory still existed in Sherman's own time, as the following Order shews: "26 June, 1635. Consensum est, ut Ornamenta, quæ in Oratorio sunt juxta Cubiculum M^ri, redimantur a D^re Beale, sumptibus Collegii, ibique maneant in usus M^ri et successorum ejus." Dr

have already seen that this passage was near the south end of the range up to 1688, and that the room under the " Conference Chamber," part of which is now the Hall of the Lodge, was added to it in 1637. This room was bounded on the north by the wall *g h* (fig. 20). The passage was therefore north of that wall; and as there is a second wall (ibid. *e f*) at a distance of eight feet further north, it is evident that it was originally between the two. The position thus assigned to it is exactly in accordance with Sherman's description, and agrees fairly well with Loggan's plan. We do not know when it was altered; but it may very likely have been about 1784, under the direction of Essex, from an Order, dated 12 March, 1785, directing a payment of five guineas to his widow in consideration of "his Trouble in surveying the late Alterations in the Principal Court." The room north of the wall *e f* was added to the Lodge at some period subsequent to 1785, but no College Order on the subject appears to have been preserved.

It is possible that the three rooms, of which the central one is the " Conference Chamber," may have been the original chambers of the Master; and that the external staircase may have been intended, as in other Lodges, to provide convenient access for him to the rest of the College. The doors at *d* and *d'* in the south wall, the original extent of which is shewn by dotted lines (fig. 20), are modern; as also is that in the west wall (ibid. *a'*) leading to the Drawing Room; but that at *a* is ancient, as part of the opening at *b* may also be. This must have been reduced to its present dimensions when the door to the staircase was blocked. Above the " Conference Chamber" there are now several rooms, subdivided by stud-partitions. The tradition that these rooms have been made out of one large room used by the Master as a study, is rendered extremely probable by the presence of a door into the College Library which appears to be original.

The rooms at the extreme west end of the building made out of the nave of the Conventual Church, one of which had a picturesque oriel window when Loggan's print was taken, appear to have been part of the Lodge from very early times; and

Beale was Master 1632—33. The Conference Chamber was used as a bedroom in 1849, when Dr Corrie became Master. It is now a sitting-room]

the ground-floor of the remaining portion, as far as the Chapel, has long been used as the kitchen of the Lodge. It was first assigned to the Master in 1663[1]. The rooms on the first and second floors, however, originally approached by a staircase out of the south walk of the cloister, of which the door (E, fig. 2) is now blocked, were not completely annexed until 1866[2]. These rooms occupy just two-thirds of that wing of the Lodge, extending on both floors from the second window shewn by Loggan to the Chapel. They had probably been used as College chambers from the beginning, for in 1579—80 we find the following entry on the occasion of a fire in "Mr Murgetrode's upper chamber," and Dr Worthington (Master 1650—60) notes that his rooms were "between the Master's Lodgings and the Chappell."

"Itm to vj. laborers to make cleane the leades where the fyer was, to cast the rubbishe downe into o^r. m^{rs}. garden and into the Cloyster yeard ij^s."

This record disproves the theory that has been often set up that these rooms were not built until 1617, by Fulke Greville, Lord Brooke, who in that year addressed the following letter[3] to

[1] [College Order, 17 September, 1663. "Concessum est a Sociis ut Magister Collegii habeat in suos usus Cameram istam infimam quæ propriis ejus ædibus proxime adjacet versus Orientem ; ita tamen ut ad singulas Anni quartas, solvat alicui Scholari (cui juxta consuetudinem debetur) tres solidos et quatuor denarios."]

[2] [College Order, 28 Jan. 1851. "That the Master be allowed to annex to the Lodge the two sets of Rooms in the Chapel Staircase, adjoining the Lodge." Ibid. 18 Dec. 1866. "Agreed that the Master have permission to annex the rooms in Staircase K to the Lodge, upon the express condition that he and his successors maintain the same in repair, and pay to the College the rent which has hitherto been paid for these rooms."]

[3] [The letter, preserved in the College Muniment Room, is endorsed: "To the Right wor^{ll}: his very lovinge Frend m^r Dr Duport, Master of Jesus College in Cambridge." He entered Shrewsbury School 17 October, 1564, on the same day as Sir Philip Sidney; matriculated as a Fellow Commoner of Jesus College 20 May 1568; held various high offices of State; when Chancellor of the Exchequer in 1618, advocated the interests of the University against a scheme for draining the Fens; founded a History Lecture (since lost) by a codicil to his will dated 6 Sept. 1628; was murdered by one of his own servants 30 Sept. in the same year; buried in S. Mary's Church, Warwick. His epitaph is: "Fvlke Grevill, Servant to Queene Elisabeth, Conceller to King James, Frend to Sir Philip Sidney. Trophæum Peccati." Cooper's Annals, iii. 131, 209; Baker's Hist. of S. John's ed. Mayor, i. 212, and notes; Works, ed. Grosart, 1870. He appears to have visited his college in 1611—12, for we find in that year: *Reparaciones et Exp. necess.* "Item a par gloves for S^r. fulke Gruell xvj^s."]

the Master, Dr Duport. It is probable that the scheme therein suggested refers to what is now, as in his time, the nave of the chapel, and that it was never carried out :

" S^r,

I intended to have seene you in Cambridge shortly. But I finde my selfe engaged into so manie busienesses in this his M^{ties} absence, that I feare I shall not have anie such opportunity. Yet my love is such to my old nurse, that I would not have her good neglected by my absence. Let me therfore entreat you, with all speed, fullie and particularly to enforme your selfe by some honest, and skilfull workman what the charge will be of convertinge the west end of your Chappell into lodginge chambers. And I pray you send me a bill of all particulars, viz. of the precise heigth, length, and breadth of the platt; of the certayne number, cizes, and prices of the Sommers, Juistes, and Bordes (wch I wish to be well seasoned) for the floores ; of the transoms and studdes for the partitions; of the lights with theyr irons, casements, and glasse; of bricke for chimneyes, and all other materialles, with the severall charges of the workmanshippe.

Let me entreat you farther, that a Platt may be drawne to shewe the contrivinge of the lights, stayre-cases, chimneyes and studies, with the severall charges of them, to the intent, that by conference with some workmen here, I may see if anie thinge may be altered for the better. The worke I would have to be substantiall, and comely ; fitt (if occasion require) for my selfe to lodge in. And therfore I desire that, by the consent of your company, the disposinge of those chambers may be confirmed to me, duringe my life. I would have the dores made more strong and seemly then ordinary Colledge dores, and the lockes aunswerable. I thincke that two stories wilbe sufficient, for so (I suppose) there may be six large chambers, of faire heigts, wheras, if we make nine, I doubt they will all be too lowe roofed; and moreover by that meanes, the lights (as I take it) may stand vnaltered. As I remember, the estimate of three stories, wch you sent me, was 160^{li} or 170^{li}: wherfore makinge but two (w^{ch}, in regard of the number and maintenance of the Colledge I hold sufficient) the buildinge may be much more substantiall, and the roomes fayrer, with equall or not much greater charge. But upon the viewe of your platt, and bill of particulars, I will soone resolve ; and whatsoever I shall see requisite will cause it to be payd, anie time the next terme, vnto whomsoever you shall send or appoynt to receive it ; vpon the receipt wherof I pray you appoint some of the discretest of your Society to vndertake the oversight of the worke. This busienesse I doe seriously entend, and ernestlie desire the speedie dispatch therof. The onely scope wch I ayme at in it is the good of the Colledge ; Let me therfore entreat you to suppresse my name vntill all things be fully determined. This expectinge your speedy aunswer with my hartie commendacions I commit you to gods protection.

your very lovinge freind

White-Hall Maij 27°.   Fulke Grevyll."

A further proof that the Lodge did not originally extend so far as the Chapel is afforded by the position of the door leading into the nave from the Master's garden (C, fig. 2), which would doubtless have communicated directly with the Lodge, as was usual, had not these chambers intervened.]

RANGES OF CHAMBERS.—The chambers in the cloister-quad-rangle, and in the range forming the western half of the south side of the entrance court, sufficed for the accommodation of the college until 1638, when, during the mastership of Dr Richard Sterne (Master 1633—44), the first stone was laid of the range on the north side of the entrance court. It seems to have been finished in about five years. The expense was defrayed partly by the College, £200 being contributed in five years, at the rate of £40 in each year[1]; and partly by subscriptions, which in many cases were collected by the personal solicitation of the Master and some of the Fellows. The charges of their "Journeys to present letters to Benefactours for the new buildinge" occur in the Audit-Book for 1637—38[2]. The principal subscribers are set down as follows in the Commemoration Book :

"Christopher Lord Hatton gave all the freestone necessary for the whole work, and added moreover £100. Sir John Baker of Sissenhurst in Kent, Baronet, gave £100. William Lord Allington of Horseheath in this County gave £50. Sir Thomas Hatton, Baronet, Sir John Brampton, Lord Chief Justice of the King's Bench, Sir Richard Hatton, one of the Justices of the Court of Common Pleas, and John Browning, B.D., sometime Fellow, gave each of them £40. Sir Anthony Cage, Knight, gave 30 Loads of Timber, valued at £50. Sir William Boswell and William Beale, D.D., sometime Fellow and Master here, gave each of them £30.

Thomas Westfield, D.D., Fellow here, and afterwards Bishop of Bristol, Sir William Bowyer, Sir Richard Onslow, Sir Heneage Proby,

---

[1] [College Order, 16 February, 1638—39. "Decretum est Unanimi consensu M^{ri} et omnium Sociorum ut in quinque annos proxime sequentes conferantur ad extructionem novi Ædificii ad septentrionalem partem Areæ Exterioris singulis annis £40 (viz., e communi cista £4 per annum, ex dividendis inter magistrum et socios £36 per annum) in toto ducentæ libræ: et ut prima solutio fiat ad Computum 1639."]

[2] ["Mr Gatfords and Mr Lants journey into Essex March ye 16. xxxv^s. ix^d. Mr Boilstons and Mr Taylers horses to Stanton iiij^s. Mr Boilston's journey to Sr Christopher Hatton and my L^d of St Asaph iiij^{li}. Mr Anscells journey to Mr Payton and Mr Jocelin Ap. 17. iiij^s. vj^d. Mr Boilstons journey to Dr Troigden and Mr Willen xxij^s. x^d. Mr Anscells and Mr Boylstons journey into Surrey to Sr Richard Onslow and Sr Ambrose Browne June. 6. lvij^s. iiij^d." Similar charges occur in the Audit-Book for 1638—39.]

Sir Ambrose Brown, D^r. Phineas Hodgson, M^r. John Squire, M^r. Robert Owen, and M^r. Thomas Buck, Esquire Bedell of this University, gave each of them £20.

John Boilston, D.D., and Jeffery Watts, B.A., both Fellows, gave each of them twenty marks.

Sir Richard Everard, Sir Robert Hatton, Sir William Butler, D^r. Thomas Dod, D^r. Edward Proby, D^r. John Twickenden, M^r. William Pyott, M^r. Francis Vernon, M^r. Thomas Overman, M^r. William Short, M^r. Robert Levett, M^r. William Warren, M^r. Richard Taylor, and M^r. Henry Hutton gave each of them £10.

Several other sums were advanced by D^r. William Fairfax, M^r. Henry Willis, M^r. John Lynch, M^r. Martin Warren, M^r. William Clarkson, M^r. John Gerard, M^r. Abraham Gates, M^r. Edmund Thornton, M^r. Morden, Rector of Foulmire, and M^r. Westfield, Rector of Islip.

To which was added by the then Master and Fellows, £332 [1]."

The sums here specified amount to £1198. 13s. 4d., but the entire charge was £1544. 16s. 4½d., besides the stone, from Weldon, and the timber, given by the Lord Hatton and Sir Anthony Cage [2].

This addition to the buildings is a range of chambers in three floors 125 feet in length, with a low-pitched leaden roof like the older parts of the College. When Loggan's print was taken a large sun-dial occupied the centre of the battlement on the south side. The coping of the battlement rising above it shews it to have been part of the original construction. The architect of this range had the good fortune to build it in a style so nearly the same as that of the range on the opposite side of the court that there is no striking discrepancy between them.

[The whole of the range westward of the Gate of Entrance, which, as it had once contained the Grammar School on the

---

[1] [This sum probably represents voluntary contributions.]

[2] These particulars are taken from the College Book, p. 75, which contains also the List of Benefactors to this undertaking from 20 Dec. 1637 to 17 Jan. 1641. [In "Excerpta e Registro," preserved in the College Treasury, the following note occurs: "1641. Mar. 11. Computus Receptorum et Expensarum pro novo Ædificio a Dec. 20, 1637, usque ad Jan. 17, 1641, examinatus et approbatus per M^{rum} et majorem partem Sociorum. Summa ejusdem existente £1544. 06. 04½." It is worth remarking that the quarries at Weldon supplied the stone for all the work executed under Bishop Alcock's superintendence—the great Tower-gate, the door-case into the cloister, the arcades of the cloister, the jawms and window-heads of the Hall, are all constructed in Weldon stone, and all have been mended and patched at one time or other with Ketton stone. The Chapel, on the other hand, so far as the original work is concerned, has no samples of stone from the Weldon quarry.]

ground floor, was sometimes called the Grammar School Range, was applied to the use of members of the College, after the suppression of the School by the Commissioners of Queen Elizabeth in 1570[1]. This change, in all probability, did not affect the exterior.]

The need of still further accommodation has unfortunately destroyed the picturesque and unique arrangement that the south front of the College presented when Loggan's print was taken (fig. 3). In his view the gateway rises proudly in three stories, surmounted by a lofty battlement in stages, and crowned by three detached ornamental chimney-shafts on each side wall; the lateral building to right and left is of two stories only, with a plain parapet, and two groups of molded brick chimneys; while the gateway, being twice as high as the adjacent buildings, produces the effect of a tower. The chamber on the second story to the right has a large window of three lights with tracery, and had evidently been intended for some official purpose. The addition of a story to this range has smothered the tower, and moreover the whole of the southern face of the buildings up to the chapel has been provided with modern sash-windows; the ornamental chimney-shafts have been removed from the tower, as well as from the whole of the front, and replaced by a set of uninteresting chimney-pots, no two of which are alike. These changes have been described in a very amusing style by Henry Annesley Woodham, LL.D., formerly Fellow:

"It will be noticed that the style of the windows corresponds but ill with the character of the gate, a discrepancy which was occasioned by the following exploit. In the last century measures were contemplated and tenders received for beautifying the whole College, by transforming its Gothic features into as perfect Venetian as might be practicable; but the demands of even the most reasonable contractor were so much beyond the means of the Society, that the design was reluctantly abandoned; its originators, however, changed into sash-windows all such as faced the public road, excepting those on the ground floor, which were concealed by the garden walls, while all the interior windows of the court were left in their primæval rudeness, in order that the cursory glance of the traveller might deceive him into an opinion of academic

[1] [The Visitors of Queen Elizabeth in 1569 had specially excepted Jesus College: "Nemo Grammaticam ullo in collegio doceat nisi in collegio Jesu tantum et in collegiis Trinitatis et Regio quoad choristas." In the later code however the words "nisi—tantum" are omitted. Dr Lamb's Documents, pp. 303, 351. The position of the school is shewn by the following entry: Audit-Book 1573—74. "Item...for ij pecks of tyle pines bestowed upon the chamber over the schoole-howsse viij^d."]

enlightenment and that posterity might recognize their liberality, and imitate their example[1]."

These changes were begun in 1718; but, as the cost was defrayed by subscription, there is no allusion to the work in the Audit-Books. The Commemoration Book thus records it :

"The New Building, on the south side of the Outer Court, was erected in the year 1718, towards which The Right Honourable William Lord St John, Baron of Bletso, sometime Student and B.A. here, gave £50; Robert Newton, D.D., and John Brooke, B.D., Fellows, gave each of them Ten Guineas; Charles Proby, D.D., Rector of Tewing in Hertfordshire, Fellow, gave Twenty Guineas; Thomas Bates, B.D., Fellow, gave £20; Sir Charles Sidley, Baronet, of this College, gave Thirty Guineas; Samuel Brearey, D.D., and Benjamin Hollingworth, M.A., Fellows, gave each of them £20; Nathaniel Hough, D.D., Fellow, gave £15; William Grigg, D.D., John Brooke, B.D., and Andrew Glen, M.A., Fellows, gave each of them £10; George Lawson, esquire, Pensioner of this College, gave £20; the Honourable Thomas Willoughby of this College, and Member of Parliament for the University, gave £50."

[The subscriptions here enumerated amount to £298. 10s. 0d. The work done was probably limited to the addition of an upper story to the Grammar School range ; and the brickwork and stringcourses were so arranged that there was no incongruity visible between the new and the old work. Sash-windows were not introduced into this portion of the façade until 1791[2], when the following order was made :

"January 10, 1791.   Agreed that new Sashes be put into the front of the College from the Master's Lodge to the end of the building to the West, including the windows at the West end."

The original windows, as Dr Woodham says, were left on the ground floor.   The effect produced by the introduction of the sash-windows will be understood from the accompanying sketch of the Great Gate (fig. 21).   In the summer of 1880 they were all replaced by windows in the original style.

The alterations to the range containing the Gate of Entrance were preceded, so far as we can ascertain, by others, not less

---

[1] [See Dr Woodham's paper, quoted above, p. 88.]

[2] [Audit-Book, 1790—91. "Averley for Sashes 58. 14. 4 " Sash-windows had however been introduced into the college before, for in 1794—95 we find " From Averley, Carpenter, for old Sashes 2. 10. 0."]

destructive of ancient appearance, to the Cloister-quadrangle.
In Loggan's print the Cloister is enclosed by a wall, which on
the north side is pierced by four square-headed windows, each

Fig. 21.   The Gate of Entrance, previous to the alterations of 1880, shewing the sash-
windows inserted in the 18th century.

of three lights. It may be presumed that the other sides were
treated in a similar manner. At the present time there are four
arches, rising from the ground, on the north and south sides,

and five on the east and west sides. No record of this alteration
has been preserved, but it may be presumed that it was at least
commenced in 1762—63, in which year the Audit-Book contains the following entry: "Jeffs, Stone-mason, a bill for the
West-Cloyster £30. 1. 0.:" and in 1764—65 "Jeffs, Stone-
mason, for the South Cloister £24. 10. 8.[1]"]

No further addition to the buildings took place until 1822,
when the following order was made:

"22 May, 1822. It was agreed that owing to the great Increase in the
Number of the Members of the College, it would be highly desireable
to add to the present Buildings."

Shortly afterwards a range of twelve sets of chambers, in
three floors, was built in what was then called the "Pump Court,"
in prolongation of the range forming the east side of the cloister-
quadrangle[2].

[The latest addition to the buildings is the range of chambers
forming the north side of this court, erected in 1869—70, under
the superintendence of the Rev. E. H. Morgan, Fellow, from
the designs of Alfred Waterhouse, Architect, at a total cost of
£9874. 3s. 1d.[3] They were commenced at the beginning of
May, 1869, and being pressed forward with all reasonable haste
were partially ready for occupation 20 April, 1870, when the
rooms on two staircases (the easternmost, and that next but one
to it) were occupied by undergraduates. The rest of the building
was occupied in October, 1870. At the same time the offices
north of the building of 1822 were rebuilt, partly on new ground,
after the design of the same architect.

The court, of which these new buildings form the north side,
is now called "The New Court." In order to provide convenient

---

[1] [The description of Cambridge called Cantabrigia Depicta, publ. 1763, says,
"There is a Cloister like those we find in the Convents and Nunneries abroad, which
surrounds a small Court." The Cambridge Guide, however, for 1799, which is
clearly based on the earlier work, says, "A cloister like those at Queens' College, and
in the convents and nunneries abroad, surrounds a small court, lately beautified, and
rendered more open and airy." The change had evidently taken place in the interval
between the publication of the two works.]

[2] [The contract was with James Webster, Builder, of Cambridge, for £2290.]

[3] [The thanks of the College were conveyed to Mr Morgan by an Order dated 20
December, 1870. The erection of the range had been decided by an Order dated
2 February, 1869. The contractor was John Loveday.]

access to it, the old fence along the west side of the entrance-
court was removed, and a new fence carried in an unbroken line
from south to north (as the plan, fig. 2, shews), so as to leave
room for a passage round the west end of the building of 1638—
41. The archway through which access to the Pump Court was
obtained (W, fig. 2), was rebuilt during the course of these works
of larger dimensions and of a more handsome design.

It should also be mentioned that the chimneys throughout
the College, having been rebuilt separately at various times, as
occasion required, were of various and most incongruous patterns
until 1871, when they were all reconstructed after the pattern of
those on the building forming the north side of the entrance-
court, which fortunately had not been altered.

GATES, GARDENS, GROVE, ETC.—The gates at the opposite
extremities of the road by which the college is entered[1] are distinguished in 1573—74 as the "vtter great gate" and "the hither
great gate." The former is called in 1609—10 the "gate next
the street ;" and in 1615—16 "the foregate." At that time these
gates were of wood[2], and the boundary wall of the College rose
over them in a gabled arch, as shewn in Lyne's plan of Cambridge, dated 1574. The present piers, of red brick and stone,
were made by Grumbald in 1703, and the iron gates are probably of the same date[3].

The garden to the east of the entrance to the College was
assigned to the Master, that on the west to the Fellows from
very early times. The north-east corner of the latter was laid
down as a Bowling-Green, which is first mentioned in the Audit-
Book for 1630—31. The brick wall round this garden was
made in 1608—9 ; that round the Master's garden in 1681—82[4].

---

[1] [This road was called "the angiporte" in the 16th century, as is proved by many
entries in the Audit-Books: e.g. "Item the ix^th of August to Barraker for vj daies
worke in Jesus weeke laying brickes vppon the angiporte next the fellowes gardein
and rough laying the same vj^s." It is now called "the chimney."]

[2] [Audit-Book 1609—10, "Item to Mr Atkinson for ye great gates next ye street
xxxix^s. iij^d. Item for nayles and iron worke about ye new gates xlix^s. viij^d."]

[3] [Ibid. 1702—3. "To Mr Grumbald for ye Peers and ye Hall 79. 16. 05." The
cost was in part defrayed out of the benefactions to the Hall recorded above.]

[4] [Ibid. 1608—9. "Item layd out this yeare for ye new bricke wall about y^e
fellows orchard and towardes ye levelling of ye grownde cxl. lib." Ibid. 1681—82.
"For building ye new wall about M^rs garden in part 15. 00. 00."]

The Master had also assigned to him a portion of the close, bounded by a fence, as shewn by Loggan.

Loggan shews a large tree in the principal quadrangle. This was a walnut-tree, which is first mentioned in 1589—90. It was once protected by posts and rails, which had perhaps been taken away before his drawing was made[1]. The Cloister Court— called "the cloister yard" or "the inner courte," in the sixteenth century, and subsequently "the further court," "the little quad-rangle" or "the inner quadrangle"—was also laid out as a garden or shrubbery[2]. Loggan also shews a garden behind the building of 1638—41, laid out in regular walks, with a fir-tree in the centre. It was first planted in 1657[3]. It subsequently became a

[1] [Ibid. 1592—93. "Item ..for making...yᵉ rayle about yᵉ walnutt tree ijˢ." Ibid. 1620—21. "Posts about yᵉ walnutt tree." Uffenbach, who visited Cambridge in 1710, was evidently much struck by the enormous extent of this tree: 12 August. "After dinner we went first to *Jesus College*, which lies quite out of the town. It looks just like a monastery. In the great square or court of the college stands an exceedingly large walnut-tree, with very wide-spreading branches. Our servant was ordered to measure the extent of ground covered by them, and found that it was 96 ft. across from side to side." It is also referred to in the following amusing lines, Works of John Hall-Stevenson, Lond. 1795, iii. 28 :

> "At Cambridge, many years ago
>   In Jesus, was a Walnut-tree ;
> The only thing it had to shew
>   The only thing folks went to see.
>
> Being of such a size and mass
>   And growing in so wise a College
> I wonder how it came to pass
>   It was not call'd the Tree of Knowledge.
>
> It overshadow'd every room
>   And consequently, more or less,
> Forc'd every brain in such a gloom
>   To grope its way, and go by guess."

There was also an Arbour in the court. Ibid. 1596—97. "Item to Nadde the car-penter for 10 dayes worke makinge the frame of the vyne in our mʳˢ Gardene and the frame of the Arbere in the quadrangle and mendinge the frame in the fellowes gardene......xˢ."]

[2] [Ibid. 1655—56. "For sweet-bryar in yᵉ cloyster-court 00. 01. 00." Ibid. 1662—63. "It. for cleansing yᵉ inner quadrangle and laurells there 00. 14. 04." The two courts are thus distinguished in the 16th century: Ibid. 1570—71. "Item the makynge cleane of the cloysters yarde and thother yarde when my L. Burley with the Counsayle came to the towne...viijᵈ."]

[3] [Ibid. 1656—57. 2nd Quarter. "To the Gardiner for worke in the Garden, 02. 0.5. 00. For 500 Quicsetts 00. 03. 00. For box 00. 06. 00. Item for a firre tree 00. 02. 06. Item for more box and sweett bryer wood binds 00. 07. 00."]

kitchen-garden; and then again a pleasure-ground. As such it was retained after the completion of the new building in 1870.

The ground to the north and west of the College, called " the Grove" or "the Close," was first planted in 1590—91 with ash-trees; and in subsequent years the planting of additional trees is frequently recorded. It was at that time much more inter-sected with watercourses than it is at present. That which crossed it from east to west, and then flowed round the west and north sides of the garden beyond the building erected 1638, was made in 1606—7. Seats were set up in it in 1717; and be-tween 1780 and 1782 upwards of 400 young trees were planted, and a new walk made. At this period it was evidently used almost as a public promenade, for in 1763 we find a statement that

" The Grove, which lies North of the College, is deservedly admired, being of a semicircular Figure, and of a great extent; which frequently invites the Gentlemen of other Colleges to take the Air here[1]."

There was also a Tennis Court, but all record of its position has been lost, and its existence is only known from the entries in the accounts for repairs done to it. The first of these occurs in the Audit-Book for 1566—67. It was apparently rebuilt in 1603—4, and is last mentioned, so far as we have been able to discover, in 1623—24.

There was also a Pigeon House, the position of which is equally uncertain. It was first built in 1574—75, and stocked in the following year. It stood in a close, called after it "the dovehouse close," adjoining the great close. In 1633 it was let on lease at an annual rent of £3. 10s.[2] As Loggan does not shew it, it had probably been pulled down before his time.]

---

[1] [Cantabrigia Depicta, p. 63. The other details are from the Audit-Books for the years referred to.]

[2] [Ibid. 1574—75. "Item laid out about the dovehouse vt patet per billam ix^{li}. vj^d. ob. Item to Robert carpenter for takinge paynes about ye barganynge for our Dove-howsse xijd." Ibid. 1575—76. "Item for ij locks for the greatt gate going out of the dovehowsse closse into the greatt closse xx^d." College Order, 1633. "Concessum est Johanni Seeli Columbarium solvendo 3^l. 10^s. per annum."]

CHRONOLOGICAL SUMMARY.

1495—96.   Bishop Alcock begins to alter the Nuns' buildings (Sherman).
1497.   12 June.   Charter granted by Henry VII. to Bishop Alcock.
1498.   William Chubbes appointed first Master.
1499.   E. Greigson and W. Plumme admitted first Fellows.
1500.   1 October.   Death of Bishop Alcock.
1503—7.   Contributions to the buildings west of the gate of entrance by Lady
            Catherine Bray, and Lady Joan Hastings.
1570   Grammar-School suppressed by the Commissioners of Queen Elizabeth.
1590—91.   Grove planted.
1608—9.   Wall built round the Fellows' garden.
1634.   New Organ made for the chapel by Robert Dallam.
1638—41.   Erection of a building on the north side of the entrance-court.
1660—62.   Restoration of the chapel.
1663—79.   Dr Edmund Boldero, Master, refits the Library.
1676.   Chapel paved with black and white marble by help of legacies from Dr
            Sherman and Mr Gibson, Fellows.
1679.   Gift of £20 from Dr W. Saywell, Master, to wainscot the east end of the
            chapel.
1681—82.   Wall built round the Master's garden.
1692.   Combination Room altered; Dr Lewis' legacy.
1703.   Piers and gates next the street set up by Grumbold.
  ,,   Hall paved and wainscoted.
1718.   Alteration to the building west of gate of entrance.
1718—20.   Alteration to building east of gate of entrance.
1762.   Combination Room altered; Lord Middleton's legacy.
1762—65.   Alterations to the cloister-court.
1785.   Essex does work to the entrance-court.
1789—92.   Alterations to the chapel in consequence of gift of £300 from Rev. Robert
            Tyrwhitt.
1790.   Remains of the Organ given to All Saints Church.
1791.   Building along the south side of the entrance-court sashed.
1801.   Alterations to Hall; windows lengthened.
1815.   Piscina discovered and repaired by Mr Hustler.
  ,,   Exterior of the chapel cased with Roman cement.
1822.   Building on east side of the Pump Court erected.
1846.   The restoration of the chapel commenced.
1849.   1 November.   The chapel opened for service.
1850.   Eastern triplet of the chapel filled with stained glass.
1851.   Two sets of rooms east of the Master's Lodge added to it.
1852.   Two windows on the south side of the chapel filled with stained glass.
1853.   Lancets on the south side of the chapel filled with stained glass.
1858.   Lancets on north side of chapel repaired and filled with stained glass.
1864—67.   Tower of chapel strengthened; roofs of nave and transepts restored and
            painted.
1866.   Two sets of rooms east of the Master's Lodge added to it.
1867—70.   Walls of nave and transepts plastered; new pavement laid down; nave
            panelled with oak and seated; south-west tower-pier reset.
1869—70.   Building on north side of the Pump Court built by Waterhouse.
1873.   The filling of the windows in the nave and transepts with stained glass by
            Morris undertaken.
1875.   Hall enlarged and new entrance to it made; new Lecture-room and new
            Muniment-room built.
1880.   Sash-windows inserted 1791 replaced by new ones in the original style.

APPENDIX.

A. *Letter from Richard Gravesend, Bishop of Lincoln, 1258—1279, to the Archdeacons of Lincoln, Northampton, and Huntingdon, directing them to allow collections to be made for the nuns of S. Radegund in all the Churches within their jurisdiction; the permission to be valid for two years only.* 21 *May*, 1268.

R. miseracione diuina Linc' Episcopus dilectis in Christo filiis Lincoln', Northampton', et Huntingdon' Archidiaconis salutem graciam et benedictionem.

Mandamus vobis quatinus cum Nuncii dilectarum nobis in Christo Priorisse et Conuentus Sancte Radegundis extra Cantebrig' ad vos accesserint pro fidelium elemosinis colligendis, ipsos beningnius admittatis, negocium ipsarum in singulis ecclesiis Archidiaconatuum vestrorum per tres dies dominicos seu festiuos per Capellanos locorum et non per alios diligenter exponi et pecuniam inde collectam ipsis fideliter et integre liberari facientes; presentibus literis post biennium minime valituris. Quas per questuarios deferri prohibemus, eas si secus actum fuerit viribus carere decernentes. Valete.

Dat. apud Huntingdon' . xij . Kal . Junii . pont' . nostri . Anno . decimo.

B. *Letter of Roger de Skerning, Bishop of Norwich 1266—1278, to all people, lay as well as clerical, in his diocese, desiring them to facilitate the collection of subscriptions for the rebuilding of the steeple of the Church of S. Radegund, which had suddenly fallen down.* 27 *April*, 1277.

R. dei gracia Norweycensis episcopus dilectis in Christo filiis Abbatibus Prioribus Archidiaconis et eorum Officialibus, Decanis, Rectoribus, Vicariis, Capellanis paroch' et aliis ac ceteris omnibus et singulis tam laycis quam clericis per Ciuitatem et Dyoces' Norwyc' constitutis salutem, gratiam, et benedictionem.

Quum in conspectu altissimi quam placid' sit et acceptum ecclesias construere et constructas fovere, in quibus laus Dei extollitur, sanctorum honor excolitur, et venia peccatorum postulatur;—ac Ecclesia sancte Radegundis Cantebrig' Eliensis diocesos (vbi sanctimoniales Deo dedicate vigiliis oracionibus et ieiuniis ac aliis misericordie operibus nocte dieque in dei laudem et honorem insistunt) per Campanilis sui subuersionem et subitam ruinam tot et tantos patitur defectus, quod nisi fidelium eleemosynis subueniatur eidem diuinum ministerium more solito (per paupertatem dictarum sanctimonialium prefatos defectus supplere non ualentium) honorifice et debito modo non poterit exequi in eadem.

Vobis mandamus in virtute obediencie firmiter iniungentes, quatinus cum nuncii dictarum sanctimonialium ad vos venerint fidelium elemosinas petituri, ipsos benigne admittatis, negocium ipsarum per sacerdotes ecclesiarum parochianis vestris diligenter exponi facientes. Et quod collectum fuerit ipsis fideliter et sine qualibet diminutione sub pena anathematis liberari faciatis. Eo magis dictarum sanctimonialium negocium cordi nobis existit quod earum penuria non paucis innotescit.

Dat' apud Hoxne . v . Kal maii . anno gratia [m°] cc°. lxx°. septimo Pont : nostri anno duodecimo.

C. *Letter of the Official of the Archdeacon of Ely to the parochial clergy of the diocese, directing them to assist in every way the collection of alms for the nuns of S. Radegund, reduced to extreme poverty by a fire which had destroyed their house. 29 September, 1313.*

Officialis domini Archidiaconi Elien' vniuersis et singulis Rectoribus et Vicariis ac Capellanis paroch' per dioc' Elien' constitutis salutem in domino.

Quia domus et bona quasi omnia quibus sanctimoniales monasterii sancte Radegundis Cantebrigg' per annum sustentari solebant casu fortuito per incendium sunt consumpta cuius pretextu pro victu querendo quasi publice mendicare quodamodo compelluntur. Quocirca vobis omnibus et singulis in virtute obediencie firmiter iniungendo mandamus quatenus cum dictimoniales procuratoresve aut certi nuncii earundem ad vos venerint pro fidelium elemosinis colligendis ipsos benigne admittatis eorum negocia clero et populo fauorabiliter exponentes, ac subiectum vobis populum fauorabiliter inducentes vt humanitatis intuitu dicti monasterii pressure pie compacientes de bonis a deo sibi collatis dictis sanctimonialibus aliqua conferant subsidia caritatis. Et quia dominus noster dominus Elien' Episcopus ac conuentr' et Lichef' octoginta dies indulgencie omnibus benefactoribus dicte domus nuper concesserunt, volumus et mandamus quatenus dictas indulgencias sic concessas clero et populo exponatis vt eo cicius indulgenciarum allectiuis muneribus populus ad elemosinarum largicionem deuocius excitetur.

Dat' apud Herdwyk iiij^to. Kalend. septembr' Anno dni millesimo. ccc°. tercio decimo.

D. *John de Ketene, Bishop of Ely 1310—1316, confirms certain indulgences granted by his brother Bishops in favour of those who should contribute to the rebuilding of the house destroyed by the aforesaid fire. 28 June, 1314.*

Vniuersis sancte matris ecclesie filiis presentes literas inspecturis Frater Johannes permissione diuina Elyen' Episcopus salutem in domino.

Vt Indulgencie per venerabiles patres Coepiscopos nostros regni Anglie omnibus et singulis ad subuencionem domus monialium sancte Radegundis iuxta Cantebrig' et reedificacionem domorum eiusdem nuper combustarum quicquam de bonis sibi a deo collatis conferentibus rite concesse et imposterum concedende nostris valeant parochianis prodesse ipsas ratas habemus pariter et acceptas.

In cuius rei testimonium litteras nostras fieri fecimus has patentes sigillo nostro communitas.   Dat' apud Hatfeld iiij^{to}. kalend'. Julii. Anno domini . milesimo . Trescentesimo . Quartodecimo . Consecracionis nostre . Quarto.

E.   *Letter of Thomas de Arundel, Bishop of Ely* 1374—1388, *granting an indulgence of forty days to those who should relieve the necessities of the nuns of S. Radegund, whose house and property had been destroyed by fire. 2 April,* 1376.

Vniuersis christi fidelibus presentes literas inspecturis Thomas permissione diuina Episcopus Elien' salutem in omnium saluatore.

Obsequium credimus deo gratum tociens impendere quociens fidelium mentes ad caritatis et pietatis opera allectiuis indulgentiarum muneribus propensius excitamus. De dei igitur omnipotentis misericordia et beatissime marie virginis matris sue ac beatorum Petri et Pauli apostolorum necnon sancte Etheldrede Virginis omniumque sanctorum meritis et precibus confidentes Omnibus parochianis nostris et aliis quorum diocesani hanc nostram indulgenciam ratam habuerint et acceptam de paccatis (*sic*) suis vere penitentibus et confessis qui Religiosis mulieribus pauperibus monialibus Prioratus sancte Radegund' extra Cantebr' nostre dioceseos quarum domus diuerse infra Prioratum predictum nuper situate miserabili et ineuitabili ignis incendio vna cum aliis rebus et bonis suis iam tarde quod dolendum est fuerant consumpte et etiam anullate. Ad quarum refeccionem siue reparacionem et ad supportanda alia onera eisdem Religiosis mulieribus incumbencia minime sufficiunt proprie facultates quicquid de bonis eis a deo collatis dederint seu in testamento suo legauerint aut in dictarum pauperum monialium releuamen alia quecunque contulerint seu conferri procurauerint sub[si]dia caritatis Quadraginta dies indulgencie de iniunctis eis penitenciis misericorditer in domino relaxamus qui bonorum omnium retributor pro hiis et aliis piis operibus amplam est eis largiturus mercedem.

In cuius rei testimonium sigillum nostrum fecimus hiis apponi. Dat' apud Dodyngton secundo die Aprilis Anno domini Millesimo ccc^{mo}. Septuagesimo Sexto et nostre consecracionis secundo.

F.   *A similar letter from William Courtenay, Archbishop of Canterbury, the nunnery having been ruined by a storm. 6 April,* 1390.

Universis sancte Matris ecclesie filiis ad quos presentes litere peruenerint Willelmus permissione diuina Cantuarien' Archieps̄ tocius Anglie primas et apostolice sedis legatus Salutem in domino sempiternam.

Pietatis operibus tociens credimus inherere quociens mentes fidelium ad caritatis opera allectiuis indulgentiarum muneribus propensius excitamus. Cum itaque domus monialium Monasterii sancte Radegundis Cantabrigg' Elien' dioc' nostre Cantuarien' prouincie adeo ruinose existant et per vim ventorum ac alias aduersas tempestates prostrate quod dictarum monialium ad refeccionem et reparacionem huiusmodi domorum et supportacionem aliorum eis onerum incumbencium facultates non suppetunt nisi illis aliunde caritatiuis elemosinarum largicionibus succurratur: Nos igitur mentes fidelium ad tante deuocionis et caritatis opera quantum cum deo possumus excitare volentes et omnipotentis dei immensa misericordia beatissime virginis marie genitricis eiusdem ac beatorum Petri et Pauli apostolorum necnon Sanctorum Alphegi et Thome martirum patronorum nostrorum omniumque sanctorum meritis et precibus confidentes vniuersis Christi fidelibus per nostram Cantuarien' prouinciam vbilibet constitutis de suis peccatis vere penitentibus et confessis qui ad refeccionem et reparacionem dictarum domuum aliqua de bonis eis a deo collatis grata contulerint legauerint seu quouis modo assignauerint subsidia caritatis Quadraginta dies de inunctis eis penitenciis tociens quociens misericorditer in domino relaxamus.

In cuius rei testimonium sigillum nostrum fecimus hiis apponi. Dat in manerio nostro de Croydon sexto die mensis Aprilis Anno domini millesimo . ccc^{mo}. Nonogesimo Et nostre translacionis Nono.

XI.

Christ's College.

CHAPTER I.

[HISTORY OF THE SITE[1].

THE site of Christ's College is bounded on the west by S. Andrew's Street, originally called Preacher Street, from the Dominicans or Friars Preachers, whose house stood on the ground now occupied by Emmanuel College; on the north by a narrow street now called Hobson Street, but originally Walles Lane[2], and by dwelling-houses, a portion only of which are the property of the College; on the east by dwelling-houses; and on the south by a piece of common ground called Christ's Pieces, and by a lane now called Christ's Lane, but originally Hangman's Lane or Rogues' Lane. These boundaries, and the ancient distribution of the site, which we are about to explain, will be understood from the ground-plan (fig. 1) and the plan of the whole site (fig. 2) which forms part of Loggan's map of Cambridge.

The western portion of this site—the ground namely which is now occupied by the buildings of Christ's College (with the

---

[1] [Professor Willis had made no collections for the site of this college. I have done my best to supply the deficiency by a careful study of the original conveyances and other documents, all of which were most kindly placed at my disposal by the Rev. J. Cartmell, D.D., the late Master. I have also been much helped by the Rev. C. A. Swainson, D.D., the present Master.]

[2] [The watercourse called "The King's Ditch" ran eastward along the street now called Pembroke Street, which it left at a point opposite to the eastern limit of the site of Pembroke College. Thence, taking a north-easterly direction, it ran past the west side of S. Andrew's Churchyard, and along Walles Lane. It is shewn as open in Lyne's plan, made 1574 (Hist. of Corpus, Vol. i. p. 246), but the portion of it in Walles Lane had been closed before 1688, when Loggan's plan was made. The gate of the town called "Barnwell Gate" was in S. Andrew's Street, at the N.E. angle of S. Andrew's Church-yard.]

exception of the Fellows' Building)—was the site to which the
Grammar-College of God's House was removed by the Founder
William Bingham in 1446, after he had surrendered his original
site near Clare Hall to King Henry the Sixth, at his special
request, because it was found that without it the king would be
unable to proceed with the erection of his own college[1].

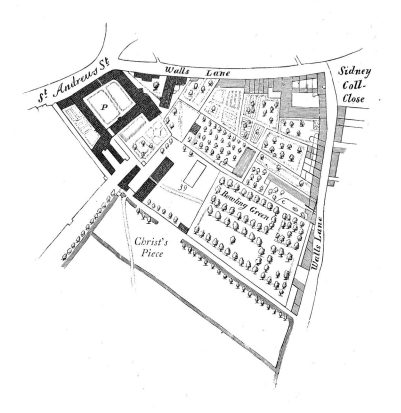

Fig. 2.   Ground-plan of Christ's College, from Loggan's plan of Cambridge.

Bingham's first purchase (18 June, 1446) was a property
belonging to the Abbot of Tiltey, described as "one tenement
otherwise two cottages."   It was situated in "le Prechour strete"

[1] [Charter of God's House, 26 August, 1446. (Commiss. Doc. iii. 162.)   The
foundation of God's House and of Christ's College has been related in the Historical
Introduction.   See also the History of King's College, Vol. i. p. 338.]

in the parish of S. Andrew, between a house formerly belonging to John Fysshewyk, Bedell of the University, on the south, and a house belonging to the Abbess and Convent of Denney on the north. This last was not formally conveyed to him until nearly two years afterwards (28 March, 1448); but he had clearly been in possession of it for some time previously, for it is spoken of as his property in the charter granted to him by King Henry the Sixth, 26 August, 1446. These two properties had a frontage to the street of 90 feet, and a mean breadth of $307\frac{1}{2}$ feet from west to east, where they abutted on land called "le Nunnesfeld," "le Nunnescrofte," or "Gerton Crofte," belonging to the convent of S. Rhadegund[1]. The northern abuttal of the property belonging to Denney Abbey was a messuage belonging to William Herrys or Herry, who was sometimes called, from his occupation, Fisher. He conveyed it to William Fallan, clerk, probably one of the Fellows of God's House[2], 8 October, 1458. It extended, like the other pieces, from Preacher Street to the Nuns' croft; and it abutted north on the messuage of Stephen Warwick.

Ten years elapsed before any further additions to the site were made. In 1468 (7 August), Brian Fysshewyk, heir to John Fysshewyk, sold to William Basset, Proctor or Master of God's House, the messuage mentioned above as the south boundary of the property belonging to the Abbey of Tiltey; and on 27 August in the same year the tenement and garden which occupied the angle between Preacher Street and Hangman's Lane. Between these two pieces there was a strip of ground belonging to the Priory of S. Edmund of Sempringham[3]. This was conveyed

---

[1] [In the conveyance from the Abbot of Tiltey no dimensions are given; in that from the Abbess of Denney the dimensions of that property are given as follows: "extendit se in longitudine C et iiij^or virgas de virgis ferreis domini Regis a predicto vico [Precherstrete] versus terram Monialium Cantebr' vocat' le Nunnesfeld alias le Nunnescrofte ex parte orientali, et continet in latitudine vndecim virgas et vnum quartum virge de dictis virgis ferreis eiusdem domini Regis." The charter states the latter piece to be 11 yards long next the street, and 101 yards broad; of the former it sets down the length only as 19 yards, without giving the breadth, which we may assume was considered to be the same as that of the previous piece. For Tiltey, a Cistercian Abbey in Essex, see Vol. i. p. 342: for Denney, an abbey of nuns Minoresses of the order of S. Clare, near Waterbeach, in Cambridgeshire, see Hist. of the Parish of Waterbeach, Camb. Antiq. Soc. 8vo. Publ. p. 100.]

[2] [He is mentioned as Proctor of God's House in 1462.]

[3] [See Vol. i. p. 1.]

to Basset by the Prior, James Bolton, on Easter Day, 1474. It is minutely described as measuring along the west border next the street 11 yards and 4 inches; and along the south border 102 yards and 15 inches. The breadth of Fysshewyk's two houses from west to east is not given, but as the ground belonging to S. Edmund's Priory is set down as the limit of both of them, the breadth of all three pieces must have been the same. The northernmost of Fysshewyk's houses, and the ground bought from the Priory, are described as extending as far as "a common watercourse in the direction of the Nuns' croft[1]."

The site of which we have traced the acquisition was sufficiently extensive to provide a certain amount of garden-ground beyond the quadrangle to the east, as the plan (fig. 1) shews. At the beginning of the sixteenth century, however, a lease for 99 years at an annual rent of 6s. 8d. was obtained from Jesus College of the croft which lay eastward of the site. The following quotation from the lease, dated 28 January, 1507, describes the position of the ground:

"This indenture made the xxviij[th] day of Januarie the xxij[th] yere of the Reigne of King Harry the vij[th] between John Eccleston Clerke Maister of the Collegge of oure blyssed lady seynt John Euangelyste and seynt Radegunde commonly called Jhus Collegge in Cambrigge .. and the Felowes of the same Collegge on the oon parte

And Richard Wyatt Clerk Maister of Cristes Collegge in Cambrigge aforesaid by harry late kynge of yngland the vj first begon And by margaret Counteisse of Richemond and Derby modir to oure soueraigne lorde the kinge Augmented fynisshed and stablysshed and the Scolers of the same Collegge on the oder parte Witnessith

that the said Maister [etc] haue demised betaken and to ferme leten to the said Maister and Scolers of the said Collegge called Crystes Collegge A certeyn parcell of Grounde lying on the bakesyde of the said Collegge called Crystes Collegge As it is meryd and staked by the maisters of both the said Collegges And moreouer it is agreed bytwen the said partyes That the said Maister and Scolers of Cristes Collegge shalhaue a Balke[2] withoute the said Stakes conteyninge viij foote brode and lying in lenght by the said stakes...."

---

[1] [The words in the conveyance from the Prior are: "Super communem diuisam versus croftum monialium sancte Radegundis Cantebr' vocat' Gerton Crofte;" in that from Brian Fysshewyk: "Super communem cursum aque versus croftum [etc.]." In the conveyance of the corner tenement the eastern abuttal is simply the croft, without any mention of the watercourse.]

[2] [This "balke," which was sold to Christ's College with the croft in 1554, is marked in Lyne's plan of Cambridge, dated 1574, as "Christes Colledge walk."]

Fig. 3. Christ's College, reduced from Loggan's print, taken about 1688. A, Chapel; B, Library; C, Hall; D, Master's Lodge; E, Kitchen; F, Master's Garden; G, Fellows' Garden; H, Tennis Court.

Vol. II.

This ground, now the Fellows' Garden, was purchased from Jesus College, 20 September, 1554. It was then called "le grett orchard."

The next addition to the garden was made 25 February, 1566 —67, when Dr Edward Hawford (Master 1559—81) bought for £20 from Thomas Henrison of Waresley in the County of Huntingdon,

"all that his close conteyninge by estimacion one acre be yt more or lesse lienge and beinge in a certeine Lane called Walles Lane...in the parishe of the holie Trinitie there bitwene ye Tenement apperteyn-inge to the college of corp' christi comonlie called Bennet College... on the southe parte   And the berne late of Robert Raie in parte and the grove late of Richard Brashye also in parte on the northe parte; One hedd thereof abuttinge vpon the said Lane called Walles Lane towardes ye west, The other hedd vpon the college called Christes College...towardes theast..."

The document is endorsed "Thomas Henrison his sale of the douehouse close belonging to the maister's house of Chr. Colledg." The position of the dovehouse being determined by Loggan (fig. 3), and the area of the close being given in the conveyance, it is not difficult to lay down this ground on the plan (fig. 1).

In the same year (12 March, 1566—67), the Master obtained a lease of a second small piece of ground from Corpus Christi College for 60 years, at a yearly rent of three shillings. It is described as follows:

"A certein garden grownde late in ye tenure of on Roger Peyrson burges of the Towne of Cambridge and nowe in ye tenure of ye saied Edwarde Hawford as it is enclosed and lyith betwene the grownde of Christes colledg in Cambridge on the south side, and the grownd late of Roger Peyrson afore saied on the north side; and on hed thereof abutteth vppon the stone wall of the said Christe his colledg ageinst th' Est, and the other hed thereof abutteth vppon A common lane leding towardes the late Greyfriers wall ageinst the west, and conteineth in lenght vj^{xx} and x foote according to ye standard, in bredth xix foote[1]."

It is unfortunately impossible to determine the exact position of this piece, as the conveyance from Peyrson has been lost. It is evident, however, that it must have been a portion of the triangular space between "The Dovehouse Close" and Stephen Warwick's house, the date of the acquisition of which is equally

[1] [This ground was purchased 16 August, 1570.]

unknown.   This space seems to have been occupied by a number of small houses and gardens, of no importance or interest.

In 1587 Dr Edmund Barwell (Master 1581—1610) acquired for £50 from Thomas Manning of Cambridge, burgess and haberdasher, and Agnes his wife, "a piece of pasture ground lately a grove."   It appears to have been situated at the north end of the Dovehouse Close, as shewn on the plan (fig. 1)[1].   By this purchase the site was brought to its present dimensions.]

CHAPTER II.

Description and general history of the Buildings.

[The extent and the arrangement of God's House are unknown; but as the revenues were never sufficient for the maintenance of more persons than a Proctor and four scholars, it is evident that the buildings required for their accommodation could not have been extensive.   From a building-account of Christ's College which will be described below, it may be gathered that they included a chapel[2].

[1] [Manning had bought from Edward Brassey, 13 Feb. 1587, for £120 "totum illud Tenementum cum pomario et groveto bosci adiacent'...Quod tenementum...abuttat super Walles lane...ex parte boriali; et super tenementum nuper in tenura...Willelmi Bradborne ex parte orient'.   Et grovetum predictum abutt' super collegium Christi... ex parte australi et super terras modo vel nuper in tenura Aule Trinitatis ex parte occident'."   Manning kept the tenement, which, from comparison of the price paid for the whole property and that received from Christ's College, was evidently the larger and more valuable portion, and sold the grove, which is thus described in the conveyance 22 March, 1586—7: "Totum illud clausum pasture nuper grovetum bosci, iacent' in parochia Sancte Trinitatis...iuxta collegium predictum ex parte orient', et pomaria nuper Willelmi Bozom et Willelmi Monsey ex parte occident', vno capite inde abuttante supra Clausum collegii predicti nuper Edwardi Hawford versus austrum, et altero partim super pomarium pertinent' ecclesie sancte Trinitatis predict', et partim super curtilagium pertinent' Collegio Jhu in Cantabrigia versus Boream."   The Walles lane mentioned in the first document is clearly the branch of the lane which runs nearly at right angles to the former and is now called King Street.   The position assigned to the close is further confirmed by the following entries in the Audit-Book: 1586—87: "Item to M[r] Manninge for the purchase of the close lately a grove on the Westsyde of the fellowes orcharde lj[li]."   Ibid. 1587—88: "Item to M[r] Maior and M[r] Ball for the acknowledging and recording the new purchase on the backside vj[s].iii[d].]

[2] ["Item to Thomas Ward for the hyre of a howse to ley in the slate y[t] couered the old chapell for j yere and an halfe vij[s]. vj[d]."   By "old chapell" the chapel of God's House is evidently meant.]

We will now describe the buildings of Christ's College, and afterwards collect the few notices that illustrate their history.]

The area of the quadrangle (fig. 2) is an irregular trapezium, placed in such a direction that the meridian line coincides very nearly with one of the diagonals. But, if we assume that the Chapel, instead of pointing to the north-east as it does, shall be directed to the east, the arrangements of the quadrangle may be easily described[1]. The entrance gateway [placed, as usual, neither in the centre of the façade towards the street, nor in the centre of the west side of the court within] is on the west side; the opposite side is assigned to the Master's Lodge, and to the Hall. At the south end of the latter are the Butteries, and beyond them is the Kitchen, external to the quadrangle. The Chapel occupies part of the north side, but extends beyond the outer line of the buildings eastward, into the garden beyond, in the manner of the chapel of Trinity College. The remainder of the north side, the whole of the south side, and the greater part of the west side, is occupied by chambers. The Library is on the west side, to the south of the gateway, on the first floor. These are the primitive arrangements, with very little change; and the walls are those which were built either by the Foundress, or immediately after her death. Their outward appearance, however, has for the most part been changed from the architectural style of her period to a pseudo-Italian.

The charter of foundation granted by Henry the Seventh, is dated 1 May, 1505, and the buildings were begun immediately [from the following entry in one of the Household Books of the Lady Margaret, preserved in S. John's College. The account runs from 13 January 1504—5 to 13 January 1505—6, and is headed "Croydon. Thaccompt of James Moryce clerke of the Warkes there of the most excellent prynces, Margarete" etc. The leaf is torn, so that the commencement is imperfect.

"...by Jamys Morice to master Sikcling M' of crystes collage in the vnyuersite of Cambrigge towardes the making of the newe bildinges there by the comaundement of maigarett moder vnto our soueraigne lord king henry the vij[th] countess of Richemond and Derby.

---

[1] The north and south sides are nearly parallel, and at a mean distance of 120 feet from each other. They are also very nearly at right angles to the east side. The irregularity is produced by the west side, which is so oblique as to make the length of the north side of the court 104 feet and that of the south side 128 feet.

Firste paid to the said M' Sikcling the xxvij[th] daye of June as apperith by a bill of his owne handwriting   Summa lxvj[li]. xiij[s]. iiij[d]."]

Two allusions in subsequent documents shew that the buildings of the College were in a forward state about that time. In the licence for performing divine service in the Chapel granted by James Stanley, Bishop of Ely, 12 December, 1506, it is stated that the Lady Margaret "has constructed in the said college a certain suitable chapel and has caused it to be solemnly consecrated[1];" and in the statutes which the Foundress gave in the same year she "permits the master for the time being to occupy those lower chambers which are below the primary chambers built for our own use, and in our absence for John [Fisher], Bishop of Rochester, so often as he may choose to visit the College, and for so long a time as he may desire to reside within it[2]." I may also quote Fuller's well-known tale:

"Once the Lady Margaret came to Christ's College to behold it when partly built, and looking out of a window, saw the dean call a faulty scholar to correction; to whom she said '*lente, lente*,' gently, gently, as accounting it better to mitigate his punishment, than procure his pardon: mercy and justice making the best medley to offenders[3]."

These are all the allusions that I have been able to discover concerning the first building of Christ's College, but they are sufficient to shew that the plan was completely formed by the Foundress; and from the uniformity of style, as shewn by Loggan (fig. 3) before the original design had been altered, the quadrangle must have been rapidly carried on to completion.

[The death of the Foundress took place 29 June, 1509; and there is evidence that individual buildings were still far from complete at that time, both from the accounts of her executors, and from a volume of building-accounts which has fortunately been preserved in the Treasury of S. John's College. We will consider the former first, and we shall see that upwards of £490

---

[1] " Quia ut accepimus...Domina Margareta...Fundatrix præfati Collegii Christi, in eodem Collegio quandam decoram Capellam in honorem Christi construxit, erexit, et ædificavit, eandemque Capellam solemniter consecrari fecit &c."—MSS. Baker ix. 225. [Bishop Stanley was stepson to the Foundress, being one of the sons of her third husband Thomas, Lord Stanley. Cooper's Memoir of Margaret, Countess of Richmond and Derby. 8vo. 1874, p. 18.]

[2] [Statutes of Christ's College, cap. VI. Commiss. Doc. iii. 179.]

[3] Fuller, 182.

was paid for building-work in the course of 1509, 1510, and 1511. The series of these accounts extends from 1 Henry VIII. (1509—10) to 10 Henry VIII. (1518—19[1]). The earliest entry having reference to Christ's College is the following, from an account which extends "from the day next after the Natiuite of Seint John Baptest the ffyrst yere of the reigne of kyng Henry the viij[th]. vnto the xxiiij day of Januarye the secounde yere of the reigne of the said kyng," that is from 25 June, 1509 to 24 January, 1510—11. The payments were made through D[r] Nicholas Metcalfe, afterwards Master of S. John's College:

> "Item money delyuerd to Maister Scotte toward the byldyng of Crystez collage at dyuers tymes, that is to say, the ffirst tyme xlj*li*. xv*s*. iiij*d*., the secunde tyme by thands of Symond Glasyer xj*li*. v*s*. viij*d*., the thyrd tyme lx*li*., the ffourth tyme xxiij*li*. vj*s*. viij*d*. the ffyfte tyme xx*li*., and the sexte tyme xl*li*., which amounteth in the hole to the summe of... .... ciiij[xx] xvj*li*. vij*s*. vij*d*.
>
> Item payd to Maynerd Waywyke[2] for makyng of an ymage for crystez collegge .... xl*s*."

Further on, under the separate heading "Money delyuered for the Byeldyng of Cristez collage," we find:

> "Item delyured to Jamez Morez toward the Byldyng of the said Collagge after the deth of the forsaid princez of such money that was ffounde in hur coffers the tyme of hur ffirst sekenez, at ij tymes by thands of my lord of Rochester and other of thexecutours, that ys to say at oon tyme C*li*. another tyme by the handes of Maister Thompson clerke lxvj*li*. xiij*s*. iiij*d*. ouer and bysyd cccxxv*li*. ij*s*. ij*d*. delyured by Robert Fremlyngham byfore the deth of the said princez
> clxvj*li*. xiij*s*. iiij*d*."

Again, in the next account, which extends "ffrom the xxiiij[th] day of January in the secunde yere of the Reigne off kyng Henry the viij[th] vnto the xix[th] day of June in the iiij[th] yere off the seide kynge," that is from 24 January, 1510—11, to 19 June, 1512, we find, under the date 16 February, 1511:

> "Item paiede to M. Skote the xvj[th] day off February the seconde yere off the reigne off kynge Henry the viij[th]. ffor diuerse buyldynges with other necessarez belongyng to the same college, as it apperith by a boke delyuerde by the same M. Skote signede with his owne hande, ouer and aboue ciiij[xx] v*li*. ij*s*. to hym delyuerde the laste yere, as it apperith in the accompt of the same yere ....iiij[xx] iiij*li*. vij*s*. vij*d*.

---

[1] [They will be found in Cooper, ut supra, pp. 186, 191, 197.]

[2] [In a document lately found in S. John's College Treasury he signs himself "Meynnart Wewyck," and is described as "of London, paynter."]

Item delyuerde to M. Edwarde ffouke one of the ffelowes off Crystys college by my lordes commaundement, by the handes of M. doctour Metcalff, ffor buyldynge with other necessariez belongyng to the same college, as it apperith by a bill signede with his owne hande

xlli."

These accounts shew an expenditure of upwards of £1000 on the buildings only. We do not, however, know how much the Lady Margaret may have spent during her life. Besides the sum above mentioned, the executors estimate the value of the plate, books, vestments, "beddyng and necessarye stuff," silk, linen, standards, and chests as £1504. 15. 4¾. The special bequests of plate in the Lady Margaret's will amount to 1632 ounces and a quarter.

The building-account extends from 5 January, 1509—10, to 8 February, 1510—11, and therefore gives particulars of the employment of some of the above funds. It begins with "the superplusage of the last accompt xlli," which shews that it does not relate to the beginning of the work, and then proceeds with

"Paymentes made there [in Christ's College] the vth. daie of the monyth of Januarie in the friste yere of the Regne of Kynge Henrie the viijth by thandes of John Scott clerc abowte the perfitement and fynysshynge of the chapell with in the said College and other to dyuerse artificers and laborers as heraffter folowith."

The sums paid being set down week by week, it is easy to estimate the progress of the work. The walls and the timbers for the roof must have been finished by the beginning of 1510, for in February six thousand tiles are bought; and in the following month the pavement is laid down. From a payment made in June we learn that this was partly of marble; and it must have been extremely elaborate, for it cost in all rather more than £35, equivalent to at least £400 at the present value of money[1]. The glazing of the windows was also proceeding in March:

[29 March.] "To Thomas Peghe glasier for viij^{xx}xv fotes di' of glasse with Imagerie at xij^d the fote...viij^{li} xv^s vj^d. Item to the same for the settynge vp of all the old glasse in the chapell by hymselffe and his seruant by viij dais at vj^d the day...viij^s. Item to the same for lxxvij fotes of white glasse with roses and portcullises at v^d the fote...xxxij^s j^d."

[1] [[3 March] "To John Killyngworth for xxix lodes sande to the pauynge of the chapell vj^dob." [22 June] "Item to William Malson for xv^c fote of marble in steppes and other for the pauyng of the chapell ouer and be side xxv^{li} to hyme paid by a booke in the kepynge of Mr James Morice xij^{li}iij^siiij^d."]

The number of square feet in the first entry would be nearly that required for the east window; and the price paid per foot shews that the glass was to be of superior quality[1]. The "old glasse" was probably brought from the chapel of God's House.

The exterior of the Chapel was apparently completed by 1 June 1510, from a payment made in that week to "laborers clensynge the courte of thoffall leffte by the masons;" and it was consecrated either then or shortly afterwards, from the following:

[1 June.] "Item for iij lodes of sand at the halowyng of the chapell ixd.

[22 June.] Item to William Geffrey for the takynge downe of iij wyndowes and settynge vp agen of the same at the consecracion of the chapell .... xjˢ viijᵈ.

[3 Aug.] Item to [Thomas Peghe, glazier] for the makynge of xxiiij crosses at the halowynge of the chapell.................................. ijˢ."

In addition to these entries, which concern the fabric of the Chapel, there are others having reference to the furniture and decoration. The organ—apparently an old one—is being mended in March; and in the same month the high altar with its curtains, and the presses in the vestry for the vestments, are mentioned[2]. The following entries refer to the imagery:

[1 June.] "Item to John Grandon of Euersdon for iij tonne of the said ston [Eversdon stone] at iiijˢ viijᵈ the tonne for thymages of cristes resurreccion and of oure ladie .... xiiijˢ.

[30 August.] Item to Nicholas aprice for the cariege of thymage of crist with the iiij knyghtes and the sepulcre with themage of oure ladie from the white friers to the college affter they were fully fynysshed and mad by Raffe Bolmone fremason .... xviijᵈ."

The woodwork of the Chapel was not undertaken before the month of July. Under the head of "Paymentes made there by me John Scott clerc the xvijᵗʰ daie of the monyth of Julie to dyuerse persones as ensuyth," we find "Joyners werkynge on a portall in the chapell and stallys." Among them occurs the

---

[1] [The contracts for the windows at King's College specify sixteen pence per foot; a price which, having regard to the great size of the windows, and the difficulty of glazing them, was probably exceptionally high. One of the windows at Christ's College contained an image of S. Christopher: Audit-Book, 1531—32, *Expense infra sacellum.* "Item to yᵉ glazyer for mendyng and makyng vp the cristofer iijˢ."]

[2] [[10 March] "Item for j skynne for the organs iiijᵈ. Item for charcoll at the mendyng of thorgans ijd." [29 March] "iiij lowpys for curtens at the hie aulters ende iiijᵈ. Item a lokke with Gemows for another presse in the Revestrie (for ther be iiij new presses) iiijˢ."]

name of Dirike Harrison, probably the workman who was employed at Queens' College to make the woodwork for the hall
in 1531[1]. Timber for the seat in the ante-chapel, extending
from the door to the turret, or "vise," is paid for in August; but
it is not until September that we find an attempt made to buy
wainscot for the panelling of the quire. No purchase of wood
is recorded, but that some was procured is evident from the
payments to workmen[2]. In the week ending 5 October three
carvers are employed; and in the following the same number.
There was evidently some difficulty in obtaining more, for in the
next week we find :

> "Item to Steven Weder for his costes rydynge with the commyscion
> for caruers by iiij dais at the commaundement of M^r hornbie ...... iiij^s.
>   Item to the same for prestes yoven to iiij of them at ther comyng
> to Cambrege to the werkes .... ij^s."

The "commission" was evidently a royal order to impress
workmen, such as we have found issued for King's College and
Eton College, from a previous entry dated 14 September:

> "Item costes of John Nicholson to Elye for to fech with the kynges
> commyscion brykleiars.. xij$d$."

In the next week, that ending 19 October, five carvers are
employed, and afterwards between six and seven in each week
till the end of the account. One of their principal works was a
tabernacle for the image of Christ, for which a tree, forty-six feet
long, is bought in October; and it is specially mentioned as
proceeding in January 1510—11[3]. It appears that two particular
carvers were wanted for this work, for we find :

---

[1] [History of Queens' College, p. 45. He and another carpenter, Henry Plow-
man, came from London. Under the same date we find "Item to the said Dirike
and Henry Joyners for ther costes and cariege of ther tolys from London to Cambrege
with rewardes for lettyng of certen daies werke or ther toles came iij^s iiij^d."]

[2] [[17 August] "Item to Thomas Goddynge for j lode of tymber for groundcellys
for the seette betwix the chapell dore and the vise v^s. [21 September] Item costes
of Nycholes Joyner to london to bie waynscott to performe the selynge of the quere
of the chapell by v dais, and bowt none by cause of the grett prices then v^s." There
is no evidence to shew when he went to London.]

[3] [[12 October] "Item...for j grett tre of xlvj fotes for the tabernacle of crist
vj^s viij^d." [13 January] "Item paymentes...to caruers on the tabernacle for cristes
Image as ensuyth."]

[25 January.] "Item costes of Hughe Wedre rydynge with the commyscion for certen carvers Henrie Norton and Ric' Fliemynge by the space of ix dais .... vj^s viij^d.
Item costes of the said ij carvers comynge to there werke ...... iij^s."

In each of the last two weeks of the period over which the account extends, we find seven carvers employed. There is no other entry, to shew upon what part they were engaged, or whether the fittings were then fully completed. In the absence of more precise information we can only suppose that the work would proceed without interruption, and be finished early in 1510—11.

The painting of the woodwork and images, and probably of the walls also, was proceeding between September and October. We find that £3. 18. 9 was then paid for

"Paynters to cast in coloures all the Batons in the bodie of the chapell, the ij litill chapelles with the payntynge of the Images of the crucifix Marie and John and gildynge of the same w^t other"

with £2. 16. 3 for the colours used. They began their work in the week of S. Cuthbert (September 4, Translation) and concluded it in that of S. Etheldreda (October 17, Translation)[1]. In the latter month charges for images made of stone (clunch) first occur. Those already mentioned doubtless stood on the rood-loft, as on 22 June a payment occurs "for ij dogges of yerne for thymages of the roode."

The money required for the buildings was supplied by Bishop Fisher through John Scott, who perhaps acted as clerk of the works. The James Morice mentioned above was also sent by the Bishop to Cambridge in June 1510, to give advice respecting some new works then about to be undertaken[2]. The design

---

[1] [The colours used were the following : " Item to Paule Smyth for certen coloures as in whiteled redled generall mastyke vernysch yelowe moty orpment roch vermylyon vergres Bisse oyle coperose white vitriall wex Ceruse Synoper red okyr yelowe oker Inde ffyne gold iiij C di' with other as by the bill thereof made parcelly apperithe lvj^s iiij^d."]

[2] [[21 September] "Item costes of John Scott from Cambrege to Bromleie to receyue money of my lord of Rochestre for the paymentes of this boke by iiij dais viij^s." [22 June] "Item to Mr James Morice for his costes comynge from Roidon to Cambrege by commaundement of my Lord of Rochestre for dyuerse causes concernynge the buyldynges and to dyuyse newe werkes abowt the chapell by v dais...... ....xvj$s$. viij$d$."]

appears to have been given by William Swayne, from the following most interesting entry :

"24 August. Item to William Swayn for the makynge of a thress-hold at the chapell dore in cristes college An holywater stokke the largienge of the vestrie dore And the makynge of A wyndowe in the M' studie And the enbatillenge of the clokke toure and for his reward for the lenghthenge of the chapell by halffe a fote and in height ij fotes ouer and beside his old couenantes and for the makynge of xviij chap-trelles with other necessaries as apperith by his indenture .... x*li*."

By "his old covenant" the original contract for the Chapel is probably meant ; and the sum paid, equivalent to about £120 at the present value of money, is evidently an architect's fee. We have seen that a William Swayne, probably the same person, was employed as "comptroller" of the works at King's College chapel in 1509[1].

The account further refers incidentally to the Library, the Hall, the Kitchen, the Muniment-Room over the gate of entrance called "the tower," and "the great chambers," by which the Master's Lodge is probably meant, as completed buildings, to which additions of minor importance are being made. We may there-fore conclude that these portions of the College had been com-pleted, or nearly so, by the end of 1509, whereas the Chapel, as we have shewn, could not have been ready before 1511, though a licence for performing divine service in it was granted in 1506. Such licences, however, were often granted soon after the founda-tion-stone was laid, or even before ; and here the Chapel might well be undertaken last, as the Society could in the meantime use the parish church of S. Andrew, which was opposite to the College, or possibly the old chapel of God's House.

No additions were made to the College until 1563, when charges for "the newe chambers" occur. They appear to have been only four in number, and no record of their position has been preserved[2].] In 1613 John Atkinson, no doubt the builder whom we have found employed at Caius College and at Queens'

---

[1] [History of King's College, Vol. i. 475.]

[2] [Audit-Book, Mich. 1563—Mich. 1564: "Item for rede to sele yᵉ newe chambers ijˢ. viiiᵈ. Item for iij casementes and iij paier of gemose for them vˢ. iiijᵈ. Item to Richard for claieing of yᵉ newe staiers ijˢ." Ibid. 1564—65 : "Item for yᵉ selinge of fower newe chambers xxxijˢ. Item vnto ij carpenters makinge studies iij daies worke vˢ. viijᵈ."]

College, was paid for a "new building[1]," which is alluded to in a letter written 23 April, 1625, by the celebrated Joseph Mede, in his capacity of tutor of the College, to Sir Martin Stutevile, whose son was about to come into residence:

"For chamber, the best I have in my power, that John Higham sleeps in, hath 4 studies, and neere me; and I had thought to have devised some change that they [John Higham and John Stutevile] might keep together, otherwise I must dispose of your son in the *new building* where I have a study voyd in one of the best chambers[2]."

This new building must be the structure shewn by Loggan (figs. 2, 3) to the east of the kitchen, extending northwards about ninety feet from the south boundary wall. It was evidently a timber building in two stories, with garrets above, consisting wholly of chambers, of which there were four sets on each floor. In fact, it was one of the Pensionaries which were built in so many of the colleges in the seventeenth century to accommodate the increasing number of students. [In a list of the chambers, studies, etc., taken in 1655, it is called "The little Building;" in a similar list taken in 1665 it is "The little Old Building called Rats Hall;" and in a third list, undated, it is "The new Buildinge[3]." It was pulled down in 1730.]

The next addition, however, was a more ornamental and durable structure, of which, strange to say, no building-account or written history has been preserved in the College. It is therefore by indirect allusions, and by lists of subscriptions alone,

---

[1] [Ibid. 1612—13. "Item layd out to Jhon Atkinson for the new building Octob. 10. xx li." Ibid. Annun. 1613—Mich. 1613. "Item to the bricklayer for paving before the new building 3 li—10^s—4^d."]

[2] In the margin he writes "The new building hath but 2 studies in chamber and 2 beds." See the chapter in Vol. iii. on "College Chambers." The letter is printed in Heywood's Cambridge University Transactions during the Puritan Period, ii. 326: from MSS. Harl. 389, fo. 428.

[3] [The arrangement of the chambers in the Old Court is a curious example of the way in which a large number of students was accommodated in a small space, and the volumes of "Study Rents" give unusually full information on this interesting subject. We shall refer to it again in the chapter on "College Chambers." Some of the rooms were distinguished by curious names, as we have found at King's College (Vol. i. p. 331). The garret at the N.W. corner of the court was called "Lancashire Chamber;" the ground-floor room on the same staircase "Slovens' Inn;" and the first-floor room in the next staircase towards the Chapel "Bob-Hall." The "Lancashire Chamber" was so called in 1587—88: "For the buildinge of a studye in the lankeshire chamber and for other thinges xxvj^s. iiij^d."]

SECTION THRO'
JAMB & MULLION

SCALE TO ELEVATION

10   5   0   10 FEET

SCALE TO MOULDINGS

2" 6" 0   1   2   3   4   5   6 FEET

Fig 4. Elevation of one bay on the west side of the Fellows' Building.

that the date can be fixed.   It is a remarkable piece of architecture, as a specimen of its period, consisting of chambers only,
in three floors, with a garret-story in the roof, extending in
length 150 feet.   There are four sets of chambers on each floor.
It presents a façade of masonry on both sides, the design of
which is traditionally attributed to Inigo Jones.   It is scarcely
in his style, but nevertheless is manifestly the work of a great
architect within and without; and is so completely detached from
the older quadrangle as to preclude the slightest effect of incongruity of architectural style.   Evelyn, writing in 1654, characterises this College as "a very noble erection, especially the
modern part, built without the quadrangle towards yᵉ garden, of
exact architecture."   Had Inigo Jones designed it, his name
would scarcely have been omitted here[1].

[This building is divided into two equal portions by the
passage leading into the Fellows' garden (fig. 1).   The doorcases at the east and west ends of this passage are finished by
angular pediments; those at the entrances to the staircases by
circular pediments (fig. 3).   In the western façade the window
on the first floor over the passage has the circular pediment
(fig. 5); the windows over the staircases the angular pediment.
In the eastern façade the same arrangement is repeated, except
that the doorways leading to the staircases are replaced by
windows of the same design as those shewn in the elevation of
the western side (fig. 4).   The other windows are of the same
design on both façades.]

The history of this building must be gathered from the following notes.   The inscription under Loggan's view relates that
"The liberal munificence of many noble and learned persons
constructed in 1642 a splendid Edifice;" and in fact the list,
entitled "A Catalogue of the names of our Benefactors for the
New Building," in the Library, registers sums amounting on
the whole to £2589. 17. 2.   In 1638 Joseph Mede, Fellow,
bequeathed "An hundred pounds to be employed towards
their intended building;" and in the same year letters

---

[1] [Inigo Jones was born 19 July, 1573, died 21 June, 1652.   In 1631—35 he had
built the arcades and porticos of the inner quadrangle, together with the garden-
front, of S. John's College, Oxford, for Archbishop Laud.   Ingram, Memorials of
Oxford, ii. 49.]

were sent out from the College soliciting subscriptions for the buildings[1]. It was therefore in contemplation in this year; and, according to Dr Covel (Master 1688—1723), the foundation was laid in 1640[2]. The stonework at least must have been finished by 1642, when (8 November) "Orders for the new Building" were made by the Master and Fellows[3]. It is therein enacted that "Every Chamber shall be made hand-somlye habitable by the Colledge, or by those who desyre to inhabit it;" and that "there shall not be allowed at once to inhabit the new Building more than foure Fellowes." The memoran-dum which follows, in the handwriting of Michael Honywood, one of the Fellows, illustrates the manner in which the funds for fitting up the chambers were supplied, and shews also that some consider-able delay in getting the building ready had taken place. After setting down a bill of particulars of ex-penses for "wainscotting and fitting up some Cham-bers in the new Building," amounting on the whole to £40. 11s. 10d., he adds:

Fig. 5. Window over one of the staircases on the first floor of the west side of the Fellows' Building.

"This I laid out upon hope that in noe long time the building would be inhabited, and so meant to receive it as they came into yᵉ Chambers, which now, when it will be, God knows. If the Colledg were able I

---

[1] One of these, addressed to Robert Gray, Rector of Mashburye in Essex, dated Feb. 10, 1638, is preserved in MSS. Baker, xix. 209. [It is printed in the Appendix. Receipts for two subscriptions of £10 each, dated 8 May, 1640, are preserved among the MSS. of Sir Charles Isham at Lamport Hall, Northamptonshire. Third Report of Hist. MSS. Com. p. 254.]

[2] [See his memoir on the Master's Lodge in the next chapter.]

[3] [Register of Leases, i. 31. They are printed in the Appendix]

should be glad now to receive it, and yᵉ Colledg to receive it in time, of yᵉ Incumers, but I believe it is not; Patienza. Jan. 16th. 1644. Mich: Honywood[1]."

[In the earliest volume of "Study-Rents," however, we find "An Account taken of the Chambers in the New-Building, The Studdies in them, the Inhabitants, and yⁱʳ Incomes. Feb. 12, Aᵒ. Dom. 1644—45;" which shews that it must eventually have been prepared for occupation much sooner than Mr Honywood expected.]

It only remains to mention that in 1823 a range of chambers, in the plainest so-called Elizabethan style, was erected for the accommodation of students, extending from the Kitchen 95 feet along the lane which bounds the College to the south[2].

CHAPTER III.

HISTORY OF PARTICULAR BUILDINGS:

Chapel.   Master's Lodge.   Hall.   Library.   Alterations in the Great Court.

CHAPEL.—The Chapel is handsome and well-proportioned, being fifty-seven feet long by twenty-seven feet broad. There is an east window of five lights with tracery in the head ; two windows at the east end of the south side, beyond the Master's Lodge ; and five windows on the north side. These lateral windows are now undivided by mullions. The Chapel has been completely Italianised, although it retains in part the medieval ceiling. It is approached through an ante-chapel of the same breadth and nearly square (fig. 1). At the north-west corner is an original turret-staircase (ibid. A) which gives access to a room above the ante-chapel, to be described below. Attached to the north wall of the Chapel are two original projecting build-

---

[1] [It should be mentioned that this sum was repaid to him by a College Order dated 27 August, 1649.]

[2] [Towards the expense of erecting this building the Right Rev. John Kaye, D.D., Master (1814—30), and successively Bishop of Bristol and of Lincoln, gave £200 ; and the Rev. Bernard Gilpin, late Fellow, and Rector of Burnham Westgate in Norfolk, gave £100.]

ings (fig. 1)[1]. One of these was the ancient vestry, and is entered from the ante-chapel; the other, near the east end of the chapel, rises as high as the roof, and serves at present as an organ-chamber, for which purpose it was probably constructed from the first, the lower floor being a priests' vestry and treasury, as at S. John's College.

[We have seen that the original Chapel was finished before the end of 1511. The Foundress made ample provision for the adornment of it by her will, dated 15 February, 1509, in which the images, plate, and altar-furniture, which she bequeathed to it are minutely described[2]. The earlier volumes of Bursar's Accounts contain only occasional references to the organ, to the eagle of brass which serves as a lectern (first mentioned in 1540—41[3], and frequently in subsequent years), to the stained glass, and to other articles of furniture, with entries for small repairs. In the first year of the reign of King Edward the Sixth a workman was paid "for helping downe with Images and mendyng the payvment under christes ymage by the space of two dayes[4]." Three years afterwards the high altar and two tabernacles were taken down, and a carpenter supplied a communion-table of wood,

---

[1] These buildings are now connected together by a wall, and communicate with each other by openings in their east and west walls respectively, as the plan (fig. 1) shews. [In a very interesting MS. diary of a visit to Cambridge made in 1768 by Sir John Cullum, Bart., and lent to me by my friend G. G. M. G. Cullum, B.A., Trin. Coll., the following notice of this building occurs. "On the N. side [of Christ's College Chapel] are two small Chapels, in the windows of which is some painted glass well preserved. In 1st window is a person kneeling, in armour, crowned: his sword (with St George's cross at the end of the scabbard) and helmet lying behind him; beneath him, a rose entirely red. 2. A person kneeling, head uncovered, sword on, his helmet with a dragon upon it, behind him; beneath him a rose, with the outward leaves red, the inward white, seeded yellow. 3. A person kneeling, crowned, and in robes of state. 4. A person standing, crowned, scepter in his right hand, and globe in left. 5. A person standing, crowned, with a circular glory round his head: a ring on his right hand, and staff in his left. The well-known story of the ring makes it probable that this figure was designed for St Edward. 6 and 7. Have each of them a Lady kneeling and praying, crowned: beneath each of them such a rose as in the 2d." See also Blomefield's Collect. Cantab. p. 216.]

[2] [Cooper's Life of the Lady Margaret, p. 130.]

[3] [Audit-Book, 1532—33. *Expense infra sacellum*. "Item payd to...the orgayne maker for y e residew of hys bargen of y e newe orgayns viij[li]." Ibid. 1540—41. *Expense forinsece*. "Item to Cyryle Jhonson for dyghtyng the egle and candyllstykkes x[d]."]

[4] [Ibid. 1547—48. *Expense infra sacellum*.]

with additional panel-work to fill up the space left vacant by
the removal of the altar, which shews that even at that time
the east end was panelled[1]. In the first year of the reign of
Queen Mary the altars were set up again, under the direction
of Mr Shaw, one of the Fellows[2]; but they were evidently
again removed at the beginning of the reign of Queen Elizabeth, when the setting up of "the communion-table" is paid for[3].
In 1569—70 the altar-furniture, probably that given by the
Foundress, was sold, for we find among the "extraordinary
receipts" for that year, "Item received for copes, vestmentes,
tunicles, and aulter-clothes xv^{li} [4]." Between Michaelmas 1636
and Lady Day 1637 considerable repairs were executed in the
Chapel. Work done to the vestry by John Atkinson the builder
is specially mentioned; and from payments "for wood for the
organ," to the organist, and to Woodroff, doubtless the carver
who was employed at King's College, we may gather that a
new organ was being then set up[5]. The diary of William
Dowsing contains the following entry:

"Christ's Colledg. Jan. 2, 1643.
We pulld downe divers Pictures & Angells, & the Steps D. Bam-
bridge have promised to take them downe. " *Orate pro animabus* " on
the brasen Eagle."

The organ evidently escaped destruction, from a payment
in 1650 "for mending the organ-pipes and putting them in
tune." In September, 1658, it was "patched up" by Thamar,

[1] [Ibid. 1550—51. *Expense infra sacellum.* "Item to ye Joyner for ye lordes
table vj^s. Item to ye Joyner for syling to fill up ye vacant place where ye high altare
stode." *Expense forinsece.* "Item yeuen to ye carpenter and his .ij. seruants for
taking downe the .ij. tabernacles and the hye aulter ij^s. Item to a cart y^t. carried
away stone from vnder ye tabernacles vj^d. Item for pavynge in ye chapple where
ye tabernacles and alter stoode iij^s."]

[2] [Ibid. 1553—1554. *Expense forinsece.* "Item for making vp two altars of
wodd and dressing vp other thinges in ye chappell iiij^s. Item to William Barns for
iiij daies in building vp altars of stone for him and his man iiij^s. iiij^d. Item yeuen to
Mr Shawe for his paines taken in ye chappell xx^s."]

[3] [Ibid. Mich. 5 and 6 Philip and Mary to Mich. 1 Elizabeth. Mich. 1558—Mich.
1559. *Expense forinsece.* "Item to him that set vpp the communion table vj d."]

[4] [Ibid. 1569—70. *Recepta forinseca.* Similar articles were sold at the Manor
of Malton (for which see Cooper, ut supra, p. 121): "Item received for Malton bell,
ij greate candlesticks, A crosse and the rest iiij^{li}. xix^s. ix^d."]

[5] [Ibid. Mich. 1636—Annunc. 1637. *Expense forinsece.* The payments to
Woodroff were made through Mr Forster, one of the Fellows.]

the celebrated organ-maker of Peterborough, and placed in the Parlour; but in June, 1661, it was restored to the Chapel, and Thamar was again employed, together with Austin the joiner, to repair it[1]. It remained in use until 1705, when it was replaced by a new one, by Charles Quarles, the cost of which, £140, was chiefly defrayed by subscription. It was repaired by Messrs Hill in 1865, after having been disused apparently since 1785[2].

The four pillars that support the roof of the Ante-Chapel were first placed there in 1661. The following entries shew that they were of wood, resting on stone bases:

"To Batty for 4 Pillars in ye Outer Chappell ... 5. 14. 2
To ye Free Mason for Bases for ye Pillars of y^e
Chappell and mending ye Floore 0. 16. 0
To ye Painter for ye Pillars in ye Chapp. ... ... 1. 2. 4 "

The space between the organ-chamber and the altar is occupied by a monument (K, fig. 1) by Joseph Catterns of London, to the memory of Sir John Finch and Sir Thomas Baines. It consists of two pedestals of white marble rising from a common plinth, and united by a common cornice. Above each pedestal there is a medallion bust of one of the persons commemorated. Prominence is given to the pedestals and medallions by making the plinth and background of black marble. A long and interesting inscription, written by their tutor, Dr Henry More, records the virtues, the acquirements, and the history, of these devoted friends[3]. Sir Thomas Baines died at Constantinople, 5 September, 1681. His body was brought

[1] [Ibid. Annunc.—Mich. 1650. *Expense forinsece.* Ibid. Annunc.—Mich. 1658. "Sept. 18. To Mr Thamar the Organist towards setting vp of the Organ in ye Parlour .5. 0. 0." Mich. 1658—Annunc. 1659. "Dec. 28. To ye Organist Themar (*sic*) more for setting vpp Organ 16. 17. 00." Annunc.—Mich. 1661. *Exp. infra sacellum.* "To Austin ye Joyner for Work about ye Organ .10. 14. 0. To Thamar for setting vp ye organ Jùne 6th 17. 18. 6." A small organ, as we learn from Dr Covel's memoir, was at this time brought from the Master's Lodge into the Combination Room, where it remained for many years. The following entry refers to it: Annunc. —Mich. 1668. "For mending and tuning ye Chapple and Parlor Organ 2. 10. 0."]

[2] [Ibid. Annunc.—Mich. 1705. "Apr. 14. To the musitians at the opening of the Organ a Guinea 01. 01. 06." The subscriptions received, amounting to £92. 15. 0, are set down at the end of the account for 1705; and 19 Aug. 1707 we find "Paid for the new Organ to Mr Charles Quarles (at severall times as by his Receipts appears) in All £140. 0. 0." The Organist and Organ-blower were paid regularly down to 1785, when the payments cease.]

[3] [It is printed in the Appendix.]

home, as the epitaph records, by Sir John Finch, who came to Cambridge in the spring of 1682, when he was entertained with much ceremony, the room in the Master's Lodge called the "Foundresse Chamber" being newly furnished for his reception, and a dinner in his honour being given in the Hall[1]. He died 18 November following, and leave to set up the monument was granted in the following month :

"4 December 1682.   Then Agreed that as much Rome (*sic*) as my Lord ffinch thinks convenient for a monument shall be allowed in the chappel where he pleases."

It was not however finished before Michaelmas 1684.   The cost was defrayed by the Earl of Nottingham[2].

We now come to the extensive alterations carried out in 1701 and 1702, by which the interior was brought to its present appearance.   The first work undertaken was the laying down of a marble pavement at the beginning of 1701, for which Robert Grumbold was employed[3].   In order to obtain the funds

---

[1] [Ibid. Mich. 1681—Annunc. 1682. "Febr. 13. To Mr Austin Joyner for Wainscot in ye Foundresse Chamber and for a Bedstead 14. 03. 10.   For the New Furniture of the Foundresses Chamber (Bedding and Curtains excepted which are my own) to make it fit for ye Reception of Sr John Finch all ye Particulars whereof are entered in ye Registry Book 24. 9. 0."   Annunc. 1682—Mich. 1682.   "For the wine Spent in ye Coll. at ye Dinners in ye Hall when Sr John Finch was here 2. 11. 6."]

[2] [Ibid. Annunc.—Mich. 1684.   "Pd for Work occasioned by ye Monument, besides 1. 14. 4 wch ye Earl of Nottingham payd 1. 7. 3."   This entry must refer to Daniel Finch, second Earl of Nottingham (the "Comitis filius primogenitus" of the epitaph, and the "Lord Finch" of the College Order of 4 Dec. 1682), who succeeded his father as second Earl directly after this date, 18 Dec. 1682.   The first Earl (Sir Heneage Finch, created Baron Finch 1674 and Earl of Nottingham 1681) and Sir John Finch were both sons of Sir Heneage Finch, the Speaker of the House of Commons.   The Admission Book of Christ's College contains the following entries respecting Baines and Finch : "Anº. Dom. 1639.   Thomas Baynes, Filius Richardi natus in pago Whaddon in Comitatu Cantabrigiensi Literis institutus Starfordiæ a Magistro Ley, admissus est Pens. minor annum agens ætatis 15. sub Magistro Gell Octob: Non: 3º.   Solvit pro ingressu 10s."   "Mich. 1644—L. Day 1645.   Iohannes Finch, filius Heneagi, Londini natus, literis vero institutus Ætonæ primum a Mro. Norris, dein vero Oxonii ab Edvardo Sylvestre anno ætatis 18º admissus est Pensionarius minor sub Mro. Potts.   Solvit pro ingressu 10s."   Baines proceeded A.B. 1642, A.M. 1646; but Finch appears not to have taken any degree.   The Book of Study-Rents shews that in February 1644—45 they were joint occupants of the "second upper chamber" in the southernmost staircase of the New Building.]

[3] [College Order, 3 March 1700—1701.   "Then agreed that Mr Robert Grumbold, Freestone Mason, should have fivety pounds advance-money of the College towards ye paving ye Chapple with Marble."]

necessary for further works, a subscription was set on foot at the beginning of 1702, by which £888. 4s. 11d. was raised. Among the items we find: "Sir R. Temple 10 Guineas;" "Mr Isaack Newton, maister of the Mint, 19 Guineas." Dr Covel, Master, gave £100, "besides his charges to London for 10 weeks," which he visited twice on business connected with the Chapel. The first of these visits he describes as "My journey to London March 3ᵈ and stay there till Apr. 25 about taking the benevolence of Gentlemen formerly of our Coll. towards rebeautifying our Chappell[1]." Subscriptions were therefore obtained by his personal solicitation. He stayed again in London for five weeks in August and September 1703[2]. The sum obtained by subscription was evidently insufficient, for in October 1701 it was decided to sell certain pieces of plate, which realized £203[3]. Other subscriptions, amounting to £118. 15s., were paid afterwards, and a legacy of £100 from the Rev. Mr Crosse was applied to this purpose, so that the total at the disposal of the College became ultimately £1309. 19s. 11d. A separate account was kept of the disbursements, headed "Laid out about the Prayer room[4] and the Chappell," from which we learn that the "beautification" cost £1340. 16s. 4½d. The following extracts give useful information respecting the work:

"Apr. 11.   To Mʳ Capon for a piece of Hanging in
                  the Prayer room 00. 06. 00
Aug. 19ᵗʰ. To the Carpenter his bill for work in the
                  prayer room &c. from March 3ᵈ to Aug. 13   22. 14. 09
Aug. 17   To the carpenter for work about the new
1702   staires behind the chappel, and boarding
                  the gutturs, etc. 13. 11. 03
Feb. 5ᵗʰ 170⅔   Paid Mʳ Joh. Mitchel for coming
                  from London and surveying and
                  valuing the wainscoting, and paint-
                  ing, carving, and paving the Chap-
                  pel 05. 07. 06

¹ [Audit-Book, Annunc.—Mich. 1702.]

² [Ibid. Mich. 1703—Annunc. 1704. *Expense forinsece.* "Sept. 25. My charges at London 5 weeks about yᵉ chappel 00. 00. 00."]

³ [College Order, 25 October 1701. "Agreed...that Two hundred pounds worth of Plate be taken out of the Treasury to be melted down towards the Repair of the Chappel...and that the Master and three of the Fellowes take out yᵉ sᵈ Plate." Among the receipts we find: "The Plate from the Treasury melted down and assay'd at the Tower and Goldsmith's hall 203. 0. 0."]

⁴ [This is a room on the first floor of the Master's Lodge, to be described below.]

Mart 5th 170⅔	Paid Loader for mats and pesses in the Chappel	02. 01. 06
May 4th 1703.	Paid Phillip Prigg in full for Glazing the Inner and outward Chappel ...	51. 03. 00
June 3d.	Paid Joh. Austin in full his two bills for wainscotting the inner and outward chappel, and vestry	639. 13. 05
	To Mr Wardall the Smith his bills, for ye balcony, bars in the windoes and other Iron work	58. 05. 05
March 16. 170⅔	To Mr Herring for Crimson Morella mohair for the Curtains and two cushions	06. 09. 0
June 18. 1703.	To Mr Wiseman his bill for painting and gilding &c.	51. 14. 0
Oct. 23. 1703.	Paid the Carver in full for his work in Chapel and ante chapel ...	145. 00. 00
Oct. 25. 1703.	Paid the freestone Mason his bills in full	196. 00. 00"

The interior has been but little altered. The panel-work, which reaches as high as the cills of the windows, is in much the same style as that which Austin placed in King's College Chapel in 1678—79[1]. At the east end there are two engaged Corinthian columns on each side of the altar. The cornice which surmounts the panel-work is raised over the monument described above, so as to form a canopy, supported on carved brackets. There is also an organ-gallery of wood, projecting into the Chapel, with a projecting semicircular seat for the player in the centre. There are two rows of stalls, with a bench in front. They are quite plain, and not sub-divided into separate seats.

The glass in the east window was given in 1847 by Miss Caroline Burney, in memory of her brother, Richard Burney, M.A., formerly Fellow Commoner. It was executed by Messrs Clutterbuck of London, in imitation of old Flemish glass. Before this time the original four-centered window had been made to consist of a central light with a semicircular head, with a lower square-headed light on each side, by filling in the arch with brickwork; and a semicircular pediment of wood, as wide as the two panels behind the altar, obscured the lower third of it[2].]

[1] [History of King's College, Vol. i. p. 525. We learn from Adam Wall that the carver was Francis Woodward. MSS. Univ. Lib Camb. Mm. 5. 47, f. 92.]

[2] [A view of it in this state is given by Ackermann, ii. 50. The stained glass, representing the Foundress, her son Henry VII., and others of her family, had evidently been brought from elsewhere.]

The tower at the north-west corner of the Chapel (A, fig. 1) was still terminated by a battlement in the original style when Loggan's print was taken (fig. 3), as may be seen by comparing it with the turrets of the Gate of Entrance. The present termination, of wood, in the style of the Renaissance, is due to the munificence of Dr John Covel (Master 1688—1723), of whom the Commemoration-Book records that he "built the Tower of the Chapel and furnished it with a Clock and Bell." [It seems to have been finished in 1720, when it was painted[1].]

MASTER'S LODGE.—The Master's Lodge occupies the whole space, sixty-two feet in length, between the Chapel and the Hall. [The rooms over the ante-chapel also form part of it. Besides this building, Loggan (fig. 3) shews another, beyond the limit of the quadrangle to the north, which is equally designated by him *Magistri Hospitium*. The extent of this latter building will be better understood from his ground-plan of the College (fig. 2). It was taken down in 1748[2]. Before commencing a description and history of the existing Lodge, we will quote, by way of preface, a memoir drawn up in 1719 by Dr John Covel[3], called "An Account of the Master's Lodgings in ye College and of his private Lodge by it self." It contains many interesting particulars respecting the Lodge, the Combination Room, and the College generally.

"The Foundresse's Statutes plainly give all ye Lower Rooms to ye Master, during her own Life, and the Life of Bishop Fisher[4]. But they mention nothing of ye Disposal of ye upper rooms after Her own and ye Bishops Decease. Therefore it seems most probable that they fell to ye Master then, as well as ye lower ones, which were assign'd to him by Her before.

And this Addition to what was his own by Statute before, can no

---

[1] [Ibid. 11 October 1720. "To the Painter. The Fane, the Belfry, the Cornish of the Lanthorne, per bill. 02. 13. 00." This tower had been taken down by Grumbold in 1671, but it was evidently rebuilt in the same style. Ibid. Annunc.—Mich. 1671. "May 20. For Work vpon ye Tower by ye Chappell. June 3. For Ladders...and taking down ye Tower 4. 02. 00. To Grumball ye Free Mason for Work about ye Turret 1. 15. 00."]

[2] [College Order, 15 March, 1747—48. "Agreed...that ye Old Lodge be taken down and that ye Materials be applied to ye building of convenient Offices for ye Master and other Purposes of ye College."]

[3] [Copied MSS. Univ. Lib. Camb. Mm. 6. 50, f. 322. The original is in the Correspondence of Dr Covel, ii. 311. MSS. Add. Mus. Brit. 22, 911. It is written by a clerk, the signature only being in Covel's own hand.]

[4] [This extract from the statutes was quoted in Chapter II.]

ways seem Extravagant compar'd with yᵉ Master's Lodgings in King's, Trinity, Sᵗ John's; Christ College being ever reckon'd as the Fourth Royal Foundation in all Elections or other particular Concerns mention'd in yᵉ publick Statutes of yᵉ University.

It does no where appear but yᵗ yᵉ first Master of yᵉ College after yᵉ Death of yᵉ Foundresse and yᵉ Bishop, enjoy'd them to himself entire, as also did all his Successors; The Masters of Peterhouse, Magdalen, Queens, Pembroke, Catherine Hall, Jesus, Cajus, Benedict, Clare Hall, and Trinity Hall, have all very ample Lodgings to themselves.

A very considerable part of yᵉ Schollars of Christ College lodged in yᵉ Brazen George[1]; and yᵉ Gates there were shut and open'd Morning and Evening constantly as yᵉ College gates were. In the year 1640 yᵉ Foundations of yᵉ new Building were laid; and yᵉ College at that time added a room or two to yᵉ Master's private Lodge, which before was only a washhouse or Laundery with a Close or two for Drying-yards. All was encompassed at first with only Hedges or Mud-wall, but afterwards they were made of Brick as they now stand; That part only at the very Corner next Walls Lane, lying between my Kitching Garden, and Captain Pepys his Stable was left even till my time, as a Stud-Clay-Wall which supported yᵉ South end of that Stable. But in June 1693 the lower part of that Stud-wall was by consent of yᵉ College and Captain Pepys pulled down, and built up again so high as it now stands at the Equall Charges of yᵉ College and yᵉ Captain, so that now all is encompassed quite round with Brick.

Dʳ Bainbrig [Master 1620—45] removed all his Women and part of his Men Servants down into this private Lodge; and to encrease yᵉ number of Schollars in yᵉ College still beyond yᵉ Chambers in yᵉ new building, he let all his Chambers in yᵉ College Lodgings, which he could spare, to Noblemen, Fellow-Commoners, and Gentlemen Pensioners that came to be admitted; always reserving and receiving their Rents to himself; as it appears by an old College Book of yᵉ Study Rents from his time downwards for many years; and all yᵉ succeeding Masters enjoy'd yᵉ same Priviledges to yᵉ Death of Dʳ Cudworth [Master 1654—88].

The old Court till after yᵉ Return of K. Charles yᵉ Second was rail'd in and there was no common Combination Room below Staires, for yᵉ Fellows every day to meet in; But at dinner and supper in Summer they met upon yᵉ Regent Walk, and there they waited till they knew what Seniors would come down, and then they went into yᵉ Hall. In Winter they always met in yᵉ Hall and stood about yᵉ Fire 'till they knew what Seniors would come down, and then they sate down at their Table.

After Dinners and Suppers they had no common Combination Room, but went into yᵉ Orchard in Summer, or at other times to one anothers Chambers, or elsewhere, as they thought fitting. Many of yᵉ

---

[1] [This Inn stood in Preacher Street, on the south side of the churchyard of S. Andrew the Great. It was given to Christ's College by Dʳ Thomas Thompson, Master 1510—17, when Vicar of Enfield, Middlesex, 7 May, 1539. In the reign of Henry VI. (2 February 1445—46) it became the property of Geffrey Neville, who had sold his house to the King for the site of King's College, on condition of another, equally good, being found for him. Vol. i. p. 339.]

Fellows when I was a Freshman[1] were Musical, and old Robt. Wilson taught them, and often bore them Company in some of their Chambers where they diverted themselves with Singing.

Dr Moor, Dr Outram, and others of ye Senior Fellows desired Dr Cudworth to spare them ye Parlor in ye College Lodgings for a Combination Room a little before I was made Fellow; And ye Master having never but once opportunity before, let ye parlor, and there being no convenience of a Study or Bedchamber to it, ye little low-Chamber next to it was at that first Time let with it. But the Income and Rent being so high none afterwards would take them at that Charge.

Some years before I was Fellow ye College Organ was taken down in ye Chappel, as ye like was done in all other Colleges; but after ye Parlor was made a Combination Room, ye old Organ pipes were patcht up and by Consent of ye Master and Fellows ye whole was set up in that Corner next ye Old Court where now the Great Map of the World hangs; and ye Wall was broken down into part of the next Chamber for ye Organ-blower, and ye Anthem books and Services to be dispos'd of in it. After K. Charles ye Second's return the old Organ was again set up in ye Chappel, and ye little Organ, which before stood in ye Masters private Parlor, was brought into ye Combination room and set where it now stands. It was always thought to belong to ye College, and ye Master never (as far as I could learn) laid any claim to it, neither doe I know how we came by it; It was always kept in Tune at ye College charge; but ye Fellow-Commoners and Young Men would break open the Locks, and abused it, so it is now worth but little.

When ye Master did eat in ye Hall, he came always down Mr Maynards staires; and then if he took any of ye Fellowes home with him they all return'd ye same way. There remains yet a door way (now walled up) by which ye Master and his Family went down into his private Garden whilst he kept in these Lodgings; but when he remov'd to his private Lodge the Stone Staires were made down from ye Sizar's Chamber under ye South side of the Chappel.

In ye Room where Mr Maynard keeps there was acted (whilst it stood empty) a Pastoral by Dr Cudworth's Children and some others, contriv'd by Mr John Andrews afterwards Fellow; To which I my self was courteously admitted as a Spectator; afterwards ye two Mr Finch's and after them Mr Lovet kept there; and though they all were Fellows yet they constantly paid ye Master their Rent without ye least dispute. When Mr Lovet died I paid his Executor his Income, and therefore Mr Maynard's Rent is higher because all ye Hangings and Furniture are all my own.

My Lord and Lady Conway and their whole attendance were entertain'd by Dr Cudworth many dayes, and were lodged partly at his private, and partly in ye publick Lodgings; and they all supped (at a Commencement night) in ye Publick Hall; and several other Persons of Quality have been many times so lodged and entertain'd likewise by him. I could add much more to ye same purpose of my own occasions for

---

[1] [Dr John Covel was admitted to Christ's College 31 March, 1654, B.A. 1657—58, M.A. 1661.]

Lodging many of my Acquaintances, Merchants, Travailers, and my numerous Relations and Friends. But I shall let that passe, for perhaps to some it may be made an Instance of my Prodigality rather than of my Necessity.

Whilst yᵉ Master lived in yᵉ Publick Lodgings, the Vicechancellor and Heads of Colleges, and all others who came to visit him, after Notice, came up yᵉ Regent Walk and were entertain'd in yᵉ Great Parlor, which is now yᵉ Combination Room; and there is not a Master of a College in Cambridge (as is abovesaid) but he hath appropriated to himself many Chambers for his own use or at his disposal; and where one hath fewer than I have, several have many more, and much more splendid.

This is a Faithfull and True Relation of this whole affair, witnesse my hand

JOHN COVEL."]

The portion of the Lodge between the Hall and the Chapel is in two floors, 27 feet wide, with a garret-floor above. The ground and first floors are each divided by original partitions into three chambers, unequal in size. The partitions on the first floor stand exactly over those on the ground floor, so that the chambers on both these floors are of the same size, as the plans shew (figs. 6, 7). The room on the ground floor next to the Hall, nearly square, is the Parlour, which ultimately became the College Parlour [as Dr Covel records]. It was entered from the Court by a separate doorway (fig. 3), now replaced by a window (A, fig. 6). This doorway was exactly opposite to the Great Gate, and the walk leading to it from the gate is "the Regent Walk" mentioned above[1]. The room has now become the Master's dining-room. A narrow passage divided off from it on the south side leads to the turret. This passage, however, is modern; for beams of the ancient ceiling run completely through it, as the dotted lines on the plan (fig. 6) shew; and, although disguised by modern carving to represent Italian forms within the room, they retain their medieval moldings in the passage. The two other rooms on this floor were evidently the original chambers of the Master, assigned to him by the Foundress. The larger, that next to the Parlour, was entered from the court by a door in the same position as at present; and the smaller, that next to the Chapel, was probably divided into a bedchamber and a study. This modest Lodge was in convenient contiguity

---

[1] [It was paved in 1657: "To yᵉ Freemason for 188 foote of freestone for yᵉ Regent Walk 6ˡⁱ. 5ˢ. 4ᵈ."]

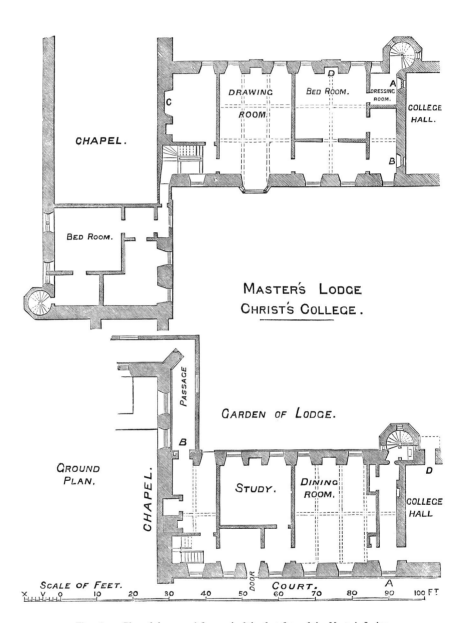

Figs. 6, 7. Plan of the ground-floor and of the first floor of the Master's Lodge.

with the Chapel on one side, and the Hall on the other. The chamber next to the Chapel now contains the staircase leading to the first floor; and it has a small room behind, in connexion with a modern external passage which is carried round the east end of the Chapel in communication with the carriage entrance (L, fig. 1), the Kitchen, and the servants' offices. The doorway through which this passage is entered (B, fig. 6) is of stone, and appears to be ancient[1]. The room between this and the parlour is now divided into entrance-hall and study. In one of the lists of chambers, etc., taken at the beginning of the 17th century, these two rooms are described as "The chamber vnder the Lodgings next yᵉ Chapple," and "The chamber vnder yᵉ Lodgeings next to yᵉ Parler."

The three chambers on the first floor were those of the Foundress. The largest had two small windows (A, B, fig. 7), now blocked, looking into the Hall. A turret-staircase on the garden side, and entered from the garden, gave access to this floor as well as to the garret above, which still retains its ancient roof with embowed braces, and appears to have extended in the manner of an open gallery over at least two of the three chambers below. This turret is placed opposite to the end of the wall which separates the Hall from the Parlour. The Foundress and the episcopal Visitor had therefore private entrance to their chambers without coming through the quadrangle, and could descend to the Hall, dryshod, upon occasion of festivities. [When the Hall was altered in 1876, a door, blocked, was found in the east wall, close to the foot of the staircase (D, fig. 6). The doorcase, which by the style and ornamentation clearly belonged to the period of the Foundress, was removed, and fitted to the opening in the north wall of the Hall (ibid. E), which had doubtless been made when the Great Parlour became the Combination Room. It is probable that there was originally a small vestibule adjoining the staircase (as shewn by dotted lines on the plan) out of which the door opened.] It is quite consistent with ancient customs to suppose that a window or hagioscope (C, fig. 7) enabled the service of

---

[1] [A "gallery" eastward of the Chapel formed part of the Lodge in 1608—9: "Item for Tymber to repayre yᵉ old gallerye at the Chappell end in the Mʳˢ garden 3*li*. 5*s*. 5*d*." A new gallery in the same place was set up in the same year.]

the Chapel to be witnessed from the small chamber which was next to its south wall. [This room was subsequently called "The Prayer-Room." It is panelled, and has a ceiling of wood and plaster-work, which is continued over the modern staircase; so that it evidently once extended through the whole breadth of the Lodge. The panel-work was ornamented with gilt stars, whence the room was called "The Star Chamber" in the last century[1].] Loggan's view (fig. 3) shews a hanging gallery leading from this chamber along the wall of the ante-chapel, and thus conducting to the room or rooms above the latter, which has always been divided into two floors, as at present, as the molded beams supporting the present floor sufficiently shew. The gallery has disappeared, but in its place a passage has been wrought in the thickness of the wall which answers the same purpose (fig. 7). A staircase in the tower at the north-west corner of the Chapel, described above, descends into the ante-chapel from one of the rooms on the first floor. Traces of two windows looking into the Chapel have been found in the east wall of the bed-room on this floor (fig. 7). The central chamber, which still has the oriel window over the entrance-door, as shewn by Loggan, serves as a drawing-room; and the great chamber over the parlour is cut up into sitting-room, bedroom, and dressing-room. It still however retains its ancient ceiling of molded beams over-riding the intrusive partitions. The woodwork, surmounted by a pediment, above the fireplace (D, fig. 7), is probably that put up by Austin in 1681—82, as related above (p. 209). The garret floor is now divided into a number of small rooms for domestic use[2].

[In 1719 the rooms in the Lodge, or, as the list calls them, "In the Master's," which were at that time let out as chambers,

[1] [Remains of these decorations were found in 1881, soon after the election of the present Master, Dr. Swainson. The name derived from them occurs in one of the volumes of "Study-Rents."]

[2] [The Master had an Oratory in the Lodge, from a payment in 1531—32 "for the alter in the M^rs closset." In 1606—7 the "masters dyneinge chamber" and the "master's outward chamber" are mentioned; and in 1658 "ye Outer roome of ye lodgings next the Hall." There was also a porch, of which the leads were repaired in 1654. It is again referred to in 1680 as "the Great Porch in ye house." Loggan (fig. 3) shews a line of battlements rising above the roof of the Lodge on the east side, which may belong to this porch. In that case it would have been in two stories, like that at King's College Lodge.]

are thus enumerated : " Over yᵉ Parler the Hon. Mʳ. Maynard ;
Over him, Beart ; By yᵉ Parler, Wheller ; In yᵉ Starr Chamber,
Mʳ. Stephens ; In yᵉ Sizer Chamber, Pennington ; Over yᵉ Ante
Chapel, North." This list, it will be observed, omits the large
room on the first floor now used as the Drawing-Room. It is
probable that this is the "Meeting-Room" which is mentioned
in the seventeenth century as part of the Lodge. In 1656 we
find "for painting yᵉ meeting roome in yᵉ lodging 01.04.00 ;"
in 1677 "for two carpets for yᵉ meeting-roome and sixe cushions
1.12.0 ;" and in 1685 "for mending and cleaning a piece of
hangings in yᵉ Meeting Room 1.0.0." It may have been fitted
up to hold college meetings in when the Parlour became a Combination Room[1].

The offices of the Lodge are modern. The passage leading
to them round the east end of the Chapel was made by Dr John
Barker (Master 1780—1808). The ancient panelling with which
it is now lined was brought from chambers in the College by Dr
John Graham (Master 1830—49).]

HALL.—[The Hall is fifty-three feet long, including the
screens, by twenty-six feet broad. When Loggan's print was
taken (fig. 3), there was an oriel, and two square-headed windows,
each of three lights, on the west side, with a small window of
two lights in the gallery above the screens. The lights were
all cusped. The battlement which surmounted the walls round
the court was continued along the Hall at the same level. There
was a louvre in the usual position, and a second turret over the
screens, in which there was probably a bell. As the audit-books
previous to 1688 contain entries for unimportant repairs only,
we may conclude that Loggan's print shews the Hall in its
original state, with the exception of the louvre, which from its
style is of later date, and seems to have been first made in 1544
—45, when we find a payment "to a carpenter for makynge yᵉ
lover in yᵉ hall vijˢ. iiijᵈ.[2]." In the course of the alterations

---

[1] [In an Inventory made 1688, among the goods "In the Maisters Lodgings and
House," we find "A long Turkey Carpet in the Meeting roome. A long table there."
It was therefore a large long room, which exactly suits the Drawing Room.]

[2] [Provision for a fire in the Hall had been made by Dr Tompson, as the name
is spelt in the Audit-Book, 1561—62, "Item for the fiers in the Hall geven by
Dʳ Tompson, xxˢ." This was probably Dr Thompson, Master 1510—17. Further

begun in 1876 a fireplace was found in the north wall (I, fig. 1) under what was then the central window. There was a lofty chimney-stack with two flues on either side of this window.

In 1723 the "repairing and beautifying the Hall," to quote the heading of a separate account kept by the Master, Dr William Towers (Master 1723—44), was undertaken. The work had been determined upon in 1721, by the following Order:

"9 December, 1721. Then agreed that John Austin shall be ordered to prepare Materials for new wainscotting the Hall, and Wm Fichet stone for paving of it."]

The interior was completely Italianized. A plaster-ceiling, in the shape of the segment of a cylinder, was attached to the timbers of the original roof, and the gallery over the screens was closed in by a lath and plaster partition which rose to the ceiling. The total spent was £316. 00. 09[1], of which sum £150 was contributed by the Rev. Sir George Wheler, Knight, Prebendary of Durham; and £100 by the Hon. and Rev. Henry Finch, Dean of York 1702—28. The exterior was probably not altered until 1770, as will be related below.

[No further alteration was made to the Hall until 1875, when George Gilbert Scott, Architect, was invited to examine it. The following passages may be quoted from his Report:

"I find the Hall to be substantially the same building which was erected at the foundation of the College. Notwithstanding the modern appearance of the exterior of the West Front and of the entire interior, the original fabric remains in a very complete state, though overlaid by the work of the last century. The East wall remains almost entirely in its original condition, though in indifferent repair and faced on the exterior with stucco. It is very possible that it was plastered in the first instance, as was the case with many old buildings. The gable walls North and South remain as originally built. The West wall has

provision was made for them 1 May, 1598, when the College agreed with Mr Richard Bunting to expend £5 yearly out of his estate at Burnham Westgate, in Norfolk, "to the end that in the time of Winter and cold seasons the common Fire and Fires in the Common Hall or parlour of the said College should be the better maintained and the charges thereof supported for the common use and benefit of the Master Fellows and Scholars of the said College for the time being from time to time for ever after the death of the said Richard Bunting."]

[1] [The first payment was made 31 July, 1723, and the last 19 January, 1724. The principal sums set down are: "James Essex, Joyner, £30; J. Woodward, Carver, £48 (in all); Austin and Essex (in all) £61;" and 27 October, 1724, "To Mr Porter who survey'd the work in the Hall £02 . 02 . 00."]

been re-faced externally, and the Oriel and windows renewed in what is but a poor caricature of the original design; but the wall itself is ancient. The original roof remains complete from end to end, concealed by a ceiling of lath and plaster, though the Louvre which once surmounted it, and which appears in Loggan's view, has been removed.

The roof over the Combination Room is of the same pitch as that of the Hall, and is also of the date of the Foundation. It is of much simpler character than the Hall roof, and was designed to be open to the room which is now the Combination Room, the attics above having been formed within it at a later date.

The screen of the Hall is a mere casing of deal, within which remains the original screen. This is of oak and of elegant design, though simple. From its character it seems to me somewhat earlier in date than the screen which was discovered in the same manner at S. John's. In the same way the original oak panelling of the side walls remains, though in a bad state, behind the 18th century deal framing.

In spite therefore of the modern character which the Hall now presents, the medieval design remains almost complete, and it would be easy to restore the whole with accuracy to the state in which it was left by the Foundress."

The first work undertaken was the removal of the original roof, which was replaced by a temporary one, so that the Hall could still be used. At the beginning of 1876 a temporary Hall was erected in the garden south of the College, and the old Hall was entirely taken down, and rebuilt, the old materials being used again. The walls were raised six feet, and a new oriel was built on the east side, in order to give additional space. The original roof, having been thoroughly repaired, was replaced; and the interior was panelled, by Messrs Rattee and Kett, with linen panelling exactly copied from the remains of the original panelling that had been discovered behind the modern woodwork. The original screen was cleaned and restored, and the gallery was again thrown open. At the same time a new approach was made to it and to the Combination Room (B, fig. 1). These works were completed in the course of 1879.

The Buttery is in the original position, to the south of the Hall. The Kitchen was always a detached building, as Loggan shews. It has been nearly doubled in size by the addition of offices on the west side (fig. 1).

COMBINATION ROOM.—We have seen that the large room on the ground-floor, which is now the Dining Room of the

Master's Lodge, was granted to the Fellows as a Combination Room or Parlour during the Mastership of Dr Cudworth (1654—1688).

Accordingly "The College Parlour" is first mentioned in the accounts for 1657[1]; an entry which probably marks the year in which the destination of the room was altered. We learn from Dr Covel's memoir, quoted above, that the small room next to it on the west side was given up at the same time by the Master. In 1747 the room over the Buttery became the Combination Room, and the former Parlour was given up to the Master, an arrangement which still subsists[2].

LIBRARY.—The Library was originally confined to the first floor in the centre of the range to the south of the Gate; and was lighted by five equidistant windows (fig. 3). In consequence of the increase in the number of books, the rooms beneath it, and those beyond it on the ground-floor, have since been added to it. There are no garrets above it. In 1735 the room on the ground-floor, between the Library staircase and the Gate, was assigned to the Library-keeper[3].

TREASURY.—The room on the first floor over the Gate of Entrance has been used as a Treasury from the earliest times.]

EXTERNAL CHANGES.—The external walls of the College were originally built of blocks of clunch in courses, alternating with red brick, and consequently, from the perishable nature of that material, had become so sordid and decayed as to make repair imperative. The north and south sides of the College, which being out of sight have been simply patched and pointed from time to time, and retain many of the original windows and details, give an excellent idea of the state to which the whole must have arrived at the end of the seventeenth century;

---

[1] [Audit-Book Mich. 1656—Annunc. 1657. "For mending Windows in ye Coll. Parlour Mar. 3 . 00 . 04 . 00."]

[2] [College Order, 27 March, 1747. "Agreed...y^t ye Room over ye Butteries be fitted up at ye College Expence (ye Income being first paid off by ye College) for a Combination Room: and y^t the Present Parlour be added to the Master's Lodge."]

[3] [College Order, Feb. 5, 1735. "Then agreed y^t ye Income of ye Ground Chamber on ye right hand in ye Library Stair Case be paid off, and y^t ye Chamber be assign'd to ye Library Keeper for ye time being Rent-free."]

indeed it is said to have presented so ruinous and repulsive an appearance that persons were deterred from entering students therein[1]. From this time the ashlaring of the College began, and was carried on in successive stages through the greater part of the last century until it was brought to its present aspect.

The work was begun in 1714 by Dr Thomas Lynford[2] [who defrayed the cost of casing the Gate House with freestone[3]; and in the following year of casing a portion of the northern half of the west front for a distance of 24 feet from the north-west corner (CD, fig. 1)[4]. He further paid for the casing of the next 24 feet (DE, fig. 1) in 1716, as recorded by Dr Covel in the following terms:

> "Memorandum. The Reuerend Dr Lynford, besides what is set down at seuerall Times in this Book, did also pay Robert Grumbold for the facing of the middle part between the two Gates, with Freestone, a bill May 5th 1716, of £53 . 3 . 0 which because it went not through my hands in being received and paid was not here set down before as part of my account, but it must never be forgotten, as being a noble part of his most generous Benefaction. Joh. Covell Apr. 3d 1717."

Dr Lynford further paid for what Dr Covel calls the "out-work" of the chambers[5], so that this portion of the College is

---

[1] [The late Master, Dr Cartmell, was told this by Dr John Doncaster (A.B. 1794, A.M. 1797, D.D. 1816) who was curate to the Rev. Dearing Jones (A.B. 1740, A.M. 1744), Fellow, and Vicar of S. Andrew the Great. He remembered the first court before it was faced with stone. The walls were of clunch patched with brick.]

[2] [He proceeded A.B. at Christ's College 1670 : A.M. 1674 : D.D. 1689 : elected Prebendary of Westminster May, 1700; died 11 August, 1724.]

[3] [Audit-Book, Mich. 1713—Annunc. 1714. 22 July, 1714. "Paid Robert Grumbold by two several bills upon Mr Will. Herring (£16 11. 4, £16 10. 0), in all £33 1. 4, being the money which was giuen by the Reuerend Dr Lynford for casing the Gatehouse wth freestone."]

[4] [27 May, 1715. "Paid Mr Grumbold the freestone Mason for the new wall, from ye Gate to the Lodge, towards the Coll. gate, 24 foot, £42.06.00." A marginal note records: "Dr Lynford's Gift in all £48. 7. 0." The balance was absorbed in sundry minor expenses.]

[5] [Jan. 25, 1716—17. "From Dr Lynford by Mr William Herring for the workemen in fitting up the six chambers their out work, in his new Addition to his Refronting the Coll. wth freestone, £17. 19. 3." Lady Day, 1717. "To Randal the carpenter for what he did in the Inside of the six chambers in Dr Lynford's new building, besides what the Dr paid for the windowes and outsides and casements, and must be allow'd the Coll. from the respective Inhabitants and be put to their Incomes. His bill £09 . 12 . 04."]

referred to in the accounts as "Dr Lynford's new building;" and we shall see that subsequent works are executed according to the pattern set by him.

No record has been preserved of the casing of the next portion, as far as the gate (ibid. EF).] The façade south of the gate (ibid. GH) was cased in 1738[1], at the expense of the Reverend Christopher Clarke, who "laid out upwards of £200 in new fronting that part of the College where the Library is next the street," to quote the Commemoration Book[2]. The contract, dated 10 March, 1738, is with William Pitcher of Cambridge, who agrees to ashlar the walls with Ketton stone, "after the pattern of the work already done for the College commonly called Dr Lynford's work." He further covenants to provide 88 feet of "stone ground-table," that is basements, which exactly coincides with the length of the street front from the gateway southwards, and shews that the whole of that part was now undertaken. The last payment to the contractors is dated 9 September, 1740[3]. The work therefore occupied rather more than two years.

[The interior of the court was next undertaken. The progress of the work will be best understood from the series of College Orders which sanctioned it:

"12 April 1758. Agreed that the South side of the first court be new cased with stone according to the plan and under the direction of Mr Essex."

"5 May 1760. Agreed that the part of the College where the Library is, to the Gateway, be new cased with stone According to the plan and under the direction of Mr Essex."

---

[1] [College Order, 13 March, 1738. "Agreed...y^t ye outside of ye College next ye street between ye Gate and Mr Harwell's Garden be cas'd with Free Stone." Thomas Harwell (A.B. 1718, A.M. 1721) was Fellow, and his garden is evidently that south of the College.]

[2] [Clarke proceeded A.B. at Christ's College 1691; A.M. 1695; was "ordain'd Priest in Lambeth Chappel 27 February by the R^t Rev. John [Moore] Ld Bishop of Norwich in the presence of that Renown'd Emperor Peter the First Czar of Muscovy," as the inscription under his print records; elected Archdeacon of Norwich 22 February, 1721—22; Prebendary of Ely 14 March, 1731—32; died 19 May, 1742.]

[3] [Professor Willis found this contract among the College Muniments. The sum to be paid for the work was £136, which the contractors received as follows: Sep. 9. 1740. "Rec^t of Mr T. Green by the hands of the Master of Christ's College £56; which with £30 rec^d 6th June 1739, and 50 l. on the 9th May last, makes £156."]

"22 May 1761.   Agreed that the part of the College where the Porter's Lodge is be new cased with Stone according to the plan and under the direction of Mr Essex."

"15 May 1766.   Agreed that the North side of ye first Court be inspected and repaired if it shall be thought necessary."

"Nov. 29 1769.   Agreed that the remainder of the first court be new fronted."

The Audit-Books shew that the payments to Mr Essex, and to Messrs Jeffs and Bentley, the stonemasons employed, were not concluded until Michaelmas 1775, up to which date, from

Fig. 8.   Bath in the Fellows' Garden, looking east.

Michaelmas 1761, £1180. 10s. 4½d. had been spent.   The Lodge was altered in 1770, from a payment to "Cotton and Humfrey for sashes and frames at the Master's Lodge," in that year, and the Hall was probably done at the same time.]

In these works the design of the exterior front of the College was respected to a certain extent.   The façade of the gate, and the battlements, are as shewn by Loggan (fig. 3). The windows of the ground floor remain in their original positions and retain their mullions. Those to the south of the gate retain their cuspings also. Sash-windows, however, with Italian dressings, spaced at regular intervals, were introduced into the Library and other rooms of the first floor. In the interior of the court antiquity was less respected. Not only were the windows altered, but the battlements were replaced by a solid parapet, and the doorways became rectangular openings surmounted by a classical pediment. The only medieval portion allowed to remain is the rich carved corbel of the Lady Margaret's oriel above the entrance to the Master's Lodge.

[The Audit-Books shew that there were once rails in the court, as we have found in other Colleges. They had however been removed before Loggan's time[1]. The rails that he shews in front of the new building were put up in 1670. He further shews a lofty wooden post on each side of the gate, connected with a line of rails, with a similar post at each end. These posts are first mentioned in 1559—60, when we find a payment "to ye Joiner for squaringe ye heades and inbowinge ye feet of ye greate postes at ye gate," and to labourers "at ye settinge vp of ye greate postes." The tops of the posts were covered with lead, and had iron spikes fixed in them. They and the rails were painted in colours. They are last mentioned in 1705—6, when a carver was paid "for carving ye Posts at ye Coll. gate," and a painter for painting them, and, apparently, for blazoning the Arms over the Gate[2].

Loggan shews a Dial in the court, interrupting the parapet at the junction of the Hall and Master's Lodge. It seems to have been put up in 1670—71[3]; and was probably removed when the court was ashlared.

---

[1] [Audit-Book, 1614—15. *Exp. forinsece.* "It' for paynting the rayles in the court viij^li." Ibid. 1651. "M^r. Oliver upon bill for timber to rayle the court 50—18—0."]

[2] [Ibid. 1603—4. "Item to the plummer for layeing the lead of the head of the postes without the gates, and for the pykes iiij^s. viij^d." "13 February 1705—6. To M^r. Wiseman for painting the Posts and gates and the Armes over the Great gate etc. 12—3—0."]

[3] [Ibid. Mich. 1670—Lady Day, 1671. "To ye Free Mason for work about ye Diall 00. 08. 00. For ye Diall-Place, Brickwork, and Plastering 2. 16. 0." Ibid.

GARDENS, etc. The Fellows' Garden now extends from the New Building to the eastern limit of the College. In Loggan's time, however (fig. 2), the western third of it, in which the Tennis-court stood, was divided off from the rest of the ground, which was planted with trees, and contained the Bowling-green. Butts for archery were set up in 1610—11. The wall along the south side was first built in 1614, and rebuilt in 1663; that along the east side of the "Dovehouse Close" and the Master's Kitchen garden, in 1673. The whole of the ground now called the Fellows' garden was sometimes termed the orchard; but in the seventeenth century part of it is called the "Ashyard." Both orchard and ashyard were planted with ash and elm in 1614—15; and limes were added in 1681[1].

The tennis-court was apparently built in 1564—65, from a charge in that year "for fynishinge ye tenis court." It was extensively repaired in 1597—98, and in subsequent years; and was not pulled down until 1711. In 1763 the garden is thus described[2]:

"The Fellows Garden is well laid out, and one of the pleasantest in the University: There are both open and close shady Walks, beautiful Alcoves, a Bowling-green, and an elegant Summer-house: beyond which there is a Cold-bath, surrounded with a little Wilderness."

The Bowling-Green is first mentioned in 1686. The Bath is near the south-east corner of the garden; a view of it, taken from the summer-house, which still exists, is here given (fig. 8). Of the three busts on pedestals at the east end, the middle one is that of John Milton. On his left hand is that of Ralph Cudworth, Master 1654—88. The name on the third pedestal is obliterated, and the bust cannot be identified with certainty. Probably it represents Nicholas Sanderson, Lucasian Professor of Mathematics 1711—39. The urn on the north side commemorates Joseph Mede. The date of the construction of the Bath

Lady Day—Mich. 1671, "To M^r. Skinner for making ye Diall 1. 15. 00. Sept. 14. To ye Painter Wiseman for ye Diall, Coll. Armes, and an outward Border 1. 16. 0." The same painter repainted it in 1693.]

[1] [In 1608—9 we find: *Exp. forin.* "Item for 300 mulberrye plants xviij^s." May not that traditionally connected with Milton be one of these? Milton was admitted a Pensioner of Christ's College, 12 February, 1624—25.]

[2] [Cantabrigia Depicta, p. 66.]

has not been preserved; but the "Summer house in yᵉ Coll. Orchard" had six chairs and a table provided for it in 1682. In Loggan's time there was a pond at the east end of the Dove-house Close. It was repaired, and protected by a brick wall, chiefly at the Master's expense, in 1673[1].]

CHRONOLOGICAL SUMMARY.

GODSHOUSE.

1446.	(18 June.) Purchase by William Bingham of messuage from Abbot of Tiltey.
,,	(26 August.) Charter granted to him by Henry the Sixth.
1448.	(28 March.) Purchase of messuage from Abbess of Denny.
1468.	(7 August.) Purchase from Brian Fysshewyk of messuage south of that belonging to Abbey of Tiltey.
,,	(27 August.) Purchase from same of messuage between Preacher Street and Hangman's Lane.
1474.	(Easter Day.) Purchase of ground from Priory of Sempringham.

CHRIST'S COLLEGE.

1505.	(1 May.) Charter granted to Christ's College by Henry the Seventh.
1506.	(12 December.) License to perform service in chapel granted by Bishop of Ely.
,,	Statutes given by Foundress.
1507.	(28 January.) Lease from Jesus College of croft eastward of site.
1509.	(29 June.) Death of the Lady Margaret.
1510.	(February.) Tiles purchased for roof of chapel; windows glazed (March); pavement laid down, exterior completed, and ceremony of consecration performed (June). Stall-work proceeding (July—October); painted during same time.
1511.	Completion of woodwork.
1554.	(20 September.) Purchase from Jesus College of croft, eastward of site, then called "le grett orchard."
1563.	New chambers built.
1567.	(25 January.) Purchase of "dovehouse close" by Dr Hawford.
,,	(12 March.) Lease from Corpus Christi College of a garden-ground.
1587.	Purchase of ground "lately a grove" from Thomas Manning.

---

[1] [Audit-Book, Lady Day—Mich. 1673. "For scowring yᵉ Pond 1. 00. 00. Memᵈᵘᵐ, That besides this 20 shillings, the Master hath himself disbursed for Digging and New making of yᵉ Pond, and for making Two Channels to carry yᵉ Water to and from the Pond, Ely Bricks, and Tiles, and Morter, for raising yᵉ Ground behind yᵉ Pond and in yᵉ Close etc. 20ˡⁱ. 11ˢ. 5." The details recorded above are taken from the Audit-Books for the years mentioned.]

1613.	A new building erected by John Atkinson.
1638.	Rev. Joseph Mede bequeaths £100 to "intended building." Letters soliciting subscriptions towards it are sent out.
1640.	First stone of Fellows' Building laid.
1642.	Orders made for the New Building.
1657.	Parlour of Lodge made a Combination-Room.
1661.	Four pillars placed in ante-chapel.
1684.	Monument set up in chapel to Sir Thomas Baines and Sir John Finch.
1701—2.	Alterations to interior of chapel.
1714.	Great Gate-Tower ashlared at expense of Dr Lynford.
1715.	Northern portion (24 feet) of front of College ashlared by same.
1716.	Portion south of this (24 feet) ashlared by same.
1720.	Bell-tower of chapel repaired by Dr Covel.
1723.	Alteration of Hall.
1738.	Portion of front of College from Gate to corner of Christ's lane ashlared at expense of Rev. Christopher Clarke.
1747.	Room over Butteries made a Combination Room.
1748.	Master's private Lodge taken down.
1758.	South side of Court ashlared.
1760.	East ,, from S.W. corner to gate ashlared.
1761.	,, ,, from gate to N.W. corner ,,
1766.	North ,, ,,
1769.	West ,, ,,
1847.	East window of Chapel filled with stained glass by Miss Burney.
1875.	Hall rebuilt by G. G. Scott.

APPENDIX.

1. *Letter to Rev. Robert Gray,* 10 *February,* 1638, *soliciting a subscription towards the college buildings.*

Letter endorsed: Ornatissimo Viro, Magistro Roberto Gray, S. Theologiæ Baccalaureo, Ecclesiæ de Mashburye in Comitatu Essexiæ Rectori, Amico nostro meritò charissimo.

Qui privatis in rebis (uti par est) modestiam colimus, cùm publica res agatur impudentes evasimus: satius opinantes brevem audaciæ culpam, quam perpetuam indigentiæ pœnam pati. Intempestivum utique esset silentium in hoc fæcundo beneficentie sæculo, et verecundia sine fructu. Verum ita se res nostræ habent, Vir Dignissime. Collegio conditoribus Regiis, et suis (dicto absit invidia) meritis illustri, dolemus id commodi splendorisque deesse quod exoptare nobis in promptu est, præstare neutiquam. Multa subruit vetustas; nec minori damno sunt ea quæ adjecit necessitas, minuente decorem copiâ. Quippe in angustum coacta Studiosorum Domicilia; et sudantibus Musis liberioris auræ suavitas negatur. Molem aut majestatem suam aliis non invidemus. Nos tantùm honestamenta quædam, salubres recessus, et elegantiam æquabilem cupimus. Sanè nos nobis non defuimus. Etenim quæ suppetebant, in Sacelli, Bibliothece, Aule, ornatum, aliàs denique ubi usus postulabat,

alacres profudimus. Sed ingenti onere victi succumbimus, animosque ad magnifi-
centiorem apparatum surgentes egestas deprimit. Spe solâ subsidii erigimur. Atque
inter cæteros ad Te accedimus (Vir Humanissime) de affectu et benevolentiâ securi;
Nec illarum ædium honori, in quibus virtutis ac eruditionis semina, quæ virum etiam
nunc ornant, hausisti, defuturum confidimus. Quibus modò auxiliatricem manum
admovere dignatus fueris, Illæ instaurationem suam Tibi inter alios deberi agnoscent,
et successores nostri, ad quos tanti Beneficii auctores transmittendos curabimus,
nominis Tui memoriam ad omne ævum gratâ recordatione prosequentur.

Dignitatis tue studiosissimi

Cantabrigiâ   Magister ⎫
   Feb. 10, 1638.*   et   ⎬ Coll. Christi.
                                               Socii   ⎭

* The date is in a different hand and ink.

2. "*Orders for the new Building made by the Master and Fellowes of Christ's
College. Novemb. 8, 1642.*"

1. Every Chamber (except it be a Fellowes Chamber) shall pay a Rent to the
Colledge, towards the Reparation of the Building; viz. a lower chamber, three pounds
a yeare : the Chamber in the second story, as also in the third, foure pounds a yeare :
the Chamber in the highest story, fourty shillings a yeare. These Rents to be
gathered quarterlye.

2. Every Chamber shall be made handsomlye habitable by the Colledge, or by
those who desyre to inhabit it : and the Charge shall be an Income, to be enterd into
a Booke.

3. Every Inhabitant, after foure yeares enjoying his Chamber, shall abate a
third part of the Income, at his leaving it : and if he leave it, before he hath held it
foure yeares, then he shall abate only a fourth part Excepting notwithstanding Fellowes
of the Colledge, who must abate according to the customs of the old Building, viz. a
Tenth.

4. The Income of every Chamber, when by often abatements it is much diminished,
shall be raysed by consent of the Master and Fellowes to a reasonable rate; towards
the discharge of the Debts incurred by the Colledge by reason of this Building.

5. No encrease of Income shall be allowed, without consent of the Master and
Fellowes.

6. There shall not be allowed at once to inhabite the new Building more than
foure Fellowes.

[Signed by] Thos. Bainbrigg. Willm. Power. Mich. Honywood. Will. Brearley.
Tho. Wilding. R. Widdrington. Gerard Wood. Ra. Tonstall.
Hen. More. Ed. Knightley. John Potts.

3. *Epitaph on Sir John Finch and Sir Thomas Baines.*

EFFARE MARMOR
Cuja sunt hæc duo quæ sustentas Capita :
Duorum Amicissimorum, quibus Cor erat unum, unaq Anima,
D. IOANNIS FINCHII et D. THOMÆ BAINESII
Equitum Auratorum.
Virorum omnimodâ Sapientiâ, Aristotelicâ, Platonicâ,
Hippocraticâ,
Rerumque adeo gerundarum Peritia Plane Summorum,
Atq hisce nominibus et ob Præclarum immortalis amicitiæ
exemplum
Sub amantissimi Tutoris HENRICI MORI auspiciis
hoc ipso in Collegio initæ
Per totum terrarum orbem celebratissimorum.
Hi mores, hæc studia, hic successus, genus vero
si quæris et necessitudines
Horum alter D. HENEAGII FINCHII Equitis Aurati filius erat
HENEAGII vero FINCHII Comitis Nottingamiensis Frater,
Non magis Juris quam Justitiæ Consulti
Regiæ Majestati a Consiliis secretioribus summiq
Angliæ Cancellarij
Viri prudentissimi, religiosissimi,
eloquentissimi, integerrimi,
Principi, Patriæ, atq Ecclesiæ Anglicanæ Charissimi,
Ingeniosâ, numerosâ, prosperâq Prole præ cæteris
mortalibus, felicissimi :
Alter D. IOANNIS FINCHII viri omni Laude
majoris Amicus intimus,
Perpetuusq per triginta plus minus annos
Fortunarum ac Consiliorum particeps
Longarumq in exteras Nationes Itinerationum
indivulsus Comes ;
Hic igitur peregrè apud Turcas Vita functus
est, nec prius tamen quam alter
A serenissimo Rege Angliæ per Decennium Legatus
præclarè suo functus esset munere,
Tunc demum dilectissimus BAINESIUS suam et Amici
FINCHII simul Animam Byzantii efflavit,
Die v. Septembris H. III. P.M. A.D. MDCLXXXI Ætatis suæ LIX
Quid igitur fecerit alterum hoc Corpus animâ Cassum rogas,
Ruit ; sed in amplexus alterius indoluit ingemuit,
ubertim flevit
Totum in lacrymas, nisi nescio quæ Communis utrique Animæ
Reliquiæ cohibuissent, Diffluxurum.
Nec tamen totus dolori sic indulsit nobilissimus
FINCHIUS
Quin ipsi quæ incumberent solerter gesserit
confeceritq negotia,

Et postquam ad Amici pollincturam quæ spectarent
curaverat
Visceraq telluri Byzantinæ, addito marmore eleganter
a se pieque inscripto, commiserat
Cunctasque res suas sedulo paraverat ad reditum in
optatam Patriam,
Corpus etiam defuncti Amici a Constantinopoli usq
(Triste sed pium officium) per longos Maris tractus
Novam subinde Salo e lacrymis suis admiscens salsedinem
ad Sacellum hoc deduxit:
Ubi funebri ipsam oratione adhabitâ mæstisque sed
dulcisonis Threnodijs,
In Hypogæum tandem sub proxima Area situm
Commune utrique paratum hospitium solenniter
honorificeque condidit.
Hæc pia FINCHIUS officia defuncto Amico præstitit,
porroque, cum eo, in usus pios
Quater mille libras Anglicanas huic Christi Collegio
donavit
Ad duos socios totidemque Scholares in Collegio alendos
Et ad augendum libris quinquagenis reditum
Magistri annuum.
Cui rei administrandæ riteque finiendæ Londini
dum incumberet
Paucos post menses is morbum incidit Febrique ac Pleuritide
Maximè vero Amici BAINESII desiderio adfectus et afflictus
Inter lacrymas luctus et amplexus charissimorum
diem obiit
Speq beatæ immortalitatis plenus piè ac placidè in
Domino obdormivit
Die XVIII Novembris H. II. P. MN. A.D. MDCLXXXII Ætatis suæ LVI
Londinoq huc delatus ab illustrissimo Domino D. FINCHIO
HENEAGII Comitis Nottingamiensis filio Primogenito
Aliisque ejus filjus ac Necessariis Comitantibus
Eodem in sepulchro quo ejus Amicissimus heic conditus
jacet:
Ut Studia, Fortunas, Consilia, immo Animas vivi qui
miscuerant
Iidem suos defuncti sacros tandem miscerent Cineres.

*** They are buried in front of the tomb, within the Altar Rails, under a slab of black marble, with this inscription:

HERE LIE THE BODIES,
OF S^R JOHN FINCH
AND S^R THOMAS BAINES
KNIGHTS.

XII.

S. John's College.

CHAPTER I.

HISTORY OF THE SITE. HISTORY AND DESCRIPTION OF THE FIRST BUILDINGS.

HE site of S. John's College eastward of the River Cam is bounded on the east by part of the High Street, sometimes called S. John's Street; on the south by Trinity College; on the west by the River Cam; and on the north by dwelling-houses, a portion only of which are in the possession of the College. It had been bounded on this side, until 1863, by a lane (figs. 1, 4), called, from time immemorial, S. John's Lane[1].

We know nothing of the history of this site before the Hospital of S. John was founded upon it[2]. By the Great Inquisition taken 7 Edward I. (1278—79), it was found that the Master and Brethren held a certain area of the fee of the Lord the King, whereon the Hospital aforesaid, with the Chapel of the same Hospital, was founded; which area Henry Frost, burgess of Cambridge, formerly gave to the town, to construct thereon a certain Hospital for the use of the poor and infirm[3].

Before the ground was acquired for this purpose, it is

---

[1] [The site is so large, and of such a peculiar shape, that it cannot be conveniently shewn on a single plan. The general disposition of it, however, will be understood from Loggan (figs. 3, 4); and the details of the eastern and western portions from the plans (figs. 1, 2), based on those made under the Award Act, 1856. It should be further mentioned that when Baker's History is quoted, the reference is to the edition by J. E. B. Mayor, M.A., Fellow, 2 vols. 8vo. 1869.]

[2] [See Historical Introduction.]　　　　　[3] [Rot. Hundred. ii. 359.]

described in another Inquisition, taken in 1275, as "a certain very poor and waste place of the Commonalty of the Town of Cambridge."[1]   From this expression we may conclude that no buildings, except those of the Hospital, had been erected upon it before it became the site of S. John's College.   The consideration of its history is thus rendered very simple ; far more so indeed than that of any other college except Jesus College.

In the fourteenth century the site of the Hospital was bounded on the south by a lane which ran from High Street to the River, for the convenience of the inhabitants of some of the houses which then occupied part of the ground where Trinity College now stands.   This lane became the property of King's Hall in 1339 ; and we learn from the conveyance that the garden of the Hospital extended down to it.   In 1392—93 (27 January) the Master and brethren of the Hospital, in token of their friendly feeling (*amicicie causa*) towards their neighbours, gave leave to the Warden and Scholars of King's Hall to take down a certain wall, which stood upon the Hospital ground. and to build a wall of stone in place of it.   Part of this wall still forms the southern boundary of the site of S. John's College.   The deed shews that the Kitchen and Library of King's Hall abutted on this wall ; and also that probably certain buildings of the Hospital extended up to them, but their nature is not specified[2].

The space to the north of this site, included between S. John's Lane on the south, S. John's Street on the east, Bridge Street on the north, and the River on the west. was occupied, until 1863, by a great number of dwelling-houses, some of which were entered from the lane.   The greater part of these houses had become the property of the college.   There was also a thoroughfare called " The Globe Passage " (fig. 1) extending from the lane to Bridge Street, in which the college brewhouse stood.

---

[1] [Borough Rate Report, p. 48.]

[2] [The deeds here referred to are among the Muniments of Trinity College, and will be further explained in the History of that College, together with those relating to the composition between the Colleges of Trinity and S. John's in 1516.   In the later of the two, after leave given to King's Hall "vnum murum [etc] prosternere," it is provided that they shall take upon themselves "onus reparacionis duorum parietum dictorum Magistri et Confratrum [Hospitalis sancti Johannis Euangeliste] abuttant' super coquinam et Librariam Aule predicte, quatenus predicti parietes racione stillicidii a dicto edificio cadentis deteriorati fuerint."]

In 1862, when an extension of the buildings had been determined, an Act of Parliament was obtained by joint petition of
the Town and the College, in virtue of which the latter obtained
possession of the lane, except a small portion at the east end
containing about 75 square feet; and of so much of " The Globe
Passage" as was bounded on both sides by the college property;
on condition of giving up to the former the aforesaid portion of
the lane, together with a triangular piece of considerable extent,
the whole amounting to 1795 square feet, for the widening and
improvement of the street. The ancient and modern boundaries
of the site have been laid down on the plan (fig. 1)[1].

We must next relate the history of the extensive gardens to
the west of the River Cam. A glance at Loggan's plan (fig. 4),
and his general view (fig. 3), shews that, for convenience of
description, they may be readily separated into three divisions:
" St John's fish-ponds"; " St John's Coll: Meadow"; and the
Bowling Green with its surroundings. When his plan was made,
the grounds were bounded on the north and north-west by a
brook, called then, as now, " Bin Brook." A branch of this,
called S. John's Ditch, divided off a piece of ground which,
with the exception of a small piece at the north-east corner,
was occupied by nineteen fishponds, and is in consequence
frequently referred to as " the pondyards" or " the fishponde close." This had been given to the Hospital by Henry
the Sixth in 1448. His letters patent, of which there is a copy
in S. John's College Treasury, describe the ground as a garden
with ponds, bounded on the north and west by a stream called
Bronne brooke, on the east by a garden belonging to the Hospital, and on the south by another garden, belonging to the same[2].

---

[1] [An application to the Town Council was made by the College 29 April, 1862,
proposing to define the boundary by a line drawn from the N.E. corner of S. John's
Lane to a certain point in Bridge Street. This was afterwards altered, in deference
to the wishes of the Town Council, so that the ground ceded should include the east
end of the lane, as described above, and also a small piece of the College site. An
agreement between the Town and College, for the purposes described in the text, was
sealed by the latter 17 Oct. 1862; and a joint petition to the House of Commons for
leave to bring in a Bill, 17 Oct. 1862. The Act received the Royal Assent 4 May, 1863.]

[2] [The "fishpond close" was always let on lease. In an Account Book of the
Hospital, dated 1485, we find "Johanne Bell pro stagnis nostris iuxta Riveram xiiij^s";
and subsequently in the Audit Books of S. John's College in each year "pro firma
Piscarii vocat' le pondyarde per annum xv^s." On the map of Cambridge by Cus-

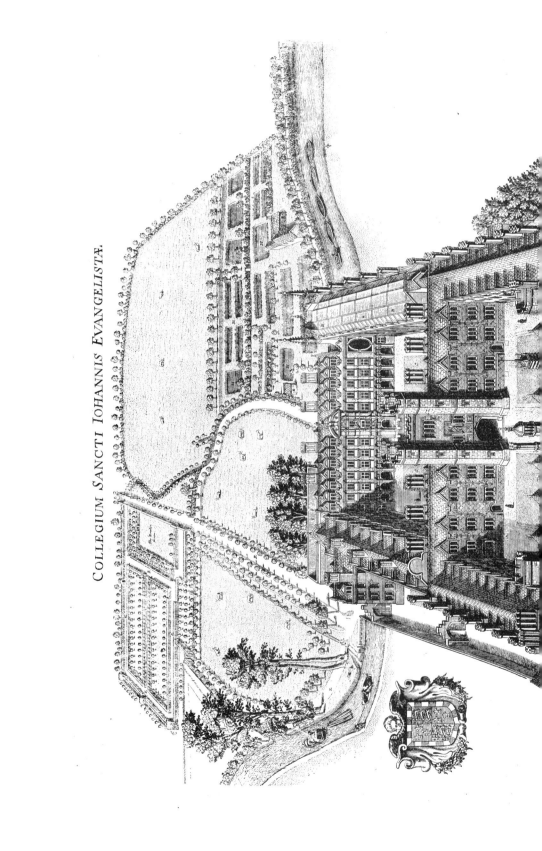

COLLEGIUM SANCTI IOHANNIS EVANGELISTÆ.

Fig. 3. S. John's College, reduced from Loggan's print, taken about 1688. A, Chapel; B, Library; C, Hall; D, Master's Lodge; E, Kitchen; F, Old Court; G, New Court; H, Fish-pond; I, Tennis Court; K, Walks; L, Gate leading to the Fields.

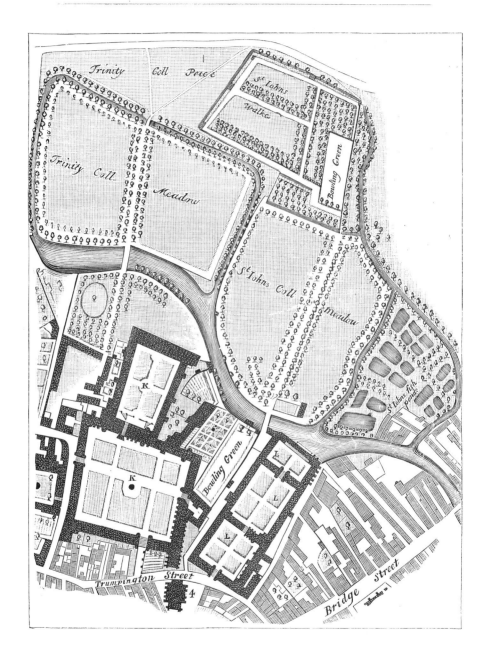

Fig. 4. S. John's College and Trinity College, from Loggan's map of Cambridge, 1688.

The first of these two gardens is no doubt the above-mentioned piece of ground at the north-east corner, and the other is the ground called by Loggan "St Johns Coll. Meadow" (fig. 4). This therefore, which we have called the second portion of the grounds,

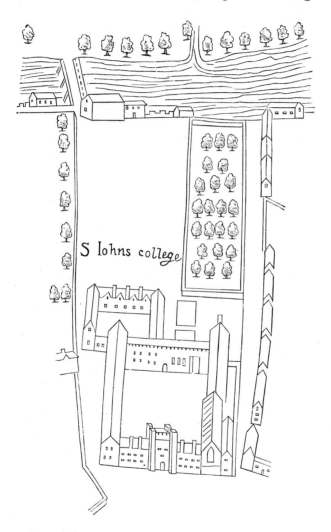

Fig. 5. S. John's College, from Hammond's map of Cambridge, 1592.

tance, 1798, only 4 fishponds are shewn, and the north-east corner is fenced off, and has a large building on it. In 1827 the eastern third of it was leased to Mr Nutter, a corn-merchant, and called Nutter's yard.]

was also the property of the Hospital, but we do not know when or how it was obtained. In Hammond's map, 1592, "S. Johns Walkes" are limited to this meadow, which is surrounded on all sides by water, and is divided into two nearly equal parts by an avenue, at the west end of which there is a gate[1].

The acquisition of the ground westward of this meadow was commenced by purchasing from the Town of Cambridge, 24 April, 1610, the piece on which the Bowling Green was after-wards laid out (fig. 2). No dimensions are given, and it is merely described as "a piece of pasture or waste ground, in the field called 'Colledge Feild' or 'West Feild' behind S. John's College, between a close belonging to that College on the east, and a highway on the west."[2] At this time the piece to the south of the above belonged to Corpus Christi College. It is thus described in a lease granted in 1611 :

"one parsell of pasture ground or laies most parte whereof now being grauell pitts, but sometime arrable land, Conteining by estima-cion three akers more or less, lieing and being in the ffeilds of Cam-bridge on ye west parte of Cambridge Carmefeild, betweene ye landes now belonging to Kings Colledg in Cambridg, sometime to the prior of Huntington, towards the South[3]; And a parsell of wast ground towardes the North: The Easte hed abbutting vppon long greene, in parte inclosed and now belonging to Trinitie Colledg; And the west hed extendeth over the Common waie and abutteth vppon binbrooke."[4]

The narrow walk between the Fellows' Garden and the grounds of Trinity College, and a small triangular piece at the north-west corner of the garden, between Bin Brook, the public road, and the avenue, were allotted to the college in 1805[5].

---

[1] [Want of space compels the omission of this portion of Hammond's map in the woodcut, fig. 5.]

[2] [The deed is in S. John's Coll. Treasury, endorsed " Bowling Green."]

[3] [In a subsequent lease from Corpus Christi College to S. John's College, dated 13 April, 1640, we find this ground in the occupation of Benjamin Prime. It is now called "Trinity College Piece"; but is the property of King's College.]

[4] [A lease from Corpus Christi College for 20 years, dated 25 Jan. 1688, states that it is granted in consideration of leases from S. John's College of two Holts in Trumpington Fields; and in the Audit Book of S. John's College for 1657—58, we find : "Item to Henry Brown for his lease of the Holts to pleasure Bennet Coll' in exchange for the upper walkes 20^{li} More to him giuen by the Coll' 5^{li}: in toto 25. 0. 0." As no further lease seems to have been given, it may be concluded that the properties were tacitly exchanged.]

[5] [This allotment resulted from an Act of Parliament (42 Geo. III.) for enclosing the Parish of S. Giles. " Borough Rate Report," p. 49.]

At the same time, by exchange with Merton College, Oxford, the field to the north of the avenue was obtained.]

The buildings of S. John's College consist of four quadrangles disposed in succession from east to west, and extending to a length of 880 feet. The eastern or primitive quadrangle contained all the essential buildings of a college, as Hall, Chapel, Master's Lodge, Library, and chambers for the Fellows and Scholars. The other quadrangles have been added from time to time in order to provide additional chamber-room, and a larger Library. It is unnecessary to attempt a description of the buildings and arrangements of the Hospital, for no part of them can now be traced which could throw any light upon the plan. They had no influence upon the disposition of the college which succeeded them, except that the retention of the chapel of the Hospital as the chapel of the college fixed the position of the north side of the college quadrangle. This chapel, of which the south side is shewn by Loggan (fig. 13), underwent a transformation similar to that of the conventual church of S. Rhadegund, as related in the History of Jesus College. [The only other building forming part of the Hospital which was retained for the college is that sometimes called the " Infirmary" (fig. 6). It stood north of the chapel, and was fitted up as a range of chambers in 1584—85. It is shewn by Hammond (fig. 5), and in greater detail by Loggan (figs. 3, 13). It will be described at length, together with the old chapel, in a subsequent chapter.]

The first or original court was nearly square, having a mean breadth of 135 feet from north to south, by 131 feet from east to west. A slight obliquity in the position of the eastern buildings made the north side two feet shorter than the south side. The entrance was through a lofty tower-gateway, in what was then the centre of the east side, as Loggan's ground-plan (fig. 4) shews. The first floor of the building to the south of this tower was occupied by the Library. On the north side was the Chapel, as already mentioned, and part of the Master's Lodge. On the west side were the Hall, the Butteries and the Kitchen. The latter had chambers over them. Chambers in two floors with garrets in the roof occupied the whole of the south side. The Combination Room, or college parlour, was to the north of the Hall, in the angle of the court, and consequently

lighted only from the north, as shewn on the ground-plan
(fig. 1). The Master's Lodge had no rooms on the ground-
floor, except his private kitchen, which occupied the base of the
wing which projected towards the north (E, fig. 6).

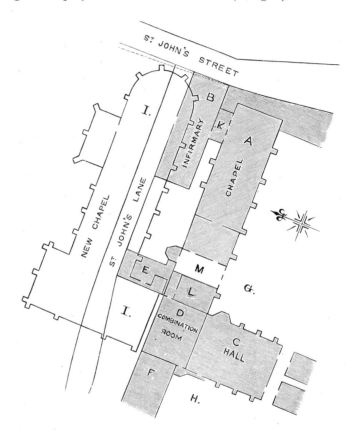

Fig. 6. Block-plan of old and new chapel and adjacent buildings, from Professor Babington's work
on S. John's College Chapel.

A. Old chapel.   B. Building used by the college as a Pensionary, and considered by Prof.
Babington to have been the Infirmary of the Hospital.   C. Hall, before the enlargement.   D. Large
Combination Room.   E. North wing of Master's Lodge.   F. North range of Second Court.
G. First Court.   H. Second Court.   I. New Chapel.   K. Bishop Fisher's Chantry.   L. Small
Combination Room.   M. Vestibule of Chapel and Master's Lodge.

It is evident, from the similarity of Christ's College to S.
John's College in plan and arrangement, in the design of their

tower-gateways, the oriels of their Halls, and other details, as preserved by Loggan, that the two colleges had a common architect as well as a common Foundress and Visitor. Unfortunately their materials were different; the former being built of clunch-rubble, the latter of brick, which was adopted in all subsequent works at S. John's as the college material, except in the New Court. To this cause it is principally owing that the one has been miserably transformed, while the other has preserved its ancient aspect completely in every part, with the exception of the first court, of which the south side was altered by Essex in 1772, and the north side was pulled down in 1869.

[The erection of the original court is thus related by Baker:

"The fabric of the college was undertaken about the same time [as the charter of foundation, dated 9 April, 1511], which was made equal to the design, and capacious enough to receive the number intended [a master and fifty Fellows and Scholars]....The first payment towards it was made at Christmas in the second year of Henry the Eighth [1510] (though it could not well be begun till the spring following, which falls in with the date of the foundation), and the last payment towards it was made in the seventh year of the same king [1515—16]...

The expense and charge of the whole building...amounted in all (some deductions made for other uses) to betwixt four and five thousand pounds (a round sum in that age). For so much was paid by the executors towards the building to Robert Shorton, master of the college, and so much was paid by him to Oliver Scalis, clerk of the works, at several payments, as appears by their several accounts."[1]

The work was evidently begun in February, 1510—11, from the following extracts from the Accounts of the Executors of the Foundress[2]:

"First paide by my lorde off Rochester commaundement, on off the seide executours, by the handes of Mr doctor Metcalff the iiijth day of ffebruary the seconde yere of the reigne of kyng Henry the viijth to on Reculver of Grenewich Brikmaker, At the begynnynge of his werke in seint Johns College at Cambrige as it apperith by a bill.....Cs.

Item paide ffor the costes off the seide Brikmaker ffrom Grenewiche to Camberige at the same tyme..................................vjs. viijd."

The same accounts shew that £2000 was paid to Dr Robert Shorton between July and November, 1511; and in the course

---

[1] [Baker's History, p. 69. Shorton's payments while Master (1510—1516) to Oliver Scalis for the "new works" amounted to £4876. 7s. 5½d. The extracts from his 5-years account relating to these payments are printed below in Appendix II.]

[2] [Cooper, Life of the Lady Margaret, p. 193.]

of the same year we find a charge "for thexpences of Benet
Curwen rydynge from Bromlegh to Camberige to ouersee the
new buyldyngis and reparacions of the seide college," language
which may perhaps imply the adaptation of buildings already
standing on the site.   The Building-Accounts having been
unfortunately lost, we are without information as to the progress
of the work.   The Chapel, Hall, and Master's Lodge, however,
must have been completed, or nearly so, by the end of 1513, for
a contract has been preserved between Dr Shorton and Richard
Wright of Bury S. Edmunds, Glazier, dated 17 December in
that year, wherein it is specified that the windows of the chapel
are to be glazed with " Imagery werke and tabernaclis" according to Dr Shorton's discretion; the windows of the hall with the
devices of the Foundress, and the Bay Window with her arms
and a figure of S. John; and the windows in the Master's Lodge
with her devices.   Among the latter windows two at the west
end of the chapel within the master's lodging are specially
mentioned.   The whole work is to be completed before Midsummer, 1514[1].

Whatever may have been the condition of the buildings here
specified, the formal opening of the college was delayed for
more than two years, for it was not until 29 July, 1516, that
the Bishop of Rochester performed that ceremony in the presence of Dr Henry Hornby, Master of Peterhouse, and one of
the Lady Margaret's executors.   On this occasion Mr Alan
Percy was elected Master, Dr Shorton having resigned, and
thirty-one Fellows were admitted[2].   A license from the Bishop
of Ely to the Bishop of Rochester empowering him to consecrate altars, vestments, and all other ornaments to divine
worship appertaining within S. John's College had been issued
three days previously; but the actual date of the consecration
of the chapel has not been preserved.   From these dates it is
evident that the buildings were so far advanced that the regular

---

[1] [The contract is printed in the Appendix from the original in S. John's College
Library.]

[2] [An account of these proceedings, drawn up at the time, and attested by Thomas
Stacy, notary public, who was present, is preserved in S. John's College Treasury.   It
has been printed in the Appendix to " The Funeral Sermon of Margaret Countess of
Richmond," etc., ed. Hymers.   8vo.   Cambridge, 1840.   See also Baker's History,
p. 76.   For the Bishop's License see MSS. Baker, xxx. 111.]

business of a college could be commenced in them[1].] They
were still, however, by no means completely finished, as we
learn from two interesting documents preserved by Baker.
The first of these is an indenture dated 20 June, 1516, between
Dr Shorton and Thomas Loveday, Carpenter, by which the
latter engages to make the stalls in the quire, the rood-loft, etc.,
according to the pattern of those in Jesus College and Pembroke Hall; also three pairs of broad gates: one for the tower-
gate, one for the gate next King's Hall, and the third for the
water-gate; also ten doors, five for the Chapel, and five for the
Hall, viz. two hall doors, a buttery door, a pantry door, and
a door leading to the Master's Lodge. Further he is to floor
all the chambers, and to make all the desks in the Library according to the pattern of those in the Library within Pembroke
Hall. These works are to be completed by 1 November, 1516,
and he is to receive for them £100. 17s. 8d. This indenture is
as follows[2]:

"This Indenture made between Mr Rob. Shorton Clerke, Doctor
in Divinity and Maister or Keper of the College of St John the Evangelist in Cambridge on the oon parte, and Thomas Loveday of Sudbury
in the County of Suffolk Carpenter on the other parte, wytnessyth
    that the said Thomas covenaunteth, and also byndeth hym hys
Heyres and Executours by thes presents, that he shall make and cause
to be made all the Staulls within the Qwier of the said College, that is
to say, 24 Staulls on eyther syde of the said Qwyer; the Desks wyth the
Bakke halfe, wyth Creests over the Seats and Staulls, as is in the southe
parte of the Qwyer in Jhesus College in Cambr', or better in every
poynt; and the Seats therof shall be made after and accordyng to the
seats within the Qwyer of Pembroke Hall in Cambr' aforesaid, or
larger and better in every poynte; and the oon halfe thereof on every
syde shall be double staulled, wyth lyke lettours, Staulls, and Seats, accordyng to the said patrone, as is before specyfied, of good substanciall
and hable Tymber of Oke, and waynescot:
    and a Rodeloft after and accordyng to the Roodelofte and Candell
beame in the said Pembroke Hall in Camb', or better in every poynt,
wyth Imagery and howsynge, such as shall be mete and convenient for

---

[1] [In the Bursar's Book for the year ending at Michaelmas, 1516, we find the
following entry: "Item sex laborariis mundantibus et scopantibus cameras, aulam,
coquinam, et curiam collegii...erga aduentum domini camerarii xvj^d." In the same
year "the grett gardyn" and the "maistrys gardyng" are mentioned.]

[2] [MSS. Baker, xii. 44. MSS. Harl. Mus. Brit. 7039. In order to save room
the amount to be paid, and the times at which the several payments are to be made,
have been omitted. Baker notes that his transcript was made "Ex originali instru-
mento sub sigillo."]

the same werks and such as shall be advised by the discrecion of the said Mr Rob. Shorton :

and also shall make 3 payr of broode Gats, wherof oon shall be mete and convenient for the Tower Gatte, and two goodly Posts byfore the said Gate, which Gate shall be made with a wykket; and the oder Gate shall be mete and convenient for the Gate next unto the Kynges Hall agaynst the Kyngs hygh way; And the thyrde Gate shall be mete and convenient for the gat at the water syde wythin the said College and which gate shall be made also wyth a wykket of good and able Oke and waynescott, better than ony Gats be wythin ony College in Cambr' :

and also tene Doors, wherof fyve shall be in the Chyrche wythin the said College, that is to say two Chyrche doores, a doore into the Revestry, a doore into the Roodeloft, and a doore into the perclose there ; and 5 other doores shall be in the Halle in the same College, that is to say two Halle doores, a Botery doore, a pantere doore, and a doore leadynge towards the Maister's Loggyng ther of lyke oke and wayneskotte wyth 2 Portalls, wherof one shall be at the parlour doore and the oter at the great Chamber doore wythin the said College of lyke oke and waynescotte, mete and convenient wyth the same, also aftur the best workmanshyp and proportion :

and also a Lantorn over the vice of the Tower wythin the said College of good substanciall and abyll Tymber of oke, mete and convenient for to hange therin the Bell of the said College :

and also shall plancher all the chambers belongyng to the said College wyth goode and abyl boorde of oke which wyll amounte to 51 hundred boorde, when it is plancherd :

and also shall make all the Desks in the Library wythin the said College, of good substanciall and abyll Tymber of Oke mete and convenient for the same Library, aftir and accordyng to the Library within the foresaid Pembroke Hall :

and clerely and holy shall fynishe all the premisses aftir and accordyng to the best warkmanship and proportion a thys syde the Fest of All Saints next comynge aftir the date herof."

The other document is as follows[1]. Unfortunately it is not dated, but, as it includes all the articles in the above contract, it must have been drawn at an earlier date, or at about the same date. Again, as it makes no mention of chambers, excepting the three next to the Hall, the rest may be supposed to have been already made habitable. It shews that the walls and roofs of the Chapel, Hall, Parlour, Kitchen, and Butteries were finished, but that they were not yet paved ; and it mentions the glazing of the Chapel, Hall, and Library, as works yet to be done.

---

[1] [Baker, ut supra, fo. 15. He terms it "A Draught or Account of charges concerning S^t. John's College, which seems to have been taken about the year 1515. *Ex Cistâ Fundatricis.*" At the end he notes "etc. torn."]

"First, for dyvers Implements to be provyded in the Chapell; as Crosses, Chalices, Candylstiks, Sensors, Alter Clothes, Curtens, vestements, Copys, and all maner of Boks, and lykewise in the Lybrarye, Hall, Boterye, and Kechyng, by estimation ....

	lib	sh	d
	1000	0	0

Divers necessary thyngs yet to be made wythin the said College.

Fyrste, for glasynge of all the wyndose in the Chapell, Hall, and Lybrary, by estimation 140 0 0

Item, for makynge of Stalls in the Chapell, seyling the same, and makyng the Roodlofte, and of Stalls and Setts in the Library, by estimation 140 0 0

Item, for makynge of 3 grett Gatts, with Loks, etc. belongyng to the said Gatts................................. 040 0 0

Item, for worke of Stone of a grete Gate, and for ston wall to be mad, etc. 040 0 0

Item, for ston wall to be devysed, and closed to the garden of the said College and the gret Ryver, on which wall shall be mad a Hows for the comyn wyddrowght of the said College, and for a wall of Ston to devyd the Masters gardyn from the comyn gardyn 050 0 0

Item, for 16 new dores to be mad in the Chapell, vestrye, Hall, Buttrye, Kechyng, etc. 010 0 0

Item, for pavyng wyth Ston the Chapell, Hall Parlor and Kechyng 050 0 0

Item, for alteryng the Kechyn and other Howses and of divers necessaryes perteynynge therto........... 040 0 0

Item, for planchyng wyth thyk bords the Pantrye, Buttre, and 3 Chambers next the Hall, etc. 020 0 0

Item, for paving the Curtte of the College 020 0 0

Item, Payd for makyng with Tymberworke of a Steple wherin shall hang the Colleg Bell 007 0 0

Item, for makyng the vestre wyth Stoneworke and tymber and other necessaries 040 0 0

Item, ther is owyng to Mr Thos. Baybyngton of Derbyshire for leyd, wherwyth the Chapel is covered, and the Masters Chamber therto adjoyning, and to cover the vestrey and divers small Towrs 140 0 0

Item, for payment of debts yet owyng by the said Hows of St Johns, which dette my said Lady willyd in any wyse to be payd 200 0 0

	lib		
Summa	937	0	0 "

[The contract with Thomas Loveday shews that the first court could not have been completed before the end of the year 1516; and Baker's statement that the last payment towards the cost of the fabric was made in 1515 must be understood to refer to some payment made by the executors to Dr Shorton or Dr Metcalfe; for he admits in another place that it was not until 1520 that the clerk of the works, Oliver Scales, "signs a full release to Dr Metcalf as Master, attested by Alan Percy and Robert Shorton[1]."]

A few years afterwards a small additional court was erected at the south-west corner, during the mastership of Dr Nicholas Metcalfe (Master, 1518—38), and partly at his expense[2]. It appears to have been begun at the end of 1528[3]. Hammond (fig. 5) gives an outline of it, from which its relation to the older buildings can be easily understood[4]. The south side was nearer to the boundary-wall of the college than the same side of the original quadrangle, and the interval was filled by a wall, in which there was a doorway. The north side, containing a gallery, probably of wood, assigned to the master, was so placed as not to interfere with the passage through the screens. Hammond further shews the master's garden on the north side of the ground westward of these courts; and a wooden bridge, in the same position as the present bridge of stone, with some houses close to the river, the largest of which may have been the stables.

In the mastership of Dr William Whitaker (1586—95) a further increase in the number of students led to the fitting up for their accommodation of an ancient building, part of the Hospital, which stood on the north side of the chapel, at about 11 feet from the north wall. We do not know what use had been made of this building previous to the mastership of Dr Leonard Pilkington (1561—64), when the east part of it was turned into a storehouse for the College, and the west part

---

[1] [Baker's History, p. 87.]

[2] [Baker's History, pp. 107, 183. His words are: "pretty large buildings behind the kitchen, the work and gift of Dr Metcalf when the college was then crowded, which with the master's gallery on the north side did then go by the name of the other court." The Inventory of 1528 mentions "xl^li by hym geven towardes the buylding of the newe Chambers on the bake side the College" (Inventories, &c., 1516—95, leaf 44^b).]

[3] [Audit-Book, Mich. 1528—13 Jan. 1529, "Item for a lyne to measure the courte with vj^d." Ibid. Hilary term, 1529, "Item delyured to Cok the fremason for the new byldyng in part of payment xxxvij^s. vj^d."]

[4] [A more accurate copy of Hammond's plan is given in the History of Trinity College.]

into a stable for the master's horses[1]. Its position and appearance, after it had become a range of chambers, will be readily
understood from Loggan (fig. 3). The alterations—which
consisted of the insertion of the windows and chimneys required, and the addition of a roof containing garrets, by which
means three stories of chambers were obtained—were begun in
1584—85, when we find, among other entries, a charge "for 12
loade of Lime for the roughcast in the new Buylding iij^{li}. xij^s";
and the rooms were occupied in 1587—88, when the rents
derived from "the new tenement" (*hospitium novum intra
precinctum collegii*) first appear in the Audit-Book[2].

[It is clear that at first no access could have been obtained
to these chambers from the college; for the wing containing
the Master's Lodge extended up to the north boundary wall
of the site, and besides, there was no appearance of a door
on the south side, or at the west end. On the other hand,
there was a door, blocked, near the west end of the north wall[3];
and in 1560 permission had been obtained from the town to
set up gates at the east end of the lane, so as to close it up,
and make it part of the college[4]. The building was therefore at
first distinct from the other ranges of chambers, like the Pensionaries and Hostels which we have found attached to other
colleges. In 1636—37 the passage round the east end of the
chapel was made (*N*, fig. 15), as the following entry shews:

"Payd M^r. Broxolme the income of his Chamber by the east end
of the Chappell where the new passage was made to the lodgeings
behind the Chappell .... ix^{li}."

Yet further accommodation was provided in some houses

---

[1] [Baker's History, p. 153. The original architectural features of this building,
which were discovered when it was pulled down in 1863, will be described in Chap.
IV. Dr Caius (De antiquit. Cantab. Acad. i. 106) calls it "vetus sacellum fratrum
sancti Ioannis Euangelistæ quod iam Collegii sancti Ioannis stabulum est."]

[2] [Baker's History, p. 184. The entry is as follows: "Recepta tenementorum
Cantabrigie. Parochia omnium Sanctorum. Diuers' tenent' Hospitium novum intra
precinctum Collegii vbi olim erat hospitale diui Johannis per annum [no sum set
down]." In 1589—90 the rent is set down as vj^{li}. ij^s.]

[3] [This door (*s*, Fig. 15) is shewn in a sketch of the north side by Essex: Add.
MSS. Mus. Brit. 6768, p. 247. The lancet-windows shewn by Essex have not been
laid down on the plan, as Prof. Willis left no measurements to shew their position.]

[4] [Baker's History, p. 462. There is, however, no evidence that this permission
was ever acted upon.]

opposite the college, on the site of which the New Divinity
School partly stands. This was called "The Pentionary"; a
name by which it is frequently referred to in the Audit-Books.
The rent derived from the "New Hostel opposite the College
(*hospicium nouum Collegii ex aduerso prope Collegium*) lately in
the occupation of Roger Harrison," is first set down in the
Audit-Book for 1588—89[1]. In 1580—81, however, when it is
mentioned for the first time among the payments, its gates are
being repaired, an entry which shews that it could not then
have been new. It contained a barn, stable, fish-house, bakehouse, and other conveniences. The name occurs last in the
Audit-Book for 1789—90[2].]

The building of the second court, the next work undertaken,
must be related in a separate chapter.

CHAPTER II.

HISTORY OF THE SECOND COURT.

THE erection of this court, the cost of which was in part
defrayed by the Countess of Shrewsbury, is thus related by
Baker[3]:

"The second court, the great work of this master [Richard Clayton,
Master 1595—1612], was begun by his persuasion[4], through the un-

---

[1] [Harrison had paid xxvj^s. viij^d. for it; in 1589—90 the rent was iiij^{li}. x^s.]

[2] [Audit-Book, 1580—81. *Exp. necess.* "It' for halfe a thousande bricke to
mende ye pensionarie gates vj^s. viij^d. It' for settinge on of ye great barre on the
pensionarie gate on St Mathewes daye...xij^d." Ibid. 1582—83. *Reparationes.*
"For thatchinge the barne and stable in Pensionary...xlvj^s. vj^d." Ibid. 1604—5.
Recept. forinseca. "Receyved of Mr Billingsley for the fishehouse in the Pensionarie
x^{li}." Baker's History, p. 184. In Baker's time the house was used only as a stable;
for he mentions (History, p. 43) "the present stables...on the other side of the street,
opposite to the old buildings." He further shews that a cemetery had once been
there: a statement corroborated by the discovery of a quantity of human skulls and
bones when the foundations of the Divinity School were dug in 1877. A plan of
the site will be found in the Cambridge University Reporter for 11 May, 1875; and
a view of the houses at the corner of All Saints Passage and S. John's Street in Old
Cambridge, by W. B. Redfarn, Plate XXIII.]

[3] [Baker's History, p. 191.]

[4] [Robert Booth of Cheshire, A.B. 1570—71; admitted Fellow 12 March, 1572—
73; A.M. 1574; admitted Senior Fellow 6 April, 1584; was Senior Bursar in 1589; in
1612 writes to Dr Gwyn, Master, to tell him that Mrs Ashton, sister to Dr Clayton,

wearied agency of Mr R. Booth our best solicitor, in 1598, being put into the hands of two undertakers Wigge and Symons (a way of building not so allowable in works intended for posterity) who for the sum of £3,400 obliged themselves in four years to erect a court in the same (or better) manner than it now stands, to be completely finished in 1602. The materials of the old building were thrown in to mend their bargain, and this first sum of £3,400 the foundress obliged herself to make good. By a second contract the undertakers were to receive further £205 for some additional buildings and ornaments, viz. for making the buildings half story etc.[1]; and this it was hoped the foundress would allow. The foundation was laid Octobr. 2^{d2}, 1598; the north side of the court was finished an. 1599, that side being first undertaken, either because it was designed for accommodating the master, or because the old buildings on the other side were to stand till more room was made. The rest of the building rose more slowly, though, bating some small particulars, the whole was finished in the year 1602, in a manner ruinous to the undertakers and not overadvantageous to the college. The undertakers were undone (for soon after I meet with Wigge in prison petitioning the society) and the college had a slight and crazy building left them, which can never live up to the age of the first court, though that court be older by almost 100 years: and yet the contract was punctually performed on their side by the payment of £3,605 with somewhat over, the whole charge amounting to £3,665, a good part whereof was never received by them, by the foundress' misfortunes coming on soon after, which disabled her to make good what she so well intended[3]. Only £2,760 appears to have been received of her, the rest is placed to account as due, and was either made good by the college, or does not appear to have been paid by the foundress. In 1620 she was in arrears, and being then in some disorder, there could be little hopes left of payment. Part of Mr Rob. Booth's legacy seems to have been applied to that use. However she is justly entitled to the foundation of the whole, what she did being wholly owing to her favour, and what she left undone being owing to her misfortunes.

late master, had taken away, as part of his property, a picture of the Countess of Shrewsbury which she "at my humble sute bestowed vppon the Colledg, and desyred y^t D^r. Clayton would cause it to be hanged vpp in the gallerye there." He had died before March, 1616—17, when a correspondence took place between the college and his representatives about his will. Baker's History, *Index:* Cooper, in Camb. Antiq. Soc. Communications, i. 348.]

    [1] [In one of the statements of Accounts between the College and the builders this alteration is described as "the bringinge vp of the half story."]

    [2] [Audit-Book, 1597—98. "For a Supper bestowed upon the Seniors and woorkemen when the foundacion of the Colledge was laide Octob. 2^d. xviij^s. j^d."]

    [3] [Mary, daughter of Sir William Cavendish, second husband of the celebrated "Bess of Hardwick," married Gilbert, son and heir of George Talbot, Earl of Shrewsbury, her mother's fourth husband. She was aunt to William Cavendish, Duke of Newcastle, and to Lady Arabella Stuart, whose misfortunes she shared. Baker's History, p. 613.]

The payments that were made by her or her order were made sometimes to the master at London or Lincoln, and sometimes to him or the several bursars in college, and though the countess of Shrewsbury be never named otherwise than as foundress, yet the payments being made by so many different hands, to so many several persons, at different times and in different places, there could be no such mystery or secrecy in the thing as has been imagined. It is certain the secret was out before the building was up, and that both she and the lord her husband were known to be at the bottom of the design, though from a clause in the contract it seems to have been at first a secret, where the undertakers oblige themselves to leave room over the gate for such arms as the college should afterwards set up there, which are now the arms of Talbot and Cavendish. Her statue was given by the late duke of Newcastle out of respect to the society as well as with regard to his name and family.

Thus the court was finished by this excellent lady with the consent, countenance and assistance of the earl her husband: her faults or misfortunes are foreign to my purpose, occasioned by her intriguing in the match betwixt her kinswoman the lady Arabella and Sir William Seymor, and afterwards reporting that that lady had borne him a son, for the which she was first imprisoned and afterwards, refusing to answer, was fined very heavily, viz. £20,000, and again imprisoned during the king's pleasure.

That she had ever any thoughts of endowing her court (as has been said) is more than I know, and much more than I believe. In all the papers there is nothing said of such a design, but there is enough said to contradict it.

The court being finished was to be divided out, and the proportions adjusted betwixt the master and the fellows, wherein the master had a large share, as reasonable, most of it having been built upon his ground, either where his garden or his old gallery stood, and all of it under his conduct and by his and Mr Booth's persuasion, and there being now room enough, several of the scholars that were willing to keep in them had likewise chambers, somewhat whereof continued till of late years, and somewhat (though very little) till the building of the last court; when (as one would imagine) the scholars lost their shares for want of room."

The agreement with the builders, dated 7 August, 1598, is as follows[1]:

"ARTICKLES INDENTED AND AGREED vpon by and betwixt the master Fellowes and schollers of the Colledge of St John the Evangelist in the vniuersity of Cambridge on thone parte and Ralph Symons of Westminster free mason and Gylbert Wigg of Cambridge[2] in the County of

---

[1] [Audit-Book, 1597—98, "For wrytinge of the Articles betwixte Simmons and ye Colledge vjˢ. viijᵈ." The Articles are in S. John's College Treasury.]

[2] [In a receipt dated 2 May, 1605, Wigge describes himself as of Histon in the county of Cambridge.]

Cambridge free mason on thother parte, for the building and perfectinge of their new building to be erected on the backside of their Colledg by the same Ralph and Gilbert in manner and forme followinge.

1.　FYRSTE the said Ralph Symons and Gilbert Wigg and their Assignes doth Covenaunte to build and ioyne to their ould Colledge three other sides which makes a Court that shall conteyne in lenght from Easte to West one hundreth three score and fiue foote, and in breadth North and Sowth one hundred thyrty and sixe foote.

2.　THIS building shall Conteyne within the mayne walls of the first story ninetene foote and within the walls of the second story twenty foote and shalbe devided into seuerall romes with large staires accordinge to the platts and vprights drawen by the said Simons or Wigg or their assignes, and subscribed with their owne hands and shall rise two stories highe besides the Roofe and within the said Roofe ther shall be made soe conuenient studdies as the Master and Seniors shall appoynte with convenient lightes particions doores and hingells.

3.　THE firste storye shall ryse tenne foote and a halfe betwixt the flowers ; the second story Eleaven foote betwixt the flowers ; and those roomes contayned within the rooffe shall be eighte foote at the leaste betwixte the flowers and the windbeames.

4.　BOTH sydes of this whole buildinge viz. both the inwarde and the outwarde walles of all the three newe Raunges of this buildinge, shall be raysed with gable endes of bricke, and every of the gable endes must be betwen seven or eighte foote brode one the inside of the courte and eight foote hie from the flower to the Cuming on of the Roofe, and on the backside proportionable as the building will receave and acording to the plotts, and shalbe also battelled betwixt the gable endes in such manner and fashon as the master Fellowes and schollers shall appoint; which battlement with his Crest shall rise fowre foote and the whol side of the owld building towards the new Court shall likewise be battelled and Raysed with gable ends of equall scantling in all respects with those in the new raunges and the Chimneys now standing in that wall shalbe taken dowen and Raysed in some other Convenient place without disgrace of the new court according to the direction of the master Fellowes and schollers aforesaid. Also the kytchin shalbe made vp and finished according to the plott yf it shall like the maister and Fellowes to haue it stand as the plott doth mencon; and the kytchin shalbe finished within such Convenient time as the master Fellowes and schollers shall appointe, with faire pavement of Cliff ston on the flower, and the Raunges, ovens, boyling places, and a convenient sinke and Currant to clense the same, and with a larder howse and pastrey, with other howses of office necessarie for a kytchin paued with bricke where anie sellering shalbe.

5.　THE walls of this building shalbe of bricke and ston the sayd brick to be provided in Stow in the County of Norffolk, or in some other place where very good bricke is to be had, and shalbe from the vpper part of the grownde to the fowndeacion fowre foote and a half in thicknes ; from the grownd to the water table three foote fowre ynches ; from them to the first flower three foote ; from the first to the second flower two foote and a half; the battelmentes one bricke lenght and the gable endes one brick and a half thick.

6.   THE Windoes of this building shalbe all of ston and so much of
them of Cliff free ston as shalbe subiect to take harme by weather, and
all of them without transomes; the height of euery light shalbe fiue
foote and the bredth of the windoes fiue foote and a half, that is to saie
in euery windoe three lights of eightene ynches wide and five foote hie
and for the mollions of the windoes one foote All the said new windoes
shalbe fashioned in all respect like vnto the windoes in the vpper
court obseruinge the number of three lights to euery windoe as is aforesaid; for the gable ends on the in side of the court three light to be in
euery gable windoe and euery light conteyning fowre foote at the
least in height and eightene ynches in breadth; and on the out side of
the Colledge euery light to carry the same bignes in height and bredth
as on the foresyde and as many light as the building will permitt and
according to the plotts.

7.   THE water table, cornish, and Crest, with the Corbell table
awnswerable to the vpper court, shalbe all of Cliff free ston with gates
and doores made in the mayne wales.

8.   ALL the windoes of ston throw this whole building shalbe well
splayed on the inside towards the romes, and shall haue substanciall
barrs of iron, that is to saie in euery light one vpright barr and fiue
Crosse barrs or locketts, and shalbe well glazed and simonted, and
euery chamber shall haue two casements and euery studye one,
all of yron; the said Casements to be in height two foote and three
ynches.

9.   ALL windoes dores gates and Chimneys shalbe well arched ouer
both in the ston worke and with brick aboue the ston ; and euery dore
and windoe shall haue his Cornish well wrought by the freemason and
the Chimneys with their becketts shalbe of good whit ston commonly
called Barington ston well wrought by the free mason.

10.   THE Flowers, particions, and Roofes shalbe of substanciall oake
tymber, and euery flower shalbe well layed with good seasoned board
of oake and euery roome shall haue a sufficient dore with hingells And
all the timber of this new building shalbe for bignes proportion and
euery respect awnswerable to the timber vsed in the buildinge of the
vpper Court.

11.   THE stayres shalbe made of good oake plankes one ynch and a
halfe thick.   All the roomes of this building shalbe well plaistered
ouerhead with good reed lime and hare and the particions betwixt euery
fellowes chamber on both sides of the same to be double latched with
good lath lyme and hare as allso all other places wher plasteringe is
needefull, and all that is playstered shalbe well whited ouer.

12.   IN THE west side of this buildinge as parcell therof shalbe built
a fayre gate howse with fowre turrets and chambers according to the
vprights and plotts drawen, and shalbe couered substancially with lead,
and all so all those gutters betwixt the Roofe and the battelments shall
have so many spouts as shalbe thought needfull for Carriage of the
water in euery respect awnswerable to the owld buildinge yn the vpper
Court aswell for the side of the owld building which shalbe towards
this new building as for euery parte of this new buildinge ; and theise
turrets and battelments shalbe raysed in height aboue the ridge of

the building adioyning proportionable as the gatehowse and turrets are in the owld court; and as the gatehowse in the owld building towards the streete is bewtified and set out with fownders armes so this inward side of this west gate shall haue a place left to be supplyed hereafter at the charg of the said master Fellowes and schollers with armes and such Colors as the master and Fellowes shall appointe ; the said place to be proportionable to the scantlinge of the armes and other ornaments now being in the owlde gate howse (And the sayed gatehouse shalbe vaulted vnderneath with arches and other woorkmanship in every respect answerable to the gatehouse in the vpper Court).

13. THE grownd of the Court and of this whole building shalbe raysed and levelled as hie as the grownd at the hall doreys.

14. FOR the manner of proceeding in this buildinge the said Ralph Symons and Gilbert Wigge doe Couenaunte that it shalbe sett vp and perfectly finished within Fowre yeares after the date of theise artickles in manner and forme following; that is to saie in this first yeare to be ended the first of August 1599. The sayd Ralph Symons and Gilbert Wigge doe Couenaunte to laye the fowndation of the whole side at least which is towards the North and to provide so much stuffe of all sortes as will suffice to the full acomplishment and finishing of the sayd north side. In the Second yeare to be ended 1 August 1600 they doe Couenaunte to finish and acomplish the said north side; to laye the fowndation of the West side, and to provide so much stuffe as will suffice for the finishinge and acomplishment of the West side. In the third from thence they doe Couenaunte to finish the West side, to laye the fowndation of the south side, and to provide so much stuffe for the finishinge and acomplishment of the said south side and also the eeste side; and in the fowrth yeare to be ended 1 August 1602 to finish and acomplish thyse whole building accordinge to the true entent and meaninge of this bargaine, and acordinge to the plotts subscribed with the said Ralph Symons and Gilbert Wigge ther handes.

15. ALL this building in manner and forme aforesayd shall god-willing be performeed and finished acording to the time limitted in the next aboue artickell by the said Ralphe Symons ; And the master Fellowes and schollers ther successors and assignes doth Couenaunte to deliuer and paie vnto the said Ralph Symons in consideracion therof three thousand fowre hundred pownds of lawfull inglish money in forme following; And to performe all theise Couenauntes vnderwritten on their behalfe to be performed.

FIRST they shall suffer the said Ralph Symons to convert to his owne proper vse without accompt two brick walls the one enclosinge the master his ortcharde and the tennis court; the other parting ortchard and garden, leavinge of the longer wall so much standinge as shalbe without the bowndes of the new buildinge betwixt that and the water side ; and also all such stuffe as shall arise of the chimneys to be taken downe on the west side of the ould court next vnto the new buildings and of the alteracion of the romes in the plott apointed for the kytchin and larder howse and all the owld bord and timber which doth enclose the tennis court and the pavement ther together with the two chimneys in the kytchen.

SECONDLY they shall paye to the sayd Ralph Symons two hundred powndes before michaellmas next after the date hereof wherwith to make his provisions at the best hand and further also from time to time so much money as shalbe due to him for the stuffe layd vppon the grownde of the said Colledge accordinge to the proportion of provisions to be yearely made by him sett downe in the fowretenth of the former artickells on his parte to be performed and respecting aswell the quantitie of the said stuffe by him layd on the grownde as the worth therof acording as such stuffe is to be bought at Cambridge; and the receipt of euery such summe must be by him acknowledged vnder his owne hand. And further when the building is in hand thei shall deliuer to him monthly somuch money as will sufficiently defray the monthly charge of workmanship acording as it is proportioned in the aforesaid fowrtenth artickle. Prouided alwayes both stuffe and workmanship to be paid for doe not exceede the somme of one hundreth pownds for the first quarter next after the date hereof; nor the somme of two hundred pownds for euery one of the next three quarters followinge; Nor the somme of seauen hundred pownds to be paid quarterly in the second yeare viz: not aboue one hundred pownds for the first quarter nor aboue two hundred pownds for euery other quarter of the second yeare; Nor aboue the some of two hundred twenty fiue pownds for euery quarter of the two last yeares Saving whatsoeuer shalbe vnreceiued by him of the said sommes in euery former quarter of euery of the said yeares maye be receiued by him at euery time after, as his provisions and work appearing as is abouesaid shall require.

THIRDLY it shalbe indifferent to the Colledge to make the aforesaid paiments at their owne choise either in money or in stuffe at such rates as stuffe in euery kinde is to be had at Cambridge at the time of the deliuery therof so that the said Ralph Symons hath notice vpon the conclusion of this bargaine, or within a quarter of a yeare after the conclusion of this bargaine what wilbe deliuered in stuffe of that which ought to be layd in the aforesayd fowretenth article in the first yeare: And within one quarter after this yeare expired to haue like notice what shalbe deliuered in stuffe in the second yeare for the third yeares provision; and so likewise during the whole time; and all such stuffe to be deliuered there in the place of buildinge at such times or before as such sumes ought to be paid as they are deliuered for; Provided alwaies that the Colledge have notice a quarter of a yeare before vnder Ralph Symons his hand what stuffe he shall vse in euery yeare that they maie have the quarters respite to make ther note of such stuffe as they will deliuer.

LASTLY yf at anie time hereafter anie doubt shall arise in or concerninge anie thing agreed vpon or sett downe in theise artickles or Couenaunts or in any of them, or if anie defect either in theise said artickels of anie thinge in anie kinde which should haue bene agreed vpon or sett downe concerninge this building to be made shall hereafter be fownde, it is agreed and concluded by consent of both parties that the most reverent father in God the lord Archbisshop of Caunterberry and the lord bisshop of London for the time being vpon the entreaty of either partie maie at all times hereafter interprete or sett downe indifferently for both parties what to them two shall seeme most equall and most agreeable to the meaneing of either parties meaninge in this aforesaid bargaine; And what theise two bishops shalbe pleased to sett downe vnder their hands shalbe obserued and kept, as well by the said master fellowes and schollers on ther partie as by the said Ralp Simons and Gilbert Wige on ther partes and behalfe, in as strict manner as anie thinge in theise articles comprised and specifyed.

In witnes wherof the parties aforesaid to theise artickels have putt their hands and seales the seauenth daie of August in the ffortith yeare of the Reigne of our souereigne lady Elizabethe by the grace of god queene of England Fraunce and Ireland defendour of the faith, &c.

Sealed subscribed and deliuered in the   RAF. SIMONS
presence of Willyam Ogden, John Palmer   GILBERT WIGGE
et mei Thome Smith Notarii publici."[1]

(Seals almost gone.)

A year afterwards a supplementary Article was drawn up between the same parties :

Aug. 9°. 1599.

" Memorandum y^t it was agreed vpon ye daye and yeare above written betwixt the m^r. fellowes and schollers of ye colledge of s^t John ye evangelist one ye one part and Raulff Symons and Gilbert Wigg fremasons on ye other part

y^t ye newe buyldinges of ye coll. afforsayd should be halff story and y^t ye sayd Symons and Wigge should have for ye woorkmanship thearof over and besides their formar covenants concerninge ye sayd buyldinges ye summ of 205^{li}. y^t. is to say 5^{li}. to be payed vnto them in hand, and ye rest att 3. severall tymes : every tyme one hundreth markes as ye thre severall sides of ye buyldinges shalbe finished to ye good like of ye company;

the wch 205^{li}. is to be payed out of ye colledge stock except ye funders (sic) of ye newe buyldinges will allowe ye same as we hope they will[2]."

The "plotts" that belong to the Articles consist of three plans, on paper, shewing (1) the first story, or ground floor ; (2)

---

[1] [The builders gave two bonds of £500 each for the faithful performance of these covenants. In the first, dated 4 September, 1598, Edward Lucas, gentleman, of Triplow in Cambridgeshire is joined with them; in the second, dated 24 October in the same year, John Simmons of Arberfield in Berkshire, Bricklayer.]

[2] [The £5 was paid Aug. 11. The signed receipts for the remaining sums follow immediately upon this memorandum in a book in which the receipts given by Symons and Wigge from time to time are regularly entered.]

the second story, to which is appended a flap to shew an alternative arrangement of the Lodge rooms on the north side; (3) the roof story. There are also three "uprights" or elevations shewing (1) the interior of the west side of the court; (2) the exterior of the north side next to the lane; (3) the interior of the same side. Each of the six sheets is signed by Simons and Wigge, and attested, like the articles, by Ogden, Palmer, and the notary. The plans are drawn to a scale of one sixteenth of an inch to a foot, not very precisely, but the dimensions intended are written across the principal parts. No scale of feet is appended. The elevations are very rudely drawn to the same scale as the plans, in ink outline tinted. The roof slates are yellow, to indicate Collyweston rag; the stonework either yellow or white; and the brickwork coarsely shewn with large lattice-work of grey bricks on a red ground (fig. 7). The grey is rubbed in with a lead pencil, and the red with red chalk. The plans are drawn in outline, the preparation lines inserted, not, as now, in pencil to be rubbed out when done with, but by scratching or indenting them in the paper with a dry point, or blunt instrument shaped like a spatula, which is to be found in old cases of drawing instruments. Color is slightly applied to the windows, fireplaces, and stairs, and not to the walls or partitions, which are left in outline[1].

[The Articles provide, § 14, for the completion of the whole court in four years, that is, by August 1602; and further, § 15, for the proportional payments to be made during that period until the whole £3400 had been received by the contractors. It appears, however, from a statement drawn up by Mr Billingsley, Senior Bursar, in 1601 (19 January), that up to that time £3290 had been paid to them. It is possible that this might have been in consequence of the quantity of material which they had stored up, for the whole work does not appear to have been finished sooner than had been expected. The commencement at the appointed time is recorded by the date 1599 being placed on the cistern-head above the first door on the north side commencing from the Hall, and, though two workmen came from London in 1601 to "oversee" the buildings, for

---

[1] [These important, and almost unique, documents have been lately bound, and are preserved in S. John's College Library.]

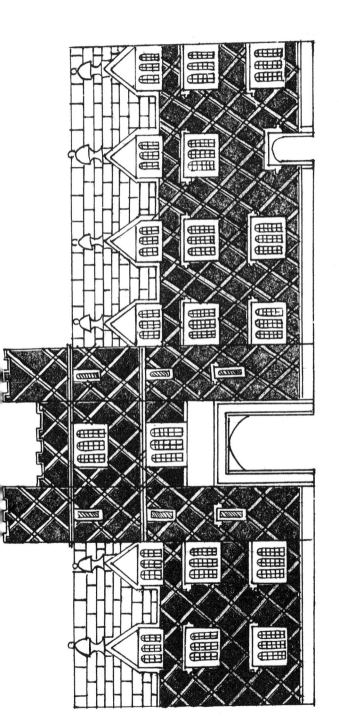

Fig 7. Facsimile of part of the design made by Ralph Simons for the west side of the second court of S. John's College. Endorsed. "Raf. Simons. Gilbart Wigge. Subscribed and delyvered in y⁶ presence of us Willyam Ogden, John Palmer, and me, Thomas Smyth. Notarie publique."

which they received a fee from the college[1], it must not be concluded from this that they were then completed, for in 1602 we
find the alteration to the old kitchen proceeding, which was to be
undertaken last[2]. The "old buildings," by which the small court
previously described is meant, had been partially pulled down
in 1601; but the removal of a larger portion is not charged for
until the following year[3]. Part of them had therefore been left
standing within the area of the new court until the last moment.
The last payment to the contractors was made 31 July, 1602.
The court was not paved until 1603. In the Audit-Book for
1602—3 we meet with a separate heading, "Layd out aboute
the new Courte, and the Courte by the water side." The total
spent was the large sum of £156. 2s. 5½d. The laying down of
the pavement is only one among a number of items which afford
evidence that attempts were made, even at that early date,
to remedy some of the defects in the construction of what
Baker calls "a slight and crazy building," a remark justified by
the fact that there is scarcely a single party-wall in the whole
structure :

"To Jeremy for .162. fote of pavinge stone in the length of the Court,
    and for .70. fote in the breadth at vj^d. the fote .... v^l. xvj^s.
For 5000 of Stow bricke for the vnderpinninge rownde aboute, and for
    the vaultes .... iij^{li}. vj^s. viij^d.
To the Masons and theire Laborers for worke done aboute the Cant
    windowes, the steps, iambes, and buttrices............ x^{li}. xvij^s. ix^d.
For pebbles for the Courte by the water side .... vj^{li}. vij^s. vj^d.
To Richard Knockle for painting of the brickworcke .... xxiiij^{li}.
To the Bricklayers for paintinge of the gable endes................. xij^s."

In the course of the work Ralph Symons lost the use of one
of his hands, and he appears to have left soon afterwards, for in
a summary of accounts dated 9 April, 1605, Gilbert Wigge
speaks of him as "late of Cambridge." When the work was
finished the builders had some difficulty in obtaining a settle-

---

[1] [Audit-Book, 1600—1601. *Exp. necess.* "To two workmen wch came from
London to oversee the newe buildinges iij^{li}. x^s."]

[2] [Ibid. 1601—1602. *Exp. necess.* 3^d. quarter, Mids—Mich. 1602. "To Simons
and Wigge for the two chimneyes in the kitchin wch they were to haue by Couenante
liij^s. iiij^d. To Bray for makeing of the Kitchin Chimneyes vj^{li}. xiij^s. iiij^d."]

[3] [Ibid. "For pulling downe the old buildings, in toto iij^{li}. xv^s. vij^d." Ibid. 1601—
1602. *Exp. necess.* 3^d. quarter; i.e. Mids.—Mich. 1602, "for pulling downe the old
building viij^{li}. xj^d. ob."]

ment with the college, and actually drew up the following petition to the King. It is neither signed nor dated, and was
probably never sent[1]:

"In most humble manner shewethe vnto your Royall Majestie

That whereas the M^r and Seniours of St Johnes Colledge in Cambridge did bargaine with your oratours for certaine buildinges to bee
erected in that Colledge accordinge to Couenauntes and Articles passed
betwixt them, which hath bene accordinglie performed by your sayd
oratours on there behalfe, wher the sayd Symondes lost the vse of one
of his handes. Uppon the finishinge whereof there grewe due to your
sayd oratours from the said M^r and Seniours the some of one hundreth
and fower score poundes. But vppon difference happeninge the de-
mande of your said Oratours was by mutuall assent referred to certaine
Arbitratours and skilfull workemen. The sayd workemen vpon vewe
of the Articles and buildinges did moderate there said demaundes, re-
ducinge the same to the somme of one hundreth and twentie poundes,
to which Award, your sayd Oratours condiscendinge cannott obtaine
paiment of that money so allowed by the sayd workemen, but have
bene dreven of from time to time, for the space of vi or vij yeares to
ther greate losse and hinderance, and cannott without sute in lawe
obtaine the same. Who beinge of power in the Uniuersitie and privi-
ledged that your Oratours cannott sue for the same out of the Universitie.

May it please your gratious Majestie in tender consideration thereof
to vouchsaife your highnes lettres vnto the sayd M^r and Seniours for
the satisffiinge of your sayd Oratours who shall bee daylye bound to pray
for preservation of your Majestie longe to continue."

The college, however, pleaded that Wigge and Symons
were indebted to them in the sum of £200 advanced to them on
a bond dated 21 February, 1600—01; and obtained judgment
against Wigge in the Vice-Chancellor's Court, 23 March, 1603[2].
We do not know what happened during the next two years;
but in 1605 (9 April) a statement of accounts was drawn up by
which it appeared that £19. 7s. 8½d. was still owing to the college.
Possibly Symons had left in the interval, for Wigge alone signs
the following appeal, written at the end of the account:

---

[1] [It is endorsed "To the Kings most excellent Majestie. The humble petition of
Raphe Symonds and Gilbert Wigge ffreemasons." This document, and the others
referred to here, are in S. John's College Library, bound up with the plans of the
New Court.]

[2] [Audit-Book, 1602—3. *Expense in lege.* "Spent in M^r. Vice-Chauncellors Courte
about the suite betwixt the Colledge and Gilbert Wigge, to the Judge and Reg.
xxxiij^s. 4^d. To M^r. Turner our Proctor for his fees xxxviij^s. 4^d. To Pryme the Bedle
xvj^d." From the copy of the sentence we learn that the partner joined with Wigge was
John Atkinson, probably the builder employed at Caius College in 1618. (Vol. i. 186.)]

"I do confesse and acknowledg it to be very tru that which is heer set downe and do most humbly besech your worships that ye wilbe pleased out of a christian comisseration to geve me tyme for the payment of the remaynder in such sorte as shall seeme meet vnto your selves my self protesting that out of myne owne hability it is very littell that I shalbe able to do therin which notwithstanding I will most willingly inforce my self by my continuall travell and labour to give you satisfaction for it after the rate of fyve pounds by ye yeare with such assurances that I may by any meanes procuir which favour I do most humbly desyre at your hands even for his sake who is mercifull vnto all with out desert and for the which your goodnes both I my wyfe and children shalbe dayly bound to prayse the lord god and to pray vnto hym for the long and happy continvance of the florishing estat of that most worthy and renowned colledge.

Your worships poore and most miserable aflicted prisoner Gilbert Wigg."

The college appears to have been moved by this appeal, and to have forgiven a portion of the debt, and accepted Wigge's proposal for the payment of the remainder; for on 3 May, 1605, he gave them a bond for £40, which he engaged to pay by yearly instalments of five pounds: and on the previous day he had signed a receipt in full for all his claims against them[1].]

The court measures 137 feet from north to south, by 165 feet from east to west. The eastern side is formed by the Hall buildings; the other three consist wholly of chambers. [Those on the ground-floor are now 10 feet high; those on the first floor 11 feet; and the garrets between 8 and 9 feet. These dimensions are of course affected by modern floors and ceilings. They are, however, so nearly those provided for in the Articles, § 3, that the increase in height of the third story, alluded to by Baker, could not have been great[2].] The centre of the west

---

[1] [It should however be mentioned that the question does not appear to have been finally settled before 1609—10, when we find: *Exp. necess.* "To M^r. Tabor for a coppie of the sentence against Wigge ij^s. vj^d." *Exp. in lege.* "For charges in the sute in answering of Simons xxxvj^s."]

[2] [Mr Booth made the following suggestions to the Master in a letter dated 6 June, 1600. As it is written from Broad-street, London, where the Countess of Shrewsbury had a house, we should perhaps be right in concluding that the scheme had been sanctioned by her: "In this rawng now erecting in your new court, and so in the next, it wilbe well that the tymber be so provyded as that the thyrd story may be 11 foote high at the least and that the second or midle story may notwithstanding be 12 foote high at the least between floare and floare; all which (as I think) may fitly be, by thrusting the seeling of the third story high into the roofe, and by raysing the floare of that third story a foote or more higher then it is in the north rawng, which may be

side has a lofty gate-tower with side-turrets. In the architectural style of this court, the doorways and windows are copied in form and moldings from those of the original quadrangle, as directed, § 6; but the battlemented parapet of the latter, which Loggan shews, is replaced by a series of gables in the former. Gables were also added to the upper part of the western wall of the Hall buildings, so as to give perfect uniformity of effect, § 4. The Master's Tower, which at first was carried only to the level of the parapet, was now raised high above it as at present; and the appended projection, once roofed as a lean-to of the Hall, was now provided with a battlemented parapet; and a corresponding tower was built at the south-east corner of the new quadrangle[1]. By these skilful arrangements the original style of the eastern side was very slightly changed, and all appearance of incongruity avoided. An oriel window, combined with a door below, is placed in the middle of the north side, and a similar combination on the south side, of the quadrangle. These were not stipulated for in the Articles.

The whole of the first floor of the north side of the court, the length of which, according to Symons' plan, was 187 feet 6 inches, was assigned to the Master. The principal portion of this was the Long Gallery, which originally extended from the west wall, in which Symons places an oriel window, for a length of 148 feet, as shewn by the ceiling, which is ornamented with plaster enrichments in relief[2]. The remainder was subdivided into rooms for the Master's use. The plaster-work of the ceiling of the gallery, of which a portion is shewn in connection with the staircase at the west end (fig. 8), was executed in the course of the year 1600, when we find an Account dated 19 January, 1601 :

"Payde also vnto Cobbe for frettishinge the gallerie and the great chamber 30^{li}."

The wainscoting was not completed until about three years afterwards, as shewn by an entry in the Audit-Book for 1603—4:

without charg to the workemen and will greatly bewtifye the chambers..." Camb. Antiq. Soc. Communications, i. 343.]

[1] [These details can be made out by observing the different styles of brickwork.]

[2] [A ground-plan of the gallery will be given in the chapter headed "Master's Lodge" in Vol. iii.]

"To the ioyner in full discharge for the wainscottinge of the gallerie, and for the . 2 . chimney pieces there, and for the rounde table in the baye windowe..................... ....xlviij^s."

Most of this panel-work, which reaches as high as the roof, still remains. Unfortunately this noble room has been much mutilated. In 1624, about 42 feet at the west end were absorbed in order to obtain a staircase and vestibule to the Library. This alteration, however, was evidently so managed that the gallery still presented a clear space from the Lodge to the Library door, uninterrupted even by a partition to separate the staircase, for Carter, writing in 1753, says:

"The Master's Lodge hath many good and Grand Apartments, but especially the Long Gallery, which is the longest Room in the University, and which, with the *Library* that opens into it, makes a most charming View."

At some subsequent time this staircase was continued above the first floor by a small ascending flight to the chambers over the gallery, which are assigned to students. The old ceiling was broken through to allow these stairs to reach the upper story.

In the last century, part of the west end was divided off by partitions to furnish additional bed-rooms for the Lodge; and more recently other rooms were taken from it in the same way, leaving only a Drawing Room about 50 feet long, which included the oriel and a chimney piece.

[After the new Lodge had been built (1863—5), the gallery was partially restored by removing some of these partitions. One of the bed-rooms at the west end was retained as a lecture-room, and the remainder now forms a fine Combination Room, 93 feet long.

The plan of the college (fig. 1) shews a projection (*F*) on the north side of the gallery, extending up to S. John's Lane. This was a modern addition, for the purpose of providing a carriage entrance to the Lodge. It contained an entrance-hall and stair-case, which were removed in the course of the alterations of 1863—69, and the projection restored to the dimensions shewn on Symons' plan. The stairs, as arranged by him, did not begin until the level of the gallery, and were evidently intended to provide access from the gallery to the rooms above. The extension of the stairs to the ground-floor is modern. According to Symons' design the gallery could be approached either at the east end, by the staircase in the Master's Tower (ibid. *G*), or at the west end, by one of the same breadth as the others in the court[1] (ibid. *H*).

It should be further mentioned, in connection with the New Court, that Mr Booth wished to commemorate himself by building a conduit in it, for which purpose he bequeathed £300. The following extract from a letter to the college, written apparently in March 1616—17, explains his wishes. The writer is Mr Charles Markham, who had married Mr Booth's sole executrix, Mrs Bridget Hord:

"It was his [Mr Booth's] wyll, to gyve £300 to your Colledg to be bestowed vppon the building of a Conduyte in your Courte. To which end it is, and ever shal be, ready, when it shall please you to beginne the worke. For it seemes Mr Boothes desyre was to bestow it soe, as it might continue as a Memoriall, and himself not forgotten.

Notwithstandinge, hearing that you arre not willing for some reasons best knowen to yourselves: To avoyd all suspicion that we intend not to make any vse of this mony by any delay: If it shall please you to bestow it vppon the mayntenance of some poore schollers, or some such lyke purpose as you out of your wisdomes and better experience shall think fitting, allways provyded that it goe not in darkenes, but that he may be admitted as a Fownder, or a Bene-factor, so as he may continue vppon reccord,...the mony shalbe ever ready when it shall please you to demand it."

The college replied (21 March, 1616—17) that they should be most willing to spend the three hundred pounds on a conduit, "did they in any proportion æquall the charge of such a worke"; and suggested that Mr Booth's chief friends should be consulted on the disposal of the bequest[2]. We shall see below that it was spent on an organ for the chapel in 1636—37.

The erection of the Second Court entailed certain alterations in the Old Court, or Upper Court, as it is called in the following extract from the Audit Book for 1604—5[3]. The work was executed in the summer of the latter year:

---

[1] [His alternative design—that which shews an oriel at the west end of the gallery—shews also a staircase leaving the gallery at a point just within the western range of the Court, and apparently intended to lead down to the garden which inter-vened between the Court and the river. There is, however, no evidence that this staircase was ever carried out.]

[2] [Baker's History, p. 479, where abstracts of the two letters are given.]

[3] [In this year some members of Lady Shrewsbury's family visited the college: Audit-Book, 1604—5. *Exp. necess.* "Three payre of gloves to two of the Earle of

" Layde out for the buildinge of the new windowes in the vpper courte;
    for the digging of the courte lower ; and carying out all the
    rubbish ; for paving the whole courte a new, and for peeble and
    sande to the pavinge ; for steppes at the gate, hall doore, chap-
    pell doore, and chamber doores............ij^c. iiij^{xx}. viij^{li}. viij^s. j^d."

The following extracts from a separate account kept for this
work, give useful indications of its nature and progress:

"To the carpenter in working about the framing of the new windowes in
    the vpper courte, and the making of the winding staires, where a
    waye is made into the lane, for 7 weekes together from Jun. 3. to
    July 20 .... v^{li}. xiij^s. ix^d.
To the free masons the same weeke [that ending 31 Aug.] about cantes
    and coynes for the hall side .... xv^s.
For 17. thousand of slate bought of one Yates of Duddington at diverse
    times and of diverse prices .... xv^{li}. xvj^s.
To the glasier for new glasse to .27. windowes and for altering the
    glasse, when it was appoynted to be set within the pillers
    Decemb. 7 .... xiij^{li}. xix^s."]

CHAPTER III.

HISTORY OF THE LIBRARY, AND OF THE THIRD AND FOURTH COURTS.

[IT has been already mentioned that the Library was originally on the first floor to the south of the Gate of Entrance,
where there are still five equidistant windows, each of two lights,
pointed, with a quatrefoil in the head (fig. 3)[1]. These windows
are of a larger size than all the others in the front of the college,
and of a different pattern. It will be seen that there is also a
sixth window of similar design separated by an interval from

Shrewsburies daughters and Sir Henrie Graye one of their husbandes being heere
Julij 29 xviij^s." The Earl of Shrewsbury came six years afterwards : Ibid. 1610—11,
Mids.—Mich. 1611. "For wyne sugar cakes and other banquetting dishes for the
Earle of Shrewsburye xx^s. For a payre of gloves for the earle of Shrewesburye xxx^s."]

    [1] [This is the Library of which the windows were broken in a quarrel between the
undergraduates of Trinity and S. John's. Audit-Book, 1601—2. *Exp. necess.* "For
warning of Trin. Coll. Scholers before the Vice Chancellor for breaking the library
windoes vj^s. For glassing the Library windoes xxvj^s. vj^d." Ibid. 1602—3. *Recepta
forinseca.* "Receuid of Trinity Colledge scholers for breaking o^r. Library wyndowes xl^s."]

the last of the preceding five. This interval was probably always occupied, as at present, by a fire-place, and the sixth window marks the termination of the Library southwards, and shews that it did not extend beyond the eastern range. That it extended so far is seen on the side next the court, where there are six windows, like those on the opposite side, and a half window next the gate-turret. The original entrance to it was through a molded stone doorway at the north-west corner, approached by the south-west turret-stair of the gateway tower[1]. Originally, as at Christ's College, there were no chambers over it; and the braces of the roof are still to be seen in the modern garrets, and in the passage leading to them, which is approached by a door broken through the wall of the above-mentioned turret-stair at the level of the third floor.]

This Library was turned into chambers, or, as Baker calls it, "cantoned out into tenements[2]," in 1616, and the books removed into "the middle chamber over the kitchen," that is, the room on the first floor, the windows of which were altered on the occasion[3]. This, however, was only as a temporary expedient, until a permanent building could be erected; and with this view the following letter was addressed in 1617 to the Countess of Shrewsbury[4]:

" May it please your Ladishipp,

Wee arre so deeply indebted allready to your Ladishipps bounty, as to press you further with our present necessityes wer a point of Incivillity not beseeming gratefull mynds, Especially att this tyme when with greif we heare of your Ladishipps great trobles and expenses in securing your owne estate and fortunes.

---

[1] This stair has a radius of 4 feet 9 inches; that in the corresponding turret to the north-west a radius of only 3 feet 6 inches.

[2] [Baker's History, p. 208.]

[3] [Audit-Book, 1615—16. *Reparaciones.* "P^d. the Carpenters for ther work in turning ye old library into chambers per billam June 8th xviij^s. vj^d. P^d. Atkinson for tymber for ye old Library per billam xxix^{li}. iij^s. vj^d. P^d. for xvj tonne of whyte stone for ye wyndowes of ye new Library at 7^s. the tonne v^{li}. xij^s." The destination of the books is known from the " Prizing" i.e. "appraizing" Book of S. John's College. The room to which they were transferred is there mentioned in 1628 as "the chamber over the kitchen in which the old Librarie books were kept"; and again as "the great middle chamber over the kitchen looking towards both courts in which the old library books were kept."]

[4] [Printed in Baker's History, p. 620.]

Notwithstanding being charged beyond our ability with the building of a new Library, adioyning to your Ladyshipps Courte, and intended for an ornament thervnto, we cowld not be so farre wanting in dutye as not first to acquaynt your Ladishipp therwith before we resolve vppon the worke, the rather for that it carryes show of presumption for vs to alter any parte of your Ladishipp's building without your liking and consent. To this end we arre become humble suitors to your Ladishipp, to approve of this our purpose, and countenance it so farre, as shall stand with your good lyking; and so recommending your Ladishipp to the protection of the Almighty we take leave, and rest

Your Ladyshipps most bounden
the Master and Seniors."

St John's in Camb'
   July 9th 1617.

The answer of the Countess has not been recorded, nor do we know what steps the college proposed to take to obtain the necessary funds. Baker[1], after mentioning the sending of the letter, proceeds as follows:

"The situation, as then intended, was to be from the gate to the river (with loss of one or more chambers in the second court), the building to be erected upon and supported by pillars: but funds were yet wanting, to which purpose several persons were applied to, without meeting with sufficient encouragement to lay the foundation; when unexpectedly a letter [dated 26 April, 1623] came from Dr Carey bishop of Exeter, signifying that an unknown person had promised £1200 to that use, if it were sufficient, but would neither advance higher, nor yet was willing to admit a partner. By this and other letters, an estimate was desired to be made of the expense, and a computation was taken from the two wings of Dr Nevill's court at Trinity, each of which cost in building about £1500; and the allowance being found to be short, the same unknown person was at last prevailed with to advance further £200, provided room could be made for two fellows and four scholars that were likewise designed by him to be founded. What further advances were made does not appear from these letters, excepting £200 or £250 (afterwards promised towards perfecting the work). But the first site and model was disliked, the present plan and situation was agreed on, the lord keeper bishop Williams[2] (hitherto very artfully concealed) owned and declared himself to be the founder by another letter [dated 10 October, 1623] from the bishop of Exeter, and the case of the building was finished by Michaelmas 1624."

[1] [Baker's History, p. 208.]

[2] [John Williams, born at Aberconway in North Wales 25 March, 1582; adm. at S. John's under Owen Gwyn, afterwards Master, 1598; adm. Fellow 14 April 1603. After holding various ecclesiastical preferments he was made Bishop of Lincoln, and Lord Keeper, in 1621; Archbishop of York 1641; died 25 March 1650. Baker's History, pp. 261, 485, 531.]

This Library, built in continuation of the north side of the
Second Court, is 110 feet in length and 30 feet in breadth.
Access to it was provided through the last doorway on the
north side of that Court, by sacrificing a portion of the west end
of the gallery, as explained in the last chapter, and by diminish-
ing one of the rooms beneath it.   The staircase (fig. 8), and the
door through which the Library is entered, over which are carved
the arms of Bishop Williams, and of the see of Lincoln, are rich
and characteristic specimens of the style then in fashion.   The
staircase was finished early in 1628[1].   It has fortunately never
been altered, though there is evidence that a scheme for decorating
it was considered in the middle of the last century[2].   The west end
of the Library is terminated by an oriel window (fig. 9), and its
foundations are laid in the river which washes its walls.   The
ground floor was until recently occupied by chambers [intended
for the use of Bishop Williams's Fellows and Scholars].   The
style is Jacobean Gothic.   The windows of the oriel are large,
lofty, and pointed, divided by a transom, and having tracery
in the heads.   Angle-buttresses with pinnacles flank the river
gable.   In the court there are no buttresses, and the mixture
of Renaissance details is much greater ; the windows, however,
are pointed, of two lights, and have tracery.   [There are large
buttresses between the windows on the north side.]   This
building is a valuable example.   Its interior fittings, as in all
college Libraries, have unfortunately undergone many alterations, from the continual and pressing necessity of providing
shelf-room for new acquisitions, but the original forms may
still be traced by comparison with similar examples[3].   Recently
these fittings have to a great extent been restored to their
original state by the removal of unsightly additions and judicious reproduction of old work.

---

[1] [Audit-Book.   Lady-Day—Mids. 1627—28.   *Expens. necess.*   "Item for
paintinge the Librarie staircase xxxiij[s]. iiij[d].   Item for paintinge stone arch (*sic*) in
the Librarie, and whitinge the gallerie staires at the Commencement xl[s]."]

[2] [Ibid. 1744—45.   *Expens. necess.*   "Burrows for a Plan and Estimate of Stucco
Work for the Library Staircase o. 10. 6."]

[3] [These alterations were begun in 1741 ; Coll. Order 1 June : "Agreed to raise all
the middle classes in the Library " ; and continued in the following year ; Ibid. 12 July
1742, "Agreed to raise all the classes in the library, except the two classes next the
door." They will be further described in the chapter on College Libraries in Vol. iii.]

[A separate account was kept, apparently by the Bursar, for the receipts and expenditure, headed, " Expences for the Librarie in the yeers 1623. 1624." The first item, " My charges with Henry Man Carpenter 5 daies to buy Timber and Bricke for the Librarie" is dated 7 August, 1623. He appears to have made the design, for we presently find, under the same date :

"To Henry Man for drawing of Plots for the Librarie, and his iorneyes to London and North-Hampton shire 7. 7. 0."

The first entries are mainly for the purchase and carriage of bricks[1]; of clunch from Barrington, which was probably used for the foundation ; and of freestone. A scaffold is first mentioned in March, 1624, by which time we may presume that the walls had risen high enough to require one ; in April stone from Peterborough is paid for; and in June the writer of the Account goes into Derbyshire to buy lead. In October the chimneys are built, the walls plastered, and the spouts fixed[2]. By this time the building must have been roofed in, and the date, 1624, which appears on the south gable of the western oriel (fig. 9), therefore marks the conclusion of this part of the work. The name of the founder is commemorated on the central gable by the letters I. L. C. S., the initials of *Johannes Lincolniensis Custos Sigilli*. Large quantities of stone were brought in July and August, 1624, evidently for the windows, from a payment of £1. 0s. 0d. in September "to Ashly for his p^t. working a tracery window." The wooden floor however was not laid until March or April, 1625[3]. On the last page of the Account we find the following record of the glazing of the windows :

[1] [After an entry dated 3 December, 1623, we find : " Here endeth my first bargaine with Widdow Dale for one hundred thousand of Brickes at fourteene shillings the thousand, wch is six score to the hundred ; and all the rest at fifteene shillings ye thousand."]

[2] [9 October 1624. "To Long and Miton in p^t. of their bargain for ye chymneies £30. 0. 0. For haire for the seeling of the walles 4. 0. 0. To Long for ye remainder of our bargain for ye chymneys and end £1. 10. 0. To John Cooper for his eleuen daies worke about the spoutes and gutters, and sixe daies coming and going to his worke 2. 0. 0."]

[3] [March 1625. " To ye Watermen for bringing 300 of Deale boord from Linne and ye Porters here 1. 6. 6. To the Naileman for 1000. of 8^d. Nailes, and 200. of 4^d. Nailes 0. 5. 4." April 1625. " For Broades to naile the Librarie floore 2. 10. 0."]

"To the Glasier in p^t. of payment for the Librarie 20. 0. 0.
Giuen them to drinke at the setting vp of the great window 0. 0. 8."

Fig. 8.   Staircase leading to the Library, shewing part of the ceiling of the Gallery.

From a payment to Grumbald, made apparently in February 1625[1], we ought perhaps to conclude that he had been
employed upon the stone-work, which, being for the most part

---

[1] [To Grimball the free mason feb: 4 for himselfe and his man 11. 19. 7.]

at the upper part of the building, would be executed last. The
cost of the portion of which we have been examining the
history, was £2509. 8s. 6½d. This sum, however, did not include either the ceiling, the fittings, or the glazing of the

Fig. 9.   West oriel of the Library.

windows, notwithstanding the sum already charged under that
head. The total of receipts and expenditure was as follows,
according to a summary preserved by Baker[1]:

[1] [MSS. Baker, xii. 166.   MSS. Harl. Mus. Brit. 7039.   Printed Camb. Antiq.
Soc. Communications, ii. 54.   An accompanying letter says "Mr. Bodurda...
gather'd the account out of Mr. Spell's Books, conferred with Mr. Joh. Symons, who
about that time was Sen. Bursar.   I have it under Mr. Bodurda's hand, who was my
Ld's Chaplain, and without doubt, would do him all right."]

"The building of the New Library in two years,
viz. 1623, 4, besides the roofe within, the Seats, and
the Glazing, which were done severally afterwards,
cost   2509 8   6 ob.

    Item, the Roof within,   160   0   0
    It., promisst to Hen. Man, If he did well, which
was given   010   0   0
    It., for the greater Seats, and lesser Seats   245   0   0
    It., for the glazing   066 13   4

                  Sum Total   2991 1 10 ob.

Sr Ralph Hare[1] gave, which was spent in the
foundation,   0192 00 00

My Lord of Lincoln gave	At severall times	1550	0	0	
	For the roofe within	0160	0	0	
	It. unto Hen. Man	0010	0	0	2011 13 4
	For the great Seats	0200	0	0	
	Towards the lesser Seats	0025	0	0	
	For glazing	0066	13	4	

The rest of the money (besides Jusses &c. all the
time, which must amount to a great Summe) the Col-
lege did pay, being   0787 08 06 ob.

                                  2991 1 10 "

The ceiling, fittings, and glazing, were undertaken immediately, and occupied nearly three years, for the books were not
finally placed in the new library until the spring of 1628[2]. In
the summer of that year, between Midsummer and Michaelmas,
the Bishop came to inspect his gift. His picture had been previously painted at the college expense, and placed in the Library[3].

[1] [The Liber Memorialis (Baker's History, p. 338) says that he gave £300 to
the building of the Library. In the Audit-Book for 1623—24, at the end of *Expens.
necess.*, we find " Layd out towards yᵉ building of yᵉ library Sir Raph Hares whole
yeares rents lxiiijˡⁱ." ; and under *Expens. in lege* " Pᵈ. to D. Spicer for Law-charges
about Sʳ. Raph Hares donation per billam vˡⁱ. xiijˢ."]

[2] [According to Baker the work was retarded by proposals made by Bishop
Williams for founding two fellowships and four scholarships which the college hesi-
tated to accept. Baker's History, p. 209.]

[3] [Audit-Book, 1627—28. 2ᵈ quarter (Lady Day—Midsummer). " Paid for
remouinge the bookes into the newe librarie ijˢ. Pᵈ.... for sweepinge the Librarie
and rubbinge it seuerall times iijˢ. Pᵈ. to Mʳ. Gilbert Jackson for the Bishoppe of
Lincolne's picture for the Librarie xˡⁱ. Item to Hobson for bringinge it from London
and the porter that brought it to the Colledge ijˢ. iiijᵈ." Ibid. 3ᵈ quarter (Mids.—
Mich.) " For remouinge Tables at the Commencement and when the Bishoppe of
Lincolne was here jˢ. iiijᵈ. Item for the banquet at the Bishoppe of Lincolne's
cominge jˡⁱ. 9ˢ. Item wine then jˡⁱ. iiijˢ. Item gloues for the Bishoppe of Lincolne

His arms, which are on the east wall, above the door of entrance, were probably put up at about the same time.

When it became necessary to provide further accommodation for books, the two sets of chambers under the Library, nearest to the river—the westernmost of which is lighted by an oriel window, forming part of that which lights the Library above—were connected with the Library by a spiral staircase of iron. This was done in 1858[1], and in 1874—75 a third set of chambers adjoining to the former were added to the Library, and the remaining chambers on that side of the court were altered so as to form Lecture-rooms. The whole of this floor has been shut off from the adjoining buildings by a strong party wall to remove some of the danger from fire to which the Library had previously been exposed.]

Two sides of a third quadrangle having been provided by the buildings of the Second Court on the east and the Library on the north, the remaining sides were added about fifty years afterwards. The foundations were laid, according to the Commemoration Book[2], in 1669; and the work was finished in exactly four years, at an expense of £5256. 6s. 3d., of which sum £1929 was given by various Benefactors, whose names are duly recorded. The date on the west gable, and on one of the spouts at the south-east corner of the court, is 1671. In architectural style this edifice is a good specimen of Sir Christopher Wren's period, without the smallest attempt at harmony with the previous work, except in the battlements, which are copied from those of the Library. They are worked, however, on a lower level. On the south side next to the back lane the windows are copied from those in the second quadrangle, so that in this part, which is out of sight, uniformity of style is preserved (fig. 12).

ij^{li}. xij^s." The ceiling was commenced between Mids. and Mich. 1626, when we find "P^d. for removing the scaffold poles into the Library ij^s." The books, or some of them, had been brought in previously, and had to be put away while the work was proceeding, for the next entry is "P^d. to Lewys for removing the bookes out of ye new library into ye study xij^d."]

 [1] [College Order, 26 March, 1858. "Agreed to devote the two sets of Rooms under the West End of the Library to the purposes of the Library, and to have the same fitted up for the reception of Bookcases, under the inspection of M^r. Smith of the Fitzwilliam Museum."]

 [2] [MSS. Baker: MSS. Harl. Mus. Brit. 7028, p. 485.]

[The court thus formed measures 87 feet 10 inches along the north side; 122 feet 6 inches along the west side; 73 feet along the south side; and 121 feet along the east side. The western

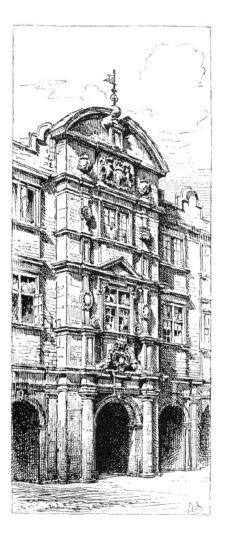

Fig. 10. Central archway on the west side of the Third Court. From The Portfolio, 1880.

and southern ranges are quite distinct (fig. 1), the former abutting against the latter at the south-east angle only. Both are in

towards the river and threatened to fall; an Order was therefore made (13 March) to have the "foundations and superstructure" repaired[1]. A completely new foundation was laid, and
the stacks of chimneys were rebuilt. In front of the northern
half of the building there is a projecting ledge or quay, now
built over (*ab*, fig. 1), which in the seventeenth century was
called the "Foot wharfe."

The southern range has an irregular ground-plan, imposed by
the direction of the river at this point, as the plan (fig. 1) shews.
It consists of two distinct portions; that forming the south side
of the court, which terminates with a lofty and picturesque
gable next the river (fig. 11), and a lower and separate portion,
to the south of the former, which, together with the above-mentioned gable, forms a second portion of the river-front, more
inclined to the east than the former. In this second portion the
floors and windows, except on the ground-floor, are on different
levels from those in the former portion, and the string-courses,
except the lowest, are not continuous. Uniformity is maintained
by the form of the battlements, and of the gables.

Until the fourth court was built, the only way to the walks
was by a passage 8 feet wide, through the south range of the
third court into the lane separating S. John's College from
Trinity College (*cd*, fig. 1)[2]. Loggan (fig. 3) shews that in his
time there were two gateways of brick with stone dressings,
closed with wooden gates, in this lane[3]; one at the south-west
corner of the range forming the west side of the second court;
and a second at the east end of the wooden bridge which then

[etc.]." The foundation of this building seems to have been badly laid from the first:
Audit-Book, 1688—89. *Reparationes*, "To James Nottingham for Materialls and
worke done in repairing yᵉ foundation of yᵉ New Building towards yᵉ River...
14. 17. 05." Ibid. 1693—94. "To James Nottingham for worke done at yᵉ new
building next the River £51. 10. 4. To Mʳ Longland and directions about the new
building by order £5. 10. 0. To Will. Grissell Smith for Iron Worke about the Foot
Wharfe without the new building...£12. 18. 10."]

[1] ["13 March 1841. Agreed that the expense of repairing and restoring the
foundations and superstructure of the western range of buildings in the third Court be
paid out of the funds bequeathed to the College by the late Dr Wood."]

[2] [The building west of this passage (that which terminates with a gable next the
river) is marked "Rath Hall" on the plan described above, p. 274.]

[3] [The gateway nearest to the Bridge had been made by Grumball (as the name is
spelt) in 1687: Audit-Book, 1686—87: "To Robert Grumball for yᵉ stone Cornish
Archetrave and other stonework over yᵉ great Bridge gate 14ˡⁱ."]

crossed the Cam at the end of the lane (fig. 12). The beautiful
stone bridge of three arches by which the older structure has
been replaced (fig. 11) was begun 20 April, 1696[1]. It was exe-

Fig. 12. Part of the Third Court, with the wooden bridge over the Cam, the Tennis Court,
and the fish-ponds : reduced from Loggan.

[1] [The following particulars are derived from an Account at the end of the
division *Reparationes domi* in the Audit-Book for 1711—12. It is headed "An

cuted by Robert Grumbold, freemason; but he did not give the
design, for we find, "spent with Mr Longland and others in ad-
vising about a modell for yᵉ Bridge o. 19. 9." The work proceeded
regularly until 21 April, 1698, up to which time £319. 19s. 3d.
had been spent. It was then suspended until 8 May, 1709, when
it was resumed, and completed before Christmas, 1712. Robert
Grumbold was again employed for the stonework; the carving
of both bridge and gate was executed by Francis Woodward.
The "total expended about this Bridge and Gate Adioyning"
was £1353. 6s. 7d., of which £500 was a legacy from Henry
Paman, M.D., Fellow, who had died in 1695[1]. The gateway
farthest from the bridge (*I*, fig. 1), each of the piers of which
bears a stone eagle, was set up in 1712. The following extracts
from the Audit-Book for 1711—12 record the names of the
artists employed:

"To Robᵗ. Grumbold Free mason his bill for worke and stone vsed
about yᵉ peers at yᵉ end of yᵉ Back Lane next Trinity College 1. 17. 3.
    To Nicholas Biger and John Woodward for cutting two Eagles
placed upon yᵉ peers in yᵉ Back Lane..............................15. 8. 9.
    To Berry Smith his Bills for Iron worke about yᵉ new gates at yᵉ
end of yᵉ Back Lane .... 5. 0. 0."

In 1825 it was determined to increase further the accommodation for students. An attempt was first made to secure a
site on the east side of the river Cam, so that the proposed
buildings might be placed in close proximity to the older ones.
This, however, having been found impossible[2], it was decided
to place the new building on the west side of the river, and the
following Orders were made:

Account of money Layd out per Dʳ Berry sen. Bursar for work and materialls used
in Building the new stone Bridge Leading into the walkes from Apr. 20ᵗʰ 1696 to
Apr. 20. 1698." The first portion of the account contains chiefly payments to
Grumbold for work and materials. We next find "Spent more in Building yᵉ Bridge
from May yᵉ eigth 1709 to [left blank]." Similar entries follow, of which the most
important are quoted in the text.]
    [1] [Lives of the Gresham Professors : by John Ward, fol. Lond. 1740. He
was admitted as a sizar at Emmanuel College, 22 June, 1643; migrated to S. John's
22 July, 1646: adm. B.A. in the same year; M.A. 1650; Public Orator 1672—81:
Gresham Professor of Physic.]
    [2] [College Order, January 29, 1825. "Agreed that we cannot procure in a
reasonable Time a proper site for the erection of additional Buildings for the College
on the East side of the River."]

"February 25, 1825. Agreed to apply to M[r] Wilkins, M[r] Browne, and M[r] Rickman to furnish us with plans and estimates of a Building to be erected on the North Side of the college walks, sufficient for the accommodation of Fellows and Scholars from 100 to 120, and that a plan of the proposed site be furnished to each of them.

Agreed that it be an instruction to the Architects to follow as nearly as may be the style of the present Second Court, with such Improvements as the Architect may suggest. And further to consider the most advisable plan of connecting the new Building with the third Court."

At that time it was not only intended that the style of the Second Court should be followed, but the material also, and in 9 July, 1825, the Bursar was "authorized to take measures for preparing Brick-earth." The following Orders give useful information respecting the history of the proposed building. It will be seen that up to February, 1827, the intention of employing brick was adhered to :

"8 March 1826. Agreed that Mess[rs] Rickman[1] and Hutchinson be employed as architects for our proposed new Buildings.

1 July. Agreed that Mess[rs]. Rickman and Hutchinson be authorized to advertize for contracts for the completion of the basement story of the additional buildings to the College upon the plan this day approved by us.

Aug. 24, 1826. Agreed to accept the Tender of Mess[rs]. T. and J. Bennett for the completion of the basement story of our proposed new Buildings.

Jan. 6, 1827. Agreed that we adopt in general the elevations for the new buildings now before us.

Agreed that the staircases in the new buildings be of stone. Agreed that the exterior of the new buildings be brick of an uniform colour with stone dressings mouldings and ornaments.

Feb. 15. Agreed that the color of the bricks to be used for the facing of the new building be as nearly as possible that of the specimen of red brick now fixed upon, and left in the possession of the master.

Agreed also that the bridge connecting the third court and the new building be of stone.

June 5, 1827. Agreed to accept M[r] Thomas Phipps's tender for executing the New Buildings in Stone.

May 18, 1829. Agreed to adopt the recommendation of the Architects that the roof of the new cloister be constructed of Clunch instead of wood and plaster."]

[1] Mr Thomas Rickman, the celebrated author of An attempt to discriminate the styles of architecture in England, 8vo. Lond. 1817, was then at the height of his reputation and influence in the University. [His partner, Mr Hutchinson, died in 1831, aged 31.]

The buildings were partially occupied in 1830, and completed in 1831. They consist of chambers in four floors disposed about three sides of an oblong quadrangle, to which the names "Fourth Court" and "New Court" have been applied. The length from east to west is 125 feet; and the breadth from north to south 80 feet; but it is narrowed in the middle to 50 feet by the excessive projection of the centre. The material, as ultimately decided upon, is white brick, faced with stone on the south, east and west sides, but left bare on the north side, which cannot be seen from any part of the college grounds. The style is Perpendicular Gothic. The south side is closed by a low cloister having open arches next to the court, and open tracery next to the walks. This cloister is vaulted with clunch. An ingeniously contrived bridge, whose passage is roofed, and enclosed at the sides by open tracery, forms the communication from the older quadrangles. By this device the nocturnal inclosure of the students within the walls is preserved without interfering with free communication between the courts. [It was designed by Mr Hutchinson[1]. There is a handsome gateway in the centre of the cloister, opening into the walks. Very great difficulty and expense was incurred at the commencement of this work by the necessity of creating a foundation in the peaty ground on which it is placed. The foundation was formed by removing the whole of the peat, laying out timber upon the underlying gravel, and building an enormous mass of brickwork upon it until the level of the river was attained. A large substructure of vaulted cellars was then added so as to raise the floor of the lower rooms considerably above the level of the ground. By this means they are rendered perfectly dry though placed in so damp a situation. Much expense would have been saved if the modern concrete foundations had then been understood. The cost of this court was £77,878.]

---

[1] [By the kindness of T. M. Rickman, Esq., Architect, I have been favoured with extracts from his father's diary. It is there noted that a Suspension Bridge was first intended, secondly one of Iron, and lastly, 8 Feb., 1827, "the price of stone being found to be less than we expected, we have nearly determined to make the Bridge of St John's of stone, which will look much better. H. H. has made a beautiful design for it." Some alterations were introduced at the beginning of 1829. The diary unfortunately gives no hint of the reason for using stone instead of brick for the façade.]

CHAPTER IV.

HISTORY OF THE OLD COLLEGE CHAPEL, AND OF THE BUILDING ADJOINING IT ON THE NORTH.

[THE position of this chapel, and its relation to other buildings, will be readily understood from Loggan's general view (fig. 3); and from the ground-plans (figs. 1, 6, 15). The aspect that the

Fig. 13. South side of the First Court, shewing the chapel, with the chantries of Dr Thompson and Dr Keyton; the roof of Bishop Fisher's chantry and of the northern building; and part of the Master's Lodge with the turret-stair leading to it, and the roof of the north wing. Reduced from Loggan. A. Chapel and chapel-door. D. Master's Lodge.

south side presented in 1688 is shewn in Loggan's second view of the college (fig. 13); which may be compared with a view of the west end of the same side taken just before it was pulled down in 1869 (fig. 14). A view of the interior, taken about 1847, is also given (fig. 16).

Before we investigate the original architectural features of the chapel, and of the building adjoining it on the north, it will be convenient to describe, and trace the history of it while used as a College Chapel. We must, however, premise that originally it consisted, as we shall shew presently, of a quire and nave separated by a central tower (fig. 15). The quire (*A*) was enlarged by the removal of the easternmost of the two arches which supported this tower, so as to add to its area the space included between those arches (*B*); and the nave was divided into two parts, of which the easternmost

Fig. 14. North-west corner of the First Court, shewing part of the south side of the Chapel; the oriel window of the Master's Lodge ; and part of the Hall. From a photograph taken before 1863.

(*C*) became the antechapel, and the westernmost (*D*) part of the Master's Lodge. This latter part was divided by two floors into chambers, with very late Perpendicular windows and doors (figs. 13, 14), inserted so as best to afford light and access to them. The ground-floor formed an approach to the Chapel, to the Master's Lodge, and to the Combination Rooms. For this purpose three doorways were made in the old walls: one to the first court of the college (*E*), one to the turret-stair leading to the Lodge (*F*), and one at the north-east end of the western wall as a way to the Combination Rooms (*G*). The original chapel was further altered by inserting Perpendicular windows of three lights each in the north and south walls, and a similar window of seven lights in the east wall; under which a low building (*N*), lighted by three small Perpendicular windows, and finished with a battlement like the rest of the college, was erected. It is clear from Loggan's view (fig. 3) that this was built at the same time as the east front of the college, for the pattern with which that front is ornamented passes across the wall of the portion in front of the chapel. Lastly, the original roof was replaced by a flat panelled roof (fig. 16), and the quire was fitted with a new rood-screen, and new stall-work, the contract for which has been quoted in the first chapter, to suit its extended dimensions. These stalls commemorated Bishop Fisher, as Baker records[1]:

"All the stalls' ends in the Queere of that College had graven in them by the Joyner a Fish and an Eere of wheat. But after he [Bishop Fisher] had suffered at London, my Lord Crumwell then commanded the same Arms to be defaced, and ugly Antickes to be put in their places."

Four chantry-chapels were added at different times to the outside, two on the north, and two on the south, of which those on the north side remained until the final removal of the whole edifice. These chantries commemorated respectively Bishop Fisher (*I*), Mr Hugh Ashton (*K*), Dr Keyton (*L*) and Dr Thompson (*M*). The two latter are shewn by Loggan (fig. 13).

Bishop Fisher's chantry was built by himself between 1525 and 1533, as we learn from Dr Metcalf's Account-books for those years, which have fortunately been preserved. It was commenced 16 June, 1525, and was intended from the first to contain his tomb, as is shewn by the following extract from an Account extending from Michaelmas 1524 to Michaelmas 1525:

"Item gyffin to the Master mason of Ely for drawing a drawght for my lordes tumbe and for his avyse of the chapell.................iij^s. iiij^d.
Item paid to William Wryght lawburer for iij days warke in brekyng downe the Foundacon of the chapell the xvj day off June ....xij^d."

The work proceeded slowly, for it is not until 1528—29 that the stone for the tomb is bought; and the completion of it is not recorded until 1532—33:

[1] [MSS. Harl. 7047. f. 15 b. Baker's History, p. 567.]

"Item to M' Lee the fremason for makyng and settyng vpp the tumbe ....vj^{li}. xiij^{s}. iiij^{d}.

Item to M' Lee the fremason in full payment for my lordes tumbe and for stone to the same tumbe...iiij^{li}."

The chantry occupied the whole space between the chapel and the building to the north of it (fig. 15), part of the south wall of the latter being made to serve as the north wall of the chantry. Its east wall was blocked by the building which stood between it and the street, and therefore the only wall in which an opening could be made was the west wall, where there was one small window. The chantry communicated with the quire by three four-centred arches (fig. 16), of which the central arch is the widest. Each arch has a square head[1]. Above the chantry there was a room, probably intended for an organ-chamber, like the room in a similar position at Christ's College. It opened to the chapel by a large arch, subsequently blocked, 10 ft. 5 in. high, and 7 ft. 11 in. wide, placed directly over the central arch below. There was also a window at each end of the chamber, and one on the north side (fig. 19). No trace of a staircase from the chantry to the chamber could be discovered. The door to the chamber shewn in the illustration is a modern opening made when it was used as a student's room.

The further history of this building need not detain us long. In 1557 we find the altar in it repaired[2]; in the mastership of either James Pilkington (1559—61) or his brother Leonard Pilkington (1561—64) the organ-chamber was "turned into a room or apartment for the advantage of the master"[3]; in 1635—37 the chantry was "adorned and beautified" by Dr William Beale (Master 1633—44) with the additions of a new roof and a window

---

[1] [These arches are now at the south end of the south transept in the New Chapel. See below, p. 343. Baker records (MSS. Harl. 7047. f. 156) "Above his chapell and tombe was graved in Romayn fair letters the sentence '*Faciam vos fieri piscatores hominum,*'" but he does not mention the position of the inscription. A Latin letter of thanks from the College to Bishop Fisher for his Chapel is printed by Mr Mayor, p. 343.]

[2] [Audit-Book, 1557—58. *Exp. nec.* "Item to Bell for settynge vp the table in my lord of Rochester's chappell, and makyng a pece of the frame newe viij^{d}."]

[3] [Baker's History, p. 153. That some material alteration or repair took place in this part of the chapel about 1580 is shewn by a stone with the name of Thomas Pilkington (adm. Fellow 1580) twice scratched upon it being found on the inside of the wall between the above-mentioned arch and the next window westwards.]

in the east wall[1]; in the mastership of Dr John Arrowsmith (1644—53) it was desecrated, and turned into a chamber[2] for the chapel-clerk[3], when the chimney shewn by Loggan (fig. 3) was

Fig. 16.   Interior of the Old Chapel, looking east; reduced from an engraving by Mackenzie in Le Keux's Cambridge.

[1] [These details are taken from the Audit-Books, and Baker's History, p. 218.   In an Inventory taken at Audit 1642 (MSS. Baker, xx. 253, MSS. Harl. Mus. Brit. 7047) we find "In Bp. Fisher's Chappell.   Hangings of red and green Serge round about the Chappell, with white and green lace.   It. one Table covered with ye same. It. 2 Formes.   It. 2 Wooden Casements."]

[2] Baker's History, p. 226.

[3] [In a list of chambers at the end of one of the "Prizing Books," we find "The chapell clarkes chamber which is the lower chamber adjoyning to the north side of the chapell.   The higher chamber [do. do.] called the organ chamber."   This upper room was used as a chamber until it was pulled down.]

probably built; and lastly, it was fitted with seats (apparently not for the first time) in 1671[1]. At some subsequent period the arches were completely blocked, for in the drawing of the interior of the chapel, in Ackermann's History, taken by Mackenzie about 1815, no arches are visible. The stalls on the north side of the chapel are terminated by a pulpit rising as high as the cornice of the panel-work behind them, which was immediately beneath the cills of the windows. Under the pulpit is a reading-desk; and behind it a niche, rising some feet higher, which may have contained a staircase by which the pulpit was approached from Fisher's chantry. This must have covered nearly the whole of the westernmost arch. Nearer to the altar is a piece of panel-work, exactly similar to that still remaining on the south side in 1847 (fig. 16), which must have covered the easternmost arch. The chantry appears to have been disused in Cole's time, if it may be identified with the "old disused chapel" mentioned in the following passage, written in 1773, to record the discovery of the tomb, intended by Bishop Fisher for himself, but removed after his execution 22 June 1535[2].

"Mr. Ashby the President of St John's calling upon me on Friday Morning at Milton, June 4. 1773, told me that in clearing away some Rubbish in an old disused Chapel, at the East End of their College Chapel, in Order to lay aside in it some of their Materials they were now preparing and using in casing with Stone the South Side of their first Court, they lit upon an old Tomb of Clunch, which had the Appearance of having been only prepared in Order to be set up, but never connected together. The 2 Shields at the Head and Feet, are elegantly shaped, but seem never to have had any Thing either carved, or painted on them, being as fresh and neat as if out of the Workman's Hands, and both encircled in a Garland or Chaplet, exactly like those on the Tomb of the Foundress of the College in the Chapel of Henry 7 at Westminster; The 2 Sides are ornamented in great Taste with Figures of Boys supporting an Entablature, where, no Doubt, Inscriptions were designed, but never executed: and the Mouldings at the Top and Bottom, as also the Pilasters, are all finished in a Grecian Taste that

---

[1] [Audit-Book, 1670—71. *Exp. ecclesie.* "To Cornelius Austin for making new seates in Bp. Fisher's Chappell 14. 9. 11."]

[2] [In a note to the following passage Cole adds: "Nov. 1, 1773. All Saints. Mr Ashby calling upon me informed me, that the Chapel, in which this Monument was found, was built by Bp. Fisher, on whose Execution the Tomb was taken to Peices and thrown aside: for in some of the old Accounts, a trifling Sum is charged for Defacing Bp. Fisher's Tomb." Baker also mentions (History, p. 92), that "some venerable fragments [of the tomb] are yet lodged near his chapel, and preserve his memory in their ruins."]

was in Fashion in Henry 7 and 8th's Times ; so I should be apt to
suppose it was designed for one of the first Masters of the College.   Mr
Essex, who drew the Draught in Lead Pencil, spoiled by me, by roughly
scratching it over in Ink to preserve it, on the opposite Page, thinks,
from the Hollow on the Top, that an Image or Figure was designed to
be laid upon it: the Figure however, if there was one, is not yet discovered.   The Monument is now removed to a small vacant Bit of a
Court on the North Side of the Chapel, to the East, and to come at it,
you pass thro' that dismal dark Passage called the Laberinth, which
surrounds the East Part of the Chapel, and that little Chapel at the
East End of the great one, which was probably designed as our Ladys
Chapel, and now of no Use".[1]

According to the measurements written across the sketch, of
which a reduced copy is here given (fig. 17), the sarcophagus

Fig. 17.   Bishop Fisher's tomb : reduced from a rough pencil sketch by Essex.

was about 6 feet 8 inches long, by 2 feet 4 inches broad.   Cole
thus records its fate[2]:

"In 1773, these Parts of the Tomb, quite fresh as new, were displaced out of the Chapel into the Weather, under the Dripping of the
Roof of the Chapel, where I saw them perfect: but the Wet utterly
perished and mouldered them to Peices next Year."

[1] [MSS. Cole, xlv. 89.   Add. MSS. Mus. Brit. 5846.]
[2] [Notes to Baker's History, p. 74.   Add. MSS. Mus. Brit. 5850.]

The other chantry on the north side of the chapel was attached to the antechapel, with which it communicated by an arch under which was the monument of Mr Hugh Ashton. Baker's reference[1] to this chantry is too interesting not to be quoted :

"The last chapel was Mr Hugh Ashton's, well known by his monument, and his rebus upon it, a thing then much in fashion, and must be forgiven to the humour of the age. It has long since lost the face of religion. Many years after its desecration, in Dr Beal's time, it was restored to sacred use, but the times coming on when little regard was had to sacred things and less to sacred places, it was again desecrated, and has not since been restored to such uses, as the other two chapels yet standing have been. It may, 'tis hoped, one day recover that right, and might I choose my place of sepulture, I would lay my body there[2]; that as I owe the few comforts I enjoy to Mr Ashton's bounty, so I might not be separated from him in my death: wherever his body lies, may his ashes rest peaceably! and may I wish him that happiness, which I dare not to pray for, but which my hopes are he now enjoys! I daily bless God for him, and thankfully commemorate him, and could I think he now desired of me what his foundation requires, I would follow him with my prayers and pursue him on my knees."

This chantry (K, fig. 15) was a low oblong rectangular building with a nearly flat roof and a fine oak ceiling. It had a window to the east, another to the west, with a small door by its side, and two to the north. It had long since been separated by a wall from the antechapel, the doorway which led into it and the arch behind the tomb having been built up, and the chantry itself appropriated as an outhouse for the Lodge. Ashton's tomb, however, was allowed to retain its place until it was removed to the north transept of the new chapel (D, fig. 25).

---

[1] [Baker's History, p. 93. For Ashton's Life see Cooper's Athenæ, i. 27. He died 23 November, 1522. Baker (MSS. xii. 58) gives the following extract from his Will, proved 9 March 1522 : "My body to be buried in S^t. Johnnes the Evangelists college at Cambridge, before the awter, where the priests of my foundation shall synge, ...Also I gyve to ye buyldinge of my chapell, where my Body shall rest, with two Awters, wherat my s^d Felowes and Scolers shall say Masse, when they shall be disposed : And there in the wall to be made my similitude in two ymages, one lyvely and another dedely, in the perfourmynge of ye same, over and besides suche money, as afore I have gyven thereunto 20 lib. in caas I fynyshed not my self."]

[2] [On this Cole remarks, Notes to Baker's History, p. 75 : "M^r. Baker had his Wish : for I saw his Body put into a Grave very near M^r. Ashton's Tomb, in the Antichapel. I was at his Funeral, which was very solemn, with Procession round the first Court in Surplices and Wax Candles, the Funeral Service performed by D^r. Phil: Williams, and the Service chanted to the Organ. His Nephew, a Fellow Commoner of the College, George Baker Esq., was cheif Mourner. M^r. Baker lived up one Pair of Stairs in the 3^d. Court on the South Side." He died 2 July, 1740.]

On the "ledger" lies a painted recumbent effigy of Dr Ashton
vested in his academic robes.   Beneath is a second effigy
representing him as an emaciated corpse, according to the directions in his Will.   Round the edge of the "ledger" is an inscription on a bronze label, recording his benefactions and the date
of his death.   Over the whole tomb is a stone canopy, formed
of two four-centered arches, joined by panel-work; in the
spandrils of which Ashton's rebus, an ash leaf growing out of a
tun, is carved.   The whole is finished above by a stone cresting.
A grating of contemporaneous iron-work, also bearing his inscription[1], protects the sides of the tomb.   The rebus occurs again at
the four corners of this grating, and in the middle of each side.

A few notices respecting the history of this chantry and
tomb are worth recording.   During the mastership of the two
Pilkingtons (1559—1564), according to Baker, it was "converted
to profane uses."   The tomb however was carefully preserved[2].
Between 1634 and 1636 it was thoroughly repaired, within and
without, and refurnished as a chapel, as the following entry from
the Audit-Book for 1635—36 shews[3]:

"Payd to Mr Nicholson the Income of Dr Ashton's chappell heretofore vsed for a Chamber, but now vsed and adorned as a Chappell,
besides xv^s wch some old wainscott there did yeild ....iiij^{li} xv^s."

In the record of the general restoration of the chapel in
1636—37, to be quoted below, Ashton's chapel and tomb are
mentioned; and in the following year a repair to the iron-work
about the tomb is specially commemorated[4].   It was however
again desecrated by the Puritans, by whom it was brought into
the condition that Baker deplores.

[1] [The two inscriptions will be found in the Appendix.]

[2] [Audit-Book, 1561—62.   *Exp. ecclesie.*   " Item to a painter for newe greeninge
the trees on Mr Ashtonnes tombe xvj^d."]

[3] [Ibid. 1635—36.   *Exp. necess.*   4th *quarter*, i.e. Mich.—Christmas 1636.   In
the Audit-Book for 1634—35 we find "To Abraham Evans by our M^{rs} appointment
for the hangings in Ashton's Chappell v^{li}. v^s."; and the Inventory mentioned above,
records: "In Dr Ashton's Chappell.   Hangings of red and green Serge round about
the Chappell, of half yard broad, with white and green Lace."]

[4] [Ibid. 1637—38.   *Exp. ecclesie.*   " Payd to John Graves the Colledge Smith for
worke about D^r. Ashtons Tombe, viz. 4 flower de lyses vj^s.   Item for 22 iron pikes
xxij^s.   Item a new Crowne ij^s.   Item iron worke for the 6 Tunnes vij^s.   Item for
making cleane the barres taking them downe and setting vp twise xiij^s.   Item making
cleane the 6 great postes iij^s. .... ij^{li}. xij^s. iiij^d."]

Opposite to Ashton's chantry was that of Dr John Keyton (*L*, fig. 15), of which Baker speaks as "now demolished[1]." It had probably been erected soon after 1533[2]; and in size and plan closely resembled that of Ashton. It was an oblong rectangular building (fig. 13), the east and west sides of which abutted upon the fifth and sixth buttresses. There was a buttress at each of the angles and one in the middle of the south side. There were also two small windows of three lights each on the south side. It opened into the antechapel by a door and a low four-centered arch. The arch was $7\frac{1}{2}$ ft. wide, but only 4 ft. 2 in. high, nearly flat, ornamented with a finial and crockets. The slab beneath it, which may have borne an effigy or have been intended for one, was 5 feet above the old pavement, and had a panelled space below it with three large shields with much-defaced heraldic bearings. The door was 7 ft. high and 2 ft. 9 in. wide. In the spandrels was the rebus of Keyton, a key springing out of a tun[3]. The roof of this chantry was extensively repaired in 1635[4], and Loggan shews that it was in existence in 1688. The period of its destruction can only be conjectured, as will be shewn below.

Dr Thomas Thompson's chantry (*M*, fig. 15) was opposite to that of Bishop Fisher. Loggan (fig. 13) shews it to have been a small low building, fitted into the angle between the west wall of the range of chambers forming the front of the college, and the south wall of the chapel. It did not extend beyond the second buttress. It had an oriel on the south side, and one small window on the west side, and it communicated with the chapel by a narrow doorway (*g*, fig. 15, fig. 18) placed quite close to the second buttress. Eastward of this doorway there was a large

---

[1] [Baker's History, p. 92. Notwithstanding this statement, Blomefield, writing in 1750, says (Collect. Cantab. p. 122) "The *Vestry* here was formerly a *Chapel*, founded by Dr *Heton* (or *Keyton* as *Fuller* calls him)...; he lies buried under the old arched Tomb between that and the Antichapel, as Mr *Baker* informed me." At the time of the destruction of the chapel there was no vestry.]

[2] [In this year Keyton conveyed £300 to S. John's College for the foundation of certain fellowships and scholarships. Cooper's Athenæ, i. 48.]

[3] [Some Account of S. John's College Chapel, [etc.], by F. C. Woodhouse, S. John's College [B.A. 1850; M.A. 1853]. 8vo. Camb. 1848.]

[4] [Ibid. 1634—35. *Exp. ecclesie.* "Paid Kendall the plummer in money besides old lead allowed him for new leading the Vestry in the outward Chappell toward the Court Aug. 31. xv[li]. xj[s]. iij[d]."]

altar-tomb (*h*, fig. 15), and over it perpendicular work, like that of a window, 7 ft. 5 in. wide, but only 4 ft. 9 in. high, divided into five panels[1]. The door to the chantry was four-centered. It was 5 ft. 9 in. high, and 2 ft. 3 in. wide. On its eastern side the jamb of an earlier doorway remained, and the space between was filled with rough red brick-work. Over the more modern door there was a broken space in the wall, which may have formed a niche for a statue; and between the top of the door and that space there was a horizontal rough stone, from which an inscription had evidently been removed. These details will be readily understood from the woodcut (fig. 18).

Fig. 18. Part of the south wall of the quire of the old chapel; shewing the door to Dr Thompson's chantry, altar-tomb, hagioscope, etc.

The materials for the history of this chantry are exceedingly scanty. It was already in existence when Fisher built his chantry, for, in the letter of thanks addressed by the college to

---

[1] [Professor Babington, St John's College Chapel, p. 14, considers that "these panels may have been brought from some other place, for they bore the matrices of small brasses, apparently turned upside down. On one of the panels the name IOHN. OVERALL and also C : I : C : R were rudely cut as with a pocket-knife." The presence of Overall's name, who is stated by Baker (p. 172) to have been eighteen years old in 1577, proves that the tomb must have been open at the end of the 16th century. In the present century the remains shewn in the woodcut (fig. 18) were "blocked up with stones and mortar, and quite covered by wainscoting of the Tudor period."]

him, it is spoken of as surpassed in beauty by the new structure; but the precise year of its erection is not known[1]. Baker speaks of it as still standing in his own time; and we have seen that Cole, writing in 1773, says that it had to be traversed in order to get round the east end of the chapel. It is not known when it was pulled down, but the removal was so complete that only very slight traces could be found of the foundations of it when the new lecture-rooms were commenced in 1869. It was then discovered that it occupied the site of an older rectangular building, perhaps the sacristy. These foundations extended into the court for a distance of 9 feet from the eastern side of the second buttress, and were then carried parallel with the wall of the chapel up to the college buildings. Probably the additions made to them when the sacristy was altered into a chantry for Dr Thompson were very slight, or consisted only of the bay window, and were easily removed when the chantry was pulled down, for no indications of the former existence of that window were observed. On the western side of the foundation of the sacristy, and external to it, a small portion of pavement formed of glazed tiles was met with at a depth of $2\frac{1}{2}$ feet below the present level of the ground. It is not known how far this pavement extended, as further excavation could not be made.

The building of which we have been describing the plan was probably arranged as a college chapel between 1516 and 1519. In the former year the heading "Cost of the Chapel" (*Custus capelle*) occurs for the first time in the Accounts, and in the latter payments are recorded to stonemasons, carpenters, and glaziers, for their work upon the chapel[2]. In the earliest Account preserved, that extending from Christmas 1510 to Michaelmas 1511, we find that mass was celebrated for the first twenty-three weeks of the period of the Account in the Church of S. Sepulchre, and for the last sixteen in what is called "the church of the College[3]." As no payments to workmen are set down,

---

[1] [On Dr Thompson see Cooper's Athenæ, i. 76. He resigned the mastership of Christ's College in 1517, and became vicar of Gateley in Norfolk. The chantry was probably built before he left the University.]

[2] [Audit-Book, 1518—19. *Custus capelle.*]

[3] [Ibid. Christmas 1510—Mich. 1511. "Item domino Barkar pro celebracione misse in ecclesia sepulcri per viginti tres septimanas xxiij[s]. Item domino Weste [one of the Fellows] pro consimili in ecclesia collegii per sedecim septimanas xvj[s]."]

we may conclude that in June 1511 the Society was sufficiently organized to require a chapel of their own, and that the chapel of the Hospital was at first made use of without alteration.

For the history of the building down to 1869 several interesting particulars may be selected from the Audit-Books. Those for the years in the reigns of Henry the Eighth and Edward the Sixth, when the altars, rood, etc., were probably taken down, have unfortunately not been preserved. In the reign of Philip and Mary we find the rood, and the altars—apparently three in number—being set up again, and vestments and furniture ordered. The "organ in the quire" is also mentioned[1]. In the first year of the reign of Elizabeth these ornaments were all removed—as we have observed was the case elsewhere. We find the following entries between Midsummer and Christmas 1559, which give a more than usually full account of what then took place:

> "Inprimis to Baxster the stationer for xij englishe saulters　　xxix^s.
> Item to hym for twoo Communion books　　　　　　　　x^s.
> Item Mr Kalke for xij papers conteninge ye lordes prayer　　vj^d.
> Item to Johne Waller and his man for a dayes workinge pulling down the hye Alter and caring it awaye xx^d.
> Item to a poore fellowe wch helpede to carie awaye ye stone of ye alter iiij^d.
> Item to ye glasier for settinge xxj paines of newe glasse in ye windowes of chappell and for alteringe ye crucifixe ij^s. ix^d.
> Item for pulling downe ye aulter in doctor Ashton chappell vj^d.
> Item to the mason for leyinge downe certaine stones aboute the hie alter vj^d.
> Item to Underwood and other for pulling downe ye alter on ye southe side of ye lower chappell and caryinge ye grauell to ye causye of ye backe side xij^d."

This was followed in 1561 by a thorough whitewashing, which occupied nine days; and in 1564 the commandments in English were set up[2]. In 1597—98 the "border of the chapel"

---

[1] [Audit-Book, 1555—56. *Exp. ecclesie.* "Item to the Joyner for setting vp ye Roode ij^d." 1556—57. "Item to Bell the Carpenter and his three men for mending the Aultars...iiij^s j^d ob." 1557—58. "Imprimis for xv elles of fyne Canvas to staine for the lowe alters in the chappell xv^s. Item for a table of the passion of chryst for the hye alter xxxiij^s. iiij^d. Item for makynge a lecturne for ye orgaines in the quere iij^s."] The list of benefactors drawn up in 1528 tells us that "Sondry and diuers marchauntes in London gave emongst theyme x^{li} towardes the byeing of the newest Orgaynes."]

[2] [Ibid. 1560—61. *Exp. ecclesie.* "Item to Waller for ix dayes worke in whitynge the chappell and for plasteringe it in many places xiiij^s. iij^d." Ibid. 1563. "Item to

was repaired. This consisted of a crest of woodwork above hangings of green say, of which 38 yards were bought in the same year[1]. Unfortunately the part of the chapel where it was placed is not specified; but the length mentioned would have been sufficient for the backs of the stalls together with the return of the same at the west end. Five years afterwards—between Michaelmas and Christmas 1605—the "wainscoting of the chapel" is paid for, but, though the sum is large, the whole building can hardly be meant, and again no particulars are given. At the same period the antechapel was paved, and a new door made on the north side[2].

We now come to the important beautification carried out during the mastership of Dr William Beale (Master 1633—44). Much of the work then executed remained until 1868. It is thus summed up by Baker[3]:

> "His zeal herein appeared further in his private college in the solemn offices of religion and in the ornaments of the chapel, which having been left very naked by some of his predecessors was adorned and beautified by him. The east end of the chapel was faced with a decent wainscot, the rest hung with sixteen pieces of hangings containing the story of our Saviour, the roof painted at no small expense; the bare charges of painting and pictures amounted to £100 and upwards. A decent table was placed for the communion, with rails and tapers and plate...with rich coverings of velvet and cloth of silver, besides the cost that was bestowed about the organ, cherubims and other furniture; thus far pretty unexceptionable, had not the dove and glory been added to the account, that furnished Mr Prynn[4] with an objection, and might as well have been let alone. Mr Ashton's chapel (formerly used as a chamber) with Bishop Fisher's, were now likewise adorned and beautified at a considerable expense, the particulars too

Mr Baxter for x geneva psalters and sixe service psalters bought at Chrystmas laste xxij^s. Item for the tenne commaundementes in Englyshe x^d."]

[1] [Audit·Book, 1597—98. *Exp. necess.* "To Mathewe ye Carpenter for makinge and mendinge some of the carved creste in the Border of ye Chappell viij^s. For thirtie eyght yards of Greene Saye at xvj^d. a yarde for the borderinge of the chappell l^s. viij^d. For fyve pillers in the Creste of the Chappell border [and other charges] v^s."]

[2] [Ibid. 1604—5. *Exp. necess.* (4re quarter). "Payde to Goodman Betson the ioyner for wainscottinge the chappell, and for mending the old seates there...xxviij^li. x^s. viij^d. To 3 masons Decemb. 14. for a weekes worke aboute the setting of the paving in the lower chappell, and the working of a new doore into the woodyarde xxij^s. To Longe and his labourers Decemb. 14 in plastering and whiting the lower chappell and making vp the wall where the olde doore was into the woodyard...xxvij^s. ix^d."]

[3] [Baker's History, p. 217.]

[4] [Canterburies Doome, Ed. 1646, p. 74.]

minute to be insisted on. But that the chapel furniture might be placed in a better light, a new window was struck out towards the east, the large window at the east end being somewhat obscured by painted glass then added for its greater beauty."

The total sum expended, as set down in the Audit-Book for 1636—37, was £435. 7s. 6½d. This however does not include the donations of individuals, who were solicited in Latin letters to contribute[1], nor the cost of the organ, which was put up in 1634—35[2]. The carpentry work about "the Organ loft and staires to it" was done by Henry Man, who had been already employed about the Library. While the work was proceeding, prayers were read in the Hall[3].

It was not long before some of these decorations were removed, for in the Audit-Book for 1642—43 we find:

"Item payed by Mr Heron the Ju. Bursar for taking down the pictures and the organs and whiting the walls £2. 8. 6."

and in the following year:

---

[1] [Specimens of these are given in the notes to Baker's History, pp. 517, 518. The college also sold 214 ounces of plate, which realized £52. 10s. 6d., about which we find at the end of the Audit-Book for 1635—36: "Memorandum that these pieces of Colledge plate hereafter specifyed being growne old and vselesse were sould att London by order of the Master and Seniors who did then purpose y^t the money should goe towards the Organs, wch since was wholy payd for with Mr Bowthe's money."]

[2] [The name of the maker has not been recorded, but in 1636—37 we find "To Mr Dallam for tuneing and repayring the Organs xl^s." He is employed again in 1638—39. After the Restoration it was tuned in each year by Thamar.]

[3] [The following extracts from the Audit-Book for 1636—37 give useful information about the details of the work: "Raysing the seats in the Chappell...xlvj^li. xij^s. iij^d. To Edward Woodroofe for 4 new statues in the fellowes seats, and 12 heades for the old statues in the seates in the chappell xx^s. To Jane for sweeping the Hall when Prayers were read there iij^s. For 34 brasse Candlestickes to be fastened in the fellowes and schollers seates v^li. xiij^s. iiij^d. To Hopwood & Luttiehuis...xl^li. vj^s. viij^d. Payd to Woodrofe for the wainscott worke at the east end 23^li. Item for angells and wings 30^s. 8^d. Item to Lambe for plates to fasten the angels 3^s. 8^d. To Knuckells for the roofe 32^li. 17^s. 10^d. for the seates 5^li. Payd more by Dr Allot to Luttiehuis for painting the new wainscott worke at the east end 9^li. 10^s. Item more to him for the Pictures about the Chappell 56^li. 1^s. 3^d. Item more [to] Knuckells for paynting the seates 20^li. 10^s. Item more to him for the roofe for Bish. Fishers Chappell, for Dr Ashton's Chappell and Tombe, etc. 48^li. 14^s. 7^d. ob. wherof 26^li. 18^s. was repayd to Dr Allot out of Mr Boothes money, sic remanet 21^li. 15^s. 8^d. ob. Item payd by him to the free-mason in Dr Ashton's Chappell 6^s. Item to the Turner for 3 Tunnes 3^s. Item to Betson for the 2 railes at the ends of the Altar 40^s. Item to Billop for frames for the pictures 6^li. 1^s. 5^d. Item for 6 candlesticks to Tabor 10^s. Item to Woodrofe for the Dove of glory 25^s. Payd in all by Dr Allot [Senior Fellow] cxviij^li. ij^s. iiij^d. ob."]

" For taking downe the Crosse over the bell Tower, March 22....
o. 4. o."

"Paid to old Dowsy when the Organ case was taken away...o. 6. 8."

In 1660—61 repairs to the chapel are mentioned, but no details are given, except the setting up of the altar; and in 1671 a piece of tapestry-work of gold and silver was provided for the east end.   The donor's name has not been recorded[1].

In 1661—62 the organ is mentioned in a way which shews that it had not been destroyed when taken down eight years before.   The organ-screen, probably part of Dr Beale's work, blocked the chancel-arch, and concealed its fine proportions.   A seat was provided in it for the Master, approached from the Lodge by a passage carried across the antechapel.   We will quote the following description of this curious arrangement[2]:

"Opposite this entrance [to the Chapel, fig. 15, *E*] is a staircase which now leads to the apartments [of the Master] before mentioned, and on the right is the partition-wall [ibid. *c d*] with two apertures which serve as doors, one for the Master, and the other for the rest of the College.   On passing through these, the scene is remarkably un-ecclesiastical; for...we perceive, supported on unsightly wooden pillars of some undiscovered order, the end of a room which extends four or five feet beyond the supporting wall.   To make the appearance still more extraordinary, something which, for want of a better name, I should call a flying gallery, extends from the rood-screen to the end of this same intrusive chamber."

The stall-work, which has been removed to the new chapel[3], was in the main that contracted for in 1516.   There were, however, more modern seats at the east end, put up in

<hr/>

[1] [Audit-Book, 1671—72. *Exp. Ecclesie.* "For materialls and work about ye Hanging at ye East end of ye Chappell £4. 7. 2." Ibid. 1672. " For Carriage of ye Hanging at ye East end of ye chappell from London 6^s.; for Cords, matts, and packing up 5^s.; for silk and mending of it o. 10. o.; for making up ye Sarcenet Curtain before it (wch was Given by ye Master), for Curtain-rods and rings, tenter-hooks, silk Ferret-ribbands &c. paid to Mr Shuter per bill. 6. 4. o.   In toto 07. 05. 00.   For silk-twists, brasse Pulleys, &c. for ye Curtain over ye Hanging...06. 04. 00." Ibid. 1715—16. " Paid to Mr Hutt for Cleansing a piece of Tapestry of Gold and Silver containing 102 Ells at 3^s. per Ell, 15. 16. o."]

[2] [Woodhouse, ut supra. The Master's seat in the Organ Loft was in existence in 1691: Audit-Book, 1691—92: "For a Turkywork Carpett for ye Master Seat in ye Organ Loft 5^s." The room which projected into the antechapel is called in the Audit-Book for 1633—34 "Our Master's Gallery over the lower chappell."]

[3] [The rood-screen is now in the south transept of the church of Whissendine in Rutlandshire.]

1647—48[1]; and plain cross-benches in the centre aisle, added in the present century.

The high "linen" panel-work at the east end—of which the portion on the south side alone remained when our illustration was taken (fig. 16)—was Jacobean in style, and was probably part of the work done in 1647—48. The same illustration shews that the tapestry on the east wall had then been taken down, and replaced by a picture, to accommodate which the lower part of the east window had been blocked. This work, representing "S. John Preaching in the Wilderness," by Sir Robert Ker Porter, was put up in 1799[2]. It was replaced in 1841 by a "Pietà," by Antony Raphael Mengs, presented by the Hon. Robert Henry Clive, M.A.

It should be mentioned that the outside of the chapel was stuccoed in 1784, and again "faced with patent stucco in imitation of stone" at the beginning of the present century, when it is probable that Dr Thompson's chantry was removed[3].

The history of the college chapel having been related, we will next investigate the style and arrangements of the older buildings. These had unquestionably formed part of the Hospital, but the use to which they had been put by the brethren cannot be determined with equal certainty. Professor Babington considers that the northern building was the Infirmary. Professor Willis, writing, it must be remembered, before these buildings were pulled down, and therefore before he had had the opportunity for examining them in detail which afterwards presented itself, spoke of the northern building as "chapel, or refectory, or dormitory"; and noted it in his sketch-book as the "Bede-house[4]." The style was assigned by him to the

---

[1] [Audit-Book, 1647—48. *Exp. ecclesie.* "Item to M[r] Ashley for 2 pieces of Seeling on each side of y[e] Chappell at the East, and containing 7 yards 7 foot at 6[s]. 6[d]. per yard 2[li]. 10[s]. 6[d]. ; for a freize about the topp of the seeling 3[li].; and for an arcatrive and linings betwixt the sieling 3[s]. : 5. 13. 6. Item to M[r] Ashley for making the seats at the East end of the chappell, for timber, nayles, and Workmanshipp per billam March 8th. 11. 13. 0."]

[2] [Audit-Book, 1799—1800. "J. Harris. Frame of Painting in Chapel £69. 6. 6. Harraden; putting up Painting £3. 18. 0."]

[3] [College Order, 15 July, 1784. Baker's History, p. 1088. Harraden's Cambridge, p. 131. He adds that the stucco cost between £400 and £500.]

[4] [His plan of the chapel, here reproduced (fig. 15), is endorsed "measured and

Early English period. Again, with reference to the college chapel, he says, "the walls of the chapel......are of Early English construction, as may plainly be seen on the north side, and on the east side, where the buttresses remain with Early English string-molds, and corbel-table along the wall, and traces of the heads of the Early English windows. The proportion and projection of the buttresses next the quadrangle are also of that period. It is scarcely necessary to add that it must have been the chapel of the Hospital."

This passage proves that, when he wrote it, he held that the two buildings ought to be assigned to the same architectural period. The style of the chapel of the Hospital—as it will be called in deference to his opinion—is again discussed by him in the following passage. After quoting the opinion of Baker, that it was "a great mistake" to suppose that the college chapel had been the chapel of the Hospital, because "whoever considers the state of the old house will hardly imagine that such a chapel was intended for a master and four or five brethren, for they were usually no more[1]," he remarks: "Baker discusses the point concerning the chapel of the Hospital in a manner that offers a very instructive example of the use of the architectural knowledge of the present century. By the aid of this it was seen at once that the present chapel is an earlier chapel altered; for on the north side two Early English buttresses remain, and the traces and fragments of the hood-molds of windows, of different form and dimension from the existing ones, which are thus shewn to have been inserted in the walls. The north wall of the chapel is therefore that of the old one. Again, the Early English arch which still spans the organ-loft proves that the south wall also is in the same place as in the

laid down by me, June 1869." Unfortunately his health gave way at the end of that year, and he was unable to write out the description of the buildings, for which he had made copious notes and sketches. These, which it is not easy to decipher or understand, have been carefully studied by myself and my friend the Rev. D. J. Stewart, who had examined the building on several occasions with Professor Willis, in the hope of giving such a description of them as he would have approved. I have also to thank my friend Prof. C. C. Babington for permission to use his History of the Infirmary and Chapel of the Hospital and College of St. John the Evangelist at Cambridge, 8vo. Cambridge, 1874, from which a number of passages have been borrowed, almost without alteration.]

[1] [Baker's History, p. 69.]

old chapel, and that the two were of the same breadth. Moreover, the size of a chapel or church is no index to the number
of endowed members of a collegiate establishment. Baker himself was compelled to modify his opinions upon this point;
for in a note he adds: 'Upon further enquiry, only the ante-
chapel with the chambers above it seem to have been new
built; the rest old; and yet the lead, stalls, glass, vestry, etc.,
were all certainly new.'"

Had the building which afterwards became the chapel of
the College been the chapel of the Hospital and nothing more,
it would hardly have required an alteration so thorough as to
amount almost to a new construction, as has been recorded in
Chapter I., and as Baker admits. It is only by the study of
ancient structures similar in intention to S. John's Hospital
that an accurate idea can be formed of the original destination
of these remains. The principal differences of arrangement
observable in such buildings have been well stated as follows:

"The component parts that appertain to nearly all [the charitable
institutions of the 14th, 15th, and 16th centuries remaining in England]
will be found to consist of an audit-room, occasionally with a muniment room adjoining; a suite of apartments, more or less extended,
for the master or chaplain; an infirmary for the sick; a common hall;
a suite of living-rooms for the inmates; and, lastly, a chapel, which,
with becoming significance, was always more ornamental in character
than the other buildings. In the relative position of these, four principal kinds of arrangement present themselves.

The first, and that of which the characteristics are, perhaps, the
most definite, is to be found in those instances where the abodes of the
inmates were all under one spacious roof; the area being subdivided
into small dwelling-rooms or dormitories. This hall communicated
directly with the chapel beyond, from which it was only separated by
an open screen, thereby affording an opportunity to the sick and aged
of hearing the recital of the Church's Offices, from which, supposing
the chapel to be a distinct building, they would otherwise have been
debarred. The *motif* of this wise and thoughtful arrangement may
probably have originated with the ancient monastic infirmaries, and
among the examples will be found the Bede Houses at Stamford and
Higham Ferrers, and S. Mary's Hospital at Chichester.

The second kind is where the dwelling-rooms for the inmates were,
as before, under one roof; but the chapel, though immediately contiguous to the hospital, was a distinct building, and entered from without; an example of this kind is to be found at S. John's Hospital,
Northampton.

A third variation is where the abodes of the inmates formed one

W. Hodson Phot.

Hudson & Son, e. Photogr.

Fig. 19. South wall of the Hospital of S. John the Evangelist, with Bishop Fisher's Chantry, and part of the old Chapel; from a photograph taken in 1863. From Professor Babington's work on S. John's College Chapel.

Vol. II.

continuous suite of buildings, sometimes within a quadrangle, but not, like the foregoing, included under one roof, the church or chapel being altogether distinct, but connected with the hospital buildings by an ambulatory or cloister, or by a short covered way only. Examples of this kind exist at S. Cross, near Winchester, Ewelme in Oxfordshire, and Cobham in Kent.

A fourth mode of arrangement, differing somewhat from the foregoing, is to be met with in the case of Ford's Hospital at Coventry, where the plan consists of a central open court, on each side of which are the almoners' abodes, at one end of the quadrangle the common hall of the hospital, and facing it, at the other end, the chapel."[1]

The building next S. John's Lane (*H*, fig. 15) was fitted up to accommodate students in 1584—85, as already recorded. On the side next the college all the old work had been destroyed or hidden by modern alterations. On the side next S. John's Lane there were the outlines of an old doorway which had manifestly been altered at least once, and of two or three lancet-windows. The east end presented to view in S. John's Street a wall of red brick terminating in a gable, and pierced by three very late windows giving light to three floors (fig. 3). An Early English triplet was discovered in this wall. The west end, so far as we know, was always plain and devoid of any openings. The removal of the floors shewed that the whole building had formed one long room, 71 feet in length by 17 feet 6 inches in breadth internally. The walls were 2 feet 2 inches thick[2].

Fortunately it was necessary to retain a part of the south wall, to prevent the back of Bishop Fisher's chantry (*I*, fig. 15), which was full of seats used in connection with the chapel, being laid open. This part of the wall had recently formed one side of the passage (ibid. *N*), made to give access to the rooms called "The Labyrinth," and had therefore been plastered, and whitewashed. The removal of this plaster exposed to view some beautiful remnants of the old edifice as shewn in the accompanying plate (fig. 19)[3], taken from a photo-

---

[1] [Examples of Ancient Domestic Architecture. By F. T. Dollman, 4to. London, 1858. Preface, pp. xiii.—xv. The Hospital had certainly a Hall, for in one of their Accounts, dated 1485, we find "Item pro j .C. cirpis pro Aula ..iiij d."]

[2] The eastern wall had been reduced to 1 foot 7 inches, and again thickened by the brick-facing, so as to become 2 feet thick, like the rest.

[3] [Prof. Babington describes this plate as follows, p. 51: "This plate represents the inner side of the eastern end of the south wall of the Infirmary, as it appeared after

graph. We may perhaps judge of the original state of the
north and south walls by these remnants of the south wall,
which we will now proceed to describe.

The Early English windows were not spaced at equal
intervals in the wall (fig. 15), neither were they all similar.
The easternmost of the
series had more elaborate
moldings than the rest, and
the "escoinson" rib was carried by shafts (fig. 19). The
other windows were plainer,
as shewn by the sketch (fig.
20) of the fourth window,
the only one of which the
cill had not been destroyed.
Beyond this there were
traces of only two more
windows; but as the wall
extended 25 feet 5 inches
to the west of the sixth
window (the last observed),
it may be reasonably con-
cluded that at least three
more windows originally
existed in it.

Between the fourth and
fifth windows there were
traces of a doorway (*i*, fig.
15) from which the stone
jambs had been removed;
and opposite to it there was
a similar opening (ibid. *k*).
Between the first and se-
cond windows a piscina

Fig. 20,   Fourth lancet-window (counting from
the east end) on the south side of the northern
building : from a sketch by Professor Willis.

the coat of plaster by which all the details were hidden had been removed, and the
rubbish that filled the arches taken out....We see the range of Early English windows
and the square opening [between the 1st and 2nd] ; below them the modern doorway
in which the man is standing, which was driven through the wall to afford access to
the building after its conversion into rooms ; next to it the Piscina, now in the new

was found (ibid. *r*, fig. 21), much resembling the examples at Jesus College and at Histon, as has been explained above (p. 136). The

Fig. 21. Piscina. From Professor Babington's work on S. John's College Chapel.

Chapel; further on an older doorway, which must have once communicated with Fisher's chantry; again, further to the right, the mere outline of the ancient south door of the building. Beyond these remains another modern doorway had been made to give access to the small court between the building and the Chapel. On the face of the wall above the early windows are traces of several successive roofs: the upper one crossing the Perpendicular window of the supposed organ-chamber, access to which was obtained by a staircase leading to the square-headed doorway to the right, shewn as recently bricked up. To the right and left of these buildings parts of the Chapel

piscina at S. John's College is wider than that at Jesus College, but not so lofty; the two side shafts stand free from the wall, and their bases, as well as the base of the central one, rest on a table in which two shallow basons are rudely hollowed out. The central shaft is connected by a bracket with the back of the niche, which is 9 inches from the face of the wall. The two side-spandrels are only partially open. The western bason has a plain circular shape; the eastern, that of a quatre-foiled circle. Barnack stone was used for the table, the shafts, and the bases; but the capitals and arches were worked in clunch. The piscina occupied a space of about 5 feet 6 inches square on the face of the wall. It was probably enclosed, like that at Jesus College, in a circumscribing frame, which has been almost wholly destroyed[1]. The presence of the piscina ought perhaps to be taken as an indication that there was an altar at the eastern end of the building, and the more elaborate character of the easternmost of the observed windows strengthened this view. Above the piscina there was a rectangular opening (fig. 19), passing quite through the wall, 3 ft. in height by $1\frac{1}{2}$ ft. wide. It was almost entirely plain and had been closed by a shutter. The masonry of its quoins differed from that of the piscina, and therefore it could not have been part of the original design.

We will next consider the building which we have agreed to call the chapel of the Hospital. While it was being pulled down it became evident that the walls belonged to the original construction, and that such repairs and alterations only had been made in them as would render the building fit and convenient for the use of the college. They had originally been built of squared blocks of excellent clunch, of which material the moldings of the doorways, the windows, and the great quire-arch had also been constructed. Among these blocks, however, many pieces of much harder stone occurred. These must have formed parts of an older building, as amongst them there were some very fine bold specimens of the dog-tooth ornament. These walls had

are seen. The portion to the right shews one of the Perpendicular windows, and above it a portion of the pointed arch of the Early Decorated window, which had preceded it."]

[1] [The arches of the piscina, but not the table, have been removed to the new chapel. When first discovered it exhibited traces of colour.]

been repaired by Bishop Fisher with any materials that could be procured; and they therefore presented a very ruinous appearance in some places, when the plaster was removed. It appeared, however, that though a large part of the original nave or ante-chapel had been found to be so dilapidated at that time, as to require an almost complete rebuilding; yet that use had been made of every fragment of wall that would stand; for portions of the north door and of the west window were found in their original positions. The remains of the latter afforded conclusive evidence of the length of the original building.

It has been already mentioned that the west end of the quire of the college chapel was terminated by a transverse wall. This was 3 feet 3 inches thick (*ab*, fig. 15), pierced by a fine Early English arch, 14 feet 6 inches wide, and about 30 feet high, the lower portion of which, on the south side, is here shewn (fig. 22). At about 10 feet to the east of this, the foundation of a second transverse wall (*ef*, fig. 15), with the base moldings, was discovered. These moldings corresponded exactly with those of the western arch, and traces of the attachment of the transverse wall to the north and south walls could be seen quite up to their top. It is probable therefore that the chapel was spanned in this place by a second arch, similar in every respect to the western arch; and that these two parallel arches carried a lantern-turret of stone or timber, of which the north and south walls were supported by transverse arches abutting on the spandrel walls of the great arches. Further, traces were observed upon the piers which led to the conclusion that the western archway had been closed by a stone screen, 9 feet 3 inches high, set flush with the western face of the arch; whence it was conjectured that a similar screen had been carried across the eastern archway also[1]. In the south wall, close to the western transverse wall, there was a doorway (*l*, fig. 15, fig. 22) 4 feet 2 inches wide, and 8 feet high internally. At a short distance to the east of it there was a holy-water stoup. No traces of original windows were found in the space between the transverse walls.

The original approach to the rood-loft was from the north-west corner of the central space, where the remains of the

---

[1] [The existence of these screens is stated on the authority of Professor Babington, ut supra, p. 17.]

doorway were discovered (*m*, fig. 15). This access to the stair must have been done away with when the quire was extended to the western quire-arch, for the stalls used by the Master and Fellows of the College extended over it. When they were put up, it was closed with rough brick-work, and a new entrance made at the north-east angle of the antechapel (ibid. *n*). This new opening remained in use as long as the chapel

Fig. 22. South door, with part of the pier of the western arch (*b*, fig. 15). From a photograph.

existed, and gave access to the rood-loft, on which the organ had been placed.

This chapel was about 121 feet long, by 25½ feet broad. It consisted of three divisions; the central space above described; the quire to the east; and the nave to the west.

The quire—which it will be seen was originally about 13 feet shorter than it became when used by the College—had three fine Early English windows in the north and south walls[1], and a large east window.   The side windows—the top of one of which is shewn in the view of the south wall of the northern building (fig. 19)—were 8 feet wide and 20 feet high.   Their cills were 7 feet 7 inches above the floor, with the exception of the window on the south side nearest to the east, the cill of which was 11 feet above the floor.   This height indicates that some building had originally abutted against the wall of the chapel in this place, to which the doorway mentioned above gave access.   It may have been a sacristy, which was removed when Dr Thompson's chantry was built.   These original windows were altered in Bishop Fisher's time, by the insertion of narrower and lower Perpendicular windows in their places.   Each of these was put centrally in the old window-space; the old moldings being left untouched, but embedded in the wall.   This applies also to the inserted windows on the south side, with the exception of that over Dr Thompson's chantry, which was placed as far to the west as the opening would allow (fig. 13), so that it might be clear of the domestic buildings of the college, which had just been erected.   Soon afterwards, on the occasion of the erection of Bishop Fisher's chantry, the most eastern of the northern windows was wholly removed, but its former existence was shewn on the destruction of the wall, by a small part of one of its sides remaining embedded in the wall, in the original position.   The east window, of six lights, was about $19\frac{1}{2}$ feet wide and at least 30 feet high.   This is known from a curious elevation of it, drawn upon a piece of clunch, which was found in the eastern wall[2]; and the bases of shafts remained to shew its width.

At the east end of the south wall there was a small ambry, 17 inches wide by 2 feet 3 inches high, and 30 inches from the ground (*o*, fig. 15).   At the same level, and 5 inches to the west of the ambry, there were the remains of a double piscina (*ibid. p*) which had apparently been about 3 feet 6 inches high, and 3 feet 2 inches wide.   Through this piscina a squint had been made

[1] [Traces of these were most visible on the north side, west of Bishop Fisher's chantry.]

[2] [Figured in Prof. Babington's work quoted above, Plate 9.]

(ibid. *q*), apparently for the convenience of the occupant of the room next to the chapel on the south.

The nave, which was 44 feet long, had certainly two Early English windows similar to those in the quire; one to the

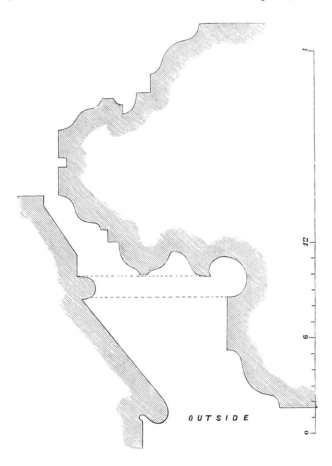

OUTSIDE

Fig. 23.   Molding of jamb and cill of west window.   From a sketch by Professor Willis.

north over Ashton's chantry, and one to the south over that of Keyton, occupying the same position as the later windows. There may have been windows similarly placed in the bay to the west of these, but no traces of them were found.   It was estimated, from the discontinuance of an external stringcourse, that the west window had been about 12 feet wide. A small portion of the cill and part of the jamb remained (fig. 23), but the height could not be ascertained, owing to the alterations made in the wall when the Master's Lodge was built.

There was an original entrance to the chapel on the north side, nearly, but not exactly, in the same place as the door to the stairs leading to the Master's Lodge (*F*, fig. 15). The south doorway which formed the modern entrance (ibid. *E*) was of late Perpendicular date, and was not an altered older doorway. It was closed by a fine original oak door, which, together with the arch, now forms the entrance into the space to the north of the second court (fig. 1, *F*).

Again, when the exterior wall west of the stairs leading to the Lodge was examined, it was found that much of it was modern, that is, that it had been built for the College, not for the Hospital (as was also the turret itself), and had had modern openings made in it to suit the convenience of the Master. But sufficient traces of the original wall remained, to shew that it had not been wholly rebuilt. Fragments of two Early English stringcourses were also in their original places; one at the level of the old window-cills, and the other at that of the springs of their arches. When the brick turret was taken down, it was found that the lower of those stringcourses suddenly rose 13 inches, so as to pass over a doorway. This was apparent only on the west side, as more of the wall had been removed on the other side of the door, to form the larger opening required for the turret. When the wall itself was taken down, the two lowest stones of the eastern jamb were found in their original place, and shewed by their moldings that this doorway belonged to the Early English building. The lower stringcourse was 9 ft. 4 in. above the ground, but where it passed over the door it rose to 10 ft. 7 in., and afterwards fell again to the original level, which it retained until it reached the north-west angle of the building. It then again rose 4 inches to pass close under the west window. It should be further mentioned that between the turret and the north gable of the Master's Lodge the wall was finished with an Early English coping and corbel-table.

The walls had once been decorated with fresco paintings.

Traces of them were found in various places, and especially the remains of a large and elaborate painting of S. Christopher behind the wainscot in the secularized part of the nave.

The chapel was dismantled in June 1868, "for the purpose of removing whatever materials are to be used either in the New Chapel or in the College Hall"; after which it was "put into a fitting temporary condition for the celebration of Divine Service" until the new one was consecrated. It was pulled down in the summer of 1869. The foundations have been left, level with the ground, so that the outline of the old building can still be traced, except at the east end, where the new lecture-rooms extend into the area. The slabs covering the graves of those interred within it have been left in their places; the monuments attached to the walls have been removed into the new building[1]. The fragments of stained glass removed from the East window have been placed partly in the central window on the west face of the new Tower; partly in the tracery of the windows of the Hall.]

CHAPTER V.

HISTORY OF PARTICULAR BUILDINGS: HALL; COMBINATION ROOM; MASTER'S LODGE; TREASURY. ALTERATIONS TO THE COURTS; THE GARDENS AND WALKS.

HALL.—The Hall before its enlargement was about 70 feet long and 30 feet wide including the screens. It had, and still has, an oriel window on the east side and a bold open-timbered roof with a lantern turret, beneath which the ancient charcoal brazier continued to perform its office until the occupation of the enlarged Hall in 1865. [The side-windows, of which there are two in the east wall, and three in the west wall, still preserve their original height and form. Loggan (fig. 3) shews five dormer windows on the east side. These had been placed there for the sake of uniformity; for it is evident that the original open roof has never been altered. The addition of

---

[1] [College Order, 17 March, 1868. The inscriptions on the slabs remaining unmoved are given by Prof. Babington, ut supra, p. 29.]

gables to the west side when the Second Court was built has been already recorded.

A few notices referring to the Hall may be selected from the Audit-Books. In 1518—19 the walls were hung with green say, of which five pieces were then purchased[1]. The wainscoting is first mentioned in 1528, and was not concluded before 1539, when 23 yards are paid for[2], but as the Accounts for the intervening years have not been preserved, we are without details of the work. From an allusion to a repair done to the screen, however, we may conclude that it was already in existence. In 1725 Cornelius Austin supplied new wainscot, and repaired the old; and John Woodward executed some carving. In the same year the Hall was painted; a process frequently repeated in the course of the century, as we learn from the Conclusion Book[3].

In 1862 it was decided to extend the Hall forty feet towards the north. The portion thus added not only occupies the site of the large Combination Room (fig. 6, D), but projects slightly beyond the north range of the Second Court, so as to admit of a small window at the west end of the dais. A second oriel has been thrown out towards the east, and the dais has been removed to the new north wall, which is lined with the rich and lofty screen of "linen" panel-work which ornamented the north wall of the old Hall. This beautiful work, which is probably original, is divided into four compartments by elaborately carved pilasters. It rises as high as the corbels of the roof, where it terminates in a crest, which projects forwards with a coved surface subdivided by ribs, at the intersections of which with the cornice are coats of arms. Above this are the Royal Arms, supported by the Lion and Unicorn. Beneath the

---

[1] [Audit-Book, 1518—19. *Custus aule.* "Computat in denariis solutis pro quinque peciis de Say viridi (*sic*) coloris empt' ad vsum Aule…iiij^li. vj^s. viij^d."]

[2] [In 1528 Maister Fenrodex (Penruddock?) is mentioned as having given £6. 13s. 4d. "towardes the sealing in the hall" (Inventories, 44^b). In an Account beginning at Christmas 1538, we find: *Expense Aule.* "Yren worke for ye selyng xvj^s. To Lambert jun' for selyng ye hall xxiiij yardes, xiiij yardes iij^li. x^s. and x yardes xx^s. iiij^li. x^s. For byse paper for ye selyng xvj^s. Mendyng ye screne vj^s." A workman of the same name was employed to wainscot Queens' College Hall in 1531—32, Vol. i. 60.]

[3] [Audit-Book, 1724—25. "Mr Corn. Austin's bill for New Wainscott, Repairs of ye Old, and Work in the Hall £63. 10. 0. For J^n. Woodward Carvers work in the Hall £8. 0. 0." See also Baker's History, pp. 1037, 1083, 1087.]

Arms is the motto EXVRGAT DEVS DISSIPENTVR INIMICI. The atchievement is enclosed in a rich frame, ornamented with pinnacles and arabesque enrichments. It is of course later than the panel-work below it, and resembles the arms in a similar position in Trinity College Hall so closely, that it may be with probability assigned to the same period. It is not unlikely that it displaced the arms of the Foundress, with her crest and supporters, which,

Fig. 24. Panel of the screen at the south end of the Hall.

admirably carved in wood, now hang in the new lobby on the west side of the Hall.

A screen with two doorways separates the passage between the courts from the body of the Hall. This screen, which had no doors in its original state, had been altered by the addition of modern doors with fan-lights over them and a regular entablature with a cornice. Both sides of it were lined with modern "linen" panel-work, put up to conceal the parts that were out of repair. This was perhaps part of the work done by Austin in 1725, when the entablature also was probably added by himself and Woodward. When this was removed, there was found beneath it fine linen panel-work of an earlier type (fig. 24); and the moldings of the doorjambs were identical with those of the roof. The whole has been carefully repaired, and the 18ᵗʰ century entablature replaced by a more suitable cornice. The side-walls of the Hall are also covered by " linen " panelling, to which a modern cornice has been added copied from the bookcases in the Library. The panel-work along the sides is of different framing from that already described, and the manner of its junction with the ends of the screen at the south end shews that it was not contemplated when the latter was erected. It was evidently wrought in the latter part of the reign of Henry the Eighth; and is doubtless that of which part was done in 1535, before which time hangings had been employed. The Hall was decorated by Messrs Clayton and Bell in 1868, and the new panel-work was put up in that year by Messrs Rattee and Kett.

It should be mentioned in connexion with the decorations of the Hall, that a piece of tapestry was given by the Countess of Shrewsbury in 1615[1]. In 1643 it is spoken of as " the cloth which vsed to hang in the hall," as though it had by that time been discarded ; but in 1648 it is mended and hung up again, a payment which is met with occasionally in subsequent years. It is last mentioned in 1722.

COMBINATION ROOM.—Before the enlargement of the Hall, there was a door (a, fig. 1) near the north-west corner, which opened into a vestibule at the foot of the tower in the north-east corner of the Second Court, called "the Master's Tower," because it led up to the chambers assigned to the Master. A second door (ibid. b) opened out of the vestibule into the Large Combination Room, which occupied the whole of the ground floor of the Hall-range to the north (D, fig. 6). It was of necessity lighted by windows on the north side only. The room on the ground-floor to the east, at the west end of the north range of the First Court, into which its two small windows looked, was used as a Lesser Combination Room (ibid. L).]

The Large Combination Room was lined with ancient panel-work. The panels, of which there were five ranges, were larger than those of the gallery, and were subdivided by fluted Ionic

---

[1] [Audit-Book, 1614—15. *Expense Aule.* "Item bestowed vpon yᵉ countesse of Shrewsbury's man yᵗ brought yᵉ cloath for yᵉ hall xxxiijˢ."]

pilasters. There was a low dado in continuation of their plinth;
and a cornice decorated with roses and portcullises. The doors
were of coeval panelling. The ceiling had plain cross-beams
with roll molds. The joists were concealed by a plaster ceiling.

[After the destruction of the old Master's Lodge and the
enlargement of the Hall, the Gallery on the first floor of the
Second Court was assigned to the Fellows as a Combination
Room, and an approach was made to it by removing chambers on each floor of the north side of the court adjoining
the Hall, and putting in their place a handsome lobby and
staircase, the walls of which are lined throughout with panel-
work, a great part of which was brought from the old Lodge.
The oak ceiling is also old. The communication between this
and the Hall is made by a new doorway (*c*, fig. 1).

The room on the ground-floor adjoining the large Combination Room on the west was used as an Audit-Room, and is
frequently alluded to in the Accounts under that name. When
not wanted for an Audit it formed part of the set of College
chambers, now removed to form the lobby above described.

MASTER'S LODGE.—Although the original Master's Lodge
has been destroyed, the arrangements of it were so interesting,
that they must be briefly described. The following passage
occurs in Bishop Fisher's second code of statutes, given in 1524:
"I reserve for my own use, whenever I may happen to come to
the College, those chambers which have been built for the
Master, as the Foundress, in her gracious kindness, allowed me
to do with respect to Christ's College, which she built in the
same manner at her own expense. After my death, however,
the Master may retain possession of the upper chambers for his
own use; of the lower ones, the larger shall be given to pensioners, or, if none require it, to some of the Fellows; the
smaller we have assigned as a Treasury."[1]]

The "upper chambers" here mentioned consisted of the
"great chamber" over the Combination Room to the north of
the Hall, a lesser chamber to the east of it, which was lighted by
an oriel window looking into the quadrangle (fig. 13); and a

[1] Early Statutes of St John's College, Cambridge, ed. J. E. B. Mayor; 8vo. Camb.
1859, p. 273. "Post decessum vero meum magister ipsa cubicula superiora possideat
in usum suum. Porro duorum inferiorum id quod capacius est cubiculum vel pensio-

third, over the vestibule described in the last chapter, and therefore within the walls of the original Chapel. [The inventories of 1546—1595 mention also an inner chamber, a long study or chamber over the chapel containing as late as 1559 an altar of wood, and a lesser study with a chimney, all on this floor.] The access to these rooms when first built was by the tower-staircase on the west side of the Hall. This tower was placed opposite to the partition wall which separated the Hall from the Combination Room (fig. 1). The alterations which it underwent when the Second Court was built were described in Chapter II. The whole set of rooms, with the turret-stair, was identical in disposition with the Foundress' apartments at Christ's College. The order, however, in which these rooms presented themselves to the visitor at S. John's College in recent times was reversed, because what had been the Master's private staircase down to the Chapel had become the principal entrance to the Lodge (P, fig. 15). This opened into a long passage which had been separated from the north sides of the oriel chamber and bedchamber by panelled partitions, and terminated at the door of the great chamber or dining-room.

The two lower chambers could only have been that under the oriel chamber, which subsequently became the Lesser Combination Room, and the vestibule. This arrangement may be explained by supposing that in 1524 the latter was divided into two by a partition which left a passage on the south. This passage would give access to the antechapel on the right, and to the chamber under the oriel on the left, of a person entering from the Court; while the treasury, or northern part of the vestibule, would communicate with the antechapel by the second doorway (C, fig. 15), which existed to the last, in the wall which bounded it on the east. After the Reformation a chapel-treasury became unnecessary, and therefore a more convenient access to the Lodge was obtained by removing the partition and erecting the tower-staircase on the north side of the vestibule.

---

nariis, vel si nulli tales fuerint, quibusdam e sociis accommodetur; nam alterum quod angustius est pro thesauraria deputavimus." The code given by Bishop Fisher in 1530 omits the word "superiora," and the sentence "porro—deputavimus." The statutes of Henry VIII. (1545) prescribe: "Magister vero collegii cubicula quæ pro magistro constructa sunt in suos usus possideat."

The oriel-chamber and "great chamber" had handsome oak ceilings with molded beams and joists. The former was lined with rich "linen" panel-work, leaving the above-mentioned passage on the north side, which exhibited plain traces to shew that it was the result of an alteration. The initials R. L. and the date, 1567, indicate the mastership of Richard Longworth (Master 1564—69) as the period of its construction[1], and probably of the alterations beneath also. The date of the panel-work in the "great chamber" has not been preserved[2].

The floor above these rooms, containing bed-chambers, was also assigned to the Lodge, with the exception of the part over the "great chamber," which was occupied by a set of college rooms entered from the Tower-staircase on the west side of the Hall. There were no rooms on the ground floor, except the kitchen, which was contained in a wing that projected from the north side (fig. 3). This wing contained a chamber-floor also, and a back-staircase leading to the above-mentioned passage.

This Lodge must have been inconveniently small; and in consequence we have found the Master building for himself a "gallery" on the north side of the small court to the west of the First Court. After the building of the Second Court the gallery which occupies the whole of the first floor of the north side was assigned to the Lodge, as has been explained in Chapter II., together with a chamber at the east end of the gallery, for which hangings were provided in 1631—32[3]. The Master had also a chamber over the gallery[4]. At this time the entrance to the Lodge from the Master's Tower in the north-east corner of the

---

[1] [Audit-Book, 1566—67. *Exp. necess.* "Item for v. score yeardes of wainescott selinge for oʳ. mʳˢ. chamber at 4ˢ. a yard xxijˡⁱ. ijˢ. Item for the creastes 34 yeardes 34ˢ. Item to yᵉ Joyner woorkinge of the portalls xijˢ. Item for the table and formes iijˡⁱ. Item for mendinge the olde hanginges in oʳ mʳˢ chamber iijˢ. iiijᵈ. Item for paintinge in his greate chamber xijˢ."]

[2] There is a tradition that a fine oak chimney-piece, which was in the old Combination Room, and is now in the Hall of the new Lodge, came from Audley End. Lord Braybrooke (Hist. of Audley End, p. 92) seems to think that it was removed while the house was in possession of the Crown between 1669 and 1701.

[3] [Audit-Book, 1631—32. "Paid for hanginges for oʳ. mʳˢ. bed Chamber and the Chamber at yᵉ end of yᵉ Gallery ixˡⁱ. xvjˢ."]

[4] [Audit-Book, 1602—3. *Reparaciones.* "To Longe and his man for plaistering of the Master's chamber over the Gallery xxᵈ."]

court was changed. It was originally by a door into the "Great Chamber," but was then made by an opening into the passage which connected that chamber with the gallery, and as they were on a different level there was a step up to the chamber.

[The Statutes of 1530 further assigned to the Master the garden and orchard near his chambers, to which those of 1545 added a pigeon-house[1]. The garden is evidently the enclosure shewn by Hammond (fig. 5) at the north-west corner of the site on the east bank of the river; and the little building by the side of the water may be "the gallerie over the river" which appears in the inventories of the Master's chambers in 1580 and 1595, but not in 1564.[2] The orchard stood on a piece of ground adjoining the site of Jesus College[3].

In the course of the works begun in 1863 a new Master's Lodge was erected on the ground north of the Library (fig. 1), with a separate entrance from Bridge street[4]. The entrance-hall is lined with panelling brought from the old Lodge; and the Master's study on the first floor is an exact reproduction of the former one, with the identical panelling, and the oriel-window which looked into the First Court.

TREASURY.—The statutes of 1530 direct that the muniments are to be kept "in the upper chamber of the tower"; by which the gate of entrance is evidently meant. This chamber has been assigned to that purpose from the earliest times. It is approached by the staircase in the north-western turret.

GREAT GATE, RANGES OF CHAMBERS, ETC.—The eastern front of the college preserves its ancient aspect more completely than almost any other, except Queens' College. The Chapel and the buildings adjoining it have been pulled down—as will be related in the next chapter—; but the range extending from the old chapel to the lane dividing S. John's College from Trinity College has been but little altered since Loggan's time. The picturesque chimneys—no two of which

[1] [Early Statutes, etc., pp. 168, 169.]

[2] [Inventories, &c. 1516—1595, pp. 72, 145, 146.]

[3] [History of Jesus College, p. 116.]

[4] [College Order, 21 March, 1863. "Agreed to adopt the plans for a new Master's Lodge now before us, provided that on receipt of Contractor's tenders it appear that it can be erected for a sum not exceeding seven thousand pounds."]

were alike—have been replaced by modern stacks; and the long sloping roofs of the dormer windows have become almost flat; but the battlements are the same; and the windows preserve their original variety of form and size.

The space between the arch and the stringcourse on the east front of the Great Gate is ornamented with the arms of the Foundress, crowned, between her usual supporters; in the centre of the finial, beneath the shield, there is a rose, and in the spandrels there are bunches of daisies; above which, on the right, there is a portcullis, and on the left a rose, both crowned. Between the windows there is a niche containing a statue of S. John; and beneath the two uppermost windows a rose and portcullis, crowned like those below. These ornaments were damaged during the Civil War. Baker[1], after describing the treatment of the Fellows, gives the following account of what took place:

"Before this reformation in the members of the society, the walls and house itself was regulated and reformed as a preparation to that which followed. All the decent furniture in the chapel was now removed, organs and pictures, etc. were taken down, and so much is placed to account on the books for whited walls, and so much for closing up Fisher's and Ashton's sepulchres, now again, one or both of them, turned into apartments, and the dead and living were lodged together. The cross upon the tower was likewise removed, and the statue or image over the gate towards the street was taken down, and St John was banished once more to Patmos; with good providence, as it happened, for had it not been timely and seasonably displaced from its niche, it might probably have been thrown down afterwards in a ruder manner, to prevent idolatry, that was then the only sin we were afraid of. But most of this, as I said, happened some time before the master's [Dr John Arrowsmith's] accession to the government, and is not to be placed to his account. For some time the sequestrators had possession of the lodge, and having polluted it, (as they had done the chapel), so much is placed to account for sweeping and washing it after it had been quitted by that sort of vermin."[2]

In this passage, so far as it concerns the Gate, Baker seems

---

[1] [Baker's History, p. 226.]

[2] [Audit-Book, 1643—44. (Lady-Day—Mids. 1644.) "Item for sweeping and washing the Lodging after the Sequestrators had left it o. 6. 6." The following extracts from the Audit-Book for 1642—43 illustrate Baker's narrative. Christmas, 1642 —Lady Day, 1643: "It. payed for the iron worke stolen by the souldiers when they brake open the gates o. 1. 6. Item to Miton Hebbe and others for helping about the bridge when it was taken downe by violence of the souldiers and laying vp the timber o. 15. 7." Mids.—Mich. 1643. "It. taken by violence out of the Bursers studye by

to be referring to a story that the statue of S. John was taken down and concealed to save it from destruction. It is usually stated that after the Restoration it was brought out of concealment and put up again. In the Audit-Book for 1662—63, however, we find the following entries:

> "Stone cutter for 2 Crownes over yᵉ Coll. gate 1. 10. 0
> Georg Woodroff for Cutting St John's Statue   ...   ... 11. 0. 0."

The present wooden gates were put up in 1665—66[1]. The gate-tower used frequently to be painted; and from the mention of gold in connection with the "forefront of the Colledge next yᵉ street" on one of these occasions, it is probable that the arms were once emblazoned and gilt[2].

Loggan (fig. 3) shews a cupola, surmounted by a lofty vane, over the south-western turret, similar to the bell-turret of the Hall. The date of its removal has not been ascertained.

In 1855 the triangular garden shewn by Loggan in front of the college was diminished by setting the gate leading into the back lane nearer to the College, and the brick wall was replaced by an iron railing. The posts and rails outside the gate have been long since removed.

The interior aspect of the courts has been but little altered from that shewn by Loggan. The first court has suffered most; from the removal of the north side, and from the unfortunate changes perpetrated in 1772, when the college was seized with the prevailing mania for Italianizing the surface of their buildings, which happily exhausted their means when they had

Captaine Mason, who broke open his chamber and studie doores in the presence of diuers fellowes Apʳˡ. 8. 1643, the sum of eleuen pounds six shillings and foure pence, wherof 8ˡⁱ—15ˢ—4ᵈ was Austen Lin's rent for Steeple Morden payed by one Deuereux then a minister of S. Albons before of Foxton in Leicestershire 11ˡⁱ. 6ˢ. 4ᵈ. It. there was taken out of his chamber by the same Captaine the same day fouretene pounds eight shillings and eleuen pence, brought him by Mʳ Bacon for his rent for Holbeach in Lincolnshire wᶜʰ is not accounted for because he hath no acquittance, and he forfeited his feof for non-payment of his rent the Mich. following, and is iustly suspected to haue a hand in sending the Captain to take away the money as well as the other."]

[1] [Ibid. 1665—66. "To John Adams for one hundred and three foot of Oake borde for the new great Gate 1. 0. 6.; for timber for the gate 2. 13. 6.; for making the gate 1. 10. 0; for...nayles 8ˢ. 4ᵈ.; for other nayles 2ˢ. 10.; for carrying the gates 1ˢ. 6ᵈ.; pᵈ. by him to Woodroff for cutting two Antilopps heads 14ˢ.; for the Timber of them 5ˢ. 6ᵈ.: pᵈ. John Adams in toto for the gate 06. 16. 2."]

[2] [Ibid. 1702—3.]

completed the south side of the first quadrangle. The order for
doing this was made 20 February 1772:

"Agreed that the side of the first court opposite to the chapel be
covered with stone, sashed, and otherwise improved agreably to a plan
given in by Mr Essex."[1]

The work began soon after Christmas in that year, but apparently it was not concluded before 1775—76, when £135 was
paid to the architect for "Interest at 5 per Cent. on £2700 laid
out on the new Building." A new facing of stone had been
imposed upon the old south wall of the court, and the garrets
replaced by an additional story of white brick, as may be
seen in the lane. On this work Cole, writing in 1773, remarks[2]:

"In my Opinion, when the College was set about Improvements, it
is Pity, as the Society has always found the Inconvenience of the
Smallness of their Chapel, not capacious enough to contain the vast
Numbers of their Society, tho' a large and handsome Room, that they
did not take down their old Chapel, and rebuild an elegant one in its
Place, fully capacious to hold their Society without Crowding. That
might have been done with the £10,000 which they have in Hand for
Repairs, and which will go but a little Way in the idle Scheme they are
now about, and which all the Society was averse to; yet the Master had
Address enough to bring them all into his Project, he generously subscribing on his own Share £500. The Plan they have just now began
is casing the South Side of the first Court with Stone, and putting
in Sash Windows, and giving a new and better Air to their Garrets: at
the same Time they weaken their original Building, which was handsome and uniform, in the true collegiate Stile, and add no convenience
to any of their Apartments, and must occasion an infinite Expence
if they go thro' their whole large College; and if they do not, it will be
Patch-Work."

The statue of the Foundress over the door leading from the
Court into the Hall Screens was put up in 1674[3]:

"Payd for ye Foundresses Statue (erected over ye Hall-doore) toge-

---

[1] [Other architects had apparently been consulted: Audit-Book 1772—73. "M^r
Sandby for Plans of the first Court, Journies, etc £45. 3. 0."]

[2] [MSS. Cole xlv. 89. Add. MSS. Mus. Brit. 5846. In a note to Baker's History,
dated 2 Aug. 1777, he speaks of "the foolish Scheme...of new casing Part of the first
Court with Stone, to the great weakening of the original Building; defacing the Uniformity of it; and at such an expense as it would be preposterous to go on in the
same Manner; so only the Face of the South Side of that Court looks elegant, to disgrace the other Parts, which now look worse." In 1775 £300 is set down as the "gift
of George Osbaldeston Esq. towards the Expence of continuing the New Building in
the first Court." This sum however was invested for future use.]

[3] [Audit-Book, Lady-Day—Mids. 1674.]

ther wth Her Arms and Supporters 40ˡⁱ. o. o.   For Casing and Carriage of yᵐ from London 4. 9. o.   For Stones and yᵉ Masons work about yᵉ Niche 15. 3. 7.   To Nottingham and his Labourers for work, slime, sand and Haire £3. 3. 10. to Kerdall yᵉ Plummer for Lead, solder, and work about yᵉ Gutter be hind yᵉ Statue 1, 15. 9.   To yᵉ Stone-Cutters man for his Journey and other appendent charges 2. 3. o.   In toto 66. 15. o."

This statue took the place of a Dial, the original position of which, at a slightly lower level than that of the statue, may be detected by a scar in the brick-work.   The Accounts shew that there were Dials in both courts; but we have no means of ascertaining the position of those in the Second Court.   The extracts given below shew that they were last repainted in 1712—13[1].   The stonework round the doorway leading into the Screens is a rather elaborate composition (fig. 3); and appears to have been originally painted, from a charge of £4. 13s. 4d. "for gilding and payntinge the hall doore" in 1605—6.   The wooden door is probably that contracted for in 1516.

The two lecture-rooms at the north-east angle of the court were built after the designs of Mr G. G. Scott in 1869, as soon as the old chapel had been removed[2].

The architectural character of the Second Court has been respected up to the present time, except that the picturesque and uniform blocks of chimneys which Loggan shews have been altered, as elsewhere, into a variety of unpleasing forms.   The spouts, which in Loggan's time discharged the water from the roof on to the ground from a point at about the level of the first floor, were brought down into drains in 1754—55.   The windows kept their small panes of glass until 1768, when it was "agreed that the stonework in the middle court" should be

---

[1] [Ibid. 1648—49. "To Jo: Ivery for paynting yᵉ Dyall over yᵉ Hall doore Aug. 23. 2ˡⁱ." 1667—68. "To Mʳ Broughton for making a New Diall in yᵉ Old Court and renewing a Diall in yᵉ New Court, Aug. 17, 08. oo. oo." 1712—13. "To Nottingham for raising yᵉ scaffolds for yᵉ 3 new Dialls in yᵉ middle court o. 6. o.   To Thomas Pretlove Carpenter for materialls used and worke about yᵉ dialls 6. 9. 11.   To Tho. Whitaker for drawing yᵉ dialls 5. 7. 6.   To Robert Palton for painting and gilding yᵉ dialls 6. o. o.   To Berry Smith his Bill for the three Gnomons and other Iron worke about yᵉ same 2. o. 9."]

[2] [College Order, 9 February, 1869. "Agreed to request Mr Scott to complete his design for two Lecture Rooms, and for iron fencing contiguous thereto, with the view of closing in the North East angle of the first court in the course of the next summer, on the removal of the old Chapel."]

"cleaned and painted and large crown glass be put into the windows."[1]

The statue of the Countess of Shrewsbury, by Thomas Burman, the cost of which, according to Baker, was defrayed by her nephew the Duke of Newcastle, was put up over the gateway on the west side of the Second Court in 1671:

"To Mr Drake, for drawing Articles between ye College and Tho: Burman sculpt^r, o. 6. 8.

Payd for ye Countess of Shrewsbury's Statue, (erected in ye Gate of ye middle Court) together with her Armes, o^r Rose, and o^r Portcullis, 40^{li}: For putting them up into Boxes and carriage from London 6. 6. o: For ye Masons work about ye Niches 7. 5. 6: To ye Labourers (with other appendent charges) 4. 9. 6.   In toto 58. 02. 00 [2]."

An Observatory was erected on the top of the gateway in 1765[3], which remained until 1859, when, having ceased to be required, it was removed.

The principal alterations to the Third Court have been already noticed. It must be further recorded that the two buttresses on the east side (f, g, fig. 1) were set up in 1691, when we find a payment to "Robert Grumball Freemason for stone and worke about the two new Butteresses in the Library Court to support the Building of the Midle Court."[4]

When Loggan's print (fig. 13) was taken, the only rails in the First Court were those in front of the Chapel, joining the chantries of Dr Thompson and Dr Keyton. These are first mentioned in 1613—14. Those shewn by Loggan were put up in 1674[5].

---

[1] [Baker's History, p. 1073. One of the old casements may still be seen in a blocked half of a window in the back lane.]

[2] [Audit-Book, 1670—71. Baker's History, p. 192. A brief notice of the sculptor is given by Walpole, "Anecdotes of Painting in England," Ed. 1827, iii. 151.]

[3] [College Order, 29 Jan. 1765. "Agreed that a surveyor be sent from London... to examine whether the building in the 2nd court will support the intended observatory; and if he thinks that it will, that [it] be begun immediately by Stevenson and Forster under the direction of Mr Dunthorne." Mr Dunthorne had given some astronomical instruments to the College, and defrayed the cost of the Observatory. For an account of the method of construction see "Astronomical Observations made in St John's College, Cambridge, in the Years 1767 and 1768. By the Reverend Mr Ludlam. 4°. Cambridge, 1769." A view of this Observatory is given in one of Storer's "Illustrations."]

[4] [Audit-Book, 1690—91. *Reparationes.*]

[5] [Ibid. 1673—74. "To Adams for new Rayles and Balisters in ye first Court along ye side of ye Chappell 14. 04. 02."]

In 1561—62 this court, then the only one, was furnished with elaborate rails—with posts spiked with iron at intervals, and a pair of gates to admit within the enclosure[1]. They are again mentioned in 1604—5, and rails in both courts are alluded to so late as 1684—85; Loggan, however, shews none in the Second Court; and those round the grass-plots in the First Court had been removed before his time. In his print they are bounded by a low hedge, which appears to have been of rosemary and sweetbriar[2], of which the former is frequently mentioned, and the latter in 1604—5. Paved walks in the First and Second Courts were laid down in 1667—68[3].

Some curious names were applied to parts of the College. A "Rats Hall"[4] is found here, as at Christ's College, and also a "Stangate Hole"[5]; but we do not know where either was situated.

TENNIS COURT, GARDENS, ETC.—The Tennis Court first stood on the ground now occupied by the north side of the Second Court, as we learn from the Articles agreed upon between the college and the architects, § 15. It was built in 1573—74. It was rebuilt in 1602—3[6] on the west side of the river, where Loggan gives an excellent view of it (fig. 12).

---

[1] [Ibid. 1561—62. "Item to Robert Bell for part of his bargaine for makinge the Railes for the Coorte xl[s]." Ibid. 1562—63. "Item to the Painter for leyinge the Irons of the greate Postes in oyle and red leade iij[s]. Item for xij pikes of yron for the postes in the Courte wayinge lxxvij pound...xxxij[s]. j[d]. Item for twoe...hinges for the gates of the Rayles...xvij[s]. vj[d]."]

[2] [Ibid. 1558—59. *Exp. necess.* "Item to Underwoode for settinge a peace of Rosemarye in the Courte...xiij[d]." Ibid. 1562—63...."for settinge the southe syd of the courte with rosemarye vj[s]." Ibid. 1564—65. "To Thomas the poore gardiner for digginge and settinge the courte withe Rosemary...v[s] ij[d].]

[3] [Ibid. 1667—68. "To George Haines for 690 feet of Purbeck Stone, and y[e] Laying of it in y[e] two Courts...34[li]. 10. 0."]

[4] [Ibid. 1651—52. *Reparaciones.* "Item to Myton for slateing ou[r] Ratts Hall 00. 12. 2." Similar entries occur in 1664—65, and in 1666—67.]

[5] [Ibid. 1593—94. *Reparaciones.* "For mending [a] chamber in y[e] stangate hole ij[s]. ix[d]." 1759—60. "Ceiling Kitchen and Cleaning that and Staincoat Hole, 21. 8. 4." College Order, 3 Aug. 1759. "Agreed to clean, plaister, and whitewash the kitchin and staincoat hole at the expense of £8. 10s." On 8 May 1765 it was agreed to repair a window in stain*court* hole: and on 23 Oct. 1782, it was "Agreed that at the end of Stain coat [*originally written* court] passage doors be put up under the direction of M[r] Essex." Baker's History, pp. 1039, 1087.]

[6] [These details are taken from the Audit-Books for the years mentioned. The

The extent of the walks and gardens is shewn in Loggan's general view (fig. 3); and the part nearest to the college in greater detail in his second view (fig. 12). The bridge led to a broad walk along the river-bank, which was there strengthened by piles, terminated by a parapet. This walk extended northwards as far as a stream which joined the river at a point close to that at which the bridge to the New Court now crosses it (fig. 1). A flight of wooden stairs there led down to the river. This stream was partly a branch of that which still forms the eastern boundary of the close containing the Bowling-green, popularly termed the Wilderness. Beyond this stream in 1688 there were nineteen fish-ponds, the largest of which communicated with the river by a sluice (fig. 12). There was no bridge leading from the college into this part of the grounds, which was called "the pondyards" or "the fishponde close" in the seventeenth century, but Hammond shews one at the north-east corner, erected probably for the convenience of the lessee[1]. The walk followed the course of the stream until it reached the central walk, which led in a straight line from the bridge to the public road, where there was a gate and bridge called " the Bridge towards the feilds." These walks were all bounded by trees, and the ground between them was pasture-land[2]. The ground to the south of the central walk was laid out in 1688 just as it is at present, except that the gate at the south-west corner stood close to the north-west corner of Trinity College walks, where the grounds then terminated, instead of at the north-east corner of the Bowling-green, as at present, where the iron gate was put up in 1780. The walk leading to it was then called " Bachelors Walk."[3] In 1688 the Wilderness was enclosed with wooden palisades and clipped hedges, except on the north side, where there was a wall. The Bowling-green was on

Tennis-court was a source of revenue to the College, and the money received from it is set down in the *Recepta Forinseca*.]

[1] [It has been found impossible to shew this part of his map. A more carefully executed copy of his view of S. John's College than that given in the text (fig. 5) will be found in the History of Trinity College.]

[2] [Several of the trees that bounded the central walk were cut down in 1825, to make way for the New Court, and others after its completion, "to give air and effect to the beautiful new building" (Cam. Chron. 9 March, 1830). They had grown by that time into a fine avenue, and were much regretted.]

[3] [College Order, 19 Feb. 1780. Baker's History, p. 1086.]

the north side, and the rest of the ground was divided into two regular oblong divisions, bounded by hedges, within which there was a row of trees.

These walks seem to have been first laid out in 1602—3, when we meet with numerous charges under that head, and for making the "gallery in the garden."[1] The ground where the Bowling-green afterwards was, was enclosed in 1610—11[2], probably immediately after the purchase of it from the Town; and the Bowling-green itself is first mentioned in 1625, when it was planted with elm and sycamore. In 1634—35 it was secured by a hedge of willows on the west side. New walks, of which some were "in the Bowling-green," and one was probably that which led to the road, were made and planted in 1630, 1631[3], and subsequent years. The planting of ten young elms is specially recorded in 1685—86[4]. The wall of the Bowling-green is first mentioned in 1648—49, and buttresses were added to it in 1666—67. As these are not shewn by Loggan, they were probably on the inside. They were repaired by Gromball in 1686—87. There were three arbours on the south side of the Bowling-green, and one on the west side, when Loggan's print was taken. A new one, called "the long Arbour," was made in 1686. It was raised higher in 1692, and repaired in 1731. It is described in 1763 as "an elegant Summer-house."[5] As Loggan does not shew it, we ought perhaps to conclude that his print was drawn before it was built.

Towards the end of the last century the Society wished

[1] [The Fellows had a gallery, as in other colleges, before this was built, which was close to the river: Audit-Book, 1604—5, "To the glasier for repayring decayed glasse in the fellowes gallerie over the river:" and apparently on the right bank, for it was pulled down when the Library was built. Ibid. 1627—28. *Recept. forinseca.* "Received of H. Man for the olde buildinge (explained afterwards to mean 'the olde gallerie') by the waterside iij^{li}. xiiij^s. viij^d." The Master's "Gallerie over the river" has been mentioned above (p. 315).]

[2] [Audit-Book, 1610—11. *Exp. necess.* "For 10^m. 5^c. of quick sett for the new inclosure beyond the walkes iij^{li} ix^s iiij^d."]

[3] [Ibid. 1629—30. (Mich.—Christ. 1630) "For 86 trees and 600 setts, and setting of them in the new walkes iij^{li}. xij^s. ij^d." Ibid. 1630—31 (same quarter) "For makinge of one grasse walke, and finishinge that walke towards the high way, and setts of Oake and hollye, and hayseede xviij^s."]

[4] [Ibid. 1685—86 (Mich.—Christ. 1686). "To Kings Colledge gardiner for 10 young Elmes to set in ye High walks...1^{sh}."]

[5] [Cantabrigia Depicta, p. 71.]

to improve their gardens, and various plans were submitted to them. In 1765 Mr Miller was consulted; in 1772 Mr Freeman; and in 1773 the celebrated Mr Lancelot Brown. His plan was apparently adopted, for we find that in 1778 " a piece of plate of the value of £50 " was presented to him " for his services in improving the walks."[1]]

CHAPTER VI.

[HISTORY OF THE NEW CHAPEL.

[THE erection of a new Chapel appears to have been contemplated so far back as 1687, when Robert Grumbold was paid 3^{li}. for " a new ground plott modell of ye old and new designed Chappell."[2] Nothing, however, was done at that time; and, in the following century, though the want of a larger Chapel was fully recognized[3], no definite scheme for enlarging the old one, or building a new one, seems to have been proposed. The subject, however, continued to be a topic of conversation among members of the college; and in 1861 began to be more loudly and generally discussed. At the annual Commemoration of Benefactors in that year, held on the festival of S. John *ante portam latinam* (6 May), the usual sermon was preached by William Selwyn, D.D., Lady Margaret's Professor of Theology, formerly Fellow. The occasion was one of unusual solemnity, for in that year the college celebrated what the preacher called "its seventh jubilee," just 350 years having elapsed since the charter was given, as related in the first chapter. He selected his text from the second chapter of the prophet Haggai:

"Yet now be strong, O Zerubbabel, saith the Lord; and be strong,

---

[1] [Baker's History, p. 1085. See also pp. 1047, 1056, and 1071. Mr "Millar" may perhaps be Philip Miller, author of The Gardener's Dictionary, published in 1731. Mr Brown, better known as "Capability" Brown (Walpole's Anecdotes, Ed. 1827, IV. 296), "told them that his plan would cost them at least £800." Baker's History, p. 1048. Some of the planting in 1777—78 was done by John Forlin, who had planted the walks at Queens' College in 1749 (Hist. of Queens' Coll. p. 55).]

[2] [Audit-Book, 1686—87. *Reparationes domi.* Robert Grumbold or Gromball was employed at Clare Hall in 1669. See History of Clare Hall, Chap. IV. Vol. i. 102.]

[3] [See Cole's remarks, quoted in the last chapter, p. 318.]

O Joshua, son of Josedech, the high priest ; and be strong, all ye people
of the land, saith the Lord, and work : for I am with you, saith the
Lord of hosts.

The silver is mine, and the gold is mine, saith the Lord of
hosts.

The glory of this latter house shall be greater than of the former,
saith the Lord of hosts : and in this place will I give peace, saith the
Lord of hosts."

In the course of the sermon the following passage occurs :

" And is there not one improvement more to be desired than all ?
long-talked of, long delayed, for which perhaps the time is now come.

*   *   *

Magnum opus et arduum.   But what if the time be come, and God
be with us !   *Deus adjutor noster.*   What if that public spirit that
breathed in the old Commonwealth of Rome, *Privatus illis census erat
brevis, commune magnum*—But why go so far as Rome for example ?
What if that same public spirit that breathed within these walls when
Craven gave £3000 for buildings ; and again, when a late master,
James Wood, gave £2000, and every Fellow the fourth part of his
Fellowship, for the building of another court beyond the Cam (I speak
from experience): what if that same spirit should still live and breathe
within these walls, and fill all hearts with zeal like David's, to find
a fitting place for the temple of the Lord ?   The silver and the gold are
thine, O Lord ; we will not rest until we have raised a Chapel more
worthy of our College, more answerable to the bounty of our benefactors, and to thy manifold blessings.

How soon would the work be done ! ... How glorious beyond all
former time would be the fabric of our ancient House !"[1]

In consequence of the feeling excited by this sermon, a
meeting of the Society was held in the Hall, 28 May, at which
a Resolution was adopted requesting the Master and Seniors
to undertake the work without delay.   No time was lost, as
the following Orders shew :

" 27 January, 1862.   Agreed that Mr G. G. Scott be requested to
consider the present Chapel, Hall, and Master's Lodge, and advise us as
to the best plans in his opinion for a New Chapel."

" 2 May, 1862.   Mr G. G. Scott having prepared for our consideration two ground plans of a new Chapel and of other Buildings for the
College :

Agreed to request Mr Scott to complete plans in conformity with
that scheme which involves the erection of a Chapel on a new site ;

---

[1] [The New Chapel of St John's College. 4°. Cambridge, 1869. In a second
edition, written after the Chapel was built, the author described the sermon as "a word
spoken at the Annual Commemoration of Benefactors, May 6, A.D. 1861, by William
Selwyn, Lady Margaret's Reader in Theology, and now Lithographed by the College."]

and to furnish us with estimates of the probable cost of the Chapel and
the other Buildings separately : it being understood that the sum to be
expended by the College shall not exceed £40,000."

" 5 December, 1862. Agreed to adopt the plans for a New Chapel
recommended in Mʳ Scott's Report, dated Nov. 24, 1862, now before us ;
provided that on receipt of contractors' Tenders it appear that this
Chapel, a new Master's Lodge, and the enlargement of the Dining Hall
mentioned in the same report can be executed without involving an
expenditure of more than forty thousand pounds from the Corporate
Funds of the College."

The Report referred to in the above Orders explains so fully
the alternative plans suggested, and the architect's reasons for
selecting that which was finally adopted, that it is subjoined :

" *To the Master and Fellows of St John's College, Cambridge.*

GENTLEMEN,

I have the honour to lay before you my designs for the rebuilding of your Chapel, with such alterations in other buildings as are
rendered necessary, or suggest themselves as desirable in consequence
of the same.

I have already submitted to your choice two general schemes
which required your consideration before any actual design could
advantageously be made. One of these was founded on the idea of
preserving, so far as possible, the more ancient features of the present
Chapel, and making it form an aisle to a larger one, to be built
on its north side. The other was for the erection of an entirely
new Chapel.

The first of these schemes was suggested to my mind by finding
that the present Chapel, though mainly to the eye a building of the
fifteenth or sixteenth centuries, contained in reality, though for the
most part concealed, a large proportion of the building of the thirteenth
century, which formed the Chapel to the ancient Hospital of St John.
This, added to the desire to preserve some other portions of the old
buildings, the removal of which will be rendered necessary by the
erection of an entirely new Chapel, led me to offer this as an alternative; but I have no doubt that the practical uses of the Chapel will
be better provided for by the erection of an entirely new structure, as
you have determined.

In selecting the style to be followed in designing the new Chapel,
we may either adopt the best variety of pointed architecture, irre-
spective of the history of the College; or we may choose between
the date of the College itself and that of the preceding establishment—
the Hospital of St John—the preceding Chapel being an admixture of
the work of both dates. Had the date of the College itself coincided
with that of the highest perfection of pointed architecture, there would
have been no room left for doubt; as, however, this was not the case,
it is satisfactory that such a coincidence does exist as regards the date
of the older Chapel, which forms the nucleus of that now existing, and

which belongs to the latter half of the thirteenth century. I have therefore adopted that period as the groundwork of my design.

The type of Chapel I have chosen is that so frequent at Oxford,
having an ante-chapel placed in a transverse position, something like
a transept, at the west end. This form was, perhaps, first suggested by
the Chapel of Merton College, being the choir of a large cross church
of which the nave had not been erected. The convenience of the type
thus furnished, would seem to have suggested its systematic adoption as
a customary form of a College Chapel. It was accordingly adopted by
Wykeham at New College and Winchester; by Waynflete at Magdalene
College; by Chichele at All Souls; and in a modified form by King
Henry VI. at Eton[1]. In most of these instances the transeptal form of
the ante-chapel was agreeably modified internally by parting off each
of its wings by coupled arches; thus rendering it essentially a perfected design, instead of being, like its prototype, an incomplete
structure.

In adopting this type I have not been actuated by any desire to
introduce an Oxford model, but have done so because it happens to
be particularly well suited to the position. The requirements of the
Chapel itself render it necessary that its length should occupy the whole
of the distance from the street to the line of the front of the Hall. It is
therefore clear that there is a difficulty as to obtaining an entrance to the
ante-chapel from the quadrangle, unless it projects beyond the south
wall of the Chapel—a difficulty which is at once avoided by the adoption of the transeptal form for the ante-chapel.

The eastern termination may, of course, be either square or apsidal.
I have made my design on the last-named form, as being a variety on
the more usual type.

I have not ventured upon stone vaulting, excepting in the ante-
chapel, for fear of incurring undue expense. It may seem at first sight
inconsistent to use a superior covering for the ante-chapel to that used
in the Chapel itself; but the reason is this, that stone vaulting being
much lower than an arched timber ceiling, involves, if it is used for
a large building like the Chapel, an increase in the height of the walls,
and of the entire building. In the ante-chapel, however, the divisions
being small, a reduction of height is desirable, so that the stone vaulting
not only does not necessitate an increase of height to the walls, but is
wanted for the express purpose of reducing what would otherwise be too
great a height for the size of the parts. In the Chapel I have adopted
an arched timber ceiling. The form of this demands the use of a
certain amount of colour, which I propose to obtain in great measure
by the use of inlaying with variously coloured woods. This applies, of
course, only to the plain surfaces between the mouldings. These may
be enriched to a very great extent in this manner, both by borders,
diapers, and even by medallions containing figure subjects; and I cannot help thinking that the novelty and durability of such a mode

---

[1] [The History of Eton College has shewn us that Sir G. G. Scott is quite wrong
in supposing that King Henry the Sixth was in any way responsible for the present
plan of the Chapel.]

of decoration will render it, to say the least, more interesting than a stone vault.

I propose to make use of the stalls of the present Chapel so far as they will go, making up the required number with new ones.

The Organ I propose to place in a projection on the north side, opening by two lofty arches into the Chapel.

I have introduced a timber leaded *flèche* as a belfry, placed at the intersection of the roofs of the Chapel and ante-chapel. This description of belfry seems suitable to the general form of the Chapel, but an enlargement of the corner turret of the ante-chapel could be substituted for it, if thought preferable.

As regards materials, I would propose the Ketton, Ancaster, or Clipsham stone, relieved internally by a moderate use of marble.

The internal facings, &c. would be of clunch.

The roof may be covered with either Westmoreland or Collyweston slates. The details would be carried out with a degree of richness about parallel with those of Exeter College Chapel at Oxford, though I should endeavour to avoid too great similarity, and to give this Chapel as much individual character as I am able to do.

As regards the other alterations in the College, I need only enumerate them. They consist of the elongation of the Hall, the adaptation of the adjoining Gallery to the uses of a greater and lesser Combination Rooms, with the necessary staircase leading to them, and the erection of a new Master's Lodge.

As regards the latter some difficulty has been found in determining its site. In my general plan I had proposed so to place it, as to render possible the future addition of a Court immediately to the north of the present second Court. If, however, it were placed to the west of such future quadrangle, a fear is entertained that it would be too near the river, while if placed to the east of that quadrangle it would necessitate the purchase of some property not yet obtained. I have therefore made a design for the Lodge in an intermediate position, connected with the projection which is in a line with the centre of the second Court. I have not yet matured this design, thinking it best in the first instance that the position and the internal arrangement should be determined; but I send plans of the two stories.

As regards the cost I am of opinion that that of the Chapel would be about £36,000, and that with an expenditure of this amount the new Chapel would be left complete in all its features, with the exception of Statues for the external niches and stained-glass windows.

That of the alteration of the Hall, &c. would be about £3,000.

And that of the Lodge about £7,500 or a little more.

If the Chapel were to be vaulted with stone throughout, the additional cost, including the necessary increase of height, would probably be about £4,500 to £5,000.

I have the honour to be,

Gentlemen,

Your most obedient Servant,

Nov. 24th, 1862.   (*Signed*)   GEO. GILBERT SCOTT."

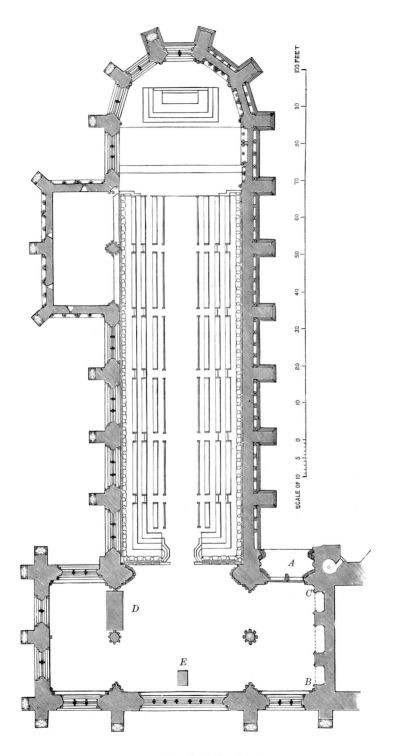

Fig. 25. Ground-plan of the New Chapel.

The court alluded to above would have measured 165 feet from east to west, by 232 feet from north to south; the east and west sides being prolongations of the east and west sides of the Second Court (fig. 1). The Master's Lodge would have been on the west side. This design, however, was not carried out, and the new Master's Lodge was placed as shewn on the plan.

The contract, with Messrs Jackson and Shaw, of Westminster[1], was signed 15 June, 1863, and the workmen commenced operations on the ensuing Midsummer day, with the removal of the houses on the site, and the building sometimes called the Infirmary, the old chapel being retained for service until the completion of the new one. On 6 May, 1864, after the Commemoration Service, at which Professor Selwyn again preached the sermon, the foundation-stone was laid by Henry Hoare, M.A., formerly Scholar[2]. The stone is at the base of the south wall of the south transept, and bears the following inscription on a brass plate: IN . NOMINE . PATRIS . ET . FILII . ET . SPIRITUS . SANCTI . HUJUS . SACELLI . FUNDAMENTA . POSITA . SUNT . PRIDIE . NONAS . MAIAS . A.S. MDCCCLXIV. GEORGIO . GILBERTO . SCOTT . ARCHITECTO.

Mr Scott's design, as accepted by the college, had provided for a flèche at the intersection of the chapel and ante-chapel. In August 1864, Mr Hoare offered " to erect a stone tower as a substitute for the flèche, and to provide for the cost of the alteration by yearly contributions of one thousand pounds until the work be completed, subject to the condition of his living so long." This act of " princely munificence" was thankfully accepted ; and Mr Scott was authorised to make the requisite change in his design, which involved an additional outlay of £6100[3]. Of this sum Mr Hoare had contributed

---

[1] [College Order, 4 June, 1863. 'Agreed to accept the tender of Mess'rs Jackson and Shaw dated 1 June, 1863, for the erection of a New Chapel for the College in Ancaster Stone; and also their Tender for the erection of a New Master's Lodge with exterior Dressings in Bath Box Ground Stone." Ibid. 12 June, 1863. "Agreed to set the Seal to a Contract with Mess'rs Jackson and Shaw, of Earl Street, Westminster, for the erection of a New Chapel and Master's Lodge in conformity with the order of 4 June, 1863, we agreeing to pay for the two Buildings the sum of forty-one thousand seven hundred and eighty-six pounds." Of this sum the Chapel was estimated to cost £34,586: the Lodge £7,200.]

[2] [The stone was to have been laid by Lord Powis, but he was prevented by illness.]

[3] [College Orders, 9 August, 1864; 8 March, 1865.]

£2000, when he met his death by an accident[1], and the rest of
the outlay was defrayed by the college.   The Chapel was
completed by the beginning of 1869, and was consecrated
(12 May) by the Right Reverend Edward Harold Browne,
D.D., Lord Bishop of Ely.   The sermon was preached by the
Right Reverend George Augustus Selwyn, D.D., Lord Bishop
of Lichfield, formerly Fellow.

The New Chapel[2] is built of Ancaster stone, in a style intended to be that which was prevalent in England about 1280,
and was used for the Hospital which preceded the College.   The
ground-plan (fig. 25)[3] shews a long and somewhat narrow quire,
with a transeptal antechapel, over the central bay of which the
tower is placed.   The principal entrance is in the east face of
the south transept (A, fig. 25); a smaller door, for the use of the
Master, is in the west face of the north transept, beneath the
window.   The organ-chamber, which contains the old organ,
altered and enlarged by Messrs Hill[4], is on the north side of the
quire.   The principal dimensions are as follows in feet and inches :

	Length	193	1
	Breadth	52	0
	Length of transeptal antechapel	89	0
	Breadth ,, ,, ...	50	0
EXTERIOR	,, of tower from north to south	42	0
	,, ,, from east to west	41	0
	Height to top of parapet	50	0
	,, to ridge of roof	80	0
	,, of tower to top of parapet	140	0
	,, to top of pinnacles	163	0
	Length	172	9
	Length from quire-arch to east end of apse	137	10
	Breadth of quire	34	0
INTERIOR	Height to ridge of vaulted ceiling	63	0
	Length of transeptal antechapel	74	8
	Breadth ,, ,, ...	32	0
	,, under tower from east to west ...	29	8
	,, ,, from north to south ..	30	8

[1] [He was severely injured on the Great Eastern Railway, 30 March, 1865, and
died 16 April, 1866.]

[2] [The general account of the new chapel here given has been mainly derived
from an excellent paper in a College Magazine called The Eagle for June, 1869;
which should be consulted by those who wish for more detailed information.]

[3] [This plan has been reduced from one signed by Sir G. G. Scott, preserved in
S. John's College.]

[4] [College Order, 12 June, 1867. "Agreed to authorize the Bursar to enter into

The interior of the tower is open to the top of the second stage of windows, a height of 84 feet from the pavement. The upper stage of the tower forms a chamber, of which the interior dimensions are :

	ft.	in.
From north to south	34	3
From east to west	33	3
Height	40	o

The tower opens into the quire by one large arch, and into each of the transepts by two arches. The piers are of Ketton stone. The piers which subdivide the arches opening to the transepts to the north and south have each four detached shafts of red Peterhead granite. The other piers have clusters of shafts of Devonshire, Irish, and Serpentine marbles. The abaci of all the piers are of black Derbyshire marble. There are shafts of Devonshire, Irish, and Serpentine marbles at the sides of the windows in the antechapel, except of those in the second stage of the tower.

The quire is of seven bays, with a five-sided apse. The vaulting-shafts are of different British marbles, like those in the antechapel. Their capitals are on a level with those of the window-shafts ; and above each capital is an ornamental niche, containing statues of the following Saints, taken in order from east to west :

NORTH SIDE.	SOUTH SIDE.
S. John, as Evangelist.	S. John, as Apostle.
S. Luke.	S. Paul.
S. Mark.	S. Peter.
S. Matthew.	S. Thomas.
S. Bartholomew.	S. Philip the Apostle.
S. James the Great.	S. Andrew.
S. Jude.	S. James the Less
S. Matthias.	S. Simon.
S. Stephen.	S. Barnabas.
S. Philip the Deacon.	S. Silas.

The " sacrarium " is enriched by an arcade, formed of pairs of arches placed within larger ones, and decorated with shafts of Devonshire, Irish, and Serpentine marbles. The abaci are of

a Contract with Messrs Hill and Son of 261 Euston Road, London, for the enlargement of the present Organ and the erection of new work in addition to the same in the New Chapel, in accordance with the correspondence now read, for the sum of One Thousand Pounds."]

the red marble known as the Duke of Devonshire's marble, and were presented by him, then Chancellor of the University. Within each of the larger arches, and above the two included smaller ones, is a quatrefoil bearing an angel, issuing from a cloud, and playing on an instrument of music. The spandrels of the larger arches are carved in diaper work.

The roof of the quire, of a very high pitch, is composed of quadripartite vaulting in oak. This is decorated by a continuous line of full-length figures. In the central bay at the east end is Our Lord in Majesty. The other bays contain a series of figures illustrative of the eighteen Christian centuries, proceeding in order from east to west, those of an even number being on the north side; and those of an odd number on the south side. The following is a list of the persons represented. The numbers prefixed denote the century.

II. S. Ignatius, Bishop of Antioch.
S. Polycarp, Bishop of Smyrna.

III. Origen, of Alexandria.
S. Cyprian, Bishop of Carthage.

IV. S. Athanasius, Patriarch of Alexandria.
S. Ambrose, Archbishop of Milan.

V. S. Chrysostom, Patriarch of Constantinople.
S. Augustine, Bishop of Hippo.

VI. S. Gregory the Great, Bishop of Rome.
S. Augustine, first Archbishop of Canterbury.
S. Æthelberht, King of Kent, Founder of the See of Canterbury.
S. Columba, Founder of Iona.
S. Benedict, Founder of the Benedictine Order.

VII. S. Paulinus, first Archbishop of York.
S. Edwin, King of Northumbria, Founder of the See of York.
S. Etheldreda, Foundress and first Abbess of Ely.
Sigebert, King of the East Angles, Founder of the first school in East Anglia.
S. Theodore, Archbishop of Canterbury, first Primate of England.

VIII. Winfrith (afterwards S. Boniface), first Archbishop of Mainz.
The Venerable Bede.
S. Frideswide, Foundress of a nunnery at Oxford, which ultimately became the college of Christ Church.
S. John Damascene, Doctor of the Eastern Church.
Alcuin, of York, Counsellor of the Emperor Charles the Great.

IX.   King Alfred the Great.
       Photius, Patriarch of Constantinople.
       S. Adelard, Abbot of Corbie.
       Bertram or Ratram, Monk of Corbie.
       S. Edmund, King of the East Angles.

X.   Otho the Great, Emperor of Germany.
       S. Dunstan, Archbishop of Canterbury.
       S. Vladimir the Great, called the Apostle of Russia.
       Olga, his grandmother.
       S. Edward the Martyr, King of England.

XI.   S. Edward the Confessor, King of England.
       Peter the Hermit, Preacher of the First Crusade.
       Godfrey of Bouillon, Leader of the First Crusade.
       Lanfranc, Archbishop of Canterbury.
       S. Anselm, Archbishop of Canterbury.

XII.   Adrian IV., the only English Pope.
       S. Thomas of Canterbury.
       S. Bernard, Abbot of Clairvaux, *Doctor Mellifluus*.
       S. Hugh, Bishop of Lincoln.
       Matilda, Queen of Henry I.

XIII. S. Louis IX., King of France.
       Roger Bacon, *Doctor Admirabilis*.
       Hugh de Balsham, Bishop of Ely, Founder of Peterhouse.
       Robert Grostete, Bishop of Lincoln.
       Stephen Langton, Archbishop of Canterbury.

XIV.   William of Wykeham, Bishop of Winchester.
       Edward II., King of England, reputed Founder of Oriel Col-
          lege, Oxford.
       Marie de Valence, Foundress of Pembroke Hall.
       William Bateman, Bishop of Norwich, Founder of Trinity Hall.
       Thomas Bradwardine, Archbishop of Canterbury, *Doctor Pro-
          fundus*.

XV.   Henry Chichele, Archbishop of Canterbury, Founder of All
          Souls' College, Oxford.
       Margaret of Anjou, Queen of Henry VI., Foundress of
          Queens' College.
       Thomas à Kempis.
       Henry VI., King of England, Founder of Eton College and
          King's College.
       John Alcock, Bishop of Ely, Founder of Jesus College.

XVI.   Sir John Cheke, Fellow, first Greek Professor.
       John Fisher, Bishop of Rochester.
       THE LADY MARGARET.
       Dr Nicholas Metcalfe, Master 1518—37.
       Roger Ascham, Fellow, and Public Orator.

XVII.   George Herbert, Public Orator, Rector of Bemerton.
         Jeremy Taylor, Bishop of Down and Connor.
         Thomas Ken, Bishop of Bath and Wells.
         Robert Leighton, Bishop of Dunblane, Archbishop of Glasgow.
         Blaise Pascal, philosopher and mathematician.

XVIII.   William Beveridge, Bishop of S. Asaph.
         Joseph Butler, Bishop of Bristol, afterwards of Durham, the
              author of the *Analogy.*
         Fenelon, Archbishop of Cambrai.
         C. F. Schwartz, Danish Missionary to South India.
         Sir Isaac Newton.

XIX.   Henry Martyn, Fellow, Missionary to India.
         William Wilberforce.
         William Wordsworth, Poet.
         Thomas Whytehead, Fellow, Missionary to New Zealand.
         James Wood, Master 1815—39.
         (These five were all members of the College.)

The windows in the quire, with one exception, have been
filled by various donors with stained glass executed by Messrs
Clayton and Bell. The subjects represent scenes from Scripture at which S. John was present. His figure, vested in ruby
and green, will be seen in each picture. The windows on the
north and south sides of the quire are of three lights. There
are two pictures in each window, extending across all the lights.
The easternmost window only on each side has a descriptive
text beneath the upper subject. In the following list of subjects
the numbers (1) and (2) designate the upper and lower subjects respectively. The commemorative inscription is placed
just above the cill. The series begins at the west end of the
north side of the quire.

NORTH SIDE, WINDOW I.

In . majorem . dei . gloriam . p. c. Gulielmus . Cunliffe. Brooks . A.M. hujus . collegii .
alumnus . A.S. MDCCCLXXI.

1. The Marriage at Cana. [Joh. ii. 1—11.]

2. The Testimony of S. John Baptist to Christ. [Joh. i. 36.] Attached to the
    Baptist's staff is a scroll with the words *Ecce Agnus Dei.*

NORTH SIDE, WINDOW II.

In . piam . memoriam . Gulielmi . Selwyn . pro . dna . Margareta . in . S. Theol.
Lectoris. ob. A. S. MDCCCLXXV.

1. The raising of Jairus' daughter. [Mark v. 35.]
         On a label over our Lord's head *Talitha cumi.*

2. The Call of S. John. [Matth. iv. 21, 22.]

NORTH SIDE, WINDOW III.

In . piam . memoriam . Henrici . Hebblethwayte . benef. p. c. Josephus . Hindle . S.T.B. Coll. olim . socius.

1. The Transfiguration.

    On the border of the "vesica" behind Christ are the words:
    Hic est filius meus dilectus in quo mihi bene complacui ; ipsum audite.

2. S. James and S. John, with their mother, ask Christ for the highest places. [Matth. xx. 20.]

NORTH SIDE, WINDOW IV.

In . piam . memoriam . Gulielmi . Pakenham . Spencer . Gulielmus . Selwyn . A. S.
MDCCCLXXI.

1. The raising of Lazarus. [Joh. xi. 43, 44.]

2. S. Peter and S. John sent to prepare the passover. [Luke xxii. 8.]

NORTH SIDE, WINDOW V.

In . memoriam . Augusti . Vaughton . Hadley . socii . et . tutoris.

1. The Last Supper.
    Nisi manducaveritis carnem filii hominis et biberitis eius sanguinem non habebitis vitam in vobis. [Joh. vi. 54.]

2. The Manna in the Wilderness. [Exod. xvi. 14.]

*** On a brass tablet beneath this window is the following inscription :

To . the . glory . of . God . and . in . memory . of . the . Reverend . Augustus . Vaughton . Hadley . M.A. formerly . Fellow . and . Tutor . of . this . College . born . September . 27 . 1833 . died . March . 24 . 1867 . this . window . was . dedicated . by . pupils . and . friends . †'*Fervent . in . Spirit . serving . the . Lord.*'†

There are five windows in the apse, each of two lights, with a sexfoil in the head. The sexfoil in each contains a half-length figure of Christ, except in the central window, in which it contains the Lamb and Banner. Each of the two lights below contains three pictures, the upper representing figures in contemplation, the two lower, scenes from the Passion, Crucifixion, and Resurrection, of Christ. The central pictures are somewhat larger than the others. The glass in these five windows was given by the Earl of Powis in 1869, as the following inscription records: IN . MAJOREM . DEI . GLORIAM . ET . IN . HONOREM . DIVI . JOHANNIS . EVANGELISTÆ . FENESTRAS . HUJUS . APSIDIS . VITREIS . ORNARI . CURAVIT . EDVARDUS . JACOBUS . COMES . DE . POWIS . L.L.D . SUMMUS . ACADEMIÆ . SENESCHALLUS . A.S. MDCCCLXIX. The following list gives the subjects, with their legends, beginning with the window on the north side. The subjects are counted from the top of each light.

WINDOW I.

Christ the Light of the World. In his left hand he holds a lantern; in his right a label containing the words "Ego sum lux mundi." [Joh. viii. 12.]

1. Patriarchs contemplating the Saviour.
    Te deum laudamus.

2. Christ washing the feet of the Disciples.
    Si non lavero te non [habebis partem mecum. Joh. xiii. 8].

3. Mary anointing the feet of Jesus.
    Fides tua te salvam fecit. [Joh. xii. 3.]

4. Kings contemplating the Saviour.
    Te deum laudamus.

5. The Agony in the Garden.
    Non mea voluntas sed tua fiat. [Luke xxii. 42.]

6. The Betrayal.
    Osculo filium hominis tradis. [Luke xxii. 48.]

WINDOW II.

Christ the Bread of Life, with sheaves of wheat before him. [Joh. vi. 48.]

1. Prophets contemplating the Saviour.
    Te deum laudamus.

2. Christ before the High Priest.
    Tanquam ovis ad occisionem ductus est. [Acts viii. 32.]

3. Christ taken prisoner.
    Illi manus injecerunt in eum, et tenuerunt eum. [Matth. xxvi. 50.]

4. Priests contemplating the Saviour.
    Te deum laudamus.

5. Pilate shewing Christ to the people.
    Ecce rex vester. [Joh. xix. 14.]

6. The Flagellation of Christ.
    Percutiebant caput eius arundine et conspuebant eum. [Mark xv. 19.]

WINDOW III.

The Spotless Lamb.

1. Apostles contemplating the Saviour.
    Te deum laudamus.

2. The Crucifixion.
    Consummatum est. [Joh. xix. 30.]

3. Christ bearing the Cross.
    [Et] baiulans sibi crucem [exivit in eum qui dicitur Calvariæ locum. Joh. xix. 17.]

4. Men of Apostolic Times contemplating the Saviour.
    Te deum laudamus.

5. The Deposition.
    Venit ergo et tulit corpus Jesu. [Joh. xix. 38.]

6. S. John leading the Virgin home.
    Et ex illa hora accepit eam discipulus in sua. [Joh. xix. 27.]

WINDOW IV.

Christ in Apocalyptic Vision, with a sword, and seven candlesticks. [Rev. i. 12—16.]

1.   Martyrs (Men) contemplating the Saviour.   In the centre of the group is
     S. John Baptist holding a banner inscribed "*Ecce Agnus Dei.*"
                        Te deum laudamus.

2.   The Body of Christ prepared for burial.
                        Acceperunt ergo corpus Jesu. [Joh. xix. 40.]

3.   Joseph of Arimathea begs the Body of Jesus.
                        Rogavit Pilatum ut tolleret corpus Jesu. [Joh. xix. 38.]

4.   Martyrs (Women) contemplating the Saviour.
                        Te deum laudamus.

5.   The Entombment.
                        Ibi ergo posuerunt Jesum. [Joh. xix. 42.]

6.   Nicodemus bringing spices.
                        Nicodemus ferens mixturam myrrhæ et aloes. [Joh. xix. 39.]

WINDOW V.

Christ as the Good Shepherd, bearing a lamb on his shoulders. [Joh. x. 11.]

1.   Bishops and Doctors contemplating the Saviour.
                        Te deum laudamus.

2.   The Resurrection.
                        Ego sum resurrectio et vita. [Joh. xi. 25.]

3.   S. Peter and S. John come to the sepulchre.
     Exiit Petrus et ille alius discipulus, et venerunt ad monumentum. [Joh. xx. 3.]

4.   Priests and Deacons contemplating the Saviour.
                        Te deum laudamus.

5.   Christ appearing to Mary Magdalene.
                        Noli me tangere. [Joh. xx. 17.]

6.   Mary Magdalene at the sepulchre.
     Tulerunt dominum meum et nescio ubi posuerunt eum. [Joh. xx. 13.]

SOUTH SIDE, WINDOW I.

In . piam . memoriam . Radulphi . Hare . Eq. Aur. p. c. exhib. sui. A.S. MDCCCLXIX.

1.   Christ appearing to his Disciples.
                        Insufflavit et dixit eis accipite spiritum sanctum. [Joh. xx. 22.]

2.   The Consecration of Aaron.   [Levit. viii. 12.]

SOUTH SIDE, WINDOW II.

In . honorem . dei . p. c. Carolus . Bamford . A.M. *hujus . coll. alumnus .* MDCCCLXIX.

1.   The Ascension.   [Acts i. 9.]

2.   Elijah carried up to Heaven.   [2 Kings ii. 11, 12.]

SOUTH SIDE, WINDOW III.

In . honorem . dei . p. c. Franciscus . Sharp . Powell . A.M. *hujus . Coll. nuper .*
                        socius . MDCCCLXX.

1.   The Descent of the Holy Spirit.   [Acts ii. 1—4.]

2.   Moses with the Tables of the Law.   [Exod. xxxii. 15.]

SOUTH SIDE, WINDOW IV.

In . dei . gloriam . et . in . piam . memoriam . Rogeri . Lupton . scholæ . Sedbergh fundat . p. c. Henricus . H. Hughes . S.T.B. Coll. olim . socius.

1. S. Peter's inquiry touching S. John. [Joh. xxi. 21.]
2. The great draught of fishes. [Joh. xxi. 6.]

SOUTH SIDE, WINDOW V.

Given by Rev. A. C. Haviland, M.A.

In . honorem . dei . et . in . piam . memoriam . Johannis . Haviland . Med. Prof. Reg. olim . socii . ob. die . VIII. Jan. MDCCCLI.

1. S. Peter and S. John heal the Lame Man at the Beautiful Gate of the Temple. [Acts iii.]

    A label over S. John's head is inscribed: *In nomine Jesu Christi Nazareni surge et ambula.*

2. The Lame Man, with S. Peter and S. John, before the Council. [Acts iv. 5—14.]

SOUTH SIDE, WINDOW VI.

In . piam . Memoriam . fratris . dilectissimi . p. c. Stephanus . Parkinson . S.T.P. Coll. Soc. A.S. MDCCCLXXI.

1. S. Peter, S. James, and S. John, give to S. Paul and S. Barnabas the right hand of fellowship. [Gal. ii. 9.]

    One of the Apostles holds a scroll inscribed: *dextras dederunt mihi et Barnabæ societatis.*

2. S. Peter and S. John confirming at Samaria. [Acts viii. 14—17.]

SOUTH SIDE, WINDOW VII.

This window has not yet been filled with stained glass.

The glass in the great West Window, also by Messrs Clayton and Bell, representing "the Last Judgment," was given by the Bachelors and Undergraduates. It bears the following inscription : AD . HONOREM . DEI . ET . IN . MEMORIAM . DOMINÆ . MARGARETÆ . HANC . FENESTRAM . P. C. IUNIORES . HUJUSCE . COLLEGII . ALUMNI . A. S. MDCCCLXIX. The fragments of stained glass that were in the east window of the old chapel[1] now fill the central window of the three on the west face of the Tower immediately above the great west window.

There are two windows on the north face of the north transept, each of two lights. These have been filled with stained glass by Wailes, in memory of Ralph Tatham, D.D.,

---

[1] [This glass had been preserved by Dr Beale (Master 1633—44): Audit-Book, 1634—35: "Paid to Robert Taylor, whom our Master set on work to place some old painted glass in the great window £2. 1. 0." Woodhouse, *ut supra*, p. 9.]

Master 1839—57. In the upper part of each window the subject (1) extends across both lights; in the lower part there is a single figure in each light (2, 3). The windows and subjects are numbered from west to east.

NORTH TRANSEPT, WINDOW I.

In . mem . Radulphi . Tatham . s.t.p. Academiæ . olim . oratoris . Coll. magistri . qui . obiit . XIX°. Jan. MDCCCLVII. æt . LXXIX. frater . et . soror . superstites . posuerunt.

1. S. Michael and his angels fighting against the Dragon.

     Prælium magnum in cælo ; Michaël et angeli ejus præliabantur cum dracone. [Rev. xii. 7.]

2. The Angel clothed with a cloud. Over his head are the words *"quia tempus non erit amplius."* [Rev. x. 6.]

     Vidi Angelum amictum nube. [Rev. x. 1.]

3. The woman clothed with the sun.
     Apparuit mulier amicta sole. [Rev. xii. 1.]

NORTH TRANSEPT, WINDOW II.

The Memorial Inscription is repeated.

1. The Lamb with his company.

     Hi sequuntur agnum quocunque ierit. [Rev. xiv. 4.]

2. The Angel preaching the Gospel. He bears a scroll inscribed : *" Evangelium æternum Iesus Christus Hominum salvator."*

     Vidi alterum Angelum volantem. [Rev. xiv. 6.]

3. The descent of the heavenly Jerusalem is shewn to S. John.
     Vidi Ierusalem novam descendentem. [Rev. xxi. 2.]

On the east face of the same transept is a window of three lights filled with stained glass by Hardman, in memory of the Reverend John James Blunt, B.D., Lady Margaret's Professor, 1839—55, at the expense of his widow and family. It was first placed in the old chapel ; and on its removal to its present position, was increased in size by the addition of a border, and of the devices in the tracery. The inscription, which extends across the three lights, is as follows : IN . MEMORIAM . JOHANNIS . JACOBI . BLUNT . COLL. SOC. S. THEOL. BACC. ET . PRO . DNA . MARGARETA . PROF. QUI . OBIIT . DIE . XVII. IUNII . ANNO . DNI. MDCCCLV . ÆTATIS . LX. The glass is intended to commemorate S. John as the writer of the Gospel, the Revelation, and the Epistles ; and also the Lady Margaret as Foundress of the Theological Professorship held by Mr Blunt. In the central light S. John

is writing the Revelation; above him is Christ in Majesty (Rev.
i. 13—16); in the light on the left S. John is writing the Gospel;
in that on the right he is addressing little children, to indicate
the author of the Epistle. Over his head, in each of the side
lights, is an Angel. Beneath these subjects the lights contain
respectively a Tudor rose, crowned; a portcullis, crowned; and a
daisy, crowned; and above them, a daisy crowned; M.R. crowned,
for Margaret Richmond; and a Tudor rose, crowned. Of the
three sexfoils in the head the highest contains a white rose;
that on the left a cup from which a demon is issuing; that
on the right an eagle.

The quire, from the screen to the "sacrarium," is paved with
Purbeck and Sicilian marble and encaustic tiles. The six steps
leading up to the altar are of Devonshire marble. The space
between the first and second steps is paved with Purbeck,
Sicilian, and black Derbyshire marbles, with a border of encaustic
tiles. The space between the second and third steps is elaborately decorated with a series of subjects in inlaid work. The
figures are of white marble, on a ground of black Devonshire
marble. Each subject is so arranged as to form a square,
set lozenge-wise, round which an inscription runs; and encaustic tiles, of the same colour and pattern as those used in
other parts of the chapel, form borders round the subjects, and,
intermixed with marbles of other colours, a general groundwork
to the whole composition. In the central portion of the pavement the above-mentioned subjects are set in two rows, five in
each row; and round the outer edge, in the small triangular
spaces which intervene between the squares, are the signs of the
zodiac, also in white marble on a black ground. The subjects
with their legends are as follows, beginning with the left-hand
corner of the upper row:

UPPER ROW.

1. Abel watching his burnt offering.

    *Abel [quoque] obtulit de primogenitis gregis sui, et de adipibus eorum; et respexit
    Dominus ad Abel, et ad munera ejus.* [Gen. iv. 4.]

2. King Solomon.

    *Sapientia immolavit victimas suas. Miscuit vinum, et proposuit mensam suam:
    [et locuta est] Venite comedite panem meum et bibite vinum quod ego miscui
    vobis.* [Prov. ix. 2, 5.]

3. Melchisedeck blessing Abraham.

Melchisedeck rex Salem Sacerdos Dei summi obviavit Abrahæ et benedixit ei [Hebr. vii. 1] *proferens panem et vinum ait Benedictus Abram deo excelso.* [Gen. xiv. 18, 19.]

4. King David.

Ascendisti in altum, cepisti captivitatem, accepisti dona in hominibus; etenim non credentes inhabitare Dominum Deum. Dominus in eis in Sinai in sancto. [Psalm lxviii. 18, 19.]

5. The Sacrifice of Isaac.

Ecce ignis et ligna, ubi est victima holocausti Deus providebit sibi victimam holocausti. [Gen. xxii. 7, 8.]

LOWER ROW.

1. The Prophet Moses.

Quæ est ista religio Victima transitus Domini est, quando transivit super domos filiorum Israel in Ægypto. [Exod. xii. 26, 27.]

2. The Burning Bush.

Non appropries huc: Solve calceamentum de pedibus tuis; locus enim in quo stas terra sancta est. [Exod. iii. 5.]

3. The Prophet Zechariah.

Quid enim bonum ejus est, et quid pulchrum ejus, nisi frumentum electorum, et vinum germinans virgines. [Zech. ix. 17.]

4. The manna in the wilderness.

Panem de [in] cælo præstitisti eis [sine labore] omne delectamentum in se habentem. [Wisd. xvi. 20.] *Panem angelorum manducavit homo; cibaria misit eis in abundantia.* [Psalm lxxvij. 25.]

5. The Prophet Malachi.

Ab ortu solis usque ad occasum magnum est nomen Meum in gentibus et in omni loco sacrificatur et offertur nomini meo oblatio munda. [Malachi i. 11.]

The quire is separated from the transeptal antechapel by a screen of oak. Eastward of this are the stalls and seats, extending as far as the bay immediately preceding the apse. There are 98 stalls; 44 of which, 22 on each side eastward, were removed from the old chapel. The new stalls, designed by Mr Scott, and executed by Messrs Rattee and Kett[1], have been made to correspond, as far as possible, with those of older date.

[1] [College Order, 7 December, 1863. "Agreed to accept the Tender of Messrs Rattee and Kett for the execution of the Wood Fittings the Stalls and the Screen for the New Chapel for the sum of four thousand pounds (£4000) subject to the settlement of the particulars of the contract at a future meeting."

13 February, 1864. "Agreed to set the Seal to a Contract with Messrs Rattee and Kett for the execution of (the above)."]

The altar is of oak, with deeply carved panels; a single slab of Belgian marble forms the top. The brass lectern had been given to the old chapel in 1840 by the Rev. Thomas Whytehead, Fellow. The pedestal is copied from the wooden lectern in Ramsey Church, Huntingdonshire, the finials which are there wanting having been restored. The wooden desk has been replaced by an eagle[1].

The position of certain objects removed from the old chapel remains to be noticed. The arches through which Bishop Fisher's chantry was entered have been placed in the south wall of the south transept of the antechapel (*BC*, fig. 25). The central arch has been left in the original condition; the lateral arches are new, in exact reproduction of the old, which were found to be in bad condition. The shield in the right spandrel of the central arch has been defaced. It probably contained Bishop Fisher's arms, the removal of which is thus commented on by Baker:

"This [Bishop Fisher's original chapel] was situated on the north side of the college chapel near the altar, where the arms of the See of Rochester are yet remaining, and had been quartered with the paternal arms of the bishop's family, now erased: in the old books, an. 32 Hen. 8[vi], there is 3[d]. placed to account *for taking down D[r] Fisher's arms*, whether it was for erasing these arms or taking them down somewhere else I cannot say; but it was an expense that might very well have been spared[2]."

The monument of Hugh Ashton, described in a former chapter, now stands under the easternmost of the two arches through which the north transept is entered (ibid. *D*). The seated statue of Dr James Wood (Master 1815—39) by E. H. Baily, R.A., which had been placed in the old chapel by Dr Wood's friends, occupies a central position at the west end (ibid. *E*).

The commemorative decoration of the building has been further carried out on the exterior. On the north side of the porch is a statue of the Lady Margaret, on the south side, of

---

[1] [The Ecclesiologist, Vol. i. p. 143. The lectern was cast by Mr Sidey of London. It bears the inscription: IN. USUM. SACELLI. COLL. DIV. JOHANN. AP. CANT. DICAVIT. VNUS. E. SOCIIS. A. S. MDCCCXL. The Ramsey example is figured in the Glossary of Architecture, ed. 1850, Pl. 104. Though dated 1840, the lectern was not formally accepted until 1842. Coll. Order, 6 May, 1842.]

[2] [Baker's History, p. 91.]

Bishop Fisher. The lower stage of each buttress bears a canopy, under which is a statue. The persons commemorated, beginning with the buttress next the transept on the south side, are:

1. Sir William Cecil, Lord Burghley.
2. Lucius, Viscount Falkland.
3. John Williams, Archbishop of York.
4. Thomas Wentworth, Earl of Strafford.
5. William Gilbert, physician to Queen Elizabeth.
6. Roger Ascham, instructor of Queen Elizabeth.
7. Mary Cavendish, Countess of Shrewsbury.
8. Richard Bentley, Master of Trinity College.
9. Edward Stillingfleet, Bishop of Worcester.
10. John Overall, Bishop of Coventry and Lichfield, and afterwards of Norwich.
11. Peter Gunning, Bishop of Chichester and afterwards of Ely.
12. Sarah Alston, Duchess of Somerset.
13. Thomas Clarkson, opponent of the Slave-trade.
14. Brook Taylor, natural philosopher and mathematician.
15. Thomas Linacre, founder of Physic lecture.
16. } Vacant.
17. }
18. Thomas Baker, historian of the College.

The total cost of the chapel, inclusive of the stained glass, was £57,955; that of the Master's Lodge, the enlargement of the Hall, and other matters incidental to the various alterations was £27,915; making a total of £85,870.]

CHRONOLOGICAL SUMMARY.

1448.	Henry the Sixth grants to the Hospital "a garden with ponds."
1510.	(Christmas). First payment made towards the buildings.
1511.	(9 April). Charter of foundation granted by Henry the Eighth. Build ings commenced.
1513.	(17 December). Contract for glazing Chapel, Hall, and Lodge.
1516.	Last recorded payment made towards the buildings.
,,	(20 June). Contract between Dr Shorton and Thomas Loveday, carpenter, for stalls, roodloft, gates, etc.
,,	(29 July). College formally opened by the Bishop of Rochester.
1516—19.	The chapel adapted to collegiate service.
1520.	Oliver Scales, clerk of the works, signs a receipt in full.
1523.	(9 March). Will of Hugh Ashton proved. Probable date of commencement of his chantry.
1525.	(16 June). Bishop Fisher's chantry commenced.
1528.	A small additional court built by Dr Metcalfe.
1533.	Dr John Keyton conveys £300 to the College. Probable date of commencement of his chantry.
1561.	Leave obtained from Town of Cambridge to close S. John's Lane with gates.
1573—74.	Tennis court built.
1584—85.	Building north of Chapel fitted up as Chambers.
1588—89.	The Pentionary opposite to the College fitted up.
1598.	(7 August). Contract signed with Ralph Simons and Gilbert Wigge.
,,	(2 October). Foundation of Second Court laid.
1599.	(9 August). Supplementary contract signed with Simons and Wigge.
1601.	(19 January). Ornamental plaster-work of the gallery executed.
1602.	(31 July). Last payment made to the contractors for the Second Court.
1602—3.	Walks laid out. Tennis-court rebuilt west of river.
1603.	The Second Court paved.
1605.	Alterations to the First Court.
1610.	(24 April). Purchase of the Bowling Green from the Town.
1610—11.	Bowling-Green enclosed.
1611.	Lease from Corpus Christi College of three acres to the south of the Bowling Green.
1616.	Library removed to a Chamber over the kitchen.
1623.	(26 April). Proposal from Bishop Williams to give £1200 to build a Library.
1624.	Walls and roof of Library completed.
1628.	Library-staircase completed. Books moved in.
1636—37.	Chapel beautified by Dr William Beale.
,,	Passage made round east end of Chapel.

1662—63.	Statue of S. John over Gate of entrance carved by Woodroff.
1665—66.	New wooden gates put up at Gate of entrance.
1669.	Foundation of the Third Court laid.
1671.	Statue of the Countess of Shrewsbury placed over the gateway leading into the Third Court.
,,	Stonework of the third Court completed.
1674.	Statue of the Foundress placed over the door leading into the Screens.
1691.	Two buttresses built by Grumball in the Third Court to support the west side of the building of the Second Court.
1696.	(20 April). Bridge leading to the walks begun.
1712.	(Christmas). Bridge completed. Piers at the west end of the back-lane set up.
1725.	Hall wainscoted and repaired by Austin.
1772.	(20 February). Decision to ashlar the south side of the first court under the direction of Essex.
1777.	Third Court altered by Essex.
1784.	Outside of chapel stuccoed.
1805.	Two small pieces of ground adjoining the walks allotted to the College. Exchange with Merton College, Oxford.
1825.	(25 February). A new building west of the Cam determined upon.
1826.	(8 March). Messrs Rickman and Hutchinson employed as architects.
1827.	(5 June). Decision that the new buildings shall be of stone.
1830.	New building partially occupied.
1831.	,, completed.
1841.	Foundations and superstructure of the Third Court repaired.
1858.	Rooms under the west end of the Library added to it.
1862.	The Globe Passage closed.
1863—65.	Lengthening of the Hall.
1863.	Contract for new chapel signed (15 June). "The Labyrinth" pulled down.
1864.	(6 May). Foundation-stone of the new chapel laid.
1865.	(Christmas). The Fellows used for the first time as a Combination Room that part of the Gallery which had been the Drawing-Room of the Lodge.
1867.	(13 Nov.). The Fellows used for the first time the restored Long Gallery.
1869.	New Chapel consecrated (12 May). Old chapel pulled down.
1874—75.	Rooms under the east end of the Library partly added to it, partly formed into a Lecture-room.

APPENDIX.

I. *Contract between Robert Shorton, Master of S. John's College, and Richard Wright, of Bury, Glazier.* 17 *December,* 1513.

This indenture made bytwen Maister Robert Shorton Clerk, doctor of Diuinite Maister and Keper of the Collegge of Seynt John Theuangeliste in Cambrigge on that oon partie

And Richard Wryght of Bury Seynt Edmund in the Countie of Suffolk Glasyer on that other parte, Witnessyth

that the said Richard couenaunteth...that he shall Glase with good and hable Normandy Glasse All the Wyndowes belongyng to the Maisters loggyng within the said Collegge with Roses and purcholious conuenyent for the same

And also all the Wyndowes within the halle of the said Collegge also with Rosez and purcholious and the Bay Wyndowe within the said halle with the pyctour of seynt John Theuangeliste and with Tharmes of the Excellent pryncesse Margaret late Countesse of Rychemond and Derby Welle and Workemanly made conuenient for the same

And also all the Wyndowes belongyng to the Chappell within the Collegge afore-said with Imagery Werke and Tabernaclis suche as the said Maister Robert Shorton shall appoynte and assigne for the same after his discression

And also ij Wyndowes atte the Weste ende of the said Chappell within the said Maysters loggyng also with Rosez and purcholious all thyse premyssez with as goode and hable normandy Glasse of colourz and pyctourz as be in the Glasse Wyndowes within the Collegge called Cristes Collegge in Cambrigge or better in euery poynte

And clerly and holly shall fynysshe all the said Wyndowes in fourme as is aforesaid after and accordyng to the beste workemanshipp and proporcion a thisside the feste of midsomer next cummyng after the date herof

for the whiche premissez so to be accomplisshed and doon The said Maister Robert Shorton couenaunteth...that he shall pay...to the said Richard...That is to Wytte for euery foote of the said Wyndowes within the said Maisters loggyng and halle aforesaid iiij^d ob the foote; and for euery Rose and purcolious within the said wyndowes viij^d.; And for Thymage of seynt John theuangeliste and tharmes aforesaid ij^s.; And for the foresaid Wyndowes within the said Chappell xlv li of good and lawfull money of yngland whereof the said Richard knowlegeth him silf to haue resceyued and hadde the day and yer of makyng herof of the said maister Robert Shorton x *li.* sterlinges and therof vtterly acquiteth and dischargeth the said maister Robert Shorton ...And xxxv *li* Residue of the said summe of xlv *li* the sayd maister Robert Shorton couenaunteth...to pay...to the said Richard...in maner and fourme folowyng

That istosey as the said Richard maketh expedicion of the said workes and nedeth to haue money for the same The said maister Robert Shorton shall pay to him the said xxxv li after his discression as he nedeth yt

And wher as the said Richard by his wryting obligatorie beryng date the day and yere of makyng herof is holden and bounden to the said mayster Robert Shorton in the summe of l. *li* sterlinges payhable atte the feste of Estir next cummyng after the date herof as in the said obligacion more pleynly doth apper   Neuerthelesse the said Maister Robert Shorton wylleth and graunteth by thise presentes that yf the said Richard dothe holde kepe perfourme and fulfille all and singuler couenauntes condicions promysys graunts and Articlis aforesaid…That than the said Obligacion to be voyde Orelles yt to stonde and be in the hole strenght and effecte

Into witnesse wherof to thise Indentures the parties aforesaid Interchaungehably haue sette their Sealles.

yoven the xvij^th day of Decembre the fyueth yere of the reigne of oure soueraign lorde kynge henry the viij^th.

Appended to this contract is a bond for £6, dated 31 December, 1512, on the back of which the following condition is written:

The condicion of this obligacion is suche that if the within bounde Richard well and workemanly doth make or cause to be made as many glasse Wyndowes apperteynyng and belongyng to the Collegge withinwretyn as it shall please the withinnamed Maister to assigne and appoynte after suche pricez as ensuyth

Thatistosay shall haue oonly for euery foote whyght glass called Normandy Glasse good and hable withoute fawte or deformytyf bought and provyded atte propre Costes and Charges of the sayd Rychard iiij^d ob for euery foote of the sayd wyndows so to be made.   And for euery foote of whyght Glasse of the sayd Wyndowes to be made with the olde glasse of the sayd Collegge after the best wormanship oonly j^d ob the foote

And shall fynysshe as many of the sayd wyndowes as may be conuenyently doon suche as the sayd maister will assigne and appoynte to be made ther clerly and holly Athisside the fest of seynt Mychell tharchaungell next commyng after the date withinwretyn atte propre Costes and Charges of the sayd Rychard after and for pricez afore rehersed Towarde the whiche charges the sayd Mayster hath delyuered and payd vnto the sayd Rychard the day and yere of makyng herof C*s* sterling yf the sayd Rychard accomplysshe the premissez in fourme as is aforesaid That than this present obligacion shall be voyde or elles is to stand and be in the hole strenght and effecte.

II.   *Dr Shorton's Building Account.*

A copy of the account rendered by Dr Shorton to the Lady Margaret's Executors for the five years ending Jan. 21, 1515—16, is preserved at the beginning of a volume which was used throughout the sixteenth century for various College Inventories.   It is called on the outside "Registrum omnium bonorum Collegii Sancti Johannis Euangeliste in vniuersitate Cantebrigie."   Shorton first states the money received by him, amounting to £5432. 9. 11½, and then his payments, amounting to £5249. 16. 7, leaving a balance due from him of £182. 13. 4½ accounted for to the Executors.

The first two extracts here given are from his ordinary payments; the third occurs in the statement of the distribution of the balance, and may therefore be presumed to belong to the period from January 1515—16 to his resignation of the Mastership in July 1516.

* * * * * *

Et [computat] in consimilibus denariis per ipsum similiter liberatis Oleuero Scalis clerico operum dicti Collegii pro diuersis prouisionibus et solucionibus ad vsum dictorum operum fiendis ad diuersas vices infra tempus huius compoti vide-licet a festo Natalis domini anno secundo Regis predicti vsque diem Sabbati proxi-mum post festum sancte agnetis virginis anno tercio Regis predicti M^{l}M^{l}xxiiij^{li} et a dicto die sabbati anno tercio predicto vsque festum sancte agnetis anno quinto Regis predicti M^{l}M^l lv^{li} xviij^s iij^d vt patet per diuersas billas inde super hunc com-potum ostensas et restitutas ac per recognicionem eiusdem Oleuery super hunc compotum M^{l}M^{l}M^{l}M^{l}lxxix^{li} xviij^s iij^d.

Et in consimilibus denariis liberatis Oleuero Scalys causa predicta ad diuersas vices a festo sancte agnetis anno quinto Regis predicti vsque idem festum anno 7mo eiusdem Regis infra tempus huius compoti accidens videlicet per manus dicti magistri Shorton CCCCxliiij^{li} ix^s iiij^d per manus Christoferi Jeneson lx^{li} et per manus Magistri Ricardi Sharpe Ciiij^{xx} viij^{li} xvj^d in toto vt patet per billas predictas ac ex recognicione dicti Oleueri super hunc compotum DCiiij^{xx} xij^{li} x^s viij^d

* * * * * *

Item in redy money by the said Mr Shorton delyuered to Oleuer Scalis clerke of the new warkes in parte of recompens of a more summe to hym due vpon a super-plusage as in the fote of his accompte of the said workes de anno vij^{mo} Regis predicti more planely aperith Ciij^{li} xviij^s vj^d ob'

* * * * * *

The Executors' accounts preserved in St John's College mention the payments made to Dr Shorton which appear on the receipt side of his 5-years account. From these we learn that the whole surplusage or balance due to Oliver Scales at the foot of his account "de anno septimo," that is, for the two years ending on St Agnes' Day (Jan. 21), 1515—16, amounted to £210. 5s. 7¼d. Of this we have seen that £103. 18s. 6½d. was paid by Shorton. An intervening payment of £27. 12s. 2d. does not appear, but the Executors cleared off the balance or surplusage due to Scales on this account by a payment of £78. 14s. 10¾d. This entry is printed in Mr Mayor's Appendix to C. H. Cooper's Life of the Lady Margaret, page 213:

"Item paide to Oliuer Scalis clerk of the newe buyldinges at Seynt Johns colege in Cambrige in ffull contentacion and payment of CCx^{li} v^s vij^d q^a of a surplusage due to hym, as aperith in his accompte of the saide buyldynges made and determynede for two hoole yeris endide at the feast of St Agnes the virgyn in the vijth yer of kynge Henry the viijth ouer and besides lxxviij^{li} xiiij^s x^d ob q^a"

This final payment on the year ending Jan. 21, 1515—16, is made out of money received at Midsummer, 1516. The Executors' accounts are preserved down to May 23, 1518, but no further payments to Scales are recorded; and we may assume therefore that the buildings were in some sense finished when the College was formally opened, July 29, 1516. Baker's mention of the receipt in full (for what sum is not stated) given by Scales to Dr Metcalf in 1520 must refer to additional work, of which the loss of the accounts prevents us from having any record. It would probably include what was done by Loveday under the contract printed in App. I.

III.   *Inscriptions on the tomb of Hugh Ashton.*

On the ledger: HIC . SITVS . EST . HVGO . ASSHETON . ARCHIDIACONUS . EBOR . QUI . AD . CRISTIANE . RELIGIONIS . AUGMENTUM . SOCIOS . DUOS . EX . LANCAS-TRIA . TOTIDEMQUE . SCHOLARES . SOCIUM . ET . SCHOLAREM . EBOR . COM . SOCIUM-QUE . ET . SCHOLAREM . DUNELM . DIOC . ORIŬNDVS . SUIS . IMPENSIS . PIE . INSTI-TUIT . ATQUE . SINGULIS . A . SE . INSTITUTIS . SOCIIS . CONSUETUM . SOCIORUM . STIPENDIUM . SOLIDIS . XL . ANNUIS . ADAVXIT . OBIIT . IX . CALEN . DECEMB . AN . M.D.XXII.

On the iron railing: PRIDIE NONAS JANUARI PERPETUO ANNVIS EXEQVIIS CELEBRATIS PRESES MAGISTRO AC SENIORI V.S SOCIUS QVILIBET XII D SCHOLAS-TICVS ITEM QUILIBET VI D EX PIA DEFUNCTI INSTITUCIO[NE].

XIII.

𝔐𝔞𝔤𝔡𝔞𝔩𝔢𝔫𝔢 𝔆𝔬𝔩𝔩𝔢𝔤𝔢.

CHAPTER I.

HISTORY OF THE SITE.

[THE site of Magdalene College is bounded on the west by Bridge Street, on the south by the River Cam, on the east by dwelling-houses and their gardens, and on the north by the highway leading to Chesterton[1].

The principal portion of this site was granted by Henry the Sixth, 7 July, 1428, to the Benedictine Monks of Croyland[2], in consequence of a representation made to him by the Abbot, which may be translated as follows from the letters patent which contain the grant[3]:

"Those who belong to any particular Religious Order in England are usually in the habit of finding monks of the same Order as themselves studying Canon Law and Holy Scripture in the University Schools. The Abbey of Croyland however, and the Benedictine Order in general,

---

[1] [Professor Willis had made no collections for the History of the Site of this College. He assumed that it had inherited the site of the Benedictine Hostel without diminution or addition. I have done my best to supply additional facts for the History, both of the Site and of the Buildings, from a study of the College records, which have been most kindly placed at my disposal by the present Master, the Hon. and Rev. Latimer Neville. I have also received much valuable information from the Rev. Samuel Wilkes Waud, M.A. 1828, formerly Fellow; and Ralph Neville-Grenville, M.A. 1837.]

[2] [There is a legend that the college was called *Monks' Corner* and the highway to the north of it *Monks' Lane*, long after monasteries had been suppressed. In the plan of Cambridge made by W. Custance, 1798, this designation is applied to the bend of the river at the S.E. corner of the College garden.]

[3] [Patent 6 Hen. VI. p. 2, m. 21.]

has no hostel or manse of its own in Cambridge, set apart for those monks of their Order whom they have themselves sent to the University Schools as aforesaid. They are in consequence obliged to occupy hostels in company with secular persons, and cannot be managed and directed in conformity with the rules of their Order, as it would be their duty to be if they had a definite place of their own to reside in."

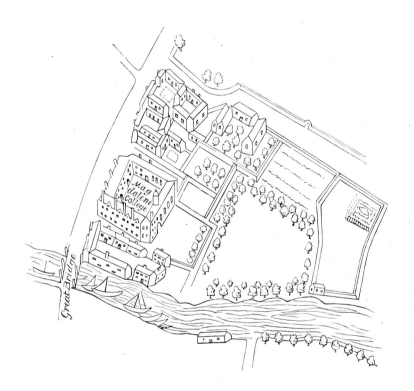

Fig. 2. Magdalene College, from Hammond's map of Cambridge, 1592.

The document then proceeds to describe the site as "two messuages with their appurtenances situated in the parish of S. Giles, of the yearly value of forty-six shillings and eight-pence." No dimensions or abuttals are given, and the garden-ground eastward of the existing College is not alluded to. In 1483 the whole establishment is mentioned as "the Hostel called Bokyngham College," belonging to the Abbot of Croy-land; and the Accounts of the Corporation of Cambridge

shew that between 1432 and 1521 he paid an annual rent for
"lez pondyerds" behind the same College[1]. A few years
later, in the charter granted by Henry the Eighth to Thomas
Lord Audley (3 April, 1542), this part of the site is described
as "those two gardens or parcels of ground together with
the ponds therein, called two pondyards, lately belonging to
Buckingham College[2]." A lease, dated 30 November, 1577,
and endorsed "Lease of our fish ponds[3]," describes the
ground as

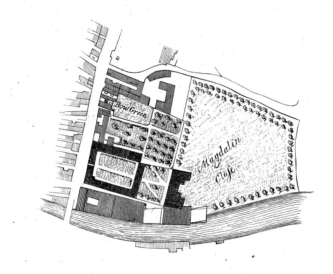

Fig. 3. Magdalene College, from Loggan's map of Cambridge, 1688.

"All that their ponyard conteyninge in it seaven pondes as it is
nowe inclosed set lyinge and being in the towne of Cambridge...
betwene the ground pertayninge to the said Colledge on the west side
and the common of ye towne of Chesterton on the east side the one
head abbuttythe vppon the common Ryver there towardes the southe
thother vppon the Queene highe waie leading to Chesterton aforesaide
towarde the Northe."

The ponds are known to have been filled up in 1586[4],

---

[1] [Treasurer's Accounts : quoted in Cooper's Annals, i. 184 : Cambridge Borough
Rate Report, p. 34.]   [2] [Commiss. Doc^{ts}. iii. 343.]

[3] [" Old Book " of Magdalene College, fo. 11.]

[4] [Audit-Book, 1585—86. "It' to Knocker for fillinge the ponds and allies
xxxix^s." Ibid. 1586—87. "It' to Cotton for fillinge the ponds xl^s."]

but the division of the ground into two gardens still existed in 1592, when Hammond's map was made (fig. 2).

We will next notice the additions made to the site, beginning from the south. Hammond's plan, and, more distinctly, Loggan's plan of Cambridge (fig. 3), shew that a thoroughfare extended under the south wall of the College from Bridge Street to the College Brewhouse. This was called "Salmon's Lane[1]." The ground between it and the river, belonging partly to Jesus College, partly to the town of Cambridge, was acquired during the mastership of Dr Peter Peckard (Master 1781—97). The piece belonging to the former, which had originally been a brewery[2], was bought 3 April, 1790; and is described in the conveyance as a

"Messuage or Tenement and the Site and Ground thereof, together with the Warehouses Granaries [etc.]...all which said Premises are situate...near the Great Bridge: Between the River towards the South East, and a Common Lane towards the North West; one head whereof abutts on the Street called Bridge Street towards the South West, and the other head thereof abutts on a piece of Waste Land (said to belong to the Corporation of Cambridge) towards the North East: And which said Premises extend in length from the said Street called Bridge Street to the said piece of Waste Ground One hundred and eighty-five feet be the same more or less, and in breadth from the said Common Lane to the River sixty-five feet be the same more or less."

The piece belonging to the Town was bought in the following year (6 July, 1791)[3]. It is described as

"Waste Ground lying and being in the parish of Saint Peters in Cambridge behind the Brewhouse belonging to the Messuage or Tenement now or late of Jesus College,....containing in length from the said Brewhouse towards the Ground belonging to Magdalene College... twenty-four yards; and in breadth between the river and the said College twenty yards and an half; together with the houses barn and other buildings now thereupon set and builded.

---

[1] [A College Order, dated 4 May, 1757, regulating the distribution of rooms in "ye old Court," mentions "ye Roome in ye corner Staircase which looks into Salmon's Lane, or that next thereto, being ye Corner Room looking into ye Street." Register ii. 753. The lane existed within the memory of persons still living.]

[2] [The property had been leased to Magdalene College by Jesus College for some years previous to the sale, and in one of the leases, dated 13 February, 1781, it is called "all that their Tenement formerly a Brewhouse." The price paid for it was £511. 1. 3, the equivalent for £650 Consolidated Bank Annuities.]

[3] [The price paid for this latter piece was £81. 8. 7. The dimensions of both have been laid down on the plan (fig. 1). It will be observed that they do not exactly correspond with those of the ground in its present state.]

And also all that Lane lying between the said Messuage...on the one part, and Magdalene College on the other part, extending and leading from the Common Street unto the said piece of Ground before mentioned together with one porch at the entrance of the Messuage."

We will next investigate, very briefly, the history of the ground bounded on the east and south by the College, on the north by the road to Chesterton, and on the west by Bridge Street, the whole of which now belongs to the College, but has only partially been used for College purposes.

The statutes, drawn up in 1554—55, mention a "garden into which the Master's chamber looks." It will be shewn below that the Master's chamber was at the north-west corner of the quadrangle. The garden therefore must have been immediately to the north of the College, in which position a narrow strip of ground enclosed by walls is shewn by Hammond (fig. 2). On the north side of this garden there was an Inn called "The Star," originally belonging to Trinity College. It is described in the earliest deed relating to it, a conveyance dated 4 September 1550, as bounded by "mawdelyn college" on the south, a tenement belonging to John Denham on the north, the west head abutting on the public highway, and the east head on a watercourse belonging to the said College. It was sold to Thomas Howard, Earl of Suffolk, 1 November, 1605, and was probably given by him to the College[1]. No dimensions are set down in any of the documents referring to it, but we shall see that the eastward extent of it at least may be estimated with sufficient accuracy from the abuttals of the property next to it on the north, also an inn, called "The Green Peele." The following description of the latter is translated from a conveyance dated 2 October, 1596:

"a tenement called *le Greene Peele*, together with the garden thereto adjoining, next to a tenement called *le Starre* on the south, and containing in length on that side from the King's high-way to Magdalen College 232 feet; on the north lying partly next the tenement of Robert Russell commonly called *le Blacke Boy*, and partly next a ditch commonly called *le Kynges Dytche*, and containing in length on that side from the King's highway to Magdalen College 232 feet; the west head of the said messuage abuts on the King's highway, and contains in breadth between the aforesaid tenements called *le Starre* and *le Blakeboy* 52 feet; the

---

[1] [He was grandson to the Founder. Lord Audley.]

east head of the aforesaid garden abuts upon Magdalen College, and contains in breadth between the aforesaid tenement called *le Starre* and the ditch called *le Kynges Ditche* 52 feet."

The "Green Peele" was bought for the College by Dr Barnaby Gooche (Master 1604—26), 6 October, 1615, for £156. 18s. 0d. The house immediately to the north of the buildings which will be shewn below to have formed part of the Master's Lodge, is just 50 feet wide, and probably represents the "Green Peele." Part of it subsequently became another Inn, called the "King's Head." The garden, evidently the walled enclosure containing six trees shewn by Hammond (fig. 2), was subsequently used by the College partly as a bowling-green, partly as a garden. The garden shewn on the same plan to the south of that above-mentioned probably belonged to the "Star."

At the north-west corner of the "Green Peele" we find a tenement, which in 1596 was called the "Black Boy[1]." It was bounded on the north by a "watercourse called Cambridge," and its garden ran back for some distance, as we shall see below, but no dimensions being given, the extent of it can only be conjectured. If we may identify the tenement with the house next to the "King's Head," it had a frontage to the street of 24 feet. It was purchased for the College by Dr Gooche, 6 October, 1615.

The watercourse mentioned as the northern boundary of both the "Black Boy" and the "Green Peele" had become a lane by the end of the eighteenth century. It belonged to the Town of Cambridge, and was sold to the College by the Corporation 10 April, 1792. The property conveyed is described as

"two messuages or tenements situate…on a piece of ground (formerly parcel of a lane which heretofore abutted upon an ancient Bridge called Cambridge Bridge) containing in breadth at the West end next the street nine feet, and from the said West end towards the east 52 feet 6 inches; with a small piece of garden ground now inclosed lying at the

---

[1] [In a conveyance dated 9 June, 1457, it is described as "inter mesuagium Warini Jugrith ex parte australi et communem cursum aquaticum vocat' Cambrigge ex parte boriali; et abuttat ad vnum caput super Regiam viam, et ad aliud caput super gardinum predicti Warini Jugrith."]

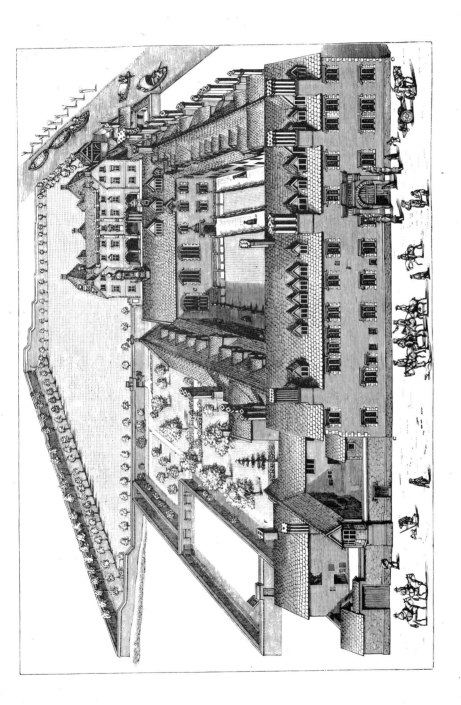

Fig. 4. Magdalene College, reduced from Loggan's print, taken about 1688. A, Chapel; B, Library; C, Hall; D, Master's Lodge; E, Kitchen;
F, Master's Garden.

east end of the said messuages....containing in length from the tenement at the said east end 13 feet, with the Passage, Yard, and part of a Blacksmith's shop there, containing next the street 8 feet, to the said Premises belonging...

and also all that...other parcel of the said Lane, formerly part of a Bowling Green, but lately converted into and used as a Garden by the said Master and Fellows, and divided by a wall from the east end of the small Garden before mentioned, containing in length from the said wall on towards the East 100 feet, and in breadth at the east end 14 feet...

And also all that their other piece or parcel of ground formerly other parcel of the said Lane since converted into and now also used as a Garden by the said Master and Fellows...and divided from the East end of the piece of Ground last abovementioned by a wall, with a door through the same, containing in length from the said East end of the said piece of ground on towards the East 100 feet, and in breadth at the East end 12 feet....''

The united length of these pieces is 265 feet 6 inches, with a mean breadth of nearly 12 feet. The length is sufficient to reach as far as the wall which bounded the large garden on the west when Loggan's print (fig. 4) was taken; and the existence of a bridge shews that the depth of the dyke, or watercourse, must have been considerable. From the nature of the ground it is difficult to believe that water could ever have run through it. It may possibly have been a dry ditch, in connection with the fortifications of the Castle. The position of it can be determined with tolerable accuracy. We have seen that a portion of the lane is described as "part of a Bowling Green;" and a lease of it, granted by the Corporation in 1762, assigns as the southern boundary the "Black Boy which was formerly, and now is, part of the Bowling Green." This Bowling Green is of course that shewn by Loggan (figs. 3, 4), the position of which can be easily laid down. Moreover, one of the houses in Bridge Street, immediately to the north of that which we have identified with the "Black Boy," is of the same breadth as the ground conveyed in 1792, namely 17 feet; and in all probability marks the position of "Cambridge Bridge." The conveyance of the "Star" shews that a branch of this watercourse ran south across the College garden towards the river.

The house at the corner of Bridge Street and Chesterton Road was an inn, which at the beginning of the seventeenth century was called the "Chequers," but soon after the "Three

Swans," a name which it retained until a few years since[1]. It was bequeathed to the College, with two tenements belonging to it, by Dr John Smith, Senior Fellow, in 1637. Between it and the above-mentioned lane there was a garden belonging to S. John's College, about which nothing further is known. As, however, it is described as the southern boundary of the "Chequers" and the northern boundary of the property bought from the Corporation in 1792[2], it is clear that no other ground intervened between those two pieces, and that its width is represented by that of a modern house of which the street front measures 34 feet; but its extent eastward is not known. The eastern boundary of the "Chequers" was a house, the name of which is written in earlier documents "coped hall," and "copped halle." It belonged to Merton College, Oxford, and was purchased by Magdalene College, 29 July, 1835. The name was probably applied originally to a single house; but in 1835 the estate comprised at least three dwelling-houses. Unfortunately the conveyance merely describes them as "part of a certain estate called Copped Hall," without entering into particulars, or giving dimensions. It probably extended up to the next piece, "a parcel of land heretofore part of a Farm called Saint Giles Rectory" which was bought 9 April, 1835, from the Bishop of Ely, as Impropriate Rector of the Parish of S. Giles. At that time it was used as a farm-yard. It is shewn very distinctly by Hammond (fig. 2), and also by Loggan (fig. 3)[3].]

---

[1] [The earliest deed preserved, dated 26 Sept., 1557, describes it as "inter venellam que ducit a Cantebr' vsque Chesterton ex parte boriali et quoddam gardinum Collegii Sancti Johannis Euangeliste...ex parte australi; et abuttat ad vnum caput super regiam viam...que ducit a castello ..vsque magnum pontem...versus occident', et super coppedhalle versus orient." In 1608 it is described as "vulgariter voc' siue cognit' per nomen de le Checker;" and in 1613 as "tenementum quondam Clarehalls ...modo vocat'...per nomen de le three swannes." The name "Coped Hall," variously spelt, is found in conveyances and leases down to the end of the last century.]

[2] [A lease granted by the Corporation of Cambridge, 11 January, 1762, gives as the northern abuttals a garden belonging to the College of Saint John the Evangelist, and a "tenement called Copy Hall."]

[3] [The dimensions have been laid down from a plan attached to the conveyance.]

CHAPTER II.

HISTORY OF THE BUILDINGS OF THE QUADRANGLE, AND OF THE PEPYSIAN LIBRARY.

MAGDALENE College has a single quadrangle, entered from the street by a gateway which opens into it near the south-west corner. This quadrangle measures 80 feet from north to south, by 113 feet from east to west. The Hall, Butteries, and Kitchen occupy the east side; the Hall being at the north end, and the Kitchen extending to the external south boundary of the buildings. The north side contains the Chapel next to the Hall; and the remainder was formerly occupied by the Master's Lodge. The south and west sides consist of chambers. The screens lead to a second court to the east of the first, bounded only by a wall on the north and south sides; but the east side is formed by a detached building, in the fashion of a mansion, most commonly designated " The New Building," but occasionally, " The Pepysian Library." The Master now resides in a modern house erected for the purpose in the garden to the north of the quadrangle, from which it is entirely separated, as the plan shews (fig. 1).

The buildings appear to be mainly those of the Benedictine House known as Buckingham College[1] [to which the present Foundation succeeded after an interval of only two years. The notices which have come down to us respecting the earlier house are very scanty, but by a careful comparison of authorities it may be possible to trace the extent of it, at least partially.

We have seen that the original establishment of a Hostel for the Benedictines began with a grant by Henry VI. to the Abbot of Croyland in 1428 of two messuages for a dwellingplace for the monks resorting to Cambridge for study; the condition of which was that all students of the Benedictine Order should have their quarters there. It may therefore be presumed that some house was provided for them, without much delay. Abbot Litlyngton, who applied for the grant in 1428, died in 1469, and was suc-

---

[1] [The following account of Buckingham College has been most kindly drawn up for me by my friend Henry Bradshaw, M.A., Fellow of King's College, and University Librarian.]

ceeded by John de Wisbech, who died in 1476. John de
Wisbech was a great benefactor both before and after he became
Abbot, and the Croyland historian who, writing in 1486, enumerates his good deeds, tells us that "in the monks' college of
Buckingham he erected chambers convenient for repose and
study[1]". The Buckingham from whom the College took its
name—which occurs in the Borough Accounts of Cambridge as
early as 1483[2]—seems to have been Henry Stafford, second
Duke, beheaded by Richard III. in 1483. A tradition preserved by Dr Caius, during whose own student-time (1529—45)
the monks still occupied the place, connects it with this Duke;
though it is evident that he confounds him to some extent
with his son and successor, Edward, beheaded in 1521. He
says that

"not many years since, the work was begun in brick by Henry,
Duke of Buckingham, from whom the college took its name, and was
continued by the monks, different monasteries building different portions; thus Ely built one chamber, Walden a second, and Ramsey a
third[3]."

It was precisely in this manner that the chambers of the
similar Benedictine house at Oxford, called Gloucester College,
now Worcester College, were built[4].

That some considerable buildings existed in the fifteenth
century is beyond question. When the present Chapel was
restored in 1847, as will be related in the next chapter, the oak
roof of the time of Edward IV. was exposed, with other remains,
shewing that Buckingham College had had a Chapel on the
same site. The Prior's chamber probably stood west of the

---

[1] [Continuatio Historiæ Croylandensis, in Fulman's Scriptores veteres (fol.
Oxon. 1684). The words are "in Collegio monachorum Bokynghamiæ cameras ad
quiescendum et studendum convenientes erexit."]

[2] [Cooper's Annals, i. 227.]

[3] ["Et postremum Collegium diuae Magdalenae est quod in transcantino vrbis
parte, ad Cantae ripam, diximus esse constitutum. Ei ante paucos annos, nullis
datis possessionibus, ex opere lateritio initium dedit Henr. Buckinghamiae dux,
vnde Buckinghamiae Collegii nomen adinuenit, incrementum monachi, dum aliam
partem alii aedificarunt. Nam Eliense monasterium vnum cubiculum, alium Waldense,
3. Ramisense monasterium fabricarunt. Monachi enim per nostra tempora locum
occupabant, qui ex variis Angliae monasteriis disciplinae gratia huc conuenerant."
Hist. Cant. Acad. p. 77. The fact that the College itself belonged to Croyland Abbey
may account for that House not being named among the other contributors.]

[4] [Ingram, Memorials of Oxford, Vol. ii.]

Chapel, a position subsequently occupied by the Master's Lodge. The doorway at the north-west corner of the court (fig. I, F) retained the arms of the Monastery of Ely (three keys, the wards in base) so late as 1777, when they were described by Cole[1]; pointing to the portion built by the monks of Ely, and tending strongly to confirm the tradition preserved by Caius. The south side of the court bears many marks of having formed part of Buckingham College (as will be noticed further on); and of the Hall we have no reason to doubt that it was built in 1519 by Edward Stafford, Duke of Buckingham, as stated in the account of the College drawn up for the use of Queen Elizabeth when she visited Cambridge in 1564. We are there told that the Duke "coming to Cambridge, put up at Magdalene College, where he remained for several days, and built the Hall, in the year 1519, the tenth year of the reign of King Henry the Eighth[2];" a story confirmed by the Borough Accounts, which shew that he was at Cambridge early in that year.

As Buckingham College was destitute of any endowment except the site and the buildings, it naturally ceased when the superior house, Croyland Abbey, surrendered to the King in December, 1539. But the continuity seems never to have been sensibly broken, and within two years and a half from the surrender we find it re-founded, under the new dedication of S. Mary Magdalene, by Thomas Lord Audley of Walden, to whom the King had granted it for the purpose. Audley, as Lord Chan-

---

[1] [MSS. Cole. (Add. MSS. Mus. Brit. 5876, f. 110): "In the North-West Corner of the first Court in Magdalen College next the Master's Lodge, on a Stone Door Case leading up to M[r] Hey's Chambers, I observed, Oct. 19, 1777, these Arms in one corner of the Arch Turning, much filled up with Whiting and Paint, but they seemed to me to be designed for Keys: viz. 3 Keys, the Wards in base." A sketch of the shield is appended.]

[2] [MSS. Baker vi. fo. 94, 117. MSS. Harl. 7033. The MS. is headed: "Transcripts from My L[d] Chief Justice's Hale's Papers some of wch are now in the Custody of y[e] Rev[d]. M[r] G. Harbin. The accounts of Colleges were these, that were taken and given in, when Queen Eliz. was at Cambridge, 1564." The account referred to in the text is stated as follows (fo. 117 b). "Collegium Mariæ Magd. Buckinghamense dictum est, a Duce ipso, qui Cantabrigiam accedens, ibi divertit, et ad aliquos dies commoratus est, et ex monachorum Hospitio Studiosorum Collegium fecit, atque Aulam ipsam aedificavit An. Dom. 1519, anno vero Regni Regis H. 8. 10." See also Parker, De Antiq. Brit. Eccl. Ed. 1729, p. xxvi. Dr Caius, in the passage cited above, has evidently confounded the earlier buildings with the Hall built by the Duke in 1519.]

cellor, had been for some years much occupied with the affairs
of the University, and as Buckingham College had latterly
ceased to be confined solely to monks (some notable laymen, as
Sir Robert Rede, having studied there), the new Master and
Fellows of Magdalene College would readily fall into their
places, as occupants of the then existing buildings. Lord Audley
had become possessed, among his other spoils, of the whole property of the Abbey of Walden, which had taken its part in the
building of Buckingham College, as we have already seen.   His
unexpected death, however, early in 1544 (30 April) prevented
any endowment except the site, and an income of £20 arising
from two pieces of property in London which he conveyed to
his new College.   The returns of the Commissioners of Henry
the Eighth in 1546 shew that the Society was then in a state of
extreme poverty.   There were only four Fellows instead of the
eight directed by the Founder "because the College is not as
yet sufficiently endowed[1]."   A Bible-clerk waited on the Fellows
in Hall[2].   A cook appears to have been then their only servant ;
and when Caius wrote in 1574 there were only three, for whose
maintenance the corporate funds were insufficient, and they had
to be paid by a tax levied on the Fellows and pensioners[3].   It is
clear therefore that there was no money to be spent on buildings.   In August, 1564, the young Duke of Norfolk came to
Cambridge with Queen Elizabeth, and great hopes were entertained that he would do something substantial to assist the
College[4], to which he had in the previous January sent the
Statutes drawn up in 1554—55 by Lady Audley and her hus-

---

[1] [Commiss. Doc[ts]. i. 165.]

[2] [Ibid. ii. 358.]

[3] [Hist. Cantab. Acad. p. 78.   In another passage (ibid. p. 54), when contrasting
the Colleges of recent foundation with the older and poorer Halls and Houses, and
the still less pretentious Hostels and Inns, he speaks of Magdalene as in every respect
the least of all: "Collegium vero diuæ Magdalenæ est hodie omnibus nominibus
omnium minimum, futurum maius cum bonis viris visum fuerit."]

[4] [MSS. Baker, ut supra.   "Tandem Vir Ornatissimus Tho. Audley Angliae
Cancellarius, per ipsum Regem munitus, ex datâ authoritate Parliamenti an. Regni
sui 30 Fundator dicti Collegii factus, atque unum Magistrum et 8 socios ibidem
stabilire satagens, repentinâ morte praeventus, quicquid instituerat inchoatum reli-
quit.   Sed maxima spes est, generum suum Excellentem Principem, Clarissimum
Icenorum Ducem cumulate brevi absoluturum quicquid honorandus Socer tam pio
animi proposito instituerat."]

band's executors[1]. His wife was the daughter and sole heir of the Founder, Lord Audley, and his own grandmother had been daughter to Edward Stafford, Duke of Buckingham, whose interest in the earlier College has been already recorded. In the narrative of the Queen's visit the following passage occurs. On Thursday, 10 August, 1564,

"The duke of Norfolke accompanyed her Majestie out of the Town, and then returning, entred Magdalen College, and gave much money in the same. Promising 40.l. by year till they had builded the quadrant of their College. And further promised, 'That he would endow them with land for the encrease of their number and studys[2].'"

The language here used shews that the buildings—which from the facts we have gathered together must have been practically those of Buckingham College—did not form a complete square. The site however contained in 1555, before the Duke of Norfolk's visit: (1) a Hall, built in 1519 by Edward Stafford, Duke of Buckingham, on the northern half of the east side of the court; (2) a Chapel, built at least in Edward the Fourth's reign (before 1483), on the eastern half of the north side, and mentioned as the *Capella ibidem* in 1545—46; (3) a Master's Chamber, at the western part of the north side, looking out, in 1555, upon (4) the Master's Garden (*Hortus major*), evidently on the north side of the College, with (5) a stable for the Master, also on this side; (6) Chambers for Students at the northern part of the west side, built by the monks of Ely, and bearing the arms of the monastery on the doorway; (7) an entrance from the street in the middle of the west side; (8) a small garden (*Hortulus omnium multo minimus*), assigned to the President, and situated close to the gate (*juxta ipsas portas atque januas*) and therefore also on the west side; (9) a chamber occupied by the President, presumably at the south end of the west side; (10) other chambers for students, who, when Caius wrote, amounted to 23 pensioners and 17 sizars. These chambers presumably occupied part of the south side, as well as part of the west side, and possibly the portion of the north side between the Chapel and the Master's chamber; and they con-

---

[1] [The letter prefixed to the Statutes (Commiss. Doc^ts. iii. 344) is dated 20 Jan., 1564, which may of course mean either 1564 or 1565.]

[2] [Nichols, Progresses of Queen Elizabeth, Ed. 1823, I. 182.]

sisted, in 1555, like the chambers in other Colleges, of celars (*inferiora cubicula*) with two studies (*musæa*) in each for juniors, and solars (*superiora cubicula*) for seniors[1]; (11) the kitchen, presumably in the same position as at present, south of the Hall. The plan (fig. 1) shews that the above enumeration has left sufficient room on the site to accommodate the building erected, or at least begun, by the Duke of Norfolk, during the eight years that elapsed between his visit in 1564 and his execution 2 June, 1572; as well as for that which a subsequent benefactor, Sir Christopher Wray, Knight, Lord Chief Justice of England, a former student of Buckingham College, is known to have contributed.]

The next historical facts that we are able to collect are furnished by the Audit-Books, of which the first is that for the year ending at Michaelmas, 1576. In this we find only small repairs being executed to the Chapel, Hall, Buttery, Master's Chamber, etc.[2]; but in that extending from 28 December, 1584, to 17 December, 1585, Sir Christopher Wray contributes £5. 13. 8 towards making the gates, and Thomas Parkinson, B.D., £6. 13. 4 for the same purpose, together with £6. 0. 0 from Mr Edward Lucas, part of a donation of £13. 0. 0, of which the remainder was given in 1586, for wainscoting the Hall, with £1. 0. 0 more "for painting his Arms sett up at the Lower end;" and among the expenses are charges for paving the gatehouse and bringing timber for the gates. This part of the College was therefore unfinished at that time, and tradition assigns to Wray the porch in the style of the Renaissance which forms part of the west front[3]; and further, that "before the year

---

[1] [Commiss. Doc^ts. iii. 358.]

[2] [Audit-Book, 1575—76. "It' for beatinge out a windoe in ye m^r. his vpper chamber, and for tymber to ye fishe chamber 5^s. It' for glasinge ye hall and chapple 5^s. 6^d. It' mendinge ye racke in ye stable 10^d. It' a key to ye great gate and mendinge ye locke 8^d. It' for glasinge ye Buttrie 5^s. i^d. It' glasinge ye windoe betwixt ye M^r. and president's chamber 10^d."]

[3] [These particulars are derived from an MS. called the "Master's Private Book." It contains extracts from the documents, and original memoranda. It was commenced by Dr Daniel Waterland, Master 1713—46. Mr Lucas placed a stained glass window in the Hall of Corpus Christi College. Vol. I. 290. Sir Christopher and Lady Wray seem to have visited the College in 1586 and 1587, from the following entries in the Audit-Book: 1585—86 "It' a march-pane to my Ladie Wraye x^s." Ibid. 1586—87 "It' March panes for my lorde xx^s."]

1587 he had improved the Building by the addition of twelve chambers with Studies[1]." These chambers are enumerated, and assigned to the Fellows and Scholars of his foundation, in a deed drawn up between himself and the College 16 July, 1587[2]. It is there stated that:

"wheras...ser Christofer Wray for the zeale he beareth to thencrease of learninge and especially of Divinitye and gods worde to be preached, hath lately at his proper costes and charges erected and newe builded a porcion of buildinge in Magdalen Colledge...

it is agreed betweene the said parties, and the intente of the said Christofer Wray is, that the said Fellowes...shall alwaie haue the vse and preferment of two of the midle chambers builded by the said ser Christofer Wray, and likewise two of the vpper chambers or roomes for ther pupilles the said pupilles payeinge yerely tenne shillinges for either of the said two chambers towardes the reparacion and charges of the said house and lectures as is aforsaid...

And likewise that if the said ser christofer Wray...shall heerafter giue and graunt landes [etc.] to the yerely value of Twentie markes or neare theraboutes for the stipend and exhibicion of two other fellowes in the said house, that they shall likewise haue the vse, and be placed in, the other two of the said midle chambers buylded by the said ser Christofer Wray and the other two of the saide vpper chambers or roomes for ther pupilles...

And that the said six schollers called the schollers of the saide ser Christofer Wray and Thomas Parkinson shall alwaie haue the vse and be placed in the nether lodginges buylded by the saide ser Christofer Wray[3]."

It is evident from this that he had either built, or rebuilt, a range of chambers in three floors, having four sets on each floor; and also that by this time a new roof, containing garrets, had been added to the ancient range which, as we have shewn, was in two floors only.

The buildings have been so disguised by cement, and by the addition of new windows, and of battlements instead of the ancient eaves, that it is impossible to determine their relative ages with certainty. The doorways to the staircases however seem to have been tolerably respected in these repairs. There are three of these on the south side (A, B, C fig. 1), besides the doorway

---

[1] [The deed prescribes the distribution of the rents of the Rectory of Gainthorpe in Lincolnshire, conveyed by him to the College, for the maintenance of certain Fellows and Scholars.]

[2] [History of Cambridge, by Richard Parker, p. 134.]

[3] ["Old Book" of Magdalene College, fo. 13.]

in the turret at the south-west corner (ibid. D); two on the west side (ibid. E, F); and the chapel doorway on the north (ibid. G); and these are all different. Those on the south side appear to belong to the period of Buckingham College, and their dissimilarity corresponds with the independent manner in which we have seen that the Monks' buildings were erected. The chapel doorway is earlier than the other door-ways[1]; but [the wide, four-centered arch of entrance] on the west side is decidedly Elizabethan. [This therefore must have been erected either by the Duke of Norfolk or by Sir Christopher Wray; but probably by the former, for had it been the work of Wray it would most likely have been made to correspond in style with the porch which he erected on the west side.] It should be added that Wray's two Fellows were formerly located in the staircase at the south-east corner of the court above the kitchen; and that by college tradition this was the range of chambers built by him.

The building at the extremity of the second court (fig. 5) is a valuable example of the architecture of the seventeenth century, and it is greatly to be regretted that neither the name of the archi-tect nor the exact date of the design has been preserved. No building accounts or contracts remaining in the College, its history depends only on subscription lists and incidental allu-sions. It is said to have been projected during the Mastership of Dr Henry Smyth (Master 1626—42); and a letter has been preserved from him to Dr Bridgeman, Lord Bishop of Chester, dated 16 August, 1640, soliciting a subscription

"towards some buildings in our Colledge (wch is not now able to lodge with conveniency all students and members thereof); for our incouragement wherein one of o^r. late fellowes hath given £200, and others y^t. have beene students in o^r. House have given hopes to some of o^r. society of their charity to follow so faire gifts and intencions[2]."

There is a further tradition that it was begun during the Mastership of Dr John Peachel (Master 1679—90), and finished

---

[1] [Since Professor Willis wrote this passage the chapel doorway has been moved, and completely changed. In the view of the north-west corner of the quadrangle at the top of the University Almanack for 1821 it is shewn as a pointed archway of three orders, with a hood-mold resting on carved corbels. The doors leading to the two staircases in the western range (fig. 1, E, F) are plain arches with square hood-molds.]

[2] ["Old Book" of Magdalene College, fo. 43.]

in that of his successor Dr Gabriel Quadring (Master 1690—1713). [The former tradition is confirmed by a letter from Mr John Maulyverer, Fellow, to Mr Pepys, dated 29 November, 1679. After thanking him for a loan on bond, and apologizing for delay in payment, he says :

"We had made a tender of it before this time, had not some of our benefactours been very slow in paying their subscriptions. We have not yet finished the inside, and I know not when we shall; however, we will rather let it stand unfinished than suffer our just debts to be unpay'd."

This language can only refer to the building for which subscriptions had been solicited in 1640, and shews that the work had been delayed for want of funds ; and a letter from Dr Peachel to Mr Pepys, dated 11 January, 1680—81, mentions a visit to London in the previous October, apparently for the purpose of asking for further assistance. After thanking Pepys for his own liberality, he adds :

"I hope to have some good view of our concerne by next Easter Terme ; and, if the Parliament give His Majesty money, I doubt not but our friends will be more free to supply us [1]."]

The troublous times of the Commonwealth had intervened between the Masterships of Dr Smyth and Dr Peachel, during which period of thirty-seven years five Masters in succession had held office; Dr Peachel not having been appointed until nineteen years after the Restoration. The design must therefore have been made in the reign of Charles the Second ; for a design made in the previous reign would hardly have been sufficiently esteemed to be carried out so long afterwards, at a period when the change of taste had been so great [2]. It must have been nearly, if not quite, finished by 1703, when Samuel Pepys bequeathed his Library to the College, from the way

---

[1] [Diary and Correspondence of Samuel Pepys. Ed. Rev. Mynors Bright, 1879, vi. 132, 133.]

[2] [The subscriptions amounted to £2029. 8s. 4d. ("Old Book," fo. 43, 126). Among them is one of £60 from Mr Secretary Pepys, to which a note is appended that £50 had been subscribed in the Masterships of Dr Duport and Dr Peachel, and £10 in that of Dr Quadring. This shews that the project had been revived by Dr Duport, Master from 1668 to 1679, who is said to have given £235 "towards the erecting the new building." MSS. Baker iv. 210, MSS. Harl. Mus. Brit. 7031. The sum subscribed in Dr Peachel's time is probably that referred to in the letter quoted above.]

Fig. 5. West front of the New Building. From The Portfolio, 1880.

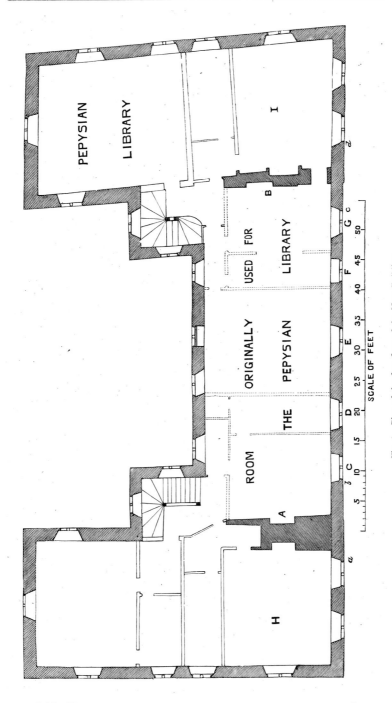

Fig. 6. Plan of the first floor of the New Building.

in which it is spoken of by him in the following document, appended to his Will[1]:

" Sam. Pepys, Esq., his Disposition and Settlement of his Library.

For the further settlement and preservation of my said Library, after the death of my nephew John Jackson, I do hereby declare

That could I be sure of a constant succession of Heirs from my said Nephew, qualify'd like himself for the use of such a Library, I should not entertain a thought of its ever being alienated from them: But this uncertainty considered, with the infinite pains and time and cost employed in my collecting, methodizing, and reducing the same to the State it now is; I cannot but be greatly sollicitous that all possible provision should be made for its unalterable preservation and perpetuall Security against the ordinary Fate of such Collections, falling into the hands of an incompetent Heir, and thereby being sold, dissipated, or embezelled.

And since it has pleased God to visit me in a manner that leaves little appearance of being my self restored to a condition of concerting the necessary measures for attaining these ends, I must and do with great confidence rely upon the sincerity and direction of my Executor and said Nephew for putting in execution the powers given them by my forementioned Will relating hereto, requiring that the same be brought to a determination in twelve months time after my decease; and that speciall regard be had therein to the following particulars, which I declare to be my present thoughts and prevailing inclinations in this matter, viz.:

1.   That after the death of my said nephew, my said Library be placed, and for ever setled, in one of our Universities; and rather in that of Cambridge than Oxford.

2.   And rather in a private College there, than in the Public Library.

3.   And in the Colledges of Trinity or Magdalen preferably to all others.

4.   And of these two, *cæteris paribus*, rather in the latter, for the sake of my own and nephew's education therein.

5.   That in wch soever of the two it is, a fair Roome be provided therein on purpose for it, and wholely and solely appropriated thereto.

6.   And if in Trinity, that the s^d. Roome be contiguous to, and have Communication with the new Library there.

7.   And if in Magdalen, that it be in the New Building there, and any part thereof, at my nephew's election.

8.   That my s^d. Library be continued in its present form, and no other Booke mixt therein, save what my nephew may add to them, of his own collecting, in distinct Presses.

9.   That the s^d. Room and Books so placed and adjusted be called by the name of *Bibliotheca Pepysiana.*

---

[1] [MSS. Baker vi. 208, MSS. Harl. Mus. Brit. 7031. Printed in Hartshorne's Book Rarities of the University of Cambridge, 8vo. Lond. 1829, where also an interesting account of the Pepysian Library is given. Pepys had made his Will in May 1703, and died 26 May following.]

10.   That this *Bibliotheca Pepysiana* be under the sole power and custody of the Master of the College for the time being, who shall neither himself convey, nor suffer to be conveyed by others, any of the s^d. Books from thence, to any other place, except to his own Lodge, in the s^d. College; nor there have more than ten of them at a time; and that of those also a strict entry be made, and accompt kept, of the time of y^t. having been taken out and returned, in a Book to be provided, and remain in the s^d. Library, for that purpose only.

11.   That before my s^d. Library be put into the possession of either of the s^d. Colleges, that College, for wch it shall be designed, first enter into Covenants for performance of the foregoing Articles.

12.   And that for a yet further Security herein, the s^d. two Colleges of Trinity and Magdalen have a reciprocall Check upon one another; and that College, wch. shall be in present possession of the s^d. Library, be subject to an annuall visitation from the other, and to the forfeiture thereof, to the like possession and use of the other, upon conviction of any breach of their s^d. Covenants.   S. PEPYS."

The appearance and arrangement of the building will be understood from the general view of the façade (fig. 5), the plan of the first floor (fig. 6), and the view of the north wing from the garden (fig. 7).   On this side it has the appearance of a gentleman's house.   Two projecting wings enclose a small court, with square towers for staircases at the junction of the centre and the wings.   These wings are curiously irregular.   The south wing is rather shorter than the north wing, and is more inclined towards the central part.   On the west side the wings project beyond the central wall only seven inches on the ground, and four inches on the first floor.   Here again the construction is irregular.   The middle window is not in the centre of the façade, and the space between the second and third windows counting from the north (*ab*, fig. 6), is greater than the corresponding space between the seventh and eighth windows (ibid. *cd*).   The wall of the central part rests on a cloister of five arches, and rises high enough to provide a range of well-lighted chambers above the first floor.   Over these it is terminated by a balustrade of stone, except at the north and south ends, where it is carried up nearly as high as the ridges of the lateral roofs, so as to mask the stacks of chimneys.   The carved enrichments in the spandrels of the arches of the façade, together with those above and below the five windows of the first floor, are evidently additions to the original design, in order to give greater beauty and importance to a building which had been originally projected merely to contain ordinary chambers. It is shewn by Loggan (fig. 4) without these embellishments[1]. The arms of Pepys in the pediment of the central window, his motto MENS CUJUSQUE IS EST QUISQUE, and the inscription

Fig. 7. North wing of the New Building, from the Garden.

BIBLIOTHECA PEPYSIANA, 1724, above the central arch of the cloister, were evidently added when the books arrived after the

[1] The inscription under his plate implies that the building was not then finished. After mentioning the celebrated men who had been educated at the College, he proceeds: "Quorum sumtibus etiam novum Ædificium, in ornamentum juxta ac incrementum Coll: incæptum, bono cum Deo, et tranquillâ patriâ, Coronidem tandem adipiscetur. Gabriel Quadring A.M. hujus Coll: præfectus."

death of the donor's nephew, Mr Jackson; and the arms of Wray and Peckard long afterwards. The arrival of the books is recorded in the following memorandum[1]:

"July 1724. Received of the R[t]. Hon[lbe]. Arthur Earl of Anglesea the Sum of two hundred pounds; of which was expended in removing and settling M[r] Pepy's Library as follows:

For Boxes, Workmen, Necessary Expences and Carriage from Clapham to London	22.	18.	11
Carriage to Cambridge	18.	03.	10
Chamber Income	26.	05.	0
Wainscoting the Chamber etc	44.	18.	7
Necessary Expences	02.	11.	8
Herald-Painter	02.	02.	0
	117.	00.	0"

[The plan (fig. 6) shews that there are no party-walls in the building, and that the only well-marked divisions are the masses of brickwork which contain the fire-places (ibid. *A, B*). The room in which the Library was placed was that which occupied the whole of the first floor between them. It was fifty-five feet long, twenty-one feet broad, and eleven feet high, and was lighted by five windows on the west side, and four on the east side[2]. The twelve bookcases belonging to Pepys, of red oak, wherein their original possessor had carefully arranged his treasures, while in his own house, were duly transferred to their new depository in strict and literal observance of the articles, § 8. These cases, which still exist, are probably those of which Pepys records the arrival in his diary, 24 August, 1666:

"Up, and despatched several businesses at home in the morning, and then comes Sympson to set up my other new presses for my books; and so he and I fell to the furnishing of my new closett, and taking out the things out of my old; and I kept him with me all day, and he dined with me, and so all the afternoone, till it was quite darke, hanging things—that is my maps, and pictures, and draughts—and setting up my books, and as much as we could do, to my most extraordinary satisfaction; so that I think it will be as noble a closett as any man hath, and light enough,—though indeed, it would be better to have had a little more light."

---

[1] [Register of Magdalene College, ii. 400. The charge for "income" shews that the room selected had been already used as a College chamber.]

[2] [It should however be mentioned that in the Audit Book for Mids.—Mich. 1799 we find "Income of M[r] Kerrich's Room added to the Pepysian Library 0. 19. 0;" and in that for the same period in 1806 "Fire-place for the Pepysian Library and Carriage 8. 3. 0."]

The Library still occupied the greater part of this room in 1823, a small piece, lighted by a single window (*G*, fig. 6), having been partitioned off from the south end to contain the Library of Dr Peckard (Master, 1781—97) and another smaller Library. Soon afterwards a second piece, lighted like the former by a single window (*C*), was partitioned off from the opposite end, to suit the convenience of the occupant of the room next to it (*H*). In 1834, however, the following order was made:

"22 Jan. 1834. It was agreed that the following arrangements should be made to enable the Society to receive more undergraduates within the College walls.

1st. It was agreed that the present Master's Lodge (except that part of it adjoining the Master's garden and stable-yard) should be converted into College rooms.

2nd. That the Pepysian Library should be moved into the new Master's Lodge, the space it now occupies being converted into College rooms.

3rd. That a sum not exceeding £4000 should be raised for the purpose of building a new Master's Lodge."

We shall see below that the new Lodge was not begun until 1835. The Library, however, was at once removed into the old Lodge[1]. The room selected was that next to the Chapel, which had been used as the Dining-room (*H*, fig. 1). It remained there until about 1847, when it was removed into the new Lodge. Soon after the election of the present Master in 1853, it was taken back to the New Building, and placed in a room in the south wing[2]. For the sake of additional security this room was provided with a fire-proof casing in 1879, under the direction of F. C. Penrose, M.A., architect[3].

[1] [Audit-Book, 1833—34. "Paid to Mr Waud for fire-place and blinds for the room in the Lodge hereafter to be the Pepysian Library £7. 16. 0." The consent of Trinity College had been asked before the above order was made, and conveyed in the following terms: "May 6, 1833. Agreed by the Master and Seniors that the consent of the College be given to the removal of the Books, &c. of the Pepysian Library from their present situation in Magdalene College to an apartment in the Master's Lodge of the same College. Chr. Wordsworth, M.C."]

[2] [The following memorandum in the College Order-Book, dated 19 May 1849: "In conformity with the College Order of 22 January 1834, the Pepysian Library has been removed into the Master's Lodge," was evidently made to record a change which had been already carried out. The dates given in the text rest on the testimony of the present Master, and others who remember the alterations referred to.]

[3] [Audit-Book, 1878—9. "Outlay on Fireproof casing to Pepysian Library, £380. 6. 10."]

After the removal of the Library, as above recorded, the rooms lighted by the two windows at the north end (*C, D*) were thrown together[1]; a set of rooms for an undergraduate was made next to it, lighted by the two next windows (*E, F*); and the small room where Dr Duport's Library had been was added to the set next to it on the south (*I*). The present divisions have been indicated by dotted lines[2].]

CHAPTER III.

HISTORY OF PARTICULAR BUILDINGS.

Chapel.   Hall.   Library.   Master's Lodge.   External changes.
Gardens.

CHAPEL.—The Chapel is about 65 feet long by 23 feet broad. The first building of it has not been recorded ; and we know but little of its ancient arrangement. The walls seem to have been frescoed, and the windows filled with stained glass, from the notice in the Journal of William Dowsing :

"Madlin College, Dec. 30, 1643.
We break downe about 40 Superstitious Pictures, Joseph and Mary stood to be espoused in the Windowes[3]."

In 1677, Dr Duport (Master 1668—79) gave an Organ to the Chapel. This was probably part of the repair which took place, as elsewhere, after the Restoration. It was used until 1693, when

[1] [The room thus made was panelled, before it was again subdivided, in a style cleverly imitated from that of the last century.]

[2] [These details have been most kindly communicated to me by the Rev. Samuel Wilkes Waud, B.A. 1825, M.A. 1828, formerly Fellow, and now Rector of Rettendon, near Chelmsford. He resided in Magdalene College from 1823 to 1843, and, as shewn in a former note, superintended the removal of the Library in 1834. His reminiscences are confirmed by the Cambridge Guide from 1763 to 1820, all the editions of which mention " the Library over the cloister in the second Court."]

[3] [Blomefield, writing in 1751, mentions (Collect. Cantab. p. 108) that "In a Window on the Glass is 'Praye to the Lorde, and Praye with the Hearte and Minde.'"]

"the Charge of the New Building increasing upon the College, and it being necessary to retrench the expences, it was thought proper to spare the charge of the Organist for the Future. So that from that time to the present no Organ has been used in The College[1]."

Before the alterations commenced in 1847 there was an ante-chapel at the west end, interposed between the dining-room of the Master's Lodge and the Chapel. This ante-chapel had a door of entrance from the court (G, fig. 1); and another from the Lodge (ibid. I). Above it there was a gallery, to which the Master had access from the first floor of his Lodge.

At some period anterior to 1688 a room had been contrived in the roof, approached by a staircase from the ante-chapel. Loggan (fig. 4) shews that this room was used as a Library.

In 1733 a general repair and "beautification" of the Chapel was begun, and continued at intervals, by which the interior was brought to the Italian aspect which has been preserved in various engravings[2]. The cost was in part defrayed by subscription[3]. In 1734 a pavement was laid down, at a cost of £104. 17s. 4d.; after which no further works were undertaken until 1754, when the following order was made:

"Memorandum. At the Audit this Day, March 26, 1754, it is agreed, that the Master [D[r] Thomas Chapman] be empowered to contract with Jeremiah Robinson for fitting up and beautifying the Chapel according to a Plan deliver'd; for a sum not exceeding three hundred, seventy one Pounds, and ten Shillings.   WM. BEATY, Register."

The work occupied rather more than two years, as the dates of the following items of expenditure shew:

"Oct. 4, 1754.   Paid the Bricklayer for bricking up the
                  East Window ....£ 5. 4. 0
July 19, 1755.   Paid Robinson for drawing the Designs
                  in the Chap. 5. 5. 0
June 25, 1755.   Paid Bricklayer for turning the Arches
                  in the Chap. 18. 5. 6½

---

[1] [Register of Magdalene College, ii. 363. The Order thanking Dr Duport for his gift is dated 20 July, 1677.]

[2] [There is a view of the interior, looking eastward, by Mackenzie, dated 1815, in Ackermann, ii. 151. This view is reproduced in 1848, by Le Keux, ii. 57. By that time the arches of plasterwork above the windows had been taken away; and each of the three lights is shewn as foliated.]

[3] [The total collected was £653. 7s. 2d. Of this sum £231 was "given by the Master and Fellows in common, being the profits of the Norfolk Travelling Fellowship, during its vacancy."]

May 21, 1756.   Paid Mr Collins for the Bas Relief for
                    the Altar 3l. 10. 0
June 12, 1756.   Casfoy for the Altar Table ....   7. 19. 4½."

[The mullions were allowed to remain in the windows, but
the tracery was either removed, or concealed by ogee arches
of plaster-work.   The ceiling was flat, ornamented with plaster
scrolls and a large central rosette.   The cornice was of similar
work.   The east end, as far as the first windows in the north
and south walls, was spanned by a nearly flat arch, ornamented
in the same style as the ceiling.   The walls of this space were
panelled.   Over the altar was the bas-relief above mentioned—
a group in plaster, representing the Maries at the Sepulchre
after the Resurrection.   This was surmounted by a pediment,
which rested on fluted columns.   There was a single row of
stalls along the north and south walls, with a bench in front, in
a plain semi-classical style.   The pavement laid down in 1733
was not thought sufficiently good, and chapel and ante-chapel
were in consequence repaved with large squares of stone, with
small squares of black marble at their intersections[1].   The
whole work cost £639. 14s. 10½d.

Between 1847 and 1851 a complete restoration of the Chapel
was carried out.   The nature of the work done will be best
understood from the following description drawn up at the
time by the Rev. Mynors Bright, Fellow[2]:

"In 1847, the College Chapel being very much out of repair, it was
determined to restore it to its original beauty, by removing the ceiling
and the three sets of rooms that were over the Chapel, thereby displaying the ancient oak-roof of the time of Edward IV.; by opening the
East window, which had been bricked up about 1752; and by refitting
the woodwork in accordance with the rest of the building.

On removing the panelling at the East End of the Chapel, four
niches with remains of richly decorated canopies were discovered, and

---

[1] ["Septr. 2, 1755. Paid Thompson for paving Chapel and Antechapel £47.
6. 7½." The work was much admired at the time. In Cantabrigia Depicta, publ.
1764, we find (p. 77) : "The Chapel is a handsome Oratory...the Whole is extremely
neat, and the Altar-piece of Plaister of *Paris* representing the History of the *Resurrection* in *Alto Relievo*, by the Ingenious M^r. *Collins*, is reckoned well worth the
Observation of the Curious:" and Dyer, writing in 1814, remarks that the chapel has
"been put into elegant order." The bas-relief is now in the Library.]

[2] [Mr Bright's account is written out in the College Order-Book. See also The
Ecclesiologist, ix. 147.]

also an Elizabethan doorway on the South side of the Altar communicating with the Hall.

This restoration was effected in 1847 and the following years, from designs by Mr Buckler the Architect, and at a cost of upwards of £2000, which was defrayed partly by Subscriptions and the remainder from the College Funds.

In 1850 the Undergraduates, with the assistance of a Donation of £40 from the Master and Fellows, presented to the College a painted East Window by Mr Hardman, of Birmingham, from a design by Mr Pugin.

In 1851 the window at the South end of the Chapel was presented to the College from a design by Miss Cleaver, who painted the figures in the window, the remainder being painted by Mr Raven, President of the College, and Messrs Kershaw, Cleaver, and Newton, Undergraduates."

The subjects of the stained glass in the windows, all of which have now been filled, by Messrs Hardman, are the following. The lights are numbered from left to right, and the windows from east to west.

EAST WINDOW.

1. Mary Magdalene anointing the feet of Christ.
2. The Deposition.
3. MARY MAGDALENE: a single figure.
4. Mary Magdalene weeping at the tomb of Christ.
5. Christ recognized by Mary Magdalene.

> *₊* In the lower part of each light is a small half-length figure of an angel bearing a scroll with a text illustrating the subject of the light.

FIRST WINDOW, NORTH SIDE.

1. Mary Magdalene anointing the feet of Christ.
2. The Raising of Lazarus.
3. Christ addressing Mary and Martha.

> *₊* On a brass tablet beneath this window is the following inscription :

> *In piam memoriam viri honorabilis et admodum reverendi Georgii Neville Grenville hujus collegii per annos xl præfecti, necnon regiæ apud Wyndesoram capellæ custodis, et nobilissimi ordinis a periscelide scribæ. De vita decessit A.S. mdcccliv. annum agens sexagesimum quartum.*

SECOND WINDOW, NORTH SIDE.

1. Joseph and the two Maries at the tomb of Christ.
2. Mary Magdalene at the tomb of Christ.
3. Christ with the Apostles and Mary Magdalene.

> *₊* On a brass tablet beneath this window is the following inscription :

> *In Memoriam Philippi Hamond A. B. Hujus Collegii olim Alumni Qui mortem obiit in India Orientali die xxiii Sextilis A. S.* MDCCCLXI *annum*

agens vicesimum tertium. Ob virtutem ac fidem desideratam Hoc monu-
mentum P. C. Plurimi Amici.

THIRD WINDOW, NORTH SIDE.

(Given by Mrs Lyell, 1880.)

The Procession to Calvary.

FIRST WINDOW, SOUTH SIDE.

Each light has small figures in circular medallions illustrating with Latin sentences, the petitions in the Litany, "*By the Mystery of thy Holy Incarnation, Good Lord, Deliver us,*" etc. The remaining space is occupied by borders of foliage.

SECOND WINDOW, SOUTH SIDE.

1. The Transfiguration.
2. The Baptism of Christ.
3. Christ among the Doctors.

THIRD WINDOW, SOUTH SIDE.

1. The Annunciation.
2. The Salutation.
3. The Nativity.

In the course of the alterations the thick wall (*a b*, fig. 1) which separated the ante-chapel from the Chapel was pulled down, and replaced by a light oak screen; and the door (ibid. *G*) was blocked and the doorcase removed. By this means the length of the Chapel was increased by about ten feet. At the same time a new west wall was built (ibid. *c d*), nearly on the site of the old east wall of the Lodge, with a buttress at the end next the court; and a new vestibule was made by cutting off about ten feet from the dining-room of the Lodge, then used as the Library. This vestibule, or passage, is approached from the court by a door which replaces the easternmost of the three windows; and it also contains the doors to the Chapel, Library, and garden; and a staircase leading to some of the sets of rooms made out of the old Lodge. In 1876 the west gable was rebuilt, with the addition of a canopied niche containing a statue of S. Mary Magdalene. The architect was Mr F. C. Penrose.]

HALL.—The Hall is 24 feet 6 inches broad, and 45 feet long, including the screens. Loggan (fig. 4) shews a large perpendicular window of four lights divided by a transom, at the north end of the west wall, and two windows, each of three lights, southward of it. There are three similar windows in the east wall. The architectural character of these windows has not been disturbed. Loggan further shews a large louvre over the middle window, rising from an hexagonal base, with a sundial on each of its sides; a bell-turret over the butteries; and a sundial, under a small pent-house, over the northernmost window of the two which lighted the room over the butteries. At this period the Hall had an open roof, the braces of which may still be seen in the garrets which were contrived within it during the last century.

The Hall—the erection of which is ascribed, as we have seen, to the Duke of Buckingham—was wainscoted in 1585, at the expense of Mr Lucas, as recorded in the last chapter. His arms were set up and painted shortly afterwards[1]. The louvre was made between 1586 and 1588, the cost being in part defrayed by cutting down nine "elme trees in the backside comonly called the grove." They "were soulde vnto Harry Flamson of Cambridge baker for ix[li] and that mony by the maister bestowed towardes the makinge of a great lover for the Colledge hall[2]." The Belfry was made at the same time[3].

In 1714 the "Hall was new ceiled, paved, glazed, and wainscotted at the expence of £265." It was no doubt at this time that chambers were contrived in the roof, though the change is not specially recorded. The wainscoting then put up has been painted in imitation of oak. It rises to the cills of the windows, and consists of large single panels projecting beyond the styles, and having a low plain dado beneath, which is hidden by the seats and tables. The wainscoting rises higher behind the high table, but has no additional ornament except two pilasters, in which are encased two

---

[1] [Audit-Book, 28 Dec. 1584—27 Dec. 1585. "It' laid out for M[r]. Lucas his wainscott vj[li]." Ibid. 28 Dec. 1585—28 Dec. 1586. "It' M[r]. Lucas his armes paintinge xx[s]."]

[2] [Note at the end of the Accounts for 1586—87.]

[3] [Ibid. 1585—86. "It' timber for the bellfraye xij[s]. vj[d]." (with numerous other entries). "It' 7 Vanes from London xl[s]. It' timber from Hinningham for a new loover iiij[li]. xvij[s]." Ibid. 1586—87. "It' tymber and leade from Hinningham xvj[li]. xiij[s]. x[d]. It' colours, oyles, gould leaves, for dyalles vanes, etc. and bringinge it home xlix[s]. viij[d]." Ibid. 1587—88. "It' layed out more about the louer…xxij[li]. 7[s]. 2[d]."]

smaller pilasters with ionic capitals, and bunches of fruit and other ornaments on their faces. These latter pilasters are manifestly remains of the previous decoration of the Hall in 1586. The wall at the north end is occupied by a large painting representing the Royal Arms in the centre, with the mottoes SEMPER EADEM and HONI SOIT QUI MAL Y PENSE, flanked by the arms of Lord Audley; Sir Christopher Wray; Howard, Earl of Suffolk; and Stafford, Duke of Buckingham[1].

COMBINATION ROOM.—We know nothing about the position of the Combination Room until 1712, when it is recorded that "the part of the first Court that is over ye Butteries and Kitchens, being decayed, it was repaired at the College charge, and a Combination room fitted up for the use of the Fellows, the whole charge amounting to £100." It was probably at this time that the small window over the Hall door shewn by Loggan (fig. 4) was blocked, and the four windows between that door and the corner of the court replaced by four large sash-windows. The dial, bell-turret and louvre were all removed, and in their place a new bell-turret was built directly over the Hall door. Its base carries a clock[2].

In order to provide convenient access to this room a complex staircase was built within the Hall at the south end, in combination with the screen and gallery above. A flight of stairs rises from the floor on either side the door of entrance, and ascends to the gallery, which is as usual over the screens. The floor of the Combination Room is on the level of the gallery, from which it is entered by a door in the middle. Two pilasters, or square pillars, rise from the gallery front to the ceiling, and are connected together by an arch, so as to form a handsome piece of architectural scenery in connection with the ascending stairs and the entrance door between them. The length of the Hall, however, is abridged by seven feet. All this work belongs to the alterations of 1714, but two more of the early pilasters, in addition to those noticed over the dais,

---

[1] [These, and the rest of the Heraldry in the College, have been kindly identified for me by my friend, Lionel Henry Cust, B.A., Scholar of Trinity College. His description will be found in the Appendix.]

[2] [These details are shewn in Harraden's View, dated 2 April, 1810. Harraden's Cambridge, p. 137.]

are worked into this screen; and over the door some smaller portions of Elizabethan carved work are fixed, which appear to have been parts of a chimney-piece. The whole of this peculiar arrangement is so similar in principle to that which Sir John Vanbrugh introduced into the Hall at Audley End in 1721, that, considering the intimate connection between the College and that mansion, it can hardly be denied that he was consulted concerning the fitting up of these apartments.

[The interior of the Combination Room was not brought to its present appearance until 1757. It was then wainscoted; a chimney-piece of Portland stone was put up, with scrolls and ornaments carved by Woodward; the floor was relaid; and a new ceiling made[1].] It is now lighted by a Perpendicular window intended to correspond with that of the Hall at the other extremity of the range. It reaches from the base-mold to the parapet, and is divided by a transom, the upper half being devoted to the Combination Room, and the lower to the pantry.

LIBRARY.—The ancient position of the Library over the Chapel has been already mentioned. When Uffenbach visited Cambridge in 1710 he remarks of Magdalene College[2]:

"It is a very old, and, as I said, mean building; the library, which stands at the top under the roof, is very small, and may perhaps consist of 600 volumes. All the books, with hardly one single exception, are entirely overgrown with mould. By the door in a little cupboard were some poor MSS."

The books remained there until 1733, when we meet with "An Account of the Expences of removing the Old Library from the Room over the Chapel, and fixing it in the Room adjoining the Master's Lodge." This is the room on the ground floor, in the angle between the north range and the west range (fig. 1). It was entered by the door which also gave access to the Lodge (ibid. F). The conversion of the Library into chambers, mentioned above, did not take place for many years. It

---

[1] [Jan. 15, 1757.] "Pᵈ. Bricklayer for Cieling, altering Chimney, and Windows £10. 19. 5. Woodward for carving Scrowls, etc. 1. 10. 0. Dᵒ. for Ovolo round the Chimney £0. 12. 6." Octʳ. 21, 1757. "Pᵈ. Stone-Mason for Portland Chimney Piece, Slab, Ketton Stone in Windows £7. 9. 6." Nov. 15, 1757. "Pᵈ. Newling's Bill for new Wainscot, new Floor etc. £93. 0. 5½." The total expended was £166. 12. 1.]

[2] [Herrn Zacharias Conrad von Uffenbach Merkwürdige Reisen: dritter Theil. Ed. 1754, p. 18. Translated by Rev. J. E. B. Mayor, p. 139.]

is described by Cole in 1773, as disused, and he terms it a
"Garret, now used as a Lumber Room, and to dry Clothes in[1]."

The room in which the Library was placed after its removal
from the garret over the Chapel is now a College Chamber;
and the Library occupies a room made out of the drawing-
room and dining-room of the old Lodge (fig. 1). This change
could not have taken place until after the Lodge had been
vacated by the Master[2].

MASTER'S LODGE.—[The Master's chamber is shewn by
Loggan (fig. 4) to have been situated at the north-west corner
of the quadrangle[3]. In subsequent times the wing (K, fig. 1)
which projected northward into the garden, and contained a
staircase, and the buildings in two floors which formed the
north and east sides of a small court entered by a separate door
from the street (fig. 4), formed part of the Lodge, but no record
of their construction has been preserved. Cole, writing in 1773,
notes that "In the Master's Study, at the end of the Gallery,
is a large handsome Bow Window, which looks towards Chesterton, and commands the River." This gallery must be the
long narrow building, apparently of wood, like the similar
structures in other colleges, which forms the north side of the
above-mentioned court. We know from Loggan that it had a
bow-window at the west end next the street, in addition to that
at the east end mentioned by Cole. The Lodge was entered
from the court by the door at the north-west angle (F, fig. 1);
and from the street by a door (ibid. L), in the space where
Loggan (fig. 4) shews three small windows. The Lodge was
gradually extended so as to occupy the north range of the
quadrangle as far as the Chapel, on both floors. The drawing-
room and dining-room were on the ground-floor (fig. 1).

---

[1] [Add. MSS. Mus. Brit. 5876, f. 109 b.]

[2] [It was directed by the following Order: "22 Jan. 1834. It was also agreed
that the Peckard Library be placed in the same room with the Foundation Library,
and that the dining room of the late Lodge be appropriated to this purpose." We
have seen, however, that the Pepysian Library was actually placed in this room in
1834. The Order must therefore be understood to refer to a change which was
intended to be carried out as soon as the Pepysian Library had been removed into the
new Lodge.]

[3] [One of the original windows, of two lights, with the cusps still undestroyed, may
be seen in the north wall.]

We have seen that the erection of a new Lodge for the Master was determined at the beginning of 1834. On 8 July, 1835, the foundation of the new Lodge was laid by His Royal Highness Prince George, now Duke, of Cambridge, who deposited a brick at the south-east corner. It is a large ornamental mansion of brick in a plain Elizabethan style. The architect was Mr Buckler. The site selected was principally that of the Rectory Farm, the purchase of which has been already recorded, with the addition of a small piece of the "great garden [1]." In order to provide convenient access to the new Lodge a carriage entrance was made in the wall between the small door mentioned above (M, fig. 1) and the west range of the College, the intervening buildings and the staircase (K, fig. 1), being pulled down to make way for it. The original door, however, remains; and the space occupied by the gable of the gallery may readily be seen to be that of a modern door through which the stable yard is now entered, the former doorway having been bricked up. These changes have been indicated on the plan (fig. 1). The gallery, however, which was standing, as we have seen, so late as 1773, had been pulled down before the erection of a new Lodge was thought of; and some rooms, approached by a passage between the Foundation Library and the drawing-room, had been erected on part of its site, and of that of the wing connecting it with the College, so as to increase its area to nearly twice the extent shewn by Loggan (fig. 3). These rooms extended eastward as far as the staircase (K, fig. 1). Most of them are still in existence, and are used as a dwelling-house.]

EXTERNAL CHANGES.—The appearance of the College at the end of the seventeenth century has been preserved by Loggan (fig. 4). At the beginning of the eighteenth century a series of repairs and alterations began. In 1702 "the Old Building or First Court was stripped and new covered, and several Chymneys repaired. The charge amounted to £149 [2]." Further alterations to the east side of the Court in

---

[1] [This enclosure of part of the garden was thought to be opposed to the xxxix[th] Statute, and a College Order 9 Feb. 1836 directed that the consent of the Visitor should be asked. This was obtained 4 May.]

[2] [Register of Magdalene College, p. 767.]

1712 and 1714 have been already recorded. In 1759—60 we meet with "Receipts for Beautifying the Old Court," amounting to £164. 17s. 6½d.; and the disbursements shew that this sum was laid out in applying stucco to the four sides of the court:

"P^d. to Cotton for Stucco on ye Side next ye Street...... 12. 3. 4
,,   ,,   ,,   Hall-side 13. 12. 2
,,   ,,   ,,   Chapel side 18. 18. 6
,,   ,,   ,,   side opposite ye Chapel 19. 17. 0½
,,   ,, work on ye East Side of the Hall
                    and Gateway 3. 6. 9
To Stanley the Carpenter 23. 15. 0½
To Cotton for tiling over ye Barber's shop............. 5. 0."

This work did not destroy the eaves shewn by Loggan, for they appear in Harraden's view, dated 1810. By that time the wooden railings shewn by Loggan had been removed, and shrubs planted all round, close to the walls. These were put in in 1781[1]. Between 1812 and 1815, however, the interior of the first court was again stuccoed, and possibly the exterior also, for the work was evidently considerable, the payments to the plasterer extending over four years. It was probably at this time that the eaves were replaced by battlements. The remarks of Dyer on these alterations are worth quoting, as shewing the admiration with which they were regarded at the time:

"The north side of the western court has been lately faced with Roman Cement, and the chapel been put into elegant order. The whole court, I understand, is to be faced in like manner, with the Roman Cement, an expensive way of casing, but which is proportionably neat and elegant[2]."

[In 1873 the houses which intervened between the College and the river were pulled down, and the ground laid out as a garden[3]. At the same time the south front was admirably restored under the direction of Mr F. C. Penrose, architect; and a picturesque gateway, with steps leading down to the river, which had probably belonged to one of the houses, was

<hr />

[1] [Audit-Book Mich.—Christmas 1781. "Trees in the 1st Court 5. 2. 3."]

[2] [Dyer's Cambridge, ii. 278. Audit-Book, Mich. 1812. "To Clabbon for facing part of the first Court 75. 14. 0." Mich. 1813. D°. £75. 0. 0. Mich. 1814. "Clabbon on account (Plasterer) £83. 5. 5." Mich. 1815. "To Clabbon in full £83. 0. 0."]

[3] [Alterations on this side had been contemplated in 1845. College Order, 6 Nov. 1845, "All the buildings on the south side of the College to be pulled down." 19 May, 1848, "That the Master direct Mr Bradwell to draw out plans and estimates for a new building on the frontage between the College and the 'Bridge House.'"]

rebuilt. The whole work might well serve as a model for future collegiate restoration. In 1875 the west front was similarly treated, under the direction of the same architect. These works cost £4717. 5s. 2d.

GARDENS, ETC.—The statutes[1], given in 1564, mention three gardens: (1) "The largest garden, otherwise called the Orchard, situated behind the College;" (2) "the smallest garden of all, close to the door of entrance;" (3) "the larger garden, into which the Master's chamber looks." Of these the first and third are assigned to the Master, together with the pasture, hay, and timber of the first; in which, however, the Fellows are allowed to take exercise and refreshment. The second is assigned to the President.

The first of these gardens can be easily recognised at the present day. The wall of red brick along the north side, built in 1667—68[2], is still standing; as is also part of that which originally bounded it on the west side (fig. 3). The north wall stands a few feet from the edge of the river-face of the "vallum" of the Castle, along which a terrace-walk has been made[3]. Loggan also shews (fig. 4, F) the extent of the Master's garden (3). The enclosure to the north of it is the Bowling Green, as we learn from his map of Cambridge (fig. 3). The probable position and extent of it have been laid down on the plan (fig. 1)[4]. It has been shewn above that the President's garden (2) probably occupied a portion of the ground on which the west front now stands; but it is of course impossible to fix the exact locality. His garden is now the small enclosure to the north of the Brewhouse.

The building shewn by Loggan between the Pepysian Library and the river was a Brewhouse, built in 1629. The Stable, as already mentioned, was north of the Master's gallery. It was built in 1589. There is still a stable in the same position, of rather smaller dimensions.]

[1] [Statute *De Commeatibus et Stipendiis.* Commiss. Docts. iii. 357.]

[2] [In "A list of Benefactors to Magdalen College," preserved by Baker (MSS. Harl. 7031, p. 210) we find: "John Howorth, D.D., Master [1664—68] gave 40 lib. towards the Brickwall about the Backside."]

[3] [Ancient Cambridgeshire: by C. C. Babington, M.A. Camb. Antiq. Soc. Octavo Publ. No. III.]

[4] [In 1734 we find let on lease with three tenements in the Parish of S. Giles, "a certain piece of ground commonly called or known by the name of the Bowling Green."]

CHRONOLOGICAL SUMMARY.

1428.	(7 July.) Grant of a site to the Monks of Croyland by Henry VI. for a Benedictine Hostel.
1483.	The Benedictine Hostel known as Buckingham College.
1519.	Edward Stafford, Duke of Buckingham, builds a Hall.
1539.	Buckingham College shares the fate of the other monastic houses.
1542.	(3 April.) Charter granted to Lord Audley by Henry VIII. for founding Magdalene College on the site of Buckingham College.
1564.	(10 Aug.) Visit of the Duke of Norfolk, who gave money for the buildings.
1585.	Sir Christopher Wray and Mr Parkinson contribute to the gates.
1586.	Mr Lucas contributes to the wainscoting of the Hall.
1586—88.	Louvre of Hall and Belfry made.
1587.	(16 July.) Deed drawn up between Sir C. Wray and the College.
1589.	Stable built.
1605.	(1 Nov.) Purchase of the "Star" by the Earl of Suffolk.
1615.	(6 Oct.) Purchase of the "Green Peele" and the "Black Boy" by Dr Gooche.
1629.	Brewhouse built.
1637.	The "Chequers" bequeathed to the College by Dr Smith.
1667—68.	Wall along north side of garden built.
1702.	Extensive repairs to the First Court.
1703.	Mr Pepys' "Disposition and Settlement of his Library."
1712.	Combination Room fitted up.
1714.	Hall new ceiled, paved, and wainscoted.
1724.	(July.) Arrival of the Pepysian Library.
1733.	Removal of Library from room above the Chapel.
1733—56.	Beautification of the Chapel.
1757.	Combination Room fitted up as at present.
1759—60.	First Court stuccoed.
1790.	(3 April.) Purchase of ground from Jesus College.
1791.	(6 July.) Purchase of ground from the Town of Cambridge.
1792.	(2 Oct.) Purchase of a lane from the Town of Cambridge.
1812—15.	First Court stuccoed.
1834.	(22 Jan.) College Order directing the removal of Pepysian Library.
,,	A new Lodge to be built for the Master.
,,	Removal of the Pepysian Library into the old Master's Lodge.
1835.	(9 April.) Purchase of the site of the Master's Lodge from the Bishop of Ely.
,,	(8 July.) First stone laid of new Master's Lodge.
,,	(29 July.) Purchase of "Copped Hall" from Merton College, Oxford.
1847.	Removal of Pepysian Library into new Master's Lodge.
1847—51.	Restoration of the Chapel.
1853.	Pepysian Library taken back to the New Building.
1873.	Houses on south side of College pulled down, and south front restored.
1875.	West front of College restored.
1879.	Pepysian Library rendered fire-proof.

APPENDIX.

HERALDRY OF MAGDALENE COLLEGE.

In the Hall.

Over the High Table: *Queen Anne.* Quarterly, 1 and 4, Great Britain (England impaling Scotland); 2, France; 3, Ireland. All within a garter and supported by a lion and unicorn. Motto: "*Semper Eadem.*"

On the Right, above: *The College.* Quarterly per pale indented or and azure, on a bend of the second between two eagles displayed or, a fret between two martlets of the last. Supporters, two antelopes gules horned chained and collared, or. Motto: "*Garde Ta Foy.*"

On the Right, below: *Sir Christopher Wray, Knight.* Azure on a chief or, three martlets gules. Motto: "*Juste et Vrai.*"

On the Left, above: *Stafford, Duke of Buckingham.* Quarterly, 1, France moderu and England, within a border argent, *Woodstock;* 2 and 3, azure a bend cotised argent between six lions rampant or, *Bohun;* 4, or, a chevron gules, *Stafford.* Supporters two swans proper chained or beaked gules. Motto: "*En lui plaisance.*" N.B. In the third quarter the bend is charged with three mullets gules.

On the Left, below: *Lord Howard de Walden, Earl of Suffolk.* Quarterly 1, gules a bend between six cross crosslets fitchée argent, thereon a crescent sable, and the Flodden augmentation, *Howard;* 2, England, with a label of three points argent, *Brotherton;* 3, Gules a lion rampant argent, *Mowbray;* 4, *Audley of Walden* as given above. Supporters a lion proper collared argent and a lion argent. Motto: "*Non Quo sed Quomodo.*"

*** This work must all have been done when the Hall was decorated in 1714.

Over the door at the top of the staircase leading to the Combination-room are the following arms: *Edward Lucas.* Quarterly 1 and 4, argent a fess between six annulets gules, *Lucas;* 2 and 3, gules a bend argent billeté, *Morieux.* On the fesse-point a crescent sable. Crest, on a helmet azure a dragon's head gules. Motto: "*Sic nobis eluxit Edwardus Lucas.*"

On the New Building.

On the west front, in the centre: *Samuel Pepys.* Quarterly 1 and 4, sable on a bend or between two nag's heads erased argent three fleur de lys of the field, *Pepys;* 2 and 3 gules a lion rampant within a bordure engrailed or, *Talbot.*

On the west front, on the left: *Wray.* Azure on a chief or three martlets gules, in pretence a hand of Ulster gules in an escutcheon argent. Intended for Sir Christopher Wray, who died in 1592; his son William was created a Baronet on 15 November 1611.

On the west front, on the right: *Dr Peter Peckard.* Quarterly 1 and 4, Gyronny of eight argent and azure on a canton gules a fleur de lis or, *Peckard;* 2 and 3 argent on a bend sable three horseshoes or, *Ferrar.* Dr Peckard was Master 1781—1797. He married a descendant of Nicholas Ferrar ("Nicholas Ferrar," ed. J. E. B. Mayor, M.A., p. 378).

*** These two shields were probably added when the College was "beautified" about 1813.

In the First Court.

Over the Entrance Gateway: *Neville-Griffin, Lord Braybrooke.* Quarterly 1 and 4, sable a griffin segreant argent armed and unguled or, *Griffin;* 2 and 3, *Neville of Abergavenny;* quarterly 1 and 4, gules on a saltire argent a rose seeded and barbed proper, *Neville of Raby;* 2 and 3 or fretty gules in a canton per pale ermine and or a galley sable, *Neville of Bulmer.*

*** This coat, put up between 1852 and 1854, probably stands for the second Lord Braybrooke, who assumed the name of Griffin in 1797, and died in 1825.

Over the arch leading from the First Court into the Screens are the Audley arms, per pale, not indented, with two lions couchant as supporters. The motto *Garde ta foy,* nearly obliterated, may be traced beneath the shield.

XIV.

Trinity College.

CHAPTER I.

HISTORY OF THE SITE.

THE site of Trinity College on the right or eastern bank of the River Cam is bounded on the north by S. John's College; on the east by Trinity Street and Trinity Hall Lane; on the south by Trinity Lane and Garret Hostel Lane; and on the west by the River Cam.

When Trinity College was founded by King Henry the Eighth in 1546 this site was occupied by two Colleges, Michael House and King's Hall, and by seven Hostels for students, namely, Garret Hostel, Oving's Inn, S. Gregory's Hostel, S. Margaret's Hostel, Physwick Hostel, S. Katherine's Hostel, and Tyled, or Tyler's, Hostel, besides Common Land, belonging to the Town of Cambridge. The relative positions of these structures and places have been laid down on the accompanying map (fig. 1), by the help of which we shall attempt to explain the gradual formation of the above-mentioned Colleges and their subordinate Hostels. The ancient arrangement, however, was so different from the modern, that the detailed history of it must be prefaced by some general considerations[1]. In these,

---

[1] [The materials for the History of Trinity College are described in the Appendix, No. I. It is therefore sufficient to state here that "Otryngham" denotes the chartulary of Michael House compiled by John Otryngham, Master, in the fifteenth century; and that "Parne" and "Mason" denote the collections made by Dr Parne and Dr Mason respectively.]

and in the subsequent history, the ancient names will be given
to the streets which bound the site as: High Street for the
present Trinity Street; S. Michael's Lane[1] for Trinity Lane;
and Milne Street for Trinity Hall Lane. [The course of the
River Cam was, at least in historic times, the same as it is at
present; but] the Town Common, called Garret Hostel Green,
was separated from the rest of the ground by a boundary ditch,
which joined the river at each end. The remainder of the site
was divided by a lane which, starting from a point in the High
Street nearly opposite to the present Great Gateway of Trinity
College, ran westward to the boundary ditch, which it reached at
a point near its junction with the river. Another lane, which
started from S. Michael's lane at the place where the Queen's
Gateway of Trinity College now stands, ran north to meet the
first lane. At the junction of the first lane with the ditch and the
river there was anciently a landing-place called Dame Nichol's
Hythe[2], whence both the lanes are called "road to Dame
Nichol's Hythe" up to the middle of the fourteenth century;
but after 1341, when this hithe became the property of King's
Hall, the name is no longer employed to designate them. When
King's Hall was originally built, it wholly faced the first lane,
for its site did not then extend to High Street, and its great gate
was built opposite to the intersection of the two lanes. Hence
the lane from High Street to the water is called "King's Hall
Lane," "King's Childer Lane," or "Lane of the King's Clerks
(*venella clericorum Regis*)." The part of this lane from High
Street to the intersection was enclosed by King's Hall in 1433,
after which time the second lane, that running northward from

---

[1] In Lyne's map (fig. 2), S. Michael's lane is called Find-silver lane. This name
does not appear in any document that I have seen. "Venella Sancti Michaelis" occurs
as early as 1312—13, in a document quoted by Mason, No. 157, and also in the
muniments of S. Katherine's Hostel in 1317—18, Otryngham, p. 52. In 1432—33
it is "venella vocat' Michel lane," ibid. p. 76. "Vicus S. Michaelis" is the name used
by Caius, although included in his list of "viculi." Hist. Cantab. Acad. ii. 119.

[2] Hyth or Hithe is a Saxon word signifying a little port or haven to load or unload
wares, and often occurs in topography in combination with some epithet, as Queen-
hyth, Rotherhythe, and so on. Along the river Cam there existed, at the period we
are now considering, several of these Hythes, as Salthythe, Flaxhythe, Cornhythe, as
well as Dame Nichol's hythe, not to mention the well-known Clayhythe which still
exists. The names of these landing-places indicate their respective appropriations to
different commodities. Ely had Stok-hithe, Brod-hithe, Monkes-hithe, Castel-hithe;
Chatteris has The Hithe. (Stewart's Ely, Chap. VIII.)

S. Michael's Lane, together with the western half of the first lane, became the only way from the town to Dame Nichol's Hythe. This thoroughfare receives various names in the ancient deeds[1]: it is called "Milne Street," as being a continuation of that street; "S. Michael's Street (*vicus*)," as forming the east boundary of Michael House; or simply a Highway (*via regia*). Dr Caius calls it "le foulelane," and describes it precisely in a passage which may be translated as follows[2]:

"In ancient documents belonging to Phiswick Hostel, it was called the lane of the King's clerks (*venella clericorum domini regis*) and *le foule lane*, that is, the muddy alley (*cænosus angiportus*). It started from the place where the second and larger gate of Trinity College, which opens into S. Michael's Street (*vicus*), now stands; and it was continued in a straight line to the inner gate, where the lavatory[3] (*lavacrum*) now is. From this point it turned to the left, and so reached the neighbouring brook."

These two lanes divide the site into three districts; which may be termed the Northern, the South-western, and the South-eastern.

The northern district, bounded on the north by S. John's Hospital, on the south by the "road to Dame Nichol's Hythe" or "King's Hall Lane," and extending from the High Street to the river, may be described as consisting of three principal divisions, each extending from the north to the south boundary. The first division next to the river was called Cornheth, and

---

[1] In 1294 "regalis via que ducit versus Damenicholeshethe," Otryngham, p. 5, 10 b. Also in 1336 ibid. p. 57 1 h. In 1278 "vicus molendinorum," ibid. p. 34, 2 d. In 1309 "mellestret," ibid. 7 d. In 1327 "vicus de mellestret," ibid. 11 d. In 1332 and 1355 "via regia," ibid. p. 76. In 1348 "vicus sancti Michaelis," ibid. p. 58, 3 k. Ibid. p. 49, 1. 9 etc. It must be observed that Foul Lane is anciently termed merely "*vicus*," and "*via regia*," and that "*venella*" is used for S. Michael's Lane, which was therefore of inferior size. A note in Otryngham (p. 72) signed "M^r. Ball. 1605. Decemb. 12°," describes this lane as extending "a Porta Elizab. ad Turrim Edwardi 3."

[2] Hist. Cantab. Acad. i. 48. I have not been able to discover the name "Foul Lane" in any of the documents which I have seen. Dr Caius, however, is excellent authority for all matters concerning the Hostels, and especially for Trinity College, because during the period of his student-residence, "*nostro tempore*" as he terms it (which he defines to have been between 12 September, 1529 and 29 September, 1545, ibid. i. 53), the Hostels were still employed for the residence of students, and Trinity College had not been founded; but when he returned to the University as Master of Caius College and was writing his book, which was published in 1574, Trinity College had been established, and the Hostels had all fallen into disuse.

[3] This lavatory must not be mistaken for the present conduit, built in 1602.

had at the south-west angle the landing-place termed Dame
Nichol's Hithe, and a group of small cottages and a granary
attached to the same. It was separated from the second or
middle division by a common ditch, termed King's Ditch (*fossatum regis*). This middle division, between which and the garden
of S. John's Hospital there was a lane, was made up of three
pieces, each occupying the whole breadth from east to west.
The first, on the north, was a garden of the Priory of S.
Edmund, afterwards of Henry de Gretford; the second was a
garden of Edmund de Walsingham; and the third, next to
King's Hall Lane, was the messuage of Robert de Croyland, the
original site of King's Hall. This last had a small house belonging to John de Cambridge at the south-west corner. The third
division, that next to High Street, was occupied by five houses
and their gardens, which, from the names of their tenants, may
be called, in order from north to south, S. Edmund's, Pyke's,
Totington's, Walsingham's, and Atte-Conduit's.

The south-eastern district, included between King's Hall
Lane on the north, Foul Lane on the west, High Street on the
east, and S. Michael's Lane on the south, may also for the sake
of description be considered as consisting of three principal
divisions, each extending completely from west to east. The
first or most northerly was occupied by a garden of the Priory
of S. Edmund to the west, and a garden of the Priory
of Chiksand to the east, next the High Street. The second
was separated into three lots, of which the first to the
west was the property of S. John's Hospital, the next a small
piece belonging to S. Katherine's Hostel, while the third,
next High Street, contained another garden of the Priory of
S. Edmund on the north, and Tyled Hostel on the south.
The whole of these two divisions in process of time were added
to the site of King's Hall. The last and largest division consisted of three parts, of which the most westerly was occupied
by S. Margaret's Hostel on the north, and Physwick Hostel on
the south, both eventually united under the latter name. The
second piece was called S. Katherine's Hostel or Refham's
messuage ; and the third division, next the street, was occupied
then, as now, by a row of houses and gardens which then
belonged to Corpus Christi College, S. John's Hospital, and the

Priory of S. Mary de Pratis respectively. These, as they have never formed part of the sites of the collegiate institutions whose history we are following, do not require further attention.

The south-western district, bounded on the north by King's Hall Lane, and on the south by Trinity Hall, and lying between Foul Lane and Milne Street on the east, and the Town Ditch on the west, consisted of five principal divisions, each extending from the Town Ditch to Foul Lane or Milne Street. The first on the north was S. Gregory's Hostel; the two next were occupied by Michael House, the fourth by Garret Hostel and Ovyng's Inn, and the fifth by the garden called Hennably.

The whole of the northern district, and half of the south-eastern district, were ultimately occupied by King's Hall. The buildings and gardens of Michael House were placed in the middle of the south-western district. The remaining space in the south-eastern and south-western districts was all appropriated to hostels, excepting of course the private houses next the street at the south-east corner. Garret Hostel and Ovyng's Inn were entered from Milne Street. Michael House gates faced south at the corner of Milne Street and S. Michael's Lane. S. Gregory's Hostel opened into Foul Lane. S. Katherine's Hostel was in S. Michael's Lane. These four Hostels were the property of Michael House. Physwick Hostel, in S. Michael's Lane, belonged to Gonvile Hall, which then had its entrance on the opposite side of the same lane. S. Margaret's Hostel, which was once the property of Michael House, and was entered from Foul Lane, was sold to Gonvile Hall and incorporated with Physwick Hostel, forming its garden. Tyled Hostel in High Street belonged to King's Hall. Now Dr Caius includes all the above in his list of the seventeen hostels which were standing in the time of his student-residence at Cambridge[1]. But as every hostel in his list was, as he relates, appropriated to students who paid their own expenses, and lived under a Principal who hired the hostel, it follows that the Hostels above enumerated were kept distinct from the Colleges to which they belonged to the last, and were let to such Principals as a source of

---

[1] Hist. Cantab. Acad. i. 46.

revenue[1]. We shall see presently that Physwick Hostel was an exception to this rule.

The general survey of the site being now completed, we may proceed to the detailed history of it, beginning with the south-western district, containing Michael House, founded by Hervey de Stanton in 1324[2], and the contiguous Hostels of S. Gregory, Ovyng, and Garret.

The Architectural History of Michael House, like that of other Colleges, must be considered under the two heads of the acquisition of the site, and the erection of the buildings. The first is so bound up with the history of Trinity College that it must be examined in detail, and there are ample materials to illustrate it. The muniments of this College were all collected by the care and diligence of John Otryngham, master at the beginning of the fifteenth century, and copied into a parchment folio which is still preserved by the name of the Otryngham Book. This however, although an invaluable record of its kind, is a mere chartulary, and beyond a few explanatory notes, concerns the soil of the .College estates alone. Bursars' books and other records of expenses, from which Architectural History seeks its authorities, are, in the case of Michael House, wholly wanting; and as the buildings have equally disappeared, it will be easily supposed that their history is extremely imperfect, and need not detain us long. But to begin with the site.

The "largest and most important part of the College," as it is termed in the Otryngham Book[3], was a house which stood at the corner of Foul Lane and S. Michael's Lane. It is described in a conveyance dated 2 June, 1294, as

"a messuage in Henneye in the parish of S. Michael, between the messuage of John de Welles, Chaplain, on the one part and a highway

---

[1] In the Commissioners' Returns to Hen. VIII. for Michael House (Commiss. Docts. i. 120), the rents of these Hostels are of course included under the general head of "Rents of divers tenements and cottages," which, exclusive of the Rectory of S. Michael, amount to £16. 13s. 2d. annually.

[2] [See the Historical Introduction.]

[3] [The documents relating to the messuage about to be described are headed (Otryngham, p. 4) "Sequuntur carte principalis partis Collegii in ordine sicut fiebant;" and again (ibid. p. 8, 19 b), Stanton's conveyance to Michael House is headed: "Sequitur carta per quam dictus dominus Heruicus dedit collegio predicto tenementum Buttetourt quod est maior pars mansi collegii et principalis."]

(*via regalis*) on the other, and extending from the highway which leads to Dame Nichol's Hythe to the King's Bank (*ripa domini Regis*)."

The stream thus designated was evidently navigable at that time, for in the conveyance to Hervey de Stanton a quay is specially mentioned as belonging to the house. The highway which formed the south boundary was partly S. Michael's Lane, partly a narrower thoroughfare, which led in continuation of it down to the river. The possessors of the house, two brothers, Roger and Robert Buttetourte, had obtained a royal license, 28 May, 1306, to enclose and keep the said lane for the enlargement of their property[1]. The house was sold, 16 March, 1323 —4, for one hundred silver marks, by Roger Buttetourte, who describes himself as son of Guido Buttetourte, a man of noble birth (*nobilis vir*), to Hervey de Stanton[2], and by him conveyed to his College 26 September, 1324.

The next acquisition, which was completed 11 November, 1326, is noted in the margin of the Otryngham Book as "the second part of the college manse," and is related as follows :

"About a year and a half had elapsed from the foundation of the College when the aforesaid Founder purchased, conjointly with Master Walter Buxton, then master (*custos*) of the College, from Adam de Trumpyngton, formerly rector of S. Michael's Church, two messuages in the parish of S. Michael, of which one is situated in S. Michael's lane, on the north side of the principal part of the College, namely between the Hall and the kitchen of the aforesaid College; and the other is situated opposite the west end of S. Michael's Church, on the north side of the glebe belonging to the church, and is the principal part of the messuage of William Syda[3]."

It appears from the muniments which follow this piece of history, which serves as a heading to them, that these two messuages cost 40 silver marks, and the first is described in the transfer to Stanton, 12 March 1325—6, as lying in Milne Street, between the House of the Master and Scholars of S. Michael on the south, and the messuage formerly of Simon Goodman on the north, and abutting on the highway to the east,

---

[1] [Otryngham, p. 6, 12 b. The deed is dated 28 May, 34 Ed. I. and headed, "Sequitur licencia Regis de quadam venella inter collegium et hospicium Ouyng."]

[2] [Otryngham, p. 6, 13 b; 19 b. The property is described in the first conveyance as "mesuagium meum cum edificiis, gardinis, kaya, et redditibus."]

[3] [Otryngham, pp. 34—39, 1 d—16 d. The ground on which this second messuage stood is now part of the site of Caius College. Vol. i. 161.]

and on the common bank (*communis ripa*) to the west. This last boundary is termed in the earlier deeds of the series "the water," or the "running water."

These two pieces of ground, which, as the plan shews, were contiguous to one another, were probably sufficient for the establishment of the College, as some years elapsed before any other purchases were made. It will, however, be convenient to trace the history of the rest of the site before we attempt a description of the extent and position of the buildings.

Hervey de Stanton died in October 1327, and the next acquisitions were due to the zeal of his executors Alexander Walsham and John de Illegh, who conducted the negotiations, and then sold the property they had obtained possession of to the newly constituted Society of Michael House. The first property bought in this way was the tenement at the corner of Michael House lane and the lane to Dame Nichol's Hythe, purchased 28 September, 1337, from John de Illegh, to whom it had been sold in the previous year by Cristina, daughter of Walter de Fulborne. The heading in Otryngham speaks of it as "The Corner Hostel (*hospicium angulare*) next to King's Hall where there is now a stable[1]:" and in the conveyance it is described as "Crouched Halle[2], between the messuage formerly belonging to Adam de Ayrmynne, Archdeacon of Norfolk, on the south, and the lane to Dame Nichol's Hythe on the north, with one end abutting on the highway (*regia via*)." It appears to have extended westward as far as the King's Ditch[3].

Sixteen years afterwards the house which intervened between

---

[1] [Otryngham, p. 57. The stable in question probably belonged to Michael House, for a marginal note in the same hand as the deed says, "Nota de stabulo juxta Aulam Regiam," to which a writer in a later hand adds, "quod vocabatur hospicium Angulare sive Crouchedhalle." To this name the following note is afterwards appended: "pars extima hospicii gregorii iuxta venellam attingentem aulam regiam."]

[2] *Crouched* used in the sense of bearing a *Cross*—"Hospitium S. Crucis." Thus Edmund Crouchback was so called from the cross he wore in his voyage to Jerusalem, whence also *crouched friars*. Fuller's Holy War, p. 215 (ed. 1651).

[3] [MSS. Mason: Add. MSS. Mus. Brit. 6397, p. 50. Mason gives the following abstract of a deed relating to this piece. It is undated, and he supplies no information of the source whence he obtained it. "John de Fulburne concedit Ric. de Morden mess. cum edificiis in Sᵗ Mic. inter terras Sim. Godeman versus Austr. et venellam versus Aquil. et abuttat super viam regiam versus orient, et super fossatum Regis versus occid."]

the last purchase and Buttetourte's messuage was bought.   The
heading to its title-deeds in Otryngham[1] describes it as

"the messuage formerly the Archdeacon's but now called S. Gregory's
Hostel, concerning which it is to be noted that the said messuage did
once belong to one Simon Goodman, a burgess of Cambridge; who had
no legitimate son, but two daughters, of whom the one was named
Matilda, and was married to John Nasyng a burgess of Cambridge, and
the other was called Johanna.   Which John Nasyng with Matilda his
wife, and Johanna her sister, did, after the death of Simon Goodman,
sell the said messuage to master Adam de Ayrmynne, Archdeacon of
Norfolk."

This sale took place in 1332, and after passing through various hands the house became, 28 January 1353, the property of
Ralph Langley, Thomas Sutton, and John Clipesby, who conveyed it to the College, after the royal license in mortmain had
been obtained, on 3 February in the same year.   It is described
in 1337, as " in the Parish of S. Michael, between the messuage
of the Master and Scholars of Michael House on the south, and
the messuage late of Walter Fulborne on the north, extending
in length from the highway on the east to the King's stream
(*aqua Domini Regis*), on the west[2]."

It would seem that the Archdeacon's house and Crouched
Hall were taken down in after times, before the Otryngham
Book was written, and that a single edifice was erected on the
same ground, which bore the name of S. Gregory's Hostel, or
Mawmarkyd Hostel, otherwise Newmarket Hostell[3], extending
as far as King's Hall Lane.   Dr Caius records that this Hostel,
which had then been pulled down, stood where the Master of
Trinity's bedroom was at that time placed[4].

In 1434, the Corporation of Cambridge leased to Michael
House for one hundred years[5] a piece of waste land called

---

[1] [Otryngham, p. 49.   The deeds are marked 1—10 g; the license in mortmain,
the "breve de Ad quod dampnum," and the final conveyance, 21—23 g.]

[2] Otryngham, p. 50, 5 g.   [The " King's stream " was probably a continuation of
the King's Ditch, which separated Croyland's House from Cornhythe (p. 422).]

[3] In some extracts from the Account-Books of the Hospital of S. John for 1465
given by Baker (MSS. Harl. 7046, p. 132) the name is written " Mimarkyd Hostell
alias vocat' Hosp^m S^ti Gregorii:" and " Hospitium Mawmarkyd."   " Newmarket
Hostell" occurs in the Town grants of the Millstones dated 1434 and 1542.

[4] Hist. Cantab. Acad. i. 48.   It will be seen in the history of Trinity College that
the present bedroom of the Master was built circa 1555, and there is every reason to
suppose that it has always been appropriated to the same purpose.

[5] [Otryngham, p. 72.   The conveyance is in the Treasury of Trinity College,

"le Millestones," measuring 99 feet from east to west, by 82 feet 6 inches from north to south, lying between the garden of the College to the south, the common lane leading to the river on the north, the garden of Newmarket Hostell on the east, and the Town Common on the west. In 1542 it became the property of the College[1]. The conveyance, in English, describes the ground as follows:

"Thys Indenture made the ffyrst daye of the monethe of August in the xxxiiij[th] yere of the Reygn of our Soueraygn lord King Henry the viii[th] [1542] bytwen William Gylle maior of the Town of Cambrige... And ffrauncys Mallett doctor in dyvynyte m[r]. or keper of the College or house comenly callyd Michell house in Cambrige...Wytnessythe

That the sayd maior...haue covenanted gyven graunted and alye-natyd...oon voyde ground or Gardeyn comenly callyd mylstones in Cambrige as yt lyethe bytwixt the Orteyarde of the sayd College on the southe parte ; and the comen lane equall with the sestroll pertaynyng vnto the Kyngs halle Cundytte on the northe parte ; the oon hedde a buttyng vpon a pece of the comen of the sayd Town callyd mylstones hylle towards the West[2]; and the Garden ground pertaynyng to the sayd m[r] and ffellowes lately callyd Newmarkett hostle towards the Est.

The wyche voyde ground or Garden conteynethe in lengthe ffrom the Est vnto the West vj perches and in bredythe ffrom the northe vnto the Southe v perches, and the sayd comen lane ys in Breadithe at the West ende xvj ffoote of the kyngs standerd and in breadythe at the Est ende of the sayd voyde grounde xiij ffoote of the kyngs standerd."

The description shews that the garden of S. Gregory's Hostel did not extend so far to the west as the College garden did. This piece was intended to lengthen it, and a marginal note in Otryngham, apparently contemporary with the lease, terms it "the west part of the garden of S. Gregory's Hostel."

By this last acquisition the site of Michael House was so far completed that we may proceed to investigate its buildings.

The records of building operations, and allusions to build-ings, are, as I have already explained, extremely scanty. It may be supposed that for many years the mansion of the

"Michael-House." The measurements given in the lease are slightly different, as follows: "et continet in longitudine iuxta venellam predictam quinque perticatas et duodecim pedes de Standard [94 ft. 6 in.], ex alia parte iuxta gardinum Collegii predicti quinque perticatas [82 ft. 6 in.], et in latitudine ad caput orientale quinque perticatas et duodecim pedes de Standard [94 ft. 6 in.]."

[1] [The Town received in exchange "ffoure selyons of lande arrable conteynyng two acres as they be and lye in a certeyn ffeld of Grauncester in the county of Cambrige commenly callyd Newnhams croft."]

[2] [For the change which takes place in the direction of the ditch westward of this piece see below, p. 405.]

nobleman, Roger de Buttetourte, served for the members of the College and took the name of the manse thereof. In the list of Benefactors William de Gootham, master circa 1380, between fifty and sixty years after the foundation of the College, is recorded as having spent £130 on twelve chambers and a kitchen, of which chambers "eight were built on the north part, and four on the south part[1]." In 1425 exequies were granted to Richard Holme, Warden of King's Hall, for having expended a large sum on the repair of the Library, and given many theological books to it[2]. In 1429 a set of rules were made by John Otryngham, the master, and his "consocii" and scholars[3], which shew, by inference, that there were but twelve chambers at that time in the house fit for fellows, and that two fellows were not lodged in one chamber unless there were more than twelve in residence. The rules in question are, that if there be 13 fellows in the house, including the master, then two of the fellows must be lodged in the "lower chamber" (*bassa camera*) on the south side of the garden-door of the House. If there be 14, then other two fellows must occupy the lower chamber on the south side of the buttery (*promptuarium*). If there be 15, similarly two are to be in the lower chamber beneath the master's chamber; if 16, two in the upper chamber (*alta camera*) over the buttery; and if 17, two in the upper chamber contiguous to the principal gate of the House, to the east. In 1441 an annual mass was ordered for William Ayscough, Bishop of Sarum, master, and in 1444 he was solemnly enrolled among the Benefactors, because, amongst other benefits bestowed on the House, he had given £100 "towards the building of it[4]." John Fisher, Bishop of Rochester, master in 1497, gave £110 to "a new building," the nature of which is not mentioned[5].

[1] Otryngham, p. 21.

[2] [Otryngham, p. 21. "Notabilem pecunie summam dicto collegio contulit ad reparaciones librarie in eodem, necnon plures preciosos et solempnes sacre theologie libros eidem caritatiue contulit, ac plura alia bona fecit, et fieri procuravit." The "exequiæ" were to be celebrated on April 23. The order is dated Easter, 1425.]

[3] Ibid. p. 74. They are printed in the Appendix, No. II.

[4] [Otryngham, pp. 75, 78. The words, in the second deed, are "nobis centum libras ad opus fabrice et edificacionis dicte domus nostre...donauerit."]

[5] [Otryngham, p. 24. Bishop Fisher's name occurs in a list of benefactors added in a later hand; and his benefaction is noted in the margin. His name is succeeded by those of two Fellows, Richard Nelson and John Retforth, each of whom gave 20 nobles "ad nouum edificium."]

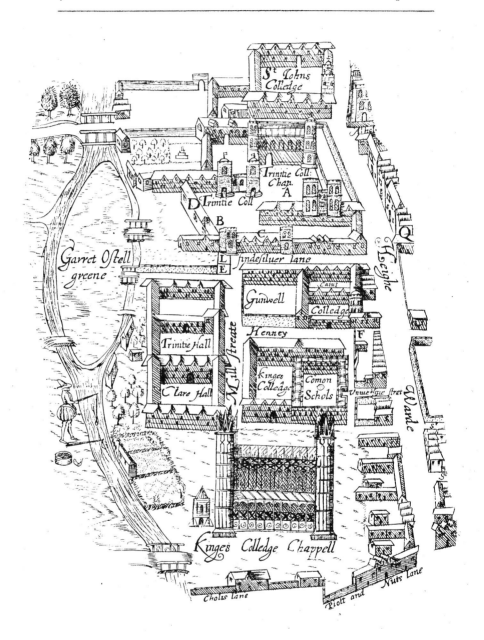

Fig. 2. Trinity College, from Lyne's Map of Cambridge, 1574. A. Kinges Hall. B. Michaell howse. C. Physwicke Ostell. D. Gregorye Ostell. E. Garett Ostell. L. Ouins Inn.

In Lyne's plan dated 1574 (fig. 2), the buildings of Michael House are shewn as consisting partly of a tower at the corner of Milne Street and Find-silver lane. This tower is part of the same range as Physwick Hostel, and beyond it to the west is a range of chambers belonging to Michael House. Ovyng's Inn and Garret Hostel stand next to it on the south. A range of building running northward from a point to the west of this tower gateway is lettered "Gregorye Ostell," but part of this range seems intended to be included in the reference to Michael House. This range stops short of the Trinity buildings, and is drawn in outline. This is however the case with all the buildings in this plan that exhibit a face to the west. To understand this plan, however, it must be remembered that at the time of its date Michael House had become part of Trinity College; and further that, though some of the buildings were retained and occupied for many years, all those which projected into the area of the Court had been pulled down, and the ground levelled. S. Gregory's Hostel also had been pulled down. The lane which, in the olden time, separated Michael House from Physwick Hostel, had been enclosed, and the end of it next Trinity Lane had been built up by a wall joining the corresponding corners of Michael House and Physwick Hostel, and containing a gate on the site of the present Queen's Gate. This accounts for the continuity of the buildings marked Michael House and Physwick Hostel.

From a comparison of these imperfect data, I conjecture that in Michael House the tower gateway, standing in this plan at the end of Milne Street and facing south, gave access to a court, of which the south side next to S. Michael's Lane, and the north side, contained the chambers recorded as the work of Gotham. On the west were the Hall, Master's Chamber, Common Chamber, Library, etc. The Chapel was in this College wanting, for, like Peterhouse and Corpus Christi College before the Reformation, the Society of Michael House attended service in the parish church. There is no evidence that any building stood on the east side of the Court, which was probably closed by a wall only next Foul Lane. West of the Court a garden extended to the stream; and on the north a small kitchen-court was probably reserved, between the north chambers and

S. Gregory's Hostel. [Here also was the stable (p. 396) and perhaps other offices.]

Having now traced the history of the buildings and grounds of Michael House as far as the lane which formed its northern border, we may proceed to the land which lay immediately to the south of the College and its garden.

The Otryngham Book informs us[1] that "after the death of Alexander de Walsham, John de Illegh purchased at great trouble and expense two hostels (*hospicia*) in Cambridge, called Ovyng's and Garyte, of which the muniments follow;" and from one of these it is shewn that these two messuages were sold to him in 1329 by the son-in-law and daughters of William de Ovyng of Berton. The property conveyed is described as

"two messuages in the parish of S. Michael, between the messuage of the scholars of S. Michael towards the north, and a tenement of John de Cambridge called Henneye on the other side; and abutting on a highway towards the east, and a stream towards the west[2]."

From the rest of the muniments I gather that the principal part had been sold in one lot to William de Estdene parson of the church of Leverington in Cambridgeshire, and John de Ovyng his nephew, in 1310, by Robert de Orford parson of the church of Cottenham. As for the remainder of it, it appears that at the south-west corner there was a landing-place termed Flaxhythe, to which a lane from Milne Street gave access[3]; and on the north side of the lane, and on the bank at Flaxhythe, there was a group of four or five small

---

[1] Otryngham, p. 40.

[2] [Otryngham, p. 44, 16, 17 f. Another deed (ib. p. 42, 9 f) describes the property as "between the messuage of Roger de Bouttetourte and the lane called Heneye."]

[3] This lane, which forms the south boundary of the whole, receives in the documents the various names of "*vicus qui vocatur flaxhyd*," and "*venella qua itur apud le flaxhethe*," "*regalem viam in Henneye*," and "*venella que vocatur Heneye*." In the final transfer of the whole to John de Illegh, the south boundary is simply the tenement of John de Cambridge, "*que vocatur Henneye*," whence it may be inferred that after Ovyng had bought up all the ground at Flaxhythe, he proceeded to enclose the lane, in imitation of his neighbour De Bouttetourte, who a few years before had obtained license to enclose the lane which was then the boundary between them. The grant of one of these small pieces of ground at the bank concludes with granting "a common passage from the street to the water-course for a cart of sacks (*communem viam a strata vsque ad filum aque ad carettam et saccos*")" (Otryngham, p. 40, 1 f). Perhaps the lane was merely an occupation road, for it is styled a highway (*via regalis*) in only one document of the whole set. [It has not been laid down on the map (fig. 1)].

cottages and gardens, some of them occupied by fishermen, the whole of which were bought up by Estdene and Ovyng one after the other, after the first purchase mentioned above, so that in 1317 John de Ovyng seems to have obtained the whole estate, which his heirs transferred, as above related, to John de Illegh in 1329. All the lesser pieces are said to be in Henneye, or at Flaxhythe in Henneye, but the principal piece is not so characterized. The royal license[1], by which John de Illegh is authorized to give the two messuages to Michael House, states that they were to be applied as part of the endowment of a chantry lately founded by Hervey de Stanton.

On this site in after times we find two Student-Hostels bearing the same names of Ovyng and Garret. The first, as Caius and others record, was an Inn for law students, and stood opposite to the western back-gate of Gonville and Caius College, in contact with Michael House. The second, also opposite to the same gate, was nearer to Trinity Hall, as Lyne's plan (fig. 2) indicates. [In Hamond's plan (fig. 3) two houses are shewn in this place, one westward of the other, which probably represent these Hostels.] These descriptions apply to the buildings. The ground behind them, extending to the Town Ditch, the old King's Ditch (*fossatum Regis*), appears to have been principally used as the garden of Garret Hostel, for no mention of Ovyng's Inn occurs in any document of Michael House subsequent to those already quoted ; but the name of Garret Hostel is perpetually applied to the whole of the south border of the Michael House property in a variety of deeds. That it was of some size and importance is shewn by its having given its name to the common or island which lay to the west of it, and which was known as *Garret Hostle green* or *Garret Hostle waste* until it was enclosed by Trinity College. Lastly, Dr Caius describes Garret Hostel as having been situated on the bank, "*ad ripam positum,*" and that it joined the south side of Michael House, meaning that its grounds extended to the bank. But of Ovyng's Inn he says only what I have quoted above, and I therefore imagine that it had little or no ground attached to it. The ordinary name of the former Hostel was probably derived from "garyte," a watchtower, look-out place, or high window, which may have charac-

[1] Dated 20 October, 3 Edw. III., 1329. Otryngham, p. 45, 20 f.

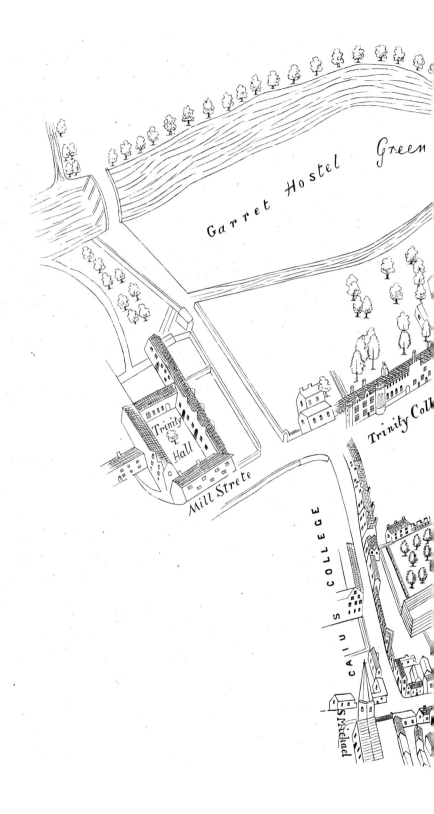

Fig. 3. Trinity College, from Hammond's map of Cambridge, 1592.

terized its early form; but it is sometimes called S. Gerard's Hostel, and in one document quoted by Baker it is mentioned as "the Hostel of S. William of York called garret Hostle[1]." How often it was rebuilt or repaired we know not, but it stood in some shape or other until the latter half of the seventeenth century, when it became so ruinous that it was taken down, and Bishop's Hostel was erected in its place, as will be related in Chapter IV.

The ground south of Garret Hostel was a garden called Hennably, belonging to the Prior and Convent of Anglesey. They had leased it between 1316 and 1338 to John de Cambridge, his wife, and his son and daughter, for their lives[2]; and in 1447 they sold it to King Henry the Sixth, who, 26 July 1448[3], conveyed to Michael House a

"parcel of a certain garden called Henabbay, according as it is divided off (*metis et bundis separatur*) from the rest of the garden, which parcel abuts at one head towards the east on *le mylnestrete;* and at the other head towards the west on the King's Ditch."

[1] "Hospitium sancti Wilhelmi Eboraci vocat' garret Hostle." MSS. Baker, MSS. Harl. Mus. Brit. 7046, p. 133, from parish papers of S. Michael, undated. Dr Caius, in his enumeration of the Hostels (Hist. Cant. Acad. i. 47) mentions them as follows: "Sextum Divi Gerardi Hospitium, ad ripam positum, et Collegio S. Michaelis iunctum ad meridiem. Septimum Ovingi diversorium erat, utrumque positum è regione portae posticae Collegii Gonevilli et Caii quae ad occidentalem solem spectat, sic ut illud Aulae S. Trinitatis propius accederet, hoc Collegio divi Michaelis, nunc S. Trinitatis, iunctum sit:" and in Parker ("σκελετος Cantabrigiensis," in Leland's Collect. v. 189), "*S. Gerardi* ubi nostro seculo pons, garut Ostle dictus. *Ovingi* ubi aedificia illa subter quae canalis inter Collegia Caii et Trinitatis sese evacuat." The contract for building Bishop's Hostel, dated 1669, prescribes: "Bishop's Hostel to be built upon that piece of ground . . . . which is lying between the said College and the College stables, called "Garratt Hostle." [The meaning of the word "garyte" is discussed in the "Promptorium Parvulorum" Ed. Camden Soc. p. 187.]

[2] [Hailstone, History of Bottisham, p. 270, quoting MSS. Cole.]

[3] [A portion of the same ground had been granted by John Langton, Chancellor of the University, and Richard Wright, Mayor of Cambridge, to Michael House in 1445, "for the enlarging of garit hostell, as hit is now staked out." Borough Rate Report, p. 16. We have seen in the History of King's College that Langton transacted the business of the acquisition of the site; and we may conclude from this deed that the King had obtained possession of the ground before the actual conveyance was signed. According to Otryngham (p. 181) Michael House had sold to King's College a certain house in School Street containing three Schools, without a formal conveyance. This house, together with a part of Hennably, was given by King's College to King Henry the Sixth, 26 June, 1448; and in the same year (4 July) he issued letters patent, giving the house and part of the garden to Michael House, out of pure charity.]

Before leaving Michael-House, it will be convenient to narrate the acquisition of the ground interposed between it and the River Cam. This was a piece of common land containing about two acres and a quarter, known in the seventeenth century by the name of Garret Ostell Greene, or the Town Common, and then separated from the site of Michael House by a ditch called the Town Ditch. As this joined the river at its northern and southern extremities, and was curved towards the west in a direction opposite to the flexure of the former, the Green became an island, as shewn in the maps of Lyne (fig. 2) and Hamond (fig. 3).

But from the expressions used in the deeds of the fourteenth century it is plain that the ditch in question had at that period not only a free current of water through it from the river, but was navigable for barges. We have found it described as "running water (*aquam currentem*)," "stream of water (*filum aque*)," "King's stream (*aquam Domini Regis*)," etc.; and it had the landing-place called Flaxhythe near its southern extremity. Roger de Buttetourte's ground, a little further to the north, had also a quay on its bank; and near the northern extremity was another landing-place, called Dame Nicol's Hythe, or Corn-hythe. But when the hithes had become the property, the one of Ovyng in 1317, and the other of King's Hall in 1341, as will be related below, the canal fell into disuse for navigation, and became merely a boundary ditch, called "Kyngs Dyche" (*fossatum Regis*), or "common ditch," names employed for the ordinary ditches by which the commons were fenced in, as well as for the great ditch which King Henry the Third made for the defence of the town[1]. That this particular ditch had ceased to be navigable is proved by the following grant dated 30 September, 1423, by which the Corporation of Cambridge granted permission to Michael House

"to make at their own costs and charges a certain ditch, twelve feet broad, extending from the common ditch (*fossatum commune*) at the west end of their garden to the river (*alta ripa Domini Regis*); through which ditch the aforesaid Master and Fellows and their successors may

---

[1] [These designations of the ditch have occurred in the deeds quoted above, and in those referring to Hennably, now part of Trinity Hall (Vol. i. pp. 213, 214).]

be enabled to have fuel and other goods brought in and taken out without let or hindrance for the term of one hundred years, reckoned from
the day of the making of these presents; provided always that the
aforesaid ditch be common to all the burgesses of the said Town
of Cambridge.

And the aforesaid Master and 'Fellows shall make and keep in
repair a foot-bridge across the said ditch three feet wide, fixed at both
ends, with a 'lenyngtre' on one side; and one '*vadum sufficiens* Anglicè
a forde' for the passage of carts, cattle, and other articles belonging to
the said Corporation. Moreover they shall keep the ditch clean; and
further, the nearest point of the said ditch to the wall of the King's
College shall be distant from it eighty feet[1]."

[Seven years afterwards (8 May, 1430) the Corporation leased
to Michael House, for one hundred years, at a yearly rent of
twelve pence, a strip of land on the same Common described as

"a certain parcel of ground, part of the common of the said Town
of Cambridge, with power to block up the east end of the common
ditch there, according as the aforesaid parcel of ground lies and extends
itself in length partly from a certain property of the said Master and
Scholars called *le Garet Hostell*, partly from a certain property of the
Prior of Anglesey called *le henne Abbey*, as far as the River of the aforesaid Town of Cambridge; and it extends itself in breadth, at the east
head of the said parcel of ground, from the common ditch which is
situated to the north of the garden of the College of the Holy Trinity for
30 standard feet over the common of the said Town towards the north;
and at the west head from the aforesaid ditch for 24 standard feet over
the aforesaid common towards the north[2]."

This piece must have been opposite to the north-west side
of Trinity Hall garden. The plan (fig. 1) shews that it is
represented, in part, by the ground at the west end of Garret
Hostel Lane, between the wall of Trinity College, and the space
originally occupied by the Town Ditch.]

The probable direction of the new passage from the north
part of the Town Ditch to the river has been laid down on the
map (fig. 1). After it was made the original north extremity of
the Ditch would be allowed to dry up altogether. The field

---

[1] [Translated from the copy of the original in Otryngham, p. 68. The measurements are set down in "pedes pauli." An annual rent of sixpence was to be paid to
the Town Treasurers for it.]

[2] [Translated from Otryngham, p. 72. The document is headed "super conces-
sione fossati iuxta Collegium sancte Trinitatis," and noted in the margin, in a late
hand, "Trin: hall ditch." The words "le henne Abbey" are noted in the same hand
"Trin: hall stables."]

called the Millestones, leased, as we have seen, to Michael Hous
in 1434, eleven years after the canal was made, is said to lie next
to a piece of the town common on the west called Millstones
Hill, which seems to have been the original northern extremity
of Garret Hostel Green; and is shewn by Hamond (fig. 3),
as a triangular space external to the boundary-wall of the
College gardens. It came into possession of Trinity College
very early, for in 1546—47 we find a record of the removal of
"the hill of the backe syde[1]."

The canal of which the formation has just been told brought
Garret Hostel Green to the shape which it retained until the
beginning of the seventeenth century. On the opposite side
of the river there was another common, called Long Green[2],
separated from the fields beyond by boundary ditches, much in
the same position as at present. A bridge over the river in the
position of the present Garret Hostel Bridge led from the south-
west corner of the Green to a road across this common; and
another bridge at the end of the straight portion of Garret
Hostel Lane was then the only access left for the townspeople to
Garret Hostel Green[3]. Lyne's plan, dated 1574 (fig. 2), shews
that Trinity College had also a small bridge over the Town
Ditch to the Green; and that Trinity Hall had another, so as to
give these Colleges easy access to the Town Bridge over the
river, and thus to the common and to the fields beyond it.

The northern two-thirds of Garret Hostel Green, and the
field on the west side of the river, called by Loggan (fig. 4)
"Trinity College Meadow," were obtained from the Town by
exchange, 23 March, 1612—13. They are described in the
deed drawn up between Thomas Nevile, Master of the College,
and Edward Cropley, Mayor of the Town, as:

[1] [Senior Bursar's Accounts, 1546—47. *In edificiis.* "Item to a poore fellowe
working on the backe syde in carying awaye ye hill iij^d." Ibid. *In reparacionibus.*
"It' for breking of a spade on the backe syde when ye Scholers worked ther iij^d. It'
to John Cooke ye beadman for breking his spade when the hill of the backe syde was
pulled downe iij^d."]

[2] [See History of S. John's College, p. 238.]

[3] [Speed's plan, made about 1590, shews Long Green in its original state, and the
bridge leading from Garret Hostel Lane on to the Green. It is on too small a scale
to be reproduced with advantage, but has been used as an authority for the construction of the plan (fig. 1).]

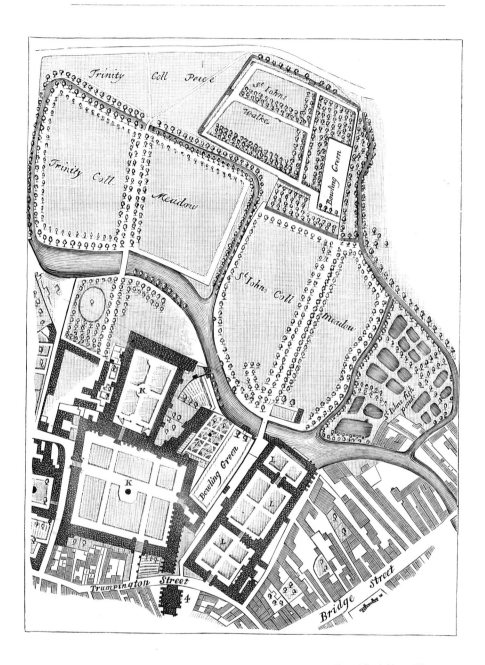

Fig. 4.   Trinity College and S. John's College, from Loggan's Map of Cambridge, 1688.

"two parcells of Ground, viz. one parcel of Pasture and Meadow which heretofore did lye in Common at all times in the year in Cambridge Westfields containing by estimation Eight Acres...lying and being on the West side of the River and High Stream, and is now Ditched and Fenced in, and lieth between a Cawsey which leadeth from the Bridge called Garrett Hostle Bridge unto the Field on the one side, and the Ground pertaining to the College called Saint John's College on the other side :

and one other parcel of pasture Ground late parcel of the Green called Garrett Ostle Green, lying on the east side of the River or High Stream, as it was then lately likewise severed from the other part of the said Garrett Ostle Green with a great Ditch, wherein now a Drain is made to run from the Backside of the said College, and the same is vaulted and covered over ;...

And whereas the said Master Fellows and Scholars...do intend and purport to inclose the foresaid part of Garret Ostle Green next the said College with a Brick Wall, and on the inward side of the said Wall to make one great Bridge over the said River and Common Stream from the said part of the Garret Ostle Green next the said College into the said Pasture and Meadow containing Eight Acres...and one other Bridge over the Ditch next the Common Field wherewith the said Eight Acres ...is enclosed, the said Bridges to be used for a Common passage for the said Master, Fellows and Scholars...from the said College into the Common Fields ; And to that end and purpose have made a Drain from the said College in the said great Ditch, and covered the same Ditch which did divide that part of Garret Ostle Green before mentioned... from the residue of the said Green ; And have already began to make the foundation of the said Brick Wall on the South part of the outside of the said great Ditch or Drain lately filled up, which Brick Wall is to contain in length twelve score feet or thereabouts directly from the wall of the said College to the said River, and have also made the foundation of a Wall or Foot of the said Bridge on the East side of the same River next the said Green

Now this Indenture witnesseth, [etc.][1]... "

The Corporation received in exchange for these Commons £50 in money, a messuage and farm called Michael Grange or Michael Dole, in the parish of S. Andrew, and various pieces of ground, of which the most important was the open space containing about twenty-five acres, now known as "Parker's Piece," from Edward Parker, to whom the estate had been leased, 16 December, 1587[2].

---

[1] [From a copy in the Treasury of Trinity College.]

[2] [The lease, copied in the Register of Trinity College, describes him as "sonne of Martin Parker of Retcheford [Rochford] in the countie of Essex ;" and a terrier of lands in Cambridge, quoted by Baker (MSS. xxxvi. 129), as "of Cambridge, Cook." According to Otryngham, p. 4, the "dola sancti Michaelis" lay to the south

[The negotiations which were thus concluded had commenced in the year succeeding the foundation of Trinity College[1], and were prolonged over a period of 66 years, as the date of the final deed shews. We do not know the whole history of the transaction; but Baker has recorded that the consent of the Town, Merton College, Oxford, Trinity Hall, Jesus College, and S. John's College had to be obtained, and that Archbishop Whitgift, Master 1567—77, "was vehement in the thing[2]." The part which he played in overcoming the opposition of S. John's College, whence the most strenuous resistance to the scheme proceeded, has been thus recorded in a contemporary document[3]:

"The M^r. and Fellowes of S^t. Johnes saye that Trinitie Colledge began to inclose that wast without their priuitie or their good will requiered, and that after the same was begon to be inclosed my L. of Canterburyes Grace wrote his lres. vnto them, requesting them that Trinitie Colledge might quietlie inclose the said wast, wherevnto they made answeare that the same parcell of wast was an inheritance belonging to their howse; And that by their statutes (as they took y^m) and by their oathe, they might not suffer the same to be inclosed: Wherevnto his Grace replied that he had [had] conference with Lawyers, and that they were resolued, that the M^r. and Fellows of S^t. Johnes might suffer

of the House of the Friars Preachers, now Emmanuel College; and the "grangia sancti Michaelis," the precise situation of which is not recorded, was the barn in which the grain grown on the said dole was stored. The terrier above quoted describes the messuage and farm as abutting "on the High Street East, and upon the Field called St Thomas Leas (otherwise Swinescroft) west." "Dole" signifies a part or portion of a meadow in which several persons have shares. Cowell's Interpreter, Ed. 1727.]

[1] [Cooper's Annals, iii. 58. Senior Bursar's Accounts, 1546—47. *Extraordinarie expensæ.* "Item expendyd by o^r m^r and other of ye fellowes upon Mr Mayre at Mr Adams whan as they commoned for ye bakesyde xij^d."]

[2] [MSS. Baker, xi. 298. MSS. Harl. Mus. Brit. 7038. He adds that there are several letters from Archbishop Whitgift at S. John's College "inter archiva." These unfortunately cannot now be found. The townspeople also disliked the proposed exchange. The following complaints, made at the Insurrection of 1549, illustrate their feelings at these inclosures (Lamb. Orig. Documents, etc. p. 158).

"Item we find...that Trinity Coll. hath inclosed a common lane which was a common course both for cart horse and man leading to the ryver unto a common grene and no recompense made therefore.

Item we fynde that the seyde College dothe commonlye use to laye ther mucke and meanor on ther backe syde apon the foreseyde common grene wher thei wyll suffer no man ells to do the lyke and have builded a common Jakes apon part of the same."]

[3] [State Papers: Domestic, Elizabeth, 1581—90, p. 709, No. 32. The document is unfortunately imperfect, ending abruptly in the middle of a sentence.]

that inclosure without breache of their Statutes or damage to their oathes; and presantlie after his Grace wrote another lre to the said M[r] of S[t] Johnes and thereby did giue them to vnderstand that yt was her ma[ts]. pleasure, (and so he was comaunded to signifie vnto them) that Trinitie Colledg should quietly inclose the said wast, wherevnto they returned answer that they did submitt themselves to her ma[ts]. pleasure, yet humblie intreating that her ma[tie]. would be pleased that their rights which they pretended to the said wast might be vnderstoode, and the Statutes of their Colledge considered of, which bound them (as they took yt) not to yield to the same, and which their peticion they likewise intreated his Grace might be made knowen to her ma[tie]."

The same document preserves the case for Trinity College, and the conditions which S. John's College tried to impose:

"The difference betweene Trinitie Colledge and S[t]. Johns Colledge in Cambridge about the inclosinge of A peece of Comon grownde.

Trinitie Colledge (the greatest for number of Students within that Vniuersitie,) having not anie seuerall place of walke or recreacion for the Students of the same, either within or without the walls of that Colledge, did (at the earnest request of the Master and Seniours) lately obtaine of the Maior, Bayliffes, and Burgesses, of the Towne of Cambridge, and other the Meane lords there, A smale plott of Common Grownde, next adioyninge to the Colledge on each syde of the Ryver to be inclosed for their private ease and vse.

It hath bene vsually called by the name of Trinitie Colledge greene, contayninge .7. Acres or there abouts, and is in the winter time overflowne with water, and beinge the place where the Scholars in the Somer season haue their ordinarie recreacion, thinhabitants of that Towne nether haue, nor can make any benefitt of feedinge for their Cattle there.

Yet in consideracion for the same we haue layde out of our owne private lands about the same Towne .25. acres at the least, to the Common vse of the inhabitants: so as they in generall hould themselues not only well satisfied, but also much benefitted by the exchaunge.

The like inclosure by the consent of thinhabitants of that Towne hath heretofore bene made by the next adioyninge Colledges: King's Colledge on the one syde, and S[t] Johns Colledge on the other syde. And the Towne doth receaue of ech, an anuall regard for the same. And there are besydes sondry precedents of the like granted inclosures made by the Maior Bayliffs and Burgesses, to other Colledges, as doth appeare by the Records both of the Towne and also of the said Colledges.

Not anie Colledge (to our vnder standinge) did euer oppose themselues againste the like inclosure, (so meete and necessarie for anie their neighbor Colledges,) vntill that nowe at this time the Master and Societie of St Johns Colledge do expresse themselues much greived, and dampnified herewith. Nothwithstandinge their contentment hath bene sought by the most effectuall meanes that by vs can be procured.

They pretend their locall Statute *de non alienandis Collegii terris etc* but havinge receaved satisfaccion on that behalfe, they now require to be compounded withall for their interest and stand vpon these particular demaundes.

First in acknowledgement that we hould the benefit by their consent, and to satisfie posteritie the [they ?] require the regard of xij^d. per annum to be paid for ever vnto their Colledge.

Secondly they would haue lefte vnto their private vse out of that grownde wch nowe by vs is to be inclosed A particion balke (as they so terme yt) of .16. foote breadthe.

Thirdly in consideracion of our large allowance made vnto the inhabitants of the Towne vpon this exchange they require that the said Towne should allso graunte (but freely) vnto them, one little plott of grownde to be allso inclosed, leadinge from their backsyde gates vnto the Feildes.

And lastlie in more full recompense, and to pleasure them withall they do require A Quill to be brought from our Condiute pipe to serve that Colledge with water[1].

Which demaundes we (in opinion) thinke not to be reasonable in regard that themselues (as a Colledge) can challenge no more proprietie in that grownde, then may euery seuerall Colledge of that Vniuersitie and Common inhabitants of the Towne."

The objections of S. John's College were probably silenced by their own success in purchasing from the Town of Cambridge 24 April, 1610, the piece of ground which they subsequently laid out as a Bowling Green[2]; for on 16 August, 1611, the Corporation made an Order intimating their readiness to effect an exchange with Trinity College on certain conditions; and on 14 December, 1612, the Master and Seniors of Trinity College made the following Order, which shews that the ground was already regarded by them as their own:

"Agreed that ye great Bridge be finished, and a wall on garret greene, and the bridge on the farr side of the green in to the fields, and that the best meanes be vsed to compound with the Towne for their graunte for peaceable injoying the same."

The terms of the deed of exchange above recited shew that Trinity College had commenced the work of enclosure before the deed was actually signed; and when the College Walks are described we shall see that part of the Common beyond the river had been planted before the end of the previous century.

---

[1] [Baker says (ut s̓upra) that this was for Mr Booth's conduit "intended in the Countess of Shrewsbury's Court." See History of S. John's College, p. 262.]

[2] [History of S. John's College, p. 238.]

The south part of Garret Hostel Green however still remained waste, and was in 1659 leased by the Corporation for 40 years to Gonville and Caius College; but, not proving so convenient for use as was expected, their lease was assigned to Trinity College in 1662. A fence, which afterwards became a wall, was evidently at once built along the south border of it, from the south-west angle of the Brewery to the river, as Loggan shews (fig. 4); an appropriation which gave offence to the townspeople, for in the same year the Senior Bursar charges for " 3 warrants about breaking downe the new wall, and for men watching to prevent mischiefe[1]." The leases were renewed regularly until 1790, when a lease for 999 years was granted, on payment of £400; and in 1823 the Town enfranchised, for £150,

"that piece or parcel of Common or Waste Ground lyeing and being at or near a place commonly called Gerards Hostle in Cambridge, containing in length next Trinity College...thirteen poles; and in length next the way to the river eight poles and three feet; and in breadth next the Brewhouse of the said College six poles and eight feet; and in breadth next the river eight poles and three feet;
And also one other piece of waste ground thereto...adjoining towards the river side, the whole parcel of ground containing...in length next the College fifteen poles and six feet, and in length next the way to the river ten poles and ten feet[2]."

The " way to the river " was a prolongation of Garret Hostel Lane to the water's edge, across a piece of ground called the " Stoneyard," whereof a lease for 999 years was granted in 1802, and it was enfranchised in 1823, for £50. It is then described as :

"All that...piece of common void ground lying on the outside of Trinity College wall near Gerard's Hostle bridge containing in breadth from the said wall at the west end fifty five feet, and at the east end from the said wall ten feet, and in length on the south side one hundred and forty seven feet, (including the Dock and Island) together with the Crane or Engine and all the houses, outhouses ... [etc.] thereupon erected...
And also all that piece or parcel of waste ground, adjoining the said piece of common void ground on the south side thereof, and containing in width from north to south next the river fifteen feet, extending

[1] [Sen. Burs. Accounts, 1661—62. *Extraordinaries.*]

[2] [These dimensions, reduced to feet, are 253 feet 6 inches along the north border, 175 feet along the south border, 107 feet along the east border, and 135 feet along the river side.]

eastward in a perpendicular line forty two feet, and then diagonally one hundred and five feet, terminating at the extremity of the aforesaid piece of Common void ground on the east side thereof..."

These dimensions enable us to lay down the southern portion of the Green with tolerable accuracy; but allowance must be made for changes in the ground since 1823. The map of Trinity Hall, dated 1731, reproduced in the History of that College, shews that the wall which was the south boundary of the part of Garret Hostel Green then held by Trinity College, was a continuation of the north wall of Garret Hostel Lane; and gives the length of it as just 180 feet. The same authority further shews that the ground purchased in 1823 was the triangular piece external to that wall on which part of Trinity College Brewhouse now stands; but the river bank has been artificially extended, so that the measurements given above do not quite fit the ground in its present state.

The width and direction of the Town Ditch can also be determined. The ground sold to Trinity Hall in 1545 was 296 feet long, measured from Milne Street, and was bounded on the west by the King's Ditch[1]. The interval therefore between this ground, and that purchased in 1823, from fifteen to twenty feet, represents the width of the Ditch. Again, the strip at the north-west corner of Trinity Hall garden is said to be bounded on the north by "our brook, now in the tenure of Michael house," by which the same Ditch is evidently meant. The exact extent of the northern part of the Green acquired in 1613 is not specified. The length of the wall along the south border, 240 feet, is the only dimension given, and that is rather less than the true distance, as we have seen from the conveyance of the next piece to the south, purchased in 1823, where the same dimension is stated to be 253 feet 6 inches. It is possible, however, to lay down the extent of this northern portion approximately, for the Senior Bursar's Accounts for 1562—63 specify the total length of the Ditch, from Garret Hostel Bridge to the river, to be 627 feet[2].]

[1] [History of Trinity Hall: Vol. i. pp. 212, 213.]

[2] [Sen. Burs. Accounts, 1562—63. *Repararationes in oppido.* "Item paied to vj men of Trumpington for casting oure dytche behind the college from garret ostle bridge to the riuer nighe the bake house ende xxxviij pole at xviij^d. the pole and iiij^d. ernest ... lvij^s. iiij^d."]

The history of what we have agreed to call the south-western district having been related, we will next proceed to that of the south-eastern. The arrangement of this has been already described in general terms. The northern half of it presents no history worth dwelling upon in this place. The boundaries given in the deeds sufficiently define the relative positions of the pieces composing it, and the little that remains to be said of them may be postponed until we come to the history of King's Hall, into the site of which they were absorbed. But the hostels in the southern part of this district require to be examined more particularly. The most important of these is Physwick Hostel, which stood at the corner of Foul Lane and S. Michael's Lane.

The ground on which it was built was made up of three pieces, one at the corner of Foul Lane and S. Michael's Lane, belonging to the Priory of S. Edmund of Sempringham; another to the east of it in S. Michael's Lane, described as a tenement and garden, together with a plot of vines; and, lastly, a piece on the north of these, on which stood the dwelling-house of William Physwick[1], bedell of the University, which he bequeathed to Gonvile Hall, "4 Kal. April. A° D^{ni} 1393," as Dr Caius has recorded in his History and Annals. The other two pieces also became the property of Gonvile Hall. Physwick's house was leased to his widow Johanna for her life by that College[2], and was afterwards altered and enlarged for the reception of students; moreover its site was increased by the acquisition of S. Margaret's Hostel on the north.

The house and grounds which were so called became the property of Michael House 30 September, 1396; and were sold to Gonvile Hall 20 March, 1467. The dimensions are fortunately given in the latter conveyance, whence the description may be translated:

"A messuage or hostel in the parish of S. Michael called *Saint Margaret Hostell*, now enclosed with walls; between a certain other hostel belonging to the same [Gonvile Hall] called *Fyshewick hostell* on

---

[1] [This name is variously spelt, Physwick: Phissewyche: Fyssewicke: Fisswicke: Fysshewik: Fysshewyk: Fhyshewyk: Fyshwyk: etc. In the History of Christ's College, p. 189, the form Fysshewyk, which was found in the muniments, was adopted.]

[2] [Caius College Treasury, "College Box," No. 30.]

the south, and a certain void ground now belonging to the King's Hall on the north; one head thereof abuts on the garden of a certain tenement of ours called *Le Mighell Angell* towards the East; and the other head abuts on the high-way towards the West. This messuage contains in length from the outside of the west wall inclusive to the outside of the east wall inclusive along the aforesaid void ground 32 yards, and along the aforesaid hostel called *Fysswicke Hostell* 33 yards; in breadth along the aforesaid highway, from the same hostel to the outside inclusive of the boundary wall of the aforesaid void ground 30 yards and 2 feet; and along the garden of the aforesaid tenement belonging to Michael House to the outside of the aforesaid wall inclusive 30 yards and 2 feet[1]."

As the ground thus minutely described is bounded on the south by Physwick Hostel, and on the east by another property, it follows that the two Hostels had the same breadth from east to west, and have accordingly been so laid down on the plan (fig. 1). S. Margaret's Hostel was united by Gonvile Hall to Physwick Hostel, and became its garden. Physwick Hostel was evidently rebuilt in collegiate form after this union had been effected. Dr Caius relates how the north

---

[1] [MSS. Mason, Add. MSS. Mus. Brit. 6397, f. 26 b. Mason notes that he copied the deed "ex munimentis Coll. Gonvilli Caiensis." The previous history of the property may be briefly recounted. It was bought by Richard de Betelee, Bedell of the University, in 1354 (Otryngham, p. 58, 4 k, where we find the heading "Sequitur de hospicio sancte Margarete"); and by him sold to John de Burgh 6 Feb. 1368 (Ibid. p. 59, 5 k). He in turn sold it 23 March in the same year to Henry Granby and John Wesenham (Ibid. 6 k) who seem to have been employed in buying property for Michael House, for in the next year they obtained from Richard de Betelee and Juliana his wife their house in School Street called the "School of S. Margaret" (Ibid. 7 k). They conveyed the two properties together to Michael House 30 Sept. 1396 (Ibid. p. 60, 9 k), the royal license in mortmain having been obtained four years previously, 26 April 1392. It is difficult to understand how Juliana Betelee was concerned in enabling Michael House to acquire S. Margaret's *Hostel*; and yet " exequiæ " were granted to her by the Master and Fellows because she had given them "gratis" S. Margaret's Hostel and "the Schools of Theology commonly called S. Margaret's Schools" (Ibid. p. 20). The "School of S. Margaret" with a building adjacent thereto, containing three other schools, was given by the College to King Henry VI., in exchange for part of Henably. See above, p. 404, and History of King's College, Vol. i. 320. The three schools, which had been purchased by William de Gotham for Michael House in 1377 (Otryngham, p. 57, 1 k), were likewise transferred to the same persons, and included in the Royal license and conveyance to the College above-mentioned. On the north side of S. Margaret's Hostel lay a garden of irregular shape (Otryngham, p. 77, where the measurements are given) leased to Betelee by the Priory of S. Edmund, 28 October, 1355. A marginal note informs us: "est pars gardini hospicii sancte margarete," but we do not know when Betelee bought it. It was evidently included in the Hostel when he sold it in 1368.]

part, and the south part as far as the gate, by which we ought perhaps to understand two sides of a quadrangle, were built in 1481[1]; Fuller mentions its "fair buildings;" and some portion of it was used by Trinity College as chambers[2]. It was evidently of great importance, from the particular description of it by Dr Caius. This we will proceed to translate:

"Physwick Hostel, situated opposite to the north side of Gonevile and Caius College, from which it was separated by a road, now forms part of Trinity College, but formerly belonged to Gonevile and Caius College. It was not let out to hire, as the other hostels were, but was the private property of Gonevile and Caius College. It was afterwards converted into a hostel (*hospitium*) or rather into a tiny (*pusillum*) College, into which, as into a colony, they could banish the too great abundance of their younger members. To provide for their management and instruction they set over it two Principals, called respectively External and Internal, of whom the former resided in the College, the latter in the Hostel. The former was a Fellow of the College chosen by the master; the latter was elected by the 'commensales' of the Hostel and the Exterior Principal conjointly. Both of them lectured in the Hostel and presided as moderators at the exercises of the students, for which they received and divided between them 16 pence quarterly from each resident in the Hostel. The like sums were paid to the Exterior Principal for chamber rent, but applied to the use of the College. In those days more than thirty or forty "commensales" resided in that Hostel. It stood and flourished for many years, and put forth many eminent and learned men, of whom some were selected for College honors, and became resident therein, others were called away to fill offices of state. This Hostel was never deserted like the others, but was taken possession of in 1546 by his serene Majesty King Henry the Eighth for the augmentation of Trinity College, in exchange for a rent of £3 annually to be paid by the Treasury until some other provision in recompense for the same should be made by himself or his successors[3]."

The house eastward of the two hostels which we have been describing is termed S. Katherine's Hostel in the Otryngham

---

[1] [History of Caius College, Vol. i. 169.]

[2] [The "tower and gatehouse in phisicke ostle," and the hall of the same, are mentioned in the Senior Bursar's books of Trinity College for 1550—51.]

[3] [Hist. Cantab. Acad. i. 48. "Annales a Collegio condito" MS. p. 6. The description in the text has been derived partly from the History, partly from the Annals. Dr Caius was appointed Principal 12 November, 1533 (Cooper's Athenæ i. 312) but whether "Exterior" or "Interior" is not stated. The grant to Trinity College was confirmed by Edward the Sixth, 12 June, 1550. Fuller (p. 235) has recorded the discontent of the Gonvillians at the whole arrangement, "who are still grumbling thereat as not sufficient compensation."]

Book, and by Dr Caius. It included several shops and gardens, and extended from S. Michael's lane on the south to the garden of the Prior of S. Edmund's on the north, which will be hereafter described, and from Physwick Hostel and S. Margaret's Hostel on the west, to the gardens of the houses in High Street on the east. It was bequeathed to Michael House in 1349 by Johanna, widow of John Refham, apothecary and burgess of Cambridge[1]. The subsequent changes must be briefly noted. In 1433, the north part of the ground was sold to King's Hall to complete the site, as will appear in the history of it, and, 25 March, 1473, Edward Story, Master of Michael House and Bishop of Carlisle, sold to William Malster and others a further portion, at the south-east corner, described as

"a cottage together with a void ground, part of our tenement called The Angell, in the Parish of S. Michael, between a tenement of the Priory of our Lady of the Meadows (*beate Marie de Pratis*) near S. Albans in Hertfordshire, and part of our aforesaid tenement called *The Angell* on the north; and a lane called *Michel-lane* on the south; abutting on the aforesaid tenement of the Priory towards the east; and on *The Angell* towards the west: which void ground together with the tenement contains in length on both sides 45 feet; and in breadth at both ends, east and west alike, 21 feet[2]."

Three years afterwards, 29 August, 1476, the remainder of the estate was sold to Matthew Chambre and others. It is then described as

"a certain messuage of ours, with the shops adjacent to the same, and other houses and gardens, situated in S. Michael's Lane, Cambridge, between a certain external wall of the newly-built Almshouses called *Reynoldes-ely-elmeshouses*, a garden of the Priory of our Lady of the Meadows, a garden of the College of Corpus Christi and S. Mary in Cambridge, a garden of the Hospital of S. John the Evangelist in Cambridge, and a garden of the College or Hall commonly called *the kyngeshalle* on the east; and a hostel lately built called *Fysshewykeshostell*, with a garden adjacent, and extending along our aforesaid messuage, on the west; the south head abutting on the aforesaid lane; and the north head on *the Kyngeshalle*[3]."

---

[1] For this pious act her name and that of her husband were duly inscribed amongst the benefactors with exequies. Otryngham, p. 19. The muniments of the property (Ibid. p. 52—55) are headed "Sequitur de mesuagio quondam Johannis Refham," and a marginal note in the same hand records "nota de hospicio sancte Katerine."

[2] [Translated from the conveyance in Trin. Coll. Treasury. A yearly rent of nine shillings was to be paid for the ground, though said to be conveyed "in perpetuum."]

[3] [Translated from the conveyance in Trin. Coll. Treasury.]

In 1493, however, Dame Edith Chambre, widow of Matthew
Chambre, bequeathed it to her kinsman Thomas Ayer or Ayeray
for his life, and after his death to the Master and Fellows of
Michael House, on condition that they should pray for her
soul, and for the souls of her husband and of all her relations[1].

The almshouses mentioned in the above quotation were built
upon the piece sold in 1473. These houses, three in number,
were founded by Reginald Ely, a freemason of Cambridge[2], and
subsequently passed into the hands of Caius College as trustees.
They were sold to Trinity College in 1864 for £200, and soon
afterwards were pulled down, additional lecture-rooms being
built on their site.

It appears from various deeds that this tenement was not
always denominated "S. Katherine's Hostel." We have seen
that it was called "The Angele" or "le Mighell Angell,"
and in 1508 it became "The Gramer Hostell now in the
tenure of Maister Thomas Ayera, Clerke[3]." Ayer therefore
occupied it as Principal of a Hostel. Lastly, it acquired the
name of Edith Chamber's house, which eventually was corrupted
into Edith's Chamber, under which name it was leased by
Trinity College in 1552 for forty years, at 53s. 4d. per annum[4].

---

[1] The will is dated 10 Dec. 1493, but she survived for some years, for in 1497
an agreement was made between the parties, Edith Chambre, Thomas Ayer, and the
authorities of Michael House, in which the latter engage for a solemn obit. She was
to be buried in S. Michael's Church. The will and the agreement are in Trinity
College Treasury, "Michael House."

[2] [Reginald (spelt Regnald or Regnaldus in the documents) Ely, by will dated
14 October, 1463, desired his executors (one of whom, John Brokeshaw, is one of
the parties to whom the property had been conveyed in 1473) to found an Almshouse
for 3 poor persons, endowed with land in Barton and Comberton. His wishes were
duly carried out, and the Almshouse built, "in a certen lane called Michaell lane,"
charged with a yearly rent of 9 shillings to Michael House for the ground. In 1539
Dr William Buckenham, Master of Caius, the representative of one of his executors,
conveyed the trust to his College. The documents are in Caius College Treasury,
Box 21. Ely was evidently a man of note in his own trade, as he was selected by
Henry VI. to conduct the works at King's College in 1444 (History of King's, Vol. i.
323). The houses were rebuilt in 1864 on ground near S. Paul's Church, exchanged
by Caius College with the Ely Trust.]

[3] [Lease to King's Hall from the Priory of S. Edmund of their void ground in
High Street, described in the History of King's Hall below.]

[4] It is remarkable that in Dr Caius' History, in the description of the Hostels,
the names of S. Margaret and S. Katherine are interchanged. His words are,
p. 49: "*A parte orientali Phiswici hospitii, hospitium erat S. Margaretae...Pone*

It is worth remarking that Michael House reckons in its list of Benefactors no less than three pious widows who gave houses and lands for the good of their husbands' souls and their own. The soil of the south-eastern portion of Trinity Court was consecrated to learning by their liberality, and the staircase-turret at that angle would, in a more poetical age, have assuredly been denominated the Widow's Tower, for the ground on which it stands, first given by Dame Refham, and then alienated by Michael House, was again given to them by Dame Edith Chamber.

We have now traced the history of Michael House, and the gradual acquirement of the south-western and half of the south-eastern district; and in the next place we shall shew how King's Hall similarly became possessed of the whole of the northern district and the remainder of the south-eastern, with some trifling exceptions. There is, however, this difference between the acquisitions of the two Colleges: those of the latter were made to enlarge their site, and those of the former to increase their revenue.

The first acquisition for the site of King's Hall was made 24 October, 1336, when King Edward the Third purchased of Robert de Croyland, Rector of Oundle,

"a messuage with appurtenances in the Parish of All Saints in Cambridge hard by the Hospital of S. John, situated between the tenements of Edmund de Walsyngham and William Atte Cundite on the east, and a place (*placea*) called Cornhythe next the river (*aqua currens*) on the west,"

hospitium Phiswici quo loco hortus ejus erat, hospitium S. Katarinae fuit...." Yet the muniments of these hostels in the Otryngham Book as well as the deed by which Michael House sold to Gonvile Hall the "hospitium vocat' St Marg^ts Hostell," are conclusive against the doctor's appropriation of these names, which is probably a transcriber's error. As the muniments further shew that Tyler's Hostel (to be described below) was contiguous to S. Katherine's Hostel, as Caius has stated, it seems that the description must be corrected as follows;

"10. Ponè hospitium Phiswici, quo loco hortus ejus erat, hospitium S. Margaretae fuit, quod decimum est, ante tamen Phiswici hospitium longè constitutum.

11. A parte orientali Phiswici hospitii, hospitium erat S. Katherinae, et haud procul ab eo tegulatum, seu tegularii hospitium, vulgo the tyler's and tyled hostell vocabatur, etc."

S. Margaret's Hostel is evidently older than Phishwick's, for it is named in the royal license of 1392, whereas Phiswick Hostel was built long subsequent to Phishwick's bequest of his house in 1393. S. Katherine's Hostel appears to be later still: but its history is vague.

and immediately put Thomas Powys, the master of his intended College, into formal possession of it[1]. The patent of foundation of the College of thirty-two scholars was issued in the October of the following year[2], and from this period the journal of the proceedings begins. The Master and Scholars with their servants were removed into the house as it stood ; and an order for the assignment of the chambers to the scholars by name, preserved at the end of the Account-book for the first year, shews that the mansion was of considerable size. [The description, however, of the probable arrangement of the rooms, and the history of the repair and enlargement of them which took place, had better, for the sake of clearness, be postponed until we have completed the history of the site.]

An immediate enlargement of this was evidently necessary, and accordingly letters patent were issued, 20 March, 1338—39, empowering the Mayor of Cambridge and Thomas Powys to buy in the King's name " any places and houses in Cambridge which might be for sale, and necessary and suitable for the enlarge-ment of the house of our Warden and Clerks whom of our bounty we are maintaining in our Hall at Cambridge." In less than two years the result of their labours appeared in another patent, dated 17 January, 1341, by which the King granted to his College a series of pieces of land enumerated in order, which they had purchased for him. The portions of the deed which are necessary for our purpose may be translated as follows, omitting all needless technicalities :

"Whereas we have acquired from divers persons in Cambridge a messuage and sundry pieces of ground, to wit, one messuage in the parish of All Saints from Edmund Walsyngham, and one garden from Henry de Gretford which formerly belonged to the Prior of the Chapel of S. Edmund in Cambridge, and one piece of ground at Damenicoles-heth in the same town from Bartholomew Peryn, and one piece in the same town from Robert de Sygesford, and one piece at Dameni-colesheth from John son of William de Comberton, and one piece at Damenicolesheth from William de Clacton, and one piece at Dameni-colesheth from Stephen son of Bartholomew Morys ;

---

[1] [It is remarkable that the King's order to Thomas de Lacy and others to put the scholars into possession is dated 12 April, 1336, while the formal conveyance from Croyland is dated 28 October in the same year. The originals of these and of the other documents which will be quoted are in the Treasury of Trinity College, unless otherwise stated.]

[2] [See the Historical Introduction.]

We, from the great affection which we feel towards our beloved Warden and Scholars of our Hall in Cambridge, have, of our special grace, granted and made over to the aforesaid Warden and Scholars the aforesaid messuages and pieces of ground, for the enlargement of their dwelling-place there.

Moreover we have pardoned the said Warden and Scholars the fault they have committed in acquiring for themselves and entering into without our license a certain portion of a certain lane between the garden of the Hospital of S. John the Evangelist, and the tenement which formerly belonged to the Prior of S. Edmund, which portion of a lane extends from the dwelling-house of the aforesaid Prior opposite to the Church of All Saints de Trumpington Warde to the end of the same lane in the direction of *le Cornheth*; and further, a piece of void ground at *le Cornheth* called the King's Ditch (*fossatum Regis*) containing 200 feet in length, and 14 feet in breadth; and we have granted the aforesaid portion of a lane and piece of ground to them and their successors for ever."

This dimension, 200 feet, enables us to set out approximately the direction of the west half of King's Hall lane.

It will now be interesting to describe more particularly the original nature of these acquisitions, by which the site was carried northwards to the wall of the Hospital, or in other words, to its present boundary. Their probable extent has been laid down on the plan (fig. 1).

The lane under the wall of the Hospital Garden extended from the back of the most northerly of the street houses to the open space called Cornhythe, by crossing which the river was reached. It must be remembered that the street houses were occupied in order from north to south by John Godyn (whose house probably stood beyond the north boundary of the site), the Prior of S. Edmund, Dame Mabilia Pyke[1], Totyngton, Walsingham, and Atte Conduit. In the deed by which the lane was conveyed to Thomas Powys, dated 17 November, 1339, the Prior and Canons of S. Edmund state that they had had a right of way along it to the river from their house, situated between John Godyn's and Mabilia Pyke's. As they had been the previous owners of the garden which the King purchased of Gretford, it was probably merely an occupation-road; and when the garden was sold, it ceased to be of use to them[2]. The garden

---

[1] [Her name is spelt Mabilia and Amabilia in the deeds in which she is mentioned. In one she is described as of Haukestone.]

[2] [The Prior had sold the garden to Powys alone 1 November, 1339; and Powys to Gretford 4 March, 1340. The Society of King's Hall lost no time in taking

in question is described in Gretford's conveyance to the King, dated 3 January, 1341, as extending from the west end of Dame Pyke's garden along the south side of this lane to the King's Ditch, which formed the east boundary of Cornhythe. The space between Gretford's garden and Croyland's messuage was occupied by the garden attached to Edmund de Walsyngham's house, which he sold to the King 22 September, 1339. This garden also was bounded on the west by the King's Ditch. It extended eastward far enough to be bounded in part on the north by Mabilia Pyke's house, while on the south it covered the whole north border of Croyland's messuage[1]. It was however distinct from the house of Walsyngham next the street, which he sold 17 April, 1343, to Thomas de Totyngton, already the possessor of the smaller house adjoining it on the north, by whom it was transferred to the King 15 April, 1344[2]. By this last purchase the site was extended up to High Street.

The five tenements at Dame Nichol's Hythe were all small pieces. Comberton's is described as "le Cornhouse;" Peryn's was eighteen feet long by twenty-two feet broads; Sygesford's was bought for 6s. 8d.[3]; and the other two pieces were probably of the same trifling character.

Nine years, reckoning from the royal grant of 1341, elapsed before any further additions were made to the site. In 1350 (12 March), however, a house which had formerly belonged to Sir John de Cambridge was sold to the King by his son Thomas. It stood in King's Hall Lane, at the south-west corner of the site, and was bounded east and north by the said site, and west by "a void ground next to the river,"

possession of the lane (Accounts 1338—39): "Item in stramine pro muro ad finem venelle xvj[d]. Item factura eiusdem muri ad finem venelle Summa xxv[s]. iiij[d]. ob."]

[1] The Accounts of King's Hall for 1338—39 shew that twenty marks were paid for it. "Item soluebantur Magistro Edmundo de Walsyngham pro vno Gardino ab eodem empt' viginti marc'." From this and similar entries we may conclude that the payments for these premises and grounds, purchased for the extension of the site, were made from the College Chest.

[2] [Walsyngham's house is described as "bounded on the north by the houses of Totyngton and Mabilia Pyke; and on the south by the house of William Atte Conduyt and the manse of the King's Scholars."]

[3] [King's Hall Accounts, i. 49 (1338—39): "M[d]. de quadam placea empt' de domino Roberto de Segeford pro di' marc' de quibus soluebantur eidem R' de cista iiij[s], et postea eidem in plenam solucionem ij[s]. viij[d]."]

evidently that called Cornhythe. This was obtained 22 May, 1351, from Thomas, son of Sir Constantine de Mortimer. It is described as

"the whole extent of my void ground, lying in the Parish of All Saints, in the Borough of Cambridge, near the Hospital of S. John; which ground extends in length from a certain common lane leading from the highway called *Le heyestrete* to the river (*aqua currens*) on the south, as far as a small ditch under the garden of the aforesaid Hospital of S. John on the north; and in breadth from the garden of the Master and Scholars of King's Hall, and from a house which formerly belonged to Sir John de Cambridge deceased on the east, to a stream derived from the aforesaid river (*filum aque currentis supradicte*), on the west[1]."

In this same year (9 June) the house of Thomas de Totyngton in High Street was bought.

There are no documents to shew exactly when the Prior's tenement and that of Mabilia Pyke were bought; but as the conveyance from Totyngton describes his north boundary as "a messuage formerly Mabilia Pyke's," it is probable that her house had been already acquired. On similar evidence we may conclude that the Prior's house had been acquired before 21 December, 1362, when the Prioress of S. Rhadegund grants to King's Hall an annual rent of 8s. which had been paid out of it. In 1376 (1 February) the purchase of William Atte Conduit's House at the corner of High Street and King's Hall Lane, or, as it is

---

[1] [Translated from the conveyance. One of the deeds speaks of it as "the garden of the Master and Scholars;" and it was probably put to that use as soon as it had been bought.] As the western boundary of Robert de Croyland's messuage is "Placea que vocatur Cornhythe super Aquam currentem," and the "fossatum Regis," the western boundary of Gretford's and Walsyngham's gardens, is said to be "apud le Cornheth," and the lane under the Hospital garden to terminate "versus le Cornheth," this name must have been given to Mortimer's land, the boundaries of which shew that it occupied the whole space between the site of King's Hall, as enlarged by the grant of 1341, and the "aquam currentem." The "fossatum Regis" must have formed its eastern boundary as well as its northern, but, as the former portion of that ditch had been enclosed in the garden of King's Hall before Mortimer's ground was purchased, that garden is set down as the eastern boundary instead of the ditch in his transfer. [It was mentioned in the History of Michael House that the north end of the ditch which bounded Garret Hostel Green on the west was altered in 1423. The difference of designation in the above description may have been used to shew that Cornhythe was bounded in part on the west by that ditch in its original state, in which case the lane to the south would have crossed this ditch by a bridge, and so reached the river; or the western boundary may have been merely a ditch, like that which had once divided it from the rest of the site.]

called in the conveyance "kyngeschilderlane," gave to King's Hall entire possession of the site north of that lane.

The site, as thus completed, was so circumscribed by highways, by the river, and by the Hospital of S. John, as to render any further increase apparently hopeless. But in 1417 the Prior and Canons of S. Edmund leased to King's Hall their garden at the corner of King's Hall Lane and Foul Lane for 99 years, at a yearly rent of 12*d.*, and their "void ground" in High Street, at an annual rent of 6*s.* 8*d.*[1] In 1430 the Prior and Canons of Chiksand leased their garden, at the corner of King's Hall Lane and High Street, for 60 years, at an annual rent of one mark ; on 14 January, 1433, S. John's Hospital sold, for an annual rent of 2*s.* 1*d.*, their messuage on the south of the garden of S. Edmund[2]; and, 12 April in the same year, Michael House sold, for an annual rent of 1*s.* 8*d.*, the remaining piece of land on the south of the same garden. It measured 60 feet from north to south by 37 feet from east to west, and is described in the conveyance as part of the garden of S. Katherine's Hostel. In the same year (8 April) the Town of Cambridge granted to King's Hall, for a red rose at Midsummer, if demanded, the portion of King's Hall Lane which separated the site from the above grounds. It is described as

"part of a certain common lane lying in the parish of All Saints in the Jewry between the Hall or College of our lord the King on the north, and a tenement formerly belonging to the Prior and Convent of Chyksand, and a tenement formerly belonging to the Prior of the Chapel of S. Edmund on the south ; and extending in length from the highway leading from the aforesaid Hall or College towards the College of S. Michael on the west to the highway called *le hyestrete* of Cambridge on the east."

[1] [We learn from documents in the Treasury of Trinity College that the Priory leased the ground in High Street, 30 August, 1429, for 99 years, at an annual rent of 6*s.* 8*d.*, and that the lease of both pieces was renewed in 1508 for the same term. But the Accounts of King's Hall for 1417—18 (Vol. vi. 122) shew that the former ground was leased at this earlier date. The amount of rent paid proves that it, and not the garden in Foul Lane, is meant : "In primis pro factura indenturarum gardini Canonicorum Ordinis de Sempyngham xiiij*d*. Item pro firma eiusdem pre manibus solut' vj*s*. viij*d*."]

[2] [After the foundation of Trinity College this property is thus referred to in a list of rents due to S. Michael's Parish: "Item de M*ro*. etc. Coll. Trin. pro redditu terrarum quondam jacentium inter Turrim et Cameras Aulæ Regis ex opposito Hospitii S. Gregorii ubi nuper erat murus lapideus 2 sh." MSS. Baker xix. 133. MSS. Harl. Mus. Brit. 7046.]

This grant was made apparently at the request of the King, for in the King's Hall Accounts for 1431—32 we find a remuneration to the messenger of the Duke of Gloucester, despatched to the Corporation of Cambridge about the lane lying next to the south side of the College[1]. Lastly, the tenement called Tyled Hostel, which stood in High Street, south of the "void ground" belonging to S. Edmund's Priory, and had formerly belonged to Richard Tylere, Cooper, was sold by its then possessor, Richard Pyghtesley, to King Henry the Sixth, 9 May, 1449, and by him transferred to King's Hall[2]. It was bounded on the south by the tenement belonging to Corpus Christi College, which we have already met with as one of the eastern boundaries of S. Katherine's Hostel. Tyler's house was let by the College, and became a Hostel for students, as recorded by Dr Caius[3]:

"Not far from S. Katherine's Hostel, was the tiled Hostel, or the Hostel of the tiler, commonly called *the tylers*, and *tyled hostell*, because, as I imagine, it differed from the rest of the Hostels both in its possessor, and in the material of which it was built. A former possessor of it had been one John Tyler, and it was roofed with tiles, a material other than that used for the rest of the Hostels."

These three properties in High Street have never been included within either King's Hall or Trinity College, excepting probably the western parts of their gardens[4].

[1] The deed in the Treasury of Trinity College is endorsed, "Concessio venelle:" and, in a later hand, "for the bake lane to Physix ostell." By a clerical error, corrected in the translation, the words "north" and "south" have been interchanged. Hence the grant has been usually considered to apply to the lane on the north of the College. But the position of the tenements of S. Edmund and the Prior of Chiksand are so clearly defined in the muniments relating to them that the determination of the true position of the lane cannot be doubtful; and it is distinctly defined in the following passage from the Accounts for 1431—32: "Item pro Remuneracione fact' nuncio domini Glowcestre miss' ad communitatem Cantebrigg' pro venella iuxta collegium ex parte australi pro se et famulo xv^s. Item in expensis eorundem per iij dies ij^s." Ibid. 1432—33: "Me^d. quod solutum est Ricardo Parys clerico communitatis ville Cantebr' pro scriptura evidencie venelle concesse collegio ex consensu dicte communitatis viij^s. iiij^d."

[2] [Patent, 27 Hen. VI. p. 2. m. 15. The patent is dated 8 May, although the house was not formally conveyed until the following day. The cost was apparently defrayed by the College. Accounts of King's Hall, 1448—49: "M^d. quod solutum est magistro Ricardo Pyghtsley pro manso suo cum certis tenementis in parochia omnium sanctorum in Judaismo Cantabr' xxxiij^li. vj^s. viij^d. Item pro ij tenementis Cs."]

[3] [Hist. Cant. Acad. i. 49.]

[4] [It should be mentioned that the two pieces of ground leased from S. Edmund's Priory, and the Tyled Hostel, are stated in the documents relating to them to be in

When King's Hall Lane was taken possession of a remarkable Aqueduct was enclosed, the history of which must detain us
for a moment.

The first construction of this aqueduct is recorded by an
Inquisition held at Babraham, 22 October, 1434, whence it appeared that the Warden (*gardianus*) and brethren of the Convent
of Friars Minors (that is, the Franciscans or Grey Friars, who
then occupied the site of Sidney College) had purchased, 5 November, 1325, of various persons enumerated, certain pieces of land,
all of two feet in breadth, for the purpose of making a subter-
ranean aqueduct to convey water from a place called Bradrusshe
to the manse of the said convent; and that they had proceeded
to construct an aqueduct with leaden pipes not only in the aforesaid pieces of land, but also through the common grounds, high
streets, and others of the King's highways, and banks of the
river, extending from the west part of the town to the east
thereof. For it appeared that they dug a long trench in the
aforesaid common grounds, 1 May, 1327, and laid therein a
leaden pipe for the conveyance of the water, and that ever since
that time, whenever the aqueduct has required repair, they have
dug up heaps of earth and sand, and made great openings in
the streets and lanes, in contempt of the King's authority, and to
the great damage and annoyance of his subjects in their passage
along the said highways. The purchases also of the pieces of
land were made without the royal license.

The document[1], which I have abridged of its technicalities,
contains an enumeration of the seventeen persons from whom
the ground was purchased, with the length of each piece in
tailor's ells (*virgas cissoris*), the total length amounting to 1467
ells. If the ell be taken at 45 inches, this length will amount to
5501 feet 3 inches. From an accurate survey of the course of the
conduit-pipe as it exists, made for Trinity College by Mr John

the Parish of All Saints. The parish of the gardens belonging to S. John's Hospital
and Michael House is not noted in the documents, but a note in Otryngham (p. 76)
states them to be in the Parish of S. Michael, as also the piece obtained from the
Priory of S. Edmund. This, however, was certainly in the Parish of All Saints.
These discrepancies shew that parish boundaries were uncertain in the fifteenth
century. S. Gregory's Hostel is stated to be in S. Michael's Parish. The present
direction of the boundary has been laid down on the map (fig. 1).]

[1] [Printed, Appendix, No. III., from the original in the Treasury of Trinity College.]

Edlin in 1842, it appears that the length from the present
Conduit House to the western side of the road behind the
Colleges, which formerly bordered the common ground, is 5510
feet, which is certainly a very remarkable coincidence.

The source of the water is in a marshy field, in the parish of
S. Giles, Cambridge, near the gravel pits on the right of the road
leading to Madingley, about 300 yards to the west of the Observatory[1]. Here the Conduit House stands. Thence the pipe runs
nearly S.E. to the Madingley Road, which it crosses at nearly the
same point as the brook. Here its course is abruptly changed
to one nearly east, and it runs through the fields in a straight
line to the N.W. angle of Trinity quarters, crossing S. John's
College grove in its way. It then passes along the southern
edge of the north walk of the quarters, crosses the river, and
runs near the north side of Neville's court, and so, under the
oriels of the Hall, passes to the Fountain. This course, with the
exception of the portions within the College, may be supposed
to be exactly the same as when it was laid down in 1325. But
there can be no doubt that the Friars, after passing the pipe
over the river at the present spot, and crossing Garret Hostel
Green, led its course along the lane which passed south of
King's Hall, at the corner of which, in the High Street, stood
the house of William Atte Conduit, for the name of this person
shews plainly that he was near to the conduit in question[2].
After the purchase of the lane in 1433, and the extension of
King's Hall to the south of it, the Friars' pipe ran through the
middle of the quadrangle. In consequence, the following petition
was addressed to the Franciscans by the College:

[1] [The field in which the Conduit House stands was not bought by Trinity College
until 7 May, 1834.]

[2] [We do not know the course of the Conduit between Trinity Street and the
present Sidney Street, called in the 16th century Conduit Street, as we learn from a
lease of part of the Grey Friars' ground, now the site of Sidney College, granted by
Trinity College in 1562 (Register of Trin. Coll. i. 86) in which the ground demised is
described as bounded on the north by Jesus Lane, and on the west by "the kinges
highe way called the Conduit Street." The name was possibly derived from the
fountain which existed near the Grey Friars, as shewn by a lease dated 1571, when
the same College demised, with particular covenants, "one pece of grounde where
vpon is nowe buylte and made one comen well and a pompe set lying and beyng in
Bridgstret otherwise called Preachers Strete within the Parish of All hallowes, in a
wall called the Grayefriers wall belonginge to the saide Colledg."]

" Memorandum that the desir whiche the Kyng oure souerein lord by thaduis of my lordes his vncles of Bedford and of Gloucestre and the Cardinal and the Remenant of his counsail desireth of the Wardein and Couent of the Freres Menours in his Vniuersite of Cambrugge for theese and weel of his College in the same Vniuersite is in this manere that foloweth and in noon other wise, that is to wete

that it like vnto the said Wardein and Couent at the Reuerence of the speciale prayer of the Kyng, my said Lordes of Bedford, of Gloucestre, the Cardinal, and the Remenant of my lordes of his counsail, and alle other Lordes of this his Reaume, and knyghtes of the Shires, Citezeins, and Burgoises, assembled for the Commune of his land in this his parlement at Westmynstre whiche haue and wol sende theire speciale lettres vnto the seid Wardein and Couent accordyng vnto the kynges said desir to graunte vnder theire commune seel licence vnto the Maister and Scolers of the said College and theire successours, that thei mowe take oonly to their vse a qwil out of the pipe of the conduyt belonging vnto the said Wardein and Couent rennyng thorough the myddes of the court of the said College.

So that the said Maister and Scolers lede the said qwil no ferther, but that thei be holden to rere it euen ouere the grete pipe in the middes of the said College ; and so that the course of water commyng in the grete pipe vnto the hous of the said Freres be in no wyse therby hindred nor letted from hem.

And if it happe that the said course be letted now or at eny tyme hereafter by the said qwil, that thanne the said Maister and Scolers be bounden vnder their commune seel in a somme resonable to be paied vnto the said Wardein and Couent and their successours, o lesse than that knoweⁿ vnto the said Maister and Scolers thei anoon forthwith do the said qwil be broken and take awey, and also do make ayein the grete pipe of the said conduyt in wyse as was afore the said graunt desired

for the whiche graunt the said Maister and Scolers offre by the kynges licence to binde theim and their successours vnto the said Wardein and Couent and theire successours, that at alle tymes that it shall happe the grete pipe of the said conduyt to breke bytwix the heed and the said College, thei shul helpe and bere theire part of costes vnto the making of it ayein.

And ouer that that thei shul haue the said Wardein and Couent and theire successours afore all other Freres in singuler loue and affeccion and be holden not oonly to promote hem where as thei may best but also to yeue hem at alle tymes of their ovne propre after theire power."

The document unfortunately is neither dated nor sealed. It is clear, however, that it must belong to this period, and the Inquisition held in 1434 may have been the result of a refusal on the part of the Friars to accede to the request of King's Hall. This view is confirmed by the issue of letters patent, 5 May, 1439, " at the request of our beloved Richard Caudrey, Master

of our College of our Scholars," rehearsing the above Inquisition.
Lastly, the lane and the aqueduct were confirmed to the Scholars,
and their transgression in obtaining them without leave was
pardoned, by letters patent, dated 31 May, 1441[1]. This grant
appears to have given them possession of that part of the pipe
only which passed through their own court, so that they held
the aqueduct jointly with the Friars. This necessarily led to
disputes, of which a trace occurs in a memorandum in the
Accounts for 1466—67, that they had given to the Friars for
the repair of the aqueduct 20s. in pure alms[2], accompanying
an item of 2s. for the "Repasta" of three friars and four
workmen about the aqueduct for two days. Finally, King
Henry VIII. granted to Trinity College the aqueduct from its
source to its termination, with all the rights appertaining thereto
as they had been held by King's Hall and by the Friars[3].

CHAPTER II.

ARCHITECTURAL HISTORY OF KING'S HALL.

[WE have now traced the gradual acquisition of the site of
King's Hall, and may proceed to investigate the history of the
buildings which occupied it, and which were altered and increased from time to time as the extension of the site gave the
Society room for expansion.]

It was mentioned in the last chapter that in the first instance
the Master and the thirty-two scholars were moved into Croyland's house as it stood. It was evidently situated near the south-

---

[1] [Patent, 19 Hen. VI. p. 3. m. 33. The words used are "quandam vacuam
peciam terre ac soli eidem aule contiguam...ingrediendo et includendo ac acqueductum
nostrum ibidem ad eorum vsum capiendo." In the Accounts of King's Hall for this
year, Vol. ix. 305, we find "Item in expensis Willelmi Sole equitantis pro litera
patenti pro aqueductu xxvj[s]. iiij[d]. Item remuneratum est eidem pro labore xx[s]."]

[2] King's Hall Accounts xiii. 238. "Notandum quod erogavimus Fratribus minoribus pro reparacione aqueductus in puram Elemosinam et non ex aliquo debito xx[s]."
A similar entry occurs Ibid. xviii. 111.

[3] [Charter of Dotation, 24 December, 1546: Commiss. Doc. iii. 407. The rights
of Trinity College were fully recognized in the S. Giles' Parish Inclosure Act, 1802:
Cooper's Annals, iv. 473.]

east corner of the site, with garden-ground to the north and west, and was entered from the lane leading from the High Street to Dame Nichol's Hythe, opposite to the end of Foul Lane. The arrangement of the house can be made out with tolerable accuracy from a list of rooms and their occupants written out at the end of the first Audit-Book, that for the year 1337. The substance of this list is here given, illustrated by a diagram (fig. 5)[1]. It must be premised that the building was in two floors, as usual at that time, and that every upper chamber was termed a solar (*solarium*), and the chamber beneath it a celar (*celarium*).

		Number of occupants.
A.	Solar next Cundyt[2]	2
	Celar under it	2
B.	Middle solar	2
	Celar under it	2
C.	Solar next to it	2
	Celar under it	2
D.	Two rooms next following	4
E.	Solar over the gate	2
F.	Great solar	3
	Celar under it	3
G.	Under the Master's study	3
	Under the Master's chamber	6

It is probable that the house was in the form of a central portion with wings, occupying three sides of a court, of which the vacant side was on the south next to King's Hall Lane. The Hall, the existence of which in 1337 is proved by the charges for lengthening it in 1338, was probably in the central portion. Besides this, thirteen chambers are enumerated. The Master had a chamber (*camera*) to himself, and also a study (*studium*) ; each of the other chambers was occupied by from two to six scholars. Beginning with the east wing the "solar next Cundyt" (A) would be that at the south end next to King's Hall Lane, and the middle solar (B), and the solar next to it (C), the two completing that side. The two rooms next to them (D) were probably over offices at the east end of the Hall,

---

[1] [The dimensions of the house have been determined by the scale of the plan (fig. 6), on which it has also been laid down. The lists are printed in full in the Appendix, No. IV.]

[2] [This expression probably refers to the house of William Atte Cundyt ; just as "Annable Pyke" in the next list evidently denotes the house of Mabilia Pyke.]

and the kitchen was next to them. The western wing had a gatehouse next to the lane, with a chamber (E) over it ; northward of these were the Master's chamber and study (G), and the great solar (F) at the west end of the Hall, which we shall find described in the next list as "the principal chamber next the Hall." These rooms would be next to the garden.

This is the usual arrangement of a large medieval house, in which the Hall has commonly the best apartments at one end, and the kitchen and the inferior rooms at the other.

But although the community (*comitiva*) contrived to squeeze themselves into the newly acquired premises, these were confessedly too small for their permanent residence, and inadequate

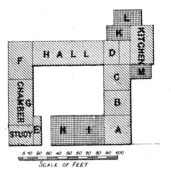

Fig. 5. Diagram to shew the probable arrangement of Robert de Croyland's house ;
from Notes by Professor Willis.

to the dignity of a royal college. The Master therefore immediately undertook extensive repairs, the nature of which may be gathered from the minute Account which he rendered to the Exchequer of the way in which he had laid out during the year 1338 a sum amounting to £30. 3s. 4d.[1]

The Account shews that the whole house was of wood ; for the only other material purchased is a small quantity of stone, and of lime for making mortar for the foundations, and to mend all the walls—by which the walls round the garden are probably meant ; for the various terms of carpentry-work used indicate that the outer walls as well as the partitions were wholly of wood. The works definitely indicated are the lengthening of

[1] [This Roll is in the Public Record Office, No. $\frac{858}{7}$.]

the Hall, apparently by about sixteen feet, the making of a screen (*speer*), and a porch, and the thatching of the roof. Repairs are also done to the pantry and buttery, and to a room called simply "the chamber," but which the next list shews to be identical with "the great solar" (F) of the list of 1337.

The work, however, did not proceed fast enough to satisfy the impatience of the Master, for early in the following year (23 April, 1339) a royal order was issued to the Sheriff of Cambridge, the terms of which indicate the necessity for using the utmost despatch:

" Whereas our beloved clerk Thomas Powys, Master of our scholars at Cambridge, is bound to get certain houses there rapidly repaired for the aforesaid scholars to dwell in, and others built, We enjoin you to provide the said Thomas with sufficient carriage for the timber which he may require from different parts of your county, for the repair and construction of the aforesaid houses."

A second order, dated 10 May in the same year, records the gift of six oaks in her forest of Sappele near Huntingdon by Philippa, Queen of England, and of four oaks in her park of Hundone by Elizabeth de Burgh, for these repairs and buildings; and the Sheriff is commanded to cut them, carry them, and deliver them to Thomas Powys[1].

It is unfortunate that no further accounts dealing with building work during the mastership of Thomas Powys should have been preserved among those sent by him to the Exchequer; and that the series of Audit-Books also should be imperfect for the next few years. In 1342, however, we meet with a second list of rooms and their occupants, which shews that some additional buildings had been erected in the mean time. The number of scholars had increased, for the total has now become 36, exclusive of the Master.

---

[1] [These documents are printed in the Appendix, No. V., from the originals in the Public Record Office. Sappele is now represented by a hamlet called Sapley or "The Sapleys," consisting of about half-a-dozen cottages lying a mile or so north of Huntingdon, and attached to the parish of Hartford. It contains about 360 acres, a small portion of which is still woodland. Camden (Britannia, Ed. 1607, p. 366) mentions that Huntingdonshire was disforested by Henry II. "præter Waybridge, Sapple et Herthei, qui fuerant Bosci Dominici et remanent Forestæ." Hundon is in Suffolk near Newmarket.]

Number of
occupants.

F. { Solar next the garden.......................2
{ Celar under it..................................3

E. The garret 2

H. { New solar next the garret....................2
{ Celar under it 2

I. { New solar next the last.......................2
{ Celar under it..................................2

A. { Solar next to it................................2
{ Celar under it..................................2

B. { Solar next to it................................2
{ Celar under it..................................2

C. { Solar next to it, and last 2
{ Celar under it 2

K. Small chamber next the kitchen............2

L. Chamber next Annable Pyke..............2

G. Celar under the Master 5

The "garret" (*garitum*) of this list is clearly identical with the "solar over the gate" (E) of the former list; and the two new solars (H, I) connected it with the old series of three solars on the east (A, B, C), thus completing the quadrangle. This explanation of the position of these rooms is confirmed by a charge for the repair of "seven chambers next the lane" between 1375 and 1378[1]; and of "the old chamber next the new gate" between 1430 and 1431[2], after King Edward's Gate-House had been built. The "two rooms next to these" (D) do not occur in this list, having probably been destroyed by the lengthening of the Hall. They are replaced by a "small chamber next the kitchen" (K) and "a chamber next Annable Pyke" (L), the position of whose house has been already indicated. The "solar next the garden" is clearly identical with "the great solar" (F), from the number of its occupants, and this way of describing it proves that it has been rightly placed on the west side. The "celar under the Master," containing 5 scholars, is evidently the "room under the master's chamber" (G) of the previous list.

There is yet a third list, dated 1344. The number of occupants is not always given, and the list omits the rooms under the Master (G).

[1] [Roll (in Public Record Office) extending from Mich. 49 Edw. III.—Mich. 1 Rich. II. "Idem computat in vadiis duorum tegulatorum ad reparand' vij cameras Aule predicte iuxta viam existent' per xxvij dies vtroque capiente per diem vj^d. xxvij^s."]

[2] [Roll (ibid.) extending from 6 July 2 Hen. VI.—2 July 9 Hen. VI.]

Number of
occupants.

F.	{Solar next the garden..2	
	{Celar under it...3	
E.	The garret...2	
H.	{Solar next the garret..	
	{Celar under it..	
I.	{Another new solar next to it.... 2	
	{Celar under it..	
A.	{Solar next to it[1]	
	{Celar under it..	
B.	{Solar next to the last....................	
	{Celar under it..	
C.	{Solar next to the last.......................................	
	{Celar under it..	
M.	Room beyond, namely, in Edmund Walsyngham's house ...	
K.	Room on the other side of the Hall next the kitchen	
L.	Room next to it, next Annable Pyke's garden.................	

The only fresh piece of information afforded by this list is that part of Edmund Walsyngham's house, acquired as we have seen in 1344, had been at once utilised.

In the previous year (25 July, 1342) the king had granted to his scholars the advowsons of the churches of Felmersham in Bedfordshire, Hyntlesham in Suffolk, Grendon in Northamptonshire, and S. Mary the Great in Cambridge, with leave to appropriate them, "because their revenues were insufficient for the proper maintenance of so important a College." The reason for the grant of S. Mary's however was different, though classed with the others in the royal letters patent. This appears from a letter addressed by the Bishop of Ely to the Master and Scholars, 19 October, 1343. He tells them that he sanctions the appropriation, "because, as you reside in the same University, you will be able to attend the celebration of mass, and other services, in that Church, with less danger of interruption." This language shews that Great S. Mary's was to be used as a college chapel[2].

The College buildings, as completed in 1342, appear to have sufficed for the wants of the scholars for more than twenty years, as no alterations of any importance are recorded in the Accounts.

---

[1] [This mode of enumeration confirms the position at the south end of the east side assigned to this solar.]

[2] [The appropriation of S. Mary's appears to have been effected at once; that of Hyntlesham however was not sanctioned by the Bishop of Norwich until 11 Jan. 1349; and a Roll of Accounts sent to the Exchequer for 1365—7 shews that the negotiations respecting Felmersham and Grendon were difficult and protracted.]

In 1346 part of Walsyngham's house, bought in 1344 (p. 423), was fitted up as a brewhouse, furnished with leaden boilers, mash-vat, coolers, and other vessels, all of which are enumerated. A pigsty was also constructed, no doubt that its tenants might be fed with the grains; and between 1366 and 1370 the cost of a wooden bakehouse and granary is recorded[1].

Throughout the Accounts for these years there are numerous entries respecting the garden; beds are made, and vines and saffron are planted and cultivated. This garden was to the west of the College, as we have shewn above, and was bounded on the side next the river by a wall. Part of this, sixty feet in length, was destroyed by a flood in 1362, and in consequence the scholars became involved in litigation, but wherefore, or with whom, does not appear. In 1362 (31 September) the Sheriff came to measure the ground next to the bank; and in 1365 the Master and two of the Fellows made a journey to London and to Windsor; they paid fees to counsel and clerks, etc., at an expense of about five pounds, and, finally, the case was heard at the assizes. When the business was settled, a wall of enclosure was built at the place where the bank was, at a cost of £10. 13s. 6d. We may easily imagine that the College had so tampered with the bank of the river, their western boundary, as to trench upon the rights of the Town, or of the Crown[2].

In 1375 a rebuilding of the entire College on a new site was undertaken. The heading of the Account sent to the Exchequer by Richard Ronhale, Warden, for money laid out between Michaelmas 1375 and Michaelmas 1377, mentions only the construction of a new Hall and Chambers, as well as the repair of other buildings and chambers; but from expressions used in the body of that Account, as well as from particulars in subsequent Accounts—both in those sent to the Exchequer, and in those preserved at Cambridge—it may be concluded that these works were part of a general scheme of rebuilding, which had been contemplated from the first[3]. There is some ambiguity in the

---

[1] [Roll sent to the Exchequer, extending from Mich. 1366—Mich. 1370.]

[2] [King's Hall Accounts, ii. 140 (1362—63). "In xxxi Sept' primo in expensis vicecomitis venientis ad mensurandum prope ripam vj^s j^d ob." Ibid. ii. 238, 1365—66. Roll sent to Exchequer Mich. 1366—Mich. 1370: "It' in factura vnius muri vi fluminis deiecti continent' in longitudine lx pedes vj^s."]

[3] The Roll, which extends from Mich. 1375—Mich. 1377, is headed "Particule

expressions used during the earlier years of the work[1]; but in a Roll sent in by Thomas Hethersete for money expended between 1388 and 1390, the headings "Repair of buildings" and "Rebuilding of the Hall" both occur; and to the latter work the king contributes £40. The word "Hall" unquestionably refers to the College, and not to the Refectory, as will be seen by comparing the terms used in the Roll with those used in the order to the Treasurer and Barons of the Exchequer to furnish the money. In the latter document, which is in French, "mestre Thomas Hetersed gardein de notre sale de nos escolers en luniursitee de Cantebrigg" is to be allowed "quarant liures desterlings...sur la reedificacion de notre sale auantdite[2]." The buildings, when completed, surrounded a small Cloister-court (fig. 6) on the north side of the present Chapel, the west end of which stands on the site of this Hall, which was pulled down in 1557 to make way for it. The portion of the original buildings left after that date is shewn by Hamond (fig. 3). So slowly, however, was the College work carried on, that the erection of this little irregular quadrangle occupied nearly fifty years, for we shall find that it was not finished until the beginning of the reign of King Henry the Sixth.

The Accounts for some years subsequent to 1375 are imperfect, and except the building of a single chamber, recorded in the Roll for 1375—77, which was evidently a large "solar," from the mention of more than one chamber or "celar" under it, we are without information of the progress of the work until 1386—87, when we meet with a contract for building a kitchen, evidently

compoti Magistri Ricardi Ronhale [for vadia, etc.] necnon de misis et expensis per ipsum factis circa construccionem noue Aule et Camerarum ac reparacionem et emendacionem aliarum domorum et camerarum ibidem." Then, after several other entries, "Idem computat se soluisse vni tegulatori pro coopertura vnius Camere Noue aule ibidem facte...lxvj[s]. viij[d]....Et in luto et stramine empt' ad cameras inferiores sub camera predicta pro area in eisdem facienda v[s]."

[1] As in the phrases "*constructio noue Aule et camerarum,*" "*vij cameras Aule predicte,*" in which the first refers to the Refectory, the second to the College. The phrase "*Reparacio Aule et camerarum in manso Collegii*" is plain.

[2] [Memoranda Roll (Exch. Q. R.) 13 Rich. II. Trinity Term. "Brevia directa Baronibus," Roll 5. In the margin of Hethersete's Roll we find "Reedificatio Aule"; and in the text, recording the king's gift of £40, are the words "et in reedificacione dicte Aule Regis," etc., which shew distinctly that the whole College is meant.]

an entirely new structure. The contract, which is wholly for carpenters' work, is with Stephen Hoore of Wykembrok[1], and John Payn of Depden, in the county of Suffolk, for the construction of certain houses[2] enumerated below. They consist of: (1) A kitchen of the same excellent timber in quantity and workmanship as that of the kitchen of the Friar Preachers at Cambridge; (2) A larder annexed to it on the east side; (3) A "solar" (*solarium*) on the west side of the kitchen, built after the fashion of the cloister next the kitchen of the aforesaid brethren, with a covered staircase leading to the "solar." The whole is to be completed at least by the Feast of the Nativity of S. John Baptist next, and for the sum of thirty marks, to be paid in three equal instalments—the first at the signing of the indenture, the second at Pentecost, and the third at the completion of the work. Each of the two contractors is to receive in addition a tunic and hood[3].

The yearly accounts of the College do not mention the kitchen until 1394—95, when two full pages of payments to carpenters, bricklayers, tilers, etc. occur[4]. Among other items the making of a portion of the fireplace called "le coporowne[5]" is recorded. Either therefore the carpenters' work contracted for eight years before had been postponed, or this entry relates to the completion of it by building the great chimney and making up the tiling of the roof.

While this rebuilding was going on, an agreement was concluded with the Hospital of S. John, 27 January, 1393, of which we will translate the most important passages, as they throw considerable light on the arrangements of the buildings of King's Hall. The kitchen therein mentioned is evidently the new one.

---

[1] Wickambrook is in Suffolk, 6 miles N. by W. of Clare, and Depden is close to it. We find Suffolk carpenters frequently employed in Cambridge.

[2] The word "domus" is used in all College contracts for all structures which are not either chambers or such distinct buildings as the Hall or Chapel. Thus it is here employed for a kitchen, larder, etc.; and is in similar contracts applied to the Buttery, Pantry, etc., which are usually at the kitchen-end of the Hall.

[3] The contract is dated on a feast of the Virgin Mary in 10 Richard II., but the name of the feast is illegible. As the work was to be finished on June 24, and the regnal year began June 22, 1386, it is plain that the completion of the work is thrown into the 11 Richard II., 1387—88.

[4] King's Hall Accounts, iv. 105.

[5] Ibid. iv. 105, "Item pro factura le coporowne camini ij[s]." See below, p. 446, n. 3.

"The Master and brethren of the Hospital of S. John the Evangelist, in token of their friendly feeling, have given leave to the Master and Scholars of King's Hall, to pull down and remove a certain wall now standing close to the ground belonging to the aforesaid Hall upon soil belonging to the aforesaid Hospital; and on the foundation of the said wall to erect another wall of stone seven rods [115 feet] in length, and at least eight feet in height; in which wall they shall not make any doors or apertures, except glass windows, nor place leaden gutters upon it, so that the said Master and Brethren may not be annoyed by the said Master and Scholars looking into their ground, or discharging water upon it.

And should a hole happen to be broken in any glass window that may be made in the aforesaid wall, through which any person could look into the ground belonging to the Master and Brethren, unless the said hole be effectually repaired within one month after notice thereof has been given, the Master and Scholars aforesaid shall pay to the Master and Brethren forty pence, by way of punishment.

Moreover the aforesaid Master and Scholars shall be held responsible for the repair of two walls belonging to the Master and Brethren, and abutting upon the Kitchen and Library of the aforesaid Hall, so far as they shall have been damaged by water dropping from the aforesaid building.

To have and to hold the foundation of the said wall, for ever; yielding and paying in each year to the Master and Brethren aforesaid a red rose on the feast of the Nativity of S. John Baptist, should it be demanded."

The work of building the new Hall had meanwhile been proceeding, so far as we can make out from the fragmentary nature of the Accounts. In 1387—88 we find a heading: "Expenses in the construction of the new Hall," which seems to have been begun 15 August, 1387. Workmen are employed for 15 weeks, and materials are bought, the total outlay amounting to £67. 1s. 8d.[1]; and in 1389—90 there are a number of weekly payments to John Maidston, who may have been the master-mason, amounting to £25. 1s. 8d., with the purchase of materials which ends with a charge for two locks and rings for the doors. This Account probably indicates the date of the completion of the Hall[2]. After this date we hear no more of the Hall until 1399—1400, when a leaden lavatory

---

[1] [King's Hall Accounts, iv. 13. "Expense facte circa construccionem noue Aule a die assumpcionis beate Marie anno Regni Regis Ricardi post conquestum xj°."]

[2] [The entries record many curious words: ibid. iii. 49, 1389—90: "Item pro vij tuntyght de ragg vijˢ. Item pro v pedibus de fenestre. Item pro xiij pedibus de vouser xixᵈ. Item pro xj pedibus de caminis. Item pro ij coynis ijᵈ. Item pro ij seris ijˢ. Item pro anul' et basis ad hostia aule vjˢ. iijᵈ."]

was made, and also a porch, which occupied a mason and two labourers (*famuli*) for five or six weeks[1]. In the same year a wall was built along the river-bank (*circa ripam*) at a cost of £19. 15*s*. 9½*d*. The materials used were brick, rag, and clunch from Hynton and Barrington[2].

In 1411—12 a new Bakehouse was begun of stone, the old one having been of wood. This was carried on in the succeeding years, and completed about 1414—15, in which year the last entries appear. Thus the construction of this apparently trifling edifice occupied at least four years. The Accounts are sufficiently detailed to shew the manner in which the scholars proceeded with their buildings, and on this ground are worth examining.

In the first year two masons, one or two labourers, and two "leyers" receive wages, and a special payment is recorded to a master-mason (*magister operis*) named Dodington, who may have given the design, for we find him entertained at dinner and supper, together with his wife and servant. Materials are bought, such as rag, slate, brick, clunch from Burwell and Barrington, and hurdles to make a scaffold. Towards the expenses four new students paid 20*s*. each in lieu of their entrance feasts (*jentacula*)[3]. No regular contract was made for the whole building, as in the case of the kitchen, but small agreements with different workmen for materials or labour, as required. In the second year (1412—13), the masons' work goes on with one labourer and three leyers, and a steelyard is bought to weigh the stone, among which that for the steps leading to the oven is specially mentioned[4]. Arrangements for the woodwork were now made. Richard Wryth is sent to Brandon, 8 June, 1413, to view timber, and a contract is drawn up with William Reyner, carpenter, of Wyrlyngton[5], and Robert Strut, of Herthyrst; but

---

[1] [King's Hall Accounts, v. pp. 51, 73.]   [2] [Ibid. v. 76.]

[3] [Ibid. v. 319. "Item remuneratur dodyngton magistro operis xiij^s. iiij^d; et pro prandio suo et sue uxoris et famuli viij^d. Item pro vino ad cenam predicti iiij^d." Ibid. p. 321. "Infrascripti soluerunt ad fabricam noue pistrine loco gentaculi in introitu faciend': In primis Rogerus Greneford xx^s. Item dominus Johannes Petyt xx^s. Item Willelmus Lake xx^s."]

[4] [Ibid. v. 328. "Item pro statera ad ponderand' petras v^s. Item pro Centum pedibus et ix et di' de tabyll et gabyll wall...xliij^s. et ij^d. Item pro xix pedibus de kyngstable ad gradum fornacis iiij^s viij^d."]

[5] Worlington is in Suffolk, 1 mile W.S.W. of Mildenhall.

the document has unfortunately been lost.   Reyner also undertook to convey all the timber required from Brandon Ferry or Tot-
rynghethe. In 1413—14, the third year of the work, the masonry
goes on.   An item "freestone for gable-walls" implies that the
top had been nearly reached, and the expenses of "Walton and
his horse for two days, to inquire after Reyner our carpenter and
his bondsman;" and of "Richard Wrythe riding to Myldenale
for the carpenter," indicate that the walls were nearly ready for
the roof; and accordingly in this and the following year the
carriage of various pieces of timber is entered in the accounts
by name, as "dormant," "pendant," "brace," "joppy," "joist,"
and the like[1]. In this year the slates contracted for in the
first year of the work arrived, and two tilers are employed
to fix them.   In the fourth year (1414—15) the slating is
still going on, and the ironwork for the doors is provided.
In this year the building seems to have been practically
finished, for in the next the only entry of importance is for
"a glass window for the bultinghous," probably an appended
building for bolting or sifting the flour.

A pigeon-house (columbare) is first mentioned in 1414—15,
when a regular heading "expenses of the dovehouse" appears in
the Accounts.   The first construction of it is not recorded. The
purchase of four dozen pigeons in this year indicates the stock-
ing of it[2].

We have now to describe a more important work, namely, a
new Library, with chambers adjoining it (noua libraria et Camera
contigua), begun in 1416—17, and completed in 1421—22[3].
We have seen that in 1393 an agreement had been made with

---

[1] [King's Hall Accounts, v. 166. "Item pro cariagio vnius trabis cum j jopy vˢ."
Ibid. p. 167. "Imprimis pro iij peciis meremii empt' in nundinis natiuitatis sancti
Johannis...iiijˢ viijᵈ. Item pro xv Jestys longitudinis xiij ped'; latitudinis in quadro
viij pollic' et vij pollic' xvjˢ. iijᵈ." Ibid. vi. 57. "Item pro j magno ligno vocat'
dormavnt. ij. pendavntys et . ij. brasys emptis de Smith de Brangtre xxvjˢ. viijᵈ."]

[2] [Ibid. vi. 53. "Item pro remuneracione portatorum columbarum ad columbare
iiij dussen iiijᵈ ob. It' pro vno salcath vᵈ. ob." The dovehouse subsequently became
a source of profit. In 1416—17 for instance it brought in £1. 3s. 9½d. Among the
entries we find "Imprimis pro iij duodenis et vj pipionibus xvijᵈ. ob. Item vj duodenis
columbarum ijˢ. vjᵈ."]

[3] [The Library was built partly by subscription. The Bishop of Rochester [Dr
Richard Yonge] gave £20 (King's Hall Accounts, vi. 69); and Henry Somere £2
towards the glazing of the windows. Ibid. p. 158.]

S. John's Hospital, by which King's Hall was permitted to rebuild the wall of boundary, and the mention of a Library in
that deed, as well as the expression "new Library" applied to
the work now taken in hand, shews that a Library was already
in existence, as, indeed, is proved by the Accounts for previous
years[1]. The first item in these new Accounts is a payment of
6s. 8d. to the Hospital for the foundation of the wall of the
Library and chambers[2]. Evidently the former wall, part of
which was a boundary wall, had now to be pulled down, and a
higher building erected upon the site, which required new per-
missions and conditions—now lost. Moreover the Accounts for
the first year shew that a new Library was not the only work
undertaken, but that a cloister[3] also was being built at the same
time. The items for materials bought, and especially a contract
for a supply of timber, shew that it was of wood, and that it was
carried round two sides of the court.

The Library was begun, as above mentioned, in 1416—17, in
which year the usual entries occur for a supply of clunch and
bricks, called "walletyle," besides large quantities of worked
stones, the names of which are exceedingly curious[4]. In the first
year's Account we again meet with the mason named Dodington, to whom 6s. 8d. is paid, but the precise service rendered by
him is not recorded[5]. In 1417—18 the cost of "the chambers

---

[1] Ibid. iv. 172. 1394—95. Under "*Expense circa librariam*" we find "Imprimis
pro xxiij chatenis viij^s. Item pro j cera et xxxiij clauis v^s. vj^d. Item pro j hangedax
et ij stapul' iiij^d." The 33 keys were for the Master and 32 Fellows. At the
beginning of this volume there is a catalogue of the books, amounting to 87.

[2] [Ibid. vi. 98. "*Expense facte circa nouam librariam et Camere contigue.*"
" Item dat' domui Sancti Johannis pro fundamento parietis librarie et camere vj^s. viij^d.
Item pro factura indenturarum predicti fundamenti et pergameno xv^d."]

[3] [The word "claustrum," which also means "court," is proved to mean cloister
in this instance by such entries as the following (ibid. vi. 99), "Item pro j magno
ligno ad platys et tribus postellis pro claustro xxiij^s iiij^d."]

[4] [King's Hall Accounts, vi. 98. The following words refer to stones: "Item pro
xl. peciis de doblettes xviij^s. iiij^d. Item pro x nowelles pro gradibus xv^s. Item pro
xxviij pedibus de moynell v^s. xj^d. Item pro vectura vj pedum de jambes et j Wawcer
xiij^d." Ibid. p. 99. "Item pro lviij pedibus de lapid' vocat' seerghys ij^s. v^d. Item
pro tabula ad moolde petre vocat' nowell ij^d. Item pro xij pedibus de fenestris ij^s. vj^d....
et pro ij bekettes xx^d." Ibid. p. 149. "Item pro ij bekettes hostii maioris xx^d. Item
pro ij bekettes minoris forme xij^d. Item pro vij^{xx}. pedibus vocat' sewlys et vaucers
xvij^s. vj^d. Item pro forme pecis vj fenestrarum ij^s. vj^d."]

[5] [In this year the heading "conuenciones noue librarie" appears in the Account-
book, p. 100; but it is followed by a blank page.]

adjoining the master's chamber" is joined with that of the Library, and Roger Wrythe goes into Essex to select timber; in 1418—19 the heading is simply "the new building," the Library not being specially mentioned ; in 1419—20 the " cost of the Library" heads a blank page[1], but is followed by three closely written pages headed " cost of the new building of the cloister." The Accounts for 1420—21 have not been preserved ; but by 1421—22 the Library was evidently finished, for in that year we find a curious Account for its interior fittings, and for the binding and arranging of the books, which occupied two carpenters, a bookbinder (*ligator librorum*), and his man, for about sixteen weeks. It contains charges for skins for covering the books, red skins and calf-skins ; entries for various pairs of clasps, with their parchments ; wages of a "joyner." probably to make the boards for the sides of the books ; the cost of chains, with locks and keys, and so on ; and finally, the superscription of the books.

We are not able to determine precisely when the cloister was finished, but the contract " for certain timber for the roof of the new chambers and two sides of the cloister" (for which 20½ marks were to be paid) is dated 16 October, 1418, and the last payment to the contractor was made 26 January, 1420[2]. This contract is followed by another for timber for an Oratory (*oratorium*), then mentioned for the first time ; and it is provided that the said timber be delivered before 1 August, presumably in the same year, 1420. In that year the Oratory is mentioned in conjunction with the Cloister, whence we may conclude that it was in the Cloister Court; and payments for the ironwork for the windows, and for wood to make an altar, shew that it must have been nearly finished. A payment for the ironwork of the joists under the leads, apparently of the cloister-roof, indicates that it also was now being completed[3]. The Oratory was fur-

---

[1] The appearance of blank pages, which is not uncommon in these volumes, arises from the practice of employing a clerk to write out in the new volume for a given year the headings which he found in the volume for the preceding year. The difference of handwriting between the headings and the items proves that such was the mode employed.

[2] [King's Hall Accounts, vi. 198.]

[3] [Ibid. vi. 238. "Item pro forratura jestys sub plumbatura viz. xxxvj peceis vj^s. viij^d. Item pro ij stodys angularibus oratorii iij^s." Ibid. p. 239. "Item pro duobus peceis ligni empt' de Johanne Essex pro altari et fenestris oratorii x^s."

nished with painted hangings in 1422—23; and in the following
year it and the Parlour (then mentioned for the first time) were
wainscoted[1]. This work occupied two workmen, each with a
servant, for six weeks, but no particulars are given. The Parlour
occupied two or three carpenters for about six weeks in 1424—25;
was glazed in 1425—26; and the purchase of 500 tiles for its
pavement in 1426—27 completes its history. This last particular may imply that it was on the ground-floor.

In 1426—27 a new building is begun, and continued for
about ten years, but as the headings of the Accounts give no
clue to the nature of it, that must be gathered from scattered
allusions in the Accounts themselves. which plainly shew that
it consisted of a great gateway-tower with four turrets, and
a range of chambers, one or more of which were assigned to
the Master. The gateway can be no other than the so-called
King Edward's gateway, which now stands at the west end of
the Chapel, having been removed, as will appear below, in the
year 1600, from its original site, which was about ninety feet to
the south of its present position.

The workmen, as usual in important building operations,
were fed, paid, and also, as it would appear, housed and partially
clothed by the College. A principal mason (*latamus principalis*)
and a second mason (*latamus secundarius*) are mentioned[2]. The
former received, in addition to his weekly wages, an annual
salary of 15s. 7d. In the first year the only thing done was the
erection of a lodge or workshop for the masons, at the latter
end of the year 1427. It was covered with sedge, as usual, to
protect the walls from frost during the winter, and finished early
in 1428. In that year—the second of the work—the foundations
are laid; old chambers are pulled down[3]; the masons' work

Ibid. p. 240. "Pro opere ferreo pro fenestris oratorii viz. CC iiij li et di. xxviij^s
vij^d."]

[1] [Ibid. vii. 59. "Expense circa celaturam oratorii et Parlore."]

[2] [Accounts of King's Hall, vii. 210 (1427—28). "Item pro ij napronys de correo
et ij par' cyrothecarum pro principali lathamo et secundario xij^d. It' pro iiij antiquis
couerlytis pro lectis lathamorum vij^s." Ibid. p. 211. "It' in x polys de Walyssh
blankett pro lectis operariorum vj^s. x^d. ob." Ibid. p. 212. "It' pro xvj ulnis pro
linthiaminibus viij^s. iiij^d." Ibid. p. 247. "Item solut' principali lathamo pro
liberatura sua...xiij^s. iiij^d."]

[3] [Ibid. vii. 211 (1427—28). "It' in prandio ij laborant' circa facturam fundamenti noui operis per v dies xv^d. It' remuneratum est Dowce carpentario pro sub-
traccione antiquarum camerarum xx^d."]

begins in earnest, and we find a mass of small items for wages and materials set down alternately, the whole sum spent amounting to £89. 6s. 7½d. In the third year (1428—29) the sum amounts to £134. 2s. 1d.; in the fourth year (1429—30) to £110. 18s. 7d. In the following years the pages are not summed. The items which shew the nature of the building are scattered sparingly through the mass of technical terms, of which some are quoted in the notes[1]. The stone came from Burwell and Hynton, and usually had been worked before it arrived, the number of pieces of each description brought in being carefully specified. The great gate is first mentioned in 1427—28, when stone to make the jambs is bought. In the following year a carpenter makes the "centering" of the vault, and stone for the ribs is bought. Two pieces for the King's arms are also charged for, and 68 feet of "Crestys pro le embataylmentes," the provision of which shews that the top must then have been nearly reached[2]. In this year lead "to cover the new gate with" is mentioned; and in the next (1429—30) timber from Haverell, doubtless for the floors and roof. Ironwork for the windows is also supplied in this year, and the stones brought in are chiefly various descriptions of crests, corbel-tables, etc.[3] In 1430—31 the great gate is roofed and leaded, and 4000 tiles are bought, probably for the floors[4]. In 1431—32 a painter "paints the

---

[1] [Ibid. p. 212. "Item solut' Thorlby querreour…pro iiij^{xx} xj dowblettes xlij^s. v^d. ob. It' pro lj ped' de joyntable vj^s iiij^d ob. It' pro xxviij ped' de leggement xj^s j^d. It' pro vj ped' de dowble vowcers iiij^s. It' pro xl ped' de single vowcers xiij^s. iiij^d. It' pro xix ped' de chamerantz pro magna porta ix^s. vj^d. It' pro xxxiij ped' de perpoynt' xvij^s." Ibid. p. 246 (1428—29). "It' solut' Henrico Jekke de Baryngton pro iiij^{xx} xiiij ped' de square peces…xxiij pedibus de serchis…iiij^{or} formepeces." Ibid. p. 248. Among stone from Burwell we find "Et iij somerpecys xij^d. Et vj docelettes xv^d." Ibid. viii. 29 (1430—31). "It' lxxxij et di fott of perpendaschler vj^d. Item venttes crest xij fott et di v^s. ij^d. ob. It' gargulles iiij vj^s. viij^d."]

[2] [Ibid. vii. 247 (1428—29). "It' pro ij peciis pro armis Regis viij^s." Ibid. 248. "It' pro iiij ped' de Oggez viij^d." Ibid. 249. "It' pro lxviij ped' de Crestys pro le enbataylmentes xxviij^s. iiij^d. It' in prandio Johannis Dowce carpentarii per iiij^{or} dies circa facturam cynctouris pro magna porta vj^d. It' in clauis pro Cynctoures xj^d."]

[3] [Ibid. vii. 286 (1429—30). "It' pro ij Crestis super Arma regis ij^s. iiij^d. It' pro xix ped' et di' de Corbel tabyl xj^s j^d. It' pro xij ped' de ventes pro enbatylment' v^s. ij^d." Ibid. p. 288. "It' pro xvij ped' et di de sqwynchuncrest v^s. j^d."]

[4] [Ibid. viii. 29 (1430—31). "Item vni plumbario pro coopertorio magne porte cum iiij^{or} turribus xx^s. Item pro cirotecis viij^d." Ibid. p. 27. "It' pro M.Ṁ.Ṁ.Ṁ. tegul' precii M^l. v^s. xx^s. It' pro cariagio earundem a lynn x^s."]

King's Arms," and "oils all the windows of the great gate and of the Master's chamber[1]." From this date the entries concerning this room or rooms occupy a considerable space in the Accounts, and shew that it was being carried forward coextensively with the great gate. The timber for the roof is specified in 1432—33, and the terms employed shew that it was large and ornamental[2]. By this time the stonework of the gate had evidently been finished; the battlements and vault were put up in 1431—32[3]; the wooden gates were made in 1432—33, and were mounted with ironwork and varnished in 1433—34. Lastly, in 1434—35, the principal stonemason carves King Edward's statue; in the following year colours are bought to paint it; and in 1436—37 it is painted[4].

Besides the Master's chamber it is clear that other chambers were being built at the same time, from the number of entries for windows, fireplaces, doors, woodwork for studies[5], and the like, which occur in these Accounts. An entrance to the garden, and a wall round the same, are also mentioned[6]. The chambers may be identified with the range which extended from King

[1] [Ibid. viii. 62 (1431—32). "Item solutum est pictori pro pictura Armorum Regis et vnccione aliarum fenestrarum magne porte et magne fenestre camere custodis xl[s]."]

[2] [Ibid. viii. 111 (1432—33). "Item solutum est Dowce pro diuersis parcellis meremii pro camera custodis. In primis pro vj joppyes precii joppe xij[d]. summa vj[s]. It' viij joppyes maiores xvj[s].... It' ij wyndebemys et j keye pro camino xvj[d]. Item pro iiij ekys pro iiij joppys iiij[d]. It' pro iiij wyndbemys...xij pedes de euysbord...."]

[3] [Ibid. viii. 62 (1431—32). "It' viij copporons peces...iiij[s]." The word "copporon" signifies the rising part of a battlement, as distinguished from the "crenels" or "spaces." Arch. Nom. p. 32.] The vault of the Gateway is indicated by: (ibid.) "Item v fott pro principali key archiis noue porte magne precii pedis iiij[d]. ob. It' iiij keyes siue nodi magne porte 1 key iij fott...iiij[s]. vj[d]." Thus we learn that the word "key" was applied to the bosses of a vault. (Arch. Nom. p. 65.)

[4] [Ibid. viii. 212 (1434—35). "Item solutum est cuidam principali lathamo pro sculptura et factura ymaginis Regis stantis ad magnam portam xxvj[s]. viij[d]." Ibid. p. 265 (1435—36). "It' pro coloribus ad pictacionem Regis ymaginis iij[s]. iiij[d]." Ibid. ix. 39 (1436—37). "It' pro pictura Imaginis Regis iiij[s]."]

[5] [Ibid. viii. 62 (1431—32). "Item pro popill bord pro coopertoriis studiorum xv[s]. iiij[d]." Ibid. p. 66. "Item pro xv mensulis pro coopertura studii Alani Pyke." Ibid. ix. 39 (1436—37). "Item in remuneracione Johannis Douce pro studiis xiij[s]. iiij[d]."]

[6] [Ibid. vii. 249 (1428—29). "It' pro ij magnis bekettis pro ostio in introitu ad gardinum ij[s] viij[d].... It' pro ij[bus] magnis jambes pro porta in introitu ad gardinum xij[d]." Ibid. viii. 66 (1431—32). "Item pro construccione muri lapidei iuxta turrim et gardinum," is the heading of a list of expenses.]

Edward's Gate to the Cloister Court, as shewn by Hamond (fig. 3), and as laid down on the old plan of Trinity College (fig. 10) to be referred to presently; and the garden is that to the west of the College, a passage to which through the range of chambers is shewn on the same plan. A "wall near the new gate" is also mentioned in 1433—34. This was probably built to enclose the additions to the site made in 1433.

During the thirty years which succeeded the completion of the entrance-gateway, no new work of importance appears to have been undertaken. We are able, however, to gather some curious hints respecting the arrangement of the buildings, and some interesting small works, from such headings in the Accounts as: "Repairs of the House" (*reparacio domorum*), and "New building" (*nova edificacio*).

In 1438—39 a new kitchen is first mentioned, called indifferently "new kitchen" (*nova coquina*), or "royal kitchen" (*coquina regis*)[1]. Neither the commencement nor the conclusion of the work is precisely recorded; and it does not appear to have been a large or important structure. It may have been a private kitchen for the King's use, either in expectation of a parliament being held at Cambridge[2], or of a royal visit, for the Accounts shew that Henry the Sixth visited the College in October 1445[3]; between Lady Day and Easter

---

[1] Ibid. ix. 137. "Item pro v. C. segge pro Coquina Regis xviij^d. It' pro prandio duorum segge thakkers xvj^d. It' pro tectura noue coquine x^d." Ibid. x. 253 (1445 —46). "Item pro iij. C. seget' pro coopertura noue coquine ij^s. xj^d."

[2] The only Parliament actually held at Cambridge was in 1388, when King Richard the Second lodged at Barnwell Abbey, and our College was constructing its early buildings (Cooper's Annals, i. 133). A Parliament was however convened at Cambridge in 1436, and again in 1446; but the place of meeting of the former was changed to Westminster, and of the latter to Bury S. Edmund's (ibid. i. 186, 198).

[3] On 25 July in the following year the first stone of King's College Chapel was laid, in all probability by the King in person, as shewn above (Vol. i. 465), and this visit may have been connected with the acquisition of the site, or the design for the buildings, of that College. [On this occasion he seems to have stayed some days, for the words "In presencia Regis" are noted in the margin of the third week of the Fellows' Commons (*communes sociorum*). As these are reckoned from Michaelmas, the third week would fall between October 13 and October 20. Some of the King's retinue were in College for two weeks, for in the *Expense extrauagantes* for that year we find (Accounts x. 247) "In primis in expensis circa familiares domini Regis xx^s. It' circa famulos Regis vj^s. viij^d. It' pro famulis armigeri Regis per ij septimanas iij^s. iiij^d."]

1447[1]; in 1448—49[2]; and in 1452—53[3]. It is probably to some of these visits, or to the preparations incidental to them, that Dr Caius alludes in the following passage[4], which, though it cannot be accepted literally, shews that the buildings of King's Hall must have exceeded those of other colleges in extent and convenience.

"In King's Hall there were buildings sufficiently extensive for the reception of the King at a parliament which was intended to be held at Cambridge, chambers sufficiently numerous, a parlour (*conclave*), a wine-cellar, and a kitchen, newly built and all lying apart, so as to be private to the King without inconvenience to the College, except in the entrance to the kitchen. Wherefore they induced the Master and Brethren of the house of S. John to grant to them for an annual rent a passage through their ground, seven feet wide and fifteen long."

While the kitchen was proceeding, a "tower near the new gate[5]" is mentioned, but here again there are no particulars to shew the exact nature of it. [As it was built, at least in part, at the expense of the Master, and as we have seen that the Master's chambers adjoined the new tower-gateway, it may have been an external staircase, like those in the old court of King's College, which were built soon afterwards.] It was begun in 1438—39, and finished in 1440—41, as we learn from a payment "for a ball and vane at the end of the new work" in the Accounts for that year. In the year in which it was begun, 29 November, 1438, some old wooden buildings were sold[6]. These may have been those originally erected just a century before; some of which had been pulled down when

---

[1] [King's Hall Accounts x. 331 (1446—47). *Expense circa Aulam.* The first item in this Account refers to Christmas; the second to the Purification (2 Feb.); then: "Item in cirpis erga aduentum Regis iiij[d]. It' pro cirpis in aduentu Regis iiij[d]"; after which there is an item "in tempore Pasche." There is unfortunately a break in the Fellows' Commons between the 25th and 38th week.]

[2] [Ibid. xi. 77 (1448—49). "It' in expensis famulorum domini Regis in tempore aduentus sui ix[s]."]

[3] [Ibid. xi. 247 (1452—53). *Expense extrauagantes.* "Item in aduentu regis xx[d]."]

[4] [Hist. Cant. Acad. i. 66.]

[5] King's Hall Accounts ix. 179 (1438—39). The expenses are headed "Communes lathamorum cum seruientibus per custodem pro turre iuxta nouam portam." The same heading occurs in the following year. Ibid. p. 310 (1440—41). "It' pro vno bolle et fane in fine noui operis vj[s]. viij[d]."

[6] [Ibid. ix. 183. "M[d]. quod recepimus per manus Stephani Lucas pro meremio antiquarum domorum venditarum Chirche mercer' et Willelmo Wylflete clerico in die veneris antepenultimo die Novembr' [November 1438] anno presenti vj[li]."]

the foundations of King Edward's Gate were laid. After the completion of the cloister-quadrangle, and the new range of chambers to the south of it, they would no longer be required. In 1443—44 a wooden Bridge was made, probably from the back-gate of the garden over the ditch to the common; and in 1449—50, a new building (*nova edificacio*) occupies a full page, with wages, carriage of timber, stone from Hynton and Barrington, freestone and worked stones as before—a provision of material for some edifice which the loss of the next year's account has perhaps prevented us from defining more particularly[1]. Among these minor works we may mention a watercourse to the buttery and kitchen, with a drain thence to the river, made in 1448—49[2]; repairs to the hay-house and the stable, which shew that the buildings included those offices; and lastly, in 1452—53, the erection of a brick-wall, for which masons were fetched from Felmersham in Bedfordshire. As trees were cut down to make way for it, it was probably to the south of King's Hall Lane, where certain gardens had been acquired a few years before, as related in the last chapter. It was evidently a work of importance, for Reginald Ely and William Ruskyn were consulted. As the former was headmason at the old court of King's College, and the latter was one of the clerks of the works, it is probable that they were employed at King's Hall in a similar capacity[3]. In this same year the "gallery between the Chapel and the Library" is mentioned[4].

We have next to record the construction of a separate chapel[5]. This was begun in the fourth year of the reign of

---

[1] [The terms which we have met with before recur again in this Account. As many as 208 loads of clunch were brought in (Accounts, xi. 156).]

[2] [It was a considerable work, for 276 feet of stone are mentioned, and Ruskyn and Ely were consulted, as below. Accounts, xi. 115.]

[3] [Ibid. xi. 131. "It' in prandio Raginaldi Ely, Ruskyn, et Johannis Brokeshaw viij^d." Compare Vol. i. 323.]

[4] [Ibid. xi. 277. "It' pro factura x lateys in deambulatorio inter capellam et librariam v^s."]

[5] It must be remembered that the community had an Oratory, which is sometimes called a Chapel (*capella*). When the building of the new Chapel was interrupted, the Oratory was repaired. King's Hall Accounts, xiv. 85 (1469—70). Under the heading, *Expense circa Oratorium*, painters are employed for 8 weeks; and in the following year (ibid. 134) the same heading is repeated, and the roof is repaired. In

King Edward the Fourth (1464—65), interrupted for about ten years, from 1469—70 to 1478—79[1], and finally completed at the beginning of the reign of King Richard the Third, having been twenty years in building. The Accounts relating to this new work shew that three of the Fellows, Belamy, Wylkynson, and Cossey, were appointed as Ediles to pay the workmen and manage the building for the College; and various sums were delivered to them for that purpose from time to time as required[2]. In 1466—67 a quantity of freestone, most of it ready worked for use, was purchased. The Account for the following year is unfortunately imperfect; but in that for 1468—69 we find £75 given out "for the construction of the new building" (*pro construccione novi edificii*) to two of the Fellows, Fylay and Gyrton, in sums varying from £10 to £20 in each month from April to September, 1469. The master-mason was John Wolrych, who was afterwards employed on King's College Chapel, when the works there were resumed in 1476[3]. In the following year the Ediles handed in their Accounts to the Bursars, and received a donation of twenty shillings. During their tenure of office £19. 12s. 7d. had been spent[4]. After this the work ceased, and was not resumed until 1479—80, when an

1468—69 (ibid. 11) an organ is bought; and in 1472—73 (ibid. 201), under the heading *Expense circa capellam*, it is repaired. In 1494—95 (ibid. xix. 21) "capella nostra magna" is mentioned, as though to contrast it with the small one of former days.

[1] In those years the headings *Nova edificacio*, or *Expense circa novam capellam*, are either omitted altogether, or are followed by a blank page.

[2] An entry under the heading *Nova edificacio* in the Account for 1464—65 (xiii. 190) shews that they were paid for their work: "Item remuneratum est Willelmo Wylkynson pro labore suo circa nouum opus iij[s]. iiij[d]." Dr Caius relates (Hist. Acad. p. 117) that the materials of the great Hall of Cambridge Castle were given by King Henry the Fourth to the Master and Fellows of King's Hall, at their request, towards building their Chapel. We have seen, however (Vol. i. 323), that the Hall in question was granted by King Henry the Sixth to King's College, 14 February, 1441.

[3] [Ibid. xiv. 46. "Item allocat' est Johanni Wolryche latamo et superuisori ipsorum latamorum pro labore suo viij[s]. iiij[d]. per manus M' Fylay." In this year King Edward the Fourth visited the College, perhaps for the purpose of inspecting the Chapel: ibid. p. 21. *Expense circa Aulam:* "Item in cirpis erga aduentum Regis viij[d]."]

[4] [Ibid. xiv. 106. *Noua edificacio:* "Item xxvij die mensis Julii Anni presentis Magistri viz. Fylay et Gyrton computauerunt cum senescallis super omnibus pecunijs receptis ad nouam edificacionem, et omnibus allocatis nihil remanet in manibus ipsorum. Summa expensarum xix[li]. xij[s]. vij[d]. Et remunerat' est eisdem xx[s]."]

agreement with a carpenter is mentioned, and as much as
£27. 16s. 1d. is spent. In the following year the Accounts
occupy a whole page, and the wages paid to plumbers and two
glaziers indicate that the roof and the glazing of the windows
was proceeding, or at least was being prepared for. In 1481—82
an agreement respecting the quire is made, and lead and
wainscot are bought[1]. In the next year twelve oaks[2] from
Walden, the gift of the Queen, are received and sawn up; and
in the next there is a full page of wages to carvers working at
the stalls, with further payments for "waynscot," and to masons
for making the wall under the stalls, and sinking a well in the
north part of the Chapel. In 1483—84 a bargain is made with
"John Say, Carvar" for the completion of all the work that
remains to be done in the Chapel; and various masons, carpenters, sawyers, carvers, and glaziers are paid. In 1484—85 the
pavement is laid down, the walls plastered and whitewashed,
and a high altar made, of wood. This marks the conclusion of
the work, for we find no more entries referring to it, with the
exception of an occasional small item for repairs, until 1498—99,
when the expenses incidental to the consecration of the Chapel
are set down[3].

Some other building was being carried forward at the same
time as the Chapel, the nature of which is shewn by an entry
which marks its completion, in 1489—90, "for levelling the
court about the new chambers[4]." These new chambers are
probably those which stood on the southern boundary of the site
(fig. 3); and the buildings pulled down may have been some of
the ancient chambers which were built facing King's Hall Lane
before the erection of the King's Gateway tower. The other

---

[1] [Ibid. xvi. 192. "It' pro Fabrica novi chori per manus Repham xl[s]. It' pro
indentura et obligacione circa plumbum xij[d]. It' pro factura indenture et obligacionis
pro Coro capelle viij[d]."]

[2] These oaks may have been intended for the new chambers that were carried on
at this time, for they are entered under *Nova edificacio*, p. 148; and not under the
Chapel account at p. 146.

[3] King's Hall Accounts, xix. 226. *Expense circa novam Capellam.* "Expense
circa consecrationem eiusdem, viz. pro prandio xxv.s. It' pictori qui fecit cruces
circa eiusdem xvj.d. It' laborantibus circa eiusdem per quatuor dies et di' xv.d.
It' pro duorum librorum catenacione xiij.d."

[4] Ibid. xviii. 135 (1489—90). *Expense extravagantes.* "It' pro certis laborantibus
circa planacionem Curie circa nouas cameras iij[s]. ij[d]."

works were a porter's lodge with walls and towers, begun in 1490
and finished in 1492[1]; and the erection of a new wall of
enclosure, the foundation of which, and the pulling down of
old building, is charged for between 1497 and 1500. After this
date no work of importance was undertaken until 1518—19,
when the great gateway-tower, which now forms the principal
entrance to Trinity College, was commenced. The history of
this I shall give in detail.

The heading "Cost of the New Tower" (*Expense circa Nouam
Turrim*) appears first in the Accounts for 1518—19. A masons'
lodge, as usual, was built; and fifteen tons of stone were bought
from a quarryman at King's Cliff. No particulars of the progress
of the work are given, except that by the end of the year the
walls had risen high enough to require protection during winter.
In the two following years very little work is recorded, but in the
Audit-book for 1522—23 we meet with the "cost of the new
gates" (*expense circa nouas fores*). A contract is made with a
carpenter named Bucston to deliver the gates complete before
All Saints' Day, 1523; and with a smith of Thaksted in Essex
to supply the nails and ironwork[2]. The latter articles, including a lock and key, were paid for on Passion Sunday
(29 March), 1524[3]. A charge for the pavement, and for the stones
to set the hinges in, is mentioned at the same time.

The building was now so far finished as to perform its office
as a gateway. The tower above it, which was to give dignity
to the Royal College, was not so immediately required. Subscriptions, from Fellows and others, are recorded in successive
years, but the work was not renewed until 1528—29, under the
auspices of Dr Geoffrey Blyth, Master 1528—36, when the
money in hand, with new subscriptions from the Fellows,
amounted to £67. 7s. 2d. The following particulars give useful
information as to what was then done. They are extracted
from an Account headed "Cost of the Great Tower" (*Expense
circa Magnam Turrim*)[4].

[1] [Ibid. xviii. 296 (1491—92). *Noua edificacio.* "It' pro coopertura pro le
porters logge cum muris et turribus cum cera pro eodem vij[s]. v[d]."]

[2] [Bucston was to be paid £6. 13s. 4d. for the gates; and the smith at the
rate of 2¼[d] per pound for nails, and 2[d] per pound for the rest of the ironwork.]

[3] [King's Hall Accounts, Vol. xxiii. 205.]

[4] [Ibid. xxiv. 68.]

" Inprimis to yᵉ Fremason vpon an ernest peny .... xˢ.
It' to Thomas Loveday the carpentar For makynge the tymber warke
    to yᵉ same tower yn party off payment off viijˡⁱ..................... xxˢ.
It' For An ernest peny and yn party off pament off xijᴹˡ brycke to
    Browne off Ely .... iijˢ iiijᵈ.
It' payd to yᵉ Fremason For yᵉ Fyrst payment at the sealynge off the
    Indenturs .... xˡ.
It' payd to yᵉ Towne clarke For makynge a payre of Indenturs and
    oblygatyons .... xxᵈ.
It' for yᵉ hole payment off yᵉ xijᴹˡ brycke above rehersyd iijˡⁱ. xvjˢ. viijᵈ.
    per manus Custodis.
Item iij dosen hurdellys .... xˢ.
Item for xj tonne of stonne .... lvˢ.
Item for scaffolde tymber yᵉ ernest .... xijᵈ."

The nature of the bargain with Thomas Loveday is further
explained by a subsequent entry:

" Barganyd with Thomas Loveday for makyng ij floyrs [over which
is written 'one floyr and a roff'] of the tower, fyndyng tymber bord and
warkmanshipp viijˡⁱ. wheir vpon he hath recevyd xxˢ.[1]"

The work, however, lingered, and was not finished until
1535, for which year there is preserved a paper memorandum-
book, measuring four inches by twelve, of ten leaves, entitled:

"Annuus computus pro turri edificando qui annus fuit 28ˢ Hen. 8.
Anno Dni 1535. The bouk of the receytes and also off the exspenses
mayd vppon the byldyng off the new tower ouer the gret gattes off the
kynges haull in Cambrige. The wych receytes and exspensyns weyr
takyn and leyd owt by the Mʳ off the same house or hall. Anno 28.
Hen. 8. The Mʳˢ. booke: Summa totalis 109*li*. 9*s*."

The receipts, amounting to £118. 17*s*. 10*d*., are set down
first. They consist partly of the funds set apart for the work,
" receyd owt off the bagge that was ordynid for that purpos";
partly of the college stock, taken " owt off the lytyll tower," by
which the treasury is evidently meant; partly of subscriptions
and chamber-rents. The expenses amounted to £109. 10*s*. 0*d*.,
chiefly for materials, stone, clunch, brick and timber.
The following entries shew the nature of the work:

" Inprimis for oon lood of stagyng tymber .... iijˢ.
Item to...carpenters with the servants and laborers for syttyng vp the
    stage...xxiijˢ. ijᵈ.
Item payd [to the same] removing the stages....................... iijˢ. vjᵈ.
Item for a bosse .... xijᵈ.
Item to ... smyth for the yeryn for the windowse .... xlˢ.

---

[1] [Ibid. Vol. xxiv. 76.]

Item payd to Lovfday for the too flowerys in ful peyment off viij^{li}. .... vj^{li}.
Item For xv tonne off coyne.. iij^{li} xv^s.
Item payd to Lovfday For fyrste floweres of iiij turrettes and battyl-
    mentes for the same... iiij^s iiij^d.
Item payd to Bukston for syttyng vp the dovres .... iiij^d.
Item the plummer for castyng and leying the leyd .... xxxj^s.
Item the seyd plummer for thre days work off hym seylf and vij of his
    servantes abovt the turrettes .... v^s."

The remarkable way in which this work had lingered is
shewn by the payment of 6$li.$ to Loveday for the two floors, in
full payment of the 8$li.$ for which he had bargained seven years
before; and again by a series of payments to a workman named
John Shereff, manifestly the freemason who had contracted for
the work at the same time with Loveday, and had then received
his first payment of 10 $li.$[1] It will be observed that the materials
were provided by the College, and that no masons' wages are
entered, but only those of a few labourers, carpenters, and
plumbers. This is the first time that a contract for masonry
has occurred in the history of this College. Contracts with
carpenters were common, and several have been recorded,
beginning with that for the woodwork of the Kitchen in
1386—87.

Before proceeding farther, we will endeavour to determine the
relative positions of the buildings of which we have been tracing
the history. These are: (1) Kitchen and larder (1386—87);
(2) Hall (1387—88); (3) Bakehouse (1411—15); (4) Library
(1416—22); (5) two sides of a cloister (1418—20); (6) Oratory
(1420); (7) Parlour (1424—27); (8) King Edward's Gate and
Master's Chamber (1426—37); (9) Gallery between Chapel
(Oratory) and Library (1453); (10) Chapel (1464—85); (11) a
range of chambers, completed in 1489—90; (12) Great Gate,
begun 1519—24, resumed and completed 1528—35.

Of these buildings the first seven either formed part of a
small cloister-quadrangle (fig. 6^2), the internal area of which

---

[1] [The following are the entries referring to Shereff: "Item payd to Shereff at
his second payment [amount torn and illegible]. Item at his therd peyment xij^{li}.
Item I payd hym pre manibus off his last peyment v^{li}. Item payd to Jhon Shereff
at london vj^{li}. Item afterward I payd hyme as hit appeyrs by his quittans iij^{li}. iiij^s."]

[2] [This plan has been laid down from a careful comparison of two made by
Professor Willis, in which the arrangements of the buildings of King's Hall differ
slightly.]

could hardly have measured more than 40 feet square, or were immediately adjacent to it. This quadrangle was situated to the north of the existing Chapel of Trinity College. The west side is still standing; the west, north and east sides are shewn by Hamond (fig. 3), and, less distinctly, by Loggan (fig. 7); the latter also gives their ground-plan (fig. 4). The south side is now occupied by the west end of the Chapel of Trinity College, which was begun in 1554—55. The Junior Bursar's Book for 1555—56 is unfortunately lost; but in that for 1556—57, under the heading "Takers downe of buyldinges," we find a number of entries which explain the old arrangements. The labourers took down "the pyke wall in tholde Hall, and a part of the north wall," "the porche and the wall vpon the south syde of tholde Hall to Sir Burton his chamber": unslated "a part of tholde Hall, and from tholde Hall to tholde Chappell": took down "the north wall of the Chambers from tholde Buttrye to tholde Chappell"; "the south wall so far as then was thought mete"; "the south wall to the soyle of the nether windowes"; "the north wall of tholde Buttrye," "the northe wall of tholde Hall"; "yᵉ reede over the cloyster and yᵉ gystes of the same"; "and the south wall of tholde Hall." The carpenters also took down the roof of these buildings. In 1561 we find a payment to John Brewster for "ij dayes comminge ouer to the Colledge to take downe the roof of the owld Chappell ijₛ." These memoranda shew that this range of buildings stood in the following order: Hall, Buttery[1], Chambers, Chapel. The chambers consisted of a small range, interposed between the east end of the Buttery and the Chapel.

The dimensions of the Chapel have not been recorded, but the position of it is fixed at the eastern extremity of the south range by the documents relating to a dispute between King's Hall and S. John's College, concerning the right and title to a "certain ground lying on the northe party of the Chappell," which was settled by dividing it with a brick wall; King's Hall to have all the ground on the south, and S. John's the residue of the ground on the north, in consideration of which piece the latter body agreed to remit an annual rent of 5s., which the Hall

[1] [This arrangement is confirmed by an entry in the King's Hall Accounts for 1438—39 (ix. 137) for repairs done "camere in fine Aule supra promptuarium."]

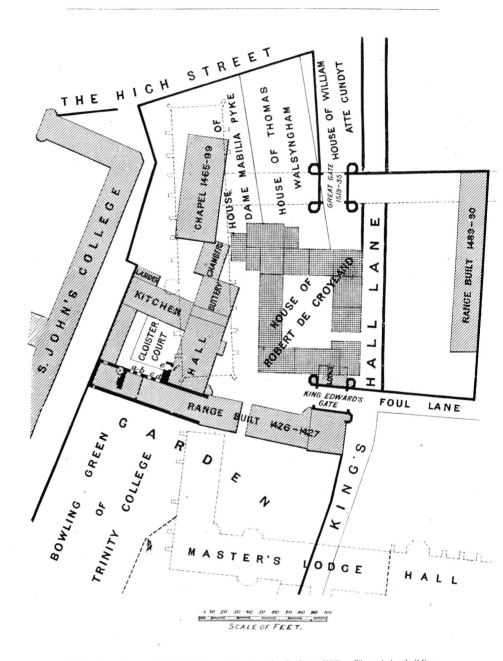

Fig. 6. Ground plan of King's Hall; as determined by Professor Willis. The existing buildings
of Trinity College are indicated by a dotted line.

had constantly paid for the said ground[1]. There are two deeds relating to this dispute. In the first, dated 28 March, 1511, the distance of three points of the intended wall from the Chapel of King's Hall is set down in feet. The second, dated 2 August, 1516, is similar to the former, but the distances of the wall, then actually built, are set down with slight differences, but of course with more precision. As the wall itself existed entire up to 1855[2], the position of the Chapel of King's Hall can be laid down from these data on the map, a reference to which will at once explain the necessity for the negotiation.

The College of S. John, the charter of which is dated 9 April, 1511, only twelve days after the first deed was drawn, was, from the nature of its site, so placed that the south-east corner of its buildings was driven into an inconvenient contiguity with the Chapel of King's Hall. The College was therefore compelled to obtain from the Hall a piece of ground sufficiently large to carry this corner of the street front, and to give room for the entrance of the lane which it was proposed to make along the southern wall of the College buildings. King's Hall was evidently unwilling to give up an inch more ground than was absolutely necessary, and in consequence the division-wall is set out with an abrupt angle opposite to the corner of the College front, which it approaches so closely as to have made it necessary to chamfer the south-east corner of the buildings. We will now quote that part of the second deed which contains the dimensions, adding in brackets the corresponding dimensions as given in the first.

"This Indenture made the secund day of the monythe of Auguste the viij[th] yere of the Reygne of Kynge Henry the viij[th] betwyne the Reuerend Fader in God Geffrey byshope of chester and master or keper of the college called the kynges halle in Cambrige and the felowes of the same on that on party, and master Alane Percy clerke master or keper of the College of saynt John theuangeliste in Cambrige and the fellowse of the same on that other party witnesithe that where variances striffes and debattes were late hade mouede and depending betwene the saide partes for and vpon the right titelle and interesse of a certayne grownde lying on the northe party of the

<hr>

[1] [Further particulars respecting this controversy are given in the Appendix, No. VI.]   [2] [See below, p. 498.]

Chapell of the saide college callede the kynges halle for the whiche
grownde or party of the same the saide master and fellowse of the
kynges halle of long continuaunce he[r]unto haue payde vnto the saide
master and fellowse of the college of saynt John and to their prede-
cessores of the same college v^s yerly

and nowe, by theagrement of bothe partes the saide grownde ys
devidede and inclosede with a breke walle whiche conteynethe in brede
at the est ende ther of betwixthe the saide chapell and the saide breke
wall xxxij^{ti} foote [25 foote]. And also yt contenythe in brede in the
myddes of the same wall fro the saide chapell to the saide wall xxij feet
[21 foote from the said Chapell unto the said new walle ageinst the
south est corner of the new Buyldynge of the said College of St Johns].
And it contenethe in brede at the weste ende of the same walle nexte
to the kychyne of the saide kynges halle xliiij feete of the kynges
standerde [41 foote from the said Chapell towarde the said new walle
of St John's by the est parte of the Kechyn,] and the saide breke
walle strechythe in lengthe towarde the est frome the kynges hygh
waye ledyng frome the high stret towarde the breg stret vnto the saide
kychyne againste the weste.

whiche breke walle the saide master and felowse of saynt Johns
college grauntethe by these presentes for them and ther successores to
kepe sapporte sustayne and maynteyne as ther owne proper walle at
ther owne proper costis and chargis for euer."

By laying down these dimensions on an accurate plan of the
ground, it appears that King's Hall Chapel was inclined more
towards the south than the present one by about six degrees,
and that it projected beyond the eastern walls of the quadrangle towards the street as the Chapel of Trinity College does,
but about twelve or fourteen feet less. It was also farther
distant from S. John's than the present chapel is by fifteen feet
at the east end, and by three or four feet at the west end.

The deed above quoted shews that the Kitchen of King's
Hall was on the east side of the quadrangle, north of the
Buttery. As from the nature of the ground this side was
somewhat shorter than the opposite, or western side, it is probable that it was wholly occupied by the kitchen. This view
is confirmed by the language of the deed, which speaks of the
ground north of the Chapel as extending from the High Street
on the east to the kitchen on the west; and by the agreement
made with S. John's Hospital in 1393, from which it is evident
that the kitchen extended up to the boundary-wall which then
divided King's Hall from S. John's Hospital. The contract for
building it mentions a larder to the east, and chambers to the

west[1]. These latter were perhaps on the ground-floor of the
north side of the quadrangle, for the above agreement alludes
to a Library which at that time evidently occupied a portion,
probably the first floor, of the north side. [The position of the
new Library, begun 1416—17, is more difficult to define. It is
not mentioned in the Accounts referring to the building of the
Chapel of Trinity College (1557—64), and therefore was not on
either the south side or the east side of the quadrangle. When
it was begun a payment was made to S. John's Hospital (p. 442),
which shews that one of its walls must have extended along
the boundary between the two foundations; and an entry in
the Accounts of the Junior Bursar of Trinity College in 1612,
for "making cleane ye longe entrey betwene the ould Liberarie
and S^t. Johns," suggests that the new Library occupied the same
position as the older one had done[2]. This, however, is of itself
improbable: and besides there are reasons for placing the
Library on the west side of the quadrangle. It was near the
Master's Chamber, for the cost of "the chambers adjoining the
Master's chamber" (*expense facte circa cameras contiguas camere
magistri*) is joined with that of the Library (p. 442), and it is
in accordance with ancient collegiate arrangement that the
Master's chamber should be close to the Hall; with the Oratory (p. 443), and the Parlour (p. 444), easily accessible from it.
If therefore we place the Master's Chamber on the first floor at
the west end of the Hall, with the Parlour beneath it, and the
Oratory near it, there will still be room for the Library along
the west side of the quadrangle. The cloister, begun 1418, is
described as extending round two sides of the quadrangle (p. 443).
These were probably the north and west sides, on the latter of
which six arches are distinctly shewn by Hamond. It would
thus provide convenient access from the chambers on those
sides to the Hall; and it would not be required on the east
side, if we are right in supposing that side to have been exclu-
sively occupied by the kitchen.]

---

[1] [One of these was called "the squire's chamber": Roll sent to the Exchequer
1424—31, "pro emendacione vnius guttur inter coquinam et Cameram eidem coquine
annexam voc' le squyerschaumbre iij^s. ij^d."]

[2] [It may be argued that a tradition of the position of the first Library would
naturally survive; and that this entry, notwithstanding its date, may have no special
reference to that of the second.]

Between 1426 and 1437 the west range was prolonged towards the south for a distance of about ninety feet, as far as the lane which, as shewn in the last chapter, then bounded the site on the south. At the same time a new gate of entrance, called King Edward's Gate, was built opposite to the north end of Foul Lane (fig. 1); to the east side of which a porter's lodge was added between 1490 and 1492. These buildings are all shewn by Hamond (fig. 3). A new Master's Chamber was built at the same time as King Edward's Gate, and perhaps a new Oratory also. If we place these together at the south end of the new west range, we shall obtain space enough to the north of them for the gallery which is described as joining the Oratory to the Library. The chambers completed in 1489—90 are probably those which Hamond shews projecting in a westerly direction from a point south of the Great Gate of Trinity College.

Before leaving this part of our subject it will be interesting to quote a passage translated from the Statutes given to Trinity College by King Edward the Sixth in 1552, when the buildings of King's Hall were all in existence, and before a new lodge had been built for the Master of Trinity College. It must be remembered that the Master's chamber therein mentioned is that situated in the range built 1426—37, and not the old one within the quadrangle.

"The Master is to have all the chambers and buildings situated round the cloister, together with the old Hall, Buttery, Pantry, Brewhouse, Kitchen, and all the yards appertaining to the kitchen; besides the orchard to the east, and the garden to the west, with the walled yard which lies close to his own chambers, together with the Pigeon House, all of which originally belonged to King's Hall; also the stable and the hayloft. The chamber in the lesser tower is to be reserved for a Treasury, and the parlour on the ground-floor within the cloister for an Audit-room[1]."

This passage seems to imply further that the Pigeon-House was in the west garden, and that the whole of the space be-

---

[1] Statute *De ambiguis interpretandis et regulis quibusdam generalibus.* " Præses habeat omnia cubicula ac ædificia claustro circumfusa cum veteri aulâ cellâ panariâ et cerevisiariâ culina omnibus areis culine adhærentibus preterea pomarium ad orientem et hortum areamque totam ad occidentem ipsius cubiculis subiectam vallo clausam et columbarium quæ olim Regiæ Aulæ erant item stabulum pro equis et cameram pro feno. Cubiculum vero in minore turre pro ærario libellis codicibus tabulis cæterisque monumentis Collegii et conclave illud inferius infra vetus claustrum pro Ratiocinario reservetur."

tween the Chapel and S. John's was occupied by the yard and garden belonging to the kitchen. There was an entrance to it from the High Street opposite All Saints Church[1].

[The subsequent history of the buildings of King's Hall need not detain us long. It has been already mentioned that the south side of the quadrangle, with the buildings which extended beyond it towards the east, including the Chapel, were pulled down to make way for the Chapel of Trinity College between 1554 and 1561; and in the next chapter it will be shewn that the ranges which stood on the ground now occupied by the Great Court, including King Edward's Gate, were pulled down in the course of the works directed by Dr Nevile. Three sides of the small quadrangle, however, were left standing, which, with the present Chapel on the south side, formed a small court of about the same size as the original one. This is sometimes called the " Inner Court[2]." Loggan (fig. 7) terms it *Hospitium Regis*, a name which evidently represents the *King's Hostell* of the Audit-Books, references to which are found occasionally throughout the seventeenth century. The cloister is last alluded to in 1619—20, when we find a payment "for whiting the Cloisters in the King's Ostell[3]." In 1694 the following conclusion was made:

" 24 April. 1694. Agreed by ye Master and Seniors y^t ye ruinous p^t of ye hostell be puld downe, ye timber sold to the best advantage for ye Coll: and ye slates to be made vse of for ye repaires of ye College, and any other materials that may be vsefull for ye College to be improved for that vse or to be sold.

Jo: Mountagu Mr Coll^{ij}."

The identification of the building here referred to with the remains of King's Hall is rendered certain by entries in the Junior Bursar's Accounts for the same year for "pulling down the old Hostle"; and for " Repayres in the old Hostle on the Bowlingreen side." This last entry shews that when the east and north sides had been pulled down the west side was repaired. The name *King's Hostell* does not occur again, this

---

[1] [King's Hall Accounts, xi. 189 (1451—52). "Item pro claue porte versus ecclesiam omnium sanctorum vj^d."]

[2] [Jun. Burs. Accounts, 1556—57.]

[3] [Ibid. 1619—20. *Extraordinaries.*]

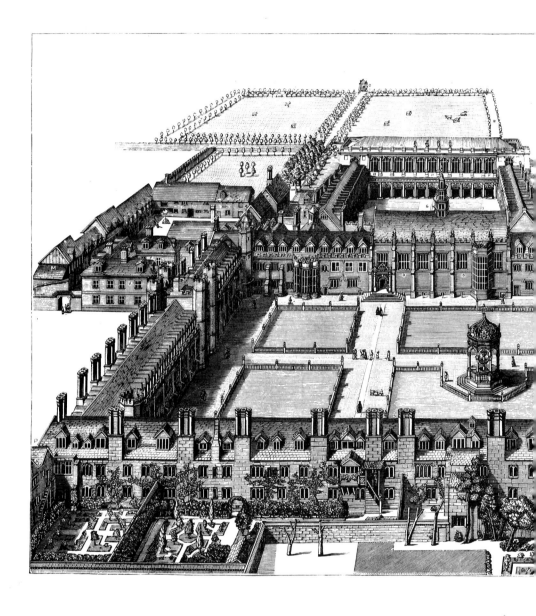

Fig. 7. Trinity College; reduced from Loggan's print, taken about 1688. A, Chapel; B, Old Library; C, Master's Lodge;
I, Kitchen; K, Bakehouse; L, Brewhouse; M, Stable; ⅃

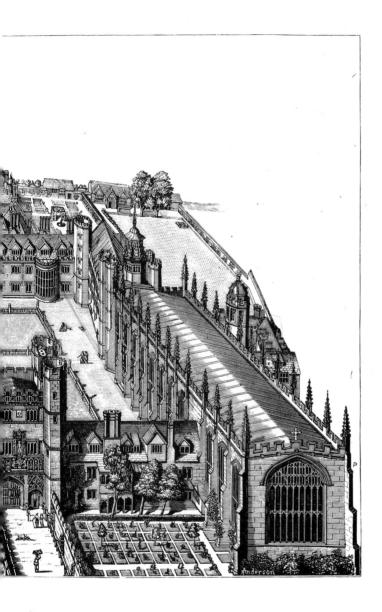

's Hall (*Hospitium Regis*); F, Bishop's Hostel; G, Nevile's Court; H, New Library; leading to the Fields.

range being described as the "building at the east end of the
Bowling Green[1]" in the following century.

A few remains of the west side of the Cloister Court of King's
Hall still exist. These have been indicated by a deep black
tint on the plan (fig. 6). Near the north end of the range there
is a newel staircase, with part of a door-jamb at its foot, shewing that it was entered from the court. Its position therefore
determines the width of the north range. South of this are two
windows (*a*, *b*), each of two lights, of good design, one of which,
with the mold of the jamb, is here figured (fig. 8). They lighted
a large room, the north and south walls of which appear to be
original. South of these again there is a large and handsome

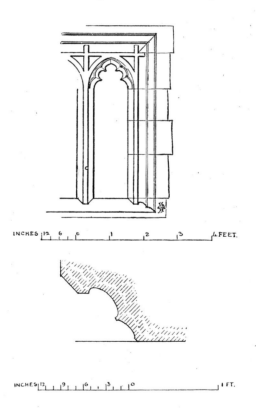

Fig. 8. Window in King's Hall.

[1] [Jun. Burs. Accounts, 1763—64. *Bricklayer.*]

door (c), four centered, with a hood-mold, and close to it a smaller door (d), of plainer design. The original purpose of these doors cannot now be ascertained. Close to this second door the wall is returned, and the north-east angle (e) has original stone coins, shewing that it was an external angle. The doorway on the south (f) appears also to be original. This door gives access to a space which is now used as a passage to the cellars, but which originally appears to have been a sort of tower or turret, lighted by at least one window on the east side. It may be conjectured that it was a belfry to the Hall, entered through a door in the north wall. If this be the case, we can determine the length of the west side of the court with tolerable accuracy. The position of the Hall and adjoining offices has been already discussed, but their actual size cannot be exactly determined.]

CHAPTER III.

GENERAL HISTORY OF THE BUILDINGS OF TRINITY COLLEGE.

[WE have now to trace the steps by which the buildings described in the preceding chapter were adapted to the use of Trinity College. When the site was delivered over to the community created by the charter of King Henry the Eighth, dated 19 December, 1546, they found themselves in possession of one chapel, that of King's Hall; three halls, those of King's Hall, Michael House, and Physwick Hostel; and the chambers of these three bodies, besides those of the subordinate Hostels [1].

The series of Account Books of Trinity College is unfor-

---

[1] The number of these in 1574 is given by Dr Caius (Hist. Cant. Acad. i. 79) as 359, exclusive of servants. In 1548, the College books already exhibit the names of 50 Fellows and 60 Scholars and Bible-clerks; but it is probable that few of these were resident. Michael House was a small community of 21 persons, and King's Hall of 50 persons (Commiss. Docts. i. 120, 150). The numbers lodged in Physwick Hostel were from 30 to 40. This is enough to shew that the number of persons to be lodged in the new College was more than the old buildings could possibly accommodate without enlargement.

tunately imperfect for the first three years after the foundation[1]. It appears probable, however, that the existing buildings were occupied without alteration during that period; for in 1550—51 we find that part of Michael House was being pulled down[2]; and in 1551—52 the same work proceeded, and Physwick Hostel was being similarly treated[3]. In this year the gates of Michael House and Physwick Hostel were walled up; Foul Lane, which separated them, was closed; and a new gate was made across the opening of that lane into Michael House Lane, in the position now occupied by the "Queen's Gate" of Trinity College. The following extracts from the Accounts for 1550—51 illustrate these changes:

"Item to W^m. Hardwicke ye xxvjth. of Marche for .v. dayes, makyng vp Mighell house gates, and settyng vp a payer of gates betwixte Mr Mans chambre and fisicke ostle .... iij^s. iiij^d.

Item...for iij. dayes dawbyng Mighell house gates, and makeng holes for ye other gates.. ij^s. vj^d.

Item for .v. dayes to Ambrose and .v. to W^m. Barnes in wallyng vp of phisicke ostle gates and the new gates .... vj^s. viij^d."

It is clear, however, that part of both Michael House and Physwick Hostel, probably the south side next S. Michael's Lane, was retained, and fitted up as chambers, among which the chamber over the gate in Michael House is specially mentioned; and in 1551 part of Physwick Hostel was repaired for the entertainment of the Duchess of Suffolk[4], sister to King

---

[1] [For 1547—48, 1548—49 the Senior Bursar's Accounts only have been preserved, and for the first of these years they are imperfect; for 1549—50 there are no Accounts; and it is not until 1550—51 that both the Senior and Junior Bursar's Accounts are complete. These Accounts extend from January to January.]

[2] [Sen. Burs. 1550—51. *Recepta casualia.* "It' receaved of Christofer Adeson of benet paryshe in parte of payment of xv^{li}. vj^s. viij^d. for a peace of tholde buyldyng in Mighels house vij^{li}. It' of the same Christofer for an yle Joynyng to ye same house covered with leade vij^{li}. It'...for a pece of thold buyldyng in Mighels house, nexte vnto M^r. Manes chambre vij^{li}." *Expense promiscue.* "It' ... for takynge downe of a wall and ye foundatyon therof and planyng ye grounde in Mighel house corte...xiij^s. iiij^d."]

[3] [Jun. Burs. 1551—52. "It' for reasyng ye fundacyons of ye walles in phisicke ostle x^s."]

[4] [Sen. Burs. 1548—49. *Expens. promiscue.* "It' to M^r. Baggot for glasse and ye hanginges of his chamber in fysicke ostle vj^s. viij^d." Ibid. 1550—51. *In reparationibus.* "It' to W^m. Hardwicke...mending y^e. chamer ouer ye gates in Mighell howse vj^d. ob." Ibid. 1551—52. *Expens. extrav.* "It' for caryng of slate tyle and tymber owt of physyke ostell when my lady of suffolk came thyther xv^s. It'...for

Henry the Eighth.   In fact the Accounts for these years present a mixture of charges for repairing and altering the buildings which were to be retained, and for pulling down those which were condemned, with the old walls of enclosure, and for levelling the ground.   Besides this kind of work, new buildings were undertaken even in the first year, 1547, for a total sum of £229. 17s. 11d. is charged in the Senior Bursar's book under the head of building, unfortunately without particulars, excepting that about £165 is for wages, and that the materials purchased consist of timber, lath, nails, glass, lead, and iron work. Stone and lime came from the Grey Friars[1], whose buildings were pulled down as material was required, and the stone either brought to the College, or converted into lime on the spot. The only items which shew the nature of the work that was being done are a few charges for glazing the windows of the Hall and Buttery in 1547, and for repairing the conduit.   In the following year, 1548, £46. 8s. 4d., was spent under the same head, apparently on repairs and alterations only.

In addition to the buildings left along the south border of the College, the east portion of which would belong to Physwick Hostel, and the west portion to Michael House, it appears probable that part of the west range of Michael House, which contained the Hall and Butteries, was also retained.   The first new work undertaken would be the completion of this range northward, and the connexion of it with the buildings of King's Hall by a second range making nearly a right angle with the former range[2].   The history of these two ranges can be made out from the Accounts; but before we collect the notices concerning them, we will describe a manuscript plan of the College, now preserved in the Library, of which a reduced copy is here given (fig. 10).

glasyng of Simsons chambre in phisicke ostle...It'...for xl dayes worke...abowte ye tower and ye gatehouse in phisicke ostle...xl^s.   It' for a partycyon at ye entrye of phisicke ostle haule..."]

[1] [The site of the Grey Friars, upon which Sidney Sussex College now stands (see the History of that College below), was granted to Trinity College by King Henry VIII, 24 December 1546; but the buildings had been used by Trinity College as a quarry before that date.   The charges for carrying stone and other materials are too numerous for quotation.]

[2] [The probable direction and extent of this second range has been indicated by dotted lines on the plan (fig. 9).]

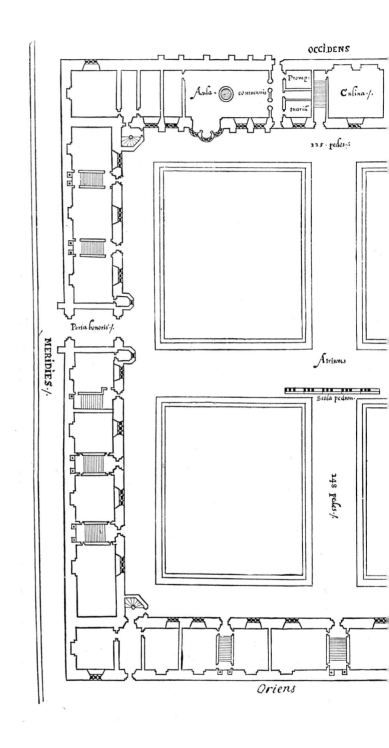

Fig. 10. Scheme for laying out the Great Court of Trinity College

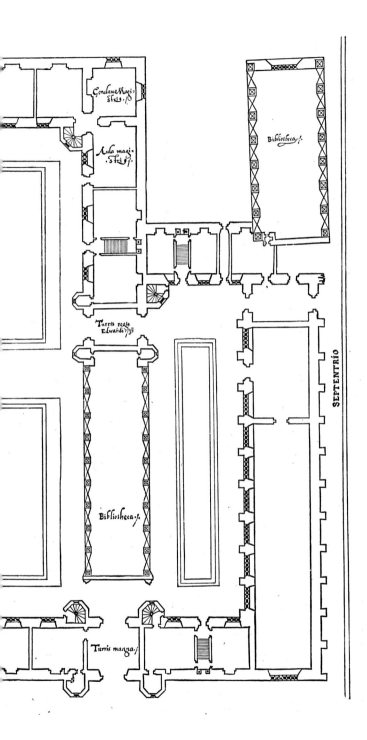

Conclaue Magi-
stri·j·

Aula maai-
·stri·j·

Bibliotheca·j·

Turris regis
Edwardi·j·j·

SEPTENTRIO

Bibliotheca·j·

Turris magna·j·

...an preserved in the College Library, probably made about 1595.

It is an architect's plan, on paper, drawn to scale, but unfortunately without date. Like all early plans, and many modern ones, the lines are all drawn at right angles to each other, although actual measurement shews that the real area of the quadrangle is an irregular trapezium. It must also be observed that the walls are made of the preposterous thickness of five feet throughout. One of the most striking points of this drawing is the representation of a Hall on the west side of the quadrangle, with an oriel corresponding exactly in position, form, and arrangement with that shewn by Loggan (figs. 7, 11); and in "A Perspective View of y^e Great Court of Trinity College in Cambridge, from y^e South," published in 1740, on which it appears to belong to "The Combination, or Publick Room[1]." A comparison, however, of these plates with the plan

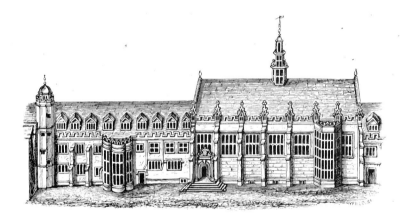

Fig. 11. Hall and south-west corner of the Great Court, after Loggan; from Le Keux's Memorials of Cambridge, ed. Cooper.

before us shews plainly that the windows represented belong to the same building. The present Hall and Kitchen were built in 1604—5, as will be related below; and among the entries in the Building-Accounts we find "Diging the foundacion of

[1] [The letter of reference to the Combination Room is on the building between the oriel and the Hall, and it is therefore uncertain whether the oriel was preserved for the use of that room or merely because it was a picturesque feature of the court. The oriel is also shewn by Hamond (fig. 3), but less distinctly, his plan being on a much smaller scale.]

ye Kitchen wall that goeth thorough ye Old Hall," and "diging at ye old Hall walles." This shews that the old Hall stood to the east of the present Kitchen, and thus identifies its position with the Hall shewn in the plan. When the new Kitchen was built it was intruded into the area of the old Hall (fig. 9), of which the back, or western, wall had to be taken down, but the front, or eastern wall, together with the oriel, was preserved, and made to serve for the Combination Room. Thus far, then, the plan before us is correct, and we may therefore trust it in other particulars. There are, however, some minor differences between these buildings, as shewn there, and in other representations, which deserve notice. There are only two windows between the oriel and the turret at the south-west angle of the court, while Loggan and Hamond (fig. 3) agree in shewing three. Loggan agrees with the plan in shewing two buttresses on this wall. Again, the plan shews only two windows between the oriel and the door to the screens, while Hamond shews four. The door to the screens is succeeded, in his plan, by a high chimney-stack, manifestly belonging to the Kitchen, and by two doors, one of which would belong to the Kitchen, the other to a staircase. The general disposition is the same, but Hamond probably shews that which was actually carried out, while the plan gives the original design which was changed in execution.

The court is entered through a great entrance-gatehouse, inscribed *Turris magna*. Directly opposite to this is a gateway inscribed *Turris Regis Edwardi tertii*, standing about ninety feet south of the present position of that tower. It is placed at the intersection of two ranges of chambers, one of which extends westward for about eighty feet, to join the west side of the court, while the other extends northward. This latter range is clearly a portion of that which was built for King's Hall in 1426—37, as explained in the last chapter.

The plan also shews the quadrangle completed on the south and east sides by a range of chambers, with a gatehouse on the site of the "Queen's gateway" inscribed *Porta Honoris ;* and it also shews a Chapel on the north side, separated by a through-passage from the above-mentioned range belonging to King's Hall. Two positions are assigned to the Library, both drawn on separate paper, and pasted on to the plan. In one of

them the Library connects King Edward's Tower with the great
Tower, so as to cut off a narrow court, 170 feet long by 50
feet wide, between itself and the Chapel, and leave a large
quadrangle on the south, measuring 248 feet from east to
west by 225 feet from north to south; in the other it is placed
to the west of the Chapel, nearly in the position where it was
subsequently built. These designs are sufficient to shew that
the plan in question was made before the old Library, that
namely which preceded the existing one, was begun. The
Chapel, moreover, differs from the existing one in not projecting beyond the street front. It may be concluded, therefore,
that the plan was drawn before the present Chapel was begun.
The plan of the *Porta Honoris* also, and that of the south and
east ranges, differs altogether from the real ones. On the
whole it may be fairly concluded that the plan was made
when the new buildings for the nascent College were commenced, and that it exhibits the general system which was
acted upon in the first instance[1]. At that time it was proposed to set out a quadrangle considerably smaller than the
present one; preserving King Edward's Gate with the range of
chambers between it and the quadrangle of King's Hall.

We may now proceed by the help of the above map to
trace the building-work undertaken after the foundation of
Trinity College. It is clear, as shewn above, that the Hall
was being repaired, or rebuilt, in 1547. As this building is
so essential to the daily comfort of the members, it is very
natural to find it the object of their first attention. According
to the plan (fig. 10), it was only 52 feet long including the
screens, and 25 feet broad, nearly corresponding in dimensions
with the Hall of Peterhouse. It had the Screens, Butteries, and
Kitchen at the north extremity.

The repairs recorded above were continued in subsequent
years, for in 1551—52 the Junior Bursar's Account contains

---

[1] In the Senior Bursar's Accounts for 1594—95, we find: "Item layde out for
divers plottes of the Colledg xlix^s. vj^d.;" an item which implies that when Nevile had
determined to finish the College various schemes were proposed for that purpose. I
should have referred the plan above described to this item, had not the Chapel been
represented so differently from the real one. [It will be shewn however in Chapter V.
that the contract for the Chapel, drawn in 1556, provides for an eastern termination as
indicated on the plan.]

several pages of wages to carpenters, sawyers, bricklayers, and labourers, headed "Expenses of buildings within the College" (*Expense edificiorum intra Collegium*)[1]. An entry " for carrying rubbyge owt of ij chambers by the newe gattes" shews that the south side of the College was being repaired. In 1552—53, there are no entries relating to new buildings, and the Junior Bursar's Account for the next year is lost; but in 1554—55 we find ourselves in the middle of a new building-account, which must have been commenced the year before, and is the subject of a special heading: "Extraordinarye Expenses abowt o^r buyldynges." The position of the building then undertaken is determined by an item dated 18 August, 1554: "gyven vnto father foord for ouer seyng the buylding nextt vnto thold towre x^s;" and by many others in which the chambers next the old tower are mentioned. The "old tower," so repeatedly occurring, is proved to mean King Edward's Gateway-tower by the smith's charge in 1555, "for a keaye of thold towre doore to the treasurye:" for the treasury was placed in this Tower by the statutes of King Edward the Sixth, in 1552, and has always remained there, and the "new building" must be the range of chambers which the old plans (figs. 3, 10) shew to have extended from this Tower westward to join the western side of the court.

The construction of this range was evidently the commencement of a scheme for building the College now definitely adopted, from the terms of the following commission issued 24 October, in the same year, 1554:

"Philipp and Marye by the grace of God Kyng and Quene of Englond and Fraunce, Naples, Jerusalem and Irelond, Defenders of the Faithe, Prynces of Spayne and Cicill, Archedukes of Austridge, Dukes of Millayne Burgondie and Brabant, Counties of Haspurge Flanders and Tiroll

To all and singler oure Justices of peax, Mayers, Shireffes, bailliffes, Constables, and all othere oure Offycers Ministers and faithfull Subiectes to whome thies presentes shall come, gretyng:

We lette youe wite that we haue auctorised and appoynted, and by thies presentes doo auctorise and appoynte, oure trustie and welbeloued George Redmayn, Richard Burton, Thomas Forde Carpentere, Anthony Frenche Carpentere, Robert Baker, and Wyllam Gybbes, and euery of theym, not onely to take vp and prouyde from tyme to tyme for vs and in oure name in all placis aswell within Franchesies and liberties as withoute, all maner of wood, waynscote, Clabbourd, Tymbre, Stone,

---

[1] [These Accounts extend from January to January.]

Tyle, brick, Iron, bourdes, quarters, lathe, Nayle, lime, Sande, Claye, and plastere and all othere thinges requisite and necessarye for the newe edyfiying, buildyng, arreryng, and settynge vpp of oure newe Colledge in Cambridge called Kinge Henry theightes Colledge; but also to take all manere of Carpenters Fremasons Carvers Tylers briklayers and all othere artificers woorkmen and laborers requisite and necessarye for the spedye Fynysshing of the same.

Withe all maner of Caryages for all and singler the premisses as well by water as by lande for oure reasonable prises and paymentes to be made in that behalfe.

Wherfore we woll and commaunde youe and euery of youe by thies presentes to be aydynge helpyng and assystynge the saide George Richarde Thomas Anthony Robert and Willyam and euery of theym in the due execution of this oure Commission. As ye and euery of youe tendere oure pleasoure and woll aunswere to the contrarye at your vttermoste perilles.

In witnes wherof we haue caused thies oure lettres of Commission to be sealed withe oure greate Seale. Witnes oure selfez at West-minster the xxiiijth daye of Octobre the Fyrste and secunde yeres of oure Reignes."

During the year 1554 the work done consisted principally in the collection of materials, mainly stone from the Grey Friars as before; in making special agreements; and in taking down those portions of the old buildings which interfered with the new range. Among the agreements may be cited[1]:

"Covenauntted with Scott the ruyghe mayson to make vpp the new wall and chimnays in ye chambers by thold towre, for eyghtt powndes, xiij^s. iiij^d.

Covenauntted with Samson to make vpp the turrett in the new buylding, for ten pounddes.

Covenauntted wyth Odam to slaytt the new Buylding by thold tower for thre pownddes.

Covenauntted with Robert Wylliamson, to take downe the turrett, ij wyndooys in o^r m^r hys grett chamber, and a pece of the gable end, to Mr Asheton hys chamber, for xlvj^s. viij^d."

The turret mentioned in the last agreement may be identi-fied with that through which access was obtained to the Master's old chambers, as shewn in the plan of King's Hall (fig. 10); and the "Master's great chamber" with one of the rooms in that range. The "new turret" is evidently that at the north-west corner of the court, as shewn in the plan (fig. 10), and by Hamond (fig. 3)[2]. We also meet with a payment "for carry-ing the stones furth of the corner chamber," probably that

---

[1] [Junior Bursar's Accounts, 1554—55, *Extraordinarye expenses about buyldinges.*]

[2] [It did not give satisfaction when first built, for in the Jun. Bursar's Accounts for

entered from the turret, and marked Master's parlour (*Conclaue Magistri*) on the plan.   In the following year, 1554—55[1], we find the new turret being slated, and some of the new chambers boarded and wainscotted; so that the completion of the northern range of chambers from King Edward's Tower westward may be assigned to the end of 1555.

Besides this range, however, it is clear that the portion of the west range, extending from the corner-chamber above-mentioned to the Hall, had been undertaken at the same time. In the Accounts for 1554—55 the new Buttery and the new Kitchen, the position of which is known from the plan (fig. 10), are both frequently mentioned[2]; and in the same year, among the new works, we find the Master's study, bed-chamber, corner-chamber, lowest corner-chamber, middle corner-chamber, outer chamber, kitchen, and buttery alluded to as parts of a structure which is being completed.   These rooms would of course be near the Hall and Parlour assigned to the Master on the plan (fig. 10).   It will be shewn in the history of the Master's Lodge below that the Parlour is now the entrance-hall; the room next to this on the south is now, in part, the kitchen of the Lodge, and was probably always so.   Beyond this, still proceeding southwards, the old plan shews two sets of ordinary chambers, with a common staircase between them, opening into the court.   The southernmost of these was destroyed to make way for the new Hall in 1604.   The windows of the other, and the door to the staircase, are shewn by Hamond (fig. 3), and by Loggan (fig. 7).   This room is now part of the Lodge.

The buildings erected at this time include a gallery, commenced between July and October, 1554.   It was in two floors, and extended in a north-west direction from the Master's corner-chamber[3].   It is shewn by Hamond (fig. 3), and by Loggan (fig. 7), who also gives the ground-plan of it (fig. 4).

1554—55 we find (8 June): "It' payd vnto Robertt Wylliamson as to hys ij men for setting vpp ye stage the new turret, to amend ye topp of y^t xx^d."]

[1] [In this year the Accounts begin to be reckoned from Michaelmas to Michaelmas. The Account for 1555 therefore terminates at Michaelmas in that year.]

[2] [Jun. Burs. Accounts, 1554—55, *The Plummar:* "It' payd vnto Coptt James for plastring ye buttrey new wall...for whytting all the new kytching,..." etc.]

[3] [Ibid. Jan.—Mich. 1554.   "Covenauntted wyth Father Fourd for to buyld the galarye, vnto o^r m^r hys new chamber, for thyrtye powndes."]

The new Chapel was undertaken next. The contracts for it were made in 1555, and the walls were completed in 1564. Its history will be given in detail in a subsequent chapter; for the present it will be better not to interrupt the general architectural history of the College.

There is evidence that a new Library was in contemplation at the same time as the new Chapel; for the two buildings are mentioned together in a commission to provide materials and workmen, which Queen Elizabeth issued in the third year of her reign, 14 December, 1560[1]. It is nearly identical in substance with that issued by Queen Mary in 1554, but the preamble sets forth that "within the College of the holie Trinity ... of the foundacion of our moste Noble father of famous memorye kinge Henrie theighte, there was a Chappell and librarye lately begonne in the tyme of our late deere syster Quene Marye which remayneth at this presente vn-fynished." This preamble is perfectly true as far as the Chapel is concerned; but the Library certainly existed only in inten-tion when this document was issued. The old plan of the College (fig. 10) gives two designs for it, as already mentioned, both raised upon open cloisters. The one between the Great Gate and King Edward's Gate is 110 feet long by 34 feet broad; the other is 93 feet long by 40 feet broad; both being measured externally. The Library however, which was ultimately erected, was 75 feet long by 30 feet broad, and occupied the upper floor of the range between the Chapel and the Master's Lodge (fig. 9). The architectural style of the windows, and still more that of the doorways, enables us to assign the date of it to the master-ship of Dr Nevile. The exact time of the foundation of this range of building is hidden in one of the lost books, but we shall presently see that it was not completed until 1601.

The new Chapel was not the only work proceeding in 1556—57, for in the Junior Bursar's Accounts for that year we find the following entries:

"7o. Augusti [1557] William Carpenter 4 dayes in framing tymber for ye upper floore of ye Chamber at ye newe Chappell ende iijs. viijd.

14o. Augusti. William Hardwyke 5 dayes in setting vpp ye vpper Ruffe of ye chamber at ye newe Chappell ende and burding part of ye same iiijs. vijd."

[1] Printed in Rymer, Foedera, xvi. 605.

The chamber referred to can scarcely have been at the west end of the Chapel, for that stood detached in its original state, as is proved by the presence of a west window, the tracery of which may be seen in the inside of the Chapel, and the hood-mold on the outside. It must therefore have formed part of the range between the eastern portion of the Chapel and the great Gateway, which range has an architectural connexion with the Chapel. An item in the Junior Bursar's Accounts for 1583—84 concerning the pipe "cominge downe from the tower of the greate gates ouer Mr Williams' studye," coupled with another in the previous year "for takinge downe and new lathing and slatinge the whole side towards the streete ouer Mr Bennett's and Mr Williams' chambers," shews that chambers had existed for some time next to the great Tower; and probably those next to the Chapel are meant, as they seem to be the oldest. In Speed's plan the indistinctness of the engraving makes it difficult to decide whether chambers or walls are intended to be represented on each side of the great gate; but in Hamond's plan (fig. 3) chambers are more clearly shewn. They extend southward only so far as the east gable of the range erected by King's Hall in 1489—90.

The Accounts for the years between 1564 and 1593 are very difficult to interpret, from the absence of particulars. The work carried on seems to have been principally ordinary repairs, with the internal completion of the previously-erected chambers[1], and of the Master's Lodging. A few works of minor importance may however be recorded. In 1567 and 1568 a new Brewhouse and water-mill were built[2]; in 1571 a wooden gallery for the Fellows replaced an older one, and alterations to the Master's gallery were carried out[3]; and in 1577 a new parlour, "graunted by M^r.

---

[1] [Some new construction must however have been proceeding at this time from the following entries: Sen. Burs. 1590—91. *Extraord. Charges.* "To Martin for hewing xxx^{tie} windowes at xvj^s. ... xix^{li}. x^s." Ibid. 1591—92. "To ffree masons for windowes and chimney worke, water table, and such like worke vj^{li}. xvij^s."]

[2] [Jun. Burs. Accounts, 1566—67. *Charges aboute the brewhouse etc., and the myllhowse.* "It' for lxxij^{tie} cogges for the mylle wheele at ob' a peece iij^s. It' for vij staves for the myll tryndle xiiij^d."]

[3] [Ibid. 1570—71. *Carpenters.* "To Thomas Watson and some of his men v payre of gloues at the raysing ye fellows gallere ij^s. viij^d." *Sclaters and Masons.* "To Thos. Thacker for taking downe the tyle and the brick of the ould gallerie iij^s." *Ioyners.* "To Pinknei for caruing the gables and frontes of the fellows gallere xxx^s. To Pinckney for caruing the windows and gables of our M^{rs} gallerie xv^s."]

Vicem^r. and the seniors," is mentioned[1]. This parlour was probably over the kitchen, from the mention of "ye windowe y^t openeth out of the vpper buttrie into ye parloure to take pottes in at[2]." In 1585—86 the Tennis court was repaired. Hamond (fig. 3) shews that it then stood at the south-east corner of the College, nearly on the site of the present Lecture-Rooms[3].

In 1593, a fresh impulse was given to the building-work by the appointment of Dr Thomas Nevile to the Mastership[4]. He remained in that office for more than 20 years. The following account of his labours is translated from the "Memoriale[5]" of Trinity College:

"When he first came to the College, he was struck by the remarkable absence of beauty in the buildings, and the want of regularity in the ranges of chambers. Ardently desiring as he did the extension of the College, he conceived a plan which was not unworthy of so grand an object; namely, that the period of leasing lands and rectories should be extended from ten years—a limit which he thought too restricted—to twenty years. When he had had the good fortune to obtain this concession from her serene Majesty Queen Elizabeth[6]—for his object could not be attained by any other expedient—he lost no time in increasing the College with new buildings arranged in quadrangular form, so that it could be said in all truth of him, as was said of Augustus Cæsar, that

[1] [Jun. Burs. Accounts, 1576—77. *Extraordinary Expenses.*]

[2] [Ibid. 1581—82. *Layde forthe to ye locke smithe.*]

[3] In the same year there are entries concerning the "rotten rowe;" "poynting and new laying the rotten rowe on the streete side;" "slating over the rotten rowe;" "work over the rotten rowe in the court side, &c. &c." All this relates to the houses in Trinity Street, south of S. Michael's Church, for by original marginal notes in the Otryngham Book (18 d, 24 g), we learn that these tenements were distinguished by the epithet "Raton Row," of which "Rotten Rowe" is plainly a corruption. They had been the property of Michael House.

[4] [Nevile matriculated at Pembroke College in February 1564—65; proceeded B.A. 1568—69, M.A. 1572. He was Master of Magdalene College from 1582 to 1593; Vice-Chancellor from October 1588 to October 1589 in which year he proceeded D.D.; Dean of Peterborough from March 1590—91 to 1597 when he was made Dean of Canterbury; and Master of Trinity College from 1593 to his death in 1615. He was buried 7 May 1615 in Brenchley's Oratory on the south side of the Nave of Canterbury Cathedral, a chapel which he had restored as a burial-place for himself and his relations. His liberality is commemorated by Bishop Hacket who says (Life of Archbishop Williams, p. 24) that "he never had his like in that Orb, I believe, for a splendid, courteous, and bountiful Gentleman." See also Fuller, p. 236.]

[5] [The history of this volume is given in the Appendix, No. I.]

[6] [Sen. Burs. Accounts, 1595—96. *Extraord. charges.* "Imprimis ye charges of procureing her Maties graunt vnder seale concerning Leases xliij^s. iiij^d."]

when he came to Rome it was built of brick, when he left it it was built of marble.

When he had completed the great quadrangle, and brought it to a tasteful and decorous aspect, for fear that the deformity of the Hall, which through extreme old age had become almost ruinous, should cast as it were a shade over its splendour, he advanced £3000 for seven years out of his own purse, in order that a great Hall might be erected, answerable to the beauty of the new buildings.

Lastly, as in the erection of these buildings he had been promoter rather than author, and had brought these results to pass more by labour and assiduity than by expenditure of his own money; he erected at a vast cost, the whole of which was defrayed by himself, a building in the second court, adorned with beautiful columns, and elaborated with the most exquisite workmanship, so that he might connect his own name for ever with the extension of the College."

To this narrative the epitaph on Nevile's monument in Canterbury Cathedral adds that he caused the buildings which were badly placed to be pulled down. In these alterations he acted under the advice of Ralph Symons, who had already built Emmanuel College, and was afterwards the architect of the Second Court of S. John's College[1]. A portrait of Symons hangs in the gallery at Emmanuel College, and the inscription beneath it records that "he built that College and Sidney College, and thoroughly reformed a great part of Trinity College[2]." Moreover, an entry in the Building-Account for the Hall and Kitchen in 1604: "Inprimis to Ralph Symmons for a module, xv^s," supplies further evidence of his work at Trinity College.

It unfortunately happens that the Junior Bursar's books are missing from 1592 to 1598 inclusive, so that the first six years of Nevile's work are unrecorded[3]. The general nature of his plans however is easily explained, and the dates of some of the best portions of his work can be ascertained, but it may be well to begin with a summary of his labours. When he came into office the court of the College, as shewn by Hamond (fig. 3),

---

[1] [History of S. John's College, Chapter II.]

[2] [The picture shews the head, and the right hand grasping a large pair of compasses. The inscription, of which half is below the head, half above it, is: "Effigies Rodulphi Simons, architecti sua ætate peritissimi, qui præter plurima ædificia ab eo præclare facta, duo collegia Emmanuelis hoc Sydnii illud extruxit integre. Magnam etiam partem Trinitatis reconcinnavit amplissimè." There is also a portrait in the Master's Lodge at Sidney College, without inscription, which is said to represent Symons.]

[3] [The Senior Bursar's Accounts for 1595—96 record £583 spent under the head of new building; and those for 1596—97, £870; but no particulars are given.]

might well be called confused in plan. The old Hall, Kitchen, and Master's Lodge formed the western side, from the northern angle of which the new chambers, including the rest of the Lodge, ran eastward to King Edward's Gateway. From the back of the latter the old western chambers of King's Hall extended northwards to join the Chapel. The latter ran eastwards to meet the small range of chambers which on the east side of the court connected the Chapel with the great gate, and extended beyond it as far as the old south chambers of King's Hall, which still projected into the middle of the intended court[1]. The southern side was occupied by portions of the old buildings of Michael House and Physwick Hostel, with a temporary gateway on the site of the present Queen's Gate. In the south-east corner of the ground the buildings named Edith's Hostel remained undisturbed[2].

Nevile's first work was the completion of the range of chambers on the east side of the Quadrangle, followed by the southern range beginning from the eastern angle, and including the Queen's Gateway tower, which bears its date, 1597, engraved upon its front. In 1599 the range of chambers belonging to King's Hall built 1489—90 (fig. 6), was cleared away, and the great Entrance-tower was "heightened," as the Accounts say. The construction of the north-western part of the quadrangle was the boldest part of Nevile's improvements, because it involved the destruction of previously erected work, and especially the demolition of the evidently venerated gateway of King Edward the Third. In 1600—1, after the completion of the Library with the two floors of chambers beneath, and the prolongation of the Lodge northwards, including the erection of the two great chambers, this Gateway was taken down, and the façade re-erected in its present position. The chambers which had connected this tower with the northern and western sides of

---

[1] [Hamond shews a tree in the portion of the court which originally belonged to King's Hall. We learn from the Accounts that this was a walnut-tree with a seat round it: Jun. Burs. Accounts, 1590—91. "Item for making railes about the trees in the Court, and mendinge the seate about the Walnutt tree iiij^s. viij^d. Item quarters and postes for the railes about the twoe walnutt trees vij^s. vj^d." The walnut-tree was cut down when the great court was laid out: Ibid. 1598—99. *Extraordinaries.* "Item for sawing and squaring out the walnuttree into tymber that stood in the Courte xij^s."]

[2] [Chapter I. p. 419.]

the court having also been pulled down, the area of the noble quadrangle was completed. This was the process of "reconcinnation" attributed to the architect Symons, and the moldings of the doorways, especially those of the southern chambers, and of the north-western chambers under the old Library, as well as those of the Hall, indicate a great change of style. The Fountain was begun in 1602, the new Hall in 1604, and the new Kitchen in 1605. The entrance-porch of the Lodge is also part of Nevile's work. The commencement of the Second Court, or "Nevile's Court," has not been recorded; but it was probably the last in date. Nevile's share in the acquisition of Garret Hostel Green, and of the grounds beyond the river, was recorded in Chapter I. By these works the College was in its principal parts brought to the state of magnificence in which it has, with very few changes, remained to the present day. At the conclusion of these works, it happened that King James the First visited the University for the first time. He came, accompanied by Prince Charles, on the 7th of March, 1615, and was lodged in the College. Two months afterwards, the King repeated his visit, but in the interval Dr Nevile had departed this life, and Dr Richardson had succeeded him. We must now enter into the details of the works thus rapidly reviewed.

The Junior Bursar's Accounts for 1598—99, which, as mentioned above, are the first preserved for this period, contain entries which shew that by that time the east and south sides of the quadrangle were practically completed. Under the heading: "Expences about the Finishing of the last yeres newe building," we find charges which relate entirely to the finishing of chambers, their studies, chimneys, &c. The entries which fix the position of these chambers are the following:

" Inprimis for a staye for ye spoote on ye newe tower .... xviij^d.

Item for taking downe the studd wall that stood at the further ende of the teniscourte and the carridge of y^t. and other Tymber y^t. laye in ye teniscourte vnto ye storehouse .... iij^s.

Item to M^r. Symons for making a stone wall at the ende of M^r. Dickinson's garden where parte of the Teniscourte stoode .... xx^s.

Item to M^r. Symons for making a bricke wall betwene Mr Harrison's and Dr Heron's gardens .... xxx^s.

Item to goodman Peere for making M^r. Harrison's staires to his garden .... ij.

Item for iiij^c and a halfe of Inche borde for Mr Creekes chamber in
the newe building.. xlj^s."

The position of the tennis-court has been already mentioned;
and the "newe tower" mentioned in this Account is of course
that which is still standing at the south-eastern corner of the
quadrangle. The tennis-court stood clear of the walls of the
chambers, and between them and the street, but so near that its
high walls would have obscured the windows. We may therefore feel certain that the "newe building" referred to in these
entries[1] is part of the range on the east side of the court ; and
the gardens are those shewn by Loggan (fig. 7) between the
east wall and the houses in Trinity Street. He also shews stairs
leading down into one of these gardens from the chamber on
the first floor, which probably represent those here mentioned.
This range was therefore completed by the end of 1598 or the
beginning of 1599.

The south side of the quadrangle could not have been begun
in 1594, for in that year (14 September) Richard Cosin, LL.D.,
bequeathed £40 to the College[2]:

"wishing that when they shall builde vp the south rowe of that
Colledge next to Gerrards Ostle and Gunvile and Caius Colledge, or
otherwise, to make the site and platte of the said Trinitie Colledge
more vniforme, that they would bee pleased to bestowe the said Fortie
poundes towardes the erreccon of one whole Chamber there of three
heights, wth mine Armes and mott vppon yt...viz. of an vnder Chamber,
a middle Chamber, and of an vpper Chamber aboue them."

This range must, however, have been begun soon after this
date, for we know that the Queen's Gate, or "Porta Honoris," as
the old plan terms it, because, like the gate built at Caius College
in 1575, it led towards the Schools, was finished in 1597, in which
year the statue of Queen Elizabeth was set up[3]. This position

---

[1] Among these entries we find "Item ..for sawing of stone for the topp of M^r.
Harrison's Baye windowes xvj^d.   Item...for the overcasting of M^r. Harrison's baye
windowe and soe muche of the stone wall as belonged to his chamber and y^t. wch. is
vnder him iij^s. iiij^d." These entries are perplexing, because there are no traces of
such an appendage throughout the College. They might have referred to one of the
projections from the eastern range on the street side; but those appear to be all built
of wood.

[2] [A copy of D^r. Cosin's will is in the Treasury of Trinity College.]

[3] [Sen. Burs. Accounts, 1596—97, *Extraordinarie charges*.   "Item to Cuchey for
carring the Queens personage from London xxxiij^s. iiij^d."]

for the gateway was evidently chosen to place it opposite to King Edward's Tower. The chambers on that side are referred to in an item in the Accounts for the last quarter of the year 1598, "for setting vpp wether bordes over the vpper Chambers towardes Keyes Colledge[1];" and again in 1601—2 the Senior Bursar charges for the plumbers making the "gutters betweene the Hall and the Queenes Tower[2]," which marks the completion of the portion of chambers thus described.

Besides the work done to the south and east sides of the quadrangle, we meet with charges referring to the removal of certain "timber chambers." These were probably the old south chambers of King's Hall; and it appears from such entries as "for overcasting of the tymber chambers that weare removed," that they were set up in some other place. It is not easy to discover their new position; but it probably was in the kitchen-yard, for one item mentions the "making vpp the ende of the bridge by the backhouse of the newe building[3]" and we know from the extract quoted above (p. 414), which defines the length of the great ditch, that the bakehouse stood near the northern end of that ditch, on the ground behind the old kitchen. Mention is also made of "that building wch. was sett vpp by Dr Barrowe[4]." It was of stone, for among the charges for heightening the Great Gate in 1598—99 we find a payment "to Dr Barrowe for freestone of his that was spent in making Cantes for the Tower and iaumes for the windowes." We meet with charges for plaster-

[1] [Jun. Burs. Accounts, 1598—99, *Dayes Worke to Carpenters.*]

[2] [Sen. Burs. Accounts, 1601—2, *Wages paid to Plummers.*]

[3] [The term "new building" in the Accounts for this year is very perplexing, for it sometimes refers to the chambers in the quadrangle, but more frequently to an edifice in some other place, as for instance in the following entry: "Item...for the carring a waye of the Rubbishe that laye behind the newe building, and for the bringing of stone and bricke from thence into the greate Courte at sundrie tymes xxviij^s. viij^d."]

[4] Dr Barrowe may be identified with "Isaack Barrowe of Cambridge, Doctor of Physick," to whom the lease of Mildenhall in Suffolk was granted by Trin. Coll. 21 April 1614 (Conclusion Book). He was admitted Fellow 29 September 1561, held various College Offices, and proceeded M.D. 1570. He married and resided in Cambridge, where he died, and was buried in All Saints' Church, 22 Feb. 1616. He lent money to the College to defray the expense of the new buildings. In one of the MSS. Parne there is a pedigree of the Barrow family, in which he is described as "a benefactor to Trin. Coll.;" and it is shewn that his elder brother Philip was great grandfather to the celebrated Isaac Barrow.

ing Dr Barrowe's building on both sides; and "for slating the
windowes y[t] weare sett vpp by D[r] Barrowe and poynting all that
syde to make it aunswerable to the rest[1]." This entry, taken in
connexion with others quoted below, seems to shew that the
chambers set up by him formed part of the range on the east
side of the Court, but in the absence of certain information, we
can only form conjectures about their position.

In this same year, 1599, we find labourers employed in
digging up old foundations, in levelling the Court, in clearing
away the timber which had not been used, and in removing the
sawpit—entries which shew that the work which had been going
on up to that time was then completed. Two years afterwards, in
1600—1, the rails shewn by Loggan were set up; and battlements were added to the ranges of chambers[2]. The garret
windows were added at the same time[3].

We must next consider the history of the building in three
floors at the north-western corner of the quadrangle, the uppermost floor of which was used as a Library until 1694—95,
when the books were removed into the present Library on the
west side of Nevile's Court.

A new Library had been contemplated so far back as 1556,
when Dr Christopherson (Master 1553—58) bequeathed his
books and manuscripts to the College, to be placed in the
library "as sone as it shall be buylded[4];" and again in 1567
Dr Beaumont (Master 1561—67) bequeathed £40 "towards
y[e] buildinge of a librarie[5]." Moreover two plans for it were
suggested in the old plan of the College (fig. 10). The

---

[1] [The work undertaken at this time evidently included the alteration of some
previously existing chambers: Jun. Burs. Accounts, 1598—99. "Item ... in sawing
of stone vsed about the newe chymneyes and windowes that weare sett vpp and
altered in M[r] Barkers and M[r] Pasfeilds chambers iiij[s]. For altering a windowe in
M[r] Pasfeilds chamber towardes the garden xiij[s]. iiij[d]."]

[2] [These works are thus summarized in the Senior Bursar's Accounts for 1600—1:
"Item...for finishing the last yeres buildinges, for the Courte Rayles, for the imbattell-
ments, and newe windowes on the Hall syde ... vj[c]. iij[li]. v[s]. viij[d]." The Junior Bursar's
Accounts contain numerous entries for the same work.]

[3] [Jun. Burs. Accounts, 1600—1. *Dayes Worke to Carpenters.* "Item to Francis
Hurbie carpenter and Johnson helpinge 5 dayes work about y[e] vpper windowes aboue
y[e] new battlementes x[s]."]

[4] [Dr Christopherson's Will is in the Treasury of Trinity College.]

[5] [Sen. Burs. Accounts, 1566—67.]

Accounts for 1589—90 shew that stone was being collected for it, and that the situation was being again debated[1]. In the Accounts for 1598—99 the Library is not mentioned, but in those for the succeeding two years it is alluded to as a building which had been previously erected though not completed[2]. We must therefore conclude that the range of which it forms part had been begun in one of the years for which the Accounts have been lost, and that it was being finished between 1599 and 1601. In the latter year the stairs leading up to it and the battlements on the north side were plastered, the interior was painted, and the ironwork required for it and the adjoining chambers in the

Fig. 12. Statue of King Edward the Third; from LeKeux's Memorials of Cambridge, ed. Cooper.

[1] [Sen. Burs. Accounts, 1589—90. *Extraordinary charges.* "To on y^t. came from Mr Hall to see the place for the librarie vj^s. viij^d. Paid to Mr Hall for freeston provided for the librarie xxiij^{li}. vj^s. v^d."]

[2] [Jun. Burs. Accounts, 1599—1600. *Layd out to the Blacksmyth.* "It. for a lock y^t. standeth at the farr end of the new library in a lower chamber xviij^d. Item for a new key for the library dore viij^d."]

Master's Lodge was paid for. The following entries illustrate this work :

"Item for 12 double quarters of 12 foote a piece and 10 quarters of 9 foote to the seelinge of the Library staires .... xiiij^s. x^d.

Item for castinge ouer the battlement of the Library next the garden and pointing the Crest.. x^s.

Item to the couper for makinge a tubb for the sealers in the Library......... .... xviij^d.

Item to Nicholson ye Smyth for Iron work belonginge to ye new buildinge, viz. in o^r Mrs Lodginge, the Vicem^r his chamber^1, the new Library, and ye rest of ye chambers [etc.]....................xxxj^{li}. xij^s. xj^d.

Item...for mendinge ye new leads y^t. were cutt away ouer the new Library end next ye M^{rs}. Lodginge, and ouer ye new Tower next ye chappell [etc.] .... xxxij^s. viij^d ^{2}."

The "new Tower next ye chappell" is King Edward's Gateway, otherwise the Treasury-tower, which had been pulled down in the previous year, 1599—1600, and rebuilt in its present position. At the same time the chambers adjoining to it were pulled down also, and the foundations were laid of the great dining-room of the Master's Lodge and of the chambers to the north of it, as the Accounts shew :

"Item to Litle for helping to remove M^r. Cookes thinges out of his Chamber when it was pulled downe ... . iiij^d.

Item to him more for helping to Remeve the boxes and Coffers out of the Tower .... iiij^d.

Item to Hughe the Brewer for removing of boxes out of the Tower .... viij^d.

Item to Chapman the Joyner for taking downe the presse in the Tower and setting it vpp againe .... vj^d.^{3}

Item after the walls weare digged, for digging the foundacion of the Tower and our Mrs Hall and the rest of the Chambers to .v. laborers for the space of .x. weekes for carring greate stones forthe of the Courte and storing of them vpp for the next yeres building .... x^{li}.^{4}"

In the following year, 1600—1, the niche containing the statue of King Edward the Third^5 (fig. 12) was set up; and in

---

^{1} The Vice-Master had his new rooms under the rebuilt King's Tower. Jun. Burs. Accounts, 1600—1. *Dayes Worke to Carpenters.* "Item to a carpenter for 13 dayes worke in makinge Mr Vicem^r his new studies and roumes vnder the new tower by the chappell xiij^s." The "tower by the chappell ende" is frequently contrasted with "the tower next to the Mrs Lodginge."

^{2} [Jun. Burs. Accounts, 1600—1. To the entries quoted in the text may be added: "Item to a labourer sweeping the new Librarie, carryinge forth Reed, helpinge to carrie home ye haires y^t were vsed by the Painters ij^s."]

^{3} [Ibid. 1599—1600. *Extraordinaries.*] ^{4} [Ibid. *Layd out to Bricklayers.*]

^{5} [Jun. Burs. Accounts, 1600—1. *Extraordinaries.* "Item to the Caruer for

1610 Thomas Tennant, citizen of London, added a clock and bell[1].

We learn that the Master's Lodge was proceeding at the same time, from such items as: "mending ye cante window on the garden syde and bringinge vp of the wall vnder the window in the M^{rs} garden;" "for 33 flaunders tyles to paue the chimney in the M^{rs} great chamber;" and, lastly, from the following, which serves as a general summary of points to which the work was directed:

" Item payd to diuerse labourers for 161 dayes at 8^d ye day...in carry-inge Rubbish and mouldes out of ye master's garden, digginge and leuell-inge in ye masters lower roumes, parlour and hall, Mr Wright's chamber, and Mr Hunt iunior his chamber, fetchinge wainscotes, clayboardes from Mr Whartons, carryinge of Reed, boardes, and vnloadinge great tymber, carryinge of Lyme, Lathe, Brickes, and other thinges...v^{li}. vij^s. ij^{d2}."

A tower, called "our Master's Tower", is frequently mentioned in connexion with the work at the Lodge. This is the turret-stair at the north-west angle of the court (fig. 7). It will be re-membered that a similar turret stood in the angle of the chambers that were pulled down (fig. 3). An item in the Accounts for 1599—1600[3], "setting vpp ye staires in our M^{rs} lodgyng to vse when ye other weare taken awaye" refers to a temporary stair erected when the above demolition took place, and also shews the use of the older staircase, and possibly of that which re-placed it.

The documentary evidence we have now collected shews that the foundations of the prolongation of the Master's Lodge north-wards were dug in 1600, and that the walls were carried up in the following year; that the walls of the Library and chambers

makinge 2 pillers about King Edwards Picture vj^s. Item to the same Caruer Paris Andrew in ye time of his sicknes for his releif v^s."]

[1] [Sen. Burs. Accounts, 1609—10. *Extraordinaries*. " Item to a workman that brought Mr Tennantes clock and diall to the College xx^s." The *Memoriale* thus records his gift: " Thomas Tennant Ciuis Londinensis commune aliquod huic augustissimo Collegio beneficium deferre summopere desiderans, septentrionalem structuræ plagam Horologio suis impensis ornandam curauit Anno 1610." His bell is still in use, bearing the following inscription, the words being divided by Fleurs de lis:

TRINITAS . IN . UNITATE . RESONAT . 1610.

RICARDUS . HOLD . FELD . ME . FECIT.]

[2] [Ibid. 1600—1. *Layde out to Bricklayers*.]

[3] [Jun. Burs. Accounts, *Dayes Worke to Carpenters*.]

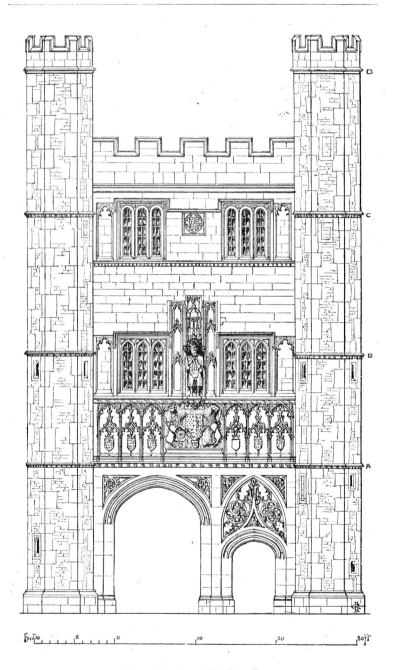

Fig. 13. East front of the Great Gate.

Fig. 14.   West front of the Great Gate.

beneath it had been erected in the earlier and unrecorded part
of Nevile's period, but were completed as to the structure in
1601 ; and lastly, that King Edward's Tower was taken down
and removed to its present position in 1600. The staircase
referred to as "the Library staires" is the present square staircase, next to King Edward's Gateway (fig. 9, *B*), and the
evidence that it was meant for the Library, and not merely
for the chambers, explains its unusual size.

Between the years 1600—1, and 1612—13 no Junior Bursar's
Book has been preserved except that for 1605—6, so that we
have to depend on the Senior Bursar, Mr Gregory Milner, for
information. His Account for the year 1601—2 records the
construction of the Fountain, the particulars of which we will
postpone to a future chapter, and quote here only the summary
of the work done, in which other matters are included :

"Item ther is paid by Mr Milner for the buildinges of this yere,
the Fountaine, Imbatlements, wainscottes in the Liberarie and
glasing .... v^{c}xl^{li}. xiij^d.

Item paid to diuers massons for taske worke at Barrington Quarrey
working 1400 foote of white stone for the batlementes .... vi^{li}. xij^s.

Item paid to diuers bricklayers raising in-worke of the imbatlements,
laying foundacions of the fountaine, and diuers vaultes; and to laborers
diging foundacions and vnloading freestone and seruing the setters at
the fountaine and imbatlements all sommer ; and to Swayers [sawyers],
conteyning the whole yere.. xxix^{li}. xiij^s. iiij^d."

We will next consider the work done to the Great Gate. It
was shewn in Chapter II (p. 453) that this Gate, begun in 1519,
had been completed, so far as was then thought necessary, in
1535 ; but now, as part of the improvements to the Great Court,
the height of some portion of it was increased, and a uniform
appearance was given to it on the north, west, and south sides
by the application of stucco. The following entries are the only
ones which throw any light on the work done, the precise nature
of which will be discussed below :

" Item laid out to John Symes and his laborers for the sawing, working,
and setting vpp of the Cantes[1] that weare made for the hightning of the
greate Tower, and plastering the same on the insyde .... v^{li}. xviii^s.

Item to John Symes for .v. Tunn of freestone sawed out for the
Cantes for the Tower and Jaumes for the windowes .... iij^{li}.

Item...for the overcasting of the greate Tower 10 dayes xx^s.[2]"

---

[1] These are the obtuse-angled stones which form the edges of the octagonal turrets.

[2] [Jun. Burs. Accounts, 1598—99. *Extraordinaries. Layd out to Bricklayres.*]

The statue of King Henry the Eighth in the central niche on the east front of the gate was commenced at the same time[1]; but the death of the carver—evidently the artist called above Paris Andrew, who had already executed the niche for King Edward's statue, to whom the work had been entrusted in the first instance—caused it to be laid aside, and it was not resumed until 1614—15, when a general ornamentation of the gate was undertaken, probably to commemorate the two visits of King James the First, which took place in March and May of that year. The Accounts are fortunately unusually minute, and we can identify most of the details of the decoration. The stone for one of the statues, apparently that of King James, was quarried at Barrington[2]; but they were all carved in London, and sent to Cambridge when finished. On their arrival the canopies on the west side of the gate were set up, with the three coats of arms above them. In the Senior Bursar's Accounts for 1613—14 we find:

"Item to Goodman Smyth of Barrington for ye mending of his Cart broken with a great stone brought from thence for the king's statue .... v^s. vj^d;"

and in those for the following year, 1614—15:

"Item to John Smythe the caruer for caruing the Kinge's statue...x^l.
Item to him for goeing to London to helpe to carue yt............ x^s.
Item to 8 porters halfe a day carring the statue .... vj^s.
Item to Ides bringing the Queene and Prince's statues from London weighing 2500^li at 3s. 4d. .... iiij^li. iij^s. iiij^d.
Item to Ides bringing King Henrie's statue from London with the Queene and Princes Armes weighing 2400 di. at 3s. 4d. ...... iiij^li. xx^d.
Item to Mr Ouer for caruing the Queene, Prince, and King Henrie's statues and the Queene and Princes Armes, and packing them vpp .... lxii^li. xv^s. ix^d.
Item to Ireland prouiding Cartes, raiseing loades of white stone at Euersden pittes, for the Queene and Prince's statues, creastes, and healping to scaffle and load y^t 4 dayes at 16^d .... vs. iiij^d.

[1] [Sen. Burs. Accounts, 1600—1, *Extraordinarie Charges*. "Item to Parris caruer deceased for his caruinge King Henrie and for his releefe in his sicknes xxxvij^s. vj^d."]

[2] [The reigning King would be described simply as "the king;" and "the king's statue" therefore denotes that of King James. As the arrival of it is not specially mentioned in the Accounts, it had probably been finished in the previous year, for which the Junior Bursar's Accounts are missing; for in the next year we meet with numerous references to "the Kinges picture," such as, under the head *Laid out to the Smyth:* "Item for lenthning a wymble to boare a hole throughe the kinges picture viii^d. Item for a boult to make the kinges picture fast ij^s."]

Item for caruing the Kinges armes on the topp of the in syde of the great gates to John Smythe.. iij^{li}. x^s.

Item to Thorpe about the nessetes[1] pictures and Armes 6 days at 18^d .... ix$s$.

Item for a horne of Iron for the Kinges Armes .... xij$d$."

The decoration of the outside of the gates proceeded at the same time:

"Item to Thorpe .6. dayes making of 6 crownes for the out syde of the gates [etc].. ix$s$.

Item to Thorpe .6. dayes about the Armes and batlementes at 18^d .... ix$s$.

Item to Kendall and his man .2. dayes sodering crownes and brest plates for the pictures .... ij$s$.

Item to Kendall's man .2. dayes laying the leads after the masons, setting on flashes and sodering on the greate Tower .... ij$s$.

Item to Kendall and his man one daye laying a gutter of lead over the Kinges picture .... xij$d$.

Item to him for sodering .6. other Crownes for the outsyde of the gates and for soder .... iiij$s$.

Item to Kendall's man for setting on those Crownes .... xij$d$.

Item for sodering King Henrie's George and for soder .... x^d.

Item .2. laborers bringing down stone and clensing the greate tower leades .... xvj^{d}[2]."

Lastly, "the gates," by which expression the whole gatehouse is evidently meant, were painted on both sides, and the crowns were gilt[3]. The posts in front of the gate were set up at the same time[4].

[The history of the Great Gate has brought us down to the

---

[1] [This word occurs frequently in this Account: "Item to John Symes his wyfe for 3 tunn of Freestone vsed about the Nessitts at 14^s the tunn xlij^s. Item to Thorpe .61. dayes about the Nessitts ix^s." This is followed by the wages of 5 other labourers for the same time; and by a similar charge for a period of 5 days.]

[2] [Jun. Burs. Accounts, 1614—15.]

[3] [Sen. Burs. 1614—15. *Buildings and out Workes.* "Item to Newton for paynting the outsyde of the gates 20^{li}. for guilding 6 crownes ouer the ·6· Armes [etc.] xxv^{li}. Item to Robert Streatter for paynting the insyde of the gate xxxj^{li}." Jun. Burs. 1614—15. *Extraordinaries.* "Item to Preist the paynter for Spannishe white and size for the greate tower xv^s." "Item for whiting the front of the greate tower before the painters begun...x^s. Item to Mr Parris for the hier of .16. double haircloathes for the insyde and outsyde of the greate gates xxxij$s$." The Queen's Tower and the Hall were similarly treated.]

[4] [Sen. Burs. 1614—15. *Buildings and out Workes.* "Item to John Smyth for caruing the .8. eschochions on the postes at the greate gates at 3^s. and finishing them xxxiiij^s. Item to John Smythe .6. dayes caruing the greate postes...xv^s."]

year 1615. We must now return to the year 1604, in which
the Hall (fig. 15) and Kitchen (fig. 16) were commenced.] The
history of their construction has fortunately been completely
preserved in a separate Account-book now kept among the
manuscripts in the College Library.

Fig. 16. Interior of the Kitchen, looking west.

The architect was Ralph Symons; but the dimensions were

settled by the sensible plan of examining existing Halls. The writer of the Account makes the following entries:

" Inprimis to Ralph Symmons for a module .... xv[s].
Item for horshier to London for my self and John Symmes   xv[s].
Item giuen at London to Carpenters and Keepers of dyvers Halles to viewe and measure them .... x[s]."

The Hall selected was that of the Middle Temple, which is precisely the same in length, breadth, and height, as the Hall of Trinity College[1], a general view of which is here given (fig. 15). Both of them measure 100 feet by 40 feet, including the screens, and are 50 feet in height[2]. Their roofs differ entirely in framing and decoration, as might be expected from the change of taste which had taken place between 1572 and 1604 (the respective dates of the two), and also from the different architects employed. John Symmes or Symes, who accompanied the Bursar, was the builder, and appears in the Account as overseeing and setting out the work. He began working about the Hall on Friday, 9 April[3], 1604, and the last payment for slating the roof was made 3 October, 1605[4], which marks the substantial completion of the structure.

---

[1] [Dugdale, Origines Juridiciales, fol. Lond. 1666, p. 188, says: " The fairest structure belonging to this House [the Middle Temple], is the Hall, it being very large and stately; the first preparation whereunto was in the year 1562 (5 *Eliz.*) though not finished till the year 1572 (14 *Eliz.*)...In 17 *Eliz.* [1574—75] the new Skreen in the Hall was made." For these dates he quotes the Register of the House, and Stow's Survey of London. Compare also a Memoir on the Hall of the Middle Temple, in Weale's Quarterly Papers on Architecture, Vol. ii. 4to. London, 1844; where a ground plan, elevation, view of the interior, and details will be found.]

[2] The other large Halls which the Bursar was likely to visit on this occasion were:

Westminster,	239 feet	× 68 feet and 42 feet high.	
Guildhall,	153 ,,	× 48 ,,	
Hampton Court,	106 ,,	× 40 ,, and 45 feet high.	
Lambeth,	93 ,,	× 38 ,,	
Lincoln's Inn,	62 ,,	× 32 ,,	
Crosby Hall,	54 ,,	× 27 ,, and 40 feet high.	

Christ Church Hall, Oxford, is 115 feet × 40 feet and 50 feet high, but it does not appear that this was inspected upon the occasion.

[3] [The first payment under the head: "Wages payd to freemasons and to Brycklayers Anno d[ni]. 1604" is: "Aprill xiiij[th]. Imprimis paid to John Symes for fiue daies worke beginning to worke about y[e] Hall v[s]. x[d]." In 1604 Easter Day fell on April 18; and April 14 was therefore a Wednesday. On the assumption that Saturday was included in the five days, work began on Friday, April 9.]

[4] [The commencement of the slating is set down as follows: "An[o]. 1605, Aprill

J.A.Bell.   J.Le Keux.

Fig. 15.   Interior of the Hall of Trinity College, looking north; from Le Keux's Memorials
of Cambridge, ed. Cooper.

The foundation of the Kitchen was begun on Thursday, 7 July, 1605, and the last payment to the slaters, for work on it and on the Buttery, was made 24 November in the same year.

[The stone used was "white stone" (clunch) from Barrington and Eversden, limestone from Clyffe, that is, King's Cliffe in Northamptonshire[1], and "ragge" from Cambridge Castle. No materials from the Grey Friars are mentioned. The slates came from Northamptonshire. The stone for paving the Hall was provided by Gilbert Wigge, probably the same person who was partner with Ralph Symons in building the Second Court of S. John's College; that for the steps was purchased from a quarry called the Earl of Lincoln's quarry[2]].

For the history of the woodwork we have the following particulars. A bargain was made with the master-carpenter, Francis Carter, 27 February, 1603—4, to execute the carpenter's work of the Hall, Butteries, Kitchen, etc. for £230. The first payment was made to him 14 June, 1604, and the last 14 September, 1605, when he had received £212. On 21 September, 1605 he agreed to roof the Kitchen for £37, the last payment for which was made 23 October[3]. He had then received £28. 10. 0. We do not know when the rest of the money was paid.

The panel-work of the interior was executed by Andrew Chapman, with whom an agreement was made 21 February, 1604—5, of which the following note has been preserved :

"Item given to Andrew Chapman in earnest to seele ye Hall with waynscott and worke in such sort as is set downe in a covenant betwixt vs and for such prises ………………………………… iij^li. vj^s. viij^d."

The payments to him began 14 March, and ended 11 July,

xx^th. Item given in earnest to Thomas Yates to slate ye Hall at xiij^s. ye pole, every pole to conteyne xvj foote dj according to covenantes drawne betwixt vs, v^s."]

[1] [5 January, 1605. "Item paid to John Symes for his man going to Clyffe Quary to provide stone vij^s. iiij^d." See Vol. i. p. 178.]

[2] ["Item given to Richard Crispe for bringing in a sample of ye Earle of Lyncolnes stonne for steppes xij^d. Item given to him for going to Mr Receavor and from thence to the Earles quarry and set men on worke iij^s. iiij^d."]

[3] "Feb. 27, 1603. Item given to Fraunces Carter in earnest to finish ye Carpenters worke of ye Hall, Butteries and Kitchen, and other roomes according to ye Covenants drawne betwixt us for ye somme of ccxxx^li ; xl^s." "21 Sept. Item paid to him vppon a bargayne to frame finish and set vp ye roofe of ye kitchen and for other workes specified in a certenne note betwixt vs for ye somme of xxxvij^li in parte thereof xl^s."

when they had amounted to £40, exclusive of the earnest-money. The wood had been previously purchased at Lynn[1]. Subsequently, 19 October, 1604, we find:

"Item to him for altering certenne pannelles of his worke for the splaies of ye greate wyndoes wch worke was besides his bargayne ... xxx^s.'

The Screen, which is the most beautiful part of the woodwork, was executed by Francis Carter, as we learn from the following entry dated 27 April, 1605:

"Item paid to Fraunces Carter for parte of his bargayne for the workmanship of a skreene for ye hall .... v^li."

Unfortunately we have no further information respecting the woodwork, except that £100 was contributed by Mr Hide[2]; whose share in it is commemorated by his arms being placed over the Screen on the west side, opposite to those of Nevile. It is probable however that Andrew Chapman had, at any rate, a share in the execution of it, for we find that £6. 10s. 0d. was paid to him "in full discharge of his bill for sealing of the hall" in 1607—8[3]; and as he had been paid three years previously for the panel-work along the sides of the Hall, the work then completed must have been either the panelwork over the dais, or the screen; but it was most probably the latter, for the wall behind the dais would hardly have been left bare, when the other walls were decorated.

The Building-Account for the Hall makes no mention of the glass for the windows. This was not finally completed until 1607—8, partly at the expense of the College, partly from the gifts of benefactors. Sir Robert Wroth gave £20 "to glaze the east oriel of the Hall, and decorate it with coats of arms"; and Sir Ralph Hare, formerly Fellow, gave £8 towards a similar

---

[1] [2 February, 1604. "Imprimis paid for one hundred waynscottes bought at Lynne Marte xxvj^li." Subsequently, under the head of *Extraordinaryes*, we find: "Item paid for horshier for my self and one to goe with me to provide waynscottes Lead and Deale planks, being abroade vj daies at Lynne xiiij^s."]

[2] [The "Memoriale" records: "Mr Hide armiger, quondam firmarius Rectoriæ de Eaton in Comitatu Bedfordiensi, Centum libras Collegio munificentissime elargitus est, ad incrustandos Aulæ parietes opere intestino."]

[3] [Sen. Burs. Accounts, 1607—8, *Extraordinaries*. The Account for 1606—7 is unfortunately lost.]

treatment of the west oriel. Other benefactors gave smaller sums towards other windows, not specified[1].

The following curious items from the Accounts refer to the construction of the lover in the centre of the roof. They shew that it was originally ornamented with a vane at each angle of the six sides of both the stages:

> "Item given in earnest for y[e] making of one greate fayne for y[e] Lover at iij[li] and xij lesser faynes at v[s] a peece .... ij[s]. vj[d].
> Item to y[e] Payntors for coullering y[e] Lover vppon a bargayne... iij[li].
> Item for vij[li] Tynn to Tynn y[e] spire of y[e] Lover .... v[s] x[d].
> Item for quicksilver vsed in y[e] same worke...... .... v[s]. iiij[d].
> Item to John Atkynson for 50 foote half ynch bord to cover y[e] type[2] of y[e] Lover .... iij[s]. ij[d]."

In order to complete the history of the structure, a careful summary of the expense, drawn up from the Account-book by Dr William Linnett[3] at the latter end of the seventeenth century, is subjoined:

	£	s.	d.
"Wages to freemasons and bricklayers............	304.	10.	6
To labourers of all sorts	185.	10.	1
Scaffolding	021.	06.	6
Carting and carriages	038.	14.	4
White stone, Rag, and freestone.......................	196.	04.	3
Timber, board, plank, and Carpenters work	546.	18.	11
Wainscote and Joyners work	075.	17.	8
Sand and Clay	079.	15.	4
Brick	103.	07.	2
Lime and filling-stone	171.	17.	8
Slate, tile, pauing-stone, slating and tiling	067.	08.	7
Lead and Plombers work	092.	14.	1
Lath, Hair, Tile-pins, mortar, tubbs, pails, Hodds, Wheelbarrows, skepps, ladders, sieves, and other necessaries	014.	14.	4
Ironwork of all sorts	084.	19.	4
Extraordinaries.........................	009.	13.	1

Summa totalis £1993. 11. 10."

The Hall as thus completed has descended to us with very slight alterations. [On the side towards the Great Court the

---

[1] [Ibid. 1607—8, *Extraordinaries.* "Item, paid to Charles the Glasier in full discharge and payment for all the glasse in the hall windows xvj[li]. iiij[s]. iij[d]." The donations are recorded in the *Memoriale.*]

[2] A "type" is a small cupola.

[3] [A note by Prof. Willis in another place says that Linnett's handwriting was identified by Dr Edleston.]

steps are now semicircular, whereas in Loggan (fig. 7) they are shewn as square. This change had been made previous to 1740[1]. At some period subsequent to that date the square panel above the cornice of the porch, together with the decorative work which flanked and surmounted it, was removed; and the cresting over the eastern oriel, similar to that over the Fountain, was replaced by a parapet.

The relation of the new Hall to the older buildings was discussed at the beginning of the chapter, and it was shewn that the west wall of the old Hall was pulled down to make way for the new Kitchen (fig. 16). The plan (fig. 9) shews that the present Buttery forms part of the Hall-building, and the different offices erected are thus enumerated in the Building-Account:

"Item paid...for finishyng ye wall worke and chymnyes of ye kitchen, butry, surveying place, with the Chambers over them and for paving ye Cellers and seeling them, and making a wall to inclose the Kytchen Yard, in parte of xxxj^{li}. for this worke .... vj^{li}. x^s."

The room over the Buttery—part of which is now the small Combination Room—extended through the whole width of the building, from an entry respecting "ye wyndoes on ye Court side in ye chamber over ye buttrie." These are probably the three windows shewn by Loggan, and the room which they lighted was approached by a staircase entered from the court by a separate door, also shewn by him, next to the oriel of the old hall. Again, besides the buildings already enumerated, a building containing a staircase for the use of the Master is mentioned. This was an independent structure with a separate roof[2]. An examination of the Lodge shews that it may be identified with the staircase at the north-west corner of the Hall (fig. 9, O).

The erection of the Hall completed the arrangements of the Great Court. As the buildings which surround it have not been materially altered since that date, with the exception of the Master's Lodge, and the range which intervenes between the Hall and the south-west corner, it will be

---

[1] [They are shewn as semicircular in the engraving by West dated 1 Feb. 1740.]

[2] [9 October, 1605. "Item given in earnest to Thomas Yates to Slate and Tyle ye Kytchen, Buttery and Staire case...ij^s": and among the payments to the Plumbers we find a charge "for laying one gutter at ye Kitchen and one at ye M^{rs}. Staircase."]

best to narrate at once the few changes which have taken place, reserving for a future chapter the history of the Chapel, Master's Lodge, and Conduit, and then to compare the existing structures with their recorded history[1].

The Great Court remained as Nevile left it until 1700—1, when sash-windows were inserted into the front of the Master's Lodge by Dr Bentley (Master 1700—42), followed, in 1723, by a similar alteration to the chamber on the first floor over the Queen's Gate[2]. This was succeeded, in 1750—51, by a general application of stucco, under the direction of a Mr Denston, from Derbyshire. He brought his own workmen to Cambridge, and, to judge by the number of square yards paid for, they stuccoed the whole court, with the exception of the south side, and the clock-tower—neither of which have ever been so treated[3]. At the same time the ruinous portions were repaired. In the following year new frames were placed in the windows. As this repair is charged under the head " Plumber and Glazier," and sash-frames are specially mentioned, it evidently consisted in the removal of the old leaded casements, and replacing them by wooden frames.

In 1753—54 we find that the whole south side, including the Queen's Gate, underwent a repair so extensive as almost to amount to a rebuilding. The following extracts from the Junior Bursar's Accounts under the heading "Great Court," give detailed information respecting what was done:

"To Mr Woodward for the New Arms in the Queen's Gate...... 2. 2. 0
"A Bill for new facing and repairing ye Wall from the Bell Turret to the Queen's Gate: viz. New Ashler under all ye Basements, New

---

[1] [In the following narrative those repairs only will be noticed which have affected the architectural character of the Buildings.]

[2] [Sen. Burs. Accounts, 1722—23. *Extraordinaries.* " Paid several Bills for work done in ye Chamber over the Queen's Gate 39 . 03 . 00."]

[3] [Sen. Burs. Accounts, 1750—51. *Extraordinaries.* "To Mr Denston his Expences for Advice about Stuckoing the Great Court 2. 2. 0." Jun. Burs. *Courts.* " Repairing many Ruinous Parts of the Front of the Great Court, lately plaistered, and providing Tiles and Spikes for the Plaisterers 40. 4. 2½. To Mr Denston, from Derbyshire, for Stucco-Work in the Gt Court in part of his Bill of £115. 5. 10 for 2767 Square Yards, at 10d per sq. yard 104. 10. 0." *Extraordinaries.* "To Mr Denston's Men after finishing their Work, towards bearing their charges Home 0. 10. 6." The total expended was £300. 11. 8.]

Window Heads and Jambs; new Ashler between the Window Heads
and Cornice; new Parapet in ditto over the Cornice: and facing and
pointing the whole, etc............................. .... 120. 7. 7

"For repairing the Queen's Gate, viz. 2635 feet new faced and
pointed; 71 feet of New Ashler; 15 D° in New Battlements; 13 D°
in the Jambs; 52 D° in Window Cases; 71 D° in the Base; and for
Scaffolding, Mortar, etc..60. 11. 1

"The Wall from the Queen's Gate to Mutton-Hall[1] finish'd as in
the former account above; viz. 3066 feet new faced and pointed;
310 feet of Parapet in Ashler; 304^{ft} Cornice D°; 373^{ft} in Window
Cases; 20^{ft} new Base; 351^{ft} under the Base; Scaffolding, Mortar,
etc. 204. 3. 1

"For Mutton-Hall-Turret finish'd as above; viz. 729 feet new
faced; 7^{ft} new Coping; 25^{ft} of ashler; 79^{ft} Window-casing and 39^{ft}
under the Basement, etc.......... ....21. 10. 8."

Between 1770 and 1775 the turret at the south-west corner
of the court, in which the hall-bell hung, was pulled down;
and the range extending thence to the Hall was rebuilt in an
Italian style, under the direction of Mr Essex; as will be related
in the history of the Combination-Room below. The change
was greatly admired at the time, and shortly after its completion the building is described as in an "elegant stile, and
a specimen of the manner in which it is proposed to rebuild
the whole quadrangle[2]."

[1] [The place thus designated seems to have been a chamber on the ground floor
at the end of the east range, which subsequently gave its name to the corner in which
it was situated, and to the turret at the S.E. angle of the Court. Before the new
Lecture-Rooms were built it had a garden, as Loggan shews (fig. 7). In 1656 a
passage was made to it from one of the houses in the street: "6 August 1656.
Order'd then by ye Master and Seniors y^t Thomas Muriall haue leave to change his
present chamber for Mutton hall and to make a passage to Robt. Muriall's house,
so to continue unlesse it proouve a prejudice to ye fellowes or any inconvenience be
found by y^t passage to ye Town: if so y^t he return to his present chamber next
ye chappell" (Robert Muriall was a tallow-chandler who lighted the College);
and in 1725 another Conclusion determines: "That whereas Mr Parne Hath been
at very Great Expence in Repairing and Beautifying The Chamber, Commonly
call'd Mutton Hall," he shall be allowed to keep it, etc. Another Conclusion in the
same year calls it "Mutton's Hall," and fixes the rent at £6. The name first occurs in
the Jun. Burs. Accounts for 1648—49, where "worke in Mutton Corner" is charged
for; and out of those for subsequent years the following notices may be collected.
Ibid. 1650—51, "worke in Edelen's chamber next Mutton-hall:" 1652—53, "P^d
Mr Akehurst for repayring the windowes in Mutton Hall when he kept there:"
1697—98, "a plate to a door-post in Mutton-hall corner:" 1760—61, "repairing the
painting of the room over Mutton Hall:" 1768—69, "work at Mutton-Hall-Turret."
In 1797—98, it had become "Murton Hall;" and in 1853—54, "Merton Hall."]

[2] [Cambridge Guide, 1791.]

In 1810 the north-east angle of the Great Court was repaired by Mr Bernasconi[1]; and in the same year the following Conclusion of the Master and Seniors directed that the eastern range, the Great Gate, and the range between the Chapel and the Master's Lodge should be again cemented:

"July 6th 1810. Agreed...that the Plinth and water Table of the Eastern side of the Great Court be repaired with Roman or other Cement: that the west Part of the northern Side (being the old Library) be new fronted with Roman Cement, and that the Plinth on that side also be done in the same manner as that on the eastern side. It is also agreed that the inside of King's Gate be lined with Cement, and that the Clock Dial be fresh painted and gilded.
W. BRISTOL, M.C."

This work was carried out in 1812—13[2].

It should be further mentioned that in 1756—57 "a new parapet Wall from the Master's Lodge to the Chapel on the side next the Bowling Green" was put up; and "Mutton Hall" was plastered on the outside[3].

The Sun Dial (*P*, fig. 9) was set up in 1704:

"For 39 feet of Step Circuler under ye Diall at 16d per foot; for ye Basis, pillar, and capitall; for setting up ye Diall and finishing ye worke; for Iron worke; for 58 pounds of lead used at 2d per pound...06. 19. 08[4]."

It is not recorded whether this Dial replaced an older one. Dials are frequently mentioned in the Accounts, but their position is usually undefined. In 1672 we meet with a charge "for painting and gilding ye diall ouer ye Hall Staires and ye Hieroglyphicall Triangle by Mr Rotheram's Chamber." The former appears to be intended in Loggan's view (fig. 7); but nothing is known about the latter.

The sash-windows on the first floor of the Queen's Gate were

---

[1] [Jun. Burs. Accounts 1809—10. "To Mr Bernasconi his Bill for repairing the North East Angle of Great Court 215. 10. 3¾." Bernasconi did similar work at Jesus College Chapel in 1815: see above p. 147.]

[2] [Ibid. 1812—13. "To James Clabbon his Bill for work in the Great Court, including Eastern side of the Building, Queen's Gateway, and Old Library; for cement, scaffolding and colouring £159. 3. 2¼ .... £260 14. 10."]

[3] [Jun. Burs. Accounts 1756—57. *Bricklayer*.]

[4] [Jun. Burs. Accounts 1703—4. *Free-Mason*. The Dial here recorded was replaced by a new one in 1795: ibid. 1794—95, *College Smith*. "To J. and E. Troughton for a Dial, 8. 10. 0."]

removed in 1866 when the room was made fireproof and fitted up as a Muniment Room.

We will next consider the east front of the College. The Great Gate remains as shewn by Loggan (fig. 7)[1], except that the band of ornament along the eastern parapet has been removed; but the approach to it has been considerably altered. When Loggan's print was drawn it was not more than 26 feet wide, bounded by high battlemented walls with posts and rails in front of them; the probable direction of which has been laid down on the plan (fig. 9). They were taken down in 1786—87, and replaced by high walls of red brick with a stone coping, set a short distance farther back[2]. That on the north side extended as far as the Great Gate of S. John's College, interrupted only by the gate leading to the passage between the two colleges. In 1855 the portion of this wall which formed the eastern boundary of the College ground was pulled down, S. John's College having made a similar change in the position of their fence; and in the following year it was decided to remove the last traces of the picturesque façade which Loggan shews between the Great Gate and the Chapel, together with the brick-wall on the right hand of the approach to the College[3]. The following Conclusions shew exactly what was then done:

"July 4, 1855. Agreed that the wall running from the Great Gate northwards, and including the garden from the gate eastward of the

---

[1] [There have been frequent repairs both to the statues and to the structure, as in 1843—44: Jun. Burs. Accounts. *Mason.* "Repairing Turrets and Parapets at the Front-Gateway £201. 1. 6."]

[2] [Jun. Burs. Accounts 1786—87. *Bricklayer.* "Taking down the old wall and cleaning bricks at the Front Gate... ..building the new wall £153. 9. 2½. *Freemason.* For coping new wall next the street 38. 3. 9."]

[3] [The rooms on the first floor to the north of the Gateway were occupied by Sir Isaac Newton from 1679 to 1696: Correspondence of Newton with Cotes, ed. Edleston, XLIII. The wooden lean-to on the east side contained a small room and a staircase to the garden which is frequently referred to in the Junior Bursar's Accounts from 1682—83 to 1688—89 as "Mr Newton's garden." Neither staircase nor garden had been much altered down to 1856. It is worth recording that William Makepeace Thackeray occupied the rooms on the ground-floor under those which had been Newton's; and Thomas Babington Macaulay those on the other side of the staircase, next to the Chapel. The Earl of Essex (1576—80) and the Marquis of Granby (1771—74) had rooms on this side of the College, as appears from several entries in the Junior Bursar's Accounts.]

Chapel, be pulled down and rebuilt further back, so as to open the east end of the Chapel to the street; and that the fence north of the Chapel be thrown back to correspond with a similar opening of the space in the front of St John's College which that College are understood to contemplate.

W. WHEWELL, M. C."

"June 4, 1856. Agreed that the front of the College towards Trinity Street, between the Great Gate and the Chapel, be restored by new stone dressings, chimneys, etc.; and by a building with stone facing in the place of the present wooden building; according to a plan prepared by Mr Salvin; the brick wall in front of that building being pulled down and the railing continued to the Gate.

W. WHEWELL, M. C."

The wall on the opposite side was set back at the same time or shortly afterwards.

The façade between this wall and the new Lecture Rooms is still not so very different from that shewn by Loggan; but the remaining portion has disappeared, together with the two gardens, on the site of which the Lecture Rooms were erected in 1833—34[1]. They cost upwards of £5500.

It should be mentioned that an Observatory for the use of the Plumian Professor was constructed on the Great Gate during the Mastership of Dr Bentley (Master 1700—42). It was decided that the Gate should be devoted to that purpose by the following Conclusion, dated 5 February 1705—6:

" Orderd by the Master and Seniors, That Roger Cotes Fellow of this College, now nominated Professor of Astronomy and Experimental Philosophy, and his Successors after him in the said Professorship, of what College or Place soever they shall be, have ye Rooms and Leads of ye Kings Gate for a dwelling and Observatory, so long as ye Trustees or Electors for ye said Professorship shall think fit; The Professor paying ten pounds per annum to ye Fellow of this College, whose Chamber it is in ye College Course.

Provided always, while they shall use ye Kings Gate for ye Observatory, yt the Scholar appointed to be ye Professor's Assistant and to lodg in ye same Dwelling with him, be one of this College to be chosen by ye Professor with ye consent of ye Master of this College.

Orderd by ye Master and Seniors, yt Mr William Whiston, Mathematic Professor of ye Foundation of Mr Lucas shall have ye 2 Chambers middle and uppermost, next ye Kings Gate to the South, for his use and Property, as long as he shall think fit, He paying for ye

---

[1] [The Conclusion respecting them is dated 15 June 1833. The work was to be superintended by Mr Humfry.]

rent of ye said Chambers Eight pounds per annum to ye Fellow, whose Chambers they are in ye College Course.

Orderd also That while he rents ye said Chambers, he shall have ye use of ye College Library in ye same manner, as ye Fellows of ye College have[1].

RI. BENTLEY, Mag^r Coll."

This assignment was confirmed by an instrument under the College Seal, dated four days later; and the Observatory was probably begun soon afterwards, but, as the cost of it was defrayed by subscription, the precise date does not appear in the College books. In Dr Bentley's Letter to the Bishop of Ely, dated 13 February 1709—10, he draws attention to "the College Gate-house rais'd up and improv'd to a stately Astronomical Observatory, well stor'd with the best Instruments in Europe"; but Mr Thomas Blomer, Fellow, in his "Full View" of this letter published in the same year, inquires: "does not the finishing of it go on very slowly for want of Money to pay the Work-Men?"; and in 1717, in the year following the appointment of Dr Robert Smith to the Professorship, it was decided that "the Payments of the Doctors of our College for their degrees, be for the present applied to finish" it; and it was not completed until the beginning of 1739, when Dr Smith produced his Accounts and shewed a deficit of rather more than £47, which was discharged by the College[2]. The appearance which it then presented will be understood from the woodcut (fig. 17) taken from the view of the College, dated 1740, which has been already cited. Carter, writing in 1753, describes it as "a Noble and Lofty Room, both well situated, and furnished with variety of Instruments for Observations[3]." In 1792 (May 30) the Plumian Trustees, finding that the Professor had "neither occupied the said rooms and leads, nor fulfilled the conditions, for at least 50 years"; and that "the observatory and the instruments belonging to it were through disuse, neglect, and want of repairs

---

[1] [The word was originally written "hathe," but is corrected into "have" in the same hand.]

[2] [Conclusions: 8 June 1717, 12 May 1739. Dr Robert Smith was elected Professor 16 July 1716.]

[3] [History of Cambridge, p. 338. Mr Edleston (ut supra, p. LXXIV.) quotes Flamsteed's opinion that "Trinity Gatehouse is not fit for" an Observatory "and that that of S. John's is preferable, and that the Virtutis Gateway at Caius is better than either."]

so much dilapidated as to be entirely unfit for the purposes intended"; agreed to give up all claim to it, and allowed the Master and Fellows to take it down, or convert it to any use they thought proper[1].   It was taken down in 1797[2].

It appears to have been the intention of the original builders of the Gate to vault it with stone ; for stone corbels existed in each of the four angles, and on the centre of each side, from which the commencement of stone groining originated. The vault however had never been constructed, but a flat

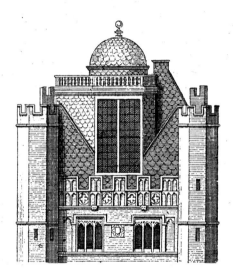

Fig. 17.   Upper story of the east front of the Great Gate, with the Observatory ; from a view taken in 1740.

ceiling had been substituted for it.   The present lierne vault, of oak, with shields at the intersection of the ribs, was put up in 1845, chiefly at the expense of the Master, Dr Whewell[3].   It

---

[1] [Edleston, ut supra, p. 200.]

[2] [Ackermann ii. 181. In the Jun. Burs. Accounts for 1796—97 a sum of £68. 9. 2 is charged for repairs to the King's Gate, which evidently refers to this work.]

[3] [See a letter from Dr Whewell to his sister, dated 20 November 1844. Life, etc., by Mrs Stair Douglas, p. 311.   Dr Whewell notes in his diary for 1844 : " Nov. 19. Mr Bradwell to make a vaulting of English oak for the great gateway with carved bosses £327. 10."]

was designed by Professor Willis and himself. The shields bear the arms of the sovereigns who have been specially connected with the College, and of the Masters.

The present Clock and Dial-Plate were put up on the Clock-Tower in 1726—27. Two new bells were provided for the chimes, and the old bell was utilised for the striking, as shewn by the following items:

" Paid for Carriage of the Dial Plate and two Bells
from the Wagon to ye Chappel .... 00. 03. 00 [1]
   To Mr Stubbs in part for the new Clock 42. 00. 00
   To Mr Ritts for Gilding the Dial Plate 26. 07. 00
   To Mr Stubbs ye Remainder of his Bill for ye Clock and
in full of the Bell founder's, Copper-Smith's, Blacksmith's,
and Painter's Bills 235. 17. 04
   To Mr Stubbs for fixing ye Hammer to ye old bell...... 01. 01. 00 [2]."

These charges, with others which are not worth quotation, amount to £358. 7. 11½. The only other important work done to this Tower is recorded as follows in the Junior Bursar's Accounts for 1752—53:

" To Charles Bottomley For repairing and Beautifying the Turrets and Great Gate of the Clock, and for new Stone, new Clunch, and fixing the Iron Cramps, pointing, etc. .... 88. 18. 2."

The Court of which we have traced the history measures 340 feet along the west side, 288 feet along the south side, 325 feet along the east side, and 257 feet along the north side. It may be further remarked that the conduit is not placed at the intersection of the diagonals, nor is it equidistant from the north and south, or east and west sides.

The chambers on the south and west sides, and also the Master's Lodge, are in two floors with garrets in the roof; and the range containing the Combination Room (fig. 7) was on the same plan until 1770. The range between the Master's Lodge and the Chapel, which it will be convenient to call the Library-range, is in three floors. All these ranges are finished with

---

[1] [Sen. Burs. Accounts 1725—26.]

[2] [Ibid. 1726—27. The inscription on the Clock Bell has been given above (p. 483). The 1st quarter Bell has merely the date, 1726: the 2^d: THOMAS OSBORN DOWNHAM NORFOLK FECIT 1795. CUM VOCO VENITE. Blomefield (Collectanea, p. 114) says: "On the large Bell put up with a new Clock. These 3 Bells and Clock were made A.D. 1726. RIC. BENTLY D.D. Master."]

battlements on the side next to the court, of the same pattern as those over the Great Gate (fig. 13). They were put up, as we have seen, in 1601—2. The eaves which preceded them were left in the east and south ranges on the sides next to Trinity Street and Trinity Lane respectively.

The stucco with which the side of the eastern range next to the Court was covered in 1751 and 1811 renders investigation into the structure of the walls impossible. Moreover the molds of the window-jambs have been cut off, and the cusps taken out of the lights. On this side there are no hood-molds.

The range between the Chapel and Great Gate is narrower than that to the south of the Gate, the respective widths being 17 feet 6 inches and 19 feet 6 inches[1]. The windows are deeply recessed. The wall is about 33 inches thick, and the distance from the outer face to the window-frame is 22 inches. The lights are 17 inches wide. Windows on this plan are found as far as the first staircase south of the Gate, D, but not elsewhere. On the east side the wall north of the Gate, MN, was entirely rebuilt by Salvin in 1856; that south of the gate, however, $M'N'$, remains to a great extent unaltered. It is built partly of clunch rubble, partly of red brick, and has never been stuccoed. The three windows on each floor next to the gate, as shewn by Loggan (fig. 7), still exist. Of this part Professor Willis remarks: "On the garden side, original windows are seen, which have deep jambs and good profiles, so as to lead one to suspect that they were either worked up from the materials of the butteries and chambers of King's Hall, taken down when the Chapel was built, or perhaps derived from the Friars' buildings." These windows closely resemble those on the ground-floor of the north side of the Library-range (fig. 18). The doorways at C, D are four-centered, but earlier in character than any of the others in the court. The one drawn (fig. 19) is that at C.

The rest of the eastern range, DA, has very different windows and doors. The windows are set much nearer to the outer face of the wall, the distance from it to the frame being about 12

---

[1] [In the following comparison it will be understood that the references are to the ground-plan (fig. 9) unless it is otherwise stated. The notes by Professor Willis, which have been incorporated in this part of the text, were either appended to his history of the buildings, or written on the margin of sketches and ground-plans.]

inches; and the lights are narrow, being not more than 14 inches wide[1]. The head of the doorways at E, F (fig. 20) is a depressed ogee arch, with a suit of very shallow moldings.

Proceeding to the south side of the court we find but little difference between the range to the east of the Queen's Gateway and that to the west of it. In the former portion the windows are 4 feet 5 inches from the ground, and each of the doorways has two steps; in the latter the windows are 3 feet 5 inches from

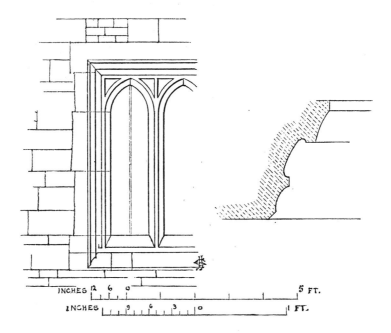

INCHES 12 6 0   5 FT.

INCHES   9   6   3   0   1 FT.

Fig. 18.   Window on the ground-floor of the north side of the Library-range.

the ground, and the doorways have no step. The windows, however, are all of the same pattern. They are of three lights or two lights, pointed, each of which is 2 feet wide, and they are set very near the outer face of the wall. Those in the lower range have hood-molds like those of the doorways, of which there are five, at G, H, I, K, L, all precisely alike (fig. 21). The wall of the

---

[1] [The state of the wall makes it impossible to record these measurements with minute accuracy.]

whole of this range is built of large blocks of stone, much chipped at their edges, and evidently brought from some older building; but in the absence of Accounts for the beginning of Nevile's Mastership we are unable to obtain further information. The windows were so much altered in 1753—54 that no conclusion as to age can be based upon them.

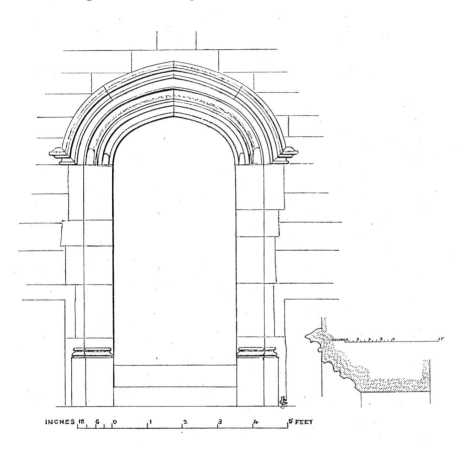

Fig. 19. Doorway on the east side of the Great Court (C, D, fig. 9).

The conclusion to which this examination has led us is that the northern half of the eastern range is the oldest. It was begun, as the Accounts shew, at about the same time as the Chapel, in 1556—57, and is spoken of as complete in 1583—84.

It extended as far as *D*, whence the north wall of the old chambers of King's Hall projected into the court. The remainder of the eastern range is next in date; and the southern range is

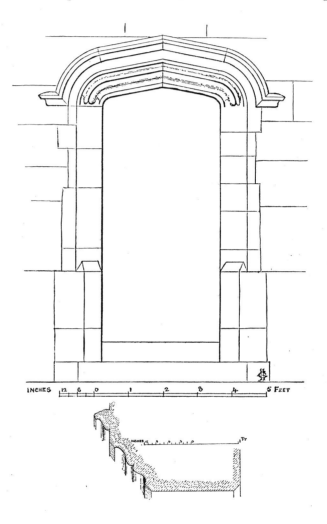

Fig. 20. Doorway on the east side of the Great Court (*E*, *F*, fig. 9).

evidently much later. The recorded dates have shewn us that work was being done to the south-east corner of the eastern range in 1598—99, and that the southern range was not completed until 1602, though the Queen's Gate was ready for the statue in 1597, and the walls, windows, and doorways may perhaps belong to the same date[1]. The difference of style, however, between these two ranges is so great that it seems probable that the prolongation of the eastern range, DA, had been begun

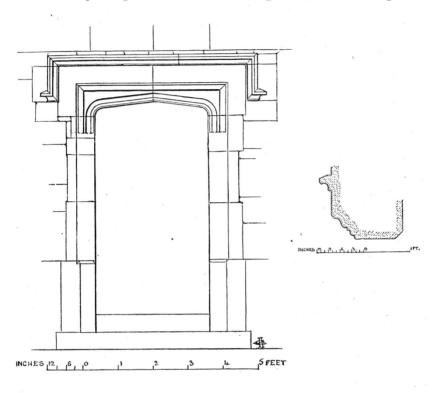

Fig. 21.   Doorway on the south side of the Great Court (G, H, I, K, L, fig. 9).

some time previously, and that it was only being altered and finished in 1598—99.

The Library-range, as mentioned above, is in three floors. The recorded date of completion is 1600—1. The windows, on

---

[1] [Professor Willis considers that the chambers between the Queen's Gate and the S.W. corner of the court "by the architectural style of their doors and windows were the last built of the southern range." The eastern range is certainly earlier, and it is probable that the building of the southern range would be commenced from the S.E. corner.]

the two lowest floors, next the court, of two lights or three lights, have peculiar polygonal heads (fig. 22) and deep jambs; those on the third floor were inserted in 1873. The doorways at Q, R (fig. 23), are more elaborate than those in the opposite range, and are clearly of somewhat later date. This furnishes an additional argument for assigning the stonework of the former range to 1597, as suggested above.

The south wall of the Library building was stuccoed so effectually in 1812—13, that its composition cannot be discovered. The north wall, next the Bowling-Green, which, as being out of sight, has never been stuccoed, is a curious piece of patchwork. The lower part, according to Professor Willis, "shews remains of an earlier stone wall, composed of large blocks of clunch divided by courses of red brick, with deep-set windows (fig. 18) of one or two lights. Above these the wall has been altered by the conversion of the old Library into chambers; the windows on the second and third floors are all insertions, and the wall containing them has apparently been rebuilt. The buttresses, of old white Ely brick, with Ketton stone quoins, are a modern addition." In another note he suggests that these buttresses may have been built after the fire of 1665—66 (p. 531), which destroyed the roof, and possibly damaged the walls. The parapet is now of the same white brick as the upper part of the wall and the buttresses; the stone coping looks as though it might be composed of the molded edges of the original battlements.

We will next examine the three Gates.

The Great Gate consists of a central portion, divided into two floors, with a turret at each of the four angles. The turret at the south-west angle contains a staircase; the others contain closets entered either from the chambers over the gate, or from those in the ranges north and south of it. Each front is divided into two compartments by a string-course of peculiar pattern, similar to that which marks the subdivisions of the flanking turrets A, B, C (figs. 13, 14); but these compartments are arranged very differently on the two sides of the gate.

The east front (fig. 13) presents the unusual arrangement of a large and small gate side by side, separated by a stone pier. On the west side (fig. 14) there is a single arch, through which the court is entered by descending three steps. This arch being loftier than that on the opposite side, it follows that there is a considerable wall-space on the east side between the crown of the arch and the floor of the chamber above it. This space is divided into seven panels. In the central panel, on a stone shield and supported by two lions, are the arms of France ancient and England quarterly[1]. Beneath this large shield is a very small one, on which are three stags trippant, for Geoffrey Blythe, Master of King's Hall (1498—1528) and Bishop of Coventry and Lichfield (1503—34)[2], during whose mastership the gate was begun. Beneath the panel, on a sheet of metal, are the words: EDVARDVS TERTIVS FVNDATOR AVLE REGIS. MCCCXXXVII. The six other panels contain small stone shields for the arms of the six sons of King Edward the Third. Each shield is surmounted by a ducal crown in gilt metal; and beneath the panel is a plate of metal for the name of the Prince, similar to that for the name of the King. The arms and names are as follows, counting from left to right:

I.	II.	III.
France ancient and England quarterly, label of three points each charged with a torteau. EDMONDUS D. EBOR. C. CANTABRUGIE.	France ancient and England quarterly, label argent; on each point a canton between two roses. LEONEILUS D. CLARENCIE. C. DE VLSTER.	France ancient and England quarterly, label of three points argent. EDVARDUS P. WALLIE. V° BLACK PRINCE. On the stonework on each side of the shield are painted three ostrich-feathers, with the motto "*Ich dien.*"

IV.	V.	VI.
Blank shield. GUILL'MUS DE HATFELD. DEMORTUUS INFANS.	France ancient and England quarterly, label ermine. IOHANNES D. LANCASTRIE. V° JOHN OF GAUNT.	France ancient and England quarterly, label of three points argent; on the points a fleur-de-lis and two crosses, all in a bordure argent. THO^s. D. GLOVCESTRIE. C. ESSEXIE.

¹ [The supporters are those of Edward the Fourth, but the shield is evidently intended for that of Edward the Third, because Edward the Fourth quartered France modern with England; and Edward the Third is plainly indicated by the inscription.]

² [In some of the repairs of the gate the field has been altered from ermine to vert, and the stags painted white, thus converting the arms into those of Thomas Rotherham, Archbishop of York 1480—1500.]

Above this band of ornamentation there are two windows of three lights, and between them a stone canopy containing a statue of King Henry the Eighth. The spaces between the windows and the turrets, and between the windows and the canopy, are decorated with panelwork. The upper compartment has two windows of three lights, with panel-work in the spaces between them and the turrets ; and in the central space is a square panel containing a quatrefoil and a shield bearing the arms of France modern and England quarterly.

The west front of the Gate is quite different. In the first compartment above the arch—the spandrils of which are richly ornamented—there is a window of four lights, above which, interrupting the hood-mold below it and the string-course above it, is a niche of classical character, containing a statue of King James the First. There are two other niches: that on the left contains a statue of his Queen, Anne of Denmark; that on the right a statue of his son, Prince Charles. Beneath each of these side-niches there is a square panel, in the centre of which there is a blank shield; and there is a similar panel and shield below the window. In the upper compartment there is a window of four lights, above which, interrupting the string-course below the battlements, are the Royal Arms, supported by the Lion and Unicorn ; and on each side is a stone shield with supporters. These are probably "the Queene and Princes Armes," put up 1614—15 (p. 487), but they are now so much decayed that the arms cannot be made out; the supporters of the shield over the Queen's statue seem to be two human figures[1]; those of the shield on the opposite side to be the lion and the unicorn.

The history of the Great Gate has shewn us that it was begun in 1518—19, and finished, so far as to be ready to receive the wooden gates, in the beginning of 1524 (p. 452) ; that the work was then abandoned for four or five years ; that it was resumed in 1528—29, and carried on slowly until 1535, when it was completed (p. 454), but in what manner has, unfortunately, not been recorded ; that in 1598—99 it was heightened ; and lastly, that in 1614—15 it was ornamented with statues and shields, which can be easily identified. On the other hand, however, it is

---

[1] [Her father's shield was supported by two savage men, bearing clubs. Willement's "Regal Heraldry," p. 91.]

exceedingly difficult to determine what part of the Gate is to be referred to the original work of 1519—35, and what is to be understood by the term "hightning of the greate Tower," applied to the work done in 1598—99.

The present appearance of the Gate is that of a structure begun on a well-conceived plan consistent with its importance, and finished hastily on a much more limited scheme. The east façade of the body of the Gate shews a well-ashlared elevation (fig. 13), richly decorated from the ground-line to the top, for so late as 1740 (fig. 17) the battlements were worked in panels after the fashion of the 16th century. This ornamentation was probably taken away in the course of the works incidental to the removal of the Observatory in 1797 (p. 501). The same drawing, and the earlier view of Loggan (fig. 7), shew that the lights of the windows on both floors had cusps like the blank panels which join them. We are therefore entitled to contend that we can represent the original design of the façade from these authorities with fair accuracy, and that the semicircular heads which are at present to be seen in the lights of the upper windows were inserted during some of the repairs of the Gate, and do not represent the alterations and additions of Nevile.

The west façade of the Gate, on the other hand, corresponds with the east façade only so far as the arch of entrance is concerned. Above this there are two imperfect courses of clunch, and two stone brackets in the angles. These are the only portions which seem to indicate a commencement of an original design; the rest of this front consisting of a brick wall without a trace of original decoration except the string-course above the statues[1], or any breach of continuity except where two windows have been inserted.

This substitution of brick for the stonework which, we may presume, was originally contemplated, and the abandonment of the stone vault which was actually begun, are facts which suggest that enforced economy compelled the builders to give up some features of their original plan[2]. The brick angle-towers

---

[1] The panels under the statues are perhaps original; the panel under the lower window belongs to the same period as the other two, but it appears to be an insertion in this position.

[2] It is possible also that the west façade was left without ornament because it was intended to erect some building to abut upon it. The old plan (fig. 10) shews a Library in this position as explained above (p. 467).

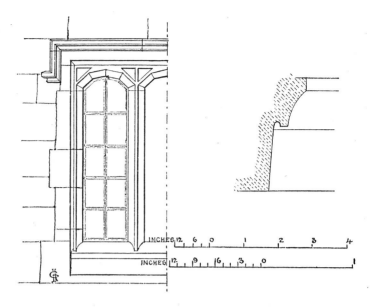

Fig. 22. Window in the Library-range.

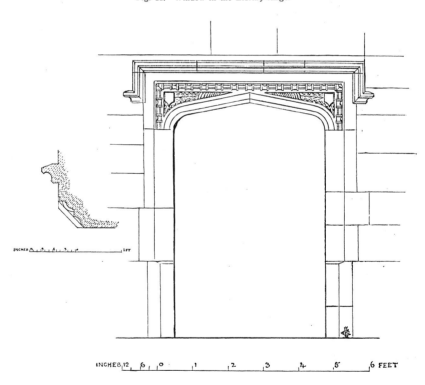

Fig. 23. Doorway on the north side of the Great Court (Q, R, fig. 9).

may naturally be assigned to this second period; and possibly, when funds ran short, they were not carried up to their full intended height.

The work of Nevile is stamped with an individual character, as may be seen in the niches which he inserted in the west façade of the Gate we are considering, in the Queen's Gate, and in King Edward's Gate. The three niches mentioned above, with their arms, are the only features of the Great Gate which, from their style, can be distinctly traced to him. Had he raised the body of the Gate House we may feel sure that he would

Fig. 25. Upper story of King Edward's Gate, from a photograph.

have followed the prevalent taste, and made some insertions on both sides which would have betrayed his interference. Again, the small quantity of stone used "for the hightning of the greate Tower," only five tons, is in favour of the theory that the work then done was not extensive; and the special mention of "cantes" seems to limit it to the angle-towers[1]. Moreover, the peculiar molding which subdivides the stages of the angle-towers *A, B, C* (figs. 13, 14), and the subdivisions of the body of the Gate, is distinctly shewn by Loggan beneath the ornamented battlement on the east façade above described; but it is not

---

[1] [On the other hand it must be remembered that some of Dr Barrow's stone was used for this purpose besides what had been bought. See above, p. 479.]

shewn by him beneath the corresponding battlements of the angle-towers, where it is replaced by a much plainer molding, similar to that used on the Hall and on the sides of the Great Court. On the whole therefore it seems probable that Nevile's "hightning" was limited to adding a few feet of brickwork, and perhaps the battlements, to the angle-towers.

The position and general arrangement of King Edward's Gate, or Clock-Tower, will be understood from the engraving (fig. 24), and from the ground-plan (fig. 9). It is in three floors: on the first there is an ordinary chamber; on the second the old Muniment Room; and on the third a chamber containing the works of the clock[1]. The old plan (fig. 10) shews that it had originally four turrets. Three of these, at the south-west, south-east, and north-east angles, contained studies or closets which, like those of the Great Gate, opened into the adjoining chambers. The turret at the south-west angle was much larger than the others, and contained a staircase providing access to the different floors. When the gate was removed this staircase was not rebuilt. The first and second floors are now approached by the Library-staircase (B, fig. 9); and the third floor by a wooden stair in the south-west turret, entered through a door close to that of the Muniment-Room. The north face of the gate is now finished off with a plain wall of red brick, set flush with the north face of the turrets, neither of which is carried down to the ground. The four turrets are now of different sizes, that at the south-east angle being the largest. The stone—a coarse shelly oolite— probably from Northamptonshire, appears to be of the same formation throughout; and the larger turret may perhaps represent the original staircase-turret. The whole gate appears to have been rebuilt carelessly and hastily, for the mullions of the four-light window on the second floor do not correspond with the "beginners" on the sill; and the vault (p. 446) was not replaced. It is probable also that the Gate is somewhat narrower than it was originally; for the hood-molds of the windows on the first floor are now cut off on the side next to the turrets, and there is only just sufficient space left for the jamb.

[1] [This is probably the room formerly appropriated to the Chapel-Clerk, and called Sky-Parlour.]

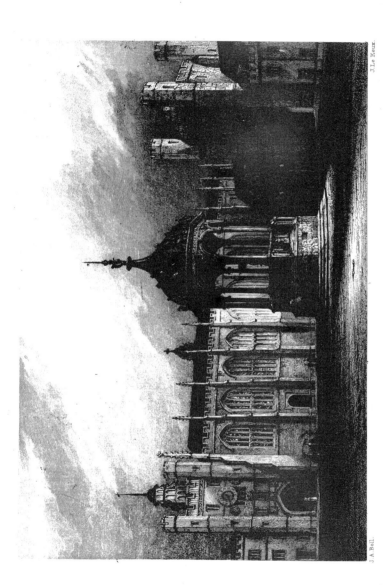

J.A.Bell.

J.Le Keux.

Fig. 24. The Great Court of Trinity College, looking towards the north-east corner; from Le Keux's Memorials of Cambridge, ed. Cooper.

Vol. II.

among Sir Christopher Wren's drawings in the Library of All
Souls College, Oxford.

A few interesting notices may be collected respecting
Nevile's Court while it remained thus restricted in size. In
1650—51 the King's arms over the gate were taken down, and
replaced by those of the State[1], which in turn again gave way
to those of the King in 1659—60. These latter, with the usual
supporters, were carved by Woodroffe in stone[2], from which we
may conclude that the whole gateway was a substantial structure of stone, harmonizing in style and ornamentation with the
buildings of the court. A paved walk led from the Hall steps
to the gate on the west side, crossed by another; and the
intervening spaces were laid out as a garden[3].]

When the Court was completed by the addition of the great
Library at the western side, the latter was placed at such a
distance as made it necessary to prolong the cloisters by adding
on each side two more compartments, or, in other words, eight
arches. The north side was undertaken first. The foundation
of the Library was laid 23 February, 1676, and in the following
April Sir Thomas Sclater, of Cambridge, Baronet, formerly
Fellow, undertook at his own charge the building of four of
these arches on the north side, with the chambers over them
(*bc*, fig. 9).

The deed drawn up between the Master and Fellows and Sir
Thomas Sclater[4], dated 18 April, 1676, contains so many curious
particulars, that the important parts of it are here subjoined:

---

[1] [Sen. Burs. Accounts, 1650—51. *Extraordinaries.*]

[2] [Jun. Burs. Accounts, 1659—60. "P^d G. Woodrofe...for ye armes in ye New-
court 05. 00. 00. Item for stone and scaffolds for ye King's Armes in ye new-court."
Ibid. 1667—68. "To John Ivory for adding a Unicornes horne to ye Kings Armes
in ye new court o. 2. o."]

[3] [This appears from charges in the Junior Bursar's Accounts for 1662—63 for
laying new stone "from ye Hall staires in the newe Court towards ye greate Gate"; and
for laying pavement "in ye crosse walke in ye newe Court." In the same Accounts
for 1673—74 there are charges "for planting new box in ye New Court."]

[4] [The original deed is in the Treasury of Trinity College. Sir Thomas Sclater is
buried in the Chapel. The following is the inscription on his grave: "Hic jacet
THOMAS SCLATERUS Baronettus Hujus Collegii Prosperis Ecclesiæ et Regni temporibus Socius. Æstu Belli Civilis hinc ejectus Prudentia Consilio Cura Rem Nomen
Dignitatem Auxit. Eandem erga suos quam olim habuit Benevolentiam Retinuit:
Vivus Moriensque Munificentia cumulata Collegio Benefecit. Obijt Dec. 10 1684
ætat. 69."]

" WHEREAS Sr Thomas Sclater out of his great respect, and to per-
petuate his good intencion and affeccion to the said Colledge (whereof
himselfe was sometime Fellow) hath declared and promised to lay out
give and bestow to the said Colledge (reckoning in what hath already
bin by him laid out and expended in and about the building herein after
mencioned) the Summe of eight Hundred pounds for the building of
two Chambers, with a little roome or Cockloft over the Staircase, and
of a Cellar under the same building, in the New Court called Nevill's
Court in the aforesaid Colledge, next adjoyning to the building and
Cloysters there now standing, of the breadth of Fower Pillars or Arches,
and deepe Five and twenty foote and eight inches. It is therefore concluded condiscended and agreed by and betweene the said parties as
followeth vizt :

1. " IMPRIMIS the said Master Fellowes and Schollers...doe...cove-
nant...by these presents... That hee the said Sr Thomas Sclater shall
or may have the free disposeing of the said two Chambers [etc.] for and
during his naturall life to such person and persons, and to such use
and uses as hee shall appoint ; and under such Condicions and limitacions as hee shall think fitt, with power in his life time to revoake and
alter from time to time any such his disposicion and appointment
relateing to the disposall of the said Chambers [etc.] for the life of the
said Sr Thomas Sclater.

2. "ITEM that from and after the decease of the said Sr Thomas
Sclater Then as to the Lowermost of the said two Chambers and the
said little roome or Cockloft over the Staircase and Cellar the same
shall allwayes...be inhabited and enjoyed freely by one of the Relations of the name and neerest of bloud of the said Sr Thomas Sclater
being of the Degree of a Master of Arts or Fellow Commoner then
liveing in the said Colledge dureing his or their stay in the Colledge
onely (if any such shall then be in the said Colledge).

3. " AND IN CASE such a person soe quallified as to name and bloud
or either as aforesaid shall not be of the Degree of a Master of Arts
nor Fellow Commoner Yet notwithstanding that, the said lowermost
Chamber, little roome or Cockloft and Cellar by the advice of the
Master of the said Colledge (for the time being) to be lett and the
profitts thereof to be paid to such relacion of the said Sr Thomas Sclater
quarterly for his use dureing such time as hee shall continue under the
degree of a Master of Arts or Fellow Commoner of and in the said
Colledge for the time of his stay there onely.

4. " AND IF it soe happen that there shalbe of and in the said Colledge of the degree aforesaid such a person of the name of the said S^r
Thomas Sclater and not soe neere of bloud and kindred as some other
then there being of the degree aforesaid Then those allwayes of the
neerest of bloud to the said Sr Thomas to be preferred and have the
said lowermost Chamber [etc.] before any other.

5. " AND as to the upper Chamber next over the said lowermost
Chamber the same to be allwayes and from time to time inhabited and
enjoyed freely by one such person, being admitted a Student in the
said Colledge, whether a Graduate or not, dureing his stay in the
Colledge onely, who is of the name and kindred or relacion of the said

Sr Thomas Sclater or either or any of them, if any such bee there, and who is not in soe near relacion to him as those which doe inhabit in, or enjoy the profitts of the said Lowermost Chamber.

6. "AND in case any of the said Relacions of the said Sr Thomas Sclater one or more of them being then in and a member of the said Colledge, haveing the said Chambers as aforesaid, shall judge it more for their or his advantage to lett the said Chamber or Chambers [etc.] the Profitts ariseing therefrom shall duely and entirely be paid to them or him quarterly, for their or his use, dureing their or his stay in the Colledge onely.

7. "ITEM it is concluded and agreed...That when and soe often as it shall soe happen that there shall not bee any such of the name and bloud or relacion or any of them of the said Sr Thomas Sclater as aforesaid in the said Colledge who shall by the true meaneing hereof have and enjoy the said Chambers, Then allwayes dureing the time of such vacancie the profitts of the said Chambers [etc.] shalbe disposed of by the Master and Seniors of the said Colledge...for the buying and placeing of Bookes for and in the new Library now intended and designed to be built in the said Colledge neere the Common River ; which said Bookes and the Seates or places where the same Bookes are to be putt according to the Modell of the said Library to be made, shall have the name of the said Sr Thomas Sclater putt upon them from time to time, and all those Bookes bought by the moneyes raised out of the said Chambers to be kept together in one or more Seates or places and not mixt with other Bookes.

8. "PROVIDED allwayes...That it shalbe lawfull for the said Sr Thomas Sclater by his Last Will and Testament in writeing, or other Deed or Writeing by him or in his life time sealed, published, declared, and executed, in the presence of two or more credible witnesses, to dispose of the said two Chambers [etc.] or any of them to any other beside his kindred that he shall thinke fitt or appoint to have the same, for and dureing onely the stay of such person or persons in the said Colledge, for the first time onely next after the decease of the said Sr Thomas Sclater...

9. "ITEM it is agreed...That the repaires of the said two Chambers ...as often as any shalbe wanting, the same shalbe paid and done allwayes out of the rents and profits ariseing therefrom, or by such person or persons who shall inhabitt the same, and not to be any wayes otherwise chargeable to the said Colledge.

10. "AND LASTLY it is condiscended, concluded, and agreed...That if any doubt difference or controversie shall at any time or times after the decease of the said Sr Thomas Sclater arise concerning any matter or thing in these Articles of Agreement conteined, or about the true sence and meaneing thereof, That then and soe often the same shalbe examined expounded and determined by the Judgement onely of the Master and Seniors of the said Colledge (for the time being) or the greater part of them, according to the true intent and meaneing of this gift and Agreement."

Sir Thomas Sclater's building was completed by the Audit of 1679, when the following memorandum was drawn up :

"At the Audit At Trinity Colledge in Cambr' The Tenth day of December Anno domini 1679.

Whereas in and by certaine Articles of Agreement in writing bearing date the Eighteenth day of Aprill Anno Domini 1676 Sr Thomas Sclater Baronet did promise and declare that he would freely give and bestow the summe of Eight hundred poundes for the building of certaine chambers in the New Court called Nevill's Court in Trinity Colledge...Which said Chambers then begun, the said Sr Thomas Sclater at his onely charges hath now finished, and heere this day produced his accompts of the disbursements which he hath laid out in the building the said Chambers: By which Accompts It appeares, the said Sr Thomas Sclater hath disbursed the summe of Eight hundred nynety and six poundes thirteene shillings and one halfe penney: Which Accompts this day being at the said Audit examined, they are hereby declared adjusted approved and allowed: And the said Sr Thomas Sclater, being then present, out of his further bounty to the said Colledge doth remitt and give unto the said Colledge the said overplus money of the said eight hundred poundes being Nynety six poundes thirteene shillings and one halfe penney.

Memorand' that the said Accompt doth not at all referr to any expence the said Sr Thomas Sclater hath bin at and bestowed in the Common Chamber over the Butteryes in the said Colledge; And Further, that a Leanto adjoyning to the New Library Staircase not included in the said Articles was built at the onely charge of the said Sr Thomas Sclater and belongeth to the said Chambers by him built in the said Nevills Court.

THOMAS SCLATER[1]."

In 1681, the south side being still incomplete, Doctor Humphry Babington, Senior Fellow, undertook to build the four easternmost arches of that side with the chambers (*fg*, fig. 9), opposite to those built by Sir Thomas Sclater. The important passages of the agreement between the Master and Fellows and Dr Babington, dated 18 May, 1681, are the following[2]:

"Whereas the New Library in Trinity Colledge aforesaid lately erected next or neare the Comon River at the end of Neviles Court, and the new building thereunto adjoyning standing on Eight Arches of stone on the Northside of the said Court as it is now enlarged, hath by the benefaccion of many worthy persons proceeded soe farr, as that the said Eight Arches of building on the Northside of the said Court is

---

[1] [It is endorsed by Mr Samuel Newton, Auditor of the College, and countersigned by the Vice-Master and seven Fellows.]

[2] [College Order, 6 April, 1681. "Order'd and agreed...that Dr Humphry Babinghton undertaking an answerable building to Sr Thomas Sclaters on ye opposite side in Nevills court have ye same conditions with Sr Thomas, and just such an Instrument to secure them to him as also ye ground adjoining on ye back side, between ye high way and those buildings, enclosed. Jo. North. M.C."]

wholly finished and inhabited, and the said New Library haveing the roofe thereof now covered is in some good forwardnes towards perfecting and finishing. But the Southside of the said Court extending from the old building and Cloysters in the same Court to the said New Library is yet lyeing open and unbuilt standing at a stay,

"The said Humfry Babington therefore mindeing the honour of the Colledge, and usefullnes of the said building soe happily begun and thus farr promoted and to further soe good a worke, And alsoe to manifest his great affeccion to the Colledge hath undertaken and promised at his owne proper Costs and Charges to raise and build for the said Colledge, the first foure Arches of Building with Cloysters on the Southside of the said Court called Neviles Court, the same to begin at and adjoyne to the old Cloysters there, and the building and Chambers over the same now in the use of Do^r George Chamberlaine, (the present Vice-Master of the said Colledge) to goe from thence Westward towards the said New Library, to bee of the breadth next the Court of Fower pillars or Arches, and deepe Twenty and five foot and eight inches, and to conteyne Two Chambers, the one over the other, with a little roome or Cockloft over the staire case, and alsoe a Celler to bee under some part of the same building, the said Foure Arches of building to bee made answerable to those fower Arches of Building opposite thereunto on the otherside of the said Court lately built by Sr Thomas Sclater Baronett.

"And Whereas the said Master Fellowes and Scholars (well resenting the said undertaking and benefaccion of the said Humfrey Babington) Have granted to lay to the said foure Arches of building to bee raised as aforesaid by the said Humfrey Babington, a certaine peece of ground for a garden lyeing in part on the backside of the same building to bee freely used and enjoyed forever with the same, and to bee always a part thereof, Which said peece of ground is lyeing next the Wall of the Garden now in the use of the said Do^r George Chamberlaine towards the east and from thence in a right line extends and goeth in length towards the Southend of the said New Library, and conteynes in breadth at the east end thereof next the said wall from the north to the south forty and foure foot, Excepting onely at the Southeast corner there a passage of fower foot from the Vice-Master's garden, and in breadth at the west end thereof from the north to the south Thirty and three foot, and in length on the northside thereof from the east to the west fifty and foure foot, and in length on the southside thereof from the east to the west Fifty and foure foot, Excepting the aforesaid passage from the Vice-Master's Garden, the same peece of ground to bee enclosed with a sufficient Brickwall of a convenient heigth at the proper costs and charges of the said Colledge, Itt is therefore now concluded condiscended unto and agreed upon by and betweene the said parties to these presents as followeth vizt :

1. "IMPRIMIS the said Master Fellowes and Scholars in consideracon of the said foure Arches of building to bee erected and built by and at the proper costes and charges of the said Humfrey Babington as aforesaid Doe....covenant....in manner and forme following vizt That hee the said Humfrey Babington shall or may have the free disposeing of the

said Twoe Chambers [etc.] with the said peece of ground to bee enclosed as aforesaid, and of all the profitts of the same for and during his
life to such person and persons and to such use and uses as hee shall
appoint, and under such condicions and limitacions as hee shall think
fitt, with power in his life time to revoake and alter from time to time
any such his disposicion and appoyntment, relateing to the disposall of
the said Chambers [etc.].

2. "ITEM That from and after the decease of the said Humfrey
Babington, Then as to the Lowermost of the said Two Chambers and
the said Little roome or Cockloft over the Staire case, and the said
Cellar and peice of ground aforesaid to bee enclosed, the same shall
allwayes, and from time to time, bee inhabited and enjoyed freely by
one of the relacions of the name and neerest of bloud of the said
Humfrey Babington, or of the name of Cave, soe related to the said
Humfrey Babington, being of the degree of a Master of Arts or Fellow
Comoner then liveing in the said Colledge, during his or their Stay in
the Colledge onely (if any such shall then bee in the said Colledge).

3. "AND IN CASE such a person soe qualifyed...shall not bee
of the degree of a Master of Arts nor Fellow Commoner, Yett notwithstanding that, the said Lowermost Chamber, little roome or Cockloft, Celler and peece of ground aforesaid by the advice of the Master of
the said Colledge (for the time being) shalbe lett and the rent and
profitts thereof shalbe payd to such relacion of the said Humfrey
Babington quarterly for his use during such time as hee shall continue
under the degree of a Master of Arts or Fellow Commoner of an in the
said Colledge (for the time of his stay there onely).

4. "AND IF it soe happen that there shalbe of and in the said
Colledge of the degree aforesaid such a person of the name of the said
Humfrey Babington or of the name of Cave of the bloud or kindred of
the said Humfrey Babington and not soe near of bloud and kindred as
some other then there being of the degree aforesaid, Then those allwayes
of the neerest of bloud to the said Humfrey Babington to bee preferred
and have the said Lowermost Chamber [etc.] before any other.

5. "AND as to the upper Chamber next over the said Lowermost
Chamber, The same to bee allwayes and from time to time inhabited and
enjoyed freely by one such person being admitted a Student in the said
Colledge whether a Graduate or not during his stay in the Colledge
onely who is of the name and kindred or relacion of the said Humfrey
Babington as aforesaid or either or any of them, if any such bee there,
and who is not in soe neere relacion to him as those which doe inhabit
in, or enjoy the profitts of the said Lowermost Chamber.

6. "AND in case any of the said relacions of the said Humfrey
Babington...being then in and a member of the said Colledge haveing
the said Chambers as aforesaid, shall judge it more for his or their
advantage to lett the said Chamber or Chambers [etc.], the profitts ariseing therefrom shall duely and entirely bee payd to them or him quarterly
for their or his use during their or his stay in the Colledge onely.

7. "ITEM it is concluded and agreed...That when and soe often as
it shall soe happen, that there shall not bee any such of the name and
bloud or relacion, or any of them, of the said Humfrey Babington as

aforesaid in the said Colledge, who shall by the true meaning hereof, have and enjoy the said Chambers, Then allwayes during the time of such vacancye, the profitts of the said Chambers...shalbe disposed of by the Master and Seniors of the said Colledge (for the time being) for the buying and placeing of bookes for and in the said New Library Which said Books and the seates or places where the same Bookes are to bee putt according to the Modell of the Seates and places of the said Library to bee made, shall have the name of the said Humfrey Babington putt upon them from time to time, and all those Bookes bought by the moneyes raysed out of the said chambers, [etc.] to be kept together in one or more seates or places and not mixed with other bookes.

8. "PROVIDED allwayes and it is agreed betweene the said parties That it shalbe lawfull for the said Humfrey Babington by his Last Will and Testament in writing or other deed or writing by him in his life time sealed, published, declared, and executed...to dispose of the said Two Chambers [etc.] to any other beside his kindred that hee shall thinke fitt or appoynt to have the same for and during onely the stay of such person or persons in the said Colledge, for the first time onely next after the decease of the said Humfrey Babington....

9. "ITEM it is agreed...That the repayres of the said Two Chambers [etc.] and walls of the said peice of ground...shalbe payd and done allwayes out of the rents and profitts arising therefrom, or by such person or persons who shall inhabit the same, and not to bee anywayes otherwise chargeable to the said Colledge."

Dr Babington's building was erected between 1681 and 1682, under the supervision of Robert Grumbold, master-mason of the Library, as we learn from a page in one of the volumes of Accounts for the Library; and the room on the first floor, called in that Account "the Great Roome," was wainscoted by Cornelius Austin at the same time[1]. The four arches which intervene between those built by him and the Library (*gh*, fig. 9) seem to have been built at the same time as his, for in the Building Accounts for the Library between January 1681 and January 1682 we find:

"To Robert Grumball, Tho. Silke, and Matthew Fitch upon Account of ye agreement with them for ye new building on ye south side of ye Court .... 83. 00. 00.

[1] [The Account, kept by Grumbold, is headed "Dr Babington's Account for Building of four Arches on the south side of the Cloystor next the Vice Master in the year 1681 and 1682." The room wainscoted by Austin is that now (1883) occupied by Sir W. G. G. V. Vernon Harcourt, Whewell Professor of International Law. The woodwork, of oak, is a splendid specimen of the style of the time. It has lately been cleaned of paint at the expense of Professor Harcourt. Austin is paid "for 171 yeards of windscoot at vi^s per y^d. For the Caruing work of the Great Roome 016. 10. 03. For 50 yeards of fir winscot in ye Bed Chambor' 015. 17. 08": etc.]

To Grumbold, Silke, and Fitch for building the Chambers on the South side of the New Court continued to the New Library, according to Articles .... 100. 00. 00."

The four arches intervening between Sir Thomas Sclater's building and the Library (*cd*, fig. 9) were erected "by the benefaction of many worthy persons," as stated in the deed between the College and Dr Babington; and they had been completed before May 1681, when that deed was drawn. This, however, is the only record which has been preserved respecting this piece of building.

The two ranges of Nevile's Court, as thus completed, were in a florid style of Jacobean architecture, raised upon the arcades of a cloister[1]. Each side of the court was divided by pilasters into five compartments, each including four arcades resting on columns, with chambers in two floors above (fig. 28)[2]. [These pilasters, as the elevation shews, were enriched by the addition of a column resting on a projecting plinth, which was richly ornamented. The cornice above the arcade was returned over each of these columns, so as to break the uniformity of the line, and form a base for a second column which marked the subdivisions into compartments on the first floor. In each compartment there were four windows, each of three lights divided by a transom; and between each pair of windows a half-pilaster, terminating below in a lion's head, which served for the transmission of a spout. The upper floor had smaller windows, also of three lights, placed exactly over those in the floor below, and over each window was a gable, ornamented with finials. On the north range, between two of the upper windows, there was a sun-dial (*i*, fig. 9). The portions erected by Sir Thomas Sclater and Dr Babington, respectively, were each distinguished by two large stone shields, placed at the top of the columns

---

[1] [Professor Willis makes the following note on the style of masonry employed by Dr Nevile: "The walls of Nevile's building [on the north side, next the Master's Garden] are of coursed rubble with alternate sloping courses, very small and neat. This rubble-work occurs with larger stones in his College Kitchen, and in the range of south chambers, next the lane, at the corner of Mill Street."]

[2] [The lengths of the north, south, and west sides of the court, measured with a tape along the kerb, are: North side, 222 feet; South side, 230 feet 3 inches; West side, 148 feet 6 inches. The length of the East side, taken along the wall of the Hall and Buttery, is 132 feet.]

dividing them from the next compartment. These shields bore
the arms of the benefactors who had erected those portions[1],
and of Dr Nevile. Sir Thomas Sclater's building, and that next
to it on the west, were further distinguished from the rest by a
wall of much greater thickness (fig. 9). The large room on the
first floor, lighted by three windows (k, l, m, fig. 9) is a splendid
specimen of the ornamentation of the time; being wainscoted
in oak, which appears never to have been-painted, and having a
ceiling of plaster-work in high relief with wreaths of flowers and
fruit, Sir Thomas Sclater's arms, and other enrichments.]

The present aspect of these buildings is very different from
the original. By the middle of the century succeeding that in
which they were built, the front wall had decayed, and the
columns upon which it rested had become dangerous, for in
1755 the Conclusion Book contains the following entry:

"April 7, 1755. Whereas the Workmen employ'd to survey the
North side of Neville's Court have reported, that all the Columns with
their Bases and Capitals and all the Windows must be new; that the
Spandrels of the Arches, the Friezes and upper Pedestals are all Clunch
and must be taken out; that the Ston Work to the Bottom of the
Upper Windows must be taken down; and in general, that it will be
difficult, if not impossible, to make the Wall sound and good without
taking down the Front and rebuilding it; It is agreed by the Master
and Seniors that the said wall be taken down and rebuilt in a substantial manner."

Accordingly, under the direction of Mr Essex, the fashion-
able architect of the time, the work was undertaken, and the
Junior Bursar's books shew that the north and south sides of
the older portions of the court were entirely rebuilt[2]. [The

---

[1] [These details are derived partly from Loggan, partly from "A Perspective View
of Nevile's Court, Trinity College, Cambridge, from ye East," drawn by R. West,
August, 1739, and published 1 February, 1740. Among the charges for building
Dr Babington's portion we find "Pd to Rob: Grumbold for A coat of Armes
003. 00. 00." The shields are still to be seen, built in to the wall at the S.W. corner
of the College grounds, near Garret Hostel Bridge.]

[2] [At the end of the Day Book for 1755—56 the Junior Bursar makes the following entries: "The Masons whole Bill for finishing the Wall of the North Cloister
£652. 8. 3. D° for the Front Wall in the south cloyster exclusive of the Day work
Bill not yet brought in £560 1. 1." If to these sums are added the cost of the back
wall £92. 10. 0, and the amount of the bill for Day work £111. 4. 0, we get a total
of £1416 for this part of the work.]

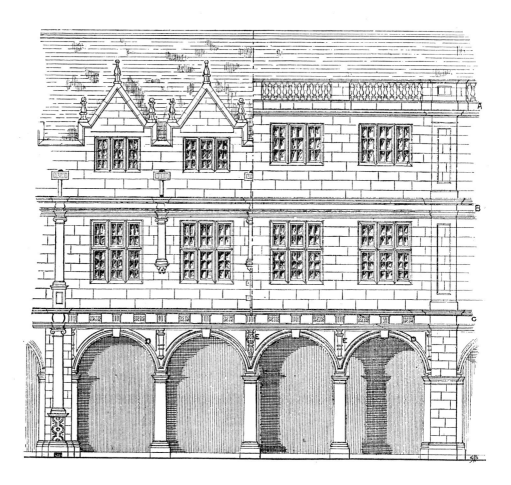

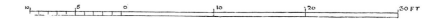

Fig. 28. Nevile's Court, shewing the original design, from Loggan, and the changes introduced by Essex in 1756. Suggested by a lecture-diagram by Professor Willis.

north side was undertaken first, and in the Accounts for the year ending Michaelmas, 1755, we find:

"To M[r] Bottomley for 403½ feet of Window casing, 9 Bases for Columns, and 63 foot of Cube Stone; and circular moulded Work to ditto 30 feet, and plain work 96 feet. Nine caps for ditto, 15 foot of Cube Stone, 54 feet of strait moulding and 16 foot and ½ of circular moulding to ditto .... £55. 8. 2½.

To W[m]. Elsden his Bill for new Stone for the Building at the north Side of the Second Court .... £329. 15. 2.

To the Workmen on laying y[e] 1st Stone .... £1. 1. 0."

In the Account for 1755—56 we find the same work proceeding[1]; the old wall is taken down to the ground; new foundations are dug for the staircases; new window-frames are fitted to all the front windows in both floors; and lastly, the balustrade along the north side is put up. It is stated that the cost of this was regulated by Sir James Burrough[2], Master of Caius College, an entry which may perhaps indicate that he had had some share in designing the alterations. The south side also of the court was commenced in this year; the front wall and the back wall were both entirely rebuilt, with new door-cases, and new stonework for the windows[3]. At the end of the Account for this year the following interesting memoranda occur:

"1. The old Stone on the South side of Nevils Court proved in general much worse than the North Side, particularly Cornices and Architraves; so that a considerably greater Quantity of new Stone was used on the South Side on that account only.

2. The lower cornice on the North Side lies only 6 Inches into the Wall, but that on the South Side goes quite thro y[e] whole thickness of y[e] Wall.

3. There are a great many more Cube feet of bond Stone on the South Side, than on the other.

4. The ashler under the Plinth of the Ballustrade on the South Side is parpin ashler, but on the North Side it is thinner Stone backed up with Bricks.

5. The Wall between the end of the Cloister and y[e] Butteries on the South Side is longer than that on the opposite.

---

[1] [For this year the Junior Bursar's Day Book only has been preserved.]

[2] [Ibid. *Ballustrade in Nevil's Court, North Side.* "To W[m] Elsden his Bill for D[o]: work being measured by M[r] Essex, and price set by M[r] Burrow £89. 3. 6."]

[3] [Ibid. *Nevil's Court. South Cloister in D[o].* "12 Nov. For the new front wall...£542. 16. 0¼. For the back wall, viz. for new Door Cases and Top Stones, Coping of the Gables and parapet Wall, stones to y[e] Chimneys; and for Jaumbs, Transums, Heads, Mullions &c to y[e] Windows..£92. 9. 10."]

6. The said wall on the South Side is all new Stone, but that on the north side all old Stone."

The stonework had evidently been nearly completed by the end of 1756, for in the Account for 1756—57 the entries relate chiefly to internal work and fittings. Under the heading "*East end of 2ᵈ Court*" we find :

" For the new Ceiling, and repairing the Wall in the Cloyster, also for all the new ceilings, and plaistering of Partition Walls in all the Chambers over yᵉ East End of the Cloyster; and for rendring the Walls of the Stair-cases and ceilings of the same : The whole being measur'd by Mʳ Essex, and the prices according to the Artickles of Agreement .... £117. 11. 6."

There are further charges for "making new doors, window-cases, shutters, cornices, etc., in the Chambers over the south Cloyster"; for "fitting and putting up all the old Wainscot in the upper Rooms of yᵉ South Cloyster"; for "new wainscot done in the four lower chambers in the South Cloyster[1]"; with a general payment to Bottomley for the stonework, similar to that quoted above for the opposite side[2]; and, in the next year, "for new Floors in all the Upper and Lower Chambers over the South Cloyster (East End), and Garrets over the Stair-cases." These entries shew that at the east end at least the structure was entirely rebuilt; and the expense of alteration was so great that, on the completion of the work, the rent of the four rooms on the first floor was raised[3]. The work was finished at Michaelmas, 1758[4]. The external changes will be understood from the elevation (fig. 28), where a bay of the new work has been drawn by the side of a bay of the old. It is clear that the two compartments at the west end of the court, on both sides,

---

[1] [Jun. Burs. Day Book, 1756—57. "Oct. 19. Paid to Mʳ Essex for new wainscott done in the four lower Chambers, bed Places, and Studies of the South Cloister as by Articles with the College £213. 0. 0."]

[2] [Under the head of *Extraordinaries* we find "For Rents of Chambers taken down £71. 10. 0": an amount which shews that the number must have been considerable.]

[3] ["Dec. 14, 1758. Agreed...that an additional Rent of two pounds per annum be laid upon each of the four first low Rooms on the South side of Nevile's Court... on Account of the extraordinary Expenses in Wainscotting, and fitting up the said Rooms."]

[4] ["Dec. 14, 1758. Agreed by the Master and Seniors that one hundred and twenty pounds be paid to Mʳ Essex in full for surveying the Repairs of the College and New Buildings for the last four years ending at Michˢ. last."]

were only faced, to make them correspond with those which were rebuilt; for the rooms on the second floor are still arranged garret-wise, with sloping sides carried down to within three feet from the floor; whereas in those at the east end the vertical height of the side-wall represents the full height of the room. The total cost of these works was £6064. 8s. 10½d.[1]

We have next to relate the history of the Library which forms the west side of Nevile's Court.]

The origin of the great Library is not very distinctly recorded. We have seen that from the beginning of Trinity College a Library, as one of the necessary elements of collegiate arrangement, had been intended; and that it was finally carried out in Dr Nevile's time. But in 1665—66 a fire broke out in the Library which destroyed the roof[2], and probably damaged the walls, for they are at present sustained by buttresses on the north side which are evidently of a much later structure, and besides have been thoroughly cased and repaired. This, and the gradual increase of books, which in all Colleges has made it necessary to rebuild and enlarge the Libraries from time to time, seems naturally to have led to a project for a new and more spacious structure in a different position, which assumed a definite form during the Mastership of Dr Isaac Barrow (Master, 1673—77). The following tradition is given in the biography of Doctor John North, Dr Barrow's successor in the Mastership[3]:

"When the doctor entered upon the mastership of Trinity College, the building of the great library, begun by his immediate predecessor Dr Barrow, was advanced about three-quarters of the height of the outward wall; and the doctor most heartily and diligently applied his

---

[1] [This sum is copied from two papers in the Muniment Room, headed: "Money paid by the College in rebuilding two-thirds of the South Side and new Fronting two-thirds of the North Side of Nevils-Court"; and: "To Cash paid by yᵉ College for Altering and reparing that Part of the North and South Cloisters in Nevils-Court next the Library." The former work cost £5486. 4s. 8¾d.; the latter £578. 4s. 1¾d.]

[2] Jun. Burs. Accounts, 1665—66. "Carpenters. For girt, sparrs, ioists, oaken board, nailes, ironworke, mens wages and carriage of timbers for the Library roofe after the fire 07. 14. 00. Extraordinaries. To Mʳ Blomer for wine after the fire at the Library 00. 03. 06." Sen. Burs. Accounts. "Gratuita. To Mʳ Griffith by order of a meeting for his paines and charge in ordering the Library after the fire 10. 00. 00." Steward's Accounts. "Distributed among such as did yᵉ best service when yᵉ Library was on fire 2. 00. 00."

[3] [Life of the Hon. and Rev. Dʳ John North. Ed. 1826, iii. 364.]

best forces towards carrying it on; and, besides his own contributions, most of his friends and relations, upon his encouragement, became benefactors; the particulars whereof will appear in the accounts of that noble structure. The tradition of that undertaking runs thus. They say that D[r] Barrow pressed the heads of the university to build a theatre; it being a profanation and scandal that the speeches should be had in the university church, and that also be deformed with scaffolds, and defiled with rude crowds and outcries[1]. This matter was formally considered at a council of the heads; and arguments of difficulty, and want of supplies went strong against it. D[r] Barrow assured them that if they made a sorry building, they might fail of contributions; but if they made it very magnificent and stately, and, at least, exceeding that at Oxford, all gentlemen, of their interest, would generously contribute; it being what they desired, and little less than required of them; and money would not be wanted, as the building went up, and occasion called for it. But sage caution prevailed, and the matter, at that time, was wholly laid aside. D[r] Barrow was piqued at this pusillanimity, and declared that he would go straight to his college, and lay out the foundations of a building to enlarge his back court, and close it with a stately library, which should be more magnificent and costly than what he had proposed to them, and doubted not but, upon the interest of his college, in a short time to bring it to perfection. And he was as good as his word; for that very afternoon he, with his gardeners and servants, staked out the very foundation upon which the building now stands; and D[r] North saw the finishing of it, except the classes, which were forward, but not done, in his time; and divers benefactions came in upon that account; wherewith, and the liberal supply from the college, the whole is rendered complete; and the admirable disposition and proportion on the inside is such as touches the very soul of any one who first sees it."

[Whether this story be literally true or not, it is certain that Dr Barrow actively promoted the building of the Library, by personally soliciting subscriptions. In the words of his biographer, Abraham Hill:

"Besides the particular assistance he gave to many in their study, he concerned himself in everything that was for the interest of his College. Upon the single affair of building their Library, he writ out quires of paper, chiefly to those who had been of the College, first to engage them, and then to give them thanks, which he never omitted. These letters he esteemed not enough to keep copies of; but by the generous returns they brought in, they appeared to be of no small value."

---

[1] [Dr Barrow alludes in his Vice-Chancellor's Speech, delivered in S. Mary's Church in 1676, at the close of his year of office, to the want of a Theatre "quod disputantium jurgiis hoc templum exoneret, et quo sanniorum ineptiæ religentur"; of a larger Library; and of Public Schools. Works, ed. Napier, ix. 222. The circumstances which attended the building of a theatre for University ceremonies referred to above will be related in the History of the Senate-House.]

One of those letters has been preserved[1]. The writer gives a definite reason for the construction of a new Library at that particular time, namely, the bequest of Bishop Hacket: "who hath given us fifty pounds a-year for ever to be expended in buying books, which our present Library (being already filled and overburdened with those we have) can neither contain nor support[2]."]

Sir Christopher Wren is known to have been the architect of this noble building, and the inscription at the foot of Loggan's plate of the Library records that his services were rendered gratuitously[3]. [This liberality may have been caused by friendship for Dr Barrow, whose praise of Wren in his inaugural lecture in 1662 as Professor of Geometry at Gresham College, London[4], reads as though dictated more by personal feeling than by appreciation of his talents. Two designs for this Library have been preserved among Wren's drawings in the Library of All Souls' College, Oxford[5]. The first of these was made before the lengthening of the court was contemplated. In the centre of the west side there was to have been a circular building, about 90 feet high, by 65 feet wide, rising from a square plinth, and covered with a dome and cupola. On the east side a double staircase gave access to a hexastyle portico of semi-engaged columns, supporting a pediment. Through this portico the

---

[1] [MSS. Harl. Mus. Brit. 7001. Printed in Barrow's Works, ut supra, 1. lxvi.]

[2] [Bishop Hacket died 28 October, 1670. The particulars of this bequest are related below in the History of Bishop's Hostel.]

[3] ["Operis vero totius accuratam designationem Societas acceptam refert D⁰. Christophoro Wren equiti aurato, qui ad structuræ elegantiam curas suas omnes sponte et gratuito contulit, Vir omnium sermone propter summam animi bonitatem et ingenii solertiam merito celebratissimus." Loggan was employed to print the design of the Library, probably with the view of obtaining subscriptions. Library Accounts, 1676. "To David Loggan for yᵉ plates-cutting and 450 Cutts, by yᵉ. Sen: Burs: 21. 12. 0." Ibid. 1677 "For reprinting yᵉ schemes, with alterations by yᵉ Senior Bursar 04. 10. 0." An item in the Junior Bursar's Accounts for 1690—91: Glasier. "for mending...the chamber where Mʳ Loggan's Press stood formerly," shews that he was in Cambridge at that time, and was provided with a work-room in Trinity College.]

[4] [Works, ut supra, ix. 176.]

[5] [These drawings are bound in four folio volumes. They were presented to the Library by Sir W. Blackstone, and arranged and catalogued by James Elmes. His catalogue is contained in a letter "To the Editor of the General Chronicle," dated Chichester 4 Sept. 1812. The drawings for Trinity College Library are in Vol. i. Nos. 39—51. The drawings for the rejected design are Nos. 39—42.]

central area was entered, round which there was a stone seat and stone tables. The wall-space was divided into compartments by composite pilasters. Above the floor there were three galleries, approached by a staircase in each of the four angles. Light was obtained through large semicircular openings in the drum of the dome, and through the central cupola. This structure was connected with the sides of the court by a dwarf wall, support-ing iron railings. It was set back so far that the east wall of the staircase by which it was entered would have been in a line with the west gables of the north and south sides of the court; and the boundary wall, after prolonging the gable-walls north-wards and southwards for a short distance, curved westward to join the Library.]

The design which was executed is accompanied by the fol-lowing explanation, contained in a rough draught of a letter to some gentleman of Trinity College, probably the Master. [It is not signed, but internal evidence shews that it must have been written or dictated by Wren.]

"S^r.

A building of that consideration you goe about deserues good care in the designe and able workemen to performe it, and that he who takes the generall management upon him may haue a prospect of the whole and make all parts inside and outside corresponde well together. To this end I haue comprised the whole designe in 6 Figures.

Fig. I.

Shews halfe the Ground plot of the Substruction Cloister and first Flightes of the Stairecases. I haue chosen middle pillars and a double porticoe and lightes outward rather then a middle wall, as being the same expence, more gracefull, and according to the manner of the auncients who made double walkes (with three rowes of pillars or two rowes and a wall) about the forum.

Fig. II.

Shewes halfe the ground plot of the upper floor, the entrances from the stairecases, and the disposition of the shelues both along the walls and breaking out from the walls, wch must needes proue very con-venient and gracefull, and the best way for the students will be to haue a litle square table in each Celle with 2 chaires. The necessity of bringing windowes and dores to answer to the old building leaues two squarer places at the endes and 4 lesser Celles not to study in, but to be shut up with some neat Lattice dores for archives.

Fig. III.

Shewes the face of the building next the court with the pavillions for the stairecases and the Sections of the old buildings where they joyne to the new.   I chose a double order rather then a single, because a single order must either haue been mutilated in its members or haue been very expensiue, and if performed would not haue agreed with the lownesse of the porches, which would haue been too darke and the solids too grosse for the openings.   I haue given the appearance of arches as the Order required fair and lofty: but I haue layd the floor of the Library upon the impostes, which answar (*sic*) to the pillars in the cloister and the levells of the old floores, and haue filled the Arches with relieues of stone, of which I haue seen the effect abroad in good building, and I assure you where porches are lowe with flat ceilings is infinitely more gracefull then lowe arches would be and is much more open and pleasant, nor need the mason freare (*sic*) the performance because the Arch dis-charges the weight, and I shall direct him in a firme manner of executing the designe.   By this contriuance the windowes of the Library rise high and giue place for the deskes against the walls, and being high may be afforded to be large, and being wide may haue stone mullions and the glasse pointed, which after all inventions is the only durable way in our Climate for a publique building, where care must be had that snowe driue not in.   I haue giuen noe other Frontispeece ["ornament" erased] to the midle then Statues according to aunctient example, because in this case I find any thing else impertinent, the Entrances being endwaies and the roofe not suiting it.   This may be don if you please, you may make the three middle Arches with 3 quarter columnes and the rest with pilasters of a third of their Diameter, which will saue some charge in stone, but it is best as it is designed.

Fig. IV.

Shewes halfe the outside of the building next the River which I de-signe after a plainer manner to be performed most with Ashler, the three portalls one against each cloister and one in the middle and the pavillions for the staires giue it grace enough for the viewes that way.

Fig. V.

Shewes halfe the section the longest way and discovers the insides of the stairecase, the porticoe belowe the Library, the disposition of the shelues, the side dores from the old building, the division of the ceeling, and the roofe.   The staires are soe carried they [may be] made of Marble or hard stone with Iron rayles, and if the middle ally of the Library were paved with small marbles you would much consult for the quiet of the place, and for the cleanesse of the bookes from dust ; the Celles may be floored with wainscote.   I haue added thin pilasters to the walles, which are easily performed in rendering upon brickworke; the cornices divide the ceeling into three rowes of large square pannells answering the pilasters which will proue the best fret, because in a long roome it giues the most agreeable perspectiue.   I made the pavillions of the staires soe as I might not loose my end Lightes; and least the Lightes next the old buildings should be cut of [off] within I would ad-uise to loose the 2 last roomes in the Garrets and lay a covering of lead upon the 2^d story, which may be ordered not to be discovered in the Court, the stone worke continuing.

Fig. VI.

Gives the transverse section through the middle Arche with the thicknesses of the walles, the manner of the roofe, and the insides to be compared with the other designes.   I haue given the auncient forme of roofe, which the experience of all ages hath found the surest, noe other

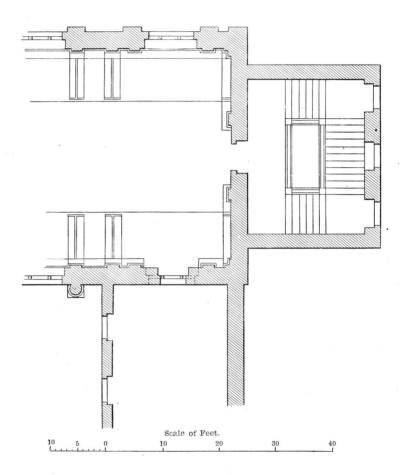

Scale of Feet.

Fig. 29. Designs of Sir Christopher Wren, Fig. II. Part of his plan of the Library, shewing the staircase at the north end, part of the first floor of Nevile's Court, the door of communication from it to the Library, and the arrangement of the bookcases.

is to be trusted without doubling the thicknesses of the walles.   The Statues will be a noble ornament, they are supposed of plaister, there are Flemish artists that doe them cheape.

I suppose you haue good masons, how ever I would willingly take a farther paines to giue all the mouldings in great, wee are scrupulous in small matters and you must pardon us; the Architects are as great pedants as Criticks or Heralds. And therfore if you approue the designes let the mason take his measures as much as is necessary for the present setting out the worke and be pleased to transmit them to me again, and I shall copy out partes of them at large more proper for the use of the workemen, and giue you a carefull estimate of the charge, and return you again the originall designes, for in the handes of the workemen they will soon be defaced that they will not be able from them to pursue the worke to a conclusion. I haue made a Cursory estimate and it is not that at which you will stumble as not exceeding the charge proposed[1]."

[Of these drawings Figs. II. III. VI. are here reproduced (figs. 29, 30, 32) by the kind permission of the Warden and Fellows of All Souls College, Oxford. Wren further gave designs for the woodwork. Among his drawings is one for one of the classes, dated 1686, shewing the cupboard beneath to contain MSS., and a table, desk, and two stools. The Building Account shews that he was constantly consulted during the progress of the work. We find that the master mason went to London to visit him in 1676; twice in 1680, "to speake with Sr Christopher Wren," and "to consult with Sr Christopher Wren"; three times in 1683; twice in 1685; and Cornelius Austin, who made the woodwork, went twice to London "to Sr Christopher Wren," in 1690[2].]

The work was begun 23 February 1675—76[3] in pursuance of an Order made on the previous day :

---

[1] [The text has been collated with the original in All Souls College Library. This memoir has been printed, but with many errors, in "Memoirs of the Life and Works of Sir Christopher Wren," by James Elmes, 4°. Lond. 1823, p. 174.]

[2] [The following entry, from the Account for the period between 29 Dec. 1687, and 21 Dec. 1688, is curious: "Deliver'd to the Master tenn Guyneas for Sr. Christopher Wren's servant 10. 15. 00."]

[3] [The authorities for the History of the Library are (1) a volume preserved in the Treasury of Trinity College, entitled : "A just Accompt of the Particular Summes of Money contributed by our Noble and Worthy Benefactors towards the Erecting of a New Library in the Colledge of the Holy and Ind. Trinitie in Cambridge and received of Dr Humfrey Babington then Senr Bursar of the sayd Colledge from the 23th of February in the yeare 167⅝ upon wch day that Building was begun": (2) a record of the sums expended in each year, kept by the official, probably the Senior Bursar, to whom the supervision of the building-work was entrusted : (3) a separate Account Book kept by Robert Grumbold, the master-mason, which

"Agreed then by the Master and Seniors, that the ground for the foundation of our designed Library shall be digged forthwith.

Also that the Teniscourt shall forthwith be taken downe.

Also that the Junior Bursar, Mr Bainbrigg, and Mr Brattel be desired to take care of seeing these particulars performed.

Also that the Teniscourt-keeper shall have a reasonable consideration for his losse upon this occasion[1].

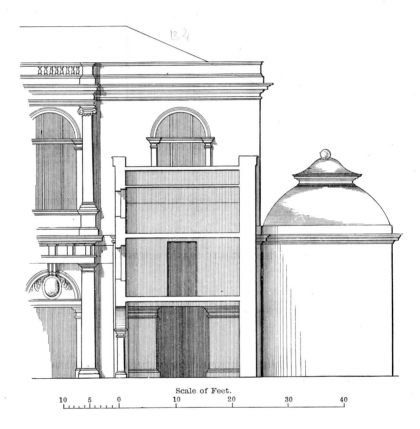

Scale of Feet.

Fig. 30. Designs of Sir Christopher Wren, Fig. III. Part of his elevation of the east side of the
Library, with a section of the north range of Nevile's Court, shewing the door to the Library
from the first floor.

supplies several particulars not to be found in the former two. These two volumes are among the MSS. in Trinity College Library.]

[1] [College Order, 19 July, 1676. " Agreed...that twenty pounds be given to the late keeper of the Tenis Court Bolton." The Building Account of the Library for the

Fig. 31.   Elevation of one bay on the east side, drawn to scale from the
existing building.

Also that the two Bursars, or either of them, shall receive and give discharges for any money contributed to this work.

Also that these Fellows D[r] Babington, M[r] Hawkins, M[r] Pulleyn, M[r] Corker, M[r] Bainbrigg, M[r] Brattel, M[r] Ekins, M[r] Bridge, M[r] Lane, M[r] Spencer, M[r] Wickins, M[r] Petit, M[r] Harrison, M[r] Battely, M[r] Chare be particularly desired to oversee the workmen and promote the work.

Also that D[r] Babington, M[r] Bainbrigg, and M[r] Ekins shall be empowered to bargain for and buy materialls with allowance of Master and Seniors.

ISAAC BARROW."

The building-work occupied about twelve years. The master-mason was Robert Grumbold, who built the Hall and part of the south range at Clare Hall[1]. He received £4. 4s. 0d. per month for his services. The stone came from Ketton. The erection of the walls must have occupied between four and five years, for it was not until 1680 that lead for the roof was bought, and agreements made with the plumber[2]. The "upper floore above the Ceiling" was laid down in 1683, and the scaffold was struck 31 January, 1684. The timber for the floor was provided in 1685—86; the internal walls and the ceiling were plastered in 1686 and 1687 by workmen from London, apparently under the direction of a Mr Banks[3]; and on 5 March 1686—87 the following agreement was made with Grumbold for the marble pavement and entered in the Conclusion Book :

"Agreed...with Robert Grumbold that he shall haue two shillings and three pence a foot for pauing the Library with black and white Marble, and laying of it in plaster of Paris, he standing to all charges, and liable to be abated the odd penny, in case the work should not giue satisfaction. Jo: Mountagu M[r] Coll[ij]"

The pavement was laid down in the course of 1688[4]; and

same year contains the following item : "To Bolton in recompense of his losse of y[e] Tennis-Court pulled down and employed in y[e] new-building 20. 0. 0."]

  [1] [History of Clare Hall, Chapter iv. In the Library Account for 1676 we find : "To Rob. Grumbold for his Modell 02. 00. 00."]

  [2] [Building Account, 22 Dec. 1679—22 Dec. 1680. "To M[r] Newton Regester for Drawing of Couenants Between John Kendall Plummer And the Colleg In reference to y[e] New Liberary 00. 10. 00."]

  [3] [Grumbold's Account Book, 1676. "P[d] to M[r] Groue and M[r] Bancks for ther Modells 31. 13. 04." Building Accounts, 10 Jan. 1686—29 Dec. 1687. "P[d] to M[r] Groue part of his debt for plaistering worke 100. 00. 00. For wine att the entertainment of M[r] Bancks and gifts to the London plaisterers this and y[e] last yeare 00. 09. 06."]

  [4] [Ibid. 29 Dec. 1687—21 Dec. 1688. "P[d] to Grumbold for the pauement of the

before the end of 1690 that work and all others requiring masons had evidently been completed, for Grumbold was paid in full.

[We will next compare the building, as thus completed, with the recorded history, and with the designs of Wren. The Library is 150 feet long on the inside, by 38 feet broad. It is

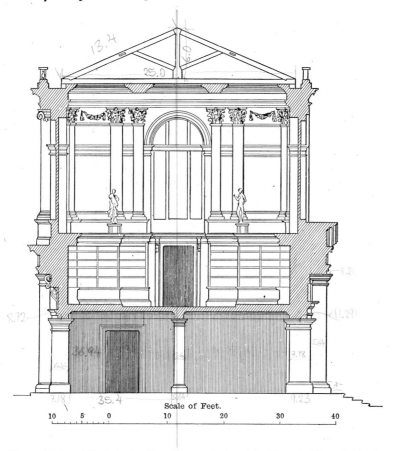

Scale of Feet.

| 10 | 5 | 0 | 10 | 20 | 30 | 40 |

Fig. 32. Designs of Sir Christopher Wren, Fig. vi. Section of the Library, looking south, shewing the intended entrance from the cloister; the bookcases, with statues on the ends of those projecting from the east and west walls; and the roof.

at present approached by a single staircase at the north end (fig. 9), but the Memoir quoted above shews that a staircase at

library in black and white marble; for the stone steps and pavement of the cloysters with Free stone in part 360. 00. 00.''']

each end was originally intended; and Fig. I. of Wren's designs is a ground-plan of the south end, with a door out of the "Substruction Cloister," as he calls it, and a staircase, similar to the door and staircase at the opposite end. These doors are also shewn in his transverse section (fig. 32). Each staircase was to have been surmounted by a cupola (fig. 30). Their height, as he says, was determined by his wish to have space for a window in the north and south walls. The reason for the abandonment of the staircase at the south end is not known. The door to it remains, precisely similar to that at the north end. It now gives access to an iron balcony put up between March 1693 and July 1695 [1].

The arrangement of the cloister will be understood from the general plan of the College (fig. 9); and the style from the elevation of one of the eleven bays of the east side (fig. 31), which has been drawn to scale from the existing building. If this be compared with the original design (fig. 30. Fig. III. of Wren's designs) it will be seen that the style there indicated has been closely followed. The only change introduced is that the sculpture in the tympanum of each of the arches to the right and left of the central arch has been slightly altered (fig. 31); and that the tympanum of the central arch, which in Wren's design was treated in the same way as the others, now contains a bas-relief representing King Ptolemy the Second receiving the Septuagint from the Translators. It was executed in 1679 [2]; but the name of the artist has not been recorded. The four statues, representing Divinity, Law, Physic, and Mathematics, which stand on the central piers subdividing the balustrade on the east side, were executed in 1681 by Mr Gabriel Cibber, a sculptor much patronised by Wren, who probably approved the design. Cibber came to Cambridge with his men, and personally superintended the placing of them [3].

---

[1] ["To Wm. Grizell for the Iron Work of yᵉ Ball Coney 20. 08. 04."]

[2] [23 April, 1679. "Pᵈ to yᵉ Caruer at London for cutting of yᵉ Midle pees in yᵉ Midle Arch...£38. 12. 04."]

[3] [Walpole's Anecdotes, ed. Dallaway, iii. 152. Grumbold's Accounts, 7 May, 1681. "Pᵈ to Mʳ Gabriell Cibber for cutting four statues 80. 00. 00." 27 June. "Pᵈ to yᵉ widdo Bats for Mʳ Gabriel Cibbers and his mens diatt 05. 18. 11. Pᵈ to Mʳ Martin [for the same] 12. 03. 03." This sum shews that they must have stayed for some time, so that possibly the statues were carved on the spot. The following

J.A.Bell.

J.Le Keux.

Fig. 33.   West front of the Library of Trinity College; from Le Keux's Memorials of Cambridge, ed. Cooper.   Vol. II.

Fig. 34. Interior of the Library of Trinity College, looking south; from Le Keux's Memorials of Cambridge, ed. Cooper.

Wren has explained (in the description of Fig. III.) the reasons which determined the proportions of his elevation ; and the section of the north side of Nevile's Court appended to his design for his own building, of which part is here given (fig. 30), shews how he was fettered by the necessity for adaptation to the levels of the old floors. The idea of entering the Library from the rooms on the first floor at each end was never carried out, but the modifications in the position of the bookcases (fig. 29) which, as Wren explains in the description of his Fig. II., were made to suit that scheme, were not altered when it was abandoned. The west front (fig. 33) was carried out in accordance with Wren's intention, "designed," as he says, "after a plainer manner." The only difference between his design (Fig. IV.) and the existing building is that he shews the central portico surmounted by a semicircular pediment, and the whole composition raised on four steps. This latter detail is also shewn in his transverse section (fig. 32).

The general design seems to have been borrowed from that of the Library of S. Mark at Venice, built by Sansovino in 1536. The Italian architect, like Sir Christopher Wren, raised his Library on a cloister, which is in the Doric style, while the superstructure is Ionic. The Venetian example is more ornate, and there are statues upon every pier of the balustrade. The arcades are left open, probably because there was not the same necessity for accommodating the levels of the floors to those of older buildings.

We will next consider the history of the woodwork. The Memoir quoted above shews the care taken by Wren to provide sufficient space for books along the east and west walls (Fig. III.); and the actual arrangement of the bookcases, as we see them at present, was suggested by him in his description of his Fig. II. as being convenient (1) for study, and (2) for the safe keeping of valuable papers. This arrangement will be understood from the general ground-plan (fig. 9) on which the bookcases have been indicated by dotted lines, and from the drawing of the north-east corner of the Library (fig. 35), which shews one of the "celles," as he terms them, furnished with a table, desk, and

entry is worth preserving : " Payd for the Carridg of a Larg Block Stone Giuen by John Manning to yᵉ Coll. for one of yᵉ Figures 01. 00. 00."]

two stools, and also one of his "lesser celles," closed, as he
intended, with "neat Lattice dores." It will be seen from
the section (fig. 32) that Wren intended to return the bookcases along the north and south walls. This was never
carried out, but whether the change received his sanction or not,
has not been recorded. These walls were panelled in the same
style as the rest of the woodwork, and evidently at the same
time; and instead of a bookcase a bust is placed on each side

Fig. 35.   Interior of the north-east corner of the Library.

of the north and south doors. The same design shews the
statues with which Wren intended to ornament the projecting
portions of his bookcases (Fig. VI.). The pedestals designed by
him were executed, but the statues were replaced by busts.

Preparations were made at the end of 1685 for the construction of these bookcases, or "classes," as they are uniformly

styled in the Accounts[1]. The work was entrusted to Cornelius Austin. He had executed nineteen "classes" by the beginning of 1691[2]. In the two following years he received further sums, in which payments for the wainscot at the north and south ends of the Library, and on the walls of the staircase, are probably included; and subsequently he was paid for a pair of carved doors for one of the four lock-up classes. Two other pairs were made by John Austin and Francis Woodward in 1699[3]. The busts in plaster which stand over the classes, in place of the statues suggested by Wren, were put up in the course of 1691 by Mr Grinling Gibbons, who also executed the beautiful wreaths of fruit, flowers and arabesques in lime wood, with coats of arms[4] in the same material, which adorn the ends of the classes and other portions of the fittings, between March, 1691 and March, 1693. During the same period the statue of the Duke of Somerset, usually ascribed to Rysbrack, was placed in the westernmost of the two niches at the south end (fig. 33). These niches were not originally contemplated, but were made by Grumbold in 1691, after the walls had been plastered. The following extracts from the Accounts between December, 1690 and March, 1693 illustrate these various works:

[1] [Seven of these "classes" had been the subject of special donations. It is recorded in a note at the end of the list of subscriptions for 1690—91, that each of the following persons gave £28: "Bp. Pearson, Dr Mountagu, Sr Thomas Sclater, Dr Chamberlaine, Dr Babington, Dr Lynnet, Mr Drake senior Steward of our Courts." In the Accounts ending 10 Jan. 1686 we find "To Corn. Austin towards buying of wainscote 050. 00. 00"; and in 1687—88 the Senior Bursar is repaid for "expences for sawing, carriage, and wharfage of Cedar, and Mr Austens journie to London 8. 3. 0."]

[2] [Ibid. 22 Dec. 1690—23 March, 1691. "To Mr Corn. Austen for Ten Classes 280. 00. 00. Pd him for Five Classes more 140. 00. 00. Pd Him also for His journie to London and 1 Guinee to Sr Xtophs Man 3. 1. 6. For erecting four Classes 112. 00. 00."]

[3] [Ibid. 23 March, 1691—23 Feb. 1692. "To Cornelius Austen in part for ye Classes etc in the Library 110. 00. 00." Ibid. 23 Feb. 1692—2 March, 1693. "To Cornelius Austin 245. 05. 06." Ibid. 23 Dec. 1695—23 Dec. 1698. "Corn. Austin his bill for a pair of dores for ye MS class 22. 10. 00." Ibid. 23 Dec. 1698—30 Dec. 1699. "Pd to John Austin and Francis Woodward for 2 pair of Doors for ye Manuscript Classes 45. 00. 00."]

[4] [A description of these coats is given in the Appendix, No. VII. The benefactors commemorated are Dr Babington, Dr Barrow, Dr Chamberlaine, Mr Drake, Bp Hacket, Sir Robert Hildyard, Dr Lynnet (?), Dr Montagu, Dr Pearson, Sir H. Newton Puckering, Sir Thomas Sclater, Duke of Somerset.]

"Given to the Waggoners that brought down the
    Statue 0. 02. 06
To M[r] Gibbon's men who set up the Busto's 1. 00. 00
To Will: Fitch for Scaffolding and cutting the Niches ... 1. 14. 00
To M[r] Grumbold for drawing up and placing the Statue... 1. 00. 00
P[d] M[r] Grumbold for Stone and Work for the Niches...... 024. 1. 00
To M[r] Gibbons for the Duke of Somersets Statue Coats
    of Arms and Cifers and Bustos 200. 0. 00
To M[r] Gibbons [without particulars] 100. 0. 00
To Gibbons for these 4 Coats of Armes p[d] by y[e] Coll:
    viz. Bp. Hackett, D[r] Barrow, D[r] Mountague, and
    S[r] Rob[t] Hilliard ; 5[li] each 020. 00. 00
Payd to Gibbons by them selves or others for them for
    these 5 Coates of Armes viz. S[r] Tho. Slater, D[r]
    Chamberlayne, D[r] Babington, D[r] Lynnett, and Bp.
    Pearson ; 5[li] each 025. 00. 00
To Gibbons more in full for the Rest of y[e] things in the
    Library .... 060. 00. 00."

The iron gates in the cloister, and the iron rails for the staircase, were put up between March, 1691 and February, 1692 :

" Paid to M[r] Partridge the London Smith in part for the
    Gate and other worke........................ .... 80. 00. 00
Paid to M[r] Partridge in full for the three Iron Gates in
    the Cloyster and Iron Railes in the Stair Case
    besides £80 formerly paid .... 320. 00. 00."]

The entire building, however, was not completed until 1695,
when the subscription-list was closed, and the books were moved
in[1]. The subscriptions had amounted to £11,879. 2s. 1d. and
the expenses to £16,425. 15s. 0d. This sum, however, includes
the cost of four arches of the Court on each side, as already
explained. The difference was made up partly by the College,

---

[1] [Jun. Burs. Accounts, 1694—95. *Extraordinaries.* "To the Porters for remouing the Books into the New Library 03. 06. 00." The delay in the completion of
the room was evidently caused by the workmen who made the bookcases, for Austin's
bills were not discharged until 1693. College Order, 20 March, 1692—93. In the
Sen. Burs. Accounts for 1698—99 is the following entry : "Paid to M[r] Rotherham
[one of the Chaplains], by order of the Master and Seniors, for his trouble in removeing the bookes out of the old Library into the new 10. 00. 00." This probably
refers to the rearrangement of the books removed four years before. Thoresby, who
visited the College 16 May, 1695, speaks of "the stately Library, which is the noblest
case of any, but not yet furnished." Diary of Ralph Thoresby, 8vo. Lond. 1830. The
old Library was fitted up as a set of rooms, of which the first occupant was the Earl
of Hartford, son of the Duke of Somerset, then Chancellor of the University. He
took his Master of Arts degree in 1703. The rent, £12 per annum, was added to the
salary of the Librarian. College Order, 8 March, 1719—20.]

partly by loans from various persons which were gradually repaid in subsequent years.

The ceiling was left perfectly plain, although in the original design (fig. 32) it is represented as trabeated, in accordance with the pilasters which decorate the walls; and Sir Christopher Wren, in his description of his Fig. V., mentions his intention of subdividing it into "three rowes of large square pannells." The trabeation was supplied in 1850—51 under the direction of Dr Whewell, Master, 1842—66.

[A few additions and alterations remain to be noticed.

A note at the end of the Building Account for 1682—83 records that "Samuel Price, Goldsmith in Lombard Street gave the King's Armes in painted glasse." This entry must refer to the Arms and supporters which occupy the space above the transom in the north window, as there are no Arms in any of the other windows. The Arms are those of King William the Third, and were no doubt put up at the above date; the letters A. R above them, and the motto SEMPER EADEM beneath them, were probably added in 1706, to accommodate them to the reigning Sovereign, Queen Anne[1]. The window at the south end was filled with stained glass in 1774—75 by Peckitt of York, after a design by Cipriani[2]. This strange composition represents Sir Isaac Newton led into the presence of King George the Third by a female figure representing the University. The King is seated on a throne, under a canopy; in his right hand he holds a wreath, which he extends towards Newton. Lord Bacon, in his robes as Lord Chancellor, is seated at his feet, preparing to write down in an open volume an account of what is taking place. Britannia stands behind the King, and in the clouds above is Fame, blowing a trumpet.

---

[1] [Jun. Burs. Accounts, 1705—6. *Library.* "To Richardson for yᵉ Carriage of yᵉ Queens Arms in glass oo. 14. 10."]

[2] [Sen. Burs. Accounts, 1772—73. *Extraordinaries.* "To Mʳ Cypriani for a Painting for the South Window in the Library 105. 0. 0." Ibid. 1774—75. "To Mʳ Peckitt for painting and staining the South Window in the Library 315. 0. 0." The cost was defrayed out of monies bequeathed by Dr Robert Smith (Master 1742—68). "Dec. 15. 1770. Orderd by the Master and Seniors that £2000 in the Old S. S. Annuities left by Dʳ Smith be sold and applied towards the new Building in the great Court, and the painted Window in the Library.　　　J. Peterborough M.C."]

In 1840 dwarf bookcases of oak, with a sloping desk on the top, were placed in some of the classes. The design was supervised by C. R. Cockerell, Architect[1]. As the number of books increased, other cases were added from time to time; and lastly, two parallel rows of dwarf cases were placed in the central area in 1864. They contain the books bequeathed by Archdeacon Hare, William Grylls, M.A., and Dr Whewell. These collections arrived in 1855, 1864, and 1866.

A marble statue of Lord Byron, by Thorwaldsen, was placed near the south end of the Library in 1845. It had been commenced by the sculptor in 1829, and was then intended for Westminster Abbey. The Dean and Chapter having refused to admit it, it lay in the vaults of the Custom House until 1843, when it was presented to Trinity College by a vote of the subscribers, on condition that it should be placed in the Library[2].

Marble busts of distinguished members of the College are ranged round the room. There is no evidence that this system of decoration was sanctioned by Wren; indeed it appears to have originated in a wish to find some decoration for the wall on either side of the doors, where he had intended to place a bookcase. At the south end of the room these spaces are occupied by the busts of Bacon and Newton; at the north end by those of Ray and Willoughby. These four busts, all of which are by Roubiliac, were the first placed in the Library. Their pedestals are of white marble; those of nearly all the others are of oak, copied from the former. The following list of these

[1] [College Order, May 12, 1840. "It appearing, that a considerable addition is wanted for the reception of Books in the College Library, and a Plan and Estimate having this day been laid before the Board: It was agreed that the same be approved of, the Plan before it being carried into effect being submitted to M[r] Cockerell for his judgment respecting the proportions of the cases, and their ornamental mouldings." Mr Cockerell gave his services gratuitously. Sen. Burs. Minutes, 17 May, 1841.]

[2] [College Order, 19 February, 1845. "The subscribers to a Monumental Statue of Lord Byron which has been executed by Thorwaldsen having offered to present it to the College on condition of its being placed in the College Library; agreed...that this offer be accepted, and the thanks of the College be returned to the Subscribers." The acquisition of the statue was due to the exertions of C. de la Pryme, M.A. The correspondence between Mr Hobhouse and Baron Thorwaldsen in 1829, and between Mr Pryme and Dr Whewell in 1843, will be found in Notes and Queries for 26 Nov. 1881, p. 421. See also Stanley's Historical Memorials of Westminster Abbey, ed. 5, p. 281. The statue is said to have been finished 2 April, 1834.]

busts, arranged alphabetically, gives the name of the person represented, with that of the sculptor and donor, and the date of donation [1]:

BACON LORD CHANCELLOR VISCOUNT S^T. ALBANS	L. F. Roubiliac Sculp^{it} 1751	Ex Dono Danielis Lock Hujus Collegij AM. [1762]
BARROW	L. F. Roubiliac Sc^t. 1756.	Pos^{it} Edv. Montagu Armig. MDCCLVI.
BENTLEY	L. F. Roubiliac Sc^t. 1756	Pos^{nt} Bentleii Filiæ MDCCLVI.
GUL^S BOLLAND EQ. AURAT. BARO SCAC-CARII. 1829—1840.	Sievier Sc.	
Gul. Clark, M.D. Anat. Prof. 1817—1866	[Timothy Butler, London, 1866.]	Don. Conjux et Filius, 1882.
WILLIAM GEORGE CLARK	T WOOLNER SC. LONDON. 1879.	[Presented by subscription, 1879.]
E. COKE Summus Judex.	L. F. Roubiliac 1757	Posuit Comes Leicestriæ. 1757.
ROGERUS COTES.	P. Scheemakers Fecit: 1758	Posuit ROBERTUS SMITH Magister Collegii 1758.
ROB. COTTON Baronettus	L. F. Roubiliac 1757	Posuit Eliab Harvey. 1757.
ROBERT LESLIE ELLIS	T. WOOLNER. SC. LONDON. 1867	[Offered by Rev. John Grote, M.A., Fellow. 1862.]
JULIUS CAROLUS HARE, M.A.	T. WOOLNER. SC. LONDON, 1861	E DONO H. M. BUTLER, M.A. [1862]
IACOBUS. IURIN. M.D.	P. Scheemakers F^t.	IACOBUS. IURIN. F. POSUIT. [1762]
JOH. MITCHELL KEMBLE, A.M.	T. WOOLNER. SC. LONDON. 1865	[Presented by subscription, 1866.]

---

[1] [The names, dates, etc. are derived from the busts themselves, except when enclosed in square brackets.]

LORD LYNDHURST.	W. BEHNES SCULP^t 1844	Presented to the Lord Chancellor Lyndhurst, High Steward of the University of Cambridge. Given to this College of which Lord Lyndhurst was formerly Fellow, by his widow Georgiana Lady Lyndhurst, February 24 1876.
NEWTON	L. F. Roubiliac Sculp^{it}. 1751	Ex Dono Danielis Lock Hujus Collegij A.M.
JOA^S. RAY.	L. F. Roubiliac Sc^t.	POSUIT EDM. GARFORTH A.M. 1751.
PROFESSOR SEDGWICK 1860.	T. WOOLNER, SC. LONDON.	[Presented by subscription, 1862.]
ANTHONIUS SHEPHERD, S.T.P. PROFESSOR PLUMIANUS, 1760—1796.	J. Bacon R.A. Sculp^t. 1790.	IPSE LEGAVIT, 1796.
ROBERTUS SMITH S.T.P. COLLEGÎ S. TRINITATIS APUD CANTABRIGIENSES MAGISTER :	P. Scheemakers Fecit: 1758.	PRÆSENTI TIBI MATUROS LARGIMUR HONORES. A.D. 1758. ÆTAT. 68
ALFRED TENNYSON 1857	T. WOOLNER, SC. LONDON.	[Presented by subscription, 1859.]
TH^S. BARO TREVOR	L. F. Roubiliac Sculpsit. 1757.	Posuit ELIZABETHA FILIA, CAR : Duc : MARLB : conjux MDCCLVII.
GULIELMUS WHEWELL, S.T.P.	E. H. BAILY, R.A. *Sculp.* 1851.	LEGAVIT IPSE [1866]
C. WHITWORTH. Baro de Galway	L. F. Roubiliac Sculpsit: 1757.	Dono Dedit. RI : WHITWORTH Nepos.
FR^{us}. WILLOUGHBY.	L. F. Roubiliac. Sc^t.	POSUIT EDM. GARFORTH A.M. 1751

A classical composition, consisting of a stone screen, containing three semicircular niches surmounted by a classical cornice and pediment, placed upon a stone terrace approached

J. Le Keux

J. A. Bell.

Fig. 36. East end of Nevile's Court, Trinity College, shewing the Hall and the "Tribunal," built 1682: from Le Keux's Memorials of Cambridge, ed. Cooper.

Vol. II.

by three flights of steps, was built by Grumbold on the west
side of the Hall in the course of 1682[1] (fig. 36). It was probably
designed by Sir Christopher Wren, as three of Grumbold's
journeys to London took place during that year. The court was
laid out at the same time with four grass plots separated
by gravel walks (fig. 4).]

Having now followed the history of Nevile's Court to the
end, we must go back to a work which preceded the Library
by a few years, namely the building of Bishop's Hostel, on the
site of the old Gerard's or Garret Hostel.

[It was shewn in Chapter I. (p. 403), that the ground between
Garret Hostel Lane and the kitchen of Trinity College was
anciently occupied by two hostels standing close together, called
Ovyng's Inn and Garret Hostel. Their history is extremely
obscure. Previous to 1552, Garret Hostel had been let to a
Mr Bicardike, whose lease of it was redeemed in that year[2].
During his occupation the buildings seem to have been used
for the dwellings of artisans[3]. It is probable that soon after it
came into the hands of the College it was fitted up as a dwelling-
house, and occupied by Anthony Rodolph Chevallier, a French
Protestant, better known by the Latin form of his name, Ceval-
lerius, who was Hebrew Lecturer in the University from 1569
to 1572, but who was residing in Cambridge in 1551[4]. The
Accounts contain numerous charges for repairs to his house,
and in 1576, soon after his departure, it was fitted up to contain
eight sets of rooms, and became "the new hostel[5]." It was
then agreed that a rent of £7. 14s. 0d. should be paid annually
to the College for it. Two years afterwards this building be-

---

[1] [The charges for it are found in the Building-Account for the Library extending
from 10 Jan. 1682—20 Feb. 1683. It was subsequently called "the Tribunal."]

[2] [Sen. Burs. Accounts 1551—52. *Expense promiscue.* "Redempcion of a lease.
Item to Mr Bycardike...for a recompense for garrett ostle, as it was agreed by ye M^r
and senyors iiij^li. v^s."]

[3] [Ibid. 1550—51. *In reparationibus.* "It' to a poore felowe of ye ostell for
caryeng in to ye lyme house xvj loodes of lyme viij^d." Similar entries occur frequently
in subsequent years.]

[4] [Cooper's Athenæ, i. 306.]

[5] [Sen. Burs. Accounts 1575—76. *Recepts.* " Rec. for chambers, Studyes, etc.
within the Colledge of that parte that was Mr Cevalerious house in mychell parishe
[then follow eight names] vij^li. xiiij^s." *Reparationes in oppido.* "For foure days in
tyling about the new hostell vj^s. viij^d."]

came known by the strange name of " Edithes hostell or
hovynes Inne," an appellation evidently derived partly from
Ovyng's Inn, partly from Dame Edith Chamber's messuage,
which was situated near the south-east corner of the College
site as shewn above (p. 419). The identification of the chambers so called with those made out of Chevallier's house
is rendered certain by the amount of rent being exactly the
same in the two cases. This rent is set down regularly in the
Senior Bursar's accounts down to 1600—1, after which year all
rents were collected by a receiver, and special items are no
longer recorded. The identification of these sets of rooms with
the building afterwards called Garret Hostel is, it must be
admitted, somewhat uncertain. The name itself disappears from
the Accounts after 1584—85 [1], except in connexion with Garret-
Hostel Bridge, until 1644, when a charge for " carrying rubish
out of Garet Ostle" occurs. In 1648 we find a small charge
for work " in yᵉ Garrett Ostle " ;] and in 1662 (9 June), by which
time it had evidently become ruinous, the following Conclusion
was made :

"Agreed that the Chambers inhabited in Gerhard's Hostel be at
present covered, and that what is like to suffer this Winter, be pulled
downe, and yᵉ Materialls secured till yᵉ next Summer

JOHN PEARSON [2]"

At this time it happened that Dr John Hackett, Bishop of
Lichfield and Coventry, who had been Scholar and Fellow of
the College, and resident there about 13 years, had a design of
giving to the College £1000 for the Library, which being inti-
mated to the Society by Dr Antony Scatergood of Yelvertofte
in Northamptonshire, who had known the Bishop intimately for
thirty years, they got him to acquaint the Bishop with their
desire of rebuilding Garret Hostel, which would enlarge the
College and its rents, and be a more lasting benefaction to
the Library [3]. Upon his giving encouragement they sent him

---

[1] [Ibid. 1584—85. *Reparationes in oppido.* " For 4 dayes worke in making vp the
wall at Garrett ostell vˢ. xᵈ."]

[2] [The following curious entry occurs in the Junior Bursar's Accounts for 1664—65.
"For 2 staples vsed at yᵉ Kings gate, to secure from passage to Garret Ostle
oo. oo. o6."]

[3] [Professor Willis says that he "abridged this narrative from Parne's MSS. No. 2,
4to. p. 288." It has therefore been left as he wrote it. In the Chancery suit which

a plan of the building, and deputed two of the Fellows, Mr
Pullen and Mr Gale, to wait upon him at Lichfield in the
beginning of August, 1669 ; upon which he enlarged his benefaction to £1200, for which sum it had been computed that the
proposed building might be completed ; [and in the matted
parlour of his Palace at Lichfield he paid £600 to the two
Fellows who had been sent to him, "on or about 10 August,
1669[1]."]   On the next day he wrote the following letter[2] to the
Master and Seniors of Trinity College:

   " Right Reuerend
                         and most worthy Gouernors of that Societie,
which is more precious to mee, next to the Church of J. Xt, then anie
place upon Earth.
   I was once an vnworthy member of your Bodie, and will be euer a
most affectionat deuotee vnto it.   But a little, that is real, is better then
long protestation of words.   And it is but little that my meaneness is
able to afford, to express a thankefull retribution to my dearest Nurse.
Your two messengers, excellent persons, Mr Pullin and Mr Gale, are as
welcome to mee, as anie persons that euer came to my Palace, fit to bee
employd vpon a greater arrand.   I haue deliuered vnto them six hundred pounds, and will send six hundred more, if God assist, before

took place in 1671, Dr Scatergood deposed that he had heard Bishop Hackett
declare "that he intended to give vnto the Master Fellowes and Schollers of Trinity
Colledge the summe of one thousand pounds for the rebuilding of Garrett hostle
there, and that hee hath often heard the said Bishopp say soe And that this deponent acquainted the Colledg therewith
   And further hee deposeth that in or aboute the Month of August one thousand
six hundred and sixty nyne one M[r] Pullen and one M[r] Gale two of the Fellowes of
the said Colledg comeing to the Bishopps pallace in the Close at Lichfeild by the
appoyntment of the said Bishopp to receiue the Moyety of his said intended Guifte,
the said deponent being there present acquainted the Bishopp therewith vpon notice
whereof the said Bishopp told the deponent that hee was gladd they were come and
said words to this purpose viz[t]. That whereas I intended to giue but Five hundred
pounds att this tyme now I will giue them six hundred pounds and six hundred
pounds at Candlemas Day next and that after the payment of the said twelue
hundred pounds aboute two monthes before the decease of the said Bishopp this
deponent saith that the said Bishopp ordered him that if hee either went to the said
Colledg or did write to the Master or any of the Fellowes thereof [to] tell them that
hee would giue them noe more for theire Liberary till they had fynished the house of
God meaneing the pinicles of the Chappell there."]
   [1] [This is the date given in the document dated 19 December, 1670, and sealed
with the College Seal, in which the receipt of the £1200 was acknowledged.]
   [2] [It is endorsed: "For the verie Reuerend and right Worsh[l]: Doctor John
Pearson Master of Trinitie College in Cambridg, and to the Reuerend and right
Worsh : the Senior fellowes of the same Societie."]

candlemass next, or sooner, as I can procure the summ, when I am at London to attend the Parlament.

My proposition to you, and my desire is, that the whole summ together may bee expended to rebuild the Hostle, formerly calld Garrets Hostle, and vtterly ruined, as I heare, as your own iudgments with skillfull serueyors shall thinke fit, no way prescribing the mode of the Structure, but leauing it absolutely to your vnquestion'd discretions. Neither will I prescribe anie conditions to bee dictated by my autoritie, but moue it with all submission, that from henceforth the new raised Structure may bee called Bishops Hostle, without anie more addition of my remembrance. And I wish hartily that the Title may bee auspicious to the learned and pious that shall studie in it.

Also I propound, that the rents of the respectiue chambers in the said Hostle may bee expended yearely vpon the College Library, either for bookes, or desques, or for the fabrick and structure of the said Library. Which rents, vnder the manage and conclusion of your better iudgments, I suppose may bee most prouidently sett and appointed by the Reuerend Master, and Vice-Master, the Seniour Dean, the Seniour Burser, and the third or Juniour Burser, or anie three of those: and bee receiued by them, or by such as they shall appoint, at such times as in their prudence for the payment, they shall like best: and euerie yeare, within six weekes after Michaelmass, they bee pleased to audit the said receipts of rents, and to expend them as they shall thinke fit, either in bookes, desques, or the necessary workes belonging to the fabrick of the said Library. Whatsoeuer question may, or shall arise, vpon that which I haue not clearely expresst, I leaue it absolutely to the determination of the Master and Seniors. So God prosper it, as wel as I intend it.

And when the worke is finisht, or in some forwardness, I will with great complacency accept of your kind inuitation to bee your guest, who humbly craue your praiers, and God knowes how often you are rememberd in the praiers of

Your humble Seruant, and the great louer of You
and Your Societie
Joh: Lich: and Couen:

Lichfield. Aug. 11. 1669."

There now happened a very extraordinary case. Although this excellent friend and benefactor had paid one-half of his gift to the deputation, he bequeathed to the College the whole sum of £1200 for the building by a codicil dated 31 August in the same year[1]; and although the remaining £600 was paid by his

---

[1] [By will dated 9 January 1665 Bishop Hackett had bequeathed to the College "the summe of one hundred poundes to bee bestowed in bookes vppon the Librarie of the said Colledge." The passage in the codicil is as follows: "And whereas I haue bequeathed in my will the summe of one hundred pounds to the Librarie of Trinity Colledge in Cambridge I revoake it and instead thereof I doe Bequeath the summe of Twelve Hundred pounds to that Noble Societye to bee paid in one yeares space after my decease to build vpp the Hostle now lying in its owne ruyne hereto-

order to the College in or about the month of November then next following, he never cancelled the codicil.

Upon his decease (28 October 1670), this gave some concern to his son and executor Sir Andrew Hackett, who thinking it a matter not to be neglected, sent Mr Greswold, formerly Fellow of the College and chaplain to the Bishop at his death, to shew them the codicil, and assure them of what he thought the design of it, and if possible to obtain a general release. The question turned out to be a more difficult one than at first appeared; it led to much discussion and disputation, and it was finally determined by a suit in Chancery in 1671 that the £1200 received was that meant in the will. Amongst other things it came out that the Bishop had been heard to say in conversation that it was most prudent for men to be their own executors, and that he had been so himself, for having given Trinity College £1200 for a building by will, he had paid it already, and the building was finished, so that his executors would have no trouble or concern with it.

The entire building, which remains to this day with very slight alterations from its pristine form, was erected by Robert Minchin, of Blechington in the county of Oxford, carpenter, in accordance with an agreement made between him and the Master and Fellows of the College, 15 January, 1669—70. This same individual was employed by Sir Christopher Wren in his works at Trinity College, Oxford, in 1665[1], and the design of the Bishop's Hostel is so much in Wren's manner that it may possibly have been revised by him. It is merely a stack of chambers, but is thrown into the form of a separate mansion, unconnected with the other buildings of the College. The ground-plan (fig. 37) has been copied from that appended to the contract, which runs as follows:

"Articles of Agreement indented and made the fifteenth day of January, in the one and twentith yeare of the Reigne of our Soveraigne Lord Charles the Second...Annoque Domini 1669

fore called Garret Hostle, but vppon the rebuilding of it, at the Charge of the summe which I bequeath in this Codicill to bee henceforth called Bishoppes Hostle Provided that the Rent of the severall Chambers thereof soe rebuilt bee yearelie ymployed to furnish the publique Librarie of the said Colledge with bookes at the discrecion of the Master, Vice Master, Senior Deane and Senior Bursar of the saide Colledge."]

[1] "History, etc. of Oxford. By Anthony Wood, M.A. Ed. John Gutch, M.A. 4th. Oxf. 1786." P. 526.

Betweene...John Pearson...Master of the Colledge of the holy and vndevided Trinity...of the one part; And Robert Minchin of Blechington in the County of Oxford Carpenter of the other part as followeth vizt :

Imprimis it is agreed by and betweene the said partyes, And the said Robert Minchin for the consideracion hereafter in these presents expressed doth...agree...

That the said Robert Minchin.. shall...before the first day of November next ensueing the date hereof well and sufficiently frame,

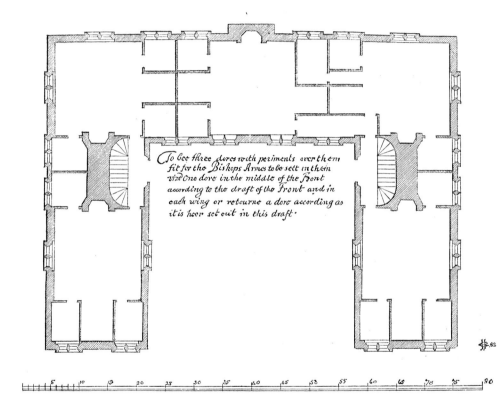

Fig. 37. Ground plan of Bishop's Hostel, reduced from that appended to the original contract.

make, build, perfect and finish, for the said Colledge, One good, sufficient, substantiall, and hansome brick-building uppon that peice of ground of the said Colledge which is lyeing betweene the said Colledge and the Colledge Stables called Garratt Hostle according to a draft thereof made which is hereto annexed and according to the particulers thereof herein after mencioned...Vizt

The said Building to conteine in length on the Southside thereof from the east to the west Seaventy and three foot, and to have two wings or retournes, each wing or retourne of the said building from the Coigne to conteyne in length fifty and two foot, and the said building in every part thereof to conteyne in breadth Eighteene foot.

The said Building to be hansomely and sufficiently Coigned with good freestone, and to conteine above ground two storyes to the roofe, each of which storyes to be full ten foot high between floore and floore, and a hansome gallary of a sufficient heighth to bee all under the roofe of the said building to conteine and be devided into five roomes or gallaryes, and every of those to have one chamber and one Studdy to them with hansome particions and dores, And uppon the Groundfloore there shalbe five outward chambers, and each of those chambers to have made and belonging thereunto two bedchambers and two Studdyes, each of which bedchambers to conteine in length seaven foot and in breadth five foot and a halfe, and each of the said Studdyes to be six foot long and five foot wide, Alsoe uppon the Second floore there shalbe five outward chambers and every of those chambers to have two bedchambers and two Studdyes to them, of the same likenes proporcion and bignes as they before mentioned below are of:

That the walles of the said building shalbe all of well burned Stow-brick to be well laid in good morter made with lime and sand, and to bee from the foundacion to the watertable (which shalbe of a convenient height) two bricks and a halfe in thicknes, and from the watertable to the first floore two bricks in thicknes, and from thence to the roofe one bricke and a halfe in thicknes;

And that there shalbe hansome convenient and sufficient lights and windowes in all the said building and to all the roomes and studdyes therein, as alsoe to the Staircases thereof.   Alsoe for the Uniformity and better grace of the said building there shalbe a hansome moulding of Freestone well wrought with a hansome Architrave to every window in the said building with a Coving round the whole building hansomely wrought, and the Three outward dore cases shalbe arched and done hansomely with freestone vniforme to the windowes.

The roofe of the said building shalbe a sufficient strong French roofe to be made after the best manner hipt of (sic), and with hansome Lutheran windowes in the roofe answerable to the fashion of the same roofe.

Alsoe there shalbe three sufficient Stacks of brick chimneyes all of well burned Stowbrick to be made and raised in the said building to a sufficient height vizt: Two double stacks and one single stack, in such sort as that there may bee fifteene chimneyes in the said building: That is to say, in every of the said outward chambers and gallaryes a chimney to carry smoake away, after the best manner, and that there shalbe hansome and well wrought jaumes and becketts of white stone for every of the said chimneyes, and all the hearthes to be freestone well laid and close jointed and to be laid even with the floores.

The wall plates of the roofe to bee all of good heart of Oake, and to be nine inches one way and seaven another   The principall sparrs and rafters to bee all of good heart of Oake and to bee at the lower end eleaven inches broad and seaven inches thick,   The purloynes or Side peices to bee all of good heart of Oake and to bee eight inches one way and six inches another,   All the rest of the roofe except the windowes to bee of good and well seasoned Firr timber, and the single rafters to be fower inches one way, and three another.

All the Lutheran windowes to bee of good heart of Oake, and all the roofe withoutside to be well and sufficiently lathed with good heart lath, well nailed, and to be well and sufficiently covered with well burned tile, to be well laid with the best morter made with lime and sand.

All the Summers of all the floores in the said building to bee of good and well seesoned firr timber and a foot square well wrought; All the joice [joists] to bee of firr and to be five inches one way, and three another.   The ground floore...to bee all floored, laid, and well done with timber and boards of good heart of Oake, the bordes to be well shott and plained, and close laid and well nailed, and all the other floores...to be close and well laid with well seasoned deales without waine or sapp, of a sufficient thicknes, to be well shott and plained, and to be sufficiently nailed

All the particions of all the said roomes and studdyes to bee of good firr timber, all the posts of the same to bee six and fower inches, and all the studds to be of a sufficient thicknes.   All the said particions...to be well and sufficiently lathed with good sound lath, heart and sapp to be mingled.

All the walls and seilings...to be well and sufficiently seiled and plaistered with good morter made of lime, sand, and haire.

All the Gallaryes, and all other roomes, chambers, stairecases, entryes, and passages...to be well and sufficiently seiled (noe reed to be vsed in anie part of the said building) but all the seilings...to be well and sufficiently lathed with good heart lath well nailed, and all the seilings and particions to be well and sufficiently made and done with good morter..

All the windowes in all the said building to bee of good heart of Oake, well seasoned, to be well wrought and close iointed, and for fashion to be all transome windowes for all but the roofe and to be answerable to the said building in the most hansome and vniforme manner, and of sufficient largenes and substance, and all the lights in all the said windowes not to be les then eighteene inches wide and heights proporcionable.

To every of the said windowes aswell to the Lutheran Windowes as to the transome windowes, there shalbe one hansome iron casement, with a hansome and sufficient fastning, and iron Stayes for all the said casements   And that there shalbe sufficient vpright iron barrs in all the lights of all the lower windowes, and for all the other windowes...to be sufficient iron splay barrs: All the said Casements, stayes, and iron barrs to be sufficiently laid over in a hansome couller in oyle: All the windowes and lights in and about all the said building to be well and sufficiently glaised with good square cleare glasse well and sufficiently leaded and soadred with good lead and sodder.

And in such places where there shalbe need there shalbe hansome and sufficient gutters and spouts of lead well laid for the conveyance of the water from the said building.

Alsoe there shalbe two paire of hansome easy convenient and sufficient Stayres to lead and carry into all the roomes, chambers, and gallaryes...soe large and spatious as the roome will afford.

And that there shalbe a hansome and sufficient dore to every roome, chamber and studdy, ... to be well and sufficiently hanged with good and sufficient joints, hookes and hingells, all the outward dores to have good and hansome locks to them well scrued on, and hansome keyes to all the same.

All the said windowes...and all timber that shalbe to the weatherside to be well and sufficiently painted layde and done in oyle in stone couller, and the inner side of all the said windowes to be painted in the same couller in good size

And that hee the said Robert Minchin ... will ... before the said first day of November ... frame erect sett upp perfect and finish for the said College all the said building ... And at the onely proper costs and charges of him the said Robert Minchin ... will finde and provide all and all manner of...materialls whatsoever which shalbe fitt and needfull to be vsed in or about the said building.

And that the said building shalbe raised, and the roof thereof covered on this side and before the nyne and twentith day of September next ensueing the date hereof

And for the better satisfaction of the said Colledge concerning the said building, Itt shalbe free and lawfull for the said Master Fellowes and Schollars...and all and every other person...who they shall appoint at all times hereafter at their pleasure to view and oversee the whole proceedings of the said building, and uppon any default or miscarriage in any part of the said worke or building to admonish and give notice thereof to the said Robert Minchin ... uppon which notice or admonition the said Robert Minchin ... doth hereby covenant and agree that all the said defaults shall be forthwith sufficiently rectifyed and a-mended ... "

It appears by the receipts at the back of the deed signed by Minchin that he was paid by thirteen instalments, generally of £100 each, and about a month apart; the first, of £100, at the sealing of the deed 15 January, 1669—70, the last, of £150, on 10 April, 1671; the whole sum amounting to £1200. The total however named in the contract is £1180. [The building therefore cost more than was originally expected, and, moreover, there is evidence that Minchin was thought to have lingered over it; for there was an interval of three months between the last payment and the last but one; and on 21 February, 1670—71, we find the following Conclusion:

"Agreed by ye Master and Seniors yt if Minchin doe send in a tun and ½ of stone within a fortnight, he shall receive money for ye same, and ye workemen imployed by him shall be pay'd weekly till it come to ye last hundred pounds, and then it shall be further considered what is best to be done, y^t ye College suffer no more in ye building.   JO. PEARSON."

A special heading "The Bishops Ostle" first appears in the Junior Bursar's Accounts for the year ending at Michaelmas 1670, up to which time £89. 13s. 10d. had been spent, chiefly in pulling down old buildings, and in digging foundations; and in the following year £267. 3s. 10½d. was spent under the same head, making a total of £356. 17s. 8½d., beyond the sum given by the Bishop.

The building must have been completed by the end of 1671, in which year we find a payment "for cutting and ingraving the Bishop's Armes[1]."   These are on a stone shield in the centre of the pediment which surmounts the façade.   The inscription over the central door "BISHOPS HOSTEL, 1670," records the date of foundation[2].

In 1874 it was proposed to pull down Bishop's Hostel and the stables, and to build a new court[3]. It was finally determined to preserve and thoroughly repair the Hostel, and on the ground obtained by the removal of the stables to erect two ranges of chambers in red brick, with some additional offices for the kitchen. The architect employed was Mr A. W. Blomfield. The ground was cleared in June, 1876; and the new buildings were completed at the beginning of 1878. Mr Blomfield further superintended the repairs done to the Hostel.]

---

[1] [Jun. Burs. Accounts 1670—71. *The Bishops Hostel.*]

[2] [It may be mentioned that a sundial formed part of the decoration of Bishop's Hostel : Jun. Burs. Accounts, 1671—72. *Extraordinaryes.* "To Wisdom for painting ye Diall in Bishop's Hostil 2^s. 10^d." Ibid. 1697—98. *Painter.* "Painting and gilding Sun-diall in Bishop's Hostel 02. 00. 00."]

[3] [Sen. Burs. Minutes, 8 May, 1874.]

CHAPTER V.

HISTORY OF PARTICULAR BUILDINGS: CHAPEL; HALL;
COMBINATION ROOM; MASTER'S LODGE; FOUNTAIN;
TENNIS COURT; TREASURY; BREWHOUSE, ETC.; GAR-
DENS AND WALKS; BOWLING GREEN.

[THE chapel of King's Hall was used by Trinity College
for some years after the date of the charter. It was probably
fitted up on an enlarged scale for the new foundation, for in
the Accounts for 1547—48 a new organ and new lectern are
mentioned[1]; and the quantity of plate, vestments, and service
books sold in 1550[2], with the sum they realised, £140. 8s. 8d.,
prove that the services must have been conducted with much
pomp of ritual.

It was shewn above (p. 469) that Queen Mary gave an
impulse to the building of the College soon after she became
Queen; and that a new chapel was one of the first works
undertaken. An agreement to build the walls for £80 was
signed with a mason named Perse at Michaelmas 1555; and
in the second week of October Mr Burton, one of the Fellows,
spent four days with a carpenter at Thorney Park selecting

---

[1] [Sen. Burs. Accounts, 1547—48. *Pro Sacello.* "Inprimis payd to yᵉ orgayne
maker whan he sett vp the orgaynes xvjˢ. viijᵈ.   Item for a lectrone in the chapell iijˢ.
iiijᵈ."]

[2] [Jun. Burs. Accounts, 1549—50. "Recevid of John Scarlett for the churche
bokes contayninge DDDD in weyght after vjˢ. viijᵈ. the hunderithe xxvjˢ. viijᵈ.
Recevid the [blank] of July for ij silver basins contayninge in weyght lvij ounces
sould after vjˢ. ounc'; the hole xvijˡⁱ. ijˢ.   Recevid for the kandlestickes of the
chappel contayning in weyght DDdi' xiiijˡⁱ at xxˢ the hunderithe lijˢ. vjᵈ." Ibid.
Sen. Burs.   "Receved of Mʳ Strache of Walden for certayne copes and vestmentes
iiijxxˡⁱ.   Item received of James Andrewe Goldsmyth for C. xliij vnces of plate after
vˢ. vjᵈ. an vnce xxxixˡⁱ. vjˢ. vjᵈ." Jun. Burs. 1550—51. "Payed to Mʳ Meres and
James Goldsmyth for yer paynes in prasyng yᵉ churches stuffe iijˢ. iiijᵈ." At the
same time the altar and altar steps were taken down, and a communion-table
was set up.]

timber[1]. The Account for 1555—56 is wanting, but in that for 1556—57 the work is in full progress. A special heading, *Thexpenses of ye new chappell*, contains an Account for wages to workmen extending over 36 weeks, from the week ending 6 January, to that ending 9 October. Eleven workmen, on the average, 7 freemasons and 4 rough-masons, were employed in each week; and by the end of the year the ironwork was ordered for nineteen "nether windows," that is, the half of the window below the transome. There are 25 windows in the Chapel, including the east and west windows and the westernmost window on the north side, where there is now a blank wall (fig. 9); and this entry shews that about three-fourths of the whole length of the building had then been carried up to half its height.

The materials used in this first year were brought from the Grey Friars, and from Peterhouse. Under the heading *Stonne from the fryers at iij^d ye lood cariage*, we find that 2950 loads were brought from the former place; and 192 loads from the latter.

In the previous year an indenture had been drawn up for the stalls, quire doors, and ornamental work of the roof, but not for the roof itself, with Stephen Wallis of Cambridge, burgess and joiner, who was to receive £300 for the whole work. The stalls were to be in two rows, sixty-eight in the upper row with misereres, and divided by pillars; and a lower row, which was not to be so subdivided. The whole work was to be after the pattern of the stalls at King's College. Wallis agreed to make a "fret" to the roof, of oak, ornamented with eighty-one pendants, each two feet long. When the contract was drawn it was evidently intended that the work should go on without interruption, and be completed soon after 30 November, 1557, when the last payment but one was to be made. We shall find however that in fact the last payment was not made until April 1566. The delay was caused in great measure by Wallis having fallen into

---

[1] [Jun. Burs. Accounts, 1554—55. The year ends nominally at Michaelmas; but a note at the bottom of the title-page states that "the accomptt doth run from December vnto December." The following are the entries referred to in the text: "Michaelmesse. Item, gyven in ernest money vnto good man Perse, ye rughe mayson, at the bargen makyn of the chappell walles to be mayd and buylded vpp for thre score poundes xij^d. Octobris 5°. Item payd vnto S^r. Burton, Octobris. 12°. for hys charges in riding vnto thornay parke to vue tymber there for o^r chappell and haueyng a carpenter with hym for . 4 . days xviij^s. ix^d."]

pecuniary difficulties, which compelled him to sell the materials which he had bought for the College work, as appears from a long and incoherent letter (neither signed nor dated) which he wrote to the Master[1]; but it may partly have been caused by a change of plan. It will be observed that in the following contract the roof is to be 33 feet broad by 157 feet long. The former measurement gives the exact width of the present Chapel, but the actual length is 205 feet. The distance, however, from the west end to the east wall of the College is just 157 feet; and the old plan (fig. 10) shews that it was not originally intended to extend the Chapel beyond that line. It is possible therefore that the extension of the Chapel eastward was an afterthought: a view which is corroborated by the large purchases of materials recorded in the years subsequent to the date of the contract, and by entries for the employment of workmen other than Wallis to execute pendants and ornaments. The contract, dated 30 April 1556, is as follows:

"THIS INDENTURE made the laste daye of Apryll In the seconde and thirde yeres of the Raignes of Philipp and Marye by the grace of god Kinge and Quene of England France Naples Hierusalem and Irelande, Defenders of the Faithe, Princes of Spaine and Sicile, Archedukes of Austriche, Dukes of Myloyne, Burgundye, and Brabante, Countes of Haspurge Flaunders and Tirolle,

Betwene Mr John Christoferson Bachelor of Diuinite, Maister of Trinite College in Cambrige of King Henry theighthes foundation, And the Fellowes and scholers of the same College on thone parte, And Steven Walles of the Towne of Cambrige in the counte of Cambrige burgesse and Joyner on thother parte,

WYTNESSETHE that wheras the said Maister Fellowes and scholers entendeth by the grace of god to erecte and buylde a newe churche within the precynte of the said College, to thentent that the Companye of the said College may haue more convenient places and Rowmes for the setting furthe and mayntenance of godes seruyce and true catholike religion, It is fully condescended and agreed betwene the said partes by thes presentes in maner and furme folowing:

That is to saye the said Steven Walles for and in consideracion of the Summe of thre hundrethe poundes of good and lawfull money of England wherof is paid in hand vnto the said Steven Walles, by the said Master Fellowes and scholers, fourescore poundes, of the whiche the said Steven by thees presentes acknowlege hymselfe to be

[1] [This letter, with the documents drawn up between Wallis and the College, are preserved in the Muniment Room of Trinity College.]

fully contented and paid   And the resydue to be paid at certaine dayes hereafter in thes presentes declared,

THE said Steven Walles covenauntethe...that he...shall worke, make, frame, and holly and fully buylde and sett vpp a newe Threscore and eight stalles with stayers belonging thervnto, and the same stayers to be according and after the maner of the Kinges College quere in Cambrige aforesaid for the Master Fellows and scholers of the said College for the tyme being in suche fourme sorte and workmanshipp in all and euery poynt and condicion as hereafter by thes presentes shall be particularly sett owte and declared.

FIRSTE vppon euery of the said stalles a border of antique with a double creste one greter above and an other lesse benethe   And the said crestes to returne aboute the throwen pyllers of waynscott, the backe playne of waynscote, with an haunce above cutt with antique, the vpper seetes to be rysing and falling as they be at the Kinges College, and after the same fourme, and betwixe euery seete a turned pyller of ooke, and ye vaute ouer ye said seetes to be playne, the bought of the seetes to be after the same worke they be at the King College   The grete deskes to be of fayre ooke and thre inches thicke, and of brede to be halfe a yerde besydes the crestes, and to haue a border of antique runnyng vppon the fore ege of the said deskes, and vnder the said deskes to be turned pyllers to bere theym vpp through owt ; and thende of the partitions to be with turned pillers as they be at the Kinges College.

The nether stalles to haue a playne seete of fayre ooke the holle lenght of the partition and the backe behinde vnderneth the turned pilleres of the stalles to be frenche pannell   The deskes of the same stalles to be halfe a yerde brode and two inches thicke with turned pylleres vnderneth to bere theym vpp.   Thendes of the partitions to be with turned pilleres as they be at the Kinges College.

AND further the said Steven Walles...dothe convenaunt and graunt ...that he...shall make the doore into the quere of the said Churche with turned pillers vpp to the toppe and to sele the vaut ouer the entrye and the sydes therof with two doores of frenche pannell to the vtter ege of the rode lofte ; And thentry to be IX or x feete from the backe of the stalles to ye ege of the rode lofte.   Towardes the furnysing wherof the said Master Fellowes and Schollers to fynde the gymmers for the said doores.

AND also the said Steven Walles convenaunteth...that he...shall worke make and frame a frette to hange vppon the rooffe with croked battones and strayte battones thorowe the holle rooffe of ooke inbowed with foorescore and one pendauntes hanging downe two foote from the said rooffe, the brede of the said rooffe to be xxxiiij foote and in lenghth one hundrethe and fyftie and vij foote.   And the said rooffe to be made and framed at the propre costes and charges of the said Col-lege for the foresaid Steven to sett his worke vppon.

AND further the said Steven Walles convenaunteth...that he the said Steven Walles...shall fynde all maner of stuffe aswell apte and mete belonging to the said stalles as to ye said frettes battones and pendauntes as tymbre nayles workmanshipp and all other thinges neces-

sary for yᵉ said Joyners worke, and the same worke and euery parte
and parcell therof to be holly and fully wrought and fynished at the
propre costes and charges of the said Steven Walles...according to
the pattron shewed to the Master and other of the said College for the
said frettes battones and pendantes. And the said Master Fellowes and
Scholers conventeth and grauntethe by thes presentes to make redye
the place to sett the Stalles apon, and a scaffold or stagge of tymbre
for the erecting and framyng of the said frettes battones and pendantes
at the costes and charges of the said Master Fellowes and Scholers and
theyr successors.

AND the said Master Fellowes and Scholers in consideracion of the
premisses and for the sure Payment of the said Summe of money convenaunt...that they...shall content and paye or cause to be contented
and paid vnto the said Steven Wallis...The summe of two hundreth
and twenty poundes the resydue of the said summe of thre hundrethe
poundes in maner and fourme folowing: That is to saye at the feaste
of Pentecoste nexte ensuyng the date hereof fourscore poundes; And
at the feaste of seynt Andrewe the Apostle then next ensuyng thirtie
poundes; And at the feaste of Pentecoste, then next ensuyng after
that other, thirtie poundes; And at the feaste of Saynt Androwe, whiche
shalbe in the yere of our lord god a thowsande fyve hundrethe fyftye
and seven fourtie poundes; And whan the said stalles frettes battones
and pendauntes shalbe fully framed sett vpp and fynished other fourtie
poundes in full contentacion and payment of the said summe of thre
hundrethe poundes [1].

AND for further consyderacion that all convenauntes, articles, and
agrementes above declared and mencioned in thes presentes on the
parte and behalfe of the said Steven Walles...to be done obserued
perfourmed fullfylled and kept, The said Steven Walles staunde bounde
with one John Howell of the said towne burgesse and chaunlour.
And one Zeyger Nicholson of the same towne berebruer by theyr
wryting obligatory Ioyntly and seuerally bering date the day of the
date of these presentes to the said Master [etc.] in the sume of Foure
hundreth poundes.

IN WYTNES wherof to thone parte of thes indentures remayning
with the said Steven Walles The said Master Fellowes and Scholers
haue putto theyr comen seale, And to thother parte remayning with

---

[1] [Wallis was paid as follows: 4 October, 1555, £20; 21 November, 1555, £50
(both for Stalls): 20 February, 1555—6, £10 (for Roof), making up the £80 due 30
April, 1556; 7 May, 1556, £40 ("due at the feast of Penticost next followenge"); 16
July, 1556, £20 ("for the last parte of payment of the summe of foure score powndes
dew to be payed vnto me at the feast of penticost last past," a statement which shews
that one receipt must have been lost, and that the money paid up to this date was
£160); 4 December, 1556, £30 ("due at yᵉ feast of Seint Andrewe thappostell last
past"); 5 June, 1557, £30 ("to me due at the feast of penticost in the yere of oʳ lorde
god a thousand fyve hundredthe fyftie and seaven"); 7 May, 1558, £40 ("to me due
at the feast of Seint Andrewe thapostle last past"). No further payments were made
to him for at least five years, for when he signed an acknowledgment in full for all
previous payments, 16 April, 1563, they amounted to £260.]

the said Master Fellowes and scholers The said Steven Walles hath putto his seale. Yeven the daye and yere abovesaid. [Signed] by me Steuen Walles."

The Accounts for 1557—58, 1558—59 are lost, but in those for 1559—60 we find :

" To Mr Russell for his paynes in commynge from London to devise the chappell worke liij^s. iiij^d.

To hym which went to sette Forde the carpenter to conferr with Mr Russell viij^d.[1]

Item to Jhon Fridaye in part of paiment of ye bargaine for ye working of ye Corbet table at . iiij^d. ye foote xxvj^s. viij^d.[2]

Item to Henry Dyckenson for his paynes in comming to se the stone work of the Chappell ij^s. vj^d.[3]"

The other entries referring to the Chapel in that year are so few and so unimportant that we may conclude that the work had been almost entirely suspended. The allusion to the corbel-table, however, implies that in some part of the building the upper portion of the wall had been reached, or at any rate that it was near completion.

In the following year, 1560—61, the work proceeds more rapidly. Wages are paid to freemasons[4] for forty-one weeks, with an average of six men in each week ; besides carpenters, "carvers of the chapel roof" who charge for "beames, crosse somers, and pendentes," rough-masons, and a large staff of labourers. Building-stone is brought in from various localities ; from the Grey Friars in Cambridge, Ramsey Abbey in Huntingdon-shire[5], and the quarries of Barrington and Weldon. The latter was for the corbel-table. By virtue of Queen Elizabeth's com-mission[6], the villages near Weldon provided carts to convey it to the Ouse at Gunwell, whence it was brought by water to Cambridge. The following extracts illustrate this :

"Inprimis paid to William Frisbie for xxxij^{ti} toone of free stone at ij^s ye toone hauinge before received of Mr Lee xx^s in parte of pay-mente.................. ....xliiij.^{s}

---

[1] [Sen. Burs. Accounts, 1559—60. *Rewardes.*]

[2] [Jun. Burs. Accounts, 1559—60. *Thinges done by great.*]

[3] [Ibid. *Extraordinary Expenses.*]

[4] [This Account is headed *Fre masones aboute the chappell.* The destination of the Carpenters and Labourers is not specified.]

[5] [Jun. Burs. Accounts, 1560—61. "Item paid to William Aungier for A bar-gaine of Ramsaye stone to the nombre of iij^{xx} lodes at iiij^s. iiij^d. ye lode xiij^{li}."]

[6] [See above, p. 472.]

Item paid to diuers persones for cariage of the said xxxij^{ti} toone of freestone from Weldone vnto Goonwoord ferry at iiij^s the toone iiij^d.
   ouer in ye hole ....vj^{li}. viij^s. iiij^d.
Item to ye highe constable at Weldone to warne the townes for cariage
   of o^r stone .... ij^s.
Item giuen to ye highe constable to warne ix townes neare Weldone to
   bring ther cartes .... xviij^d.
Item to Robert Lukas for cariege...of hewene stone for corbell table
   bie water from Goonward ferrie to Cambridge .... xv^s. ij^d."

In addition to the provision of stone for the corbel-table, the
progress made with the walls is shewn by the erection of scaffolds
in February and April, 1561, and by the exertions made to
procure a supply of timber. John Brewster, who seems to have
been the master carpenter, made several journeys into Essex,
armed "with the commyssione for prouysione of Timbre"; and
the Bursar, Mr Oxenbridge, went there also to see the wood
which had been provided. In this year the roof of the old
chapel was taken down[1]. Some windows also were glazed[2].

The Accounts for the following year, 1561—62, are wanting;
but in those for 1562—63 the work is proceeding actively. Freemasons are employed for 48 weeks, and the average has risen to
nearly nine in each week. Eight labourers also are employed
in each week of the same period, and a few carpenters. It is
however possible that some of these workmen may have been
employed in other parts of the College, for charges for the
Chapel are mixed up with others for the Conduit, and certain
" new chambers," the position of which is not specified. Materials were brought from the same localities as before. The Grey
Friars supplied 108 loads of stone, part of which was "laide in
the dores of the new chappell," part was "new wrought by
Peeres to ashler and quenynge," that is, to make "coins" with;
while Ramsey supplied 342 loads. The Bursar rode thither on
three occasions, and superintended in person the destruction of
part of the church. The entries referring to his first visit are so
curious that they shall be quoted at length:

---

[1] [Jun. Burs. Accounts, 1560—61. "Item to John Brewster Jun. . ij . dayes
comminge over to the colledge to take downe the roof of the owld Chappell ij^s."]

[2] [Ibid. *The Glasier.* "To hym for x foote of newe glasse at vj^d. ob. the foote
for ye newe windowe at the end of the newe chappell v^s. x^d. It' to hym for settinge vp
and leadinge oulde glasse in the other windowes xij^d."]

"In primis paide to Aunger for three greate buttrises in the Este ende of the chauncell at Ramsei and of the northe side v^{li}. iij^s. x^d.

Item the . xix . day of Januarie my breakfaste and Homfrey carters when we went to see the ston viij^d.

Item our dinners at Ramsei and Aungers xx^d.

Item our suppers at nyght and the baliffes ij^s.

Item for ij horses ij dais at x^d. the day and breade for theme iij^s. iiij^d.

Item to Williamson of Barnwell for casting downe the three buttrises xx^s.

Item to Clarkson of Ramsei in regarde of cariedge to the water side vj^d."

The same church supplied stone for the floor, and lead for the roof. Lead was also brought from Mildenhall in Suffolk. In the course of this year the Bursar went again into Essex to get timber; and also into Suffolk, where he bought "x greate tries at xxviij^s. the trie." Part of the Chapel must have been covered in, for Wallis the joiner receives £11 "for selyng the weste ende of the newe chappell[1]"; and agreements are made for glazing fifteen windows, of which seven are stated to be on the north side, and we may presume are counted from the west:

"Item to Blithe of Thackstedd for his charges when he was first sende for to measure the windows and to take his instructions......ij^s. vj^d.

Item paide to William Blithe of Thackstedd in part of paiment for glasing eight windows in the newe chappell wth wyght glass at v^d. ob. the fote and painted glass as apperethe bi a bill indented xx^{li}.

It' paide to Miles Jugg for the glasing of vij windows of the northe side, I meane in parte of paiment at like price for wyght glass and painted ....xx^{li}.

It' to William Blithe and Miles Jugg in regarde of the bargen for painted glasse by master Oxenbridge consent .... vj^s. viij^d.

It' for my charges and horshier ij dais to thackstedd for to intreate wth Blithe for paintedd glass .... v^s. ij^d.[2]"

In 1563—64 a still larger staff of workmen was being employed, amounting to nearly 30 in each of forty-two weeks. This number was composed of 15 freemasons[3], 4 bricklayers, and 11 labourers. Besides these 4 carpenters were at work for each of

---

[1] [Ibid. 1562—63. *Seling wth halfe inche borde in the newe Chappell.*]

[2] [Ibid. *Glass in the newe chappell.*]

[3] [At the end of the Accounts for 1562—63 we find under the head *Extraordinarie expenses:* "Item to Thomas Warde going with the commission into Northamptonshire and Lincolne for fre masons iiij^s viij^d," and sundry masons receive "press money or charges coming to Cambridge."]

31 weeks. Materials were still being brought in, consisting of stone from the Grey Friars, Ramsey Abbey, and the quarries of Weldon and Cliffe; lead; and timber. A note appended to the carpenters' wage-book for 22 July 1564: "gyuen to the carpenters for gloues at the raysinge of the Rofe of the chappell ij^s," shews upon what work they were employed; while under the headings *Caruyng and the charges their of* and *Iron worke for the newe chappell* we find the following items:

"In primis paide to Andrewe Storme for caruyng nyne beames at eightene shillinges the beame viij^{li}. ij^s.

Item to Andrewe Storme for caruyng the example or paterne to folowe in caruyng the rest of cross sommers vij^s. vij^d.

Item...for caruyng the sommers, pendentes, etc by greate viij^{li}. xij^s.

Item paide...for one greate transom bar for the east wyndowe wiche weied fyue score pownde and seuene at iij^d. ob the pownde xxxj^s. ij^d. ob.

Item for scoweryng and newe trimmyng fowre stories of olde yron at ij^s. vj^d. the storie .... xj^s.

Item for foure score and ix barres for the wyndowe in the est ende of the chappell .... xiij^s."

The employment of numerous masons and few carpenters, with the references to the east window and to the carving of nine beams for the roof, suggests that the eastward prolongation of the Chapel had now been undertaken, if not completed; a conclusion strengthened by the employment of workmen other than Wallis, whose contract, as explained above, deals only with the western portion of the existing building, which had been finished, roofed, and panelled in previous years.

In 1564—65 a still larger staff of freemasons is at work. The stonework, however, must have been practically finished, for the painter charges "for coloring wth fyne blacke that scriptur wch is graven in the east end of the Chappel," by which is evidently meant the inscription on the east gable: "ANNO 1564. DOMVS MEA DOMVS ORATIONIS VOCABITVR"; and the finials at the east end are alluded to as completed[1]. Moreover, under the heading *Tymber for the false Roofe of the chappel*, we find agreements for preparing the timber required, and for bringing it to Cambridge, upwards of £95 being paid under this head. The panelwork at the east end

---

[1] [Jun. Burs. Accounts, 1564—65. *Iron worke for the newe chapple.* "Item for Irons for the ij fynialls at the east ende of the chapple xij^s. x^d."]

of the interior was also being executed by a joiner named Arnold Pinckney[1]; workmen were laying the foundation of the stalls ; and paving-stone was being brought in from Croyland.

In the following year, 1565—66, the "partition of the chapple" as it is called, or in other words the rood-loft or organ-screen, is being set up. It occupied six carpenters for eleven weeks. The only entries which give any indication of the design are :

"Item for turning of viij postes at vj^d. the post for ye porch .... iiij^s.
Item to Jhon Dymmock for turning of fower pillers at viij^d. ye piller
                      ij^s. viij^d.
Item for paper to make mowles for the pillers .... ij^d."[2]

The stalls and scholars' seats were evidently completed in the course of this year, for Wallis received the last instalment of the £300 due to him on 28 April 1566; and on the same day gave a bond of £20 to complete the stalls before All Saints' Day (1 November), and further, to "set vp a freitte to hang vppon the rouffe ... with in sixe weekes space at any time after he shall by anie officer of the Colledge be warned and called therunto." The "false roof" was still unfinished, for in the course of 1566 the workman with whom the agreement for a supply of timber had been made brought it to Cambridge, and "placed it together in th' vpper court of the college"; and in 1567 fifteen carpenters are employed for six weeks to set it up. Charges for the leadwork also occur in this year. The roof was executed, in part at least, by a Mr Byse from London, who brought five workmen with him[3]. In this Account we find a separate heading: *Labourers about the Chappell*, the last pay-

---

[1] [Ibid. 1564—65. *Seling wth halfe inch bord in ye newe chapple.* "Payd to Arnold Pynckneye Joyner for seling the vpper end of ye chapple being xxiiij Rovmes at v^s a Rowme vj^{li}."]

[2] [Ibid. 1565—66. *Extraordinary expenses for the particion of the chappel.* The total cost was £19. 6. 0. Some of the seats of the old Chapel were used again, for charges occur under the heading *Slaters* "for vnderpinninge th' ould seates of ye chapple." The following entry is valuable as shewing that old materials were used in every part of the Chapel: "To Thomas Barnardiston and William Wytton Chirch wardens of Barton for xxvj hundrethe and one quarter of Lead at viij^s. vj^d. the hundreth xj^{li}. iij^s. Paid to them for iij hundreth and xx powndes more xxvij^s."]

[3] [Ibid. 1566—67. *Other Extraordinarie Charges.* "To Mr Byse for comminge downe from London to viewe the chappell roufe xij^s. For carryeng his tooles frome London and home agayne viij^s. iiij^d. For vj paire of gloves to Mr Byse and his . v . men iij^s. To Mr Byse at his departure v^s."]

ment under which is for the week ending 27 September, 1567. This entry marks the conclusion of the work, which had lasted for just eleven years. No record of the consecration exists.

We must now describe the glazing of the windows; for though the glass then put in has long since disappeared, it will be interesting to notice the system of decoration followed in the first instance. The agreements made in 1562—63 with the two glaziers, William Blithe of Thacksted in Essex, and Miles Jugg, apparently from the same place, have been already quoted. In the Accounts for the following year, 1563—64, under the heading *Glass for the newe chappell*, we find the following items:

"In primis paide to William Blithe of Thacksted for xvi Top pieces for the west wyndowe whiche drewe to xxi fote of glass at v^d. ob the foote...ix^s. vij^d. ob.

Item paide to hym for iiij^{xx} xix fote of white glass sett vpp in the xj lightes of the seconde storie in west wyndowe at v^d. ob. the fote
xlv^s. iiij^d. ob.

Item paide to hym for fyue score and eight fote of white glass at v^d. ob. the fote set vp in nyne lightes of the loweste storie in the west wyndowe .... xlix^s. vj^d.

Item paide to hym for iij fote of glass cut in x pieces for the corneres of the loweste storie at v^d. ob. the fote .... xvj^d. ob.

Item for a greate Rose A flowerdelice and a purcholis at vi^s. the piece set vp in the weste wyndowe and iij letteres in golde iij$s$ ...... xxj^s.

Item for ij Tables for Sentences at vj^s. viij^d. a piece .... xiij^s. iiij^d.

Item for xii small Ranges .... vj^s. viij^d.

Item paide for eight score and eight fote of white glass, and half a fote, at v^d. ob. the fote for the firste wyndowe of the sowthe side
iij^{li}. xvij^s. ij^d. ob: quar:

Item for the ij Armes in the saide wyndowe xij^s.; for the ij Ranges iiij^s.; and for xii panes of the foures (?) hauyng flowers, letteres, or prynces Armes in them. Summa xii^s. .... xxviij^s.

Item for the white glass of six other wyndows on the sowth side euerye wyndowe conteinyng eight score and eight fote et dimid'...and for xij Armes and xij Ranges and three score and twelfe quarrels paynted wth gold worke..............................xxxj^{li} xj^s iiij^d. ob.

Item to Miles Jugg the glasier for the paynted glasse of syx wyndowes of the northe side the chappell, vizt for xij Arms and lxxij greate paynted quarrels and xij Ranges .... viij^{li} viij^s.

Item to hym for syx wyndows of glass for the north side of the chappell
xxiij^{li}. iij^s iiij^d. ob.

Item my charges and horshier to Thacksted when I wente to bargen wth the glasier for the wyndowes yet to glase .... ij^s. vj^d.

Item to two glasiers iiij dais takyng downe the glass of the olde chappell
viij^s.

Item gyuen to William Blithe of Thacksted in ernest of a bargein for glassing the wyndows of the new chappell wth burgundye glass at vj^d. the fote, to be don betwen this and easter if passedge by sea be had before the feast of the natiuitie next comyng ; if yt happen that passedge be not concluded before y^t feaste, but betwixt christ-enmas and fastingham, than o^r. wyndowes to be glassed before pentecost next ensewyng ....ij^s."

In the Account for 1564—65 the charges for glass are :

" In primis for glasynge of ix wyndowes v on the north syde and iiij on ye sowth syde for glasing of them wth whyt glasse at vj^d. ye foote beinge eyght score and eyght foote and dimid' for everie windowe
xxxvij^{li} xviij^s. iij^d.
Item for ij armes in everie of the said windowes at vj^s a peace   v^{li}. viij^s.
Item for ij Ranges in everye one of the ix windowes at vj^s. and for the Rose pvercholys flowerdelice name of kinge henrye at xij^d a peace being xij in everie one of the ix windowes .... viij^{li} ij^s."

These extracts shew that in the course of 1564, six windows on the north side were glazed by Jugg, and the west window, with seven windows on the south side, by Blithe. In the following year five windows on the north side were glazed, making a total of eleven, and four on the south side, completing the series on that side. The glazing of the twelfth window on the north side, and of the east window, is not recorded [1].

The decoration of these windows was evidently extremely simple, being limited to coats of arms, heraldic devices, and a few inscriptions, on a ground of white glass. Even these, however, were considered objectionable by the reformers of that day, for in 1565—66 we find the following curious entry [2] :

" Novemb. xvj^{th}. Item for reparinge of the places wch wer Broken furth in all the windoes whearin dyd appeare superstition......xvj^d."

The Chapel, as thus finished, is 205 feet long by 33 feet broad. It is divided into twelve bays of equal size, each lighted by a window on the north and south sides, except the westernmost bay, in which there is no window on the north side; and the fourth bay from the east end, where the east range of the Great Court abuts against the Chapel. The original division into quire and ante-chapel is indicated by a space 12 feet wide

[1] [The former may have been paid for by the following donations recorded in the Senior Bursar's Accounts for 1564—65. *Recepta extraordinaria :* " Imprimis received of Sr Edward Warner knight toward the glasyng of a window in o^r chapell xx^s. It' of Mr Barwick toward the glasyng of a window in o^r chapell iij^{li}. vj^s. viij^d."]

[2] [Ibid. 1565—66. *Glasse in the chapple and other places.*]

between the fourth and fifth bays from the west end; and by an external turret-stair on the north side, which was evidently intended to give access to a rood-loft (fig. 9).

The general appearance of the exterior will be understood from the engraving (fig. 24). The buttresses are shallow, in three stages, and surmounted by pinnacles. The walls are terminated by battlements, similar in design to those of the Hall and Court. The windows in the north and south walls are all exactly alike. Each consists of four lights, trefoiled, and subdivided by a transom. The east and west windows are each of nine lights, but there is a considerable difference in their design. This is probably due to their having been constructed by different architects, for, as mentioned above, it is evident that the prolongation of the Chapel beyond the east range of the College was not intended in the first instance.

The roof is divided into 24 bays, equally spaced, an arrangement which causes the corbels on which the roof-brackets rest to fall irregularly with respect to the windows. The general design is shewn in the two views of the interior (figs. 38, 39). On the tenth principal, counting from the east end, are the letters " R. B. Mʳ.", with a rudely cut face, evidently for Robert Beaumont, Master 1561—67; and on each side of the ridge-piece in the tenth bay is the date 1561. It is very difficult to reconcile the existing roof, which has evidently not been altered since it was completed, with that which we are led to expect from the contract with Wallis; for not only is it entirely flat, instead of being coved ("inbowed") at the sides; but in style it appears to be somewhat earlier than the known date of the building which it covers. On referring to the facts collected above we find that in 1559—60 a Mr Russell came from London "to devise the Chapel work," and conferred with Ford the carpenter, while a Mr Dickenson came "to see the stone work." May we not conclude that the latter suggested the prolongation of the Chapel, and the former a new treatment of the roof? In the next year, 1560—61, John Brewster, the master-carpenter, took down the roof of the old Chapel. It appears not improbable, when we consider that the existing Chapel was almost wholly built of old materials, that this old roof would be used up again as far as it would go, with, of course, the alterations necessary to make it fit a larger building; and that the nine beams carved in 1564 were required to supplement it. According to this theory Wallis never executed that part of his contract which refers to the roof; he took money from the College, which, as he admits, he spent for his own purposes; and so late as 1566 we find him giving a bond to "set up a fret" when called upon, but there is no evidence that he ever was so called upon.

The arrangement of the fittings has fortunately been preserved. The memorandum[1] recording it evidently belongs to the period of the Restoration, but as there is no appearance of any change having been made in the interval, it may be regarded as representing in the main at least the system followed out at the first construction.

> "Y^e Measure of ye Chappell.
> From ye East End to ye Backside of ye present Altar piece 36 feet long
> From ye present Altar to ye present Seats   24 „ „
> From ye east end of ye Seats to ye Organ Screen   70 „ „
> Y^e Screen it self   8 „ „
> Y^e Antichapell   65 „ „
> Y^e Breadth of ye Quire   18 „ „ "

These measurements, which have been laid down on the plan (fig. 9), give a total of 203 feet, which is very nearly correct. They shew that a space equal to the width of two bays was left behind the altar, as was the case at King's College Chapel previous to 1774[2]; and that the stalls terminated in the centre of the fourth bay from the west. The extent of the stalls, and their distance apart, were nearly the same as at present. The screen, which was only eight feet wide, was so placed as to be accessible from the staircase in the turret on the north side.

An organ, probably on the screen, is first mentioned in 1593—94, when a maker named Hugh Rose did work to it; and a new case, or "frame" as it is called, was constructed by Andrew Chapman, the carpenter who subsequently wainscoted the Hall[3]. Additional decorations, new curtains of blue cloth, etc. were

---

[1] [It is written out on a paper pasted into the second "Conclusion Book."]

[2] [There seems to have been a door into this space, for in the Sen. Burs. Accounts for 1615—16 we find: *Expences in the Chappell.* "For a locke, a key, a staple, and a hindge for the Chappell East doare towardes ye garden ij^s. viij^d."]

[3] [Sen. Burs. Accounts, 1593—94. *Expences in the Chappell.* "Item to Hughe Rose for the Organe vj^{li} xiij^s iiij^d. Item to Andrewe Chapman for the frame of the Organe xxiiij^{li}."]

added in 1603—4, and the Royal Arms, blazoned in colours, were set up on it[1]. This organ had probably been used in the Chapel of King's Hall, for in 1609—10 it is spoken of as "the old organ," and is mended, painted, and gilt at a cost of £50. 10. 0. In the same year a maker named John York constructed a new "chaire organ[2]." The organ was thoroughly repaired, and again painted and gilt, in 1637[3]. There was also a brass lectern with branched candlesticks, and a pulpit. The former is first mentioned in 1579—80, the latter in 1592—93. The pulpit had probably, like the organ, been brought from the old chapel, for it was replaced by a new one, by Chapman, in 1609—10[4].

In 1636 the Senior Bursar was entrusted with "ye beautifying of ye Chappell, and ye decent adorning of ye Communion Table"; and in June of the same year the following Order was made:

"June 15 1636. Agreed by ye M^r and ye Seniors to set o^r Communion-table in o^r Chappell as it is in Cathedrall Churches and Chappells, at ye upper end, and ye ground to be raysed; and y^t ye chappell be adorned accordingly."

A special heading, *Expenses in the Inward Chappell*, records the outlay of about £500[5]. A new pavement of Ketton stone and marble was laid down, the walls were wainscoted with deal, the frieze of which was gilt, and new altar-cloths and hangings were provided. The last were probably for the east end. The material, which seems to have been unusually rich, was given to the College, and the hangings were made up and painted in London, at a cost of nearly £200[6]. A new Vestry

---

[1] [Ibid. 1603—4. "Item to the Joyner for a Perriment on the topp of the Organs wth the scrowles and 7 bowles for the same, xlj^s viij^d. Item for the Kinge his armes cuttinge and colouringe and bringinge from London iiij^li xij^s vj^d." Their position on the organ-loft is assumed from a charge in the Sen. Burs. Accounts 1673—74. " For ..gilding and painting ye King's Armes on the Organ Loft 03. 10. 00."]

[2] [Ibid. 1609—10. "Item to John York for making the newe chaire orgaine xl^li. Item to Knuckle the painter for painting and guilding therof xiij^li vj^s iiij^d."]

[3] [" 26 July 1637. Aggreed that Mr Greeneberry and Mr Knuckle shall have for the paynting and guilding of the Organ 50^li. Item that Mr Hallam shall have for the mending and the tuning of the Organ xx^li."]

[4] [Sen. Burs. Accounts, 1609—10. "Item to Chapman the Joyner for making a newe pulpet out of Dr Grayes vale given him by the Coll. xiij^li vj^s viij^d."]

[5] [Ibid. 1636—37.]

[6] [In the Senior Bursar's Accounts for 1639—40 we find: " To Mr Willis [one of the Fellows] for expenses in his Journey to London, and about ye causing of ye stuff that Mr Rijchaut bestowed on the Colledge to make ye rich hanginges, to be peeced,

is mentioned as having been fitted up at the same time out of
a room which had previously been a College-chamber[1]. The
only room which could have been used for this purpose must
have been one of those in the east range of the Cloister-Court
of King's Hall, which abutted upon the Chapel (figs. 6, 7), and
was not pulled down until 1694 (p. 461).

In the course of the year 1643, the Chapel was "reformed."
Dowsing's journal[2] records that "we had 4 Cherubims & Steps
levelled"; and the Senior Bursar makes the following entries[3]:

"To Chambers for not blowing ye organs a whole year xl^s.

To Mr Knuckle for whiting over ye Figures and for his paines and
his servants l^s.

To George Woodruffe for taking downe ye organs and hanginges xv^s.

To Mr Jenings for taking downe ye Organ pipes xlv^s.

Given to free Masons, bricklaiers, carpenters, and vpholsterers for
remouing ye hanginges and railes in ye chappell xxviij^s."

The following entries, from the Steward's Accounts, refer to
the first quarter of 1644:

"To diuerse souldiers at seuerall times that behaued themselues
very deuoutly in the chappell 00. 05. 00. To some of Major Scot's
souldiers who defended the chappell from the rudenesse of the rest
00. 05. 00."

At the Restoration the organ was set up again, and Thamar,
the organ-maker of Peterborough, was employed to construct a
new one, or to repair the old one on an extensive scale. At the
same time a "transome," a word which probably denotes the
screen behind the altar, was made, and the altar-furniture,
Litany-desk, etc. were replaced[4]. In 1685—86 an agreement was

---

and fringed, and lined, and fitted as they now are, to each place in the Chappell, and
for seuerall expences about the fitting up of the new vestrey...Cj^li xiij^s iiij^d." The
Senior Bursar had made the following entry in his Account for 1636—37. "For the
Hangings and painting them xcv^li vj^s viij^d."]

[1] [Sen. Burs. Accounts 1639—40. *Chapell.* "To Mr Trot for ye Income of his
Chamber wch is now the vestrey xviij^s."]

[2] [Cooper's Annals iii. 366.]

[3] [Sen. Burs. Accounts 1642—43. *Chappel.* In his Account for 1641—42, under
the heading *Extraordinaries*, we find the following curious entries: "Given to those
that carried ye university Plate into o^r Tower ij^s. Spent at ye intertainment of
Captaine Cromwell and his gentlmen Soldiers ix^s v^d." In 1651—52 he charges "Item
for an hour glasse 00. 01. 00."]

[4] [The following entries from the Accounts illustrate these changes: Sen. Burs.
1659—60. *Chappell.* "For removeing, setting vpp, and tuneing the Little Organ

made with Mr Bernard Smith, commonly called Father Smith, to make an entirely new organ, which was completed, and solemnly opened, in 1694[1].

The following curious narrative[2] incidentally describes the arrangement of the east end after the Restoration:

"On the 30th of *November*, being *Advent Sunday*, a very sad accident came to the *High Altar*, newly erected in *Trinity Colledge Chappel* in *Cambridge*, which according to the information we have received from divers Letters written from some of the Fellows of that House, was as followeth.

"*Evensong being ended, the Chappel Clerk put up the Candle-ends in a Box ; and not being careful enough in extinguishing them, and placing the Box very irreverently too near the* Sanctum Sanctorum, *it took fire, which was* so prophane *as* to burn down the *Traverse, which was made of most rich* Mosaick-work, *and the new Errected Altar, with all the costly Furniture wherewith it was Adorned, which were all sacrificed in the flames : Yea, it spared not the Book of* Common Prayer, *which lay upon it, nor the* holy Vestments *belonging to the Choristers and Singing-Men, nor the* Consecrated Plate, *not only that which was then upon the Altar, but a great Chest of other Chappel Plate also ;* which (as most of the Letters say) was melted.   *   *   *   One Circumstance is most remarkable in this Accident, *viz.* That this High Altar was the first that was set up in *Cambridge*, yea, as it is believed in all *England* since the late Revolution ; and the reason of it was, because Mistress *Cumber*, Wife to the former Master of that Colledge[3], did, about twenty years ago, out of great Piety, Zeal, and Devotion, secretly convey away

01. 10. 00.   For an embroidered Carpett 06. 10. 00."   The work on the organ was directed by Mr Loosemore, the College organist. Ibid. 1661—62.   "Paid Shuter's bill for worke about the hangings about the Communion Table 03. 16. 02.   Paid to Stephens and other workemen for the Transome and other worke done in the Chappell ...86. 11. 11."   Ibid. 1662—63.   "To Mr Thamar towards the makeing of the Organ 15. 00. 00."   He receives in all £110 ; and, 18 December, 1674, it was "Agreed that Mr Thamar be allowed 20 shillings annvally for keeping the Organ."   "For deales planke and timber for the transome 02. 19. 08.   For coullering the Transome and Railes 01. 02. 00."   Ibid. 1664—65.   "For painting the Letany deske etc. 00. 04. 06."]

[1] [Sen. Burs. Accounts 1685—86. *Chappell.* "To Mr Denson ye First paymt upon ye Articles betweene him and Mr Smith towards makeing an Organ 10. 00. 00." Ibid. 1693—94.   "For Symphonys, one at ye opening of ye new Organ, and ye other on Trin. Sunday at 10s a time 01. 00. 00.   To Mr Bernard Smith at seuerall times for ye New Organ 111. 00. 00."]

[2] ["MIRABILIS ANNUS SECUNDUS: OR, THE SECOND PART Of the SECOND YEARS PRODIGIES. Being a true Additional *Collection* of many strange SIGNS and APPARITIONS, which have this last Year been seen in the HEAVENS, and in the EARTH, and in the WATERS.   Together with many remarkable *Accidents*, and signal *Judgments* which have befel divers Persons who have Apostatized from the Truth, and have been Persecutors of the Lord's faithful Servants."   4°.   Printed in the Year 1662. p. 53.]

[3] [Thomas Comber, D.D., was Master from 1631 to 1644, when he was ejected.]

this Altar, with all its appurtenances, that it might escape those most Sacrilegious hands, which at that time did both in *Cambridge,* and everywhere else, destroy those Sacred Shrines, as Badges of Superstition, and Introductions to Popery."

It is evident that at the beginning of the eighteenth century the Chapel was in need of a thorough repair[1], and that the College was not wealthy enough to charge the expense to its corporate funds, for in the spring of 1702 the Reverend William Corker, one of the Senior Fellows, gave £500 "to repair and adorn" it[2]. This munificent gift probably suggested the idea of defraying the entire cost by subscription. We do not know how soon a systematic effort was made to get funds together in this way, for the list which was subsequently opened is unfortunately undated. A few donations are recorded by the Senior Bursar in the years 1705 and 1706; and in the latter year the following Order was made:

"July 11th, 1706. Orderd and agreed by the Master and Seniors, yt Mr Roger Coats, fellow of this College, be ye Officer to receive the Money given to repair and Beautify the Chapell, and yt he do pay from time to time the several workmen concernd therein, and keep a Book of Receipts and Disbursments, and exhibit ye accounts to ye Master and Seniors from time to time, as he shall be required."

It seems probable, from the terms of this Order, that it was made in view of subscriptions to be subsequently contributed; and we may therefore refer to this year the commencement of the formal subscription-list[3], which is headed as follows:

---

[1] [Dr Monk, without giving authorities, says (Life of Bentley i. 205): "the fabric itself was dilapidated, the roof being decayed and dangerous, and one of the walls in imminent danger of falling."]

[2] ["April 16, 1702. Orderd by the Master and Seniors that the thanks of ye College be returnd to ye Revd Mr Corker senior fellow of this College for his Gift of Five hundred pounds to repair and adorn ye College Chapel." Mr Corker died 30 April 1702, and was buried in the Chapel at the expense of the College. Sen. Burs. Accounts, 1709—10. *Chappell.* "To Robt Grumbold for a Marble Gravestone with the Inscription for ye late Reverend Mr Wm Corker as an extraordinary Benefactor to ye Coll. Chapel 14. 10. 0." The Inscription is: "H. S. E. Gulielmus Corker Art. Mag. Collegii hujus Socius Senior, qui septuagenarius moriens Aº Dni. MDCCIIº. Mense Apr. die XXX. Sacello et Bibliothecæ Libras DCC Testamento donavit. Viro doctissimo et munificentissimo Monumentum hoc Collegium posuit A.D. MDCCIX."]

[3] [A further reason for assigning it to this year is afforded by the fact that the subscriptions to which dates are prefixed are dated 1707 and 1708, and occur at the end of the list. There are only six of these, representing a total of £120.]

"In consideration, that the Master Fellows and Scholars of ye College of the holy and undivided Trinity in the University of Cambridge ...have resolved to repair and beautify the Chappel of the said College, the charge of which may amount to about three thousand pounds; Wee whose names are hereunder written do hereby severally oblige our Selves our Executors and Administrators to the Master, Fellows, and Scholars of the said College, to pay, or cause, or procure to be paid, the Sums of money herein by us respectively subscribed, into the hands of the College Officer appointed to receive the said money, before Michaelmas day which shall be in the year of our Lord God one thousand seven hundred and seven, towards the charge of repairing and beautifying their Chappel, in such manner as the Master and Senr Fellows of the said College shall think fit."

The sums recorded in this list amount to £2744. 15s. 0d. The Master contributed £200, and the Fellows, with very few exceptions, the amount of their yearly dividend. Besides this sum other subscriptions and legacies were paid to the Account of the Chapel at the end of 1707, which, together with £1000 which had been lent by the Master in 1706[1], raised the total available at that time for the repair and decoration of the Chapel to £4820. 18s. 5½d.[2] As the estimated cost had been £3000, the Master and Seniors were fully justified in undertaking the work; and as we shall see that very few expenses were

---

[1] ["Sept. 6, 1706. Orderd also, y^t the summe of one thousand pounds be borrowd at Interest of five per cent, and appropriated to ye repairs of ye College Chapel."]

[2] [There are two lists at the end of the account of the Senior Bursar, Mr George Modd, for 1707—8, the first of which is headed: "A particular Account of severall Benefactions Rec^d for the use of the Chappell and Library by the R^nd Mr Nicholas Spencer late Sen. Bursar never yet accounted for to ye College from the Sen. Bursar's Office." Mr Spencer had held the office of Sen. Bursar in the years 1702, 1703, 1704 and 1705, and died suddenly in 1706 while still in office (Present State of Trinity College, p. 19). The total received by him amounts to £936. 3. 5½. Among these subscriptions is "The Gift of Mr Isaac Newton 60. 0. 0." The whole sum was paid over to Mr Cotes for the use of the Chapel in 1709 and 1710. The second list is headed: "Memd. the following Gifts towards ye adorning ye Chapell here inserted were rec^d by Mr Modd and accordingly accounted for to the College in his 2 last Years' Books pro Annis 1705 and 1706." It contains sums amounting to £140, exclusive of £20 from Dr James, whose subscription has been included in the general list. The receipts for the Chapel therefore are:

List of subscriptions headed by the Master	2744. 15.	0
,, ,, in Sen. Burs. Book 1706—7	1076. 3.	5½
Amount borrowed (6 Sept. 1706)	1000. 0.	0
	£4820. 18.	5½]

charged to the account of the College, except of course the interest of the money borrowed, it is difficult to understand why the scheme excited so much indignation. It was however from the first unpopular with the party opposed to the Master, probably for no better reason than because he had been active in promoting it, and in the "Articles against Dr Bentley[1]," exhibited to the Bishop of Ely 11 July, 1710, we find it made the subject of grave accusation :

> "WHY did you waste great Sums of the College Money in buying a new Organ, and making great and unnecessary Alterations in the College Chapel, without the Consent, and contrary to the Advice of the Senior Fellows, and at an unseasonable Time, when the Price of Corn was low, and the College poor? AND, to involve them into greater Necessities, WHY did you cause them to borrow Money at Interest to carry on the said Work, and lend them 1000*l.* your self, and that contrary to the College Statutes concerning Usury?"

The history of the work executed is unfortunately most imperfect. As so often happens in the case of an outlay which was principally defrayed by subscription or by loan, without any direct charge on the corporate funds of the College, it was not thought necessary to preserve the records of receipts and expenditure. The Account-book which Mr Cotes undoubtedly kept has disappeared, and we are therefore completely without information as to the names of any of the persons who directed the alterations. Moreover the Senior Fellows were evidently not consulted ; for the only Orders entered in the Conclusion-Book are the following :

> "July 26th. 1706. Orderd...y[t] Prigg y[e] Plumber do new cast and work y[e] Lead of y[e] Chapel, and Brewer y[e] Bricklayer do build up y[e] East Window, and new plaister y[e] South side of y[e] Chapell ; upon such terms as are agreed between them and M[r] Coats fellow of this College."
>
> "May y[e] 3[d]. 1708. Agreed by the Master and Seniors, y[t] M[r] Christopher Schrider do finish the Organ by tuning and voicing it ; and that he be allowd so much out of y[e] Total sum agreed for with the late M[r] Bernard Smith for making y[e] whole Organ, as Her Majesties Organists shall think reasonable[2]."

---

[1] [They were thrown into the interrogative form because the Statute *De Magistri Amotione* directs that the accused shall be examined (*examinatus*) before the Visitor.]

[2] [Schrider was son-in-law to Bernard Smith, and succeeded to his business after his death at the beginning of 1708. It is stated by Dr T. A. Walmisley in a paper in the Cambridge Portfolio, p. 194, that this organ cost £1500 ; but he does not give his authority. The sum seems to be an extravagant one, when compared with that

"Nov. 24th. 1715. Agreed...That Mr Bursar pay to Mr Schrider 30 pounds for cleaning and voicing ye Chapel Organ, and 20 pounds for the swelling stops; and yt henceforward Mr Schrider have 5 pounds a year for ye keeping the Organ in good tune and Order."

These Orders shew that the work had been begun in 1706, that the organ was nearly finished in 1708, and must have been in use for some time in 1715. It is probable that the indispensable repairs were finished in 1713, at the end of which year the Senior Bursar pays the plumber in full. Much of the work however still remained unfinished; and we shall see that it was not brought to a conclusion for more than twenty years. When Professor Cotes died, 5 June, 1716, his Accounts had not been audited, and some subscriptions were still unpaid[1]. When the audit was held, after more than a year had elapsed, the following Minute was entered in the Conclusion Book:

"August 31, 1717. Whereas ye Revd Mr Roger Coats Professor of Astronomy and Experimental Philosophy and Fellow of this House was appointed (by Order July 11th 1706) Officer to receive and pay all Money towards ye Repair of ye College Chapell; and being since to ye great loss of ye College and ye Learned World deceasd, His accounts are laid before ye Master and Seniors by Mr Robert Smith His successor in ye said Professorship and Fellow of this House, and being examind, The Accounts are found to stand Thus:

Receipts in all	5653	03	01
Disbursements in all	5498	01	06
Due on this account from Mr Coats	0155	01	07
Add his own Subscription yet unpaid 25 0 0	0180	1	7

Ri. Bentley."

The receipts, as entered here, exceed the sum stated to be available from subscriptions, promised and paid, and from other sources, at the outset of the work, by £832. 4s. 7½d. We do not know to what this difference was due, except that in 1717

paid to Smith for other organs. The contract between him and the Dean and Chapter of Durham in 1683 (Rimbault, The Organ, 8° London, 1855, p. 78) specifies £700, and the materials of the old organ, as the price of the organ for that Cathedral; and it is hardly likely that the Cambridge organ could have cost more.]

[1] ["Aug. 31, 1717. Orderd..., That Dr Ayloff Senior Bursar do gather the Remaining Subscriptions due to the Chappel, and account them to the said Master and Seniors. Ri. Bentley."]

the Duke of Somerset had given £100 "towards further beauti-fyeing yᵉ Chapell[1]," which is probably included among the other receipts.

In 1718 a fresh subscription was set on foot, and in that year and the following £150 was collected. Out of this sum a bricklayer received £27. 01s. 00d. "for work done to yᵉ East end of yᵉ Chappell" in 1717—18, and Woodward the carver £79. 0s. 0d., for work which is not specified, in 1719—20, and 1720—21[2]. After this date the Chapel is not mentioned in the Accounts until 1724—25, when under the heading *Extraordinaries for the Chappell*, the Senior Bursar enters £100 received "of his Grace the Duke of Somersett towards adorning the Altarpeice," together with an equal sum "of the Rev. M. Banks for further Ornaments in the Chappell." The payments record an outlay of £444. 0s. 0d. for elaborate altar-furniture, a "Gilded Frame," velvet, damask, and the like, but woodwork is not mentioned[3]. It is clear, however, that the woodwork could not have been completed for at least ten years after this date, because over the Vice-Master's stall are the words "R. WALKER V. Mᴿ," commemorating Dr Richard Walker, who was not elected Vice-Master until 17 May, 1734; and moreover the Junior Bursar's Day-book for 1755—56 contains the following entry, headed *Coats of Arms in Chapel*:

"July 19.   Paid to John Woodward for carving 26 Coats of Arms at £1. 0. 0. each, also mending the freize and other Parts of yᵉ carving £28. 7. 6."

There are seventeen shields on each side of the Chapel, commemorating the following persons, beginning from the west end and including the two shields on the organ-screen. The words in capital letters are copied exactly from the woodwork; the names and the dates of degrees have been obtained from the records of the University. A star prefixed to a name denotes that it occurs in the first list of subscribers.

---

[1] [Sen. Burs. Accounts, 1716—17. *Extraordinary Receipts.*]

[2] [The balance £43. 19. 0 is not accounted for.]

[3] [The total charged on the side of payments is £544; but this includes "The D. of Somerset's Gift accounted for in the Bursar's book pro Anno 1717, £100. 00. 00," an entry which shews that the Duke's donation had probably been included in the estimate of receipts made in 1718.]

NORTH SIDE.

R. WALKER. V. M^r: for Richard Walker, Trin. Vice-Master 1734.

M^R. PERRY: for William Perry, Trin. Fellow, A.M. 1675.

CAR. BARRINGTON.

* DR CRESSAR: for Stephen Cressar, Trin. Fellow, D.D. 1708.
* MR BATHURST: for Edward Bathurst, Trin. Fellow, A.M. 1673.
* MR EDEN: for Henry Eden, Trin. Fellow, A.M. 1704.
* MR BURRELL: for William Burrell, Trin. A.M. 1673.
* ROG. COTES, A.M.: for Roger Cotes, Trin. Fellow, A.M. 1706.
* MR STVBB: for Edmund Stubbe, Trin. Fellow, A.M. 1707.

IAC. MONTAGU. EQ. AVR.: Trin. adm. "socio-commensalis" 1683.

IS. NEWTON. EQ. AVR.: for Sir Isaac Newton, Trin. Fellow, knighted 1705.

* DR IAMES: for Henry James, Queens', D.D. 1679, President of Queens' College 1675—1717.
* IOH. HACKET, D.D.: for John Hacket, Trin. Fellow, D.D. 1717.
* CAMPION: for Henry Campion, adm. "commensalis" 1697; or William Campion, adm. "socio-commensalis" 1724.
* TREVOR: for Thomas Trevor, Trin. eldest son of Thomas Lord Trevor, A.M. 1712.
* SAM. KNIGHT, D.D.: for Samuel Knight, Trin. D.D. 1717.
* EDW. RUD, D.D.: for Edward Rud, Trin. Fellow, D.D. 1717.

SOUTH SIDE.

R. BENTLEY: for Richard Bentley, Master 1700—42.

PIEREPONETE[1]: for William Pierpoint, Trin. Fellow Commoner, matriculated July 1706.

I. MOUNTAGU, D.D.: for Dr John Mountagu, Master, 1683—1700.

* MR BACON: for Montagu Bacon, Trin. A.M. 1734.
* MR MODD: for George Modd, Trin. Fellow, A.M. 1669.
* MR CHAMBERLAYNE: for William Chamberlaine, Trin. Fellow, A.M. 1704.
* MR MILLER: for Edmund Miller, Trin. Fellow, A.M. 1693.
* IAMES IURIN, M.D.: for James Jurin, Trin. Fellow, M.D. 1716.

MR EKINS: for Thomas Ekins, Trin. A.B. 1704 (?).

* DR AYLOFFE: for William Ayloffe, Trin. Fellow, LL.D. 1705.
* M. HUTCHINSON: for Michael Hutchinson, Trin. Fellow, A.M. 1691.

MR MOYLE: for Robert Moyle, Trin. Fellow.

* DR MIDDLETON: for Conyers Middleton, Trin. Fellow, D.D. 1717.

DR SMITH: for Robert Smith, Trin. Fellow, LL.D. 1723.

* COLEMAN. D.D.: for Henry Coleman, Trin. D.D. 1712.
* IOH. FULLER. ARM: for John Fuller, Trin. A.B. 1699 (?).
* IAM. BANKS. A.M.: for James Bankes, Trin. A.M. 1686.

The above list shews that Dr Jurin became Doctor of Medicine in 1716; that Dr Knight, Dr Hacket, Dr Rud, and Dr Middleton became Doctors of Divinity in 1717; that Dr Smith

[1] [The name is arranged on a label so as to make the three words: PIE. REPONE. TE.]

became Doctor of Law in 1723; and that Mr Bacon became Master of Arts in 1734. Their shields therefore could not have been put before those dates; and there is such a complete uniformity of treatment in the shields and their ornamentation, that we may conclude that they were all executed at the same time and by the same artist. They are usually ascribed to Grinling Gibbons, who executed the wreaths and other devices in the Library, as shewn above (p. 545), and they are unquestionably in his manner. He however died in 1721, thirteen years before Dr Walker's title or Mr Bacon's degree could have been recorded. Moreover it has been shewn above that Woodward worked in the Chapel in 1720 and 1721, and moreover carved 26 shields in 1756. It seems probable therefore that he executed the shields and their ornaments at the earlier date; and that in 1756 he repaired his previous work, and carved the shields, most of which had until then been left blank.

The arrangements made by Dr Bentley have not been materially changed. Certain alterations, to be hereafter described, were made in 1832, and a well-considered scheme for providing additional accommodation, decorating the roof and walls, and filling the windows with stained glass, was carried out between 1870 and 1875. In these works, however, the general plan of Bentley's fittings was respected. We will therefore give a description of them, illustrated by the accompanying engravings (figs. 38, 39). The former, by Storer, shews the way in which the seats were arranged previous to 1832; the latter, from Le Keux's Memorials of Cambridge, published in 1847, shews the changes introduced in 1832, and, further, the original form of the organ-case, which was altered in 1870.

Dr Bentley began his work in 1706, by blocking up the east window, and placing the altar against the east wall. At some subsequent period, the precise date of which, as explained above, cannot now be ascertained, a lofty baldacchino of oak was erected over the altar. It consists of a semicircular arch, springing from four Corinthian columns, and surmounted by a pediment, richly decorated with arabesques, vases, cherubim, and other devices in fashion in the last century. We do not know how the wall-space beneath the arch was treated originally, the picture of S. Michael binding Satan, by West, having been given by Dr

Fig. 38.   Interior of Trinity College Chapel, looking east, by Storer, shewing the
arrangement previous to 1832.

Hinchliffe, Master 1768—89, and there is no tradition that it replaced an older work. The wall above the baldacchino was undecorated, but on each side of it, occupying the space which had originally intervened between the jamb of the east window and the north and south walls, there were two large figures under canopies, painted in fresco on the wall. Similar figures occupied the contiguous spaces on the north and south walls. The subjects on the east wall were Our Lord, and the Virgin Mary; on the north wall S. James the Great; on the south wall S. Mary Magdalene[1]. The history of these paintings is unknown; but, from their style, they were older than the period of Dr Bentley, and may perhaps be the "Figures" which were "whited over" in 1643.

The ancient fittings, with the exception of the panelwork in the Antechapel, were all removed[2], and replaced by new wood-work—similar in character to the baldacchino over the altar. The organ-screen, about 17 feet wide, occupied the whole of the fifth bay, counting from the west end ; the stalls extended over the next five bays; and the last two formed the "sacrarium." The stalls are in two rows, without any subdivisions ; and originally, as the older view shews (fig. 38), the line was unbroken by any projection or elevated seats. In front of the lower row of stalls there was a fixed seat ; and a bench in the same style which seems original, stood a few feet in advance of it. The woodwork rises as high as the cills of the windows, and behind the stalls is divided by Corinthian pilasters into ten spaces of equal width, each of which is again subdivided into two large panels. The molding below the pilasters, and the enta-blature above them, are carried across the intervening spaces, so as to form a deep border, ornamented with coats of arms, and wreaths of fruit and flowers. The whole is surmounted by a projecting cornice supported upon brackets. This cornice is

---

[1] [These figures are determined differently in The Ecclesiologist ix. 146; in Le Keux, ed. Cooper, ii. 319; and in The New Cambridge Guide, by M. Watson, 1804, as: Our Lord, S. John Baptist, S. Mary, and S. Elizabeth.]

[2] [According to ancient tradition, some of these fittings were taken to S. Michael's Church, where stalls still exist which correspond very well with those described in the contract. No confirmation of the tradition can however be found in either the College Accounts or the Parish Books.]

returned across the organ-screen; and over the seats of the
Master and Vice-Master is elevated into a curvilinear pediment,
resting on detached Corinthian columns. The panelwork above
described is prolonged along the north and south walls beyond
the stalls, and along the portion of the east wall not occupied
by the baldacchino. The different members of the composition
are worked at the same level; but variety is produced by a
different entablature, and by subdividing the vertical spaces by
pairs of small disengaged columns instead of by pilasters. On
this woodwork Professor Willis remarks: "The work was designed and carried out in a noble and admirable style; and
although it be out of harmony with the traceried windows and
the roof, the discrepancy is amply compensated for by the great
beauty of the fittings."

During the remainder of the eighteenth century, and for the
first quarter of the nineteenth, no changes of importance are
recorded in the Chapel. It may be mentioned that the organ
was frequently repaired and improved[1]; that in 1787—88 the
roof was painted in white and gold[2]; and that in 1804—5 additional seats were provided on a platform near the altar[3].

In 1831—32 extensive alterations were carried out under the
direction of Mr Edward Blore, Architect. The walls were thoroughly repaired within and without, and the stonework of the
east window renewed. Hitherto each bay of the roof had been
subdivided into four square spaces, with a circular ornament in
the centre of each (fig. 38). Each of these spaces was now subdivided into four, with new ornaments at the angles and intersections; and the whole was grained in imitation of oak[4]. The
elevated seats for the Senior and Junior Dean, the pews for the

[1] [The chief repairs are the following: Jun. Burs. Accounts, 1766—67:
Organ. "To Mʳ Parker Organ Maker in London, for repairs and improvements
in yᵉ Organ, by Order of and Agreement with the Master and Seniors 185. o. o."
Ibid. 1800—1801, *Extraordinaries* "Paid J. Avery for work at Organ (on advance)
60. o. o." Ibid. 1801—2. "Paid J. Avery for work at Organ (on advance) 60. o. o.
Paid J. Mills Solicitor to the Commission for J. Avery 117. 6. o." Ibid. 1818—19.
"Paid into Court £147, Flight's Bill for repairing the Organ."]
[2] [Ibid. 1787—88. *Painter.*]   [3] [Ibid. 1804—5. *Carpenter.*]
[4] [The roof is described as follows in Le Keux (1847): "The ceiling of the
Chapel, which was formerly worked in compartments of white and gold, and was
much too delicate for the distance at which it was necessarily viewed, was entirely
renewed a few years ago, and is now of a much bolder design."]

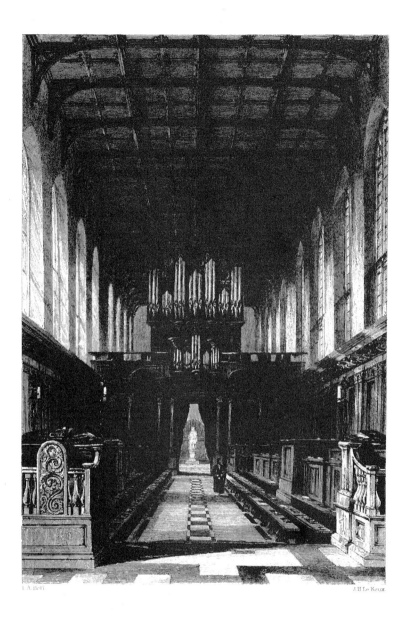

Fig. 39. Interior of Trinity College Chapel, looking west, shewing the changes made 1832,
and the original form of the organ; from Le Keux's Memorials of Cambridge.

choir, and the desks at the east end (fig. 39) were constructed at this time, and a new system of lighting was adopted[1]. The Antechapel was similarly repaired[2]. The total cost of these works was £2511. 7s. 11d.[3]

No definite proposal to change these arrangements was made until 1865, although it had been felt for some time that the Chapel stood in need of repair, decoration, and, if possible, enlargement. At the General Meeting of the Fellows held 15 December 1865 the question of providing increased accommodation was formally debated[4]; and an affirmative vote having been taken at the same meeting in the following year, the Master and Seniors took the matter seriously in hand in February 1867. A wish was expressed by some that an entirely new Chapel should be built, but this idea was dismissed as undesirable and impracticable, and it was determined to preserve and improve the existing fabric. The more substantial and necessary portions of the work were undertaken first. In 1867 the roof was repaired; in 1868 the two westernmost bays on the south side (fig. 9) were ashlared; in 1869 and 1870 the six bays next to them were similarly treated; and in 1873 the remaining three bays, and the east end. Meanwhile (13 February, 1869) Mr Blomfield, Architect, had been consulted "as to the best mode of enlarging and increasing the accommodation," and after a long and careful consideration, and the rejection of various proposals, as the building of a north aisle, a chamber on the north side to contain the organ, etc., it was determined (25 March, 1870) to retain the organ-screen, but to diminish it in depth by seven feet, and to remove it, with the stall-work, seven feet

---

[1] [The principal feature of this scheme was a lofty standard of bronze, about ten feet high, bearing eight large candles. It was placed directly in front of the altar, in a line with the reading-desks, on a large square pedestal. It is shewn in one of Storer's views; but, though much admired when first put up, it evidently was soon removed, for it does not appear in Le Keux's view, taken about 1847.]

[2] [The contract (preserved in Trinity College Muniment Room) provides that the canopied tomb of Thomas Seckford, who died 26 June, 1624, ætat. 16, which stood against the north wall of the antechapel, shall be removed to the vestry.]

[3] [Sen. Burs. Accounts, 1831—32. The contract is dated 19 August, 1831.]

[4] [The proposal submitted to the Meeting, signed by 16 Fellows, was: "That, the College Chapel having become inadequate for the requirements of the College, measures be taken to ascertain whether the present Building might not conveniently be altered and enlarged."]

further to the west; to provide new seats for the undergraduates with backs and kneeling-desks; and to build a new vestry and a practising-room for the choir on the north side. At the same time an agreement was entered into with Messrs Hill for the enlargement of the organ; and, lastly, the whole building was lighted with gas.

The decoration of the walls and roof, and the filling of the windows with stained glass, was undertaken next. The cost of the previous work had been defrayed out of the corporate funds of the College; but for the decoration an appeal was made to the resident and non-resident Members of the College, who, as suggested in the circular soliciting subscriptions, "might be glad of an opportunity of contributing to the adornment of a building so closely connected with the history of the College, and in which the remains of so many great and good men are deposited." In consequence of this appeal upwards of £11,000 was subscribed between 1871 and 1875, besides special gifts, which will be noticed below. The general scheme for the decoration of the quire was suggested by Dr Westcott and Dr Lightfoot, and carried out by Messrs Heaton, Butler, and Bayne, under the direction of Mr Blomfield. The figures in the windows were designed by Mr Henry Holiday. Before describing the different portions in detail it should be premised that the decoration of the roof represents the Hymn of Creation—the praises of the different elements of Nature and the representatives of Humanity—leading up to the manifestation of the Divine Glory (Rev. iv.). The decoration of the walls represents, advancing from west to east, the preparatory discipline of the patriarchal, legal, and prophetic periods, leading up to the figures of S. John the Baptist and the Blessed Virgin on the eastern wall. The altar-piece, between these figures, represents the completed Triumph of Christ, in the Entombment crowned by the Ascension. The windows, advancing from east to west, represent the historical development of the course of Christian Life, gradually confined within narrower limits till it closes in the representatives of the College.

The subdivisions of the panels of the roof introduced in 1832 were removed, leaving four large panels in each bay. The ribs, purlines, and cornice, were decorated in gold and colour, so as to

give prominence to the original moldings and enrichments, and
the panels were filled with subjects illustrating the *Benedicite*,
the words of which, in Latin, were painted along the walls, as
a frieze immediately below the cornice.   The representations of
the powers of Nature occupy the westernmost panels.   These
are succeeded by the "Children of Men" (Adam, Noah, Abraham,
the Queen of Sheba, Pharaoh, Cyrus); "Israel" (four central
panels each containing three figures typical of the twelve
Tribes); "Priests of the Lord" (Melchisedec, Aaron, Jeshua,
Moses, Joshua, Samuel); "Servants of the Lord" (Solomon, Ezra,
Judas Maccabeus); "Spirits and Souls of the Righteous" (Samuel,
Elijah, Enoch); "Holy and Humble Men of Heart" (Job, David,
Isaiah); "Ananias, Azarias, and Misael"; and lastly, four Arch-
angels bearing a scroll on which the Doxology is inscribed.
The four easternmost bays are differently treated.   The sixteen
panels into which they are divided form a square, in the centre
of which is a glory of radiating golden beams, round which
are angels bearing scrolls, with the inscription: DIGNUS ES
DOMINE DEUS NOSTER ACCIPERE GLORIAM ET HONOREM ET
VIRTUTEM, QUIA TU CREASTI OMNIA, ET PROPTER VOLUN-
TATEM TUAM ERANT ET CREATI SUNT.   Rev. iv. 11.   The
corner panels of the square contain the Evangelistic symbols;
the remaining eight panels contain groups of elders casting
crowns before the central glory.   There are three figures in each
panel, so as to make up the required number, twenty-four.

The wall-spaces between the windows have medallions containing heads of Patriarchs, Priests, Kings, and Prophets of the
Old Testament dispensation, with suitable emblems and decorations beneath; while the large interval on the south side, against
which the eastern range of the Court abuts, is occupied by a
representation of the Holy Family, with the adoration of the
Shepherds and the Magi, to symbolize the offerings of culture
and simple faith to the new-born Saviour.   The subjects of the
wall-paintings between the windows are as follows, beginning
from the west end:

SOUTH SIDE.

ADAM: the Apple, freshly tilled ground, and the four rivers of Paradise
    below.
MELCHISEDEC: the Vine, wheat below.   Gen. xiv. 18.

JACOB: the Palm.

DAVID: the Cedar, as the royal tree.　Psalm xcii. 12; Ezek. xvii. 22—24.

JOSIAH: the Oleander: selected as being one of the most striking shrubs of Palestine, to symbolize the reform under Josiah.

EZRA: the Almond: intended to mark the fresh organization of the law under Ezra.　Numbers xvii. 8; Jeremiah i. 11.

NORTH SIDE.

NOAH: the Olive; a rainbow, dove and olive branch above; a dead raven lying in the water below; a pair of peacocks stand under the olive-tree.

ABRAHAM: the Oak; beneath is a ram, caught in a bramble by his horns.　Gen. xii. 6, xiii. 18, xxii. 13.

MOSES: the Papyrus; a pair of the sacred Ibis, with the Nile, below.

AARON: the Acacia; a species of Acacia (*Acacia seyal*) has been identified with the tree called *Shittah*, out of the wood of which the Ark and the table for the shewbread were constructed.　Exodus xxv. xxvi.

JOSHUA: the Pomegranate, Fig, and Vine.　Deut. viii. 8.

ELIJAH: the Juniper; the waters of the brook Cherith, below.

DANIEL: the Willow; the waters of Babylon, below.

MALACHI: the Frankincense Tree, in reference to the prophecy of Malachi (i. 11), which foreshadows an abiding and universal worship.

** The wider wall-space opposite to the organ bears, on each side, an angel carrying a scroll.　On these scrolls is inscribed the first verse of the Latin hymn *Jesus dulcis memoria*, generally attributed to S. Bernard, with the old tune in plain-song notation.　Above is a square medallion, in which is an angel blowing a trumpet.

The east end was considerably altered.　The figures on the east wall, described above, were replaced by paintings representing the Virgin Mary and S. John the Baptist.　Several of the more obtrusive ornaments of the baldacchino were taken down, and the arch which contained the picture was made coextensive with the great arch above it.　The space thus obtained was filled by two pictures: the lower representing the Entombment, the upper the Ascension[1].　The baldacchino itself was enriched by a judicious application of gold.　These decorations and paintings were given by the Rev. William Hepworth Thompson, D.D., Master; and the altar-cloth, worked in Belgium, by the Architect.　The rest of the woodwork was enriched in a similar style, and above the stalls a gold ground was introduced behind the delicate carvings round the coats of arms.　The brass

[1] [The picture of S. Michael was removed to the vestibule of the Library.]

lectern in the centre of the quire had been given by the Master and Mrs Thompson in 1866.

The large panels of the woodwork with which the walls of the "sacrarium" are lined were decorated with intarsia work, at the expense of A. J. B. Beresford Hope, M.A., M.P. for the University. In the centre of each panel is a medallion head, and the remaining space is occupied by arabesques, flowers, fruit, and birds. The subjects are the following, beginning at the east end:

South Side.	North Side.
Levi	S. Peter
Judah	S. James the Less
Joseph	S. John
Benjamin	S. Andrew.

On the east wall: SYNAGOGA.   On the east wall: ECCLESIA.

The fifteen windows of the quire contain the following figures, eight to each window, arranged as nearly as possible in historical sequence. The order of the windows, and of the figures, is from East to West, the lower lights preceding the upper lights in each window. In order to obtain an exact historical sequence the windows on the north side must be considered in conjunction with those on the south side; but the grouping of each individual window is mainly determined by unity of subject. The figures in the different periods are chosen with the view of representing characteristic features or movements of the time in which they lived. For instance, in the window illustrating Latin Christianity, Charlemagne represents Empire; S. Thomas Aquinas, Scholasticism; Louis IX., the Crusades; Dante, Medieval thought; Columban, Missions; Gregory VII., Ecclesiastical Organization; S. Francis, Devout Life; Giotto, Art. In the following list the first column contains the Latin inscriptions, in capital letters, copied exactly from the glass; the second column the names in English, with illustrative particulars.

NORTH SIDE, WINDOW I.

Disciples of Christ.

1	S. ANDREAS	S. Andrew the Apostle (John i. 40).
2	S. PHILIPPVS	S. Philip the Apostle (John i. 43).
3	S. NATHANIEL	S. Nathaniel (John i. 43).

4	NICODEMVS	Nicodemus.
5	S. MARIA MARTHÆ SOROR	S. Mary, sister of Martha.
6	S. MARTHA	S. Martha.
7	S. THOMAS	S. Thomas the Apostle.
8	S. MARIA MAGD.	S. Mary Magdalene.

Given by Thomas Jodrell Phillips-Jodrell, M.A., formerly Fellow.

SOUTH SIDE, WINDOW I.

Evangelists and Teachers.

1	S. MATTHAEVS	S. Matthew.
2	S. MARCVS	S. Mark.
3	S. LUCAS	S. Luke.
4	S. JOHANNES	S. John the Evangelist.
5	S. JACOBVS MI.	S. James the Less.
6	S. PETRVS	S. Peter.
7	S. PAULVS	S. Paul.
8	APOLLOS	Apollos.

Given by the Rev. Hugh Andrew Johnstone Munro, M.A., Senior Fellow, formerly Tutor.

SOUTH SIDE, WINDOW II.

The Church of the First Days.

1	S. BARNABAS	Barnabas, the companion of S. Paul.
2	S. STEPHANVS	Stephen the Deacon (Acts vi.).
3	S. TIMOTHEVS	Timothy (Romans xvi. 21).
4	PHŒBE	Phebe (Romans xvi. 1).
5	CORNELIVS	Cornelius the Centurion (Acts x.).
6	S. DIONYSIVS	Dionysius the Areopagite (Acts xvii. 34).
7	LYDIA	Lydia (Acts xvi. 14).
8	S. ONESIMVS	Onesimus (Colossians iv. 9).

Given by the Rev. Henry John Hotham, M.A., Senior Fellow.

NORTH SIDE, WINDOW II.

The Ante-Nicene Church.

1	S. CLEMENS ROM.	Clemens Romanus, Pope Clement the First, died *circa* 100.
2	S. IGNATIVS	Ignatius, Bishop of Antioch, died 107.
3	S. JVSTINVS MAR.	Justin Martyr, died 165.
4	S. PANTÆNVS	Pantænus, president of the Alexandrian School, died *circa* 216.
5	S. PERPETVA	Perpetua, martyr of Carthage, died 202.
6	TERTVLLIANVS	Tertullian, died *circa* 220.
7	ORIGENES	Origen, died 253.
8	S. CYPRIANVS	Cyprian, Bishop of Carthage, died 258.

Given by the Rev. William George Clark, M.A., Senior Fellow, formerly Tutor.

SOUTH SIDE, WINDOW III.

The Eastern Church.

1	S. ATHANASIVS	Athanasius, Archbishop of Alexandria; died 373.
2	S. BASILIVS. M.	Basil the Great, Bishop of Cæsarea; died 379.
3	S. EPHRAEM. SYRVS	Ephrem of Edessa in Syria; flourished 370.
4	S. JO. CHRYSOSTOMVS	John Chrysostom, Archbishop of Constantinople; died 407.
5	EVSEBIVS PAMPH.	Eusebius Pamphili, Bishop of Cæsarea; died 340.
6	IMP. CONSTANTINVS M.	Constantine the Great; died 337.
7	HELENA AVG.	Helena, mother of Constantine; died 328.
8	IMP. JVSTINIANVS	Justinian the Great; died 565.

Given by Mrs Thrupp, in memory of the Rev. Joseph Francis Thrupp, M.A., formerly Fellow.

NORTH SIDE, WINDOW III.

The Western Church.

1	S. AMBROSIVS	Ambrose, Bishop of Milan, died 397.
2	S. HIERONYMVS	Jerome, translator of the Vulgate, died 420.
3	S. MONNICA	Monnica, mother of Augustine, died *circa* 387.
4	S. AVGVSTINVS HIP.	Augustine, Bishop of Hippo, died 430.
5	S. MARTIN. TVR	Martin, Bishop of Tours, died 397.
6	S. LEO MAGNVS	Leo the Great, Pope Leo the First, died 461.
7	S. BENEDICTVS	Benedict, founder of the Benedictine Order, died 543.
8	S. GREGORIVS M.	Gregory the Great, Pope Gregory the First, died 604.

Given by the Rev. Spencer Mansel, M.A., formerly Fellow; in memory of William Lort Mansel, D.D., Master 1798—1820.

SOUTH SIDE, WINDOW IV.

The Anglo-Saxon Church.

1	ALBANVS MARTYR	Alban, protomartyr of Britain; died 303.
2	AVGVSTINVS ARCH. CANT.	Augustine, first Archbishop of Canterbury; died 607.
3	BERTHA. REG. CANT.	Bertha, Queen of Kent; died *circa* 600.
4	THEODORVS ARCH. CANT.	Theodore of Tarsus, Archbishop of Canterbury; died 690.
5	BONAFACIVS AP. GER.	Boniface, Apostle of Germany; died 755.
6	BEDA VENERABILIS	The Venerable Bede; died 735.
7	ALCVINVS	Alcuin, disciple of Bede, Abbat of S. Martin of Tours; died 804.

8 ALFREDVS REX.   Alfred the Great, King of England; died
                            901.

Given by Mrs Mathison, in memory of the Rev. William Collings Mathison, M.A., formerly Senior Fellow and Tutor.

NORTH SIDE, WINDOW IV.

Latin Christianity.

1 IMP. CAROLVS M.   Charles the Great, Emperor, died 814.
2 THOMAS AQVINAS   Thomas Aquinas (*Doctor Angelicus*), died 1274.
3 LVDOVICVS . IX.   Louis the Ninth, King of France 1226—1270.
4 DANTES ALLIGH   Dante, died 1321.
5 COLVMBANVS   Columban, founder of the Monasteries of Lux-
                      euil and Bobbio, died 615.
6 GREGORIVS VII.   Pope Gregory the Seventh, died 1085.
7 FRANCISCVS ASSIS   Francis of Assisi, founder of the Franciscan
                      Order, died 1226.
8 GIOTTVS   Giotto, painter, died 1336.

Given by the Rev. Coutts Trotter, M.A., Fellow and formerly Tutor.

SOUTH SIDE, WINDOW V.

English National Life before the Reformation.

1 SIMON DE MONTFORT   Simon de Montfort, sixth Earl of Leicester;
                       died 1265.
2 MATTHÆVS PARIS   Matthew of Paris, Monk of S. Albans;
                       died 1259.
3 EDWARDVS PRIMVS   Edward the First, King of England, 1272—
                       1307.
4 FR. ROGER BACON   Roger Bacon, Franciscan Friar; died 1292.
5 EDWARDVS WALL PR.   Edward the Black Prince; died 1376.
6 JO. DVNS SCOTVS   John Duns (*Doctor subtilis*); died 1308.
7 GALFR. CHAVCER   Geoffrey Chaucer; died 1400.
8 GVLL. CAXTON   William Caxton, first English Printer; died
                       1483.

Given by Joseph Barber Lightfoot, D.D., formerly Fellow and Tutor, now Lord Bishop of Durham.

NORTH SIDE, WINDOW V.

English Ecclesiastical Life before the Reformation.

1 LANFRANCVS ARCHIEP. CANT.   Lanfranc, Archbishop of Canterbury,
                               died 1089.
2 ANSELMVS ARCHIEP. CANT.   Anselm, Archbishop of Canterbury,
                               died 1109.
3 THOMAS ARCHIEP. CANT.   Thomas of Canterbury, died 1170.
4 STEPHANVS ARCHIEP. CANT.   Stephen Langton, Archbishop of Can-
                               terbury, died 1228.
5 HVGO EP. LINCOLN   Hugh, Bishop of Lincoln, died 1200.

6	ROBERTVS EP. LINCOLN	Robert Grosseteste, Bishop of Lincoln, died 1253.
7	GVLIELMVS EP. WINTON	William of Wykeham, Bishop of Winchester, died 1404.
8	WOLSEY CARDINALIS	Cardinal Wolsey, died 1530.

Given by Augustus Arthur VanSittart, M.A., formerly Fellow.

SOUTH SIDE, WINDOW VI.

The English Reformation.

1	IO. WYCLIFFE.	John Wycliffe, Translator of the Bible; died 1384.
2	DES. ERASMVS	Desiderius Erasmus, Editor of the Greek New Testament; died 1536.
3	W. TYNDALE	William Tyndale, Translator of the Pentateuch and New Testament; died 1536.
4	T. CRANMER ARCHIEP.	Thomas Cranmer, Archbishop of Canterbury; died 1555.
5	H. LATIMER EP. VIG.	Hugh Latimer, Bishop of Worcester; died 1555.
6	EDWARDVS. VI.	Edward the Sixth, King of England 1547—1553.
7	N. RIDLEY EP. LOND.	Nicolas Ridley, Bishop of London; died 1555.
8	ELIZABETH REG.	Elizabeth, Queen of England 1558—1603.

Given by the Rev. Robert Burn, M.A., Fellow and formerly Tutor.

NORTH SIDE, WINDOW VI.

Founders and Benefactors of the University and College.

1	SIGEBERTVS . ANGLOR . REX	Sigebert, King of the East Angles, died 635.
2	ETHELDREDA ABB.	Etheldreda, founder of the Monastery of Ely, died 679.
3	HENRICVS III.	Henry the Third, King of England 1216—1272.
4	H . DE . BALSHAM EP . EL.	Hugh de Balsham, Bishop of Ely, died 1286.
5	HERV . DE . STANTON.	Hervey de Stanton, founder of Michael House, died 1327.
6	EDWARDVS III.	Edward the Third, King of England 1327—1377, founder of King's Hall.
7	HENRICVS VIII.	Henry the Eighth, King of England 1509—1547, founder of Trinity College.
8	MARIA REG.	Mary, Queen of England 1553—1558, foundress of the Chapel.

Given by Benjamin Gray, M.A., formerly Fellow.

NORTH SIDE, WINDOW VII.

University and College Worthies.

1	GV. DE BVXTON	Walter de Buxton, Master of Michael House 1324—1328.
2	IO. DE. BAGGESHOTE	John de Baggeshott, first Warden of the King's Scholars, 1316.
3	IO. FISHER EP. ROFF.	John Fisher, D.D., Bishop of Rochester, died 1535.
4	C. TVNSTALL EP. DVN.	Cuthbert Tunstall, D.D., Bishop of Durham, died 1559.
5	IO. REDMAN	John Redman, D.D., Master of King's Hall 1542—1546; Master of Trinity College 1546—1551.
6	M. BVCER	Martin Bucer, Regius Professor of Divinity 1550, died 1551.
7	IO. WHITGIFT ARCH.	John Whitgift, Archbishop of Canterbury, Master 1567—1577, died 1604.
8	T. NEVILLE	Thomas Nevile, Master 1593—1615.

Given by the Rev. Edward William Blore, M.A., Senior Fellow and Vice-Master, formerly Tutor.

SOUTH SIDE, WINDOW VII.

Worthies of the College.

1	FR. BACON	Sir Francis Bacon; died 1626.
2	IO. DONNE	John Donne, poet; died 1631.
3	G. HERBERT	George Herbert, fellow, poet; died 1632 —33.
4	E. COKE	Sir Edward Coke, Lord Chief Justice; died 1634.
5	H. SPELMAN	Sir Henry Spelman, antiquary; died 1641.
6	IO. DOM. CRAVEN	John Lord Craven, founder of the Craven Scholarships; died 1650.
7	A. MARVEL	Andrew Marvel, dramatic poet; died 1678.
8	IO. HACKET EP. LICH.	John Hacket, Bishop of Lichfield; died 1670.

Given by M. R. Cope, Esq., in memory of his brother, the Rev. Edward Meredith Cope, M.A., formerly Senior Fellow and Tutor.

NORTH SIDE, WINDOW VIII.

Worthies of Trinity College.

1	IO. PEARSON	John Pearson, D.D., Master 1662—1673.
2	IS. BARROW	Isaac Barrow, D.D., Master 1673—1677.
3	A. COWLEY	Abraham Cowley, fellow, poet, died 1667.
4	IO. DRYDEN	John Dryden, poet, died 1701.
5	IO. RAY	John Ray, fellow, died 1704—5.

6	R. COTES	Roger Cotes, fellow, Plumian Professor, died 1716.	
7	IS. NEWTON	Sir Isaac Newton, fellow, died 1727.	
8	R. BENTLEY	Richard Bentley, D.D., Master 1700—1742.	

Given by Joseph Prior, M.A., Senior Fellow and Tutor; by Mrs Thompson, in memory of the Rev. George Peacock, D.D., formerly Senior Fellow and Tutor, Lowndean Professor of Astronomy 1836—58 and Dean of Ely; and by Charles de la Pryme, M.A., in memory of George Pryme, M.A., formerly Fellow, and Professor of Political Economy 1828—63.

These works cost nearly £20,000; of which £11,000 was spent out of the corporate funds of the College upon substantial repairs; the cost of the decorations was defrayed by the subscriptions.

The decoration of the quire having been completed, that of the Antechapel was undertaken. It was begun in 1875 and finished in the course of the following year. The west window was opened out on the inside, so as to display the tracery[1]; the walls were coloured; the mural tablets were rearranged; the panelwork was enriched with a suitable cresting; an inner wooden porch was constructed; and the roof was decorated in a style corresponding to that of the quire. The subjects selected are the arms of the following founders and benefactors[2].

John Whitgift.	Thomas Allen.	John Redman.	The College.
The College.	Hervey de Stanton.	Michael House.	King's Hall.
William Whewell.	Thomas Nevile.	Isaac Barrow.	John Hacket, as Bishop of Lichfield
Queen Victoria.	Queen Elizabeth.	King Henry VIII.	King Edward III.
King James I.	Queen Mary.	King Henry VI.	King Edward II.
A. J. B. Beresford Hope, M.P. for University.	S. H. Walpole, M.P. for University.	Duke of Devonshire, Chancellor.	W. H. Thompson, Master.
The College.	Regius Professorship of Hebrew.	Regius Professorship of Greek.	Regius Professorship of Divinity.

Five of the windows had been filled with stained glass by Wailes between 1846 and 1858. The following list gives the subjects with their legends, counting from the east end. The numbers (1) and (2) designate the upper and lower subjects respectively, except in the first window, where the figures are counted from left to right, beginning with the upper row, and the inscriptions are on scrolls borne by kneeling angels.

[1] [When the stucco was removed from the west wall a small two-light window was discovered below the west window. It may be conjectured that it had belonged to one of the King's Hall buildings; and that the wall containing it had been utilized when the Chapel was built.]

[2] [The spectator is supposed to stand with his back to the west wall.]

SOUTH SIDE, WINDOW I.

1.   SANCTVS PETRVS.

    † Alexander Chisholm Gooden Discip. ob. MDCCCXLI
Annos XXIII natus.

2.   SANCTVS ANDREAS.

    † Duncan Farquharson Gregory Soc. ob. MDCCCXLIV
Annos XXX natus.

3.   SANCTVS IACOBVS.

    † Alexander Fredericus Merivale quondam Soc. ob.
MDCCCXLII Annos XXVII natus.

4.   SANCTVS IOHANNES.

    † Henricus Goulburn Soc. ob. MDCCCXLIII Annos XXX
natus.

5.   SANCTVS LVCAS.

    † Gulielmus Josephus Bayne M.D. natus est A.D. IIIII
Kal. Dec. 1796. ob. Id. Junii 1844.

6.   SANCTVS MATTHEVS.

    † Ioannes Henricus Renouard A.M. Socius Coll. et
V.M. ob. Die XXX Mart. 1830. Ætat. 71.

7.   SANCTVS MARCVS.

    † Robertus Hodgson Greenwood A.M. Socius Coll.
ob. Die 5. Decem. 1839. Ætat. 70.

8.   SANCTVS IOANNES BAPT.

    † Georgius Adamus Browne A.M. Socius Coll. et
V.M. ob. Die 4. Iunii 1843 Ætat. 68.

The glass in lights 1—4 was put up by the relatives of the
persons commemorated in 1846; that in light 5 by the widow
of Dr Bayne; and that in the remaining three lights by the
College in 1849.

SOUTH SIDE, WINDOW II.

1.   The call of S. James and S. John.   [Matth. iv. 21.]

On a label at the bottom of the lights:

† Jacs. Hemery M.A. olim Soc. Decan. Cæsariensis
natus est prid. Kal. maias A.D. 1814 obit v Kal.
Decembris A.D. 1840.

Given by the relatives of James Hemery, D.D., Dean of Jersey,
1850—51.

2.   Mary Magdalene anointing the feet of Christ.

On a label at the bottom of the lights:

† She hath chosen that good part which shall not be taken away from her.   [Luke x. 42.]

On a scroll above this text are the following lines from "The Temple" § 16:

> Whereas my birth and spirit rather took
>   The way that takes the town
> Thou didst betray me to a lingering book
>   And wrap me in a gown.
> And as I threatened oft the siege to raise
>   Not simpering all mine age
> Thou often didst with Academic praise
>   Melt and dissolve my rage.

Given by the College in memory of George Herbert, 1852[1].

SOUTH SIDE, WINDOW III.

1.   Christ and the woman of Samaria.

On a label at the bottom of the lights:

IN MEMORIAM RICHARDI PIKE MATE A M OLIM SOC: VICARII DE WIMESWOLD QVI NATVS EST XI^{MO} DIE MARTII 1818 OBIIT VI^{TO} DIE IVNII 1856.

Given by Mr Maté's sister.

2.   Christ appearing to Mary Magdalene.

On scrolls at the bottom of the first and fourth lights respectively:

† But unto you that fear my name shall the Sun of righteousness arise with healing in his wings.
                              [Malachi iv. 2.]

† Robert Leslie Ellis Born August 25th 1817 Died May 12th 1859.

SOUTH SIDE, WINDOW IV.

1.   Christ among the Doctors.

IN MEMORIAM GVLIELMI HODGE MILL S.T.P. QVONDAM SOCII LING. HEBR. PROF. REG. QVI OBIIT IN DIE NAT. N.N.I.C MDCCCLIII ÆT. 63.

Given by the Rev. W. C. Mathison, Senior Fellow and Tutor, 1862.

---

[1] [The following note occurs in the Minutes of the Senior Bursar, 24 January, 1852 : "The memorial window to late Mr Hemery approved generally; and at the suggestion of the Master the other half of the window to be filled up at the expense of the College with a window to commemorate George Herbert, notice of whom had lately been brought before the College by Mr E. W. Benson's [now Lord Archbishop of Canterbury] English Speech on the Commemoration Day."]

2.   S. Paul at the feet of Gamaliel.

> IN MEMORIAM GVALTERI CAMPBELL DISCIPVLI QVI
> OBIIT IVLII DIE XXIII MDCCCLX ANNO ÆTATIS XXII.
> *Given by Mr Campbell's relatives,* 1862.

NORTH SIDE, WINDOW I.

1.   The Marriage Feast at Cana of Galilee.

2.   Diaper-work.

> *At the bottom of the lower lights:*
> What shall I render to the Lord for all His benefits.
> [Psalm cxvi. 12.]
> July 1, 1858 William Whewell Frances Everina Affleck.
> *Given by Dr Whewell to commemorate his marriage with
> Lady Affleck,* 1 *July,* 1858.

Five memorial statues have been placed in the Antechapel, as indicated on the plan (fig. 9):

1.   Sir Isaac Newton, by Roubiliac, presented in 1755 by Robert Smith, D.D., Master.

NEWTON.

> Qui genus humanum ingenio superavit.

On the back of the plinth are the words:

> Posuit Robertus Smith S.T.P. Collegij hujus S. Trinitatis
> Magister MDCCLV.   *L. F. Roubiliac inv^{it} et sc^{it}.*

2.   Lord Bacon, by Weekes, presented[1] by William Whewell, D.D., Master.

FRANCISCVS BACON

> BARO DE VERVLAM S^{TI} ALBANI VICECOMES
> SEV NOTIORIBVS TITVLIS
> SCIENTIARVM LVMEN FACVNDIÆ LEX
> SIC SEDEBAT.
> QVI POSTQVAM OMNIA NATVRALIS SAPIENTIÆ
> ET CIVILIS ARCANA EVOLVISSET
> NATVRÆ DECRETVM EXPLEVIT
> COMPOSITA SOLVANTVR
> AN^{O} DNI. M.DC.XXVI
> ÆTAT^{S} LXVI.[2]

On the right side: H. WEEKES. SC. 1845.

3.   Dr Isaac Barrow, by Noble, presented in 1858 by the Marquis of Lansdowne.

---

[1] ["The Master requests permission to present to the College a copy in marble of the well known statue of Bacon in [S. Michael's Church, Gorhambury]. Allowed with thanks." Sen. Burs. Minutes, 16 March, 1842.]

[2] [This is the original inscription written by Sir H. Wotton.]

ISAACUS BARROW
VIR SUO TEMPORI
PIETATIS PROBITATIS FIDEI ERUDITIONIS
MODESTIÆ SUAVITATIS EXEMPLUM:
PROFESSOR MATHESEOS IN HAC ACADEMIA
ET EO QUIDEM NOMINE NEWTONI ANTECESSOR
SED MELIORE TITULO OB PRÆCLARA SUA
INVENTA MATHEMATICA ;
THEOLOGUS ARGUMENTORUM GRAVITATE
ET SERMONIS COPIA PRÆCELLENS ;
COLLEGIUM HOC PRÆFECTUS ILLUSTRAVIT
JACTIS BIBLIOTHECÆ FUNDAMENTIS AUXIT.
OBIIT IV. DIE MAII ANNO DOM. M.DC.LXXVII.
ÆTATIS SUÆ XLVII.
MONUMENTUM HOC FACIENDUM CURAVIT
HENRICUS MARCHIO DE LANSDOWNE
AMORIS ERGO IN COLLEGIUM SUUM.[1]

On the right side : M. NOBLE SC. 1853.

4. Lord Macaulay, by Woolner, presented in 1868 by the Committee of Subscribers[2].

THOMÆ BABINGTON BARONI MACAULAY
HISTORICO DOCTRINA FIDE VIVIDIS INGENII LUMINIBUS PRÆCLARO
QUI PRIMUS ANNALES ITA SCRIPSIT
UT VERA FICTIS LIBENTIUS LEGERENTUR
ORATORI REBUS COPIOSO SENTENTIIS PRESSO ANIMI MOTIBUS ELATO
QUI CUM OTII STUDIIS UNICE GAUDERET
NUMQUAM REIPUBLICÆ DEFUIT
SIVE INDIA LITTERIS ET LEGIBUS EMENDANDA
SIVE DOMI CONTRA LICENTIAM TUENDA LIBERTAS VOCARET
POETÆ NIHIL HUMILE SPERANTI
VIRO CUI OMNIUM ADMIRATIO MINORIS FUIT QUAM SUORUM AMOR
HUJUS COLLEGII OLIM SOCIO
QUOD SUMMA DUM VIXIT PIETATE COLUIT
AMICI MÆRENTES S.S.F.C.[3]

On the right side : T. WOOLNER. SC. 1868.

---

[1] [Written by Dr Whewell. Senior Bursar's Minutes, 20 November, 1858 : "Inscription for Noble's monument of Barrow suggested by the Master. Approved by the Seniors."]

[2] [College Order, 29 May, 1868: "Agreed that the Statue of Lord Macaulay, offered to the College by the R^t Hn. Sir F. Pollock, Bart., the Chairman of the Committee of Subscribers, be accepted, and that a site be assigned for it in the Ante Chapel." The Statue was first offered in 1861, when "a niche in the Library, or the Vestibule of the Library," had been suggested by the Master and Seniors for its reception. Senior Bursar's Minutes, 14 November.]

[3] [Written by Richard Claverhouse Jebb, M.A., Fellow, afterwards Public Orator; and now Professor of Greek in the University of Glasgow.]

5. Dr Whewell, by Woolner, executed for the College in 1872[1].

IN MEMORIAM

GUILELMI WHEWELL S.T.P. R.S.S.

VIRI INGENIO SAPIENTIA ANIMI ROBORE ET MAGNITUDINE
INTER ÆQUALES CONSPICUI
SCIENTIARUM QUOTQUOT FUERUNT INTERPRETIS DISERTI
VERITATIS INDAGATORIS STRENUI VINDICIS IMPIGRI
MAGISTRI DENIQUE OPTIMI
HANC STATUAM PONENDAM CURAVIT
BENEFICIORUM MEMOR COLLEGIUM

OBIIT A.S. MDCCCLXVI. ÆTATIS LXXII.
PRAEFECTURAE XXV.[2]

On the left side : T. WOOLNER SC. LONDON 1872.

The Porch on the south side was built by Mr Blomfield in 1872. It bears the following inscription : DOMINUS CUSTODIET INTROITUM TUUM ET EXITUM TUUM EX HOC NUNC ET USQUE IN SÆCULUM. [Psalm cxxi. 8.]

HALL.—The building of the Hall in 1604—5 has been already related (pp. 488—490). It should be noted, however, that some portions of the buildings which formed the west range of the quadrangle seem to have been retained. We know from Loggan (fig. 7) that part of the east front of the older hall was preserved; and the archways through which the screens are entered, one of which is here drawn (fig. 40), are proved by the style to be of much earlier date than any part of the existing Hall. There is also a door in the north wall opening into the Lodge (Z, fig. 41) which cannot have been intended as a communication between the two buildings in their present state, as there is a difference of 4 feet between the levels of their respective floors.

The architecture of the Hall, both within and without, has been carefully preserved from serious alteration. Some slight changes have been already noticed (p. 494), to which it may be added that in 1751—52 the west side was stuccoed by Mr Denston, who had been employed in 1750—51 to treat the Great Court in a similar manner; and that in 1753—54 the east side was "faced

---

[1] [College Order, 10 April, 1869. "Woolner to execute marble statue of Dr Whewell for Ante Chapel."]

[2] [Written by William Hepworth Thompson, D.D., Master.]

and repaired[1]." The south window, blocked in 1773—74, was reopened in 1862. The glass with which it is filled was executed by Messrs Heaton, Butler, and Bayne, and given by W. H. Thompson, D.D., Master, in 1869. The vaults under the Hall were made in 1751—52[2].

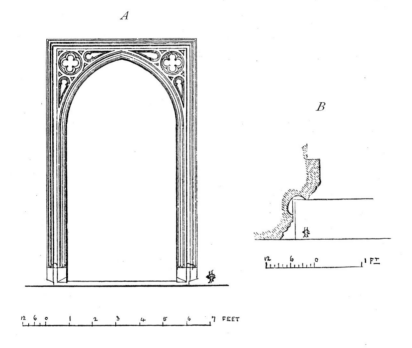

A

B

Fig. 40. *A*. Archway leading to the Screens. *B*. Section of the arch-mold.

Occasional charges for repairs to the woodwork are met with, but none are sufficiently important for quotation. In 1650—51 the arms of the State were carved and set up. They were replaced in 1659—60 by those of the King[3]. The arms

---

[1] [Jun. Burs. Accounts, 1751—52. "To Mr Denston for Stucco-Work at the West-Side of the Hall and Combination." Ibid. 1753—54. "To Mr Bottomley his whole Bill for new facing and repairing the East Front of the Hall £305. 7. 0."]

[2] [Ibid. 1751—52.]

[3] [Sen. Burs. Accounts, 1650—51. *Extraordinaries.* "To John Woodruffe for carveing the States arms and setting them up in the Hall. 07. 00. 00." Jun. Burs. Accounts, 1659—60. "P^d G. Woodrofe for cutting ye kings armes in ye hall 08. 00. 00."]

then put up are probably those still over the dais. They are the Royal Arms, supported by the Lion and Unicorn, with the motto SEMPER EADEM.

In 1866 the interior was thoroughly renovated. The paint was removed from the screen, and from other portions of the woodwork where practicable; the width of the dais was increased; and gas chandeliers were suspended from the roof.

COMBINATION ROOM.—A room called "the parlour" is mentioned in the Accounts of Trinity College as early as 1564—65[1], but no hint of the position is given; and in 1576—77 furniture is provided for "the newe parlour graunted by Mr Vicemaster and the seniors." This parlour was probably over the old kitchen, as explained above (p. 474). When the new Hall and kitchen were built, a new position would have to be found for it, and it is reasonable to suppose that it would be placed, as in other Colleges, as near the Hall as possible. It is not, however, alluded to in the Accounts until 1650—51, when a table is ordered for "the Fellowes Combination Chamber," and "the lesser Combination Chamber" is wainscoted[2]. The latter was evidently on the first floor, from a payment in the following year for making the staircase leading to it[3]. In 1740 the Combination Room was at the south end of the Hall, as explained above (p. 466), and as the appearance of that part of the College, as shewn in the print there referred to, does not differ from that shewn by Loggan in 1688 (figs. 7, 11), we may safely conclude that the Combination Rooms referred to in the seventeenth century were in the same position as those referred to in the eighteenth. They were then on the same floor, separated by a passage, as shewn by an Order made 18 December, 1721, "that a Place in ye Passage betwixt ye 2 Combination Rooms be fitted up, to keep the College Plate in." These rooms were probably approached from the court by the door next the old oriel, and the small two-light window above that door lighted the passage between them; but, as men-

---

[1] [Jun. Burs. Accounts, 1564—65. *Ironworke*. "for mendyng a locke of the parler doore v^d."]

[2] [Sen. Burs. Accounts, 1650—51. *Extraordinaries.*]

[3] [Jun. Burs. Accounts, 1651—52. *Extraordinaryes.*]

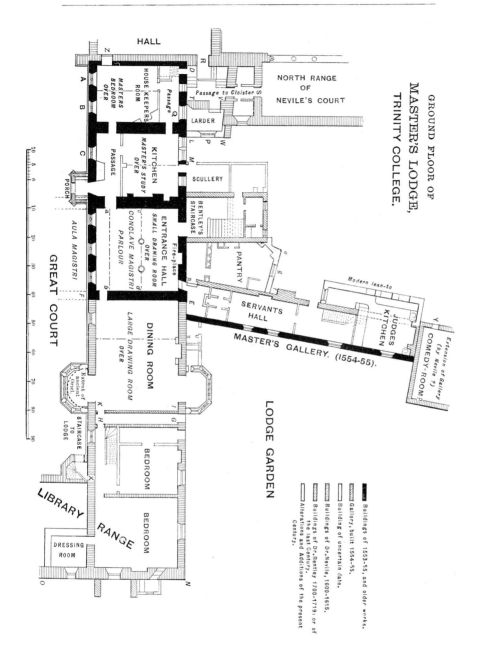

Fig. 41.   Ground-plan of Master's Lodge.

tioned above (p. 466), their exact arrangement cannot now be recovered. This staircase would also provide access to the garrets which then existed in the roof.

This Combination Room was evidently considered inconvenient, from the language used in the following clause of the will of Francis Hooper, D.D., Senior Fellow, who bequeathed £1000 (2 December, 1762)[1]

"to be laid out at the Discretion of the Master and Seniors in rebuilding or altering and ornamenting the Combination, that that Room may in some degree answer to the Grandeur of their College, which the disinterestedness and Generosity of that Society has rendered so superb and Magnificent."

We shall see below that Dr Hooper's legacy was spent upon a new Bridge in 1764, but, notwithstanding, the new Combination Rooms were decided upon in 1770, commenced in 1771, completed in 1774, and occupied in 1775. The whole range from the Hall southwards, with the exception of the Kitchen, was taken down, and rebuilt in white brick, faced with stone on the side next the court[2]. The new building is in three floors, without garrets. The large Combination Room occupies the central portion (*ik*, fig. 9), lighted by three windows facing east. The west side abuts against the Kitchen, and is therefore without windows. This room is 36 feet long, 30 feet broad, and 18 feet 7 inches high. The smaller Combination Room, over the Buttery, has two windows facing west. These rooms are approached by a staircase from the screens (*l*, fig. 9). There are two sets of rooms for undergraduates over the small Combination Room and the Manciple's room, but the larger room rises to the roof. The total cost of this work was between £4700 and £4900. The architect was James Essex, who received, "for his Trouble as Surveyor etc. of the new Combination Room, etc." £223. 4. 0.]

MASTER'S LODGE.—It was mentioned above (p. 471) that the work done in 1554 included a new Master's Lodge. It had three rooms on the ground floor, according to the old plan

---

[1] [Dr Hooper's Will was proved 4 August, 1763. Part of the cost of rebuilding the Combination Rooms was defrayed out of the bequest of Dr Robert Smith, Master 1742—68 (p. 547.)]

[2] Jun. Burs. Accounts, 1770—71. *Bricklayer.* "To Wm Wells his 3 Bills for Carts in digging the Foundation and carting away the Rubbish for the new Combination etc. £171. 3. 1½."]

(fig. 10); a Parlour (*conclaue magistri*) occupying the corner between the north and west ranges; a room of about the same size to the south, the destination of which is not noted; and a hall (*aula magistri*) east of the Parlour in the north range. The entrance to this Lodge was directly from the court into the hall, through which access was obtained to the two other rooms, and to a turret in the angle of the court which contained a staircase leading to the upper floors.

When these rooms were completed in 1553—54 a gallery (fig. 41) was built for the Master, advantage being taken of an existing wall for one side up to a certain height[1] (*mn*, fig. 9), and a foundation being dug for that on the other. This part of the work cost only £5; while Ford the carpenter was to receive £30 for the woodwork (p. 471). It is evident therefore that the gallery was a wooden structure on foundations of brick or stone, probably the latter, for in 1583—84 "the stone gallery that goeth into the M^r. his garden" is mentioned. It was in two floors, to each of which access was provided from the garden; to the upper one by a staircase, to the lower one by a flight of steps[2]. It was finished in the following year, as shewn by various entries. The carpenter makes four gable-ends of windows in the new gallery; the smith supplies locks and hinges for the doors, twelve casements and "eight bars of iron for the clerestorye"; "Yong the glasear" provides glass for the same, and "for the clerestorye in thupper galarye"; several thousand bricks arrive by water for the chimneys; and lastly, ledges are made to fasten the hangings to. A glimpse of the Master's Lodge at this date is afforded by the

[1] [Jun. Burs. Accounts 1553—54: "Covenauntted with Scott [a 'rough-mason'], to make vpp ye wall for ye new galarye, and cast a fowndacion on the other syde, with ij wavtts, furth of ye chambers, in to ye galarye, for fyve powndes." Ibid. 1554—55. "'It' vnto Copt James, for plastring both the sydes of ye new studd wall in the lower galarye, and for ouercasting and piastring thold wall in ye saym lower galarye...and for mending ye brekes on thowt syde of ye galarye wch was hurtt wth stageing x^s." *Extraord. exp. abowtt Buylding* "For laying the stepps furthe of ye garding in to ye vpper galarye. For hewyng stones for ye stares furthe of ye garden in to the low galarye. Item for ij barres of Iron for the ij litle lyghtes in ye stares of ye galary."]

[2] [It has been already shewn (p. 422) that the west portion of the site of King's Hall measured 200 feet from north to south. As the distance between this wall and the wall on the north side of the Bowling-Green is just 200 feet, it is probably part of the south boundary-wall of that site.]

Will of Dr John Christopherson (Master 1553—58) who makes
the following bequests 6 October 1556:

> "I gyve vnto ye College all the hangynges in my studie, in all the
> chamers, and in the galery, with the borders joyned thervnto; And
> therwithall I gyve the bedstedes, the tables, the fourmes, the stooles
> and chares that be in all the said chamers; And the waynscotte and
> seling to remayne in the said chamers for ever, to the vse of my suc-
> cessors; Moreouer I gyve vnto the College all the Stuffe in my Kytchyn
> of what sort so ever it be...And of the same stuffe a perfytt Inventory
> to be made, and so to be delyuered vnto my successor..."

Notices of repairs and alterations occur in subsequent years,
of which a few are worth quotation. In 1570—71 "the dore
to the water out of our Master's gallery" is mentioned, with
other expressions which shew that in that year a building
which is subsequently termed "our master's water-gallery," or
"our master's gallery over the river," was being built or extensively repaired[1]; and Hamond (fig. 3) shews two structures, one
beyond the other, of which the westernmost extends as far as
the ditch which then formed the east border of Garret-Hostel
Green. The Accounts for this year, however, are exceedingly
perplexing, for it is evident that there were in all three galleries,
two for the Master and one for the Fellows, and it is often
impossible to determine to which building a particular entry
refers. In 1589—90 the gallery, evidently that built in 1553—54,
was wainscoted, and sundry articles of furniture were bought
for it[2]; in 1591—92 "our master's parlour" was similarly
treated, and hangings of "dornick," provided in the previous
year, were put up[3]; and in 1592—93 "a silke curtaine for y^e
picture of Kinge Henry in our master his galery" is charged for.

The last entry has brought us to the commencement
of the Mastership of Dr Nevile. His plans, as already related
(p. 476), involved the destruction of the range of chambers, the
western extremity of which contained part of the Lodge. To

---

[1] [Jun. Burs. Accounts 1570—71. *Laborers*. "To Thomas Key ij daies about the
stank of our m^{rs} gallerie xvj^d." *Smith*. "for a locke to the dore to the water out of our
m^{rs} gallerie iij^s iiij^d" etc.]

[2] [Sen. Burs. Accounts 1589—90. *Extraordinarye Charges*.]

[3] [Ibid. 1590—91. "For iiij^{xx}. and ij. yardes of dornixs at ij^s. provided for the M^{rs}.
Parler viij^{li}. iiij^s. Ibid. 1591—92. "The wainscot seeling of o^r. M^{rs}. parler xij^{li}. iiij^s.
Hanging of the dornixe and x yeardes of border xxvj^s. ij^d.]

amend this mutilation the Lodge was extended northward to join the Library-range, this extension including the great Dining-hall, with the Drawing-room above, and chambers beyond. These operations were commenced in 1599—1600, and continued in the two following years. The Accounts contain various items relating to them, the most important of which were quoted above (pp. 482, 483), to illustrate the general Architectural History of the College. In addition to those it may be mentioned that in 1599—1600, Chapman, the carpenter who was employed on the woodwork of the Hall, took down the wainscot, and in the following year replaced it with additions. The sum paid shews that the work done by him must have been extensive[1]. In 1600—1601 "the partition beyond the great chamber" was plastered ; the chimney in the same chamber was paved with "33 flaunders' tyles"; hangings of "greene sea" were provided; and lastly, three labourers "made cleane the hall in the Lodging." These entries indicate that some of the rooms at least were now ready for occupation. The Lodge, however, was by no means finished, for in the next year Chapman continued his work there and in the adjoining Library, partly at the expense of the Master[2]; and in 1612—13 we find the fitting up of "the great parlour," the audit-chamber, and "our master's bed-chamber" still proceeding. These entries shew that the finishing of the rooms added to the Lodge was not carried on continuously, but the want of a continuous series of the Bursars' books necessarily makes it impossible to recover a complete history of the building, although enough remains to shew its general progress.

In 1614—15 we find charges for "turning the great stairs," and for "diging a dore out of the lodging into the hall[3]," with

---

[1] [Jun. Burs. Accounts 1600—1601. *Dayes Worke to Carpenters*. "Item to Chapman the Joyner for fittinge the wainscott in 2 of the old chambers in the M^{rs} lodginge and addinge new wainscote vnto it, for the work and the stuffe iiij^{li}. Item to Chapman the joyner in wages for worke done in ye Masters Lodgynge xxvj^{li}. v^s. iiij^d."]

[2] [Sen. Burs. Accounts 1601—2. *Extraordinaries*. "Inprimis paid to Chapman ye Joyner for wainscote worke in the liberarie and our Mrs Lodging Cxv^{li} whereof I receaued of our Maister xxx^{li} and of Dr Morrice [Senior Fellow] 20^{li} and soe is paid by me vltra lxv^{li}." During this period the Junior Bursar's Accounts are missing for 11 years: from 1601—2 to 1611—12; and the Senior Bursar's for 1602—3 and 1606—7.]

[3] [Jun. Burs. Accounts 1614—15. *Layd out to Tylers, Bricklaiers [etc.]*.]

an incidental reference to "the porche at the entrance to the lodging[1]," which shews that the porch by which the Lodge is entered from the Court may be assigned to the Mastership of Dr Nevile.

After the death of Dr Nevile no work of importance was done to the Lodge until 1700, when Dr Richard Bentley became Master. He was installed 1 February, 1699—1700, and shortly after commenced the alterations which were not removed until the Mastership of Dr Whewell (1841—66). Under the direction of Dr Bentley the Lodge not only underwent a thorough repair, but important structural changes were introduced. The rooms were new ceiled, wainscoted, floored, fitted with marble chimney-pieces and sash-windows; and the present noble staircase built instead of the old one. In all the rooms wainscot was substituted for tapestry with the exception of the already wainscoted dining-room[2]. In this Bentley complied with the fashion of the day, as he did in the introduction of the marble chimney-pieces and sash-windows. Yet even at that period the incongruous appearance of the latter in a Quadrangle of Gothic character led to complaints, and he could find no better defence than the utilitarian principle that they admitted more light than the old ones. These works were so extensive, and the arbitrary way in which the Master carried them out gave rise to so much dissension, that it will be well to relate them in detail.

[The Master's project for modernizing and beautifying the Lodge was sanctioned by the following Order subscribed by the eight Senior Fellows:

"April ye 11th 1700. Orderd then by the Mr. and Seniors, That the Master's Lodge be repaird and finishd with new Seeling, Wainscot, Flooring and other convenient improvements; towards which Expense the Master will contribute *de proprio* the Summ of one hundred pounds Sterling.

R. Bentley Magr. Collegii."

The Master was subsequently accused of having obtained this Order by assuring the Seniors that the entire outlay would

---

[1] [Ibid. *Extraordinaries.* "Item [for whiting] or Mrs. lower hall, the stayres vpp to the lodging, the long gallerie to or. Mrs. kitchin, with the porche at the entrance to the lodging...xxiiijs."]

[2] [Professor Willis has made this statement on the authority of Dr Monk, Life of Bentley, i. Chapter vii. The only notice of tapestry for the Lodge in the Audit-Books is the following: Jun. Burs. Accounts 1663—64. *Expences extraordinarie:* "In ye Lodge for a peice of tapestrie...02. 10. 00."]

not exceed £300, and of having purposely entered the Order
in general terms to conceal his own intention of spending a
larger sum; and moreover of having stated that it was incum-
bent upon them to fit up the Lodge in a suitable style for the
reception of the Queen's son, the Duke of Gloucester, who would
shortly become a member of the University[1].

The work began in May following, and was continued until
October. A new heading: "*Extraordinaries for the Master's
Lodge by Order of a Meeting*," now appears annually in the
Accounts, but unfortunately the sums expended were for the
most part entered in gross, and we are left without information
as to the special work undertaken. The total expended in the
first year was £91. 0s. 0d. for materials and labour, the only
entry of special interest being a small payment to Austin the
joyner " for taking down the wainscutt in ye Judges Chamber."

While the work was going forward the Master obtained leave
to add a room to the Lodge :

"Septemb. 2^d 1700. Agreed by the Master and Seniors, That y^e
Ground chamber next ye Master's Lodg be made ye Master's chamber
in exchang of ye ground Room in ye passage to ye Bishop's Hostel.

Agreed y^t Mr Hanbury's Income in ye said ground Chamber be paid
to him by ye College.   Ri. Bentley Mag^r Coll."

This room must have been that which intervenes between the
Kitchen of the Lodge and the College Hall, to which Loggan
(fig. 7) shews a separate entrance from the Court.

In the course of the following year—that ending at Audit
1701—Cornelius and John Austin were paid for 178 yards of
wainscot, and 3 sashes; and Robert Grumbold "for 268 feet of
window stuff in nine windows" and for "setting up ye marble
chimney peices in ye new Roome"—the total amounting to
£229. 5s. 3d. It is evident, however, that this by no means
represented the sum for which the College was liable, for at
the end of this same year the following Order was made :

"Dec. 24, 1701. Orderd by the Master and Seniors, that the
Bills towards the repair of ye Lodg be paid by the Senior Bursar, as

---

[1] [Some Remarks upon a Letter entitled "*The Present State of* Trinity *College
in* Cambridge: written by Richard Bentley D.D. now Master of the said College, to
the Right Reverend John Lord Bishop of *Ely*." By Mr Miller Fellow of the College.
London, 1710, p. 51.]

they are brought in for work done there in all ye rooms above and below on ye right hand of ye Hall; being supposed to amount to about seven hundred pound.

Orderd by ye M^r and Seniors that a sum not exceeding one hundred and fifty pound, be laid out on ye rooms on ye south end of ye Lodg; besides ye M^{rs} hundred pound.   R. Bentley Mag. Coll."

The necessity for this last Order appears in the Senior Bursar's Account for the year ending at Michaelmas 1702, when, under the heading "*Extraordinaryes for the Master's Lodge as appeares by bills*," the large sum of £742. 7s. 0d. is charged for, but, as usual, without particulars. By adding together the totals in the Accounts kept by the Senior and Junior Bursar respectively to Michaelmas 1703, it appears that up to that time £1193. 2s. 4d. had been spent; and the Seniors no doubt concluded that the work was now complete[1]. This however was by no means the case. Hardly a year had elapsed before the following Order had to be made:

"Dec^{ber} the 20th 1704. Orderd by the Master and Seniors, That a summe not exceeding three hunderd and fifty pounds be paid by the Senior Bursar for ye work done and to be done for repairs and improvements of ye Lodge above ye sums of former Conclusions; and that the Master lay out the 270^l in his hands upon furniture of ye Lodg;[2] and that an Inventory of ye said furniture with the old furniture be enterd in the Junior Bursar's Book, as Goods belonging to ye Lodg.

Ri. Bentley Mag^r Coll."

The money allotted at this time was not spent immediately. It passed, as usual with extraordinary grants, through the hands

---

[1] [Of this sum £835. 5. 6 was paid by the Senior, and £357. 16. 10 by the Junior, Bursar. At Michaelmas 1703 the former enters his Account under the heading "Extraordinaries for the Master's Lodge" as follows: "To Mr Grumbold... £92^{li}. 18^s. 6^d. wch. wth. 15^{li}. 4^s. 6^d. charged by Mr Bathurst Junr. Bursar in his yeares booke 1702 is in full of what was granted at the conclusion of the Audit 1701 £92. 18. 6."]

[2] [This sum consisted of the £100 originally promised by the Master in 1700; and of £170 about which there had been a great controversy. It was the Master's dividend for the year 1699, and had been claimed by Dr Bentley. It however clearly belonged to his predecessor, Dr Montague, who had resigned in November of that year, on his promotion to the Deanery of Durham (Monk's Bentley, i. 146). Ultimately Dr Montague allowed his successor to keep the money, provided he spent it on the Lodge; and the following Order was made: "April 16, 1702. Orderd...that the thanks of ye College be returned to ye late Master the Revd Dr Montague now Dean of Durham for his Gift of one hundred and seventy pounds to the College to be laid out in adorning ye Master's Lodge as the present Master in his judgment shall think fit; R. Bentley."]

of the Senior Bursar, who paid £21. 13s. 0d. in the course of the
year ending at Michaelmas 1705 ; and the remainder in the
course of that ending at Michaelmas 1706. Of this sum £160
was paid at various times to Grumbold the mason, to a carpenter named Silke, and to other workmen ; £1. 13s. 0d. to a
plasterer in 1705 "for stopping and whiting the Great Staire
Case"; and the remainder in one sum to the Master, but for
what purpose is not recorded. It is probable that the greater
part was spent on the staircase, which, as will be seen presently,
had been demanded by Dr Bentley after the first alterations
to the Lodge had been completed. The provisions respecting
the purchase of furniture and the drawing up of an inventory
seem never to have been carried out. In the course of the
six years ending at Michaelmas 1709 the Junior Bursar records
the expenditure of small sums under the heading : "*Extraordinaries for the Master's Lodge*," amounting in all to
£159. 3s. 11½d., after which no further entry for the Lodge was
made by either official until 1719, when the whole matter was
concluded by the following Order :

"Decemb. 5, 1719. Item, That ye said Master have the sum of Two
Hundred Eighty Four pounds paid him out of the College Treasury for
Goods bought by him for ye Master's Lodg above all Accounts with
former Bursars, wch are hereby on both sides Dischargd; And that an
Inventory of ye College Goods in the Lodg be made and kept in the
College Treasury."

The money was not paid until 1722—23, when the Master
received £384, instead of the £284 directed in the Order[1].
The work done to the Lodge had cost the College £1702. 6s. 3½d.,
or, if this last payment be included, £2086. 6s. 3½d.[2]

[1] [Sen. Burs. Accounts 1722—23. *Extraordinaries*. "Paid to the Master Two
hundred Pounds due to him (according to an Order dated December 5th 1719) at
Mich. 1721, £200. 0. 0. Paid to the Master One hundred and Eighty-four pounds
due to him (according to an Order dated Dec. 5, 1719) at Mich. 1722, in full of the first
Order, £184. 0. 0."]

[2] [Total to Mich. 1703.

	Sen. Burs. £835. 5. 6	
	Jun. Burs. £357. 16. 10	£1193. 2. 4
Spent 1704—1709.	Jun. Burs.	159. 3. 11½
Order, 20 Dec. 1704.	Sen. Burs.	350. 0. 0
,, 5 Dec. 1709.	,, ,,	384. 0. 0
		£2,086. 6. 3½]

The following extracts from the "Articles against Dr Bentley" exhibited to the Bishop of Ely, 11 July 1710, not only shew the deep resentment which had been excited by this large expenditure, but give useful particulars of what had been actually done up to the date of their publication.

"WHEN your Lodgings in the College were very good, and served two Noblemen your Predecessors, WHY did you upon false Suggestions prevail with the Senior Fellows of the said College, to consent with you to the wasting and expending any College-Money, in vainly beautifying and adorning the same? WHY did you do the same to the Damage and Detriment of the said College, and wasting their Goods and Revenues, since the College-Statutes do not oblige the College to be at any Charge in doing thereof?

AFTER you had proposed to the Senior Fellows of the said College, and assured them, that the beautifying and adorning the said Lodgings would cost but 300*l.* whereof you would contribute 100*l. de proprio,* upon which Considerations only they consented; WHY did you fraudulently and deceitfully draw up the Order or Conclusion concerning the same in general Terms, expressing that you would contribute 100*l. de proprio,* or to that Effect, without mentioning that the said College should expend but 200*l.* and then procur'd them to set their Hands to the said Order in an unusual manner; and afterwards by Colour of the same demanded, and by violent and unworthy Methods exacted of the said College, and afterwards took and wasted 1500*l.* or some other great Sum or Sums of the said College-Money thereupon? AND WHEN they often refused to pay the same, WHY did you audaciously threaten them not only with Resentment from the Crown and Court, but that the Workmen should bring Actions at Law against them for the Money so expended?

WHEN even by the same Order or Conclusion, only convenient Improvements ought to be made in your said Lodge, WHY did you, according to your own extravagant Fancy, cause between 30 or 40, or some other great number of Sash-Windows to be made in the same, which was not only an excessive Charge to the said College, and a wasting of their Money and Goods, but besides broke the Uniformity of the rest of the Quadrangle, contrary to a former Order or Conclusion?

WHY did you according to your own Will and Pleasure, cause so many and so large Rooms to be wainscotted in your said Lodge, which could be only designed to entertain Boarders therein for your private Gain, and make many other costly and needless Alterations and Additions, and that without the Advice, Consent, or Direction of the Senior Fellows, or the Bursars, or either of them, as the said College-Statutes require?

WHY did you take divers and great Sums of the said College-Money into your Hands, on pretence of paying the Workmen in the said Lodge, or other Pretences, and did not duly pay them the same, or never gave an Account thereof to the said College, or their proper Officer or Officers, or to the Senior Fellows; but misapply'd, wasted or embezled the said Money, or great part thereof?

WHY did you not lay out 270*l.* upon Furniture of your said Lodge, and enter an Inventory of that with the old Furniture in the Junior Bursar's Books, according to an Order or Conclusion made about 5 or 6 years since by your self, and the then Senior Fellows; but on the contrary, waste and embezle, or convert the same to your own Use, and claim it as your own?

WHY did you, without any Authority, take into the said Lodge, or appropriate to your own Use, a great deal of room never before used with it, particularly one Room, which was formerly used for the acting of Comedies; which the Lecturers of the College, are by the Statutes obliged to make against *Christmas*, besides other Rooms?

WHEN by false and base Practices, as by threatening to bring Letters from Court, Visitations, and the like; and at other times, by boasting of your great Interest and Acquaintance, and that you were the Genius of the Age, and what great things you would do for the College in general, and every Member of it in particular, and promising that you would for the future live peaceably with them, and never make any farther Demands, you had prevailed with the Senior Fellows to allow you several hundred Pounds for your Lodge, more than they first intended or agreed to, to the great Dissatisfaction of the College, and the wonder of the whole University, and all that heard of it: WHY did you the very next Year, about that time, merely for your own Vanity, require them to build you a new Stair-case in your Lodge? AND WHEN they (considering how much you had extorted from them before, which you had never accounted for) did for good reason deny to do it; WHY did you of your own Head pull down a good Stair-case in your Lodge, and give Orders and Directions for building a new one, and that too fine for common Use? AND WHEREAS the Work in the beginning, was so much against the Consent of the Seniors, that the proper Officer, the Bursar, forbad the Workmen to go on with it; WHY did you in plain Contempt of the said Seniors, and in direct Violation of the said College Statutes, and wasting their Goods, cause the same by your own sole Authority to be continued, and the said Stair-case to be finish'd, at the Expence of 300*l.* or thereabouts? Which Sum you soon after demanded, and took of the said College, or some or one of their Officers.

WHEN the said Seniors judged the aforesaid Demand of 300*l.* on the College so unreasonable, that they several times refused to comply with it; WHY did you use base and unworthy Methods, to extort their Consent to the Payment of it? Particularly when Mr *Hanbury*, the late Dr *Cressar*, Mr *Drury*, and Dr *Hutchinson*, or some or one of them had performed all the statutable Exercises required for their Election and Admission into the place of College Preacher, and did frequently solicit you for your Consent to their Election and Admission; WHY did you without any colourable or statutable Objection against them, refuse for many Months to elect and admit them, or either of them; threatning in plain terms you would never part with your Club (meaning your Power of electing and admitting) unless they would use their Interest with the Seniors, to gain their Consent to the Payment of the Money for the said Stair-case, and unless such of them as might be accidentally of the Seniority, would promise to vote accordingly; which Refusal was a Violation of the College Statutes, in refusing to put them in Execution, but according to your own Interest?"

Dr Bentley, on the contrary, was well satisfied with his work. He describes what he had done for the fabric of the College in the following passage of his letter to the Bishop of Ely, dated 13 February, 1709—10:

"It has been often told me by Persons of Sense and Candour, that when I left them I might say of the College, what *Augustus* said of *Rome, Lateritium inveni, marmoreum reliqui.* The College-Chappel, from a decay'd antiquated Model, made one of the noblest in *England;* the College-Hall, from a dirty, sooty Place, restor'd to its Original Beauty, and excel'd by none in Cleanliness and Magnificence. The Masters Apartment (if that may be nam'd without Envy) from a spacious Jail, from want of room in an excess of it, made worthy of that Royal Foundation, and of the Guests it's sometimes honour'd with: An elegant Chymical Laboratory, where Courses are annually taught by a Professor, made out of a ruinous Lumber-Hole, the thieving House of the Bursars of the old Set, who in spite of frequent Orders to prevent it, would still embezle there the College-Timber: The College-Gatehouse rais'd up and improv'd to a stately Astronomical Observatory, well stor'd with the best Instruments in Europe. In a word, every Garret of the House well repair'd and inhabited, many of which were wast and empty before my coming [1]."

Uffenbach, who came to Cambridge in the summer of 1710, gives the following description of the Lodge, as altered by Bentley:

"In the afternoon [31 July] we visited *D* Bentley*, who is Master of *Trinity College*, and has built himself an excellent house, or wing, to live in, so that he is as well lodged as the queen at *S* James's*, or better. The rooms are very large, and of extraordinary height, the floors curiously inlaid with all kinds of wood, the panels in every room very fine (as now in England tapestry is no longer in fashion, but all is panelled at great cost), the window-panes of extraordinary size, and the windows themselves very large and high [2]."

We will now compare the information we have collected with the existing Lodge, by the help of the accompanying ground-

[1] [THE PRESENT STATE OF Trinity College IN CAMBRIDG, In a LETTER from Dr *Bentley*, Master of the said College, To the Right Reverend John Lord Bishop of Ely. Publish'd for general Information by a Gentleman of the TEMPLE. The Second Edition, Corrected. 8vo. London, 1710. p. 60.]

[2] [Herrn Z. C. von Uffenbach Merkwürdige Reisen. Dritter Theil. Ulm 1754, p. 15. The translation is by Rev. J. E. B. Mayor, S. John's.]

plan (fig. 41); on which the parts built at different periods are distinguished by a change of shading.

The plan is exceedingly simple. Proceeding from the College Hall northwards there are six rooms on the ground-floor distributed in the following order: Housekeeper's Room, Kitchen, Hall, Dining-Room, two Bedrooms. On the first floor there are the same number of rooms, placed exactly over those below: Master's Bed-Room, Master's Study, small Drawing-Room, Large Drawing-Room, two Bed-Rooms. Above these there are garrets, of which the set at the north end are now assigned to an undergraduate. It is evident that the rooms at the west end of the Library range, which are entered from the staircase in the corner of the court, once formed part of the Lodge[1].

It may be stated in general terms that the Lodge was commenced during the mastership of Dr Christopherson (1553—58), and completed in that of Dr Nevile (1593—1615); and it was shewn above, on the authority of the old plan (fig. 10), that the former Lodge had three rooms on the ground-floor, one of which was in the north range, and certain other rooms, the precise position of which it is now impossible to identify. Between the door of the room used as the Housekeeper's Room—now replaced by a window (A),—and the angle of the court, Hamond (fig. 3) shews two windows, as at present (B, C). The angle-turret shewn by him stood partly on the same ground as the present porch, and the range which extended from that turret to King Edward's Gate was evidently a prolongation of the north and south walls of the Master's Hall, as indicated on the plan by dotted lines; and in fact, foundations were discovered in this position in the course of some excavations made shortly after the election of the present Master. In confirmation of the view that this Hall and the room above it represent the western termination of a range which once ran at right angles to the present west side of the Court, Professor Willis points out that this part of the building has a lofty gable on the west side, the chimney in which is a fine piece of masonry, of freestone laid in regular

---

[1] [This is evident from an entry in Dr Bentley's Ephemeris: "July 26, 1701, Saturday. Mr Hutchinson, Mr Green, and Mr Laughton played at bowls in the College bowling-green all Chapel time, in the evening service: seen out of my window by me (who was then lame and could not be at Chapel) and Will. Saist."]

courses, evidently the termination of the range; that the plinth which appears at intervals along the west side DE is returned along the north side at E, shewing that the building to the north of that point is of a subsequent construction; and lastly, that the beams in the hall (ab, cd) rest on the north and south walls, instead of on the east and west walls, as those of the other rooms do[1].

It may be concluded therefore that the older Lodge was terminated by the north wall of the entrance-hall (EF); and that the portion north of that wall may be assigned to Dr Nevile. Professor Willis indicates several further differences between the two portions; "the wall of the Kitchen (LM) is of clunch, accurately laid in courses to the top, although decayed on the face[2]. The wall EN, which is much defaced by the insertion of Bentley's sash-windows, is of random clunch masonry mixed with brick, and has a plinth of red brick. This plinth is covered with cement on the west side, but it remains in its original state along the north side, NO. The same random clunch-work runs along the whole north wall of the Library range as far as the Clock-Tower. The chimney-shafts in the wall EN are wholly of brick, from the ground upwards[3]."

The east front of the Lodge, as completed by Dr Nevile, is shewn by Loggan (fig. 7). The windows which lighted the rooms to the right of the porch were alternately of two lights and three lights. The window over the porch was of three lights; next to it on the left hand there was a window of two lights both on the ground-floor and on the first floor; and between these and the College Hall there were two windows on the first floor, and one on the ground-floor, each of three lights. The windows in the lower tier only had hood-molds. It may be conjectured that these windows, or at least those in Nevile's portion, resembled those in the Library range (fig. 22); for the window in the west wall of the Kitchen (LM), and those at P and at Q (the latter of which is now a door), are of precisely that pattern. The Kitchen is part of the older building, as the plan shews; and it is therefore probable that Nevile altered the older portion so as to

---

[1] [The direction and position of the beams in the Dining Room, Kitchen etc. have been indicated on the plan (fig. 41) by dotted lines.]

[2] [The rest of this wall is hidden by the scullery, staircase, and pantry.]

[3] [From a page of notes by Prof. Willis, endorsed "Trinity College, August, 1860."]

make it uniform with the rest. Besides these windows there was a semicircular oriel, in three stages, to give additional light to the Dining-Room and Drawing-Room; and in the roof there were twelve dormers of various sizes. The original state of the west side must be a matter of conjecture. Loggan's ground-plan (fig. 4) indicates a semicircular oriel on that side exactly similar to the one on the east side; but on the other hand the Accounts imply the existence of a single oriel only[1]. In 1841, when Dr Whewell became Master, there was a shallow bow-window on

Fig. 42. East front of the Master's Lodge in 1740.

the west side on the site of the present oriel; but we do not know when it had been constructed, and it did not rise to the Drawing-Room above. Dr Bentley removed all the windows in the east front, with the exception of the dormers and the oriel, which was in existence so late as 1740 (fig. 42), and replaced

---

[1] [Jun. Burs. Accounts 1605—6. *Iron work*. "For 2 casements in o^r. m^{rs}. lodging for the round window into the Court o. 5. o." Ibid 1679—80. *Carpenters*. "For 60 foote of peeces...to lay the Lead upon in the Round window in the Lodging oo. 18. oo." Ibid. 1685—86. *Extraordinaries*. "For whiting the Bow window in ye lodge oo. 11. oo." Ibid. 1711—12. "To Grumbold for mending ye Battlements of ye round window in ye Lodge." Ibid. 1753—54. The "stone work over the Bow Window" is repaired.]

them by two rows of sashes, ten in each row, inserted in the old openings, which were enlarged to receive them[1].

The rooms added to the Lodge by Nevile were probably always of the same size, or of nearly the same size, as they are at present. The Dining-Room evidently extended as far as the brick wall *GH*, which is the north limit of the Drawing-Room above; and the panelwork which lines it is, by the style, that introduced by Dr Bentley. It is carried along the wall *GH* behind the more modern partition *IK,* the panelwork on which has been imitated from it.

The Drawing-Room, or, as it is sometimes called, King Henry the Eighth's Room, from the picture of King Henry the Eighth which now hangs in it, is exactly over the Dining-Room. It has an elaborate coved ceiling of plaster-work, divided into compartments, with pendants (fig. 43); and a carved stone chimney-piece, surmounted by a stone cresting, similar to that of the Fountain, which was begun, as we have seen, in 1601—2 (p. 486). In the centre of the chimney-piece are the arms of the College, flanked on the right by those of Nevile, and on the left by those of the Deanery of Canterbury. Above are the arms of Queen Elizabeth: England and France modern quarterly, supported by a Lion and a Dragon. No record of the decoration has been preserved; but the presence of these supporters shews that it must have been executed before the death of Queen Elizabeth (24 March 1602—3). The ceiling may be compared with that of the old Chapel of Corpus Christi College, put up between 1602 and 1617[2]. Dr Bentley added a flat ceiling to this room, by which the older roof was effectually concealed. The rooms to the north of the Drawing-Room are those usually occupied by Royal Visitors, and those beneath them by the Judges of Assize. Their destination has probably been always the same.

The staircase at the north-west corner of the College Hall was made for the use of the Master when the Hall was built, as was mentioned in the history of the Hall above. At present it

---

[1] [The exact number of sash-windows inserted by him seems to have been 34: 20 on the east side, 8 on the west side, and 6 on the north side. Two of the latter are now covered by a modern lean-to; and 2 of those on the west side, which lighted the drawing-room and dining-room respectively, have been filled up. The date of the destruction of the eastern oriel has not been preserved.]

[2] [History of Corpus Christi College, fig. 18.]

terminates at the door into the Hall (*R*), and a narrower stair
leads down through a modern door (*D*) to a passage cut off from
the Housekeeper's Room.   It is clear however that it originally
turned, as shewn on the plan, and led down to a passage communicating directly with the north cloister of Nevile's Court,
through the door (*S*) which is still in use[1].   The wall *TV* is of
the same date as the staircase; and the window at *P* was probably once inserted in it, so as to light the lowest flight and the
passage, for the wall *L W* is of white brick, evidently erected not

Fig. 43.   Ceiling of the Drawing-Room in the Master's Lodge.

long since, when it was necessary to provide a larder.   Besides
this staircase there was the turret-stair in the north-west corner
of the Great Court.   At the foot there is a door into the Lodge
(*X*), and on the first floor a second door opening into the passage
beyond the Drawing-Room.   By this second staircase the rooms
at the northern extremity of the Lodge could be approached by
their occupants without inconvenience to the Master; and he

---

[1] [Jun. Burs. Accounts 1614—15.   "Item for a locke for o^r. M^r., at the stayres
head at the ende of the cloyster ij^s. viij^d."]

could reach the Library without descending into the Court. The door into it from the staircase still exists[1]. The staircase on the west side of the entrance-hall is known to be the work of Dr Bentley; and the Articles against him state that he destroyed an older one to make way for it, but about this staircase nothing more than the fact, as there stated, is known, and statements in controversial pamphlets must be received with caution.

The gallery occupied the oblique narrow line of building which extended from the Lodge in the direction of the river. It is evidently somewhat later than the older portion of the Lodge, for the plinth of the wall ME, which was shewn to have been once an external wall, is partially covered by it. The portion next to the Lodge still exists, and the south wall of the remainder. Loggan's ground plan (fig. 4) shews that this latter portion was the largest and broadest. The exact dimensions of it were discovered a few years ago by excavations in the Master's garden, and have been laid down on the plan (fig. 9). It is remarkable that no record of its destruction should have been preserved, as so large a building could hardly have been pulled down without authority[2]. Loggan (fig. 7) shews that it had a lantern turret, and external stairs on the south side, leading to what was then a garden. Professor Willis notes that "the upper storey of the portion still standing is of wood and plaster, and that the walls on which it rests have been underpinned with modern white brick. These walls are built principally of blocks of clunch; but the building between Bentley's staircase and the gallery, now a pantry, seems to belong to a different construction, for the wall ef is of random Barnack stone, perhaps built out of old materials brought from elsewhere. At g there is a low four-centered door leading to a cellar; and at V there is an external door of Nevile's time, with a rose or poppy in one spandril, and a snail in the other." This door may indicate that the western extension of the gallery was one of Nevile's works. The upper storey, or

---

[1] [The staircase was evidently regarded as itself part of the Lodge. Jun. Burs. Accounts 1614—15. "Item for altering the lock coming out of the Maister's lodging into the Liberarie vj^{d}."]

[2] [The following Conclusion seems to imply that it was in existence in 1752. "Apr. 20. 1752. Agreed that the small building adjoining to the south west corner of the Master's old gallery be pulled downe, as having been useless and ruinous for some years past. Rob. Smith."]

"upper gallery," is slightly wider than the lower storey, and rests upon a molded beam, like the gallery at Queens' College, which it closely resembled. It was of nearly the same width[1], and once had oriel windows. On examining the north side it appears that the beam was returned under one of the windows, but that subsequently it was abruptly cut off at a few inches from the face of the wall, into which the old window-frame has been inserted. The window opposite to it on the south side has apparently been altered in a similar manner. One of the rooms in the gallery was called "the Bow window room" so late as 1784—85[2].

When the gallery was first built it seems to have been used as a reception-room, from the purchase of furniture and hangings for it, and the allusion to the picture of King Henry the Eighth which hung there. When the Lodge had been increased by Dr Nevile, it is probable that the large room on the first floor would be used as a reception-room instead of it; and in fact we find that in the last century, this room was called the "Dining Room above stairs[3]"; a use to which it appears to have been put as early as 1667—68, from a payment in that year for repairs to the "roof between the dining-room and the gallery[4]." The gallery however was still used, for it may be traced through the Accounts down to 1800[5]; after which date it is not again mentioned, and the larger portion of it was most probably pulled down soon afterwards. The plan (fig. 41) shews that it overlaps Nevile's building by a few feet; and on the first floor there is a door out

---

[1] [The internal width of the gallery at Queens' College is 12 feet, see above, p. 28: of that at Trinity College 10 feet.]

[2] [Jun. Burs. Accounts 1784—85. *Carpenter.*]

[3] [Sir John Cullum's MS. diary (see above, p. 206), written in 1768, contains the following notes on Trinity Lodge: "In the Master's Lodge, in the Dining Room above stairs, is a fine whole length picture, large as life, of Henry 8" [etc.]: and, "In the parlor with the bow window is an original of the famous Robert Earl of Essex." Moreover the Cambridge Guide for 1799, giving a list of the pictures in the Lodge, enumerates the rooms as follows: "DINING ROOM, ABOVE STAIRS; THE FIRST BED CHAMBER; THE SECOND BED CHAMBER; STUDY; LODGE HALL; DINING PARLOUR." The first of these rooms is certainly the present Drawing Room, for it contains the pictures of Queen Elizabeth, King Henry VIII. etc.]

[4] [Jun. Burs. Accounts 1667—68. *Bricklayers.*]

[5] [Jun. Burs. Accounts 1619—20. "For .22. yardes and halfe a quarter of say for yᵉ lodginge gallerie lixˢ." Ibid. 1664—65. *Upholster.* "For 158 yards of Matt for yᵉ upper Gallery in yᵉ mʳˢ Lodg 02. 10. 00." Sen. Burs. Accounts 1688—89. "To Mʳ Shuter for matting yᵉ Lodge Gallery for 461 yards of Matt 06. 09. 00." Jun. Burs. Accounts 1799—1800. "For whitewashing staircase and long Gallery."]

of the small sitting-room at the east end of it into the Drawing-
room. In the Accounts for 1670—71 we find a charge for
making "two dores into the Acting-roome out of yᵉ Auditt
Chamber"; and other entries occur which lead to the conclusion
that the Audit-Chamber was some room in the Lodge[1]. We have
seen that it was the practice in other Colleges to use one of the
best rooms in the Lodge for the double purpose of Dining-Room
and Audit-Room, and if such was the practice here, we may
identify a portion of the Gallery with the Acting-Room or
Comedy-Room, the permanent addition of which to the Lodge
was made one of the charges against Dr Bentley. It has been
usual to identify the "Comedy-Room" with the large Drawing-
Room; but it is difficult to believe that a room in that position
could ever have been regarded as not properly belonging to the
Lodge, which was evidently the case with the room annexed by
Dr Bentley. Moreover, there are notices of the place in which
plays were acted which indicate a room in quite a different
position. When Cosmo dei Medici, Duke of Tuscany, visited
Cambridge in 1669, it is stated that the Master and Seniors
"brought him to yᵉ Master's Lodge, and then they went to yᵉ
Comedy House where they had a Comedy[2]"; and in another
account: "The evening coming on, his highness was introduced
into the theatre, a room rather small than spacious, where was
represented by the scholars a Latin comedy[3]." Moreover Dr
Thomas Parne, whose college career extended from 1714 to
1749, has left the following description of the Comedy-Room[4]:

"Ye Comedy room included both yᵉ long Room where yᵉ bow
windows are and some of yᵉ present Master's Parlour, when they used
to have leave to keep Christmas; yᵉ Senior Soph and Bachelor were
masters of yᵉ Revels and ordered all things in College. One came
with drums, the other with trumpets before him; yᵉ fellows dined and
supped promiscuously with yᵉ scholars. They had a Pole or Colestaff

<hr>

[1] [It was evidently of some size and importance: Jun. Burs. Accounts 1672—73.
"For making a freestone hearth in yᵉ Auditt chamber eight foot long and almost 2
foot broad o. 10. o." Ibid. 1673—74. "To Mʳ Shuter for hanging the Auditt
chamber o8. o8. oo."]

[2] [Alderman Newton's Diary, quoted in Cooper's Annals, iii. 533.]

[3] [The Travels of Cosmo the Third, Grand Duke of Tuscany, in England in the
Reign of Charles II., with Memoir of his Life. Edited by Robert Stewart: 4°
London, 1821, p. 229.]

[4] [MSS. Parne ii. 165, quoted by Professor Willis.]

which they called yᵉ Stang on which servants and Scholars were carried by way of Punishment, the latter chiefly for missing Chapel. Stangate Hole was yᵉ Place where this instrument of discipline used to be deposited."

This description does not apply to the large Drawing-Room, but it suits the gallery, part of which was called "the Bow-Window Room" as shewn above; and in the portion farthest from the Lodge there was space for a room about 75 feet long by 25 feet wide, lighted, as we learn from the Accounts, by four windows[1], ventilated by a louvre, and sufficiently remote to be called "the Comedy House" and "the theatre."

There was also a room called "the Attyring chamber:"

"Item to Thompson one day in making vpp harthes and mending the Chymney in the Attyring chamber xvjᵈ."
"Item a locke for a dore going out of the tyringe house into the hall xvjᵈ.[2]"
"For a bolt for the doore that cometh out of the tyreing chamber into the Mʳˢ lodginge xijᵈ.[3]"

The only room which fulfils the required conditions of being accessible from both the Hall and the Lodge is that on the ground floor at the north end of the Hall, which was added to the Lodge in 1700. The door at the north-east corner of the Hall (Z, fig. 41) opens into this room; and the difference of level between the floors of the Hall and of the Lodge might have been easily obviated by a small staircase. A small window looks into the Hall, as at Christ's College, from the Master's bedroom.

We must now trace briefly the subsequent history of the Lodge from the death of Dr Bentley to the present time.

In 1757—58 some work was done by Essex; but it does not seem to have been extensive. A new wainscoted partition and a new servants' hall are specially mentioned[4]. The partition is probably that which cuts off a narrow passage from the north side of the Dining-Room; the servants' hall is on the ground floor,

---

[1] [Jun. Burs. Accounts 1668—69. *Bricklayer* "For yᵉ hire of 4 haircloaths for yᵉ windows in yᵉ Comedy Room 8ˢ."]

[2] [Jun. Burs. Accounts 1614—15.]   [3] [Ibid. 1619—20.]

[4] [Jun. Burs. Accounts 1757—58. "To Mʳ Essex, his Bill at Mich. for putting up the Wainscott in the Master's Lodge, the new Partition, Window Shutters, Cornices, Architraves, Lintels, etc. £32. 1. 8½." In the same Account the Painter charges "for painting the doors and passages in the Servants new Hall."]

beneath the gallery. In 1785—86 a new roof was constructed, upwards of £400 being spent on timber. It was probably at this time that the dormers were altered. In subsequent years we find entries referring only to repairs and new furniture, until we come to the Mastership of Dr Whewell.

Dr Whewell was appointed Master in October 1841, and before the end of the month Mr A. J. B. Beresford Hope, who had taken his degree in that year, in writing to congratulate him, made the following proposal :

"Allow me to beg that you will in the name of the College accept as a slight token of affection and gratitude from one of her *alumni* the sum of 300 *l.*, to be devoted to the purpose of restoring to the Lodge the Oriel and Mullioned windows, exactly as they stood before Bentley's alteration, and thus in some measure giving back its antique character to the Old Court. Of course if it can not be done for that amount I do not mean to confine myself to it."

At the beginning of the following year the work was entrusted to Mr Salvin. Dr Whewell records in his Journal, 19 January 1842 :

"Mʳ Salvin, architect, arrived, and under his direction and in his presence we made attempts to discover traces of the oriel which formerly existed as a part of the front of the Lodge. We found the foundation of the wall of the oriel immediately below the surface of the ground. The plan was semicircular, the diameter of the semicircle 13 feet 7 inches, exactly opposite to the oriel which exists towards the garden. By examination of the upper storey of the Lodge it appeared that there are no lodging-rooms over Henry VIII.'s Drawing-Room, but only a blank garret, to which there is no access except through the windows. The key of the window was given to me by the Butler."

The plans for the restoration of the eastern façade were submitted to the Master and Seniors 12 April, 1842, and we may presume approved, for the work was put in hand at once. As it progressed, it was found that it would be much more costly than had been originally supposed, and Mr Hope most generously increased his donation to £1000. In September 1842 it was decided to rebuild the western oriel. The whole was not finished until the beginning of 1843[1]. At the end of that year the Accounts were audited, and the total cost of the restoration,

---

[1] [The Bursar's Minutes of the Meetings of the Seniority shew that on 16 February, 1843, the Master made a statement, detailing the work done to the Lodge. It must therefore have been nearly finished by that time.]

Fig. 44. The Fountain in the Great Court of Trinity College.

which is written out on a separate page at the end of the book, was found to have amounted to £3765. 19s. 6d.[1]; of which sum Mr Hope paid £1000, and the Master £250.

The sash-windows were replaced by windows of two lights and three lights alternately, with hoodmolds; and a stone oriel was built on both the eastern and western façades. It is much to be regretted that Dr Whewell and Mr Salvin determined to make the eastern oriel polygonal, instead of semicircular, as it had originally been. The lofty gable by which it is surmounted is also an addition for which there is no authority. The restoration of the picturesque dormers does not seem to have been thought of. The work is commemorated by the following inscription on a stone label immediately beneath the battlements of the eastern oriel: MUNIFICENTIA . FULTUS . ALEX . J . B . HOPE . GENE-ROSI . HISCE . ÆDIBUS . ANTIQUAM . SPECIEM . RESTITUIT . W . WHEWELL . MAG . COLLEGII . A . D . MDCCCXLIII.[2]

The garden of the Lodge will be described below in connection with the Walks and Gardens of the College.

THE FOUNTAIN IN THE GREAT COURT.—The history of the aqueduct which supplies the Fountain in the Great Court was related in Chapter I., and it was mentioned in Chapter III. that the Fountain itself (fig. 44) was begun in 1601—2. We now have to investigate the details of the original construction, and then to narrate the subsequent history. It should be premised that it was rebuilt in 1715—16, and that several details of the older structure were not reproduced.

It was shewn above (p. 428) that the conduit-pipe probably passed originally along the lane which formed the south boun-

---

[1] [Besides this there were other expenses, by which the outlay on the Lodge in 1842 and 1843 is brought up to £5268. 9. 11½.]

[2] [This inscription was severely criticised at the time, on the ground that the College was not sufficiently honoured in it. Dr Whewell, after an interview with Professor Sedgwick on the subject, writes in his Journal, Feb. 16, 1843: "I stated that I conceived the Inscription was correct, Mr Hope's gift having been made to me, and the selection of the Inscription being one of the details of the work which I was obliged to decide; that I had done so, framing the Inscription at the suggestion of the architect, and with the consent of Mr Hope; but that if the Fellows were dissatisfied I regretted that the matter had not been brought before the Seniority; that I had no wish of avoiding to consult them; and had shewn the Inscription before it was put up to the Dean and the Bursar."]

dary of the first site of King's Hall (fig. 6). If this theory
be correct it would have crossed the Great Court a few feet
to the north of the present Fountain ; and in fact in 1560—61
a charge occurs "for mendinge and sawderinge the cunditte
pipe in the sesterne beside the chappell[1]." In 1553[2], however, a
fresh extension of it from the kitchen is specially recorded :

"Item to the plummer for making out the Cundythe owt of the
kytchyn into ye courte ; for the workmanship and sauder......xv^s."

It must be remembered that the kitchen here mentioned is
the old kitchen, on the west side of the quadrangle (fig. 10),
so that as far as that range the pipe must have followed the
same direction as at present. The above entry marks the
first project for the erection of a Fountain. Nothing more
appears to have been done until 1601—2 ; for which year the
Senior Bursar's Accounts only have been preserved. At the
end of the Account proper, which is distributed under the usual
heads, it is noted that the Bursar, Mr Gregory Milner, has spent
£540. 13s. 0d., on the buildings of the year, of which the
Fountain is stated to be one. The remaining pages contain
the details of this expenditure, not divided between the works
undertaken, but arranged under the heads of wages, and materials of various kinds. It is therefore impossible to do more
than select the items of interest which may be undoubtedly
assigned to the Fountain. The work began 1 February 1601—2,
and was continued until 1 December. After a page and a half of
wages, the following entries occur:

"Item for caruing the eight beastes by taske to Wyat and Thorpe
and ye lion on ye top v^{li}.
Item to Robert Masson for plaister wth frett worke vnder the
flower of the fountaine xlij^s.
Item paid this yere to diuers Carpenters making and setting vpp
the newe Rales about the Coundite, for working and laying the tymber
flower of the fountaine [and other charges] vj^{li} xv^s vj^d."

These are succeeded by the following, under the heading,
Layd out for Tymber :

"Inprimis paid for vj loades and xxx^{tie} foote of tymber to flower
the fountaine and to inlarge the Rayles at xxv^s......viij^{li} viii^s ix^d.

---

[1] [Jun. Burs. Accounts. *The Cundette.*]

[2] [Sen. Burs. Accounts, 1553—54. *In reparationibus.* In this year the Accounts
run from January to January. The extract is noted in the margin *Cundit.*]

Item paid for lyntalls at the fountaine iiij^s viij^d.
Item for boardes laid vnder the leades of the fountaine vj^s viij^d."

The stone for the superstructure was brought from the quarries of Clyffe and Clipsham; the foundation was of brick;

"Item payd to Lyllie and Baylie for sixe thowsand of Bricke spent in foundacions and vaultes for the fountaine, [and other works]...iiij^{li} x^s."

Lastly, under the heading, *Extraordinarie charges*, we find:

"Item for a phaine for the peremint of the Coundite and coullering the same.
Item paid for viij cockes of brasse for the Cundite and carridge xxvj^s viij^d."

The Senior Bursar's Accounts for 1602—3 are lost, and in those for following years no entry referring to the Fountain occurs until 1611—12, when a charge for the stone for the steps shews that they at least had been left unfinished[1]. There is a charge for setting them in the following year, when the space round the Fountain was paved[2]. In 1614—15, when the whole College was cleaned and decorated for the reception of King James, the Fountain was repaired and painted:

"Item to Thorpe one daye setting on the Lions faces on the Cundite xviij^d.
Item to John Newton for paynting the Cundite and King Edwardes picture xij^{li} vj^s viij^d."

It may be concluded from the above extract that the original Fountain—as it may conveniently be termed—was finished in 1615. We do not know who furnished the design, for the names which occur in the Accounts are obviously those of workmen only[3]. Whoever he was, he must have been an artist of first-rate ability, for the work is one of singular originality and beauty. The original Fountain is shewn by Loggan (fig. 7), and though his print is on a small scale, a study of it, assisted by the above extracts, reveals certain differences between the original and the existing structure (fig. 44), as stated above. The octagonal base was approached by four

---

[1] [Sen. Burs. Accounts 1611—12. "To Persiuall for the Condit staires 492 foote at 18^d xxxvj^{li} xviij^s."]

[2] [Jun. Burs. Accounts 1612—13. *Layd out to Tylers, etc.*]

[3] [Thorpe, who carved the figures of animals, is no doubt the workman who was employed to decorate the Great Gate in 1614—15 (p. 488).]

steps instead of by three; there were taps for water on all the eight sides instead of on one side only; there was a floor of wood across the central cistern, with a small circular aperture in the centre for the water to flow through; the crowns of the arches were ornamented with lions' heads instead of human faces; the stone ribs at the top were plain; and the lion on the summit had a metal crown and tongue, and bore a weathercock. Moreover it should perhaps be concluded from the mention of "plaister wth frett worke vnder the flower" in one of the above extracts; and of "foure moulds to frame ye plaistering on the top of the Conduit" in a repair carried out in 1673, that there was a ceiling of plaster-work under the stone canopy, where there is now a floor of wood. Lastly, the whole was painted, probably as much for preservation of the stonework as for ornament. It appears from the Accounts of subsequent years that some of the decorative portions were gilt[1].

The Conduit, like most of the work done by Dr Nevile, appears to have been insecurely built, for extensive repairs took place in 1661—62, and 1672—73[2]; and in 1716 it was necessary to rebuild it completely. Mr Edward Rud, Fellow, notes in his diary[3], 4 June 1716: "We began to take down our conduit in order to rebuild it;" and the Junior Bursar's Book has a special heading: *The Accounts for Re = building the Conduit.* The work, which was entrusted to Robert Grumbold,

---

[1] [Jun. Burs. Accounts 1645—46. *Extraordinaries.* "For Oiling and Coloring y^e Lions heades at the Cunduit o. 4. o." Ibid. 1661—62. "To John Wisdome for painting y^e Conduit [and other work] 015. 00. 00." Ibid. 1692—93. *Extraordinaryes.* "For paynting and Guilding the Conduit 17^{li}. *College Smith.* For a New Crown and Tongue for the Lyon on the Conduit oo. 10. 04."]

[2] [The extent of the work done is shewn by the remark of Thoresby, who saw it 16 May 1695, and speaks of "the delicate fountain lately erected." Diary, ut supra, p. 546. The Order for a previous repair to the pipes in 1656 is sufficiently curious for quotation: Conclusion Book 28 May, 1656. "It was this day ordered by ye Master and Seniors that Goodman Page...doe forth with provide Cockes and Pipes for ye Conduit, and put it into such a condicion y^t ye Vpper Pipes may run constantly. And the Porter is hereby ordered to see y^t ye Pipes doe run accordingly. And if any of ye Colledge servants sell water in to ye Towne whereby ye observation of this order may be prejudiciall The Porter is to give information thereof That the Master and Seniors may take an Effectuall course therein as the case requires." The last provision in this Order is illustrated by Carter (p. 338), who, writing in 1753, speaks of the "beautiful Fountain of excellent Water (which is used by great part of the Townsfolks for Tea)."]

[3] [Camb. Antiq. Soc. 8vo. Publ. No. v.]

occupied 25 weeks, and cost £183. 13s. 6d. The Account unfortunately contains no particulars of what was done, the items being for wages, and for new stone. The changes introduced, so far as it is possible to distinguish them, have been enumerated above. The view of the Court published in 1740 shews a sun-dial on the top, immediately beneath the lion. It appears to have been triangular, from a charge in the Accounts for 1693, "for painting and guilding the 3 dyalls Lyon and Ball 5li." The same view shews a row of three pine-apples on each of the stone ribs. At the conclusion of the work, the whole was painted and gilt[1]. A further repair, which, to judge from the expense, must have been nearly as extensive as the previous one, took place in 1766—67[2]; the steps were renewed in 1821—22; and in 1842 the pipes were "entirely repaired and replaced throughout[3]."

The following coats of arms occur in the cresting, and in the spandrels of the arches. The uppermost shield is marked (1), that in the left spandrel (2), that in the right spandrel (3).

North face. The See of Canterbury impaling on a cross flory 5 bezants; for Archbishop Whitgift, Master 1567—77; died 29 February 1604. 2. Blank. 3. Archbishop Whitgift, as above.

North-west face. 1. Blank. 2. The See of Canterbury. 3. Dr Thomas Nevile, Master 1593—1602.

West face. 1 and 2. Trinity College. 3. The See of York, to commemorate Matthew Hutton, D.D., formerly Fellow, Archbishop 1595—1606.

South-west face. 1 and 3. Blank. 2. A defaced shield.

South face. 1. The See of Chester, impaling per bend indented : for Henry Ferne, Master 1660—62 ; he was made Bishop of Chester 1662 and died in the same year. His arms were put up in the course of the repair which was then proceeding[4]. 2. A chevron between 3 heads? erased. 3. A defaced shield, See of Canterbury?

---

[1] [Jun. Burs. Accounts 1718—19. *Painter.* "To Charles Adams, for painting and guilding the Conduit 35. 0. 0." A Dolphin appears to have formed part of the decoration, but its position cannot be identified. It is first mentioned in the Junior Bursar's Accounts for 1716—17, when Grumbold is paid, "For putting in ye Cock at ye Conduit for ye Dolphin"; again in 1768—69 when "a new Portland Stone Dolphin at the Conduit" is mentioned ; and a similar charge occurs in 1792—93.]

[2] [Ibid. 1766—67. *Free Mason.* "To Jeffs and Bentley for Work and Stone to the Conduit to Octob. 31st 1767. £136. 5. 9¾."]

[3] [Senior Bursar's Minutes, 24 May, 1842. It was on this occasion that the course of the aqueduct was surveyed by Mr Edlin. The cost was upwards of £1800.]

[4] [Jun. Burs. Accounts 1661—62. *For worke on ye top of ye Conduit.* "To Spakman for cutting ye Bppe of Chesters Armes, and other worke cutt att the Conduit 000. 19. 03."]

South-east face. Blank.
East face. 1. Dr Thomas Nevile. 2, 3. Blank.
North-east face. Blank.

The shield held by the lion on the top bears France modern and England quarterly.

The House at the Conduit-head on the Madingley Road (p. 428) is evidently of considerable antiquity. It is a small oblong building, constructed of large blocks of stone, chiefly oolite, intermixed with a few blocks of sandstone. The pent-house roof is formed of slabs of the same material, fastened to the gable-walls, and to each other, with leaden cramps. The present square-headed doorway is evidently a modern insertion; but the masonry shews signs of having been disturbed; and the original doorway was probably arched.

TREASURY.—The Statutes given by King Edward the Sixth direct that money, account-books, and muniments are to be kept in a chamber in the lesser tower (*in minore turre*); and that a chamber on the ground floor (*cubiculum inferius*) in the old cloister is to be used as an Audit-Room. The Statutes given by Queen Elizabeth in 1559—60 assign the same destination to the muniments, in the same words. As these Statutes were given before the Queen's Gate was built, it is clear that by the lesser tower the gateway of King Edward the Third is meant. A chamber in this Gate had been used as a Treasury before the removal (p. 469); and, when the Gate was rebuilt in its present position, the chamber on the second floor was again fitted up for that purpose, to which it is still applied.

The position of the Audit-Room, after the room above-mentioned ceased to be used as such, has been discussed in the History of the Master's Lodge.

TENNIS COURT.—The first Tennis Court was situated at the south-east corner of the College (fig. 3). It was pulled down in 1598—99 to make way for the range of chambers forming the east side of the Great Court (p. 477); and in 1611 a new Tennis Court was built between the end of the north range of Nevile's Court and the river (p. 518). It is indicated in this position in the rough sketch of the College (fig. 45) which forms part of the plan of Cambridge dated 1634, prefixed to Fuller's History.

The building was entrusted by the Master and Seniors to three Fellows, who were directed to borrow £100 for the purpose :

"10° April 1611. Concluded that the Tenniscourt building is referred to Mr Cheeke, Mr Roan, Mr Stanhope; to be accomptable to the M^r and SS^rs when they shall be called.

3 June 1611. It is also concluded that ye overseeres of ye Tenise courte buildinge...doe procure 100^li for y^e furtherance of y^e same, and y^e Senior Burser to be bownde wth them for y^e repaiemente of y^e same in y^e Colledge behalfe; to be repayd to the Coll: by fellow commoners admissions and commenssments."

Fig. 45. Trinity College, shewing Nevile's Court in its unfinished state, and the Tennis Court : from the plan of Cambridge (dated 1634) prefixed to Fuller's History.

The Senior Bursar's Accounts for 1610—11 are lost, and therefore we cannot trace the progress of the building. It must however have been nearly finished by June 1611, for two tennis court keepers were appointed on that date ; and the Accounts for 1611—12 record only the payment of the last instalment of the £100, and of some few extras. The total cost appears to have been £120[1]. This building was pulled down to make way for the Library (p. 538), and was not rebuilt on any other site.

BREWHOUSE, BAKEHOUSE, STABLES, ETC.—It is probable that in the first instance these buildings were placed between the west side of the Court and the ditch which separated the College

---

[1] [College Order, 1 October, 1612. "This day it was concluded that...120^li be repayde to the Coll: wch was layd out by the sen. Burser for finishing the Tennis court."]

ground from Garret Hostel Green. A separate heading in the Junior Bursar's Accounts for 1566—67: *Charges aboute the brewhouse etc, and the myllhouse*, which is continued in succeeding years with the addition of the Bakehouse and the Fish-house, though not recording particulars, points to a rebuilding on an enlarged scale. In 1611—12, after the building of the Hall and Kitchen in their present position, the Senior Bursar lays out £635. 15s. 6d. "for all manner of out-buildings." Again no particulars are given, and the loss of his Accounts for the preceding and succeeding years, and of the Junior Bursar's Accounts from 1606—7 to 1611—12, prevents our knowing what was being done at that time. It is however probable, from the amount then spent, and from the absence of any subsequent reference to the building of those offices on a new site, that they were then placed where they are shewn by Loggan (fig. 7). According to him the Stable was on the south side, and the Brewhouse on the west side, of a yard which occupied part of the site of the ancient Garret Hostel. The Bakehouse was on the north side of the same yard, in continuation of the south side of the Great Court. They remained in this position until the New Court was built; when the Stables were curtailed in extent, and the Brewhouse was transferred to its present position on the opposite side of the river. The Bakehouse was then pulled down, and was not rebuilt. We do not know the position of the Fish-house.

Before leaving this part of our subject it should be mentioned that the following offices are referred to in the Accounts: Woodyard, Slaughter-house yard, Poundred meat house, Capon house, Hen-house, Malt-chamber, Limehouse, Storehouse, Horsekeeper's chamber, Barber's shop, Swan-house. These buildings are not of sufficient importance to detain us longer in attempting to trace their history or define their position; but their existence is worth noting as shewing the provision made for keeping within the precincts of the College everything required for the inmates. There was also a "Stangate-Hole" here, as at S. John's College (p. 321); and a building called "Spice house[1]."

---

[1] [Jun. Burs. Accounts, 1598—99. "Item for ij dayes worke in mending...Mr Dickensons Spice-house...ij^s." Ibid. 1612—13. *Glazier*. "Item in the spice house one casement vj^d. Item in Sr Walton's spice house 2 foote of newe glasse xij^d." A similar charge occurs in the same Account for 1614—15.]

WALKS AND GARDENS.—It was explained in Chapter I.
that when Trinity College was founded the site was bounded
on the west by the King's ditch; and that beyond it was the
Common called Garret Hostel Green, which was acquired partly
in the seventeenth, partly in the eighteenth century.

The disposition of the College ground between the west side
of the court as it then stood, and this boundary-ditch, can be
made out with tolerable distinctness from Hamond's map
(fig. 3). Beginning from the north we find (1) a garden west of
the King's Hall quadrangle, in the same position as the present
Bowling Green, and of nearly the same size; (2) a garden corresponding generally with the present Master's Garden; (3) a few
scattered trees indicating a garden west of the Kitchen and
Hall, and separated from some buildings, evidently representing
Garret Hostel, by a wall, of which, owing to the damaged
condition of the map, only a fragment is seen. The first of
these gardens belonged to the Fellows, and in 1568—69 the
wooden palings by which it was separated from the Master's
garden (2) were replaced by a wall[1]. The third garden may
be identified with ground first planted in 1551—52, when a
charge occurs "for 1000 setts for ye garthen in ye kitching
yarde[2]." In subsequent years it is variously described as "the
cook's garden," "the kitchen garden," and "the orchard."

Garret Hostel Green was evidently regarded as the property
of the College almost from the beginning. The boundary-
ditch—described as "the great ditch," "the ditch in the backside," and "the Colledge ditch"—was cleaned and kept in repair
at the expense of the College; and it was crossed by two, if not
by three, bridges, of which the construction and the repairs are
paid for by the College Bursar. The southernmost of these
provided access to the Green at the end of Garret Hostel Lane,
as explained above (p. 407). It is referred to as "the common
brydge on the bakesyde[3]," and more precisely in the Junior
Bursar's Accounts for 1554—55 :

[1] [Jun. Burs. Accounts 1568—69. *Extraordinarye receptes.* "Inprimis of William
Spicer for ye olde pale betwene o^r. m^{rs}. garden and the fellowes xxxiij^s. iiij^d." *Carpenters.* "Thomas Watson 6 dayes about the wall betwene o^r. m^{rs}. garden and the
fellowes vj^s."]   [2] [Sen. Burs. Accounts, 1551—52.]
   [3] [Ibid. 1552—53. As the charge for its repair is entered among the *Expense
forinsece* it clearly refers to a bridge which was not the property of the College.]

"Item payd vnto Wylliam Carpenter februarii primo for mendyng the .ij. bridges at yᵉ duffhowse and at yᵉ layn end vnto Trinite Hall .... iiijˢ. viijᵈ."

The second bridge mentioned in this extract must be that shewn in Lyne's plan (fig. 2); and, as we know that one of the walls of the dovehouse abutted on the Master's garden[1], we may suppose that it crossed the ditch out of the kitchen-garden, a position which would place it about midway between the former bridge and the point at which the ditch falls into the river, as laid down on Lyne's plan. This bridge is evidently identical with "the bridge by the backhouse," first mentioned in 1598—99; and as we find "the backehouse ende" used to denote a place near the north end of the ditch, just as Garret Hostel bridge is used to denote the south end of the same, we may place the bakehouse and dovehouse in the yard west of the kitchen. It should be mentioned that in the Accounts for 1552—53 "the brydge besydes our mayster's stable" is mentioned. This may either have been a separate bridge built for the convenience of the Master's servants, or only another name for the bridge last described.

The planting of Garret Hostel Green was commenced so early as 1552, when the Junior Bursar charges "for settyng willows on the grene"; and subsequent entries for planting ash and willow "on the backsyde" probably refer to the same place, for there would hardly have been room for large trees elsewhere. Not only, however, was the green treated in this way, but also the common-ground on the opposite side of the river, which is always spoken of as "the fields," or "the field," in contradistinction to "the green" or "the backsyde." In 1554—55 a carpenter repairs "yᵉ fooyt bridge in to yᵉ feyld yᵗ was broken downe with the flooyd." This was evidently the bridge over the river, called in subsequent years "the great bridge[2]" or "greater bridge[3]," to distinguish it from "the little

---

[1] [Jun. Burs. Accounts 1598—99 "Item for ij dayes worke over that syde of the douehouse that is next our Mʳˢ. garden xxᵈ."]

[2] [Sen. Burs. Accounts 1589—90. *Reparationes.* "Paid for tymber to make the stopp and barre vppon the great bridge iiijˢ." This bridge must not be confounded with Garret Hostel Bridge, which is referred to as "the great bridge called Garrett bridge," or "the great bridge next Trinity Hall."]

[3] [Ibid. 1607—8. *Extraordinaries.* "Item to Carpenter for mending the greater bridge into the feildes xvjᵈ."]

bridge," first mentioned in 1560—61[1], or "furthest bridge," which crossed the ditch at the west end of the avenue. In 1599—1600 the "ij feild bridges" are repaired at the same time.

The "causey into the feilds" is first mentioned in 1589—90, but as it is repaired in that year, it must have been made in some previous year for which the Accounts are lost. In 1598—99 "the causey that was made into the feildes," called also the "greate causey," is heightened by the addition of 204 loads of rubbish and 60 loads of gravel; after which it is paved, and protected by rails. In the Accounts for 1599—1600, and for the years immediately succeeding, we find the following entries respecting the enclosure and planting of the walks:

"Item disbursed by Mr Milner [Senior Fellow] for enclosing of ye greene on bothe sydes ye Ryuer wth a deepe ditche and for xxx. settes .... xij^{li}. xiij^s. iiij^d.[2]"
"Item paid for XLIX settes of Ashes for the newe enclosure
xxiij^s. iiij^d.[3]"
"Item...for XL^{tie} setts of Ashes for the Close and bushing them with thornes .... xx^s.[4]"

In 1603—4 an extensive planting of the close with willows took place; and a considerable sum was spent "in dichinge the close and hedginge the river[5]."

The deed of exchange in 1613 between the Town and College, by which the grounds were finally acquired (p. 407), describes the fencing off of the south end of Garret Hostel Green by a ditch and wall, the great Bridge over the River, and the smaller bridge over "the ditch next the Common Field," as works about to be undertaken. We have seen, however, that bridges of some sort had existed long before; and the language of the deed must therefore be understood to refer to a rebuilding, at least of the great bridge, which was then in pro-

---

[1] [Jun. Burs. Accounts 1560—61. *Extraordinarye expenses.* "It' to Cornelis Shelylote for mending ye lytell bridge half a daye vij^d." This bridge is sometimes called "the furthest Bridge."]

[2] [Jun. Burs. Accounts 1599—1600. *Extraordinaries.*]

[3] [Sen. Burs. Accounts 1600—1601. *Extraordinarie Charges.* In this year Mr Milner was Senior Bursar.]　　　[4] [Ibid. 1601—1602.]

[5] [Ibid. 1603—1604. The planting with willows was continued through most of the eighteenth century. So late as 1659—60 a charge occurs "for 30 willow setts for the Outer walkes."]

gress. This work had been begun in 1611—12[1], and was ordered to be finished, together with the other works mentioned above, in December, 1612 (p. 412). They were probably completed in the course of 1613. The bridge was in the same place as the present one, and the "causey," on the same ground as the present avenue, ran past the wall on Garret Hostel Green, then the southern limit of the College ground, and over the bridge to the newly-built "feild bridge."

This bridge, built in 1613, was replaced in 1651—52 by the one shewn in Loggan's print (fig. 7)[2]. It had two arches, separated by a massive triangular buttress in the centre of the stream. This bridge lasted for just a century. In 1763 it was found to have become ruinous, and attempts were made to repair it. These having failed, it was decided to build a new one (fig. 46) with the money bequeathed by Dr Hooper[3]. The work began at Midsummer 1763, probably with the attempts to repair the old bridge, and ended at Michaelmas 1765. A statement of the disbursements for the bridge, appended to the Junior Bursar's Accounts for 1764—65, shews that the total cost was £1500. 3s. 0¼d. The old materials were used for the piers and abutments, the superstructure being built of Portland and Ketton stone. The architect, Mr Essex, received £50 for the design, and supervision of the work[4]. The shields on the bridge bear the arms of the College and of Dr Hooper[5].

We will now return to the ground on the east side of the river. It was mentioned in Chapter IV. (p. 518) that the ditch which formed the east boundary of Garret Hostel Green was filled up in connection with the building of that portion of Nevile's Court which was due to the liberality of Dr Nevile

---

[1] [Sen. Burs. Accounts 1611—12.]

[2] [Jun. Burs. Accounts 1651—52. *Extraordinaryes.*]

[3] ["Jan. 18, 1764. Agreed by the Master and Seniors that a New Bridge be built out of the Money left to the College by the late Dr Hooper, as the old Bridge is reported by the Workmen to be incapable of a durable Repair. Rob: Smith."]

[4] ["June 16, 1766. Agreed...that the Junr. Bursr. pay Mr Essex the sum of Fifty Pounds for giving in a Plan of the Bridge, surveying the Works there, and other business. Rob: Smith."]

[5] [Dr Hooper's arms are (Burke's General Armoury): "Gyronny of eight, ermine and azure, over all a castle, argent. *Crest:* a demi-wolf couped, holding in the dexter paw an oak branch fructed, all proper."]

himself. This took place in 1605—6[1]. The ground between the New Court, or Nevile's Court, was called "Tennis Court Green," "Tennis Court Yard," and "Tennis Court End." In 1650—51 it was planted with trees, which subsequent entries shew to have been elms[2]. After the acquisition of the south part of Garret Hostel Green in 1662 (p. 413), the "new grounds,"

Fig. 46. Bridge built by Essex, 1763—65: from Le Keux's Memorials of Cambridge, ed. Cooper.

as they are termed, were laid out[3], and a "new wall by the river," called also "the water-wall," was built[4]. The arrangement of this piece of ground in 1688 is shewn by Loggan (fig. 7). There was a high battlemented wall, strengthened by buttresses, along the south border; and a second wall, somewhat lower,

---

[1] [Sen. Burs. Accounts 1605—6. *Extraordinary charges.* "Given by appoyntment to M[r] Brookes for y[e] town ditch vj[li]. 13[s]. 4[d]. To Jhon Powell for fillinge y[e] ditch about the greene in y[e] inside for mayntenaunce of y[e] trees xxij[s]. Tarr bought to dresse y[e] trees in y[e] Green 18[d]."]

[2] [Jun. Burs. Accounts for 1650—51 and subsequent years. This ground was evidently laid out afresh after the new bridge was built as related above.]

[3] [Jun. Burs. Accounts 1663—64.]　　　　[4] [Ibid. 1664—65.]

extended along the river-bank as far as the bridge[1]. A walk, planted with trees, ran along the south and west sides, and in the centre there was a raised bed. An avenue, planted on the same ground as the present one, extended from the bakehouse to the bridge. The trees are evidently older than those in the avenue beyond the bridge, and are perhaps intended to represent the elms which were planted in 1667—68.

The ground which intervenes between the walks and the high-road on the west side of the College, called by Loggan (fig. 4) *Trinity Coll. Peice,* belonged, in the seventeenth century, partly to King's College, partly to Corpus Christi College, and partly, as it would seem, to St John's College also, and had been leased to different occupiers. It was obviously of great importance to Trinity College to acquire this ground, or at least to prevent others from taking permanent possession of it. Moreover, it was intended at that time to lay it out as a pleasure-ground, as the following Order shews:

"14 May, 1663. Agreed...y^t ye Senior Bursar doe speedily enquire of ye Owners of ye Land by ye back Gate, that there may be a purchase made of it, and imployed for a place of Recreation."

Accordingly, in 1663—64 the leases were acquired[2]. That of the part to the north, belonging to King's College, was bought from a Mr Moulton "to make a bowling green[3]"; that of the part to the south, belonging to Corpus Christi College, from Mr Edward Green, butcher, of Cambridge. In 1677, on the expiration of Moulton's lease, a fresh lease was obtained from King's College, in which the property is thus described:

"all those theire three acres of pasture ground more or lesse lyeing and being on the Backside of Trinitie Colledge aforesaid & late in the occupacon of William Moulton his assignee or assignes, abutting East on the Comon highway leading towards St Johns Colledge walkes[4] and west upon Bin Brooke and sideing South next the land of

---

[1] [This wall was extensively repaired in 1697—98. Jun. Burs. Accounts 1697—98 *Free Mason.* "12 foot of stone to mend ye Buttrisses next ye River 00. 12. 0. 157 foot of coping upon ye wall next ye River" etc.]

[2] [Professor Willis mentions, on the authority of Parne, that "about 1664 the College had formed a design for fine groves gardens and a bowling green beyond the road over against the field gate. This was the beginning of the 'Paradise'."]

[3] [Sen. Burs. Accounts 1663—64. *Extraordinaryes.*]

[4] [By this "highway" the footpath leading to the gate which now stands at the N.E. corner of S. John's College Wilderness must be understood.]

Corpus Christi Colledge in the Universitie of Cambridge aforesaid late in the occupacon of Edward Green or his assignes[1]."

The extent of Green's land is not mentioned, but the amount of the annual rent paid for it shews that it must have been much smaller than that belonging to King's College.

The scheme for making a pleasure-ground was evidently abandoned, for Loggan shews it as an open field, intersected by paths, and destitute of trees. It probably remained in this state until 1748—49, when "the new Improvements behind the College[2]" are mentioned. No details are given, but as in the Accounts for 1757—58[3] we find entries for the purchase of 160 "Elms Plants," and also for protecting "the Young Elms before the Field Gates," it may be concluded that the former entry refers to the preparation of the ground, and the latter to the planting of the trees now growing there.

The "great walkes[4]," by which expression the central avenue, usually called the "high walk," is evidently meant, were planted with limes in 1671—72; and in 1674—75 the south-west walk was similarly treated. The old willows, the planting of which at the beginning of the century was recorded

[1] [King's College Ledger Book, vi. The lease, for 20 years from 1 March 1677, at an annual rent of £3. 0. 0, is dated 28 May, 1677. An annual rent of £2. 0. 0 is still paid to King's College for this ground. The following entries among many others refer to these purchases: Sen. Burs.: 1663—64. *Extraordinaryes.* "To Mr Moulton for land bought of him to make a bowling green 40. 00. 00. To Mr. Greene for ye purchase of a peece of ground behind ye Colledge 35. 00. 00. For one yeares rent for ye ground behinde ye Coll. bought of Moulton 03. 00. 00." Ibid. 1677—78. "Paid the Rent for a parcell of ground lyeing beyond the Red Gates wch the Colledge hath taken by lease from King's Colledge for one year ending at Michãs 1677, 03. 00.00. Mr Greene for our Leyes and Lands at the Red Gates 00. 16. 00." Ibid. 1688—89. "To St John's Colledge their Rent for ye Land behind ye Redd gate 01. 08. 00. To King's Colledge their Rent for Land wee hold of them in ye Feild on the backside of our Colledge 03. 00. 00." Ibid. 1700—1701. "Bennet Coll. Ground rent for ye ground behinde ye Fieldgate 0. 16. 00."]

[2] [Jun. Burs. Accounts 1748—49, *Extraordinaries.* "For removing Soil from Sidney Coll. to ye new Improvements behind the Colledge 0. 15. 0."]

[3] [Ibid. 1757—58. *Carpenter. Backyard and Quarters.* In the same Account for 1761—62 we find: *Walks.* "for propping the Young Elms next the Road and in the Quarters"; and in that for 1763—64: *Extraordinaries.* "For Advertisements relating to the Young Elms behind ye Field-Gate 0. 13. 0."]

[4] [Sen. Burs. Accounts 1671—72. *Extraordinaries.* "For ye Lime trees on ye great walkes and planting them 10. 06. 00. For ye carriage of them from London 01. 04. 00."]

above, were now cut down and sold[1]." We learn incidentally, in connection with this work, that the two square plots into which the ground was then, as now, divided were termed "the quadrangles." In this year the planting was unusually varied and extensive. Elms are charged for, with a great number of other trees and shrubs; as "Spanish Firs," holly, "tameresse trees," juniper, Spanish broom, honeysuckle, philerea, evergreen oak, and an enormous quantity of quick. Of many of these shrubs the seeds only were bought, and a plantation of them was made "behinde the Brewhouse." The quick was set "in the New walkes," but the place in which the other shrubs were planted is not mentioned[2]. This planting was continued in the following year; and in 1676—77 "a new walk next St John's" was planted with horse chestnut, and a quickset hedge on "the South bottome of the High walke goeing to the Red gates was made." The walk itself had evidently not long been planted, from a charge in 1678—79 for "watering the trees on both sides the Great Walke from the bridge to the Red Gate." Between this date and 1684 charges occur for horse chestnuts, firs, and "18 Dutch Lime Trees," and in 1684 a new walk, secured by a wall, was made under the direction of Robert Grumbold along the bank on the west side of the river[3]. A charge for "the stone stepps descending to the New walke" shews that it was on a lower level than the rest of the walks; and there is also a curious entry for "painting the barrs and Turnepikes in the entrance to the New walke, and towards the great old walke[4]."

Shortly after the making of this walk Loggan's print was drawn (fig. 7); and the narrative which we have tried to put together shews how the grounds were gradually brought to the appearance there shewn. In his view the west end of the "high walke" is ornamented with a handsome stone archway

---

[1] [Sen. Burs. Accounts 1674—75. "Thirty Lime Trees for the South west Walke 04. 10. 00. Two thousand two hundred of Quicksetts and Prim-print 00. 18. 04. For plashing the Hedge and levelling the said Walke, more than the old willow trees were sold for 00. 09. 04."]   [2] [Jun. Burs. Accounts 1674—75.]

[3] [24 March 1684. "Agreed then by the Vice Mr and Seniors that a wall be made on the other side of the river to secure the walk: and that the Senior Bursar take care of it. Geo. Chamberlaine: V. Mar."]

[4] [Sen. Burs. Accounts 1684—85. *Extraordinaries.*]

Fig. 47. East front of Nevile's Gate, Trinity College.

of Jacobean architecture (fig. 46) which in the last century was called "Nevile's Gate[1]." In Loggan's print, however, it is simply the "Gate leading to the fields" (*janua que ducit ad agros*); and in the Accounts the gate at the end of the avenue is uniformly referred to as "the Red Gate." Had it been placed in this position by Dr Nevile himself, it would probably have been referred to in the Accounts under his name; or at least the existence of it would have been made manifest by charges for repair. Again, Loggan shews that it stood on the west side of the ditch, outside the college ground, a position which it could hardly have occupied until after the purchase of the leases recorded above. On the whole therefore it seems probable that the following entries in the Accounts for 1680—81 record its first construction, at any rate in this place:

"To the Smith for iron worke to the New Redd Gate that leads to the Fields 3^{li}. 19^s. 10^d. To the Carpenter Mr Silke for worke at the same Gate 3^{li}. 6^s. 11^d. To Mr Grumball for worke and materialls at ye same gate 22^{li}. 9^s. 5^d. To Matthew Fitch [a bricklayer] for materials and workemen's wages 19^{li}. 13^s. 3^d. And to the Painter 2^{li}. In all £51. 09. 05^2."

The following arms appear upon the Gate. Their relative positions will be understood from the woodcut (fig. 47).

East front. The Royal Arms, as in the Hall, encircled with the garter, and supported by the lion and the unicorn. On the south side is a rose, and on the north side a thistle; the badges of England and Scotland respectively. On each pier of the gate, below these badges, is a shield: that on the south side bears Trinity College, that on the north side Magdalene College; both impaling Nevile. In the spandrels of the arch are two smaller shields; one charged with the saltire; the other fretty with a canton ermine, being the first and second quarter of the Nevile arms.

West front. The arms of Nevile, quartered as follows: 1 and 2 Nevile, 3 Bulmer, 4 Alban of Middleham, 5 Glanville, 6 Clavering. On each side is one of the Nevile crests; on the north side a pied bull's head charged with a red rose, on the south side a galley. On the piers, below these, are two shields: that on the north side bears the Deanery of Canterbury, that on the south side the Deanery of Peterborough, both impaling Nevile. In the spandrels of the arch are the arms of Trinity College on the north side; and on the south side a bend raguly

---

[1] [It is thus designated in the view of the College dated 1740 (see above, p. 466), where an elevation of the east front of the Gate is given.]

[2] [Sen. Burs. Accounts 1680—81. *Highwayes.*]

with a portcullis on a canton, for W. H. Thompson, D.D., Master; impaling three annulets on a bend cotised (the Selwyn arms), for Mrs Thompson.

It is evident that these arms, with the exception of those of the College, and of the present Master, were selected to commemorate the preferments and the family relations of Dr Nevile. It was mentioned above (p. 519) that there was a gate called "the Red Gate" in the wall which bounded Nevile's Court on the west until 1680—81; and that there was evidence that this gate was of stone, and surmounted by the Royal Arms. It may be conjectured that when the wall was pulled down, the gate was removed to the end of the avenue, and that the above Account may refer to this change of position. This stonework, or part of it, may have been copied by Grumbold, and other coats of arms may have been added to those already in existence on the old Gate.

Nevile's Gate remained in the position shewn by Loggan until 1733, when the Hon. Henry Bromley, of Horseheath, M.P. for Cambridgeshire, presented the handsome pair of iron gates which now serve as the termination of the avenue[1], and Nevile's Gate was removed to what subsequently became the entrance of the Stable Yard, but was then the entrance to the College from Trinity Hall Lane. In 1876 it was placed in its present position.

With the exception of a new plantation, in "the Horse Chestnut Walk" next St John's College, which Mr Harrison the gardener laid out in 1749—50, no change has been introduced into the arrangement of the walks on the west side of the river since 1688 (fig. 7); nor is any renewal of the trees alluded to[2]. We may therefore conclude that the lime-trees, at

---

[1] [Sen. Burs. Accounts 1732—33. *Extraordinaries*. "To Gillam for the carriage of the iron Gates given to the College by the Hon[ble] Henry Bromley Esq[r]. 23. 12. 10." The Junior Bursar charges for fetching them from Mr Bromley's seat at Horseheath; "for work about the new iron Gates next the Field"; and "for Stone and Workmanship at the Gate remov'd from the end of the high walk to the Back Yard."]

[2] [The following entries are worth quotation, as defining certain parts of the walks: Jun. Burs. Accounts 1754—55. "*Expences...behind Frying-Pan-Walk*. For digging planting, [etc.] 4. 4. 6. To M[r] Harrison for Plants 5. 11. 6." Ibid. 1757—58. *Carpenter*. "For fixing Guards to the Young Trees in the Master's and Fellows Quarters." Ibid. 1759—60. *Walks*. "For work in...Planting the Shrubbery in Frying-Pan-Walk 7. 9. 8."]

least in the central avenue, are those planted in 1671—72.   In 1873 it was determined "to plant an Avenue of Oriental Planes outside the present Lime Avenue, with the view of replacing it at a future time."   At the same time plane-trees were planted outside the gates, between the walks and the Fellows' Garden[1].

The grounds on the east bank of the river were laid out in a very different manner in 1688 from what we see at present. Loggan's ground plan and his general view shew an avenue in the same position as the present one, but considerably longer, extending past the south end of the Library, and Dr Babington's addition to Nevile's Court, as far as the Bakehouse.   The ground between the Library and the river appears to have been a meadow, without walks, and partially planted with large trees. South of the avenue, between the Brewhouse and the river, there was a grove of trees planted in regular rows, with a large oval bed in the centre.   Between the Bakehouse and Nevile's Court there were two or three small gardens which certain Fellows had been allowed to make in 1615—16[2].   One of them had belonged, in 1681, to the Vice-Master Dr Chamberlaine ; and another was assigned to Dr Babington and his heirs by the deed executed with him in the same year (p. 523).   A comparison of Loggan's plan with one of later date, as for instance that of Custance, dated 1798, shews these private gardens still in existence.   There was an entrance from the Great Court to Garret Hostel, but it was surrounded by a wall, and there was no passage from it to the walks, or entrance to it from the street. The walks were entered from the College through a passage between the south end of Nevile's Court and the Library.   The ground between the Library and the river was laid out as at present, except that there was no back way into the Master's Lodge ; and the ground to the south of the avenue had become a grass-plot, bounded by a row of trees ; and the Brewhouse was masked by a plantation.

A few notices of the alterations made between 1688 and the present time are worth recording.   They began in 1716—17, when we meet with an "Account of Expenses upon yͤ College Walks and Plantations, done by Dr Hacket by order of Master

1 [Minutes of the Seniority, 28 Nov. 1873.]
2 [College Orders, 18 October 1615, 27 March 1615—16.]

and Seniors[1]." A contemporary narrative of the work, which occurs in the diary of Mr Edward Rud for February 1716—17, is valuable as fixing the date of the plantation of the avenue of lime-trees eastward of the bridge:

"Feb. In this month all the old Elms behind our Library and on each side the walk leading to the bridge were rooted up or fell'd, and a new walk of limes planted there. The hedge towards the river on the south side of the bridge was then also planted, and the walk towards Garret-Hostle lane was then widen'd in order to be planted next year. The north hedge also, and the hedges on each side of the terrasse or high walk were then plash'd, and the western and part of the north ditch piled and planked. Next year not only the south walk was planted on each side, but also the west walk had the old hedges on each side stubb'd up, and new ones planted."

The alteration of the grounds to the north and south of this avenue began in 1746—47, when a plantation of lime-trees was made behind the Brewhouse, and the ground between the Library and the river was levelled[2]. The "New Piece between the Brewhouse and the River" was however not laid out until 1765 —66[3]. In 1758—59 a "new wall on the east side of the River" was built; and in the following year the ground between the river and the Library was laid out with turf and gravel walks. Two years afterwards an attempt was made to ornament the river-bank, as we learn from a payment "to Harrison the Gardner for Planting North-American Poplars, weeping-willows, and other Aquatics, under y[e] wall next the River." These later alterations in the grounds were probably due to the influence of Dr Richard Walker, founder of the Botanic Garden, who was Vice-Master from 1734 to his death in 1764. His taste for horticulture is thus commemorated in a contemporary work[4]:

"And tho' there be no public Garden belonging to the University, *Cambridge* is not destitute of exotic Plants, the *Trinity* Gardener, M[r] *Harrison*, having, by the Direction of D[r] *Walker* the Vice-Master, introduced several Species of foreign Fruits and Flowers, Natives of the warmest Climates; particularly the *Anana* or Pine-apple, the *Banana*, Coffee-shrub, Logwood-tree, the Torch-thistle, the Red Jessamine of the *West Indies*, &c. which are brought to great Perfection

---

[1] [Jun. Burs. Accounts 1716—17. *Extraordinaries.*]

[2] [Ibid. 1746—47. *In the Back part.*]   [3] [Ibid. 1765—66. *Back yard, etc.*]

[4] ["The Foreigner's Companion Through the *Universities* of *Cambridge* and *Oxford.*" By Mr Salmon. London, 1748, p. 67.]

by the Help of a Green-house and Stoves, which Mr *Harrison* has erected in the Doctor's Garden."

The "New Court," or "King's Court," stands upon a considerable portion of the piece between the Brewhouse and the river; but in other respects these grounds have not been altered.

It should be further mentioned that the Fellows' Garden, or "Roundabout," was leased from the University in 1803—4. It was then called the "New Inclosure." It was purchased in 1871[1] for £4,000. The avenue of elms on this ground, in continuation of the central avenue in the walks, was planted by Dr Whewell, Master, at his own expense, in 1843[2].

GARDEN OF THE MASTER'S LODGE.—The extension of the Master's Lodge northwards by Dr Nevile curtailed the garden of about one-third of its area, as may be seen by comparing the map of Hamond (1592) with that of Loggan (1688). The latter further shews some trees growing close to the Lodge on the ground between the gallery and Nevile's Court; and also some cultivated ground, probably a kitchen-garden as at present, at the west end of that ground close to the river.

The pleasure-ground between the gallery and the bowling-green was planted in 1647—48; when, under the heading *Lodgeing*, a charge occurs for "Apple trees, Peare trees, Cypress trees, Vines, Bayes, Woodbinde etc.[3]" When Loggan's print was taken, this ground was laid out in regular flower-beds, with an arbour in the centre, and a fountain containing a statue, placed there in 1677—78[4]. On the west side there was a wall as high as that which divided the garden of the Lodge from the bowling-green. Between this wall and the river-bank sufficient space was left for a building which may be identified with "the Master's Summer House," built in 1684—85[5].

The alterations made in the garden by Dr Bentley, though

---

[1] [Grace, 11 May, 1871. Reporter, pp. 292, 341. Documents in the Registry of the University shew that this ground (with other pieces in Cambridge, Barnwell, and Trumpington, amounting in all to 27 acres) had been given to the University by Nigellus Thornton in the reign of Edward I. In 1555—56 the whole estate was leased as "the Vniuersitie landes"; and in a Terrar, dated 1703, the portion subsequently sold to Trinity College is stated to be "in Carmefield."]

[2] [Sen. Bursar's Minutes 3 Nov. 1843.]   [3] [Jun. Burs. Accounts 1647—48.]

[4] [Sen. Burs. Accounts 1677—78. *Extraordinaries.* "To Francis Hurrey for a Statue in the Master's Garden 02. 10. 00."]   [5] [Ibid. 1684—85.]

most of them have been removed, must be briefly noticed. In 1718—19 the old summer-house was replaced by a more spacious building, containing a bath, supplied, as it is said, from the Conduit. At the same time the high wall next the river was pulled down, and the ground laid out as a terrace, which became Dr Bentley's favourite walk for the remainder of his life. The cost of these alterations, and Bentley's manner of conducting them, were severely criticised, especially by Dr Conyers Middleton, who wrote in 1720:

"But to shew how well he can preserve his Character, and that he is still the same Man he was near twenty Years ago; the very last Year he squander'd at least *five hundred Pounds of the College Money*, in the improvement of his Garden, the building a sort of a Banquetting-house there, the making a Terrass-walk upon the River, and some other things of great Expence and no Use to the College; and tho' it is the *express Command of the Statutes*, and has always been the Custom of the College, that the junior *Bursar* shall not expend any considerable Sum, even in the most necessary Repairs of the House, without the *particular Order of a majority of the Seniors*, and shall himself be oblig'd to pay for all the Expence he makes without such Authority; yet all this was done not only without *their Order*, but without their being so much as *made acquainted* with it[1]."

The charges for these works, and for a subsequent undertaking of Dr Bentley's, when he built, or fitted up, "*a spacious Granary* near his own Lodgings at the expence of the College[2]," occur in the Junior Bursar's Accounts from 1718—19 to 1721—22, but as they are intermixed with those for other buildings, the total cannot be estimated. The Bath-house, which seems to have been constructed principally of wood, was pulled down in 1771—72[3]. It was probably situated on the west side of the garden, in such a position as to leave room for the terrace between it and the river[4].

The present arrangements of the garden are due to Dr Whewell. The geometrical flower-beds on the north side were designed by Professor Willis.

BOWLING-GREEN.—This ground, which was the garden of

---

[1] ["A TRUE ACCOUNT OF THE PRESENT STATE OF TRINITY COLLEGE IN CAMBRIDGE, Under the Oppressive Government of their Master RICHARD BENTLEY late D.D." 8vo. London 1720. p. 19. Compare Monk's Bentley, ii. 24.]

[2] [Middleton, ut supra, p. 31.]   [3] [Jun. Burs. Accounts 1771—72. *Bricklayer*.]

[4] [The position assigned to it on the plan (fig. 9) has been determined by foundations discovered in the garden at the same time as those of the Gallery.]

King's Hall, as explained in Chapter II., naturally became the
Fellows' Garden of Trinity College; and the various charges
for planting that garden may be referred to it. It should be
mentioned, however, that there are also entries for work done
to "the Seniors' Garden" and "the Seniors' Orchard" which
seem to imply a separate piece of ground, the position of which
cannot now be ascertained.

The bowling-green was first made in 1647—48, when a
payment is made "to ye Workemen in earnest for ye Bowling
Greene[1]"; and various entries in subsequent years shew that
it was always in the same place. On the west side, next the
river, there was a summer-house (fig. 7), in front of which were
two seats, put up in 1667—68[2], and on the north and south sides
there seem to have been flower-beds as at present. The summer-house was pulled down in 1796.

Dr Bentley was desirous of annexing the bowling-green to
the garden of the Master's Lodge, to which it would have made
a very convenient addition. His attempt was made one of the
Articles against him presented to the Bishop of Ely in 1710:

"Why did you endeavour to take away from the College and apply
to your own use the College Bowling-green and Summer-house, and other
convenient Houses in or near the said Bowling-green?"

The scheme was steadily opposed by the Fellows; and the
Master, after vainly trying to obtain their consent by privately
soliciting individuals, was obliged to abandon his design[3]. It was
in this part of the College that the "Lumber-Hole," as Dr Bentley
termed it, was situated, which he fitted up as a laboratory for the
use of John Francis Vigani, who in 1703 was created the first

---

[1] [Jun. Burs. Accounts 1647—48. *Extraordinaries.*]

[2] [Jun. Burs. Accounts 1667—68. *Extraordinarys.* "For making ye two seat
in ye garden and ye garden dore 8. 17. 0.   For Hony suckles and sweet brier to sett
in ye garden Hedge o. 5. o."]

[3] ["Some remarks upon a letter entituled *The Present State of* Trinity
College in Cambridge. By Mr Miller Fellow of the College," 8vo. London, 1710.
p. 68. "The College, as most other Colleges, have had for many Years a bowling
Green, which costs about 5*l.* a Year, where there is a Summer-house, and other
Conveniencies, this he had a Mind to have to enlarge his Garden, and when he
closeted and teaz'd a great many for their Consent, and could not get it that way; he
said, *he was Lord of the Soil,* and would have it: But his Head being taken up with
more advantagious Projects for himself, the College do yet enjoy their Bowling
Green." See also Notes and Queries, 13 Aug. 1881.]

Professor of Chemistry[1]. The following Order, the terms of which are said to have been selected with the express purpose of preventing any future encroachments by the Master, shews that the laboratory occupied the ground floor of the old buildings of King's Hall, on the east side of the bowling-green.

"Febr. 11th 1706—7. Orderd...yt the low Chamber under ye Old Hostle adjoyning to ye Gate be made and fitted into a Laboratory for ye use of Chymistry, and Physic and Philosophical Experiments; and yt it never be converted to any other use."

The following quotation from a contemporary pamphlet illustrates the feeling excited by the fitting-up of this room:

"I'll tell you, Sir, a piece of secret History concerning this *Lumber-Hole*. This *Lumber-Hole* you must know, Sir, lies just upon the edge of a *Bowling-Green* that belongs to the *Fellows;* which *Bowling-Green* that belongs to the Fellows, is parted but by a Brick-Wall, from a certain *Garden* that belongs to the *Master;* Which Master, Dr *Bentley* by Name, having, as appears, a very notable projecting Head, thought it wou'd be a mighty pretty thing if he cou'd contrive it so as to justle out the *Fellows,* and lay this same *Bowling-Green* into his *Own* Garden: But the Fellows were not then in a Humour to be so serv'd. Cou'd it have been brought about, nothing in the World wou'd have been more Commodious than this *Old Lumber-Hole*. For if the Design had not miscarry'd, Then had this old *Lumber-Hole* been an *Elegant Green-House* for Dr Bentley: But since they wou'd not do *That,* He resolv'd He'd be even with 'em for their *Stubbornness;* and if it cost them a *Hundred Pounds* the *Lumber-Hole* shou'd be made, and Constituted, and for ever after call'd, an *Elegant, Chymical Laboratory*. I am none of those who glory in despising and running down *Chymical* Observations and Experiments; but yet with regard to this so famous *Laboratory* of Ours, I have talk'd with those that have gone the Courses, and they *All* seem to be of Opinion, That as those Matters are manag'd, the *Learned* World is not like to reap any mighty Profit or Advantage from any thing that is *There* taught[2]."

It may be concluded from these extracts that the chamber fitted up as a Laboratory was on the ground floor in the old west range of King's Hall. Part of this space is now used for wine cellars; part is still a lumber-room.]

---

[1] [Bentley's own version of this affair has been quoted above, p. 616.]

[2] [Blomer's Full View, p. 119. See also Articles against Dr Bentley, § xxiv.]

CHAPTER VI.

HISTORY OF THE KING'S COURT, OR NEW COURT; AND OF THE MASTER'S COURTS.

[AFTER the completion of Neville's Court, as related in Chapter IV., no addition to the College buildings was made, or, so far as we know, even suggested, until the beginning of the nineteenth century. The duty of providing additional rooms for undergraduates, the number of whom had largely ᵼncreased after the peace of 1817[1], was urged upon the College by Dr Christopher Wordsworth, immediately after his appointment to the Mastership in 1820; and the following Order was entered in the Conclusion Book:

" December 14, 1820. The expediency of making an increase of Chambers in consequence of the great increase of admissions, and with a further view of bringing the Students to reside wholly within the Walls of the College, and of remedying the inconveniences now experienced from undefined and excessive admissions, having been taken into consideration :

It was ordered that Mr Watford be employed to take a ground plot of the present site of the College, and of the contiguous premises.

Ordered at the same time, that it be referred to the two Bursars, and the Steward (in conjunction with the Master, and, in his absence, with the Vice Master) to procure information, and to report to the Board, their opinion of the best means of carrying the above design into effect.

Chr. Wordsworth, M.C."

Three sites presented themselves for consideration : (1) the Scholars' Green, as the southern half of Garret Hostel Green was then called ; (2) the Bowling Green[2]; (3) the space between the Great Court and Trinity Street. The last of these having been dismissed as impracticable, the College officers mentioned in the above Order proceeded to consider the two former. The following passages from a draft Report drawn up by the Master

---

[1] [History of Corpus Christi College, Vol. i. 302. The number of undergraduates who matriculated at this period was: 1817, 299; 1818, 334; 1819, 423; and in each of the next ten years an average of 439.]

[2] [A scheme for building on this site was suggested by Daniel Cresswell, M.A., Fellow.]

in February, 1821[1], are valuable as shewing the care taken in preparing the scheme:

"It appears to us upon an inspection of the Ground Plan, made by Mr Watford according to the directions of the Board at the last meeting, that only two spots present themselves as eligible for additional buildings; which are, first the Scholars' Green; and secondly, the Bowling Green.

That we prefer the former; and are of opinion that it is desirable that the whole increase of buildings should take place there, unless it be found, on further examination, that it is necessary for want of room to occupy both situations.

In order to form some judgment on this head we next considered what number of sets of chambers it may be desirable that the College should possess, the number at present being taken at 120.

It appears to us that the Hall and Chapel respectively are sufficiently capacious for the reception of a body in commons of 300 or thereabouts. The largest number in commons in the October Term 1820 amounted to 354; in the October Term 1821 to 374.

On this basis, and to secure the important result, that none should be in Lodgings in the Town for any longer time than the first term, we think it desirable that the whole number of sets of chambers should be raised to 280 or thereabouts.

With respect to this part of our inquiries, we are inclined to think it probable that a Quadrangle might be built on the Scholars' Green, by taking in the addition of a small portion of the Stable Yard, which, if consisting of two stories, together with a basement-floor, and garrets, might contain 160 sets of rooms, or thereabouts."

It was further suggested in the Report that a competent architect should be consulted; that the building should be "of a handsome stile, substantial and durable"; and that subscriptions might be resorted to as a means of raising the necessary funds. The following Orders resulted from this Report. The execution of the work was not submitted to competition, but was entrusted to William Wilkins, Architect:

"March 9, 1821. Ordered that Mr Wilkins, the Architect, be instructed to inspect the Ground Plan of the College, and to report his opinion of the site or sites most suitable for new buildings, and to give a plan or plans for 160 sets of rooms or thereabouts.

With respect to the Buildings he is to be instructed that they should be of a handsome, appropriate stile; substantial and durable, and of the best materials—the estimate being given first in Brick, plain—secondly in Brick, faced with cement—thirdly in Brick, with stone casings.

Chr. Wordsworth, M.C."

---

[1] [This paper is in the Master's handwriting, and endorsed by him "Draft of Report to the Board, agreed on at a meeting of Master and Bursars, Feb. 12, 1821."]

Mr Wilkins prepared his plans without loss of time, for he sent them to the Master in May, 1821[1], and the Orders made after they had been considered shew that they were generally approved :

"June 9, 1821.   The plans for the new Buildings being taken into consideration ;

It was ordered that, with a view of ascertaining the probable expence as nearly as may be, Mr Wilkins be directed to prepare a Specification, and estimate, together with the Working Drawings, if necessary, for such parts of the Plan, as respect the additional accommodation for Students—reserving the questions with respect to the stile of the Stables and Brew-House, for further consideration.

Chr. Wordsworth, M.C."

"June 13, 1821.   Mr Wilkins attended, and received his Instructions, according to the directions of the last meeting, of the Master and Seniors."

The scheme, however, notwithstanding this rapid progress at the commencement, was not finally adopted for nearly two years.   It encountered serious opposition from some of the Senior Fellows, who not unnaturally were alarmed at the magnitude of the undertaking, as revealed by the estimate.   It was objected[2] that a quadrangle on that particular site would do "irreparable injury to the beauty of the College"; that it would be detrimental to the Society in general by entailing the destruction of buildings essential to their convenience and comfort, as the Brewhouse, the Stables, and other offices, and to those Fellows in particular who resided in the South Cloister; that it would violate "a solemn compact for Dr Babington's Garden[3]"; and lastly, that the possession of Scholars' Green was doubtful.   Moreover, reasons were brought forward against commencing any new work of such importance at that time on account of the general distress of the country and the consequent diminution of the College revenue; the want of any resources except an unwarrantable advance in room rents; and a "probable diminution of the number of Admissions, arising (1) from the aggravated expenses of the University; (2) the not improbable preference which may be given to a foreign

---

[1] [Mr Wilkins' letter, describing and justifying his plan, is dated 12 May, 1821.]

[2] [These objections are taken from a "Copy of the paper produced at the meeting of the Master and Seniors Dec. 29, 1821, by Mr Lambert."]

[3] [The agreement with Dr Babington was quoted above, p. 523.]

education." Under these circumstances the Master felt obliged
to withdraw the scheme for a time, in the hope that by allowing a longer period "for consideration and conversation, some
of the disinclination which was apparent in the minds of several
of the Seniors might be abated, and the Plan be adopted with
general concurrence [1]." This result was achieved in May, 1823 [2].
The following Order marks the adoption of the scheme, and
defines the method of obtaining the necessary funds:

"May 17, 1823. The Plans for new Buildings, prepared by Mr
Wilkins, in pursuance of the Order of the Board, having been taken into
consideration, it was

Agreed by the Master and Seniors that the same be approved of,
and that the necessary steps be taken for carrying them into effect—the
eight sets marked 29 and 30 being omitted [3].

Agreed at the same time,

That the money requisite for the completion of the Design be
raised partly by subscription, and partly by Loan under the authority of
Parliament if found necessary.

That the money to be procured by Loan, be raised on Bonds under
the College Seal, the Bonds being drawn transferable and redeemable
at the pleasure of the College (the order of redemption to be determined
by Lot) on twelve months notice given to the Holders, and paying an
interest not exceeding 5 per cent per annum; or, that the money be
borrowed in such other way as shall be judged more expedient.

That in regard to the Subscription to be promoted among the present and former Members of the Society and the Public in general: it
be a condition of such Subscription that the Rents of a number of Sets
of the new Apartments bearing the same proportion to their whole
number, as the money so subscribed shall bear to the whole cost of the
undertaking, shall be appropriated to the augmentation and improvement
of the Ecclesiastical Benefices in the Patronage of the Society, through
the medium of Queen Anne's Bounty or otherwise—and to the establish-

---

[1] [These words are quoted from a speech which the Master made to the Seniority,
of which a rough draft has been preserved.]

[2] [The Master's scheme had been submitted to the Board in nearly identical terms,
29 December, 1821 and 25 June, 1822. He notes in a Journal which he kept of what
took place with reference to the New Buildings:

"May 17, 1823. Brought forward my Propositions for the New Buildings (a
third time). All carried. *For.* Master, Messrs Greenwood, G. A. Browne, Carr,
John Brown, Judgson. *Against.* V. Master [J. H. Renouard], Messrs Pugh, Mac-
farlan. In the Evening saw the Architect Mr Wilkins and communicated to him the
result, reading to him the Orders out of the Conclusion Book. Gave him the specification to transcribe and return to me."]

[3] [The part of the plan thus designated was a detached building, containing eight
sets of rooms, which Mr Wilkins proposed to erect between Bishop's Hostel and the
east range of his new Court.]

ment of a Domus Fund to be applied in aid of any extraordinary and extensive reparation or improvement of the College ; and

That the sum of £2000 sterling be subscribed in the name of ' The Master Fellows and Scholars ' from the Old South Sea Annuities in the possession of the College, as a benefaction to the above Subscription Fund.

That the rents accruing from the remainder of the new Apartments, and from a reasonable advance upon the Rents of such of the existing sets of Rooms as are not occupied by members of the Foundation, be set apart for the payment of the Interest of the sums to be borrowed, and for the gradual liquidation and discharge of the Principal.

That, for further protection against any undue risk in this great undertaking, no Work be entered upon until a contract be signed by a competent Builder, with full and sufficient security for the accomplishment of the whole, according to the specification, and with the best materials. at a charge not exceeding forty thousand Pounds.

That the College having entered into a Lease with the Corporation, bearing date June 21, 1791 for part of the Scholers Green, at an annual rent of a Pepper-Corn for 999 years, application be forthwith made to the Corporation to enfranchise the Ground comprised under that Lease[1]."

A circular soliciting subscriptions was at once issued. It was drawn up by the Master; and the following passage may be cited, as shewing the reasons which influenced him and his supporters in urging the scheme upon the College at that particular time:

" They [the Master and Fellows] have been led to undertake this extensive design (which cannot be executed without personal sacrifices on their own part), by a consideration of the serious evils arising from the Lodging of great numbers of Young Men in the Town ; which evils, briefly, are : *increased expence ; scanty accommodations*, and consequent *unhealthiness* in some of the Lodging-Houses ; and the impossibility of preserving the same degree of salutary *superintendance* and *discipline*, and the same undisturbed *opportunities* for *study*, which are in an eminent degree, the advantages and privileges of an English University."

The answers, of which a large number have been preserved, shew that those who had been educated at the College were much gratified at the prospect of an immediate increase in its buildings ; and notwithstanding the agricultural distress then prevalent, which is mentioned in several letters as a reason for not subscribing at all, or for sending a comparatively small sum, rather more than £9000 was collected in the course of a few months, in addition to the sum given by the College in its

---

[1] [The acquisition of this ground was related above, p. 413.]

corporate capacity.   King George the Fourth gave £1000;
whereupon the Master, in writing to Lord Liverpool to acknowledge the donation, preferred a request on behalf of the College
that the new Quadrangle might be "designated either by the
name of 'Brunswick Court' or of 'King's Court' in honour of
His Majesty[1]."   The latter name was selected; but the court is
now usually known as the " New Court."

The circular was not issued until the end of May, 1823; but
it was determined not to wait for subscriptions, but to begin at
once, probably in order to take advantage of the summer.   A
contract was signed 26 June, 1823, with Mr Spicer Crowe,
Builder, of London, who bound himself to begin on or before
the first day of July; to have the buildings roofed by 10
November, 1824, and "wholly completed, finished, and ready for
occupation" by 10 October, 1825.   Mr Crowe came to Cambridge with his men on Thursday, 10 July, and commenced
operations on the following day by cutting down the trees
growing on the ground[2].   The formal ceremony of laying the
first stone took place on the King's birthday, Tuesday, 12
August.   His Majesty was represented by the Speaker of the
House of Commons, the Right Honourable Manners Sutton,
M.P.   The following description of what took place has been
abridged from The Cambridge Chronicle:

" The members of the University assembled in the Senate House at
half-past one o'clock, where fruit and wine was provided for their refreshment.   At two o'clock, the academic body, in full costume, left the
Senate House in procession.

On arriving at the King's Gate, the procession was received by the
Master, Dr Wordsworth, the Fellows, and all the resident members of
the college.   A band of music, stationed within the gate, instantly
struck up *God save the King;* and the collegiate procession having advanced, the academic body joined the train.   The whole then proceeded
through the Great Court into Nevile's Court, where, turning to the right,

[1] [The Master and Seniors returned their formal thanks to the King for this donation, 8 August, 1823, when it was further agreed "that a humble request be made that
his Majesty would be graciously pleased to permit the New Quadrangle to be designated by the name of Brunswick Court, in honour of his Majesty."   In a letter of the
same date, however, to Lord Liverpool, the Master suggests the alternative names as
above related; and Lord Liverpool in his reply (15 August) states that the King " has
no objection to the New Quadrangle at Trinity College being designated as The
King's Court."]

[2] [These dates are supplied by the Master's diary above quoted.]

and passing under the Library, time was given for a very numerous assemblage of ladies, who had witnessed the procession from the Master's Lodge, to occupy the south cloister.

The members of the procession having taken their respective stations on the ground, the Rev. James Scholefield, M.A., Fellow, delivered a Latin oration. The Speaker, addressing the Master of Trinity, then delivered an appropriate oration in English.

The upper part of the foundation-stone having been elevated, the Master presented the gold, silver, and copper coins of the present reign to the Speaker, who placed them in the cavity prepared for their reception, and covered it with a plate bearing this inscription :

QVOD . FELIX . FAVSTVM . QVE . SIT
IN . HONOREM
SANCTÆ . ET . INDIVIDVÆ . TRINITATIS
ATQVE
AD . ECCLESIÆ . ET . REIPVBLICÆ
EMOLVMENTVM
EX . DECRETO . MAGISTRI . ET . SENIORVM
FAVENTE . ITEM . RELIQVO . SOCIORVM
ET . DISCIPVLORVM . CŒTV
HÆC . NOVARVM . ÆDIVM . FVNDAMENTA
JACIEBAT
VIR . HONORATISSIMVS
CAROLVS . MANNERS . SVTTON
JVSSV . REGIS . AVGVSTISSIMI
GEORGII IV.
VICEM . IPSIVS . GERENS
PRIDIE . IDVS . SEXTILIS
M.DCCC.XXIII.

The two parts of the stone having been fastened together, and the whole raised to a proper height, the architect, William Wilkins, Esq., handed a silver trowel to the Master, who presented it to the Speaker. The latter having spread the mortar, the stone was lowered, the band playing *Rule Britannia.* He next applied the level, the square, and the plumb-line, in the customary form, and concluded the ceremony by striking the stone with the mallet. The Master then offered the following prayer :

' O Lord God Almighty! holy, blessed, and glorious Trinity! three persons, and one only true God ; the fountain of all wisdom, and giver of every good and perfect gift; who stretchest out the heavens like a curtain, and layest the beams of thy chambers in the waters; thou without whose blessing the builder labours but in vain; hear us, we beseech thee, according to thy great goodness, in heaven thy dwelling place, and sanctify this work, which in an humble dependence upon thee, we have now auspiciously begun. Further, we pray thee, the labours of our hands with thy continual help; and accomplish the same to that good end for which they are designed—the encrease of thy honour and glory. May the enlargement of our borders tend, through thy grace, to the promotion and stability of the true Christian religion in this realm and in foreign lands ; to the extirpation of errors and false opinions ; to the growth of sound learning, virtue, and piety; and to the common welfare and prosperity of this Church and Nation.

Bless, we beseech thee, those benefactors who contribute to this good work. We implore an especial blessing upon thy servant our Sovereign; let his days be many, and his reign happy and glorious to himself and his people. Continue him in thy fear and love: and, this life ended, crown him with unfading glory in the life to come, through Jesus Christ our Lord.

Together with these our supplications, we offer unto thee our humble and hearty thanks for thy manifold mercies, bestowed continually upon this ancient house, dedicated to thine ever-blessed name. We praise thee for our Royal founder, and for all our Royal and pious benefactors, humbly beseeching thee that as they in their times charitably bestowed for our comfort the temporal things thou gavest them, so we, in our time, may faithfully use the same to the setting forth of thy Holy Word, thy laud, and praise: and that, finally, we with all thy servants departed this life in thy true faith and fear, may dwell with thee in glory; having a building of God, a house not made with hands, eternal in the heavens. Grant this, O merciful Father, for Jesus Christ's sake, thy Son our Saviour. Amen.'

The anthem *Praise the Lord O Jerusalem,* was then sung by the choir; after which the Vice-Chancellor [Henry Godfrey, B.D., President of Queens' College] pronounced the benediction; and the ceremony concluded with the national anthem of *God save the King,* in which the assembled multitude enthusiastically joined, following it by hearty cheers[1]."

The buildings were occupied in the Michaelmas Term, 1825, notwithstanding delays occasioned by unforeseen circumstances: as, the difficulties of obtaining secure foundations; additions ordered during the progress of the works; and an accidental fire which broke out 10 December, 1824[2].

The dimensions and position of the new quadrangle will be readily understood from the plan (fig. 9); and the style from the engraving (fig. 48). Mr Wilkins had prepared an alternative design in a classical style, at least for the west front, to harmonize with the Library, but it does not appear to have met with any support. We are, however, without information as to the steps by which the present design came to be adopted, or whether it was much modified before it was finally approved. The north side is formed by the south range of Nevile's Court;

---

[1] [See also Dr Whewell's Life, by Mrs Stair Douglas, p. 90, and Memoir of the late Rev. James Scholefield, 8vo. London, 1855, p. 32.]

[2] [Cooper's Annals, iv. 545. The contractor tried to obtain an extension of time, which was refused by the Master, 11 July, 1825. Some of the rooms appear to have been occupied in 1824, as the Accounts set down £342. 5s. 0d. for rent received at Christmas, 1824; but it is evident that the whole must have been finished at the specified time, as £3154. 2s. 6d. was received for rent at Christmas, 1825.]

I.A.Bell.

J.Le Keux.

Fig. 48.   Interior of the King's Court, or New Court, Trinity College, looking north-west : from Le Keux's Memorials of Cambridge, ed. Cooper.

Vol. II.

the remaining three sides by ranges of chambers, each in three floors, with garrets in the roof. These three ranges contain 110 sets of rooms, including the garrets. Mr Wilkins intended at first that the arch on the west side of the court should be exactly opposite to that on the east side ; and with the view of attaining that exact symmetry which he considered essential for the success of architectural compositions, he divided his west front into a central portion with wings, and pierced the former with two arches, one of which was to serve as a carriage-way, the other to be merely ornamental.

The south side of Nevile's Court was ingeniously remodelled so as to make it harmonize in style with the new buildings. The windows of the chambers were slightly altered by the addition of drip-molds ; those of the staircases were increased in size, and richly ornamented ; the walls were subdivided by string-courses, and terminated by battlements. Lastly, octagonal turrets were added to the projecting staircases, which were connected by a cloister. In the first design this cloister extended for the whole distance between the east and west ranges of the new court, interrupted only by the blocks of building which contain the staircases ; but this arrangement was modified during the progress of the work, for the sake of obtaining additional chambers, and the cloister was limited to the space between the two central staircases[1]. We have seen that it was at first intended that the material employed should be brick or stone. This scheme was unfortunately abandoned, probably on the ground of expense ; and it was provided in the contract that the west front only should be faced with Ketton stone ; and that the east front, and the whole of the interior, should be worked in Roman cement. The south side next Garret Hostel Lane was left of plain white brick.

The extent of the new buildings required that the old Brewhouse, a Stable and Coach-house assigned to the Master, part of the College Stables, part of the offices of the Kitchen, and a Lecture Room should be pulled down, and reconstructed with the old materials. The Brewhouse and Kitchen offices were transferred to their present position; the College Stables, somewhat diminished in extent, formed two sides of a yard behind

---

[1] [This cloister, which was constructed of cement throughout, was removed in 1868.]

Bishop's Hostel until 1876, as described above; and the Master's Stables were rebuilt at the east end of the Library, on ground which had previously been part of the Master's Garden.

It was provided by the contract that these works should be executed for £37,700; but, as is usual with such undertakings, the cost considerably exceeded the estimate. When the Accounts were balanced it appeared that the expenses amounted to £50,444. 8s. 2d.; out of which total £45,401. 19s. 7d. had been paid to the builder, and £2,244 to the architect. The receipts were £50,589. 12s. 4d. The subscriptions had amounted to £12,351. 16s. 4d.; and the greater part of the remainder had been raised by loan[1].

The two quadrangles opposite to the Great Gate, called "The Master's Courts," though belonging to Dr Whewell's trust, must yet be regarded as a part of the College buildings, and their history must be briefly narrated.

The site is bounded on the east by part of Bridge Street, there called Sidney Street; on the north by All Saints' Passage, formerly called Dolphin Lane; on the west by Trinity Street; and on the south by dwelling-houses. Dr Whewell, by Will dated 17 December, 1863, bequeathed this site with the buildings erected, or to be erected, upon it, in trust to Trinity College for the "reception and habitation" of its members; and, secondly, for the endowment of eight scholarships and a Professorship in International Law[2].

Dr Whewell had commenced the acquisition of this site before 1849, by purchasing a property opposite to the Great Gate, on which "The Sun" Inn had formerly stood. He next acquired, from Jesus College, the houses adjoining it on the east; and in 1859, after vainly endeavouring to acquire the property to the south of his first purchase, which would have increased the frontage towards Trinity Street, and to induce the College to assist him

---

[1] ["Oct. 22, 1824. Agreed...that a sum of £33,000 be borrowed from the Commissioners of the Exchequer Bill Loan for encouragement of Public Works, to defray the extra charge of erecting the Kings Court, in addition to the money raised by subscriptions (£11,000 or thereabouts)." In 1826 £4000 more was borrowed from the same Commissioners. The rest was composed of small loans, with £47. 13s. 4d. derived from the sale of the trees.]

[2] [Dr Whewell's Will, in which his intentions are set forth at full, is printed in Trusts, Statutes, etc. of the University, ed. 1876.]

in his concurrent schemes of building and endowment, he determined to wait no longer, but to erect a Hostel himself. A
design was prepared, under his direction, by Mr Salvin; and
the smaller of the two courts, containing twenty-five sets of
rooms, was completed in the course of the summer of 1860.
Dr Whewell next acquired the ground intervening between this
court and Bridge Street, and before the end of 1865 the design
for the second and larger court, which contains seventy sets of
rooms, had been prepared by the same architect. The contract
was signed a short time before Dr Whewell's death, which took
place 6 March, 1866. The buildings were completed in 1868,
and occupied in the Michaelmas Term of that year. The value
of this benefaction could not have been less than £100,000[1].]

---

[1] [These details and dates are derived from the Life of Dr Whewell by Mrs Stair
Douglas, Chapter x.]

CHRONOLOGICAL SUMMARY.

MICHAEL HOUSE AND KING'S HALL.

1324.	Michael House.	Purchase of Roger de Bouttetourte's house by Hervey de Stanton (16 March).
	Michael House.	Royal license to Hervey de Stanton to place his scholars in a house which he had bought, and to assign to them the advowson of S. Michael's Church (1 June).
1326.	Michael House.	Purchase of Adam de Trumpyngton's house by Hervey de Stanton.
1327.	Michael House.	Death of Hervey de Stanton.
1329.	Michael House.	Purchase of the Hostels of Ovyng and Garyte by John de Illegh, one of Hervey de Stanton's executors.
1336.	King's Hall.	Order to Thomas de Lacy to put the King's scholars into possession of Croyland's house (12 April).
		Croyland conveys his house to the King (24 October).
1337.	Michael House.	Purchase of Crouched Hall by John de Illegh.
	King's Hall.	Patent for the foundation of the College (7 October).
1338.	King's Hall.	Croyland's house repaired by Thomas Powys.
1339.	King's Hall.	Order to Mayor of Cambridge and Thomas Powys to buy houses (20 March).
	King's Hall.	Royal order to Sheriff of Cambridge to provide carriage for the timber required for repairs (23 April).
	King's Hall.	Queen Philippa and Lady Elizabeth de Burgh present timber (10 May).
	King's Hall.	Edmund de Walsyngham sells his garden to the King (22 September).
	King's Hall.	Prior and Canons of S. Edmund sell to Thomas Powys the lane leading from their house to the river (1 November).
1341.	King's Hall.	Henry de Gretford sells his garden to the King (3 January).
	King's Hall.	Letters patent granting to King's Hall 7 pieces of ground for the enlargement of the site (17 January).
1342.	King's Hall.	Advowsons of Felmersham, Hyntlesham, Grendon, and Great S. Mary's, Cambridge, granted by Edward III. (25 July).
1344.	King's Hall.	Thomas de Totyngton sells Walsyngham's house to the King (15 April).
1346.	King's Hall.	Walsyngham's house fitted up as a Brewhouse.
1349.	Michael House.	S. Katherine's Hostel bequeathed by Johanna Refham.
1350.	King's Hall.	Thomas de Cambridge sells his house to the King (12 March).
1351.		Thomas de Mortimer sells his void ground, otherwise called Cornhythe, to the King (22 May).
		Thomas de Totyngton sells his own house in High Street to the King (9 June).

1353.	Michael House.	Purchase of the Archdeacon's house.
1363.	King's Hall.	Building of a new wall of enclosure next the river.
1375.	King's Hall.	Rebuilding of the College on a new site commenced.
1376.	King's Hall.	Purchase of William Atte Conduit's house.
1386.	King's Hall.	New Kitchen begun.
1387.	King's Hall.	New Hall begun.
1390.	King's Hall.	New Hall finished.
1393.	King's Hall.	Agreement with S. John's Hospital about a wall.
1396.	Michael House.	Acquisition of S. Margaret's Hostel.
1411—15.	King's Hall.	New Bakehouse built.
1416—22.	King's Hall.	New Library and new chambers adjoining the Master's chamber built.
1417.	King's Hall.	The Priory of S. Edmund lease a garden at the corner of Foul Lane and King's Hall Lane, and a void ground in High Street.
1418—20.	King's Hall.	Cloister and Oratory built.
1422—27.	King's Hall.	Parlour mentioned as being built.
1423.	Michael House.	Permission from the Town of Cambridge to make a ditch from the common ditch at the west end of the garden to the river.
1427.	King's Hall.	King Edward's Gate-house, Master's chamber, and other chambers and studies commenced.
1429.	King's Hall.	The Priory of S. Edmund lease their tenement in High Street.
	Michael House.	Rules for the assignment of chambers made by John Otryngham.
1430.	Michael House.	The Town of Cambridge lease part of the south-east corner of Garret Hostel Green for one hundred years (8 May).
	King's Hall.	The Priory of Chiksand lease their house at the corner of High Street and King's Hall Lane (29 September).
1433.	King's Hall.	Purchase of messuage from S. John's Hospital (14 January).
		Grant of the east half of King's Hall Lane from the Town of Cambridge (8 April).
		Purchase of part of the garden of S. Katherine's Hostel from Michael House (12 April).
1434.	Michael House.	The Town lease "le Millestones."
1437.	King's Hall.	King Edward's Gate finished.
1438.	King's Hall.	Old buildings pulled down (29 November) and sold.
1439.	King's Hall.	Tower near the new gate begun at expense of Master.
	King's Hall.	New kitchen called *Coquina Regis* built.
	King's Hall.	Letters patent, rehearsing an inquisition held at Babraham to inquire into the rights of the Franciscans to ground purchased by them 5 November, 1325, for a conduit, and to the pipe laid down by them, May 1327 (5 May).
1441.	King's Hall.	Letters patent, confirming King's Hall Lane and the aqueduct to the College (31 May).

1445.	King's Hall.	Visit of King Henry the Sixth (October).
1447.	King's Hall.	Visit of King Henry the Sixth (between Lady Day and Easter).
1448.	Michael House.	Part of Hennably granted by King Henry the Sixth.
1448—49.	King's Hall.	Visit of King Henry the Sixth.
1449.	King's Hall.	Richard Pyghtesley sells his house called "The Tyled Hostel" to King Henry the Sixth (9 May).
1452—53.	King's Hall.	Visit of King Henry the Sixth.
1453.	King's Hall.	A brick wall built to enclose the newly purchased ground.
1464—85.	King's Hall.	Separate Chapel built.
1467.	Michael House.	Sale of S. Margaret's Hostel to Gonvile Hall.
1473.	Michael House.	Sale of a portion of S. Katherine's Hostel to William Malster.
1476.	Michael House.	Sale of S. Katherine's Hostel to Matthew Chambre.
1490—92.	King's Hall.	Porter's lodge built.
1493.	Michael House.	Dame Edith Chambre bequeaths S. Katherine's Hostel.
1497.	Michael House.	John Fisher, Bishop of Rochester, gives £110 to a new building.
1498—99.	King's Hall.	Consecration of the Chapel.
1518—19.	King's Hall.	Great Gateway Tower begun.
1524.	King's Hall.	Gateway finished (29 March).
1528—29.	King's Hall.	Work resumed on Great Gateway Tower.
1535.	King's Hall.	Great Gateway Tower finished.
1542.	Michael House.	Purchase of "le Millestones" from the Town.

TRINITY COLLEGE.

1546.	Charter granted by King Henry the Eighth (9 December).
1547.	Hall and Buttery repaired.
1547.	Negotiations to purchase ground behind the College from the Town.
1550—51.	Part of Michael House pulled down.
1551—52.	The Gates of Michael House and Physwick Hostel walled up; part of Physwick Hostel pulled down; part fitted up to receive the Duchess of Suffolk.
1552.	Planting of Garret Hostel Green.
1553.	Conduit-pipe brought out into the Great Court.
1554.	Commission of Philip and Mary for the building of the College (24 October).
1554.	Master's gallery built.
1554—55.	Range of chambers between King Edward's Gate and the west side of the quadrangle, including Master's turret and chambers, built. New Buttery and Kitchen in progress at the same time.
1555.	Agreement with Perse to build the walls of the Chapel (Michaelmas).
1556.	Indenture with Stephen Wallis for the stalls and roof of the Chapel (30 April).
1556—57.	The range between the Chapel and the Great Gate in progress.
1559—60.	Mr Russell and Mr Dickenson come from London to supervise the work at the Chapel.

1560.	Commission of Queen Elizabeth for the building of a Chapel and Library (14 December).
1560—61.	The roof of the old Chapel is taken down.
1564.	The roof of the Chapel put on. Inscription at East end.
1565—66.	The Organ-screen is being set up.
1566.	Last payment to Wallis (28 April).
1566—67.	Brewhouse, millhouse, and other offices built.
1567.	Last payment to labourers for the Chapel.
1571.	Wooden gallery for the Fellows built; new Parlour mentioned.
1576—77.	Furniture provided for "the newe parlour."
1589—90.	Repairs done to "the causey into the feilds."
1593.	Dr Thomas Nevile made Master.
1597.	Statue of Queen Elizabeth placed over the Queen's Gate.
1598—99.	Great Gate heightened; east and south sides of great quadrangle completed.
1599.	Court levelled; timber removed; sawpit filled up.
1599—1600.	Library-Range completed. King Edward's gateway pulled down and rebuilt at the west end of the Chapel. Foundation laid of the great dining-room in the Lodge.
1600—1.	Work at the Master's Lodge proceeding.
1600—1.	Rails set up in the Court. Battlements added to Chambers.
1601.	Completion of the Library.
1601—2.	Fountain in the Great Court begun (1 February).
1604.	Bargain with Francis Carter for woodwork of Hall, Butteries, Kitchen, etc. (27 February).
1604.	Hall begun (9 April).
1605.	Agreement with Andrew Chapman to wainscot Hall (21 February).
,,	Kitchen begun (7 July).
,,	Last payment to Carter for woodwork of Hall, etc. (14 September).
,,	Slating of Hall completed (3 October).
,,	Bargain with Francis Carter for roof of Kitchen (21 September).
,,	Last payment to Carter for roof of Kitchen (23 October).
,,	Slating of Hall and Buttery completed (24 November).
,,	Agreement with Francis Carter for Screen in Hall.
1605—6.	Ditch forming the east boundary of Garret Hostel Green filled up.
1607—8.	Windows of Hall glazed.
,,	Andrew Chapman paid in full for wainscoting the Hall.
1611.	Tennis-court built between the Library and the River.
1611—12.	Bridge across the River Cam commenced.
1612—13.	Master's Lodge being fitted up.
1613.	The ground on the west side of the River Cam, and the northern two-thirds of Garret Hostel Green, obtained by exchange from the Town.
1614.	Probable date of completion of Nevile's Court.
1614—15.	Great Gate decorated with statues, coats of arms, etc.
1614—15.	Door made out of Master's Lodge into Hall.
1636.	Rearrangement of the east end of the Chapel.
1647—48.	Bowling Green laid down with turf.
1650—51.	"Fellowes Combination Chamber" mentioned.
1663—64.	Leases of land beyond the College Gates acquired.
1669.	Bishop Hackett offers to rebuild Garret Hostel.

1670.	Contract with Robert Minchin to build Bishop's Hostel (15 January).
1671—72.	Avenue of limes planted.
1674—75.	Limes planted in the south-west walk.
1676.	New Library begun (23 February).
1676.	Agreement with Sir Thomas Sclater for his building in Nevile's Court (18 April).
1676--77.	Chestnuts planted in the walk next to S. John's College.
1679.	Sir Thomas Sclater's building completed.
1680—81.	The Gate called subsequently "Nevile's Gate" placed at the west end of the avenue.
1681.	Agreement with Dr Humphry Babington for his building in Nevile's Court (18 May).
	The building between his and the Library proceeding at the same time.
1684—85.	"Master's summer-house" built.
1685.	Preparations made for commencing the woodwork of the Library.
1688.	Pavement laid down in the Library.
1691—92.	Iron gates in the cloister, and iron rails on the Library staircase put up.
1691—93.	Grinling Gibbons executes woodcarvings in the Library.
1694.	Part of the old buildings of King's Hall ordered to be pulled down.
1695.	Books moved into the New Library.
1700—9.	Repairs to the Master's Lodge carried out by Dr Bentley. New staircase built; sash-windows introduced.
1704.	The Sun-Dial set up in the Great Court.
1706.	Repairs and decoration of the Chapel commenced; subscription opened; East window blocked up.
1706—7.	A Chemical Laboratory fitted up in one of the chambers of King's Hall.
1713.	The necessary repairs of the Chapel finished.
1715.	Schrider paid for the new organ.
1716.	Fountain in the Great Court rebuilt.
1716—17.	Avenue of lime-trees planted on east side of River Cam.
1718.	Fresh list of subscriptions for the Chapel opened. Work done to the east end.
1718—22.	Alterations in the garden of the Master's Lodge made by Dr Bentley. Bath-house and Granary built.
1719—21.	Woodward the carver at work on the Chapel.
1722—23.	Final discharge of all bills incurred for the Master's Lodge.
1723.	Sash-windows introduced into chamber on first floor over Queen's gate.
1724—25.	Duke of Somerset subscribes £100 towards adorning the Altar-piece in the Chapel.
1726—27.	New Clock and Bells placed on King Edward's Gate.
1733.	Iron gates, given by Mr H. Bromley, placed at the west end of the avenue. "Nevile's Gate" removed to the stable-yard.
1739.	Observatory on the Great Gate completed.
1750—51.	Great Court stuccoed by Denston.
1751—52.	West side of the Hall stuccoed by Denston. Vaults made.
1752—53.	King Edward's Gate, or Clock Tower, "beautified."
1753—54.	East side of the Hall faced and repaired.
1753—54.	Extensive repair to south side of Great Court, including the Queen's Gate.

1755—56.	Woodward carves 26 Coats of Arms in the Chapel.
1755—58.	Reconstruction of Nevile's Court by Essex.
1756—57.	New parapet made on the north side of the old Library.
1764—65.	Bridge across the River Cam rebuilt by Essex.
1770—75.	Combination Rooms rebuilt by Essex; bell-turret at S.W. angle of Great Court pulled down.
1775.	Stained-glass window placed at the south end of the Library.
1786—87.	Walls bounding the approach to the Great Gate pulled down.
1790.	Lease for 999 years of part of the south end of Garret Hostel Green obtained from the Town.
1797.	Observatory on the Great Gate taken down.
1802.	Lease for 999 years of " the Stoneyard " obtained from the Town.
1802—3.	Lease of the Fellows' Garden obtained from the University.
1810.	The N.E. angle of the Great Court stuccoed by Bernasconi.
1812—13.	The East side of the Great Court, the King's Gate, and the old Library stuccoed.
1820.	Additional buildings for students suggested by Dr Wordsworth.
1823.	Plans for the King's Court, prepared by Wilkins, accepted.
,,	Contract with Mr Crowe, Builder, signed (26 June). First stone laid (12 August).
,,	South portion of Garret Hostel Green enfranchised by the Town of Cambridge.
1825.	King's Court completed.
1831—32.	Alterations in the Chapel directed by Mr Blore, Architect.
1833.	New Lecture Rooms begun.
1841—43.	Alterations to Master's Lodge; Mr Salvin architect. Eastern and western oriels rebuilt.
1845.	Oak vault at the Great Gate put up by Dr Whewell, Master.
1849.	Dr Whewell begins to purchase property opposite the College.
1850—51.	Trabeation added to the Library ceiling.
1855.	The walls bounding the approach to the Great Gate replaced by iron railings.
1856.	East front of the range between the Great Gate and the Chapel rebuilt by Mr Salvin.
1860.	Dr Whewell's first Court completed.
1864.	Site of Reginald Ely's Almshouses purchased from Caius College.
1865.	Repair, decoration, and enlargement of the Chapel proposed.
1866.	Decoration of the interior of the Hall.
1867.	Repairs to the roof of the Chapel.
1868—73.	South side and east end of the Chapel ashlared.
1868.	Dr Whewell's second Court completed.
1870—75.	Rearrangement and decoration of the interior of the Chapel. Mr Blomfield architect.
1872.	Purchase of the Fellows' Garden from the University.
1875—76.	Decoration of the Antechapel.
1876.	"Nevile's Gate" placed at the entrance to the College from Trinity Lane.
1876—78.	Two ranges of chambers built on the site of the stables. Mr Blomfield architect.

APPENDIX.

I. *Authorities for the History of Trinity College.*

The authorities for the history of Trinity College may be most conveniently considered in the following order:

1. Michael House.
2. King's Hall.
3. The book called the "Memoriale" of Trinity College.
4. The collections formed by Dr Thomas Parne and Dr Charles Mason.

1. MICHAEL HOUSE. The Account-Books of Michael House have all disappeared with the exception of a single roll of parchment headed "Custus domorum," which unfortunately is not dated, but may be assigned to the year 1326, from an entry, quoted below, recording the expense of taking possession of the glebe and advowson of Chedele, i.e. Cheadle in Staffordshire. The deed granting possession of this property (in the Muniment Room of Trinity College) is dated 20 July, 20 Edward II., 1326.

The first heading of the roll, "*Custus Cancelli*," sets forth an extensive series of works done to a Chancel, evidently that of S. Michael's Church, Cambridge; and from the total expended, £38. 18s. 4¾d., as well as from the nature of the entries— stone for the walls, glass for the windows, and lead for the roof—it may be concluded that the original construction is here recorded.

The second heading is "*Custus pistrini*"; and here again the nature of the entries and the sum expended, £20. 14s. 8¼d., indicate a first construction.

The third heading, "*Expense circa hospicium ex opposito ecclesie*," enables us to assign with certainty the first heading to S. Michael's Church; for it has been shewn above (p. 395) that a messuage in this position was purchased by Hervey de Stanton and Walter de Buxton in 1326. On this work £11. 11s. 5d. was spent.

The following headings and expenses succeed:

"*Expense forinsece.* In placito pro hospicio Ouinge contra Priorem de Bernewelle pro decimis vicarii xiiij.li. iij.s. iiij.d. ob. qᵃ. vt patet per parcellam in rotulo compoti.

Summa xiiij li. iij s. iiij d. ob. qᵃ.

Chedele. In expensis magistri Simonis versus Chedle et in Chedele pro seisyna capienda in gleba et aduoccacione de Chedele xxxj.s. Item Willelmo de Bromle attornato xx.s.

Summa Lj.s.

Monialibus. In vjˢ annui redditus empti de Priorissa et Conuentu sancte Redagund' iij.li.

Summa iiijˡⁱ.

Expense in Ecclesia. In vna noua legenda Lxij.s. Item in factura vnius casule cum duabus tunicis xv.s.

Summa iij.li. xxvij.s.

Expense circa nouas cameras xlvij.lj. Item in hospicio Ouing xlvj.lj. viij.s.

Summa iiijˣˣ. xiij.lj. viij.s."

The muniments of Michael House on the other hand have been carefully preserved; and most of the originals copied into the cartulary referred to in the text as "The Otryngham Book" are still in existence. It has however been more convenient to refer to them as there transcribed.

The Otryngham Book is a folio volume, 14½ inches high by 9½ inches broad, containing 89 leaves of parchment, a few of which have been inserted since the volume was first paged. The documents are written out very clearly and carefully, on both sides of the leaves, in various hands. The leaves are numbered in red ink as far as fol. 32, on which the earliest handwriting ceases. The subsequent leaves are numbered in black ink. The whole has been paged, probably in the last century. It was "new bound 1728" as noted on a fly-leaf at the beginning, in rough brown leather. Another note on the same fly-leaf records: "This Book being formerly bound in Black was frequently called the Black Book of Michael House Lands."

The documents are sorted in order of place; those in the earliest hand referring wholly to Cambridge. They consist of royal letters patent, licenses in mortmain, conveyances, title deeds, and the Statutes imposed by the Founder and his successors. A few explanatory headings and marginal notes were introduced by the original transcriber; to which some have been added at a later date. "These," Professor Willis notes, "require to be employed with caution, for several of them are explanatory glosses impertinently intruded by a person unacquainted with the real nature of the site, and manifestly erroneous and misleading."

The connection of the book with John Otryngham, Master 1427—33 (Graduati Cantabrigienses ed. Rev. H. R. Luard, 1873, p. 503), rests on the authority of the following deed, unfortunately without date, which is transcribed fol. 85 *b*, p. 178.

"Cum enim nostri collegii custos diligentissimus Magister Johannes Otryngham, preter omnem illam curam peruigilem quam habuit pro munimentis nostre domus, sparsim diuisis, recolligendis, ac eciam consequenter pro eorundem munimentorum in quodam libello ordinata compilacione, ad non modicam nostre domus vtilitatem; verum eciam ex sua liberalitate plurima alia dicte domui contulerit, viz: sexaginta libras in pecuniis; quinque crateres argenteos et sextum pro dulci vino deauratum; quatuor salsaria argentea ex quibus facta sunt noua; duas fiolas argenteas; Augustinum de ciuitate dei et Hugonem de sacramentis in eodem volumine; ac eciam vnum tenementum situatum juxta tenementa Denforth; nos igitur Willelmus Ascough custos dicte domus eiusdemque domus consocii dictorum beneficiorum non immemores set ea veluti justicie debito astringimur recompensare volentes vnanimi assensu statuimus et ordinamus quod singulis annis fiant exequie secundo Idus Maii in ecclesia Michaelis cum missa in crastino vel infra quatriduum sequens. Volumus eciam quod medietas firme dicti tenementi inter socios qui predictis exequiis et misse presentes extiterint aut in publicis negotiis collegii occupati fuerint distribuatur."

It was suggested by Mr H. T. Riley (First Report of the Historical MSS. Commission, Appendix, p. 82) that the word "libellus" in the above deed could hardly refer to so large a volume as that here described. But, as a matter of fact, very much larger volumes are spoken of at this period under the names of *libellus* and *opusculum*. A portion of a volume has been lately found in the Muniment Room of Trinity College which has been proved by the handwriting to have been written very few years after the foundation of Michael House. It consists of a single quire of parchment, eleven inches long by six inches broad, on which some of the same documents which are found in the Otryngham Book are written. The first four leaves contain the documents belonging to Chedle (Otryngham, p. 153); the two next those belonging

to the messuage of Adam de Trumpington (ibid. p. 37—39); the remainder a portion of those belonging to Ovyng's Inn (ibid. p. 42 foll.). The explanatory headings
and the marginal references are wanting, but space has been left for the former. It
should be remarked that the two last sets only are transcribed into the Otryngham
Book in the earlier hand; from which we may conclude that the transcription was
interrupted, and continued in a later hand.

2. KING'S HALL. The conveyances of the different pieces of property composing the site, with a number of their title-deeds, are preserved in the Muniment Room of
Trinity College, as noted in the text, except those belonging to the two houses at the
north-east corner of the site (Appendix No. VI.), known as S. Edmund's and Pyke's,
which cannot now be found.

Two series of Accounts have also been preserved.

A. *In the Public Record Office.* Twenty-five rolls of parchment, minutely recording the manner in which the master had expended the sums for which he was bound
to render an account to the Exchequer. They form a broken series extending over
rather more than a century, from 1338—39 to 1443—44. A list of them will be found
in the Commission Documents i. 63. As a general rule these Accounts are filled with
the weekly payments made to the scholars and others (*vadia*) and the cost of their
dress (*robas*); but in some few of them building operations of various kinds are recorded.
The most interesting roll on these grounds is the earliest, that for the year 1338 (see
above, p. 432). The heading, which will serve as a specimen of the headings of the
others, is as follows :

"Particule compoti Thome Powys magistri Scolarium de Elemosina Regis apud
Cant' sustentatorum, tam denariorum receptorum quam de misis et expensis per ipsum
factis circa quandam domum de nouo edificandam et diuersos defectus quarundam
domorum in eadem villa reperand' et emendand' anno regni regis Edwardi tercij post
conquestum xij°.

Idem reddit computum de .xx. li. recept' de Priore de sancto Neoto in axilium
reperacionis et emendacionis diuersarum domorum scolarium Regis ibidem moran-
tium."

The cost of every article used in the repair is minutely set down in the account;
and at the end the expenses are found to have exceeded the receipts by £10. 3s. 4d.

B. *In the Library of Trinity College.* The yearly Accounts kept by the Bursar,
extending from 11 Edward III. (1337—38) to 35 Henry VIII. (1543—44), two years
before the surrender of the college to the King, which took place 9 October, 1546.
As stated in the text (Chapter II.), the series is by no means complete, and, as so frequently happens with this class of documents, the Accounts are often wanting for the
very years for which it would have been most desirable that they should have been
preserved. The most serious of these gaps have been noticed in the text. Notwithstanding this defect, however, and the damage which some of the pages have
suffered from damp, the volumes are in wonderfully good condition, and supply an
almost inexhaustible fund of information respecting the life of a medieval College.

The Accounts are written on rough paper, the pages measuring about 10½ inches
by 8 inches, and were probably originally stitched into parchment covers. They are
now bound in 26 volumes. The exact date of this binding is not known. Mr Riley
(Hist. MSS. Comm. Report I, Appendix p. 83) conjectures that it was done between
1660 and 1680; but it is more likely that it belongs to the early part of the xviiith

century, and may be that referred to in the Senior Bursar's Accounts for 1721—22, *Extraordinaries:* "To the Bookbinder for binding Books in the Treasury, 05.07.06." Ibid. 1722—23 : "P^d. M^r. Richardson's bill sign'd by M^r. L'Isle [Denys L'Isle, Fellow, Auditor and Registrar of the College, Monk's Bentley, ii. 51] for books bound for ye use of ye College, 02.15.06."

We will now describe the arrangement of one of these Accounts, selecting as our example that for 1414—15. It is headed :

" Papirus anni secundi Regis Henrici quinti, In quo creati sunt Senescalli Magistri Johannes Tyryngton, Willelmus Asshenden, Willelmus Brygge, Willelmus Paynell, Robertus Dufford, Johannes Gryme."

After a page devoted to the receipts, the expenses are distributed under the following headings, to which, in other years, special headings are occasionally added :

" Communes Sociorum " (arranged by weeks) ; " Expense Extrauagantes ;" " Repasta communia ;" " Recepcio ecclesie Beate Marie ;" " Expense eiusdem ;" " Repasta ecclesie beate marie ;" " Recepcio Ecclesie de Hyntlesham ;" " Repasta eiusdem ;" " Recepcio Ecclesie de Felmersham ;" " Repasta eiusdem ;" " Expense ecclesie de Felmersham ;" " Recepcio ecclesie de Grendon ;" " Repasta eiusdem ;" " Expense eiusdem ;" " Empcio Focalis terricidiorum siue lignorum ;" " Empcio segetis ;" " Redditus debiti a collegio ;" " Expense de Fakendam ;" " Liberacio Facta per custodem ;" " Expense facte per eundem ;" " Expense facte circa Vadia et Robas ;" " Reparacio domorum ;" " Expense facte circa molendinum ;" " Exitus molendini ;" " Expense facte circa pistrinam ;" " Exitus pistrine ;" " Expense facte circa aulam ;" " Expense facte circa promptuarium ;" " Expense facte circa Coquinam ;" " Conuenciones Famulorum ;" " Soluciones Stipendiorum Famulorum ;" " Oblaciones Famulorum " (gratuities given to the servants) ; " Oblaciones Sociorum ;" " Expense Facte circa Librariam ;" " Empcio stauri ;" " Repasta Sociorum ;" " Empcio Frumenti ;" " Empcio Brasii ;" " Expense facte circa columbare ;" " Expense facte circa Nouam Pistrinam ;" " Conuenciones Noue Pistrine ;" " Conuenciones Collegii ;" " Exitus columbaris."

Most of the Accounts are so full of erasures that it may be conjectured that they are only rough drafts, from which fair copies were subsequently written out on parchment, and probably forwarded to the Exchequer.

3. THE " MEMORIALE " OF TRINITY COLLEGE. This is a folio volume, containing 176 leaves of vellum, 18¾ inches high by 14 inches broad, on which are painted the arms of the Founders and principal benefactors of Michael House, King's Hall, and Trinity College, with short accounts of their lives and benefactions, for which this record is often the only authority. It bears the following title, inscribed upon a richly illuminated page :

" Memoriale Collegio Sanctæ et Indiuiduæ
Trinitatis in Academia Cantabrigiensi dicatum 1614

Cura et industria Ed : Stanhope Militis Legum Doc:^ris Collegii huiusce quondàm Socii Compositum et ordinatum Eiusdemque sumptibus delineatum et exornatum, in piam gratiam et perpetuum honorem munificentiæ et olim, et nunc, et in posterum, huic Collegio Deuotorum.

Erunt Reges nutritij tui, et Reginæ nutrices tuæ."

It is difficult to determine how much of the literary portion of the work is due to Sir Edward Stanhope (for whose life see Cooper's Athenæ ii. 470). In his Will, dated 28 February, 1602—3, there occurs the following passage. It is here quoted from the copy dated 10 April, 1608, under the seal of the Prerogative Court of Canterbury, of that portion of it which concerns Trinity College, and which is preserved in the Muniment Room.

" I do further give vnto the saide Colledge of the Blessed and vndevided Trinitie in Cambridge the somme of Twentie poundes of Currannt Englishe monie to be paide vnto them by my Executor or Executors within six monethes after my decease wherewith my will is the Colledge shall provide one verie great Booke of Large Velam in severall leaves whereof shall firste be faire written and lymed the Names titles Armes and Dignities of all the Founders of the said Colledg sett out in theire proper Cullers. After them the Armes of the Colledg. After that the names of all the Benefactors who have given anie yearelie perpetuitie of maintenaunce to that Colledg since the first erection thereof, together with the perticuler induments which they have so yearelie given to that Colledg. After shalbe written the name and estate of everie Benefactor who since the erection of that Colledg [has given] anie remembraunce of theire love and kindenes to the same; wherein shalbe expressed the perticuler gifte so by anie of them given be it more or lesse. After that shalbe [written] the names of all the Masters who have governed that Colledg since the first erection thereof together with a perticuler of those places whereto anie of them have bin called in the governement of the Churche or Commonwealthe before theire Death.

This booke must further be kepte for the publicke Register Booke of all the perticuler Bookes Mappes Globes or other Ornamentes whatsoever belonging or hereafter to belonge to the saide Colledge Librarie.

The love which I am assured the M^r. and Seniors of the Colledge doth beare to the kinde remembraunce of all the good Benefactors to that blessed Societie I knowe to be such as I am assured they will see this smale portion of Twentie poundes to be imployed to the full for keepinge a perpetuall Register and Memoriall garnished in that Booke to the best and kindest encoridgement of all future frendes who shall hereafter be incorraged to do good to that Colledge.

This Booke thus written garnished and finished with leaves sufficient to add what shall hereafter by good men be supplied I desier maie with such good speede be prepared that it be one of the First bookes which should be perfected bound vp chained and affixed to theire Librarie.

So do I comende the prosperouse future state of this Famous Colledge of the blessed and vndevided Trinitie in Cambridg of king Henrie the Eight his foundation to the guide and governement of the most holie and Blessed Trinitie, I being by Dewtie of Nature bounde not to forgett the howse and Familie which I discend of. Theire estate being such as God be blessed it is, my desier is they wilbe contented with theise smale remembraunces of theire loving kinseman."

Sir Edward Stanhope died 16 March, 1607—8, and his Will was proved 25 March following. As the "Memoriale" is dated 1614, it would appear at first sight that he had had nothing more to do with it than what is stated in the above extract. In the volume itself however (fol. 63) his benefactions are stated to be the following:

"1°. Ad bibliothecæ concamerationem et coassationem Centum Libras dedit, deinde Biblia Hispanica, variosque theologicos: tum copiosa serie Librorum iuris Ciuilis amplificauit, quos index Librorum recitabit.

2°. Atque, quo diligentius bibliotheca curari possit in posterum, Septingentas Libras legauit moriens, ad procurandas terras Liberas ad annuum valorem triginta duarum Librarum in perpetuum, quibus aluntur bibliothecarius eiusque amanuensis.

3°. Neque discipulorum oblitus pauperum Quadraginta Libras per quadriennium distribuendas inter subsizatores donauit.

4°. Vtque perpetuò vigeant Fundatorum et benefactorum nomina et monumenta, Librum registrarium ipsius suâ operâ descripsit ac delineauit, et viginti Libras ad eundem conficiendum legauit."

The words used in the fourth paragraph—"*librum suâ operâ descripsit ac delineauit*" —if taken literally, would lead us to conclude that Stanhope was the author, as well as the donor, of the book. The title page, however, states distinctly that it was not put into its present shape before 1614, six years after his death. The difficulty may be got over by suggesting that he left notes and sketches from which, after his death, the biographical notices were compiled, and the arms drawn.

4. THE COLLECTIONS OF DR PARNE AND DR MASON.

A. DR PARNE. Thomas Parne was admitted a sizar of Trinity College 8 January, 1714, as shewn by the following entry in the Admission Book:

"Jan. 8, 1713—14. Admissus Thomas Parne siz. annos natus 20 filius Ri : Parne de Oxford, e schola Bedford, sub præsidio Mʳⁱ Aspinal.

Mʳᵒ Baker Tut."

He matriculated 10 July, 1714; proceeded B.A. 1717; M.A. 1721; S.T.B. 1729; S.T.P. 1739. He was elected "socius minor" 1720; "socius major" 1721. He held the College offices of head lecturer (*lector primarius*) 1740; Greek lecturer (*lector linguæ Græcæ*) 1741; Senior Dean 1742; and was Vicar of S. Michael's Church, Cambridge, from 1742 to 1747. During a part of this period he had been one of the Tutors. In 1745 he was elected a Senior Fellow. He was University Librarian from 1734 to his death in 1751. His temper, always violent, at length developed into brain-disease. For some years previous to his death his eccentric behaviour had been overlooked, but, 27 April, 1749, it was agreed by the Master and Seniors that he should not be allowed to reside in College until he had recovered, but should retain his weekly allowance, on the ground that he had been "guilty of many offences against the Statutes," which arose "from a distemper'd mind and absence of Reason, which was so notorious that we were call'd upon on all hands to put him under confinement and into a proper Regimen." The Senior Bursar's Accounts shew that the last "*stipendium*" paid to him was that for the quarter ending at Midsummer, 1751. It is therefore probable that he died in the course of that quarter.

Dr Monk (Life of Bentley, ii. 267) mentions that in 1728 Parne, then one of the Tutors of the College, joined Dr Colbatch in his scheme for prosecuting Dr Bentley in conjunction with two other Fellows, Mason and Ingram. In consequence of this action he incurred the full force of the resentment of the Master, and of those Senior Fellows who supported him. He experienced continued and vexatious interference with his duties as Tutor; and to the same cause Dr Monk attributes his failure to obtain the office of Public Orator, for which he was a candidate in 1730 (Ibid. ii. 296, 297). Through the friendly intervention of the Vice-Master, Dr Walker, he was formally reconciled to Bentley in 1734, but three years afterwards he again joined his opponents; conduct which caused Bentley to speak of him as "that rascal Parne" (Ibid. ii. 382); and it does not appear that they were again reconciled.

Dr Monk records that Dr Parne was "a person of great talents and high reputation in the University" (Ibid. ii. 267); and that as deputy to the Regius Professor of Divinity he "acquitted himself in the Schools with much ability and a graceful manner" (Ibid. ii. 420). It was his intention to write the history of his college; with which end in view he carefully studied the Accounts of King's Hall and Trinity

College. The former are frequently annotated in his hand. He filled two quarto note-books with extracts from these volumes, interspersed with remarks and recollections of his own. It is fortunate that these books had been studied, and to a certain extent transcribed, by Professor Willis, for they cannot now be found. Dr Parne also accurately transcribed many of the charters, letters patent, statutes, and other documents belonging to Michael House, King's Hall, and Trinity College, into four small folios. These, bound in two volumes, are in the Muniment Room of Trinity College.

The History of Trinity College did not proceed far. The preface, and part of the History of Michael House, are the only portions which can be said to have been in any sense of the word completed. It was the author's intention to carry the History down to the year 1700, and it was to have concluded with a passage which is worth quotation, when we remember the part which the author had played in the disputes which had done so much mischief to the College:

" I have now brought down the Account of our Society almost to the times which fall under my own knowledge and Observation, and if I should resolve to continue it it would be easy to have materials enough to swell the sequel to a Bulk far exceeding what is already delivered. But it is on many Accounts hard to be open and impartial in relating things done at so near a distance. And tho' I were exalted above Human frailty (as I am most sensible that I am not) if it were worth while to dare to praise and dispraise many Persons now living; yet I am something unwilling to record those things which, as far as they are remembered, will only expose us to the wonder and Pity of Ages to come."

The MS. volume from which this passage is quoted is in the Muniment Room of Trinity College.

B. Dʳ MASON. Charles Mason was admitted a pensioner of Trinity College 30 October, 1718, as shewn by the following entry in the Admission Book:

"Oct. 30 1718. Admissus Carolus Mason Pens. annos natus 19 filius Caroli Mason Gen: de Preed in Com. Salopiæ e scholâ de Wem in eodem Com: sub præsidio Mʳⁱ Edwards. Mʳᵒ Rob: Smith Tut."

He matriculated 17 December, 1717; proceeded B.A. 1722; M.A. 1726; S. T. B. 1736; S. T. P. 1749. He was elected "socius minor" 1725; "socius major" 1726. He held the college offices of "sublector quartus" 1726; "lector linguæ latinæ " 1729; "lector linguæ græcæ" 1736; "lector primarius" 1737; Senior Dean 1760—61. In 1751 he was elected a Senior Fellow. In 1742 he became Vicar of Barrington, Cambridgeshire. From 1734 to 1762 he was Woodwardian Professor. In 1746 he succeeded Colbatch as rector of Orwell, Cambridgeshire, where he died, 18 December, 1770. The following epitaph is inscribed upon his grave in the Chancel:

Here Lieth the Body of the Rᵈ and Learned
CHA: MASON. D.D.
Many Years Senior Fellow of Trinity
College, and Woodwardian Professor of
Fossils, F. R. S., Rector of Orwell
Departed this Life Decᵇʳ 18ᵗʰ 1770
in the 72ᵈ Year of his Age.
A truely Pious good and Virtuous Man
a sincere and Valuable Friend; as Eminent
for his Learning as his greatness of
Mind; Patient under his Sufferings and
Chearfully resigned Himself to the will
of God. Resting in certain hope to be
United with Christ.

As mentioned above in the account of Dr Parne, Mason sided with Colbatch against the Master; and it is probable that the researches into which he was thus led directed his attention in the first instance to the history of his College.

Cole has left the following account of Dr Mason (MSS. Cole xxxiii. 156. Add. MSS. Mus. Brit. 5834) in a note on a paragraph in the *Cambridge Chronicle*, 8 September, 1764, recording the appointment of Dr Ogden to be Woodwardian Professor of Fossils:

"He was Fellow of Trinity College, and marrying when he was between 60 and 70, to the Admiration of all his Friends, he being, not only far advanced in Life, but looked upon as rather unhewn, rough and unsociable, and the most unlikely Man to take a Wife, of any of his Time. He quitted Senior-Fellowship, Professorship and Liberty however in 1762 for a Lady of small Fortune, but of great Accomplishments, of the Name of Graham, and of just half his Age, and now resides at his Rectory of Orwell in Cambridgeshire, where he has built much, and this year his College has given him £90 to assist him in the Repairs of his House. He is a very ingenious Man, an excellent Mechanic, a good Antiquary and no bad Geographer: witness a most accurate Map of Cambridgeshire, which he has made from a personal Visitation of almost every Spot in the County: as it is on a large Scale, the Expence of printing it will be considerable: yet great Pity it is, that it should be lost. He has also large Collections for an History of the same County, Part of Mr Layer's, and part of Mr Rutherforth's Collections. He is a Shropshireman, and has a small Estate of his own."

It is worth while to compare with this favourable record the following amusing denunciation, which occurs at the end of a transcript of one of Mason's MSS. (MSS. Cole xxvii. 332. Add. MSS. Mus. Brit. 5828):—"in which I never had more Occasion to observe the singular *Perverseness* and *Oddity* of his *Disposition*, which urged him always to *act in Contradiction* to the *Rest of Mankind*. Thus, thro' out this Book, where-ever he has Occasion to mention the *Year* of the *Reign* of any *King* he always and uniformly puts the *Year before* the *King's Name*, thus, for *Instance*, *Egmanton, Wil. V. H.* 2. *Pulham.* in flat *Contradiction* to *common Practice*, and what would *puzzle* and *confound* extremely, was it not for the long *List* above, where the *Longevity* of some of our *Kings* makes it *impossible* to *mistake*: otherways, *v. Hen.* 2. would be taken for the *Fifth* of *Henry* 2^d according to the usual and *received Mode* of *dating*: whereas it means with Dr *Mason* the 2^d of *Henry* 5th. However I have ventured to *correct* this *way of dating* all along, whereever I have met with it: otherwise I *scrupulously observe* his *other slovenly* and *careless Way* of *Entring*, without *Authorities, Stops,* or *false ones,* and many other *puzzling Circumstances,* besides a *vile Hand,* which would almost make one believe it was done on *Design* to *perplex*. His *Dates* also and *Names* are by no Means to be *relied* on: for where-ever I have had *Occasion* to *consult,* on my *doubting* his *Authority,* my 5 *Volumes* of the *Ely Registers,* containing all the *Doctor's Authorities,* I have generally *found* them *grossly faulty*: it being *evident,* the D^r either did *not take Time* enough or *knew not how* to *decypher* the various *old Hands* the *different Registers* are wrote in. I am sorry to observe thus much in Regard to Dr *Mason's Character* of *Obstinacy, Singularity* and *Perverseness*: he was my *particular Friend*: and I believe him to have been a *most worthy, honest, and friendly Man,* and of the *most inflexible integrity*: not to mention his *Learning and Ingenuity,* in which he was *eminent* as a *Scholar* and *Virtuoso*."

After Dr Mason's death his friends tried to get the above-mentioned map completed and published. Mr James Essex, writing to Gough 9 January, 1780 (Nichols' Illustrations of Literature, i. 288), says: "I have been taking some pains to get

M^{rs}. Chettow to agree with M^r. Elstobb, an ingenious land-surveyor, to finish D^r. Mason's Map of Cambridgeshire. He has been for many years employed in survey-ing the rivers, cuts, etc. and making large maps of particular districts in the fenny parts of the county, which have furnished him with many correct materials towards filling up what is not taken by D^r. Mason, who has nothing more in his than the situations of many churches, but they are accurately laid down, and corrected by trigonometrical calculations; and if the whole is completed, as it may be by Mr Elstobb, I have not a doubt of its being one of the most accurate maps hitherto published." Similar praise is bestowed on the work in a second letter, written 7 November, 1782 (Ibid. p. 296) with regret that "what he has done, though mathe-matically correct, is consigned to the worms, who in a short time will destroy the labour of years, and deprive the curious of a work which would do honour to his memory, if preserved." In 1783 arrangements had been made to have it engraved by Faden; but the scheme was abandoned, and it was first published in 1808 by Messrs Lysons in the Magna Britannia (Ibid. p. 229).

The following description of Dr Mason is from the Memoirs of Bentley's grandson, Richard Cumberland, Fellow, B.A. 1750, M.A. 1754, and therefore 28 years junior to him (p. 106):

"When the day of examination came we went our rounds to the electing seniors; in some instances by one at a time, in others by parties of three or four; it was no trifling scrutiny we had to undergo, and here and there pretty severely exacted, particularly, as I well remember, by Doctor Charles Mason, a man of curious know-ledge in the philosophy of mechanics and a deep mathematician; he was a true modern Diogenes in manners and apparel, coarse and slovenly to excess in both; the witty made a butt of him, but the scientific caressed him; he could ornament a subject at the same time that he disgusted and disgraced society. I remember when he came one day to dinner in the college hall, dirty as a blacksmith from his forge, upon his being questioned on his appearance, he replied—that he had been *turning*—then I wish, said the other, when you was about it, friend Charles. you had *turned* your shirt."

Soon after Mason's election to a Fellowship, he fell in love with Dr Bentley's daughter Joanna, who was married in 1728 to Denison Cumberland (Monk's Bentley, ii. 267); and for a time his addresses were evidently agreeable to the lady. A copy of verses called '*A Lamentation for the loss of Mrs Joanna Bentley*,' and signed *E. Prior*, probably Edward Prior, Fellow, B.A. 1721, M.A. 1725, evidently a rejected rival, has been preserved by Nichols (Literary Anecdotes, i. 224). The writer describes Mason's personal appearance in the following savage lines:

> " Mason, to love and shape eternal foe,
> That chaos of a man, that unlicked lump of beau.
> Behold the haggard honours of his face,
> The ghastly smile, and the Cyclopean grace!
> Those harpyan claws that should the plough sustain,
> Now screened by ruffles, dare the plough disdain;
> The brawny calves in silken stockings shown,
> Strange change! to wear the best from wearing none!
> In snaky curls the stiffening wig appears,
> Bristling with all the horrors of Medusa's hairs.
> Nor disagreement through the whole we find,
> He's Mason both in body and in mind."

Like Dr Parne, he collected materials for the early history of Trinity College, but he does not appear to have had any intention of writing a detailed work. He and Dr Parne probably worked together, for one of Mason's note-books contains an index in Parne's hand. Two of these manuscript books are preserved in the Muniment Room of Trinity College. They contain the headings of evidences relating to the site of Michael House and King's Hall, which he appears to have studied with greater care than Cole gave him credit for; for his extracts are carefully sorted and indexed, and many of the original deeds in the Muniment Room are docketed in his hand. Besides these note-books, a small folio MS. of 85 leaves is preserved in the British Museum (Add. MSS. 6397). On the first leaf are these words:

"MSS. by Dr Cha: Mason, relating to Mich: House, King's Hall, Trin: Coll:, Mayors of Cambridge, &c., given to me by his Widow. W^m. Cole."

The documents transcribed in it are partly from the Muniment Room of his own College, partly from those of Caius College and Corpus Christi College; so that, thanks to D^r. Mason's industry, most of the authorities for the site of Trinity College are brought together in one volume. He made many attempts to draw a map of the site, or parts of it (fol. 56—72); and it is not improbable that the most complete of these may have suggested to Professor Willis the possibility of drawing out a complete plan. Mason has not attempted to lay down the different pieces to scale upon an accurate survey of the present College; but he has noted them correctly with reference to each other, and he has recognised the existence of the two lanes, which, as described above (Chapter I), traversed the site, and separated it into three divisions. To what was there said respecting them may be added the following note in Otryngham (p. 72):

"3^s. venellæ.
1^a. a Templo Michaelis per Garret Austell ad riueram communem.
2^a. a porta Elizab: ad Turrim Edwardi 3.
3^a. a Templo omnium sanctorum in Judaismo ad Sedgyard vocat' Milnestones.

M^r. Ball, 1605, Decemb. 12°."

These lanes are: Henney Lane (1); Le Foule Lane (2); King's Hall Lane (3). The last entry is particularly valuable as shewing the use made of the open space called Millestones, or Le Millestones Hill.

Mason also compiled a list of the members of Michael House, King's Hall, and Trinity College, copied by Cole in 1773 (MSS. xlv. 221—315. Add. MSS. Mus. Brit. 5846).

II. *Rules for the assignment of Rooms in Michael House, made* 25 *November*, 1429. *Otryngham*, p. 74, *noted in the margin* "*Camerarum assignacio.*"

Memorandum quod nos Johannes Otryngham Custos domus sancti Michaelis Cantebr' et eiusdem consocii et scolares, in festo sancte Katerine virginis et martyris Anno domini millesimo cccc^{mo}. vicesimonono et regni regis henrici sexti octauo, pro pace tranquillitate et quiete inter nos et successores nostros in assignacione et admissione camerarum dicte domus in posterum conservanda, statuimus et hac constitutione imperpetuum valitura de consensu et assensu omnium magistri et sociorum dicte domus ordinamus

Quod si contigerit tresdecim computato magistro in dicta domo deputari quod tunc duo de sociis bassam cameram ex parte australi porte gardini dicte domus si eis assignata fuerit admittere teneantur.

Si vero quatuordecim fuerint computando magistrum, tunc alii duo socii bassam cameram ex parte australi promptuarii assignatam admittere teneantur.

Si vero quindecim fuerint tunc alii duo preter istos quatuor in bassa camera sub camera magistri residere teneantur.

Si vero sedecim fuerint tunc in alta camera super promptuarium duo de dicte domus sociis statuantur.

Et si fuerint in numero septemdecim, tunc eciam duo de sociis dicte domus deputenter et assignentur in alta camera contigua principali porte domus ex parte orientali.

Proviso quod seniores socii dicte domus in assignacione camerarum continue preferantur.

III. *Letters patent of Henry the Sixth, dated 5 May, 1439, rehearsing an Inquisition taken at Babraham 22 October, 1434, at which the right of the Friars Minors to the soil of a certain aqueduct, purchased by them 5 November, 1325, was investigated.*

Henricus dei gratia Rex [etc.].

Sciatis quod inspeximus quandam Inquisicionem indentatam captam apud Baberham in Com' Cantebr' vicesimo secundo die Octobris Anno regni nostri terciodecimo coram Arthuro Ormesby adtunc Escaetore nostro in Com' predicto virtute officii sui penes Scaccarium nostrum videlicet in baga de particulis compoti eiusdem nuper Escaetoris de exitibus Escaetrie nostre in Com' predicto ac in Com' Hunt' a quinto die Nouembris Anno regni nostri duodecimo vsque tercium diem Nouembris Anno extunc proxime sequen' residentem ; Cuius quidem Inquisicionis tenor sequitur in hec verba.

Inquisicio capta apud Baberham in Com' Cantebr' vicesimo secundo die Octobris Anno regni Regis Henrici sexti post conquestum terciodecimo coram Arthuro Ormesby Escaetore domini Regis in Com' predicto virtute officii sui per sacramentum Simonis Wesenham, Ricardi Sutton, Reymundi Baldewyn, Willelmi atte Wode, Johannis Clement, Philippi Grove, Ricardi Joly, Johannis Catesby, Johannis Gyn, Johannis Barkere, Johannis Jekell, et Henrici Franceys :

Qui dicunt super sacramentum suum quod quidam Johannes quondam Gardianus conuentus fratrum minorum de Cantebr' et confratres sui diu post statutum de terris ad manum mortuam non alienandis videlicet quinto die Nouembris anno regni Regis Edwardi filii Regis Edwardi decimo nono perquisiuerunt sibi et successoribus suis de tunc magistro et confratribus hospitalis sancti Johannis Euangeliste in Cantebr' quandam peciam terre et soli cum pertinentiis continentem in longitudine centum virgas cissoris et in latitudine duos pedes.

Et similiter dictis die et anno perquisiuerunt...de tunc priore de Bernewell et conuentu eiusdem loci aliam peciam terre...continent' in longitudine duodecim virgas cissoris et duos pedes in latitudine.

Et similiter perquisiuerunt...dictis die et anno de Thoma Morys aliam peciam terre...continent' in se ducentos et quinquaginta virgas cissoris in longitudine et duos pedes in latitudine.

Et similiter perquisiuerunt...dictis die et anno de Willelmo Lauenham quandam aliam peciam terre...continent' in de trescentas virgas cissoris in longitudine et duos pedes in latitudine.

Et similiter perquisiuerunt...dictis die et anno quandam aliam peciam terre... continent' in se quingentas virgas cissoris in longitudine et duos pedes in latitudine de Galfrido Seman.

Et similiter perquisiuerunt...de Hugone Pyttok dictis die et anno quandam aliam peciam terre...continent' in se octo virgas cissoris in longitudine et duos pedes in latitudine.

Et similiter perquisiuerunt...dictis die et anno de tunc Abbatissa de Watirbech et conuentu eiusdem loci quandam aliam peciam terre...continent' in se viginti virgas cissoris in longitudine et duos pedes in latitudine.

Et similiter perquisiuerunt...dictis die et anno de tunc priore de Huntyngdon et conuentu eiusdem loci quandam aliam peciam terre...continent' in se octo virgas cissoris in longitudine et duos pedes in latitudine.

Et similiter perquisiuerunt...dictis die et anno de magistro Roberto Brygeham quandam aliam peciam terre...continent' in se duodecim virgas cissoris in longitudine et duos pedes in latitudine.

Et similiter perquisiuerunt...dictis die et anno de Thoma Ballys quandam aliam peciam terre...continent' in se octo virgas cissoris in longitudine et duos pedes in latitudine.

Et similiter perquisiuerunt...dictis die et anno de Stephano Morys quandam aliam peciam terre...continent' in se octo virgas cissoris in longitudine et duos pedes in latitudine.

Et similiter perquisiuerunt...dictis die et anno de Johanne Pyttok quandam aliam peciam terre...continent' in se octo virgas cissoris in longitudine et duos pedes in latidudine.

Et similiter perquisiuerunt...dictis die et anno de Willelmo Lolleworth quandam aliam peciam terre...continent' in se sex virgas cissoris in longitudine et duos pedes in latitudine.

Et similiter perquisiuerunt...dictis die et anno...de Willelmo Bekeswell quandam aliam peciam terre...continent' in se octo virgas cissoris in longitudine et duos pedes in latitudine.

Et similiter perquisiuerunt...dictis die et anno de Willelmo Marbilthorp quandam aliam peciam terre...continent' in se decem virgas cissoris in longitudine et duos pedes in latitudine.

Et similiter perquisiuerunt...dictis die et anno de Willelmo Redwode quandam aliam peciam terre...continent' in se novem virgas cissoris in longitudine et duos pedes in latitudine.

Et similiter perquisiuerunt...dictis die et anno de Ricardo Tableter quandam aliam peciam terre...continent' in se ducentas virgas cissoris in longitudine et duos pedes in latitudine.

Ad quendam aqueductum subterranium in eisdem peciis terre faciend' cum pipis plumbi, et sic cum eisdem pipis aqueductum illum vsque mansum predictorum Gardiani et Conuentus a quodam loco vocato Bradrusshe dirigendi.

Et dicunt quod post dictas perquisiciones dicti nuper Gardianus et Conuentus tam in dictis peciis terre dictum aqueductum subterranium quam in terris dominicis dicti nuper Regis Edwardi filii Regis Edwardi et in altis stratis, regiis vicis, viis regalibus, et riparia eiusdem ville a dictis peciis terre extendent' in longitudine videlicet a parte occidentali ville predicte vsque ad partem orientalem ipsius ville Cantebr' cum plumbo fecerunt, et in eisdem terris dominicis, stratis regiis, vicis, viis regalibus et ripariis quandam longam trenchiam et fossam fecerunt tempore predicti nuper Regis Edwardi...videlicet primo die Maii Anno regni Regis Edwardi tercii primo, et in eisdem fossa et trenchia pipam de plumbo ad aquam in eadem currend' tunc et ibidem posuerunt.

Et similiter dicunt quod continue post dictam facturam dicti aqueduct' subterranii dicti nuper Gardianus et confratres sui, et successores sui, et Gardianus qui nunc est, et confratres sui cum oporteret eos aliquam raperacionem aqueduct' predicti facere in dictis stratis regiis vicis viis regalibus et riparia temporibus Regum dicti Edwardi filii Regis Edwardi tercii, Ricardi secundi, Henrici quarti, Henrici quinti et domini Regis nunc foderunt et terram et zabulum inde proiecerunt et in eisdem magnos puteos fecerunt in contemptum et exheredacionem domini Regis, et magnum nocumentum tocius populi domini Regis temporibus illis per stratas vicos vias et ripariam predict' transeuntis.

Et dicunt similiter quod dicte pecie terre de dicto nuper Rege Edwardo filio Regis Edwardi tempore dicte perquisicionis tenebantur ad feodi firmam.

Et dicunt quod dicti nuper Gardianus et Conuentus nec aliquis successorum suorum de premissis seu aliquibus premissorum aliquam licenciam regiam optentam habuerunt.

In cuius rei testimonium huic Inquisicioni Juratores predicti sigilla sua apposuerunt dat' die anno et loco supradictis.

Quam quidem Inquisicionem ad prosecucionem dilecti clerici nostri Ricardi Caudrey Custodis collegii nostri scolarium nostrorum in vniuersitate Cantebr' sub sigillo dicti Scaccarii nostri duximus exemplificandam.

In cuius rei testimonium has literas nostras fieri fecimus patentes Teste J. Fray apud Westmonasterium quinto die Maii Anno regni nostri decimo septimo per Inquisicionem predictam in baga predicta in thesaurario existen' et per Barones.

_{*} The following list gives the names of the proprietors, and the number of ells of land bought from each :

S. John's Hospital	.	.	.	100
Barnwell Priory	.	.	.	12
Thomas Morys	.	.	.	250
William Lavenham	.	.	.	300
Geoffrey Seman	.	.	.	500
Hugh Pyttok	.	.	.	8
Abbess of Waterbeach	.	.	.	20
Prior of Huntingdon	.	.	.	8
Robert Brigham	.	.	.	12
Thomas Balls	.	.	.	8
Stephen Morys	.	.	.	8
John Pyttok	.	.	.	8
William Lolleworth	.	.	.	6
William Bekeswell	.	.	.	8
William Marbilthorp	.	.	.	10
William Redwood	.	.	.	9
Richard Tableter	.	.	.	200

$$1467 \text{ ells} = 5501^{\text{ft}}.\ 3^{\text{in}}$$

IV. *Lists of rooms and their occupants in King's Hall.*

a. First list, at the end of the Audit-Book for 11 Edward III. (1337—38). King's Hall Accounts, i. 34.

Pyribrok
Priour } in solario versus Cundyt

Springehense
Glaston } in celario sub eo

Gretford
Pererys } in medio solario

Coppeham
Tylneie } in celario sub eis

Contron
Adam } in solario sequenti

Fitling
Sonky } in celario sub

Stokes
Halys
Essex } in ij cameris sequentibus
Springet

Adamarus
Chestirfield } in solario supra portam

Secheuill
Pulton } in magno solario
Wyght

Milemet
Cleie } in celario sub
Harlaston

Stretford
Berkyngg } sub studio Magistri

Horslee
Pynnok
Plumpton } sub camera Magistri
Briddeport
Saunford
Englis

b. Second list, at the end of the Audit-Book extending from 1 October, 15 Edward III. to 1 October, 16 Edward III. (1341—42). Ibid. i. 131.

Disposicio camerarum facta per magistrum et per sex et per Comitivam.

In primis ordinantur Mr Walterus Milesmet et Mr Johannes Sawtry in solario iuxta gardinum. Et in selario sub eis Radulphus de Stonham, Nicholaus Horsle, et Johannes Sturton.

Item in Garito Johannes Essex et Johannes Plumton.

Item in solario nouo iuxta Garitum Mr Johannes Glaston, et Mr Symon Stratford, et in selario sub eiis Thomas Pyribroke et Thomas Priour.

Item in alio nouo solario iuxta predictum Mr Richardus Bytryng et Richardus Fitling. Et in selario sub eis Mr Robertus Wyght et Johannes Pulton.

Item in solario proximo Dominus Thomas Berkyng et Philippus Weylland et sub eis Johannes Perers et Thomas Copham.

Item in alio solario proximo Mr Adam Werlyngwort et Johannes Multon. Et sub eis Ricardus Hales et Alanus Mareschal.

Item in solario proximo et vltimo magister Thomas Paxton, et magister Johannes Ixworth; et sub eis Dominus Robertus Senky et Jacobus Beuerley.

Item in camera parua iuxta coquinam Thomas Springhet, Alexander Sawmford.

Item in camera iuxta Annable Pyke Dominus Rogerus Harliston et cum eo Willelmus Hokton.

Item in selario sub Custode Willelmus Bridport, Baudet, Rumseye, Imworth, et Ward.

　　c.　Third list, at the end of the Audit-Book for 18 *Edward III.* (1344—45).　*Ibid.*
　　　　　　　　　　　　　　　　i. 184.

Disposicio camerarum Anno xviij° die dominica proxima ante festum Natalis Domini.

Solarium iuxta gardinum.　Walter Millemete.
　　　　　　　　　　　　　　　John Sautre.
In selario sub.　Radulphus de Stonham.
　　　　　　　　Philippus Weyland.
　　　　　　　　Nicholaus Horsle.
In Garito.　Essex.　Plumpton.
H　{Solarium iuxta Garitum.
　　{Solarium (*sic*) sub.
I　{Alium solarium novum proximum.　Byttering et Fitling.
　　{Selarium sub eis.
A　{Solarium proximum.
　　{Selarium sub.
B　{Alium solarium proximum.
　　{Selarium sub.
C　{Solarium proximum.
　　{Selarium sub.
Camera vlterior videlicet magistri Edmund de Walsyngham.
Item ex alia parte aule iuxta coquinam.
Camera proxima iuxta gardinum Anabil' Pyk.

　　V.　*Orders to the Sheriff of Cambridge to carry timber for the repairs of King's Hall.*

　　a.　Order dated 23 *April,* 1339.　*Close Roll,* 13 *Edward III., p.* 1. *m.* 12. *dorso.*

Rex vicecomiti Cantebr' salutem. Cum dilectus clericus noster magister Thomas Powys magister scolarium quos apud Cantebrigg' de elemosina nostra sustentamus ex parte nostra oneratus existat ad quasdam domos apud Cantebrigg' pro inhabitacione eorundem scolarium celeriter reparari et quasdam construi faciend' tibi precipimus quod eidem Thome sufficiens cariagium pro maeremio quod pro reparacione et construccione domorum predictarum necessar' fuerit a diuersis locis balliue tue vsque dictam villam Cantebrigg' ducend' et cariand' in eadem balliua tua tam infra libertates quam extra pro denariis ipsius Thome inde soluend' habere facias quociens et quando per ipsum Thomam super hoc ex parte nostra fueris requisitus   Et hoc nullatenus omittas.   Teste custode predicto apud Berkhampstede.   xxiij die Aprilis.

> *b.   Order dated* 10 *May*, 1339.   *Close Roll*, 13 *Edward III.*, *p.* 1. *m.* 2.

Rex vicecomiti Cantebr' et Hunt' salutem.   Cum magister Thomas Powys magister scolarium quos apud Cantebrigg' de elemosina nostra sustentamus ex parte nostra oneratus existat ad quasdam domos apud Cantebrigg' pro inhabitacione eorundem scolarium celeriter reparari et quasdam construi faciend' ac Philippa Regina Anglie consors nostra carissima sex quercus in foresta sua de Sappele iuxta Hundyngdon ac dilecta nobis Elizabeth' de Burgo quatuor quercus in parco suo de hundone in auxilium construccionis et reparacionis domorum predictarum dederint et concesserint vt accepimus tibi percipimus quod quercus predictas sine dilacione succidi et vsque dictam villam de Cantebrigg' de exitibus balliue tue duci et cariari et prefato Thome liberari facias pro construccione et reparacione domorum predictarum   Et de custubus quos in hac parte rationabiliter apposueris tibi in compoto tuo ad scaccarium nostrum debitam allocacionem habere faciemus Teste custode predicto apud Berkhampstede x die Maij.

*** The 'custos' mentioned in the above documents is Edward the Black Prince, who was appointed 'custos Angliæ' during his father's absence in France.

> VI.   *Dispute between S. John's College and King's Hall respecting a piece of ground on the north side of the Chapel*, p. 455.

Our information respecting this dispute is contained in the following extract from the Accounts of King's Hall for 1511—12 (Vol. xxi. 196.   *Expense extrauagantes*): "Summa expensarum factarum per doctorem Jacson locumtenentem Londoniis super lite mota per magistrum consocium Terell super quadam parcella terre jacenti inter nostram capellam et collegium sancti Johannis iij^{li}. vij^d."

The second of the two documents referring to it,—that printed in the text,—was copied from the original in the Muniment Room of Trinity College.   The first has been preserved by Baker (MSS. Baker xii. 26; MSS. Harl. Mus. Brit. 7039).   As usual, Baker does not tell us from what source he obtained it, but as he notes that he copied it from an original, we may assume that in his time it was in the Muniment Room of S. John's College.   This first deed, dated 28 March, 1510—11, is merely a memorandum of the conditions which the Society of King's Hall were prepared to abide by, and to insert in a formal indenture to be subsequently prepared.   The text of the document is as follows:

"Memorand' That ye 28th day of ye Moneth of Marche, ye 2^d yere of ye Reign of our Sov. Ld Kyng Hen: ye 8th, we Gyffrey Blythe, by ye grace of God Bishop of Chestir and Maister of ye Kyng's Hall in Cambrige, with ye concent of My Brethren and Felowes of ye same College, whos names hereunto be subscribed, fully gif, graunte, and relesse all our interesse, title, and clayme that we have in y^t parcell of grounde lying on ye north syde of our Chapell of ye s^d College, bitwen ye said Chapell of the Kyng's Hall and the College of St John's, except 25 foote at ye est ende of ye said parcell of grounde, to be mesured from ye Chapell of ye said Kyng's Hall to ye new walle of St John's College.   And also 21 foote from ye said Chapell vnto ye said new walle, ageinst ye South Est Corner of ye new Buyldynge of ye said College of S^t

John's. And also 41 foote from yᵉ said Chapell towarde yᵉ said new walle of Sᵗ John's by yᵉ est parte of the Kechyn of yᵉ said Kyng's Hall and to us ye said Maister and Felowes of the said Kyng's Hall allweys reserved.

To haue and to hold yᵉ said parcell of grounde, except afore excepted, vnto yᵉ Right Rev. Faders in God Rychard Bishop of Wynchestir, John Bishop of Rowchestir, and to yᵉ Rᵗ worshipfull Mʳ Henry Hornby Clerk D.D. executours to yᵉ moost excellent Prynces Margaret, late Countess of Rich: and Derb:, to yᵉ use and behoffe of yᵉ Maister and Felowes of yᵉ said College of Sᵗ John's, att such tyme as they shall be encorporate, for ever, undir yᵉ maner folowyng, that is to sey, that yᵉ said Maister and Felowes that shall be of yᵉ said College of Sᵗ John's, whan it is fully erecte and corporate, shall relesse all yᵗ right, title, and Interesse that they have of and in 5ˢ of annuall Rent, late due and going out of yᵉ said parcell of grounde, to us yᵉ said Maister and Felowes of yᵉ Kyng's Hall and to our successors for ever.

And to these Articles and graunts aforesaid, well and truly to be performed and observed and kept on yᵉ behalf of us yᵉ said Maister and Felowes of yᵉ Kyng's Hall: And that Indenture herof suffycyent in yᵉ Lawe shall be made herunto, we have subscribed our names:

[Then follow 12 names, ending with]

Per me Jacobum Nycolson, locum tenentem."

It is to be regretted that the piece of ground to be given up to S. John's College should not have been described with the same precision as the piece which King's Hall stipulated to keep, for we should then have been able to lay down with accuracy on the plan (fig. 9) the north-eastern corner of the site, which it is now impossible to do. We do not know whether the lane which the Prior and Canons of S. Edmund sold to Powis in 1341 extended as far as the High Street; and we know nothing about Godyn's house except that it was situated to the north of that belonging to the Prior and Canons aforesaid. With reference to this house Professor Willis says, in addition to what was stated in the text (p. 422): "It does not appear that the tenement of John Godyn was ever acquired by King's Hall, and it must therefore have occupied the triangular garden next the street at the south [south-east] corner of the present College of S. John's."

Professor Willis further shews that the annual rent of five shillings mentioned in the above documents was charged upon a house which in the reign of Edward the First was occupied by Walter Pylat. In support of this he quotes the following passage from the Hundred Rolls (Rot. Hund. 7 Edward I. (1278—79) ii. 390):

"Item Walterus Pylat tenet unum mesuagium in parochia Omnium Sanctorum juxta Osspitale, quod emit de magistro et fratribus Osspitalis Sancti Johannis Cant'; et insuper reddit per annum dictis magistro et fratribus vs. Qualiter et quo warranto dicti magister et fratres pervenerunt ad mesuagium et ad redditum nesciunt."

Walter Pylat's house subsequently became the property of Edmund de Walsyngham, by whom it was sold to Thomas de Totyngton and King's Hall, as related above (p. 423). It had been purchased by Walsyngham from Ralph de Cumberton, and in the conveyance, dated 1 May, 1300, is described as "mesuagium nostrum integrum cum omnibus suis pertinenciis quod quondam fuit Walteri Pylet pistoris in parochia ecclesie omnium sanctorum iuxta hospitale sancti Johannis in villa Cantebr'; quod scilicet mesuagium...jacet inter mesuagium Ricardi de Marcheford ex vna parte, et mesuagium Christiane Lucas ex altera. Et extendit se in longitudine a regia via vsque ad tenementum quod quondam fuit Magistr' Johannis de Hemmingford et Petri de Welles."

VII. HERALDRY OF THE LIBRARY.

The capital letters and figures prefixed to the description of the coats are those on the classes.   On both sides of the room they begin from the south end.

EAST SIDE.

A, B.   Blank.

C.   A cross potent between four crosses pattées (*See of Lichfield*) impaling three piles in point, on a chief a lion passant guardant (*Hacket*).

> Ensigned by a mitre.
> For John Hacket, Bishop of Coventry and Lichfield (1661—71).

D.   Three mitres (*See of Chester*) impaling a chevron ermine between three oak leaves (*Pearson*).

> Ensigned by a mitre.
> For John Pearson, Master (1662—73) ; and Bishop of Chester (1673—86).

E.   Two swords in saltire between four fleurs de lys (*Barrow*).

> Crest : a squirrel gnawing a nut.
> For Isaac Barrow, D.D., Master (1673—77).

F.   Quarterly 1 and 4 three lozenges conjoined in fess within a bordure (*Montagu*); 2 and 3 an eagle displayed (*Monthermer*).

> Crest : a demi-griffin, wings displayed, gorged with a collar componée.
> For the Honourable John Montagu, Master (1683—1700).

G.   On a chevron between three trefoils slipped, the badge of Ulster (*Sclater*).

> Crest : a laurel wreath.
> For Sir Thomas Sclater, Bart.

H.   Three mullets.   In the fess point the badge of Ulster (*Hildyard*).

> Crest : a cock.
> For Sir Robert Hildyard, Bart.

I.   An inescutcheon within an orle of mullets (*Chamberlaine*).

> Crest : on a ducal coronet an ass's head.
> For Sir George Chamberlaine.

K.   Quarterly 1 and 4, ten torteaux 4. 3. 2. 1 ; a label of three points (*Babington*); 2 and 3 fretty.

> Crest : a demi griffin, wings displayed.
> For Humphry Babington, D.D.

L.   On a fess between three oak slips fructed three roundels.

> Crest: a grasshopper, or locust.
> Probably for William Lynnet, D.D.

M.   Crest : on a ducal coronet a boar's head between two ostrich feathers.

N.   Quarterly 1 and 4 two ostrich feathers in saltire between three boars' heads couped (*Newton*) ; 2 and 3 a bend fusily (*Puckering*).

> Over all a label of three points.

O.   The monogram H. P.

> These three are for Sir Henry Newton Puckering, Bart.

P. A wyvern wings displayed, and tail nowed (*Drake*).
    Crest : a demi-wyvern wings displayed.
    For Robert Drake.

WEST SIDE.

S. Crest : On a ducal coronet a phœnix in the flames (*Seymour*).
    Repeated on X, 2, 5.

T. Monogram C. S. within the Garter surmounted by a ducal coronet.
    Repeated on W, Z, 4.

V. Quarterly of six.
    1. On a pile between six fleurs-de-lys three lions of England. (*Augmenta-tion granted to Queen Jane Seymour by Henry VIII.*).
    2. Two wings conjoined in lure (*Seymour*).
    3. Vairé (*Beauchamp*).
    4. Three demi lions-rampant (*D'Esturmy*).
    5. Three roses in bend counterchanged (Mack William).
    6. A fess engrailed between three escallops (*Prynne*).

Crest : on a ducal coronet a phœnix in the flames, within the Garter.

Supporters : dexter a unicorn; sinister a bull; each gorged with a ducal coronet, and chained.

Repeated on Y, 3, 6.

These are for Charles Seymour, sixth Duke of Somerset, K.G. chancellor of the University 1688—1748.

At each end of the room over the doors are the Royal Arms of William the Third within the Garter and surmounted by the crown.

ON THE ROOF OF THE VESTIBULE.

North side. A lion passant between three fleurs de lis. Crest : a griffin's head erased (*North*).

For the Honourable John North, Master (1677—83).

On the west, south, and east sides respectively are the arms of Dr Barrow, Dr Pearson, and Dr Montague, as above (E, D, F).

XV.

𝕰𝖒𝖒𝖆𝖓𝖚𝖊𝖑 𝕮𝖔𝖑𝖑𝖊𝖌𝖊.

CHAPTER I.

HISTORY OF THE SITE. DESCRIPTION AND HISTORY OF THE FIRST BUILDINGS.

[THE site of Emmanuel College is bounded on the west by S. Andrew's Street, originally Preachers Street; on the north by Emmanuel Lane or Emmanuel Street; on the east by a piece of common ground called Christ's Pieces; and on the south by dwelling-houses, built upon ground which was anciently called Middlefield[1].]

This site—with the exception of a triangular piece of waste ground at the north-east corner (*A B C*, fig. 1) which was granted to the College by the Town in 1838[2]—is simply that of the House or Priory of the Dominicans or Friars Preachers, commonly called the "Black Friars." [3] [The history of its acquisition

---

[1] [MSS. Baker xxxvi. 129. The authorities for the History of Emmanuel College are the volumes of Bursars' Accounts, preserved in the Treasury; two volumes preserved in the Library containing MSS. Collections for a History of the College, made by Dr William Bennet, Fellow (B.A. 1767, M.A. 1770), Bishop of Cork and subsequently Bishop of Cloyne, 1790; and the correspondence between Dr Sandcroft, Dr Breton, and Dr Holbech preserved among the Tanner MSS. in the Bodleian Library, Oxford.]

[2] [The deed, dated 1 February 1838, provides that, in consideration of this grant, the College shall pay £50, and rebuild the garden-wall at the corner of Emmanuel Street and Christ's Pieces, so as to avoid an angle inconvenient to the traffic.]

[3] It is called "Domus sive Prioratus Fratrum Predicatorum vulgariter le Blacke Friers," in the Charter granted to Sir Walter Mildmay by Queen Elizabeth, 11 January. 1583—84. Commiss. Doc^ts iii. 479.

by the Founder, Sir Walter Mildmay, is thus related in one of
the College records[1]:

"First the premisses came vnto kinge Henry theight by Acte of
Parliament towchinge the dissolucion of Monasteries, And aftrewardes
the said kinge by lettres patentes vndre the great Seale of Englande
dated xvj^{to} Aprilis anno xxxv^{to} Regni sui [16 April, 1544], did graunt
the same to Edwarde Elrington and Humfrey Metcalf, and to the heires
of the said Edwarde for ever.

Aftre that the said Edwarde Elrington and Humfrey Metcalf by
their deede polde dated quarto martij anno xxxvj^{to} Henrici octaui
[4 March 1544—45] did graunt the premisses to William Sherewoode
gent' and his heirs for ever[2].

Then George Sherwoode gent' sonne and heire to William Sher-
woode by deed polde dated xxix^{no} septembris anno xxiij^{cio} Elizabethe
Regine [29 September, 1581] did graunt the premisses to Robart
Taylor esquier and his heires for ever.

And afterwardes the said Robart Taylor by deede polde dated
xij^{o} Junii anno xxv^{to} Elizabethe Regine [12 June, 1583] did graunt the
premisses to Richarde Culverwell Citizen and mercer of London and
Lawrence Chaderton and their heires for ever.

And after that the premisses were conveied to Sr Walter Mildmay
as followeth at large."

The ground as purchased by Sir Walter Mildmay, 23 November, 1583, for £550, is thus described :

"all that the scite, circuit, ambulance, and procinct of the late Priory
of Fryers preachers commonly called the blackfryers within the Towne
of Cambrige...and all mesuages, houses, buildinges, barnes, stables,
dovehouses, orchardes, gardens, pondes, stewes, waters, lande, and
soyle within the said scite...And all the walles of stone, brick, or other
thinge compassinge and enclosinge the said scite...[3]."]

The present buildings stand upon nearly the same sites as
those erected at the first construction of the College. Their
architectural aspect however is totally different from that which
they originally presented, and their arrangement has been
changed. The primitive arrangement will be understood from

---

[1] [The following passage forms the preface to a vellum book into which the early
documents of the College have been transcribed. It is called: "A booke conteyninge
the entrye or enrollment of certeine lettres patent, writinges, and evidences towchinge
Emmanuell Colleage in Camebrige latelie founded by Sir Walter Mildmay knight,
one of her majesty's most honorable privie councell, with a breif declaracion wch doth
shewe how the same Colleage was sometyme a house of Friers and came to kinge
Henry theight by dissolucion etc."]

[2] [Fuller, p. 278, records that Mr Sherwood made it his dwelling-house.]

[3] [The deed is copied in the volume described above.]

the views of Hamond (fig. 2) and of Loggan (fig. 3), compared with the ground-plan of the site (fig. 1).

The College, now as at first, has two quadrangles of unequal
size, the smaller lying to the north of the larger.   The principal
entrance is from S. Andrew's Street, through the centre of the

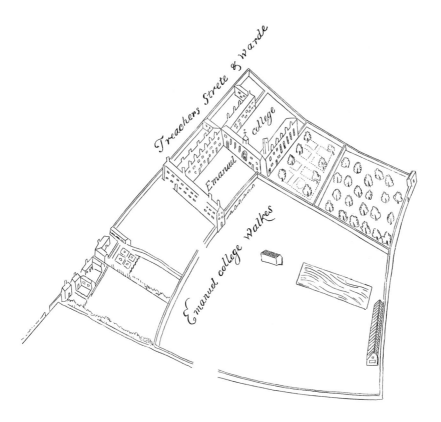

Fig. 2.   Emmanuel College, reduced from Hamond's map of Cambridge, 1592.

west side of the larger quadrangle, and the smaller quadrangle
is reached by means of two passages at the two ends of the
north side of the great quadrangle.   But in the original plan, as
Loggan shews, the College was entered from Emmanuel Lane
through the smaller quadrangle, and these passages gave access

from it to the larger quadrangle. The small quadrangle consisted of three sides only, being open to the north. The
south side was occupied by the Hall and the Master's Lodge,
of which the latter was at the east end. The east side or wing
consisted of the Chapel, with chambers over it in the roof.
The west side contained the kitchen, over which there was a
gallery[1], and some chambers. At each angle of the south side
there was a small square turret[2], one of which furnished a
porch to the Chapel, the other to the kitchen. The Parlour or
Combination-room was at the east end of the Hall, and a
passage through the building close to the eastern porch passed
between the Lodge and Combination-room, and gave access
to the larger quadrangle beyond. The entrance to this smaller
quadrangle, which, as already stated, was then the principal
entrance to the College, was in Emmanuel Lane, through an
ornamental doorway[3], in the centre of the north wall, whence a
broad path between two lines of posts and rails led straight
towards the oriel of the Hall, which the architect had contrived
to place in the middle of the façade. At this point the path
intersected a similar one, which, extending along the façade,
conducted to the kitchen on the right and to the Chapel on
the left. From the kitchen-porch the usual passage, or screen,
between the Hall and Butteries, furnished a second access to the
larger quadrangle. The latter had buildings on three sides only,
but it differed from the former in being open to the east instead
of to the north. [On that side it was closed by a wall (fig. 2),
which apparently was pierced with an arcade.] The western
side of this quadrangle was evidently erected partly upon the
ancient walls of the Friars' buildings. It had buttresses
(fig. 3), and may have been the Dormitory. Now, however,
it was converted into chambers. The south side also was
occupied by a range of chambers which is still called the
"Founder's Range," and to all appearance has no mixture of
pre-existing buildings.

---

[1] [Bursar's Accounts, 1586. "Item 6 iron barrs...for yᵉ galerie wyndows over yᵉ
kitchin ixˢ."]

[2] [The turret at the south-west corner is shewn on Loggan's ground-plan.]

[3] [Blomefield (Collectanea, p. 116) records that over this doorway was the
following inscription : "Sacræ Theologiæ Studiosis posuit Gualterus Mildmaius Aᵒ
Dni. 1584."]

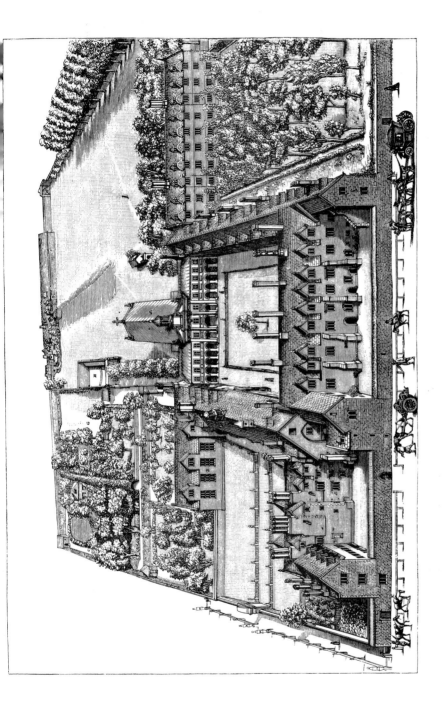

Fig. 3. Emmanuel College, from Loggan's print, taken about 1688. A, Chapel; B, Library; C, Hall; D, Master's Lodge; E, Kitchen; F, Master's Garden; G, Fellows' Garden; H, Tennis Court; I, Brewhouse.

There was a considerable interval between S. Andrew's Street and the College buildings, as at present; but three short wings projected from the latter and joined the boundary wall which then bordered the street, thus forming two narrow subsidiary courts, each, like the larger one, open on one side. [Of these, that to the west of the principal quadrangle was called Wolfenden's Court in the seventeenth century[1]; the other, which had a separate entrance from Preachers' Street (fig. 3), was called Bungay Court.]

There is no specific record of the manner in which the first buildings were carried on. [The charter, dated 11 January, 1584, sets forth Sir Walter Mildmay's intention to form a College; and declares that "when it shall have been erected, made, founded, and established," it shall be called the College of Emmanuel. At that time therefore the buildings could not have been far advanced, even if they had been commenced. At the end of the following year (1 October, 1585), the Founder sent down the Statutes, which he would hardly have done had not some buildings been ready for his scholars. In the Bursar's Accounts for 1586, the first year for which they have been preserved, work is being done to the Common Parlour and to the chamber above it, while the Hall is referred to as though it were completed[2]. The Kitchen and Gallery are also mentioned. In the following year, 1587, we meet with entries for whitewashing the Chapel; and for mending the louvre of the Hall[3]. In December of the same year the Founder issued a supplementary statute in which he desires that "a single chamber of those recently constructed, that chamber namely which is at the end of the range towards the east, between the lowest chamber and

---

[1] [A letter, dated 11 Feb., 1694—95, copied by Bennet (ii. 72) describes "a little room on the right hand in the entry through which we go from the quadrangle into Wolfenden's Court." On this Bennet notes: "Wolfenden's Court, now the space between the iron palisades and the front rooms of the College; it was once separated from the street by a high wall, and received this name, I suppose, from James Wolfenden Fellow in 1670, who might keep in or near it."]

[2] [Bursar's Accounts, 1586. "To Thomas Sendal for seeling and pargeting the common parler in part of payment for the whole xxx^s. For seeling and pargeting ye entrie at the end of ye hall...xxiiij^s vij^d. For four casements two to the common parlor and two for the chamber above it xvj^s."]

[3] [Ibid. 1587. "For whyting the chappell aboue and vpon the ends and sydes xxxv^s vj^d. For souder to mend ye hall lover x^s vij^d."]

the upper chamber next the roof, may be appropriated to such of our descendants as may be studying in the College[1]." This language implies that the chambers in question were then complete. The range called the "Founder's Range" is evidently meant, and the provision here enacted was probably the origin of the name. In 1588 there are entries referring to the Master's Lodge, the Great Gates, and the wall in which they were contained; large quantities of building-materials, stone from Cambridge Castle, and timber sent by various benefactors, were brought into College[2]; the Hall was whitewashed, the inner court was paved, furniture was bought for the Parlour[3]; and lastly, the "dedication" festival was celebrated in the presence of the Founder[4]. It may be concluded, therefore, that the two quadrangles, in the state in which they are shewn by Hamond in 1592, were completed by the Founder before his death, which took place 31 May, 1589.]

The "Benefactors' Book" records the names of many of his contemporaries who assisted him in the work. Sir Henry Killigrew gave £140 for the purchase of S. Nicholas' Hostel[5], the

---

[1] ["*Statutum de camerâ consanguineis Fundatoris reservandâ:*" "Quamobrem unicam cameram ex earum numero quæ recens extructæ sunt, quæque in eo ordine extrema orientem respicit, et inter imam cameram et supremam tecto proximam interjacet, posteris et consanguineis nostris, qui studii causa in Collegium prædictum asciscentur, dicandam esse censuimus." Commis. Doc^{ts} iii. 523.]

[2] [Bursar's Accounts, 1588. "For carters for bringing stone from ye Castle, and Tymber from Sr Giles Alrington's by Sr Francis Hynds, Mr Hutton, Mr Justice Sute, Mr Wendie, Sr John Cutts and others; in bread, beer and meate xxxv^s viij^d." The other entries for stone from the Castle are too numerous for quotation.]

[3] [Ibid. "For 4 days work whyting ye hall vj^s viij^d. For half a days work for whyting ye screene x^d. For whyting ye common parlor and ye stairs above to o^r founders chamber iij^s. To Hobson for carying ye parlor table 500 and a half xvj^s vj^d. Two fourmes for ye parlor vj^s. A bason and vre for the hall v^s vj^d. For paving the Inner court and the tarris without it xxiiij^{li}."]

[4] [Ibid. "For clensing ye street at ye dedication iij^s. To the two keepers that [brought] us two does at o^r dedication xj^s. For coales at the dedication xiij^s. For dressing all roomes agaynst o^r founders coming iij^s vj^d. For a cragg of sturgeon carying at ye dedication xxij^d."]

[5] ["Centum et quadraginta libras numeravit, ut ex sancti Nicholai Hospitio, pretii illius solutione acquisito, dignissimo Collegii Prefecto, venerabili viro doctori Chadertonio, Ædes ad habitandum idoneæ extruerentur." The Hostel is described in the conveyance as: "all that mesuage tenemente or Inne comonlye called St Nicholas hostell with all houses buildinges yardes gardens groundes and hereditamentes to the same belonginge scituat' lienge and beinge in the parisshe of St Andrewe without Barnwell gates in Cambridge aforesaid betwene the tenemente late of John Adam on

materials of which were applied to the construction of the Lodge for Dr Laurence Chaderton the first Master (Master 1584—1622). The Hostel was purchased 27 March, 1585. Sir Wolstan Dixie, Lord Mayor of London in 1585, gave £650 to the buildings. Sir Richard Ashton of Middleton in Lancashire, gave £13. 6s. 8d. to the fittings of the Library. Sir John Hart, Lord Mayor of London in 1589, gave £50 towards the College walls, and Dr Edward Leedes (Master of Clare Hall 1562—1571, and afterwards Rector of Croxton in Cambridgeshire) gave 1000 marks towards the buildings. These dates all point to the active prosecution of building-work in the years immediately succeeding the grant of the charter.

The architect is known to have been Ralph Symons, whose work at Trinity College and S. John's College has been already mentioned. [His employment here is recorded in the inscription on his portrait in the gallery of the Master's Lodge[1], and in the following piece of contemporary information which occurs in the preamble to the lease of a tenement near the College granted to him 21 October, 1586, by Dr Edward Leedes. He is to have the property on certain advantageous terms

"in consideracion that the said Raphe Symondes is a well mynded man towards Emanuell Colledge in Cambridge latelie founded and newlie buylded, The workemanship wheareof touching the stone worke hath been wrought and perfourmed by the said Raphe, whearein he hath shewed him selfe verie dilligent and carefull[2]."

This sentence implies that the portion entrusted to Symons was completely finished when it was written. As we have shewn

the one partie and the tenemente called the Chequer and a tenemente of Tho: Bredon on the other partie the one hedd therof abuttinge vpon the Quenes higheway called Preachers strete and the other vpon the Quenes highwaye leadinge towardes Barnwell..." The price paid was £150.]

[1] [Quoted above, p. 475.]

[2] [The lease is in the Treasury of Emmanuel College. The house demised stood at the north corner of Preachers Street and Emmanuel Lane; "Betwene the Tenement called the Antelopp towardes the Northe, And the Comon Lane leading by the wall of the Black Fryers now Emmanuell Colledge on the southe, and the west parte abutteth vpon ... Preachers Strete, and the part towards the East on the Tenement or ground belonging to S^t. John's College." In another document, dated 10 January, 1587, Symons describes himself "of Barkhamstedd in the Countie of Hartford Freemason." The corner-house above described was called Roxton Hall in the next century, and it adjoined certain houses which together formed a range called the Pensionary. This appears from a lease of part of it dated 1 September, 1669.]

that parts of the College were still in progress two years afterwards, the words perhaps refer to the Founder's Range.   Besides
the construction of this] he evidently adapted a portion at least
of the buildings of the Dominicans; and a tradition, which there
is no reason to doubt, asserts that the Hall was no other than
their Church.   [This is corroborated by the following interesting
piece of history, preserved by Dr Bennet[1] :

> "Our Hall was the Chapel of the Convent, and in repairing the
> Combination-room about 1762 the traces of the High Altar were very
> apparent near the present fire-place.   In 1771 the great West window
> of the old Chapel which had been long brick'd up was pull'd down to
> erect the Butteries, and by the number of bones dug up in laying the
> foundations of the Cloyster building, it is probable that the burying
> ground of the Friars extended all along the present front of the College."]

The western gable of the Church of the Dominicans, with
angle-buttresses, and the arched head of a western window,
walled up and pierced with small chamber windows, is clearly
delineated in Loggan's view.   It is said that the Puritan founder
of the College evinced his contempt for ancient tradition by
making this use of the Church, and purposely placing his
Chapel in the north and south direction.

CHAPTER II.

HISTORY OF THE BUILDINGS TO THE END OF THE SIXTEENTH AND SEVENTEENTH CENTURIES.

[THE first addition to the buildings erected by the Founder
was the small range of chambers in three floors extending from
the north end of the kitchen-range westwards to the street
(fig. 3).   As it is described as "the new building next to the
street" in a list of chambers dated 26 October, 1614, we may
conclude that it had been erected at the beginning of the
seventeenth century ; but its history has been completely lost.
It must have been about fifty feet long, by twenty feet broad[2];

---

[1] [Bennet, *ut supra*, i. 166.]

[2] [It has been laid down on the plan (fig. 1) from Loggan's plan of Cambridge.]

and the above list shews that it had three chambers on each of its three floors.]

A more important addition took place in the Mastership of Dr William Sandcroft[1] (Master, 1628—37) when, 4 February, 1632—33, the following Order was made :

"Memorandum that for the enlarging of our roome which long time hath beene, and still is, too scant to receiue the number of students in the Colledge, and for the bringing of them all to keepe and lodge within the walls (according to the expresse words of the statute Cap. 40° *nullum pro pensionario ad conuictum scholarium aut sociorum admitti uel in Collegio morari uolumus . . . qui non cameram habeat uti in dicto Collegio cubet*) It was thought fitt by yᵉ Mʳ and the Society, and accordingly agreed and concluded by ioynt and unanimous consent of the Maior part,

To haue a new range of building erected from the founders chamber to Pits garden according to a plott drawne, and couenants made, to that purpose.

And that in regard of the charge the Colledge is to be at both for the present building and continuall maintayning for time to come of the said range of building yᵉ yearely rent to be sett vpon the chambers and studies in yᵉ same (by the Mʳ being assisted by the two seniour fellowes according to the statute Cap. 4ᵗᵒ *in fine*) and accrewing theirfrom shall from time to time for euer goe to the treasury and the encreasing of the publike stocke of the Colledge, and in noe wise be conuerted to anie priuate vses. And further that for the better getting in of yᵉ sᵈ Chamber rent to the Colledge, euery Tutour shall at euery of our accounts pay to the Mʳ for euery of his pupills inhabiting yᵉ sᵈ chambers soe much rent as shall then be due from them and comming to the Colledge, and in default of such paymᵗ soe by them to be made it shalbe lawfull for the Mʳ to detayne soe much out of their owne and their schollers allowances as shalbe sufficient to satisfy the Colledge. In witnes wheirof both yᵉ Mʳ and the greater part of the present fellowes haue heereunto subscribed their names the day and yeere aboue written[2]."

The range of chambers contemplated in the above Order is the "Brick Building," which runs out southward from the eastern extremity of the "Founder's Range." The builder was John Westley, of Cambridge, bricklayer, who was employed to build Clare Hall in 1638—42[3]. The following contract, drawn up between him and the Master, Dr William Sandcroft, and the Fellows, "concerninge a range of buildeinge to be erected and sett up in Emanuell Colledge," is dated 9 February, 1632—33.

---

[1] [He was uncle to Dr William Sandcroft, Master 1662—65.]

[2] [College Order Book, p. 39. It is signed by the Master and eleven Fellows.]

[3] [History of Clare Hall, Chapter III.]

"Imprimis, the sayd John Westleye For the Consideracion hereafter expressed, doth Couenante ...... that the sayd John, his Workmen, seruants, or Assignees, shall and will, at or before, the Twelueth daye of October next ensueing the daye of ye date of these presents, at his and theyr owne proper Costs and Chardges, well, substantially, sufficiently, and workemanlike Erecte, build, and fully finish, as toucheing the Brickworke, and Tyleinge, in such sorte, as is hereafter more particularly expressed, uppon good and sufficient foundacion, makeinge A sufficient Vault, ouer the Riuer, And by the Five and twentieth daye of March, which shalbe in ye yeare of our Lord 1634 shall haue fully finished, as toucheing all other worke by him to be done

One Buildeing of an Hundred, and Fortye Foote in Length, to be Three Storyes in height, And a Garrett to begin from ye Wallplatt upward; the Fyrst Floore to lye Eighteene Inches aboue the walk before it; And betweene that, and the Seilinge, to be Nine Foote; And betweene the Floore, and the next Seileinge, to be Nine Foote, and A halfe; And betweene that Floore and the next Seileinge, to be Eight foote; The Lower Storye to be Twentye Foote wyde, within ye Walls. The other two Storyes to be Twentye Foote, and Eight Inches wide, within the Walls.

And that the outward Walls of the same buildeinge shalbe of Bricke. All the Corners thereof to be sett with Coynes of Freestone; The same Walls to be of the thicknes of Three Brickes in length under the Watertable; The same Watertable to lye three Foote or more aboue the grownd, and to be of Freestone Chamfered Fowre Inches and A halfe thicke, And from the Watertable, to the Middle Floore, the Walls to be of the thicknes of two Brickes and a halfe in length. And from the Middle Floore to the Wallplats, the Walls to be of the thicknesse of two Brickes in Length.

Both ends of the same buildeinge to be wrought Gablewise with Crosses and some Comlye finisheinge of Freestone; with an Architrave playne Fryse of Whitestone, and Cornish of Freestone, ouer the head of the Windowes on both sides.

All the Walls on the Inside to be cast ouer with Lyme, and Hayre.

And that there shalbe in the sayd buildynge Two Stackes of Chimneyes, soe placed that there be in euery outward Chamber, One; In the Whole Sixteene; with Chimneypeices of good Whitestone, Cleane, and handsomely wrought; The shaftes of the same Chimneyes, to be Caryed upp in the Ridge of the Roofe, according to a particular draught by him exhibited subsigned with his owne hand.

And that there shalbe placed two Conuenient doorsteads with Freestone Jalmes, and Whitestone heads; And Conuenient Windowes in the three Lower Storyes of three lights apeice; Euery light to be eighteene Inches Wyde; And the height to be determined by the height of the Roome with Freestone Soyles Six Inches thicke and Tenn Inches broade; The jalmes, and Munions to be of Whitestone. And in the Fyrst and second Storyes, Arches of Bricke to be turned ouer euery Windowe.

And that all the Roomes in all the Storyes, and Garrett of the sayd buildeinge, shalbe well and workmanlike Seiled with Lyme and Hayre, layd uppon Reede well fastened with harte Lathes vnto the Timber of the sayd Buildeinge. And all the Particions and studyes, to be splented and Clayed betweene the Studds; And on the Outside cast ouer with Lyme, and Hayre, on hartelath; And the Inside to be layd with Lyme and Hayre, betweene the studds.

And the buildeinge to be couered with good Tyles, layd with Morter, uppon hartlath; The Finishments ouer the Windowes to be made accordinge to the great Draught, or some other Waye Equiualente thereunto, as shalbe hereafter thought of; The Gable-ends ouer the Windowes in ye Roofe to be of Bricke; as also the Fillings upp, under ye Windowes Eues; And to Pave it with Pebble on the Fronte side, a yard from ye Wall; In the Gable-ends in each Roome, A Windowe of Two Lights apeice; Eighteene Inches Wyde, And of the same proportion for height, with the Windowes of the other Roomes respectiuelye;

And the said John Westlye doth Couenante [to] provide and haue readye for ye sayd...buildeinge, All the Brickes and Tyles, the same to be good and well burned, Freestone, and Whitestone well bedded, Lyme, Sande, Hayre, Lath, Reede, And his Morter for all purposes, to be well and workmanlike made;

And Further ... to prouide, wellplace and fasten, One Barr of Iron in euery light, of the same bignesse with those in the Parlour of the sayd Colledge, And euery studdye Windowe to haue an Iron Casemente, And euery outward Chamber, two; And euery Bedchamber one, besides two Studdyes; and the end Studye, to haue two Casements; All the length of the sayd Casements to be the same with the Casements in Katherine Hall new buildeinge; And all the same lights to be Well and sufficientlye Glazed with good White glasse in small Quarryes, well Leaded, Soldered, Semented, and sufficientlye sett into the said Windowes, and bownd to the Barrs, and for any other particulars omitted, Referringe to the great Draught aboue-mencioned. .

And for the sayd buildeinge, soe to be made, and finished, the sayd Master and Fellowes ... Doe Couenante ... that they ... shall and will well and truly Contente and paye ... to the sayd John Westlye ... the Summe of Six Hundred, Threescore, and Five Pownds of Currante Money of England, in Manner, and Forme following (*videlicet*) at thensealinge of these presents, Thirtye Powndes; puttinge in sufficient securitye for the same; When the buildeinge is brought upp to the Watertable Thirtye Pownds more; When the sayd Buildeing is brought upp to the Fyrst Floore, One Hundred Powndes more; At the Second Floore layeing One Hundred Pownds more; When the Roofe and Tyleing is ended One other Hundred; At the end of the Worke, the other Three Hundred and Five Pownds, in full payment of the sayd Six Hundred, Threescore, and Five Pownds;

And the said Master and Fellowes Doe further Couenante and agree that the sayd John Westlye in Consideracion of the performance of ye premisses; shall and may haue, take downe, and use, all the Old Wall, where the sayd New buildeing is to be erected, as beforesaid;

And also the Tyles, and Lathes of the Tennis Court and house of Office.

Prouided alwayes, that the sayd John Westlye...doe well, and sufficiently performe, and keepe, all and singular the Couenants, Articles, and Agreements by, and on his parte to be performed, according to the Intente, meaning, and order in theise presents limited and appointed.

Prouided also, that in case the sayd Worke stands at A stage, thorough the defaulte of the said John, soe that there be manifest danger that it will not be Finished by the time before limitted, then the sayd Master and Fellowes, or theyr Successors, shall be at Free libertye to procure some other whom they shall best like of, to goe thorough with and Finish the said worke.

In Witnes whereof aswell the sayd Master and Fellowes theyr Common Seale, as the sayd John Westlye his Seale, to theise Articles Indented, Interchangeably, have putt, the Daye, and yeare, Fyrst above written."

On the same day a separate contract was made with Henry Man, of Cambridge, carpenter, as follows :

" Imprimis the sayd Henry Man, for the consideracõn hereafter expressed, doth couenant...That...[he] shall...find prouide, and haue readye, All kind of Timber, necessarye for the buildeing to be erected by John Westlye in the sayd Colledge.

First For Fowre Floores, throughout the whole buildinge. The grownd Floore to be of good, sufficient, and well seasoned board of Oake, layd uppon sufficient Joyse of Oaketimber, the other three Floores, to be of good, and sufficient Summers or Dormans, Joyse, and board of Fyrrtimber ; The Boards to be well seasoned, and without Sapp ; And to be Close layd, and finely smoothed.

Next for the Roofe. The roofe to consiste and be of good and sufficient Oake Timber, with soe many principall sparrs, as can be conveniently placed wth stronge Pyrlines and Windbeames, with Seileing Sparrs of Fyrr : And to stand uppon Wallplats of Oake Seauen Inches thicke, and Nine Inches broade ;

Then for the Windowes in ye Roofe, to be of good Oake Timber, with Wether sparrs handsomely wrought. All the particons within both in Chambers and studdyes, in all Fowre Floores, to be according to ye diuisions described in a growndplott, by him exhibited, and agreeing to the Plott of that buildeinge in Katherine Hall, in which Mr Knowles now keepeth, with the Chambers aboue and beneathe him ; the particons to be by him made of studs of Fyrr timber ;

All the doores to all the Chambers, and studdyes, to be made of Fyrr-dele, handsomely and well wrought. And to prouide sufficient Lintels and Slabs to laye under and ouer them, for ye Chimneyes, and also Harthpaces.

The Stayers to be of good and sufficient Oaken Plankes, layd uppon good and sufficient Bearers; And that he wilbe readye to laye his Floores, and Roofe, at or before such tyme as the Bricklayer shalbe readye (or callith) for them.

And he, the sayd Henry Man, doth further Couenant to doe such other workes, as doe properly belonge to Carpenters, according to the ground plott aforementoned. And that he will have finished his worke by the Fyrst Daye of Maye, which shalbe in the yeare of our Lord, 1634.

And for the sayd Buildeinge so by him to be made, and finished, the sayd Master, and Fellowes, for them, and theyr Successors, doe Couenante...to and wth the sayd Henry Man,...that they...shall and will... paye, or Cause to be payd, to the sayd Henry Man...the Summe of Two Hundred, Eightye-Five Powndes,......of Currante Money of England in Manner and forme followinge, (that is to saye) One Fortye Powndes thereof, at thensealeing hereof, putting in a sufficient secureity for the same, And Threescore pownds more at and uppon the fyrst daye of March, next ensueinge: Thirtye pownds more, at the layeinge of the Fyrst Floore; Thirtye more at the next: The residue of the sayd two Hundred Eightye-Five powndes......at reasonable tymes, as the worke shall goe forwarde in Full payment of the sayd two Hundred Eightye Five pownds.

And the sayd Master and Fellowes, doe Further Couenant, and agree, that the sayd Henry Man in Consideration of ye performeance of the premisses, shall and may have, take downe, and use, in the same worke, All the Timber of the Cover of the Tenniscourt Situate in the sayd Colledge.

In Witnes whereof as well the sayd Master and Fellowes theyr Comon Seale, as the sayd Henry Man, his Seale to these Articles Indented, haue putt, the Daye and yeare Fyrst aboue written[1]."

The building was finished within the appointed time, for both Westley and Man received their last payment 22 April, 1634; and 25 October in the same year Westley received £20 as a gratuity "in regard of that which he had done in the New Buildings aboue couenantes." By this time therefore the building must have been completed. A note of some of the extra work done by Westley has been preserved, from which the following items are worth quotation :

"All the piramides upon the little gable ends			
worth	4	0	0
For carving the spandrells of the doores ...	0	10	0
Four foote more then Covenants in the length			
of the building	16	0	0
All the French Eves to keepe the water from the			
building	13	16	8 "

[The Brick Building is a range of chambers in three floors, with garrets in the roof, of the exact dimensions prescribed in the contract[2]. The west side of it is shewn by Loggan (fig. 3),

---

[1] [These two contracts are preserved in the Treasury of Emmanuel College.]

[2] [These measures are all inside measures.]

and as his view was taken in 1688, or not more than 54 years after the building was completed, we may presume that it faithfully records the original appearance. The construction, however, seems to have been faulty, and frequent repairs have destroyed many interesting features[1]. For instance, the row of gables which Loggan shews on the west side have been removed; and if a similar row once existed on the east side, they have been removed also. The dormers of the garret windows also are no longer to be seen. Again, the doorways, the heads of which were constructed, as the contract prescribes, of clunch, have become so decayed that their primitive features have been nearly obliterated.]

The next architectural work undertaken was the provision of a new Chapel, and a new Library. The old Chapel had become nearly ruinous, and besides, the singularity of its position, the fact that it had never been consecrated, and the puritanical observances alleged to be practised in it, gave great offence. [The following statement, drawn up in 1603, gives a graphic picture of the disorders complained of[2]:

"1. First for a prognostication of disorder, whereas all the Chappells in ye University are built with the Chancell Eastward, according to ye uniform order of all Christendome, The Chancell in y^t Colledge standeth north, and their kitchen eastwarde.

2. All other Colledges in Cambridge do strictly observe, according to ye laws and ordinances of ye Church of England, the form of public prayer prescribed in ye Communion Booke. In Emanuell Colledge they do followe a private course of publick prayer, after y^r own fashion, both sondaies, Holydaies, and workie days.

3. In all other Colledges, the M^rs and Scholers of all sorts do wear

---

[1] [Dr Bennet (ii. 42) says of it : "The Plot or Plan of this (now called the Brick building) is well enough contriv'd, but the execution shamefully negligent, so that tho' the Prime Cost was £1500, and above £500 more has been since laid out upon it, the whole is already (1788) in a tottering state, and only kept together by the strength of the Chimnies."]

[2] [MSS. Baker vi. 85. MSS. Harl. Mus. Brit. 7033. It is headed "The publick disorders as touching Church causes in Emanuell Colledge in Cambridge;" and at the end Baker notes: "From my Ld. Ch. Justice Hale's Papers, now in ye custody of Mr Geo. Harbin." A similar account is given in a paper sent in to Archbishop Laud, and endorsed by him : "Common Disorders in the University. Received Septemb. 23, 1636. Certaine Disorders in Cambridge, to be consider'd of in mye visitation." MSS. Baker vi. 152—155. Printed in Cooper's Annals iii. 283. Evelyn, who visited Cambridge in 1654, notes on Emmanuel: "The chapell is reform'd, *ab origine*, built north and south, meanely erected, as is ye librarie." Memoirs, etc. ed. Bray, ii. 96.]

surplisses and Hoods, if they be Graduats, upon yᵉ Sondaies and Holydaies in yᵉ time of Divine Service.   But they of Emanuell Colledge have
not worn that attier, either at yᵉ ordinary Divine Service, or celebration
of yᵉ Lord's Supper, since it was first erected.

    4.   All other Colledges do wear, according to yᵉ orders of yᵉ Uni-
versity, and many directions given from the late Queen, Gowns of a sett
fashion, and Square Capps.   But they of Eman. Coll. are therein altogether irregular, and hold themselves not to be tied to any such orders.

    5.   Every other Colledge, according to yᵉ Laws in that behalf pro-
vided, and to the custome of the King's Householde, do refrayne their
Suppers upon Frydaies and other fastinge and Ember daies.   But they
of Eman. Coll. have Suppers every such nights throughout yᵉ year,
publickly in yʳ Hall, yea upon good Fridaye it self.

    6.   All other Colledges do use one manner of fourme in celebratinge
the Holy Communion, according to yᵉ order of the Communion Booke,
as particularly, the Communicants receive kneelinge, with the particular
application of these words, viz. *The Body of our Lord Jesus Christ, etc.;
The Blood of our Lord Jesus Christ, etc.;* as the sᵈ Booke prescribeth.

    But in Eman. Coll. they receive that Holy Sacrament, sittinge upon
Forms about the Communion Table, and doe pull the Loafe one from
the other, after the Minister hath begon.   And soe yᵉ Cupp, one drink-
ing as it were to another, like good Fellows, without any particular
application of yᵉ sᵈ words, more than once for all.

    7.   In other Colledges and Churches, generally none are admitted
to attend att the Communion Table, in the celebration of yᵗ Holy
Mystery, but Ministers and Deacons.   But in Eman. Coll. the wine is
filled, and the Table is attended by the Fellows subsizers."

It must be admitted that in "An Inventory of all things
in the Chappell," drawn up in 1589, "A Communion table with
two forms" is mentioned. In subsequent lists we find "A
Communion Table, and a carpet for it," and no further allusion
is made to the forms. From the list of 1662, which is fuller
than any of the preceding ones, it may be gathered that there
was an ante-chapel; that the Chapel was wainscotted, with
"seats thrice round about"; that it had nine windows, with
"the Q. Armes in the greatest at the end"; that it was
lighted by a brass chandelier of twelve branches suspended
from the centre of the roof, and by brass branches projecting
from the walls, and by candlesticks fixed to the seats. Lastly,
there was a pulpit and hour-glass. It must have been inconveniently small, for the room, which has not been altered, is
only 68 feet long, including the vestibule, by 28 feet broad[1].

---

    [1] [The state of the old Chapel is thus described in a letter from Dr Palmer (pre-
served by Dr Bennet) on his donation to building the new Chapel, 11 October, 1669:

The position of the Library has not been recorded, but
there are some references to it in the Audit-Books and other
documents, which, if considered in connexion with one another,
enable us to fix its position with tolerable certainty. A catalogue of the books, dated 27 April, 1637, speaks of the eastern
and western divisions of the Library, and enumerates the classes
in each. This shews that the room must have stood east and
west, and clear of other buildings, so as to admit windows in the
north and south walls, between the bookcases, as usual in
ancient libraries; and, in fact, in 1657 a charge occurs "for
ripping the north side of the Library." Moreover it was on the
first floor at least, from allusions to the staircase, and payments
for carrying books up to it. If we next proceed to consider
the different parts of the College in which the Library could
have been placed, we may reject at once the Brick Building
and the ranges which form the west sides of the first and
second Courts, for they do not fulfil the required conditions as
to aspect. Again, the north range of the principal court was
wholly occupied by the Hall and Master's Lodge, and the
south, or Founder's Range, by chambers. There remains, however, the small range which extended from the north end of
the Kitchen-range to the street (fig. 2), and formed the north
side of the small court called "Bungay Court." This building
satisfies the required conditions as to situation. It must have
been about fifty feet long, and on the first floor Loggan shews
seven windows; an unusual number in so small a space for any
other room than a Library.]

This Library was soon found to be inconveniently small;
and when Dr Richard Holdsworth (Master, 1637—44), bequeathed his books to the College in 1649, upon the condition
that a suitable room should be provided for them[1], the Society

"Ego ex quo primum tempore Collegium vestrum salutavi, notavi sacellum vetustate
bene confectum; tabulati tremorem, parietum rimas, tumores, et crustas ferro con-
strictas: mirum est tot annos stetisse, quod brevi collapsurum fuisse crediderim."]

[1] [Dr Holdsworth was ejected from his Mastership in 1645, and died 1649. He
bequeathed his Library, under complicated conditions, to the University and Emmanuel College. In 1664, after long controversy, the matter was referred to the
Archbishop of York, and the Bishops of London and Ely, who decided that the
Library should belong to the University; but that the duplicates, together with £200,
should be sent to Emmanuel College; the money to be expended in books. We find
however that it was used in the erection of the new Chapel.]

was induced to consider the question of building a new one. No definite scheme, however, was undertaken until Dr William Sandcroft became Master, in August, 1662. The following extract from a letter[1] written by him from Emmanuel College, 17 June, 1663, to his former tutor, Mr Ezekiel Wright, then Rector of Thurcaston, in Leicestershire, explains his intentions, and his active zeal in promoting them :

"I am now in Pursuit of Dr Holdsworth's numerous Library; and though the University hath long since swallowed it in a generall Expectation, yet, having lately got a Sight of his private Directions to his Executors, and consulted both Lawyers and severall of my Lords the Bishops, and the Executors themselves thereupon, I doubt not at all, the Right will prove to be ours : Provided that we erect a Case or Room fitt to receive them; the Condition upon which he give them us. For the Performance whereof, and also for the removing that great Mark of Singularity, which all the World so talks of, in the unusual Prospect and Dress of the Chapell (different from that of other Colledges,) I have it in Designe to make both a new Library and Chapell too; and as for the Manner of contriving both, I would gladly receive your particular Opinion, so I must be forct to beg the charitable and liberal Assistance of all that have been Members of it; and your's, Sir, especially, who wert once so great an Ornament, and now so true a Lover of it."

[Dr Sandcroft was Master for rather less than three years, from August, 1662, to May, 1665, when he was made Dean of S. Paul's. He was therefore prevented from carrying out these views of improvement in person; and the buildings contemplated by him were erected by his successors Dr John Breton (Master, 1665—76), and Dr Thomas Holbech (Master, 1676—80). His removal, however, promoted rather than impeded the work. The architect employed was Sir Christopher, then Dr, Wren, who at the time was actually engaged with the erection of the new Chapel at Pembroke College, begun in 1663[2]; but his employment at Emmanuel College may well have been due to his constant intercourse with Dean Sandcroft in respect of the rebuilding of S. Paul's Cathedral[3]. We shall find that the design for the Chapel, Cloister, and Gallery was

---

[1] [Life of William Sandcroft, by George D'Oyly, i. 130. The letter is printed from MSS. Cole, lix. 275. The original was lent to Cole in 1781 by Dr Richard Farmer, Master of Emmanuel, 1775—97.]

[2] [History of Pembroke College, Vol. i. p. 147.]

[3] [Parentalia, p. 278. D'Oyly's Life, i. 138.]

elaborated by Sandcroft, probably in consultation with Wren. His successors in the Mastership informed him regularly of the minutest details of the progress of the building; and sought his advice and help on all occasions. He contributed largely to the funds, and induced his wealthy friends to follow his example[1].]

The Chapel is placed with great skill at the east side of the great quadrangle, in a position precisely similar to that of Peterhouse. Its western gable occupies the middle of that side, and the Chapel itself extends eastwards from the quadrangle into the grounds beyond. Like its prototype, it is connected to the right and left with the previously existing sides of the quadrangle by means of open cloisters. Above this cloister is a long gallery for pictures, &c. attached to the Master's Lodge, from which a door opens to the organ-loft and pew for the Master's family. [The design for the façade (fig. 4[2]), preserved among Wren's other drawings at Oxford, shews that he proposed to build the gallery of red brick, with stone dressings, probably to make it harmonize with the older buildings of the quadrangle. We do not know why this intention was not carried out; but Loggan shews that the whole was ashlared from the first. It should also be mentioned that, in the course of the work, the central arch of the cloister, which in Wren's design is shewn of the same width as the others, was taken down and made wider[3].

The design for the Chapel had been under consideration by Sandcroft during the year 1666, but it had evidently not been seen by the Master and Fellows. The following letter[4] was written to him by Dr Breton, 25 January, 1666—67:

......" This whole Society ioynes with me in the thanks to be given to you for your care concirning the modell of our chapell, which we wish to receive when it is finished, but doubt whether we shall be able

---

[1] [This is expressly stated by the Fellows in a letter to Sandcroft, forwarded by the Master 9 September, 1676. After thanking him for a gift of £200 which he had just given them "in tempore maximè opportuno," they proceed: "Tu primus omnium nobis novi Sacrarii desiderio laborantibus subvenire dignatus es: Tu ad tanti operis Aggressionem animos addidisti; Te Auspice fundamenta fecimus; Tuis tuorumque præsertim amicorum Suppetiis in hodiernam tandem excrevit pulchritudinem."]

[2] [This copy, in the exact colours of the original, but slightly reduced in size, has been contributed to this work by the Master and Fellows of Emmanuel College.]

[3] [30 June, 1677. "Paid Robert Grumbold for taking downe and enlarging and building up agayne the Arch against the Chappell doore 004. 10. 00."]

[4] [MSS. Tanner: Bibl. Bodl. Oxon. xlv. 262.]

FIG. 4. FACSIMILE OF PART OF THE ORIGINAL DESIGN BY SIR CHRISTOPHER WREN FOR THE CHAPEL AND GALLERY AT EMMANUEL COLLEGE.

to lay the foundation this year as we did intend; the unexpected troubles have raised the price of Lime to be double to what it was a month since. The same may be guessed of other things that are to be prepared by fire, the price of coales being of a sudden become excessive great here, yet if it be possible we would this year make some visible appeareance of what we intend."

Other letters refer to the model, here mentioned for the first time; to Sandcroft's notes upon it; and to the difficulties which stood in the way of beginning the work during that year. The arrival of the model is announced by the Master in a letter dated 24 September, 1667:

"We are much pleased with the model of our chappel; I yet meet with nothing to be added to your obseruations concerning it; onely we wish it could be raised to a greater height, and if we haue not an East window (concerning which we are of my Lord of Duresme's[1] opinion) it is thought it will be necessary that yᵉ side windows be inlarged. I shall trouble you with any exceptions which shall be made ageinst it as it is viewed by others hereafter[2]."

At the beginning of the following year, 1668, the preparation for the foundations had begun in earnest; but the exact place in which the building was to stand had not yet been determined. The Master writes (28 January, 1667—68):

......"My Lord of Westmorelands timber is come[3]. We prepare for the Foundation of our chappell, and much desire Dʳ Wren's advise vpon the place[4]."

In the following month the Master took a journey into Northamptonshire in the hopes of obtaining a supply of stone direct from the quarry at Ketton, at a lower price than it could be purchased elsewhere. In announcing to Sandcroft (19 February) his success and the saving which would thereby be effected, he again expresses a wish that Wren could be induced to visit the College:

"Dʳ Wren hath sent me a very ciuill ansure of the letter which you was pleased to send him from me, he sayth it is possible he may be in

---

[1] [Dr John Cosin was Bishop of Durham from 1660 to his death 15 Jan. 1671-72.]

[2] [MSS. Tanner clv. 19. At the beginning of the Chapel Accounts we find: "For the module of the designe in wainscot 13. 05. 00. For its carriage from London 00. 07. 08."]

[3] [The list of contributions copied from a "Table" in the Antechapel (Blomefield, Collectanea, p. 117) records that "The right Honourable *Charles* Earl of *Westmoreland*, gave 40 Timber Trees." The Chapel Accounts put the number at "about 30."]

[4] [MSS. Tanner clv. 37.]

London by Midlent (which is now near) and that he may then make a start to come here, but desires I would not delay one day in expectation of him. Truely, Sir, though I am in some readiness to begin, I will stay many days rather then want his aduise vpon the place. His presence will be a great reputation (besides other aduantages) to the whole work. Giue me leaue to ask earnestly of you to vse your power with him, which I know is great, to procure it[1]."

The following is the contract[2] which the Master had succeeded in obtaining. It is dated 17 February, 1667—68:

"Articles of Agreement betwixt John Breton Doctor of Divinity Master of Emmanuel Colledge in Cambridge...of the one part, and Simon Wise of Dean in y[e] County of Northampton, and Nicholas Ashly of Ketton in y[e] County Rutland Free-Masons of the other part.

Imprimis. It is covenanted and agreed betwixt y[e] partyes abouenamed; That the said Simon Wise and Nicholas Ashly shall of their own proper costs and charges provide stone called Ashler white and good stone, at y[e] Quarry of Ketton aforesaid, of seaven inches at the one end and three inches and halfe at y[e] other end. And y[e] said Ashler convey to Emmanuel Colledge in Cambridge at their own costs and charges and sett it up at their own proper costs and charges upon the foundation of a Chappell there to be built to y[e] ground-table betwixt y[e] Day of y[e] Date hereof and y[e] first day of y[e] month of July next ensuing.

Item. It is agreed betwixt y[e] Partyes abouenamed y[t] y[e] said John Breton...shall pay unto y[e] said Simon and Nicholas or one of them the price of seaven pence and one halfpenny for euery foot square of Ashler soe sett up by them at their owne proper Costs and charges, And that y[e] said John Breton...shall pay them or one of them in part y[e] Summe of five pounds at or before y[e] first day of May next ensueing and ye summe of five pounds upon delivery of y[e] said Ashler in Emmanuel Colledge. In witnesse whereof y[e] said Partyes aboue named have hereunto sett their hands and seales this 17th day of February 1667."

We do not know whether Wren came to Cambridge as it was hoped he would; but the actual work began in March following[3], with the pulling down of the wall which bounded the Court towards the east[4]; and in May the foundations were dug. The Bursar, Mr Alfounder, writes to Sandcroft (26 May):

---

[1] [MSS. Tanner clv. 17.]

[2] [From the original in Emmanuel College Treasury, Box 9.]

[3] [A separate Account has been preserved, entitled: "An Account of the particulars of the expences of the chappell, cloysters, gallery in Emman. College as they were By D[r] Bright disbursed since March, 1668."]

[4] ["To 4 labourers for 3 days worke in pulling downe the old wall that stood where now the Front of the Cloyster oo. o9. oo."]

"Wee are digging for the foundation of the chappel, and had finished that peice of the worke before now, had not the springs and the great rain made us some unexpected troubles which wee shall soone ouercome by pumping and fayr wether[1]."

The work progressed regularly until November, 1672, by which time the walls had been completed, the roof put on, and the plasterers had begun to work on the ceiling. The Accounts were then audited, and it appeared that the subscriptions had amounted to £3144. 07. 04, and the expenses, "from the beginning of its foundation to Nov. 5th, 1672," to about £2975. 10. 06. After this the building-work appears to have ceased for four years; for the next Account begins in 1676—in which year Dr Holbech succeeded Dr Breton as Master—from which we learn that fresh subscriptions had been collected, and that the plastering, paving, and glazing of the Chapel, with the construction of the ceiling and the floor of the gallery, were proceeding[2]. The scheme for the woodwork was submitted to Sandcroft in June 1676. It had been designed by a Mr Peirce and a Mr Oliver[3], both of London, but was executed by Cornelius Austin, who received his first payment 26 September, 1676, and his last 7 January, 1677—8, by which time the fittings must have been completed, by payments at the end of 1677 for the altar-furniture[4]. The building had therefore occupied rather more than nine years. The total expenditure had amounted to about £3972, and the subscriptions (including nearly £600 from Dr Sandcroft), to £4116[5].

The ceremony of consecration was performed by Dr Peter Gunning, Bishop of Ely, 29 September, 1677[6]. When the day

---

[1] [MSS. Tanner ccxc. 133.]

[2] [Expenses, 1676. Sept. 12. "Pd to Mr James Flory Citizen and Mason of London as advance mony and pt of his payment before hand for the paving of the Chappell wth Marble etc. according to the Articles agreede 050. 00. 00."]

[3] [Dr Holbech to Dr Sandcroft, 17 June 1676. MSS. Tanner xl. 9. Chapel Accounts, July 1676. "Imprimis given to Mr Peirce of London for delineating the Groundplot and Wanscott and seates in 5 severall Draughts 002. 00. 00."]

[4] [Among other payments we find, 3 October, 1677: "Paid Richard Linleey for making ye cloth behind ye Altar, and for making Covers for ye septum, and ye Letany Desk, and ye 2 Crickets at ye Altar as per Bill 000. 10. 00."]

[5] [Blomefield, Collectanea, p. 117.]

[6] [This is the date of the Act of Consecration, copied MSS. Cole xxvii. 78. The Accounts from 3 May — 23 October, 1677, contain the expenses of the festivities incidental to the occasion.]

had been finally settled, the Master wrote to Sandcroft to say that he hoped his health would be such "that the most earnest desire of all this Society to see you here at the consecracion of our Chappell may not be frustrated," but we do not know whether he was able to accept their invitation. Shortly afterwards however, he gave a further proof of the interest which he took in the work by defraying the entire cost of the internal fittings. The Master's letter to him on this subject is so interesting that it must be quoted at length:

"Coll. Emman. Nov. 13, 1677.

Reverend Sir, my most approved good freind

It is not the least of my troubles that my illnesse and distempers both in head and feet have kept me from writing to you since that great work accomplished the Consecracion of our (or rather your Chappell); for I am sure I had never more need both to desire the blessing of your prayers and your favorable advice and help too in myne other concerns, especially in That, which these inclosed Papers will acquaint you with: which indeed I might be very much ashamed to offer to your Vew after soe bountyfull and most Munificent Donacions as your Piety and Goodness hath allready enriched us with, but that your self were pleased to discover to me your intentions of furnishing us with all the wanscott at your owne charge, and I am now forced to discover to you our wants after all other legacyes and guifts brought in to be such, that with your addicion upon this Bill (which I nothing doubt) we shall not soe fully discharge all our debtes, but that a porcion will still remayne to be supplyed by him who according to his poore ability hath designed That, and some further contribucion towards the accomplishing of this Work, which I the rather acquaint you with that you may thinke that I am not one that would spur a free horse either soe unreasonable or uncivill as to ask more of you than your owne pleasure prompts you to ; and yet withall not soe foolish but that according to the freedome you have bene pleased to grant me of conversing with you I would make you acquainted with all my affaires and intentions every way. For I assure you next under heaven it is you that I must and shall ever acknowledg my best and greatest freind : To whom therefore I wish and pray for all happyness, and presenting my most affectionate service and respects shall ever rest

your most truely thankfull and deepely obliged
freind and servant, Thomas Holbech[1]."

The east end was at first adorned with hangings, which were replaced in 1687 by an altar-piece of carved oak[2], consisting of

---

[1] [MSS. Tanner clv. 53. The papers enclosed, preserved with the above letter, shew that the total cost of the fittings had been £386. 10. 10.; for which sum Dr Holbech gives Dr Sandcroft a receipt in full.]

[2] [Audit-Book. *Expenses since 6 April*, 1687. "For yᵉ Joyners and Gilders Commons and Sysings whilst at work about the new Altar-piece £01. 08. 10." The

two fluted Corinthian columns supporting an entablature, sur-
mounted by a pediment. This, like the rest of the woodwork,
was given by Dr Sandcroft, then Archbishop of Canterbury[1].
The donation probably included an altar, rails, &c., for those
put up in 1677 had evidently been of the plainest description[2].
The painting, however, representing the Return of the Prodigal
Son, by Giacomo Amiconi, a Venetian artist who worked in
England from 1729 to 1739, was not presented until 734, by
Christopher Nevile, Esq., Fellow Commoner[3]. The organ, to
purchase which Burch Hothersall, Fellow Commoner, M.A.
1682, gave £120, was probably put up at the same time; for
the rents received between 1684 and 1688 from the estate given
by the Archbishop "for the repairing and Ornament of the
Chappel and Library," were principally spent in payments to
the Organist[4].

It may be mentioned that the glass chandelier which hung
in the centre was given by Edward Hulse, M.D., in 1732[5]; and
that in 1735 Mr Burrough received £7. 7s. "for his assistance in
beautifying yᵉ Chappell," but the details of the work are not
recorded. The building does not exhibit any traces of material
alteration since the first construction.

hangings which it replaced are thus described : Audit-Book, 10 August, 1677:
"Pᵈ for 22 yᵈˢ of sattin, Eleven of Purple, and Eleven of Carnacion for yᵉ Cloth
behind yᵉ Altar at 13ˢ per yᵈ 014. 06. 00. For Red Callico to fixe yᵉ same
000. 12. 06."]

[1] [The thanks of the Master and Fellows were conveyed to the Archbishop in a
long Latin epistle dated 4 May, 1688 (MSS. Tanner xxviii. 26). After stating that
the benefactions of the Most Reverend Prelate have been such as to kindle ardour in
the most frozen hearts, and make even the dumb son of Crœsus speak, they regret
that they, the recipients, do not resemble those ancient orators, who are said to have
become more eloquent when they pleaded in the temples of their Gods, for then they
should worthily thank him for all his favours past, and especially for those lately
conferred : "quibus consummatissimum Collegii nostri Sacellum, quibus ornatissimum
ejus Altare, augustissimum, et quàm maxime decorum effecisti ; atque adeò publicum
Dei cultum (quod summis Tibi erat in votis) omnibus gratiorem reddidisti."]

[2] [In the original Account for the fittings their cost is set down as follows : "Itᵗ"
one Communion Table and Rayles and 3 Cricketts, 1. 18. 5."]

[3] [The donor's name has been preserved in a note in the Admission Book. The
picture arrived between April and October, 1734 : Expenses since 22 April, 1734,
"Pᵈ for carriage of yᵉ Chappell Picture from London o. 1. 6."]

[4] [MSS. Tanner clviii. 132.]

[5] [Ibid. Expenses since 2d Oct. 1732. "Pᵈ for yᵉ carriage of 2 Boxes with yᵉ
Lustre £0. 5. 6."]

The new Chapel being completed, the fitting up of the
old one as a Library was undertaken at the beginning of the
following year, the plan, as usual, having been submitted to
Sandcroft for his approval[1]. A separate Account[2] was kept
for this work, which cost £231. 18s. 6d., spent principally in
payments to Cornelius Austin for making bookcases, rearrang-
ing the old wainscot, and providing furniture[3]. The only
structural alteration was the insertion of a new window at the
north end of the room, set up by Robert Grumbold[4]. These
works were completed in November, 1679.]

Additional bookcases were provided between 1705 and
1707, in order to accommodate Archbishop Sandcroft's library,
the bulk of which came to the College after his death, 24
November, 1693. These books were deposited partly in
new shelves put up under the windows, partly in half classes
erected between the high ones which had been set up a few
years before. This was done in accordance with his own
wishes, as recorded in a letter written by his Chaplain, M₁
William Needham, to his brother, Mr Gervase Needham, Fellow
of Queens' College, on " Sᵗ Stephen's Day, 1693," about a month
after the Archbishop's death :

"As to the Structure which his Grace designed for the Books, I don't
know that he came to any fixed Resolution about it ; neither had he
laid aside the Thoughts of it, when I received his last Blessing ; his
Mind still running on a new Fabric, tho' of lesse Dimensions than the
Ground which was measured by his first Command to me. It was, I
think, that very Morning I left him, that he caused me to be let into his
Study, (all his Books being then placed together in that one Room,

---

[1] [Holbech to Sandcroft, 14 February, 1678. MSS. Tanner xxxix. 181. The
scheme for fitting up the Library with classes and half-classes had been submitted to
Sandcroft 15 July, 1678. The letter, which deals principally with the arrangement
of the bookcases, will be found in the Chapter on " College Libraries."]

[2] [" The Accᵗ of what received and disbursed towards the making of the New
Library in Emmanuel Colledge begun Anno 1678."]

[3] [" 18 April, 1679. Pᵈ Cornelius Austin for taking downe and making up the
old Wanscot for the Walls and windowes as per Bill 002. 17. 06. 26 April. To
[the same] in pᵗ of paymᵗ of his Work about the Classes 040. 00. 00. 3 Novemb.
Pᵈ him also towards discharge for yᵉ finishing of the Classes, and for 8 Tables and
16 joyned stooles 022. 02. 00."]

[4] [" 5 April, 1679. Pᵈ John Squire for worke and timber about taking downe yᵉ
great End Window of the old Chappel 001. 02. 00. Pᵈ Robert Grumbold for the
New stone Window and setting it up at the North-end of the Library 008. 00. 00."]

great Part of which he had formerly shown me in two Garrets,) that I might view them, and give him my Opinion, whether that Share, which I judged would come to the College, would crowd your Library too full, if there were new Shelves put up under the Windows, and Halfe-Classes erected betwixt the whole ones? I told him, they might stand so, not inconveniently; but he still tooke Time to consider, whether it should be so, or a new Fabric; and I have heard nothing further since that Time[1]."

The Accounts shew that the additional bookcases were made by John Austin between September, 1705 and July, 1707[2].

[By the erection of the new Chapel and Cloister, as above recorded, the College was brought to the aspect shewn by Loggan. In the next chapter we shall relate the steps by which it was transformed into its present appearance.]

CHAPTER III.

HISTORY OF THE BUILDINGS DURING THE EIGHTEENTH AND NINETEENTH CENTURIES.

[AT the beginning of the eighteenth century the buildings shewed signs of decay, for a College Order, dated 10 March, 1714—15, decides that two Fellowships shall not be filled up, because, among other reasons, "it appeareth that y[e] Buildings of y[e] College, in y[e] Walls, Roofs, and Tilings thereof, are at this time much Decay'd and out of Repair, in so much y[t] it will require a good sum of Money to repair them as they ought to be." We do not know what steps were taken to remedy these defects; but] at the end of 1719 the Founder's Range was pulled down, and in its place the present building was erected in the French style which prevailed in this country at the beginning of the Hanoverian dynasty. [The College Order, directing the alteration, is dated 7 August, 1719:

[1] [D'Oyly's Life, *ut supra*, ii. 96. MSS. Cole, *ut supra*, p. 280.]

[2] [14 September, 1705. "Rec[d] of D[r] Balderston in part for the erecting of new Classes for Arch-Bishop Sancrofts books twenty-five pounds." The last payment was made 18 July, 1707. The total expense was £78. 11. 00. The College received only a portion of the printed books from the Archbishop's Library: his MSS. were bought by Bishop Tanner and passed with his other books into the Bodleian Library (Macray, Annals of the Bodleian Library, Oxford, p. 153). It is from the letters there preserved that so many of the facts related in this chapter have been gleaned.]

"It being necessary to pull down y^t part of the College call'd ye Founder's rang, It is resolved by ye Master and Fellows,

That Mr Whitaker and Mr Whitehead be appointed and empowred to hire, oversee, and pay ye men to be employed in ye said work.

That the workmen shall be paid every week, and to that end ye s^d Mr Whitaker and Mr Whitehead shall every Saturday after dinner in ye Parlour lay before [the] Society a particular account of ye number of workmen, and how many days each of them has been employed that week, together with ye gross sum of ye Wages, wch sum shall be then deliverd to ye s^d Mr Whitaker and Mr Whitehead, to be by them some time that day paid to ye several workmen.

That a book shall be provided and kept in ye Treasury wherein all ye expences and disburshm^t, relating to ye pulling down or rebuilding ye fores^d Founders rang, shall be particularly enterd from time to time every Saturday after dinner.

That all ye money that shall be given or appointed for ye aforesaid work, shall be lodged in ye Treasury."

This book unfortunately has not been preserved, and we are therefore without information respecting the progress of the building. The cost was defrayed, in part at least, by subscription, and the Benefactors' Book records a total of £2386. 17s., exclusive of smaller sums[1]. The most important gift was £500 from Thomas Fane, sixth Earl of Westmoreland. It is said that want of funds retarded the conclusion of the work[2]; but the rooms were evidently ready for occupation at the beginning of 1722, when the following orders were made respecting the charge of fitting up certain chambers in it:

"April 23, 1722. It was unanimously agreed by the Master and Fellows y^n pres^t, y^t the College shall be at the charge of Wainscoating, Painting and fitting up a Room in ye New building for Mr Whitehead, in the same man^r the middle Rooms in the middle Staircase in the new building shall be fitted up by Mr Banyer and Mr Holmes (at y^r own Expence) upon the following Considerations.

1st. That whereas he is now possessd of a right to the End Room in the middle Story in the Corner Staircase of the s^d Building (otherwise called ye Founders range) the Income of wch amounts to the sum of eighteen pounds, he promises that w^n he leaves the College he will resign his right to ye s^d Income to the use of ye College.

---

[1] [The Audit-Book shews that the College contributed £300, 16 October, 1722; and the rest of the money was probably borrowed, from an Order, dated 25 October, 1726, which provides for the discharge of "the debt of the new Building."]

[2] [Bennet, *ut supra*, ii. 43. It is evident that this work left the College in debt, for the following Order was made, 25 October, 1726: "'Twas then agreed by y^e Master and Fellows that all Fines now due to y^e College shall be set aside and applyed towards discharging y^e debt of y^e new Building, as long as We shall judge it proper. W$^{m\cdot}$ Savage."]

2ly. That upon his leaving the College he will give the sum of twelve pounds to the use of y^e College[1]."

"May 23, 1722. It was agreed by the Master and all the Fellows that the College shall be at the Expence of fitting up a Room for Mr Holmes upon condition that he immediately pays to the use of the College the sum of eighteen pounds and gives security for the payment of twelve pounds more when he leaves the College."]

After this reconstruction the range took the name of "The Westmoreland Building," and in 1732 the arms of the then Earl were set up over the central doorway[2]. The plan shews that the building, as reconstructed, occupies a considerably wider site than before; the thick wall *a b* (fig. 1) being evidently the south boundary-wall of the original structure[3].

In 1811 (15 October) it was gutted by an accidental fire, which originated in the centre of the building in the rooms of Mr George Thomas, a Fellow-commoner[4]. The only portion which escaped was the stone front next to the court, and part of the inside walls[5]. A subscription was again set on foot to defray the cost of rebuilding, and £4484 was collected. It was rebuilt in the same style, and with the same internal arrangements, as before the fire.

In 1752 it was decided to rebuild, in conformity with the " Founder's Range," the Butteries and the adjoining building in "Bungay Court," under the direction of Mr Burrough[6]. [His

---

[1] [It is signed by the Master and five Fellows.]

[2] [Audit-Book, *Expenses since* 20 *October*, 1732. "P^d Mr Pitches for setting up Ld Westmorland's Arms £11. 00. 00." He had visited the College in 1724. Ibid. *Expenses since* 30 *March*, 1724. "Paid for ye Entertainment of Lord and Lady Westmoreland 17. 00. 05."]

[3] [Dyer (History, ii. 374) speaks of " the old building enlarged and cased with Portland stone."]

[4] [The Benefactors' Book records that "George Thomas Esquire in whose rooms the fire originated gave £500."]

[5] [Cambridge Chronicle, 18 October, 1811.]

[6] ["June the 22. 1752. Whereas the Butteries and the contiguous Buildings are become very ruinous, and it is hop'd that Benefactions may be procur'd to defray the expence of rebuilding the same; Agreed that they be pull'd down and rebuilt so soon as money sufficient be rais'd for that purpose; and that the Butteries and the end rooms in Bungay court be the first that be gone upon.

"Agreed thereupon that Mr Burrough be desir'd to prepare a plan for the whole of the said intended new Building in conformity to that call'd the Founder's Range, and that Mr Devie be join'd to the Master in Carrying the said plan into Execution, when approv'd by the Society."]

plan, however, was not approved, for the following reason, according to Dr Bennet :

"The Master, according to the Plan, was to have had the present Combination Room added to his Lodge, and the passage between them stop'd up. The Fellows on the other hand were unwilling to go to the bottom of the Hall to a more distant and noisy room. The Scheme accordingly went off for some years, and the money, of which a large sum had been subscrib'd (one Gentleman alone, Sr Richd Chase of Hartfordshire, having sent five hundred pounds), was return'd to the Donors[1]."]

After this, no building-work was undertaken for eight years, until, 24 June, 1760, it was agreed that the Hall should be "repaired and fitted up" according to a plan sent in by Mr Essex. This work was completed in rather less than four years, the Hall being reopened 21 April, 1764[2]. The last payment was made 26 May in the same year, up to which date the work had cost £1796. 10s. 11¾d. It included a new pavement of Ketton Stone[3]. In this work Mr Essex appears to have retained the original plan and very nearly the original style, as far as the exterior of the Hall is concerned. A casing of stone was imposed upon the walls ; a parapet was substituted for the eaves ; and, in the building between the Hall and the Chapel, the original style was changed into one corresponding with that selected for the opposite side of the court in 1719.

The scheme which had been abandoned in 1752 was revived in 1769, when we find the following Order :

"March 11, 1769. Whereas the Building opposite to the Chappel is in so ruinous a condition that the Surveyor says that it can stand but very few years, Agreed that the Butteries and the Building running from thence to the street be immediately pulled down, and rebuilt according to the Plan drawn by Sr James Burroughs some years since[4]."

---

[1] [Bennet ii. 45.]

[2] [The various items of expenditure are written out at the end of the Audit-Book for 1748—1794, headed "Expence of ye Hall and Court," but, as the payments are set down in gross, it is impossible to discover the details of the work done. Among them we find: "1764 . Apr. 21 Expence of Dinner 37. 17. 4."]

[3] [College Order 3 June, 1763: "Agreed that a Floor of Ketton-Stone be laid in ye Hall; ye old Stone to be used as far as it will go; and to be laid in ye same form with ye old Floor."]

[4] [Bennet (ii. 46) notes upon this:—"This was not strictly obeyd. The Plan of Sr James Burroughs being departed from in almost every instance, and in some considerably improvd. When the great repairs of the Hall, Chapel, and now of the

Fig. 5. West front of Emmanuel College, built by James Essex 1770—75, by Storer; from Le Keux's Memorials of Cambridge, ed. Cooper.

Vol. II.

[The second building mentioned in this Order must be the small building which Loggan shews extending from the west end of the Hall to the street. The design of Burrough was not carried out after all; for in the following July it was "agreed that the Plan drawn by Mr Essex for rebuilding the West side of the Court be carried into Execution, when the College shall be enabled to do it[1]." The work was undertaken immediately, for the first payment to the New Building was made 29 July in the same year. The first operations were probably confined to the pulling down of the old structures, for it was not until the beginning of 1770 that the design was engraved, and probably circulated for the purpose of obtaining subscriptions[2]. The last payment to Essex was made 5 May, 1775. The building had therefore occupied rather more than five years. The funds required were raised, at least in part, by subscriptions, which amounted to £2857. 10s. 0d.[3]

The building, as executed, (fig. 5) differs slightly from the design. Both shew a central portion in two floors, without garrets, projecting slightly in advance of the wings, which are in three floors. The central portion has ten windows on the ground-floor, and eleven windows on the first floor; the wings have three windows in each floor. The entrance to the College is in the middle of the central portion. In the existing building the uniformity of this central portion is broken by four Ionic columns, which rise uninterruptedly from the ground to the cornice, at which level they support an entablature surmounted

front or Cloyster building (in all which £10,000 was expended) are consider'd, it reflects the highest honour on Dr Richardson's Mastership [1736—75], whose economy in College affairs provided the Funds, and whose good sense directed the expenditure. He was a most strict and unpleasant Master to his Fellows, but had a great regard for the Prosperity of the Body, with a Gentleman-like behaviour, and a liberal mind."]

[1] [College Order, 5 July, 1769.]

[2] [Audit-Book, 27 Feb. 1770. "Mr Lamborn for Plans of ye Building 4. 14. 6." 20 March, 1771. "150 Prints of ye Building 0. 6. 0."]

[3] [Benefactors' Book. In this case, as in the former one, the work left the College in debt, which was discharged in the following way: "March 16th, 1776. Whereas the College at this Time suffers an *Insigne Detrimentum* in Consequence of several Debts occasion'd by the Expences attending the Erection of the New Building: We the Master and Major Part of the Fellows have determin'd, according to the Power given us in the nineteenth Chapter of our Statutes, That none of the vacant Fellowships can be fill'd up for the present."]

by a triangular pediment. Instead of these the design shews three arches of rustic-work, projecting a few inches from the front, and rising as high as a band of stonework, which divides the vertical heights of the building into two equal portions. The columns rest upon these arches, and are merely slender shafts, equal in height to the first floor.]

In 1823 a further extension of the accommodation for undergraduates was determined on, and, 23 July in the same year, the following Order was made:

"Agreed that the College seal be affixed to the Contract with M[r]. James Webster for erecting the new Building according to the Plan and specification agreed upon."

This "new Building" is that on the north side of the small quadrangle. It was not, however, commenced until the following year, having probably been retarded by a more ambitious scheme for erecting a range of chambers in a different part of the College, near the Brick Building[1]. This having been found impracticable, the original scheme was revived, and the work was commenced towards the end of July, 1824[2]. It will be seen from the plan (fig. 1) that the building was so arranged in the first instance as to leave a space, or detachment, on each side for the better circulation of air in the Court. But four years afterwards the following Order directed the destruction of the small building which formed the north side of Bungay Court:

"1828. May 27. Whereas Bungay Building is in a ruinous State it is agreed that it be pulled down, and that the range of the Kitchen Buildings be extended towards the Lane after the Plans of M[r]. Arthur Brown, and that the College Seal be affixed to the Contract with M[r]. James Webster for the Execution of the same."

The original extent of the Kitchen building northwards is indicated by the thick wall *c, d* (fig. 1), which, with part of the

[1] ["1824. June 30th. Agreed that it is desireable to build adjoining to the brick building, and to employ M[r] Humfrey to furnish an elevation of the proposed new building and the improvements which may be made in the front of the Brick building." See also Cambridge Chronicle, 18 June, 1824.]

[2] [Cambridge Chronicle, 30 July, 1824. "We perceive that the Master and Fellows of Emmanuel College have commenced their intended improvements. The new building is to consist of 18 sets of rooms and will complete a second Court, towards Emmanuel Lane. We are assured that the rooms are to be ready for occupation in October, 1825."]

external plinth, may still be seen in the cellar. The building commenced in 1828 closed up the western detachment, and prolonged the Kitchen Range northwards as far as Emmanuel Lane. It is probable that at the same time a façade of cement was bestowed upon the entire western side, as thus elongated, of the last remnant of the original College[1]. Thus was Emmanuel College brought to its present aspect and condition, retaining of its original structure only the kitchen which was part of the Black Friars buildings, and the Library.

CHAPTER IV.

HISTORY OF PARTICULAR BUILDINGS. HALL, COMBINATION ROOM, MASTER'S LODGE, TREASURY, GARDENS, ETC.

HALL.—We are informed that the Hall was

" wainscotted, painted and new glazed and adorn'd with new tables through the Beneficence of Sir William Temple and Richard Chandler Esq[r]., and other worthy persons formerly members of this College[2],"

between April and October, 1694. It is probable that most of the woodwork then put up is still in existence, and that the alterations carried out by Essex in 1760 were chiefly confined to plastering the walls, and to concealing the original king-post roof with a flat ceiling[3].

COMBINATION ROOM.—The position of the Combination Room, or Parlour, has evidently always been the same as at present. In 1876 it was somewhat increased in size by the addition of an oriel window on the north side, erected from the design of A. W. Blomfield, M.A., Architect.

---

[1] [Dyer, writing in 1814, speaks of the "kitchens, raised of clunch-stone."]

[2] [Note at the end of the Account extending from 1 April to 10 October, 1694. The Account for the next half-year records the expenses of a dinner " at opening y[e] Hall."]

[3] [The Foreigner's Companion, etc. 1748, speaks of this Hall as "having an arched Roof." It is clear, therefore, that the present ceiling was put up by Essex.]

MASTER'S LODGE.—The original Master's Lodge occupied the two floors over the Combination Room eastward of the Hall[1]. This Lodge was soon found to be inconveniently small, and in 1648 and 1649, it was altered and enlarged by taking in two sets of adjoining chambers[2]. At the same time "the great chamber in the Lodgings" was hung with "8 peices of hangings" and new furniture was provided. The erection of the Chapel supplied the Master with a gallery over the cloister, which was furnished for him in 1680—81[3]; and other additions were possibly made to the Lodge, for Carter, writing in 1753, says that "the Master's Lodge hath many pretty apartments." It was gradually extended westward into the Master's garden, as shewn on the plan (fig. 1). A considerable part of this extension took place in 1835, shortly after the election of George Archdall, B.D., to the mastership, as the following Order shews :

" July 9th, 1835. In the alterations and repairs at the Lodge, agreed that the new Dining Room, the Passages and the Porch be erected at the Master's expence, and that the Master pay one half of the expence of the new offices, and the new entrance; the College doing the repairs painting papering &c., in the old part of the Lodge. The College to repair the Stable and Coach-House, and to make the new gravel walk. The College to pay for the new mantel pieces and the Master for the grates."

The original Lodge had been entered by a staircase in the turret in the south-east angle of what was then the entrance-court ; but after its extension it was extended through a door in the passage eastward of the Combination Room. It was inconvenient as a residence, and shortly after the election of the present Master in 1871, it was pulled down, and the present Lodge erected under the direction of Mr Blomfield.

[1] [As in other Lodges there was an opening out of one of the rooms into the Hall : *Expenses since* 26 *October*, 1636. "Item to him [a mason] for mortar and stopping up ye hole into ye hall out of ye chamber over my dining chamber, o. 1. 8."]

[2] [*Expenses since* 25 *October*, 1648. "Layd out about altering the Lodging 69. 13. 11." *Expenses since* 19 *October*, 1649. "Payd Mr Cudworth for Sr Alcocks and Mr Adams for incomes of chambers wch the Master tooke into his hands, 15. oo. oo."]

[3] [*Expenses since* 19 *October*, 1680. "Bought for the Master's Gallery by vote of ye Society 36 turky work Chairs at 7^s 6^d per chair, 2 Spanish tables, and 2 wrought carpets, o17. oo. oo."]

TREASURY.—The Treasury is a room on the ground-floor
eastward of the Combination Room or Parlour, a position which
it has occupied from the first foundation of the College.   An
Inventory dated 1589, under the heading "In the Parlor," mentions "one dore of firr going into the treasure house."

GARDENS, ETC.—The arrangement of the gardens at the end
of the seventeenth century is shewn by Loggan, both in his
general view of the College (fig. 3), and in his plan of Cambridge.
The Master's Garden was then separated from the Entrance-
Court by a wall which prolonged the west side of the Library to
Emmanuel Lane; and from the Fellows' Garden by a wall, of
which the greater part is still standing.

The Fellows' Garden, then as now, occupied the ground
between Emmanuel Lane and Christ's Pieces[1]; and both it and
the Master's Garden were separated from the meadow to the south,
called "The Close," by a wall which ran from near the south-
east angle of the Master's Lodge to the wall which bounded the
site on the east.   The direction of this wall has been shewn by a
dotted line on the plan (fig. 1).

We do not know when these gardens were laid out; but
probably soon after the first foundation of the College, for the
planting of mulberry-trees is recorded as early as 1608[2], and in
1634 the Master speaks of "the new wall" in his orchard; and in
1636 of the new wall in the Fellows' Orchard[3].

The building shewn by Loggan in the centre of the Fellows'
Garden is evidently the Summer House, built in 1680[4]. He also
shews the Bath, but without the building now standing at the
west end.   We do not know when the Bath was first made;

---

[1] [There is a piece of wall on the north side of great thickness, which is evidently
much older than the rest, and was probably erected by the Dominicans.]

[2] [*Expenses since 26 October*, 1608, "For mulbyrie plants at yᵉ king's appoyntmᵗ
300. xviijˢ." *Expenses since 22 April*, 1612. "For digging a fence dych and setting
fourtie mulbyrie trees, xiijˢ. xᵈ."]

[3] [*Expenses since 22 October*, 1634. "Item to John Westly in part for yᵉ New
wall in my orchard and yᵉ forecourt, 20ˡⁱ." *Expenses since 3 May*, 1636. "Item to
John Westly for yᵉ new wal in yᵉ fellowes orchard......being 5 pole after 3ˡⁱ yᵉ
pole 15ˡⁱ."]

[4] [*Expenses since 19 October*, 1680. "Paid for building the 2 Summer houses in
yᵉ Master and Fellows Orchard, 022. 00. 00."]

but the Bath-house had been erected before 1748, when the
following description was written:

"The Gardens are very extensive, and well planted with Fruit.
There is a Bowling-Green and Cold-Bath in the Fellows Garden, over
which is a neat Brick Building, sash'd in Front, and containing also a
commodious little Room to dress in. The Curious take notice of a
fine young Cedar-tree in this Garden[1]."

Loggan also shews a Bowling-Green in the south-east corner
of the Garden, the laying down of which has not been recorded.
It is first mentioned, as already in existence, in 1638. Various
charges occur in the Accounts for laying out the garden[2], and
planting vines and evergreens, but none of them are sufficiently
important for quotation. Dyer, who was himself educated at
this College, has left the following description of the gardens[3] as
they appeared at the beginning of the century:

"The fellows' garden, though not large, is agreeably laid out, and
diversified by many plants, a bathing-house, bowling-green, and piece
of water. The cedar-tree, once so beautiful in growth, now beginning
to wear the majesty of years, is one of the most beautiful in England.
There was formerly a mount in a corner of this garden, from which
might be seen what was going on in the neighbouring lane, and Christ
College layes; but this pert peeping ornament has been very properly
removed. This is one of the most agreeable gardens in the University.

The master's garden has in it nothing remarkable, except it may be
a summer-house, of some antiquity, surrounded with the prints of our
principal old poets, a very agreeable nook, in which either a pipe or a
poem will go very pleasantly."

The "Close," or "Great Close," as it is sometimes called,
remains in nearly the same state as shewn by Loggan; except
that it has been somewhat reduced in size by the extension of
the Fellows' Garden (fig. 1).

The position of the Tennis-court is known from Loggan's
view (fig. 3); and it has been laid down on the plan from the
more precise indications supplied in his map of Cambridge. We
have seen that it was unroofed in 1633, when the Brick Building
was erected; but we do not know when it was pulled down. The

---

[1] [The Foreigner's Companion, etc., London, 1748, p. 72. This cedar, which
no longer exists, is said, on the authority of Dr Bennet, to have been planted by John
Martyn, Professor of Botany, 1733—61. (Dyer, Privileges of the University, ii. 96)].

[2] [In 1764 "Forlin, the gardener of Queens," was employed, on whom see
above, p. 56.]

[3] [George Dyer proceeded B.A. 1778, and his History of the University and
Colleges was published in 1814.]

"great ponde" is mentioned as early as 1612; but Loggan's map shews that in his time it was considerably smaller than it is at present. In Loggan's general view the trees, especially four of those on the south side, are represented as young. They are probably those planted in 1683[1].

The small garden at the north-west corner of the College, near the kitchen, is probably the "Cook's garden," first made in 1612; and the little court between the kitchen and the street, afterwards called Bungay Court, is that designated "Kitchen Court" in 1615[2].

The garden between the Founder's Range and the Brick Building, having always been private, is not mentioned in the Accounts.

There was a Pigeon House, as usual in Colleges, in some part of the grounds, but the situation has not been recorded[3].

Loggan shews a row of rails in front of the College, with a pair of lofty posts flanking the entrance, and a similar post at each corner of the rails. These posts were first set up, apparently, in 1614, when Woodruffe is paid £5 for carving them. Those figured by Loggan were set up in 1680[4].]

[1] [*Expenses since* 25 *October*, 1683. "Paid for young trees in the great close, 004. 05. 00."]

[2] [*Expenses since* 9 *May*, 1614. "Making ye Cooks Garden, xij^s vj^d. To Midleton and others more for leveling ye kitchin court, v^s iiij^d."]

[3] [*Expenses since* 28 *October*, 1620. "Mending ye duff howse, v^s."]

[4] [New Library Accounts, 1680. "P^d Wm Redhead for the Poasts and rayles before the great Gate of the College, 020. 00. 00." Feb. 14th and 24th. "P^d out of ye Mony r^d for the Library tow^ds the making and setting up the new Posts and Rayles before the great gate of the college, 20. 00. 00."]

CHRONOLOGICAL SUMMARY.

1583.	23 November. Sir W. Mildmay purchases Dominican site and buildings.
1584.	11 January. Date of Charter.
1585.	1 October. Statutes sent down by Founder.
1588.	Dedication festival celebrated in presence of Founder.
1589.	31 May. Death of Sir W. Mildmay.
1632—33.	9 February. Contract with John Westley for the Brick Building.
1634.	22 April. Last payment made to Westley.
1668.	March. Erection of new Chapel begun.
1672.	5 November. Chapel Accounts audited: work ceases for 4 years.
1676.	Work resumed.
1676.	26 September. First payment to Cornelius Austin for the woodwork.
1677.	29 September. Chapel consecrated by Bishop of Ely.
1678.	7 January. Last payment to Austin for woodwork.
1678—79.	Old Chapel converted into a Library.
1687.	Altar-piece erected in the Chapel.
1694.	Hall wainscoted, and new tables provided.
1705—7.	New Bookcases made by John Austin for Dr Sandcroft's books.
1714—15.	10 March. Two Fellowships to be applied to the repair of the Buildings.
1719.	7 August. Founder's Range to be pulled down.
1722.	23 April. 23 May. } Orders for fitting up chambers in Founder's Range as rebuilt.
1752.	22 June. Butteries and adjoining building in Bungay Court to be rebuilt after a design by Burrough.
1760.	24 June. Hall to be repaired and fitted up by Essex.
1764.	26 May. Last payment made for work to Hall.
1769.	11 March. Butteries and building between them and street to be pulled down and rebuilt after the design by Burrough.
1769.	5 July. West side of Court to be rebuilt by Essex.
1775.	5 May. Last payment made to Essex.
1811.	15 October. Founder's Range gutted by an accidental fire.
1824.	23 July. Building on north side of smaller quadrangle to be built.
1828.	27 May. Bungay Building to be pulled down, and the Kitchen-Range extended to Emmanuel Lane.
1835.	New rooms added to the Master's Lodge.
1871.	New Master's Lodge built.

XVI

The College of the Lady Frances Sidney Sussex;

COMMONLY CALLED

Sidney Sussex College.

CHAPTER I.

HISTORY OF THE SITE.

THE site of Sidney Sussex College is bounded on the west by part of Bridge Street, here called Sidney Street, but anciently Conduit Street; on the north by Jesus Lane; on the east by the houses in Malcolm Street, some of which belong to the College; and on the south by Sussex Street and King Street, the latter of which was anciently called Walles Lane.

This site was that of the convent of the Franciscans, or Friars Minors, commonly called the Grey Friars, who settled in Cambridge in the first half of the thirteenth century.

Their Church and their conventual buildings had been so completely destroyed before the site was made over to the executors of the Foundress, that only one building, to be hereafter described, could be made even partially available for the purposes of a College. A few historical notes respecting them may however be collected.

At the beginning of the sixteenth century the University was in the habit of holding the ceremony of Commencement in the Church, the large size of which rendered it peculiarly convenient. The earliest notice of this practice occurs in the University Accounts for 1507—8, when carpenters are employed to carry the materials used for the stages from the Schools to the Church of the Franciscans, to set them up there, and to carry them back again to the Schools[1]. Similar notices are to be found in subsequent years. In 1523 a Grace passed the Senate that in that particular year the ceremonies usual at Commencement should be held in the Church of the Friars Minors, and that they should receive ten shillings yearly for the use of their Church and for the safe keeping of the stages[2].

In 1540—the House having been surrendered to King Henry the Eighth in 1538—the University took formal steps to obtain possession of the site and buildings. The Vice-Chancellor and Mr Ainsworth of Peterhouse were directed, by Grace of the Senate, to intercede with his Majesty and Thomas Cromwell, then Chancellor of the University[3]; and a draft petition to the King, rehearsing a proposed form of Grant, is preserved among Archbishop Parker's manuscripts[4]. This document is unfortunately undated, and it does not appear that it ever received the sanction of the Senate. A note at the end, in a different and later hand, records that the grant was "divers times sued for, but could never be obtained"; and Roger Ascham, in a letter to Thomas Thirleby, Bishop of Westminster, which, though with-

---

[1] [Univ. Accounts, 1507—8. "Item Magistro bedforth pro Roberto carpentario componente fabricam commensacionis in ecclesia Minorum cum seruitore suo per quinque dies iiijˢ. ijᵈ. Item eidem Roberto pro signacione partium Stagiorum quomodo componerentur iiijᵈ. Bruno Cornelio pro reparacione vitri fenestrarum in ecclesia Minorum per M. Vicecancellarium doctorem Robson xlˢ. Item Greñ fabro pro vectibus illic ferreis iijˢ. viijᵈ. Thome Robynson carpentario operanti per quinque dies apud Minores in componendis stagiis erga Commensacionem ijˢ. Item pro vectione stagiorum a scholis ad Minores fratres et illinc ad scholas Pro laboratoribus vt asseruit Magister Bedforth xˢ. viijᵈ."]

[2] [Grace Book Γ fol. 113 *b*. "Conceditur vt solennes inceptiones obseruentur aput Fratres minores hoc anno non obstante statuto sic quod mercedis loco vicissim habeant a vobis tam pro occupacione ecclesie sue quam pro tuta custodia fabrice vestre pro singulis annis quamdiu vobis videbitur vt ibi fiant xˢ."]

[3] [Grace Book Γ fol. 171 *a*. "Item conceditur vt Vicecancellarius et magister Aynesworthe de collegio petri possint agere causas et negocia vestra apud Regiam maiestatem et dominum Cromwellum Cancellarium nostrum precipue pro domo et ecclesia nuper fratrum minorum hic apud vos et pro leta proque ceteris negociis vestris quatenus expediri illis videbitur et expense circa eadem fiende possint illis allocari per doctores Edmundes, Lockward, et Malett sic quod maior pars horum consentiat."]

[4] [Printed in the Appendix from the original in Corpus Christi College Library : MSS. Parker cvi. No. 95, p. 301.]

out date, must evidently have been written in 1541 or shortly afterwards, entreats him to use his interest on behalf of the University, that, among other things, they may obtain the house of the Franciscans. "Our great toil," he says, "makes but little progress. Their house is not only a grace and ornament to the University, but presents great conveniences for holding congregations and transacting all kinds of University business[1]."

The site and buildings were formally conveyed to Trinity College by King Henry the Eighth, 19 December, 1546; but the following survey of them[2], prepared six months earlier, shews that they had been already taken possession of and partially destroyed:

"The University of Cambridge. A particular Survaye made the 20th of May, Anno Regni Regis Henrici Octavi 38o of the late dissolved House of the Grey Freers, within the University of Cambridge, as hereafter followeth, that is to saye:

The site of the said Howse of Freers with the Precincts of the same.	The Church and Cloysters with all other the Houses thereupon bilded, bine defaced and taken towards the bilding of the King's Majesties New College, in Cambridge, and therefore valued	nothing.
	The Soyle wherof, with the Orchard, Brewhouse, Malthouse, Millhouse and Garner, within the Wallis thereof, bine yerelye worth to be leten fowre Pounds six Shillings and eight Pence sterling	4. 6. 8.

Vis. et Examinat: per me, Ro. Chester, Supervis. Domini Regis ibidem."

No Account-Book has been preserved in Trinity College between that for 1542—43 and that for 1547—48, which is imperfect. We cannot therefore ascertain when the destruction of the Friars' Buildings commenced; but, having regard to the enormous quantity of materials which they provided between

---

[1] [Rogeri Aschami Epistolarum Libri Quatuor. 8vo. Oxon. 1703, p. 332. The letter is dated 19 January, but the year is not mentioned. As Thirleby was not consecrated Bishop of Westminster until 19 December, 1540, the earliest date which could be assigned to it is January, 1541.]

[2] [Commiss. Docts. iii. 598. Cole remarks upon this document: "This Survey shews that the foundation of Trinity College was contemplated, and the new buildings were actually commenced, some months before the surrender of Michael House and King's Hall." MSS. Cole xlvi. 228. Add. MSS. Mus. Brit. 5847.]

1547—48 and 1556—57[1], when the supply seems to have become exhausted, it is difficult to conceive that the damage done
in 1546 could have been very serious.   On the other hand the
following inventory[2], which could not have been taken earlier
than the end of the year 1547, shews that by that time the
Church had been destroyed.   The School-House was not taken
down until 1553—54[3].

"At yᵉ freres.

In primis eight stooles for masons to heue stone of.

Item a roofe of tymbre wᶜʰ [was] ouer yᵉ hall at [the] freres lying in
a store house next to Laignes, and an old whelebarrowe.

Item hewen stone for wyndows and for yᵉ turrett vnder yᵉ scole
howse, with old slate and an old hand barroue.   A morter tubbe.

Item a stock lock and a key of yᵉ lyme kylne doore.

Item a locke and a key of yᵉ owter gate.

Item two morter tubbes.   A whele barrow.

Item thre sowes of lede of which one lieth where yᵉ churche stode
being vᶜ. di' qᵃ. xxjˡⁱ. in weight ; and two in yᵉ corner of yᵉ cloyster
next to yᵉ steple and lyme kylne, tone xiijᶜ. xiiijˡⁱ. tother vijᶜ. vijˡⁱ."

The charges for the carriage of materials from "the Friars"
set down in the Accounts of Trinity College during the nine
years above mentioned are incessant ; but unfortunately they
give but little indication of the nature of the buildings destroyed.
The materials were either reduced to lime, or hewn into shapes
convenient for use in new buildings, previous to removal.   The
buildings specified are: the Church; the Belfry, containing a peal
of bells ; the Cloister ; the Grave-Yard ; and the School House[4].
The cloister probably surrounded the grave-yard, and the last
entry in the inventory quoted above shews that the belfry
adjoined the cloister.

Soon after the acquisition of the Grey Friars by Trinity
College, the site was subdivided into portions convenient for
letting.   The first of these leases, to William Laing, labourer,

[1] [It has been shewn above in the History of Trinity College (p. 562) that in the
course of this year 2950 loads of stone were brought from "the Friars."]

[2] [This inventory of the property of Trinity College is preserved in the Muniment
Room.   Part of it is dated 1547, and the whole appears, from the handwriting, to
have been taken at about the same time.]

[3] [The Senior Bursar's Accounts for Trinity College for this year contain a charge
"for taking downe of the scholehouse at the freres."]

[4] [The four first of these are mentioned in the petition from the University ; the
last in the Accounts of Trinity College.]

of Cambridge, is dated 24 September, 1547, and the ground demised is described as :

" the hole orchard wch belonged of late to ye house called the gray friers...wth also certaine houses that is to say a malthouse, kilnehouse, old brewhouse, being situate within the procincte of ye said friers ; with also a certaine garden plot lieng on the east side of the said kilnehouse, and joining on the south side one Walles land wth also a contened little house standing at the orchard gate on the west entring of the saide orcharde...with also so much voyd ground lieng on the north side from ye said houses as is appointed by the said M^r fellowes and schollers to be convenient for the vse of the said William Laieng for his cattel and carriage that is to say xx^tie taylors yerdes from the northe ende of the old Brewhouse and so discending eastward by a right line toward the orchard aforesaid...¹"

Two years afterwards, 24 December, 1549, the College leased to Ralph Bicardike

"a pece of ground parcel of ye ground of ye late gray friers, as it lieth next the kinge's high way called condatt strete, betwene a storehouse on the northe parte and ye ground now in ye tenure of William Layeng on the south parte wch pece of ground conteineth in lenght from the north in to the south eleven pooles ; and in bredth at the south end four pooles and sixtene foote ; and in bredth at the north end two pooles and fiften fote ; every pole conteining eighten footes of the kinges standerd²."

In 1562 (10 September) a third piece was leased to William Hedley, yeoman. It is endorsed, " A lease of the hither parte of the gray friers grounde," and is described as

" one pece of ground being the syte of the late gray friers wth certaine houses that is to say a greet store house and all thother edifices in ye said pece of ground situate and being ; the said pece of ground butting of thest side on a diche commonly called the kynges diche, ye north side on Jesus Lane, on the west side the Kinges highe way called the conduit street, and butting on the south west side vppon on parcel of the said gray friers grauntede by Indenture bering date the xxiiij^th of december in the third yere of the raigne of Edward the sixt to Rafe Bicardicke late alderman of ye towne of Cambridge, and butting of the south side on parcel of the ground and edifices late letten by Indenture bering date the xxiiij of September in the first yere of ye raigne of

¹ [Trin. Coll. Register, i. 24. The lease is for 40 years at an annual rent of £4. 6s. 8d.]

² [Ibid. i. 39. The lease is for 21 years, at an annual rent of five shillings. A subsequent lease of the same piece, dated 15 April, 1570, specifies in addition "a storehouse on the east parte," and " one house or Bearne standing at the sowthe end vpon ye said ground conteininge in lengthe x yeardes and in breadthe fower."]

o[r] soveraigne lord Edward the sixt to William Lane late laborer of the towne of Cambridg[1]."

In Lyne's plan of Cambridge, dated 1574 (fig. 1), the whole site is shewn surrounded by walls, and in the western wall there is a large and lofty gate. The King's Ditch runs across it from north to south, and at the south-west corner stands a single large building. In the more accurate plan of Hamond, dated 1592 (fig. 2), the site is subdivided in a way which explains the terms of the leases quoted above. The ground let to Lane was

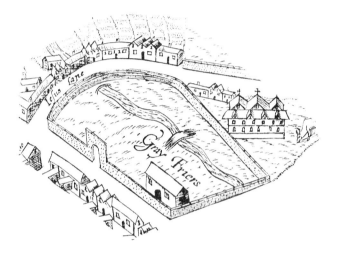

Fig. 1.   Site of the Grey Friars, from Lyne's Map of Cambridge, 1574.

evidently, from the large amount of the rent, the most extensive and valuable portion of the site. The orchard, not mentioned in any of the other leases, was no doubt situated on the east of the King's ditch. The malt-house and other offices, with a garden adjoining to them, are probably the houses shewn standing together at the south end of the site, and "the little house at the orchard gate" is that at the corner of Walles Lane and the street now called Sussex Street. Lane was also allowed a piece of ground sixty feet in length on the west side of the King's ditch, behind the closes shewn next to Conduit Street.

---

[1] [Ibid. i. 86.   The lease is for 20 years, at an annual rent of twenty shillings.]

It may be considered that the general position of his buildings
is represented by the yard and offices southeast of the Chapel
(fig. 3), but the lease to Bicardike shews that his ground extended to Conduit Street. The second portion of the site was
198 feet long next to Conduit Street, a distance equal to that

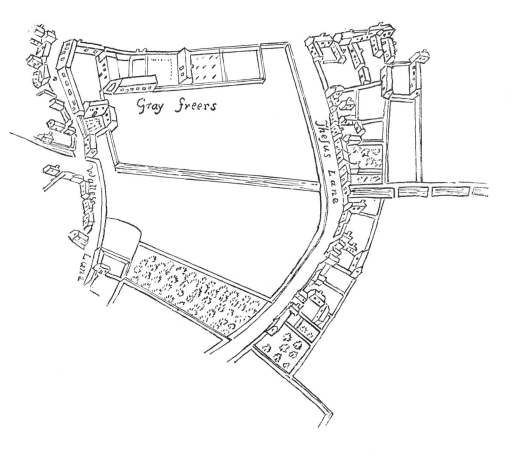

Fig. 2. Site of the Grey Friars, reduced from Hamond's Map of Cambridge, 1592.

from the entrance to the stable-yard to the north wall of the
second court. At the south end, where a barn stood, it was
88 feet broad from the street to a store-house, a distance equal
to that from the street to the Chapel; at the north end, where

there was a second store-house, it was 51 feet broad. The three buildings here mentioned are evidently the three shewn by Hamond, of which the two first stand close together. The last piece is more clearly defined in the lease. It extended eastward from Conduit Street along Jesus Lane as far as the King's Ditch ; and on the south side it was terminated by the pieces let to Bicardike and Lane respectively. The "great store-house" mentioned in the lease is probably the building which Hamond shews at the south end of two square closes next the street. We may conjecture that these closes were walled in between 1562, when the lease was granted, and 1592, when Hamond's plan was drawn.

These leases unfortunately say nothing about the church or conventual buildings belonging to the Franciscans. It may be conjectured however that the malthouse and brewhouse leased to Laing in 1547 had belonged to them ; and, as they were situated on the south side of the site, that the rest of the offices of the convent were there also. It will be shewn below that the old Chapel of Sidney Sussex College was in all probability the Refectory ; and Fuller believed that the Church stood to the north of the area of the principal quadrangle, where the Bowling Green was in his time (fig. 4) :

"The area of this church is easily visible in Sidney College garden, where the depression and subsidency of their bowling-green east and west, present the dimensions thereof, and I have oft found dead men's bones thereabouts[1]."

If this tradition be true, we must place the cloister south of the Church, between it and the Refectory, in order to provide sufficient space for it. It will therefore be represented, at least in part, by the College quadrangle.

In 1578 (29 October) the Corporation of the Town of Cambridge deputed the Mayor and others to negotiate with Trinity College for the acquisition of this site, on which they proposed to erect a Hospital for the poor, offering in exchange part of Garret Hostel Green, and the Common Ground on the west side of the River Cam, opposite to the College[2]. We do not know why this proposal was declined, for the exchange suggested would have been more advantageous to Trinity

---

[1] [History of Cambridge, p. 66.]   [2] [Cooper's Annals, ii. 366.]

College than that which they ultimately accepted ; nor whether any other persons tried to obtain possession of the ground until after the death of the Countess of Sussex, 9 March 1588—89. The negotiations with her executors, which probably began soon after her death, were not concluded until 1595. All alienation of property being expressly forbidden by the statutes of Trinity College which were then in force, it was necessary to obtain the authority of Parliament to effect the sale, and the College was probably unwilling to take this step. It will be seen from the correspondence printed below, that Archbishop Whitgift, formerly Master (1566—77), whom the Countess of Sussex had made one of the supervisors of her Will, did his best to induce the College to grant the request of her executors; and when they had procured[1] an Act of Parliament in 1593 empowering the College to sell or let to them the site of the Grey Friars "any locall Statutes of the said Colledge, or any statute or lawe of this Realme to the contrarie notwithstandinge," Queen Elizabeth wrote a letter to the Master and Fellows pointing out that the Executors had spared no pains to discharge their trust,

"And withall have been humble Suitors to us, that wee would bee pleased, for the furtherance of soe good a purpose, to write these our letters unto you, the rather to move you to graunt to their request ;

Wee, considering that their suite tendeth to a common benefite of our Realme, to the amplifying of our Universitie, and the beautifying of our towne of Cambridge, have been moved...to require you, as wee doe by these presents, that you would presently sell or graunt the said site of the Friars, for some reasonable price, to the said Executors...

Wherevnto wee doubt not, but that of your owne disposition you will shew yourselves soe ready, considering that the same tendeth to the advancement of learning, whereof you are professors, That wee shall not neede to vse any arguments, other then to move you to the speedie doeing thereof.

And whereas you may bee in doubt of the danger of the statutes and ordinances of your said Colledge, which doe forbid such alienacions, although wee doe take it, that you are sufficiently discharged and dispenced with the penalties and danger thereof by the late statute made for that purpose, Yet for your better satisfaction and contentment wee doe hereby of our mere motion and certaine knowledge and of our prerogative royall, fullie clearely and absolutely discharge and dispence with you and every of you touching all your said statutes and ordi-

---

[1] [It is expressly stated in the opening sentences of Queen Elizabeth's letter that the Act of Parliament had been obtained by the motion of the Executors.]

nances in that behalfe, and touching all and everie branch penaltie and forfeiture which you and every of you might fall into or incurre, by reason of aliening, selling, or graunting the premisses in manner afore-said[1]."

It was probably in consequence of this letter that the College agreed to sell, for in 1594 (25 July) the Queen issued her letters patent authorizing the executors to found a College on that site or elsewhere[2]. Difficulties, however, arose about the amount of compensation to be paid; and the following correspondence took place between the College and the Archbishop[3]. The letter sent to him is not dated, but the date of his reply renders it probable that it was sent in July, 1595.

"Our humble duties premised. As first at your Graces motion, and for the foundacion of a Colledge, we haue not bene vnwillinge to parte with the Scite of the late dissolued Gray Fryers in Cambridge, to no smale damage and preiudice of our Colledge inheritance, so con-sideringe the delaies, and slender recompence to be expected for so large and beneficiall a graunte as we haue entred into, we are bould eftsonnes to recommend the serious consideracion thereof to your Graces wisdome, and wonted care of our poore Colledge; well hopinge that as we haue referred our demaunds in this behalf to your Graces determinacion, so your Grace wilbe well pleased to award vs aboue the fee farme of twenty markes, some proporcion of monie answerable to the buildinges, and other comodities of stone and stuffe, aswell within as aboue the ground, which by estimacion of workemen beinge of greate valew, we are content to leaue behinde vs, or else that your Grace would be pleased to except, and reserve out of the bargaine and sale such houses lands and Tenementes to former vses as at the veiw of discreet and indifferent persons may be exempted and well spared; leavinge sufficiencie for the scite, buildinges, Courts, backsides, and other offices of the intended foundacion: or, for defaulte thereof, and to satisfye all demaundes at once, that the founders there would be pleased to procure, and purchase the same rent of assise, in anie place in England, to be anexed for ever to our Colledge which towards this new foundacion is severed from it. In hope whereof we comendinge our reasonable requestes to your Graces wise iudgment and your Grace to Almightie God. From Trinitie Colledge in Cambridge."

"After my very hartie commendacions: Whereas you haue referred to my consideracion what the College should haue in money for an

---

[1] [Registrum Magnum of Sidney Sussex College, p. 5. The letter is not dated, but it is clear, from internal evidence, that it was written after the Act of Parliament above referred to had been passed.]

[2] [Commiss. Docts. iii. 529.]

[3] [This letter and those which follow are copied from the originals in the Muniment Room of Trinity College.]

olde buylding standing within the wall of the Grey-Fryers now used
for a malting-howsse; or whether any Consideracion should be made
therefore or noe: And lykewise what Consideracion the Master should
have for his charges in commyng vp and downe to London the last
Trinitie terme, for the perfecting of the assurance of the sayde Grey-
Friers: Forasmuche as I cannot convenientlye resolve vpon these
poyntes (being notwithstandinge of no great importance) without conference with some by you authorised, which cannot well bee before
the next terme: I verye hartelye pray you for the avoyding of further
excuses and delayes in so good a purpose, that you would in the mean
tyme with as muche expedicion as may fee bee, finishe and make perfect
the assurance betwixt the College and Sir John Harrington for the sayd
Grey-Friers: And I will not fayle to give my resolucion for the two
poyntes before mentioned as neare as I can to both your Contentacions.
And so I committ you to the tuicion of Allmightie God. From Croydon
the last of July, 1595.

Addressed: Your assured loving frend

" To my very loving frendes   Jo. Cantuar."
the Master and Seniours of
Trinitie College in Cambr'."

A formal conveyance of the site to the executors was then
drawn up, dated 10 September, 1595[1], from which the following
passages may be extracted:

"WHEREAS the Ladie Frauncis Countisse of Sussex, hathe for the
mayntenance of good learning by her last will and testament, willed
and ordayned That her executours should bestowe and imploye A
certaine somme of monye for the Erection of a Colledge in the vniuersitie of Cambridge, And for the purchasing of some competent landes
for the mayntenaunce of a Master, certaine Fellowes, and Scholers as by
the said will apperethe

AND WHEREAS in the last parliament of our said Soueraigne Ladie
the Queenes Matie holden at Westminster in ye fyve and thirtithe yere
of her highnes said Raigne amongst other thinges it was enacted That
the late Scite of the dissolved howse of the Graye Fryers in or nere
Cambridge might be sould or lett in fee farme or otherwyse for the
erecting of a newe Colledge in the Vniuersitie of Cambridge

NOWE THIS INDENTURE WITNESSETHE that...

Thomas Nevill D^r in Divinitie M^r, and ye Fellowes and Scholers of
the...Colledge of the holie and vndevided Trinitie within ye towne and
vniuersitie of Cambridge...for and in consideracion of a certayne somme
of monye to them in hand paid before thensealling of these presentes
And of the yerelie rent in and by these presentes hereafter reserved
And for diuerse other good causes and consideracions them therevnto
especially moving...Haue bargained and solde...vnto...Henrie Earle of
Kent, Sir John Harrington, Robert Forthe, and Nicholas Bonde...

---

[1] [Trin. Coll. Register, ii. 254.]

ALL THAT PARCELL OF LAND conteyning by estimacion Three Acres be it more or lesse called or knowne by the name of ye late Scyte of the howse of ye Graye Fryers within or neere the Towne of Cambridge ...nowe enclosed with a stone wall, togeather with the said wall and walles; And all howses and buildinges, in or vppon ye said parcell of lande with thappurtenaunces; And all draynes watercourses wayes passages profittes commodities advantages and hereditamentes whatsoeuer, to the said parcell of land nowe belonging, or in anywyse appertayning; And ye revercion and revercions of all and singular the premisses. And all priviliges, fraunchises, and liberties to be had vsed and enioyed in and vppon ye premisses or any of them or by any Inhabitantes...in or vppon the same or any parte thereof (except one Condite sometymes belonging to the said Scyt[1]) To have and to hold ye said parcell of land...for euer...yelding and paying therefore yerelie to the said Mr Fellowes and Scholers...The yerelie rent of Thirtene powndes six shillinges eight pennce...

AND WHEREAS the said Mr Fellowes and Schollers of the said College parties to these presentes, for the furthering and spedie affecting of so good a worke, have abated very greatly of the price of the value and worthe of the said grownd wherevppon the said Colledge is to be erected and builded, Be it therefore provided alwayes that yf the said Colledge appoynted to be erected and builded by the said will of the said Ladie Fraunces Countisse of Sussex be not erected and builded within seauen yeres next emediatly ensuing the date of these presentes That then these present Indentures and all and euery thing and matter therein conteyned And euery other acte and actes, thing and thinges, hereafter to be made for the further assuraunce of the premisses to be vtterlie voyde frustraite and of none effecte...

IN WITNES WHEREOF the parties aforesaid to these Indentures have Interchangeably sett their seales the daye and yere first aboue written."

The yearly rent is specified in the above document, but the amount to be paid in hand before the conveyance was sealed is still undefined. A week later it was fixed by the Archbishop at one hundred marks:

"I haue signified to Sir John Harrington, that for furder recompence of the bargayne betwixt you concerning the Friers, hee shall yeild vnto you one hundred markes. You may signifie so muche vnto the Companie, if you thinck good. It is my order, wherevnto all parties haue promised to stand. Vale in Christo. From Croydon the xviith of Septemb. 1595.

Addressed: Y^r assured loving frend
"To my very loving frend Jo. Cantuar."
Mr Dr Nevile, Master of
Trinitie Coll. in Cambr'."

---

[1] [This conduit was in Bridge Street. See above, p. 428. It is probably represented by the pump which Loggan (fig. 4) shews in the wall just beyond the north range of the quadrangle.]

The executors sealed the conveyance in the course of the month, and at the beginning of October the Earl of Kent sent the hundred marks to Dr Nevile. His letter, and that of Sir John Harrington, are subjoined.

"Good Mr Doct^r Nevill, I haue stayed to send vnto you longer then I purposed, for that to satysfie your Counsell I haue been enforced to send to all the executors seuerally, whereof some were at Oxford, others beyonde London, and in other places distant farr from me. But now having procured them all to seale, I haue sent the assurance vnto you, not doubtinge but as you haue euer delt freindly and lyke a gentleman in this accion, you will now be contented to passe the assurance for the gray friers as it is agreed vnto by your Counsell. I doubt not but you haue intelligence of my Lord of Caunterburies order what his pleasure is should be perfourmed by vs. If you haue not, I thincke this letter which I haue sent will satysfie you therein. I suppose his Lordship hathe awarded you a farr greater somme then you either expected or would your self haue demaunded, and I haue appointed this bearer to deliuer you so much of the same somme as you will take, prayinge you to haue consideration that how much you shall abate of this somme, so much shall Sydney Colledge be furthered and bettered by your good meanes and fauour[1]. And so I commit you to God. Burley the 3 of October, 1595.

Your very assured Frend
John Haryngton."

Addressed:
" To the Right worshipfull my very good
Freind Mr Doctor Nevell M^r of
Trynitie Colledge in Cambridge."

"Good Mr Doct^r Nevill, I doe most hartely intreate your good favour and furtherance in passeing thoroughe and finnyshing the assuraunce of the Graye Friers to vs the executors of the late Countesse of Sussixe. The good purpose and commendable accion therein I leave to your good consideracion. All hir Ladyship's executors haue nowe sealed subscrybed and delyvered the counterpanies according to due corse of lawe; my erniste desire therefore is that you wilbe pleased with the fellowes of your house to seale and delyuer the other partes that is to be performed by you, according to former agreemente. The tyme hathe bynne longe, the charges and trobles very greate to the executors to bring this to passe that hathe bynne done, the money remaininge

---

[1] [It is worth notice that no receipt of this sum, or of any part of it, has been entered in the Bursar's Books of Trinity College, the series of which, for this period, is quite complete. The only references to the negotiations are the following : Sen. Burs. Accounts, 1593—94. *Law Charges*. "Item to M^r. Ellis for pervsinge the assurance betwyxt the Colledge and S^r. John Harrington xx^s." Ibid. 1594—95. "Item for drawing the first booke betwixt the Colledge and S^r. John Harrington xxxvj^s. iij^d."]

but very smale to finnyshe that which is begune.   Wherein what favour, with expedition, yourselfe and fellowes will vochsaffe to shewe us, we will be all righte thankfull vnto you; besides you shall gaine the generall good commendacion of all for your furtherance and perform-ance of so good an accion.   And so I doe commende the same with yourselfe to God's mercyfull protection.   Wrest; the xth day of October 1595.

Yo^r very assured Loveing
Frend

H. Kent."

Addressed :
" To my very assured good
frende, M^r doctor Nevell
Master of Trinitie colledge
in Cambridge be theis."

It is not likely that any further delays arose; for at the beginning of the following year, 14 February, 1595—96, the executors founded the College; and on 20 February follow-ing they gave possession of the site to the Master, Mr James Mountague, and to William Wood, M.A., and John Maynard, B.A., in the name of the rest of the Fellows and Scholars[1].]

CHAPTER II.

History of the Buildings.

THE foundation of the College was laid by the Master 20 May, 1596[2].   The buildings were completed in or about 1598, with the exception of the Chapel, which was added two years afterwards[3].   The architect was Ralph Symons, who had built Emmanuel eight years before.

---

[1] [Comm. Docts. iii. 581.   Le Keux, ed. Cooper, iii. 16.]

[2] [Le Keux, ed. Cooper, iii. 16.   The date is given elsewhere 20 May, 1595, which must be a mistake, as it was shewn in Chapter I. that the College was not founded, and Mr Mountague was not made Master, until 14 February, 1596.]

[3] [MSS. Baker x. 413.   MSS. Harl. Mus. Brit. 7037.   The MS. from which Baker quotes is headed by him : " Tabula Sidneiana sive Historia Collegii Sidneiani, ex Adversariis Johannis Sherman S.T.P. Collegii Jesu Præsidis, et Archidiaconi Sarum, concinnata.   Transcripta ex MS⁰ : Tho: Harrison S.T.B. et Coll. Sidn. Socii Dignissimi."]

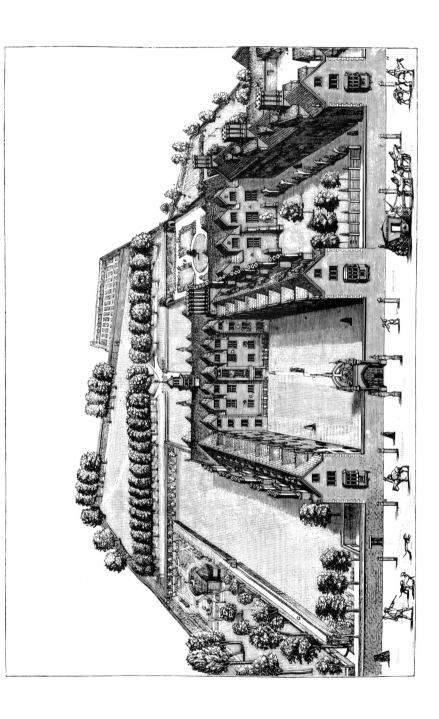

Fig. 4. Sidney Sussex College, from Logan's print, taken about 1688. A, Chapel; B, Library; C, Hall; D, Master's Lodge; E, Kitchen; F, Master's Garden; G, Fellows' Garden.

The College was built of a gloomy dark brick, with stone dressings[1], and of the plainest character. It consisted originally of only the present north court, or "Hall Court" as it is termed, which measured 78 feet from north to south, by 110 feet from east to west. The original arrangement of it is shewn by Loggan (fig. 4). It was entered through a gatehouse of fanciful design in the middle of the wall which closed it on the west side next to the street. This gatehouse was a low oblong structure; the façade had a four-centered arch flanked by two pseudo-classical columns bearing an entablature. In the centre, over the arch of entrance, was a tablet bearing the arms of the Foundress; and it was finished above by a high pinnacle and vane placed at the point of intersection of four stone ribs which curved upwards from the centre of each side. The north and south sides of the court were occupied by ranges of chambers in three floors, of which the upper one was a half-storey, with eaves and wall-dormers over every window on the side next to the court. On the north side next to the garden, there were no wall-dormers, but the dormer-gablets of the half-storey were connected by a parapet, except in one instance[2]. There were garrets in the roof, lighted by small windows, which are shewn by Loggan on the north and south sides of the north and south ranges respectively. The east side of the court was formed by a building which extended from the northern to the southern extremity. The general arrangement of this building has not been altered. The northern half is occupied by the Hall, which had at first an open timbered roof. The door of entrance, in the middle of the façade, opens, as usual, to the screens. The southern half contains the Butteries and Kitchen on the ground floor, also entered from the screens, and on the first floor the Master's Lodge, with garrets above. There was originally a square turret in each angle of the court, as at Emmanuel College. The one to the

---

[1] [Prof. Willis makes this statement on the authority of Harraden, who says (Cantabrigia Depicta, p. 161) "The whole College is built of dark coloured brick, partially intermixed with stone; the effect of the whole is so gloomy, that no correctness of form or distribution of parts can counteract its impression."]

[2] [Our only authority for the north side of the north range is a print by J. K. Baldrey, at the head of the University Almanack for 1809. It is, however, doubtful whether it represents the original arrangement; for the garret-windows shewn by Loggan have disappeared, and the parapet looks like the result of a repair.]

right served as a porch to the Lodge; the one to the left performed the same office for the College Parlour, which then was
on the ground floor at the east end of the north range, contiguous to the high-table of the Hall. A similar turret projected
from the middle of the façade, and furnished a porch for the
Hall of a more ornamental character than the others. Two
columns, like those of the entrance gate, supported an entablature, above which there was a coat of arms. Higher up, between
the windows, there was a sundial; and in the gable a lozenge,
perhaps intended to bear a second coat of arms, surmounted by
a small pediment, and decorated with arabesque enrichments.
There were wall-dormers over all the windows. Loggan's
ground plan of Cambridge shews that access from the principal
court to the garden on the north, and to the second court on the
south, was obtained by a passage near the west end of the north
and south ranges respectively.

The eastern side, facing the garden, had at each extremity a
large semicircular oriel which rose a little above the eaves. The
northern oriel belonged to the Hall; the southern lighted the
Kitchen below, and the Master's great chamber above. The
original appearance of this front will however be best understood
from the accompanying elevation (fig. 5) which has been reduced from a drawing made in 1821, before the original style
had been destroyed.

The Master's first floor consisted originally of a great chamber, 24 feet long by 26 feet broad, at the south end of the range;
a second chamber; and a third narrow chamber. The two latter
were over the Butteries. The Lodge was approached by a staircase which was either in the south wing, or, more probably, in
the turret in the south-east angle of the court (fig. 4).

The Chapel, over which was the Library, was formed by
fitting up the ruinous walls of a building which had been left
standing in the area to the south of the buildings of the court—
the sole available remnant of the Franciscan convent. It projected irregularly southwards from the south-eastern corner of
the quadrangle, standing just clear of the south gable of the
eastern range, as shewn by dotted lines on the plan (fig. 3).
The unorthodox direction of this building was not objected to
by the founders of the College; and we have already seen that

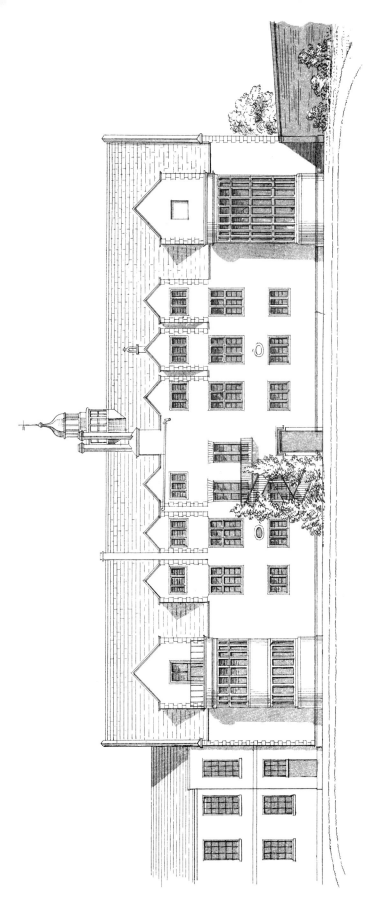

The original character of the Chapel and Library
is quite destroyed.
The Ornaments at the angles of the gables have been
nearly all omitted at the various repairs.

It appears by this drawing and on inspection of the
Building itself, that many alterations have been made.
One Bow and both gables have been rebuilt, some of the
windows have had their character changed, the spaces
betwixt some of the dormers have been closed.

EASTERN SIDE OF
SYDNEY COLLEGE IN ITS PRESENT STATE.

FIG. 5. ELEVATION OF THE GARDEN-FRONT OF THE EAST RANGE OF SIDNEY SUSSEX COLLEGE,
REDUCED FROM A DRAWING BY JEFFRY WYATT, 1821.

their architect had been expressly instructed to set the chapel at Emmanuel College in the north and south direction.

It has been already stated, on the authority of Sherman, that the Chapel was fitted up two years after the completion of the other buildings; that is, about the year 1602. On the other hand Fuller[1] asserts that the College "continued without a chapel some years after the first founding thereof, until at last some good men's charity supplied this defect"; and there is a tradition that the work should be referred to Samuel Ward, B.D., Master from 1609 to 1643, who is recorded to have been

"a most excellent Governour, and an exact Disciplinarian in his College; which flourished so much under him, that Four new Fellowships were founded in his Time, all the Scholarships were augmented, and a Chapel, together with a new Fair Range of Buildings, were Erected[2]."

It is, however, certain that a portion of the internal fittings was due to the liberality of Dr Mountague, who, having been the first Master, became Bishop of Bath and Wells in 1608. Cole, writing in 1748, has left the following description of his works[3]:

" He wainscoted the Altar End of the Chapel in a very handsome Manner : but this was done, as I should guess, when he was Bp. of Bath and Wells, for over the Altar is carved the Arms of that See impaling his own. The same Arms with a most beautiful Mitre over them in a Window of the great Dining Room of the Master's Lodge is still preserved : from wch I should gather that he also glased and finished the Windows in that part of the Lodge : however it is certain that he was a great Benefactor to it in many other Respects. Nor did he while private Master of this College confine his Munificence within the Walls thereof; for the King's Ditch in Cambridge being at that Time very offensive to the Inhabitants, he at ye Expence of an Hundred Pounds brought a clear runing Water into it, to the no small Conveniency and Pleasure both of the Town and University."

These accounts may be reconciled by supposing that the Chapel was first fitted up in or about 1602; but that afterwards, during the Mastership of Dr Ward, and at his suggestion, additional work was done to it, to which Dr Mountague contributed.

The "new fair range of buildings" which Dr Ward has the credit of erecting, is the range of chambers on the south side of

---

[1] [History of Cambridge, p. 293.]
[2] [Walker, Sufferings of the Clergy, fol. Lond. 1714, p. 158.]
[3] [MSS. Cole xx. 102. Add. MSS. Mus. Brit. 5821.]

the second quadrangle, which, like the first, has buildings on three sides only, with a wall next to the street. This building is due to the liberality of Sir Francis Clerke, of Houghton Conquest in Bedfordshire, Knight. He founded four Fellowships and eight Scholarships, and in the deed of foundation, dated 29 November, 1628, the following passage occurs:

> "And it is also intended that every of the said fower Fellows shall haue a middle Chamber in the buildinges intended newly to be built by the said Sir Francis Clerke, and to be added to the building of the said Colledg, wherein every of them shall make choise according unto his seniority.
> And every of them shall also haue a Chamber over theire heads which shalbe for twoe Scholars[1]."

The exact date of the building has not been preserved; but it is probable that it would be erected soon after this deed was drawn up. Like Sir Christopher Wray's at Magdalene College, Dr Perse's at Gonville and Caius College, and others, it was primarily intended to lodge Sir Francis Clerke's beneficiaries, who would have occupied eight sets of chambers. The actual structure, however, is in three floors, with garrets in the roof, and there are five sets of chambers on each floor, so that seven sets, exclusive of the garrets, would be left at the disposal of the College. Loggan (fig. 4) shews that this building had originally wall-dormers over the staircases only, and that the doors were square-headed, instead of being four-centered like those in the Hall Court. We see from the same authority that it overlapped the Chapel very slightly. By this arrangement both the Chapel and the Library had a window at the south end.

[The College as thus completed consisted of three parallel ranges of chambers, each with a gable-end next the street, in which was an oriel window. These, as Loggan shews, were ornamented with coats of arms. The most northern bore those of Henry Grey, Earl of Kent, with his motto, FOY EST TOUT; the next those of Sir John Harrington; and the third, in all probability, those of Sir F. Clerke. The two first have been preserved in the College.

[1] [Registrum Magnum of Sidney College, p. 168.]

At the beginning of the eighteenth century the buildings were shewing signs of decay. In November 1729[1] it was agreed not to fill up a vacant Fellowship, "the College being in a ruinous condition as to its buildings"; and in May 1730, "in considera-tion of the miserable and ruinous condition" of the buildings, it was agreed to borrow £200. This money was probably spent on general repairs, and not on the alteration of special buildings; for the Hall, Gateway, Chapel, Library, and Master's Lodge, are expressly mentioned in subsequent years.

In March, 1747, it was agreed that "two Fellowships should be kept open for the repairing and refitting of the Hall, and other repairs"; in January, 1749, £400 was borrowed "for the speedier fitting up of the Hall"; and in February 1749 another Fellowship was kept open for the same purpose, and for the College Gateway. We may therefore refer to this period the removal of the original gateway, and the alteration of the Hall.

The position of the gateway was not altered, but it was replaced by one of the same shape, but of classical design[2], which in its turn was removed, and now stands at the entrance to the Master's garden in Jesus Lane.] The Hall was thoroughly Italianized; and a flat ceiling was introduced under the original roof. When Jeffrey Wyatt was consulted with respect to the repairs of the Hall and Lodge in 1821, this roof was surveyed, and from a drawing which was then made it appears that its framing remains intact above the ceiling. It is a plain hammer-beam roof with S-shaped braces in the fashion of its period, and of the simplest kind. The only change that had been made was by bolting a pair of beams, one on each side of the hammer-beam ends, so as to form a low collar-beam, or tie, to receive the ceiling. The hammer-beams and pendant posts had been removed, and the present plaster cornice intro-duced in their place. Wyatt notes on the margin of the draw-ing that if thought desirable there would be no difficulty in restoring it to its original open character. The Hall is 27 feet broad and 56 feet long, from the door to the north wall; but

---

[1] [The dates of these several repairs have been most kindly copied for me from the Acta Collegii by my friend the Rev. Robert Phelps, D.D., Master.]

[2] [Harraden's view, dated 1810 (Cantabrigia Depicta, p. 159) shews this gateway in the same position as the older one.]

these alterations cut off nearly nine feet from the south end, for a music gallery, which is supported upon two columns, and upon a closet at each end, one of which contains the stairs leading to the gallery. The change was evidently much admired at the time, for Carter, whose work was published in 1753, says:

"The Hall is a very spacious room, and was wholly Repaired and Beautified within these two Years, and is a Grand Apartment."

The appearance of the Hall, which has not been altered since the changes we have been describing, will be understood from the engraving (fig. 6).

[The buildings next undertaken were the Chapel, Library, and Master's Lodge. In October 1774 it was agreed to keep a Fellowship open for their repair, as they had by that time become ruinous. It is recorded by Cole that " the old Chapel was quite worn out, both in its Stone Work and Timbers, and was become dangerous. The wainscote was chiefly rotten." Several plans seem to have been suggested by James Essex, the architect consulted, for though the Master, Mr William Elliston (Master 1760 —1807), " produced Essex's plans for a new chapel, and entered upon ways and means" 31 March, 1775, Essex was desired soon afterwards (18 April) " to draw a new plan for chapel and library"; and 4 July in the same year the Master "produced another plan by Mr Essex." Lastly, 3 October, the Master "produced another plan drawn by Mr Essex, according to the Master's idea of a new chapel and library, etc.: which was in general preferred to the other plans"; and, 19 April, 1776, it was agreed to take down the old chapel. Of this scheme Cole has left the following account[1]:

"In July 1776 the Chapel was pulled entirely downe, with some new Buildings erected by it by D. Paris[2] the late Master, who had well-nigh ruined the College by suppressing Fellowships for the ornamenting the Hall and his Lodge; so that 6 new Fellows were elected at one Time from other Colleges, for Want of Admissions in their own : among the rest Dr Elliston the present Master, who by his good Economy and prudent Management has much benefitted the Society, by raising their Rents and occasioning the usual Admissions. He planned the new Chapel, and means to erect it on the old Foundation, but lengthening it; having no Scruples about its irregular Position of

---

[1] [MSS. Cole *ut supra*, p. 139.]
[2] [Francis Sawyer Parris, D.D., Master 1746—60.]

Fig. 6.   Interior of the Hall, Sidney Sussex College, by Storer: from Le Keux's Memorials of Cambridge, ed. Cooper. Vol. II.

North and South: and to finish it at the College Expence, without suppressing Fellowships, or begging Subscriptions, in a plain and decent, but not costly Manner, or much ornamented."

While the old chapel was being pulled down, Essex made careful notes of it, and laid down a ground plan[1] (fig. 7). The most important passages of his memoir are the following:

"This Building...was the last remains of the ancient Religious house of Franciscans...Some have reported (says Mr Fuller[2]) that it was formerly a Stable, which is not improbable, though he will not allow it to be true, for it is uncertain what uses it was apply'd to between the time of the dissolution of the Monastery and the time of its being purchasd for the College; but, before it was converted into a Chapel, about 20 feet of the south end had been separated from the rest by a wall, and used to lay Coals in, as plainly appear'd when the foundations were digging for the new Chapel, and the other part might have been used for a stable for ought he knew to the contrary, tho' it certainly was not built for that purpose. Mr Fuller conjectures from the concavities in the walls that this building was ye ancient Dormitory of the Franciscans. This however may be doubted, because the Cavities he speaks of were only the doors, windows, and a chimney, of the room; not recesses for beds (reposing places) as he supposes them; and that it was not the Dormitory, but the Refectory, appears from the plan of it; and from the quantity of small bones of fowls, rabbits, and other animals, with spoons, etc. which were found among the rubbish when it was pulled down.

The whole building was 69ft 6in long, 23 ft 6 in wide between ye Walls, and 25ft 0in high to the top of the walls, above which the roof formed a Cieling with elliptical principals and the intermediate spaces flat in the middle and sloped on the sides...There were 3 windows and a door on the west side; on the east side there were the same number of windows and a door, with a Chimney (at *a*) 7 feet wide, placed near the Middle. On the west side, nearly opposite the chimney (at *b*) two holes appear in the wall, too low for a table or side-board, and too high for a seat; these might recieve timber to support the floor of a pulpit or desk where the Lecturer read the Scriptures to the Friars while they were at meals. At the south end there were two doors 4 feet wide, leading to an adjoining building, the foundations of which may be partly traced (*ff*). It appears by some marks in the wall about 10ft from the S.W. angle, near ye side of ye south door (at *d*), that a Cistern

---

[1] [The document is among Essex's MSS. in the British Museum: Add. MSS. 6761. A second copy, somewhat differently expressed, has been lent to me by my friend W. M. Fawcett, M.A., Jesus College. The two have been combined in the following extracts, and the spelling has been tacitly corrected.]

[2] [History, *ut supra*. "Some have falsely reported, that the new Chapel of the College was formerly a stable: whereas indeed it was the Franciscans ancient dormitory, as appeareth by the concavities still extant in the walls, places for their several reposure."]

or lavatory had been fixed there, under which, about a foot lower than the floor of the room, was a neat stone drain, about one foot square, which running obliquely (in the direction *de*) under the south end of the room, conveyed the water from this place into the King's Ditch. This drain served likewise to convey other waste water from some part of the monastery or from the Condit which belonged to it, and was served from the spring in the fields near Madingley road, before it was given to Trinity College, who cut off the pipe and retain'd the spring for their own use.

The floor of this room was made of plaister, or common mortar mixed with clay (not unlike those used in malthouses) : and lay'd 4 feet below the level of the Chapel floor. At the upper end (which was to ye North), about 10 feet above the floor, there was a moulding or cornice which ran across that end, but not round the room. There were neither windows nor doors at that end, unless the entrance into the Chapel (*g*) had been a door enlarged ; which is not improbable, for the principal apartments were on that side, but did not join to this building.

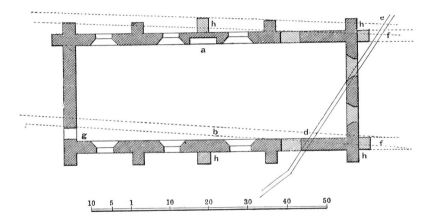

Fig. 7. Ground plan of the old Chapel of Sidney Sussex College, reduced from that made by James Essex, architect, 1776.

There is no appearance of any timber floors except that of the Library, which was afterwards added, the whole being one large room open to the Roof; which proves that this Refectory had neither the Dormitory nor any other apartment over it. At the south end may be traced the substructure of ye foundations to other buildings which I concieve were the Buttries, into which the doors at that end open'd. The floor of the Buttries was higher than the floor of the Refectory two steps, which being made of Clunch were much worn. The Cellars and other offices were ranged on the South, next Walls Lane. Where the Warden's and Friars' Apartments were situate cannot be traced, but as the Church stood about fifty yards North of this building, it is probable they were ranged somewhere between that and the Refectory. In an old plan of Cambridge other buildings appear to have joined this, running from it towards the street, where now the south wing of the College stands...

This Building, being greatly decay'd, was taken down in the month of August 1776, and on the 1st day of October following, at half an hour after eleven, the first stone of the new Chapel was lay'd in the South East angle of the Building, about 5 feet below the surface of the ground; the head of the stone, which is 11 inches square, lies towards yᵉ East, and projects 2 inches before the range of the wall. It has the date of the year, 1776, deep cut in figures 2 inches long; the length of the stone is 1ft 2in, and on the lower surface this ✠ is cut with a Chissel. The Master and Fellows being at that time engaged at the College Audit, no one was present at the Ceremony but the Master Bricklayer, and a Labourer who assisted me in Laying it. The Situation of the new Chapel is little different from the old, but not on the old Foundations. The dotted lines in the plan shew the variation. The Buttresses (*h. h. h.*) represented with [lighter shading] were not part of the original building, but added afterwards

James Essex."

The old chapel having been pulled down in July 1776 the foundations of the new one were laid; but the superstructure was not begun until the summer of 1777. The work proceeded slowly, the necessary funds being mainly provided by the usual expedient of keeping Fellowships open[1]. In May, 1779, it was agreed "to empower Mʳ Essex to employ Mʳ Clarke the plasterer to begin the ceiling and walls"; and in the following November to use deal painted for the wainscot, oak having been abandoned as too expensive. A payment of £100 to Mr Essex in March, 1782, "for superintendence of the New Building," marks the conclusion of the work.

The building erected by Essex was extended behind the gable of Clerke's building, as the plan shews (fig. 3). It consists of two parts; the southern contains the Chapel; the northern the College Library on the first floor, and beneath it the Master's kitchen and servants' offices, with a small Antechapel in the centre. A portion of the east side of this building is shewn in the elevation of that side of the College (fig. 5). The west front, of which a view is preserved in the College Library, was in

---

[1] [In 1777 (16 April) it was agreed "to continue the vacancies of 3 Fellowships for the expense of rebuilding the Chapel, Library, and Offices of Lodge": on 4 November, 1779, £40 a year was appropriated to the same purpose; and 31 March, 1781, another Fellowship was kept open.]

an equally plain style. A central portion, slightly in advance of the wings, was entered through a door flanked by classical pilasters, and surmounted by a pediment. A larger pediment, of similar character, surmounted the central portion; the wings had a plain entablature. The ground-floor had six sash windows, three on each side of the door; the first floor seven; all precisely similar to those on the east side.

A description of the College, as it appeared after the alterations of which we have been tracing the history had been completed, is worth quotation[1]:

"The entrance to Sidney is by a good Doric portico : the first court is a neat little brick building, but with nothing in it remarkable ; in the second court is the chapel, with an agreeable interior : a few years since it was rebuilt, and a new direction given to it, to make the Court more uniform, Dr Elliston, a late master, reviving the ancient character of the ecclesiastic, superintending and directing the building, according to his own taste."

We have next to record the series of alterations by which the College was brought to its present aspect. The Master and Fellows were enabled to undertake them in consequence of a bequest from Samuel Taylor, Esq., of Dudley, LL.B. 1704, who, by will dated 10 September, 1726, left certain lands to endow a Fellowship in Mathematics in the College, "which sort of study, in the Time of his being a Student there, was, as far as he did observe, much neglected." In 1818 an Act of Parliament was obtained[2] to authorize the sale of his mineral property and the investment of the proceeds in the hands of trustees ; with leave to purchase mathematical books and instruments, and also

"to apply any sum not exceeding Four thousand Pounds in erecting, building, altering, or fitting up, and preparing, a convenient and proper Place for the Reception of such Mathematical Books and Treatises and Instruments...as the Master and Fellows shall think fit."

The work was commenced in 1821, in which year we find the following Order :

"25 October 1821. The Master and Resident Fellows are empowered to seal contracts with such persons as they approve for building

---

[1] [Dyer's Cambridge, 1814, ii. 438.]

[2] [Private Acts of Parliament, 58 Geo. III. cap. 39.]

Fig. 8. Garden-front of the east side of Sidney Sussex College, after the alterations made by Wyatt in 1821, by Storer; from Le Keux's Memorials of Cambridge, ed. Cooper.

the Mathematical Library, and making other improvements in the East and West fronts of the College, agreeably to the plan and specification proposed by Jeffry Wyatt."

Before this Order was made, Wyatt had prepared a series of drawings, dated March, 1821, representing the buildings as they then stood, with alternative designs for their alteration and enlargement. Two styles of architecture were offered, the one the plain pseudo-Elizabethan Gothic which was adopted, the other the restoration of the genuine Elizabethan in which the College had been designed for its founders and benefactors, but which had been gradually deteriorated by the removal of the characteristic ornaments at the angles and crowns of the gables, of which latter one remained on the east front (fig. 5) ; the rebuilding of one of the great oriels, as the same drawing explains ; the rebuilding of the central porch-turret in a plainer manner, without the ornaments shewn by Loggan ; and other changes of form ; of which the most noteworthy is the removal of two of the wall-dormers. A parapet had also been introduced in the buildings of the Hall Court instead of the picturesque dormers of the original structure.

Before describing Wyatt's designs it should be mentioned that the main wall of the eastern front was found to overhang between eight and ten inches. It was therefore necessary to take measures for effectively supporting it. The changes introduced on the east, or garden-front, will be understood by comparing the elevation (fig. 5) with the line-engraving (fig. 8), taken after the work was completed. In order to support the wall, Wyatt added ten deep buttresses, with the connecting arches in the centre. At the same time he rebuilt the upper part of it, omitting the centre gables, and adding an embattled parapet. The windows on the first floor were made uniform, those of the original building being taken as a pattern. The windows in the third floor were made of two lights, instead of three lights, as in the original. On the court side he added the projecting structure in three floors which now connects the ancient angle-turrets, the central turret being altogether removed. The new piece, 14 feet wide, contains on the left an entrance-hall and staircase for the Master's Lodge ; on the right the "Taylor Library." In the centre is an open porch, covering the entrances to the Hall and

Lodge. Over this porch is the Master's Library. The lanthorn-turret which now crowns the centre of this work was built at this period, and the whole was clothed in Roman cement.

These changes having been completed, the same architect, now signing himself Jeffry Wyatville, submitted designs for the improvement of the chambers, Mr Taylor's trustees having been authorized, by a second Act of Parliament passed in 1823[1], to supply a further sum of £4500, for, among other things, "defraying the expenses of providing and fitting up rooms for the residence of the mathematical exhibitioners within the College." The designs are dated 1824, but they were not accepted until seven years later, when the following Order was made :

"23 April 1831. Agreed that the centre Building of the College be repaired and altered, and a new entrance into the College, and [a new] Gateway Tower be erected agreably to the plans etc, of Jeffry Wyatt-ville."

In the next year a similar Order was made :

"7 June 1832. Agreed that the North Wing of the front Court, and the South Wing of the Chapel Court be forthwith altered and repaired and that a new Combination Room be erected in the Fellows Garden, according to the plans etc, of Sir Jeffry Wyattville."

In carrying these designs into execution a new roof-story was added to the north and south wings of the Hall Court, by which four stories of complete chambers were obtained in lieu of three surmounted by small narrow garrets. Sir Francis Clerke's building received a parapet instead of its eaves, and also new dormers. An ingeniously contrived gateway-tower was built at the street end of the central wing. This, standing upon three open arches, gives equally convenient access to each quadrangle, although it may not be the most effective mode of displaying the architectural design of the courts to a spectator to set a blank wall in front of him as he passes under the arch of entrance, and thus compel him to enter each court sideways at a corner. The gateway tower is of masonry, the rest of the work is covered with Roman cement, by which the new additions and the old walls are brought to a uniform surface and colour.

[1] [Private Acts of Parliament, 4 Geo. IV. cap. 25.]

At the same time the windows and doorways were changed in style to suit the new fashions by adding hood-molds. It was at this time that the gateway, which, as explained above, had been built in 1749, was removed to the garden-entrance in Jesus lane. The position of the new Combination Room will be understood from the plan (fig. 3) on which Wyatt's work is distinguished by a lighter shading. It is in connection with the north side of the older room, through which it is approached from the Hall.

These works were completed in the course of 1832. An audit of the receipts and expenses, dated 14 August in that year, shews that the cost had amounted to £13,063. 0s. 0d., distributed as follows:

Hall, Lodge, Kitchen, Butteries and adjacent Buildings	5269 . 0 . 0
Gateway, centre wing, and walls	3600 . 0 . 0
North wing of Centre Court	2144 . 0 . 0
South wing of Chapel Court	1400 . 0 . 0
Combination Room	650 . 0 . 0
	13,063 . 0 . 0

The Chapel was "repaired and beautifyed" in the course of 1833 at the sole expense of the Master, William Chafy, D.D. An attempt was made to give a Gothic character to it by inserting windows of four lights, pointed, subdivided by a transom, and with a hoodmold over them, into the openings of the original sashes; and by adding a porch on the west side. The whole was stuccoed to correspond with the other buildings.

[LIBRARY.—The situation of the Library between the Master's Lodge and the Chapel has been already mentioned. A door at the north end opens into the Lodge; and a door at the south end into the gallery of the Chapel which is appropriated to the Master's family. The Library measures 36 feet in length, by 22 feet in breadth; and is lighted by eight windows, four on each side.

The fittings, designed by Essex in 1778[1], are in the plainest possible style, but follow older work in their arrangement. The

---

[1] [College Order, 5 June, 1778. "Agreed...that the classes for books be according to Mr Essex's plan, with doors at both ends for MSS etc, and that the ceiling be plain with only a cornice."]

classes project into the room between each pair of windows; and there are also shelves against the walls between the end of each class and the windows, and between the sill of each window and the floor. In front of each window there is a dwarf class. There are also shelves against the north and south walls, with a cupboard for MSS. in the centre of each division.

GARDENS.—The arrangement of the gardens at the end of the 17th century is shewn by Loggan (fig. 4). The Fellows' garden (G) occupied nearly the same space as at present; but it was divided into two portions, of which that nearest to the College was laid out as a Bowling Green. The Master's pleasure-garden (F) was then restricted to the space east of the chapel, but in addition to this he had a kitchen-garden, noted by the same letter, extending over the irregular space next Walles Lane, now occupied by College offices. The ground east of the Master's Lodge was laid out as a grass plat, divided by a central walk leading to the orchard beyond, the use of which is not noted. The small garden at the south-east corner was a cook's garden until a row of dwelling-houses was built upon it[1].

Dyer, whose history was published in 1814, thus describes the Fellows' Garden :

" Here is a good garden, an admirable bowling-green, a beautiful summer-house, at the back of which is a walk, agreeably winding, with variety of trees and shrubs intertwining, and forming, the whole length, a fine canopy over head; with nothing but singing, and fragrance, and seclusion; a delightful summer retreat; the sweetest lover's or poet's walk, perhaps, in the University."

The summer-house here mentioned, built by Essex in 1775, stood against the north gable of the Hall[2].]

---

[1] [This is stated on the authority of Dr Phelps.]

[2] [It is shewn in the view of the College at the top of the University Almanack for 1809. A College Order dated 31 March, 1775, directs the Steward " to procure a plan for a summer house of wood like Lord Melbourne's, a model of which was produced"; and by a second Order, dated 15 April, it was agreed " That a new summer house be erected in the Fellows' Garden, according to Mr Essex's plan, and Mr Humfrey's estimate."]

CHRONOLOGICAL SUMMARY.

1507—8.	Church of the Franciscans used by the University.
1523.	Ceremony of Commencement held in the same church.
1538.	Surrender of the Franciscan convent to King Henry VIII.
1540.	The University intercedes with the King to obtain possession of the site and buildings.
1546.	(19 Dec.) Site and buildings conveyed to Trinity College. Destruction of the buildings commences.
1547.	(24 Sept.) Part of the site leased to William Laing.
1549.	(24 Dec.) Part of the site to the north of the former piece leased to Ralph Bicardike.
1553—54.	School House at the Franciscans destroyed.
1556—57.	Supply of materials brought "from the Friars" to Trinity College apparently exhausted.
1562.	(10 Sept.) Part of the site to the north of the former two pieces leased to William Hedley.
1578.	(29 Oct.) Mayor and Corporation try to purchase the site.
1588—89.	(9 March.) Death of the Lady Frances Sidney, Countess of Sussex.
1593.	Act of Parliament empowering Trinity College to sell the site.
1594.	(25 July.) Letters patent of Queen Elizabeth authorizing the foundation of the College.
1595.	(10 Sept.) Conveyance of the site to the executors of the Lady Frances Sidney, Countess of Sussex.
1595—96.	(14 Feb.) Foundation of the College by the executors.
„	(20 Feb.) The executors give possession of the site to the Master.
1596.	(20 May.) Foundation-stone of the College laid.
1602.	An old building belonging to the Franciscans fitted up as a chapel.
1628.	(29 Nov.) Sir Francis Clerke proposes to erect a building on the south side of the Second Court for his Fellows and Scholars.
1729—30.	General repair of the buildings.
1747—49.	Hall repaired, and classical gateway put up.
1776.	(August.) Old Chapel pulled down.
1782.	Essex paid in full for the new Chapel.
1821.	Repairs to east and west façades, and erection of the Taylor Library. Wyatt architect.
1824.	Wyatt's designs for the rest of the College prepared.
1831.	South range of the principal court altered.
1832.	North range of the principal court, and south range of the chapel court, altered.
1833.	Chapel repaired and beautified by Dr Chafy, Master.

APPENDIX.

*Draft of a petition to be sent to King Henry the Eighth, praying him to grant to the
University the Church and Convent of the Franciscans.*

To the king our soueraign lorde.

Pleaseth it your hieghnes of your moost noble and haboundaunt grace to graunte
your graciouse lettres patentes in due fourme to be made accordyng to the tenour hereafter ensuying.

Rex omnibus ad quos etc Salutem.

Sciatis quod Nos de gratia nostra speciali ac ex certa scientia et mero motu
nostris dedimus et concessimus, ac per presentes damus et concedimus Dilectis sub-
ditis nostris Cancellario Magistris et Scolaribus Vniuersitatis nostre Cantebr' in
Comitatu nostro Cantebr' Scitum, ambitum, circuitum, et procinctum domus siue
prioratus fratrum minorum infra villam nostram Cantebr' in Com' predicto iam disso-
lut'; ac totam ecclesiam, Campanile cum campanis, et cimiterium eiusdem domus,
Necnon omnia et singula mesuagia, domus, edificia, terras, tenementa, ortos, gardina;
pomaria, columbaria, aqueductus ac cetera hereditamenta quecumque infra predictam
villam Cantebr' ac procinctum et libertat' eiusdem dicte nuper prioratui siue domui
pertinen' siue spectan' que ratione dissolutionis domus siue prioratus predict' in manibus nostris iam existunt, seu existere debent aut deberent.

Habend' tenend' gaudend' occupand' et percipiend' scitum, ambitum, circuitum, et
procinctum predict', ac tot predict', ecclesiam [etc., as above] a tempore dissolucionis
domus siue prioratus predict' prefatis Cancellario Magistris et scolaribus et successoribus suis imperpetuum, in puram ac perpetuam elemosynam absque aliquo compoto,
redditu, seu aliquo alio proinde nobis, heredibus vel successoribus nostris reddend',
soluend', seu faciend'.   Eo quod expressa mentio, et cetera.   In cuius rei testimonium,
et cetera.

Statuto de terris et tenementis ad manum mortuam non ponend' aut aliquo alio
statuto [etc.] non obstante.

Added in a different hand:

This graunt dyuerse tymes sued for but cold never be opteyned.

XVII.

Downing College[1].

HISTORY OF THE SITE AND BUILDINGS.

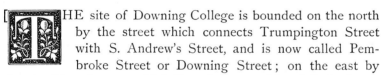HE site of Downing College is bounded on the north by the street which connects Trumpington Street with S. Andrew's Street, and is now called Pembroke Street or Downing Street; on the east by the dwelling houses which line the west side of S. Andrew's Street and Regent Street; on the south by Downing Terrace; and on the west by Tennis Court Road.

The condition of this site at the end of the seventeenth century will be understood from Loggan's Map of Cambridge dated 1688, of which a portion is here given (fig. 1). This shews that the northern division of it—that which lay immediately to the east of Pembroke College, was then called "The Lease," and the large division, to the south of the former, "The Marsh." In Hammond's map of Cambridge, dated 1592, the whole space is lettered "S. Thomas lees"; but in that of Lyne, dated 1574, the northern portion only is so designated, while the southern is marked "Swinecrofte[2]," a name which in the

---

[1] [Professor Willis had written nothing for the History of Downing College except a few sentences descriptive of the design of Mr Wilkins. These have been incorporated in the following account of the acquisition of the site and the commencement of the buildings, which has been drawn up in accordance with the system followed in the previous Histories. I have to thank my friends, William Lloyd Birkbeck, M.A., Master of Downing College, and John Perkins, LL.D., Bursar, for kindly giving me every facility for examining the minute-books, ground-plans, and all other records of their college.]

[2] [This part of Lyne's map has been reproduced in the History of Corpus Christi College, Vol. I. p. 246.]

fourteenth century was given to the whole district[1]. Fuller, whose history was first published in 1655, tells us that these

Fig. 1. Site of Downing College, reduced from Loggan's map of Cambridge, dated 1688.
17. "The hogg Market."   22. "The Spinn House."   39. "The Tennis Court."

Lees derived their name from the adjoining S. Thomas's Hostel, in Trumpington Street[2], and that they were "formerly the

---

[1] [History of Pembroke College, Vol. I. p. 122.]   [2] [Ibid. p. 124.]

Campus Martius of the Scholars here exercising themselves, sometimes too violently; lately disused, either because young Scholars now have less valour, or more civility[1]." When they were purchased for the site of Downing College the whole space, containing about thirty acres, was unenclosed pasture-ground, the property of various persons, and the subdivisions had probably been but little altered since 1688. The marshy character of the southern portion of the site was still maintained at the end of the last century, for Mr Gunning, describing the condition of that part of Cambridge when he entered the University in 1784, mentions that "in going over the land now occupied by Downing Terrace, you generally got five or six shots at snipes[2]."

The founder, Sir George Downing, by will dated 20 December, 1717, bequeathed estates in Cambridgeshire, Bedfordshire, and Suffolk, to certain trustees, in trust for his cousin Jacob Garret Downing, and his issue in strict settlement, with remainder to other relatives in like manner. In case of the failure of such issue, the trustees were directed to purchase

"some piece of ground lying and being in the town of Cambridge, proper and convenient for the erecting and building a college, and thereon shall erect and build all such houses, edifices, and buildings as shall be fit and requisite for that purpose; which college shall be called by the name of Downing's College[3]: and my will is, that a charter royal be sued for and obtained for the founding such college, and incorporating a body collegiate by that name."

Sir George Downing died 10 June, 1749, and his will was proved 13 June in that year. The trustees had all died before him; his cousin, on whom the estates devolved, died without issue in 1764; and all the parties entitled in remainder had previously died, without issue. In the same year an information was filed in the Court of Chancery, at the relation of the Chancellor, Masters, and the Scholars of the University, against Dame Margaret Downing, widow of Sir Jacob Garret Downing, and the heirs-at-law of Sir George Downing. The

---

[1] [Fuller, ed. Prickett and Wright, p. 60.]

[2] [Reminiscences, octavo edition, p. 36.]

[3] [This is the expression used in the Will of Sir G. Downing, the copy of which preserved at Somerset House, London, has been compared with the quotation from it in the charter dated 22 September, 1800, where the expression used is Downing College.]

Lord Chancellor gave judgment 3 July, 1769, declaring the will of the testator well proved, and that the same ought to be established, and the trusts thereof performed and carried into execution, in case the King should be pleased to grant a royal charter to incorporate the college; and further, that the defendants, the heirs-at-law of the testator, were at liberty to make application for that purpose[1]. The estates, however, were in possession of Lady Downing, and afterwards of her devisees, without any real title to them; and the opposition raised by them, with the further litigation consequent upon it, delayed the charter for more than thirty years; but, as the above-mentioned decree rendered its ultimate issue a matter of certainty, the question of a suitable site for the intended college began to be discussed immediately, not only among those most interested, but in the University at large. The heirs-at-law, and especially one of them, Mr Francis Annesley, who ultimately became the first Master, appear to have cooperated cordially with the University in endeavouring to get the question settled, and the college built, with the least possible delay. A letter written to Gough by Michael Tyson, Fellow of Corpus Christi College, 21 November, 1771, shews that the promoters of the college had even then selected the site ultimately adopted, and had gone so far as to choose their architect:

"Essex is come down from London with a commission to purchase, at any rate, Pembroke Leas, to build Downing College upon, and immediately to draw a plan and elevation of the new College. The charter is to be framed out of hand, and the foundation laid as soon as possible[2]."

We do not know whether Essex sent in any design, but, if he did, it was not approved of, for a letter written from Cambridge, 27 October, 1784, by Mr Michael Lort, Fellow of Trinity College, shews that by that time another architect had superseded him. It is curious to find Mr Annesley spoken of as Master of Downing College sixteen years before the college had any legal existence:

......"Mr Ainsly the new Mr of Downing has been here to fix on a site for his new College, for, though many has been proposed to him,

---

[1] [Charter of Downing College, 4to. London, 1800, p. 4. There is a tradition that the charter was drawn by Mr Pitt.]

[2] [Nichols, Literary Anecdotes, VIII. 572.]

yet objections are made to all—Mr Wyat the architect wishes much that it should be opposite to some of the colleges on the River, for then he thinks he shall not be crampt for Room, & may make four fine façades; but how will they here get an access to, & communication with, the Town? The most promising Spot seems to be that between B^p Watsons house and the Tennis Court, but here tis said they cannot dig cellars, a material object, I presume, to such a college.—The King has recommended two particulars—that it may not be a Gothic building, & that the Professors be obliged to publish their lectures—to this latter, I do not assent, Lectures thus published will do little credit to the author or his college[1]."

The site suggested in the above passage is the northern part of the present one. The dwelling-house of Richard Watson, D.D., Bishop of Llandaff, is still standing on the west side of S. Andrew's Street, near the south end of the row of houses shewn on the map (fig. 1)[2], and the Tennis-court is evidently the building at the east end of the site of Pembroke College (ibid. 39), which was not pulled down until 1880.

In, or before, 1796, the heirs-at-law petitioned the crown for a charter of incorporation; and, 19 December in the same year, they entered into an agreement with the Town of Cambridge (subject to the condition that if the charter were not granted within one year the agreement should be void), to purchase the open space called Parker's Piece for the site of the college, or to take a lease thereof for nine hundred and ninety-nine years; and on the same day an agreement to the like effect was made between the same parties with respect to a piece of ground at Castle End, known as Pound Hill, containing one acre and twenty-three poles[3]. The charter, however, was not granted

---

[1] [This letter, addressed to the Rev. Mr Ashby, at Barrow near Newmarket, is preserved among the MS. collections of Sir John Cullum, Bart., at Hardwick House near Bury S. Edmund's. Mr Ashby evidently thought the selection of an architect and a site premature, for in a subsequent letter, dated 21 December, 1784, Mr Lort replies: "As to Downing College I think with you that neither of us shall see it established."]

[2] [This house, called Llandaff House, was built by Bishop Watson on the site of an Inn called "The Bishop Blaise," the conversion of which into a private residence was commemorated in the following epigram by William Lort Mansel, afterwards Master of Trinity College, and Bishop of Bristol:

"Two of a trade can ne'er agree
No proverb can be juster;
They've ta'en down Bishop Blaise you see
And put up Bishop Bluster."]

[3] [Le Keux, ed. Cooper, III. 44.]

within the prescribed time, and the agreements therefore became null and void.

Two years afterwards, 15 March, 1798, the same parties made a third agreement with the town (subject to the condition of the charter being granted within three years), for the purchase of an acre of ground called Doll's Close, facing the open common called Butt Green, south of Jesus College; and, the Privy Council having recommended the King to grant a charter 6 June, 1800, it was conveyed to the heirs-at-law in trust for the intended college with the usual formalities, 14 and 15 July, 1800.

This charter passed the Great Seal 22 September, 1800. The Society nominated therein, consisting of a Master, three Professors, and three Fellows, began at once to hold regular meetings, the minutes of which give valuable information respecting the site and buildings. Unfortunately the proceedings of the first six years[1] were not entered as they took place, but at some subsequent period, under the heading of each year. It is clear, however, that these annals must have been reduced into their present form from notes taken at each meeting. The following extracts contain all that is required for our present purpose.

In the year 1800:

"The first Meeting was held soon after the date of the Charter, at which the Charter was read, and ordered to be printed for the use of the Members.

James Wyatt, Esq., was appointed Architect of the College.

It was resolved to apply for an Act of Parliament for confirming his Majesty's Charter, and for changing the Scite of the College, and for providing a Fund for Building the same. Dr Annesley and Mr Professor Christian[2] were requested, and undertook, to look out for a more proper Scite.

On the result of the Proceedings of Dr Annesley and Mr Professor Christian, which were reported from time to time, It was determined that the most desirable situation for the College would be the Pembroke Leys: and Dr Annesley was authorised to negotiate and contract with the Proprietors of that Ground, and he succeeded in obtaining conditional Contracts for the purchase of the greater part of it."

In the year 1801:

"An Act was passed for extinguishing the rights of Common upon Pembroke Leys; and another Act was also passed for changing the Scite

---

[1] [Dated Minutes of meetings begin 24 June, 1806.]

[2] [Edward Christian, M.A., Downing Professor of the Laws of England, 1800—23.]

of the College from Doll's Close to Pembroke Leys, and enabling them to borrow money for the purpose of carrying on the Building[1]."

In the year 1802:

"Several Contracts for purchase of Pembroke Leys were approved by the Court of Chancery."

In the year 1803:

"The enclosure of Pembroke Leys and the purchase of Lands were proceeded in."

In the year 1804:

"The Enclosure of Pembroke Leys and the Purchases and Exchanges of Lands there were settled[2]."

Meanwhile the buildings had not been forgotten. Mr James Wyatt, whom we have found mentioned as the architect of the college in 1784, prepared two designs, which were ready by the beginning of 1804. The Master then submitted them to the judgment of Mr Thomas Hope[3], with the request that he would criticise their respective merits. The result of his examination

---

[1] [These Acts of Parliament received the royal assent 2 July, 1801. Doll's Close, the actual extent of which was 1 acre, 1 rood, was sold in 1810 for £350.]

[2] [The title-deeds in the possession of Downing College shew that most of the different pieces of ground were not formally conveyed until 1807. It was at this time that the road called "Tennis-court Road" (see the plan of Cambridge) was set out. A bridle-way had previously existed, separated from Pembroke Leas by a deep ditch. The Act of Parliament "for extinguishing the Rights of Common and other Rights in and over certain Lands called Saint Thomas's Leys otherwise Pembroke Leys," appointed Commissioners, and provided, among other things, "That the said Commissioners shall, and they are hereby required, to set out a convenient Carriage Road, communicating from the Street called *Bird-bolt Lane*, along the Wall of *Pembroke Hall* Garden, to the Back Gate of *Pembroke Hall*, and also another convenient Carriage Road or Way, communicating with the said first-mentioned Road or Way at such point as the said Commissioners shall think fit (taking into Consideration the Convenience of the Owners of the said Land, and of the Persons entitled to use the said Road or Way respectively), and the Road running across at the Bottom of the said Leys from the *Trumpington* Road to the *Linton* Road, or communicating with the said first-mentioned Road as aforesaid, and the *Trumpington* Road, at some Point South of *Addenbrooke's Hospital*, as the said Commissioners shall think fit; which said Road or Way shall be used by such Persons only as are entitled to use the Road now running in the last-mentioned Directions."]

[3] ["Observations on the Plans and Elevations designed by James Wyatt, Architect, for Downing College, Cambridge; in a letter to Francis Annesley, Esq. M.P." By Thomas Hope. 4to. London, 1804. The pamphlet is in the form of a letter, dated 22 February, 1804.]

is contained in a tedious pamphlet, in which we find a great deal about himself, but very little about the designs submitted to him. In fact, all that can be gathered respecting them is, that one was larger than the other; that the style of both was Roman Doric; and that the chapel occupied the centre of the south range, with the gate of entrance opposite to it in the north range. The criticism terminates with the following passage:

"With the material defects then pointed out in the building in question, and with many lesser ones I shall pass over in silence, I do not see in it one striking feature, one eminent beauty. Neither elevations nor sections display a single instance of fancy, a single spark of genius, to make up for their many faults. Everything alike in them is trite, commonplace, nay, often vulgar. The pile has so little a character of its own, that the style of the gateway soars not above that of a park-entrance; and the rest of the building might, but for the niches within the portico, and the heavy tower over it, be mistaken for a gentleman's country residence. The decorations are such as we see every day, but behold every time, not with a renewed pleasure, but with a growing satiety and disgust. The portico is that, not of the Roman Pantheon, but of the Pantheon in Oxford Street [1]; and however much credit I am willing to give the architect of that temple of pleasure for the inside thereof, though borrowed from the very different kind of temple consecrated by the Emperor Justinian to Divine Wisdom, yet I much doubt that a man of taste would ever quote its outside portico among the fine architectonic productions of our time; why then should the same architect, so many years after, not satisfied with repeating its obsolete form in a chapel on the road to Highgate, again replicate the same in a most important addition to one of the first Universities in Great Britain?"

The minute-book is silent on the merits or demerits of Mr Wyatt's design, but we find in it the following account of the way in which he came to be superseded by Mr Wilkins, then at the outset of his career.

In the year 1804:

"A Plan for the Buildings by Mr James Wyatt being laid before the Master in Chancery, with an Estimate, he required a second to be submitted to him, in consequence of which a second plan and estimate were made by Mr James Byfield, Architect; and other plans and estimates were afterwards voluntarily made, and offered to the College, by Mr William Wilkins, Junr. Fellow of Caius College and Architect, and by Mr Francis Sandys and Mr Lewis Wyatt Architects. These plans and estimates

---

[1] [Mr James Wyatt (born 1743, died 1813) was first brought into notice as the architect of this building, opened in 1772. The portico is still standing.]

being submitted to the College at different Meetings, and to the Master in Chancery, that of Mr Wilkins was ultimately approved, and ordered by the Court to be carried into execution."

Mr Byfield's design, of which a ground-plan only has been preserved, dated 1804, places all the buildings in the area north of a line drawn from Fitzwilliam Street to Regent Street. On this ground he shews a quadrangle of three sides only, measuring 275 feet from east to west, by 145 feet from north to south. The chapel, flanked on either side by a Professor's house, and a range of Fellows' chambers, occupies the centre of the north side. The library and the hall face each other in the centre of the east and west ranges respectively. The Master's Lodge is at the south end of the east range, and the offices attached to the hall at the corresponding end of the west range. The college is entered from S. Andrew's Street, and from Tennis-court Road (Fitzwilliam Street not having been at that time set out[1]).

Mr Lewis Wyatt's design, dated 9 December, 1805, is illustrated by several elevations and sections. His quadrangle, situated apparently in nearly the same position as that subsequently commenced, measures 332 feet from east to west, by 345 feet from north to south. The east and west sides consist of ranges of chambers, with a Professor's house in the centre of each. A large building, lettered "The principal building," occupies the greater part of the south side; and a gate of entrance the centre of the north side. The "principal building" contains the chapel, and (apparently) the hall and the library. The chapel, like that designed by Mr Byfield, stands north and south, with a semicircular apse at the south end. Colonnades, with gas-lamps suspended between each pair of columns, connect the principal building, and the gateway, with the east and west ranges. The buildings, in two floors, are worked in a tame classical style, to which it is impossible to give any distinctive name.

It must not be concluded from the above minute that the design was finally settled in the course of 1804. It was not until the spring of 1806 that the designs of Mr Lewis Wyatt (that by Mr James Wyatt having, apparently, been abandoned) and Mr Wilkins were submitted by the Court of Chancery to the

[1] [This street was set out in 1822.]

judgment of three architects, Mr George Dance, Mr J. Lewis, and Mr Samuel Pepys Cockerell. These referees decided in favour of Mr Wilkins, 26 March, 1806[1]; and, 27 November of the same year, we find the following minute:

"27 November 1806. It was resolved that the Master be requested to undertake the Execution of the Order for proceeding with such part

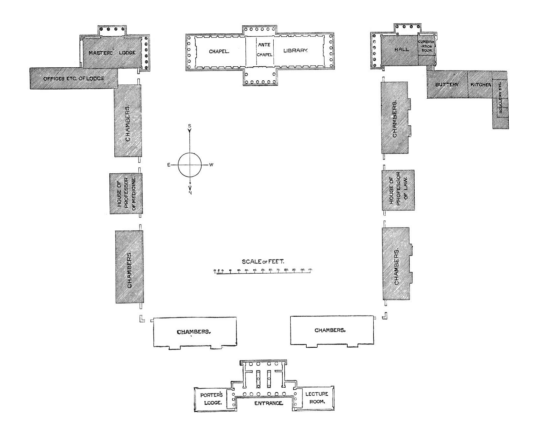

Fig. 2.   Block-plan of the buildings of Downing College, as designed by Wilkins.

of the Buildings of the College as shall serve for the Residence of the present Members, and to borrow such sums of Money upon Mortgage, pursuant to the Act of Parliament, as shall be necessary for that purpose."

[1] [Their report is preserved in the Master's Lodge of Downing College, but, as it does not give the reasons for their decision, it need not be quoted at length.]

The arrangement of the accepted design will, it is hoped, be understood from the block-plan (fig. 2), and the position of it on the site, from the plan of Cambridge. The buildings—in two floors without garrets—are disposed round a quadrangle 300 feet square, nearly equal in area to the great court of Trinity College. In the centre of each side of the quadrangle a dwelling-house is shewn, that on the east side being appropriated to the Professor of Medicine, that on the west side to the Professor of Law. The remaining portions of these sides, to the right and left of these residences, are detached blocks of chambers. The Master's Lodge is at the south end of the east side, the Hall and Combination Room at the south end of the west side. The south side of the quadrangle is formed by a detached range of building, containing the Chapel and the Library. The former is entered through an octastyle portico, which gives access to a vestibule, or ante-chapel; and it is so arranged that the altar would have been placed at the east end. The Library could be entered from this vestibule, or from a door at the west end, through a hexastyle portico. On the north side there were to be two ranges of chambers, separated by a wide interval; and northward of them again the *Propylæum*, or gate of entrance, flanked by a lecture-room on the west, and a porter's lodge on the east. The *Propylæum* is worked in the Doric style, but the buildings on the south side of the quadrangle are Ionic. An alternative ground-plan places the *Propylæum* at the north end of the avenue, opposite to the Museum of Human Anatomy; but this arrangement, if ever seriously entertained, was soon abandoned, probably on account of the obvious inconvenience of placing the porter's lodge and the lecture-room so far from the rest of the college[1].

The first stone was laid on Monday, 18 May, 1807. The ceremony was conducted in the following manner[2]:

"On Monday last the foundation stone of Downing college was laid by the Master, Professors, and Fellows first appointed in the charter. On this occasion the University assembled in St Mary's Church at

[1] [This description is derived from a study of the original plans by Wilkins, preserved in Downing College.]

[2] [The account here given is from the Cambridge Chronicle of Saturday, 23 May, 1807, corrected from a MS. account in the College minute-book; and from other sources of information.]

eleven o'clock, where a sermon was preached by the Public Orator, Edmund Outram, D.D., Fellow of S. John's College, from Numbers xxiv. 5. *How goodly are thy tents O Jacob, and thy Tabernacles, O Israel;* after which they proceeded to the Senate-House, and heard a Latin speech delivered by Mr William Frere, the Junior Fellow. From the Senate-House the procession went through the Market Place and along St Andrew's Street to the site of the future College.

When the procession arrived upon the ground, the Master (attended by the other members of Downing College), making a suitable address in Latin, deposited in the stone specimens of the different coins of the present reign; and placed over them a plate, upon which was engraved the following inscription, containing a short memorial of the origin of the foundation and the objects of the institution:

COLLEGIVM · DOWNINGENSE ·
IN · ACADEMIA · CANTABRIGIÆ ·
GEORGIVS · DOWNING · DE · GAMLINGAY ·
IN · EODEM · COMITATV · BARONETTVS ·
TESTAMENTO · DESIGNAVIT ·
OPIBVSQVE · MVNIFICE · INSTRVXIT ·
ANNO · SALVTIS · M · DCC · XVII ·
REGIA · TANDEM · CHARTA · STABILIVIT ·
GEORGIVS · TERTIVS · OPTIMVS · PRINCEPS ·
ANNO · M · DCCC ·
HÆC · VERO · ÆDIFICII · PRIMORDIA ·
MAGISTER · PROFESSORES · ET · SOCII ·
POSVERVNT ·
QVOD · AD · RELIGIONIS · CVLTVM ·
JVRIS · ANGLICANI · ET · MEDICINÆ · SCIENTIAM ·
ET · AD · RECTAM · JVVENTVTIS · INGENVÆ ·
DISCIPLINAM · PROMOVENDAM ·
FELICITER · EVENIAT ·

The stone being placed in its proper situation, with the usual forms, a benediction was pronounced by the Public Orator.　　*　　*　　*

Mr Watts, the University Printer, deposited in the foundation stone the first stereotype plate cast in this University, which was dedicated to the Vice-Chancellor and the Heads of Houses.

At the conclusion of the ceremony the University returned in procession to the Senate-House.

The weather was remarkably fine, and a large concourse were attracted, as well from the neighbouring country as from the town and University, to witness the various parts of a ceremony which has of late so rarely occurred.

An Entertainment was given at four o'clock, at the Red Lion, to the Vice-Chancellor, Doctors, and University Officers, amounting to between 60 and 70 persons, by the Master, Professors, and Fellows of Downing College."

Tradition records that the first stone was laid at the Hall; but medieval precedent was not followed in completing that edifice, with the kitchen, etc. before any other was undertaken. On the contrary, it was evidently intended from the first to begin with the east side of the quadrangle, with the exception of the northernmost range of chambers. This course of proceeding was directed by the following Order:

"May 19, 1807. That Mr Wilkins be directed to proceed with all convenient expedition to complete the Master's Lodge; the Professor's Lodge in the East side of the court, being designed for the residence of Professor Harwood; and the Six Sets of Apartments between the two Lodges, being for the temporary residence of Professor Christian, and Messrs. Lens, Meeke, and Frere."

Of the three buildings here mentioned, the Master's Lodge and the Professor's Lodge were probably the first undertaken, for in the following December a second Order directed the postponement of the range of chambers between them, until the Professor's Lodge on the opposite side of the quadrangle should be completed:

"31 December, 1807. On further consideration of the resolution respecting the order in which the buildings should proceed, Resolved that the Professor's Lodge on the west side of the Court for the Residence of Professor Christian be begun and completed before the six sets of apartments on the east side; in case the Funds of the College should not allow them to be carried on at the same time."

Notwithstanding this Order, it is clear that the portions of the east side referred to in the Order dated 19 May, 1807, were undertaken as originally intended; for we find that the two Lodges were finished by 1810, and the building between them by 1813[1]. Considerable delay had evidently taken place, from some cause which cannot now be discovered, for, 31 October, 1812, it was resolved "That the buildings already begun be proceeded in with all speed, and completed before any other be begun."

The following extracts from the minute-book shew that no part of the west side had as yet been undertaken. Unfortunately neither the petition referred to in them, nor the affidavit of Mr Wilkins, has been preserved, and we are therefore

---

[1] [The Cambridge University Calendar for 1810 says: "The Master's Lodge, and the Lodge for the residence of the Professor of Medicine, are now completed"; and the volume for 1813, after repeating the above sentence, with the addition of the words "and occupied," proceeds as follows: "A building which unites these two Lodges, and contains apartments for three Fellows, is now completed and occupied."]

unable to state what changes had been suggested. It is probable that a desire to admit undergraduates may have influenced the petitioners, for the buildings hitherto erected were for the use of the Master, the Professors, and the Fellows.

"24 January, 1818. Upon reading the Petition presented to the Court of Chancery in December last, for altering the Plan of the Buildings, and Borrowing Money to carry on the West side thereof in four years at the cost of £27,000; and upon reading the Draft of Mʳ Wilkins' proposed affidavit to be laid before Master Stratford, and inspecting the plan therein mentioned marked B: Resolved that so much of the proposed alteration......as relates to the Western side of the Quadrangle is approved, and that the same be immediately proceeded in.

Resolved that the alterations proposed by Mʳ Wilkins in the Northern side require further consideration, but that, in as much as there is no immediate prospect of proceeding with those parts of the Building which will be affected thereby, it will be convenient that the consideration of the same be postponed to a future time.

Resolved that the Law Professor's Lodge be finished as soon as possible after the Building is carried up, and before any other part of the West side is finished.

Resolved that it is desirable to have Buildings to answer the purpose of Porters' Lodges on the Eastern and Northern entrances to the College Grounds, it being found essential even to the present convenient Occupation of the College to have the Power of Locking or Opening Gates at those Entrances."

In consequence of these resolutions, the west side of the quadrangle was begun in the course of the year. Mr Spicer Crowe contracted to execute "all the works of the proposed New Buildings exclusive of the stonework," for £20,800; and Messrs Thomson, stonemasons, "to execute the stonework for the new Buildings within two years, except the two Porticoes, which are to be executed within the third year," for £7560. These contracts were drawn in August, 1818, and provided that the buildings should be ready for occupation in September, 1820. They were covered in before the winter of 1819–20, and, though considerably delayed by the severity of the season, were completed at, or soon after, the time named, for in May, 1821, undergraduates were admitted to reside and keep terms. The mention of the two porticoes, and the largeness of the sum which it was proposed to expend, £28,360, shew that the Hall was included in the works then undertaken[1].

[1] [The above details are derived from the minute-book, and from the Cambridge Calendars for 1820 and 1822.]

No further attempt to complete Mr Wilkins' design was made until 1870, as will be related below; but various necessary works were carried out, such as the boundary walls of the Law Professor's garden (1822); the wall along the north and part of the west sides of the site (1825); the Porter's Lodge and gates in Regent Street, and the rest of the wall next Tennis Court Road (1834). The avenue is mentioned in 1825 as having been already planted.

It will be remembered that among the buildings on the east side of the quadrangle completed in 1813 the northernmost block of chambers had not been included. Moreover the north end of the west range had been left unfinished, as though it was intended that some future building should abut against it. This might possibly be connected with the alteration to the north side mentioned in the Resolutions of 1818. In 1870 it was decided that "it is desirable to complete the east side of the court, and to make such improvements in the Hall and Combination Room as may be deemed necessary." The architect selected was Mr Edward M. Barry; and after a good deal of preliminary discussion extending over three years, we meet with the following Resolution:

"8 February, 1873. Resolved that the east side of the Court be completed according to Mr Wilkins' design for the elevation, and that a Committee confer with Mr Barry, and suggest definite plans for the new buildings for the consideration of the College."

The work was undertaken soon afterwards, and completed in about three years, at a cost of £21,281. It included the above-mentioned block of chambers, together with a lecture-room, on the east side; the completion, externally, of the west side, with the addition of two rooms to the Law Professor's house, contrived in the space between it and the block of chambers to the north of it; and some judicious alterations to the Hall.

It should be mentioned in conclusion that, though it had been found impossible, from lack of funds, to build the intended chapel, yet that the site was consecrated, and one member of the college, Sir Busick Harwood, M.D., Professor of Anatomy 1785—1814, was interred within it. The following account of this transaction appears in the Minute-Book:

" 24 November, 1814. The Master reported that Sir Busick Harwood [who died 10 November] had in his Life time frequently mentioned to him an anxious desire that his remains might be interred in the Scite of the College Chapel, which desire he had also expressed in his Will. That the Master had in consequence applied to the Bishop of Ely for permission, and being informed at his Lordship's Office that a Petition of the College was necessary, and the time not allowing for a Meeting of the College to be called, he had had such Petition drawn up and sealed with the College Seal, and that in pursuance thereof a Licence had been granted by the Bishop, of which the following is a Copy :

Bowyer Edward [etc.] Whereas we have received the petition of the Master, Professors, Fellows, and Scholars of Downing College in the University of Cambridge, setting forth that the Buildings of the said Petitioners College, now in part complete and inhabited, are situate in a detached part of the Parish of Saint Benedict in the Town of Cambridge, and within our Diocese, and that it is intended to erect all the future Buildings of the said College in the same Parish ; that the Burial Ground of the said Parish is already very inadequate for the Interment of the Parishioners thereof and would be entirely insufficient for the Interment of the Members and Inhabitants of the said Petitioners College :

That the said Petitioners are therefore desirous to have a Cemetery or Burial Place set apart and preserved for the use of the said Petitioners for ever; and have accordingly caused a Piece of Ground containing 40 feet in length from North to South and 20 feet in width from East to West, situate near to and on the West side of the Master's Lodge of the said College, to be fenced off and set apart for the said Cemetery or Burial Place, and which will form part of the Foundation and Scite of the Chapel hereafter to be erected in the said College, and praying that We would be pleased to consecrate the said Piece of Ground [etc.]

Now * * * We * * * being desirous of complying with the request of the said Petitioners, but being at this time unable personally to consecrate the said piece of Ground, have therefore thought fit to grant * * * our full leave licence and authority for the interment of the Bodies of the Members and Inhabitants of the said College dying in the faith of Christ and Communicants of the Church established, in the said Piece of Ground so as aforesaid set apart and appropriated as and for a Cemetery or Burial Place, until such time as the same shall be consecrated by us or our successors, or by our or their Authority, saving and reserving all fees dues and perquisites to the perpetual Curate or Minister of the Parish of Saint Benedict and their successors. 12 November 1814.

The Master also Reported that he had taken the necessary steps for forming the said Burial Ground, and constructing a Vault in the same with the concurrence of Mr Wilkins the Architect."

Sir Busick Harwood was accordingly interred in the above-mentioned vault on Thursday, 15 November, 1814[1].]

[1] [Cambridge Chronicle, 9 December, 1814.]

CHRONOLOGICAL SUMMARY.

1717 (20 December). Will of Sir George Downing.

1749 (10 June). Death of Sir George Downing.

1769 (3 July). Judgment of the Lord Chancellor in favour of Sir G. Downing's Will.

1796 (19 December). Agreement with the Town of Cambridge to sell or lease Parker's Piece or Pound Hill, for the site of the college.

1798 (15 March). Agreement with the same to sell Doll's Close, for the same purpose.

1800 (22 September). Charter of Downing College.

James Wyatt appointed architect.

New site suggested.

1801 (2 July). Acts of Parliament for enclosing Pembroke Leys, and for changing the site of the College from Doll's Close to Pembroke Leys.

1804. Mr Wyatt's design submitted to the Court of Chancery, and a second design asked for.

1806. Designs by Mr Lewis Wyatt and Mr Wilkins submitted to a committee of three architects. Design by Mr Wilkins selected.

1807 (18 May). First stone laid.

1810. Master's Lodge, and Professor's house on east side of quadrangle, completed.

1813. Range of chambers between them completed.

1814. Site of chapel consecrated, and Sir Busick Harwood buried within it.

1818. West side of quadrangle begun.

1821 (May). Undergraduates admitted to residence.

1870. Completion of east side of quadrangle suggested.

1873. Mr Wilkins' design proceeded with by Mr Edward M. Barry.

ADDITIONS TO THE SECOND VOLUME.

Queens' College.

p. 58. To the history of the walk called Erasmus' Walk it should be added, that in 1779 the Corporation of Cambridge ordered the trees to be cut down and sold[1], but the University interposed, and paid £50, with an annual rent of one shilling, to preserve them. The terms of the Grace of the Senate, dated 26 February, 1779, recommending this course of action, shew that it was believed at that time that Erasmus had walked and meditated under their shade. The trees are now (1886) still standing.

"Cum Arbores in Ambulacro Erasmiano dicto consitæ ne ex severo Prætoris Edicto excisæ penitus subruantur, quinquaginta Librarum Summâ, annuoque unius Solidi Stipendio, præcaveri possit et provideri:

Placeat Vobis, ut in Academiæ Commodum et Ornamentum, in Ulmeti objacentis Præsidium, et in justam tanti Viri, apud nos olim diversantis, et immortalia sua Opera ibidem studiosè meditantis, Memoriam, Venerationemque, quinquaginta istæ Libræ, annuumque istud unius Solidi Stipendium e Cistâ communi pio gratoque Animo erogentur."

p. 58, l. 36. The size of the college site has made it impossible to include the Brewhouse and the Stables on the plan (fig. 1).

A new range of chambers designed by W. M. Fawcett, M.A., architect, was begun 16 December, 1885, on the north side of the President's kitchen-garden, close to King's College. A glance at the plan (fig. 1) shews that a new building in this position will form the north side of an extension of the Walnut-tree court; but there will be a considerable interval between its east end and the north end of the range built 1616—18.

[1] [Cooper's Annals, IV. 389.]

The new building will be 130 feet long by 28 feet broad, in three floors, with garrets in the roof. It will contain 30 sets of rooms for undergraduates, with one set of rooms for a Fellow. In style it will harmonise with the original buildings of the college.

Jesus College.

p. 126, l. 7.   In the summer of 1884 the plaster was removed from the external west wall of this transept, and an arcade of round-headed arches was revealed, precisely similar in style to those in the east wall.   The exact number of arches could not be ascertained, as the arcade had been broken through by the insertion of two three-light windows of the Alcock period.

p. 169, l. 1.   This staircase, in the south-west corner of the room, was discovered in February, 1886, in the course of the repairs and alterations carried out in the Master's Lodge shortly after the election of the present Master.

A considerable addition to the buildings, consisting of two tutor's houses, and a range of chambers, containing rooms for 36 students, was commenced in 1883.   The foundation-stone of the range of chambers was laid by Arthur Westmorland, LL.D., President and Bursar, 7 November in that year, at the north jamb of the gate of entrance.   The architects were Messrs R. H. Carpenter and B. Ingelow, Carlton Chambers, London : the contractor, Mr Bentley, Waltham Abbey.   The tutor's houses were commenced in the following year.   The position of these buildings has been laid down on the map of Cambridge. It will be seen that the range of chambers forms the east side of a new court, which has the chapel on the south, part of the cloister-court and the chambers built in 1822 on the west, and is, for the present, open to the north.   Of the tutor's houses, one stands eastward of the chapel, the other near the north-west corner of the range commenced by Mr Waterhouse in 1869.

S. John's College.

p. 271. It appears from the "Prizing-Books" of S. John's College, that before the west side of the Third Court was begun there was already a small set of chambers, containing six sets of rooms, "by the waterside." A note added to the last account of the prizing of one of the rooms, dated 9 November, 1668, informs us that the whole building was "pluckt down in April 1670"; and a note in another place adds that "these chambers were demolished to make way for the New-buildings[1]."

p. 317, l. 12. Further proof that part of the heraldic achievements on the gate of entrance were gilt, is supplied by the verses of Giles Fletcher, which, as Mr Mullinger points out, were probably written between 1595 and 1599[2]. The poet describes the fourteen colleges which then existed. The following lines refer to Trinity College and S. John's College:

> "Quattuor inde novis quæ turribus alta minantur
> Et nivea immenso diffundunt atria circo,
> Ordine postremus, sed non virtutibus, auxit
> *Henricus* tecta, et triplices cum jungeret ædes,
> Imposuit nomen facto. Quæ proxima cernis,
> Coctilibus muris, parilique rubentia saxo,
> Quà super alta sedens portarum limina custos
> Arduus auratis tollit se cornibus Hircus,
> *Margaris* erexit, fausto quam *Derbia* partu
> Edidit."

The entries referred to in the text, which occur in the Audit-Book for 1702—3, are as follows:

"For colouring the Towers at the Forgate of the Colledge   2.   6.   8
To Robert Dalton for gilding and painting the forefront of
    the Colledge next the street .... 27.   o.   o."

p. 322, l. 26. After the words "then terminated," the sentence should have concluded as follows: "instead of at the south-east corner of the Wilderness, as at present. The iron gate was put up in 1780, where the walks then terminated, and probably

---

[1] [For this information I have to thank my friend A. F. Torry, M.A., Fellow.]

[2] [The University of Cambridge, from the Royal Injunctions of 1535 to the Accession of Charles I., pp. 372, 638. The verses occur in a poem entitled: "De Literis Antiquæ Britanniæ, Regibus præsertim qui doctrinâ claruerunt, quique Collegia Cantabrigiæ fundârunt." Cantab. 1633.]

moved to its present position soon after 1805, when the additional piece was acquired (p. 238). In 1780 the walk along the south side of the meadow was called *Bachelors' Walk*."

In the autumn of 1885 a new range of buildings, in three floors without garrets, to contain lecture-rooms and chambers for undergraduates, was begun in the open space between the west end of the chapel and the river, from the design of Francis Cranmer Penrose, Esq., architect. It is to be approached from the Second Court through the space at the foot of the staircase leading to the Library (H, fig. 1); and it will be so arranged that the lights in the range forming the north side of that court will not be interfered with. This new range will not only bring the Master's Lodge into closer connection with the college, but will also be capable of extension at a future time, so as to form part of the west side of a new court extending to Bridge Street. The following description of the design is written by Donald MacAlister, M.D., Fellow, who has taken an active part in the promotion of the building-scheme, and is therefore thoroughly conversant with the plans.

" The building will be of red brick with stone dressings, the roof being covered with plain red tiles. The length is about 130 feet in all, the width nearly 40 feet. The approach is through the archway (E Second Court) leading to the Library. The first flight of the Library staircase will be removed, and turned round, so as to form a continuation of the second flight, two archways being made in the north wall beneath the present windows lighting the stairway. All the interesting features of the present staircase will be carefully preserved, and, some think, brought out more perfectly. A few steps will then lead to a corridor 85 feet long, running along the back of the block towards the Lodge Garden. From this corridor access is had to the lecture-rooms on the ground-floor, and to the two wide staircases leading to the upper floors.

Four lecture-rooms are provided. The largest, at the north end of the building, is a handsome room 28 feet wide by some 38 feet long. The next largest is 25 feet by 35, and at the south end. Between these are two smaller rooms separated by a moveable partition, and suitable for smaller classes. There is also, intervening between the south end-wall of the block and the wall of the Second Court, a one-storey room, designed for holding physical apparatus, and capable perhaps of being used as a small laboratory. A doorway, like that in the Second Court facing towards the Master's Lodge, gives an independent entrance, from what we may call the "Chapel-front" of the block, into the lecture-rooms, and in the day time also to the upper storeys.

This Chapel-front is broken by the projection of the large lecture-room at the north-end, and, further south, by an oriel window like that in the Lodge. The windows of the lecture-room have arched heads like those of the Old Library in the First Court; those of the upper rooms are square-headed. Two gables break the roof line, and the ridge is surmounted by a hexagonal lantern like that above the Hall.

The west elevation, towards the river and the Lodge Garden, shews for part of its length the red roof of the corridor, which is only one storey high, together with 3 square or polygonal stair-towers, each with features of its own. The variety of this aspect of the building is one of its special merits, and we think it will harmonise well with the Library on the one hand and the Lodge on the other.

Nine sets of rooms are arranged for on each of the two upper floors, the sizes being nearly those of the ordinary rooms in the New Court. The gyp-rooms are on a somewhat novel plan, for while each man has a small service-room of his own, there are on each staircase two larger gyp-rooms, where washing-up, &c., can be done for several men in common.

Very ample provision is made for light and ventilation, and we can well believe that rooms in the New Building will be much sought for and highly valued. The new lecture-rooms are urgently needed for teaching purposes; but we may hope that they will also serve to accommodate, and so to bind more closely to the College, the various societies to which from time to time we have given a home. Lastly, when the finished plans are seen, we believe it will be agreed that, from an architectural point of view, the New Building will be no unworthy addition to the varied and interesting fabric of S. John's[1]."

The contract was sealed 11 November, 1885, and the contractors began work a few days afterwards.

Trinity College.

p. 474. To the account of Dr Nevile's work should be added the testimony of a contemporary, Giles Fletcher the younger, who, dedicating to him his poem, *Christ's Victorie*, first published in 1610, thus expresses himself:

"And what are the two eyes of this Land, but the two Universities? which cannot but prosper in the time of such a Prince, that is a Prince of Learning, as well as of People. And truly I should forget my self, if I should not call Cambridge the right eye: and I think (King Henrie

[1] [The Eagle, Vol. XIII. p. 369.]

the 8 being the Uniter, Edward the 3 the Founder, and your self the Repairer of this College wherein I live) none will blame me, if I esteem the same, since your polishing of it, the fairest sight in Cambridge."

p. 475, *note 2*. The portrait in the Master's Lodge at Sidney Sussex College, long believed to represent Symons, has been proved to represent William Perkins, Fellow of Christ's College, a celebrated divine, who died 1602.

p. 604, l. 19. It is probable that when the lesser Combination Room was wainscoted by the College, the larger one was similarly treated by Sir Thomas Sclater, whose work in Nevile's Court has been already recorded (p. 519). A reference to what he had done for the Combination Room appears in the *Articles against Dr Bentley*, published in 1710, No. XLVIII.:

"Why did you endeavour to deprive the College of the Combination-room, which was made or beautified for their Use at the Charge of our great Benefactor Sir *Thomas Slater*, by the Consent of the College?"

Emmanuel College.

After the completion of the History of Emmanuel College, a survey of the site and buildings, made by James Essex in 1746, was discovered in the college. A copy of this valuable record (fig. 1) now replaces a plan which had been made for this work. It is specially interesting as shewing the extent of the buildings between the principal court and S. Andrew's Street, before the alterations carried out by Essex in 1769, and also the small building called "Bungay Building," between the kitchen and the same street. In fact, if it be compared with Loggan's view, drawn in or shortly after 1688, it will be seen that the arrangement of the buildings and the gardens had not been altered between his time and 1746. In the latter, part of the north wall of the tennis-court, had been pulled down, and its south wall had been prolonged as far as the pond, so as to increase the Fellows' Garden, but in other respects no change had been made.

At the commencement of the History it was stated (p. 687) that the "site—with the exception of a triangular piece of waste ground at the north-east corner (*A B C*, fig. 1) which was granted to the College by the Town in 1838—is simply that of the House or Priory of the Dominicans." This is not strictly accurate. If the survey by Essex be compared with the outline of the existing site which is placed above it, it will be seen that a larger piece than the above-mentioned triangle remains unaccounted for.

It appears that in 1792 (15 August) the Town of Cambridge granted to the college a lease for 999 years, at a pepper-corn rent, of two pieces of ground, described as follows:

" One piece of Common or Waste ground whereon part of a Summer-house is built, lying and being on the backside towards Christ College piece * * *

And also all those Messuages or Tenements * * * with the stables and coach house thereto adjoining, situate standing and being on the North side of Emmanuel College, containing in length three hundred and eighteen feet; in breadth at the South East End twenty three feet; in the midst twenty three feet; and in breadth at the North East End twenty three feet; the South West front abuts against the said College."

The summer-house can be at once identified with the building at the north-east corner of the Fellows' Garden shewn by Loggan, and delineated by Essex; and the second piece is evidently the strip of ground between the old wall of the garden (part of which is still standing), and the modern wall which now bounds the site towards Christ's Pieces; but, in the absence of more precise information respecting the history of the dwelling-house adjoining, it is difficult to reconcile the length with the ground in its present state.

At the end of 1885 a building was commenced on the east side of the Close, occupying part of the site of the stables, and abutting at its north end upon the dwelling-house eastward of the pond, called Emmanuel House, now in the occupation of W. N. Shaw, M.A., Fellow. It has been designed by W. M. Fawcett, M.A., architect, and consists of a basement and three floors, with garrets in the roof. The material is red brick. It will be 52 feet long, by 30 feet broad, and will contain 14 sets of rooms for undergraduates, with a common breakfast-room.